The Complete Correspondence of
Sigmund Freud and Ernest Jones
1908–1939

The Complete Correspondence of
SIGMUND FREUD
and
ERNEST JONES
1908–1939

Edited by
R. Andrew Paskauskas

Introduction by
Riccardo Steiner

The Belknap Press of
Harvard University Press
Cambridge, Massachusetts
London, England
1993

Printed in the United States of America
10 9 8 7 6 5 4 3 2 1

This book is printed on acid-free paper, and its binding materials have been
chosen for strength and durability.

Library of Congress Cataloging-in-Publication Data

Freud, Sigmund, 1856–1939.
[Correspondence. Selections]
The complete correspondence of Sigmund Freud and Ernest Jones,
1908–1939 / edited by R. Andrew Paskauskas; introduction by
Riccardo Steiner.
p.   cm.
Correspondence chiefly in English; some correspondence in German
with English translation.
Includes bibliographical references and index.
ISBN 0-674-15423-1 (alk. paper)
1. Freud, Sigmund, 1856–1939—Correspondence. 2. Jones, Ernest,
1879–1958—Correspondence. 3. Psychoanalysts—Austria—
Correspondence. 4. Psychoanalysts—Great Britain—Correspondence.
5. Psychoanalysis. I. Jones, Ernest, 1856–1958. II. Paskauskas,
R. Andrew. III. Title.
[DNLM: 1. Freud, Sigmund, 1856–1939. 2. Jones, Ernest,
1879–1958. 3. Psychoanalysis—correspondence. WZ 100 F889cr]
BF109.F74A4   1993
150.19'52'0922—dc20
DNLM/DLC
for Library of Congress
92-23913
CIP

Contents

Preface   vii

Note on Editorial Method   xiii

Abbreviations of Works Cited   xvii

Introduction by Riccardo Steiner   xxi

Correspondence   1

List of Correspondence   773

References   795

Glossary   821

Index   823

Preface

❧

THE CORRESPONDENCE in this volume consists of letters, postcards, and telegrams. Jones's part of the correspondence is in English, with the exception of two postcards written in German. Freud's side is in English and German (about 120 items in German, close to 190 in English), and includes several notes which were translated or summarized by colleagues and forwarded to Jones during the war. Except for these latter pieces, one undated letter from Jones, and approximately 30 missing pieces, the items in this correspondence have been numbered 1 through 671. These numbers, however, do not agree with the count provided by Jones in his biography of Freud. In the American edition, he gives a total of 1,347 items in the Freud-Jones exchange, a figure clearly out of proportion (Jones, 1955a, p. xiii). In the subsequent British edition (Jones, 1955b), on the second page of his preface, Jones gives the total number of items in this correspondence as 898, which suggests that he might be including figures for his own and Freud's *Rundbriefe*.

Portions of this correspondence are drawn upon in the biographical and historical literature on psychoanalysis. Such use, however, is not extensive and tends to accentuate Freud's letters to Jones. It can be divided into three broad categories: letters to which Jones refers in the appended notes to his biography of Freud (Jones, 1953a, 1955a, 1957a; 1953b, 1955b, 1957b)—a little less than half of these are quoted directly; important excerpts of the correspondence contained in disparate works such as *Letters*, Schur (1972), and Steiner (1985); and selections from the correspondence incorporated in major biographical studies (Clark, 1980; Brome, 1983; Grosskurth, 1986; Gay, 1988; Young-Bruehl, 1988). With the exception of Brome, the biographical studies of Jones typically do not make use of the Freud-Jones correspondence (Girard, 1972; Davies, 1979).

The problems associated with Jones's use of this correspondence in his biography of Freud are at times quite marked, especially as regards the alteration of Freud's English. Although in his preface Jones states that he has not "ventured to amend [Freud's] grammar" (Jones, 1955a, p. xiii), there are nevertheless many dissimilarities of spelling, grammar, and punctuation between the letters quoted in Jones's published biography and Freud's originals.

Other inconsistencies pertain to citation of letters. The most glaring problems in this respect are the references to four of Jones's *Rundbriefe* as letters from Jones to Freud. Moreover, sometimes a letter from Jones to Freud may be cited erroneously as a letter from Freud. There are also discrepancies in citations between the American and British editions of the biography. Although I have not itemized all incongruities here, those that bear on historical issues are identified in the notes.

The Jones side of this correspondence, most of which was contained in the offices of the Sigmund Freud Copyrights until the spring of 1989, is now deposited in its entirety in the archives of the British Psycho-Analytical Society, in London. Each of these institutions also holds a transcript of Freud's letters to Jones (hereafter referred to as the British transcript).

A computer transcript of the extant correspondence was prepared by Frauke Voss from photocopies of the Jones holographs and the British transcript. This was proofread by me and Ilona Paskauskas.

I subsequently received photocopies of the holographs of Freud's letters to Jones from the Manuscript Division of the Library of Congress, in Washington, D.C. On these copies numerous passages had been obliterated by the Sigmund Freud Archives of New York. This procedure was undertaken because of concern with preserving patient confidentiality. However, I already had access to the British transcript, which, with the exception of typographical errors or other minor omissions and mistakes, was basically intact. In many instances, the passages blotted out by the appointees of the Archives referred to Freud's analysis of Loe Kann and had already been published in Vincent Brome's biography of Ernest Jones (Brome, 1983). Moreover, information about some of the other patients in question was already in the public domain. For example, in Freud's note to Jones about Smiley Blanton (May 8, 1930), "Smiley Blanton" had been blotted out to conceal, one supposes, the patient's identity—this in spite of the fact that Blanton's book, *Diary of My Analysis with Freud* (New York: Hawthorn, 1971), is reasonably well known to American audiences.

Further attempts on my part to gain access to the Freud holographs proved futile. Although verification of the Freud side of the correspondence was somewhat impeded, it was nevertheless possible, by collating the British transcript with the marred copies of the Freud originals, to achieve an acceptable level of accuracy.

Most of the Freud-Jones correspondence is in English; about one-fifth is in German. The passages in German that appear on the Jones side of the correspondence were translated by Frauke Voss. Albert Dickson, working from the British transcript, did the initial translation of Freud's letters written in German. Frauke Voss, working from both the British transcript and copies of the Freud holographs, verified Dickson's translation and in many instances made suggestions for revision. Ms. Voss and I then reviewed all of the translations in detail again. Darius Ornston also reviewed the translations of Freud's letters and made several suggestions for revision. Since that time, in consultation with Ms. Voss and the editors at Harvard University Press, I have made a number of further adjustments to the translations. Any remaining errors or omissions are my responsibility.

The editorial committee of the Sigmund Freud Copyrights, in conjunction with Harvard University Press, initially gave me authorization to undertake this project, and I am especially indebted to Mark Paterson, Masud Khan, Albert Solnit, Ilse Grubrich-Simitis, and of course Arthur Rosenthal, director of Harvard University Press until 1990, for their support. Mark Paterson and Christine Barnard, as agents for the Sigmund Freud and Ernest Jones estates, respectively, facilitated the handling of rights.

The members of the Jones family have been a constant source of support and encouragement. I am deeply grateful to Mervyn Jones, his wife, Jeanne, and daughter Jackie; and to Ernest Jones's niece Bridget Blundell, and his nephew Robert W. Trotter. Moreover, I would like to pay a special tribute to the members of my own family, especially to my parents and to my brother, Raymond, and sister, Ilona; their support has been crucial at critical junctures and has persistently endured. I also thank my wife, Ilona, whose devotion and forbearance were tested to the limit.

Those who painstakingly set up the archives of the British Psycho-Analytical Society know how appreciative I am for their assistance over the years. I would especially like to thank Pearl King and Jill Duncan, as well as Riccardo Steiner, not only for his sweeping introduction to this volume, but for his acute sense of what was missing in an earlier version of my manuscript.

Special mention goes to the heads of the other key repositories of the documented history of psychoanalysis, most notably David Newlands during his tenure at the Freud Museum, London, and the chiefs at the Manuscript Division of the Library of Congress, Washington, D.C., and the Sigmund Freud Archives in New York.

John Bowlby made a deep impression on me during the several occasions on which we exchanged views, and his penetrating insights have helped structure my own thinking in regard to Freud and Jones, as have the spoken and written words of John Forrester, Darius Ornston, Sander Gilman, Martin Stanton, Gerhard Fichtner, Albrecht Hirschmüller, Ernst Falzeder, Judith Dupont, and Alain de Mijolla, all of whom I acknowledge with the deepest respect.

I also extend sincere thanks to my associates at the University of Toronto, especially Charles Hanly of the Department of Philosophy and Trevor Levere, Connie Gardner, and Pauline Mazumdar of the Institute for the History and Philosophy of Science and Technology.

For funding during the various stages of this project, I thank the Fellowships Division of the Social Sciences and Humanities Research Council of Canada. I also appreciated the efforts of those who facilitated my affiliation with various academic institutions, in particular William F. Bynum of the Wellcome Institute for the History of Medicine.

My tenure at McGill University between 1987 and 1991 was especially fruitful and provided an environment that enabled me to deal effectively with the difficulties that invariably arise in a project of this scope. Special mention goes to Donald Bates of the Department of Humanities and Social Studies in Medicine, Faculty of Medicine, and Faith Wallis and her staff in the Osler Library, as well as the research assistants Fiona Murray and Elsbeth Heaman.

I also benefited greatly from utilizing the resources of various institutions in North America and would like to express my appreciation to all those who helped smooth the way to the relevant documents. In the United States I examined material in the Rare Book and Manuscript Library, Butler Library, Columbia University; the Abraham A. Brill Library, New York Psychoanalytic Institute and Society; the New York State Psychiatric Institute Library, New York; the Houghton Library, Harvard University; the Francis A. Countway Library of Medicine, Harvard Medical School; and Clark University Archives, Worcester, Massachusetts. In Toronto I made use of the archival repositories of the University of Toronto, Queen Street Mental Health Centre, Public Archives of Ontario, Clarke Institute of Psychiatry, and the Toronto General Hospital.

The editors and staff of Harvard University Press have been patient, diplomatic, and exceptionally professional. I thank them all for their insights, patience, and their commitment up to the end.

I also wish to express my deep gratitude to everybody else who in one way or another collaborated in the effort that has culminated in the completion of this volume: Elaine Iles, Celia Hirst, Ramunas Kondratas, B. W. Powe, Murray Hall, Lorenz Jung, Clifford Scott, Edward Timms, Albert Dickson, Martin Lubowski, Keith Davies, Tom Roberts, Michael Molnar, Johannes Reichmayr, Ernst Federn, Ted Carlson, Konstantinos Arvanitakis, Eugene Taylor, John Kerr, Peter Swales, Sonu Shamdasani, Barbara Gerlecz, Rudi Käser, Andrius Valevicius, Maria Szlatky, Rhian Davies, Ellen Gilbert, Elizabeth Mercer, Sandy Pritchard, Remigius Satkauskas, Carl Aboud, Tarek Abdeh, Thierry van Biesen, Paule Chiha, Leslie Knight, Danuta Berger, Liliana Gedvilla, Christine Westover, Deidra Roberts, Kaarina Kailo, Eva Lester, Audra McManus, Marielle Berthelet, Isabelle

Clément, Renée Blondin, Alexendra Esmeralda Claudel, Justine Aten, and Iman Al Ghadban.

Finally, this awesome undertaking would not have appeared in its present form without the resolute and enduring dedication of Frauke Voss. Over the years she took on different roles as translator, researcher, colleague, and friend. Her commitment to the cause *(die Sache)* and her profound understanding of life and art have in great part provided the sustaining force that allowed me to present this volume in a framework that preserves, I think, the aesthetic and intellectual power of what Riccardo Steiner refers to in his introduction as the "still beating . . . pulse" of "one of the most vital and revolutionary movements that has characterized the cultural life of our century."

R. Andrew Paskauskas

Note on Editorial Method

ON BOTH SIDES of the correspondence, a letter or word in square brackets is added occasionally to correct a spelling error or to smooth out an awkward sentence.

In general, Freud's letters written in English appear as in the original, with all their errors and idiosyncrasies. Thus Freud's use of "adress" rather than "address," "advise" instead of "advice," and "narcisstic" rather than "narcissistic," for example, is maintained, as is his characteristic disregard for the use of apostrophes; although it may be worth noting that Freud's preference for omitting the apostrophe from "dont" was perhaps not that unusual—indeed Leonard Woolf did as much in his own letters (Spotts, 1989). However, at times Freud employs constructions such as "didnt," "shant," "cant," and "dont" with an apostrophe appearing roughly above the mid-part of the word. In the present volume instances of this usage are treated as "did'nt," "sha'nt," "ca'nt," and "do'nt."

In Jones's handwritten letters one rarely finds mistakes in grammar, spelling, or punctuation. However, Jones frequently makes mistakes when employing German words or phrases, and his typed letters contain frequent typographical errors. Usually the addition of a letter within square brackets is enough to sort out the problems with the German. Minor mistakes in Jones's typed letters are often silently corrected. Jones also appears to have reread his typed letters and penned in corrections. These are sometimes noted if they reflect an important change of attitude, or display a possible moment of ambivalence.

Abbreviated words, expressions, and titles of books or journals are spelled out in many instances to facilitate readability. The "&" has been replaced by "and" in almost all instances except when it forms part of the title of a book or a company name. Where a special nuance or elegance is manifested by an abbreviation in a particular context, it is left intact, sometimes with an explanatory footnote. The frequently used Greek-letter abbreviation for psychoanalysis, for example, is preserved. Jones typically uses the lowercase ψα, except in some of the early letters; Freud uses both forms, but he prefers the uppercase ΨA.

Abbreviations for "Mister," "Mistress," "Doctor," "Number," or "volume," are employed in different ways by Freud and by Jones. Freud tends to omit the period; Jones often employs superscript letters which are underlined. The letters in numerical abbreviations are also frequently written in superscript by both correspondents. For this edition these forms have been regularized.

Words or phrases which were crossed out in the correspondence are in most cases placed within square brackets and identified by a note, as are additions in the margins or elsewhere outside the main body of text. Most ellipsis points appear in the original. At times either Jones or Freud may quote passages from external sources, in which case ellipses within square brackets indicate missing parts of the external text, and are accompanied by a note of explanation.

The Glossary contains a list of German words and expressions employed by Freud and Jones within the original context of an English sentence or phrase or retained in the translated letters. The Glossary includes psychoanalytic, editorial, and organizational terms. For the standard psychoanalytic terms, A. Strachey (1943) was used as a reference. But I also have taken into account the emerging literature on the problems of translating Freud (Bettelheim, 1982; Gilman, 1991; Junker, 1987; Ornston, 1982, 1985a, 1985b, 1992; Mahony, 1984, 1987; Pines et al., 1988; Steiner, 1987, 1991; Wilson, 1987). Thus some of the more controversial terms such as *Schaulust*, or *Besetzung* and its derivatives, are dealt with separately in the notes.

The German terms listed in the Glossary are not italicized in the text of the letters; for the most part neither are words or expressions quoted directly from Freud's German writings. Other German words or short expressions are italicized, as are words in languages other than English. Where appropriate, a translation is provided in either square brackets or a note. Lengthier passages in a foreign language are not italicized. Titles of books and journals are italicized, except in a few instances; for example, Jones's designation for the *Journal of Abnormal Psychology*, "Prince's Journal," is preserved but distinguished from the "Journal," his manner of referring to the *International Journal of Psycho-Analysis*, by the use of italics, as "*Journal*."

Dates at the head of letters have been standardized. The printed letterheads have been simplified. Freud's letterhead has been adjusted to "Vienna, IX. Berggasse 19." Freud sometimes wrote on stationery of the *Zeitschrift* or *Imago*. After the First World War, Jones frequently wrote on stationery of the British Psycho-Analytical Society, the International

Psycho-Analytical Association, and the International Psycho-Analytical Press. The letterheads of these operations usually include the business addresses of several key officers. In the case of these more elaborate letterheads, no addresses are given; the name of the organization and principal city alone appear at the head of the text of the letter, except on internal memos in which case neither address nor city name is provided.

The salutations of both correspondents in the present volume are followed by a comma, although Freud was accustomed not to use any punctuation at all in his opening, and Jones used variably a period, colon, or comma. Some of Jones's typed letters from December 1930 on contain handwritten closing phrases as well as his signature; these, however, are noted only in few cases.

The list of references at the end of this volume contains the most important books and articles cited or referred to in this volume. In the correspondence, if a work is mentioned only once by either author it usually does not appear in the list of references, but is cited in full in the appropriate note. Freud's writings and Jones's are listed separately. The dating scheme for works by Freud follows that of the *Standard Edition*, where more complete information about individual items can also be found. Apart from Jones's neurological papers and the pieces on applied psychoanalysis (Jones, 1923a, 1951), many of his articles can be found in the various editions of his *Papers*.

Throughout this correspondence there are frequent references to letters between Jones or Freud and other individuals. Wherever these references are of historical import to the issues at hand, every attempt has been made to deal with them in a note. In many cases, however, further information was not readily available because of restrictions on material in various archives, or because the material was no longer extant. The most important of these unpublished documents—such as the *Rundbriefe* and the correspondence among individual analysts (Jones, Freud, Carl Jung, Sándor Ferenczi, Karl Abraham, Max Eitingon, Otto Rank, Hanns Sachs, and Anna Freud)—can be found in the archives of the British Psycho-Analytical Society, London; the Freud Museum, London; Sigmund Freud Copyrights, Wivenhoe; Rare Book and Manuscript Library, Butler Library, Columbia University; and the Library of Congress, Washington, D.C.

The List of Correspondence contains information about the format of each item. Unless otherwise indicated, the letters between Jones and Freud were either handwritten or typed, and in most cases were signed by the authors. In some instances Jones's letters were initialed or signed in his name by a secretary. When Freud wrote in English he used Latin characters. When he wrote in German he preferred using Gothic script. But, since Jones could not read Gothic script, Freud also resorted to using Latin characters when writing in German. In a few instances Freud began a letter in Gothic, then caught himself and continued in Latin characters; openings of this sort are identified in the notes. Freud's typed letters were usually dictated to Anna Freud. Jones almost invariably, for reasons explained in letter 26, underscored his signature at the end of each letter with a symbol that stood for his younger sister Sybil:

Abbreviations of Works Cited

Alltagsleben	Freud (1901b)
Bruchstück	Freud (1905e)
Collected Papers	Sigmund Freud, *Collected Papers*, trans. under the supervision of Joan Riviere, intro. Ernest Jones, 4 vols. London: Hogarth Press and Institute of Psychoanalysis, 1924–1925.
C.W.	*The Collected Works of C. G. Jung*, ed. Sir Herbert Read, Michael Fordham, Gerhard Adler; exec. ed. William McGuire, trans. R. F. C. Hull. Bollingen Series XX, 20 vols. Princeton: Princeton University Press, 1967–1978. London: Routledge and Kegan Paul, 1953–1978.
Das Ich und Das Es	Freud (1923b)
Drei Abhandlungen	Freud (1905d)
Fünf Vorlesungen	Freud (1910a)
Gradiva	Freud (1907a)
G.S.	Sigmund Freud, *Gesammelte Schriften*, 12 vols. Leipzig: Internationaler Psychoanalytischer Verlag, 1924–1934.
G.W.	Sigmund Freud, *Gesammelte Werke*, ed. Anna Freud, in collaboration with M. Bonaparte, E. Bibring, W. Hoffer, E. Kris, and O. Isakower, 18 vols. London: International Psycho-Analytical Press; and Frankfurt am Main: S. Fischer Verlag, 1940–1952, 1968.
Ich-Analyse	Freud (1921c)
Illusion	Freud (1927c)
Imago	*Imago: Zeitschrift für Anwendung der Psychoanalyse auf die Geisteswissenschaften*, ed. Otto Rank and Hanns Sachs.

Jahrbuch	*Jahrbuch für psychoanalytische und psychopatholo-gische Forschungen*, ed. C. G. Jung, directed by E. Bleuler and S. Freud.
Jenseits	Freud (1920g)
Journal	*International Journal of Psycho-Analysis*, ed. Ernest Jones.
Krankengeschichten	Freud (1905e, 1909b, 1909d, 1911c, 1918b); *Collected Papers*, 3
Laienanalyse	Freud (1926e)
Leonardo da Vinci	Freud (1910c)
Letters	*Letters of Sigmund Freud*, selected and ed. Ernst L. Freud, trans. Tania and James Stern, intro. Steven Marcus. New York: Basic Books, 1960.
Massenpsychologie	Freud (1921c)
Metapsychologie	Freud (1915c, 1915d, 1915e, 1917d, 1917e); Grubrich-Simitis (1987)
Minutes	*Minutes of the Vienna Psychoanalytic Society*, ed. Herman Nunberg and Ernst Federn, trans. M. Nunberg. Vol. 1: 1906–1908, vol. 2: 1908–1910, vol. 3: 1910–1911, vol. 4: 1912–1918. New York: International Universities Press.
Neue Vorlesungen	Freud (1933a)
Papers	Ernest Jones, *Papers on Psycho-Analysis*, 1st ed., London: Baillière, Tindall and Cox, 1913. 2nd ed., London: Baillière, Tindall and Cox, 1918, 1920; New York: William Wood, 1918, 1919, 1920; and Toronto: Mac-Millan, 1918. 3rd ed., London, 1923; New York, 1923. 4th ed., London, 1938; Baltimore: William Wood, 1938. 5th ed., London, 1948; rpt. Maresfield Reprints, 1977; Baltimore: Williams and Wilkins, 1948, 1950.
Sammlung	Sigmund Freud, *Sammlung kleiner Schriften zur Neurosenlehre*, 5 vols. Leipzig: Deuticke, vol. 1, 1906, 1911, 1920, 1922; vol. 2, 1909, 1912, 1921; vol. 3, 1913, 1921; Leipzig: Heller, vol. 4, 1918, 1922; Leipzig: Internationaler Psychoanalytischer Verlag, vol. 5, 1922.
Schriften	*Schriften zur angewandten Seelenkunde*, a monograph series, ed. S. Freud.
S.E.	*The Standard Edition of the Complete Psychological Works of Sigmund Freud*, trans. James Strachey in collaboration with Anna Freud, assisted by Alix Strachey and Alan Tyson, 24 vols. London: Hogarth Press and Institute of Psycho-Analysis, 1953–1974.

Selbstdarstellung Freud (1925d)

Sextheorie Freud (1905d)

Studien Freud (1895d)

Traumdeutung Freud (1900a)

Vorlesungen Freud (1916–17)

Witz Freud (1905c)

Zeitschrift *Internationale Zeitschrift für ärztliche Psychoanalyse*, ed. Otto Rank, Sándor Ferenczi, and Ernest Jones.

Zentralblatt *Zentralblatt für Psychoanalyse: Medizinische Monatsschrift für Seelenkunde*, ed. Wilhelm Stekel (and Alfred Adler).

Introduction

by Riccardo Steiner

"NOW FOR A GREAT SURPRISE: among the English contingent there was a young man from London, Dr Jones (a Celt from Wales!) who knows your writings very well and does psychoanalytic work himself. He will probably visit you later. He is very intelligent and could do a lot of good" (McGuire, 1974, p. 86). Jung wrote these words to Freud on 11 September 1907 from Zurich, on arriving home from the Premier Congrés International de Psychiatrie, de Neurologie, de Psychologie et de l'Assistance des Aliénés. Freud replied on 19 September from Rome, where he was holidaying, with a certain haughtiness, as if Jung's account went entirely without saying: "The Celt who surprised you is certainly not the only one; before the year is out we shall hear of unexpected supporters and you will acquire others at your flourishing school" (McGuire, 1974, p. 88).

Jones had been discussing with Jung the possibility of organizing a congress on psychoanalysis in Salzburg. Replying from Vienna to another of Jung's letters extolling Jones's human virtues and enthusiasm, Freud adopted a slightly different tone: "Your Englishman appeals to me because of his nationality," he wrote, adding, "I believe that once the English have become acquainted with our ideas they will never let them go" (McGuire, 1974, p. 102). For the founder of psychoanalysis, the pure chance of being able to add a Welshman like Jones to the still threadbare ranks of his non-Viennese followers constituted an opportunity to project his ideas into English culture and find roots for them there, enabling him to become part of a world he had loved since his youth.

In 1908 Jones headed for Canada, where in October he would take up a post at the University of Toronto, seeking his academic and professional fortune after a brief but by no means easy or uneventful career in medicine and neurology in London and several months spent studying with Jung at the Burghölzli in Zurich. He visited Freud with A. A. Brill, a psychiatrist psychoanalyst already resident in New York, on 30 April 1908, just after the first Congress of Psychoanalysis held in Salzburg on 27 April. There, among other things, and in spite of his complete lack of personal experience in psychoanalysis, Jones had delivered a paper entitled "Rationalisation in Everyday Life" (Jones, 1908d). "Rationalisation," the neologism Jones coined for the occasion, would later enjoy great currency in the technical language of psychoanalysis.

It was at Salzburg that Jones had been able to see and listen to Freud in person for the first time. Freud had presented a paper on the "Rat man" (Jones, 1955a, p. 42; 1955b, p. 47), and significantly, in light of his exchange with Jung quoted above, he remarked that, judging by the shape of his head, Jones certainly did not seem English. Wasn't he Welsh? (Jones, 1959, p. 166). In the course of this first congress Jones had also been able to meet Alfred Adler, Karl Abraham, Wilhelm Stekel, and Sándor Ferenczi, among others, and even to perceive a noticeable tension between Jung and Abraham (Brome, 1983, pp. 53–55).

The meeting in Vienna between Freud, Jones, and Brill is described by Jones both in his autobiography, *Free Associations* (1959, pp. 168–169), and in his biography of Freud (Jones, 1955a, pp. 45–46; 1955b, pp. 50–51). It was by no means an easy encounter, in spite of Jones's enthusiasm for Freud, whom he had also had the chance to admire, surrounded by his closest associates, at one of the famous Wednesday meetings in the Berggasse on the occasion of Freud's birthday, 6 May 1908. Freud was at the height of his physical strength, having just reached fifty, and in good spirits because of the recognition his work was beginning to elicit. At their meeting they discussed how to disseminate psychoanalysis in America, but more specifically how Freud's works and technical terminology should be translated and to whom their official translation should be entrusted. Notwithstanding Jones's positive statements about Brill, at that time Freud's favorite, it is not hard to find in this meeting the first hints of the rivalry between the two that emerged shortly afterward, which Freud for a time attributed to Jones (Steiner, 1987b, pp. 57–60; 1991, pp. 385–386). More than a hint of this perplexity and awkwardness can be found in a letter, dated Vienna, 3 May 1908, which Freud wrote to Jung during the days of Jones and Brill's visit: "Jones and Brill have been to see me twice. I have arranged with Brill for the translation of a selection [*Selected Papers on Hysteria*] . . . Jones is undoubtedly a very interesting and worthy man, but he gives me a feeling of, I was almost going to say, racial strangeness. He is a fanatic and doesn't eat enough. 'Let me have men about me that are fat' says Caesar etc. He almost reminds me of the lean and hungry Cassius. He denies all heredity; to his mind even I am a reactionary. How, with your moderation, were you able to get on with him?" (McGuire, 1974, p. 145).[1]

In this light, it is worth recalling the comments Freud sent shortly afterward in another letter to Jung, who had lost his initial enthusiasm for Jones because he seemed to have grown uncertain about psychoanalysis in the course of those months. On 12 July 1908 Jung had called Jones "an enigma . . . an intellectual liar (no moral judgement intended), an adulator and an opportunist" (McGuire, 1974, p. 164). Freud replied to Jung with words that, curiously enough, are reminiscent of something Freud had written in one of his many famous letters to Abraham:[2] "I thought you knew more than I about Jones. I saw him as a fanatic who smiles at my faint heartedness and is affectionately indulgent with you over your vacillations. How true this picture is, I don't know. But I tend to think that he lies to the others, not to us. I find the racial mixture in our group most interesting; he is a Celt and consequently not quite acceptable to us, the Teuton and the Mediterranean man" (McGuire, 1974, p. 165).

In order to introduce the reader to the complexity of the Freud-Jones correspondence, I have sought to emphasize some details that slightly antedate the beginning of the exchange of letters between the two, many more of which could be found in the letters between Freud and Jung, Freud and Abraham, and in the unedited letters, such as those between Freud and Ferenczi. Even today they are indispensable if we are to reconstruct not merely the times and places, but more especially the ways in which the relationship between Freud and Jones became established, together with the complicated professional and personal links that are so prominent in these letters and in which their first meeting played such a fundamental role. Indeed, in Vienna the two men had the chance to meet and speak personally and at length for the first time.[3] Setting aside the contrast between the genius of Freud, the "conquistador" of the unconscious, and the ingenuity of Jones, who was to become its most astute and institutionally successful "entrepreneur," at least as regards the first generation of Freud's followers, we must not overlook the more than twenty years that separated them. They undoubtedly shared certain scientific interests and fascinations: Jones knew all of Freud's most important works on neurology and had read with immense enthusiasm Freud's early psychoanalytical publications. These he had discovered and devoured with his friend Trotter in London at the turn of the century, at least according to his autobiography (Jones, 1959, pp. 159–160; but see Paskauskas, 1988b, pp. 110–115), despite his patchy German—which he would improve over the years. Later, Jones and Freud would discover common intellectual passions, such as their interests in Napoleon and Shakespeare. Nevertheless, there were differences, both personal and cultural, deriving from their very different backgrounds but also from their differing literary, scientific, and sociocultural milieux. As has often been pointed out, Freud's was a culture far broader and less polarized around the medical sciences than that of Jones, and

Freud was far more familiar with English culture than Jones was with the German and Austrian world, as Jones himself was the first to admit. Yet let us not misunderstand: Jones was anything but lacking in culture. Although his upbringing was provincial and his petit-bourgeois family by no means intellectual, he had been able to study, was intelligent and capable, and had achieved excellent results, especially in the natural sciences; he could also boast a thorough knowledge of Latin and a smattering of Greek. As a boy, and later at university in Cardiff and London, he had worked his way through Charles Darwin and Thomas Huxley (who was to influence him greatly), as well as utilitarian philosophy, John Stuart Mill, and even W. K. Clifford and Karl Pearson (Steiner, 1987b, pp. 54–57), the major socialist works, and writers such as Charles Dickens, George Bernard Shaw, H. G. Wells, and so on (Jones, 1959, p. 35; Brome, 1984, pp. 158–159; Steiner, 1987b, p. 87).

But there can be no doubt that the far broader humanistic culture that typified the German-speaking countries of the period, as well as the ingenuity with which Freud and some of his followers were able to use it, must have made itself felt from the outset. In terms of the culture that was typical of the Jewish minority to which Freud and the other pioneers of psychoanalysis belonged, Jones adapted himself quite well, to the extent that he was able to remember and relate any number of the Jewish anecdotes and jokes so dear to the Viennese. There is, then, ample testimony to Jones's ability as a Welshman, and hence himself a member of a minority, to empathize with the problems of adjustment and integration and, at the same time, with the desire to maintain autonomy that characterize both cultural and racial minorities (Gay, 1978, pp. 101–120; Gay, 1987, pp. 117–154; Klein, D., 1981, pp. 40–102). One could perhaps claim that there had almost been an element of seduction in Freud's tone when, at their first meeting, he had pointed out that Jones was a Welshman and not an Englishman, as if to imply "you are a bit like one of us." But it was Jones himself who confessed much later that what had most struck him about Freud and the Viennese from the first, apart from their somewhat informal dress, was their quoting of "Latin and Greek passages by memory during their conversations and being astonished at my blank response" (Jones, 1959, p. 35).

Curiously enough, in spite of these signs of uncertainty and ambivalence toward Jones, which both Freud and Jung harbored and which can also be detected in this correspondence, we recognize that they had been right to find in the young Jones a marked tenacity and a potential devotion to the cause of psychoanalysis. But the uncertainty and ambivalence tell us something else as well. They seem to condense into nuclear form the development of the relationship between Freud and Jones revealed in these letters.

Indeed, in Freud's perceptive grasp of Jones's pragmatism and realism, as well as in their April 1908 encounter in Vienna, occur the first signs of the nature of the entire debate surrounding the strategy and direction of the dissemination of psychoanalysis in the English-speaking countries and elsewhere that would constitute one of the most important themes of the long collaboration between them. Furthermore, bearing in mind the complex network of letters between Freud and Jung, Abraham, and Ferenczi, Freud's attempts to walk the tightrope of conflicting loyalties, and Jones's subsequent appearance on the scene, we have it on the authority of Vincent Brome, in the absence of Jones's early letters to Jung and Abraham, that Freud asked Jones to mediate between them in an attempt to achieve peace immediately after the Salzburg Congress (Brome, 1983, p. 55).

Overlooking for the moment the evident rivalry between Jones and Brill, one thing is clear: the explosive mixture of, and at times enormous confusion between, scientific, professional, and personal relationships caused by the emotional tempests surrounding Freud's varying role in his first circle of followers, on the one hand as leader of the ensemble and on the other as therapist of some but not all of his colleagues. This was to constitute a leitmotiv not only of the Freud-Jones correspondence but of all the collections of letters between Freud and the other great pioneers of psychoanalysis. Jones, in point of fact, was never personally analyzed by Freud. In any case, the personalities of each of these individuals, and the emotional difficulties each of them felt with respect to Freud, also played a leading role. In addition to those already mentioned, we shall meet, in the course of these letters, Alfred Adler, Sándor Ferenczi, Anna Freud, Karl Abraham, Melanie Klein, Otto Rank, Theodor Reik, Joan Riviere, John Rickman, Hanns Sachs, Wilhelm Stekel, and Alix and James Strachey, to mention some of the most important names. At times, then, we shall bear witness to a veritable deluge of transference and countertransference responses in both Freud and Jones, based at one moment on feelings of paternal affection and protectiveness in Freud and admiration and filial devotion in Jones, and the next on Freud's need to keep his distance or on Jones's half-confessed need for possession, that is, for exclusivity in his relationship with Freud, as well as his often fierce competitiveness and rivalry toward his colleagues and less manifestly toward Freud himself. To make matters worse, these emotions were often difficult for them to understand and control, especially in view of the theoretical and clinical development of psychoanalysis during those years, when, for example, there was as yet no clear awareness of the role played by the maternal figure or of psychotic anxieties in the transference (Roazen, 1974, pp. 345–361; Steiner, 1985, p. 37; Gay, 1988, pp. 103–245).

Another thirty years, the period of time covered by this correspondence, would pass before the man Freud dubbed "der Celt," who had at first raised so many reservations and so much suspicion, would bring one of Freud's adolescent dreams to fruition: that of coming to live in England. Indeed, as these letters suggest—and the letters exchanged with Anna Freud confirm—it was Jones who persuaded Freud to leave Vienna in June 1938 and take refuge with his family in London, where, on 19 September 1939, he would die. It was Jones who greeted him at Victoria station in London and drove him "through the beautiful city of London to our new house at 39 Elsworthy Road," as Freud wrote to Max Eitingon on 6 June 1938 (Letters, p. 41), although his words were marked by a caustic bitterness at having to abandon Vienna and face the uncertainties surrounding his future, an old man by now, irremediably ill and close to death. These, I repeat, are the years covered by the correspondence collected here. Indeed, the more than seven hundred letters exchanged by Freud and Jones cover a longer period of time than the correspondence between Freud and any of his other collaborators of the first generation.

From the first months of his stay in Canada and then in the United States, Jones sustained an intense correspondence with Freud, writing almost invariably in English, with a few rare exceptions. Freud, as was his custom (E. L. Freud in Letters, pp. ix–x), and as Martin Freud (1957, p. 45), Hanns Sachs (1945, pp. 91–93), Martin Grotjahn (1967, pp. 13–18), Peter Gay (1988, passim), and Alain De Mijolla (1989, pp. 9–48) remind us, replied promptly, by return of post, making use of moments of repose, evenings, nights, and weekends when, robbing himself of sleep or interrupting his theoretical writings, he would reply to his many correspondents, whose numbers would grow immensely as the years passed. His early letters are sometimes in English and sometimes in German, handwritten and often in Gothic script. As time went by, however, he wrote increasingly in German. At first Jones too wrote by hand, although later many of his letters were typewritten. Interestingly, perhaps because they were aware of the value of their correspondence, the two authors kept nearly all of the letters. As far as we know they have not been destroyed or lost in any great number, as is the case with letters from Freud's other correspondences, for instance, with Fliess. What is more, although Freud destroyed traces that would have been of great help to his future biographers, as we know from his letter to his wife (24 April 1885 in Letters, p. 152) and from the disappearance of many of his manuscripts, he was not the only one; Jones confessed to Freud that he had done the same regarding certain events of his youth (Jones to Freud, 14 October 1913).

The letters published here have been translated, where necessary, from German to English and edited with great care, dedication, and learning by Andrew Paskauskas. He has spent many years in research, by no means straightforward, given the complexity and breadth of the matters they address.[4]

Indeed, the reader must constantly bear in mind that these letters embrace a period of time that was as intricate and dramatic as can be imagined, not only for the nascent psychoanalytic movement, but also in terms of cultural and social history. Notwithstanding the particularity of the letters that constitute this volume, this broader background remains constantly pertinent. Jones's early letters, for example, come from the late Edwardian, imperial England of the first decade of the twentieth century, and from Canada and the United States, where echoes of enthusiasm for the conquests that pushed back the frontiers seemed only recently to have faded. The pragmatic openness of American culture to new ideas from the Old World, and hence to psychoanalysis, is amply witnessed. In these same letters, however, one can sense, although it is hard to know with how much exaggeration (Paskauskas, 1988b, pp. 110–115), the dangers of the somehow superficial culture of the New World, not least in the fields of psychiatry and the newly ascendant psychoanalysis, where there was a tendency toward charlatanry and commercial gain on the part of the self-made American psychiatrist or psychoanalyst of the time (Jones to Freud, 10 December 1908, 7 February 1909, 19 March 1909; Burnham, 1967, pp. 128–134). All these are observations that were to find full support in Freud's well-known aversion to the culture of the New World (Gay, 1988, pp. 562–570). But it should not be forgotten that Freud's letters, in their turn, must be seen in their own context, illuminated by the last uncertain flickers of the Austro-Hungarian Empire, at this stage riven by all manner of insecurities and tensions under the aging Franz Josef I, and in the context of a Vienna in which Freud was beginning to reach the pinnacle of his fame and to enjoy his success while continuing to write and publish.

Jones's return to London in 1913 and the difficulties he encountered in disseminating psychoanalysis[5] and in his first attempts to found a psychoanalytic society signal his determination to create what in time would become one of the world's principal centers of psychoanalysis and lead to the establishment of the British Psycho-Analytical Society in 1919, the *International Journal of Psycho-Analysis* in 1920, and the International Psychoanalytical Library in 1921. Nor should it be forgotten that all of this was taking place against the backdrop of the First World War, which radically changed the layout of the states of Europe and whose impact was felt even within psychoanalysis itself, as the central European empires collapsed and the Russian revolution began. The reader need do no more than turn to the letters that refer to the conditions determining the development of psychoanalysis in England and in Austria and to the living conditions of the time and the difficulty of merely surviving, especially in postwar Vienna (Jones to Freud, 15 January 1917, 10 June 1919, 8 December 1919; Freud to Jones, 22 October 1914, 14 December 1914, 25 December 1914, 18 April 1919, 20 May 1919, 1 September 1919).

The general background, then, is an indispensable complement to the letters in this volume. As for the years up to the Nazi occupation of Austria and the flight from Vienna by Freud and his family and from other parts of Europe by many of his colleagues—this after the Berlin psychoanalysts had been compelled to flee in the mid-thirties—the letters speak for themselves. There are echoes, too, of the great depression that struck England during the thirties and of the successive political events that occurred during Jones's presidency of the International Psychoanalytic Association. He organized, for example, the emigration of Jewish psychoanalysts, first from Berlin after Hitler's rise to power and then from Vienna following the tribulations suffered by the Austrian republic and its fragile democracy. We also get some idea of the situation in which these psychoanalysts were living all over Europe and some notion of the difficulties psychoanalysis had to face in North America, where there were continuous disputes between medically trained and lay analysts. But at the same time, these letters, with their frequent and sometimes urgent invocations of the outside world, seem at times to want to be more than a private account of the personal details of Freud's relationship with Jones and vice versa, or a history of the psychoanalytical movement: they seem to want to draw the attention of their hypothetical reader to the many shapes and forms of the complex interactions between external and internal reality, between cultural, historical, and social facts and the theoretical elaboration of psychoanalysis as a system of research. They seem to tell us that the complex and multidimensional interactions of these factors must not be forgotten if we are to understand something of the specific nature of psychoanalysis and its development during those early formative years—as a discipline that was not only theoretical and open to scientific discussion but that was also applied literally, lived and acted upon with such freedom and sincerity, irrespective of its setting, and with such crudity that the ill-equipped reader as well as the professional analyst can at times be left perplexed.

Along with this dramatic picture of events, which I can only allude to in passing in order to suggest one interpretation, it is important to be aware of the play of factors linked to a history that is more modest and personal, more idiosyncratic, but no less important and interesting, in order to be able to understand and appreciate the human richness of these letters. I am referring above all to those references that allow us to grasp something of the habits of everyday life and of a very specific social context, which constitute precious clues to the understanding of certain aspects of the personal lives of these two pioneers of psychoanalysis and, given their stature, of the history of a certain sector of the European intelligentsia of the first forty years of this century.

In the first place, Freud and Jones were two professionals whose family commitments could be very demanding, especially in Freud's case, and they had to find time in which to write to each other. Jones, too, was a prodigious worker, and after analyzing eleven or twelve patients during the day, apart from his other obligations, he would attend to his correspondence from nine o'clock at night on, writing and studying or working into the small hours on his papers and the tasks related to the organization and management of the British Psycho-Analytical Society, the International Psychoanalytical Library, the *International Journal of Psycho-Analysis*, the translation of Freud's earliest works, and the supervision of the International Psychoanalytic Association (Jones to Freud, 24 January 1924, 28 October 1928).

Of course, there were none of the diversions afforded by a consumer society. It was the age, let us not forget, of fat fountain pens, the first mastodonic typewriters, the first telephones—a means of communication that, in Freud's case, was installed before the turn of the century—the radio, the cinema alongside the theater, the Orient Express, mail trains, and only in later years postal service by air. It is hard to say how much this communications technology, which seems so dated now, helped or hindered this avalanche of letters, which, except for the telegrams and telephone calls, depended for their timely delivery on the punctuality and speed with which the postal trains and the Orient Express crossed the Channel and Europe and on the efficiency of the K. und K. Post und Telegraphenamt in Austria (after 1919, the Post und Telegraphenamt) and the Royal Mail in England. They seem to have worked almost perfectly, to judge by the regularity with which Freud and Jones exchanged their messages.

The physical size of their letters, which rarely exceed eight pages, alone seems to give us the "internal dimension" of a definite epistolary style that allowed things it would be impossible to include in official documents and in printed works to be communicated (for example, certain judgments of colleagues or Freud's violent reprimands of Jones and his behavior) while certain other matters had perforce to be omitted or ignored. But it is also striking that external factors, such as the places where these letters were written, seem to reveal a geography and a toponymy, at the same time official and personal, of these crucial years in the history of psychoanalysis. The letters evoke the Vienna of the Berggasse and the London of Harley Street and, later, Regent Terrace; the places where the correspondents took their holidays—the country around Vienna, the Austrian lakes, the Italian Alps, or the cottage in Sussex that Jones bought at one point—but also the places they visited abroad, such as Sicily, Rome, Florence, Holland, Switzerland. It is as though we were turning the pages of an old album of fading photographs or following the tremulous rhythm of an old film through clues and reference to the roads that have become part of the mythology of the origins of psychoanalysis, the spas, the names of certain hotels and guesthouses, by now part of the memorabilia of the gossip hunters and those who study the personal history of Freud or Jones. All of this ultimately helps us to grasp the historical sense of the typically bourgeois domestic and professional universe that characterized both of these correspondents beyond their cultural and personal differences, but which was also, as I have suggested, the world of a certain Europe of the first forty years of this century, with its long visits to holiday resorts and "Grand Tours" of Italy after the not yet completely forgotten fashion of Goethe, Byron, Shelley, and other intellectuals, both German and English, who were fascinated by Rome and Tuscany.

Hence, how can one fail to recall in this context the almost adolescent pride of Jones as he announced to Freud that he was learning to operate a typewriter (Jones to Freud, 13 July 1911) or that he had just bought his "first" motorcycle and sidecar for touring England in the summer (Jones to Freud, 30 May 1916)? His pride may today make us think of the prehistory of communications. Or Freud's sense of calm achievement as he commented to Jones that he could allow himself a long holiday of two months or more with most of his large family in the countryside around Vienna (Freud to Jones, 13 August 1930), where we know that apart from writing, he continued to see his patients and was able to dedicate himself to one of his favorite activities, gathering mushrooms. There are certain other minute details these letters reveal that give us a sense of the passage of time in relation to the emotional history, the lives, and the physical health of the two correspondents, such as the hand cramps that prevented Freud from writing (Freud to Jones, 10 January 1910, 18 April 1919, 23 March 1922). Freud, as he had confessed to Silberstein in his youth (Freud to Silberstein, 30 July 1873, in Boehlich, 1990, pp. 27–28), felt compelled to write, and his correspondence at times can be seen as a sort of necessity in order to dispel boredom, the *horror vacui* to which life and the blank page itself seem, paradoxically, to have constantly led him.

And then there is the onslaught of those aches and pains, both small and not so small, like the attacks of rheumatism (Jones to Freud, 27 October 1928), that in Freud's case culminated after 1923 in the onset of cancer of the palate. Gradually, as he grew older, it affected the rhythm and volume of his correspondence with Jones, and in his last years he often left it to his daughter to attend to. The cancer, apart from the pain, would lead to frustrations that were both physical and psychical, such as, at times, the impossibility of smoking, which prevented him from thinking more freely (Freud to Jones, 2 March 1937). Undoubtedly all this could cause rivers of ink to flow among those who are interested in and have highlighted so insistently the presence of unconscious fantasies and drives in the very act of writing, in view of the sheer volume of this correspondence when it is added to the other letters they both, but especially Freud, had to write. One could discuss at length each individual passage and the unconscious identifications that mobilized for such a long period both sender and receiver (De Mijolla, 1989, pp. 37–41).

But without entering into the field of airy speculation and interpretation, this near-compulsion to write detailed day-to-day accounts of suffering great and small on which the two correspondents often seem to linger, when linked to the passing of the years, seems to render the history of this correspondence still more human precisely because it is the very materiality of the body that makes its presence and its voice felt, and in a way that can perhaps raise a smile among those accustomed to fax machines, word processors, and cellular phones. It is, then, only by bearing in mind the context and the network of echoes and allusions, and the events of history they invoke, as well as the very different personal histories of the two correspondents, that we can try to grasp the sense of these letters, which are clearly a veritable gold mine of news, judgments, information, projects, and initiatives above and beyond the personal portraits of some of the pioneers of the psychoanalytic movement. Apart from psychoanalysis as a scientific discipline, I would say it is "die Sache" (the thing, or the cause), as Freud called it more than once—that is, psychoanalysis as a movement requiring organization, and its aims—which emerges in all its importance, probably also because of the specific character and interests of Jones.

At this point, the matter I shall address may necessarily appear abstract or partial, and perhaps arbitrary more than anything else. Yet any attempt to arrange into themes and reading topics material that is characterized by and owes its vitality as much to a constant to-ing and fro-ing as to frequent changes of focus regarding themes, topics, and people and their sometimes inconceivable actions in the course of the same letter, or in a series of letters following one after the other, as if we were watching a sort of perpetual kaleidoscope, must be incomplete. This movement seems ultimately to be underlined by the stylistic freedom and the freedom of expression of the two protagonists, and the attention they granted to the news stories or questions that most interested or concerned them at the moment.

And yet, seen as a whole, these letters do indeed allow certain themes to be grasped and followed through time, and I shall try to suggest a few, although of course the reader is entirely free to select and follow others. One example is the many letters, and it is obviously impossible to quote all of them here, that bear witness to Jones's remarkable political and organizational abilities and the energy he put into them, his "Chinese rigidity," as Freud put it, expressing his ironic amusement (Freud to Jones, 27 July 1921), which drove Jones to an enormous, obsessive, and often authoritarian labor of control over and motivation of every part of the newborn British Psychoanalytical Society from 1919 onward, and to the desire to efface everything he had done prior to the First World War. One thinks of the letters in which Jones first managed to establish a relationship of almost exclusive trust with Vienna and with Freud, supporting the initiatives of the Internationaler Verlag, founded by the Viennese in order to fill the coffers of the Psychoanalytic Society of Vienna and the International Psychoanalytical Movement, which had been emptied by the financial disaster that followed the fall of the Austro-Hungarian empire. Then, one recalls the personal and political conflict between Jones and Otto Rank when Jones gradually succeeded in gaining autonomy from Vienna, publishing from 1920 the English version of the *International Journal of Psycho-Analysis* with Ballière and Tindall and from 1924 the International Psychoanalytical Library with the Hogarth Press, even as he managed at the same time to guarantee an increasingly privileged role for the British Psycho-Analytical Society with Vienna.

At the center of this extremely well-handled cultural operation was the skill with which Jones succeeded in persuading Freud, who was not without some misgivings and confusion, an echo of which can be found even in the letters written in the late twenties and early thirties, to concede him exclusive English translation rights to his works. Most of these had not yet been translated by Brill in America, and Jones's actions therefore undermined Brill's position, already weakened by personal problems, as Freud's sole English translator. Jones's reactions, which at times assumed tragicomic dimensions—as revealed in the letters in which he stalwartly defended the aims he envisaged regarding the rights of translation, even against Freud's own nephew, Edward Bernays, in America, whom Freud adopted as his translator (Jones to Freud, 27 January 1920)—constitute the basis of the Standard Edition of Freud's opus, which would be edited by James and Alix Strachey with the help of Anna Freud and Alan Tyson after the Second World War. But these very letters also show how the Standard Edition, in particular as a term referring to the works translated into English, was born in the twenties under the direction and control of Jones. He even translated parts of some of Freud's papers, as in the case of "Beyond the Pleasure Principle," while he directed and organized the famous Glossary of the technical terms of psychoanalysis based on Brill's first attempts, and those of Jones himself when he was still in America, to translate Freud's technical terms (Steiner, 1983; 1987a, pp. 187–189; 1987b, pp. 66–80; 1991, pp. 387–388; Paskauskas, 1988b, pp. 120–122).

When Jones first undertook this complex piece of cultural politics, he told Freud in one of the most human of all these letters, "You know that it is essentially for you that we are all working, which is why your inspiration and approval means so much to us all. If I can produce a Collected

Edition of your works in my lifetime and leave the journal on a soundly organized basis, I shall feel that my life has been worth living" (Jones to Freud, 10 April 1922). Jones of course could not have imagined what would happen in the thirties with the "new diaspora" of the Mitteleuropan psychoanalysts (Steiner, 1988), a result of the racial persecutions of the Nazis, which would make the English language and the Standard Edition the hegemonic language and text through which a great deal of the communication and scientific activities of the international psychoanalytic community would be channeled.

And yet the series of letters that speak of his initial efforts and Freud's responses, at first lukewarm but then increasingly receptive, to translating his works into English using the group of translators and colleagues under Jones's direction are enough to convey some sense of the acuity of Jones's intuition and of the vitality of this correspondence, but also of the differences of character and the inevitable dissymmetry in the relationship between Freud and Jones. For it is in this group of letters that we find, among other things, some of the most beautiful and amusing portraits of the young English psychoanalysts sent by Jones in the early twenties to be analyzed by Freud precisely in order to build up a body of translators who had direct experience of "the word" and "the Maestro." The Stracheys, Joan Riviere, John Rickman, and others emerge from these letters with a liveliness and a precision that, I would say, is made still more acute by the ambivalence and frequently the jealousy Jones felt toward them, and by Freud's benevolent and tolerant comments (Freud always being ready to defend and value highly those who had lain on the couch at Berggasse and who showed ability, irrespective of their personal problems, especially if they were ready to dedicate themselves to the psychoanalytic cause).

Here, once again, even if in epistolary form, Freud reveals his extraordinary gifts as a writer and humorist. I am thinking of some of his observations on the Stracheys (Freud to Jones, 12 October 1920, 7 February 1921, 14 July 1921, 9 December 1921), but in this context the letters on Joan Riviere are particularly outstanding. Jones's ex-patient, in Vienna under Freud's care, became at one stage something like a "displaced symptom" of Jones's problems. Freud defended her tooth and nail (Freud to Jones, 23 March 1922, 6 April 1922, 11 May 1922, 4 June 1922) and made her the subject of perhaps the most memorable portrait of this gallery of characters that suddenly emerges in three dimensions, breathing life into the trite details of news and the inevitable bureaucratic and administrative banalities with which the two correspondents had to busy themselves in Vienna and London.

Jones did not give up, although he was embarrassed by Freud's comments on his treatment of Joan Riviere, which also hint at a possible affair between Jones and Riviere during her treatment in London and reveal something of Freud's and Jones's approach to women and the world of the psychoanalysts, at that time still totally dominated by men. (Freud would revise his opinion of Riviere soon afterwards when she sided with Melanie Klein; see Steiner, 1985, p. 35; Hughes, 1991, pp. 23–24; Freud to Riviere, 9 October 1927, in Hughes, 1992.) At a certain point, almost intimidated by the warmth of Freud's support for Riviere and her work as one of the leaders of the team of translators, Jones accused her of being ignorant of medicine and of the technical terminology of psychiatry (Jones to Freud, 22 June 1922) in order not to lose the privilege of making all the necessary decisions and exercising full control from London over the translation of Freud's technical language into English. Through all of this, the competitiveness of the Welshman, who would write some interesting papers on female sexuality and character later on, seems to me quite clear. His most pathetic, infantile side is amply demonstrated in these letters and could be illustrated again in the case of the Stracheys and John Rickman, whom Jones seemed almost to fear on their return from Vienna and whom he constantly "supervised" in competition with Freud.

Indeed, Freud did not fail to notice these traits in Jones's character, which he too would have to negotiate later on in cases such as the conflict, only apparently administrative, between Jones and Otto Rank that led to the withdrawal of the British Psycho-Analytical Society from the Internationaler Verlag. Here, one can glimpse traces of that ill-confessed jealousy, reinforced by distance and by the privileged access of those in Vienna to Freud and his family, from which Jones felt excluded in spite of all his efforts—he went so far as to try to court the young Anna Freud when she came to England in 1914 (Young Bruehl, 1988, pp. 66–69). These personal problems reached such a point that Freud seemed almost to lose faith in his role as "pontifex maximus," as he had defined himself (Freud to Jones, 4 June 1922), attempting to achieve some sort of equilibrium between all these tensions and the intensity of Jones's more or less direct transference reactions, acted through the friends and colleagues who were in direct contact with him in Vienna, although it must be borne in mind that they too had a more or less unconscious interest in having Jones appear in an ambiguous light in Freud's eyes.

All of this, as I have said, was centered essentially on the question of translation, in which everyone seemed to stake a claim for a more or less "unique" and exclusive relationship with Freud. The letters that make up this correspondence constitute exceedingly valuable material for understanding the enormous and intricate jumble of personal, cultural, and institutional factors which characterized the project under Jones's direction, and which reflected the many difficulties psychoanalysis had to face at that time in order to establish itself in the field of medicine and

academic psychiatry and psychology in England, quite apart from the public of educated readers, whom Jones seemed to regard with much less
enthusiasm. One can find echoes of this problem even after the troubled
moments of the twenties, when Freud, highlighting, albeit with an ironic
tone, the need for elegance in English (Freud to Jones, 16 July 1920, 2
August 1920) started stalwartly defending James Strachey primarily, but
also his wife, Alix, Joan Riviere, and John Rickman as his preferred translators and as collaborators useful to the cause of nascent English psycho-
analysis (Freud to ones, 15 June 1921, 15 July 1921, 6 November 1921, 11
and 17 May 1922, 22 June 1922). Jones's preoccupation with his project
and with the leadership it would confer on English psychoanalysis (Jones
to Freud, 26 May 1922), as well as Freud's confusion, which stemmed from
his ignorance of the legal complexities of translation rights in England and
America (Jones to Freud, 20 June 1924), would also make themselves felt
later on.

But perhaps most interesting of all are the more or less conscious contributions in English made by Freud, who at times accepted the translations of his technical terms made by Brill, Jones, and the compilers of the
Glossary, for example, in his use of "ego" in his letter of 18 February 1919,
where he used both the English and the original German version of his
terminology; see also the comments exchanged between Freud and Jones
on how to translate "Es" or "Kultur" (Freud to Jones, 7 March 1926; Jones
to Freud, 11 March 1926; Freud to Jones, 25 August 1929; Jones to Freud,
5 April 1930). It should not be forgotten that, writing in English, Freud
several times used the word "soul" in its secular sense, corresponding to
the German *Seele* (to which, among others, Bruno Bettelheim [1983] has
called attention), raising a storm of polemic (Freud to Jones, 1 June 1909,
27 January 1910, 15 November 1912, 25 March 1914, 18 February 1919,
12 February 1920, 18 February 1928, 3 May 1928).

On the other hand, as I have mentioned, there is "die Sache"—"our
work," the movement, psychoanalysis as an institution and its defense at
the international, intersocietal level—which occupies so much of this correspondence (Jones to Freud, 2 April 1919; Freud to Jones, 3 April 1923,
22 December 1926; Freud to Jones, 2 June 1931). As Freud wrote to Jones
on 30 December 1925, in remembrance of the qualities Abraham brought
to psychoanalysis: "We must work on and keep together. No one can
personally replace our loss, but then for our work no one can be indispensable. I shall soon depart," he added, "the others, hopefully not until much
later, but our work must continue; in comparison with its greatness, all
of us put together are insignificant." And in the letters concerned with
this matter, the reader will find documented (Jones to Freud, 30 July 1912)
Jones and Ferenczi's famous plan to found a group restricted to those whom
Jones dubbed "Charlemagne's knights of psychoanalysis" (Jones to Freud,

7 August 1912) and to whom Freud would grant the famous "ring" as a mark of his appreciation for their loyalty and the bond that united them after 1912 (Freud to Jones, 1 August 1912).

For those already familiar with the complex relations between Freud and some of his students, as well as those who are less so, these letters furnish abundant information, together with the viewpoints of both Freud and Jones, on the events that led to the departure from psychoanalysis of Stekel (Freud to Jones, 28 October 1912), and then Jung (Jones to Freud, 18 September 1912; Freud to Jones, 22 September 1912, 5 December 1912, 8 December 1912; Jones to Freud, 29 December 1912; Freud to Jones, 1 January 1913; Jones to Freud, 4 November 1913, 9 January 1914, 29 September 1924) as well as, later, Otto Rank (Freud to Jones, 27 September 1926), culminating, after the death of Abraham (Jones to Freud, 25 December 1925), lamented by both Freud and Jones as their most loyal friend and collaborator, in the breakdown of the relationship between Freud, Ferenczi, and Jones (Jones to Freud, 15 January 1931; Freud to Jones, 13 June 1932; Jones to Freud, 9 September 1932; Freud to Jones, 12 September 1932; Jones to Freud, 25 May 1933; Freud to Jones, 29 May 1933; Jones to Freud, 3 June 1933). All of this is discussed over and over by the two correspondents, together with the thousand organizational misadventures and difficulties the psychoanalytic movement faced in the course of those years, which were vital for its survival and dissemination. Indeed, along with the internal tensions and the highly intricate play of projections, accusations, and jealousy, both conscious and unconscious, among his followers, as well as certain difficulties Freud himself encountered as he tried to negotiate their demands, given that he was by no means the most acute "Menschenkenner" at times (Brome, 1984, p. 45; Evans, 1964, p. 132), it is also important to bear in mind the objective difficulties psychoanalysis confronted during that time.

One thinks in this context of Jones's letters on Freud's sympathy for telepathy (Jones to Freud, 25 February 1926; Freud to Jones, 7 March 1926), which, he held, would compromise the image of scientific seriousness that was necessary to British psychoanalysis. This in the twenties was going through a process of integration into British medical culture that would culminate in the famous inquiry by the British Medical Association in 1928 to determine its degree of scientific credibility and the deletion in 1932 of Jones's name from the list of dangerous people (which also included that of Bertrand Russell) who could not speak on the BBC (Jones to Freud, 5 May 1932). Closely connected are the exchanges of opinion in the letters on the prickly subject of lay analysis (Freud to Jones, 25 September 1925; Jones to Freud, 23 September 1926, 18 July 1927; Freud to Jones, 23 August 1933), in which the reader will be able to see the differences in temperament and *forma mentis* between Freud and Jones, the former very much in favor of lay analysis, the latter ever concerned about the medical context in which the analysis had perforce to develop in England and America and politically more cautious. Yet it should not be forgotten that Jones himself went on to support Melanie Klein's arrival and the possibility of her practicing psychoanalysis in England—she, the lay analyst par excellence and without even a degree—as indeed he later supported Anna Freud, also a lay analyst with no degree, like several of the other refugees from Vienna and Berlin.

In these letters, Jones, who at first seems somewhat marginal, even provincial seen in the light of Vienna, often intimidated but at the same time deeply ambitious and tenacious and ready to accept Freud's reprimand, gradually begins to emerge until he appears as the dominant figure of the organization of the International Psychoanalytic Association, whose presidency he would hold from 1920 to 1949 with some long intervals.[6] Nor would I say that he emerges in these letters solely as an astute bureaucrat and executive, as he tends to be seen. One thing that is striking is his political intuition, which Freud often appreciated, for example, his judgments of Germany immediately after the First World War (Freud to Jones, 10 November 1918, 15 January 1919) and at the very beginning of the war (Jones to Freud, 3 August 1914), when he underlined the danger of the military fanaticism of the Prussians and discounted Austria (Jones to Freud, 15 November 1914), which in his opinion could no longer play a significant political role. Or, to cite another example, the pragmatism with which he would confront Freud over the American reality, because, according to Jones, in fifty years the Americans would hold the fate of the world in their hands (Jones to Freud, 29 September 1924). Or again, the speed with which he grasped the dangers Nazism would pose to psychoanalysis (Jones to Freud, 1 March 1933, 16 May 1933), even if, writing to Freud with a certain prudence given the latter's fragile health, he was by no means as explicit as in his correspondence with others (Steiner, 1988, pp. 35–37).

I have already referred to the events I consider to be Jones's diplomatic masterpiece and which revealed the depth of his generosity, that is, the rescue of the psychoanalysts from Berlin and then from Vienna in the late thirties, in spite of the ambivalence, the political compromises with the non-Jewish German analysts, and the uncertainties toward the German-speaking analysts he encountered even in England. Here, within the British Psycho-Analytical Society, Jones had to deal not only with the concerns of Melanie Klein regarding the arrival of the continental colleagues and "die Verdeutschung" of the Society itself (Jones to Freud, 23 February 1937); at the objective level, there were also the economic straits in which Great Britain was foundering at that time as it emerged from the Great Depression of the thirties (Jones to Freud, 10 April 1933), which made the lives of the refugees extremely difficult.

These letters allow us, in addition, to follow certain more specifically scientific and theoretical developments within psychoanalytic research, both in Freud's work and in that of Jones, quite apart from certain only apparently marginal curiosities, such as Freud's protracted interest in the historical investigations of Shakespeare and the various hypotheses surrounding his identity (about which Peter Gay has recently written some moving pages [1990], although Jean Starobinski's excellent essay [1970] should not be forgotten).

From this point of view, the opportunity to follow in detail the progress of Freud's elaboration of, for instance, "Totem and Taboo," which he then gave to Jones and Ferenczi to read and comment upon (Freud to Jones, 20 June 1913; Jones to Freud, 25 June 1913)—and which he discussed at the same time his letters were describing his difficult relationship with Stekel and, more imposingly, with Jung—is singularly instructive, not least because it shows us the strict links that at times connected the scientific and the extrascientific and personal reasoning behind Freud's work, leaving aside the possible speculations one might be tempted to make about Freud's relationship with his psychoanalytic children. It is almost as if the heretics of those years themselves represented a sort of primitive horde, incapable of accepting the tabu relating to the father, which could, however, stimulate Freud indirectly to consider the problem. And one could make further observations about other works: the essays "Leonardo da Vinci and a Memory of His Childhood" (1910c), "The Moses of Michelangelo" (1914b), "On Narcissism" (1914c); and the books *Beyond the Pleasure Principle* (1920g), *Inhibitions, Symptoms, and Anxiety* (1926d), *Group Psychology and the Analysis of the Ego* (1921c), *The Ego and the Id* (1923), *Civilization and Its Discontents* (1930a), and finally, *Moses and Monotheism* (1939a), which would be translated by Jones's wife and would lead Freud to write one of the most touching letters of his last years (Freud to Jones, 1 November 1938). One can find an echo of each of these works in the correspondence in one way or another, and I would say that the letters in which Jones, in his turn, discusses Freud's Lamarckianism (Jones to Freud, 1 August 1912) and, above all, those in which he expresses his objections to the death instinct (Jones to Freud, 6 September 1921, 1 January 1930, 2 May 1935), gave Freud the means by which to clarify his own thought, distinguishing between "Destructionstrieb" and "Todestrieb," a differentiation worth underlining in this context (Freud to Jones, 15 March 1935). But it is also possible to grasp Jones's scientific activity in action, from the essays on symbolism (Jones to Freud, 17 June 1913; Freud to Jones, 3 January 1914) and on Hamlet (Jones to Freud, 18 May 1909, 20 April 1910; Freud to Jones, 22 January 1911) to his ideas on female sexuality (Jones to Freud, 29 February 1920, 10 January 1932; Freud to Jones, 22 January 1932; Jones to Freud, 12 February 1932).

No moment in the course of this entire correspondence is more tense, more charged with conflicting emotions and with significance for the theoretical events of psychoanalysis and its development, however, than the letters that document the disagreement between Freud and Jones over the doctrines of the rising star of psychoanalysis in those years, Melanie Klein, who had moved to London from Berlin in 1925–26, after Abraham's death and with the support of the Stracheys and Jones, among others (Grosskurth, 1986, pp. 130–182; Meisel and Kendrick, 1985). Aside from the scientific side of the quarrel, we should not forget that Klein's ideas on infantile development contrasted with the views not only of Freud, but also of his favorite daughter, Anna, "my little daughter, the most gifted and accomplished of my children," as he has remarked some years before (Freud to Jones, 22 July 1914). Here, yet again, one can grasp almost physically the impossibility of distinguishing clearly, or rather of distinguishing absolutely, between the mixture of epistemological, personal, and emotional elements in play in the defense of certain principles in the field of psychoanalysis. It is as if the unconscious as the object of research were taking its revenge, making its presence felt as the subject, impossible to control with any assurance.

Perhaps in those particular letters it is possible to grasp one of the most dramatic moments of the entire relationship between Freud and Jones, where the ghost of Cassius seems to reemerge into full view as Freud, who would never descend to theoretical compromises, practically reproached Jones for betraying the sense of psychoanalysis as Freud and his daughter conceived of it by supporting Klein in London (Steiner, 1985, pp. 35–37). And after a brisk change in the ranks there were bitter words, too, for Joan Riviere (Freud to Jones, 9 October 1927), who had slipped out of Freud's control and whom Jones now defended against the founder of psychoanalysis (Jones to Freud, 18 October 1927) after she sided with Klein. Speaking not only scientifically but also from his innermost, most intimate feelings, Freud's fiery words culminated in the famous statement directed against those who, like Jones, held that Anna Freud had been badly analyzed and that it was for this reason that she could not understand the latest developments of Melanie Klein's psychoanalysis. This was a double-edged argument, Freud stated, and psychoanalysis used *ad personam* could not help to solve ideological disputes. And, for that matter, Freud concluded, Anna had been analyzed "more deeply and more thoroughly" than Jones (Freud to Jones, 23 September 1927), although he did not add that it had been he himself who had analyzed his daughter (Young Bruehl, 1988, pp. 80–90, 103–9).

It is interesting to follow Jones's response. On this occasion he managed to use with great sagacity the whole gamut of what one might call emotional, intellectual, and psychic shock absorbers before Freud's wrath, something he owed, as he put it in another letter to Freud, to his quick Celtic blood and quick reactions (Jones to Freud, 14 March 1923), in contrast to "the phlegmatic Anglo-Saxon temperament." In his defense of Klein, who had treated his two children, one can also perceive Jones's intention to claim, through the interest in the psychoanalysis of infants the British Psycho-Analytical Society had nurtured well before Klein's arrival in London (King, 1979, p. 282; 1983, pp. 254–255; 1991, pp. 17–19), the indigenous roots of English psychoanalysis as well as an indigenous identity from a scientific point of view, above and beyond the administrative sphere, independent of Vienna (Jones to Freud, 30 September 1927). "Our views in London," like "We in England," soon became Jones's motto (Jones to Freud, 30 September 1927, 10 January 1932, 2 May 1935), and the letters, read closely, show further moments of disagreement between Vienna and London. One instance is that of the famous lectures exchanged in 1935, 1936, and 1937 between London and Vienna (King, 1991, pp. 22–23) to clarify the divergences of their respective points of view. It is impossible not to think, in this context, of the letters of the thirties in which Jones and Freud discussed female sexuality, and Jones, using Klein's views although not directly referring to her by name, even if Freud at one point explicitly mentioned her, underlined the importance of the paternal figure in the early psychic development of the little girl, a fact Freud seemed to have obscured somewhat, Jones maintained, unleashing Freud's anger: how, indeed, was it possible that he of all people had forgotten the paternal role in the development of the little girl? (Jones to Freud, 10 January 1932; Freud to Jones, 12 February 1932).

Elaborating on this approach, one could undoubtedly say far more. There is something very striking in certain flashes of insight, certain observations thrown in *en passant*, apparently stimulated by something banal—a poor biography of Nietzsche, for instance (Freud to Jones, 4 June 1922). The reader could profitably consider Freud's argument when he cautions against finding solutions in a banal pathology for the complex problems posed for psychoanalysis by the great creators, especially when one thinks of the boom in attempts to apply psychoanalysis to the lives of philosophers, artists, musicians, and writers, as well as of psychoanalysts, to which the commercial greed of consumer culture and the narcissism of later "biographers" or critics influenced by psychoanalysis, who seek scandal everywhere, have accustomed us.

There is, however, a great deal more to be said about the personal relationship between Freud and Jones as it emerges from their correspondence. I have already referred more than once to the fact that the differences in age, and above all in culture and language, together with Jones's relative distance from Vienna and his particular creative gifts, which tended to lead him toward very practical ends, contributed to the creation of a sort of "safe distance" between them. The businesslike tone of many of these letters seems to forestall the most extreme, tragicomic, and sometimes even catastrophic convolutions that occurred from time to time between Freud and some of his other followers, who were in many respects closer to him and spoke and wrote in his language.

Nonetheless, one should certainly not pass over something Jones wrote toward the beginning of his relationship with Freud that could undoubtedly unleash a whole series of more or less legitimate psychoanalytic interpretations, especially if taken out of its historical and personal context: the passage in which Jones declared, "I am more responsive than initiative by nature and only work under an external personal stimulus" (Jones to Freud, 30 March 1910), to which he added in a letter dated 19 June 1910, "I feel it is more a sensible ideal to aim at developing one's own capacity in whatever direction that may lie than in trying to be 'original.' The originality complex is not strong with me; my ambition is rather to know, to be 'behind the scenes' and 'in the know' rather than to find out. I realise that I have very little talent for originality; any talent I may have lies rather in the direction of being able to see perhaps quickly what others point out: no doubt that also has its use in the world. Therefore my work will be to try to work out in detail, and to find more demonstrations for the truth of ideas that others have suggested. To me work is like a woman bearing a child: to men like you I suppose it is more like the male fertilisation. That is crudely expressed but I think you will understand what I mean."

In this regard one must also remember the amusing comments Jones sent in one of his first, reverent letters to Freud (Jones to Freud, 8 November 1908), in which he apologized for his almost insurmountable inability to read Freud's Gothic script, and the attempt by Freud, faced with a case of what he jokingly called "Alexia gotica" (Freud to Jones, 20 November 1908, 27 January 1910), to write in Latin characters or in English, which eventually resulted in those revealing notes on the fact that the impossibility of writing as he wanted in his own language blocked his ability to think ("All facility—inspiration is reserved for greater matters—deserts me at once." Freud to Jones, 20 November 1926).[7] Nonetheless, these minute details on Freud's preference for Gothic script might be interpreted as giving us the means of grasping a sort of "graphic container," as one might define his adoption of Latin characters in German or of the English language, which paradoxically contributed in its own way to that "safe distance" I have referred to, especially in light of his enjoyment of writing and the importance he accorded his correspondence. His capacity or incapacity to express himself in his "Muttersprache," both orally and in writing, learned during the first years of schooling, obviously helped or hindered him in gaining direct access not only to his inspiration but also to his emotions and to the connotative aspects of his language. None of this, however, detracts from the fact that these letters, even when written in Latin script or in English, bear witness to the clarity of Freud's judgments, whose sincerity leaves the reader shocked at times as well as impressed by the fact that Freud undoubtedly occupies the limelight.

Indeed, this collection of letters, like the other psychoanalytic collections of the period, could furnish a precious source for cultural historians and historians of ideas, and for those professional critics and biographers who are interested in the changes and transformations the epistolary style of European culture has seen over the years, according to the type of correspondents and the cultural and social milieu in which they lived and worked. Although it would clearly be possible to find similar examples of "sincerity" in many other letter collections (perhaps it is worth mentioning here the group of friends that surrounded Stefan George, Freud's contemporary), there is no doubt that the frankness that wild analysis could sometimes reach in these letters can give us some idea of its importance in the context of postal correspondence during those years, even if one must remember that it was a case of judgments and confessions exchanged between two professional practitioners of a discipline still in its infancy.

One might take as an example certain judgments of Jones's character, which Freud sent him and not only during the first years of their correspondence when their relationship still needed consolidating, which could well have led him to genuine psychic short circuits (Freud to Jones, 31 October 1909, 11 January 1910, 10 March 1910, 24 February 1912, 8 June 1913). Freud never hesitated to underline certain traits of Jones's character, even later on (25 June 1922, 6 November 1922, 7 January 1923, 9 October 1927). And one comes naturally enough to wonder just how far Jones's aggression ended up being displaced onto some of his colleagues, to the point of his being accused openly of anti-Semitism (Jones to Freud, 12 September 1923), through his fear of compromising his relationship with Freud, as in the lines (Jones to Freud, 21 June 1932) in which Jones refers to his "constitutional dislike, bred from schooldays, against referring to a senior authority difficulties and disputes with colleagues of one's own generation." Apart from his competitive relationship with Brill, Jung, and Otto Rank, one must bear in mind the quarrel with the Americans of the *Psychoanalytic Quarterly* (Jones to Freud, 2 June 1932, 21 June 1932) and his relationship with Ferenczi, which I have already alluded to, even if the letters also give us Freud's point of view, and not Jones's alone, on the Hungarian analyst and his last years (Roazen, 1974, pp. 356–371).

But if Freud, more than a "pontifex maximus," as I have said he sometimes liked to call himself, brings to mind an angry Jupiter launching thunderbolts, or the voice that judges and invokes what is written on the sacred tablets, in order to be able to guide or merely cope with Jones and his followers, he can also be seen at times, even with a vein of affable irony, to play the part of Cato the censor in relation to Jones. One need look no further than the letters regarding Jones's common-law wife, Loe Kann, in analysis with Freud during the years when the latter was beginning to get to know Jones and his work (for example, Jones to Freud, 17 October 1911; Freud to Jones, 14 January 1912, 24 February 1912, 8 November 1912, 8 June 1913; Jones to Freud, 6 November 1912, 29 December 1912, 11 June 1913). These were clearly not easy times for Jones: the most personal aspects of his private life were being subjected to detailed scrutiny through Freud's analysis of Loe Kann in Vienna (Paskauskas, 1988b, pp. 115–117), while he himself was dependent on ingratiating himself with Freud, intent as he was on his project of becoming the sole official spokesman for psychoanalysis in the English-speaking world. At the same time Jones spent some months in 1913 in analysis with Ferenczi, who discussed Jones in his letters to Freud. And Freud also had access to Ferenczi's private life (Dupont, 1989, pp. 190–193). Freud at times even went so far as to give Jones somewhat restrictive advice on the conduct of his sexual life (Freud to Jones, 14 January 1912, 14 January 1914, 8 February 1914), which Jones found particularly hard to swallow. He found himself in an embarrassing situation once again (Jones to Freud, 22 May 1922) on Joan Riviere's return to London after her stay in Vienna—but it should be remembered that Jones himself had in both cases asked Freud to analyze the women in question.

Nonetheless, in this prismatic relationship, there are unforgettable passages that reveal details, even if sometimes minute, of the warmth and humanity the two correspondents harbored for each other, which would gradually deepen their relationship. One thinks, for example, of Freud's reaction to the news of the birth of Jones's first daughter, Gwenith, who, sadly, would later die. Not only did Freud congratulate Jones, he also, like any good doctor, asked about the weight of the infant (Freud to Jones, 12 October 1920), having studied children as a young man in Vienna, and being an expert father with children of his own. Or one recalls the letters (Freud to Jones, 28 January 1921) in which, given the inflation and the weight of taxation in postwar Austria, Freud asked Jones's help and the use of his name in opening a bank account in Holland so as not to lose certain of his savings that he intended to leave his wife (Freud to Jones, 28 February 1921), although the operation, predictably, immediately became enormously complicated. Jones, on the other hand, in the aftermath of the First World War, was busy trying to help Otto Rank (Freud to Jones, 29 April 1920), who was in dire straits and whom Freud too had helped in his turn. And Jones (Jones to Freud, 8 December 1919) was able to send to Vienna several English patients who could pay fees no one living in the former Austro-Hungarian Empire could afford, thereby contributing substantially to easing the financial straits of Freud's family, which Freud recognized and for which he expressed his appreciation more than once (Freud to Jones, 8 February 1920).

That over the years the two enjoyed what was sometimes an affectionate friendship is attested by some rather disturbing confessions made by Freud, who, as time went by, became more open with Jones. I am thinking of the famous letters written after the death of his daughter Sophie (Freud to Jones, 12 February 1920), as well as others that reflect moments of profound sadness in the aging Freud (Freud to Jones, 7 May 1933), or the very human idiosyncracies surrounding, for instance, the subject of growing old (Freud to Jones, 11 January 1910), or relating to the celebration of his birthday, which he had at some stage begun to abhor (Freud to Jones, 21 July 1935).

From this point of view, some of the comments that Freud as an old man, and in a tone of detached fatalism, sent to Jones after the death of his aged mother (Freud to Jones, 15 September 1930), are truly "unheimlich." The letter in which Freud tried to console Jones after the death of his daughter is also extremely moving; in order to distract him, Freud immediately asked Jones to do some research on Shakespeare for him (Freud to Jones, 11 March 1928, 3 May 1928). These themes and motifs are less dazzling, but they allow the reader to follow the traces of a sort of epistolary dialogue of a more intimate, personal nature amidst the many letters devoted to official and bureaucratic matters.

It is certainly difficult to imagine Freud behaving toward Jones as he had toward Ferenczi and Jung, or to think of him writing Jones a letter starting "My dear Son and successor," as he had on 10 August 1910 to Jung.[8] Most of the time Freud limited himself to "My dear Dr Jones," "My dear Jones," or "Dear Jones." Jones almost always adopted a deferential "Dear Professor Freud" or "Dear Professor," although the ways in which the letters close might on occasion furnish some impression of the emotional state of the two correspondents, viewed within the constraints of those rhetorical and stylistic conventions that qualify definite conclusions about any writer's real intentions. In the face of all the varieties of difficulty, difference, and ambivalence I have been describing, one can perhaps conclude that, as far as this aspect of their relationship is concerned, the two could find in the practical action they undertook to promote the international psychoanalytical movement a foundation for their general approach and a healthy meeting point.

Jones helped Freud avoid the danger of letting psychoanalysis develop into a purely emotional matter linked only to the often unchecked emotional tensions within the psychoanalytic family in Vienna and Central Europe in those extremely delicate and precious years (Roazen, 1974, pp. 187–405; Klein, 1981, pp. ix–32, 138–154; Gay, 1988, 153–243; but see also Yerushalmi, 1991, pp. 41–43, and his views about what he calls "Jones's anti-Jewish bigotry," p. 54), and prevented it from becoming "a Jewish national affair," in the fraught expression Freud employed in a letter to Abraham dated 3 May 1908. Jones managed to fill the place of Jung, himself chosen by Freud precisely in order to avoid that danger, and Freud, in moments of tension between the two, sometimes tended to confuse Jones with Jung (Freud to Jones, 25 March 1914).

"We in London and Vienna must hold together; the other European groups hardly play a role and the centrifugal tendencies in our international are very strong at present," Freud wrote to Jones on 26 May 1935, at a time when both could see enormous threats to psychoanalysis brewing, threats that had political and social roots. Setting aside many other instances of mutual recognition and esteem (for example, the moving final letters of the correspondence, Freud to Jones, 7 March 1939; Jones to Freud, 3 September 1939), this seems to be the terrain on which their relationship, within the limits imposed by historical circumstance and personal capacity, yielded its greatest fruit.

In concluding this review of one possible reading of the letters between Freud and Jones, it must be remembered that their correspondence belongs to a moment in the history of psychoanalysis in which the relatively restricted number of adherents, with mainly male analysts in the key positions, the very nature of the men of science who came of age at the crossroads of the nineteenth and twentieth centuries, the often wild way in which they used psychoanalysis (one has only to think of *die Rundbriefe*), the frequently patriarchal and authoritarian methods adopted by them in order to manage the psychoanalytic movement, and many other factors in addition to the matters I have already discussed, serve to give us some sense of the distance that now separates us from them. In 1935, as preparations were being made for the occasion of Freud's eightieth birthday, the entire international psychoanalytical movement numbered hardly more than four hundred trained members, and the most important figures might still have been able to meet around a table, as they had in Freud's house during the first years of the Viennese Psychoanalytical Society. And yet, these little more than four hundred psychoanalysts left Freud quite perplexed as he thought of having to reply to all of them; by this stage he knew very few of them personally (Freud to Jones, 21 July 1935).

Today, in a global, social, and cultural context totally different from that of Freud and Jones, we can predict that within a few years the membership of the International Psychoanalytic Association will greatly exceed ten thousand, divided among a pleiad of societies, study groups, committees, and subcommittees, with enormous problems and ambitions and involved in political games related to the differences between schools, between orientations, and between languages and national cultures that are created by administrative procedures and by the requirements of control and internal democracy in such an elephantine organization and administrative machine, as well as by the specific emotional and ideological problems created by the transmission of psychoanalysis itself, its preservation inside and outside its institutions, and its relations with the medical and non-medical world.

What, then, is one to make of these letters, which document such a personalized relationship and seem to promise the possibility of being present, as if we were inside an extended family, at the birth of so many of the problems that have marked the history of psychoanalysis and the culture of our time? In view of the risk of depersonalization and anonymity run by an institutional apparatus like that of psychoanalysis today at every level, including very frequently that of local societies, these letters seem to reflect a world that should be left to the "laudatores" or "detractores" "temporis acti," as in some cases one might be tempted to qualify them.

Once their limits have been recognized, however, these letters are more than a simple curiosity to be left to the historians, as so many partisans of the "here and now" are often heard to say with an attitude of superior impatience, too often forgetting that the present emerges from the "then and at that time" and that one cannot speak of the future without coming to terms, implicitly and explicitly, with the past. The specific nature of psychoanalysis, the specific ways in which it is transmitted, and the importance the family history of each patient assumes in it seem, additionally, to give a particular value to the memory of and the traces left by the psychoanalytic family and its first members, because certain of the problems that came to light with them have since either been transmitted and matured, or have lost their earlier force or even disappeared with the physical disappearance of those who had generated them. But from all this it is possible to draw a series of salutary teachings as one learns to appreciate the merits or, indeed, to avoid the errors of even these two correspondents, something it is possible to do only by knowing them better.

The most profound lesson to be learned from these letters, then, is not to be found in miracle-working quotations from this or that letter, as if, because of the stature of the two figures concerned, it were a question of incontrovertible truths or judgments about facts or individuals, to be repeated with the attitude of the hagiographer as in the verse from Ecclesiastes, "Let us now praise famous men" (4:1), which at times tends to be transformed into "Let us now worship or belittle their famous words." The lesson we can draw from these letters should drive us toward further questioning of our present and future through the very activity of reconsidering our past, which must be seen in a problematic light.

Undoubtedly today, especially with the gradual disappearance of the

pioneers of the first generation of psychoanalysts, living documents bearing physical witness in their voices, above and beyond their texts, to a
certain code of psychoanalysis as it had been transmitted to them directly
by Freud and his circle of friends and colleagues, the need to have ever
increasing recourse to letters, archives, and documents of every sort, in
other words, to turn to writing, above and beyond the voice, for the memory of facts, events, and people, leads necessarily to increased dependence
on these traces. But more than incontrovertible truths, these letters must
be considered "monuments" (Steiner, 1988, p. 37), to use the word of a
glorious historiographical tradition, which require continued, attentive
interpretation. Among other things, in order to reach more certain or more
articulated results beyond the intrinsic importance of the points of view
expressed by Freud and Jones, it would be necessary to think of their
correspondence as being in strict contact with the whole range of their
other activities and writings, as I have tried to show through a few examples at the beginning of these introductory pages, in the context of the
entire corpus of letters exchanged by these correspondents with the other
protagonists named in these letters, or even with colleagues and friends
with whom they discussed topics and questions arising in this correspondence who are not mentioned (Fichtner, 1989, pp. 74–76). There is a great
deal of work to do, as is patent, which per se intimates the impossibility
of reaching any definite, "self-evident Truth" and above all implies the
impossibility of definitively fixing the two writers in one particular place
at one particular time. One cannot freeze them or pinpoint them in any
particular turn in their lives or in their actions or thoughts, nor in any city
or with any single view from their window. We always see them in motion,
carrying their lives, thoughts, tensions, and feelings from the past to the
present and into the future, even as they write.

These reflections are necessarily related to a series of more general considerations that are rooted in the experience of reading these letters. Any
correspondence, even the most sincere—and in the case of Freud and Jones
I have tried to draw the reader's attention to certain singular qualities
along these lines—is always the fruit of a stylistic blend of autobiographical detail and news, sometimes historical and even narrative, and of a sort
of social compromise. Behind the signatures of Freud and Jones, proper
nouns in all their social significance (Bourdieu, 1986, p. 69), despite their
nuanced emotions and the clarity of some of their epistolary exchanges,
are hidden countless aspects of their personalities, which they have chosen
more or less deliberately to obscure, disguise, model, or modularize, always
and inevitably thinking of whom they were addressing, with the idea that
the other constructed himself out of the person who wrote to him and that
the writer did not want the other to make himself out of him. If this is
especially tangible in Jones's case, it cannot be excluded in Freud's case

either (Gay, 1988, pp. 158–159). And then there arises the problem of their potential general readership.

In the case of Jones and of Freud too, in short, it is worth remembering that there is always a diffraction, a greater or lesser difference between the subject, or the various aspects of the subject who is thinking, speaking, and listening to himself, and the subject who writes and who passes from private to public dialogue. And the possibility of grasping all these different aspects of the subject in their entirety escapes us; we are reminded once again of their precariousness in this instance too by the white spaces between the lines, the margins of the pages, and the very number of pages, which in themselves, having been written on or, at times, not completely filled, have been folded and thus seem to bear witness to the intermittent nature of these messages and the frame of mind of the two correspondents. To quote Paul Valéry's "Mauvaises pensées et autres" referring to any attempt at biography, "le plus vécu de cette vie échappe" (Oster, 1989, p. 220) even in the case of those letters that dedicate a great deal of space to the correspondents' private lives.

And we should all be aware of the fact that to try to draw from these letters the key to a new and definitive hypothetical biography, which might give us the sense of "what really happened between them," would be rather like the illusion of confusing a layer of papier maché applied to the funeral masks of the two protagonists,[9] which makes their features even more stylized, with their true portraits, even if the commercial over-dose of archive information and biographical reconstructions with a psychoanalytical bent seems today to feed this illusion to the point of absurdity.

One thinks in this context of a story by Kafka, which some perhaps will find overly "uncanny" and exaggerated but which, used in its turn as a metaphor and with all due caution, expresses better than anything else the sense of the passage of time and distance that occurs between the hypothetical existence of a primum, the message of a primum—a full, immediate, original message—and she or he who is destined to receive it, bearing in mind the case of this correspondence. I am referring to the short story "The Great Wall of China" (Kafka, 1946, pp. 88–94), in which, at one point, the narrator reminds the reader that the size and the fragmentation of China is so great that the Emperor's subjects living far from Peking in the isolated villages along the Great Wall always receive messages out of synchrony with the Emperor's time. By the time the message reaches their village, the Emperor might well be dead, even if for them, so far from the Imperial Palace in Peking, he is very much alive. In our case, even though in our certainty of the physical passing of the two correspondents and of so much of the world in which they operated, we know that these letters speak to us from the past, the attempt to point out certain aspects to the reader should make us even more aware of the sense of distance that separates us from them. However, once all this has been recognized, along with the need to be able to interpret these letters in spite of all the risks and the need for critical caution, and the need for the humility that every intellectual endeavor of this type should imply, nothing keeps one from maintaining that in many of these letters the reader will be able to feel the still beating, even if intermittent, pulse of one of the most vital and revolutionary movements that has characterized the cultural life of our century.

I would like to thank P. Burke, Emmanuel College, Cambridge; J. Duncan, librarian of the British Psycho-Analytical Society; Professor S. Gilman of Cornell University; Pearl King, Honorary Archivist of the British Psycho-Analytical Society; M. Molnar of the Freud Museum, London; J. Mitchell Rossdale, London; Inge Scholz Strasser of the Sigmund Freud Gesellschaft, Vienna; and D. Toomey, London, for their help and advice. This introduction has been carefully edited by M. Rendell, whom I particularly wish to thank.

1. Freud played the part of Brutus in a reading cum recital of act 4, scene 3 of Shakespeare's tragedy *Julius Caesar* on 29 July 1871, while he was still attending the Leopoldstadter Communal Realgymnasium in Vienna (Freud, E. L., 1985, p. 64). Curiously enough, in a description of a dream in the *Interpretation of Dreams* (Freud, 1900a, p. 424), Freud identifies with Brutus's ambivalence before Caesar, in accordance with Shakespeare's rendering. He adds: "Strange to say, I really did once play the part of Brutus. I once acted in the scene between Brutus and Caesar from Schiller [Freud is referring here to Schiller's *Die Räuber*] before an audience of children. I was fourteen years old at the time and was acting with a nephew who was a year my senior. He had come to us on a visit from England." What is more, even if it can be interpreted in any number of ways, one of Freud's first impressions of Jones brought Shakespeare's play to mind, specifically the figure of Cassius; one might also add, by implication, Brutus. Both participated in the assassination of Caesar.

2. In an attempt to assuage Abraham's antagonism toward Jung by reminding him of their racial kinship, Freud had written: "Please be tolerant and do not forget that it is easier for you than it is for Jung to follow my ideas, for in the first place you are completely independent, and then you are closer to my intellectual constitution because of racial kinship, while he, as a Christian and a pastor's son, found his way to me only against great inner resistances. His association with us is the more valuable for that. I nearly said that it was only by his appearance on the scene that psychoanalysis escaped the danger of becoming a Jewish national affair" (Freud to Abraham, 3 May 1908; Abraham, 1965, p. 34).

3. According to Vincent Brome, (1984, p. 26), they had thirteen hours of personal discussions.

4. The original letters by Freud are kept with his other manuscripts in the Library of Congress in Washington, D.C. Jones's letters are in the archives of the British Psycho-Analytical Society in London.

5. A curiosity that nonetheless gives us some sense of the cultural climate of the time in England is the fact that until 1910 Sophocles' *Oedipus Rex* could not be staged in a public theater because of its preoccupation with the theme of incest (Clark and McGuire,

1989, p. 17). When the first English translation of *The Interpretation of Dreams* was published by Brill in 1913, the book circulated only among a few small groups of doctors, judges, and so on, because it was held that the public at large ought not to read it in light of its references to adult and infantile sexuality (Steiner, 1991, p. 355).

6. Jones was elected president of the I.P.A. at the sixth Congress at The Hague in 1920 and held the office until 1924. He was elected again at the end of the Wiesbaden Congress in 1932 and held the office until the 1949 Congress in Zurich. He therefore had the task of guiding the I.P.A. through the entire period of European fascism.

7. The letters Freud wrote in English could certainly be considered anything but banal from the point of view of research. If we are to understand certain aspects of Freud's expressive style and above all of his culture, these letters have to be seen in the light of his insatiable reading in English from his youth onwards, as the letters to Silberstein, with their numerous quotations and interpretations, not to mention the translations of John Stuart Mill, frequently witness. On the strength, perhaps, of these youthful readings it might be possible to shed light on certain nuances, errors, and predilections evident in Freud's English, which he himself described at one point as "rusty" (Freud to Jones, 22 December 1918) but which Jones, for various reasons, seemed always to appreciate (Jones to Freud, 22 July 1913, 22 December 1926). Andrew Paskauskas has made some interesting observations on the peculiarities of Freud's style in English in an unpublished paper entitled "Freud's English: Style, Charm and Ideology," read in London in April 1989 at the symposium "Translation in Transition."

8. One could say more in relation to Freud's letters to Oscar Pfister and especially to Arnold Zweig and to Lou Andreas-Salomé.

9. I am using here with a great deal of freedom certain ideas derived from Julian Barnes (1989, pp. 294–295).

The Complete Correspondence of
Sigmund Freud and Ernest Jones
1908–1939

1

13 May 1908
9 Glückstrasse, München

Dear Professor Freud,

I begin with[:] again[,] with warmly thanking you for the great pleasure your kind reception of me in Wien gave me. I speak only of the personal question, for only work and not words can thank you for what I owe to you in your more public capacity as a writer, and that I hope later to do. My stay in Wien, short as it was, will always be a most memorable one to me.[1]

Next as to Gross.[2] You know, no doubt, that he has definitely entered Burghölzli, so that at present, he is probably having a bad time in the early drugless days. I hear that Jung is going to treat him psychically, and naturally feel a little uneasy about that for Jung does not find it easy to conceal his feelings and he has a pretty strong dislike to Gross; in addition there are some fundamental differences of opinion between them on moral questions. However we must hope for the best. My relation to his wife is of course difficult. Gross is obsessed with the idea of my treating her and is expecting reports from both of us as to complexes etc.. It is dangerous to start on a campaign of lies with such a penetrating man as he is, and to refuse outright would be a serious thing to him in his present state and would not improve their relations to each other. It will probably end in a compromise, like most things, and at present I am just having some talks with her about their relations. Her hate against him is not at all so strong as I expected and is accompanied as usual by an opposed feeling of affection. Also her feeling for me is not so strong as you and I expected. (I do not think I am far wrong in this.) She has a whole series of nervous symptoms, but every thing seems to point to their being due simply to the difficulty of their relations to each other. For the past few months she has been—and to some extent still is—deeply in love with another man, and has had to conceal this from Gross, as the two men dislike each other. Gross gets great delight in getting other men to love her—no doubt a perverse paranoic development of his free love ideas. This she doesn't like, as she says it is her own business; in addition she has been very jealous about his relations with other women. All this I know you will treat as strictly private, but I thought you ought to know it. I should be grateful for any advice you may have time to send me.

I am working all day at the psychiatry Klinik. It will be very important for me in Canada for they think the world of Kraepelin and a government commission visited Europe recently and was most enthusiastic over his Klinik.[3] They are going to build one on its model in Toronto[4] and send their assistants over to Kraepelin to be trained. I therefore hope to get some position over there, which of course will be most important for me both as regards standing and material.[5] I hear that Kraepelin has been speaking very favourably of Jung's association work.[6] Yesterday in his lecture he made the following remarkable statement. "According to the latest views of the French School[7] there is in hysteria a suppression of certain ideas—*I might call it Verdrängung*[8]—". He is making progress, nicht wahr [don't you think], having got as far as 1886.[9] Perhaps therefore there is a little hope for him. Several of his assistants lean strongly to your views but they can of course do nothing. I asked them why they didn't study some cases of hysteria instead of talking so much about it and they said it was so rare that they never saw any! The cases are of course called catatonia, traumatic neuroses, dementia pr[a]ecox etc., etc..[10]

When I go to Canada I leave your interests and those of modern psychology in England in the hands of a young psychiatrist, Bernard Hart.[11] He is widely read in general psychology and very intelligent, but he has so far had no opportunity of studying hysteria and his German is very slight— even worse than mine. He is coming to Wien tomorrow and I asked him to call on you, for I knew how extremely kind and courteous you are. Please excuse the liberty I take, but I feel sure you will not mind.

With kind regards and warmest thanks from

yours sincerely
Ernest Jones.

1. Jones met Freud during the first international meeting of psychoanalysts at Salzburg on 27 April 1908 and presented his first psychoanalytical paper (Jones, 1908d). He then spent a few days with Freud in Vienna and attended a session of the Vienna Psychoanalytic Society; see *Minutes*, 1:389–396.

2. Otto Gross (1877–1919), iconoclastic investigator in psychiatry and psychoanalysis, who advocated sexual, political, and cultural revolution; see Emanuel Hurwitz, *Otto Gross: Paradies-Sucher zwischen Freud und Jung* (Zurich: Suhrkamp Verlag, 1979). A drug addict and patient of Carl Jung, Gross was also Jones's friend and informal instructor in the technique of psychoanalysis (Jones, 1959, p. 173). Regarding Gross's relationship with Frieda (née von Richthofen) Lawrence, wife of D. H. Lawrence, see Martin Green, *The von Richthofen Sisters: The Triumphant and the Tragic Modes of Love: Else and Frieda von Richthofen, Otto Gross, Max Weber, and D. H. Lawrence, in the Years 1870–1970* (New York: Basic Books, 1974), and *Frieda Lawrence: The Memoirs and Correspondence*, ed. E. W. Tedlock, Jr. (New York: Knopf, 1964), pp. 94–102.

3. Emil Kraepelin (1856–1926) in 1904 took charge of the new psychiatric clinic at

Munich (Nervenklinik der Ludwig-Maximilians-Universität), where he became professor and dean of the Faculty of Medicine in the university. Jones studied at Kraepelin's clinic in November 1907, and again in May and June 1908. The Canadians' visit is discussed in C. K. Clarke, "Notes on Some of the Psychiatric Clinics and Asylums of Germany," *American Journal of Insanity*, 65 (1908): 357–376.

4. After having agreed to finance the construction of the psychiatric clinic, the Ontario government yielded to pressures for prison reform and shelved the project indefinitely in 1909.

5. See note 2 to letter 3.

6. The early papers on the association method are collected in Jung (1973). See also Jung (1907a).

7. The most important exponents of the school were Pierre Janet (1859–1947), one of France's most eminent neurologists and psychologists and professor at the Collège de France (1902–1936), and Jean-Martin Charcot (1825–1893), who achieved fame for his use of hypnosis in the study of hysteria.

8. See Emil Kraepelin, "Über Hysterie," *Zeitschrift für die gesamte Neurologie und Psychiatrie*, 18 (1913): 263–264, where he discusses the concept of Verdrängung (repression) in Freud's sense.

9. Jones might have had in mind Freud's paper on male hysteria (Freud, 1886f) or Charcot's seminal work on hysteria, *Neue Vorlesungen über die Krankheiten des Nervensystems insbesondere über Hysterie* (Leipzig: Töplitz and Deuticke, 1886), translated by Freud, a product of Freud's six-month period of study with Charcot in Paris (Freud, 1886e).

10. Categories in Kraepelin's systematic classification of mental disorders as outlined in his *Psychiatrie: Ein Lehrbuch für Studierende und Ärzte*, 7th ed., 2 vols. (Leipzig: Barth, 1903–1904); 8th ed. (1909–1913).

11. Bernard Hart (1879–1966), British psychiatrist, introduced psychoanalysis to the educated public and to psychiatrists in the English-speaking world. One of the original members of the London Psycho-Analytical Society founded by Jones in 1913, he confined himself mostly to psychiatric practice.

2

27 June 1908
München

Dear Professor Freud,

First let me thank you very heartily for your exceedingly kind letter,[1] which I greatly appreciated having. I am writing this a few minutes before leaving München for Zürich. After two days there I go to London for a week, and then to Paris for six weeks with Marie at the Bicêtre.[2]

I don't know how much you know of the Gross affair. He escaped from Burghölzli last week over the wall and came back here this week. I saw him yesterday. He seems to be much worse, quite paranoiac—shut off from the outside world—and has already started taking cocaine again. He wants to provoke a lawsuit to prove the value of psycho-analysis, to drag

Kraepelin in and expose his ignorance before the world!! He is extremely *euphorisch und aufgeregt* [agitated]. It is a bad business altogether. I believe his wife is going to Graz next week.

Dr. Macfie Campbell[3] who wrote to you from London is here at present. He is the man who wrote a long and sympathetic review of Jung's D. P. [Dementia Praecox] book in the *Review of Neurology and Psychiatry*[4] of which he is subeditor. He is just going to New York to take up an important position as Director of the Psychiatry Institute there. He would be a good man to capture as an ally and he is very friendly inclined to all your work, though he has had no practical experience of it.

I send you my best greetings and thanks

Yours most sincerely
Ernest Jones.

1. Letter missing.
2. Pierre Marie (1853–1940), pupil of Charcot, M.D. Paris 1883; French neurologist noted especially for work on the spinal cord. In 1897 he established a neurological service at the Bicêtre in Paris, and in 1907 assumed the chair in pathological anatomy.
3. Charles Macfie Campbell (1876–1943), M.B., Ch.B. 1902 Edinburgh. Met Jones at Kraepelin's clinic. Went on to hold posts at the Psychiatric Institute of the State of New York, Johns Hopkins University, and Harvard.
4. C. Macfie Campbell, review of Jung (1907a), *Review of Neurology and Psychiatry*, 5 (1907): 411–420.

3

26 September 1908
85 Bloor St. East, Toronto

Dear Professor Freud,

Well, here I am landed in my new country which I like very much so far.

At present I am busy trying to pass medical examinations, for I am excused from only the Primary one in spite of our Imperialistic bombast. I have been warmly welcomed by Clarke, the Professor of Psychiatry,[1] who knows a little of your work and is eager to know more. He has promised me a university appointment and also one in the new psychiatry clinic, which will be open in two years and of which he will be the head.[2] In the meantime I am to work at hysterical cases in his asylum.

The town is very charming. It has a Deutscher Verein, which I am joining; amongst the most active members is Kirschmann, Professor of Psychology.[3] Do you happen to know him?

I am now going to ask of you a favour. A friend of mine in England has conceived the wish to translate *Die Ursachen der Nervosität* and asked me to introduce him to Stekel.[4] I haven't Stekel's address by me, and I wonder would you mind asking him to write to my friend at the subjoined address?[5] He is a good man and writes English well. By the way, do you think the new edition of *Traumdeutung*[6] (which we are eagerly awaiting) could be translated, or is the German too colloquial? Sooner or later it will have to be, of course.

I often think of the interesting times I spent at Zürich, Salzburg and Wien, and am greatly looking forward to renewing next year the friendships I made there. With my kind regards and many thanks, I am,

Yours very sincerely
Ernest Jones.

1. C. K. Clarke (1857–1924), medical superintendent at the Toronto Asylum for the Insane (1905–1911), appointed professor of psychiatry in 1907 at the University of Toronto and dean of its Faculty of Medicine in 1908.

2. Consider the account in Jones (1959, pp. 151–152): "Dr. C. K. Clarke, Professor of Psychiatry in the University of Toronto and Dean of the Medical Faculty there, had just been touring all the European psychiatric clinics and intended to found one, for which he had obtained the sanction of the Ontario Government. I chanced to hear of this and, furthermore, that he was on the look-out for a younger man to be the director of this new Institute . . . My qualifications and testimonials secured me the appointment." See also Jones (1954, p. 200), and note 12 to letter 6.

3. August Kirschmann, student of Wilhelm Wundt, was head of the psychological laboratory at the University of Toronto (1893–1909).

4. Wilhelm Stekel (1868–1940) studied medicine in Vienna, became a general practitioner, and was a close adherent of Freud until about the end of 1912; see Stekel (1907).

5. Address after Jones's signature: "Hugh Kennedy, Esq.. 13, Providence Terrace. Swaffham. Norfolk. England."

6. Freud (1900a), 2nd ed. 1909.

4

Change of address
· 8 November 1908
35 Chicora Avenue, Toronto

Dear Professor Freud,

Many thanks for your kind letter.[1] I am ashamed to say it took me two weeks to translate completely, for I am not familiar with Old German characters.

First as to Stekel. I gather your opinion from the fact that you promised to enclose his address, and then "forgot" to do so. Acting on this broad hint I have written to Kennedy advising him not to take any further steps. It is some time since I read the brochure and I gave it to Kennedy, a patient of mine, to read, first to occupy him in learning German, and secondly to shew him I was not alone in supposing that all neuroses did not come from the stomach as is generally taught. I did not like Stekel's *Angstzu-stände* much, because of its style. He quite forgets or has never thought whom he is speaking to, which is a fatal mistake. If he is writing for those familiar with psycho-analysis then he could say all he wanted to in a short article. If he is writing for those not familiar with psycho-analysis then he should be more intelligible. When he says Der [Die] Kleine steht vor der Thür = Der Penis steht vor der Hosen-Thür,[2] that may be quite true, I do not dispute it, but it certainly is not *obvious* to a lay reader, and only "puts his back up", as we say, to read what seems to him to be foolish. Such things need much longer exposition than Stekel gives, and not his airily dogmatic assumption of their obviousness. I like his classification of Angstzustände very much, and suppose it comes from you.[3] It ought to supersede Janet's psychasthenia which is a term covering cases of hysteria, neurasthenia and dementia pr[a]ecox,[4] in my opinion. I have just read Abraham's book with great interest. That subject opens up an enormous field, as I can tell from some reading I have done in English mythology and fairy tales. It is beautiful to trace the connections between different legends in the same and different countries, and in getting further and further back to see how inevitably we get back to the source of life, the old grand theme.[5] I should like to write a brochure for your series on *Wü[u]nscherfüllung im Spielen des Kindes*,[6] if I could only write German. I suppose you don't publish any in English?

I have had some interesting cases lately, one especially of hypomanie[7] in which your mechanisms shewed plainly the basis of the case and at the same time the nature of the Mass and Holy Communion as being a symbol for "Verlegung von Unten nach Oben".[8] I suppose you agree with this? I have come across an old English book on the Nightmare that would greatly interest you, for the writer relates cases that "hit one in the face", they so strikingly support your theory. I am writing an article on the subject for Prince's journal.[9] Do you take his journal, by the way? It is perhaps worth it.[10]

Now coming to the difficult subject of writing. Morton Prince wants Brill[11] and me to review your theories in his journal. He is willing to publish it after as a brochure. We have had much correspondence about it all, and I should greatly like your opinion as to the best method. The one I have proposed is as follows. A series of independent articles to be written by Brill and me separately, published in the Journal, and republished together in a book entitled "The Freudian Standpoint in Psychology" or something of the sort. I would probably take the normal and Brill the abnormal part. Thus he would write (1) Hysterie und alli[i]erte Zustände [allied conditions] (2) Dem[entia] pr[a]ecox and the outlook on psychiatry. (3) Sex development, children, abnormalities etc.. I might write (1) Origin and Interpretation of Dreams. (2) Daily Life. Wit. Versprechen etc..

(3) Symbolism in various mental processes, poetry, legends etc., etc..
(4) general introduction. The total would be about 150–200 pages.[12] What
do you think of that? We must decide soon, as there is a great call for your
work in America, especially in New York and Boston. I think, if we are
careful, that your theories can be introduced here with less prejudice being
aroused than in [America][13] Germany. (Verschreiben = Wü[u]nsch, dass
"here" Canada bedeuten mag.).[14]

Now I am going to ask you a couple of questions, if I may. I do not
apologise, for when people become founts of knowledge they must expect
that other people will want to come to them to drink. Would you kindly
tell me (1) what explanation you have found in your analyses for widely
distributed, non-localised anaesthesia, e.g. hemie- or total anaesthesia. Do
you think that withdrawing of interest by internal concentration on the
complexes is sufficient to account for it as an *Aufmerksamkeit[s]ablen-
kung* [diversion of attention], or is there a more precise reason? (2) What
mental types are there in Angstträume. I have always found the subject is
a passive, i.e. wish to be raped, whether it is a woman or a man who has
the dream. Can an active, male type have Angstträume and how does it
then work[?]

You will see my questions are very simple, but people who are afraid to
ask simple questions do not learn much, as they are often the most instructive kind of question.

And now I have bored you enough and will stop. I need hardly say what
a great pleasure it is to hear from you, and I shall be grateful for any advice
in the little difficulties mentioned above.

With kindest regards,

Yours very sincerely
Ernest Jones.

1. Letter missing.
2. The original reads "Ihre Kleine steht vor dem Tor: der Penis vor der Hosentüre";
see Stekel (1908, p. 156), translated by Gabler (1923, p. 206) as "'Her little girl was at
the gate': the penis at the gate of the trousers."
3. Stekel classified anxiety conditions with reference to symptoms as a language of
organs that symbolically expresses unconscious feelings. In his preface to Stekel (1908),
Freud gave most of the credit to Stekel for the "observations and all the detailed opinions
and interpretations" contained in the study, and limited his share of influence to recommending the use of the term *anxiety hysteria* (Freud, 1908f), a category used by Freud
to denote certain kinds of phobias as found, for example, in the case of "Little Hans";
see Freud (1909b, pp. 115–117), and Jones (1913b).
4. Janet distinguished two principal categories of the psychoneuroses: hysteria and
psychasthenia. The latter category was divided by Janet into phobias and obsessions;
see Pierre Janet, *Les Obsessions et la psychasthénie*, vol. 1, and Pierre Janet and F.
Raymond, *Les Obsessions et la psychasthénie*, vol. 2 (Paris: Alcan, 1903); and Ellenberger (1970, pp. 374–377).

5. In his early writings Karl Abraham was especially concerned with the theory of symbols and myths. In the most important of these, he connected myths with dreams and viewed both as wish-fulfillment fantasies; see Abraham (1909).

6. "Wish Fulfillment in the Play of the Child" for the *Schriften* series. Although the study was not undertaken by Jones, he did display a marked interest in neurological research and children during his early years (Jones, 1904, 1905b, 1905c, 1907b, 1907g, 1907h, 1908a, 1908c), and his curiosity about children's play at this stage in his career makes it easier to understand his support of Melanie Klein in later years, from 1925 on.

7. Jones (1909e).

8. "Transpositions from a lower to an upper part of the body"; see Jones (1909e, p. 215), and Freud (1900a, p. 387).

9. See Jones (1910m), which did not appear in Prince's journal, but which contains (p. 384) an extensive list of old books on nightmares.

10. Morton Prince (1854–1929), M.D. 1879 Harvard, taught neurology at the Harvard Medical School between 1895 and 1898, and at Tufts College Medical School between 1902 and 1912. Prince's work on dissociation phenomena was undertaken between 1898 and 1911, and he published his important study on multiple personality in 1906. Prince's relations with Freud were not good. Freud had refused to contribute to the inaugural issue of Prince's *Journal of Abnormal Psychology* in 1906. Moreover, Prince was accused by Freud and Jung of being nonpartisan: he had failed to attend the Salzburg congress and present his paper; negotiations had broken down to amalgamate Prince's *Journal* with Freud's and Jung's plan for a psychoanalytic journal; and he was especially prudish on the sexual issue. See McGuire (1974, pp. 117, 142, 175, 176, 205, 242).

11. Abraham Arden Brill (1874–1948), Austrian-born American physician, M.D. 1903 Columbia. Ardent follower of Freud, and rival of Jones in spreading psychoanalysis in the English-speaking world. Founded the New York Psychoanalytic Society in February 1911, taking priority over Jones, who was the prime mover in the founding of the American Psychoanalytic Association in May 1911.

12. Each published separate works; see Brill (1912a), and Jones, *Papers*, 1st ed. 1913.

13. Crossed out in the original.

14. (Slip of the pen = wish; I would like "here" to mean Canada.)

5

20 November 1908
Vienna, IX. Berggasse 19

My dear Dr. Jones,

Since you want me to avoid german characters I might as well try to write you in English; you are responsible for my mistakes.

1) Your critical remarks on Stekel's book are obviously true, you have hit the mark. He is weak in theory and thought but he has a good flair for the meaning of the hidden and unconscious. His book cannot satisfy us personally but it will do immensily good among the outsiders his level being so very much near to theirs. I am glad you like Abraham's work far better, he is a sharp thinker and has set his foot on fertile ground. The

next number of the collection will continue to accost the subject of Mythology which I guess is to be conquered by our views.[1]

2) Do write the *"Wunscherfüllung in Kinderspielen"*[2] for the series. Do it in English, I will get it translated here or translate it myself, if it suits my purpose as it is sure to do.

3) As for your and Brill's intention about writing those articles for M. Prince's journal, I heartily agree with you and wish you had already done it. It might be the best way to introduce my teaching to your countrymen, perhaps much more efficacious than a translation of my papers. I cannot enter into the detail of the arrangement, you propose; you will find your way through the matter yourself. The journal I will take as soon as you can announce me the first article. If you miss this wave of favour perhaps you will have to wait long time for the next. It is interesting for me that you prefer the broader aspects of the theory, the normal, psychological and cultural relations to the pathological ones; sometimes I feel the same way.

4) I am sorry you will be disappointed at my answers to the questions you put me. As for Anaesthesia I am inclined to think that it is a secondary effect of the psychical changes, brought about by withdrawal of interest *(Besetzung)*,[3] perhaps the erogene zone of the skin being particularly involved in the unconscious complexes. I know nothing better, because Anaesthesia never is a direct object of analysis, it is no "symptom" but a "stigma".[4]—As for "Angstträume" I do not think it wants a special character to explain their occurrence. I find them occasionally with all sorts of people. But I could state that dreams of painful contents (not exactly filled by anxiousness) are very frequent with *masochistic* men and women, as the chastisement is a clear "Wunscherfüllung" for these characters. I have a hint on this point in the 2nd edition of the *Traumdeutung*.[5]

I miss more news about your own position and doings and how you are satisfied by your new home.

Yours very truly
Freud

1. Rank (1909).
2. "Wishfulfillment in Children's Games."
3. See Ornston (1985b).
4. *Stigmata* are the essential, or permanent, symptoms of hysteria, as opposed to the accidental symptoms, which are not necessarily part of the disease complex itself; see Pierre Janet, *Les Stigmates mentaux des hystérique* (Paris: Rueff, 1893), where "anaesthesias" are categorized as "mental stigmata." Regarding the important influence of Janet on the young Jones between 1907 and 1909, see Paskauskas (1985, pp. 130–154).
5. See Freud (1900a, p. 159).

6

10 December 1908
35 Chicora Avenue, Toronto

Dear Professor Freud,

Many thanks for your kind letter. How I admire your facility in a foreign language! Ability to speak or write German even tolerably is one of the things I greatly desire.

I meant to go to Boston and New York this week to talk things over and sound the feeling there, but have had to postpone my visit till after Xmas.[1] I am not very hopeful of the present wave of interest, for the Americans are a peculiar nation with habits of their own. They shew curiosity, but rarely true interest (it is the difference between the itch of a neurasthenic and the [longing][2] desire of a normal lover). Their attitude towards progress is deplorable. They want to hear of the "latest" method of treatment, with one eye dead on the Almighty Dollar, and think only of the credit, or "kudos" as they call it, it will bring them. Many eulogistic articles have been written on Freud's psychotherapy of late, but they are absurdly superficial, and I am afraid they will strongly condemn it as soon as they hear of its sexual basis and realise what it means. The most we can hope for is a few practical converts who can work and spread their experience. However we must do what we can and pave the way for the future. Brill and I will of course send you reprints of our articles. I published my Salzburg paper in Prince's journal in August,[3] and from the letters I received about it it seems to have found favour. I am very eager to keep our movement strictly scientific, for that will very greatly increase its "respectability" and power of obtaining a hearing. I am going always to dissociate myself from all these quack Xian Science, and Emmanuel Church movements, for it is almost hopeless to convert these religious fanatics on a large scale, and also their pandering to the populace brings anyone associated with them into discredit in scientific circles. I have refused to write for this paper *Psycho-Therapy*[4] (which in itself is a quack word over here), and I am glad to hear that you and Jung have also refused. Morton Prince warned the editor against your sexual writings, and they do not want anything that might offend the delicate susceptibilities of the gentle ladies and clergymen that form a great part of its audience—a charming attitude for scientific work, isn't it. Prince also gave me the same warning this week when he sent me two articles of Abraham's to review for his journal.[5] One has to be very careful here, otherwise no one will listen to one. For instance even the respectable Prince is thought nothing of because of the "theatricality" of some of his work, and his dealing into such unsuitable subjects as the subconscious!! By the way I suppose you know he is opening the discussion on the subconscious at the Geneva Congress in

August.[6] He told me you were going. Is it true? You can see if it is worth while to discuss his views, for he began a series of articles on the subject in the October number of his journal.[7]

Thank you very much for your kind offer re the Kinderspielen. I should greatly like to do it, for I have for years been interested in the subject since the time when I was a school doctor and used to discuss the question with teachers, and have collected much material. I have, however, so much work on hand that I am afraid I cannot undertake it for at least another year.

Your answer to my first question explained what I wanted to know, but with the second one I did not make myself sufficiently clear. You say that Angstträume occur in all sorts of people. Is it true, however, that the majority of them (not all of course) consist in gratification of the feminine component of the sex instinct, whatever the sex of the person may be? I find namely that they consist so often in an attack [of][8] on the dreamer, and so rarely in a frustrated attack by the dreamer.

You were good enough to ask for news about the life out here, and if I have not already bored you too much I will tell you a little. In any case you can read this at some delightful Wiener Café instead of the arid discussions on Von Aerenthal's conduct in the daily papers.[9] Well, Canada is larger than Europe (including even Russia) or the United States and has the population of London. Consequently there is plenty of room here. Ontario, one of the smaller provinces, has nearly a half of the total population, and is the size of Germany. Toronto is a prettily built town, though the architecture is extremely mixed. Music is rare here, and there is not a picture gallery in the country. The people are 19 parts American, and one part Colonial, therefore are very insulted if called Americans. I have always noticed that the more difficult it is to distinguish people (e.g. Norwegians and Swedes, Flemish and Dutch, Spanish and Portuguese), the more insulted they feel at being confused with each other. They are a despicable race, exceedingly bourgeois, quite uncultured, very rude, very stupid and very narrow and pious. They are naive, childish and hold the simplest views of the problems of life. They care for nothing except money-making and sport, they chew gum instead of smoking or drinking, and their public meetings are monuments of sentimental platitudes. They are horror-struck with me because I don't know the date of the King's birthday, for they take their loyalty like everything else in dead seriousness[10] and have no sense of humour. The University has 3500 students and is well equipped. It is naturally not so good as the American or German universities. I have four appointments here. (1) Demonstrator of Clinical Medicine, which I teach twice a week at the General Hospital (2) Demonstrator of Applied Physiology ....[11] university. (3) Pathologist and Neurologist of the Lunatic Asylum. This appointment Prof. Clark[e] got the government to make for me temporarily until the Psychiatry Clinic is built—in about two years' time. He has promised me the Psychology Department there. (4) Demonstrator of Psychiatry.[12] I have to give a course on the psychological aspects of psychiatry after Xmas, which ought to be very interesting, at least for me. I have of course many other things to do. For instance, I am reorganising the medical department of the University Library, I review and abstract regularly for six neurological journals in various countries, I edit the Ontario Asylums Bulletin,[13] and am in the middle of writing a large number of articles and three books. I am at present busy house hunting for my harem, which consists of a wife, two sisters and two servants, being at present in a rented furnished house.[14] No neurology is taught here at all, for there is no one who even pretends to know anything about it. The current view about hysteria is that it is a discreditable form of imitating diseases, partly with a view to make medical diagnosis harder than it need be and partly out of a reprehensible desire to obtain sympathy by an unfair means. Treatment consists in telling them that it is no use, for they have been found out. Hysteria is not rare here, but *Angstneurosis* is much commoner.

What do you think of the picture?

It is a wonderful Abreagi[e]ren to be able to write to you, as you may imagine.

> Yours very sincerely
> Ernest Jones.

1. See note 15 to letter 7.

2. Crossed out in the original.

3. Jones (1908d).

4. William B. Parker, ed., *Psychotherapy: A Course of Reading in Sound Psychology, Sound Medicine, and Sound Religion*, 3 vols. (New York: Centre Publishing, 1909), a work devoted to the history and philosophy of psychotherapy, as well as its methods.

5. See note 2 to letter 11.

6. Sixth International Congress of Psychology, Geneva, August 1909.

7. Prince (1908–09).

8. Crossed out in the original. This passage is connected to Jones's self-analysis; see note 11 to letter 26.

9. Aloys Lexa von Aehrenthal (1854–1912), Austrian foreign minister, who was at this time involved in heated negotiations with Russia, Serbia, and the Western powers in securing for Austria-Hungary the annexation of Bosnia and Herzegovina.

10. The ties between Canada and Britain were very close at this time; see Carl Berger, *The Sense of Power: Studies in the Ideas of Canadian Imperialism, 1867–1914* (Toronto: University of Toronto Press, 1970).

11. As in original, dittoing the phrase "which I teach twice a week at the" university.

12. Jones's tenure as associate professor of psychiatry was from September 1911 until the end of 1913.

13. *Bulletin of the Ontario Hospitals for the Insane* (Toronto).

14. Louise ("Loe") Dorothea Kann, Jones's common-law wife; Elisabeth and Sybil, Jones's younger sisters.

7

7 February 1909
New York

Dear Professor Freud,

At last my American trip has come off, and very interesting has it proved. I have so many impressions at present that I must select a few that will most interest you.

I got first to Boston, and was exceedingly well received by all the University people there and was fêted hard for five days. Three things of interest happened. First we arranged a congress in Psychotherapy to be held on May 6. The President of the American Therapeutic Society is getting it up,[1] and invited what he considered to be the [eight][2] seven most prominent men on the subject in America to take part. They are Prince, Waterman, Sidis, E. W. Taylor, Tom Williams, Putnam and myself.[3] The President also will read a paper on Hypnotism, making eight. My paper is called "Psycho-analysis in Psychotherapy".[4] At my suggestion the papers will be published first in Prince's journal, and then as a brochure[5] to be sold throughout America as an official announcement of its best men, (God forgive them!).

Secondly in May there will be formed an American Society for Psychopathology *(oder so etwas)*, which will meet annually beginning in May, 1910.[6]

Thirdly a special meeting was arranged by Prince to hear me expound your theories. Wm. James couldn't come, but all the others were there, 16 of them, Prof. Münsterberg, Prof. Putnam (psychology and neurology respectively at Harvard), Prof. Dearborn (Physiology) etc., etc..[7] I had to address them and then expound and answer questions for four hours. I think that such personal work often does much more than writing, for one can instantly correct misunderstandings and false ideas that come up. It seemed to be a great success, judging from the complimentary congratulations I had. They were sympathetically inclined and very interested, especially in the sexual part. One must not hope too much however from it, for they are the only people in America at all interested in Psychotherapy, and even they are so concerned in money making as to do practically no original work or observations. The main difficulty was their colossal ignorance. So far I have not met *one*[8] man in America, except of course Brill, who has even *read* the *Traumdeutung*. Even Sidis, who has worked at dreams for six years, and who has nearly completed a big book on the subject hasn't read it, though he tells me he is "going to".[9] I think I managed to convince them of their ignorance, and some may perhaps take up the study. Putnam is the most hopeful, but he is aged 66. Isn't it absurd to criticise from their abysmal distance? The objections were of the usual order, Hineinexaminierung, phantasti[s]che Deutung, Überschätzung der sexuallen Motiven, etc.[10] that you are so familiar with. Prince is a great believer in Psychical Shock and can't understand how you came to "overlook it". He says trauma disrupt the mind with their intensity. To illustrate this, Münsterberg, who treats patients, said that he traced a case of hysterical vomiting and gastric pain to the emotional shock of swallowing a hot potato, though he confessed that the discovery had made no difference to the symptoms. I drily said that we did not regard the swallowing of hot potatoes as the kind of factor that was important in the pathogenesis of the psychoneuroses, and the audience laughed, but it needs a deal of patience to listen to things like that. Prince is not prudish on sex ideas. His main trouble is a more or less philosophic one of the Subconscious, which is worrying him tremendously, especially because he couldn't get a clear idea of your views on the subject. Your Unbewusste he divides into two, (1) Co-conscious (? verdrängte Ideen), ideas usually inaccessible to the personal consciousness but which reveal themselves indirectly as symptoms and experimentally in automatic writing, crystal gazing etc.. (2) Unconscious, which is not psychical at all, but physiological complexes i.e. physical changes in the molecules of the cortex. This comprises most of our conserved memories etc., which can enter consciousness, thus becoming psychical, by being called up through associations.[11]

Are you reading the series of articles he is writing on the subject in his Journal at present.[12] I think you ought to, for he criticises your views severely and he is a man of considerable influence here. He is personally a very agreeable man, rough, breezy, hearty, with a lawyer-like, hard and fast, cut and dried mind, fond of definitions. He does not read much, but has had considerable experience of hysteria, especially from the experimental side. He has read the *Studien*, the *Drei Abhandlungen*, and the *Sammlung*, but not the dream books, the *Witz*, or the *Bruchstück*.

Boris Sidis is a Russian, very objectionable personally, very egotistic and exceedingly shut to ideas not his own. He is 39, (Prince is 54). He is dead opposed to all your work, chiefly because he has a cure for the neuroses by hypnoidization—which consists simply in getting the patient half way to hypnotism and getting access to their stores of subconscious energy! He has just published huge articles disproving *all* the European work on the Psychogalvanic reflex and it is accepted here.[13] He says the emotional variation in the current is due not to an increase in resistance, but to a new current generated in the body, mainly in the intestines. This thesis confirms the James-Lange theory of the emotions!![14] James and Prince think an enormous lot of him.

Putnam is a delightful old man, meek, humble, learned, well-read, idealistic, but easily swayed in all directions.[15]

You see the problems here are peculiar to the Anglo-Saxon race, and one must know nicely the kinds of currents and prejudices in order to combat them most successfully. I am sure it is important to aim first at the recognised people, and not to popularise too soon. There is so much vulgarisation and exploitation of everything here, that one has a strong weapon in insisting on the exact scientific side of the subject, and that is what I mean to do. Also I want to be generally recognised in neurology and psychology or other fields, so that one's influence will be greater and one will be more readily listend to. A man who writes always on the same thing is apt to be regarded here as a crank, because to the superficial American every subject is easily exhausted except for cranks, and if the subject is sexual he is simply tabooed as a sexual neurasthenic. Hence I shall dilute my sex articles with articles on other subjects alternately. I also think it is important to give first the more elementary points and to link them with recognised psychological principles, so as to get them accepted. If one begins with the latest pinnacle of the towering edifice, it must appear in the air to the passer bye, if the supports are not also shewn. For that reason I deplore Brill's article in the Journal.[16] It created a great deal of hostility and ridicule in Boston, as might have been expected, and did no good at all. The reason was that he gave so many distant, recondite, and apparently forced interpretations, as to appear extremely uncritical to the readers. Brill is an exceedingly clever worker with patients. I greatly admire his capacity for quick interpretation and his ability in the management of patients, but I do not consider him a good scientific exponent. He is so carried away by his personal glow of satisfaction and excitement as to forget altogether his audience. He much resembles Stekel in the contrast between his personal success and his public failure—but the latter is a more important matter in America where the situation is so delicate at present and so much depends on the pioneers. Brill is also in a rather shut circle and cannot estimate the general feeling and attitude amongst psychologists and neurologists throughout the country.

Outside Boston there is little interest in psychopathology, except in psychiatry, and psychotherapy—except the Weir-Mitchell kind[17]—is regarded with much disfavour. Even the conservative Boston People are regarded with great suspicion as tending towards spiritism, quackery etc., etc..

The general quality of the neurologists and psychiatrists in America is much poorer than I expected. They are chiefly what is here called "business" people, being concerned mainly with making money. August Hoch and Adolf Meyer are the two psychiatrists that stand out from all the rest.[18] I had some hours' talk with Meyer yesterday. He fully accepts all your work and theories though I do not believe he has had much experience of actual analysis. He is a strong believer in the sex origin of the psychoneuroses and also the insanities. Like myself he holds to the full psychogenesis of dementia pr[a]ecox and does not find it necessary to draw in Jung's X factor.[19]

If there is any point about these people or about any other matter that I can give you information on, please let me know. My publications are slow, as I have a tremendous lot of routine work that takes all my time, but my nightmare article will be out in April.[20] We are looking forward greatly to the Fritz case in the *Jahrbuch*.[21] I enjoyed the reprint you kindly sent me from the *Mutterschutz* and also your article in the *Deutsche Revue* I managed to get lately.[22] I hope the second volume of your *Sammlung* will be out soon.

With kind regards

Yours very sincerely
Ernest Jones.

1. Frederick Henry Gerrish, M.D. 1869 Medical School of Maine; organized the meeting of the American Therapeutic Society, New Haven, 6 May 1909.
2. Crossed out in the original.
3. G. A. Waterman, M.D. 1899 Harvard; E. W. Taylor, M.D. 1891 Harvard; Tom A. Williams, M.B., C.M. 1896 Edinburgh; as well as Prince, Sidis, Putnam, and Jones, were all trained physicians with specific interests in psychotherapy and psychopathology. The most important of this group was James Jackson Putnam (1846–1918), one of America's most distinguished neurologists. He was head of neurology at the Massachusetts General Hospital between 1874 and 1909, and in 1893 was appointed professor of diseases of the nervous system at Harvard Medical School. He made a major commitment to psychoanalysis after Freud's appearance at Worcester, Massachusetts, September 1909.
4. Jones (1909c).
5. Prince et al. (1910).
6. German = or something like that. See note 1 to letter 32.
7. William James (1842–1910), M.D. 1869 Harvard, one of America's foremost psychologists and philosophers. He taught physiology at Harvard College between 1872 and 1876, and his researches in physiological psychology culminated in the monumental *Principles of Psychology* (1890). Hugo Münsterberg (1863–1916), German-born American psychologist, Ph.D. 1885 under Wundt, Leipzig, took charge of the psychological laboratory at Harvard in 1892; of philosophical bent, he made contributions to the psychology of learning and forensic and industrial psychology. George V. N. Dearborn, M.D. 1893 Columbia; professor of physiology, Tufts Medical School, Boston; also had research interest in experimental psychology.
8. Doubly underlined in the original.
9. Boris Sidis (1867–1923), M.D. 1908 Harvard; previously studied under William James and was awarded a Ph.D. in 1897, the first from Harvard with a specialty in psychopathology. For his book on dreams, see B. Sidis, *An Experimental Study of Sleep* (Boston: Badger, 1909).
10. Examination from the inside, fanciful interpretation, overestimation of sexual motives, etc.
11. Prince regarded the subconscious as a clinical category, derived from phenomenal facts. For Prince, the subconscious included (a) "co-conscious" ideas or processes that were dissociated from the conscious personality and that led an autonomous existence apart from it, and (b) "unconscious" memories or ideas which were temporarily inactive.

The co-conscious, which corresponded to Janet's "subconscious," was a parallel, well-organized system of awareness comparable with consciousness, whereas the unconscious was a kind of storehouse of neurograms, the physiological records of psychological behavior (Hart, 1909–10, pp. 353–354; and Prince, 1908–9, pp. 261–297). For Freud, however, the unconscious was a conceptual category devised to explain the phenomena (Hart, 1909–10, p. 365). Significantly, before 1909 the Americans debated the issues about what the subconscious represented, and Freud's concept of the unconscious was not discussed or employed on a wide scale until after his American visit of September 1909. In his early writings Jones frequently used the term *subconscious*, even in his psychoanalytically oriented papers, for example, in his first one, Jones (1908d).

12. Prince (1908–9).

13. "All" is doubly underlined. The psychogalvanic reflex is the change in the electrical resistance of the body of a human subject registered by a galvanometer after the application of external tactile, optic, or acoustic stimuli. See Jung (1907b), Jung and Peterson (1907), Jung and Ricksher (1907–8), and Sidis and Kalmus (1908–9).

14. The theory that treats emotion as the derivative of an organism's initial physical or physiological response to a situation.

15. In his historical writings Jones recalls that he met Putnam in December 1908. Consider these accounts: "In December 1908 Dr. Morton Prince invited me to be his guest in Boston, when I first met Dr. Putnam" (Jones, 1919; in Putnam, 1921, p. 462). "It was Dr. Putnam who published, in the first number of the *Journal of Abnormal Psychology* (February 1906), the first paper in English specifically on psycho-analysis, and the first adequate account of it in that tongue. His summing-up was, however, on the whole adverse. In December, 1908 I had many talks with him in Boston and induced him to revise his judgement" (Jones, 1945, p. 9). And "In the autumn of 1908, while staying with Morton Prince in Boston, I had held two or three colloquiums at which sixteen people were present: among others, Putnam, the Professor of Neurology at Harvard University" (Jones, 1955a, p. 56; 1955b, pp. 62–63). See also note 2 to letter 231.

16. Brill (1908–9).

17. S. Weir Mitchell (1829–1914), American neurologist who advocated a form of therapy typically known as the "rest cure," which included not only relaxation and bed rest but also good nutrition, daily massage, and removal of occupational pressures.

18. August Hoch (1868–1919), Swiss-born American psychiatrist, taught at Cornell University Medical School (1905–1917), and in 1910 took charge of the Psychiatric Institute, Ward's Island, New York. He was instrumental in introducing Kraepelin's classification system in North America, and made contributions to the psychological study of the psychoses. Adolf Meyer (1866–1950), Swiss-born American psychiatrist of the first rank, M.D. 1892 Zurich. He held important posts at the State Lunatic Hospital, Worcester, Massachusetts (1896–1901), the Pathological Institute of the New York State Hospitals, and after 1908 at Johns Hopkins University, where he became professor of psychiatry and first director of the Phipps Psychiatric Clinic. He remained sympathetic to psychoanalysis, although he developed his own brand of functional psychiatry.

19. Jung postulated that in the metabolism of those suffering from dementia praecox, there exist toxins that injure the brain irreparably so that the highest psychic functions become paralyzed. According to Jung, the toxin is produced not by the body, organically, but by the dementia praecox complex itself; see Jung (1907a).

20. Jones (1910m).

21. Jones is referring to the case of "Little Hans"; see Freud (1909b).

22. Freud (1908c); and Freud (1908e), which came out in the *Neue Revue*.

8

17 February 1909
407 Brunswick Avenue
Toronto

Dear Professor Freud,

You will see I have again changed my address. I have at last got a house of my own, and am happy in that I shall soon be able to get at my beloved books once more.

I found your letter here when I returned from New York. Brill told me about your daughter's marriage, and we sent you a cablegram.[1] I hope she will be very happy. I did not have the pleasure of meeting her when I was in Wien, but perhaps I may at some future date.

I read Strohmayer's article[2] with great interest. It ought to be convincing to many outsiders, as confirming many of your views and yet not being based on your method, for evidently he has not much knowledge of psycho-analysis. Jena will be the first centre to be established in Germany, and I hope it will have many important successors.

I have some beautiful cases here, with very pretty results in the analysis. I can certify that hysteria is just the same here as in Vienna, and probably at least as common.

I sent Jung recently a programme of our May congress, perhaps he will forward it to you.

With kindest regards,

Yours ever sincerely,
Ernest Jones.

P.S. You will before now have got my New York letter, describing my impressions.

1. Freud's daughter Mathilde (1887–1978) married Robert Hollitscher (1875–1959) in 1909. Freud's letter and Jones's and Brill's cable are missing.
2. Possibly W. Strohmayer, "Zur Analyse und Prognose psychoneurotischer Symptome," *Zeitschrift für Psychotherapie und medicinische Psychologie,* 2 (1910): 75–92.

9

22 February 1909
Vienna, IX. Berggasse 19

Dear Dr. Jones,

You are performing big work, accept my thanks for it and let me express the hope that the progress of our cause will coincide with your personal advantage. Yet in reading your—as usual—highly characteristic descrip-

tions of the leading persons in american Psychopathology I could not refrain from doubting your views in one point and regarding one man. You
write, Morton Prince is an upright sympathetic man, very much leaning
to our theories and you seem to get yourself into a sort of attachment
towards him. Now I have been told in Salzburg that he proclaims my views
are mostly taken from Janet and in fact identical with them, I know from
Brill and the same from Abraham,[1] that he declined papers sent him on
his demand on the account of their containing too much of sexual matter—
you say he is not prudish, but he answered Abraham that he could not
accept the term "homosexual" because he has so many lay readers (or
ladies may be)—his exposition of my remarks on the Unconscious are only
bad misconceptions, which make me surmise he has never read the book
but only looked at the special item.[2] Now how can you reconcile the words
and the deeds of this man, the judgment I must shape of him and the
impression he gave you? It might be better to keep from him and to be
prepared to his bad intentions veiled by his friendly speaking.

As for your diplomacy I know you are excellently fitted for it and will
do it masterly. But I am afraid it is easy to do too much in this way.
Consider it is a piece of psychoanalysis you are performing on your countrymen, you are not to say too much at once or at too early a moment,
but the resistance cannot be avoided, it must come sooner or later, and it
is best to provoke it slowly and designedly.

I am impatient Brill should bring out some of my writings in translation,
I will stand the blame for it and if there is true scientific interest independent from the money earning desire in your countrymen you will profit
by the reaction rising up after the wave of resistance has passed.

Dont forget that we of Europe hope to see you again in the spring of
1910 and converse timely[3] with Jung about the exact term.

Yours sincerely,
Freud

1. See H. Abraham and E. Freud (1965, pp. 61, 63).
2. See Prince (1908–9), vol. 3, passim.
3. Freud seems to be following the German here: *zeitig* = timely, in good time.

10

28 February 1909
Vienna, IX. Berggasse 19

Dear Dr. Jones,

Only to give you notice that I will come to your new country in the
beginning of Sept. next following an invitation of the Clark University,

Worcester Mass. (Stanley Hall),[1] which will celebrate the 20th anniversary of its foundation at this term. A former invitation reaching me in Dec. I had to decline, because it contained the condition of being present in the first days of July which would have involved a very considerable loss of medical work in Vienna. I am expected to give a course of 4–6 lectures in—German,[2] I am sure—before an audience of Neurologists; the invitation is couched in very honourable terms. I shall be very glad to meet you either in New York or in Worcester and hope my presence and my sayings will not interfere too much with the high diplomacy of your proceedings.

Yours truly,
Freud

1. G. Stanley Hall (1844–1924) received the first doctorate in psychology (1878) from Harvard under the supervision of William James; in 1887 he founded the *American Journal of Psychology*. His research interests encompassed sexuality, psychopathology, child development, and adolescence. In 1888 he became the first president of Clark University, Worcester, where Freud received an honorary doctorate in September 1909, constituting the first official acceptance of psychoanalysis in America.
2. Freud (1910a).

11

19 March 1909
407 Brunswick Avenue
Toronto

Dear Professor Freud,

First let me thank you for your most interesting reprint. It was like all your writings too short, in that we crave, like Oliver Twist, for more.

Then as to the great news of your coming over. I am of course delighted for personal reasons, and in addition I think it will do your cause good, for I am a great believer in the effect of personal influence and presence. What subject will you choose? I suppose you will publish the lectures in the form of a book covering more or less systematically a given topic. Why don't you speak in English. I honestly see not the slightest reason why you shouldn't, and of course if I could do anything towards the idiomatic rendering of any points or in any other way I should be most happy to do so. Is the exact date fixed? I shall be in Europe end of July and August and shall be returning (to New York) about the end of August. I wonder if it would be possible for me to have the good fortune of travelling on the same boat. Have you chosen your route, etc., yet?

With regard to Morton Prince I think, strange as it may appear, that we are both right. There are often different ways of looking at the same thing.

It is natural he should want to minimise the importance of your work, for he is 54, and it is hard for him to realise that he has been working for a quarter of a century on the surface, and has missed the essential points all the time. One can hardly expect him to behave otherwise under the circumstances. He is as upright as he can be, but is of course swayed by the influence of all those years passed on other directions. His exposition of your views on the Subconscious is hopelessly foolish, but that is because he is stupid, and because also he really finds it very hard to understand your meaning; he finds your writings very difficult.

He has not declined any [abstract][1] paper from Brill, only an abstract that was written in coarse language (I read it myself). Different countries have different ideas as to what is permissible in expression, and his journal is not a medical one, but a semi-popular one with a large female audience. He personally is not prudish. Of Abraham's article I know nothing, so cannot say. Prince accepted two abstracts I recently wrote of Abraham's alcohol and dementia pr[a]ecox articles.[2] He certainly has no "bad intentions veiled by friendly speaking", for he is simple-minded and easily seen through.

I am sorry you so disapproved of my remark on diplomacy and will say no more about it except that there are different ways of reaching the same aim and that each must work as he sees fit.

With kindest regards

yours ever sincerely
Ernest Jones.

1. Crossed out in the original.
2. Likely Abraham (1927, pp. 64–79, or 1955, pp. 13–20) on dementia praecox, and Abraham (1927, pp. 80–89) on alcohol. Jones's reviews did not appear in Prince's *Journal of Abnormal Psychology*.

12

8 April 1909
407 Brunswick Avenue
Toronto

Dear Professor Freud,

This is just a line to say how very much I enjoyed your article on Der kleine Hans.[1] It was a wonderfully finished study and also a valuable confirmation of the conclusions you had reached by other routes. The infantile theory of the resemblance between childbirth and defaecation must be very common, judging from the frequency with which it is revealed in male patients in asylum work. I am seeing manifestations of it very often indeed.

I was greatly interested in your suggestion about contempt for women and for Jews for "penis" reasons.[2] The former struck me straight away as profound, but the latter seemed stranger to me, as I would have said the general attitude towards Jews is hate (owing to their success, aloofness etc.) rather than contempt. However some lines of Browning[']s poetry occurred to me which I must confess support your view, and, in case you are not familiar with them, I will quote them. They form an epilogue to the poem Cleon, in which the Greek philosopher is answering a letter of a foreign king who has appealed to him. He expounds a very pessimistic Weltanschauung and concludes thus:

> "And for the rest,
> I cannot tell thy messenger aright
> Where to deliver what he bears of thine
> To one called Paulus; we have heard his fame
> Indeed, if Christus be not one with him—
> I know not, nor am troubled much to know.
> Thou canst not think a mere barbarian Jew,
> As Paulus proves to be, *one circumcized*,[3]
> Hath access to a secret shut from us?
> Though wrongest our philosophy, O King,
> In stooping to inquire of such an one,
> As if his answer could impose at all!
> He writeth, doth he? Well, and he may write.
> Oh, the Jew findeth scholars! certain slaves
> Who touched on this same isle, preached him and Christ;
> And (as I gathered from a bystander)
> Their doctrine could be held by no sane man".

Obviously all the scorn of the passage is concentrated on the two words I have underlined. Browning was an orthodox Christian, and although none of his writings are anti-semitic still he may have been annoyed to think that his Saviour was a Jew. Much of his writings shews strong masochistic tendencies. I wonder what the explanation might be?

I am sailing to Europe July 17 and leave there end of August (date not fixed).

With kind regards

Yours most sincerely
Ernest Jones.

1. Freud (1909b).
2. Freud (1909b, p. 36).
3. Emphasis added by Jones. From "Cleon," in Browning (1895, p. 361).

13

18 May 1909
Vienna, IX. Berggasse 19

Dear Dr. Jones,

I heartily acknowledge the receipt of a big heap of printed matter containing your valuable contributions to organic neuropathology[1] and foreshadowing another lot neither smaller nor less in value of your communications about neuroses and psychoanalysis, we do expect you will produce in the next years.

I can give you the information, that we—Dr. Ferenczi and I—intend sailing from Bremen August 21st on board "George Washington" N. D. L. I cannot know if this term may coincide with your return to America. In any case you know we are fixed.

I have not yet made up my mind about the subject of my lectures in Worcester. Sometimes it occurs to me as the best expedient to treat dreams and their interpretations. I am ready to take up your hints, if you are of other opinion.

I am with best love to you

yours sincerely
Freud

1. Likely the selections published prior to mid-May 1909 from Jones (1905a, 1907b, 1907c, 1907e, 1908a, 1908b, 1908c, 1909a, 1909b, 1910b, and 1911a), reprints of which were kept by Freud and are contained in the Sigmund Freud Memorial Collection at the New York State Psychiatric Institute Library, New York. There may be a hint of sarcasm in Freud's acknowledgment of these nonpsychoanalytic writings, for Jones at this stage had only one published paper of a psychoanalytical orientation to his credit; see Jones (1908d).

14

18 May 1909
407 Brunswick Avenue
Toronto

Dear Professor Freud,

Just a note to "report progress". The Symposium on Psycho-Therapy at New Haven came off last week and was very successful. It will be printed in the June number of the *Journal of Abnormal Psychology*.[1] Seven took part in it. I read a paper on Psycho-analysis which was very well received.[2] It created a small sensation, but a favourable one. I think you will probably like it. I hope to finish in a fortnight two articles, one a detailed sexual psycho-analysis I am sending to the *American Journal of Insanity*, and the other one on the Oedipus-Complex as an explanation of Hamlet's mystery![3] The latter is a pretty [well][4] full discussion of the question and I think it should interest you. Have you dipped much into the Hamlet-literature? It is appalling in its extent, and mostly pretty poor in quality. I shall send the article to the *American Journal of Psychology*, edited by Stanley Hall.

Which latter reminds me of your approaching visit. I found that none of the Boston men, Putnam, Taylor, Prince etc. had heard anything of it, and they had mostly already made their arrangements for that time of year. Why ever doesn't Stanley Hall send out notices of it, say to the members of the American Neurological Association etc. He is very remiss, for time is getting on. From what the men say I am afraid that you must make up your mind to be content with a small audience. They say that Americans simply will not trouble to go out of their way to hear lectures from anyone, and that the lectures ought to be given in a large town like New York or Boston. You absolutely must deliver them in English, for hardly anyone here understands German. I should be very glad if I [could do anything][5] [could] be of any assistance in this respect. Have you decided on the subject yet?

I saw Brill last week in New York. He looked ill still, as he had a severe attack of influenza, but was working very pertinaciously.

I forget if I have written to you since the *Jahrbuch* arrived, to say how much I enjoyed Der kleine Hans.[6] It was a beautifully finished study, and give [gave] me quite an aesthetic pleasure, as do all your pieces of work that are done so perfectly. What may we expect next from you? When are you going to linotype those points about technique in psycho-analysis for us?

With my kindest regards

Yours ever sincerely
Ernest Jones.

P.S. What do you think of Pfarrer Pfister?[7] It beats the American Emmanuel movement hollow.[8] What are we coming to?

1. Prince et al. (1910).
2. Jones (1909c).
3. Jones (1909e, 1910a).
4. Crossed out in the original.
5. Crossed out in the original.
6. Freud (1909b).
7. Oskar Pfister (1873–1956), Protestant pastor of Zurich, founding member of the Swiss Psychoanalytic Society in 1910. For correspondence with Freud, see Meng and Freud (1963).
8. Founded by Reverend Elwood Worcester in 1908, the movement attempted to combine religion, medicine, and psychotherapy in response to the perceived moral and psychological decay of American society.

15

1 June 1909
Vienna, IX. Berggasse 19

Dear Dr. Jones,

I enjoy the frequency of your letters and as you see I hasten to give you answering. Many thanks for your interesting news about your work, I expect you become soon a reader of the articles announced. To be sure the essay on the parallel Oedipus-Hamlet will interest me most. When I wrote down what seemed to me the solution of the mystery I had not undertaken a special inquiry into the Hamlet-literature, but I knew what the results of our German writers were and saw that even Goethe had missed the marks.[1]

Permit me to put you right as soon as possible about Pfister. He has nothing at all to [do] with Emmanuelism and the like; I know him personally by a visit he paid me last month. He is perfectly in earnest, a scientific man and a very kind character, nay a charming man, very modest too. Grant him all the rights due to one of our crew and not the worst man as far as I can see.

As for my visit in Worcester I do not know if Stanley Hall be to blame. He writes me: "We have given out no notices as yet; nevertheless, in some way the news of your coming has reached a number of people in this country who have been profoundly interested in your work and have written us expressing their pleasure and their desire to hear whatever you may have to say to us." So you see I will have some audience at least and as for those who will not be present I will be sorry, but not disconsolate. In opposition to you I expect nothing at all from the big men: Putnam, Morton Prince etc. and hope, you may not find [yourself] disappointed with them. As for myself I did not choose my place, I donot want to put anyone out of his way or his plans, I am going to where I have been invited and may securely leave arrangements to Stanley Hall.

Nor will I give my lectures in English. It would be hard to me and put me at a great disadvantage against hearers and critics. I got the University's publication at the former celebration ten years ago and could see, that none of the five foreigners (Forel, Picard, Boltzmann, Mosso, Ramon y Cajal)[2] had lectured in English; two of them in German, three in French.[3] I think they did not pretend to have come as teachers but merely as scientific guests, and I too feel free of so much pretension. As for the subject of the lectures I have not yet decided but I may settle on a purely psychological problem probably on the dream.

I could not do much written work in the course of these months. Perhaps Jung will accept the paper on the Salzburg man of the rats,[4] if the *Jahrbuch* be in want of matter. The essay on the technique is half finished, no leisure now to bring it to an end.[5] I am glad you see the importance of "klein Hans",[6] I never got a finer insight into a childs soul.

Take my best regards and give me notice of your further doings

yours faithfully
Freud

1. See Freud (1900a, pp. 264–266).

2. Auguste Forel (1848–1931), renowned Swiss psychiatrist, predecessor of Eugen Bleuler at the Burghölzli Asylum in Zurich. Émile Picard (1856–1941), distinguished French mathematician. Ludwig Boltzmann (1844–1906), Austrian physicist, greatest achievement in the application of statistical mechanics to thermodynamics. Angelo Mosso (1846–1910), Italian neurophysiologist, pioneer researcher on cerebral circulation in humans. Santiago Ramón y Cajal (1852–1934), Spanish neuroanatomist, won (with Golgi) the Nobel Prize in medicine in 1906 for establishing the neuron as the basic unit of the nervous system. Freud had also worked on the neuron theory in the 1890s (Freud, 1950a), and the historical context of his work in relation to Cajal's is dealt with in Sandra E. Black, "Pseudopods and Synapses: The Amoeboid Theories of Neuronal Mobility and the Early Formulation of the Synapse Concept, 1894–1900," *Bulletin of the History of Medicine*, 55 (1981): 34–58.

3. Clark University, *Decennial Celebrations, 1889–1899* (Worcester, 1899).

4. Freud (1909d).

5. Freud (1910d).

6. Freud (1909b).

16

6 June 1909
407 Brunswick Avenue
Toronto

Dear Professor Freud,

Many thanks for your letter and your kind remarks about my articles. I wonder whether [you][1] it has come your way to pay much attention to the dyschiria and phrictopathic sensation I have described as hysterical manifestations?[2] I am getting out a long study of the former subject in Brodmann's Journal shortly, and should be glad to hear what you think of it.[3]

My boat, the Kaiserin Auguste Victoria, sails from Hamburg three days after yours, but I hope to catch you up somewhere on this side. I am very glad Ferenczi is coming with you. I am very fond of him and shall be glad to see him again. He has been doing good work for you, hasn't he?

You will by now have got my letter with some remarks about Worcester, and my fear that your audience is likely to be small. Still perhaps, as usual, my opinion is too pessimistic. I hope so, at all events.

I am very glad you give me the welcome opportunity to say a little about the subject, though I cannot presume to expect that my opinion will be a great factor in your decision. It seems to me that the people on this side have no idea of the colossal amount of work you have done, or the mass of exact evidence you collect before carefully issuing your opinions. Those who know you know how very much the reverse you are of hasty, and that any conclusion you put out is most thoroughly sifted and deliberately weighed. But the people here, who do not know you and cannot read German, are apt to think that when you say "Dreams represent wish-fulfillments" or "Hysteria has always a sexual basis" etc., [it is only] you are only expressing an opinion, or suggesting a wild hypothesis. Freud "thinks" this, Ziehen, Oppenheim or Dubois[4] "thinks" the other thing, in no way realizing how completely you differ from the other men not only in your genius, but also in the study and work you have done before giving emitting your "opinion".

Therefore I should be strongly inclined to deal more with principles than with conclusions. Couldn't you speak on some of the psychological mechanisms in general (Verdichtung, Verschiebung, Ersatzformation, etc.), illustrating them from different spheres, dreams, psychoneuroses, daily life etc., thus making the lectures nearer to the psychologist than to the clinician. It would bring out the profound difference in your objective attitude towards the mind, as distinguished from the orthodox way in which the academic psychologist uncritically accepts the *Versuchsperson's*[5] account of his mental workings and touchingly believes that everyone knows everything that is in his own mind: "The Role of [Unu] Unconscious [mental] psychological mechanisms in various mental processes".

This would then be broader than lectures on dreams alone, and would involve less repetition of your previous writing. How does it strike you?

With kindest regards.

Yours ever
Ernest Jones.

1. Bracketed words throughout this letter were crossed out in the original.
2. Jones (1907e, 1908b).
3. Jones (1909a). Korbinian Brodman (1868–1942), M.D. 1898 Leipzig; famous for his work on the comparative anatomy of the brain; editor of *Journal für Psychologie und Neurologie*.
4. Theodor Ziehen (1862–1950), chief of psychiatry at the Charité in Berlin between 1904 and 1912. Hermann Oppenheim (1858–1919), Berlin neurologist who in 1890 founded a private clinic which became an international center of clinical neurology. Paul-Charles Dubois (1848–1918), professor of neuropathology at Bern, who considered mental disturbances in psychological terms, and advocated a rational, persuasive form of psychotherapy.
5. Experimental subject's.

17

5 August 1909
Grand Hôtel de la Métropole
Genève

Dear Professor Freud,

Greetings from the right side of the Atlantic! I hope to meet you in New York on Sept. 4 and go to Worcester to have the pleasure of listening to you. My wife and I would be delighted if you could manage to pay Toronto a visit and stay with us there. I have also asked Jung if he will come so far North, and expect to hear from him soon. He is not here at the Congress.[1]

There are a number of "Freudianers" here besides myself; Hart of London, Maeder of Zürich,[2] Schwarzwald of Lausanne, [Assagliani][3] Assagioli of Florence (who is writing a thesis on psycho-analysis for his doctorate)[4] and Szecsi of Genf (formerly of Buda-Pesta). The last two have never met any Freudians and have learnt only from reading and applications. The last named is a very clever young fellow, only 24. He is reading a paper here, entitled "Psychische Compensation"[5] on your work. He told me he would like to publish it—at greater length—in the *Jahrbuch*, but didn't know you or Jung. I offered to write to you about him, so he will now probably write to you about the matter.[6]

I am looking forward to seeing you.

With warmest regards

Yours
Ernest Jones.

1. Sixth International Congress of Psychology, Geneva, 2–7 August 1909.
2. Alphonse Maeder (1882–1971), Swiss psychotherapist, interested in both Freud and Jung, but after the break sided with Jung; later noted for his method of brief analysis.
3. Crossed out in the original.
4. Roberto Assagioli (1888–1975) of Florence, representing the Italian Society of Anthropology and Comparative Psychology, Circle of Philosophy of Florence, and the Library of Florence; his thesis "La Psicositesi" (Ph.D. diss., University of Florence, 1910) was partially published in *Psiche: Rivista di studi psicologici*, 1, no. 2 (1912).
5. See Stephan Szecsi, "Psychische Kompensation als Übergang vom Normalen ins Pathologische," which is contained in the proceedings of the congress, in Edouard Claparède, ed., *VIe Congrès International de Psychologie, 1909, rapports et comptes-rendus* (Geneva: Kündig, 1910), pp. 792–796. For Jones's contribution, see Jones (1910g). Hart, Maeder, Schwarzwald, and Assagioli did not present papers at the congress.
6. Szecsi's piece did not appear in the *Jahrbuch*.

18

17 October 1909
407 Brunswick Avenue
Toronto

Dear Professor Freud,

First let me hope that you had a pleasant voyage home, and that you enjoyed your American "trip". Any fatigue from it should be compensated by the knowledge that you have struck a powerful blow for the cause in America, and Brill and I are very grateful to you for both impersonal and personal reasons.

I hope you had a good time in the mountains, and should be glad to hear sometime as to what you made of Putnam. He does not seem to have much *practical* knowledge of psycho-analysis, but he is a useful ally. He has this month published an article, in which he enthusiastically praises your work and method.[1]

I should like to say something about my personal inhibitions, but it is difficult in a short space. I am proposing to inflict a long account of them on Jung, who spoke to me on the subject, and if he thinks it worth while he can send it on to you. The following few words give the practical side of it. So far as I can judge my inhibitions, which I know could not have escaped your sharp eye, were never against your work or conclusions, but against the advisability of joining in your method of propagandism. I felt that a more consciously organised campaign would have had better results than blind advocacy on the part of everyone who took up the work. Naturally, as you will imagine, this attitude was at bottom determined by personal complexes. However, the outcome of the story is that about six or eight months ago[2] I determined not only to further the cause by all the means in my power, which I had always decided on, but also to further it by whatever means you personally decided on, and to follow your recommendations as exactly as possible. In that I hope I am succeeding to your satisfaction, as tested, for instance, by my recent writings. Anything you may care to say to me on the subject I will give my keenest thought and attention to.

Many thanks for your comments on the Hamlet article. I made the necessary alterations in regard to the death of Shakspere's father, and to sex-repression towards Ophelia.[3] It was difficult to interpolate a full translation of the *Traumdeutung* passage without breaking the flow of the article, but I made a summary of its contents in one place,[4] and I expect that is what you intended. Then I development [developed] Rank's work[5] at much greater length, and added a good deal on the other characters in the play (especially Laertes and Polonius) from the point of view of Doubling and *Auseinanderl[[eg]ung]*.[6] This makes the article twelve pages longer. Sanford wrote to me this week asking for it as he wanted to give it a prominent place in the January number, so I have sent it off.[7]

By the way it has occurred to me in connection with what you said about Shakspere's name that it might be from *Jacques père*. It is known that the original pronunciation, and frequent spelling, was Shăxper, and that certainly proves the Jacques part of it. On the other hand I don't know of any instance of *père* being added to a name, as son is in English and German; nor do I know that *fils* is incorporated into French names. Can you enlighten me on the point?

What did you think of the "hypomania" case?[8] According to Jung it is a dementia praecox case after all. I suppose he is right, for noone knows more about the subject than he does, but I believe he would clinically include under dementia praecox many cases that Kraepelin would call manic-depressive. Brill tells me you didn't understand what I meant by "orgasm". Well, I don't know what other word to use. The patient, who of course did not touch me, would close her eyes, get flushed cheeks, breathe rapidly, make movements of coitus (she was on her back in bed), and come to a climax just as in an orgasm. It was curious, wasn't it. She did not use her hands for masturbation in it.

Do you think it would be worth while to work up any other of Shakspere's tragedys at shorter length (Lear, Othello, Macbeth) and then write a paper on Shakspere himself? There is much material about him personally from our point of view.

Next month I am to give an address on the Psycho-analytic method of treatment before a combined meeting of county societies in Canada, and the next month (Dec.) I am reading a paper on the subject before the Ontario Academy of Medicine.[9]

This week the Government has opened here a Polyclinic for nervous and mental diseases, of which I have charge.[10] Private practice has also greatly increased, and the University work has begun, so I am very busy.

I send you my warmest regards,

yours ever cordially
Ernest Jones.

1. After the Worcester lectures Freud, along with Jung, had joined Putnam at his camp in the Adirondacks. For a short account of Freud's visit, see George E. Gifford, Jr., "Freud and the Porcupine," *Harvard Medical Alumni Bulletin*, 46 (1972): 28–31. Putnam's article, which documents his personal impressions of Freud, came out in two parts; see Putnam (1909–10).

2. This coincides with the death of Jones's mother toward the end of May or early June 1909.

3. Jones (1910a, pp. 97–98, 98 n. 1).

4. Freud (1900a, p. 265), and Jones (1910a, p. 98).

5. See especially Rank (1909).

6. "Doubling of the principal characters" and "decomposition"; see Jones (1910n, p. 105, 109).

7. E. C. Sanford of Clark University was one of the principal editors of the *American Journal of Psychology*.

8. Jones (1909e).

9. Jones (1910c).

10. C. K. Clarke, preface to *Bulletin of the Ontario Hospitals for the Insane*, 2 (1909): 3–4; and "A Clinic for Nervous and Mental Diseases," ibid., 4 (1911): 73–77.

19

23 October 1909
Vienna, IX. Berggasse 19

Dear Dr. Jones,

I thank you for sending me the issue containing your paper,[1] which I read with much interest.

On the question of left- and right-handedness I only know that Stekel will be publishing something on dreams in the next issue of the *Jahrbuch*,[2] which we are expecting shortly. You are, of course, aware of Gaupp's book on right-handedness.[3] Incidentally, I will have Rank keep his eyes open in case he finds anything useful for you. That right and left should mean male and female seems quite obvious.

My time is at present quite taken up with writing out the five lectures, which you yourself had to listen to in Worcester.[4] Very inconvenient when one has so much else to do as I.

I am very curious about Putnam's future attitude. I understand he has written a laudatory paper somewhere, which, however, has not reached me; nor, incidentally, have I received the copy of the translation that Brill must surely have sent off.[5] Has he tried to have further contact with you? Or does everything need much more time?

Cordial greetings and I hope to hear from you again soon.

Yours very truly,
Freud

1. Jones (1909f).

2. Stekel (1909).

3. Ernst W. T. Gaupp, *Über die Rechtshändigkeit des Menschen* (Jena: G. Fischer, 1909).

4. Freud (1910a).

5. Putnam (1909–10); Brill (1909a).

20

31 October 1909
Vienna, IX. Berggasse 19

Dear Dr. Jones,

Your letter gave me much satisfaction (I am too busy to write in English, but will try to be clear). I did note your inhibitions and think they were the reason why you were not really in favor of my trip to America. You were afraid that I would thwart your intentions and now you admit that this trip only promoted our cause. You have a particular need for complicated plans, instead of taking a direct route, and all sorts of other things may hide behind this constitutional predilection.

You treated our good friend Brill with unmistakable hostility and disdain, no doubt also out of personal motives, in other words, *complex* related motives. Now, I think, the cause is too great and vast, and we would not accomplish anything by means of clever delaying tactics. One could too easily run the risk of becoming deceitful and hide the essentials, which is in direct conflict with the spirit of ΨA. It has always seemed to me best to behave in such a manner as if the freedom to talk about sexuality were self-evident and calmly face the inevitable resistance. Offense will here be the best defense. I believe there are hopeful signs that you will head for our way of thinking with increased confidence and conviction.

I was very pleased that the fate of the Hamlet essay was decided so favorably. A slight misunderstanding has crept in between us regarding the derivation of Shakespeare's name. I did not mean Jacques *père* but Jacques Pierre, which is not an uncommon combination of two forenames. The derivation was given to me by a very erudite old gentleman, Prof. Gentilli, who now lives in Nervi.[1] If you have anything on Shakespeare's other dramas it will certainly be worth exploring. I myself have collected some material on Macbeth. I can offer no definite opinion on your mania case.[2] The analysis seemed very fragmentary to me and the relation of orgasm to the stimulus words uncertain. Perhaps the person continued to fantasize without paying much attention to your stimulus words. Jung's view of this intended publication will certainly be more valuable to you.

Putnam was a most gracious host,[3] but the interminable climbing about brought me to the point where I finally went on strike and stayed at home, especially since I was not quite well either. Then we got deep into conversation and I noted with pleasure that he was much more at home in ΨA than I had reason to believe. He related quite skillful, though not thorough, analyses and dream interpretations to me. The practical difficulties of treatment still seemed to scare him a great deal. I should like to read the article of his that he alluded to. Of course I do not know whether it is on its way, like the Brill translation, which I have not received yet either.

Your avid activity promises the best. In the past month I received only one very appealing paper from an Italian, Dr. Modena, deputy head of the insane asylum in Ancona.[4] I have finished the work for the *Jahrbuch*[5] and the third edition of *Alltagslebens*. Most of my time is now taken up with my lectures for Clark University, which are to be translated and circulated in America.[6]

My fatigue vanished together with the stomach catarrh which I brought home with me. The memory of the trip becomes more and more wonderful.

In the meantime, cordial greetings

Yours very truly
Freud

1. In his discussion of Freud's consuming interest in Shakespeare, Jones gives Gentilli a brief mention; see Jones (1957a, p. 429; 1957b, p. 460).
2. Jones (1909e).
3. In the German original Freud had written "Gastwirt" [innkeeper], then crossed out "Wirt."
4. Possibly Gustavo Modena, "Psicopatologia ed etiologia dei fenomeni psiconeurotici (Contributo alla dottrina di S. Freud)," *Rivista sperimentale di Freniatria*, 34 (1908): 3–4.
5. Freud (1909d).
6. Freud (1910a).

21

[postcard]

3 November 1909
407 Brunswick Avenue
Toronto

Dear Professor Freud,

I have collected a number of interesting facts about superstitions and beliefs relating to the right and left side respectively. Could you give me any idea as to the relation of the subject to sexuality? I know of course Fliess' hypothesis about left-handedness, but I don't suppose you at all agree with that.[1]

Things are going well here with Brill and myself.

Yours ever
Ernest Jones.

1. Wilhelm Fliess (1858–1928), ear, nose, and throat specialist, practicing in Berlin; close colleague of Freud between 1897 and 1900. Fliess posited that bisexuality was associated with right- and left-handedness, and that secondary sexual characteristics of

the nondominant bisexual disposition are more prominent in those who are left-handed; see W. Fliess, *Der Ablauf des Lebens: Grundlegung zur exakten Biologie* (Leipzig, 1906), pp. 537–571. In a letter to Abraham of 6 April 1914, Freud denounced Fliess's theory; see H. Abraham and E. Freud (1965, p. 171). This note is also revealing of Jones's attempts at exploring his own bisexuality. See especially his comments to Putnam about right and left of 1 July 1910 in Hale (1971a, p. 221).

22

18 December 1909
407 Brunswick Avenue
Toronto

Dear Professor Freud,

I have delayed answering your letters for a singular reason arising from my defective education. I can read German quite well, and need never trouble you to write in English, but I cannot read the old German handwriting characters. After making several vain attempts I thought of a German friend in Montreal, who got them typewritten for me, and after getting them back from him yesterday I hasten to reply.

Your personal remarks to me were quite justified, and I thank you for being so open with me. I quite recognise the faulty attitude I had taken up and further recognise that a little suspicion of me on your part will be hard to avoid until I prove that I have adopted a more satisfactory one. However I cannot help that, but I will do my best in time to earn your confidence. Deeds, not words, speak best. I don't think I need bother you with a long account of my personal complexes; last month I sent a pretty full account of the matter to Jung,[1] and asked him to send it on to you if he thought it might interest you. Shortly put, my resistances have sprung not from any objections to your theories, but [from][2] partly from an absurd jealous egotism and partly from the influences of a strong "Father complex". You are right in surmising that I had at one time hoped to play a more important part in the movement in England and America than I now see is possible; it must, and should, be directed by you, and I am content to be of any service in my power along the lines you advise.

About Brill I find it not easy to write because I know you will be strongly inclined to take anything I may say *cum grano salis*. Nevertheless I will speak as honestly as possible, and you can believe me or not as you will. My hostility to Brill I of course do not deny, and the causes of it are I think clear to me (jealousy in regard to his relation with you, etc.), but I feel quite convinced that you and Brill overestimate it considerably. You and Jung have only heard one side of the case, his and not mine, and I have recently proved to Brill that he has several times misinterpreted my conduct (especially via incorrect reports). Perhaps this was due to his jealousy of me (which he fully admits) having led him to suspect me and put the worst interpretations on anything he hears of me. My attitude is as follows: I admire a number of qualities in him, especially his loyalty, honesty, and his skill in psycho-analysis, but I am not blind to certain defects that particularly strike an Englishman. I find him agreeable company, and like him personally, though I do not think it likely I could ever be quite intimate with him. He does not at all understand my nature, and in some respects our tastes also differ. However he is a good man to work with, and there is no reason on earth why we should not "pull together". Realising how extremely important for the movement it is that, especially in a new country, the workers should be in harmony I have made every effort to come to a better understanding with him, to deal with my personal complexes, and to work loyally by his side. I honestly think I have been successful in this, especially in the last three months, and hope that in the future all will go well. It is of course plain to me that in a movement such as ours it is merely ridiculous and small-minded to let personal factors play a role. I have recently suggested to him that we send each other our articles before publication in order to get each other's comments; it will be useful to both.

And so enough of these petty personal questions, which I am sorry to have had to trouble you with.

Many thanks for your remarks about right and left handedness. There are a great number of indications that the two correspond to male and female in beliefs, (e.g. that boys come from the right testicle girls from the left; also in Egyptian phallic worship that the [right][3] penis was the Father, the right testicle Horus (Christ) and the left Isis (Maria)).[4] These are of course secondary beliefs grafted on the primary recognition of the difference between the skillful—good—right, and the clumsy—evil—left. I had a few speculations, quite wild I fear, going further into the origin of the difference. I am sometimes sceptical whether the accepted explanation is true, namely that the difference is a physiological one and due to the disparateness of the two halves of the brain. Might it not possibly have originally been psychical (and therefore sexual)? I have known cases in which the man could masturbate only with the right hand and Martius stated that this was also so!! When Priapos was given a statue with his hand on the penis it was on the contrary also the left.[5] Might early auto-erotic practices not determine which was to be later skillful hand, in some cases right, in others left. Probably this is quite foolish, but if you think there might be anything in it I should be glad to know.

I am glad you found Putnam had some practical knowledge of P. A.; I was afraid it was only slight. The article of his to which you refer was one on Character-formation, published in a book called *Psychotherapeutics* (a collection of articles by eight writers, including myself). He says there, referring to my article on P. A., "I will only say that the longer I have studied the matters of which this paper treats, the more fully I am convinced of their significance". Also: ". . . persistence into later years, of mental twists and habits formed in childhood, not in their own form, but strangely altered and concealed. The principle itself is familiar enough, but it is to the keenness and genius of Freud that we owe its working out . . . ." .[6] He is writing two articles on P. A., which will appear in the Feb. and April numbers of the *Journal of Abnormal Psychology.* No doubt he will send you reprints.[7] I do not know which article of mine he spoke of to you; I have written several, and will of course send you reprints of them. He is to read a paper before the American Psychological Association annual meeting in Boston Dec. 29 on the Relation between Bergson and Freud's conceptions of the Unconscious.[8] The secretary also asked me to read a paper, and I have given as a subject "Freud's Theory of Dreams". It will be short, only 20 minutes allowed, but I will ask the editor of the *Psychological Review* if I may publish it there in extended form with examples to illustrate the points.[9] I have a good collection of dream analyses, both of patients and my own. Morton Prince is to read a paper on the same day on Dreams.[10] He wrote to me to be prepared for an attack, so I suppose we shall have a battle royal. I will send you an account of the meeting.

Adolf Meyer has asked me to write a 9000 word article on Freud's Psychology (review) for the March no. of the *Psychological Bulletin.*[11] I haven't begun it yet, but I expect I shall find it difficult. However I will do my best and shall probably call on your help, as you are always very generous with it, a fact I personally very greatly appreciate.

Last month I gave an address on P. A. before the Niagara District Association. It was excellently received, and it has just been accepted by the *Journal of Nervous and Mental Disease,* probably for March.[12] In January my Hamlet and also the Nightmare article come out.[13] I am full of plans for future work but will not speak of them, for experience has shewn me that I never carry out more than half of what I plan, although I work very hard (This year I find I have published 18 articles,[14] mostly neurological however). Private practice is satisfactory, I have four or five P. A. a day and much other work, especially teaching in the University. Last week the Government started an out-patient Clinic for Nervous and Mental Diseases,[15] and appointed me Director. I am giving (by request) a series of lectures on your work and Jung's at the asylum. They are well attended and evoke much interest.

I was very interested to hear about Modena of Ancona, for I think I can claim a little credit in his taking up the work. We spend [spent] a month together at Kraepelin's clinic ten years ago.[16] He was then averse to your work, but we had many talks and have since corresponded. He was much taken up with anatomy and I had difficulty in getting him to realise the importance of the psychological point of view. Have you heard from Assagioni [Assagioli] of Florenz?

We are greatly looking forward to your next work. The 2e Hälfte des *Jahrbuchs* has not yet arrived, perhaps it is not yet out. I sent Jung last week the review of the English literature he asked for the *Jahrbuch*.[17]

Would you like me to translate the Clark lectures, or are they doing it in Worcester?[18] It is good news that you soon recovered from the journey, and especially from the American cooking.

Is the month of the congress yet decided on?

I apologise for the undue length of this epistle, but you see there were many things I wanted to tell you.

With warmest regards

Yours ever
Ernest Jones.

1. I have not been able to track down Jones's letters to Jung. The collection at Sigmund Freud Copyrights Ltd., Wivenhoe, England, which I first examined in 1984, contained Jung's original letters to Jones, primarily between 1907 and 1914.

2. Crossed out in the original.

3. Crossed out in the original.

4. The Egyptian goddess Isis (eternal mother), symbol of fertility, was the mother of Horus, a sun god.

5. Priapus was a fertility god with extremely large genitals. Jones's preoccupation here with mythological figures in relation to the issue of right and left was linked to his self-analysis and his personal exploration of the concept of bisexuality. See the description and analysis of a dream (Jones, *Papers*, 5th ed., pp. 240–241), which refers to Priapus and the question of phallic symbolism.

6. See Jones (1909c), and Prince et al. (1910, pp. 189, 202–203).

7. Part 2 of Putnam (1909–10) appeared in the February–March 1910 issue of the *Journal of Abnormal Psychology.*

8. Putnam delivered a paper titled "Freud's and Bergson's Theories of the Unconscious" at the annual meeting of the American Psychological Association, Boston, 29–31 December 1909. For a synopsis, see *Psychological Bulletin*, 7 (1910): 44.

9. This did not appear in *Psychological Review*; see Jones (1910d).

10. Prince (1910a).

11. Jones (1910h).

12. Jones (1910c).

13. Jones (1910a) and (1910m).

14. For 1909 the bibliography of Jones's writings contains fourteen articles (Jones, 1909a–1909n). At least four others might be included for consideration as part of the 1909 series: Jones (1910a), the essay on Hamlet, which appeared in the January 1910 issue of the *American Journal of Psychology;* Jones (1910o), which was based on an address delivered at the Toronto Orthopedic Hospital, 13 November 1909; Jones (1909–10), which appeared in the December 1909–January 1910 issue of the *Journal of Abnormal Psychology;* and Jones (1910c), which was based on an address delivered before the Niagara District Association of St. Catherine's, Ontario, 24 November 1909. We might

also consider Jones (1911h), which likely dates from the 1909 period; and possibly Jones (1910d), which was to be delivered 29 December 1909.

15. A picture of this clinic, a decrepit-looking shack, is contained in Cyril Greenland, *Charles Kirk Clarke: A Pioneer of Canadian Psychiatry* (Toronto: Clarke Institute of Psychiatry, 1966), p. 17.

16. Jones's analysis of the numerical slip is contained in his letter to Freud of 12 February 1910 (letter 26) in response to Freud's letter of 11 January (letter 24).

17. Jones (1910n).

18. The translator was Harry W. Chase, fellow in psychology, Clark University; see Freud (1910a).

23

2 January 1910
407 Brunswick Avenue
Toronto

Dear Professor Freud,

First let me thank you for the interesting reprint that arrived this week. Like all your writings it opens the way to all sorts of new problems, but it leaves one with the regret that it was so short. What a store of knowledge you have to give us.

The Boston expedition was I am glad to say eminently satisfactory. The paper on dreams aroused general interest, and Stanley Hall asked me to publish it in an extended form in the April number of the *American Journal of Psychology*.[1] In the discussion Putnam unreservedly expressed his agreement with all your views, as he does in two articles in the *Journal of Abnormal Psychology*,[2] the first of which has already appeared. No doubt he has sent you a reprint. Hall spoke but did not say he agreed with your views, confining himself to generalities such as the fact that it was no longer possible for psychologists to ignore your work, that the investigation of it had become urgent, etc.. The part of my paper that aroused most opposition was, curiously enough, my statement that the Traumgedanke[n] were always egocentric.[3] One wild female flourished two dreams at me that were "entirely altruistic", and declared there was nothing selfish in her, even in her subconscious. Another one said you had no right to generalise that all dreams were egocentric because you hadn't analysed all dreams; it wasn't scientific. What was true of Austrians might not be true of Americans! I said that experience had shown that a man died if he was immersed in deep water for ten minutes. Was one not justified in generalising this statement before proving it on all men and in all seas? Another psychologist said he had been using your psycho-analysis in the study of the aesthetics of humour and found that the results of the analysis depended on the temperature of the room. As you have shamefully neglected to publish records of the varying temperature of your *Sprachzim-mer* [consulting room], your conclusions are all worthless. Of all the ingenious criticisms of P.A. I think this is the finest jewel. It beats anything from Germany, don't you agree? Boris Sidis made a fierce general attack on you, made cheap fun of the "mad epidemic of Freudism now invading America", said your psychology took us back to the dark middle ages, and called you "another of these pious sexualists". I made a passionate, but I hope dignified, reply for which Hall and Putnam warmly thanked me. Putnam was so enraged that he couldn't trust himself to speak. Fortunately Sidis is in very bad odour in the medical profession, and is in a fair way to ruining himself. A lady has just left him a country house and estate worth $600,000 to use as a sanatorium. He is foolishly calling it the Sidis Psychotherapeutic Institute,[4] and I am sure he will get into financial difficulties over it. Prince did not attack us, but merely said he had failed to find that dreams were *always* wish fulfillments. He agrees that they are psychical processes, the symbolic representation of subconscious hidden processes and accepts your mechanisms. *Dass ist schön [schon] etwas.*[5] He is trying to practise P.A. and his whole attitude is quite different from what it used to be. He is full of admiration for your theories, and says that if they are true they constitute a more fundamental discovery than is generally thought. He is reading an address on dreams in New York this month, and got me to write most of it for him.[6] I stayed at his house while in Boston and we had many talks. I may convert him yet, and that would be a great stroke in America. He talked to me pretty frankly about his resistances, the difficulty of giving up old ideas etc., and said he could see we must rely on the [new][7] younger men. I spent one evening at Putnam's and another at Münsterberg's. We held a meeting to organise an American Society of Psycho-Pathology which will meet in the spring.[8] I met Holt, of Harvard, an exceptionally intelligent man and a very clear thinker.[9] He has only used P.A. in every day life, but accepted the whole of your work as soon as he read it. It fitted in with views of his in pure psychology, on the unconscious etc., and he has a book in the press on consciousness which will expound your views.[10]

Did I mention to you an American Jew called Rochester,[11] from Rochester N.Y.? He came last month to spend a week with me talking over P. A. He had been with Brill in the Vanderbilt last year,[12] and since then had been working conscientiously at it in practice. I think he will be pretty good in time.

So you see I am satisfied with the Boston trip, and the whole movement is going forward. Putnam and I discussed the subjects of our papers before the Canadian Medical Assoc. next June. I am to take up general classification and aetiology,[13] and in regard to that have some questions I should be very glad to have an answer from you on. Do you still hold to the asexuelle

Nervosität, without any basis in the sexual constitution? If so how would you clinically differentiate it from slight neurasthenia? Do you ever get pure neurasthenia without some Angstneurose, and how is it *clinically* related to post-influenzal depression and exhaustion? I should greatly like a fuller description of the clinical symptoms of pure neurasthenia. Don't you think the gastric disturbances came from Angstneurose?

With warmest wishes for a happy and successful New Year from

Yours ever
Ernest Jones.

1. Jones (1910d).
2. Parts 1 and 2 of Putnam (1909–10).
3. See Jones (1910d, pp. 141–142).
4. Sidis's institute was located in Portsmouth, New Hampshire.
5. "That is already something."
6. See Prince (1910a), for his report to the New York Neurological Society, 4 January 1910.
7. Crossed out in the original.
8. See note 1 to letter 32.
9. Edwin B. Holt (1873–1946), American psychologist, Ph.D. 1901 Harvard, taught at Harvard and Princeton; incorporated the notion of purpose or motivation in behavioral psychology.
10. See Holt (1915).
11. Haydon Rochester (b. 1879), M.D. 1902 University and Bellevue Hospital Medical College, New York; practicing psychiatrist.
12. The Vanderbilt Clinic in New York.
13. Jones (1910k).

24

11 January 1910
Vienna, IX. Berggasse 19

Dear Dr. Jones,

The post from America brought so much good news today that I shall no longer postpone replying to your letter of 18 December. Together with Putnam's paper in Morton Prince's journal,[1] and a letter from Brill, came a very cheerful letter from St[anley] Hall, with the account of how he and Putnam dealt with Boris Sidis. Things seem to be progressing well after all, and it pleases me that your prophecies of doom do not come true.

I am even more pleased by the personal content of your letter. Do not believe that I am likely to underestimate a man of your capacity for work and intelligence, or that I would give him up easily. You have had your period of vacillation in your own way and expressed your resistance in a particular manner, but each of us had such a phase, and your elegantly phrased and honest letter puts everything right again and gives me the best expectations for the future. I also gather from Brill's account how much your relationship has changed for the better. It would also be too sad if psychoanalysis could not exert an improving influence on our own characters and move us to mutual tolerance. Let us remember the line from our Prince: use every man after his desert, and who should [shall] 'scape whipping?[2]

In the matter of left-handedness, I should be more inclined to view the organic factor rather than the psychical as the primary one, but I have no well-founded judgment in all this.

I readily believe you would have made a better translation of my Worcester lectures, but the University offered to do it and now everything has been done.[3] Hall, who very much praises your short dream lecture, wants to acquire it for a $\psi\alpha$ issue of his journal[4] and has probably done so already.

The Congress is to be held at Easter. I expect Jung to let me know the exact date within the next few days.[5] In Zurich things are quite lively too. The latest news from Russia is that Ossipow in Moscow is competing for an award in ΨA from the Moscow Academy.[6] Assagioli introduced himself to me by letter, and Modena is considering Italian translations.[7] I doubt that you could have met him ten years ago at Kraepelin's. Ten months, perhaps?[8]

I shall be brief because my writer's cramp is particularly painful today; I am afraid that you won't be able to read my writing as it is. Actually I am not fully recovered from the journey, and have been suffering since then from appendix pains. Let us hope that in exchange something respectable will emerge for our movement in America.

You are young, and I am already envious of your ceaseless activity. The bit in Putnam's essay—He is no longer a young man[9]—hurt me, and this outweighed any pleasure I was able to get from the rest of the paper.

In eager anticipation of your dispatches

with cordial greetings, Yours,
Freud

1. Putnam (1909–10).

2. Quoted in English, from Shakespeare's *Hamlet*, act 2, scene 2, lines 516–517. Also quoted in Freud (1917e, p. 246).

3. The fact that this translation was done "under Freud's supervision" is noted by Steiner (1987, pp. 71ff.).

4. Jones (1910d).

5. Held 30–31 March 1910, at Nuremberg, where the International Psychoanalytic Association was founded.

6. M. E. Ossipow was to enter a prize competition for the best essay on psychoanalysis; see Jones (1955a, p. 76; 1955b, p. 84). For Ossipow's contributions to psychoanalysis at the time, see M. Wulff, "Die russische psychoanalytische Literatur bis zum Jahre 1911," *Zentralblatt*, 1 (1911): 364–371.

7. Modena was planning to translate Freud (1905d); see Roberto Assagioli, "Die Freudschen Lehren in Italien," *Jahrbuch*, 2 (1910): 352. See also Jones's interpretation

of one of his own dreams in which Modena's name figures prominently regarding the issue of translation (Jones, 1910d, p. 290).

8. Jones examines his slip of the pen in his letter of 12 February 1910 (letter 26).

9. In English in the original. From Putnam (1909–10, p. 294).

25

27 January 1910
Vienna, IX. Berggasse 19

Dear Dr. Jones,

Your letter would have been worthy of a faster reply, but there was too much work this week.[1]—If I must use these characters I may as well write in English and you will understand me much better. My handwriting has deteriorated so very much since the American trip.

Let me first answer to your scientific questions:

1) If I still hold to non sexual nervosism?—No, I only used this as a non prejudicial name. I think, it is the same in its essence, the sexual mechanism having become attacked by a non sexual agent. But the fact is, I have made no inquiry since then, when I used to see much more patients however superficially, and so you are free to examine and to rebuild the matter as you can.

2) What with Neurasthenia? No I have not changed my mind about it, but I can give no better knowledge than I did at that time, as cases of N. did not submit themselves to Psychoanalysis. All this matter of N. has to be revised thoroughly. I still believe it to be an actuality-neurosis, the symptoms not determined by complexes but the immediate effect of intoxication (or the like) but I guess the psychical moment in N. has been underrated and wants to be introduced to a big amount into the pathogenesis of the disease.

3) Sure there are cases of N. with no anxiety at all, mostly of pollutional origin, but not very frequent, best in very young people.

4) As for exhaustion you must apply to analysis. I trust you will find it does not differ essentially from Neurasthenia. But rather dont ask me.

I am very glad you are doing so excellent work, are coming along in a very satisfactory way with Brill and I find your article on "Psychoanalysis and Psychotherapy"[2] is splendid and just the thing we want to put these Americans into the right position towards our work. The same is the case with Brills paper on my conception of Hysteria.[3] You ought not to leave off to keep together. Putnam is very nice, a true soul he seems. As for Morton Prince I am glad to see that now you impress him more in your present condition of a strong partisan than you could when you used diplomacy and compromisses.[4] You see it is only by your own determina-

tion you can convince and gain adherents: Bleuler's suggestion by affectivity.[5]

Your report of the discussion on dreams is delicious; I had to tell it on
the Wednesday meeting.[6]

Writing no[w] gets so hard for me that I hasten to put an end to this
letter. How is your Hamlet? I hope to hear soon from you and give you
my best love and good wishes for 1910

Yours
Freud

1. First line is written in German, in Latin characters.
2. Jones (1909c).
3. Brill (1909b).
4. Freud is likely following the German here: *Kompromiss* = compromise.
5. See Eugen Bleuler (1906), *Affectivity, Suggestibility, Paranoia*, trans. C. Rickener
(Utica, N.Y.: State Hospitals Press, 1912).
6. The Wednesday meeting of the Vienna Society was held on 26 January 1910. Freud's
comments on Jones are not recorded in *Minutes*, 2:412–414.

26

12 February 1910
407 Brunswick Avenue
Toronto

Dear Professor Freud,

Your last letter gave me one of the greatest happinesses of my life, and
I am still so moved by it that I cannot write about your personal remarks
more than to thank you with all my heart for your kindness.

I warmly hope that your physical ailment is now a thing of the past. It
is too bad that America should deal you a mean blow through its cooking.

I was much touched by your reference to Putnam's remark, and am sure
he did not mean it in the sense you took it. People are apt to think that
every revolutionary investigator must be "only a young man", and he
wished to indicate that you are a man of vast experience. You always have
the consolation of remembering that your mind is younger than anyone
else's, and that it will take several generations to catch up to date with
you. All we younger men can do will be to work out some of the details
of your ideas, and apply them.

Neither Brill, Putnam nor I can come to the Nuremberg congress, to our
great regret. I have a psychiatry course on just at that time, and cannot
escape from it. Do you not think the time is ripe to apply a suggestion
you made in the *Traumdeutung*, namely to make a collection of typical
dreams?[1] Why not establish a central bureau at Jung's to which short

accounts of analyses could be sent by different workers? Then after a couple of years the results could be worked up for the *Jahrbuch*. Would it not be a suitable subject to discuss at the Congress? The same applies to typical symbolisms. It has often struck me that we meet with the same symbolisms in different countries, and that associations are readily coined for these although the words are different in the various languages.[2] These must be more primitive than the other typical symbolisms which are peculiar to one language, and therefore more accidental (e.g. 8 = *in Acht nehmen*.).[3] Pardon me for my presumption in making these suggestions, for I know they must have occurred to you.

I sent the Boston Dream article to the English *Review of Neurology*, for every little counts in spreading the gospel, but I am very dissatisfied with it. I am more pleased with the extended one I recently sent to Hall, which will appear in April.[4] Brill is writing an article on Wit that will come out in the same number of the *American Journal of Psychology*.[5] If you ever see this journal look up the January number, where Hall has written a personal appreciation of you (unsigned) à propos of the *Schriften zur angewandten Seelenkunde*.[6] I am at present busy on the paper for the *Psychological Bulletin* on "Freud's Psychology",[7] and find it excessively difficult. I so much want to do it well, and realise my incapacity to do it justice very keenly indeed. I am sending you two reprints of the Hamlet article[8] in case anyone else in Wien might like a copy (? can Rank read English). It is much enlarged since you saw it.

I have just read with great pleasure the new edition of the *Psychopathologie des Alltagslebens*. May I give two little personal instances. You say that in my letter to you I talked of meeting Modena at München *ten* years ago. Assuming that you have not misread my bad handwriting this is of course a Verschreiben for *two* years (Nov. 1907). It is ten years since I qualified as a doctor. Ten years has no other relation to psychopathology, for I was interested in general neurology and psychology throughout my student days, but only became interested in psychopathology in 1903–4. I interpret the Verschreiben as indicating a wish that the München experience was longer ago; I therefore put it at the beginning of my career. It was early in 1907 namely that I just got acquainted with your work, and so am justified in calling that year the beginning of my knowledge of psychopathology. I certainly wish it were longer ago, so that I hadn't wasted the earlier years and could now have had more ΨA experience.[9]

Another more unusual instance is the following. From about the age of 12 until almost the present I had the obsession never to write anything, a letter, address an envelope, school task, etc., without under-signing it thus ⟶.[10] I always interpreted it to myself as standing for Science, which I greatly idealised. I know now that it stands for Sybil, the name of my younger sister. I have found out by dream analysis that when she was

born, when I was 3⁸/₁₂, I had the double phantasy that she was my child
(a) from my mother and myself, (b) from the doctor and myself. A masochistic dream relating to the doctor is given (in a slightly changed form) in my
dream article in Hall's journal.[11] All my life I have treated my sister as my
father treated us, i.e. very impatiently and arrogantly, and although I am
very fond of her have never been able to live with her, until last year,
without quar[r]elling,[12] on this account. In writing, which with me is very
directly sexually symbolic, I therefore put her *below* me, in a double sense
(a) as my child (b) erotically. What do you think of that?

I am collecting material for an article on *Psychopathologie des Alltagslebens* that I hope to write in about six months time.[13] Before that I have
three others to do: (1) Dreams and psychopathology for the American
Medico-Psychological Association in May. (2) ΨA and Education, I have
been asked to write for the new *Journal of Educational Psychology*. I have
as yet no idea what to say. (3) General Conception of the Psychoneuroses
for the Canadian Medical Association in June.[14] Could you perhaps spare
the time sometime to help me in this by adding a little to what you have
written on neurasthenia, especially (a) the clinical side of the aetiology.
How long after cessation of masturbation can the symptoms continue? I
suppose you make psychical conflict essential for its production? (b)
Definition of symptoms, (c) treatment.

With apologies for troubling you so much, and with my warmest regards
I am

Yours ever
Ernest Jones.

1. See "Typical Dreams" sections in Freud (1900a, pp. 37–38, 241–276, 385–404).

2. This idea is developed in more detail in his essay "Symbolic Significance of Salt"
(Jones, 1912h; 1951, pp. 22–109); but see also the important monograph on symbolism
in general (Jones, 1916a).

3. The German word *Acht* means attention, care, or heed, consideration, as well as
the number eight. In the expression *in acht nehmen* (to respect, esteem), *Acht* derives
from the same root as *der Ahn* (ancestor); *der Ahn* is someone who demands our respect.
Acht meaning the number eight, however, derives from the Greek *oktō*. For Freud's use
of *ahnen*, see note 3 to letter 209.

4. See Jones (1910d) regarding both versions.

5. The paper did not appear in the *American Journal of Psychology*; see Brill (1911).

6. See unsigned review of Freudian literature, *American Journal of Psychology*, 21
(1910): 168–170.

7. Jones (1910h).

8. Jones (1910a).

9. In his historical writings Jones suggests that his experience in the practice of psychoanalysis dates from 1905–6. Consider several passages from his later years: "I well
remember the first patient with whom I practised the new therapy [psychoanalysis],
surely the first person to be analysed outside of German-speaking countries (1905–6)"

(Jones, 1945, p. 9). "In that year, 1905, forty-eight years ago, I ventured on the practice of psycho-analysis. I well remember my first case, the first one to be analysed outside of German-speaking countries" (Jones, 1954, p. 202). "The first case [Jones's] to be analysed outside German-speaking countries (1905–6) was one of conversion hysteria" (Jones, 1955a, p. 28; 1955b, p. 31). "I began practising his method [Freud's] at the end of 1906 and well remember my first patient" (Jones, 1959, p. 162). For a discussion of the historical issues related to Jones's first attempts at practicing psychoanalysis, see Paskauskas (1985, pp. 104–120). See also the passage associated with note 3 to letter 190.

10. In fact, Jones's signature in every one of his letters to Freud is underscored with this symbol, except for those he did not sign himself, or in the few cases where space was lacking. See the List of Correspondence.

11. See Jones (1910d, pp. 301–305), and Jones, *Papers*, 5th ed., pp. 237–240.

12. In the place where the second *r* would normally appear, Jones seems either to have crossed it out or to have inserted an *r* retrospectively.

13. Jones (1911g).

14. The first paper was not delivered. For the other two, see Jones (1910f, 1910k).

27

14 February 1910
407 Brunswick Avenue
Toronto

Dear Professor Freud,

Just a line to thank you for your letter, which arrived just a day after I had written to you.

Your remarks about neurasthenia were very helpful. I am glad to hear you think the factor of psychical conflict also important in it, for I cannot help having that strong impression myself. I have seen excessive and long-continued masturbation (daily from 14–26) more than once without apparent harm in people who did not think it wrong (one, strange to say, was a clergyman). I was also glad to have my mind put at rest about the non-sexual Nervosität. As you say, there is always a basis of sexual inadequacy, and the other agents (stress of life) merely bring this out. The only remaining point I should like to ask (and I feel ashamed to bother you so much when you have so much to do) is about the *time* relation between cause and effect, i.e. how long can neurasthenic symptoms shew themselves after the cessation of masturbation. It is particularly in regard to therapy that this is important.

I was so glad you liked my ΨA article;[1] it has been well received. I think it is good to take a high scientific attitude, and to rub in words like "profound", "thorough", "penetrating"!

I liked Brill's article in the *Medical Record* exceedingly, and find it the best thing he has done.[2] He presented the theory excellently. He is at present very over-worked, like the rest of us.

The men at the Verein must have enjoyed hearing about the Boston criticisms; they were certainly very comical.

Have you anything coming out in the next number of the *Jahrbuch?* We are eagerly awaiting that, as well as the new edition of the *Drei Abhandlungen.* I hope the Congress will be a huge success, and am very sorry I cannot come to it.

Last week I read at the Detroit Society of Neurology a case that would interest you, a boy of 15 who after a slight accident developed symptoms of cerebral irritation (like after fracture of the skull) and was thought to have meningitis. I saw him two months after, and he was a beautiful simulated foolishness and childishness (like Hamlet). He spoke, behaved and felt like a boy of 4, and it proved to be determined by a strong mother complex (desire to be taken into her bed etc.). He got quite well after ΨA. If I have time I will try to publish it.[3]

With kindest regards

Yours ever
Ernest Jones.

1. Jones (1909c).
2. Brill (1909b).
3. Jones (1910i).

28

10 March 1910
Vienna, IX. Berggasse 19

Dear Dr. Jones,

I am very fond of your letters and papers. Indeed your Hamlet article is excellent and shows you from very favourable sides. I did not recognise it having read the manuscript at W.[orcester] as you remember, it is so much improved. I gave the second copy to the Verein; they are trying to get it translated and published in German if you dont object to it.[1]

I trust by the time going, your talents and your indefatigable activity have won for you the place you aspired in America, and I am sure material success is soon to follow. And you did succeed by dealing frankly with us and overcoming your own resistance, by criticizing your own character, an excellent constellation.

As for the Congress, we are sorry to have none of you amidst us but we feel compensated by this years visit. Perhaps it will be news to you, as it was to me, that Jung has left Europe for America yesterday on bord the "Kronprinzessin Caecilie"; he has been called to Chicago, has to leave the 22d of this month and be present at the Congress the 30th.[2] Smart, is he? Will you take the opportunity to see him?

Your two bits of Self-Analysis are all right. None can contradict you if such are your results.

As for Neurasthenia I must confess, this topic needs a complete reassumption by means of our modern knowledge. As regards the time between the cessation of masturbation and the appearance of symptoms, it is hard to give a general statement. I remember some cases, where the interval was very short.

Your proposition to attack the problems of symbolisms by collective investigation I willingly accept and have instigated Stekel to put it before the Congress. No doubt, it will be executed in the way you intended, but Stekel is likely to become the headman of the comitee. It is a good way to get him under control.

The 2d edition of the *Sextheorie* will come to you in a few days. I am writing a paper on Leonardo da Vinci, Heft 7 *angewandte Seelenkunde*.[3] The *Jahrbuch* is under press. I am very busy and in better health, much trouble in my family, sorry to say.[4] After all Putnam may be more correct as regards my age than you. Have you read the article of *Hart* on the Unconscious?[5] The first clever word upon the matter.

I am yours sincerely
Freud

1. Jones (1910a).
2. The Second International Psychoanalytic Congress, 30–31 March 1910 at Nuremberg, where the International Psychoanalytic Association was first formed. Freud was particularly anxious about Jung's trip to America just prior to the meeting; see McGuire (1974, p. 304).
3. Freud (1910c).
4. This may be a reference to the poor health of Freud's mother-in-law, Emmeline (née Philipp) Bernays, who would die of cancer the following autumn; see Jones (1955a, p. 78; 1955b, p. 87).
5. Hart (1909–10).

29

30 March 1910
407 Brunswick Avenue
Toronto

Dear Professor Freud,

First let me thank you for kindly sending me the *Drei Abhandlungen*. It was all the more welcome in that I lent my copy to a friend in England and never got it back, and have not been able to get another copy since it has been out of print. In fact I recently had to get Brill to lend me his so as to look up some points. The added footnotes were very interesting, especially the one on homosexuality;[1] I suppose you had good reasons for not re-writing the book, but one naturally regrets you didn't think fit to add more.

Your letter and kind remarks were exceedingly welcome; many, many thanks. Your encouragement is especially valuable to me for many reasons; first the obvious one of pupil and master, then the fact that I am more responsive than initiative by nature and only work under an external personal stimulus, then further that in my work I am very isolated, for almost all my friends and relatives have used their strongest influence to dissuade me from undertaking "such dangerous work" (sexual). It was a big break with them all for me to continue it alone, for at that time I had no personal help from you and the school, [and had][2] having various internal troubles, and only my intense conviction that your work was profoundly true and important carried me through. Fortunately things are now in smoother water, chiefly owing to you personally, so you see I am both grateful to and dependent on you.

I hope you are pleased with the result of the Congress. I hope to hear an account of it from Jung. I did not hear of his scurrying visit till it was over. He is getting quite a "world-trotter". (Now, why have I written "world" instead of the ordinary phrase "globe-trotter"? The analysis doesn't come to me straight off; I must try again later).

It is delightful to hear that your health is again all right, and I sincerely hope the family trouble will soon be past.

It is exciting news that you are writing on Da Vinci. What a superb subject! And now we shall know what were the wonderful dreams he saw behind La Vierge aux Rochers and La Gioconda, and what was the secret of his mirror-writing (you know it has recently been proved he was not left-handed?). Do you remember Walter Pater's essay on Da Vinci, published in his *Renascance*?[3] You must quote his page of description of the Monna Lisa, for it is the most [ma]gnificent[4] and beautiful passage of its kind in English literature. If you haven't it by now, I enclose a copy of it.

I should like sometime to hear further your opinion of Hart's article, and whether you agree with all of it. I suggested to him to write it last August. He was one of my best pupils in England, although I had at first some difficulty in getting him to take up your work. Ultimately he said "Freudism is strictly speaking a religion; you can't *prove* it, but you have to accept it because "it works"", which was quite clever. He has so far no practical experience of ΨA, but I have every hope he will do much valuable work on the philosophical principles of the theory. You can see he is a devoted disciple of Karl Pearson. Do you know Pearson's *Grammar of Science*?[5] It would greatly please you, though there is nowadays nothing new in it. It is the grandest exposition of the fundamental principles of science that I know of, and inspired me as a student with clear and high scientific ideals, though not so enthusiastically as did W. K. Clifford's *Essays*.[6]

I am glad you like the Hamlet article. I had a letter from Paul Tausig,[7] Wien, about translation, which I naturally should like, but I wrote to say that I first had to get permission from Stanley Hall. No doubt he will give it. The Nightmare article is to be followed by a casuistic one on cases, and then one on night terrors in children (à la Stekel). This fall I want to write a long article, which I shall offer to you for the *Schriften*, entitled "Die Mahre in der Mythologie und in der Geschichte".[8] It will contain much on fear and dreams in relation to the origin of religious belief; I have already most of the material. What do you think of the idea? In the future I feel I shall do much work on Religion, for though dangerous it is an important subject in Anglo Saxon countries. That, however, must be later; I have much to learn first. I think I told you that Meyer asked me to write a review of your psychology for the *Psychological Bulletin*.[9] I did so in February, and have just got the proofs. The last sixth (on wit and everyday life) is cut out; perhaps it is meant to appear in a subsequent number. More than half of the sexual part is cut out without asking my permission, although it was worded as acceptably as I could. I at once wrote back saying (to Prof. Warren, the Editor) that I could not consent to publishing a mutilated article, and that if he wished to exclude the sexual part I must withdraw the whole article. I expect an answer in a day or two, but it was the only thing to do, don't you think so. If they want an expurgated edition of "Freud for the Young" they must get it from a non-Freudian, which is an easy matter.[10] At the Psychopathological Society, which meets for the first time at Washington on May 2, I am reading a paper on "suggestion", à la Ferenczi and of course the *Drei Abhandlungen*.[11]

With kindest Regards

Yours ever
Ernest Jones.

1. The added footnote in Freud (1905d, pp. 144–145) concerns the psychical mechanisms of the development of homosexuality and is appended to the section which deals with the issue of bisexuality.

2. Crossed out in the original.

3. Walter Pater, *Studies in the History of the Renaissance* (1873), later called simply *The Renaissance* (1877).

4. The blotches within the brackets form the letters *si*, indicating that Jones may also have considered writing the word *significant* here.

5. Pearson (1900).

6. W. K. Clifford, *Lectures and Essays*, ed. Leslie Stephen and Frederick Pollock, intro. F. Pollock, 2nd ed. (London: Macmillan, 1886).

7. Paul Tausig translated Jones (1910a).

8. See Jones (1931b, pp. 241–340).

9. Jones (1910h).

10. For Jones's controversy with Howard C. Warren, a founding editor of the *Psychological Bulletin* in 1904, see Leys (1981).

11. Jones (1910–11a), following Ferenczi (1909).

30

15 April 1910
Vienna, IX. Berggasse 19

Dear Dr. Jones,

Your letters prove a continuous source of satisfaction to me, I wonder indeed at your activity, at the size of your erudition and at the recent sincerity of your style. I am happy I did not listen to the internal voices hinting at giving you up when the odds were against you, and now I trust we will walk[1] and work a good bit together.

You must not expect too much of Leonardo, who will come out in the next month, neither the secret of the Vierge aux rochers nor the solution of the Monna Lisa puzzle; keep your hopes on a lower level, so it is likely to please you more. Many thanks for the page from Pater, I knew it and had quoted some lines out of the fine passage.[2] I think L. was "bimanual", but that is about the same thing as left-handed. I have not inquired further into his handwriting, because I avoided by purpose all biological view restraining myself to the discussion of the psychological ones.

As for Harts paper I found it the best on the damned topic of the Unconscious I had read in the last years and enormously superior to Morton Prince's trash. It is a merit to have driven him into this line of work. As for Pearson and Clifford, both of whom I only know by name I have formed the intention to get better acquainted with them, but I have to postpone the execution of this wish until summer, my receptivity being now strained to the utmost by 11 cases of neuroses so that I must react by productive work in order to keep up my equilibrium.

Your essay on the "Mahr" I gladly accept for the *Schriften* next to Leonardo.[3] I have been promised *Pfister* on the Count of Zinzendorf and *Max Graf* (the father of Hans, our little hero) on Rich Wagner and his mother.[4] Whoever arrives first will go to the press before the others.

As regards your behaviour with Prof. Warren I feel sure you ought not to have acted otherwise and hope you will continue the same policy against any similar temptations. The Worcester Lectures are ready for appearance but I have to wait for their coming out in English before I send them off. The April number of the *American Journal of Psychology* has not yet arrived and I have got no other notice.

Nurnberg was a success. We founded an "Internat. ψα Vereinigung" containing the Ortsgruppen of Zürich, Vienna and Berlin (others to follow), giving out a *Correspondenzblatt* every month and paying 2 S or 8 mk or 10 kr every member. We took up Jung as president for the next two years and fixed an [yearly]⁵ annual congress which is to be the source of all the powers. Quite a constitution. At home I resigned as Obmann and had Adler elected in my place. Adler and Stekel are to edit a monthly *"Centralblatt"* as a supplement to the *Jahrbuch*. All are full of fresh hope and promise to work. I am retiring to the backgrounds, as behaves an elderly gentleman (no more compliments pray!)

Yours sincerely
Freud

1. At the time of the Worcester conference Freud was not yet convinced of Jones's commitment to psychoanalysis, and had taken the trouble to "walk" him to the train station to see him off to Toronto. See the first paragraph of letter 73.

2. Pater is cited several times; see Freud (1910c, pp. 110, 111, 115).

3. *Schriften* is written out in Gothic script. Jones's paper did not appear in this series; see Jones (1931b, pp. 241–340).

4. Pfister (1910), and Graf (1911).

5. Crossed out in the original.

31

20 April 1910
407 Brunswick Avenue
Toronto

Dear Professor Freud,

I hope by now you have got over the labours of the Congress, and that you feel happy at the success of it.

It was a great pleasure to read your lectures and Jung's in *The American Journal of Psychology*;¹ a *Wiederleben* [re-living] of old experiences. Your lectures were well translated, though you notice they contain many printer's errors. The only criticism I have heard of them so far is that "an ordinary reader would gather that you advocate free love, removal of all restraints, and a relapse to savagery"!! This from our Professor of Psychiatry.²

My indignant letter to Adolf Meyer about the *Psychological Bulletin* article brought forth satisfactory responses, copies of which I enclose. After getting two letters and a telegram from Meyer and a letter from Warren I again went over the parts left out of the article, and decided to compromise. I insisted on their putting in parts, about incest and about the shifting of the erogenous zone in women, and let them omit a few [matters]³ points of detail that didn't at all matter. I think you will agree after you have read the letters that it was the only graceful thing I could do. Warren was evidently in a delicate situation, and honestly doing his best to meet me. To insist on the whole lot would have meant rejection of the article and all future ones; as it is they are both in my debt, always a useful thing with editors. Meyer was pretty decent, but characteristically concerned about himself, an aspect which I must confess hadn't occurred to me. You will naturally keep secret the passage about Warren; I only enclose it because I know you want to be kept *au courant* with affairs in America. It is a damned shame. He is the leading psychologist in America, and has had to resign his professorship, editorship and even the presidency of the next International Congress of Psychology. The American public are no respectors of persons.[4]

I will of course send you a reprint of the article as soon as I get them. It was exceedingly difficult to do, and if you have the time I should be very glad to hear from you the chief errors I made, for that is the best way of learning. My dream article in the *American Journal of Psychology* I am more satisfied with.[5] It lacks the human vitality and interest of Ferenczi's delightful paper,[6] but it is an attempt to indicate the solidity and technical thoroughness of the *Traumdeutung*. Dream Nr 7 is one of my own, slightly altered; it is a masochistic birth dream.[7] Nrs 4 and 5 are from my wife.[8]

I have heard of three editorial articles on my Hamlet essay, and seen two. One favourable one is in the *Umschau* for March 12.[9] Another favourable one, written anonymously by a friend of mine, came out in The *New York Medical Journal* (six columns.). An unfavourable one, written in execrable English, appears in the April no. of the *Interstate Medical Journal*.[10] It doesn't mention your name, and classifies me in the Lombroso school[11] (Ye Gods!). After speaking of the "wilderness" of my criticism of Hamlet the writer says that I teach that natural affection for the mother "should be carefully watched, lest unawares it steals a march on us", and become sexual. "Now this note of warning, we understand from Dr. Jones' essay, was never brought home to Hamlet by any of his medical friends; hence he nurtured what was in the beginning & a natural affection into that phase of abnormal sexuality whose bitternesses are the one thing that invariably fasten the attention of the modern psychologists. . . . who add to the burdens of modern civilisation by weighting us with theories that destroy our faith in numan nature". H. was a pessimist etc., and "why incrust him with other defects that can do naught but prejudice us against the personal beauty of the poetical lines which Shakespeare puts into his mouth? Innocency need not necessarily be the dominant note of modern psychology, but is it absolutely incumbent on all its expositors that they must see sexual abnormality in nearly all the unexplained acts of the unconventional? "

If the writer had read Warren's letter to me he would be relieved of some of his anxiety about the universal preoccupation of all psychologists with "sexual abnormalities".[12]

When is Da Vinci coming out, and what are your next plans? I expect you get shoals of letters from your pupils, especially the younger ones, entreating you to write about this or that subject. May I add to these a little suggestion, which perhaps you may some day have time to consider? I should like you, namely, to write about the development of character traits, and the origin and significance of such sentiments as hate, anger, jealousy, ill-temperedness, conceit, cowardice etc. etc..

Yours devotedly
Ernest Jones.

1. Freud (1910a), and Jung (1910).
2. C. K. Clarke.
3. Crossed out in the original.
4. Jones is referring to the scandal regarding James Mark Baldwin, former editor of the *Psychological Bulletin*, and professor at Johns Hopkins, who was arrested in a Baltimore brothel in 1908, and later forced to resign his academic and other professional positions; see Leys (1981, pp. 448–449).
5. Jones (1910d).
6. Ferenczi (1910).
7. See Jones (1910d, pp. 301–305), and dream no. 8 in Jones, *Papers*, 5th ed., pp. 237–240.
8. Jones (1910d, pp. 293–296); see also Jones, *Papers*, 5th ed., pp. 227–231.
9. The review by Wilhelm Gallenkamp, "Hamlet—ein sexuelles Problem," *Die Umschau*, 9, no. 11 (1910), was already known to Freud; see Jung to Freud, 17 April 1910 (McGuire, 1974, pp. 307–308).
10. Anonymous review, "The Mystery of Hamlet's Motives," *New York Medical Journal*, 91 (1910): 605–607; and Anonymous editorial, "Psychology and Hamlet," *Interstate Medical Journal*, 17 (1910): 221–223; for quoted passages, see pp. 222–223.
11. Cesare Lombroso (1836–1909), Italian anthropologist, posited a correlation between criminality and physiognomy, and subscribed to the theory of degeneration to account for criminal behavior and sexual deviation.
12. For Warren's attitude, see Leys (1981, pp. 448–450).

32

4 May 1910
The New Willard
Washington, D.C.

Dear Professor Freud,

As this letter is being written only an hour after an exciting Freudian debate, please forgive me if the perseverating affect leads me to make it too personal a recital of my recent experiences. First, however, let me thank you for your delightful letter I got last week. It was excellent news about the movement in Europe, and the successful congress. It is a little difficult for us to see what the *two* new journals are for, but, as Brill put it: "You bet those fellows over there know what they're up to". About the American Verein: I do not wish to be conservative, but I am not sure that it wouldn't be better to postpone that for another year or so. We are too few, and too far about, to meet more than once a year, and a Verein in one place would mean the gathering of undesirable outsiders who would waste all the time in questions. Putnam and Hoche [Hoch] both think that, too. Still if it would be a help to the Internationale Vereinigung to have a sub-section in U.S.A. we could make one formally and meet once a year. Things are a little in the transition period just now, and I am sure that shortly there will be a real need for at least two in the U.S.A.

Now for news. Monday morning May 2, was formed a new American Psychopathological Association, with 40 members.[1] Papers were read as follows. Dreams, Prince. Dreams, Waterman. Sexual Symbolism in Dreams, Putnam (full of beautiful examples). Anxiety Neuroses, Brill, with a pretty analysis of a phobia by means of a dream. Action of Suggestion in Psychotherapy, self (à la Ferenczi).[2] I have found many pretty little things in relation to the latter, e.g. animal magnetism was named after metal magnets; the word magnet comes, via the Greek, from two Phoenoecian roots *mag* = powerful man, and *naz* = that which pours out, and influences something else![3] The discussion was altogether Freudian, and went quite smoothly. A committee was appointed of Prince, Waterman, Allen,[4] Meyer, Hoche [Hoch], Putnam and myself, in which you see your interests are fairly well represented. We chose a set subject for next year's meeting: The Pathogenesis of Morbid Anxiety; rapporteurs, Sidis, Donley and myself. Five Honorary members are elected: Freud, Jung, Janet, Forel and Claparède; Switzerland comes out strong.

I was elected member of the American Neurological Association, which is rather an honour, as they usually keep men waiting a few years. At their annual dinner a disagreeable incident occurred, in an after dinner speech by Joseph Collins.[5] He is a N.Y. neurologist, whose wife left him in under a year on account of his coarseness and sadistic brutality; I know about him, for I treated his wife in England by ΨA. He is notorious for his proclivity to indecent jokes. He made, in the worst taste, a personal attack on poor old Putnam, and protested against the Association allowing Putnam to read a paper of "pornographic stories about pure virgins" (another paper to which I shall refer in a minute). "It was time the Assoc. took a firm stand against transcendentalism and supernaturalism, and definitely crushed out Christian Science, Emmanuelism, Freudism, and all that bosh, rot and nonsense", etc., etc. In a recent paper he described your method which he called "Freunds",[6] and said you relied on hypnotism. He is to give a big address in Toronto next month before the Canadian Medical Association, which will be devoted to "stamping out Freudism".[7] As Canada stinks of puritanism, religion and suppression he will probably arouse some strong prejudices against me there, but I will meet him and do the best I can.

At this morning's meeting of the American Neurological Association Putnam read a most excellent paper on "Recent experiences with Freud's method", beautifully written and quite fearless.[8] There was 1½ hours debate, about 15 men. A couple, especially Sachs of N.Y., opposed it, a couple were very sympathetic, especially Llewelys Barker of Baltimore,[9] and the most sat on the fence "valuable aid in severe cases, but all sorts of dangers and disadvantages", etc. Someone said the Assoc. should be thankful that a man of Dr. Putnam's high ethical motives had probed and tested it for us, and this aroused the heartiest applause. There were many stupid things said, but nothing unpleasant or personal. Meyer and Hoch were there but didn't speak; Collins was not there (nor Brill, who had gone home.). My speech dealt chiefly with general questions of resistance etc., and was very well received; in fact quite half the meeting warmly congratulated me after. Putnam replied in detail to the points, and was very clear and persuasive. The feeling of the meeting was certainly more fair-minded than might have been expected, and, as many of the men said after, "The Freudians won hands down". Outside the meetings your work has been all the week in the centre of interest, and I am bombarded with questions. Many men are strongly in favour, and are trying hard to learn it (Coriat, Waterman, D'Orsay Hecht, etc.). I met a man, Sidney Schwab,[10] Chicago, who said he was your first American supporter, having studied under you in 1899, when you read out the *Traumdeutung* in manuscript. He says he has ever since been trying your method, but finds it too difficult, and can get no results. How would you explain that?

On Saturday (May 7) I read a paper on Epilepsy, chiefly following Maeder, at the National Association for the Study of Epilepsy,[11] which meets at Baltimore. Spiller of Philadelphia[12] then wants me to visit him there, but I don't think I shall have time. He was with you in Wien 1893, and sends his compliments to you. I spent then a couple of days at Wards' Island, with Campbell and Hoch, and shall of course see much of Brill. I am sharing a room with Hoch this week here, and like him very much indeed. He is a quite convinced Freudian and understands the work, but he recognises that he has not had enough experience to "feel the attitude", as he put it very clearly. He read an excellent paper on Psychogenesis of Dementia Praecox this morning, giving the fullest credit to you and Jung all through, and relating a neat sexual analysis of a case.[13] Jung made a valuable impression on him in Zürich this winter, but I do not think their rapport was quite perfect; still I feel sure that he has no serious resistances, and that he will be a good supporter. Probably Jung told you he suffers from a phobia. Adolf Meyer I like less and less. He bores me, which is the most unpardonable crime in civilised society. I am sure he does not understand your work at all, and I don't think he will ever overcome his resistances (ego-complex); they show themselves in the most stupid little objections. He read a paper today on D. P.,[14] very dull, obscure, and general—nothing in it. "There are two routes to investigate these matters, Freud and Jung's referring to concrete experiences, and my own dealing with *habit-reactions*".[15] It is Bezzola over again.[16]

Did I tell you I was giving 12 lectures on the Psycho-neuroses before the Hamilton Medical Society (Ontario).? They are going very well so far; it is easy to make a good impression when you have your men under your eye and can explain difficulties; especially with general practitioners who have to take what one says as the pure Gospel.

I am sure that is quite enough news for one time. The movement is bound to go forward in America, and I only wish I could do more for it in England. Perhaps, some day? I dearly long to go back there.

With warmest greetings from

Yours always
Ernest Jones.

1. Consider the various accounts provided by Jones in his historical writings regarding the founding of the association. On one occasion he wrote, "I had the idea of founding the American Psychopathological Association, and, with the help of Brill, Hoch, Morton Prince and Putnam, the first meeting was held in May, 1910" (Jones, 1945, p. 10). In his biography of Freud he referred to "the new American Psychopathological Association I was just founding" (Jones 1955a, p. 58; 1955b, p. 64). And in his autobiography he wrote, "On the whole my centre was Boston . . . I used my influence there to found the American Psychopathological Association" (Jones, 1959, p. 234). The issue of Jones's involvement in the founding of the association is treated in Eugene Taylor, "Who Founded the American Psychopathological Association?" *Comprehensive Psychiatry*, 27 (1986): 439–445. For a synopsis of the events and other personalities involved, see Samuel W. Hamilton, "Notes on the History of the American Psychopathological Association: 1910–1931," *Journal of Nervous and Mental Disease*, 102 (1945): 30–53.

2. See Prince (1910), Waterman (1910), Brill (1910b), and Jones (1910–11a), following Ferenczi (1909). Putnam's paper seems not to have been published.

3. A more elaborate discussion of the magnet is contained in Jones (1910–11a); see Jones, *Papers*, 2nd ed. 1918, pp. 340–341. The phrase "pours out" is underscored with a wavy line.

4. Alfred Reginald Allen (1876–1918), M.D. 1898 University of Pennsylvania Medical School; Philadelphia neurologist, assistant to Weir Mitchell.

5. Joseph Collins (b. 1866), M.D. 1888 New York University, prominent American neurologist. He was professor of neurology at the Post-Graduate Medical School, New York (1898–1909), and a president of the American Neurological Association (1902).

6. In Joseph Collins, "Aphasia," in *A System of Medicine*, ed. William Osler (London:

Frowde, Hodder, and Stoughton, 1910), p. 315, we find "the name optic aphasia has been given by Freud."

7. Collins (1910).

8. Putnam (1910a).

9. Bernard Sachs, M.D. 1882 University of Strassburg, president of the American Neurological Association (1894). Llewelys Franklin Barker, Canadian-born American neurologist, M.B. 1890 and M.D. 1905 (honorary) University of Toronto; he was professor of medicine, Johns Hopkins University (1905–1913), and president of the American Neurological Association (1916).

10. Isador H. Coriat (1875–1943), M.D. 1900 Tufts College Medical School, trained in neurology and psychiatry; important American psychoanalyst in Boston from 1913 onward. D'Orsay Hecht, M.D. 1898 Northwestern University Medical School, and later associate professor of nervous and mental disorders. Sidney I. Schwab, M.D. 1896 Harvard, president of the American Neurological Association (1921).

11. Jones (1910j).

12. William Gibson Spiller, M.D. 1892 University of Pennsylvania Medical School; editor of *Journal of Nervous and Mental Disease*, and president of the American Neurological Association (1905).

13. Hoch (1910).

14. Meyer (1910b).

15. In the published version the wording of this passage is significantly different, although the meaning remains roughly the same; see Meyer (1910b, p. 280).

16. Dumeng Bezzola (1861–1936), Swiss psychiatrist, studied hysterical phenomena; criticized heavily by Freud and Jung; see McGuire (1974, pp. 29, 32, 50, 53, 85, 93, 114, 115).

33

22 May 1910
Vienna, IX. Berggasse 19

My dear Dr. Jones,

I have to thank [you] for a lot of publications and two letters full of matter of high interest. But before all let me express again my conviction, that you are the most skilful, powerful and devote[d] helper, Psychoanalysis could have found in the New World. I trust your longing to go back to England will meet with no satisfaction for a long while. America will keep you and offer you enough to feel at home there.

Among the papers I liked most that on my psychology,[1] being a very unphilosophical mind myself and feeling proudly surprised to be in posession of something of that kind. Let me add that I am glad you are not one of those fellows who want to show themselves original and totally independent every time they do something in writing, but you do not despise to show yourself as interpreter of anothers thoughts. It is a proof that you feel *sure* of your own originality and subordinate easily your personal ambition to the interests of the cause. Indeed you seem to have changed in a most thorough and satisfactory manner.

I will have to give my best thanks to old Putnam. He is an honest man. As for Collins I am glad to hear you know enough of his personal life, to make one proud of his enmity. You are quite [write so]² right [. . .]³ about A. Meyer, he is unreliable and tries to turn things to his personal profit. Brill and Jung agreed about him at Worcester.

Now for our news. The *"Zentralblatt"* is a fact, Bergmann is editor, the first number to appear in Oktober, I acting as "Herausgeber".⁴ It is no rival of the *Jahrbuch,* but a supplement to it. The activity of my Vienna people wanted it as a compensation for the lost Hegemony. I hope it will do much good in educating the medical readers by smaller and easier samples of our work. You will be invited to put your name in the list of contributors.

As regards your American Section of the "International", you will make it out with Jung, who now acts as official leader of the movement. Personally I think, you ought to form something like a section, pay your contributions of S–2 a year and get the *"Correspondenzblatt"* for it, to keep in continuous relation with the European members. The work of organisation seems to go on slowly with the Zürich people too. Jung mentions difficulties, prepared for him by Bleuler and Frank.

The *Leonardo* is to come out in the last days of this month. I am very busy and by no means well these weeks, suffering from Influenza and the consequences of my American dyspepsia. So I do not much work of any value. I am preparing some smaller articles for the two Periodicals, that's all. As regards your call to write on character formation, I must confess that I feel not competent to the task. Jung could do it better as he is studying men from the superficial psychical layers downwards, while I am progressing in the opposite direction. Besides any kind of systematic work is inconsistent with my gifts and inclinations. I expect all my impulses from the impressions in the intercourse with the patients.

mit herzlichen Grüssen I am dear Dr. Jones

Ihr
Freud

1. Jones (1910h).
2. Crossed out in the original.
3. Crossed-out word is illegible.
4. J. F. Bergmann was the publisher; Wilhelm Stekel and Alfred Adler were the initial editors. The operation was "directed" by Freud.

34

3 June 1910
407 Brunswick Avenue
Toronto

Dear Professor Freud,

At last I have a defeat to chronicle, not too serious, I hope, but still unmistakeably a defeat. Hoch, Putnam and I read papers at the Canadian Medical Association this week,[1] and I don't think any of the three were very good, all being produced via complicated inhibitions. Joseph Collins spoke in the discussion, which was very animated, and on the next day read a paper.[2] He was too clever for us. I had prepared answers for the lines I expected him to take, but he surprised us by being very mild and diabolically insinuating. The feeling of the meeting was decidedly on his side, though I honestly think less so after the discussion than before it, which is something. I think it will not have a bad effect in general—it will stimulate more interest and experiment, which is what we want—but it may injure me locally. There is lately a strong prejudice in Toronto against me on account of the stress I lay on sexual matters, and it is likely to injure me especially in University and other appointments, but one can only hope for the best. I have taken a decided stand, and will stick to it—it is the easiest and most natural way.

Friedlander has sent a hostile article to Prince's Journal, but it cannot be published till next year for lack of space.[3]

Hoch, who is thoroughly convinced of all your views, Putnam and I spent a very agreeable three days together, talking hard over many matters. Hoch has a rather strong prejudice against Brill, on account of his unpopularity in Ward's Island and also some unprofessional behaviour in medico-legal cases, but I managed to do something to soften this.

There is no other news from this side, contrary to my usual budget. I had a letter from Mott[4] of London today, congratulating me on spreading the knowledge of "Freud's valuable work" in England; that is good, for he is the only scientific psychiatrist there. Unfortunately he is very anatomical.

The *Jahrbuch* has not yet arrived, but I suppose it will be out soon. Thank you very much for the reprint of your lectures,[5] which I was very glad to get. Tausig tells me you will probably write a short introduction to the Hamlet translation; that is exceedingly kind of you.

I hope to have better news next time.

With Kindest Regards

Yours ever
Ernest Jones.

1. See August Hoch, "The Relation of Insanity to the Psychoneuroses," *Canadian Lancet*, 44 (1910–11): 107–118; Putnam (1910b), and Jones (1910k).

2. Collins (1910).

3. Friedländer (1911).

4. F. W. Mott (1853–1926), M.D. 1886 London; director of the Pathological Laboratory, London County Asylum, Claybury; one of Jones's former mentors.

5. Freud (1910a).

35

19 June 1910
407 Brunswick Avenue
Toronto

Dear Professor Freud,

First let me thank you for kindly sending me the *Leonardo* book. I had followed your advice and not expected too much, so that when it came it charmed me very much to find such a delightfully delicate analysis. There is no credit in drawing conclusions when the material is so full as to make them obvious, but to trace them out, and to lighten the obscurity, when the clues are so fine and easily overlooked—that is the really wonderful. We must also be grateful that you put in so many general remarks and suggestions. What a tremendous work we have to do to follow up and expand your hints!

Also I have warmly to thank you for your very encouraging letter. I am always very happy to hear from you, for your letters mean so much to me, but I often feel ashamed of taking up your time, as there must be many of your pupils who make the same claim. As to originality, which you mentioned, I feel it is a more sensible ideal to aim at developing one's own capacity in whatever direction that may lie than in merely trying to be "original". The originality-complex is not strong with me; my ambition is rather to know, to be "behind the scenes", and "in the know", rather than *to find out*. I realise that I have very little talent for originality; any talent I may have lies rather in the direction of being able to see perhaps quickly what others point out: no doubt that also has its use in the world. Therefore my work will be to try to work out in detail, and to find new demonstrations for the truth of, ideas that others have suggested. To me work is like a woman bearing a child; to men like you, I suppose it is more like the male fertilisation. That is crudely expressed, but I think you will understand what I mean.

The kind of thing that appeals to me is taking a given subject, e.g. umbilicus, buccal erogenous zone, etc., etc., and to try to follow up all its psychological implications by means of dreams, neuroses, mythology,

folklore, everyday life, etc.; the pleasure lying in making the subject as
complete as possible, however small it is, and in the delight of finding
things fit like a child's puzzle. I well remember the ecstatic joy I used to
get by finding or being taught a beautiful demonstration of a rider in Euclid;
it used to amuse my schoolmaster greatly, and it was only by great good
luck that I never took up a mathematical career. I had no real gifts that
way, and should not have been happy in it.

I have been meaning to ask you your opinion of the value of Gross's
differentiation of two types of mind; in his last book on Minderwertigkeit
the idea seems so fruitfully and cleverly worked out that I should much
like your views on it.[1]

Since you think it would be well to make an American section of the
Internationale Vereinigung, we must certainly bring it about; I have written to Brill to ask him to arrange matters with Jung.

With Kindest Regards

Yours ever
Ernest Jones.

1. Otto Gross, *Über psychopathische Minderwertigkeiten* (Vienna: Braumüller, 1909).

36

28 June 1910
407 Brunswick Avenue
Toronto

Dear Professor Freud,

I trust that you have quite got over the influenza by now; you must get
thoroughly set up by your holiday, which I hope will be as interesting as
the American one, but less laborious and less harmful to health.

I posted the reprint to you yesterday you were good enough to ask for,[1]
and also a couple of others. There are several more "cooking".

Reading over again your *Drei Abhandlungen* yesterday I was set thinking
by your remark (about Hans) as to symbolism in early childhood.[2] You
have compared the normal with the neurotic as regards sexual traumata,
but I don't know how much material you have as regards the other matter.
I assume you have a fair amount, but in case any extra material would be
of interest, I subjoin a fragment of my self-analysis. You can postpone
reading it until you have nothing better to do, though that means putting
it off for a long time.

[In unpacking my furn][3]

I should start by saying that I consider myself fairly "normal", perhaps
not quite so much as the average. I had a number of Zwang and Angst

symptoms, especially in juvenile life, never very serious, though quite pathological.—since then analysed.

In unpacking my furniture and arranging it in this house last year I came across a single, wooden stethescope, and on thinking what to do with it was impelled to place it on the consulting-room desk, between me and the patient's chair. I never use it, and keep all other medical instruments in drawers. A few months ago a patient asked me what it was, and why I kept it there. I gave an off-hand answer, but it started me thinking. When I was house-physician ten years ago (Interne) I always used to carry it whenever I went into the wards, though I hardly ever used it—carrying in my pocket a binaural stethescope. That alone is suspicious, and I used to think it was due to imitation of my house-physician, who always did the same, and whom I greatly admired when I was a student. However, it had much deeper grounds as well.

In the last two years I have found out the motive that made me go in for medicine; to do so was a sudden decision at the age of 15, never having previously thought of it. It was a lucky decision, for I cannot imagine myself happy at any other work. As a boy I had greatly admired our family doctor, a handsome dare-devil fellow. We were in a small country-place, and he lived with us till I was three years old. He never much liked me, owing chiefly to my disturbing him then by crying etc.. One day in a rage he hung me in a high water-hutt, which with other traumata formed the later basis for a phobia of heights. Three especial memories stand out, as a sort of Deckerrinerung. (1) I was impressed by a remark of another boy's that the doctor was loved by all the women of the neighbourhood, a fact confirmed by the enormous crowd of weeping women I saw at his funeral, when I was about twelve. Now I have always been conscious of sexual attractions to patients; my wife was a patient of mine. (2) When the doctor died, my mother cried, and I heard her tell my father how kind he had always been to her, and how he had kissed her consolingly the last time he attended her. I recall feeling jealous, or, to be more accurate, wondering if my father was jealous. (3). *Intense*[4] Angst at having the doctor thrust a spoon down my throat to examine it—several times in early childhood; and also on two occasions when he pulled a tooth.

From several dreams, especially No. 7. in my article on dreams,[5] I have no doubt that I was in love with him, and that at the age of $3^{8}/_{12}$, when my younger sister was born,[6] I had the double phantasy that she was the child (a) of the doctor and myself, (b) of myself and my mother.

Now, I well remember, when about ?7 years old,[7] being examined by the doctor who used a single, wooden stethescope, and it is easy to recall the erotic sensation I got, during the rhythmic chest movements, from the pressure of the instrument. I must at that time have unconsciously symbolised it as his penis.

Further, in the dream referred to above, the doctor attacked me with a *sword*, ∴ wooden stethescope = sword = penis. ("The pen is mightier than the sword", and pen and stethescope each represent the chief weapon of two great professions.).

I was always much struck by the story of one of the British Knights of the Round Table, I forget if it was Sir Launcelot or Sir Galahad, who slept with a maiden with a drawn sword between them to keep him from temptation, and to reassure her of her safety. The meaning, therefore, of the wooden stethescope on my desk is quite clear. I still keep it there!

With Kindest Regards

Yours ever
Ernest Jones.

1. There may be a missing letter.
2. See Freud (1905d, pp. 193–194, n. 2).
3. Crossed out in the original.
4. Doubly underlined.
5. Jones (1910d, pp. 301–305), and Jones, *Papers*, 1st ed. 1913, pp. 334–336.
6. Sybil Jones (b. August 1882); Jones was born on 1 January 1879.
7. The question mark is Jones's.

37

3 July 1910
Vienna, IX. Berggasse 19

Dear Doctor Jones,

As you know Brill has been with me for some days. We had much talk about you and I was happy to find out that you continue on friendly terms and that he is full of appreciation for the richness and value of your work. He mentioned—I hope he was authorised to do so—your planning to leave Toronto for the New York State service and I quite agree with him, that you have to wait out your professorship on Canadian soil and not degrade yourself by accepting the position of a subordinate. This is even the main motive of my letter as I have little else to tell you. I begin to feel tired and look out impatiently for the 15th of this month, which is to put an end to this years hard working. From the first of August we will be at Noordwijk near Leiden, but you may go on using my Vienna adress until I give you the other.

Your essay of selfanalysis interested me deeply, it showed your character in a very favourable light. As for Gross I dont remember distinctly what his differentiation was, and I am too busy these last days to take to his ingenious but whimsical thoughts. So I beg to be excused this time. I hope you believe me that I feel my time best employed when it goes to correspondence with my friends.

You will have heard of Hoche's lecture on the new epidemic spreading among physicians, published in *"Berliner Klinik"*.[1] It is a valuable symptom of the uneasiness felt by our enemies in face of the growth of psychoanalysis.

What is the matter with your Oedipus going to be translated into German?[2]

I have written to Putnam asking him to put himself at the head of an American Section,[3] as I think he is the proper man. Is he not?

I am with best love

yours
Freud

1. Hoche (1910).
2. Jones (1910a).
3. See Freud to Putnam, 16 June 1910, in Hale (1971a, pp. 100–101).

38

25 July 1910
R.M.S. "Lusitania"

Dear Professor Freud,

You will be surprised to get a letter from me from England, or rather from the coast of Ireland, but so it is. My patience with Canadian civilisation suddenly reached a breaking point, and I fled to Europe. From London I shall go to Paris, then Brussels and Holland. I shall hope to see you in Noordwijk about August 10, that is, provided you will not too greatly resent your holiday being disturbed. My sister-in-law[1] has a house there and I have stayed with them there the past two years, so shall again take the opportunity of paying them a visit. I hope you will not mind, and will promise not to interfere too much with your well-earned rest, which I hope will do you the world of good.

In Brussels I am going to investigate this new Internationaler Congress für medizische Psychologie. It sounds suspicious with Frank playing so prominent a part,[2] and I surmise that one of its objects, like Moll's *Zeitschrift*,[3] is to counteract the *"psychische Epidemie"* [psychical epidemic] of Hoche.[4] Forel asked me to read a paper at it, and I shall do so, on Suggestion.[5] Janet is to read one on the same subject![6]

My address [till Satu][7] will be Poste Restante, Bruxelles.

With Kindest Regards

Yours ever
Ernest Jones.

1. Loe Kann's sister.
2. Ludwig Frank (1863–1935) of Zurich, author of *Die Psychoanalyse* (Munich:

E. Reinhardt, 1910), which advocated a modified version of the Freud-Breuer cathartic method. There is no mention of Frank in Jones (1910–11b) or in Ellenberger (1970, pp. 805–806), where summaries of the proceedings are to be found.

3. Albert Moll (1862–1939), Berlin sexologist, founder and editor of *Zeitschrift für Psychotherapie und medizinische Psychologie.*

4. Alfred E. Hoche (1865–1943), opponent of psychoanalysis; author of the anti-Freudian polemic (Hoche, 1910), which is given coverage in Jones (1955a, p. 116; 1955b, p. 131).

5. See Jones-Forel letters of July 1910 in Hans H. Walser, ed., *August Forel, Briefe: Correspondance, 1864–1927* (Bern: Huber, 1968), pp. 407–408; and Jones (1910–11a).

6. Pierre Janet, "Les Problèmes de la suggestion," *Journal für Psychologie und Neurologie,* 17 (1910–11): 323–331.

7. Crossed out in the original.

39

2 August 1910
[R.M.S. *Lusitania*][1]

Dear Professor Freud,

Thank you very much for your letter. I shall look forward to the great pleasure of seeing you about the 11th or 12th. I think you misunderstand my letter a little.[2] The only impulsive thing about my move was the sudden desire to take a holiday—really largely determined by hearing you would be at Noordwijk. I sail back to Canada on the 20th. Nothing is farther from my thoughts than to leave Toronto, even for the States, unless for the best of reasons and only if I got a satisfactory position.

Brussels is terribly crowded. We spend the rest of the week touring the Ardennes, Liège etc.; and return on Sunday.

This morning in the discussion I learnt that "Narcolepsy" is due to auto-intoxication favoured by auto-suggestion.[3] It is a useful piece of knowledge!

Yours ever sincerely
Ernest Jones.

1. Letterhead is crossed out in the original.
2. Freud's letter in response to Jones's previous letter is missing.
3. See Trömner (1911).

40

10 October 1910
407 Brunswick Avenue
Toronto

Dear Professor Freud,

I suppose you are by now back in the midst of routine, and hard at work. I sincerely hope that the benefit of your holiday will be an enduring one; the Mediterranean trip must have been most enjoyable.

I can hardly write about my visit to you without using superlatives that I know would be distateful. Let me, however, simply but warmly thank you for your friendliness and for the patience with which you answered all my questions. It was for me an inspiration never to be forgotten.

News here is partly good, and partly bad. We are definitely starting the branch association, and circulars are being sent out to a selected list, signed by Putnam, Hoch, Brill and myself. Hoch has been very cordial in the matter.

Brill tells me his practice is not good just now, and mine is nil. I haven't had a single patient for treatment in the six weeks since I got back, so have been forced to have recourse to patients from the Polyclinic. (One of them, a Zwangsneurotiker, has just given me the following infantile theory. Children were made by two large mysterious figures who moulded and shaped them by means of two fleshy limbs without hands; the material out of which the children were made was neither liquid nor solid, like putty; it dropped from the people *into* something! Till seven he thought women had a penis and imagined his sister's had been cut off. I suppose he must have been reading your writings, for I had given him no suggestions!! The orthodox world could have no other explanations.). The Government has forbidden our Asylum Bulletin to appear any more, as some of the articles were "not fit for publication, even in medical circles" (my own, of course).[1] That beats Germany, doesn't it? There is altogether a great deal of prejudice against me in medical circles since especially the paper I read here last June on the Neuroses.[2]

Still most things have their bright side, and one result has been that I have been able to immerse myself in the nightmare work,[3] which I intend to send to you before Christmas. I have increased my material to a colossal extent, and can only use part of it. The subject opens and broadens into such a number of side-ways that it costs an effort to keep to the main track. I have learnt a very great deal from the side paths, which are most interesting, and I hope to be able to follow some of them up later. May I ask you for help in the way of suggestions on the following two points (1) the significance of the *Hexensalbe* [witch's ointment] which was said to be used as preparation for the *Hexenfahrt* [witch's journey]. I have read that it was a narcotic plant, but suspect it has a more symbolic meaning. (2) the myth that the Sun-god (e.g. Heracles) became a [wife] woman after the turn of the year in June. This could be read in Adler's sense that the decaying God must contemptuously be a woman,[4] but there is certainly more behind it. Children have no idea of impotence in the aged, have they?

I hope you will give me the opportunity to work up the Macbeth play sometime, though I am afraid I must postpone it for a couple of years in view of other plans. I wonder if it is merely a coincidence that Beth was the name of the three German Norns who presided over childbirth, and whom Laistner traces to the jealous, childless woman?[5] Perhaps Rank could look up the etymology.

I was extremely interested to read your article in the *Jahrbuch*.[6] Abel could have strengthened one example if he had known English better. Namely "to cleave" = both *spalten* and *kleben*. "to cleave a rock" (cleft = *Kluft*), and "Thou shalt cleave to thy wife". I have noted already a number of other examples. Would it be acceptable if I sent them to the *Zentralblatt*? They would all be English, but we are beginning to find it difficult to keep to one language in ΨA work on literary and mythological subjects, even to German. I see that Ferdinand (*Sexual-Mystik der Vergangenheit*, S. 103) deals with Abel's discovery, and, as you might expect, brings it into relation with the male and female principles.[7]

The Hamburg neurologists had a stormy "Ausleben seiner [ihrer] Komplexen [Komplexe]"[8] on the subject of ΨA recently (See *Neurol. Centralbl.* June, 1910).[9] More interesting in two respects was an article by Schauer in the *Arch. f. d. ges. Psychol.* Heft 3 & 4. S. 411. First because the subject, your views on *Der Witz*, is one rarely dealt with, and secondly because he reached the very heights or depths of futility in his criticism. What do you think of the following? "Ein obszöner Witz, der in Herrengesellschaft belacht wird, verdankt seine Lustwirkung ganz sicher nicht der sexuellen Erregung. Es würde eine geradezu krankhafte Steigerung der geschlechtlichen Erregbarkeit dazu gehören, wenn jede Anspielung auf sexuelle Dinge sogleich eine Erregung der Libido zur Folge hätte." As to your remark that when a man tells a girl a *Zote* [dirty joke] the "Zuhörer durch die mühelose Befriedigung seiner eigenen Libido bestochen wird", we have the following unanswerable objection! "Das ist sicher falsch. Dieser Dritte lacht nicht wegen der m. E. s. [mühelose Erregung seiner] Libido—die Erregung der Libido [sexualis] hat überhaupt niemals lachen zur Folge—, sondern er lacht, weil er einer Neckerei beizuwohnen meint". His love of accuracy is shown in the fact that he refers to you throughout as "Freund".[10]

Your interview with our friend Friedländer does not seem to have curbed his passion for notoriety. In a violent diatribe against the ΨA *Jahrbuch* (in the *Zeit. f. Psychol.* Ht. 1 & 2) he complains bitterly of the way he is neglected, especially by you: "Ich darf wohl darauf rechnen, dass mir im

Freudschen Lager geglaubt wird, ich selbst besässe keine Komplexe, nachdem einer der glühendsten Verehrer Freuds mich analysiert und komplexfrei befunden hat. Mein Referat über die Freudsche Lehre war monatelang vorher angekündigt worden, warum bemühte sich Freud, der sogar eine Reise nach Amerika nicht scheut[e], nicht nach Budapest, um mich dort zu widerlegen, warum "fertigt" er seine Gegner in einer Fussnote ab, warum "u.s.w." [11] He is getting quite pathetic, isn't he, but I hope he will be consistently ignored, and that his ravings unto Heaven will find no answer. It looks very much as if he was personally attracted to *you*, for in his other writings he praises the value of your work and deplores that it is spoilt by the fanatacism of your supporters, while now he cries you down and praises anyone (e.g. Binswanger) [12] who dares to doubt anything of yours.

Prince tells me that F. has sent him an article which will make me feel hot all over. I must get Putnam to resist the temptation of answering it. I believe it is to appear in December, in the same number as my "Janet" article. [13]

I saw Hart in London. He is coming on slowly, but has a good deal of resistance re symbolism. He has done some good work, though very elementary, on a case by means of hypnosis. In time I think he will be all right. He published a fairly good account of your Psychology recently (read before the British Psychological Society), [14] from which however you will be sad to learn that you are a poet rather than a scientist.

Well, you will want me to bring my chit-chat to an end, but I greatly enjoy writing to you.

With Kindest Regards

Yours ever sincerely
Ernest Jones.

1. There is no significant break in the regular issues of the *Bulletin of the Ontario Hospitals for the Insane* (Toronto), which appeared more or less quarterly from 1907 well on up to the beginning of the First World War, and which frequently contained reprints of many of Jones's papers.

2. Jones (1910k).

3. Jones (1912j).

4. This theme is taken up again in Jones (1931b, pp. 284–286). The word "wife" is crossed out in the original.

5. The three Norns in Teutonic myth and folklore were demigoddesses, representing the past, present, and future, who presided over and determined the fate of man and of the gods; see Ludwig Laistner, *Das Rätsel der Sphinx* (Berlin: W. Hertz, 1889). Jones did not undertake the Macbeth project.

6. See Freud (1910e), where he deals with Karl Abel's *Über den Gegensinn der Urworte* (Leipzig, 1884).

7. Maximillian Ferdinand [Sebaldt], *Sexual-Mystik der Vergangenheit* (Leipzig: W. Friedrich, n.d.), p. 103.

8. "Demonstration of [their] complexes."

9. See *Neurologisches Centralblatt*, 29 (1910): 659–662.

10. O. Schauer, "Über das Wesen der Komik," *Archiv für die gesamte Psychologie*, 18 (1910): 411–427. Quoted passages are from p. 422. The three passages read: (1) "An obscene joke which arouses laughter among a group of men does certainly not owe its pleasurable effect to sexual stimulation. It would amount to an almost pathological increase of sexual excitability if any hint at sexual matters would immediately lead to a stimulation of Libido." (2) "The listener is being seduced by the effortless gratification of his own Libido." (3) "That is certainly false. This third person is not laughing because of the effortless stimulation of his own Libido—stimulation of Libido never leads to laughter—but he is laughing because he thinks he is witnessing some banter."

11. Anonymous review of *Jahrbuch*, 1 (1909), *Zeitschrift für Psychologie*, 57 (1910): 142–147. Quoted passages are from p. 143: "I am sure I can count on being believed in the Freudian camp when I say that I myself have no complexes, after one of Freud's most ardent admirers analyzed me and declared me to be free of complexes. My *Referat* on Freud's teachings had been announced months in advance, why did Freud, who did not even shun a trip to America, not make the effort to come to Budapest in order to refute me there, why does he 'deal' with his opponents in a footnote, why etc."

12. Ludwig Binswanger (1881–1966), Swiss psychiatrist, initially sympathetic to Jung's views, later influenced by Martin Heidegger and Freud; see his *Sigmund Freud: Reminiscences of a Friendship* (New York: Grune & Stratton, 1957); applied the principles of existentialism, phenomenology, and psychoanalysis to psychotherapy.

13. Friedländer (1911), and Jones (1910–11).

14. Hart (1910).

41

6 November 1910
Vienna, IX. Berggasse 19

Dear Doctor,

I have long forgotten I was way[1] and looked upon the orange groves of Palermo, the temples of Girgenti and site of old Syracuse dull with Scirocco. I postponed to answer your rich letter until I could give you a definitive notice about the fate of your Hamlet. Deuticke suggested to me to accept it into the Series of "*angewandte Seelenkunde*"; if you do not resist it will appear there in the first weeks of January and will be followed by your article [of][2] on the nightmare.[3] The translation by Tausig is in my hands and waiting for some corrections. The precursor in the Series, Nr 9 is to be an essay by Graf: Rich. Wagner im Fliegenden Holländer.[4] I hope you have already made some arrangement with the translator for the fee coming from Deuticke.

As regards your questions I as usually know nothing about it, but I have put Rank on the track, who will give you as much as he finds. The sexual theory of your patient deserves a short note in the "*Zentralblatt*", which will be always be[5] open to similar samples and constations.[6] As for Macbeth the subject is reserved for you for any time you choose, but I hope your usual impatience for work will not suffer to let it wait a couple of years.

I see no objection why the *Zentralblatt* should not bring english contributions or translate them or in following the hints of Abel's paper should restrict itself to the German language.

I am deep in work with the subject of Paranoia and trust I will publish next (but write before) an analysis of Schrebers *Denkwürdigkeiten*,[7] a book which I am sure you know well. I am taking great pains in superintending the *Zentralblatt* and shutting out what evil might arise from personal grimaces of the two redactors,[8] not a very thankful business.

About Christmas I might be in Zürich or Jung here in Vienna as matters are becoming urgent with Bleuler, who I am afraid will not [continue][9] stay among our ranks.[10] There is much energy which could be better expended wasted in struggling with the personal complexes and deficiencies even of our friends. It may be we have extended rather too rapidly in the last year and are passing through something like a crisis now.

Pray give me your news as soon as you can and be sure of my answer at better terms than this time.

Yours truly
Freud

1. Freud seems to be following the German here: *ich war weg* (away); *der Weg* = way, path.

2. Crossed out in the original.

3. Jones (1910a, 1912j).

4. Graf (1911).

5. Freud employs "be" twice in the original.

6. The English *constate* = to establish as certain, ascertain, or verify. But Freud may have also associated the German word *Festellungen* (findings) with *constations* because *konstatieren* = *feststellen* in German.

7. See Freud (1911c) for his analysis of Daniel Paul Schreber, author of *Denkwürdigkeiten eines Nervenkranken* (Leipzig: Oswald Musse, 1903); and *Memoirs of My Nervous Illness*, trans., ed., intro., notes, and discussion by Ida Macalpine and Richard A. Hunter (London: Wm. Dawson & Sons, 1955).

8. Adler and Stekel.

9. Crossed out in the original.

10. See especially Alexander and Selesnick (1965) for Bleuler's position on psychoanalysis.

42

6 November 1910
407 Brunswick Avenue
Toronto

Dear Professor Freud,

Three reprints at once from you, only one of which I had previously read. What a rare treat! Thank you very much. I especially enjoyed the one on psychotherapy.[1] You know that we younger enthusiasts (unwisely, I admit) sometimes complain that you don't often talk generalities, so it is the more welcome when it comes. You certainly have no illusions as to the future difficulties we must encounter, but it was good to see your sure optimism in spite of them all. I was glad you laid such stress on the importance of self-analysis (not once, but continuous); I don't think the importance of it could be exaggerated. When is your book on *Methodik* coming out?[2] There must be many people eagerly awaiting that, both friends and foes.

The symbolism you mention of climbing stairs[3] and steps I have not yet met, but in English we call a *roué* a "high stepper". Neither have I yet found the cravat symbol you told me of in Holland, but in England, and I suppose all other countries, the three following facts concern it. Certain men [have][4] attach an excessive *Affekt* to the buying of cravats, are always changing them, and proudly show *drawers* full of them. It is commonly thought to be highly significant when a young lady begins to pay attention to the cravats worn by a man friend. A man resents greatly having his cravats chosen for him by his wife or his fiancée; it is essentially a *man's* affair. Jokes on both the last points are frequent in *Punch*, etc..

There is no great news from this side. The Association will be formed, but Hoch is delaying it by not sending on promptly the circular, a preliminary copy of which I sent to him as well as to Putnam and Brill, I must write to him. Putnam was extremely proud of the warm letter you sent to him; he sent it to me to read, and it was certainly most generously worded.[5] I apologise for sending you the last number of the *Journal of Abnormal Psychology*, for after all Prince's silly article wasnt worth bothering you with.[6] I have written one in reply, for one couldn't let it pass unchallenged,[7] and I think it will appear in the next number. Friedländer's article will probably appear at the same time;[8] I hear that his quotations from you were so "filthy" that the translator had to send it in as [a] written manuscript so as to avoid soiling the mind of his New England typist! I forget if I told you in my last letter of my promotion. Dr. Clarke, the Dean, asked the President of the University to make me Professor, but the latter said that unless there was any special reason to the contrary he would prefer to go through the usual order of procedure. As

Clarke has been much accused of favouritism to me (which is quite true) he agreed, so that I am an "Associate"⁹ this year and will definitely be Professor next year. As Clarke gives only asylum demonstrations that means that I give all the University lectures in Psychiatry, which I have already started last month. He asked me to teach only general principles of psycho-pathology, leaving the clinical side to him; the result is that two hundred innocent youths are being severely inoculated with psycho-analytic doctrines under the official auspices of the University of Toronto. They are finding it very interesting, as you might expect, though naturally I have to give mild doses.

Paul Tausig has written to say that he has arranged for the Hamlet essay to come out in the *Schriften* series. Is this so? Tausig seems to be a little of a *blagereur* [*blagueur*] from what I can make of him. If it is true, and of course I should be proud to think that you found it worthy of the *Schriften*, I only wish to say that I promised Stanley Hall that the translation should state that the paper appeared in his Journal, and this is of course due to him in all courtesy.

I am paralysed by the mass of material there is in folk-lore, mythology, superstition, anthropology, etc.; there is urgent need for a great number of workers to collect and classify it. I believe that practically all your conclusions could be proved, or at least strongly supported, by this material; it is simply amazing how everything harmonises. Let me give one little instance, which perhaps you know, from Le Sage the Spanish writer. "Zador makes a Teufelspakt in a dream and in return the devil discloses in [a] gold-mine in a churchyard (i.e. bed—where one sleeps); he takes enough gold for his present needs, but is awakened by an angry wife to find he has passed motions into the bed".¹⁰

I have recently had some very gratifying results. The boy with the eye obsession I spoke to you of has remained quite well. Another much worse case I had been treating since January is hard at work and says he never knew what life was before; his main complexes were concerning the oral and anal zones, and his chief obsession that Christ was sucking his penis all the time. It was a beautiful case, as he was an excellent subject. At present I have a still better Zwang case of a young man who *believes* unshakeably that he generates electricity, that he can transfer his thoughts to other people at any distance, etc.. I told you in my last letter of one of his infantile theories. Another was that sexual relations consisted in blowing flatus into the partner's anus. This act has got in all sorts of ways connected with the ideas of breathing and speaking, and from mythology, religion etc. I have concluded that the idea of flatus is perhaps always primary to breath (psyche, anima etc.).¹¹ It is too long a topic to put in a letter, as I have so much material on it, but I should be very glad to hear your views about it.

In conclusion may I ask you one more question (I am behaving as though your patience was inexhaustible, which it seems to be)? In your list of Partialtriebe, paired off, you give of course Schaulust and Exhibitionismus.[12] The former is necessarily concerned only with the eye. Is there any reason why it should not be replaced by a more general term (you spoke to me in Holland of the investigation tendency), for it seems to be only the part (of course by far the most important part) of a more general tendency, including touch, smell and perhaps taste. I was led to think of the point by finding what an important role was played in this patient by finding things out by smell, desire to smell the anus and, later, other objects.

I liked Sadger's paper on *Analerotik*,[13] and agree with him except perhaps for one point. He differs from you in believing that miserliness is not cardinal, and may be absent in women of the well-to-do class. I find that in such women (several cases) the Geld-*complex* is always important, that is, that the question of money is always very significant, though it may not appear on the surface as miserliness. I have in mind one patient who was apparently excessively extravagant and *generous*, who hated miserliness. It turned out that her generosity was a reaction against her mother whom she intensely hated, who was very miserly (and who used to give her clysters till she was twelve years old), i.e. *Analerotik* and homosexual sadism and masochism. Geld complex was none the less strong, e.g. she hated being *made*[14] to pay a cent unless she wanted to in her own way, etc.

With very kindest Regards

from yours always
Ernest Jones.

1. Freud (1910d).

2. Freud planned to write a separate study on psychoanalytic treatment entitled *Allgemeine Methodik der Psychoanalyse*, but never completed it; see Freud (1910d, p. 142).

3. Freud (1910d, p. 143).

4. Crossed out in the original.

5. Possibly Freud to Putnam, 29 September 1910, in Hale (1971a, pp. 107–108).

6. Prince (1910b).

7. Jones (1911b).

8. Friedländer (1911).

9. Associate in psychiatry is to be distinguished from associate professor of psychiatry, a post to which Jones would be appointed in autumn 1911.

10. Alain-René Lesage (1668–1747), French novelist and dramatist; wrote *Le Diable boiteux* (1707) and *Histoire de Gil Blas de Santillane* (three installments, dated 1715, 1724, 1735).

11. These ideas were followed up in Jones (1914a).

12. Freud (1905d, pp. 166–167).

13. J. [Isidor] Sadger, "Analerotik und Analcharakter," in *Die Heilkunde*, 1910, p. 43, is utilized in Jones (1918b); see *Papers*, 2nd ed., pp. 667, 670, and 685.

14. Doubly underlined.

43

19 November 1910
407 Brunswick Avenue
Toronto

Dear Professor Freud,

Many thanks for your letter that came this morning. With regard to the Hamlet I had already written to you, after hearing from Tausig, to say that it could only be a great pleasure to me that you would think it worth publishing in the *Schriften* series. I had not arranged anything financially with Tausig, not knowing under what conditions he would publish it, but I will write to tell him to keep any fee that Deuticke may pay; it must have been a trouble to translate it. Perhaps Deuticke will let me have a few copies that I could send to friends.

It is very sad about Bleuler, and I am sure we all hope it will come right. I suppose his personal complexes are reinforced by his jealousy of Jung, and by his desire to be accepted in the respectable circle of German psychiatrists. Maeder tells me that he (B.) is just publishing a book;[1] do you know about it? It seems unavoidable that there will be a fringe of half-hearted supporters, and it is difficult to know what attitude to adopt towards them. We have a similar problem here in another form, and should be very glad of your advice. In our new Ortsverein Hoch wants to accept as members all those who have shown the slightest interest in ΨA, even when they know nothing of it. Brill and I are more inclined to be eclectic, but we must take in some like Meyer, Coriat and Onuf.[2] We have two members in India, one, Berkeley-Hill whom I mentioned to you, and Colonel Sutherland who writes in Krauss' *Anthropophyteia* under the pseudonym of Dr. S. of S..[3] Hill sent me the first ψα performed on an Indian, which the patient proudly wants to have published, but it is much too elementary—little more than anamnesis.

Putnam's Washington paper has just been published in the Nov. no. of the *Journal of Nervous and Mental Disease*,[4] and no doubt he will send you a reprint. The discussion on it was published in the Oct. no., and I am sending you a copy of it.[5] I also send a short account of a little Hamlet, whose *Dummstellen* [simulated foolishness] will interest you as coinciding with the explanation you gave me of that in the greater Hamlet.[6]

I have been invited to give an address on "some Freudian subject" before a joint meeting of the Chicago Neurological Society and the Chicago Medical Society, and have chosen as title "A consideration of some criticisms of the ΨA method of treatment";[7] it is in January. I think it is a good sign of the times, and I hope it may act as a stimulus in Chicago. Pfister's Schrift was very interesting, though he was careful not to generalise. I wonder if others of the clergy will follow his lead. By the way, this week

I had a patient sent to me from the Emmanuel Church in Boston! I shall look forward to Graf's musical memoir with great interest.[8] Can you find someone who would work up the symbolism of astrology and astronomy? It is a very promising field. My nightmare[9] is getting on slowly, as I have so much other work; it is a fearful task to select from the mass of material, but much of the work will come in useful later on with perhaps other articles.

Jung asked me to send him something for the *Jahrbuch* before the end of the year, but it will be impossible. I will try to send him analyses of some cases of Zwangsneurose by the spring.[10] One of them contains the infantile theory I spoke of, but, as that has expanded so much, perhaps it will be better to publish it in its own *Zusammenhang* [context] rather than separately in the *Zentralblatt*.

It will be very good to hear from you on the subject of paranoia; was it your Dutch case that has inspired you? Maeder has written to me much on the subject; he finds Ferenczi's presentation of *Schrumpfung* [shrinking] *und Projektion* very imperfect, and only one side of the problem.[11]

Have you analysed many dreams of exceptional and entrancing beauty (at least subjectively so)? I have had three in my own life, or perhaps more than I have forgotten. One, years ago, concerned a wonderful cliff and sea scenery—not enough details to analyse. Another, two years ago, was playing, in the Grecian way, in a meadow with a young girl, the feeling being of extraordinary innocence and purity; analysis showed it was my young sister. The third, a recent one, concerned an indescribably beautiful mass of architecture, palaces with marvellous corridors. It turned out to be an infantile one about the genitalia of my parents, particularly my mother (anal)! I wonder what is the explanation of that transcendent sense of beauty; it far surpasses anything I have experienced in waking life.

Friedländer's article and my criticism of Prince have been postponed till February. Meyer and Hoch have articles in the Dec. no. of the *Journal of Abnormal Psychology*;[12] I will send you a copy.

With my warmest regards,

Yours ever
Ernest Jones.

1. Bleuler (1911).

2. Bronislaw Onuf (b. 1863), M.D. 1884 University of Zurich; charter member of the New York Psychoanalytic Society (12 February 1911).

3. Owen Berkeley-Hill (1879–1944), British trained physician, entered the Indian Medical Service in 1907; would become a member of the American Psychoanalytic Association. Colonel W. D. Sutherland, I.M.S. of India. Both men became members of the London Psycho-Analytic Society (1913) and the British Psycho-Analytical Society (1920). For Freud's contribution to Krauss's *Anthropophyteia*, see Freud (1910f).

4. Putnam (1910a).

5. *Journal of Nervous and Mental Disease,* 37 (1910): 630–639.
6. Jones (1910a, p. 111).
7. Jones (1911d).
8. Pfister (1910); Graf (1911).
9. Jones (1912j).
10. Jones (1912–13).
11. See Ferenczi (1909, p. 48), and Jones, *Papers,* 1st ed. 1913, pp. 250–251.
12. Friedländer (1911), Jones (1911b), Meyer (1910b), and Hoch (1910).

44

20 November 1910
Vienna, IX. Berggasse 19

Dear Doctor,

I heartily rejoice at the good news of your promotion and trust you will be called professor a year hence and enjoy the increase of influence attached to this title. I am glad you did not leave Toronto for New York.

As for P. Tausig he seems to be a *blagueur* indeed. He had nothing to do with the reception of your Hamlet into the series. It was Deuticke's idea, when I asked him to publish it as a brochure, and I remember to have made the proposition to you some time ago, when you declined for modesty or what else. I am sure it will hold a high place in the collection. Tausig has delivered the translation into my hands inscribed "Hamlet— *Ein Sexualproblem*". You may be assured that I restituted the original title.[1] There are many weak and even some bad spots in his work, which I will correct one of these days, before it goes to the printer. As for the fees of publication, Tausig states you left it all to him. I beg you will notify to Deuticke directly whether this is true or which share of it you claim. The name of Stanley Hall and the *American Journal of Psychology* will be brought out at the proper place, that's my business.

The ludicrous dream in the *Gil Blas* (or *Diable boiteux?*) was known to me, when I wrote the paper on *Analerotik* and I even alluded to it.[2]

The sexual theories of your patient find a counterpart in those of a lady whom I am treating, who is all filled up with air, meaning by air sexual products, leaning to the quotation from Genesis, that God inflated Adam by his *"Odem"* [breath] and proceeding from the same infantile theory, that married intercourse consists in blowing air into each others bowels from out the anus. There is indeed some good work to be done here.

As for the sexual components the *Schaulust* and *Exhib.*[3] are only given as samples and you are free to add the other sexual interests to the list, subsuming the whole of these tendencies to an "Erkenntnistrieb", when you remember that *"Erkennen"* [to know] means *Coitiren* in the Bible. (Und Adam erkannte sein Weib . . .)

I am deep in Schrebers *"Denkwürdigkeiten eines Nervenkranken"*,[4] shaping out of it the first of my papers on Paranoia, which will come out in the third volume of the *Jahrbuch*.[5] In the mean time the *Zentralblatt* will have reached you. Perhaps next time I will give some interesting news about personal affairs in the Vienna "Vereinigung".

I am with sincere regards

ever your
Freud

1. Jones (1910a).
2. See Freud (1908b, p. 174).
3. "Sexual pleasure in looking" and "exhibitionism" *(Exhibitionismus)*. Bruno Bettelheim has pointed out that the rendering of *Schaulust* as "scopophilia" ("scoptophilia" was an earlier version) is a vulgarization of Freud's ideas: "the monstrosity contrived by Freud's translators and perpetuated in the 'Standard Edition'—'scopophilia'—certainly conveys nothing at all" (Bettelheim, 1982, p. 80). James Strachey attested to the haphazard way in which the term *Schaulust* was rendered into English when he wrote: "I must admit that the Glossary Committee disgraced itself lamentably over at least one word. The question was how to translate '*Schaulust*'—the pleasure in looking. Greek terminology was all the rage, and the word 'scoptophilia' was suggested and accepted with acclamation. It certainly looked a little odd; but nevertheless it passed into all the four volumes of the *Collected Papers* uncriticized. You might have imagined that we should have remembered telescopes and microscopes and so have suspected that the Greek root for looking was something like 'scop'. Actually there *is* a Greek root 'scopt', but what it means is 'to make fun of'. And so to this day you may still come upon references to the component sexual instinct of pleasure in derision" (Strachey, 1963, p. 229).
4. Freud had written *Nervenkrankheiten*, then crossed out *heit*.
5. Freud (1911c).

45

2 December 1910
407 Brunswick Avenue
Toronto

Dear Professor Freud,

Many thanks for your letter of Nov. 20. I am very grateful to you for taking the trouble of correcting the Hamlet. Some parts of it must have been very difficult to translate, especially for Tausig who does not know English well. That was impudent of him to change the title. I have written to Deuticke, as you suggest.

I was horrified to think I had sent you as a novelty a story *(Gil Blas)* to which you had alluded in your writings, for I know your writings as a rule in great detail. I do not find it in the Analerotik paper, unless it is the

"Dukatenscheissers",[1] a term I am not familiar with. One more proof of your terrifyingly wide reading!

That was very interesting about your lady filled up with air. The subject opens out very extensively. Partly through two patients and partly independently I have got hold of a mass of material that it illuminates. The mythological parts you probably know, and I daresay most of the anthropological also, but perhaps you are not aware of the great extent that Hindoo Yogi doctrines have taken hold of a large class of Americans. I am sending you a copy of a small book on "The Science of Breath",[2] which I am sure will interest you greatly, although the Hindoo part itself will be familiar to you. It is an interesting speculation as to the type of nonsense that will replace orthodox religion in time (a) psychical research, *Schattenseele* [shadow soul] from dreams, (b.) occultism, telepathy, *Hauchseele* [breath soul] from flatus, etc. In one patient the connection between interest in occultism and anal curiosity was as plain as possible. What impresses one of the importance of *analerotik* is its primitiveness, before the child knows of the existence of the vagina, semen etc., etc. I think of a patient's remark: "I am always trying to get to the *bottom* of things".! Will you let me write an article sometime for the *Jahrbuch* or *Zentralblatt* on the symbolism of Flatus, especially in its religious connections?[3]

I have got the first number of the *Zentralblatt,* and am delighted with it. It is full of good things, and is most promising for the future. Such a journal for short notes was badly needed. Perhaps we shall have one in English in a few years.

The American Ortsverein is going on well, though we shall not meet till May. There are about twenty members, six of whom are English. Stanley Hall and Adolf Meyer wrote to me most cordial approving letters.

Do you yet know when your *methodik* book will be out?[4] I have not yet found a translator for Hitschmann.[5] A publisher this week asked me to write a book of 400 pages on Freudian psychology, but I think it well to postpone this a couple of years.

Don't you agree?

Yours,
E. J.

1. "Shitter of ducats"; see Freud (1908b, p. 174).
2. Three books on breath by Fletcher, Arnulphy, and Durville are mentioned in Jones (1914a); see Jones (1951, 2:298, n. 1).
3. See Jones (1914a).
4. See note 2 to letter 42.
5. Hitschmann (1911).

46

18 December 1910
Vienna, IX. Berggasse 19

Dear Dr. Jones,

No I am not a *King-fu*. I regularly find as much instruction as new hints in your letter. The treasure dream I did not mention in any of my writings, because I was not sure where I had found it. I only wanted to say, that it was present to my mind, when I wrote the *Analerotik*.

Any article of yours on the Mystery and Mythology of Flatus will be welcome either to the *Jahrbuch* or to the *Zentralblatt*. You are right, there is an enormous amount of material behind these topics and none to work it up. As for Rank, who would be the right man for such a task, I have put him to work on a literary idea, you remember. You took the Macbeth problem out of this *Zusammenhang* [context].[1]

Donot take up too much work and resist the editors for the moment. You promised to give out a short manual of psychiatrics placing therein the Psychoneuroses at their due post and inoculating a new generation of American physicians by the $\psi\alpha$ Virus.

Your Hamlet will be delivered up to Deuticke in the last days of this year. I will take up correcting the translation when my own paper on Schreber (Paranoia) has gone through the last finishing in these days.[2] Will you send me a note for addition giving account of your new Hamlet, corroborating the explanation of the feigned foolishness of the old one?

Putnam's papers are excellent and his preface to the Sexual theory very kind and appropriate. You are right, that my letter on his Toronto [letter][3] lecture was rather exuberant, but I felt it at that time and felt it again at the perusal of the proofs for the *Zentralblatt*. I was very happy at his judgment, and perhaps a kind of diplomacy had a part in it. Yet I was astonished myself, that the constant depreciations I am suffering here should have rendered me so sensible [sensitive][4] to being acknowledged by some one honest and clever. It is true I had thought I had more internal resistance.

I have received all your papers whenever I do not mention them individually. You know I will always be very much [. . .][5] interested in the progress of the American branch but I think better to restrain from meddling and to leave all practical decisions to both of you.

I am *mit herzlichen Grüssen* [with warm greetings]

Ihr getreuer [your faithful]
Freud

1. Possibly Rank (1912).
2. Freud (1911c).

3. Crossed out in the original.
4. French *sensible* = German *sensibel* = English "sensitive."
5. Barely legible word, possibly "assured," is crossed out.

47

1 January 1911
407 Brunswick Avenue
Toronto

Dear Professor Freud,

Thank you very much for your letter that came yesterday. I am eagerly looking forward to your Schreber paper. Is it to appear in the *Schriften* or the *Jahrbuch*? I have just read Brill's translation of the *Drei Abhandlungen*, with Putnam's excellent preface.[1] The translation is decidedly better than the former one, though it leaves much to be desired. It will, I think, do more good than the previous volume, being a better *Zusammenhang*.[2] Certainly we owe Brill a debt of gratitude for such laborious and difficult work.

The Ortsverein here is progressing excellently so far as membership is concerned. No one so far has refused to join, and we are looking forward to the May meeting with much anticipation. Putnam is busy reading several papers at local meetings. I am afraid that all other news I have to give is only personal. I hope the enclosed note, which you asked for, will be suitable.

Now I come to a big confession! Namely it will be impossible to send you the Nightmare Schrift[3] as soon as I promised. I have worked terrifically hard at it, but had again underestimated the time necessary to overcome the difficulties of arranging so much material into a readable and logical connection. Even so it looks as though I will not be able to do it in less than 150 pages. I have definitely failed to compress it into the size of the previous *Schriften*, and must send it to you to decide how best it can be published. So far I have finished writing out the first draft of six of the twelve chapters, and have most of the rest mapped out. The work however is much interrupted. Last month I couldn't touch it for three weeks at a stretch, and now again I must lay it aside for another three weeks on account of my Chicago paper.[4] I do not see how it can be finished before the end of March. My only consolation is that it will certainly contain some fascinating and strongly confirmatory matter.

You are right in telling me not to take up too much work, but it is exceedingly difficult to know what to choose. I am bubbling with all sorts of plans for work; and I do not think they are too infantile, for it is mostly work that I feel I can do. At present I do not see how I can begin the

psychiatry book till the autumn,[5] there is so much to do first. I have
promised Jung to send him some cases for the *Jahrbuch*. February I must
give up to my contribution to the symposium on Angst at the Psychopathological Association,[6] etc. One thing I especially reproach myself for
is that I am losing some of my zest for elementary propagandism, having
greatly replaced it by the desire to work in the attractive and unexplored
fields of folklore, anthropology and mythology. They have the strongest
fascination for me, and there is so much that needs to be done.

This week I got a strange invitation from the Philadelphia Neurological
Society. They want to hold in February a Symposium on your work. The
psychopathological sides are to be presented by Prince (!) and myself, and
it is to be attacked on the neurological side (!) by the local mandarins,
Mills, Dercum, etc..[7] The prospect is not enchanting, and I am trying to
prove to myself that I would do more harm than good by going. I sent a
cold answer, asking for some days to think it over, and wrote to Brill and
Putnam to get their opinions. I feel you would not blame me for refusing,
for it is a really stupid proposal.[8]

My "Janet" paper has appeared, dreadfully mutilated by the printers.[9]
They translated (badly) many of the foreign quotations without my consent, so please excuse that; I was very angry. The reprints have not yet
come, but I expect to send you one next week.

It is my birthday today (32), and I am full of resolutions for the coming
year. My strongest wish is that it will be for you personally and for our
work a successful and happy year.

With warmest greetings

Yours always
Ernest Jones.

Footnote.[10]
In a recent paper (Simulated Foolishness in Hysteria, *American Journal of Insanity*, Oct. 1909. P #279)[11] I have connected the hysterical moria
states that show this symptom with the infantile ecmnesia described
by Pitres. In an actual psychoanalysis there recorded I was able fully
to confirm Professor Freud's suggestion referred to above, and to show
that the motive of the behaviour was, by feigning infantile innocence, to
gratify sexual sensations with the mother in ways that are denied to older
children.

1. Brill (1910c).
2. Jones likely means that the translation is "better integrated."
3. Jones (1912j).
4. Jones (1911d).
5. This was never completed.
6. Jones (1911e).

7. Charles K. Mills (b. 1845), professor of neurology, Department of Medicine, University of Pennsylvania. Francis X. Dercum (b. 1856), professor of nervous and mental diseases, Jefferson Medical College, Philadelphia.

8. "Symposium on Freud's Theory of the Neuroses and Allied Subjects," *Philadelphia Neurological Association,* 24 February 1911; see *Journal of Nervous and Mental Disease,* 38 (1911): 491–497. For Jones's letter to Putnam with his reply, see Hale (1971a, pp. 248–250).

9. Jones (1910–11a).

10. This footnote was sent in response to the request contained in Freud's previous letter regarding the German version of the Hamlet essay (Jones, 1910a); see *Schriften,* 10:61, and Jones (1949, pp. 145–146).

11. The piece was actually published in 1910; see Jones (1910i).

48

3 January 1911
407 Brunswick Avenue
Toronto

Dear Professor Freud,

Your second letter has just come, re the Hamlet paper. I apologise for giving you so much trouble; it is very good of you to take it.[1] The first passage (P. 75) "without reference to the past or future evolution of motive" is certainly very condensed, and attains a quite Nietzchean obscurity, though it has its meaning all the same. It refers to your demonstration (e.g. in the *Gradiva*) that a given piece of conduct, poetic creation etc. etc. relates to (a) *past* experiences and (b) *future* ones (Wunsch), in other words is past—one stage—of an evolution. I think that Shakspere describes conduct intuitively without consciously tracing it to either its past roots or its future connections. The idea in the next sentence is taken from Shaw, who points out that Shakspere was a blind artist rather [than] a conscious philosopher. (This is stupidly put, I know, but you will gather what I am driving at).

P. 77. "the argument, then, must remain unconvincing except to those who already accept it." I am not sure that I understand the difficulty here, but I will try to put my meaning in another way. The reasons given by critics for H's general aboulia are not adequate psychologically (H's scepticism etc.). This will be obvious to some readers. I mention shortly an argument why the reasons of the critics are inadequate, but do not fully discuss it as it is irrelevant, for I go on to show that H. had no *general* aboulia. Therefore the readers who appreciate the argument briefly hinted at are already convinced; others will not be convinced without a longer discussion which it is not worth while to enter on as it is irrelevant; they must therefore remain unconvinced—the point makes no difference.

Have you an obsolescent word in German corresponding to the last word of the paper, "eld"?[2] It sounds very appropriate in English.
With my best thanks,

Yours ever
Ernest Jones.

P.S. This morning I got an invitation to read a paper at the American Medical Association meeting in Los Angeles, Southern California, end of June. I wish you would tell me it was my duty to refuse such invitations, for I weakly accept as a rule. Do you think they do any good?

E. J.

1. See Jones (1910a, pp. 75, 77) for quoted passages which follow.
2. Jones (1910a, p. 113).

49

22 January 1911
Vienna, IX. Berggasse 19

Dear Dr. Jones,
Had I known that your birthday coincidates[1] with that of the new year I would have sent you a special greeting for the memorable day. I find you are very young and have done a great deal in your short life. I was not so far advanced in 1888. So you need not hurry in such a restless way, there is plenty of time before you.

Your Hamlet [is][2] was nearly finished by the printer when your letter arrived, so you will have to complain of two ommissions, but your note could still be added. I expect the title page in a few days and I want your decision whether to put Professor before your name or not. If you do not wire to the contrary (a single word), I will have called you "Professor".— There is no correlate to your "eld" in German. I mean to say *"des Alters"*[3] instead. You must not hustle for the Nightmare. It is time when you can send it in the course of this year. The programm of the *Schriften* is pretty rich. After your Hamlet there is enrolled an essay by a Zürich juridical student Storfer[4] on Parricide, next comes Abraham, Segantini, Rank's Lohengrin is to follow and so on.[5] I cannot claim more than 4 or 5 volumes in a year at least at the moment. When the nightmare exceeds the volume of the hitherto published numbers, perhaps Deuticke will consent to give a double one or he may condescend to publish it separately.[6]

As for your work and the invitations to medical meetings I dare say you are the best judge upon the second point, I only want you [to] remark to you as I did to Jung at Munich in Christmastime—that we are to withstand the big temptation to settle down in our colonies, where we cannot be but strangers, distinguished visitors, and have to revert every time to our native country in Medicine, where we find the roots of our powers.

I met Bleuler and Jung at Munich (separately, one after the other) on the 25th–27th Dec. rejoiced in hearing again the [first][7] second one whom I found in excellent spirits, and got on friendly terms with the former. Bleuler has to my extreme satisfaction joined the Zürich Verein since. I delivered into Jung's hands the paper on Paranoia (Schreber) for the 3rd volume of the *Jahrbuch*.[8] You will have got the second half of the second volume at this time and I am sure you will have found ample satisfaction in perusing the bold and able yet elegant apology of ΨA contributed by that curious fellow Bleuler.[9]

The new year did not behave kindly against me. I had a particularly busy and distracted time, disturbed by bodily uneasiness if not disease, and taken up by visits of Ferenczi and a new man from Stockholm Dr. Bjerre.[10] My eldest son—Martin—broke his thigh on a Ski-touring this day two weeks, had to be brought down from the mountain (2000 m) with great difficulty and we had a full share of emotion (and costs) by the accident. He is free of fever now, in good condition and [every][11] any hope for complete recovery seems justified so far.

I am with best love for you and expecting your news

sincerely yours
Freud

1. This echoes "day," as well as "date," as in the "date" of Jones's birthday, and in effect may have had more acoustic resonance for Freud than "coincides."
2. Crossed out in the original.
3. Written in Gothic script.
4. A. J. Storfer (1888–1944), Romanian-born Viennese psychoanalyst; in 1924 replaced Rank as managing editor of the Internationaler Psychoanalytischer Verlag, a post he held until 1932.
5. Storfer (1911), Abraham (1911), and Rank (1911a).
6. Jones (1912j).
7. Crossed out in the original.
8. Freud (1911c).
9. Bleuler (1910).
10. Poul Bjerre (1876–1964), Swedish medical psychologist practicing in Stockholm, who had just presented a paper on 17 January to the Society of Swedish Physicians titled "Die psychoanalytische Methode," *Zentralblatt*, 1 (1911): 375–376. On the same day Freud gave a more elaborate account of Bjerre's visit to Jung (McGuire, 1974, p. 386).
11. Crossed out in the original.

50

[telegram from Jones]

7 February 1911
Toronto

: not professor =

51

8 February 1911
407 Brunswick Avenue
Toronto

Dear Professor Freud,

Thank you very much for your letter, which arrived two days ago. That was most unfortunate news about your son Martin. Please convey to him my condolences with most cordial wishes for a speedy and thorough recovery. The only consolation I find in such experiences is that they afford one an opportunity to read literature, novels, etc., which otherwise one reads with only a guilty conscience at stealing the time. I also most warmly hope that you yourself are again quite well. Though we must not overwork you, we cannot afford to have you lose any time at all by illness. Besides you have had enough of the hard things of life, and have fully earned a happier time for the future.

That was excellent news about Bleuler; it would be a thousand pities were we to lose such a prominent man, besides being a handle for our opponents. As you well put it to me once; "of what use is $\psi\alpha$ if it cannot help us to overcome our personal complexes, and work together". I got the *Jahrbuch* two days ago, and at once devoured Bleuler's article. (I had previously read your article and Rank's, both of which Rank kindly sent me last week.)[1] It is certainly an excellent one, and very admirable in its generosity, honesty and moral courage. It is to be hoped that it will do some good. It provides further an interesting study of Bleuler's personality. I do not suppose my impressions are of any value, but I will give you a few which may perhaps amuse you. Most interesting is his constant dread of generalising, of "going too far", which seems to be a wide-spread complex among scientific men. I sometimes think more harm is done by this fear than by the opposite tendency of too hasty generalisations. Of course it all depends on the man; some should never be allowed to generalise at all. But when a man has the judgement and capacity for it then it is fine when he also has the intellectual courage not to [be] afraid of doing it. One sees further what a drawback it has been to Bleuler to have had no experience with the psycho-neuroses. If he had had he perhaps would not have been so pessimistic about what $\psi\alpha$ can do in determining nosological questions, and would have clearer views about the aetiology of dementia praecox, etc.. Also he would certainly have no doubt as to the essentially infantile and sexual character of the unconscious. Put in a very exaggerated way, he seems to have had more experience of the Vorbewusste of adults, and the Bewus[s]te of children. Hence he misses the feeling of dynamic continuity we have about the Unbewusste, from childhood to adult life. His numerous personal examples, which like those given in his former writings, lie near the surface, I should partly interpret as a compensation against secrecy. The weakest part of his paper is surely his remark (S. 725) about sleep and dreams. Fancy his quoting the fear some patients have of dreams as a proof that these do not guard against sleep.[2] I don't understand how he can fail to grasp what you so clearly discussed in the *Traumdeutung*.[3] Lastly, I see a personal complex (suppressed jealousy) in relation to you, but perhaps it is not agreeable to discuss that.[4]

Your last two papers were very enjoyable. The Wilde $\psi\alpha$[5] was so appropriate to the local situation in Toronto, that I feel like asking you and Brill for permission to translate it, or part of it, for one of the journals here (that have no circulation outside Toronto). Would you mind? I hope we are to have a series of *Liebesbedingung* articles.[6] Could you conveniently coin a term to describe each type. I have not yet seen a pure case of the type you describe, but I am familiar with the indivual traits. The *Dirnenliebe* [predilection for prostitutes] complex has specially interested me in several patients.

Rank's dream paper was also very delightful.[7] I greatly admired the clear way in which he put his material synthetically together so as to bring out the *Zusammenhang* [connection] after dissecting it. What a beautiful dream, besides. As to Silberer I don't know what to make of him. He seems to be badly infected by the philosophic virus.[8] I like Sadger's writings much more than I used to, and do not know whether the change is in him or in me, probably the latter.[9]

I have a good deal of news to give; like yours, partly good, partly bad. Let me finish with the latter first, which is personal, and which I will try to put shortly. The atmosphere is very unhealthy here for $\psi\alpha$, owing chiefly to an incredibly developed prudery, a total ignorance of and misunderstanding of your writings, and perhaps partly to some jealousy of me in certain circles. Stupid rumours keep spreading about my mode of treatment. I recommend masturbation (an old story I told you about), I send young men to prostitutes, and advise debauchery to young women. Two of the latter have become pregnant in consequence—they were three last May, but one seems to have disappeared! I stimulate sexual feeling by showing patients obscene postcards!! etc. etc. But most annoying is some trouble that has been going on for over a month. A severe hysteric whom I saw only a couple of times last September went to a woman doctor (Gordon),[10] and after much pressing declared that I had had sexual relations with her "to do her good". Unfortunately Dr. Gordon had greatly interested herself in the other stories, being the secretary of the local Purity League, so she went with the full batch to the President of the University and asked him to dismiss me, so that I should no longer pervert and deprave the youth of Toronto. The President took the matter very sensibly, although he is a parson,[11] and referred it to Dr. Clarke, the Dean of the Medical Faculty, Professor of Psychiatry, and a close friend of mine. He investigated it as far as he [good][12] could, naturally declared the stories a tissue of nonsense and gave his opinion that the patient was a paranoiac (I think he is wrong there). I had a most sympathetic interview with the President, who was very curious about your work, and also got hold of the best lawyer in the town. There the business still rests, and I am debating whether it is wise to bring a slander action—with more publicity—against the doctor. The patient attempted to shoot me, but her revolver was taken away, and she was sent to a private sanatorium. That alarmed my wife—aided perhaps by some unconscious motive, the nature of which you will have no difficulty in discerning—and she has insisted on the house and myself being guarded by detectives. I even had to take one with me on my trip to Chicago. We have also had extensive investigations made into the patient's past (she is a divorcée, a morphine-maniac, has attempted suicide, etc.), and in all probability she will be deported from the country as an "undesirable character", with which description of her I quite agree. It has therefore been an anxious and also expensive time for me (so far it has cost me over a thousand dollars).

Now to pleasanter things. My trip to Chicago was very successful and enjoyable. I found two men, one from St. Louis, working very earnestly at $\psi\alpha$, and already in possession of the main principles—both most enthusiastic. Many others were very sympathetic, and were trying the work. Dr. Patrick, the chief neurologist there, who opposed us at Washington last May, is practically converted,[13] thanks, so he says, to the talks he had with me then, and has an assistant in his private practice who devotes all his time to it. My address was well received, except by Sidney Kuh who made a very aggressive onslaught.[14] It was extremely stupid. "He couldn't agree with [Freud][15] the logic of Freud's argument that because *Frauenzimmer* in German = *Frau*, therefore to dream of a room means something sexual". I was in bad need of some *Abreagieren* [abreaction] after my Toronto experiences, and as he fortunately laid himself open in most obvious ways, I let myself go at him in a way I have never done in my life (as a rule I am rather a man of peace). Luckily he is very unpopular, so the others greatly enjoyed it.

I could write a great deal about Chicago, but will spare you this time. It is the most hideous excrescence on God's earth. Strangely enough, there are many charming men there, though.

You will be glad to hear that Baltimore promises to become a stronghold of ψα in a little time. There is a man there, whom Jung may have mentioned to you, Burrow, who seems to be an excellent fellow. I correspond regularly with him and with a student who spent two months with me here, and who is taking up the work well.[16] They both say that Adolf Meyer is working hard at ψα, having a polyclinic for psycho-neuroses, and is stimulating them all in that direction. He seems to have behaved splendidly to us of late, and as he is rather a weathercock that is a good sign. Thomas, the Professor of Neurology there, is also taking up the work very seriously, as are some others. Harvey Cushing, the famous brain-surgeon, of Baltimore, has been staying with me during the past few days, and confirms all these reports.[17]

I refused to go to Philadelphia, and advised them to postpone their discussion of the subject for a year's time. We are looking forward to the May meeting of the ψα Ortsverein, of which there are already twenty members.[18] I am very optimistic about the spread of the work in America.

Your advice to me not to be so restless was very welcome. There is no fear that I shall go to the other extreme and get lazy. I am glad you give me more time for the nightmare, which has been badly interrupted of late. When you see the amount of work in it I feel sure you will forgive my apparent slowness. I hope my telegram on Tuesday was in time, for I surely cannot use a title I have no legitimate claim to. It is good news that the *Schriften* are so "besetzt".[19] It shows how much material there is to publish, the *Schriften*, *Jahrbuch* and *Zentralblatt* certainly were very much needed.

Did you like the "Janet" paper I sent you last week? I have just sent Adler for the *Zentralblatt* a little prose counterpart to Rank's *Mitteilung* [communication] (S. 109), i.e. a pretty Versprechen out of Meredith.[20]

My most interesting case at present is one of an "over-work breakdown from business" in a very intelligent man of 40. He came with symptoms of neurasthenia, and at first I could get no history of somatic sexual disturbances. Then he told me that in coitus his wife took the upper position and "did all the work". "It always reminded him of previous experiences of being masturbated". It is instructive to note how he has linked his psycho-sexual complexes with his business, which has become a mirror of them.

I had no idea when I began that I should be so long, and trust I have not over-wearied you.

With my most affectionate respects I am

Yours always
Ernest Jones.

1. Bleuler (1910), Rank (1910), and Freud (1910h).

2. Bleuler (1910, p. 725). See also the extensive critique of Bleuler's paper in Jones (1911–12).

3. For Freud the notion that "dreams are the GUARDIANS of sleep and not its disturbers" is fundamental; see Freud (1900a, pp. 233–234, 564, 580).

4. On the relationship between Bleuler and Freud, see Alexander and Selesnick (1965).

5. Freud (1910k).

6. *Liebesbedingungen* (necessary conditions for loving) is the opening theme of the two papers in the *Liebeslebens* series on the "psychology of love"; see Freud (1910h, p. 165; 1912d).

7. Rank (1910).

8. Herbert Silberer (1882–1922) became noted for his psychoanalytic writings on dreams and occult phenomena; here Jones refers to his "Phantasie und Mythos," *Jahrbuch*, 2 (1910): 541–622.

9. J. Isidor Sadger (b. 1867), one of the first followers of Freud; published—widely—pathographies and articles on degeneration and genius, as well as on psychoanalytical topics.

10. Emma Leila (née Skinner) Gordon (1859–1949), one of Canada's first female medical doctors, was very religious, held strict views on alcohol consumption and loose living, and was a member of the Women's Christian Temperance Union. In telling James Jackson Putnam about this incident, Jones does not mention Dr. Gordon by name; see Jones to Putnam, 13 January 1911 and 5 February 1911, in Hale (1971a, pp. 252–253, 255–256). Regarding his patient, Jones adds, "I foolishly paid the woman $500 blackmail to prevent a scandal" (p. 253).

11. Robert Alexander Falconer (1867–1943), respected academic, author, minister of the Presbyterian church of Canada, and president of the University of Toronto (1907–1932).

12. Crossed out in the original.

13. Hugh T. Patrick (1860–1939), M.D. 1884 Bellevue Hospital Medical College, New York; later professor of neurology, Northwestern University Medical School; president of the American Neurological Association (1907).

14. Sidney Kuh (1866–1934), M.D. 1890 University of Heidelberg; Chicago neurologist.

15. Crossed out in the original.

16. Trigant Burrow (1875–1950), M.D. 1899 University of Virginia, Department of Medicine; in analysis with Jung (1909); charter member of the American Psychoanalytic Association. The student, whose name is written vertically in the margin, was John T. MacCurdy (b. 1886), B.Sc. 1908 University of Toronto; M.D. 1911 Johns Hopkins University School of Medicine. Both Burrow and MacCurdy later turned away from psychoanalysis; see especially Burrow (1958).

17. Henry M. Thomas (b. 1861), M.D. 1895 University of Maryland School of Medicine; clinical professor of neurology, Johns Hopkins Medical School. Harvey Cushing (1869–1939), M.D. 1895 Harvard Medical School; Moseley professor of surgery, Peter Bent Brigham Hospital, Boston; leading American neurosurgeon, as well as noted biographer of Sir William Osler.

18. The American Psychoanalytic Association was founded 9 May 1911 in Baltimore.

19. That is, filled up; but see Ornston (1985b).

20. Jones (1910–11a); Rank (1911b); a few excerpts from Meredith on dreams and forgetting were included in Jones (1913h).

52

[postcard]

12 February 1911
[Vienna]

Dear Doctor,

I have got your cable in time; sorry to have you degraded, hope to see
you elated very soon.

Got your paper on Suggestion today, guess you have never before written
anything so convincing.[1] I was not aware that things stood so favourable
to our hypothesis. Write me soon.

Herzlich yours
Freud

What's the matter with Brill?

1. Jones (1910–11a).

53

[postcard]

22 February 1911
[Vienna]

Dear Dr. Jones,

Glad to have got your Hamlet today, it is nice-looking.[1] Deuticke promised to send you the number of copies you asked.

Yours truly
Freud

1. German translation of Jones (1910a).

54

26 February 1911
Vienna, IX. Berggasse 19

Dear Dr. Jones,

Your correspondence is charming indeed. I have been very much pleased
about your remarks on Bleuler's character and who should be allowed
generalizations and who not. Of course you are perfectly right. He is a very
artificial character; *"Komplexmaske"* [phony] Jung called him one day in

his anger, but I have found out at Munich that he longs to be loved and esteemed like other people too.

I found less gratifying the news about the persecution you are suffering just now. I think, if the case stands so favourably to you, why not undertake an action for slander against the doctoressa? It would teach her a lesson and perhaps turn the tide of public opinion into a direction favourable to you. But you will decide better for yourself. I had a lady doctor called Gordon among my students, when I was a young *Sekundararzt* [assistant physician], she seemed an excellent woman and may not be identical with your prudish foe.

If you want the translation of the "wild ΨA", do it. I am sure Brill [would] have no objection against it.[1] It may serve you as a testimonial of moral intentions. The public is too stupid.

I am glad you like Rank's work. He is growing rapidly in sharpness and good forms and keeps his honest character unharmed. I gave him some help in this paper, but he wanted very little. I am of intention to use his force broadly in my next works and to make him a partner in the coming edition of the *Traumdeutung*,[2] which has to be rewritten and rearranged in the course of a few years.—I think I gave you my opinion about your excellent article on Suggestion, the letter may still be swimming.

I have got the news of the birth of a local group at New York with himself as president.[3] I guess the panamerican one which you mentioned, which is to meet in May is already formed; and both will keep good terms with eachother. Do no[t] neglect the official notice to Jung and the collecting of the contributions to get the external sign of the Society, the *Korrespondenzblatt*. There is a scheme in appearance of blending the *Korrespondenzblatt* with the *Zentralblatt*, and if so, the *Zentral*, will be the official organ of the Association and every member will get it for his contribution, which is to be raised slightly, perhaps S 2½. I am in correspondence with Bergmann on behalf of this plan which might be put into execution after the Congress, with the second volume of the *Zentralblatt*.

I am sure you know that Putnam promised to come to this years Congress at the end of September, most likely Lugano will be the place of meeting. I hope firmly that you will come too and bring as many of the fresh members as possible. I have made the remark that the Congress is the best means of captivating people and shaping them as to become reliable adherents.

I am glad and astonished at the progress won in Chicago. If ever you get hold of a lot of men, try to make them "members". Dr. Burrow I know personally, I think he came to see Jung on an evening when we were in a roof-theatre in New York, and he did assist the meeting in Nürnberg.

You are right to ask me for a good name of the type described in my last paper *"Liebesleben"*, but I have not yet found it. The matter is not to be continued immediately. Paranoia is the next subject treated in vol. III of the *Jahrbuch*.[4]

Pretty interesting things have come to pass in the Vienna group. We had a series of Adler—debates and as the incompatibility of his views with our ΨA came clearly out, he resigned his leadership, though he was not obliged or suggested to do so. But he is of a morbid sensibility. Stekel followed his example, and so I have to accept the honour he dropped on Wednesday next and will take the matter into my own hands again. Adler's views were clever, but wrong and dangerous to the spreading of ΨA, his motives and his behaviour are all throughout of neurotic source.

Did you not mention once the name of Sutherland in British East India? He has announced himself to come to Vienna in the first days of March. I wonder what this most isolated of our adherents may be like.

Do you think it a sign of rising interest in ΨA in your dear old England, that I have been invited to become a corresp. member of the London society for psychical research? The names on their list are all excellent.

My son is recovering in a satisfactory way. I am allright since I got over my chronic Gas-intoxication. I hope your troubles will come to a good end and look forward to your news about work and personal interests.

Yours truly
Freud

1. See Brill (1912b).

2. Apart from correcting proofs, Rank was to take charge of the bibliographic work for Freud (1900a). He would also contribute two papers, "Dreams and Creative Writing" and "Dreams and Myths," which were included at the end of chapter 6 in the four editions of Freud (1900a) between 1914 and 1922; Rank's name also appeared below Freud's on the title page in each of these editions. See Strachey's comments in *S.E.*, 4:xiii, xxi, as well as Freud's remarks in *S.E.*, 4:xxviii, xxix.

3. Brill preempted Jones in forming the New York Psychoanalytic Society (12 February 1911), acting before Jones, along with Putnam, could found the American Psychoanalytic Association (9 May 1911).

4. Freud (1911c).

55

[postcard]

2 March 1911
[Vienna]

Dear Dr. Jones,

I have got the *Journal of Abnormal Psychology* today. You remember our correspondence about M. P. [Morton Prince] years ago. Now you will have found out what he is, the most arrogant ass you could imagine.[1] Jung is indignant, he promises to deal·him some good blows in the *Jahrbuch*.[2]

Keep upright

Sincerely yours
Freud

1. The February-March 1911 issue of Prince's journal contained the exchange between Prince and Jones on dreams; see Jones (1911b), and Prince (1911).
2. Jung (1911).

56

8 March 1911
407 Brunswick Avenue
Toronto

Dear Professor Freud,

The Hamlet Heft arrived this morning, and has given me much pleasure to read through. I feel quite proud. I do not know how to thank you enough for the great personal trouble you have taken over it; Rank, in a letter I got today, told me something of it, and besides I think I know enough German to detect your hand in the beautiful phrases with which you have clothed and polished my work. Believe me that I am deeply grateful and appreciative.

Rank seems to be grandly active in his work. You must be proud of him as a disciple. He tells me that we may expect a third edition of the *Traumdeutung* in May. That will be a great treat.

I have told my London agents to send you some plays of Bernard Shaw,[1] and hope they will arrive safely. I do not expect you to read them all, except possibly on a holiday. The ones most worth reading are, in order: Man and Superman, Major Barbara, Getting Married, Caesar and Cleopatra, and the Devil's Disciple. The first (notably the Hell Scene in it) I can specially commend to you. Please do not take this little present as an expression of my gratitude to you, for that cannot be shown in such a way as this, though perhaps it may serve as a memento of my first contribution to your work, a contribution which I sincerely hope will be followed by other more worthy ones.

Things in general are going well in America. I constantly get letters showing interest and advancement in the work. You ask me about Brill's health. All I know is that he had some obscure trouble, with high intraocular tension, in the eyes, and that it is now again quite well. It is to be hoped that he will get no recurrence. I am at present negociating with him and Jung about the organisation in America. I think there should be a main

centralising American *branch* of the Internationale ψα Vereinigung, and
that local subsections should be subordinate to it. They both seem to agree
to this, and I expect it will be so settled at the May meeting. I have written
to Bleuler (and Jung) asking for permission to translate his *Jahrbuch* article
for the *Journal of Abnormal Psychology*.[2] Matters between Morton Prince
and myself are strained. He is an agreeable fellow, but too much of a
schoolboy, and prefers fighting to learning. I am afraid that if it comes to
a split in the camp, as is probable in May, Putnam may side with him
rather than with us. Putnam is too timid by nature, unless one can act on
his conscience, and "duty-complex". If I am still here next year, I expect
we shall have a journal of our own, which will knock out Prince's. Personally, matters are very disagreeable with me in many ways. Externally the
clouds are rolling high in Toronto, and the opposition to me on all sides
is fierce. I hear the maddest inventions and rumours of my "dangerous
teachings and influences", and all sorts of absurd lies are told about me. I
still keep a detective, but that silly couple of female doctor and patient
have done nothing more of late. They applied to a magistrate for a warrant
to arrest me, but he sent them about their business. I have enough evidence
collected about the woman's past to have her deported out of the country,
but am taking no steps as they might lead to an open scandal. My wife is
very upset, and urges me, as she has done for a long time, to retire from
private practice on account of its being "such dangerous work". If I refuse
I think she will leave me, although we are otherwise devoted to each other.
She has terribly strong complexes against the work, and I have never had
a chance of breaking her resistance, on account of the grave state of her
general health. If I give up I should have to go to London, and devote myself
for a few years to research in mythology, anthropology, religion etc.. As
you know, there is ample room for such work, but I feel I could do good
work in neurology and psychiatry, where I already have some reputation,
and do not want to give up.

It is difficult to ask for advice, for the circumstances are too complicated
to relate fully, but you know I would attach the greatest weight to anything
you could say. For various reasons I must decide one way or the other soon.

You may imagine that in this state of affairs, on top of heavy work, I have
not been able to give myself much to fresh work during the past couple
of months. The most certain thing in my mind is that I can never give myself to any other line of work than ψα; it has for me a most powerful appeal.

With Kindest Regards

Yours always affectionately
Ernest Jones.

P.S. I have found in Dr. Curran Pope a very good translator for Hitschmann,
and have written to tell him so.[3]

1. George Bernard Shaw was a favorite of Jones's.

2. Bleuler (1910), and Jones (1911–12).

3. Curran Pope (1866–1934), physician in Louisville, Kentucky, joined the American Psychoanalytic Association in 1912. Eduard Hitschmann (1871–1957), M.D. 1895 University of Vienna; member of the Vienna Psychoanalytic Society. Hitschmann (1911) was translated by Charles R. Payne of Westport, N.Y., M.D. 1906 Cornell University Medical School.

57

17 March 1911
407 Brunswick Avenue
Toronto

Dear Professor Freud,

Thank you greatly for your very delightful and welcome letter. It is excellent to get good personal news of yourself and your son.

I am afraid I cannot write a bright letter, for, as you will surmise from the one I wrote about ten days ago, things are with me very depressing. Fortunately an end is in sight for I have had to come to a definite decision. My wife said she could not stand the anxiety and suspense of the situation here, and that if I stayed on she would leave me for good. There was also reason to think that that would soon mean suicide, though she did not say so. She is very pessimistic, and suffers greatly from complicated abdominal trouble (kidney stone, etc.). I decided to accompany her, and our plan at present is as follows: I go to Europe in September and if I get my Professorship before I go, I will come back for one session only to lecture and then leave; if I do not get it I shan't come back. In the meantime I will try to get a position in the States. If I do not get one to my liking I will go to England. In any case I shall find a way to go on with the work.

I have not been able to do any work in the past two months or more, but I now feel I can settle down to it again.

A point of some little interest was the discovery this week of the following infantile theory, one no doubt familiar to you: the child grows inside and emerges per rectum; the material is food, and the fertilising fluid is medicine supplied by the doctor. In a birth dream, she called on the way to "bathe" in a milk shop, and was given several bottles of milk, [with][1] one of which was a violet colour bottle. The associations to the latter were: (1) violet = favourite flower—buds—children. (2) "poisonous" medicines are in blue bottles (3) butter-milk (semen symbol) is sold in brown bottles (brown + blue = violet). She has to take buttermilk as medicine, and it makes her feel sick.

It is rather pretty, don't you think so.

I am glad the *Zentralblatt* and *Korrespondenzblatt* will be combined. We want what we haven't yet got, namely a *Zentralblatt* that will be complete, giving an abstract, however short, of all the works that appear for and against. The present *Zentralblatt* only gives a selection of these. By the way, might I suggest that the date, month of publication, be put on the *Zentralblatt*, though perhaps you have some reason for not wishing it.

You wrote that the *Traumdeutung* was appearing in a new edition in the course of a few *years*. Rank told me it was to appear in May, so perhaps you made a Verschreiben. I hope so.[2]

That was most interesting news about the Vienna group. You see how much you are wanted in the leadership, so you must resign your personal inclinations towards leisure, and keep in the saddle. I gathered from Stekel's last writings that he had been infected by Adler. The more I think of Adler, the more obviously one-sided his views become to me. As you say, such a lack of judgement must be constellated by strong personal factors. It would be valuable to know who you consider best understand your views. Would the following order be far wrong? Jung, Ferenczi, Rank, Maeder, Riklin.[3]

The May meeting of the American ψα Association will probably be an informal one, and we shall have to discuss the relation of it to the New York Society. Brill now wants the latter to be independent, but I am afraid that would leave the other men out in the cold, and would prevent the good harmony that is necessary. Would you be so very kind as to let me know the date of the September meeting?[4] We have to get tickets ahead (it is Coronation year)[5] and make other arrangements. Putnam has given up the American Medical Association in Los Angeles in order to go, and I hope there will be a good American contingent.

I hear excellent accounts of Adolf Meyer, who seems to be whole heartedly encouraging ψα investigation. My pupil, McCurdy, who is working with him is doing splendidly, and brought me this week a pretty D. P. [Dementia praecox] analysis. He is a very level-headed fellow, and I think he will attain a high position in psychiatry.

You will by now have met Col. Sutherland, who has joined our association. I do not suppose he has done much ψα. He has done much work in the sexuality of Hindoos, some of which was contributed to *Anthropophyteia* under the synonym of Dr. S.

You ask me of the Society of Psychical Research. I am sorry to say that in spite of the good names in it, the society is not of good repute in scientific circles. You will remember that they did some valuable work in the eighties on hypnotism, automatic writing etc., but for the past 15 years they have confined their attention to "spook-hunting", mediumism, and telepathy, the chief aim being to communicate with departed souls. Did you accept the corresp. membership? It does not seem that your researches lend much support to spiritism, in spite of William James' ardent hope. Poor James. One hasn't even the consolation of thinking that he knows better by now.

You are quite right in your concise description of Morton Prince, but after all it only describes one side of him. He has been spoiled by being the pet of Boston, in both social and scientific standings, and has kept up his boyish love for fighting for the fun of it in a light irresponsible way. There is much to be said about his character, but I am fairly sure he will never understand ψα.

With my Kindest Regards

Yours always
Ernest Jones.

1. Crossed out in the original.
2. The third edition of Freud (1900a) appeared in the spring of 1911.
3. Franz Riklin (1878–1938), Swiss psychiatrist, undertook pioneering work with Jung regarding the word-association experiments; see Jung (1973).
4. The Third Congress of the International Psychoanalytic Association, Weimar, 21–22 September 1911.
5. George V succeeded his father, Edward VII, who died on 6 May 1910.

58

30 April 1911
407 Brunswick Avenue
Toronto

Dear Professor Freud,

My last letter, sent a week after the previous one, really answered in part your latest one,[1] for it stated what I had decided to do. Since then my plans are not much changed. I am told I shall probably get my professorship next month, so shall stay here through next winter to lecture. After that I may get an appointment in the States or go back to London. The hint you gave me about the unconscious seizing on wandering habits was very useful. Still I think it will be compensated by another complex—the wish to succeed in London.

As to your general advice to stay here, I hardly know what to say to you. I am immensely grateful for the concern you show in my affairs, and for the advice. I don't think I need to say that there is no one whose opinion I respect so much, or whose advice I would more gladly follow than yours. But the whole matter is so enormously complicated—in ways I cannot describe in a letter—that I feel it is not fair to expect you to judge. Perhaps I may have the opportunity of having a talk with you when I am over in

September. By the way I hear from Ferenczi that the meeting-place of the Congress is changed to Weimar. Is that definite?

Next week are all the Baltimore meetings. It will be rather a critical time in the history of American $\psi\alpha$, for the future society-organisations will be discussed. I wish Putnam and Hoch were as fervid as Brill and myself. Your footnote in the Zentralblatt had a great effect on Putnam,[2] but lately he has been off again on all sorts of philosophic tracks. Fortunately, there are a number of younger men who are taking up the work very seriously, and who should soon become proficient at it.

I have had a dreadful pressure of work of different kinds in the past few weeks. Next week I have five papers to read, one on organic neurology, the rest on different aspects of $\psi\alpha$. None of them is of any note, except one on the Pathology of Angst, which I hope may interest you.[3]

I have just read Stekel's dream book.[4] What a prolific worker he is! I suppose you agree that it will be of service to psycho-analysts, but will not convert many outsiders. I was greatly shocked at his talk about telepathy; the evidence he produces is no better than any spook-hunter. He must have an unconscious vein of religious superstition that he hasn't opened up. Isn't that so?

Your last dream paper in the Zentralblatt[5] is surely enough to convince anyone. Regarding the hat symbol, it is extremely common out here; the ordinary hard felt "bowler" hat is generally called a "Christie stiff"[6] (Christie being the name of the original maker). I have also found it as a female symbol. In England the soft indented felt hat is generally called by young men a "cunt" hat; (cunt is a very vulgar expression for cunnus, from which I suppose it is derived. Trotter[7] told me the following amusing self-analysis about the word. You know that the Norman aristocratic names Montgomery, Montmoren[c]ie, etc., are pronounced as if spelt Munt. This he had always disliked, preferring to say Mont; recently he traced this repugnance to the rhyme with the other, objectionable word.).

I was surprised not long ago to find a snake in a dream as a female symbol. Have you seen that? It shows how the most exquisitely male symbols can be bisexual, just as well as easier ones like telephone, and supports your view of primitive bisexuality. The symbolism in question arose through the resemblance of the snake with the posterior hole, and snake-skin, to a condom, which the pt. [patient] had used when masturbating to heighten an illusion of being in a vagina ("sheathed").

I hope the Vienna trouble is subsiding. It is a pity that Adler and Stekel are not the men Jung and Ferenczi are. It is too bad that you should be bothered in that way.

As to myself, be assured that however things may seem at a distance I shall devote myself whole-heartedly to helping forward the movement in the way I feel I can best do it. I will write again in a fortnight after getting back from the States (I am going to Washington and Detroit as well as Baltimore, and am taking my wife with me).

With Kindest Regards,

Yours always
Ernest Jones.

1. Letter missing.

2. Putnam (1910b) was anonymously translated by Freud, who added a footnote about Putnam's highly regarded status as a neurologist in America and his "unimpeachable character and high moral standards"; see *Zentralblatt*, 1 (1911): 137 n. 1, and *S.E.* 17:271–272 n. 2. Moreover, Freud added the phrase "although he [Putnam] has left his youth far behind him . . ." in response to Putnam's remark about Freud's age; see passage cited by note 9 to letter 24.

3. In May he read four papers; see Jones (1911a, 1911e, 1911f, 1911g).

4. Stekel (1911).

5. Freud (1911a).

6. Doubly underlined in the original.

7. Wilfred Batten Lewis Trotter (1872–1939), one of the great neurosurgeons of Britain; he was Jones's best friend, and figures prominently in Jones (1959); had married Jones's sister Elizabeth in 1910.

59

14 May 1911
Vienna, IX. Berggasse 19

Dear Dr. Jones,

I have had a bad day for writing, my cramp being on its acme I know not why but I will not postpone the letter to a next Sunday.

I did not hasten to answer your letter of the 17th April,[1] partly because it did not correspond to mine[2] and partly from the [ex][3] impression I had ventured too far into the intimacy of your motives. I see you did not resent it although it is clearly a case when a man must act according to his own mind and cannot take another man's counsel. Now I find the situation is all improved by one bit of good news in your second letter. If you get the professorship this (next) month and go on lecturing for one season you may lieve [leave] Toronto without harm to yourself. I objected seriously to your going away before gaining the title. The loss for America may be the same in both cases, but I am sure ΨA will not lose you. In England you will have to begin anew from the very beginning and perhaps this is a charm attractive to your temper.

Now for your single questions in both letters. Just today Jung proposes in N. 5 of the *Korrespondenzblatt* the terms of 16/17 or 21/22 Sept. for the Congress, which is to take place at *Weimar*. I am forced by private motives to vote for the later one, the first one being too near to a certain domestic anniversary.[4]

2. Your infantile theory (a secondary one, never treated by me in extenso) is very nice. You ought to collect some of these theories for the *Zentralblatt*. To be sure it is semen and that is poison. We must add "medicine" to the list of equivalent fluids and excretions in Stekel's symbolic Gleichungen.

3. The 3d edition of the *Traumdeutung*[5] will meet you as Rank promised in a few weeks, perhaps not later than the new *Jahrbuch*. In a paper of mine therein you will detect a sign that I did not read B. Shaw without profiting from him.[6]

4. The condition here in Vienna is not very satisfactory. I see no good coming from my personal aura or influence. Lastly Stekel made his peace and promised to behave in a nice way, but the other boy Adler fixes himself in mute resistance and ill suppressed anger. He is a paranoiac I am sorry to say. The Libido of the Oedipus-Complex is—to him—made up, "*arrangirt*";[7] can you understand why it should be so?

5. As for the list of best understanding my views, can it be complete without including your own person very far in the front?

6. Sutherland is a clever and amiable fellow. The $\psi\alpha$ power behind him is a younger man, Dr. Hunt at the same place.[8]

7. Stekels book is full of merit and full of mistakes, a progress in analysis and no honour to him. He is likely to be right in most of the interpretations, for this is his strong side. I was very much surprised at your statement the snake might be a female symbol, as I had never found it and objected to Stekels affirmation regarding the same. I begged him to give me proofs and he had none, so I hope [you] will reconsider your case and write me a word about it.

8. I was afraid I had made a mistake in that note about Putnams character. I did not know at the time, that he wanted the translation for circulation in America, else I would not have dared to give him a character where he is so much better known than I. He wrote me about his ethical aims and scruples and I am closing this letter to you in order to answer him.[9]

Yours truly
Freud

1. Freud is referring to Jones's letter of 17 March 1911.
2. This letter is missing.
3. Crossed out in the original.
4. Freud's twenty-fifth wedding anniversary 13 September.
5. "*Trdeut*" is written in Gothic script.
6. See Freud (1911b, p. 223 n. 1), and *Jahrbuch*, 3 (1911): 5 n. 1, in which he quotes a passage from Shaw's *Man and Superman* (1903). See also note 4 to letter 68.
7. "Contrived"; written in Gothic script.

8. Slip for Berkeley-Hill; see letter 61.
9. See Freud to Putnam, 14 May 1911, in Hale (1971a, pp. 121–122).

60

22 May 1911
407 Brunswick Avenue
Toronto

Dear Professor Freud,

I am enclosing two little communications and one article, in the hope that you may think them worth publishing in the *Zentralblatt*. The shortest concerns an example of sekundäre Bearbeitung that I mentioned to you, and which you asked me to send a note about for publication. Another is a pretty analysis of Namenvergessen that I got from my wife; it refers to my sister (Owlie) who married Trotter last year.[1] The article I am much more dubious as to the value of, and I will leave it quite to your judgement to decide whether it is worth publishing at all, or whether it should be altered in any respects.

Now you will want to know about the May meetings, especially the ψα one,[2] and I had better shortly recount the movement from the beginning. You had separately suggested to Putnam, Brill and myself last year that we found an American branch of the Internationale Vereinigung, and last November we sent out a circular signed by the three of us and also by August Hoch, the Director of the N. Y. Psychiatric Institute. A little later, Brill, without saying a word to Putnam and myself, founded a N. Y. branch of the I. V., of which he is President. I agreed with him that such local branches that can meet frequently must be the main thing in our propaganda, and suggested the following proposal. That a general American head branch of the I. V. be formed, to meet once a year to coordinate the work being done, and to give men from different parts of the States the chance of meeting each other, and that as many local societies as possible be formed as sub-branches of the main one. This seemed to me the only logical plan, and to be demanded by the geographical conditions. It was agreed to by Jung, with whom I have been in constant correspondence on the matter, but Brill wouldn't hear of it. He wrote me an extraordinary letter, saying that the plan would do away with local branches and that he didn't want to be independent of the I. V., thus quite misunderstanding the plan. We exchanged several letters, but I failed to move him in his objection.

At the meeting in Baltimore not a soul from N. Y. turned up, not even a representative of the society there, and Brill was unfortunately prevented from coming on account of his wife's illness.

The plan therefore fell through of necessity, and, as it was absurd to start another rival society on the same lines as the N. Y. one, I suggested that it might serve a good purpose if we founded one on the lines of the American Neurological Association, the object of which is to provide a cachet for men of good standing by admitting only those of proved competence. We shall need that in $\psi\alpha$, for already in America there are many men exploiting it for financial and other reasons, whose knowledge of the subject is minimal, and who only bring discredit on the work. This plan was accepted, and I have written to Jung to ask him to take us in as a branch of the I. V.. The annual meeting is to be open to all members of any local branch, as well as to invited guests, but no one will be elected member of the association unless he has shown some competence in the work. Under the circumstances I feel it was the best thing we could do. Putnam is President, I am secretary, and Adolf Meyer, Hoch, and Burrow form the committee. Meyer has been exceedingly friendly in the past year, and Hoch has written some good papers. Burrow, an assistant of Meyer's, was with Jung for a year, and knows the work well.

The meeting of the American Psychopathological Association this year was very disappointing. I will send you the published account of it next month. The Angst discussion,[3] thanks to Putnam, fizzled out into philosophy, and the sexual question was not mentioned. Meyer is to be President for the next year, so Prince is in the background.

At the American Neurological Association Scripture read a paper on $\psi\alpha$.[4] It was in very bad taste, nothing but cheap jokes, etc., and a vulgar caricature of the real thing. It caused great amusement in the audience, and great indignation in the minds of some of us.

I have just returned from Detroit where I read papers, on successive evenings, before the Medical Society, and the Academy of Medicine, one on the Relationship of Dreams to psychoneurotic symptoms, the other on *Alltagsleben*.[5] The latter I am expanding into an article of about 100 manuscript pages, as I have a lot of good material, and I hope to finish it this week. I will send it to the *American Journal of Psychology*, and if it does not suit them will publish it in the *Journal of Abnormal Psychology*. Then I start on the article I promised Jung for the *Jahrbuch*.[6] You will notice that my working fit has returned.

You will be glad to hear that you have ardent supporters in towns so far apart as Chicago, Omaha, Louisville and Cincinnati, and that there is quite a colony in Baltimore. Boston holds aloof, and naturally so does the organic Philadelphia, though there is one good man there taking up the work with zeal.

I am eagerly awaiting your paranoia work. By the way, is it not time that we had a Dritte Folge of the *Sammlung?*

My personal affairs are still in a flux, but I hope to have some satisfactory news when I write next. My "protector", Dr. Clarke, the head of the asylum has just resigned on account of the unfavourable conditions in the service, and has taken up a position in the General Hospital.

Yours always affectionately
Ernest Jones.

1. See Jones (1912f) and (1912e).
2. The American Psychoanalytic Association was founded 9 May 1911 at a meeting in Baltimore.
3. Concerning Jones (1911e).
4. E. W. Scripture, "Psychanalysis and Correction of Character," read at the annual meeting of the American Neurological Association, Baltimore, 11–13 May 1911; published in *Journal of Nervous and Mental Disease*, 38 (1911): 743–745.
5. Jones (1911f, 1911g).
6. Jones (1912–13).

61

1 June 1911
407 Brunswick Avenue
Toronto

Dear Professor Freud,

I am very grateful to you for your kind letter that came this week. There was no possibility of my "resenting" your excellent advice, but I felt distressed that the circumstances were so complicated that I could not do them justice in a letter. You may rely on me to do the best I can in the business. Things are slowly developing, and I hope soon to be able to write more definitely.

There are some points in your letter to answer. In regard to infantile theories I am extremely interested, and am busy collecting them. I often feel embarrassed however when I think that probably a given one is banal to all you people in Europe, and therefore not worth mentioning. Still when I have put together something I can submit it to you for your opinion, if you will be so kind. You must have noticed the interesting fact that the explanations given by adults (finding under cabbages, etc.) are only disguised versions of true infantile theories; they are worth working out in detail, I should think.

I am sorry about Adler, and cannot understand such strong fixation. In a recent letter to me he made a curious remark, about Hamlet. "Und Ihnen brauche ich es ja nicht zu sagen; Hamlet, das ist eine Herzenssache".[1] He was explaining why he didn't care to review my book himself. All I know about the Oedipus-complex is that it is exceedingly difficult to overcome.

I have found that so in my own person, although I am quite familiar with the sources of it.

I am glad you liked Sutherland. His younger friend is Berkeley-Hill, a pupil and patient of mine. Why did you come to call him Dr. *Hunt?*

With regard to the snake. I did not know Stekel had said that, for I have not had time yet to read his book in detail. My reason was as follows: the patient, who had very strong homosexual trends, had committed many acts of bestiality (sheep, dog, bird etc.), and had tried to have coitus with a dead snake *(per anum)*. What attracted him was its sheath-like appearance. He always pictured the vagina as a sheath, and used to masturbate with a condome on so as to get the illusion he was in a vagina. In a dream a snake appeared in one part as a father-symbol (penis), and in another he was putting [on][2] high boots on to a lion's foot. He was the lion, the foot was of course the penis, and the books [boots] gave the associations—condome—snake. I see that it is not a pure case of female symbolism, and it could not have arisen had not the male symbolism been also there.[3]

If I may say so, I am sure you did not make a mistake about the footnote on Putnam;[4] he was extremely pleased with it.

I have finished my long *Alltagsleben* paper, and am beginning the one for the *Jahrbuch*, which I hope will not be too late.[5] I have been exceedingly active lately, perhaps due to my buoyancy at receiving so many marks of esteem in America; I am too susceptible to such things.

If you think of publishing the name-forgetting anaylsis I sent you last week would you add the enclosed account of a little continuation, which happened only a few days ago.[6] I also enclose an interesting passage from Darwin, which might be worth putting in the Varia.[7]

I have been reading again the *Psychopathologie des Alltagslebens*, as usual with fresh profit, and should like to make the following little remarks. You speak of unconscious suicidal attempts.[8] I had one such case in London. A young lady was passionately devoted to a sister who died. Her mind was full of phantasies about rejoining her in heaven. She had a horror of funerals, churches and anything to do with death, so much so that she couldn't even hear the sound of birds' singing, as it reminded her of church bells etc.. One day when cycling in London she turned a corner and saw a funeral emerging from a side street. She at once fell under a dray-waggon, and sustained a fracture of the skull. After this she had a long hysterical delirium, with of course complete antero-retrograde amnesia. The bystanders attributed her fall from the bicycle to a sudden gust of wind, but the analysis clearly showed it was otherwise determined.

You remark (S. 130) on the feeling of conviction of free will being much more marked with unimportant action.[9] Cannot this be correlated with the way in which the unconscious seizes on unassociated indifferent material in dream making, etc.?

I have been greatly impressed with the striking frequency with which one word is replaced by its exact opposite in speech, writing, print, etc.. You give an example, S. 66. Nr. d..[10] Maeder accidentally makes the same mistake, where the motive is evident (*Coenobium*. p. 112. line 3 of the second foot-note, *"impartiellement"* for *"partiellement"*[)].[11] I think there are two similar slips in the *Psychopath.*, though I am not sure of the first one (1) S. 101. line 8 of the footnote, *'ungerecht'* instead of *'gerecht'*. (2) S. 105. line 3. *"unbeabsichtigter"* instead of *"beabsichtigter"*.[12] Don't you think it would be worth while in the next edition to correlate this tendency with your remarks on "Gegensinn"?[13] Please forgive my presumption in making the suggestion to you.

It would be an interesting thing to collect, and analyse so far as possible, the misprints in the *Zentralblatt*. An amusing perseveration occurs on S. 276, where they correct a mistake on S. 181 of *"le subconscious"* instead of *"le subconscient"*. The correction reads "soll es heissen le subconscious".[14]

On S. 197, footnote, two mistakes occur, with a fairly obvious motivation. They write "Das Freud'sche Ideogenitäts*monument* und seine Bedeutung im mani*sch*-depr. Irresein K*r*upelins";[15] it is not hard to guess which the author considers the greater man. In my paper I have some charming examples of disparagement by means of name-distortion.[16]

With Kindest Regards

Yours always affectionately
Ernest Jones.

1. "And indeed I don't have to tell you; Hamlet, that is a matter of the heart."
2. Crossed out in the original.
3. Later, in his paper on symbolism (Jones, 1916a) Jones gives up on the idea of a snake as a female symbol. After discussing the snake as a phallic symbol and mentioning the works of Stekel (1908, 1911) on symbolism in general, Jones writes that the serpent is "one of the most constant symbols of the phallus," and that "very occasionally it can symbolise the intestines or their contents, but, so far as I know, nothing else" (Jones, *Papers*, 2nd ed. 1918, pp. 143, 144 n. 1, 170 n. 1).
4. See note 2 to letter 58.
5. Jones (1911g) and (1912–13).
6. Jones (1912e).
7. See the short note Jones (1911i).
8. See Freud (1901b, pp. 178–183).
9. Freud (1901b, pp. 253–254).
10. See, for example, no. 5 in Freud (1901b, pp. 120–121).
11. Alphonse Maeder, "Une Voie nouvelle en psychologie: Freud et son école," *Coenobium*, 3 (January 1909): 112.
12. Freud (1901b, pp. 181 n. 1, 191), *G.W.*, 4:201 n. 1, 212.
13. The process whereby words are replaced by their opposites is partially discussed in Freud (1901b, pp. 59–60).

14. The attempt at correction failed. The editors made the same mistake by writing the English *subconscious* instead of the French *subconscient*. See *Zentralblatt*, 1 (1911): 181, 276.

15. *Monument,* the *sch* of *manisch-,* and the *u* of *Krupelins* are doubly underlined. The error is made in *Zentralblatt*, 1 (1911): 197, in reference to Otto Gross, *Das Freudsche Ideogenitätsmoment und seine Bedeutung im manisch-depressiven Irresein Kraepelins* (Leipzig: Vogel, 1907).

16. Jones (1911g).

62

25 June 1911
Vienna, IX. Berggasse 19

Dear Dr. Jones,

There is your working fit again. I like it better than the foregoing negative one.

Before I go on answering your interesting questions I will let you know, that the *Traumdeutung* is out and will go off to America in a few days (my lady-secretary being absent just now). I am impatiently waiting for the 8th of July to leave Vienna and make off for Karlsbad. You may go on using my Vienna address, all letters are forwarded by the Vienna post office.

I have sent your contributions to Stekel, who is sticking to my side in this crisis in a way worth of praise and remembrance. I want him to be the sole editor of the *Zentralblatt,* but Adler is not yet thrown out; he and his company (some 6–7 members of the Verein) behave in a very malicious manner. Collect whatever you can and send it to us. I dont think we will have to refuse anything you send. As for Oedipus, you will have learned since, that Adler considers the whole of the complex as a sham-construction, fabricated in order to get afraid by one's sexual appetites. He (A. not Hamlet) is not very far from Paranoia, his distortions are gorgeous.

Why did I call Hill—Hunt? I do not know. I shall subject the matter to analysis one of these days. In first thoughts I find some relation to Stanley Hall.

As for the snake I agree with you that it is no clear case. There is no fundamental opposition between us on this point. The infantile theory attributing the same organ to both sexes, there is a distinct tendency to use the symbols in a bisexual sense,—though it is not regularly [executed][1] realized.

In the *"Alltagsleben"* you are quite right as regards p. 105 *(unbeabsichtigt),* but not so in the note p. 101, as you did expect yourself.[2] I mentioned the relation to the *"Gegensinn"* in a few words *Jahrbuch* 184 (note).[3]

Your remark on the feeling of conviction in small things and the relation of the unconscious to these trifles is quite just and very clever.

The *Jahrbuch* will not come out before End of July, but it will be very strong.

With kindest regards

yours truly
Freud

1. Crossed out in the original.

2. In the first instance, mentioned by Jones in letter 61, Freud's usage is correct. Thus, "psychologisch ungerecht" (that is, "psychologically unjust") is left intact; see Freud (1901b, p. 181 n. 1), *G.W.*, 4:201 n. 1. In the second, the alteration reads "beabsichtigter Handlungen" (that is, "intended" actions as opposed to "unintended" ones); see Freud (1901b, p. 191), *G.W.*, 4:212.

3. See *Jahrbuch*, 2 (1910): 184; and Freud (1910e, p. 161 n. 2), *G.W.*, 8:221 n. 2.

63

13 July 1911
407 Brunswick Avenue
Toronto

Dear Professor Freud,

In response to the solicitations of various friends I have acquired the art of type-writing, which should make my letters easier to read. In the first place let me thank you warmly for so kindly sending me the new edition of the *Traumdeutung*. It came only last evening and already I have seen so many new things in it that I had better not start commenting on it if I am to write the other things I want to, but I warn you that you are in danger of getting a long letter from me about it as soon as I shall have read it through carefully. I was very proud to find myself mentioned in it.[1] In a recent number of the *Journal of the American Medical Association* Dercum, of Philadelphia, has an absurd article on your theory of dreams, which he controverts by the penetrating observation that it is contrary to the universal experience of mankind.[2] I wonder it didn't occur to him that aeroplanes are also. In the same number Lloyd has an extremely vulgar attack on my Hamlet article, which he says could only have been written by a sexual pervert;[3] the only argument he brings is to the effect that Hamlet knew who was his mother, while Oedipus did not, therefore the two plays can have nothing in common. To such shifts are our opponents reduced in their search for disproofs! On the other hand you will be glad to learn that two very excellent reviews have appeared. One, in the *British Medical Journal*, is an exceedingly fair-minded and sympathetic review of the translated *Drei Abhandlungen*.[4] The other is a thirty six page review in the *American Journal of Psychology*, by Rud. Acher, of your recent work and also of some other writings of the school. No doubt Stanley Hall will send you a copy of it, but in the meantime I might quote a typical sentence.[5] "So little is known about [Leonardo] da Vinci's early life that it seems a pity that some other more familiar character was not chosen in preference to him; and yet when one reads this classic analysis by that prince of psycho-analysists [psychoanalysts], one almost feels that, if more facts had been at hand, his almost magical sublety [magic subtlety] of analysis would have had less opportunity to reveal its power and penetration." He writes very clearly on the importance of the unconscious, and the evolution of racial instincts, being evidently very hopeful of the possibility of harmonising psycho-analysis with widened principles of psychology.

It is very distressing that you should be bothered by the internal dissensions caused by Adler. It is annoying that he has a following, but he has probably no influence outside Vienna, with the sole exception of Putnam, who thinks very highly of his ideas; perhaps they are similarly constellated, but Putnam's paranoic tendencies take a different direction, as you will see from his remarks in the current number of the *Journal of Abnormal Psychology*, a copy of which I will send you in a few days as soon as it comes out.[6]

With regard to the editorship of the *Zentralblatt* couldn't you broaden the basis of it by securing Jung? I hear there is some talk of amalgamating the *Zentralblatt* with the *Correspondenzblatt*. Would it be possible to make it international to the extent of publishing in English or French the occasional communications in those languages, just as was done with the abstract by Assagioli in the last number?[7] It seems to me that this would increase its sale and influence in other countries, and would promote the international aspects of the movement. The main advantage, however, would be the saving of the labour of translating foreign contributions, which must already have been considerable. I know that the thought of burdening Rank has prevented me from sending in more little contributions than I have, and the same must apply to the others.

I have always communicated with Adler on matters of abstracting, so that if he is resigning I shall have to bother you a little about them. You know that Brill and I divided up the English journals between us for abstracting purposes, each doing certain ones. I sent Adler early last October a batch of eleven reviews, none of which has yet been printed, and in the present number of the *Zentralblatt* one of these already reviewed articles is reviewed by Maeder (from an English journal).[8] Surely this sort of thing will lead to much confusion and waste of labour. I presume Adler has not been able to get anyone to translate my abstracts, which is quite understandable with such a thankless task, but it is another argument for making the *Zentralblatt* international if this is financially possible.

Many thanks for sending to Stekel my other contributions. I hope that you included the confirming postscript to the analysis of the name-forgetting, which was enclosed in my second letter.[9]

By now you must be tired of my annoying you with so many little details, and indeed it is a shame to do so on a holiday that is so much needed, and when it must be a relief to get away from things. I am afraid, however, that I must inflict on you a few personal matters, about which I had hoped to be able to write before.

The situation here has remained the same, a mixture of good and bad. My enemies in the Government circles took advantage of Dr. Clarke's resignation from the asylum to dismiss me without the shadow of an explanation. That was a blow both financially and in professional standing.[10] The promised Psychiatric Clinic has also been definitely abandoned. Further, the professorship which the President of the University had promised me was not awarded, owing to strenuous opposition from various people who thought that my views were "dangerous". On the other hand the General Hospital decided to open a neurological department for my benefit, so that I have no doubt it would be possible to make something out of the situation in time.[11]

But as you know the whole question has been greatly complicated by my wife's feelings. She is a chronic invalide, from calculous pyelo-nephritis and other complications, and suffers from severe and almost constant pain for which she has had to take huge doses of morphia, which has considerably affected her both bodily and mentally. Her life here is miserable and apart from me very lonely, for she is away from her friends and relatives, and cordially detests the Canadian people, as I do myself. She has made big sacrifices for me in the past in many ways, although she does not believe in my work and is very fearful about the dangers of it to my reputation. She has done her utmost to stand the strain here and was willing to try to stand another year of it for the sake of my getting the professor's title. As it is, however, it would be inhuman of me to ask her to stay longer, and, I expect, fruitless. My only option, therefore, is to return with her to London or to separate, which is unthinkable.

I have thus decided to leave here for good in the middle of next September. The future is of course uncertain. I have very little chance of getting much of a position in London, but I believe that there should be enough demand for my services to keep me busy in Psycho-analytic work. It is bound to get known in time even in England, though I think it will be a long while before it wins much recognition. At all events I should be able to do something for the movement there. I will try to do as much for it in America as before, for I hope to be able to cross every year and attend all the annual meetings in May as I do at present.

The work is going on well. I sent Jung last month a long paper, and took the opportunity in it of gently differing from Adler's views.[12] The problem of the nightmare book is satisfactorily solved by dividing it into two, dealing with its relation to history and mythology respectively. The former I shall certainly be able to let you have in September. I have just finished an interesting chapter on the devil, treated as an incest myth. It was a great pleasure to be able to take up this work again after more than six month's labour at other subjects.[13] This week I corrected the proofs of an everyday life paper for Hall's journal and one on dreams for the *American Journal of Insanity*; both are to appear in October.[14] The next non-clinical work must of course be the Macbeth. I wonder also if I might ask you to reserve for me the subject of Napoleon, that is, provided no one else is thinking of working at it. It has occurred to me to take it up from the point of view of his Oriental complex. I have always been interested in his character, and have read the literature in question fairly widely.[15]

Well, this is certainly a big enough dose of me for one time, so I will bring my epistle to a close.

I warmly hope that you will have an equally enjoyable and beneficial holiday.

With my very kindest regards,

yours always cordially
Ernest Jones.

1. The third edition of the *Traumdeutung* appeared in 1911 and mentioned Jones in two footnotes; see Freud (1900a, p. 266 n. 1, p. 270 n. 2).

2. Francis X. Dercum, "The Role of Dreams in Etiology," *Journal of the American Medical Association*, 56 (1911): 1372–77.

3. J. H. Lloyd, "The So-Called Oedipus-Complex in Hamlet," *Journal of the American Medical Association*, 56 (1911): 1377–79.

4. Unsigned review, "Puberty and the Neuropsychic System," *British Medical Journal*, 1 (1911): 1337–38.

5. R. Acher, "Recent Freudian Literature," *American Journal of Psychology*, 22 (1911): 408–443. The quotation is on p. 423.

6. Putnam (1911).

7. Roberto Assagioli, "Transformation et sublimation des énergies sexuelles," *Zentralblatt*, 1 (1911): 353–354.

8. The 1911 issues of the *Zentralblatt* (vols. 1 and 2) contain numerous reviews of the psychoanalytic and psychiatric literature by Maeder.

9. Jones (1912e).

10. C. K. Clarke had just taken up an appointment as superintendent of the Toronto General Hospital. Jones's position at the Toronto Asylum was that of a part-time pathologist.

11. Jones's predicament is further clarified in letter 65.

12. Jones (1912–13).

13. See Jones (1912j, 1931b).

14. Jones (1911g, 1911f).

15. The Macbeth and Napoleon studies were not completed. The latter project, a perennial work-in-progress, was to be called *Napoleon's Orient Complex*. See Jones (1957a, 191; 1957b, 204).

64

9 August 1911
Tirol, *Klobenstein* am Ritten
Hotel Post

Dear Dr. Jones,

I am very sorry you have to leave Toronto and to leave without the title you have so well deserved. You have, as it were, conquered America in no more than two years, and I am by no means assured which way things will go, when you are far. But I am glad you are returning to England, as I expect you will do the same for your mother-country, which by the way has become a better soil since you left it. I had to refuse no less than three offers for translating the *"Traumdeutung"* from Englishmen, expecting as you know that Brill will do it soon.[1] I have got to answer letters from towns like Bradford, and one of the medical men at least, Osler,[2] did actually send me a patient, who is still under care of Federn.[3] So your task may prove less hard than you seem to judge it. Let me add, that one of the three I mentioned, Dr. Eder,[4] editor of *"School Hygiene"* promised to bring before the British Medical Association the report of a case cured by ΨA.[5] Yet I confess, apart from Havelock Ellis,[6] all the applications betray german names.

Now to answer your letter point by point.

I have got the articles by Dercum and Lloyd and cried over the last; it is too stupid. I did not get the review by Acher, Stanley Hall never sends anything.

As for the internal dissension with Adler, it was likely to come and I have ripened the crisis. It is the revolt of an abnormal individual driven mad by ambition, his influence upon others depending on his strong terrorism and sadismus. I hope we will lose a good many others of little or no use who are ready to follow him. I am by no means unhappy at the event.

You are perhaps aware of the plan not only of incorporating the *Correspondenzblatt* into the *Zentralblatt* but of raising the latter to the role of an official organ of the Internationale ΨA. It will then be easy to regulate the use of foreign languages according to your hints.

Adler proved a very unable editor, so you must not be astonished at the disorder showing in the disposal of your contributions. Stekel will show an excellent one and the concentration of all responsibility in one hand will do a lot of good.

As for Napoleon I will make every one to respect your claim of priority.

No[w] for some personal news. I passed 3 weeks in Karlsbad to get some treatment for my colitis earned in New York, and since then I live here with part of my family in a delicious place in sight of the highest and fairest Dolomites of Tirol 1150 m high, but it is too hot this year to enjoy one's self as it ought to be. On the 15th of Sept. I will leave for Zürich, live there 4 days with Jung at his house and see the other men, our brethren of Zürich. It is likely Putnam will be there at the same time. Next the Congress, you know 21–22 Sept.[7] and the last days of the month I intend spending with Abraham, Brill or whoever wants me for a good talk. I need not be back to Vienna before the 30th.

My intellectual powers now slowly come back from their "vacancies" [vacation]. I am engaged in something which is likely to occupy me for years, i.e. psychology of religious faith and rites.[8] I know I am following a crooked way in the order of my works but it is the way of unconscious connections.

You will have heard of the idea of a new journal, not medical at all, "Eros und Psyche" edited by two good men *Sachs* and *Rank*. I hope it may be activated in January next. It goes with no doubt, that you are to become one of the foremost contributors of this new ψα organ.[9] As for Rank you know enough of him; Sachs is a very clever, instructed, honest man. "*Advokat*" [lawyer] yet he came out as author of an excellent translation of Kipling's "*Soldatenlieder*".[10] The condition of the existence of "*Eros and Psyche*" is of course, that the future fate of the *Zentralblatt* be assured by its becoming the official organ of the Internationale i ΨA.[11]

Now this is the last letter I am addressing to you in Toronto. Your career there was short, hard but really not unglorious.

With kindest regards, in expectation of our next meeting at Weimar

yours truly
Freud

1. Brill (1913).
2. William Osler (1849–1919), M.D. 1872 McGill University; famous Canadian physician and teacher.
3. Paul Federn (1871–1950), one of the earliest of Freud's followers, played an important role in the psychoanalytic movement; his life ended tragically by suicide.
4. Montague David Eder (1866–1936), British psychoanalyst, who on and off would

sympathize with the work of Jung, was generally regarded highly by Freud. See Freud (1945a), where Freud pays tribute to Eder as the first practicing psychoanalyst in England. The historical issues involved in Jones's angry response to Freud's post-humous publication are discussed in Paskauskas (1985, pp. 110–112).

5. Eder (1911).

6. Havelock Ellis (1859–1939), English sexologist; famous for his multivolume *Studies in the Psychology of Sex* (1897–1928).

7. Third Congress of the International Psychoanalytic Association, Weimar.

8. Freud (1912–13).

9. This became *Imago*; see Jones (1912h).

10. Hanns Sachs, translation of Kipling, *Soldaten Lieder und andere gedichte* (Leipzig: J. Zeitler, 1910).

11. Freud had actually written I. A. Ψ.

65

31 August 1911
407 Brunswick Avenue
Toronto

Dear Professor Freud,

My best thanks for your very kind letter. You will be glad to hear that yesterday we decided not to leave this country yet awhile, after all. It is a complicated story, the main points of which are these: When it became known that I was leaving, various university authorities, particularly the Chancellor,[1] whose daughter I had successfully treated, became surprisingly active in their efforts to retain me; Adolf Meyer and others also wrote strong letters about it. The result was that they have given me the professorship (in psychiatry) as well as a special department in neurology.[2] On the strength of that I have, after considerable difficulty, persuaded my wife to stay here a little longer, until next April. After then we shall settle in London, but I hope to be able to retain the position and cross over every year for four months (to Toronto) for the work of the session. It will be a decided blow to my local enemies, but I do not see how they can now do anything to prevent it. I feel that the whole episode must be looked upon as a definite triumph for our cause, since I am mainly known for my psycho-analytic work, and this was also the cause of the objections to me, which have now been defeated.

I have finished the nightmare book that has taken me so much work, and am consequently feeling in rather a self-complacent mood;[3] at present I am busy on the article that Rank asked me to write for the new Journal, and perhaps I may be able to finish it before I leave in ten days' time.[4]

I was very glad to hear your improved opinion of the better conditions in England, but I am afraid that some of them are only the result of my

continuous pricks there. I knew about the applications to you for translation rights; Eder, for example, was a student of mine, and I have managed
to interest him in the work. He got Pfister recently to write an article for
his Journal.[5] That Osler had sent you a patient was quite news to me, and
very gratifying, for he is highly "respectable".

I fancy I told you that I had enlisted the services of Davidson, the Professor of Romance Philology here, who is a patient of mine.[6] I am hoping that
he will do good work, for he is very able, has private means, and has just
resigned his position in order to devote himself to research work. After
reading Graf's book[7] he brought to me today a remarkable poem by Thomson,[8] a copy of which I enclose. I suggested to him that he send a note of
it to the *Zentralblatt*.

The news of the *Eros-Psyche* Journal filled me with enthusiasm. I am
sure it will be a good move in attracting outside workers in other fields,
and in providing an opportunity badly needed for publishing work of the
kind; of course I hope to be able to help a little myself, though I must now
think seriously of my psychiatry text-book.[9]

The most exciting news in your letter, however, was that you had determined to devote yourself to religious problems. Obviously that is the last
and firmest stronghold of what may be called the anti-scientific, anti-
rational, or anti-objective Weltanschauung, and no doubt it is there we
may expect the most intense resistance, and the thick of the fight. Religion
has been the subject that has interested me more than any other, probably
owing to frightful conflicts in youth, from which I think I am now entirely
emancipated. My reading on the subject has been, I think I may say, really
extensive, and has passed through characteristics stages. At the time when
I should have been attending to my medical studies I was mostly reading
either philosophy or apologetics. Later came the agnostic and atheistic
literature, and then the work on the psychology of religion (mostly American). Of late years it has been more the study of comparative religions,
and particularly of the savage races. Some time ago I conceived the idea
of collecting material for ten years and writing a grand book on the Biology
of Religion, much of which I have actually planned out. Last year in Holland you inadvertently discouraged me by making the remark, which
perhaps I misunderstood, that the subject was a solved one, and therefore
not worth spending time on; evidently I was curiously mistaken. Nevertheless I decided to go on with my collecting etc., for I felt that to me at
least the conflict between science and supernaturalism was one of absorb-
ing interest. Now it is grand news to hear that the matter will be dealt
with properly, and will receive the attention that I felt it deserves. Possibly
I may be able to be of some little service to you in obtaining material
otherwise difficult of access. Strangely enough my experience has been
that the most valuable material, especially in anthropology, has been

gathered in England, probably on account of their Imperial and travelling opportunities and interests; this even applies to phallic and other sexual material.

I am also enclosing some extracts from a well-known writer of over three hundred years ago, on the subject of dreams; they may interest you.

I was delighted to hear of the benefit the holiday had been to your health, and hope to see you in Weimar looking as "fit" as possible. I need a holiday very badly myself, for I have worked sixteen or eighteen hours a day for the past three months, and am feeling rather played out. The heat here has been exceptionally intense and trying this summer.

With apologies for such a long letter, which at all events will be the last for some time, and with my very kindest regards,

> yours always cordially
> Ernest Jones.

1. Sir William Ralph Meredith (1840–1923), LL.D., distinguished Canadian lawyer and politician.

2. Jones was appointed associate professor of psychiatry, a position he held until the end of 1913. What Jones refers to as the department of neurology was the nervous ward of the Toronto General Hospital, which had been under the charge of Toronto's principal neurologist, Campbell Meyers, and was closed down (*Annual Report of the Toronto General Hospital*, 1912, p. 17).

3. Jones (1912j).

4. Likely Jones (1912h), published in *Imago*.

5. Oskar Pfister, "Psycho-Analysis and Child Study: Some Introductory Considerations," *School Hygiene*, 2 (1911): 366; 432.

6. Frederic J. A. Davidson (1870–1946), M.A., Ph.D., was an associate professor of modern languages at the University of Toronto; in the 1920s, while living abroad, wrote a satiric novel in French about Toronto titled *Du vieux vin dans des bouteilles neuves* (intro. Gabriel Hanoteux), in which Jones figures as the internationally famous psychologist Dr. Sirius, appointed to the University of Torham.

7. Graf (1911).

8. See note 2 to letter 70.

9. This book was not completed.

66

> 17 October 1911
> 407 Brunswick Avenue
> Toronto

Dear Professor Freud,

Well, I am safely home again, after a most inspiriting holiday. I am glad to say I found my wife distinctly better. Adolf Meyer had done her much good by talking to her very reasonably about my work. I broached the subject of treatment to her, and in the joyful mood at my return she was surprisingly optimistic. Your opinion that there was a chance for her to get better carried very great weight, for she could hardly help living with me and not thinking highly of you. She said she would [go] do anything, [except] so long as she wasn't expected to believe things she couldn't believe, (i.e. have ideas forced on her against her will). Rather to my surprise she was very definite on the point that she would rather be treated by you than by anyone else, but I told her that very (un)likely[1] that would be impossible but that you would judge best.

I shall never forget the kind way you talked to me in Weimar, and am more grateful than I can say. I went away that night overjoyed at the thought that she might get better. To be honest, however, I must say that on the following day I had a disagreeable dream, which after a difficult analysis showed the wish that she might die instead of getting better. I felt greatly relieved after having it out with myself, and ever since have been freer and happier than for years.

We have not talked over details yet, but I will let you know the arrangements when they are made. She seems to assume that she will stay the winter here, and so soon after coming together again I didn't like to suggest her leaving, but no doubt it would be better for her to go in a couple of month's time.

I have no other special news. This year I have much less routine work than before (hospital, etc.) and can devote myself to practice and writing. I have just started with five new patients, an alcoholic, two pseudo-epilepsies, a conversion hysteria and an anxiety-hysteria.

My copy of the *Jahrbuch* has not yet arrived, which is disappointing. Fortunately, however, I had a reprint of the Schreber analysis, which was a great illumination. The relation of paranoia, paranoid dementia, and dementia praecox to homosexuality, narcissism, and auto-eroticism is an enormous clarification and simplification.[2] Was there ever a new science that progressed at such a pace? I suppose, though, that you, looking back, think of the slowness of the beginning.

I have just read Rank's Lohengrin saga[3] with great enjoyment. It seems to me to have too much material in it, if anything, but it is very beautiful.

I cannot tell you what a pleasure the congress was to me. Everything was so inspiring and resolute. I used the time of my holiday well in talking—in Munich with Seif,[4] in Berlin with Abraham, and in New York with Brill. Only those of us who are isolated know what a delight it is to meet again men in the same work.

The Congress in Munich[5] was unutterably stupid and tedious except for a few jokes that enlivened the discussions. Tromner last year read a paper on sleep,[6] and Seif said he would give him one piece of advice—to read the *Traumdeutung*. This year he read a silly paper on dreams, and frequently quoted the *Traumdeutung*.[7] Seif said he was glad to find he had taken his advice about reading the *Traumdeutung* and that he would now give him another piece—to read it again. Vogt,[8] who was President, made a beautiful Versprechen. He is exceedingly tyrannical and bullies everyone. In the discussion on hypnosis I angered him by defending Ferenczi's view re the parents, and he replied—red in the face—in words to this effect: "Es ist ein Unsinn zu behaupten, dass, z. B., meine Kraft Patienten zu hypnotisieren in *meinem* Vaterkomplex liegt.—natürlich wollte ich sagen, in ihrem Vaterkomplex".[9] Seif and I explained the meaning of the Versprechen for the benefit of the audience. If they meet often enough they will learn some $\psi\alpha$ by practical experience. In spite of my unorthodoxy they put me on the committee this time, to represent America.

I wanted to ask you about the translation of the manuscript I left with you. Rank tells me that Sachs will translate the Salt article, but what about the nightmare one?[10] I do not know if Rank has the time, as he has his examination to do, but if so (which would be a great pleasure to me to have such a competent translator) I should like to pay him suitably for the trouble. Will you perhaps let me know about this, or arrange it; I have no idea what Deuticke pays for the *Schriften*. I am of course very eager to hear your opinion of the manuscript when you have time to read it over. By the way, did you get a reprint on the Pathology of Morbid Anxiety,[11] which I sent when you were at Carlsbad? In writing it I was very shaky on the delicate question of the mind and body, and should be very much obliged to you for any criticisms of it you may feel inclined to make at your leisure.

With my warmest Regards

Yours affectionately
Ernest Jones.

1. The parentheses here appear to have been inserted at a later rereading to indicate the error. Also, the two words enclosed in brackets were crossed out in the original.

2. Freud (1911c).

3. Rank (1911).

4. Leonhard Seif (1866–1949), neuropathologist practicing in Munich; head of Munich branch of International Psychoanalytic Association; a good friend of Jones's before the war; later turned to Adlerian individual psychology.

5. Annual meeting of the International Society for Medical Psychology and Psychotherapy, Munich, 25–26 September 1911. For agenda, see *Journal für Psychologie und Neurologie*, 18 (1912): 478.

6. Trömner (1911).

7. Ernst Trömner, "Enstehung und Bedeutung der Träume," *Journal für Psychologie und Neurologie*, 19 (1912): 343–355.

8. Oskar Vogt (1870–1959), German neuropathologist; concerned primarily with pathological anatomy of the brain but also advocated a form of psychotherapy called causal analysis.

9. "I maintain that it is an absurdity that my power to hypnotize patients lies in *my* father complex—naturally, I wanted to say in their father complex."
10. Jones (1912h, 1912j).
11. Jones (1911e).

67

5 November 1911
Vienna, IX. Berggasse 19

My dear Professor Jones,

I rejoice in giving you this new title, I did not make so much of it with myself in 1902, at least openly.

I am very glad at the disposition of your wife, let us hope her spirits will keep up until the time is come to do something for her in a serious way. It is a shame that there is no such place as a Sanatorium here at Vienna, where such a patient could be treated by ΨA.

The paper you mention, on morbid anxiety, arrived safely at Karlsbad. I have no special critic to give about it, finding there the usual clearness and neatness of your mind, except hinting at the excellent way you answered some malevolent criticism on the side of . . . (I forgot the name: Donley or Donkey). Do you really find the rate of our scientific progress an uncommon rapid one? I am standing under the opposite impression sometimes. I find it hard to give a synthesis of our creed, and the single articles thereof are by no means brought together to a good agreement. There are a great many things boiling in my head, but they are very slow to come out, and I always feel it hard to conform completely to another's thoughts. Yet I cannot do everything myself, and the contributions of others, say Jung f.e. [for example] are of the highest importance.

As for your "Nightmare" I have not yet attacked the question of translating, as I am bound to submit to a pause, two pamphlets having appeared just now (Rank and Storfer)[1] and Deuticke failing somewhat in his devotion. But the time for it will soon come. D. declined to our great disappointment formally to take the new journal, which now stands foremost among my cares. I hope we will [be] able to produce it with H. Heller (our member here). Rank is already in possession of your salt.

I am working hard on the psychogenesis of religion, finding myself on the same track with Jung's "Wandlungen".[2] Business is not very lively now, but the profit is not big enough, as I feel not so strong as I used to do.

Hoping to have good news from your side in short intervals I am

yours sincerely
Freud

1. Rank (1911a), and Storfer (1911).
2. See Freud (1912–13), and Jung (1911–12).

68

26 November 1911
407 Brunswick Avenue
Toronto

Dear Professor Freud,

Many thanks indeed for your kind letter, including the complimentary remarks on my work; you no doubt suspect how important such encouragement is to me. At the same time I am sorry you did not put in some criticism; my request for such was seriously meant, for a hint from you goes a long way in correcting the errors I must make.

The news of my wife is not so good as when I wrote last. She does not want to go to Europe until next May, for she says she cannot stand being so long with the whole Atlantic between us in case of any urgent need. It looks therefore as if we shall cross together in May; I shall stay somewhere in Europe until the following Christmas. She has also had a bad recrudescence of her hostility towards analysis, and I am afraid her attitude will be one of submission to the treatment with a bad will, and with no hope. It will depend on you or Maeder if this attitude can be altered. She has been feeling very sickly, tired, and weak, and has an obsession that she will die this winter. The latter is no doubt a sign of resistance against the treatment, but I am hoping it also has an unconscious meaning of the desire for a new birth, for I know for certain that the ideas of birth *(Mutterleib)* [womb] and death are intimately associated in her mind. On the other side I am glad to say that our personal relations have greatly improved, and we have not been so happy together for a very long while. This is chiefly due to my own greater freedom on account of better self-analysis.

My copy of the *Jahrbuch* has just arrived, and I have been charmed with your *Zwei Prinzipien* article.[1] It is a perfect little cameo, just as you give us sometimes, full of condensed thought artistically polished and finished. It is the kind of article from which we shall go on drawing new ideas and fresh inspiration for many years, always finding new things in it. How well it harmonises with Jung's great production in the same number, of which I am most eager to see the continuation; I think it is the best thing he has ever done.[2] Jung sweeps over the canvas like a Rubens, you draw with the accuracy and close feeling of a Del Sarto.

May I ask one question that applies to both articles? It is easier for me to couch it in the form of a comment, though it is prompted only by the desire for enlightenment. Namely I was surprised that so much stress was laid on the differences between the two modes of mental functioning, and not more on their ontogenetic relationship; this especially applies to Jung's article, it is true, for you say a little on the matter on page 2. In the sentence "es wurde nicht mehr vorgestellt was angenehm, sondern was real war, auch wenn es unangenehm sein sollte"[3] I was puzzled by the sharp opposition of the two. I had conceived of the desire for reality as being essentially merely a more effective method of obtaining gratification than the hallucinatory method. Do I understand you to mean that it was so originally, having come into existence for this purpose, but that later on it acquires a meaning of its own—the search for reality being an aim or principle in itself, quite apart from the greater power thus won of procuring gratification? Or does it continue to serve the latter function in a more roundabout way? In other words isn't the reality principle constantly a form of sublimation, or do the two principles become secondarily entirely divorced from each other? I wonder if I have made my difficulty clear. If it is possible to give me a short answer that would not take up too much of your time I would be much obliged.

I was enormously impressed by your choice of the quotation from Bernard Shaw.[4] I know all his work and life very well, and think you could not possibly have selected a better passage for expressing the central and most fundamental point of his philosophy. In spite of his unconventionality he is at heart essentially an English Puritan of an ascetic type. I was always struck by the truth of his position that the strivings of a great man are not primarily towards happiness as such, but towards reality, and I think that in the Hell Scene there are passages that bring out the grandeur of this simple conception more forcibly than do even Ibsen or Nietzsche. When I got to know your work I had some difficulty in reconciling the two, and came to the conclusion that you must be right and Shaw wrong because of the more fundamental and biological significance of the Lustprinzip. Now you show that after all Shaw had got hold of something truly important and great. That is a permanent appeal of psycho-analysis that it does not deny the conclusions of others; it does more, it explains them. There lies one of its greatest sources of strength (take, for example, the relatively trite matter of suggestion in therapeutics).

I have done a certain amount of work in the past six weeks, but not much. I sent Stekel a couple of short things,[5] and to the *Journal of Abnormal Psychology* the analysis of a beautiful Oedipus saving dream—the heterosexual and homosexual solutions coming in two distinct halves, with very neat determination.[6] This week I finish my casuistic article for the *Jahrbuch*,[7] and next week I read a paper at Detroit on the mode of action in psycho-analysis in therapeutics.[8] I have just been very flatteringly asked to contribute a section of 40000 words on the treatment of the neuroses for a large two-volume work on the treatment of nervous and mental diseases,[9] the most ambitious of the kind yet attempted. Although it will interfere with my other plans for work I am accepting it, for it is an unusual opportunity for the propagandism of our views and otherwise it might fall into bad hands; it has to be finished by April. I hear from Rank that Sachs is translating my salt article, for which I am much obliged. The other, nightmare, one is safe in your hands; I suppose you have not had time to look them through, but will wait till they are translated.[10] I am eager to hear about the troubles with the publishers, and sincerely hope that they will be satisfactorily settled. Have you definitely decided on the title of the new journal? Are you not afraid that *Eros-Psyche* may provoke too great prejudice and ribald jests?

I have often smiled at the thought of a remark you once made to me about the French: "They are an arrogant people". Here is an excellent example. In a review in Janet's journal of a paper of mine on psycho-analytic treatment the reviewer concludes with the words: "Il est à peine besoin de noter que ces idées sont courantes en France depuis les travaux de Pierre Janet".[11] As I laid stress on the sexual aspects I am gratified, though surprised, to hear this news. It is plain that when, in the dim future, your works do reach France the authorities there will move heaven and earth to prove that the French knew and discovered them years ago, just as they amusingly did lately in the case of Ehrlich's salvarsan.[12]

Now in conclusion I am going to ask you another theoretical question. A friend, and former patient of mine, who is a pretty good observer, brought me recently the following experience. He dreamt that an Oriental woman was trying to get him to do something for her, no doubt something erotic. He put her off with the words "Now, I've done this three times". He woke up (it was in the morning) and positively heard himself saying these words aloud. His wife also heard them distinctly, but is equally positive that they were "Oh, all right, I'll do it in the morning". There are I suppose three possible explanations: (1) faulty observation on one or the other side, which their certainty seems to exclude. (2) Both sentences may have occurred in the dream and been spoken aloud, but he remembers only the one, while his wife heard the other, which may have been the only one spoken aloud. This is hardly likely, as they both refer to the same utterance, *heard* by both. (3) It is possible that an unusually great distortion took place in the secondary elaboration. This would be a remarkable occurrence. Have you any experience of such a thing? It must be a rather rare opportunity to check the point. I should be greatly interested to hear what you think of it.

You ask me abut my impressions as to the rate of progress. You will see that they are bound to be different from those of one in Vienna, for I stand outside the daily work, so to speak, and note only the results arrived at. These seem to me to be very considerable every year, both in detail and in gross. Examples of the former are various symbolisms and strikingly your work on the saving phantasy, of the latter especially the extension of your principles to the broad problems of mental evolution and cultural development, which are of the highest importance for the race in general and for civilisation in particular. I am inclined to think that not the *Traum-*

deutung but your forthcoming work on religion will be your masterpiece.[13]
Is this going on well at present, or are you feeling weighed down by the
immensity of the material and subject to be dealt with? By the way, you
will be sure to ask me if you have difficulty in getting any of the books
we spoke of at Weimar. Of course your remark is very true as to the lack
of coordination in the different articles of the creed, but how can that be
otherwise in a rapidly growing subject? The synthesis can only come later,
and it is a good thing for the progress that it has not been too prominent
up to the present. I notice the lack of coordination in quite little things:
To take quite a simple instance, I have read at least four different interpretations for Platzangst. Perhaps they are all true, but the relative significance of each has not been pointed out.

I have no impersonal news to give from this side. Brill is more in the
thick of the fight at present than I am, and he seems to be training some
very good men to help him in New York. All the members of my group
have paid their subscriptions and I have forwarded them with the addresses
to Riklin as secretary. I have heard several times from Jung since returning,
and hope to spend some time with him next summer. I am also in correspondance with Abraham, Ferenczi, Seif, and others. In London things
seem to be making a start. When I get there I shall certainly push things
hard, and ought to be able to found a branch in a short time.

yours always
Ernest Jones.

1. Freud (1911b).

2. Part 1 of Jung (1911–12), *Jahrbuch* (1913), 3:120–227.

3. Strachey translates this as: "What was presented in the mind was no longer what
was agreeable but what was real, even if it happened to be disagreeable." See Freud
(1911b, p. 219), *G.W.*, 8:232.

4. The passage from Shaw quoted in Freud (1911b, p. 223, n. 1) reads: "To be able to
choose the line of greatest advantage instead of yielding in the direction of the least
resistance."

5. Likely from among the following: Jones (1912d, 1912f, 1912g, 1912i).

6. Jones (1912c) is actually a disguised autobiographical account based on his self-
analysis.

7. Jones (1912–13).

8. Jones (1912a).

9. Jones (1913a).

10. Jones (1912h, 1912j).

11. "It is hardly necessary to note that these ideas have been current since the work
of Pierre Janet." See review of Jones (1910c) by Pierre Mendousse, *Journal de Psychologie*,
8 (1911): 477.

12. Salvarsan (arsphenamine), an arsenic compound used hypodermically or intramus-
cularly for syphilis, yaws, and other protozoan infections; developed by Paul Ehrlich
(1854–1915), German bacteriologist, who received Nobel Prize in medicine (with Elie
Metchnikoff) in 1908.

13. Freud (1912–13).

69

7 January 1912
407 Brunswick Avenue
Toronto

Dear Professor Freud,

This is to introduce Dr. D'Orsay Hecht of Chicago, a well-known American neurologist. He has shown great sympathy towards our work, and has helped on the cause considerably in Chicago, though I do not think he has had very much personal experience of ψα. He was President of the Chicago Neurological Society when I read a paper there,[1] and on that occasion and many others has shown me every possible kindness. Going to Europe for a short while he is naturally eager to have the honour of meeting you personally. Would it be against the rules of your society for him to be present at one of the meetings?[2]

Yours very sincerely
Ernest Jones.

1. Jones (1911d).
2. Hecht attended the meeting of the Vienna society on 20 March 1912, as recorded in *Minutes*, 4:75.

70

14 January 1912
Vienna, IX. Berggasse 19

Dear Professor Jones,

I dont remember I ever left a letter of yours so long unanswered. I first postponed reaction until finishing the reading of your "Nightmare", then I got into so hard a time that I could not, my regular relief on Sundays getting lost every time.[1] May be I was sorry too having heard that you got yourself into fresh difficulties with a woman. Taking a more lively interest in your private affairs since your last communication at Weimar I pity it very much that you should not master such dangerous cravings, well aware at the same time of the source from which all these evils spring, taking away from you nearly all the blame but nothing of the dangers.[2]

By ill chance I had to give you some trifle remarks, which looked as if I wanted to put you under criticism everywhere, and as you know my sympathy for your person, my esteem for your work and my gratitude to your services, you will not wonder that the letter refused itself to the pen, until at last I saw I had better not to pursue in this line.

To begin by those disagreeable trifles, I got no[t] the satisfaction from your nightmare, that almost all your contributions to science had given me. It is a tremendous amount of stuff, but less proof than I had expected and in some places only a translation of the known facts into the $\psi\alpha$ dialect. Yet the essay is now in translation by Dr. Sachs and will come out as Nr. 14 of the *Schriften*.[3]

The *Zentralblatt* begs me to inform you that the extracts from Thomas *Nashe* (The terrors of the Night) and the verses by *Thomson* (Art) seemed not fit as they wanted translation.[4] I like the little poem very much and if you will present me with it, I am very glad. But it is with dissatisfaction that I refuse *anything* coming from your pen.

Now let me answer to the singular items of your letter. I am very sorry at the worse condition of your wife; whatever I can do to influence her for improvement will be done. Indeed you hardly realize how deep my personal interest is in men who give me so much assistance and friendship as you do. It makes me positively unhappy not to be able to assist them or to detect a cloud in our personal relations. One of the weakest points of my organization yet I am too old and worn out to change.

Your question about the relation of the R. Prinzip to the L. Prinzip is answered in the paper itself in agreement to what you yourself suppose. The Reality pr. is only continuing the work of the L. P. in a more effectual way, gratification being the aim of both and their opposition only a secondary fact. Yet I am sure this paper of mine will produce much hesitation and wants a better thorough-going exposition. I was very much amused at your finding out my quotation from Shaw, as it was pointed directly to you as an indirect means of expressing my thanks to the giver.

As regards the interesting case of your friend (or yourself) dreaming "No I have done this three times", while his wife asserts having heard him say "I'll do it in the morning", I am ready to admit, 1) that both parties were right in what they asserted, 2) that there were more than one solution of the situation imagined in the latent thoughts, one of which invaded the manifest dream, the other one came to be spoken out, 3) that a care to inform or misinform his wife was the motive for speaking out of the dream to her. It is a very nice case and a good analysis might show highly amusing.

My book on Religion which you trust may become superior to the *Traumdeutung* is an unborn, I hope not a stillborn infant. Scientific work is not so easy and not so commodious to me as it was 15 years ago.

The new journal to be called *"Imago"*—we wanted a handle to its name and found no better, this name at least is indistinct, vague enough—will be issued next March or let us say: May, and I have promised a contribution to No. 1, so I had to shift my course and begin by an essay on the ψ analogies between the primitive and the neurotic mind three points a) Inzestscheu, b) Ambivalenz, c) Allmacht der Gedanken *(Magie)*,[5] but only the first point in this first number. I have been very busy besides, as you will have seen from *Zentralblatt* and will see in the *Jahrbuch*, but I am far from satisfaction by these papers. I am not up to the task of rapid and frequent production.

I know it will promote things very much, when you are in England. There is some stir in France even now, another man Hesnard a pupil of Régis at Bordeaux presenting in the name of his master to me "the excuses of the French nation" for so continued a slighting and declaring himself prone to work for ΨA in French papers. Of Morichau-Beauchant (Poitiers) who seems very good and sincere you will read a contribution in the Jan. number of the *Zentralblatt*. An other in French you may find in the *Gazette des hôpitaux* 1911.[6]

Now let me finish and express the hope that you do not resent my long delay and give me notice as soon as you feel the want.

Yours faithfully
Freud

1. Sunday was a day of relaxation for Freud, when he was free from seeing patients, and when he did most of his reading and writing (Jones, 1955a, pp. 384–385; 1955b, pp. 428–430). On this particular Sunday, 14 January 1912, Freud explains that he has not recently had available to him the regular leisure hours that would allow him to finish reading the nightmare article and reply to Jones's letter of 26 November 1911.

2. The particulars here regarding Jones's "fresh difficulties with a woman" remain unclear. But as Jones had recently been discussing with Freud the details of Loe Kann's condition and his feelings for her (at the Weimar meeting of the International in September and in letter 66), Freud's concern may possibly be related to Jones's penchant for other women; consider, for example, his affair with Loe's maid Lina (letter 114). Moreover, the fact that these "cravings" alluded to by Freud were deemed to be "dangerous" suggests that Freud's concern might also have been related to a possible infringement on Jones's part of the doctor-patient relationship; see, for instance, Jones's problems of early 1911 with a female patient (note 10 to letter 51) and his comments regarding his analysis of Joan Riviere in letter 352 of 1 April 1922: "It is over twelve years since I experienced any [sexual] temptation in such ways, and then in special circumstances."

3. Jones (1912j).

4. Thomas Nashe (1567–1601), English poet and dramatist; see Nashe (1594). James Thomson (1834–1882); his poem "Art" first appeared 17 February 1867 in the *National Reformer*, a radical weekly newspaper.

5. Parts 1–3 of Freud (1912–13).

6. E. Régis and A. Hesnard, "La Doctrine de Freud et de son école," *L'Encéphale* 8 (1913): 356–378, 446–481, 537–564. R. Morichau-Beauchant, "Le 'Rapport affectif' dans la cure des psychonévroses," *Gazette des hôpitaux*, 84 (1911): 1845–49; and "Homosexualität und Paranoia," trans. O. Rank, *Zentralblatt*, 2 (1912): 174–176. For an extensive treatment of the development of psychoanalysis in France, see Roudinesco (1986), and also Marcel Scheidhauer, *Le Rêve Freudien en France: Avancées et résistances: 1900–1926* (Navarin éditeur, 1985).

71

20 January 1912
407 Brunswick Avenue
Toronto

Dear Professor Freud,

I have for some time been hoping to hear from you, but I expect you have been very busy with your manifold tasks. Did you get my letter of November the 25th?[1]

I hear from Rank and others that you are very occupied on the religion question, and that you are also planning a new edition of the *Traumdeutung,* to be entirely re-written. That will certainly mean much work. I suppose you know that the psychological theories of the *Traumdeutung* (censor, repression, unconscious, etc.) have received the honour (?) of an article 120 pages long in the *Archiv für die gesamte Psychologie* (Heft II). The esteemed author condescendingly remarks that now since he has shown your theories to be wrong you will feel called upon to renounce them, but it does not seem to have occurred to him that there is another alternative.[2]

Your dream article in the *Zentralblatt* will surely be useful.[3] Unfortunately I had had to learn most of the conclusions by bitter experience. I have had two or three patients who definitely showed their resistance by bringing me a flood of dreams every day, so that it soon became impossible to deal with them all. I think an article that would be much appreciated would be one explaining when and under what circumstances one should interpret for the patient without his direct help.

Life has been very quiet with me of late. My wife is about the same. She will cross with me in the early part of May. My writing has been confined to some short and unimportant articles. I read a paper before the Detroit Neurological Society early in December and one before the American Psychological Association at the end of the month.[4] They will be printed, so that of course you will get copies. Probably you got safely a number of reprints some time ago. Were they satisfactory? I always like to have your opinion when you have the time to read my outpourings.

This morning I got a piece of good news that will please you; I suppose it is the immediate cause of my writing today. It was a letter from a Professor Marechau-Beauchant [Morichau-Beauchant] in Poitiers, who is very enthusiastic about your work. I fancy that, as usual, he can read English better than German, for he speaks much about my writings. He enclosed an article from the *Gazette des Hôpitaux* (1911, P. 1845) which shows a good understanding of your theories.[5] It is chiefly on the affective rapport during treatment, and the true meaning of this. It is surely time that France woke up from her lethargy. Also a number of letters from new people in different parts of America and England (even Ireland) show me the rapidly increasing interest that is being taken in the work. In Washington last month I had the opportunity of talking over things with a number of men, and was very satisfied with the way in which things are going. Stanley Hall (whose journal has lately been containing some excellently full reviews), told me that he has been running a class for the purpose of studying dreams. He said he had found it difficult to interest the men in dreams, which shows that they could not have had much expert guidance. He also said that he had great difficulty with his own dreams, and found that sexual thoughts were very rare in them, which he put down to his age. I assured him that interest in life ceased not with old age but with death only, and we had a talk about stereotyped symbolism (on the lines of your hat dream analysis).[6]

My most interesting case at present is one of cyclothymia,[7] which has given a therapeutic success far better than could have been hoped for. As far as I can see, the mechanisms seem to stand midway between those of hysteria and of the Zwangsneurose, showing some characteristics of each. The central complex was a simple Oedipus one, and perversions were not very important. Recently I had the following interesting experience. An Englishman who called on you in Vienna last year sent me from a distant clime—India—some three hundred associations which he asked me to interpret without assistance. I wrote back saying that the lady was not neurotic but normal, that she was married but was having sexual relations with the man who took the associations and was afraid of her husband discovering her, that she preferred fellatio to coitus, that she was musical and had such and such accomplishments, and such and such complexes (maternal, anal, etc.). He answered saying that the interpretations were right in every detail, that he was now convinced that the word-associations method had something in it, and of course pointing out that the communication was confidential (I am telling no one but you about him).

What strange sources we find confirmation of our views in. Who would have thought finding anything of scientific value in the *Church Quarterly Review?* Yet in the November number there is an article on Reincarnation which contains the following remarkable sentence: "Here perhaps we should mention an idea which is not uncommon among European children of tender age. The present writer, for instance, can well remember that, when a little more than three years old, he had a firm conviction that his parents would by and by grow little again and become *his* children in their turn. From observations made to him since by very little English boys and girls he has reason to conclude that the same strange fancy exists in not a few childish minds of today. He has heard a little boy say to his mother: 'Mamma, when you are little, I will take care of you'. Does this throw any light on the origin of the reincarnation doctrine? Is it natural to the childhood of the race as well as (perhaps) to that of the individual? And does its reappearance in adults among ourselves betoken the 'second childhood' of the race?"[8]

I have just been exceedingly annoyed by a review of recent work on dreams that Sidis has published in the *Psychological Bulletin* (January).[9] It contains the most offensive personal remarks about yourself, Rank, Stekel, and myself. It is beyond the limits of what I thought a scientific journal would print, both for disgusting language and venomous malice. The only consolation I can get out of it is the evidence it is of our success as felt by someone who has been ousted from a position of authority in psychopathology. I shall have a sweet revenge when I write my monograph on the treatment of the psychoneuroses, on which I am about to begin.[10]

At present my energies are altogether absorbed by the Napoleon problem, where I have collected some beautiful material as to his inner mental life. When one is internally impelled in a given direction of interest it is exceedingly difficult to divert the stream into another direction, however laudable. I am saying this by way of excuse, for I feel a little guilty at having given much time to a problem that externally is in no way urgent. Still I am trying to keep my eye on the needs of the situation in general.

With the very best possible good wishes for the New Year

from yours always
Ernest Jones.

1. See letter 68, actually dated 26 November 1911.
2. Friedrich Hacker, "Systematische Traumbeobachtungen mit besonderer Berücksichtigung der Gedanken," *Archiv für die gesamte Psychologie*, 21 (1911): 1–131.
3. Freud (1911e).
4. Jones (1912a, 1912b).
5. The article mentioned by Freud in letter 70; see note 4 to letter 70.
6. Freud (1900a, pp. 360–362).
7. Manic-depressive psychosis.
8. Quotation is from the Reverend W. St. Clair Tisdall, "Reincarnation," *Church Quarterly Review*, 72 (1911): 337–338.
9. Boris Sidis, "Dreams," *Psychological Bulletin*, 9 (1912): 36–40.
10. Jones's annoyance seems eventually to have subsided, as in Jones (1913a, pp. 368, 379 and 1920b, pp. 64, 92) Sidis is treated with deference regarding his concept of hypnoidization.

72

30 January 1912
407 Brunswick Avenue
Toronto

Dear Professor Freud,

Your eagerly awaited and exceedingly welcome letter has just come. I take the inhibition indicated in it as the best token of your kindly feeling towards me, and I was greatly moved by this. How well you understand to bind men to you with ties of affection and gratitude; many an enemy has remarked with envy on the devotion you inspire in your followers, and their observation is quite correct. This especially holds in the most difficult task of all, when, as in my case, you have to check wrong tendencies. My attitude towards this is best illustrated by the following story about my first meeting with you (at Salzburg). I need not describe my anticipatory feelings, for you can easily imagine them. Mingled with them was an affect that I had always experienced on having to do with any authority or master, from school up, namely a certain dread and especially a fear of being blamed, of being found out in wrong-doing; this arose from a strong guilt-complex, the ultimate origin I now know well, but which until of late had given me more suffering than anything else in life. Well I had of course many personal impressions of you, but none was more vivid than an acute realisation, experienced for the first time in my life, that here was a man who, in spite of his authority and rank, would understand and not blame. I expressed it at the time to Trotter by saying that you were the only man of position I had ever met who knew what it was to feel young in heart, meaning that you had the power of comprehending the trials and difficulties of youth. I felt at the same time that I would listen to criticism and guidance from you in a way that I had never before been willing to from anyone. The more I have got to know you the plainer has become that first impression, and never more so than in your last letter, so that it is an instance where I can plume myself on my intuition. I can therefore assure you that any criticism you may give me will always be taken in the sense in which I feel you mean it, namely as being not so much blame as help and guidance for the future, and I can also say sincerely that I am genuinely desirous to improve both as regards my work and knowledge and as regards my character, being well aware of the need for it in both directions.

One of the things for which I am most grateful to psycho-analysis for is that by the aid of it I have been able to get control of various wrong tendencies in myself, slowly and one after the other, and often after paying a high price for them, but in the end surely. The last year is the first that I have spent free from that terrible guilt-complex, and I cannot tell you what this has meant to me. I know well how my heart would have beat if I had some time ago read your even slight allusions to my difficulties that you now mention, but this time it had no such effect. Indeed the tendency in question is I believe a matter of the past, though I know the danger of being overconfident about such things; nevertheless I have no Angst, and can look forward to the possibility of future complications and dangers without trepidation, which I certainly never could before.

Passing next to my Nightmare work, the feeling I have about your remarks is one of genuine sorrow that it was not better in your eyes, and also of considerable interest as to the nature of and reasons for the failure, but I am glad to say hardly any discouragement. Perhaps the latter may be due to a too-great inner confidence. Namely I rarely feel satisfied with my work, but in this instance I must confess to have been pleased with the way in which some of the things came out in the investigation. Strangely enough even your disappointment with the work does not entirely shake my faith that it has some kind of value, and as it is exceptional for me to feel much pride in the things I have done I imagine that this must have some psychological foundation, and is not likely to be altogether due to conceited overestimation. I try to console myself with thinking that perhaps the aim I set out to accomplish was different from what you expected, etc.. But the important matter to me is after all the opportunity of learning as to how I should have done it better, and if you would be so kind as to amplify your remarks about it a little I should be very indebted. For instance, regarding the deficiency in proof, what *type* of proof should I have developed?

With regard to the extracts from Nashe and the poem by Thomson there is a little misunderstanding. I sent them to you purely for your personal interest, and never meant them for the *Zentralblatt*. I am glad you liked them. Possibly some of the former may be applicable in a future edition of the *Traumdeutung*, for they are curiously suggestive. It was Professor Davidson, a patient of mine, who discovered the poem, and he talked about translating it into German (he writes German poetry) for the *Zentralblatt*. However he has not yet done it.

My wife, I am very happy to say, has been of late rather better in health, etc., but this week she has been terribly upset over the following calamity. We have a little dog to whom she is passionately attached,[1] and he has been bitten by a dog in the last stages of furious rabies (diagnosis confirmed by microscopical examination). We are having him treated, at home, by Pasteur serum, sent from Philadelphia. This has to be sent twice a day for three weeks, and at present we are in a state of anxiety owing to the irregularity and mistakes of the agents. Much of our time is taken up with telegraphing and with making arrangements at the post office (where we have a special man told off to secure the packages), and so on. Luckily we have an excellent vetinarian. Unfortunately it will be several months before the danger will be past, and consequently the anxiety.

Thank you very much for your answers to my questions. There is nothing more to say about them except that I have not yet had the opportunity to make an analysis of the curious speech dream of Professor David-son's, though I will try to do so if I get the chance.

You have no doubt got the letter I sent a few days ago, so that I have no more news at present. I hope to have the pleasure of another letter from you soon.

With again my best thanks and kindest regards,

yours always
Ernest Jones.

1. The dog figures significantly as a child substitute, as reported by Jones in his disguised autobiographical account; see Jones (1912c), *Papers*, 1st ed. 1913, pp. 381–385.

73

24 February 1912
Vienna, IX. Berggasse 19

My dear Jones,
I have been very much interested by your letter of Jan. 20th but I had to wait for the next one which happily took off a load from my soul. Now I am very glad that you know how fond I am of you and how proud of the high mental powers you have put into the service of ΨA. I remember the first time when I got aware of this my attitude towards you, it was a bad one; when you left Worcester after a time of dark inconsistencies from your side and I had to face the idea that you were going away to become a stranger to us. Then I felt it ought not to be so and I could not show it otherwise than by accompanying you to the train and shaking hands before you went away. May be you understood me, in any case that feeling has proved true ever since and you have come out splendid at last.

Now let us converse on objective matters. As regards your nightmare I confess I could not justify my impression now, since your manuscript is a long while in the hands of Sachs and his clever wife, who are doing also the translation of your "Salt" and for this reason have been lazy in making up the "nightmare".[1] But if you wish I will give you my notes and objections after I get the translation.

Answers to the many topics you touch upon in your letter, would be stale at this time, except as far as M.—Beauchant is concerned the intelligent Frenchman, who is corresponding with me since ¾ of a year, and whose trace you will have found in the *Zentralblatt* since.

Otherwise I prefer to give you some information on fresh scientific work going on in this part of the world and especially with me.

"*Imago*" as you see is no longer a conception, it will have become a reality at the end of March. It brings the excellent chance into existence of being directed by two bright and honest boys like Rank and Sachs, who besides stand in excellent relations to each other. My contribution "Inzestscheu" is by no means famous,[2] but the next two articles may [Su][3] prove much better. The second is entitled "Tabu & Ambivalenz" and will I hope show up the essence of that marvellous "taboo"; it is half written and all finished in thought. The third not yet shaped in a definite form, will bear the name: Die Magie und die Allmacht der Gedanken. These three papers I conceive as forerunners of another more important one which intends to proclaim "Die infantile Wiederkehr des Totemismus".[4] I have got all the books you indicated to me, Crawley Bourke *(scatol. rites)*; Hartland *(paternity)*, Pearson *(Grammar of scI)*,[5] so I need not trouble you for sending me one of these from Toronto. I am now even in possession of the "*Encyclopedia britannica*", 11th ed. 1911.

The Society for Ψ [psychical] Research has prevailed upon me to send her a paper on the "Unconscious in ΨA", which does not contain any news but tries to explain our points of view to english readers and in english words. It has been mildly corrected by one of the Society's members and is to appear in the "Proceedings" of the Society.[6]

As I am busy now on the 8th paper since we parted in Weimar I have not the right to recommend you concentration and restraint of productivity as I might have done. All your papers sent have been received and prized by me as always.

The most interesting piece of news is the production of dreams by post-hypnotic suggestion, giving the sleepers the order to dream of such or such a kind of sexual intercourse. In doing so, the subjects made use of the very same symbols we have revealed by ψα interpretation of dreams. It is a young Vienna philosopher *Schrötter* who has succeeded in this way,[7] and yet in spite of this precious confirmation of our views he seems to be rather an opponent than an adherent.

I hope you will soon give my [me] good news about your wife and yourself (including the—symbolical?—dog) and believe me now and for ever

yours truly
Freud

P.S. "*Gradiva*" and "*Witz*" are just now undergoing the second edition.

1. Jones (1912j, 1912h).
2. Freud seems to be following the German here: *famos* = splendid or great.
3. Crossed out in the original.
4. The German terms refer to sections from Freud (1912–13): "The Horror of Incest,"

"Taboo and Ambivalence," "Magic and the Omnipotence of Thoughts," and "The Return of Totemism in Childhood." The third title is written out in Gothic script in the original; the last is in both Latin and Gothic.

5. Crawley (1902), Bourke (1891), Hartland (1909–10), Pearson (1900).

6. Freud (1912g).

7. K. Schrötter, "Experimentelle Träume," *Zentralblatt,* 2 (1912): 638. See also Freud to Jung, 18 February 1912 (McGuire, 1974, pp. 298–299).

74

15 March 1912
407 Brunswick Avenue
Toronto

Dear Professor Freud,

I was so happy to get your letter this week. It did my heart much good, and will be a source of fresh stimulus to me. Thank you again and again.

First let me talk a little about my wife. I am glad to say that she has been better in every way, except of course that the morphia is the same as before. We have been happier this winter than ever before, and have been very, very near together. She is also more hopeful about herself, and her attitude towards psycho-analysis seems to have changed to some extent, though of course one cannot be sure that this latter is deep; the resistances must still be there. Only recently she wistfully wondered whether a time would come when she might again be interested in my work and help me in it, as she used to in the days that I did only neurology. One thing I am sure of, and that is that she has a more sincere desire to get well than ever before. She has been for some time trying to overcome her inhi[bi]tion about writing, so that she might write a letter to you; I do not know what it will be about, but it will probably give you a better idea of her state of mind that [than] I can. I cannot tell you how anxious I am to get her well again if possible; there is hardly any sacrifice I would not make to achieve this. As you may imagine, her thoughts about yourself have been greatly influenced by my attitude towards you, and of late her wish has grown stronger and stronger that you should treat her, and no one else. I do not know if this could be possible, but I am afraid that if not she will be very disappointed and disheartened. I also have been doubting whether Maeder has enough skill and experience to deal with her resistances, and not to provoke them in a fatal way. Perhaps I am influenced too much by her attitude in this, and also by the natural desire to get the best for one's wife. I know it would be difficult for you to think of this, but we would make any financial arrangement in our power, including for instance the getting of a suitable suite of rooms in Vienna, with a nurse, and a doctor to attend her as often as would be necessary when the morphia is being reduced. I feel one could safely trust her honesty about the morphia, and I have the best of reasons for saying this. We are leaving here about the middle of May, and will get to Vienna by probably June the 14th, which I realise is your busiest and most fatiguing season. She finds the future suspense and indecision hard to bear, and I wonder if it would be at all possible for you to say beforehand anything about the probabilities; I know you can say nothing definite until you see her. Would it be practicable for her to go to a sanatorium until you start work in the 1st of October? I have thought of this, but she asks why she need go to a sanatorium for this interval, and points out that if the morphia is to be reduced before psycho-analysis it might just as well be done in England (the home of her heart), whereas any psycho-analysis for a couple of months by someone who is not to carry it through might not be satisfactory in many ways. It is a difficult situation. I think I have told you that I have arranged to be in Europe until the beginning of next February.

I have been in correspondance with Rank about *Imago,* and have arranged with him various ways in which I can help on its sale in America and England. The prospectus looks most promising, and the journal is bound to be a great success. It is certainly urgently needed, and even though it may not pay much at first, it will surely do so after a while. There psycho-analysis comes to its own, in demonstrating itself not a mere therapeutic measure that is to replace hypnotism, but as a key to the deepest problems of civilisation, and a task that will make all the sciences grateful to medicine as the sister who has taught them most. I often wonder how soon you began to see the distant applications of psycho-analysis, at a time when your attention had to be concentrated on such problems as hysteria. I expect it was pretty early, but you must have wondered whether you would ever see them put into existence. How you must rejoice to see those early dreams come true.

I am eagerly looking forward to your promised contributions, which I suppose are the first fruits of the work on religion. The totemism one specially interests me, perhaps because it is such an essentially English subject, most of the work having been done by Englishmen. How surprised poor Fraser will be, after announcing that "after twenty years of research on the subject my plummets have at last reached bottom", to hear how much they are still floating in mid-sea. The same would apply to Hartland's supposed demonstration that knowledge of the relation of sexual intercourse to conception is a relatively late idea in human development, whereas all the instance[s] he quotes are [all][1] simply proof of that knowledge, being symbolic additions in the phantasy. Still we must be thankful to such men for the wonderful material they provided us with, and at such labour.[2]

I heard about your contribution to the society for psychical research, for the secretary told me about it when asking me for one also. I refused to send them one, for I think that you can afford to do things that someone in my junior position cannot without being misunderstood.

I have thought much over your reference to my need for concentration in writing, and suppose it partly refers to my occasional neurological articles. They of course are written with a definite reason, which I believe to be a sound one, and have taken me hardly any time, as they all contain work done long ago, and which otherwise would be wasted. But on looking back over the past three years I see that your reproach is also just as regards my psycho-analytic writings. My excuse there is that so much of my writings of late have had to be *pièces d'occasion*, for society meetings, etc., and also that most of it has been of an elementary propagandism nature. My instincts rebel against this disordered and casual work, and I must confess to looking forward with a heavy heart to having to renew it when I go to England. I had hoped that I had finished most of this, now that there are others to do it, and could devote myself to more serious investigations. In England I shall try to get other men, more suited, to take up the more popular writing, but I shall probably have to do some myself at first. Putnam has been invaluable in this way, for he has a special talent for it and has a great gift for explaining new ideas in pleasing and persuasive language. The type of work I like doing is that of taking a small subject that can be covered completely, such as that of salt symbolism, and dealing with it fully. In saying this I am conscious that many of my articles do not support the truth of the statement, but it is so nevertheless. I shall be very glad to have any criticism that you can spare time for on the subject of the nightmare article, for I feel convinced that I should learn much from them.

I had two pieces of good luck yesterday that I must tell you about. One was a letter from the President of the next International Congress of Medicine inviting me to serve as member of the Council of the Section of Neuropathology,[3] of all subjects in the world! I don't understand why I should have received this honour, but I am very glad of it. The other, perhaps more sincere, was a visit from a patient who had come all the way from Australia to consult me; he tells me he had read about my work in several of the Australian newspapers, which appear to be more up to date than I had thought. I am to treat him here, his main complaint is timidity (father-complex), and also in England, where he will follow me in June. (I am expecting to spend two months in London this summer). I have not done much work since Christmas, chiefly owing to the rabies anxiety (I think I told you about my wife being treated), but am now getting on well with my monograph on the treatment of the neuroses, which is of course very easy to write.[4]

I often think how the length of my letters must appall you; fortunately you will soon have a good respite from them.

Yours always affectionately
Jones.

1. Crossed out in the original. The word "simply" is handwritten in an otherwise typed letter.
2. Hartland (1909–10), and Frazer (1910, 1911–15).
3. The president of the congress was Sir Thomas Barlow; the president of the neuropathology section was Sir David Ferrier; Jones is listed as a council member representing Canada. See *Seventeenth International Congress of Medicine (London, 1913): Daily Journal* (London: John Bale, Sons and Danielsson, 1913), pp. 54, 123–124.
4. Jones (1913a).

75

28 April 1912
Vienna, IX. Berggasse 19

My dear Jones,

The receipts of three of your reprints this morning which happens to be a Sunday reminds me that I am to answer your letter speedily if I am not to wait for another adress.[1] To be sure I felt the obligation many times in these last weeks, but I am so fatigued in the evenings and so busy in daytime—I had to give up even the Sunday respite—that the idea of writing an english letter has become pushed back from day to day while time went on incessantly.

As you are eager for criticism let me say that your paper on the therap. action of ΨA[2] proved me again that there are few men so fitted to deal with the arguments of others than you and that you are perfectly right about the view of resistance, while you hint at the same time at another source of therap. gain about which more could be said, the moment of the distance of times.

The dream which could easily be recognised as your own interested me highly though you may have altered some of the material relations.[3] It would be matter of much [thou][4] talk which I hope we will have together. As your wife is in the centre of interest after your passing over to Europe, I may think of seeing you again in England in Sept., after the interview in June. I promised to have a look at my brother there who is finishing his 80th year.[5] It is not yet fixed where I should travel in harvest, there is no Congress this year and so it could be made possible to see more of you and of England than I had first thought of.

To be sure the health of your wife will be the most important concern. In June my work at Vienna may be shrinking, my interest to be sure will not.

I congratulate you upon the two news showing that your work is attracting the attention it deserves. I am sorry to think that you will not yet have done with your duties of an instructor and popularizer when you come to England; it is a great sacrifice I know but you will have to wait long time before finding who did it in your stead.

I am glad you take an interest in *Imago* which I fear will not have so easy a career as the other organs have met with. Your "salt" will come out as soon as space permits, your "nightmare" is fairly advanced and proof-sheets come out rapidly as I am said [told].[6]

My second paper on the Taboo which should be finished by this time is suffering under my absolute lack of time and concentration for work. I trust it will produce a much better impression than the first one. Let us see if Frazer, Hartland etc. can agree that the solution they were looking for is being offered here. I am afraid, they will not.

Jung has been rather deeply engaged in his work on the Symbols and changes of Libido. You know he has been called to New York (Fordham Univ.) for a course of lectures in Sept.[7] It is this interesting occurrence which made us postpone the next congress until 1913.

In the New York *Times* April 5th [19]12 there appeared a short article entitled "Attacks Dr. Freud's Theory", containing a ferocious assault of Allen Starr on your correspondent, explaining his theories by the immoral character of Vienna and the immoral life I had lived there, professing that he had known me well "some years ago" and had worked side by side with me for one winter.[8] I wonder none of our people applied to me for this statememt, I had to receive it from a patient visiting New York. But it is more remarkable that I have never known the Allen Starr who knew me so well and in fact it is 23–25 years [that][9] since I was last in a laboratory. Now what does this mean? Is wilful lying and calumny a usual weapon among american neurologists?

I will be glad to hear of your news and hope they will be as favourable as your last ones were. Let me follow your journey from Toronto to the older and better mother country.

With most sincere wishes

yours faithfully
Freud

1. There is likely a missing letter here.
2. Jones (1912a).
3. Jones (1912c).
4. Crossed out in the original.
5. Emanuel Freud (1833–1914), son of Jakob Freud and his first wife, Sally Kanner, was Freud's half-brother.
6. Jones (1912h, 1912j).
7. Jung (1911–12, 1913b).

8. Moses Allen Starr, *New York Times*, 5 April 1912, p. 8. See also Putnam (1912), and Hale (1971b, 301–302).

9. Crossed out in the original.

76

7 May 1912
407 Brunswick Avenue
Toronto

Dear Professor Freud,

I have not had any answer to my last letter, and am surmising that perhaps it went down with the *Titanic*.[1] If so the sorrow of that disaster will be even more far-reaching that [than] was at first thought.

Many thanks for the reprint of the Inzest-Scheu article. My number of *Imago* has mysteriously not arrived, so that the reprint was all the more welcome, and was eagerly devoured. I noted with interest that you had found the writings of English workers of some use in your application of psycho-analysis. Let me hope that in the future they will also be of further service, in spite of their tardy beginning. Are you sending reprints of the present series to Frazer in Liverpool? I should greatly like to get some of these anthropologists and mythologists interested.

I am exceedingly sorry to hear from Riklin that the Congress may be postponed, but you will know what is best under the circumstances. I am afraid that a Spring meeting would cut off all possibility of any Americans or Canadians attending. I had meant to bring with me this time two professors of the Toronto university, who are greatly interested in the work; one, a Canadian, teaches Romance languages,[2] the other, an Englishman, teaches English literature. The latter is proposing to make with me a study of Blake, the great mystic and thinker.

I am of course exceeingly busy at present arranging things for my departure next week. Practice has been very active to the last, and I shall have at least two patients when I am in Europe. The Australian I think I mentioned to you changed his mind as he did not care to lose the month when I shouldn't be able to see him, and is taking treatment instead with Brill, whose name I gave to him; Brill tells me he is going on very well and will get better. My monograph on the treatment of the neuroses is finished and sent off to the publishers.[3] I have also had accepted the book I want to publish this summer consisting of revised reprints of various articles.[4] The Psycho-Analytic meeting in Boston[5] promises to be a success, and I expect the membership will go up from 8 to 23. Stanley Hall has promised to be present, as well as Adolf Meyer and August Hoch. We are sucking the strength out of the rival Psychopathological Association, in the same way that I hope we shall do from Prince's Journal as soon as we can get one started of our own. Still that won't be for a little while yet.

My wife is still better, is devoting great attention to dress, and is looking forward to leaving Toronto. We expect to arrive in Vienna about the 13th or 15th of June.

I sent you some reprints recently. The dream is of course my own, dating from last September.[6] I think the mosaic of it is very pretty, and I hope you will like it.

I don't think there is any more news at present. Perhaps I will write to you on the ship an account of the Boston meeting.

With my very warmest and kindest regards

yours always
Ernest Jones.

1. The *Titanic* sank on 14 April 1912. Jones is likely referring to a missing letter of early to mid-April.
2. Frederic Davidson.
3. Jones (1913a).
4. Jones, *Papers*, 1st ed. 1913.
5. The second annual meeting of the American Psychoanalytic Association was held in Boston at the end of May.
6. Jones (1912c).

77

10 May 1912
407 Brunswick Avenue
Toronto

Dear Professor,

Your very welcome letter arrived this morning. It was good of you to send me such a long one when you have so much tiring work to do. Fortunately I shan't have to disturb you in this way for a little while to come. I am always divided in my attitude towards your letters between on the one hand the thought that it is unfair of me to expect them and on the other my intense pleasure and stimulus at receiving them.

I knew nothing about Starr's letter to the *New York Times*, but Brill had told me that he had said something of the same sort at the meeting of the Academy of Medicine. I have written to Brill suggesting that he answer the letter. Brill does not keep one in good touch with local events. He is a bad correspondent, but one cannot reproach him, for he works very hard indeed and also perhaps finds writing not easy. It would be an easy thing to deal Starr a crushing blow by way of reply; there are so many means of attacking him. The only bright side to the disgraceful episode is that it

shows how hard up for serious arguments a man must be if he descends
to such low measures, and it also furnishes an objective proof of our statements that our opponents are influenced by emotional factors rather than
intellectual ones. As to your question whether wilful lying is a usual
weapon among American neurologists, I hardly think this could be generally affirmed, but it is true that such things are not rare, for I have known
several examples. Perhaps they are influenced by their electioneering
methods when they try to deal with scientific matters. At all events there
are many of them that one cannot describe as civilised beings in the European sense of the word. For some reason, probably on commercial grounds,
this seems especially to apply to N.Y.

I heard from Riklin about Jung's visit to America. I suppose it is to the
postgraduate course that they are giving at Fordham University, organised
by Jelliffe.[1] He asked me to lecture on the neuroses, but I couldn't as I
shall be at that time in Europe. It is a great pity that the congress has to
be postponed, but I suppose you have good reasons for it.

I was very interested to hear of your projected visit to England, and hope
it will be many times repeated. You should get better alimentary treatment
there than you did in America, and I hope that you will enjoy the visit. I
trust I may have the opportunity of seeing something of you there. If it
were a year later I would ask you to stay with me, but for the next year I
shall be roofless.

Many thanks for your opinion of my article on the therapeutic action
of ps-a.[2] When I republish it in my collection of articles I shall amplify the
time element you referred to. I have already found a publisher for this little
volume, and are [am] revising and extending the articles that comprise it.
With regard to the dream article I do not think I made any material alterations, so that I am quite revealed in it. I do not expound the anal complex
in the second dream, though it is plain enough to a *Kundiger* [expert].[3]

Here is a good example of a Verschreiben being determined by an affect.
Thoma, in the *Revue neurologique,* reviews my long paper on suggestion
by saying "La suggestion joue le rôle principal dans toutes les méthodes
psycho-analytiques". You observe the double depreciation effected by the
mistake: not only does psycho-analysis produce its effects via suggestion,
but there are many kinds of ps-a. I shall take my revenge by quoting it in
an *Alltagsleben* paper. On the same page he abstracts my article on the
ps-a method of treatment in the words "l'auteur précise les indications de
la ps-a [psycho-analyse] dans les psychonévroses et il indique les cas [(im-
bécillité, âge trop avancé, etc.),] où l'on ne peut guère espèrer des résultats
de la méthode." Surely my article was not quite so negative as that! In
what petty ways can hostility show itself.[4]

I read that you and Jung have contributed papers to a congress in
Australia.[5] I wonder if they are accessible; perhaps I shall be able to find

them in London. There now remains only Brazil, China, and Greenland
to be penetrated. Still I do think with all the opposition that we shall suffer
like Alexander for want of worlds to conquer.

With warmest regards

from yours always
Jones.

1. Smith Ely Jelliffe (1866–1945), New York neurologist, took up psychoanalysis in
1911 through Brill's influence, but was also highly interested in the work of Jung, Adler,
and Bergson; early pioneer in the field of psychosomatic medicine; with William Alanson
White, founded the *Psychoanalytic Review* in 1913.

2. Jones (1912a).

3. Jones (1912c); see *Papers*, 1st ed. 1913, pp. 386–390.

4. The two quotations are from *Revue neurologique*, 23 (1912): 432, regarding Jones
(1910–11a; 1909c). The first reads: "Suggestion plays the principal role in all the
psychoanalytic methods." The second reads: "The author specifies the rules of psychoanalytic treatment in the psychoneuroses and points out the cases (imbecility, mature
age, etc.), where one can scarcely hope for results from the method." The words in
brackets are part of the published version, but were left out by Jones.

5. Freud (1913m), and Jung (1913c).

78

18 July 1912
13 Princes St., Cavendish Sq.
London

Dear Professor Freud,

I hope that you had a pleasant journey to Carlsbad, and are now enjoying
your well-earned rest and change from Vienna's noise and dust. I travelled
straight through to London, except for an hour's stay at Bonn where I had
time to accompany my wife to her sister's house. She stood the journey
(21 hours in hot weather) excellently well, although we could get no *Schlaf-
coupé* [sleeping car]. It is also the first time I have seen her pack and get
ready so calmly and sensibly, without any *Reisefieber*.[1] I suggested it was
the beginning of the ψα success, but she preferred to attribute it to the
journey being in the direction of London. However when her sister asked
her about the treatment, and about you personally, she was very enthusiastic and her attitude was one of great confidence. It is the first sign of
identification when someone will not allow a stranger to attack a cause,
but reserves that pleasure for themself, just like when a man "runs down"
his own country but resents a stranger doing it. She comes on to London
(without the dog) next Monday, but will only stay a week or so. Then she
returns to Holland for a month to visit various relatives and comes back
to London early in September.

I stay here till about Aug. 20, then go to Wales and Partenkirchen (with Seif) for a week each, Zürich, and back to London on Sept. 10. I shall eagerly look forward to your visit about that time, and need hardly say that I will do everything to give you as good a time as possible.

I am enclosing a few literary excerpts of interest. Will you kindly send them on to Stekel, that is, if you think them worth publishing.

My visit to Vienna will always be a memorable time in my life, in many respects. It was for me equally instructive and enjoyable, and I am very grateful to all of you for the kindness with which I was treated.

I had a number of scientific problems to ask your opinion about, but what you had to tell me was always so much more interesting that they got put in the background. Possibly I may have the opportunity of raising them in September, but at present I will give you some peace.

Please remember me kindly to your wife and those of your family who may be with you, also to Dr. Van Emden.[2] Last, and most important, let me again try to thank you for the load you are taking off my mind and all that you are doing for my wife's future health and happiness; you know what it means to us both better than I can explain.

With very warmest regards

Yours affectionately
Ernest Jones.

1. That is, without any agitation over traveling.
2. J. E. G. van Emden (1868–1950), leading Dutch psychoanalyst, acted as intermediary between Freud and Jones during World War I; see unnumbered letters in this volume dated 26 October 1914 and 14 December 1914.

79

22 July 1912
Karlsbad, Goldener Schlüssel

Dear Professor Jones,

I was very happy about the good news from your wife and the kind words from yourself. Let us hope that the continuation will suit the beginning and that we shall earn at least a good portion of recovery, although to be sure we will struggle for nothing less than the whole of it.

Scientific news are scarce in this hot water-place. The most interesting may be that I got yesterday a letter from Jung which cannot but be construed into a formal disavowal of our hitherto friendly relations.[1] I am sorry, not more on personal motives but for the future of the Verein and the cause of ΨA, but I am resolved to let things go and not to try to influence him more. ΨA is no more my own affair but it concerns you and so many others besides as well.

If we go over to England, it will not be before the 10th of Sept. As far as I can I will stick to this project and hope to see you there both. But I might hear from you several times in the interval.

Your interesting contributions will be sent to Stekel for the *Zentralblatt*. With best wishes for your success in your own country

Yours sincerely
Freud

1. See Jung to Freud, 18 July 1912, in McGuire (1974, p. 511), with regard to the "Kreuzlingen gesture." The episode is also discussed in Jones (1955a, pp. 143–145; 1955b, pp. 162–163), and in Schur (1972, pp. 260–264).

80

30 July 1912
13 Princes St., Cavendish Sq.
London

Dear Professor Freud,

Thank you for your letter, which arrived safely. My wife was delayed a week in Bonn owing to some severe gastro-intestinal poisoning (supposed to be due to decomposition of the morphia), but got here two days ago quite recovered. She travelled alone, the first night she has been alone for $2\frac{1}{2}$ years, and was very happy to see London. The day she arrived she did not take her usual morning dose of morphia till 5 p.m., and then only half of it. Altogether she has reduced the daily dose by one fifth, which is already substantial. We are having a very happy time, seing old friends and so on.

I have been sounding the situation in London and am still optimistic about it. Last night I spent a pleasant evening with Hart. Circumstances have for the moment made him less jealous of my competition. He has just been made Superintendent of a private asylum in London,[1] with permission and time to do private practice. He is marrying in a month's time. He seems more reasonable about the respectability question, perhaps because he is now permanently settled as to position, and remarked that to be respectable in psychopathology means to make no progress. In the past year he has been very occupied with taking higher examinations, routine work, etc., and has done practically no reading. He says that he cannot call himself a frank adherent of the ψα movement, but is enormously impressed by it, and definitely means to practice it openly with his private patients. He accepts the principles but does not yet identify himself with the cause. Perhaps he will do that later, but I am afraid he will find it hard to make any personal sacrifices for an interest outside himself. Still his general attitude is much freer and better than when I last saw him.

Eder, of whom I also spoke to you, has much improved, being less pugnacious and rebellious against all the world, partly I think because he is now happily married. I treated his first wife four years ago. She committed suicide when he left her and ran off with another man's wife, whom he married after her divorce. This one is especially intelligent and well-educated. She has recently been treated by Jung, who agrees with her wish to take up treatment of children. I am treating Eder himself at present, for a few symptoms and so that he may get further into the work. He intended going to Jung for this, but took advantage of my being in England. (Also he is an old pupil of mine medically, although he is 13 years older). His general attitude is splendid and he will surely make a valuable adherent. Perhaps he will be able to influence B. Shaw and H. G. Wells, Zangwill,[2] etc., all of whom are close friends of his.

The Psycho-medical society has mostly hypnotists for members, though to my surprise Hart has joined it (out of politeness to MacDougall, the Oxford psychologist,[3] who invited him to). I do not yet know if it will be useful, but fancy it will be better to confine ourselves to a proper ψα Verein on the one hand and the Psychiatric Society (branch of the Royal Society of Medicine) on the other.

So much for news. I sincerely trust that you will be able to keep to your plan of coming to London on Sept. 10th. We shall enjoy your visit enormously, and Hart and Eder are also extremely eager to meet you. If you have heard from Ferenczi and Rank, and are in a position to decide, perhaps you will let me know your requirements in the way of rooms, and then I can arrange suitable ones in good time.

About Jung I do not know what to say except that I am very sorry, the reason being that his whole conduct is a complete puzzle to me, altogether inexplicable. As we would put it colloquially, "he has the game in his own hands, and refuses to play it". The following passage from a recent letter of Putnam's is perhaps to the point; it is à propos of some remarks of mine defending Stekel. "It makes me a little uncomfortable to find any virtues lacking in any prominent psycho-analyst. I feel as if we ought to be something superhuman, to justify our doctrines. Defects and weaknesses of character are surely to be looked upon as 'symptoms', and we ought all to be angels capable, doubtless, of seeing our shortcomings, but only slightly influenced by them."[4] ψα certainly forces one to see one's defects, and should help us to overcome them. I believe the central difficulty is that relatively few men really identify themselves completely with the cause, nothing like the extent that you do; so many put their own private personality first, in the foreground of importance, and relegate the cause to a subordinate position. What a woefully distorted perspective of the transitoriness of the individual compared with the permanent gain in progress that they might merge themselves into!

I get a little pessimistic at times when I look around at the men who must lead for the next thirty years. Jung abdicates from his throne, Stekel is obviously impossible, even Rank may be hindered by material considerations unless something can be done for him, Ferenczi is running a big risk with the Gedankenübertragung—true or false—, and so on. Perhaps I am wrong to talk like this, but I can't help wishing that things at the top, gathered around you, were more satisfactory. Still there are counterbalancing signs, and no doubt things will improve in a year or two. Ferenczi, Rank and I had a little talk on these general matters in Vienna. They were rather disappointed with the whole Zurich attitude at the moment, and even thought that their faith in the cause was not what it should be. We all agreed on one thing, that salvation could only [life]⁵ lie in a restless self-analysis, carried to the farthest possible limit, thus purging *personal* reactions away so far as can be done. One of them, I think it was Ferenczi, expressed the wish that a small group of men could be thoroughly analysed by you, so that they could represent the pure theory unadultered by personal complexes, and thus build an unofficial inner circle in the Verein and serve as centres where others (beginners) could come and learn the work. If that were only possible it would be an ideal solution.

Let me turn for a moment to one or two scientific matters. I hope that in one of your next *Imago* papers you will touch on the difficult problem of the *Ursprung der Verdrängung überhaupt*.⁶ Although this may have different sources, it seems to hang so closely with the subject of incest that perhaps it would form an appropriate section in one of your present series of papers. If we go back to a matriarchal era, or at all events to a time when the fatherhood was unknown, perhaps one great factor may have been the jealousy of older, grown men against boys who would be naturally attached to their mother. I hope that you are dealing with the problem in relation to that of tabu.

Your telling me of the *Stumm-Tod* [mute—death] symbolism had an interesting *Nachklang* [reverberation]. I dreamed that I was walking from the house of my old family doctor to the house where I was born (and lived for three years). With me was a female dog, one that the doctor gave me at the age of eight, and a frequent dream-figure for my mother. The dog spoke, to my great astonishment, and debated whether it could go with me *(coire)* in that direction.

Here there is the opposite of the *Stumm-Tod* motive. My mother died three years ago, and in the dream speaks, is alive, against all natural expectations.

The birthplace symbolism is amusingly determined by a witticism made by a London comedian at a fancy dress ball. An actress appeared with very little clothing on, and in reply to his question told him that she represented the World (Mother Earth). He stared for a while, and when she asked him what he was gazing at, he answered "I was looking for the place where I was born".

And so I end up in a light [note][7] vein, which perhaps is always best. With all kind wishes from

Yours affectionately
Ernest Jones.

1. Medical superintendent, Northumberland House Asylum, London.
2. Israel Zangwill (1864–1926), novelist, playwright, and Zionist leader; author of the play *The Melting Pot* (1908).
3. William McDougall (1871–1938), British psychologist; head of psychological laboratory at Oxford; in 1920 left for the United States and worked at Harvard and Duke.
4. This passage from Putnam's letter is not to be found in Hale (1971a).
5. Crossed out in the original.
6. "The origin of repression in general."
7. Crossed out in the original.

81

1 August 1912
Karslbad

My dear Jones,

I had just begun writing the epilogue to the Symposion on "Onanie" on Stekel's urgent admonition[1]—literary work is so hard under the action of the hot springs—when your letter arrived and threw me out of my track so that I must answer it first in order to be able to go on in that other line.

I am extremely glad at the good news about your wife to whom I have taken a strong interest in so short a time and I think on her behalf as well as on yours we shall come to London on the 10 or 11th of Sept. The particulars about our journey I will give you as soon as Ferenczi is with me, in the last days of this month. We will try to keep in connection in the interval. From the 15th of this month you can take as my sojourn Hotel Latemar, Karersee, Tirol.

What took hold of my imagination immediately is your idea of a secret council composed of the best and most trustworthy among our men to take care of the further development of ΨA and defend the cause against personalities and accidents when I am no more. You say it was Ferenczi who expressed this idea, yet it may be mine own shaped in better times, when I hoped Jung would collect such a circle around himself composed of the official headmen of the local associations. Now I am sorry to say such a union had to be formed independently of Jung and of the elected presidents. I dare say it would make living and dying easier for me if I knew of such an association existing to watch over my creation.[2] I know there is a boyish perhaps a romantic element too in this conception, but perhaps it could be adapted to meet the necesseties of reality. I will give my fancy free play and may leave to you the part of the Censor.

First of all: This committee had to be *strictly secret* in his existence and his actions. It could be composed of you, *Ferenczi* and *Rank*, among whom the idea was generated. *Sachs*—in whom my confidence is illimited in spite of the shortness of our acquaintance—and *Abraham* could be called next, but only under condition of all of you consenting. I had better be left outside of your conditions and pledges; to be sure I will keep the utmost secrecy and be thankful for all you communicate to me. I will not drop any utterance about the matter before you have answered me, not even to Ferenczi. Whatever the next time may bring, the future foreman of the ΨA movement might come out of this small but select circle of men, in whom I am still ready to confide in spite of my last disappointments with men. This plan would be another motive for our coming to London.

Now let me turn to science. The true historical source of Verdrängg I hope to touch upon in the last of the 4 papers, of which Taboo is the second, in that to be called "Die infant. Wiederkehr des Totemismus".[3] I may as well give you the answer now: Any internal—(damn my English!)— Jede *innere* Verdränggsschranke ist der historische Erfolg eines *äusseren* Hindernisses. Also: Verinnerlichung der Widerstände, die Geschichte der Menschheit niedergelegt in ihren heute angeborenen Verdränggs-neigungen.[4]

I know of the obstacle or the complication offered by the matter of Matriarchy and have not yet found my way out of it. But I hope it will be cleared [a]way. It will not be treated in the paper on Taboo which is very much restricted in its intention.

Your dream is very nice. I had no time to follow the motive while in Vienna but I think it is quite reliable.

I close from "external influences"

Yours sincerely
Freud

1. Stekel (1912b), and Freud (1912f).

2. The previous three sentences were entirely left out by Jones when he quoted this letter in his biography of Freud (Jones, 1955a, p. 153; 1955b, p. 173). For an in-depth analysis of Jones's strategy of excluding Jung from membership in the secret committee, see Paskauskas (1988a).

3. "The Return of Totemism in Childhood," part 4 of Freud (1912–13).

4. "Every *internal* repression barrier is the historical outcome of an *external* obstacle. Therefore: internalization of resistances [represents] the history of the human race as deposited in its present innate tendencies to repression."

82

7 August 1912
13 Princes St., Cavendish Sq.
London

Dear Professor Freud,

It was a charming sight, if I may say so, to catch your imagination at work, in the fire of creation, and I am very happy that the suggestion in question is in harmony with your views. It should prove a stern test of what ψα, ruthlessly and courageously carried through, can do in the way of objectivity, and if it is successful it must surely be a valuable achievement, therefore one worth a great effort. My own thought is that the council should be quite unofficial and informal, therefore necessarily secret, and in the closest possible touch with you for the purposes both of criticism and instruction. Fortunately the last condition is not difficult, for you are delightfully approachable and generous with your knowledge and advice, as I can personally bear witness with the greatest gratitude. What we shall have to do will be to purge away all excrescences of the theory, so far as possible, and to coordinate our own unconscious aims with the demands and interests of the movement. It would be impossible to do this quite thoroughly without your constant guidance, for I suppose that, strictly speaking, you, the creator of the movement, are the only person [of][1] in whom this coordination is complete.

When you have the chance of talking to Ferenczi and Rank I hope to hear what they feel in the matter. In our conversation the only subject discussed, raised I think by Ferenczi, was the possibility of a few men being analysed by you, so that they could serve as representatives in different places to teach other beginners. The idea of a united small body, designed, like the Paladins of Charlemagne, to guard the kingdom and policy of their master, was a product of my own romanticism, and I did not venture to speak about it to the others until I had broached it to you. We must surely have some serious discussion of the whole situation when you are in London.

And this brings me to a concrete demand of reality, namely the question of accommodation, which is not always easy in London in September. I am now in the most comfortable and convenient lodging-house I have any experience of. The landlady is in every way obliging, and will adapt all things (meals, etc.) to one's requirements, the cooking is excellent, and as one pays for every meal separately one is free to be either in or out to them. Now can you send me authority to take rooms here from the 10th of September, unless you have other plans. I presume you would need a sitting-room and three bedrooms. The others could also share my sitting-room. I am leaving London at the end of next week and should like to reserve the rooms before I go.

My wife had a most enjoyable time in London, and has quite recovered from her misadventure in Bonn (the poisoning). She left last night for Holland, and will return about September the 2nd. After the 17th I shall be in Wales for ten days, but letters will be forwarded from here. At the end of the month I go to Partenkirchen to Seif, and then to Zurich, returning here on Sept. 10th.

Thank you very much for answering my question about the *Ursprung der Verdrängung*. I think I see your meaning in the conclusion you formulated, for Rank had quoted it to me and we had discussed it.[2] I feel that you have captured an important and far-reaching idea in pointing to the inheritance of Verdrängung as the result of earlier racial experiences, but I am rather in the dark as to the relation of it to the Weismann principle of the non-transmissibility of acquired characters. I hope it can stand in harmony with this, and not in contradiction.[3] Some of Jung's passages are either carelessly worded or they seem to contradict the principle. Thus he speaks of inheriting the effects of various experiences, of these being "stamped in" on the race, and so on. Is it not more likely than this that the capacity to react to external obstructions by means of repression and sublimation varied in different individuals, and that this capacity has been affected (developed) through the operation of natural selection, especially perhaps sexual selection?

The work with Eder is progressing very satisfactorily. He will make a good worker for us. I have also seen something of Berkeley-Hill, who unfortunately had to return to India this week; he is very enthusiastic, and has quite a good knowledge.

I hope you are having a profitable and enjoyable time in Karlsbad.
With kindest regards from

Yours always
Jones.

1. Crossed out in the original.

2. The passage referred to from Freud's letter of 1 August 1912 (see note 4 to letter 81) is not to be found in *Totem and Taboo* (Freud, 1912–13). But a similar one appears in Freud's added note of 1915 to his *Drei Abhandlungen* (Freud, 1905d, p. 225 n. 3), where he points the reader generally to his *Totem and Taboo* without providing page references.

3. August Weismann (1834–1914), important biologist, known for his germ plasm theory and his opposition to the Lamarckian principle of transmission of acquired characteristics. Freud's statement in fact does contradict Weismann's theory. Freud's adherence to Lamarck's principle throughout his life—against the grain of standard biological thought of the time—was a great bone of contention between Jones and Freud; see Jones (1957a, pp. 309–314; 1957b, pp. 332–337).

83

11 August 1912
Karlsbad

My dear Jones,

I am glad to learn that the taste for romance is not restricted to my own phantastic self. I may drop a word on the matter to Ferenczi when I see him but in the whole I intend to leave it to you, procuring stuff for private entertainment when in London.

I hav[e] learned lately that human plans are unreliable. You remember my youngest girl, your wife met her too. I intended to send her with aunt to pass some months of the next winter in Italy to make up for the study of last year and to have some nice sights in young years. All dispositions were made, when my other girl—Sophie—came back from Hamburg as the bride of a young man she had met there among our relatives. She is to marry in next spring, aunt will not be absent during the preparations and so Italy has to be given up.[1] But let us suppose that we are passing through a phase of history where nothing extraordinary comes to happen. If so, I expect firmly to meet you in London 10th of Sept. and beg you to take up lodgings as you propose to do. At least for Ferenczi and me.

As for Brill I am still waiting for his answer. Rank I have invited today to join us at London and hope you will be glad to see him too. As he is about to pass his examination I am not sure which side will come out victoriously in the conflict aroused by my invitation.[2]

You may write me best under my Vienna adress as long as you have not got details about my September sojourns.

With best love to your wife and yourself

your affectionate
Freud

1. Sophie Freud (1893–1920) married Max Halberstadt (1882–1940) of Hamburg in January 1913. Freud had three daughters: his youngest was Anna (1895–1982); his eldest was Mathilde (1887–1978). The elaborate family tree at the beginning of Clark (1980) is very useful. The aunt referred to is Minna Bernays, who lived in the Freud household.

2. Rank was preparing for his fall doctoral examinations at the University of Vienna, but had accepted Freud's invitation to visit Jones in London; see Lieberman (1985, p. 137). In the end, however, the trip was canceled.

84

18 August 1912
Hotel Latemar, Karersee, Tirol

My dear Jones,

It was a remarkable contrast to read your clever and delicate remarks on this finest spot of the Dolomites among the big mountains, high trees in the most refreshing or rather intoxicating airs I have ever breathed. I thank you for them but I have nothing to add. My mental faculties have not yet returned since Karlsbad. The presence of my family including my daughters "friend", is not promoting to intellectual research.

Your wife I hope is continuing in good condition, or—I will not come to London.

While I was copying the intricate adress for my letter to you I resolved to recommend you using my old Vienna one until we meet.

I am nearly out of every relation to our work. The 3rd number of *Imago* was the only trece [trace] to me. I know nothing of the *Jahrbuch*, I have not got your book on the Nightmare etc.[1] and I am nearly enjoying my shameful indifference.

No news from Rank or Brill.

I am wishing you the best impressions in your country

yours truly
Freud

1. Jones (1912j).

85

[postcard]

22 August 1912
Karersee

Dear Jones,

Only to let you know that Rank will be with us at London. I have no news from Brill.

Yours sincerely
Freud

86

28 August 1912
The Woodlands, Gowerton

Dear Professor Freud,

Just a line to thank you for the news about Ferenczi and Rank. I will make arrangements in London, and if you write to my wife there she will meet your train (in case you arrive before I do, which, however, is not likely; I expect to be in London on the 8th). You have the address, 13 Princes St., Cavendish Sq..

I leave here tomorrow and go to Partenkirchen and Zurich.

The August *Imago* arrived to-day, and I am in the middle of your Tabu article.[1]

Jung sent me the proofs of my article from the forthcoming number of the *Jahrbuch*, where it appears that he is publishing only a third of it, one case out of three, the rest to appear later (next year).[2] As usual no explanation! I do not think I am specially impatient about my work being published, but I find 18 months a long time for an article written by special request, especially when it is not thought necessary to apologise for the delay.

In eager anticipation *A reverdichi* [Arrivederci]

Yours
Jones.

1. Part 2 of Freud (1912–13).
2. Jones (1912–13).

87

3 September 1912
Hotel Regina

My dear Jones,

I am sorry I must write you this letter but I cannot avoid to do so. My fears have become true, something has happened which makes it impossible for me to come to London or to say whether I shall be able to come or not. My eldest daughter, who has suffered so long from the consequences of a badly performed appendicitis-operation and had an excellent time these last two years, fell ill suddenly these days.[1] Again fever and great subjective annoyance, the provoking cause being rather an enjoyable one a beginning of gravidity after 3 years of married life. But on account of the irritation of the wound and the fever the hopeful condition had to be interrupted. I came up to Wien from Bozen[2] a short time after the operation and I had to resolve not to go away until we see the end of the fever and the illness. She feels much relieved after the delivery, but I cannot say when I will feel sure of her, and thus I have to write you that I cannot come to London. Ferenczi is here with me, as much disappointed as I and so is Rank.

The day before yesterday when I was even more anxious on account of my daughter I wrote to Pfister praying him to give you these news when you are at Zürich.[3] But it occurred to me he might be absent from Zürich at this time and I learnt here—where I arrived in the morning—your actual adress with Dr. Seif.

I hope you will give me your news from Zürich, as I am sure to stay here at least 8 or ten days.

With love to your wife

yours affectionately
Freud

P.S. Compliments to your host Dr. Seif.

1. The precarious state of Mathilde's health over the years is summarized in Gay (1988, pp. 308–309).
2. Bolzano in the Dolomites.
3. Freud to Pfister, 2 September 1912; see Meng and E. Freud (1963, p. 57).

88

4 September 1912
Partenkirchen

Dear Professor Freud,

It is a little doubtful whether you will receive this before you leave, so I write only a few lines and to wish you Godspeed on the journey.

Seif has here the Korrektur of Jung's article, which is nearly 300 pages long. I have already read most of it. He maintains that much of the Urlibido has been already sublimated in bygone ages and is therefore no longer sexual in the individual child. He does not deny infantile sexuality altogether. He distinguishes sharply between Libido and Sexualität.[1] There is little new in the work. It is a most rambling and disconnected shovelling in of mythology with occasional remarks of his own. It is written in great excitement and flurry, and exceedingly badly arranged and presented— most obscure. I cannot think that many people will make much out of it. Seif was recently with Jung and has much to say about him. He is a little inclined to be on Jung's side. He may perhaps come with me to London for a few days next week.

Adler, Stekel, Bleuler and other thorny people will be at the Zurich Congress. It should be interesting.

Glückliche Reise und Auf wieder sehen,[2]

Yours
Jones.

P.S. O. Vogt has resigned from the Congress, and Forel is ill, so there are only Bernheim, Seif and myself in the *Vorstand* [executive committee].[3] The whole thing will either die or be absorbed by ψα, like the American Psychopathological Association.

1. See Jung (1911–12), pt. 2, chap. 2, pars. 1–2. Jung had already warned Freud about his reconsideration of the question of libido in a letter of 11 December 1911; see McGuire (1974, p. 471).

2. "Have a good trip and see you again soon."

3. Third annual meeting of the International Society for Medical Psychology and Psychotherapy, Zurich, 8–9 September 1912; see *Journal für Psychologie und Neurologie*, 20 (1913): E89–E242.

89

Friday night, 6 September 1912
Partenkirchen

Dear Professor Freud,

I am happy to hear from your telegram[1] this evening that the news is already better, and I warmly trust you will soon be relieved of all anxiety. It must have been a bad blow that such a *Krankheitsanlass* [cause of disease] should have proved so unfortunate in its consequences.

I need hardly tell you how disappointed I was when I got your letter, and my wife will surely feel the same way. The reality of life deals some hard shocks to the Lustprinzip at times, and this one is not one of the least.

We leave here in the morning, and I will get your letter (forwarded) in Zurich, probably on Sunday. I am still hoping that you will be able to come in a week or so, when all goes well, and beg of you to do so if it is at all possible and convenient to you.

Seif comes with me from Zurich to London for a week or so. He had overcome many inner difficulties and is anxious to make your better acquaintance. I am sure he will be a valuable support, and he is also a good fellow personally.

I shall of course write to you about the affairs in Zurich, which promise to be interesting. I have already read the Vorträge. *Bleuler über das Unbewusste ist das* [die] *alte Geschichte, d. h. Vorbewusste.*[2] Adler's theses are an exquisite self-analysis that is most interesting. Maeder has some good thoughts on the functions of the dream. Seif and I both talk about Angst.[3]

I send my deepest good wishes for a quick recovery of the patient, and a release to you from anxiety.

Aufwiedersehen, hoffentlich bald.[4]

Yours
Jones.

1. Telegram missing.
2. "Bleuler on the unconscious, the same old story, namely the pre-conscious." See Eugen Bleuler, "Das Unbewusste," *Journal für Psychologie und Neurologie*, 20 (1913): E89–E92.
3. Alfred Adler, "Das organische Substrat der Psychoneurosen," *Zeitschrift für die gesamte Neurologie und Psychiatrie*, 13 (1912): 481–491; A. Maeder, "Über das Teleologische im Unbewussten," *Journal für Psychologie und Neurologie*, 20 (1913): E101; L. Seif, "Zur Psychopathologie der Angst," *Zeitschrift*, 1 (1913): 95–99; and Jones (1913b).
4. "Until I see you again, soon I hope."

90

7 September 1912
Vienna, IX. Berggasse 19

My dear Jones,

No sudden attack of old age makes my hand shaky. I am writing you in the train from Vienna to Italy and my hand plays the part of a seismometres needle.

Both your letters and your telegram[1] were very painful to me. It seems to be a time where I cannot keep the promises given to my friends and dear ones. I aroused all the appetites of my youngest daughter by the prospect of a winter spent in Italy and could not send her on account of the betrothal of her older sister.[2] I bade Rank prepare for a sojourn at London and I had to disappoint him as well as you owing to the illness of the eldest daughter.

It is a discomfortable feeling, if such accidents go on repeating themselves and invalidating [yo][3] one's intentions and promises.

There was a rapid improvement in my daughters condition, after pregnancy had been interrupted and my children as well as the physician insisted that I should go back into my vacancies [vacation]. But there is some fever still present I hope not for long time more. So I could have kept my date at London, neglecting slight misgivings for the next time, had I been in better condition myself.

I felt increasing fatigue and inactivity since Karlsbad, sleeping badly and spirits rather low and had looked for London as analeptic. The excitement of this last week did mightily my weakness[4] so that I feel I am in need of rest and unfit to produce myself in clever society. Even Ferenczi kind as he is, who would not leave me for his own pleasure and recreation, is sometimes too much for me. He is reading in the next compartment and must not know it. I cannot remember a similar condition which I am prone to ascribe to the strong action of the hot waters and I expect something from time and sunshine.

Eager by your remarks on Jungs paper I procured the *Jahrbuch*, which I will read in company of Ferenczi the next days. I see where its fault lies and could give you the number of the page, where he is going astray. I will do so later.

My next adress is: Hotel Seehof St. Cristof am See bei Caldonazzo Südtirol

I beg for yours to give you notice and pray to assure your wife that not seeing her at London is the most sensible [sensitive] loss of this affair.

Wishing you success and good humour at the Congress

yours sincerely
Freud

1. Telegram missing.
2. See note 1 to letter 83.
3. Crossed out in the original.
4. In the process of translating from German to English, Freud may have intended to say: "Die Aufregung dieser letzten Woche hat *mich mächtig geschwächt*" (The excitement of this last week has *mightily weakened me*). The juxtaposition *Macht-Schwäche* has interesting color and cadence in German, and there seems to be a slight hesitation in Freud's handwriting at the word *weakness*. Hence: "The excitement of this last week did mightily weaken me."

91

12 September 1912
13 Princes St., Cavendish Sq.
London

Dear Professor Freud,

It is of course a great disappointment to us both that you are not coming to London, but our feeling in this direction is quite submerged by our solicitude about the cause and I wish it were in my power to do or say something that would have a beneficial effect with you. Feeling as you do you are wise not to travel so far to such new and tiring impressions, but you must regard it as only a postponement to a more favourable occasion, perhaps next year when we shall have a private home in which to receive you and make you comfortable. The effect of the over strong Carlsbad *Kur* [spa] will surely work off before long, and then all will be again well. But is there not more than this, a psychical moment? Perhaps your solicitude about your daughter, who means so much to you, may have got identified, and strengthened, by your solicitude about your *other child*—the mental one? They are both necessarily exposed to the vicissitudes of life, over which you have not always full power and cannot always direct their steps, but in both cases there are protecting forces present that are much stronger and more tenderly careful than most such children have the privilege of.

Your daughter is I trust by now quite better, and you will next concern yourself about the other child, ψα. I spent several hours discussing Jung's views with Riklin, Maeder, etc., and understand them, though not fully, at least better than by reading the article, where they are not at all clearly expressed. I suspect that some of them are of purely personal origin, especially the rejection of the reality of incest-attraction and the replacement of sexual by excremental. But much of the work is in striking agreement with the logical development of the *Sexualtheorie* that you yourself have gone through in the last years; especially the phylogenetic aspects, the inheritance of repression and perhaps already desexualised (sublimated) tendencies. I will not say more till I hear from you, which I am most anxious to do, but my hope is that the cleft will prove to be not deep. Maeder, Binswanger, Seif and I held a private consultation about the personal question, and we think it should not be impossible to restore better relations if a good will is there. There have been misunderstandings, (perhaps on both sides?), and Jung has been over-sensitive about some things. But no more of this at present. I want greatly to talk with you, and in Vienna we must have our previously arranged consultation with Ferenczi, Rank, and Sachs.

The congress was of course not interesting, but there was no strong opposition to us. Bleuler was tedious and stupid in his Vortrag and as President. Adler was calm. He invited the congress to meet next year in Vienna, and in spite of our opposition to this it was arranged. Young Maier[1] made the amusing Versprechen of referring to Bleuler's *Schizophrenie Monographie* as B's *Biographie*, which was not very flattering to his chief. Forel was active, but fortunately could not speak much on account of the effect of his apoplexy.[2] The chief thing was naturally the private talks which were very valuable.

Seif is with me here, and stays another week. My wife is pretty well and happy, though much concerned about you.

My dearest wish is that you may rapidly benefit from the change and rest. I am most eager to hear from you, but pray do not write if you feel tired or wish to give your mind to the scenery, sunshine, and immediate environment.

Yours affectionately
Jones.

1. Hans Wolfgang Maier (1882–1945), first assistant to Bleuler at the Burghölzli asylum, which he later directed (1928–1941).

2. For reports of the meeting of the International Society for Medical Psychology and Psychotherapy, see *Zeitschrift* 1 (1913): 95–99, and *Zentralblatt* 3 (1913): 119–120.

92

14 September 1912
S. Cristof [San Cristoforo]

My dear Jones,

I have passed through some days of very bad health, now I feel recovered and intend going to Rome tomorrow to catch a last dose of beauty and selfcollection. Write me under my name (the F printed) *ferma in posta*. I got a nice letter from Maeder about the Congress and I am sure I have to thank *your* influence for it. Mrs. Jung who had been silent for a long time added some very kind lines[1] to sending her husbands famous paper in S.A. [*Separatabdruck*].[2] So the prospects seem rather clearing—if all this be not the immediate effect of your personal intercourse with the Zürich people.

My daughter seems to continue in the same condition, not bad, but some patience will be required.

I expect to meet Ferenczi on the line to Rome. He had no good time with me.

Give my best love to your wife and accept my thanks for all you are doing in the time of my weakness.

Yours truly
Freud

1. Emma Jung to Freud, 10 September 1912; see McGuire (1974, p. 514).
2. Offprint or reprint.

93

[postcard]

16 September 1912
Hotel Eden, Via Ludovisi
Rome

Dear Jones,
I am glad to be here and I feel quite recovered.
Best love to you both.

Yours truly
Freud

94

18 September 1912
13 Princes Street
Cavendish Square, W.

Dear Professor Freud,
I got today from [your] postcard from Rome, and last night your letter from S. Cristof. (The latter you curiously addressed to Partenkirchen, whence it was forwarded to me). We are exceedingly happy to hear that you are again well, and I am sure the stimulating environment of your old love, Rome, will complete the cure.

You do not say whether you got my letter safely at S. Cristof., but I surmise so from your reference to Zurich. Yes, I told Mrs. Jung that you were eager to see her husband's article, and asked her to send it as soon as possible. We have had a little correspondence since then, and also *Gegen-analyse* [counter-analysis], of some interest; I can tell you when I see you. She was analysed by Seif last autumn (this is *strictly private*), and seems to take a fairly objective view of her husband's failings. I am hoping that her influence over him will be of value to us.

My impression is that Jung's scientific divergences will not prove very serious, but you will know best about this and I am eagerly expecting to hear from you on the matter. Did I tell you that his New York lectures are to be devoted to the theoretic side of the *Libidotheorie?*[1] The English translation has been corrected by Eder in London, who has given me some account of it.[2]

Jung's relation to the Verein is another question altogether, and it looks as though this can never be satisfactory in the sense that you had hoped. He believes strongly that great men are injured by too much contact with their followers, thinks this is true of you, and is going to avoid the same danger himself by isolating himself more or less from the rest (and wrapping himself in a divine and impenetrable shroud of mystery!).[3] This explains much of his attitude towards us all. His wife thinks further that there is a competition between the personal interest in other workers (*Libidobesetzung*) and his own private work, which he regards as more important.

We cannot have a monarchy unless one man is strong enough to be king, and also willing. Perhaps the best solution after all would be to have a yearly changing President merely as *Geschäftsführer* [administrator], with a strong central committee of about six who would conduct the campaign, organise the forces, and formulate the plans. What is your view of this?

Seif left here for Munich tonight. We had an enjoyable time in the galleries, museums, etc., with much instruction to both. My wife and I leave for Holland probably on the 27th, and after two days there will proceed to Vienna. She is very happy here; and pretty well, with occasional cardiac and gastric attacks at night. I heard recently from Rank, who of course is hard at work. Please give my best regards to Ferenczi, whom I hope to see in Vienna; it was a special disappointment not to have him in London, but "better luck next time".

With all good wishes for a pleasant and beneficial time

Yours affectionately
Jones.

1. Jung (1913b).
2. Eder and Moltzer (1913–15).
3. Similar words appear in Jones (1913g), a paper directed primarily at Jung; see Jones (1951, 2:248–249).

Dear Professor Freud,

I have been meaning to write to you ever since I first heard of your daughter's illness—did in fact begin twice with the usual negative result. I was so sorry to hear of it, but happily it is all over now and you are feeling better too—as we gathered from your p.c. from Rome.

It was such a disappointment not to have you here—I did look forward to it so much—although I never guessed how much till all hope had to be given up. Still—you were quite right not to come under the circumstances—I am sure that you will find London worthy of your best health and spirits. Let us hope that perhaps next autumn we may be able to receive you in our house and make you as comfortable as you deserve.

Dr. Seif left tonight after a very busy and enjoyable 8 days—he had an appetite for sightseeing more fitted to 8 months.

I want to ask a business question (which is wicked during your holidays!)—if it suits you as well, would you give me my hour as late in the day as possible? I'm looking forward so much to seeing you again.

Sincerely yrs
Loe K. J.

95

22 September 1912
Rome

My dear Jones,
I am glad I have received all your letters as you have mine and hasten to answer the two last ones from your side before we can exchange writing for talking.

I am very sensible [sensitive] indeed to your kindness shown during my last troubles and glad to let you know that my daughter is slowly improving even above the level when I left her, while I feel strengthened and relieved by the air and the impressions of this divine town. In fact I have been more happy than healthy at Rome, but my forces are coming back and I feel

"wieder Lust mich in die Welt zu wagen
der Erde Leid, der Erde Glück zu tragen".[1]

What you construed about the Verdichtung of the two daughters sounds so ingenious that I dare not contradict it,[2] the more so as it gave you occasion for promises which touch my ear like music might another man. Of course there is a great difficulty if not impossibility in recognising actual psychical processes in [the][3] his own person. To me the physical side must be more evident, the sudden intolerance of the heart-muscle for tobacco and it seems even more for wine, of which I could not forego small doses, while in Tirol and Italy. My last improvement here is due to a great restriction of that delicious roman wine I was indulging in.

Now let it be enough of personal complaints and hopes. As for the scientific interest between us, I completely agree with you, that there is no big danger of a separation between Jung and me. I began reading his paper until I knew the plot of it, p. 174.[4] There you will find, he is simply bagging the question and misunderstanding me. I never obliterated or changed the meaning of libido, but stuck to my first definition all over. I threw up the problem whether paranoia can be explained by the retraction of the libidinous components, left it unsolved, but pointed to a certain way of solving it. He is proclaiming without further proofs, that libido theory is unable to answer for the loss of reality, as if it was *Selbstverständlichkeit* [foregone conclusion].[5] I hope we will have a good talk over it, but to be sure it is all discutable and highly interesting and there is no germ of enmity in it. The fact is he stumbled a first time in the application of libido theory on Paraphrenia[6] and now he is stumbling again to the opposite direction, but he might [con][7] do so and continue to be my friend as he was during the first of his errors. I must confess, the paper did not interest me enough after this discovery to finish it while here. I postponed the lecture to the long day of journey home.

So if you and the Zürich people bring about a formal reconciliation I would make no difficulties. It would be a formality only, as I am not angry with him and sure enough, that my former feelings for him cannot be restored. I am quite sure his friends are mistaken about my provoking his sensibility [sensitivity] in some points. I never but spoiled him and he behaved in details, which are not known to you, quite odiously against me. He wanted a dissension and he produced it.

The other side of the question I see pretty dark. The character which you give him—according to the best sources I understand—is "really too bad" for association. I have no great respect for greatness proclaiming itself, before others bow to it and I think our personal variations in intellectual and other gifts vanish before the enormity of the task before us; it is about the difference of small and big ants bidden to demolish a hill. If he thinks himself so great as you describe him he will not be fit for working with us and will become a danger for our work. When he did not answer as president with unrestricted prerogative, it is quite sure he will not do better after the restriction of his powers and it seems quite improbable that he should continue as an ordinary member.—But I think it best to leave this matter of presidency all to you and your council.[8] I seem to have arranged it badly, now you may try to succeed better.

Ferenczi kind as he always is, has spent these days with me. He seems full of good ideas now and will be glad to meet you at Vienna.

Please tell your dear wife that all shall be done that is best for her, but I am not able to make a definite promise about the hour before I know whom I will meet in the first days of October. It is a hard arrangement every time.

We will shake hands in a few days. My best love to your wife and yourself.

Freud

1. "I feel the urge to face the world again, / To bear life's happiness, to stand its pain." Translated in Jones (1955a, p. 95; 1955b, p. 108). In Goethe's *Faust*, pt. 1, lines 464–465, the verse actually reads: "Ich fühle Mut, mich in die Welt zu wagen, / Der Erde Weh,

der Erde Glück zu tragen." The meaning shifts only slightly in Freud's version, as *Leid* and *Weh* are both synonyms for "pain"; but the opening words are actually "I feel the courage." Here also the Jones version interprets *Erde,* or "earth," as "life."

2. See letter 91, where Jones speaks of Freud's eldest daughter, Mathilde, and his "other child," psychoanalysis.

3. Crossed out in the original.

4. Jung (1911–12). See *Jahrbuch,* 4 (1912): 174; Hincklw (1916, pp. 77–78); *C.W.* 5:133–134.

5. Jung is challenging Freud's explanation of paranoia in the Schreber analysis (Freud, 1911c, pp. 72–73) as a withdrawal of libido from the exterior world. Jung posits that the psychotic has no sense of reality and thus withdraws all general interest from the external world, not just libido.

6. In the Schreber analysis, Freud put forward *paraphrenia* as a substitute for Bleuler's term *schizophrenia.* Strachey's note on Freud's use of this term is helpful; see Freud (1911c, p. 76, n. 1).

7. Crossed out in the original.

8. A significant moment politically and historically: here Freud in effect passes on decisions regarding the presidency of the International Psychoanalytic Association to the secret committee.

96

28 October 1912
Vienna, IX. Berggasse 19

My dear Jones,

Your wife shows, as I expected her to be, a precious creature of the highest value. She feels very well indeed, nay much better than is compatible with our treatment. The first half of her daily dose of Morphia—or nearly so—has been cut down with very small suffering. To be sure the second half will cost dearer. She is gentle [kind] enough to let me read your letters and I am enjoying the exactness of your descriptions, the vivacity of your impressions, and the high tone of your intercourse with your wife.

There are some news here for your interest. Stekel has separated, I have resigned the editorship of the *Zentralblatt* and am preparing a new journal, worked by Ferenczi or by Abraham [the *Zeitschrift*]. I hope you will retire your name from the head of Stekel's periodical and reserve your productions for our next creation. I am so very glad for the loss; we left each other in a friendly way, but Hell knows what his dark designs are.

I am in excellent spirits and envy you for all your sight-se[e]ing but especially for what expects you at Rome.

Yours truly
Freud

97

30 October 1912
Pension White
2 Piazza Cavalleggieri
Florence

Dear Prof. Freud,

This evening I sent you two photographs of statues in the Duomo in Florence, which may interest you. The one by Donatello is said to have directly influenced Michel Angelo in the creation of his Moses. Of the other I know nothing, but it seems to resemble the Moses still more. A valuable book is a prominent feature in both. There is in the Academy here a life-size cast of the Moses. Whether it is good or not I shall know better when I go to Rome, but I surmise that the face is not a good reproduction. Do you find anything curious about the *left*[1] hand? The first two fingers are in the beard, and the others tightly clasping the clothing in a rather unneccesary way.

Of foreign news I have not much. I wrote three times to Brill to put him on his guard against Jung, but have not heard lately from him. From other sources, Dr. Payne (Hitschmann's translator), August Hoch, and Frau Dr. Jung I hear that Jung has made quite a furore and is very happy over his success. I enclose a copy of an interview which perhaps Brill has also sent you.[2] From a letter of Bleuler's that I got last week I abstract the following curious passage: "Jungs neuer Libidobegriff ähnelt meiner Meinung nach wieder demjenigen, den Freud vor einer Anzahl von Jahren hatte und seitdem wieder etwas veränderte. Sie wissen, dass für mich die ganze Libido Theorie, wie sie jetzt ausgebildet worden ist, noch der Klarheit entbehrt. Ich habe deshalb kein Urteil, das ich weiter geben möchte. Dagegen halte ich die Arbeit von Jung, wenn sie auch sehr subjektiv ist, doch für eine sehr wichtige. Es ist merkwürdig, was für ein Material der Mann in den wenigen Jahren anhäufen konnte. Auch in Nebensachen sind eine Menge geistreicher und gewiss zum grossen Teil auch guter Ideen darin. Aber wie gesagt, für jetzt und vielleicht noch für die nächsten zehn Jahre wird niemand kompetent sein, ein definitives Urteil über die grosse Arbeit abzugeben".[3]

I have just read your paper in Ht. 4 of *Imago*. The series grow, if possible, even more interesting as they progress. I wonder what Frazer will say about them. He is a splendid fellow, but it would be surprising if he had the courage to bow to an outside influence in a field that he has made his own. I give only one or two little comments: (S. 312) "[. . .] Widerspruch [. . .], dass man dem Herrscher eine so grosse Gewalt über die Vorgänge der Natur zuschreibt und sich doch für verpflichtet hält, ihn mit ganz besonderer Sorgfalt gegen ihm drohende Gefahren zu beschützen, als ob seine eigene Macht, die so vieles kann, nicht auch dies vermöchte."[4] Unless I mistake, it reads in the New Testament that one of the mockeries to Christ on the cross was "[Him][5] others he could save, himself he cannot save".[6] Your remarks on conscience are extremely interesting,[7] and make me think that we need from you sometime a clinical paper on the relation of "Angst" to Zwangsneurose and the part it plays there. By the way, in B. Shaw's "Fanny's First Play", the passage occurs "We are all sinners, *what else is religion?*"[8] The chapter on the vampire in my *Alptraum* Schrift contains much interesting *material* on the relation between the living and dead,[9] though I think I overlooked the explanation of the *Rache* [revenge] idea of the dead. Kleinpaul's book on this subject I do not know, and must get sometime.[10]

By the way, you promised me once to give me a criticism of my *Alptraum* work, but it is not likely you will have found time to read it again. As for my "salt",[11] I can say that the second part will be much better than the first, which is mainly introductory. By this time, or very soon, you will have received from London a copy of my "Papers on $\psi\alpha$". I hope you will not find the preface too lyric; it contains one sentence specially written to please you, which I am sure you will find.[12] I hesitated before venturing to dedicate the book to you, because I should have preferred something far more worthy. I did so, however, on the ground that it was my first book, so that the dedication really refers to all my future life-work as well. I trust that this book will be the beginning of a series that will go on improving in value until the end.

And now, what about Italy, a subject, which you see I have postponed as long as possible. The reason is quite plain. I have been, and still am, quite overwhelmed by the richness and depth of new impressions, and fear that any attempt to commit them to paper might risk a certain crystallising of them in a stage when they should still be fluid. You will perhaps perceive my feelings better if I try to describe some of what Italy means to me, or rather the extraordinary many sidedness of its attraction for me. From childhood up Italy has always been holy ground to me, through the close associations of our best poets, Milton, Wordsworth, Shelley, Keats, Byron, the Brownings, Swinburne and Ruskin. They sing of Italy as of heaven, with a love they give to no other country on earth, and I have always pictured it as a fairy dreamland:

> "Woman country, wooed not wed;
> Loved all the more by earth's male-lands,
> Laid to their hearts instead."[13]

Italy, where music, painting, and modern poetry had their origin, and where still the finest examples of painting and architecture are to be seen. Italy, with such a fascinating history, of rival courts and conflicts in the middle ages, and later struggles for freedom and unity. And behind all this, the grand figure of Ancient Rome towering like a Colossus.

In whatever direction I look there are interests to be experienced and things to learn. Take my latest interest, Napoleon. Here was his first magic campaign (I have been on four of his battle-fields here), from Italy he sprang, in Italy are most members of his family buried, and at every step one comes across his traces, ruins restored at his orders, pictures stolen, monasteries replaced by public gardens, and so on. Even on my first evening, in Venice, I came across a complete set of the *Revue Napolienne* in the library of a learned society, something I had never been able to find elsewhere.[14]

I am trying to learn Italian, in itself a task to such a bad linguist, and also to form some impressions of the types of modern Italians, their characteristics and differences. I am studying closely the history of the various styles and schools of architecture and painting, to repair some of the deficiencies of my early education, and this alone is an enormous undertaking. But the subject-matter, the religious symbolisms and different modes of expressing the main human themes, is, as you know, of the greatest fascination to a psycho-analyst, and I have come across the most interesting imaginable things.

Italy surpasses even my expectations in sheer beauty, and I am throughout entranced. The effort to assimilate so many new impressions, to take note of the numerous trains of thought aroused in all directions, is almost physically exhausting, and must serve as excuse for my not being able to give you at present any connected impressions. But I know that I am benefiting and developing very greatly; it is an event in my life.

The reports from my wife sound satisfactory, sometimes suspiciously too much so, as if she were masking her resistances. But she says she is making real progress with the analysis, understands the principles better, and is feeling pretty well. She is full of gratitude for the kindness you show her, and is anxious to know from me if you say that she is progressing satisfactorily. I am also of course anxious to hear some words from you. Even if you cannot say much at present, a little will mean much to me.

For all reasons, therefore, I shall look forward eagerly to a letter from you.

Yours very affectionately
Jones.

1. Doubly underlined in the original.
2. See Jung (1912).
3. "In my opinion Jung's new concept of libido resembles the one Freud had a number of years ago, which he has modified somewhat since then. As you know, in my opinion, this whole libido theory, as developed now, still lacks clarity. I therefore have no judgment that I would like to pass on. On the other hand, I consider Jung's work, subjective though it is, to be very important. It is remarkable how much material the man has

been able to amass in a few years. Even in matters of secondary importance there are many clever and certainly to a large extent also good ideas. But, as I say, for now and perhaps even for the next ten years no one will be competent to give a definite judgment about the work as a whole."

4. The passage is from Freud (1912–13, p. 48), *G.W.*, 9:62 (*Imago*, 1 [1912]: 312). Strachey's version is "[Yet another] contradiction, [and one not so easily resolved, is to be found in the fact] that the ruler is believed to exercise great authority over the forces of Nature, but that he has to be most carefully protected against the threat of danger—as though his own power, which can do so much, cannot do this."

5. Crossed out in the original.

6. Matthew 27:42.

7. Freud (1912–13, pp. 67–70).

8. Line spoken by Mrs. Gilbey in act 3; see *Fanny's First Play: An Easy Play for a Little Theatre*, in *Bernard Shaw: Complete Plays with Prefaces*, vol. 6 (New York: Dodd, Mead, 1962), p. 152. The play was first performed in London in 1911.

9. Chap. 4 of Jones (1912j); see Jones (1931b, pp. 98–130).

10. Rudolf Kleinpaul, *Die Lebendingen und die Toten in Volksglauben, Religion und Sage* (Leipzig, 1898), is mentioned in Freud (1912–13, p. 58).

11. Jones (1912h).

12. Jones, *Papers*, 1st ed. 1913, was dedicated to Freud; on p. xii Jones refers to Freud as the "Darwin of the mind."

13. From Robert Browning, "By the Fireside," verse 6; see Browning (1895, p. 185). Jones omits the first two lines of the verse: "I follow wherever I am led, / Knowing so well the leader's hand." The next line begins: "Oh woman—country!"—meaning Italy.

14. Likely the *Revue Napoléonienne*, edited by A. Lumbroso (Turin, 1901–1904), with supplements nos. 1–6 (Rome, 1906–1914).

98

6 November 1912
Pension White
2 Piazza dei Cavalleggieri
Firenze

Dear Professor Freud,

I was glad and happy to hear from you that my wife is going on well. I have not heard from her for a week, but hope her progress is being maintained. Are you satisfied also with the analysis itself?

The news about Stekel is certainly highly interesting, but I should much like to hear more details for I do not yet understand the situation. The *Zentralblatt* was officially made its organ by the Congress. What happens now? Does it continue to exist, and, if so, which will be the official organ of the Verein? It is of course a satisfaction to be separate from Stekel, who has done us much harm, and whose tactlessness always kept us on tenterhooks as to what would happen next. He has a paper of mine on Angst,[1] which I suppose he must still publish if the *Zentralblatt* goes on. What is to be the name of the new journal? I hear from Sachs that Ferenczi is to edit it, which is excellent news. Is it to contain Referate? If so, it will be an extremely difficult business to organise them, but if it is done it should be done well.[2]

My patient here is a great bore, but sometimes he brings interesting things. He has the delusion that, owing to interference by his parents in early years, his foot, and especially the great toe, is permanently bent and deformed. It will never be straight again. Here is his picture of it.

He dreamed lately that he was in school adjusting different *paper* flags to each other, to make them meet and fit properly. He drew them as follows, which I interpret as nates [buttocks].

I do not think enough attention has been called to the fact that some of the feeling that goes to make the snake-symbolism is of anal origin, derived both from faeces and from worms. I have been sure of this in several patients. It explains why disgust at reptiles and insects is often more prominent than fear. In a picture in Florence of St. Philip exorcising the dragon, many of the spectators are holding their noses, evidently from disgust at the smell emitted by the dragon.

I see many interesting things in the art in Italy from the ψα point of view. Take an instance, the crucifixion regarded as a re-birth phantasy (naturally only one of its aspects). The sorrow and swooning of the Madonna, supported by two friends, is sometimes depicted as direct *Geburtswehen* [labour pains], and in one picture here she stands up evidently in the last month of pregnancy. In the *deposizione* pictures she holds the body of Christ on her lap just like a new-born babe; in the later ones he merely reclines against her. I have many photographs of such things, which I should like to show you in January if you have the time.

With regard to the magic power of touch, that you dealt with in *Imago*,[3] there are many interesting things in Christian history, for instance the woman who was healed by touching merely Christ's garment, the various miracles of healing by the saints, the fact that religious gifts and power to perform various ceremonies can only be transmitted from one bishop to another by what we call in English "the laying on of hands". I saw this morning a picture where cripples were healed even by touching the *shadow* of St. Peter as he walked by. I suppose you wished to avoid Christian topics in your articles, but if you would like photographs of any particular idea depicted in religious art, I could surely find them for you.

I have two short articles [finished][4] ready in my head for *Imago*, one a finished cameo type, the other more general and tentative. I will write them in Vienna and submit them to you.[5]

Hoping to hear soon from you again I am

Yours always affectionately
Jones.

1. Jones (1913b).
2. The new journal, *Internationale Zeitschrift für Psychoanalyse* edited by Rank, Ferenczi, and Jones, appeared in early 1913.
3. Freud (1912–13).
4. Crossed out in the original.
5. At least one of these was published; see Jones (1913f).

99

8 November 1912
Vienna, IX. Berggasse 19

My dear Jones,

I have been so deeply emotioned by your last letter announcing the dedication of your book that I resolved to wait for its material appearance to react by a letter of pride and friendship. But it has not yet come yet, instead of the book came your second letter, and as you have a right to be answered promptly on actual events I see I must do it and owing to want of time and intensity of stress restrain myself to the most urgent points instead of entering into all the diversity of your interesting conversation.

As for your wife: We had an excellent time and have brought the morphia to half the dose (3 + 3). I know that she is showing up before me so that I see her better than you would find her, yet I am sure I was not mistaken. Analysis progressing satisfactorily, I could draw the outlines of her very interesting lifestory and make her understand some of the turning-points in it. Übertragung complete and no difficulty to make her agree to its meaning, all the great qualities of her character and the liberty of her thinking helping me therein. The only dark point in my opinion, that she had not resistance enough and felt too comfortably. When the day before yesterday (⅞th night) an attack of pain made its appearance and sad thoughts came up with it, I meant it to be a progress and entering into a new and more fruitful phase of the treatment. Yet there is a drawback to the glory.

The attack was not expected by me, I cannot deny the possibility of its being a true organic one only exaggerated by neurosis and in such a case I would have to adapt my promise to the facts of the case. She told me that Lina[1] had found the urine bloody and I eagerly wanted to see it and have it examined. Unhappily—or must it be taken rather as a good sign?— it had been spilt before I asked for it and I have to keep diagnosis and prognosis in suspension till the next opportunity appears. She was very disappointed today as she evidently had adjusted her expectation to an *aut-aut* [either-or], not wilful to comply with the necessities of life and to thank for a relief, where a restitution is impossible. But I hope confidently to persuade her, that the task of the treatment is not touched by the element of some organic necessity for pains and as much can be gained in one case as in the other, which would come out more splendid.

As for Stekel I hope I have given you the story of his separation in my first letter (writing so much about the same matter I am no more sure). He has since announced his desertion from the Vienna Verein without other provocation. All of us are happy and so Seif and Maeder seem too. I am afraid he will find life very hard and suffer the fate of the inflated frog. The *Zentralblatt* will continue to appear under his direction, whether it will bear the title of official organ of the Internationale ΨA Verein is indifferent to me, but it seems doubtful. Maeder wrote today he will bring the matter before the Verein next week. In any case it will cease to be so with the next Congress. Bergmann seems to intend to give it up at the end of this third year, but you cannot rely on Stekels informations, he is full of lies, when he is in a straight.

I think you are justified in retiring your Angstpaper from the *Zentralblatt*, the role of the periodical and all personal relations having changed meantimes and I expressed myself to the same end against Seif, who put the same question. I have taken back a paper of mine, and so Sachs and Rank have done. We want the papers for our own organ and a quick collapse of the *Zentralblatt* cannot be but most appreciable to all of us. So I beg you will do the same. I have got the translation of your Angstvortrag from Ferenczi and sent it back to him since.

As for the new periodical. It is not yet brought out, in the phase of incubation, but it must be born. I am in relation with Reiss at Berlin and with Deuticke, no definite answer so far. Heller is craving for it, when other plans miscarry.[2] Ferenczi or Abraham or both will be the redacteurs according as Berlin or Vienna may come out as the *Geburtsort* [birthplace]. Perhaps the combination: Ferenczi-Rank will prove the best. They all behave very nicely in this affair, Seif too and I hope Maeder will not be behind.

Rank has now passed his examination, he is Doctor up to the ceremony.[3] I expect him with Sachs and Heller for a supper at my house just now, 9h.

Your two photographs have shaken much of the confidence in my interpretation, I am studying a copy in the Academy here.—They are coming. Good bye and enjoy Italy as thoroughly as you can. Be not afraid of Rome, you have to pass not postpone through the hardships of first acquaintance, do it.

Yours in love
Freud

1. Loe Kann's maid.
2. The *Zeitschrift* was first published by Hugo Heller (Leipzig).
3. For Rank's Ph.D. thesis, see Rank (1911a).

100

13 November 1912
Pension White
2 Piazza dei Cavalleggieri
Firenze

Dear Professor Freud,

I got your formal circular this morning,[1] but had of course already sent my resignation to Stekel, and it is superfluous to say that I will throw myself into the new enterprise with a zest that needs no stimulation. I also told Stekel that my Angst paper could not now be published in the *Zentralblatt*.[2] It can go to the new journal if you will accept it. It is satisfactory to think that the new journal will throughout represent our views with much less admixture of error than the *Zentralblatt*. What are you going to call it? *Monatsschrist für* ψα. Can you help me out of the following embarrassment in this connection? I am just going to collect subscriptions for the American Association, most of which money is for the distribution of the *Zentralblatt*. As it is, I don't know what to do about it. Can't the new journal be made the official organ of the Verein before the meeting in next September? Perhaps you will discuss this with Jung, who arrives home next week (so I hear from his wife). This would be just the occasion to show the use and function of a Council of the Verein, if we had an effective one.

I want to thank you very deeply for the details about my wife, which were just the kind I wanted to know. It was a great relief to read them. [You][3] I agree that the gain of treatment would be almost as great even if an organic element remained, but what you called her "fanatical" character makes her wish for "all or nothing"; she finds it difficult to reconcile herself to half-results in anything. You gave me good news about the progress, but today I get a letter from her, written two days after yours, which gives the reverse side of the medal—no doubt provoked by her attack and other things. She complains bitterly about you, that you do not trust her, do not believe her statements, and twist everything until she is quite confused in her mind. I suppose the resistance had previously been concealed in a woman's deceptive way, by her pretending to agree to conclusions that in her heart she did not accept. At all events, you probably have as much resistance to deal with now as will more than make up for its previous absence. She is beginning to feel the treatment as an attack on her personality; she repeats that if she were allowed to conduct it herself, at her own speed, etc., she would be good and do her best (evidently anal-complex) but to be "forced, bullied, and teased" against her will makes her feel broken and hopeless with no heart to give herself to the treatment. And her chief cry is your want of faith in her, your doubt, disbelief and suspicion of what she says. (Personally I have always found her invariably trustworthy in her statements, though of course she deceives herself as we all do).

I did not find it easy to answer her letter, though I have done so today. I should, of course, keep out of the analysis, and leave everything to be settled between you two, but she turns to me very pityfully for comfort and help, so I had to make some *general* remarks, about the ambivalence of affects, etc..

She tells me that the urine was thrown away without her knowledge, but that Lina was sure it contained some blood. I have many times found blood and pus in it, though with less frequency and in smaller quantities in the past three years.

I hope that this week will be better than the last, and shall very anxiously look forward to your next letter (perhaps you will find time to write on Sunday?).

I shall probably leave here on the 26th, having lost the little Angst I had of Rome. Half of my Italian holiday at least will be spent in Rome, which I think is a fair proportion for a first *"Rundreise"* [round trip]. In what way did the photographs shake your confidence? The other statues could only have served for the theme and form, not for the inspiration that constructed the Moses.

I have been referring to the Bible a little recently, and came across many interesting things. Do you remember the following curious bringing-together of teeth and child-birth? It is in Solomon's Song, spoken by the man.

"Thy teeth are as a flock of sheep, which go up from the washing, whereof everyone beareth twins, and there is not one barren among them."[4]

I heard from Rank today. He must feel very relieved to get his well-won freedom.

Yours always affectionately
Jones.

1. Freud's circular letter of 11 November 1912, announcing his resignation of the directorship of the *Zentralblatt* (Archives of the British Psycho-Analytical Society, London).
2. Jones (1913b).
3. Crossed out in the original.
4. Song of Solomon 4:2.

101

14 November 1912
Vienna, IX. Berggasse 19

My dear Jones,

Again a short letter—I am too deep in business for more—as you will be anxious about your wife. You need not, I am pretty sure it was a purely hysterical attack, it came to a sudden end after she had written that last famous letter to you and she is splendid and charming since. That letter contained I am sure all that she ought to have told me what she dares not yet to do. She will behave better a next time and we will get more profit from an attack than we could on the first trial. I got the urine only yesterday, it contained nothing but the slightest trace of albumen (pus).—

You will have heard all that is going on from other sides. The new organ is born now, christened:

Internationale Zeitschrift für ärztliche ΨA

Ferenczi and Rank the working editors, Heller the publisher. We want your name and something from your pen (the Angstpaper) for Nr. 1 to appear the 15th of January.

Nearly all the collaborators of the *Zentralblatt* came over to us. The Zürich men [have][1] could not yet understand why I cast away the *Zentralblatt* instead of the person but they are now informed by my letters of the way, Bergmann took Stekels party and I have no doubt they will join too.

Your book not yet arrived. I could do nothing worth mentioning since my letter, all has gone into this mean business.

Yours heartily
Freud

1. Crossed out in the original.

102

14 November 1912
Pension White
2 Piazza dei Cavalleggieri
Firenze

Dear Professor Freud,

I got today a letter from my wife of a very different tone, full of sunniness and life, and you may imagine how much it cheered me. The other was evidently an outburst of feeling, which perhaps will do her good; she ought to pour it on to you as well, but no doubt she will do so. I find her wonderful good *("brav")*[1] in the endeavours she makes, do you also?

I have news. This morning came a long letter from Putnam, from which I make the following abstracts.: "What Dr. Jung said, in effect, was that while he still held to the importance of the $\psi\alpha$ technique, he had come to rate the infantile fixations as of far less importance than formerly as an etiological factor, and, indeed, as I understood him, as an almost negligible factor in most cases—though I hardly think he could really maintain this if he were pushed for a positive opinion. At any rate, the point on which he seems now inclined to lay emphasis is the difficulty of meeting new problems and environmental conditions which arise at the time of the actual onset of the neurosis. It seems to me that we all recognise the importance of these influences, but I cannot as yet feel anything is won through minimising the significance of the other factor. . . . . . The point which seemed to me to indicate most strongly the idea of a breaking-off on his part was that he said he thought the significance of the whole conception of infantile sexual tendencies in Freud's sense had been over-rated; that all persons, sick or well, have about the same phantasies, and that he did not any longer believe that the sensations which a nursing child *(Säugling)* has could be classified as sexual in any sense, but only as related to nutritional necessities. This does not coincide with my present beliefs, but of course it will go far (although possibly in an unfortunate way) towards gaining adherents for the $\psi\alpha$ method. Perhaps, after all, that is the important thing, because whatever ideas are really the most sound will in the end (far away) come most strongly to the front."[2]

So you see that Putnam's intelligence and intellectual honesty, with his experience of the neuroses rather than the psychoses, and possibly aided by my warning letters, seem to be bringing him in the right track. Meyer's hostility to Jung, which is even greater than that to you, may help us, and if so Hoch will follow him. Burrow I am sure I can control, in spite of his devotion to Jung, and no doubt Brill is safe. So altogether I am hopeful that we shall prevent any serious inroads being made on the theory in America. Pierce Clark is made of weaker stuff.[3] In a letter to Putnam, which the latter encloses, he says: "I think ψα in the light in which Jung formulates it is bound to have a very wide and rapid extension from now on. It certainly removes some of the disagreeable barriers heretofore impeding the progress of the movement." The aesthetic criterion is certainly a strange one for a scientific man to rely on, though unfortunately not novel.

Yours always affectionately
Jones.

1. German for "good," "honest," or "worthy."
2. Excerpt from Putnam's letter is not to be found in Hale (1971a).
3. L. Pierce Clark (1870–1933), M.D. 1892 New York University Medical College, specialist in neurology and psychiatry.

103

15 November 1912
Vienna, IX. Berggasse 19

My dear Jones,

I must answer your letter at once, it made me so glad. *Die Rechnung stimmt.*[1] It shows as I expected it would. The attack of your wife is in fact the reverse of her tender affection, you remember she recovered completely after that letter of "abreaction". As regards the contents of that [those] complaints the most striking and least justified point is my not believing her and mistrusting her statements, as it can only find a rationalisation in my doubt expressed to her whether her pains are from the kidney or from the soul. But you may take into account, what she confessed yesterday, that she was a big liar when a child. I am sure the profit of that first attack would have been greater if I had shut out the organic explanation with as much decision as I will be able to do at the next. So it is allright and her resistance can be directed to serve the treatment, what is the great aim of our technics.

Many thanks for your permissions in the Stekel affair. I am sorry to say that he is lying in a desperate shameless way about the causes of the dissension, writing to Zürich, that I wanted the comité to stifle the liberty of his and their opinions and not mentioning the Tausk-question and his assertion the *Zentralblatt* was his own property at all.[2] But the leading Zürich men behave nicely (Maeder, Riklin) and it is very likely that the "*Internationale Zeitschrift für* ΨA" can be proclaimed the official organ even before it appears. If you will use your influence to this direction with them it may help a good deal. Riklin proposes a council of the Zentrale and the foremen at Munich for the complete acquittal of the matter. I think it should be done.

I envy you for se[e]ing Rome so soon and so early in life. Bring my deepest devotion to Moses and write me about him.

A trifle of business more which I cannot arrange with her and postponed in the crowd of other interests without forgetting it. I gathered from some indications that you have paid the rooms at Cavendish Sq. for Rank and my person, which indeed you had to do, but it is my fault and I am responsible for it. You may imagine it will be only a slight addition to the costs of my daughter's illness. So I want to know the amount.

I am cheerfully yours
Freud

1. "It all adds up." The German here is in Gothic script.
2. The disputes between Tausk and Stekel centered around the fact that Freud wanted Tausk to supervise the book reviewing for the *Zentralblatt*, which resulted in attempts by Stekel to keep Tausk's reviews out of the journal. See Jones (1955a, p. 136; 1955b, p. 154), and H. Abraham and E. Freud (1965, p. 125).

104

[telegram]

16 November 1912
Vienna

Proud[1] of your dedication[2]

Freud

1. "Prond" in the original; probably an operator's error.
2. Regarding Jones, *Papers*, 1st ed. (1913).

105

17 November 1912
Pension White
2 Pizza dei Cavalleggieri
Firenze

Dear Professor Freud,

Many, many thanks for the kind thought that prompted yesterday's telegram. You must have guessed how much pleasure it would give me; I felt greatly honoured indeed.

Also let me thank you for your thoughtfulness in sending me the letter that arrived this morning. From your hard work you spare time to soothe my anxiousness. I have seen many such attacks, and they are terrible to live with. From no patient have I received a more vivid impression of the terrific forces pent up in the unconscious than I have from my wife. It is as though a horrible abyss of unalterably black despair and hopelessness suddenly yawned in front of one, and one stands paralysed and helpless before an awful *Abgrund* [abyss]. Then it closes again, and a smiling surface appears to help one forget what one would willingly forget. I trust that you will get a look inside this volcano of emotion, and teach her how to make a better use of its fires.

I like very much the title of the new *Zeitschrift*, also of course the word *Internationale*, and am delighted that you have chosen Ferenczi and Rank. About Heller I am less enthusiastic, for some recent Korrektur-Bogen from the next number of *Imago* produced a distressing impression on me; I hope he will be made to change his printer. Still we have the advantage of a pliable publisher. I am very pleased that my Angst article is to appear in January,[1] and have sent Ferenczi some corrections in accord with his suggestions. I felt that this difficult subject, which I know I have treated imperfectly, could not be left longer, for there are already false impressions being spread about it. I am happy that so many supporters have come in already for the *Zeitschrift*; the Zurich men are bound to follow. I need not tell you how completely my services are at your disposal; I only wish I were in Vienna to help a little with the organisation of the work.

I sent Rank an amusing letter that came from Stekel. It illustrates his simplicity of mind; to him no complexities exist in life.[2] Rank will probably show it to you.

Much of my interest at present is on the subject of Christian mythology (apostles, saints and martyrs). It is almost as rich and complex as the Greek mythology, especially as all the figures are derived from previous personages and invested with their attributes. The distortion in the presentation of the themes is sometimes extraordinarily involved, and there is much work for the future.

Yours affectionately
Jones.

1. Jones (1913b).
2. Possibly Stekel to Jones, 12 October 1912, quoted in Paskauskas (1985, p. 337).

106

[telegram]

21 November 1912
Vienna

Domenica 24 Mattina Saluti

Freud[1]

1. "Sunday, 24 Morning Greetings, Freud" Freud was calling Jones's attention to a meeting Jung had called for 24 November to deal with the issue of Stekel and the *Zentralblatt*, and the founding of the *Zeitschrift*. It was attended by Freud and Abraham as well as several other colleagues, including Jones, who had been given the wrong date (25 November) by Jung. See Jones (1955a, p. 145; 1955b, p. 164), and Paskauskas (1988a, pp. 13, 21–22). Freud's fainting attack, which occurred shortly after this meeting, is discussed in note 3 to letter 108.

107

5 December 1912
Pension Dawes-Rose
12 Via Gregoriana, Roma

Dear Professor Freud,

I trust you have completely recovered from your Munich adventure. It must have meant a considerable expenditure in affect, for you had a difficult task to perform.

I am quite a convert to your feeling about Immortal Rome, "this divine city", as you called it. It surpasses even my expectations, and is arousing in me all kinds of extensive thoughts about mankind. As yet, of course, my impressions are still disordered, and will need some time to get clearer.

I try to picture what are your favourite spots here. One I am sure is the Pincian, the Villa Medici, and especially perhaps the terrace below Santa Trinita, above the Spanish Square. Another would be, I wonder if you know it, in a charming old-world restaurant on the Aventine, the Castello dei Cesari by name.

My first pilgrimage the day after my arrival was to convey your greetings to Moses, and I think he unbent a little from his haughtiness. What a statue! Far finer than the copies would lead me to think. I have a strong fancy that the face bears resemblance to Michel Angelo himself, especially in the mouth and the breadth of cheek-bones. He must have felt like that at times over his "stone", when he watched the people worshipping the golden calf of a pope. What an opportunity, to be asked to supply a tombstone for one's enemy—one that falls to the lot of few. It would be rather entertaining to have to compose a suitable epitaph for Kraepelin, Ziehen, and a few others, wouldn't it.

I am hoping, after all that it may be possible to see most of the chief things here in my six weeks. At least one can see the main types, and leave the variations to future occasions. It is gloriously fine, and warm, here at present.

I enclose a curious letter from Jung which has been sent on from Wales; it was written before Munich. He gives now a new excuse for his behaviour, namely that he has had to neglect his duty towards himself (and therefore does towards his friends). There are some words I cannot read. Would you ask my wife, who has an aptitude for deciphering handwriting, to write them in, and to return the letter to me. (That is better than wasting your time). I have also had an excellently long account from Brill, which gave me many suggestions. The whole thing is fitting together like a Chinese puzzle, and it would not be hard to make a pretty full ψα of Jung's attitude. Did Brill tell you that he maintains *you* have a severe neurosis? Another beautiful projection. Jung [makes much of][1] lays great stress on making ψα more pleasant and acceptable, therefore more "workable" (Shades of William James; what an honest man to have his name invoked for the support of such an idea!). He will save ψα in your despite[2] (do you know this idiom?). A word of August Hoch's gives the key to the whole situation. He speaks of Jung's views as being a "deliverance". Jung is going to save the world, another Christ[3] (with certainly Anti-semitism combined). The world is trembling with fear because the *böse Vater* [evil father] has found out their secret thoughts, their incest wishes and infantile sexuality. But the gallant St. George steps forward and reassures the world. "Continue with your infantile sexuality, which is not sexual, and your incest wishes, which are not incestuous. Such things are quite innocent and harmless, and now that I have saved you you need no longer fear." Now I understand better the remark he made to me three years ago in Zurich, that you would destroy your own work by going to extremes but that he would save it (or words to that effect).

From which I would make the prognosis: that he will be willing to suffer at the father's hands, like Christ, and will be *scheinbar unterw[ü]rfig* [seemingly subservient]; that as ψα is now his, being saved by him, he will not desert it or break with the movement.

What do you think of all this phantasy?

I have not had a letter from my wife since the one you brought to Munich, so perhaps she is working up towards another attack, as you expected.

Have you any news of the arrangement with Bergmann? I suppose you have enough work to do in arranging for the *Zeitschrift*. By the way, I wonder if the following corollary of the Stekel affair has occurred to you, namely that it will necessitate your publishing a third series of the *kleine Schriften*,[4] for you cannot leave those beautiful articles buried in a decaying journal. Together with the *Jahrbuch* ones they would make a big enough book. I hear you groan at the prospect, for you must find the preparing of new editions trying when you want to do something else.

Yours affectionately
Jones.

This was written last night. This morning I got Jung's circular letter about Bergmann,[5] which looks satisfactory.

1. Crossed out in the original.
2. That is, Jung will save psychoanalysis in spite of Freud.
3. This is developed further in Jones (1913g); see Jones (1951, 2:263–264).
4. See *Sammlung*, vol. 3 1913.
5. See McGuire (1974, pp. 527–529).

108

8 December 1912
Vienna, IX. Berggasse 19

My dear Jones,

I have many motives to write you the first letter this Sunday: your wife, your present, your letter, the news about $\psi\alpha$, wish I could write you in German but German words in latin characters are impossible to me and I am sure you would not decipher my gothic ones.

Now for the first topic. Your wife is splendid, no trace of "kidney" pains since the first attack and no doubt, this first one was fabricated out of the monthly, which betrayed itself by definite somatic signs (no blood) at the right term and unaccompanied by pains these last days. Morphia is down to 2 + 2 (one third). I am even more contented that is she [she is] not so much "maniacal" while in good temper and even stoops to pieces of patient uninteresting analytical work. So the chance is good and the change sure to be a lasting one, though to be sure there is some doubt how far the chief point, the sexual anesthesia can be gained.

As for the book you sent me from Rome about Rome, it arrived at St. Nicholas day together with the gorgeous flower-arrangement from your wife. She is showering flowers on me and I promised to return them to her as soon as her pains were setting in. But we could not wait for them and she got some flowers from my side yesterday. I am very glad you are getting so deep an impression at Rome and quite sure you did feel pretty unhappy in the first days as every honest man is bound to do. Your enjoyments will come out clearer every day. I know the restaurant on the Aventine pretty well, but there are more curious spots on the Coelius near by. My favourite spots are on the Palatine but it is better not to begin about this miraculous city. As for the beauty of the women it needs some days to detect it.

I thank you for your very just remarks about Jung. The words you could not read are *"fordern"* and *"scil."* (*scilicet:* Schreber),[1] so I can send you the letter directly.[2] In fact he behaves like a perfect fool, he seems to be Christ himself, and in the particular things he says there is always something of the *"Lausbub"* [rascal]. But he acted nicely at Munich, got a severe chastisement there, and as he considers ΨA as his own and his position against me is far from indifference I expect as you do that he will stay with us. The letters I get from him are remarkable, changing from tenderness to overbearing insolence. He wants treatment, unfortunately by my last attack I have lost [a] portion of my authority.[3] There must be some psychic element in this attack which besides was largely fundamented on fatigue, bad sleep and smoking, for I cannot forget that 6 and 4 years ago I have suffered from very similar though not so intense symptoms in the *same* room of the Parkhotel; in every case I had to leave the table.[4] I saw Munich first when I visited Fliess during his illness (you remember: "Propyläeen" in the *Traumdeutung*)[5] and this town seems to have acquired a strong connection with my relation to this man. There is some piece of unruly homosexual feeling at the root of the matter. When Jung in his last letter again hinted at my "neurosis" I could find no better expeditive than proposing that every analyst should attend to his own neurosis more than to the others's. After all I think we have to be kind and patient with Jung and as old Oliver said, keep our powder dry.[6] I restricted myself to the remark against Jung, that I do not think *he* has been a sufferer by my neurosis. In any case, there is a suspicious amount of dishonesty, want of simplicity and frankness I mean in his constitution (Stekel would continue thus: . . . .) The business of the *Internationale Zeitschrift* seems all right. We will get rid of Bergmann by payment of 652 Mk, half of which sum I am ready to pay, leaving the other half to the funds and releasing members of all contributions. Nr. 1 is getting printed, Rank working with his regular reliability and steadiness and Ferenczi ready for his action while he seems to be ill just now. I trust all these affairs will be righted before long. The political situation in Austria seems stormy and we are prepared to meet a very bad time.

I trust you are enjoying Rome as ever man did and know you will owe more to this first meeting than you can realise now.

I will write you again as soon as your wife's condition or circumstances may ask for it.

Good bye

yours sincerely
Freud

1. Referring to Freud (1911c).

2. The sentence in question from Jung to Jones, 20 November 1912 (Sigmund Freud Copyrights Ltd., Wivenhoe) reads: "Ich dachte, Sie hätten nach der ψα Grundregel 'Nie erwarten, sondern fordern' sich das bei mir geholt, was Sie zu haben wünschen scil. das 'laut gesagt' was Sie denken." *Fordern* and *scil.* are circled. In English the sentence reads: "I thought that in accordance with the basic rule of ψα 'never expect but demand' you had obtained from me what you wanted to have *scilicet* [to wit] 'said aloud' what you think."

3. A reference to Freud's second fainting attack in the presence of Jung, which occurred during their meeting of 24 November 1912 in Munich; the first was in 1909, prior to their departure for America from Bremen. Jung's response to Jones's description of the second attack (Jones, 1953a, p. 317; 1953b, p. 348) was: "Your biographical material is very interesting although it would have been advisable to consult me for certain facts. For instance, you got the story of Freud's fainting attack quite wrong. It also was by no means the first one; he had such an attack before in 1909 previous to our departure for America in Bremen, and very much under the same psychological circumstances." Jung to Jones, 19 December 1953 (Sigmund Freud Copyrights Ltd., Wivenhoe). In volume 2 of his biography of Freud, Jones briefly mentions the second attack and elaborates on the story of the first attack; see Jones (1955a, pp. 55, 146; 1955b, pp. 61, 165). For a critique of Jones's version of these fainting episodes, see Schur (1972, pp. 264–272).

4. The phrase beginning after the semicolon is dropped from the quotation of this passage in Jones (1953a, p. 317; 1953b, p. 348).

5. The passage in parentheses is also left out of the quotation in Jones (1953a, p. 317; 1953b, p. 348). Freud refers here to the famous dream of "Irma's injection" (Freud, 1900a, pp. 106–121), and the discussion of Propyläeen is contained in the chapter titled "The Work of Condensation" (pp. 294–295).

6. "Put your trust in God, but mind you keep your powder dry" (Oliver Cromwell addressing his troops).

109

23 December 1912
Pension Rose
12 Via Gregoriana, Roma

Dear Professor Freud,

I was very happy to get your letter, a fortnight ago, and have given you a few days' intermission of peace before writing again. The good news about my wife was splendid, and was confirmed by a letter I got from her yesterday (the first for a month, one being lost en route). You know how deeply my feelings are involved, and that nothing touches me so nearly as news about her welfare. She seems to have bourne the illness first of the dog, then of the maid, with excellent spirit, though no doubt with great activity.

I hope that in the holidays you may find time to look into the book about Rome, and that it will give you some pleasure. Hutton seems to have taken on some of the mantel of Walter Pater, though with a greater sadness. I was struck by one sentence in particular, where, making light of the cheap modern ideas about "progress" he exclaims: "As if there is any progress in the human soul other than re-birth from what has always existed!"[1]

Rome, as you may expect, continually deepens her charm and her hold on one's heart. How full and rich she is, and with what lavishness she gives. I am coming to feel her peculiar secret of eternal youth and creation through destruction. She has never hoarded treasures of the past, because of her proud confidence in her ability to produce ever new ones—no doubt less wonderful in some ages than in others, but always with the stamp of her peculiar spirit. You are right, I should have placed in Palatine first as a place to dream dreams; that is the most inspiring part of Rome. I enclose two photographs of Moses. Will you tell me if they are what you wanted. You will notice that the projecting pediment interferes inevitably with the view of the tables. I examined the latter carefully, and one cannot say that there are finger-prints on them.

This week I got a letter from Putnam, from which I quote the following: "I have read carefully Jung's "Wandlungen", but cannot find any adequate justification for his differences from Freud's views. . . . J.'s visit to New York has perhaps made it harder for the more thorough-going doctrine to prevail. However, I do not really think that this will remain true to any great extent, for any man who has the scientific ability and willingness to study will soon convince himself where the truth lies. . . . Jung and Stekel, with all their virtues, incline too much to swelled head, and that they do so shows that $\psi\alpha$ has not done its full work for them."[2] I have no further news of Jung myself, except a rather significant negative piece. I wrote to him two long conciliatory letters after Munich, in reply to his. In one of them, sent nearly a month ago, I offered him a short article for the *Jahrbuch*, as in Munich he had asked me for another. I have heard not a line from him.

I was interested in your remarks about your attack in Munich, especially so as I had suspected a homosexual element, this being the reason of my remark in saying goodbye at the station that you would find it difficult to give up your feeling for Jung (meaning that perhaps there was some transference to him of older affects in you).

I send you all the "Compliments of the Season", and the heartiest wishes for a Happy New Year, which I hope will be as productive in every sense as the last one, though let us say less stormy.

Yours always
Jones.

1. The book sent to Freud was likely Edward Hutton, *Rome* (New York: Macmillan, 1909). The quoted passage is not, however, to be found in this book.
2. Putnam's letter is not to be found in Hale (1971a).

110

[postcard]

24 December 1912
[Rome]

P.S.

Would there be any objection to my publishing my Angst article later in the *Journal of Abnormal Psychology?*[1] There will probably be a debate on the subject in May in America.

E.J.

1. Jones (1913b).

111

26 December 1912
Vienna, IX. Berggasse 19

My dear Jones,

I cannot see why you should not be permitted to publish your Angst-paper in the *Journal of Abnormal Psychology,* nor do I think the other two would object to it.

As for your wife I am glad to give you full information before you come here; as you might easily find her in another comdition [condition] that [than] she has been in all these weeks. I am under the impression that you do not realise completely how well she is. There has been no other "kidney"-attack since the first which was finished in so dramatic a way by that long letter to you. The counterpart of that constellation showed itself, when she was not able to write you for nearly three weeks and at last managed to get the forced letter lost, to be sure by some unconscious error in ad[d]ress or so. We have got down to nearly $\frac{1}{4}$ of the morphia with no sacrifice at all, yet have to be prepared for some noise when the last dose is taken away. I would not accelerate the rate, for the later the more attached will she be, and I have no interest in spoiling the week you will spend with her and with us. There is not the least doubt that a big lot of good has been done to her, the greater part of it destined to be of lasting character. How far we can go in the way of recovery I cannot prophesy, it depends on her resistance against normal sexual relations, where I expect the citadel of resistance. Perhaps she will be eager to begin intercourse and feel highly disappointed when anaesthesia has not subsided, as will be the case. The rest of morphia is reserved for her consolation. The monthly made some demonstration at due time but didn't think it expedient to make its appearance.

I dare say she is enjoying her Vienna sojourn very much. I could not help leading her over to my family for some moments Tuesday evening. As for the complexes I had even cause to be satisfied by the ψα work many a time although she prefers skimming over to diving into the depths, but she seems to perform much with herself, being an independent nature and often needing no more than a hint.

The next theme is not so pleasant as the first was. As regards Jung he seems all out of his wits, he is behaving quite crazy. After some tender letters he wrote me one of the utter insolence,[1] showing that his experience at Munich has left no trace with him. He worked under a very slight provocation. I directed his attention to a certain Verschreiben in his letter, when he protested that "nicht einmal Adler und seine Spiessgesellen zählen mich zu den *I*hrigen".[2] It was after this that he broke loose furiously, proclaiming that he was not neurotic at all, having passed through a ψα treatment (with the Molzer? I suppose, you may imagine what the treatment was),[3] that I was the neurotic, I had spoiled Adler and Stekel etc.. It is the same mechanism and the identical reactions as in Adlers case. To be sure Jung is at least an *"Aiglon"*.[4] Having got over the feeling of shame this letter provoked in me I would have sent you the letter for perusal but it is now with Ferenczi. I composed a very mild answer but I did not send it. He could take so meek a reaction as a sign of cowardice and feel his importance the more. On the other hand I cannot suffer myself to be provoked as much as the letter deserves, our common interests standing in the way of an official separation. So I have fallen back on the expedient of not answering at all and am inclined to break off any private relations with him letting him rave and criticise against me as he does openly and privately at Zürich.[5]

I think you too should make no more steps to his conciliation, it is to no effect.

Abraham has been here for three days. I am not informed how far Rank succeeded in gaining him to join our band. The position taken by Putnam is highly enjoyable, you should keep him warm, so that America may be kept on the side of Libido.

You are right in supposing that I had transferred to Jung homosex. feelings from another part but I am glad to find that I have no difficulty in removing them for free circulation. We will have some good talk on this matter.

Thanks for your two photographs of Moses. They show as much as may reasonably be expected. If I may trouble you for something more—it is more than indiscrete—let me say I want a reproduction—even by drawing—of the remarkable [under][6] lower contour of the tables, running thus in a note of mine

Now as for Rome no letter could come up to the immensity of the subject.

Take my best wishes for the year to come. Who knows what it may bring to you and to your

truthful friend
Freud

1. Jung to Freud, 18 December 1912 (McGuire, 1974, pp. 534–535).
2. "Not even Adler and his cronies count me as one of yours." The pertinent sequence of exchanges between Freud and Jung can be found in McGuire (1974, p. 533). On 9 December 1912 Freud referred "to the rumours current here that you are 'swinging over' to him [Adler]." Jung objected by saying that "the Viennese prophets are wrong about a 'swing over' to Adler." And he added: "Even Adler's cronies do not regard me as one of yours" (*Ihrigen* = yours; *ihrigen* = theirs). In the German edition of McGuire (1974, p. 592) the latter quotation of Jung's reads: "Selbst Adlers Spiessgesellen wollen mich nicht als einen der Ihrigen erkennen," which differs somewhat from the version Freud presents to Jones, although the meaning in both cases is the same.
3. Maria (Mary) Moltzer (1874–1944), professional nurse, trained with Jung, co-translator of Jung (1913b); later practiced analytical psychology. In an interview Jolande Jacobi reported: "I heard from others, about the time before he [Jung] met Toni Wolff, that he had had a love affair there in the Burghölzli with a girl—what was her name? Moltzer." Jung Oral History Archive, Box 3, p. 110, Countway Library of Medicine, Boston.
4. French for "eagle," which in German is *Adler*.
5. Freud does in fact answer on 3 January 1913 (McGuire, 1974, p. 539), proposing that "we abandon our personal relations entirely."
6. Crossed out in the original.

112

29 December 1912
Pension Rose
12 Via Gregoriana, Roma

Dear Professor Freud,

Thank you very much for your full report about my wife. The favourable news was very gratifying to hear. The letter-writing question is very curious. She must certainly have mis-addressed the lost letter, for I made every enquiry for it here. That must mean a strong affect to produce such an error, for she is usually *pedantically* exact over addresses. Her subsequent reaction was also striking, showing a combination of displaced remorse and indifference that contrasts with the way she would usually react to such an occasion. On hearing it was lost she unnecessarily telegraphed "Deeply distressed. Am writing again". She took three more days to write, registered the letter this time carefully, and in it expressed first her distress and remorse that I should have suffered ("What did you think of me?", etc.) and her indifference because the lost letter was very short and contained only dry news (two respects in which it differs from her usual letters). Now I have not heard again, although there was every reason why I should have in the past week. Can it be *only* the over-compensation for the long complaining letter she sent? Having your reassuring letters has of course prevented me from being anxious, but it would be a great convenience if she could overcome this inhibition. I think the resistance is partly against the treatment, because she said twice that this inhibition is the chief thing she would like to see cured: "it would be the best test of the treatment". You will have found no doubt that she attaches the highest value to the letters she writes; they are the most precious objects, to be parted with only with the greatest difficulty.

I feel that the next month is an unfavourable occasion to test the anaesthesia matter, partly because it is unlikely to be overcome in such a short stay (don't you find that it often takes much time and practice?) and partly because it would not be wise to expose her to the risks of pregnancy when she has so much in front of her (house-settling in London), while she finds all kinds of precautionary measures very distasteful. On these grounds I do not think I will make any overtures myself, but will be guided entirely by her feelings; I anticipate she will desire intercourse. If you have any further suggestions to add to this attitude I should be glad to have them (otherwise I will not give you the trouble of answering this letter, as I shall be seeing you next week).

I can well believe that she is able to make some self-analysis also, for she is very quick and intelligent and likes to know the truth—if it is not too unpleasant. In some ways she has a very keen feeling for reality, and is no lover of the ordinary illusions.

As for Jung, I am fast losing the respect I once had for him. You may be sure I will write him no more conciliatory letters while he treats my best efforts with indifference. I have not heard from him, but I got yesterday a most annoying letter from Seif whose absurd attitude is evidently dominated by his own private emotions together with influence on Jung's part. I will say nothing more of it till I see you, which I am very eager to do for all reasons. I don't at all see how we are to retain private relations with a man like Jung, who has been behaving most dishonestly in the things he says about you, as well no doubt as in other ways.

I have had another good letter from Brill. He seems to be showing up well in the circumstances, and I shall be glad to see him when I reach New

York. Putnam will also probably come there to meet me, so we can all have a good talk and present a united front. Putnam is annoyed over the philosophy question and cannot understand our "blindness", but I don't think his reply to Ferenczi will enlighten our darkness very much.

I found Sperber's essay in *Imago* very interesting,[1] but I fear that expert philologists could find many weak points in the logic of his arguments. He must be a man rather like Pfister.

Your little paper in the Proceedings of the Psychical Research Society was very clearly but, and literally translated.[2] I "forgot" to thank you for it the last time I wrote, just as I forgot your reprint in Vienna and nearly did the one in Munich. It gave me some trouble to analyse this, but it is now all clear. I need not repeat it to you because it only concerns a reproach that I have no right whatever to make, and which could emanate only from a very inflated unconscious. What a good thing it is that a *Zensur* exists, otherwise the conceit of some of us would make us intolerable to our neighbours.

I will attend to Mr. Moses, but I am afraid it will mean only a drawing. This week I hope to finish my paper on God-men, in which there is the opportunity of saying some sweet things, quite indirectly, about Jung; it is very enjoyable.[3] Although I have only another week in this wonderful city I shall not be sorry to get back to life and work once more; too much holiday is demoralising to such a lazy person as myself, and there is much to do in the coming year.

Yours always
Jones.

1. Hans Sperber, "Über den Einfluss sexueller Momente auf Entstehung und Entwicklung der Sprache," *Imago*, 1 (1912): 405–454.
2. Freud (1912g) was first written in English, but seemingly revised in England.
3. Jones (1913g).

113

1 January 1913
Vienna, IX. Berggasse 19

My dear Jones,

Only a few lines to give you a happy new year and some notes about your wife before we meet again.

She continues allright. Lina had a second attack of pains, she nursing her. The nicest case of "Übertragung" I ever saw. The girl takes upon her the kidney stones, which have left the mistress. Morphia down to ⅓. Her difficulty in letter writing is perhaps related to resistance against treatment but more distinctly to that secret aversion against you (the reversal of that glorious medal of love), which treatment will bring to light as soon as you and morphia will have departed.

As for Jung I am resolved to give up private relations with him. His friendship is not worth the ink, and we know by his own words that he always feels hampered by kind relations to men. I want him to go his way and have no need of his companionship myself. But as long as it shows possible I want to keep up the common interests of Verein and journals.

The same politics let us follow with every other man in the circle, ready to receive them after they are sent back by him as will invariably be the case.

I hope to give the lecture on "Animism" while you are here, 15th of January.[1]

Eder has arrived, he wanted to get analyzed by me for three weeks. As I couldn't find the time I handed him over to Tausk. Maybe he is offended but I am overcharged and tired of sacrifices. He shows some reserve about the now ardent matter of Jung's.

Ferenczi seems to improve in health.

Eager to have a long talk with you in the course of this month,

yours sincerely
Freud

My best love to that grand city!
P. S. Better not to forget!! I touched the matter of sexual relations yesterday and expressed to her my opinion not to press the affair. She seemed to agree with me.

1. Part 3 of Freud (1912–13) was presented before the Vienna Psychoanalytic Society on 15 January 1913; see *Minutes*, 4 (1912–1918): 147–149.

114

30 January 1913
London

Dear Professor Freud,

I don't know if you are [in] the mood to welcome any letter of mine, and you know already all I can say, but I must write to thank you for being so good to Loe at such a critical time. I am more thankful than I can say that she has you to fall back on, and that she has decided to go on with the analysis.

The relation with Lina was an old affair (which explains the identification behind her hysterical attacks), and in Italy I was fully determined to break it off. But some devil of desire made me yield to the temptation. I do not feel very guilty about my relation to her, nor did it indicate any abnormality in myself, but something tells me from within that the continuation of it in Wien was dictated by a repressed spirit of hostility against my dear wife,[x1] and you can imagine what heart-rending remorse that is causing me. That is the secret of an otherwise inexplicable inconsiderateness and *Leichtfertigkeit* [thoughtlessness]. That I should have done something to wound her, whom I love so passionately and for whom I would do anything to save her, is almost beyond my endurance to bear.

I would beg you to do everything possible for her, did I not know that your goodness of heart would do that from itself.

Jones.

1. The notation "[x] as punishment for her anaesthesia" is written out on the left-hand side of the page.

115

10 February 1913
Vienna, IX. Berggasse 19

My dear Jones,

I could not answer your kind letter, as I had to make some observations on the woman you are so fond of and who is getting dearer to me daily. You will not have expected that my affection or my esteem will have suffered much by our last experience, the more as it turned out to be after your explications, or you know not enough of me. To be sure I cannot envy you or give you right. I did not understand your acting in this way in the most inappropriate moment, when she was rapidly approaching recovery, but even then I was sure you could not have done something simply mean and treacherous. I waited for explanation and clung to neurosis in the meantime.

Now I think I can understand it, as you exposed the matter and I may perhaps even know something more about it.

Now for her. It was a tremendous shock at first. She got the old pains, not very strong though, raised the morphia at once to 4 from 1.2 and renounced treatment. You remember, she identified ΨA, your and my own person and so she had to break off with all three of them. Yet there was a thread left undamaged between her and myself. I got hold of it and persuaded her to go on not for your sake but in her own interest. She agreed and it came to be right. We are down to 0.8 at this time, no pains at all, resistance much diminished, her behaviour almost normal in the affair which was even more intricate than you can surmise, and she lends an attentive ear to everything ψα can tell her. We did turn the accident to the side of profit, now analysis being no more an act of complaisance [agai][1] for you, it is meeting with a much better reception. At the end I will have to thank you for the dangerous experiment.

There is a change in her position against you as well as against me. She considers herself free as long as treatment lasts, and according to the rules of ΨA she has the right to do so. I am glad she took up this position herself or I would have been obliged to force her into it. I could not go on in the role of your friend as long as I am to act as her physician. I had to forget everything except this last. Now it has come natural to me, you know I am not working for you but for her delivery to the exclusion of every other aim. But I dare say you were prepared to this, when you urged her to undertake the treatment. At the end I firmly expect she will come back to you by her free will not by my influence. I will be glad at the result. She will go far in recovery, yet the chief point, the sexual abnormity, is still doubtful and only by this reason I am unable to predict if your relations will come to be the normal ones and more so than before.

So you stick to your work, do not break communication with her and hold on firmly, till I can step off the scene. There is more going on now than I can make you know, but it is unavoidable.[2]

As for less private news, none of our friends is to know what is going on between ourselves, of course. Work is smooth, Rank is doing excellent work. Jung and the Swiss people seem to feel disconcerted, our firm attitude was not without good effect apparently. The *Jahrbuch* promises the second half of your paper in the next volume,[3] it is not nice against you, although I have no intention to heat you against Jung. There is no intercourse between us except in business matters. I have a happy time in this respect and feel no longing at all for more from his side.

Congress will be fixed to 7/8 Sept. at Munich, a good date.[4]

Kraus at Berlin gave a very decided lecture in favour of ΨA, but I am sorry he may not take care to have it announced as publicly as we might wish.[5]

Now make your heart easy for work, be careful with those bad women and write as soon as you can

to your devoted
Freud

1. Crossed out in the original.
2. Freud is likely holding back information regarding Loe's recent involvement with another man by the name of Herbert ("Davy") Jones, an independently wealthy American and would-be poet (letters from Loe Kann to Freud, Freud Museum, London). The two would marry in the summer of 1914; see letter 192.
3. Jones (1912–13).

4. Fourth International Psychoanalytic Congress.

5. Friedrich Kraus (1858–1936), professor of medicine, Berlin University; corresponded with Freud regarding Abraham's attempts, which never materialized, to secure a professorship at the university. Freud heard about Kraus's lecture from Sabina Spielrein; see Carotenuto (1982, p. 119), and H. Abraham and E. Freud (1965, p. 134).

116
[postcard]

[17 February 1913][1]
321 Jarvis St., Toronto

Freud,

[Here are] more references: (1) Goldenweiser. Totemism. an Analytical Study. *Journ. of Amer. Folklore.* 1910. Vol. XXIII. Pp. 179–293. (2) Leuba. The Varieties, Classification and Origin of Magic. *American Anthropologist*, 1912. Vol. XIV. Pp. 350–367. Both are reviewed in the *Psychological Bulletin* for Dec. 1912. (Pp. 454, 475).[2]

Yours
Jones.

1. The card was postmarked on this date.

2. Edward Sapir, review of A. A. Goldenweiser, "Totemism, an Analytical Study," *Journal of American Folklore*, 23 (1910): 179–293, *Psychological Bulletin*, 9 (1912): 454–461; Alexander F. Chamberlain, review of James H. Leuba, "The Varieties, Classification, and Origin of Magic," *American Anthropologist*, 14 (1912): 350–367, *Psychological Bulletin*, 9 (1912): 475–476.

117

5 March 1913
Vienna, IX. Berggasse 19

My dear Jones,

Only a few lines written in haste, to let you know first that Lina is allright, secondly that Jung has sailed to America another time today or may be yesterday.

You will have got my letter about your wife. Not much to be added now. Condition highly promising, Morphia down to 1 grain a day or less (1/10 of the original dose). Pains beginning every now and then, not the old ones (never mentioned since Linas counterfeit!) but fresh ones wandering from spot to spot according to where opportunity invites them, bowing to analysis, showing plainly the classical mechanism and not very strong, prove very useful for her instruction. Maybe the hot fight is still to come.

Your letter was excellent. I judge you are right in every point of your analysis and confess you have done a lot of good to my task of benefitting your wife. Let me hope it will prove the same to you after a while.

The very best piece of news I [ha][1] ever heard from you was that description of the meeting where you were "lionised". You cannot easily imagine how much I rejoice in the satisfaction of your taking up an influential and highly respected position in London and nowhere else! But you must promise formally never to spoil it when you have got it at last, *by no private motive.*

Work is going on smoothly here by help of the good boys. Ferenczi is by no means healthy looking but I expect him to recover at Corfu.

I am waiting for your good news

yours truly
Freud

1. Crossed out in the original.

118

18 March 1913
321 Jarvis St., Toronto

Dear Professor Freud,

I am very grateful for your welcome letters. They were both singularly well-timed. The first one you wrote not on hearing from me from London, but after waiting a week or two to observe my wife, which was just what I wanted. And yet you didn't wait to get my regular Toronto address, but sent it earlier so that I should be relieved at my most anxious time. This was very considerate of you. Now this morning comes the second one, with the good news about Lina, at a moment when I was anxiously awaiting my wife's first letter, which cannot arrive for another week.

About my own attitude in the matter I have no more to say, for I fully described it in my last letter and you evidently quite understand it.

As to my wife I was very gratified to hear your good reports, though I shall not be happy so long as any morphia remains; perhaps it will have disappeared by the time you get this. I am in complete agreement with your attitude of making her interests not only the first consideration, but the only one, to the exclusion of all else. I know that your code would allow you to do nothing else, and I would wish it in any case. I must take my chance of her coming back to me spontaneously, and I believe she will do so (though this may be merely narcissism on my part).

I had heard that Jung was in America this week, but only for three days; it is simply a financial expedition, but he took advantage of it to act vigorously on Hoch. He and I are fighting for the possession of Hoch's soul, which is a poor thing at the best, and I think I shall win, for I have an excellent friend (MacCurdy) as assistant to him and he gives him daily pin-pricks. Jung has not written to me since Munich, and I do not intend to re-open unless he does. His behaviour about my article in the *Jahrbuch* was indefensible and petty in the extreme.[1] It is annoying, for I had planned a series of articles suited to the *Jahrbuch* (on the inter-relations of the Triebcomponente), which now I shall not be able to publish.

Thank you further for the reprints, which came two days ago. It was very enjoyable renewing my acquaintance with the animism article,[2] though as usual I wished it were twice as long. I enclose a quotation from Browning that shows an appreciation of infantile narcissism.[3] I am glad you pointed out how strongly the facts contradict the idea of primary Minderwertigkeit.[4] By the way, it is interesting that I should have traced the "God-complex" (Allmacht) to narcissism rather than simply to the Oedipus-complex.[5] I must write the article I planned in Italy on the connections between the Allmacht der Gedanken in der Zwangsneurose, narcissism, and the anal-complex (especially flatus).[6]

There is not very much news from this side. There seems to be a *"panikartige Flucht"* [panic-like withdrawal] proceeding in Boston, due to police action against the *Journal of Abnormal Psychology*. I will tell you more about it when I hear the details. Putnam is rather nervous, as you might expect. My relations with Brill are very satisfactory, but I do not want to interfere with his field of action in New York, so I have refused three invitations from there, to address the Neurological Society, the Academy of Medicine, and to give a private course of twenty lectures. To be sure, I had other good reasons. Next month I go to Baltimore to take part in the opening of the Phipps Psychiatric Clinic (Adolf Meyer).[7] Then I leave Toronto for Washington on May the 4th, and probably sail on the 10th. Of my work here I will write next week, when I expect to send you an article for *Imago*.[8]

Are you going to take an Easter holiday this year? Your mentioning Ferenczi and Corfu makes me think you are going there. I have not yet written to Ferenczi or Sachs, but must do so. Rank is a regular correspondent, and keeps me in touch. Are you going on with the *Imago* series of articles, or have you finished the first stage before proceeding to the second (Religion)?

Many thanks for your kind thoughts about England, which echo one of my deepest wishes. I do not deceive myself that it will be an up-hill fight, for, as you know, I have a black mark to my name in London,[9] but I hope that by sitting tight and behaving well something will be accomplished in time, if not for myself, at least for ψα.

Yours always affectionately
Jones.

1. Jones (1912–13).
2. Part 3 of Freud (1912–13).
3. Jones (1916c) quotes a passage from Browning's poem "A Soul's Tragedy," which relates to the theme of the egocentricity of the unconscious and the mental attitude of the child; see Jones, *Papers*, 2nd ed. 1918, p. 633.
4. Freud (1912–13, p. 90 n. 2).
5. Jones (1951, 2:246–247).
6. Jones (1914a).
7. Jones (1913d).
8. Jones (1913f).
9. There were actually two professionally embarrassing incidents, in which Jones was accused of improper behavior with children. For his own version of these events, see Jones (1959, pp. 145–151).

119

26 March 1913
321 Jarvis St., Toronto

Dear Professor Freud,

I heard yesterday from my wife, for the first time since London. It was a very friendly, kind letter, loving at times, though she evaded the main question of her attitude to me. Perhaps the most striking feature was the complete absence of complaints and pessimism in regard to the treatment, which she acknowledges is doing her a great deal of good and freeing her from one symptom after the other. She evidently feels much better altogether, and on a more objective basis than before.

As to the accompanying article, when I spoke about it to Sachs (who has the copy of the photograph referred to in it) he was a little afraid it might be too shocking for *Imago*, but advised me to write it and submit it for your opinion. I am in hopes that he could translate it into acceptable German that would not offend too much, and am very eager to hear what you think of it. It seems to me to be an important theme, which must be discussed some time.[1]

The poem I enclose, which has never been published, is by a celebrated Spanish lyricist; it was given to me by a patient. Have you ever seen it? It is remarkable that the writer should feel impelled to cast such thoughts into an artistic form—a violent ambivalency, like the theme of my article.

I have three papers yet to write in the next five weeks, to be read at

Baltimore and Washington.[2] So between these and the accompanying article, which has cost a great deal of work, poor Napoleon has not come much
farther. Still I have read much, making notes, since being in Canada, and
know now exactly how much more I have to read; I cannot begin to write
about him for several months. In searching for an explanation of his ficti-
tious origin of his name ("Lion of the Desert") I came across by accident
the following curious fact. He won a battle in Syria (1799) at a town called
"Naplons" (derived from Neapolis), which is where the holy *Joseph* (father
of Jesus) is supposed to be *buried*. This was before he invented the etymology of his name, and indeed he almost certainly knew of it at an earlier
age, 18, when he made a list of the towns of Syria. I wonder if there is any
connection?

I see you take the opportunity in the *Zeitschrift* of putting Maeder right
on the topic of dreams,[3] but from his article in the *Jahrbuch* he doesn't
seem to be able to sowe very simple ideas.[4] What do the Zürich people
think of Fortmüller's entertaining exposition in the *Zentralblatt?*[5] Who
helped him to compose it? I find Rosenstein's Kritik rather diffuse,[6] with
too much repetition; it would have gained strength by being more concise.

I leave Toronto on May 3rd or 4th, and hope to have the pleasure of
hearing from you again before then. I reach Vienna on about the 27th.
What sort of reception do you think I shall get?

Yours always affectionately
Jones.

1. Jones (1914a).
2. Jones (1913d, 1913i, 1913–14).
3. Freud (1913a).
4. A. E. Maeder, "Zur Frage der teleologischen Traumfunktion: Eine Bemerkung zur
Abwehr," *Jahrbuch*, 5 (1913): 453–454.
5. The reference is to Carl Furtmüller, "Wandlungen in der Freud'schen Schule,"
Zentralblatt, 3 (1913): 189–201.
6. Gaston Rosenstein, review of Karl Furtmüller, "Psychoanalyse und Ethik," *Zentralblatt*, 3 (1913): 162–164.

120

Imago

9 April 1913
Vienna

My dear Jones,

I received your mnscrpt on aural conception today.[1] No doubt it will be
highly interesting and good lecture[2] for our readers. I want to peruse it
myself before handing it over to Sachs.

Now for your wife. She is down to 2 injections of 0.003 each, let us say
half a centigr. daily, practically nothing, less than $\frac{1}{120}$ part of the original
dosis. Yet the most interesting part of the treatment is to come before you
arrive her[e]. It was no easy task for me, standing in this way between two
of my friends—my only consolation is, that both of them will be happier
and healthier hereafter, but if they will be together does not depend upon
my will, as you know the laws of treatment. Yet like you I hope; in any
case I expect a nice and favourable issue of the case between you.

I am not at all contented, that you bear Jungs insolence without remon-
strating. If you do so I can assist you as editor and assure to your contributions the same treatment which others find. So you must not give up your
intention of holding your grip on the *Jahrbuch*.[3]

The poem you enclose is amusing enough, happily I know enough
Spanish to understand it. Heine once expressed the same idea but in a far
more poetical, sublimated, shape.

I am now slowly composing the 4th of the *Übereinstimmungen* [ac-
cords], that on Totemism, which is to close the series.[4] It is the most daring
enterprise I ever ventured. On Religion, Society, Ethics and *quibusdam
aliis*.[5] Gold help me!

I am looking for impatiently for that end of May, perhaps the work will
be finished when you come here to strengthen the old ties.

Yours most cordially
Freud

1. Jones (1914a).
2. Freud seems to be following the German here: *eine gute Lektüre* = something good
to read.
3. Jones (1914c).
4. Part 4 of Freud (1912–13).
5. "Certain other topics."

121

25 April 1913
321 Jarvis St., Toronto

Dear Professor Freud,
Your much looked-for letter came this morning, and although it could
not tell me all the many details I wanted to know it was welcome news
to hear that my wife was still going on so well, and has lowered the
morphia to such a minimal quantity where it can serve little else than
symbolically (I shall be anxious, however, until it all goes, for it is such
an easy thing to raise the dose on any occasion when life is hard to face).

You said little about her attitude to me, but between the lines I gather than [that] you are hopeful of a reconciliation, which is what I most want. I have become a little freer and better analysed in my attitude and feeling towards her. I owe her and shall give her manfully a very hearty and honest apology, but I have much less tendency to abase myself before her as previously, and after all no woman can altogether demand this in her heart from a man, in spite of friend Adler.[1]

I wrote an account of the Baltimore meeting[2] to Rank and to my wife, which no doubt will reach you, so I need say no more about this. I am deeply impressed by the success of Jung's campaign, for he appeals to formidable prejudices. It is, in my opinion, the most critical period that ψα will ever have to go through, and we formed the Committee not at all too early; there is much to discuss about devising proper measures to meet his propagandism, and I am eagerly looking forward to coming to Vienna, if for this reason alone. I have written a strong protest to Jung at his treatment of me, but in such a form that it need not lead to an open rupture, which I am not eager to provoke. If I had written earlier it would have been much angrier. Still I do not expect he will answer me, for his recent conduct in America makes me think more than [ever][3] that he does not react like a normal man, and that he is mentally deranged to a serious extent; he produced quite a paranoic impression on some of the ψα psychiatrists in Ward's Island.

I am impatient to read your promised Totemism essay, which I hear is to appear in the June number of *Imago*. We shall see if Maeder will still think you have *"kein Verständnis"* [no sympathy] for religious problems! I enjoyed enormously Ferenczi's last essay in the *Zeitschrift*,[4] his last work, I think. He has much of your intellectual courage for facing the last conclusions of a train of thought, such a rare gift with scientific men who are generally obsessed by the fear of "going too far".

There may be four new local Vereine to add to the International next autumn, but it is quality not quantity that we need more of. I do so want to talk with you about many things, that it is difficult to wait—though now it is less than four weeks. My thoughts are occupied by the ψα movement, and I am full of schemes. It is a grand time to be alive in, better than any other period in history because it is fuller of fighting on which much depends.

Yours enthusiastically
Jones.

1. The reference is to Adler's concept of the masculine protest with respect to women; see Alfred Adler, "Der psychische Hermaphroditismus im Leben und in der Neurose," *Fortschritte der Medizin*, 28 (1910): 486–493 ("Masculine Protest and a Critique of Freud," in Heinz L. Ansbacher and Rowena R. Ansbacher, *Co-Operation between the*

Sexes: Writings on Women, Love and Marriage, Sexuality and Its Disorders [New York: Anchor Book, 1978], pp. 32–48).

2. Jones had attended the opening ceremony of the Phipps Psychiatric Clinic, Baltimore, 18 April 1913.

3. Appears to have been inserted at a later reading.

4. Ferenczi (1913).

122

3 June 1913
Pension Gerö, Lipót-körnút 10
Budapest V

Dear Professor Freud,

Well, I am beginning to settle down to the novel life here. Ferenczi seems satisfied that my German is enough for the analysis, and I hope he will also be satisfied with the analytic work itself. It is of course too soon to say much about that yet, but he has already shown me a good many new things about myself. He is very tactful and kind, and I am sure we shall get some good work done, which I both want and need.

The idea of losing my wife has not yet penetrated fully into my mind. I have difficulty in "taking it in". She has meant so much to me for years, and I held so fast unconsciously on to the *Bedingungslosigkeit* [unconditionality] of her love, that it will cost me pretty severe depression before getting over the blow of seeing her love given to another, especially her *full* love, which I had always dreamed of winning. It is of course worse for me that I know how much I have contributed to the present situation. I only hope that happiness for her will be at least a gain amidst the surrounding loss. For me the next year or two will be especially critical, in many ways, so that the help of this analysis comes just at the right time.

One thing that helps to reconcile me to the parting is that her hostility to me seems to have increased, or at all events to have become more manifest. I tried my best in Vienna, in spite of the suddenness of the blow, to behave in the best possible way to her and also to [Herbert] Jones, but it was quite without success. Every remark I would make she would at once snap up, contradict, or else twist into another meaning, and then dispute with the greatest affect. On Saturday night I made a final attempt to get into good relations with her, and succeeded a little by means of agreeing with her (which was not at all true) that our friction that week was due to my "irritability". Later we had a good talk, and she brought this to the subject of our child. She insisted with the greatest vehemence (and quite unnecessarily, for I did not contradict her) that she had never resented its loss, or reproached me in any way about it, and that she had quite convinced you of this. I have never told her of the tooth scene where she repeated in French the Paris operation, and I don't suppose she remembers this, as it was under chloroform that it happened.

You will not expect me to write a very cheerful letter, for you may imagine how grey things are seeming to me just now. I will try of course to pick up the threads again, but my *Lebenslust* [pleasure for life] is not over great.

I hope Rank is better. It is appallingly hot here; I trust it is not so bad in Vienna.

Yours always
Jones.

123

8 June 1913
Vienna, IX. Berggasse 19

My dear Jones,

I am glad you are trying to find some good points in the new situation and I'm sure they may be found. Ferenczi is strong and reliable and you may win him for life. You had a big share in my private thoughts all this year over, you know. I am indeed of opinion you have lost your wife more completely than you realise. She is a treasure of a woman, but of deep-going abnormality and I am not without misgivings about her physical health and her fate, when this business with Jones II comes to an unfavourable end, as might easily be. You see how a clever and perspicuous man can be deceived about his next ones. All the time she was revolting against you, and even now she cannot bring it out in a manner appropriate for analysis.

You will recover soon I am sure and find a compensation in the work awaiting for you and in the interest of your sincerely attached friends. As for her we will watch over her, if life does not meet her passionate wishes and you will keep up the friendship resulting from so long a partnership in life.

I could not help observing that there is some constraint between ourselves due to my role in her analysis, I felt the effect in your getting so tired on our Cobenzl trip,[1] when I grew fresher with the advancing hour. It will pass away I have no doubt when you see my part more clearly. I had to work against my own interest. Your house in London, had the treatment come to another result, would have become a regular *Absteiggquartier* [temporary accommodation] for me and so have fulfilled one of my earliest wish-fancies.

Rank is allright. I had to tremble at the idea of his getting disabled for a longer time as he is—in every department of the work—the indispensible helpmate and a most intelligent companion. If anyone of us is getting rich it will be his duty to provide for him in a satisfying way.

Now the heat will have cooled down with you as it did here. Get the story of Brill's patient told to you, who had to find Budapest the coolest town on the continent.

Yours sincerely
Freud

1. The Cobenzl was a hotel and restaurant overlooking Vienna. Jones's "Cobenzl tiredness" is brought up in the next several letters.

124

11 June 1913
Pension Gerö, Lipót-körút 10
Budapest V

Dear Professor Freud,

Thank you so very much for your kind and sympathetic letter; I echo every word of it. Like you, I feel very concerned about my wife's future, and still feel bound to her to the extent of watching over and caring for her, unless that is taken from me by Herbert Jones. I hope deeply that she will be happy, for she deserves it after so much suffering. Nothing has given me truer pleasure than the times when I have been able to make her feel happy, and it was (and is) a grief to me that these were not longer and more permanent. I shall certainly try in any event to maintain an affectionate friendship with her, and this at least should be possible. She wrote me a charming letter this week, the first real token of affection for months, and it made me so happy.

As for myself I am sure already that time will heal the wound in a healthy way, and am beginning to adapt myself to the altered situation, at least so far as consciousness is concerned. I doubt that with me work and friends (even such friends!) will fully compensate for the love I need, and feel at present inclined to marry again, perhaps in two or three years. Next time I must make a more normal choice, and shall know far better how to make a wife happy (knowledge brought by much suffering to two souls). For the immediate future, however, such thoughts must be postponed—they are day dreams—and I must apply myself to the urgent needs of the situation. There will be much to do, and I hope to have a good enough heart to do it. Then perhaps in time to come, who knows but that you may yet visit me in my house in London? That will be one stimulus the more for me to work hard.

I am satisfied that the analysis is going on well, and I hope Ferenczi is. I do not know, for he is rather reserved in the matter, and will no doubt tell you his opinion more frankly. He is exceedingly intelligent, as well as kind, and I greatly admire his technique of dealing with me.

You were of course right about an unconscious personal resistance in regard to yourself, and Ferenczi had in the first few days analysed the psychical side of my Cobenzl tiredness. As you no doubt suspect, my unconscious, with the logic peculiar to itself, had been blaming you for the loss first of my greatest friend (Trotter),[1] then of my wife, i.e. the man and woman who were dearest to me. With such a great loss it is little wonder that I mechanically sought for someone to blame, especially when I had so much self-blame that needed projecting. However there isn't any doubt but that this will be only a passing phenomenon, even in the unconscious, for consciously my attitude is quite the opposite, and has been all through. There is no question about appreciating your attitude, for the delicate correctness of this is sky-clear, and I am only sorry that you should have been placed in such a painful situation.

From outside I have no news, except that Payne and Pfister are negotiating about the matter of translation.[2] It is the best possible news to hear from you that Rank is again all right, and I cordially agree with all that you say concerning him.

I don't know when we are coming to Vienna, but I suppose this month sometime.

With kindest regards from

Yours always
Jones.

1. In *Free Associations* Jones states that "Wilfred Trotter was my best friend and— apart from Freud—the man who has mattered most in my life (Jones, 1959, p. 101). Trotter had great respect for Jones as a neurologist, but he cautioned Jones about being connected too closely with the Freudians. Two passages that are not quoted in *Free Associations* reveal Trotter's position: "You are, as I have told you fifty times, the most heavily armoured neurologist in the universe" (Trotter to Jones, undated, probably November 1907); and in a letter of 14 November 1908 Trotter wrote: "Try to keep yourself distinct *from other expositors*. There is nothing so unsatisfactory as trusting your fate to allies whose mental capacity is inferior—as that of your allies must always be to you . . . And remember you can't keep yourself clear of responsibility for other people—think of the future hanging on some of these child like Enthusiasts." (Letters to Jones from Wilfred Trotter, in the possession of his son, Dr. R. W. Trotter of Haslemere, Surrey.)
2. Regarding Pfister (1913).

125

17 June 1913
Pension Gerö, Lipót-körút 10
Budapest V

Dear Professor Freud,

Rank writes to me that you will arrange a meeting when Ferenczi and I come to Vienna. That will be next Saturday week, and we return on the Sunday night.

I am doing my best in the analysis and think it is going on satisfactorily. Ferenczi discovers in me very strong aggressive tendencies which I have reacted to by too much suppression and submissiveness, and which revenge themselves in various impulsive tendencies. It is to be hoped that in the future all this will be better balanced.

The Cobenzel fatigue was thus determined. On the evening before, my wife and I had walked up, and I had half-jokingly said that the private foot-way belonged to us—as a symbol of something between us that was left over from the wreckage. The next morning she got up at three, fetched Jones from his hotel, and took him up the same path—as if to show me that not the slightest bond was left between us. That evening I proposed to show you the path, but you preferred the road you already knew. That must unconsciously have struck my resentment at being a plaything in the hands of fate, at being allowed no independent decision or activity. What a trivial thing will affect one when it touches a sensitive spot!

The wounds are rapidly healing now, though, and I am coming to realise that this break is the best thing not only for Loe, but also for myself. It is doubtful if we could ever have made a satisfactory life of it, even apart from Jones' existence. We have both worked off our infantile sexuality at the expense of the other, and must now both face a more adult form of life. The future is at present dark for both of us, but wide open for possibilities of happiness or at least satisfactoriness. Now that I love her less, I can afford to feel more friendly and kindly towards her, and I will do all in my power to further her happiness.

I have just read your "Zwei Kinderlügen", which I had heard in the *Vorlesung* [university lecture], and am following with keenest interest the proof-sheets of the Totemism essay as they come in.[1] Frazer makes some intelligent remarks, doesn't he? I wonder how you can condense so much of the huge discussion so clearly and effectively. With the end of the last sheet the plot begins to thicken and the next batch is awaited with great eagerness. Ferenczi and I have many interesting discussions outside the analysis hours, and are especially occupied just now with the question of symbolism, origin and psychological significance. I have suggested to him to choose it as a subject for the Congress, and think he will do so. Rank and Sachs in their book[2] seem to me rather too exclusive on the phylo-genetic side—but perhaps there will be an opportunity for us all to discuss it next Sunday week. As subject for the congress I am thinking of "The attitude of the ψα physician to the questions of current conflicts and sub-limation",[3] where it will be easy to expose Jung's fallacies, and I should be glad of your opinion of this.

Jung's letter to me was quite typical.[4] Bleuler never kept my article back, and the *Jahrbuch* appeared four months after Jung's return. Then again his attitude of masked indifference to his "new theory".

With kindest regards

Yours affectionately
Jones.

1. Freud (1913g, 1912–13).
2. Rank and Sachs (1913).
3. Jones (1914b).
4. Jung's letter of 7 May 1913 appears in Paskauskas (1988a, pp. 20–21). Jung attempts to explain the delays in publishing Jones (1912–13).

126

20 June 1913
Vienna, IX. Berggasse 19

My dear Jones,

I am sure you will not yet have got so monotonous a letter as this. I am pleased with everything you wrote.

Your understanding of your marital constellation is excellent. I find your intention to speak about the subject you mention [upon][1] at the congress one which could not be chosen better. You are perfectly right about Jungs letter. Now I know of no more points of agreement.

Will you please tell Ferenczi that I donot expect him to send back the proofs of the *Totem*. I will thank both of you for any remark or criticism you will offer on the following Fahnen, as I am no more so confident in the matter as I was in the beginning. But it may be I cannot give room to far reaching modifications as the thing has to be finished.

Your wife is excellent. I do not think I will encourage her to go to Budapest next week; it might do good for the treatment but not for her, and I want her to have a quiet time. So you find me in your way this time for the last I trust.

You will have heard from Ferenczi that our proposals crossed while identical in content. I expect you both Saturday next week, to partake in our official meal.[2]

You see I have some difficulty in writing today, I am physically tired although in excellent spirits.

I am glad you learn to appreciate Ferenczi as he deserves to be.

With best love to you

sincerely
Freud

1. Crossed out in the original.
2. The dinner was held to celebrate the completion of Freud (1912–13); see Jones (1955a, p. 355; 1955b, p. 398).

127

25 June 1913
Pension Gerö, Lipót-körút 10
Budapest V

Dear Professor Freud,

Thank you very much for your kind letter. As to my wife, she will have so much to do in London this summer that she certainly deserves a quiet time now, especially after the stormy period she has passed through. Perhaps she will come to Budapest next month.

I feel a special responsibility in passing an opinion about your latest work, for I am probably the only person besides yourself who is familiar with both subjects, the totemism and tabu literature on the one side and ψα on the other; Robertson Smith's is the only book you quote that I haven't read; to be sure, an important exception.[1] Well, I feel calmly and absolutely certain that your theory is perfectly correct, and that it will stand any test the future may submit it to. What the immediate general impression produced may be is another matter, concerning which I have no opinion, and it may well be that my ready acceptance is greatly helped by personal inclinations in the direction of the theory; I have for years believed that the Oedipus situation originated in *actual* conflicts between the pretensions of the sons and the jealousy of the sire, these being later converted into inner conflicts, and that we have there the central problem of the development of civilisation (Cf. the last sentence of my Hamlet essay).[2] That being so, I can see no possible solution to the problems of totemism other than the one you offer.

I feel that I should express the following idea which forces itself on me, namely that your judgement of the value and correctness of the theory is affected by the fact of your being the author—far more than is generally the case in your work, which suggests that this one has an unusual personal significance for you. The external situation does not explain to me altogether your feeling-attitude. For instance, is it not possible that some of your doubt and diminished confidence may have arisen as a reaction to what was perhaps an overestimation of the boldness and dangerous innovation of the theory (as indicated by the initial triumphal feeling in former letters)? For, to speak quite candidly, I do not find the new theory so terribly startling to one who is familiar with your previous work. When one takes the conclusions of Frazer, R. Smith, and Atkinson[3] and fertilises them with the *Traumdeutung*, what other conclusion is possible that [than] the one you have just ennunciated? What is chiefly new *now* is the illuminating way you have linked all the various aspects of the problems together, and made a perfect whole. (I am referring, of course, to the central theory, not to the numerous other new ideas in the work). That the son wishes to murder his father and to marry his mother you showed thirteen years ago;[4] but while Jung devalues this discovery by calling the wish "merely symbolic", you on the contrary go on to point out that it is dread reality. Probably this progress on your part indicates a still further personal development in an even more absolute conviction of the unqualified truth of the discovery (*wahr; aber* so *wahr!*).[5] Hence the impression the present work makes on you. At all events that is my own opinion, and if there is any truth in it I sincerely trust you will not weaken what you have written, but will stand by every word. You have chosen the part of Mithras,[6] and must play it out with his courage, as you always have. How I rejoiced, for instance, to read the passage, so characteristic of you, that if the new factor you add is true, then it is not merely *a* new factor, but necessarily *the* central factor!

Now I come to a few details, which are all unimportant, but which perhaps you may care to consider as you were good enough to ask for any remarks that occurred to me. I have also submitted them to Ferenczi before writing them now.

(1) Fahne 15. First line of the second footnote. Is the word *"ungeheuerliche Annahme"* possibly rather strong?[7] If you purposely make it so, out of consideration to the reader, then could not the effect be softened by quoting the frequency of actual father-murder, [especially][8] or, the regular priest and king murders in the Golden Bough. (Frazer, Rank)?

(2). F. 16. end of second paragraph. The relation of the situation to the institution of mother-right. One sees clearly what you mean, but it is so briefly indicated that both Ferenczi and I had to reflect over it for a moment. Could not an explanatory sentence be added?[9]

(3). F. 19. first paragraph. That the human victims represent gods. Whether it is worth while to quote instances of this,[10] for it is an important link in the argument? You must know of many examples. I remember in Prescott's *Conquest of Mexico*,[11] it is described how at the time of Cortes the Mexicans treated their victims with the greatest honour and deference, practically as gods, for a year and a day, then sacrificing them.

(4). F. 20. The chief remark. You describe the hero of the tragedy as the Urvater, who is killed by the Bruderclan of the chorus (originally).[12] I suspect this is entirely so in some tragedies, but that in others he represents the son who kills himself (rushes on [himself][13] his doom in spite of warnings) as a punishment for rebelling against authority (which you mention in the previous paragraph), as a *Selbstopfer* [self-sacrifice] who thus becomes the God-father (confirmed by the fact of tragedies being revived in the middle ages by the Passion Plays), and that in most he represents a Verdichtung of *both* father and son. This follows from your other discussion, but perhaps it is worth while to state it so as to avoid misunderstanding, that is of course if you agree to its correctness.[14]

(5). F. 21. The continuity of the tradition, especially at the time when there was no tyrannical father present.[15] I fancy that the theory could be still further defended against this possible objection, in the following way: It is unlikely that the brothers became later on model fathers, any more than Napoleon became a tolerant ruler after he had freed his country from oppression. It is true that there was probably no one strong man who drove out the younger generation (although there may have been at times), but still all the adult men must have represented *Imagines*[16] of a wicked father to the young boy, exactly as at the present day, for the reason that they necessarily disturbed his relation to his mother or to the older women in general, even by their very presence. The unconscious understanding on his part of the strong Oedipus feelings of his elders (the brothers) must therefore have gone to strengthen a feeling-attitude that was already there, and which is universal under all circumstances. After all, you have been obliged in the presentation to imagine a simple schematic case, whereas in fact the whole affair must have been very complicated; repeated murders, fraternal strife, communities living near each other in different stages of the situation, etc..

That is all, and now I want to say what a delight it was to read the whole essay, both for the wonderful presentation, and for the precious gems one was constantly coming across.

You will have noticed that in this letter I have ventured for the first time to take it for granted that you are a human being with human reactions, and to write openly and frankly as from one man to other. My analysis is giving me more self-dependence and freedom by diminishing further what was left of my father-complex, and I think you will welcome that as much as I do. It is better to have a natural and therefore permanent attitude of respect and admiration than a kind of veneration which brings with it the dangers of ambivalency.

We get to Vienna at 6.55 on Saturday, and I am greatly looking forward to seeing you again, also my other Vienna friends.

Yours always affectionately
Jones.

1. Smith (1894).

2. Jones (1910a, p. 113): "It is only fitting that the greatest work of the world-poet should have been concerned with the deepest problem and the intensest conflict that has occupied the mind of man since the beginning of time, the revolt of youth and of the impulse to love against the restraints imposed by the jealous eld."

3. Frazer (1910; 1911–1915); Smith (1894); Atkinson (1903):

4. Freud (1900a).

5. "True; but *how* true!"

6. As opposed to Christ, who sacrificed his own life to redeem his brothers from original sin. Freud declares: "We may perhaps infer from the sculptures of Mithras slaying a bull that he represented a son who was alone in sacrificing his father and thus redeemed his brothers from their burden of complicity in the deed"; see Freud (1912–13, p. 153).

7. "Monstrous hypothesis." Freud toned this down to "ungeheuerliche erscheinende Annahme." The result reads, "This hypothesis, which has such a monstrous air . . ." See Freud (1912–13, p. 142 n. 1), *G.W.*, 9:172 n. 1.

8. Crossed out in the original.

9. See the passage dealing with the "institution of matriarchy"; Freud (1912–13, p. 144).

10. See Freud (1912–13, p. 151); explicit examples are not provided.

11. William Hickling Prescott, *The Conquest of Mexico*, 2 vols. (London: Everyman's Library, 1913–14).

12. Freud (1912–13, p. 155), *G.W.*, 9:187–188.

13. Crossed out in the original.

14. Jones argues for interpreting the tragic hero as a condensation (Verdichtung) of father and son, a suggestion which is not taken up in Freud (1912–13, p. 156).

15. See Freud (1912–13, p. 158).

16. Plural of *Imago*.

128

8 July 1913
Pension Gerö, Lipót-körút 10
Budapest V

Dear Prof. Freud,

I want to wish you a pleasant journey and an enjoyable time in Marienbad, also to thank you again for your delightful hospitality in Vienna. I enjoyed the whole trip more than any experience I have had for a long time.

I have had a long answer from your English correspondent, to whom I wrote. He is making himself useful by buying books, and seems a decent enough fellow, although very curious. He is a schoolmaster, with a remarkable interest in the psychology of stammering (very specialised), which he has been investigating by means of association words, etc.. He offers to devote a year to learning ψα which attracts him.

I hear today from Loe that she is coming to Budapest on Saturday, and am looking forward to her visit. I think we shall both enjoy it. No doubt she told you how well we got on together in Vienna. Our relations are much less strained, and hence much pleasanter.

The analysis here still makes progress. Ferenczi is very patient with my eccentricities and changes of mood, and we get ever deeper into things. We also spend much time together in scientific talks, and understand each other very well. He has a beautiful imagination, perhaps not always thoroughly disciplined, but always suggestive. He has been exceedingly kind to me here, and I shall always remember it. I have nearly a month more here, and hope to get a good deal more done in that time. Then comes London, about which I am hopeful rather than optimistic, and plenty to do in many directions.

This last year I gave you a harder and less agreeable task than I expected, but you must try to forgive me as I could not foresee its difficulty. I greatly admire the way you have performed it, and am beginning to feel more completely grateful than could be expected a month ago.

Now you will be having a thoroughly deserved holiday, and I expect you are impatiently counting the hours to it. So I will close as I began with sending you my warmest good wishes.

Yours affectionately
Jones.

129

10 July 1913
Vienna, IX. Berggasse 19

My dear Jones,

Now I too want to profit from your progress in German and give up writing to you in the poorest English. There are many heartfelt things I could say in reply to your kind letter, however, I shall limit myself to the assurance that you not only set me a difficult task but also presented me with an enormous gift. You know that one cannot be with Loe for very long before one becomes truly fond of her.

She is unfortunately now also giving me cause for concern, not with respect to a nervous condition but to an organic one. As the swelling in her legs would not subside, I finally had her consult one of our younger internists, Dr. R. Kaufmann,[1] whom I regard as excellent. He has diagnosed that the feverish condition in May, which Hitschmann and Fleischmann traced to urine poisoning caused by bending of a ureter, was due to, or led to, a thrombosis of a vein deep in the abdomen. He was very glad that no further mishap ensued, regards the process almost at an end, but insists that she should keep resting *until the end of this month.* He did not forbid all movement, but only the journey to Budapest. I do not understand too much about this and may therefore be a little more anxious than necessary, but all these abdominal matters are uncanny to me. I therefore ask you to forgo Loe's trip to Budapest and to bring your influence to bear on her not to leave Vienna before the end of this month. You can then see her before you go to London and perhaps travel together with her. She knows of her diagnosis through Kaufmann, was sad for a whole day, but then very sweet again. We don't want to make her anxious, but only urge her to be careful. When she became concerned about her future, I comforted her with the story of the *"fertige Sache"*,[2] about which Ferenczi can tell you.

I have great expectations of your settling in London. I am very sorry that Rank cannot visit you for several months, and it is very nice that you invited him. This is now the second time that he has missed London, but he will get there in the end. You may guess what pleasure it gives me that you have amicable relations with him, Ferenczi, and the other members of the committee that you yourself conceived.

Auf Wiedersehen on 6 August in Munich after you have done your congress round.

With cordial greetings

Yours,
Freud

1. Rudolf Kaufmann (1871–1927), a leading Viennese internist, and nephew of Breuer. Freud refers to a dream of Kaufmann's in support of the wish-fulfillment hypothesis in several places; see Freud to Fliess, 4 March 1895 (*S.E.*, 1:213; Masson, 1985, p. 114), as well as Freud (1900a, pp. 125, 233; 1940a, p. 170).
2. "Fait accompli" or a "sure thing."

130

[postcard]

[11 July 1913][1]
[Vienna]

Herlichen Gruss[2]

Fr.

Loe allright

1. Date of postmark.
2. "Greetings from the heart," or "warm greetings."

131

22 July 1913
Pension Gerö, Lipót-körút 10
Budapest V

Dear Professor Freud,

I have heard from Loe that she got back safely to Vienna, and has a good report from Dr. Kaufmann; she is to have the urine again analysed. We had an excellent time together and enjoyed it both very much. I find her incomparably more normal than previously, different even from May. She reacted quite normally to a very disagreeable experience of a kind that would have upset her in bygone times, namely losing a train after driving to two stations to find it. It was given wrongly in the time-table.

I am extremely sorry to tell you that my progress in German does not cover hand-writing, which is a matter not of knowledge but of years of experience especially when young. I could read only four words of your letter. In time perhaps I might improve, but it would probably always mean having to show your letters to someone else, so that you could not write freely or privately. I am very fond of your English, which has often a classic, old-world touch, but it must be more trouble for you to write than German, which means that you probably make the letters shorter than otherwise. So in any case I lose something, which seems unavoidable.

I have just read Jung's New York lectures, in the *Jahrbuch*,[1] no agreeable task. They are full of contradictions and logical errors of thought. He is very polite to you, except for occasional outburts, such as "Es gibt Ärzte, welche glauben, sie kämen mit Selbstanalyse aus. Das ist Münchhausen-Psychologie, mit der sie sicher stecken bleiben".[2] Very striking is his distrust of patients; he has evidently the feeling that the whole analysis is an artefact, and repeatedly talks of how you have been misled by patients and followed them blindly. One sees here again the effect of his paraphrenia experiences, and the lack of feeling for what is real. The silliest pages are S. 380–381, a masterpiece of nonsense.[3]

The *British Medical Journal*, which you mention in your card, I have not yet seen; Forsyth is a *Kinderarzt* [pediatrician],[4] once a friend of mine. Eder is behaving more and more suspiciously in many ways, and I am now in doubt whether the time is ripe for a Verein. At all events we must put it off until after the Munich Congress,[5] when I shall know more of what is going on in England. His latest news is that he is going to read a paper at the British Medical Association on "Jung's and Adler's modifications (!) of Freud's Theory".[6] Without denying these gentlemen the right to have whatever modifications that may please them I certainly think this is a very malapropos time to discuss them in England, before the audience knows about the theory that is to be modified. It is, to put it mildly, a highly unnecessary proceeding.

On the other side I enclose a delightfully written article taken from the *Pall Mall Gazette*, one of the leading Conservative London papers. About a dozen sentences are taken from the first three chapters and preface of my book,[7] so no doubt that is the source of the (unknown) writer's information, which seems to have made a favourable impression on him. Perhaps you will be good enough to return it to me sometime. I am going to translate eleven of Ferenczi's papers, to make a book for Prince's Monograph Series.[8] At present we are in the middle of some New York chicanerie on the matter, in which as usual Jelliffe is involved. F. has cabled to try to stop them. He has asked me to review Pfister's book for the *Zeitschrift*, and I fancy this will need some criticism.[9]

Well, my analysis is drawing towards a close, and I have found it so valuable that I am wondering if I can manage to get in another month next year.[10] It has without doubt been successful in making me face more clearly various character traits and dangerous tendencies, and I trust that it will prove its value also when it comes to be tested in actual life. I cannot praise Ferenczi too highly for his skill and tact throughout, and he has also succeeded in making it congruous with the analysis to be very kind "out of school", so that on the whole I have had a very enjoyable time in Budapest. Outside the analysis I have not done much work except German lessons and a few reports, but I hope to write my Munich paper this week.[11]

You are about to be bothered by a very troublesome lady, Frau Hoesch-Ernst,[12] who once visited me in Toronto. She sent a letter to Vienna university, which you have perhaps got, asking to see you during your holidays. She is a German psychologist, who has read most of the $\psi\alpha$ literature, and is sure she knows everything. She is a woman of 48, with very disagreeable character traits, and in a miserable current situation, with little chance of future happiness. She was to have come to me for analysis, but now wants to go to you, on condition that she need not mention the name or nationality of her lover!!

What does Marienbad feel like? I suppose I need hardly ask.

With kindest regards to yourself and the family

Yours always
Jones.

P.S. I join Loe in Vienna on Aug. 2nd, and we go on at once together to London.

1. Jung (1913b).

2. "There are analysts who believe that they can get along with a self-analysis. This is Münchhausen psychology, and they will certainly remain stuck." See Jung (1913b), *Jahrbuch*, 5 (1913): 415, and *C.W.*, 4:199. Apart from being a slight against Freud, the

comment may also have been taken personally by Jones. It surely hit a nerve, for Jones had spent a great deal of energy in undertaking his own self-analysis between 1909 and 1913, and would have resented the implication that he was practicing pseudopsychology ("Münchhausen psychology" is an allusion to Baron Münchausen, the eighteenth-century figure famed for his amusingly mendacious stories).

3. See Jung (1913b), *Jahrbuch*, 5 (1913): 380–381 and *C.W.*, 4:164–166, where he attacks Freud's notion of the latency period, between the ages of five and puberty, in which sexual desire lies dormant.

4. David Forsyth, M.D. 1903 and D.Sc. 1908 London; charter member of the London Psycho-Analytical Society, founded 30 October 1913.

5. Fourth Congress of the International Psychoanalytic Association, 7–8 September 1913.

6. Eder (1913).

7. Jones, *Papers*, 1st ed. 1913.

8. See Jones (1916b).

9. The review was not written by Jones; see E. Hitschmann, review of Pfister (1913), *Zeitschrift*, 2 (1914): 185–186.

10. Jones states in his autobiography that "I decided . . . to undertake a didactic analysis with Ferenczi in Budapest" and that "I spent an hour twice a day on it during that summer and autumn [of 1913]" (Jones, 1959, p. 199).

11. Jones (1914b).

12. Lucy Hoesch-Ernst of Godesberg bei Bonn. See her Ph.D. dissertation, "Anthropologisch-psychologische Untersuchungen an Züricher Schulkindern" (University of Zurich, 1906).

132

23 July 1913
Vienna, IX. Berggasse 19

My dear Jones,

I am sorry I must go on abusing your fine English as you have kept the Alexia gotica while giving up the Aphasia mot. and sensor.[1]

I am very glad to hear of your good news about our friends male and female, these are bright spots in life's dark disk.

I have not yet got Jungs last eluctation [elucidation] neither in the volume nor in Sonderabdruck, so I cannot react to this part of your letter. Presumably you are right.

I have got and answered already a letter from Mrs. Hoesch-Ernst postponing her to Oktober in Vienna, to be sure she betrayed neither her character nor her age in the letter, but my answer was in no ways compromising.

As for Eder's paper I am in the position to send it to you in mnscrpt, I found it full of misrepresentations but not suspicious in intention.

The cut from the *Pall Mall Gazette* you will get back after some delay, I enjoyed it very much although I am afraid the comparison with old Ch. Darwin will not hold good.

It seems an excellent idea and a good plea for expressing your thanks to
F. that you should translate some of his deep-going—I might say: inten-
sively felt and laboured—papers.

Marienbad is likely to be a splendid place—in summer. As matters stand
I must abstain from giving a judgment. I am pretty well and very far from
our work. My people (son-in-law and his wife included) are merry and
healthy. Monday I had the pleasure to talk all the day long with Eitingon
coming with an errand of Abraham's. They want me to talk on this congress while I had resolved to keep back in order to avoid an outbreak.
Eitingon is one of those who will stand any proof.

I am sorry to think after the Munich Congress there will be a time when
personal relations may be so more difficult. It was nice to know you so
near and to see you so often.

With best wishes for all your London affairs

yours truly
Freud

1. Freud refers to Jones's inability to read Gothic script (Alexia gotica) even though
he had learned to speak and understand German. "Aphasia mot." is motor aphasia
(inability to speak), and sensory aphasia is the inability to understand speech.

133

8 August 1913
13 Princes Street
Cavendish Square, W.

Dear Professor Freud,

I am very pleased with the London events and reception, from every
point of view. Jung's paper at the Psycho-Medical Society went off
smoothly, with a good discussion.[1] Of him I will write later. The debate
on ψα this morning was certainly a great success. I am sending you Janet
and Jung's *Sammelreferate* [collective papers],[2] and say nothing about them
except that it was lucky that Janet was so stupid and exposed himself so
naively to attack. I was asked to open the discussion, and found it an easy
task, as I was in excellent speaking form.[3] I pointed out that Janet's paper
was full of misrepresentations and untruths, which was easy to prove by
taking four definite examples; e.g. that ψα had two procedures (1) *advising*
regular coitus with a preservative! and (2) applying Janet's method; that
you had urged doctors to devote all their force and intelligence to discover
an ideal preservative; that coitus will always cure all neuropathic troubles;
and that the man you reprimanded for *wilde Psychoanalyse* was a disciple
of your own. I said he was merely a disciple of yours in the same sense as

Janet, namely in the capacity to misunderstand what he read. Then came some general remarks. Janet was also battered by others, and in reply had nothing to say except to apologise for his inaccurate presentation. Eder, Coriat, and Forsyth spoke for us, and Frankl-Hochwart, Bérillon, Williams and Walsh against.[4] Sir Geo. Savage, the chairman, summoned up the discussion by warning us against Janet's eloquence, which was a dangerous gift, pleaded strongly for the importance of ψα in some very intelligent words which I will quote in my report for the *Zeitschrift*,[5] and finished by urging us "Let us not be obstinate against these new and valuable ideas". Jung played a quiet part, made a few courteous generalities, and was in the background. Very few Germans were there, if any, mostly English, so he had a disadvantage in speaking German. After the meeting Sir James Crichton-Browne, the President of the Section and Senior Lunacy Commissioner, came up, shook hands and warmly congratulated me, thanking me in the name of the Committee for having made "a much needed protest against these misrepresentations", and spoke very highly of ψα. A number of other notable men did the same, and the whole attitude was very cordial and full of English "fair play". As a result, one can say that Janet is squashed,[6] and that the debate at least did no harm in England. The general impression was certainly in our favour. I am also pleased with the way I have been received otherwise, *und denke jetzt, die Sache wird schon in England gehen.*[7]

Loe is well, but much perturbed. The Jones family is in London, and she spends every afternoon with Herbert, in great apprehension of being discovered by the father. The latter is worse, and I should think definitely *geisteskrank* [emotionally disturbed]. Loe's tension and irritability are discharged on me in the most disagreeable way, so it is not a pleasant time in spite of my efforts to make things smooth. My father has been seriously ill and I must go down to Wales soon. The finding of a *Wohnung* [a flat] is also very difficult and troublesome, so that altogether this week or two is not easy, and I am sure you will excuse me for not writing more at present. I am taking advantage of the Congress to meet and talk with various people, old friends and new. When is Brill crossing? It is very curious he hasn't answered any of my letters this summer.

With kindest regards

Yours
Jones.

1. Jung (1913a).
2. Janet (1914), and Jung (1916a).
3. Later published as Jones (1915b).
4. See "Discussion No. 2: Psycho-Analysis," in *Seventeenth International Congress of Medicine* (London: Henry Frowde, 1913), pp. 13–71.
5. See Jones (1913j).

6. See Ellenberger (1970, pp. 817–819), challenging Jones's own historical accounts of his defeat of Janet (Jones, 1955a, p. 99; 1955b, p. 112; and 1959, pp. 241–242). Also see note 3 to letter 139.

7. "And now think the cause will succeed in England."

134

10 August 1913
Mbad [Marienbad]

My dear Jones,

I cannot say how much gratified I have been by your report on the Congress and by your defeating Janet in the eyes of your countrymen. The interest of ΨA, and of your person in England is identical, now I trust you will *"schmieden das Eisen solange es warm ist"*.[1]

"Fair play" is what we want and likely it may be got better in England than anywhere else.—

Brill will not come over. He writes, it is his family, wife and daughter, who want his presence this year. He has been appointed chief of the clinic of Psychiatry at the Columbia University, and so he is settled and independent at last.

I promised Loe a bad time in London which I want to squeeze out of her the last and deepest motives of her disorders. I hope matters with Herbert will not become so extricate [intricate] this summer as to defy clearing in autumn. Give her my very best regards and *please tell her* I knew difficulties were coming up when she wrote she could not finish the letter to me. There is something necessary and unavoidable in it; so she should not lose temper or courage and keep above the situation.

I am leaving Mbad tomorrow for S. Martino di Castrozza, Hotel des Alpes. We had a bad time here, it was too cold and wet. I can scarcely write from rheumatism in my right arm. Perhaps we are to have more freezing in the mountains.

Go on in giving me your good news during these four weeks. You make me feel strong and hopeful.

Sincerely yours
Freud

P.S. Loe knows how little expectation I am bringing to the promised visit of old Mr. Jones.[2]

1. "Strike while the iron is hot."
2. Herbert Jones's father did not make it to Vienna; see letter 139.

135

[postcard]

15 August 1913
S. Martino

My dear Jones,

I acknowledge receipt of the Congress Report.[1] Ferenczi arrived here today, I gave it to him; we will send it back to you as soon as he has read it. I am not so very curious.

With best love for you and Loe

Freud

1. Jones (1913j).

136

15 August 1913
13 Princes St., Cavendish Sq.
London

Dear Professor Freud,

This contains merely a few disconnected notes on points I have recently come across, and which may interest you.

Zur Theorie der Angst! Bacon writes: "We know diseases of stoppings and suffocations are the most dangerous in the body; it is not much otherwise in the minde".[1] (This might be quoted by the Baconians as proof of his psychological insight).

Relation between desire and anxiety. In English we use the latter word just as often to mean desire as to mean [fire][2] fear (e.g. I am anxious to meet him = desirous, eager, etc.).

There is no new thing under the sun. Freimark, in his book on occultism, and Wirth, in his on Somnambulismus,[3] frankly hold that hypnotism is purely a sexual rapport, and that the effect of it solely depends on this fact. Again I discover that the veteran Hughlings Jackson made this sage remark: "Find out all about dreams and then you will understand insanity."[4]

I suppose you know the passage in Boccaccio: "Who willeth thee ill dreameth thee ill."[5] It is of course also found elsewhere in proverbs.

A little philology. First re the magnetic rapport in hypnosis. The word "coition" (English for coitus) used to be used till the 17th century to indicate the attraction of a magnet for a metal.[6] Re Ferenczi on friendship! Friend comes from the Sanscrit *freond*, which meant a lover, and till 1600 the word was used indiscriminately in English in both senses. I believe the same was true of φιλος.[7]

These are a few of the additions I am making to my papers for re-publication in book form.[8]

The following phrase, of which I was reminded by hearing it in a play of Shaw's we went to see last week, is curious: A London euphemism for prostitute is "daughter of a clergyman",[9] originating in the frequency with which they tell their clients that they are clergyman's daughters. The double meaning is I suppose this: First a submerged longing for respectability, but deeper than this is one based on the identification God—clergyman—Father, and indicating the incest origin of the prostitution-phantasy (female *Don Juanismus*). They are true descendants of the "sacred whores of Babylon". Isn't it wonderful how such a connection will leak out casually and unpretentiously centuries later. I am always struck with amazement and admiration at such instances.

I am just leaving for Wales. My address till September will be: The Woodlands. Gowerton. R.S.O. Glamorganshire.

> Yours
> Jones.

P.S. Re Regression. It is interesting that the words "imagination" and "phantasy" had originally in Greek a purely *visual* meaning.

1. Francis Bacon, "Of Friendship," in *The Works of Francis Bacon*, ed. J. Spedding, R. L. Ellis, and D. D. Heath, vol. 12 (New York: Hurd and Houghton, 1864), p. 166. The passage is employed in Jones (1911e); see Jones, *Papers*, 2nd ed. 1918, p. 490.

2. Crossed out in the original.

3. Freimark's *Okkultismus und Sexualität* and Wirth's *Theorie des Somnambulismus* are referred to in Jones (1910–11a); see Jones, *Papers*, 2nd ed. 1918, p. 338.

4. This particular passage is employed in Jones (1911f); see Jones, *Papers*, 2nd ed. 1918, p. 267 n. 1. The statement that "dreaming has long been likened to insanity" appears in J. Hughlings Jackson, "The Factors of Insanities," *Medical Press and Circular*, 108 (1894): 615.

5. From Giovanni Boccaccio, *The Decameron*, ninth day, seventh story, in which Talano di Molese dreams that his wife's throat and face are mangled by a wolf. He tells her to take care, but she ignores his warning, and the dream comes true.

6. Employed in Jones (1910–11a); see Jones, *Papers*, 2nd ed. 1918, p. 341.

7. Greek *philos* = lover. Employed in Jones (1910–11a); see Jones, *Papers*, 2nd ed. 1918, p. 358.

8. Jones, *Papers*, 2nd ed. 1918.

9. Line spoken by Bobby in *Fanny's First Play*, act 3.

137

18 August 1913
13 Princes Street
Cavendish Square, London

Dear Professor Freud,

Thank you deeply for your kind remarks and encouragement.

As to Loe, I am glad to say she is better again of late. When I was down in Wales last week and she was alone she had a kidney attack and took morphia. The pain was on only one occasion. She has some physical pain in her foot, owing to the pressure of the boot on a vein, but is otherwise physical[ly] well. Herbert, who is with her three times a day, is more desperately in love with her than ever, and has no doubt at all about his intentions. She has altruistic qualms about "spoiling a young life" concerned with her age and health, and that seems to be the one conflict at present in her mind. Still she has a good time with him. I take up the benevolent attitude of blessing two happy young lovers, who are always a good sight to look on, and am really happy that Loe, who has suffered so much, should now get something positive out of life. I fancy it will go well with them, for she can do anything in the world when she loves. At the same time I rejoice now to think we are parting, for with all her magnificent character and many charms she has as well a devouring and all-absorbing personality, so that life with her is at the best a strenuous performance, and at the worst, when she does not love, a painfully disagreeable and racking experience.

I hope to settle arrangements about taking a flat in another few days, and if that is the case the installation will be complete before the end of September. Loe has generously offered to pay my expenses for the first three years, until I am *"auf sicherem Boden"* [on sure ground], but probably that will not be necessary. I began practice last week with the first patient, and hope that will be the prelude to a long medical career in London. By the way, if for any reason you decide not to accept Frau Hoesch-Ernst I should be very glad if you could refer her back to me, for I should be willing to treat her, as I know the circumstances of her life and think one could help her. I have written twice to Ferenczi and will not repeat the news he will give you, e.g. about Jung. Putnam tells me he has met Flournoy's son who is greatly interested in $\psi\alpha$, and who is going to work with Adolf Meyer at Baltimore.[1]

Now I want to ask your advice about the following matter: Havelock Ellis wants me to write a general book on $\psi\alpha$ for the Contemporary Science Series (ca. 400 pages), of which he is the editor.[2] It is important, for the series has a wide circulation, and I suppose I must do it, for I couldn't bear the thought of another writer mangling the subject, as would surely be the case. It would also be advantageous from the point of view of practice, as the series reaches the educated laity. On the other hand I am already terribly behind hand in my own work (abstracting for journals, writing articles, etc.), and in any case my first two months will be given to translating Ferenczi.[3] It would therefore mean postponing Napoleon for six months, which I hoped to finish in Canada in the spring if I could collect the material this winter, and that is already much delayed. Still I am sure you will say I must do it. The only plausible alternative would be to get Pfister's book translated,[4] and that is not well adapted for an English audience and is also confusing as regards Jung, etc.. I am just starting to write a full course on Psychiatry for a Correspondence College to which I am tutor. It will take much time, but will be useful in preparing material for my text-book, which I hope to write in two or three years time. Next summer I must certainly get out my book on the *Treatment of the Neuroses,* an enlargement of a section which has appeared in an American System of Neurology.[5] So I have enough to do, apart from routine such as heavy correspondence, reviewing, etc..

I get to Munich on the evening of the 5th. When do you arrive, and where will you stay? I hope the weather is better at S. Martino, and especially that your rheumatism is improved. Please remember me to Ferenczi, and those of your family who are with you.

With kindest regards

from
Jones.

1. Henri Flournoy (1886–1955), son of Théodore Flournoy (1854–1920) of Geneva. The father was editor (with Claparède) of the *Archives de psychologie;* the son was a Swiss physician, who spent a year at Johns Hopkins Hospital, Baltimore, and later became a committed psychoanalyst and prominent member of the Swiss society.
2. See note 4 to letter 156.
3. Jones (1916b).
4. Pfister (1913).
5. Jones (1913a, 1920b). The latter book, as well as the Ferenczi translation (Jones, 1916b), were the only books Jones completed out of all those mentioned in this paragraph.

138

22 August 1913
S. Martino di Castrozza

My dear Jones,

I am glad you are entering with full sails into english scientific life. As you are kind enough to consult me about Havelock Ellis' offer I will not postpone to answer that you cannot decline it but must do it first of all. Napoleon can wait, even the translation of Ferenczi's may; the translation of Pfister's book is no work for you, I should think. Your work is enough for one man, but your capacity for doing work is immense, it ought to be directed into the most urgent channels.

As for Loe you know no doubt that she had no kidney attack but a true and well deserved relapse. No wonder she is better with you since.

Glad to see you in a few days

Yours faithfully
Freud

P.S. Ferenczi shares my opinion about Ellis' proposal.

139

22 August 1913
13 Princes Street
Cavendish Square, W.

Dear Professor Freud,

Ferenczi, whose good letter arrived this morning, suggests that I should write combined letters to you two, so as to save time; if I hear from both of you in return I shall get the best of the bargain. By the way, he says he has told you something in a general way of my B'pest analysis. If you have any comments that occur to you, I should be glad to hear them.

Enclosed is a copy of the paper I proposed reading at Munich;[1] perhaps you would be so good as to let me know of any amendments you suggest. I am not satisfied with the part dealing with Jung directly. When I say I cannot understand why he goes on analysing phantasies that are purely secondary in nature, and not causal, he can easily reply: because the Libido and energy necessary for the performance of the *Aufgabe* [task] have got anchored there and have to be released through analysis. This is not easy to meet without overstepping the bounds of therapeutics and dealing with other parts of his "theory".

I hear with joy that you are reading a paper at Munich, and am eager to know the subject.[2]

The onesided account of the $\psi\alpha$ debate in the *Times, Neue Freie Presse* (which Rank sent me), etc., was due to the fact that no reporters were present, so that they wrote their account purely from the printed Rapporte of Janet and Jung that were handed to them.[3] I smiled to think of your lack of curiosity as regards the latter. The olympic calm of S. Martino contrasts vividly with the turmoil of London.

The chief news from here is that today I signed the lease of my flat (69,

Portland Court, London W.), so that at least my practice will again have a "local habitation and [abode][4] a name"—let us hope it will not be the "airy nothing" to which this phrase was first applied. I expect to move in by the end of September, so that Loe will get to Vienna about the same time as yourself.

Havelock Ellis wants the book for his series to be 5–600 pages long, and chiefly non-medical, so that it will be a big job to do it well as it should be done. I believe it would produce a wide impression here, for the time is very ripe. One constantly sees references to ψα in the better-class magazines and literary journals. They are usually highly complimentary, with that respect for the distant that is likely to change when matters are brought to closer quarters. However, it is good that the start is in a serious and acknowledging tone.

Loe is going on better, and there is no doubt they will marry next May; even the later movements seem decided. The Jones family all sail for America on Sept. 3rd, the father having finally decided, after much wavering, not to go to Vienna. He has fixed delusions that his children are all conspiring to injure him, and he has a J. J. P. complex in regard to his youngest daughter, who happens to dislike him.[5] Herbert Jones has behaved splendidly with him and the sisters, doing everything possible. In regard to Loe and myself he has greater difficulty, as he is still intensely jealous of me and wants to marry her at once (Please do not tell Loe that you know this, for she wants to write to you herself, though I doubt if she will do so yet awhile).

Tell Ferenczi that the Orchestral Concert season has just commenced here, and that I have a season ticket and go every evening. So even in London there is some relaxation, though in this hot weather I am greatly missing the open-air life of B'pest. Other personal news is that yesterday I had a septic tooth-root removed, which I am hoping may have been the cause of my chronic joint trouble. I hope yours is better in S. Martino. Have you thought of the possibility of this aetiology?

Other news at present have I none, so I will close with wishing you both (and all your family) a most agreeable time in the Tirol, and inspiration from mutual conversation.

Yours
Jones.

1. Jones (1914b).
2. Freud (1913i).
3. Ellenberger (1970, pp. 817–819) in fact relies heavily on the newspaper accounts in his recreation of this episode to challenge Jones's version of the story; see note 6 to letter 133.
4. Crossed out in the original.
5. That is, James Jackson Putnam's Griselda complex, referring to Putnam's incestuous attraction toward his own daughter; see Putnam (1913).

140

29 August 1913
S. Martino

My dear Jones,

Your paper is excellent, unsparingly clear, clever and just. I feel some resistance against writing you in English after reading your German. You ought to learn gothic letters too.—You are right that there is some scarcity in your remarks about an important point against Jung. You might add that there is a special interest in abstaining from decisions in the Zwangs-cases, where the patient is luring to renew his play with the precepts given from without, which he had performed hitherto with those given from within. As regards the question of the importance of the unconscious fancies I see no reason why we should submit to the arbitrary judgment of Jung instead of the necessary one of the patient himself. If the latter values those productions as his most precious secrets (the off-spring of his day-dreams), we have to accept this position and must ascribe to them a most important role in the treatment. Let aside the question if this importance be an etiological one, that's out of joint here, it is rather pragmatical.

Your remarks on the esteem ψα is enjoying from afar in England, made me laugh heartily; you are quite right.

In a few days I will have the pleasure of talking with you upon more topics. Dont forget: it is Bayerisch. Hof and we hope to arrive Friday 5th in the evening (9h). I will bring a letter from Pfister with me which will strike you dumb, an *"document humain"*.

I received a good paper "on ΨA" by one Becker of Milwaukee.[1] The first papers of the newcomers seem always pretty good, now let us wait, what the man may write two years later.

Au revoir

yours
Freud

1. W. F. Becker, "Psychoanalysis," *Wisconsin Medical Journal*, 11 (1913): 384–391.

141

13 September 1913
13 Princes Street
Cavendish Square, London

Dear Professor Freud,

My thoughts are very much with you in the splendid city, recuperating in that sublime atmosphere from the passing pettinesses of a few days ago.

Still, on looking back, I think we have every reason to be satisfied with the events. We achieved the main object of bringing some light into the muddled confusion of the Zurich people, and also demonstrated that there was more vital activity in the Vienna school than they seemed to imagine. Our next task will be to go on with the clarification, and define the Zurich point of view more sharply, a task which they themselves should have fulfilled. We shall not be able to devote ourselves freely to the progress of ψα until we have shaken these impediments off. It must be many years since you last had to defend in a public meeting the elementary principles of ψα and I hope it gratified you to see that this time you had an active bodyguard to support you.

I want to thank you again for your personal kindness to me. To it I owe in a great measure the confidence I felt at the congress, also partly to the greater freedom from Angst resulting from my analysis, and partly to the considerable experience I have already had of such discussions.

I enclose a *"petit document humain"* from Putnam, which you might send on to Ferenczi, as I think it will interest him also. The passages I have marked with a cross need no comment. His tough stomach unhesitatingly rejects Jung's mish-mash, inspite of the sprinkling of philosophy and ethics which might have deceived Putnam's palate. He also sends me a dream of his own relating to incest with his daughter, thus confirming your surmise about the Griselda paper.[1]

Eder and I have arranged to found a London group next month, and expect to have perhaps a dozen members with the British members of the American Assoc. (Berkeley-Hill, etc.). In order not to leave the selection of new members to the society we will arrange that all names must first be passed by a committee, consisting of the President, Secretary and Vice-President (who will probably be Bryan of Leicester).[2] We will be fairly strict, but at first shall have to pay as much attention to character and intentions as to "orthodoxy", and thus include men like Eder and Hart. I think of inviting also Havelock Ellis and McDougall (Prof. of Psychol. in Oxford). What would you say to this?

I am busy making arrangements for the English and American abstracts for the *Zeitschrift*, and hope that before the New Year this will be thoroughly organised.

Loe has been very much better and is throwing herself vigorously into the work of furnishing. But she seems to have the need of an occasional explosion. She brought home a stray kitten when I was away, overfed it, and then late last night gave it an overdose of purge as well as an enema. The cat got a little twitching—nothing in the least serious—and because I took this at first lightly she flew into a most violent temper and outburst of hate. Then she kept me for three hours running "urgent messages" as a punishment. Bromide had to be fetched and a special syringe procured to administer it. The weakest kind of morphia must be got in case it was needed—it was safer to dilute weak morphia than the strong kind she had already! Then hydrocyanic acid *in case* we wanted to kill the kitten quickly, etc., etc.. She certainly has the power of gratifying and developing the masochistic side of a man, but there are other love-components that also have to be thought of!

I don't think Frau Hoesch-Ernst will go to Vienna after all. She seems to have transferred her affections to Ferenczi, and will perhaps go to him, as her lover, whom I know, refuses her permission to come to me, being afraid of my discovering his secret!

Please convey my salutations to the Palatine. You will find that much work has been done there in the past year.

With kind regards to your sister-in-law and yourself

from Jones.

1. That is, that Putnam (1913) is largely autobiographical.
2. C. A. Douglas Bryan, M.D. 1900 London, especially interested in hypnotism; honorary secretary of the Psycho-Medical Society, London, and charter member and first vice president of the London Psycho-Analytic Society, founded 30 October 1913.

142

21 September 1913
Eden Hotel, Rome

My dear Jones,

I am glad to be here, yet most thankful for letters if they contain so much of information and of good prospects as yours. We are to expect much, very much of your zeal and energy and hope to be able to give you something for it in return. Your principles about the selection of members seem to be right. In no case could I advise you better than yourself.

Putnams letter was very amusing. Yet I fear, if he keeps away from Jung on account of his mysticism and denial of incest, he will shrink back from us (on the other side) for our defending sexual liberty. His second-thought pencil-written question is very suggestive about that. I wonder what you will answer to it. I hope no denial that our sympathies side with individual freedom and that we find no improvement in the strictness of american chastity. But you could remind him that advise plays no prominent part in our line of treatment and that we are glad to let everyman decide delicate questions to his own conscience and on his personal responsibility.

I am allright here at Rome, like it better every year. Not so much sight-seeing this time on account of my sister in law, but we cannot help enjoying [old]¹ ancient Rome and I am filling up gaps of my experience. So I am coming this day from the delicious *Tombe latine* missed hitherto. I am sorry she (Minna) does not like the Palatine as I did. I have visited old Moses again and got confirmed in my explication of his position, but something in the comparative material you collected for me, did shake my confidence which is not yet restored.

I say nothing about Loe as I am impatient to see her in a few days. I intend to leave Rome Saturday next.

Now go on writing me and believe me to be—now more than ever—

yours truly
Freud

1. Crossed out in the original.

143

Internationale Zeitschrift für Ärtzliche Psychoanalyse

1 October 1913
Wien

My dear Jones,

Here I am after 17 delicious days of Rome. Work is beginning fast. I will have to work 5 hours tomorrow and nine this day week. This Wednesday is unofficial, Cafe Landtmann. The two books, *Totem and Tabu*, and the third series of *Kleine Schriften zur Neurosenlehre* may appear in this very month.[1]

I have not been shaken in any point by the growing distance from the Munich impressions, they only appear [to] me even more ludicrous and pitiful than when fresh. I would prefer a neat division as soon as possible but for your London group, which ought to march safely before this event comes on.

I have been consulted by Heller about some practical discussions between you and him which I trust will arrange themselves to no damage for you. If you know H. you will not be astonished at his ups and downs, fit of enthusiasm followed by fits of caution. But at the whole he is an honest fellow and driven by intellectual interests as well as by material ones. He is awfully impressed by you and afraid, you might be angry for his want of propensity to translate your book on ΨA into German.[2] I think he is wrong about it. You know I am sure that this translation is not neces[s]ary or desirable, the book being intended to adress directly an english audience with no other path to ΨA open to it: a french translation would suit us much better.[3] To the german public you have become known by your more original productions and so let it be.

At Rome I began to do some work, I attacked the matter of Narzissm and wrote a first paper on it.[4] I would be glad to talk it over with you the same as with Rank and Sachs. The personal relations between the members of the Comité are the most pleasant feature of these serious times.

I have learned that I shall not see Loe before some days later. So you may give her my love once more.

I am with the most intense wishes for all your beginnings in this time of your life

yours truly
Freud

1. Freud (1912–13), and *Sammlung*, 3.
2. Jones, *Papers*, 1st ed. 1913.
3. Did not appear until much later; see Jones (1925b).
4. Freud (1914c).

144

4 October 1913
13 Princes Street
Cavendish Square, W.

Dear Professor Freud,

The question I raised with Heller is in no sense a dissension, and I quite appreciate what you say about his character. It was simply this. Now that we hope to get more and better English abstracts I did not think it right that Rank should be burdened with the translation of all of them, as he has been doing up to now, so I thought of finding some suitable person in London to translate them regularly under my supervision, and then to submit them to Rank for a final correction. I asked Heller if the *Zeitschrift* could bear *part* of the expense entailed in this plan, and he tells me the only money available is the Honorar, which of course goes to the reviewer only. I then wrote that I would pay the whole cost if necessary, but that when the funds of the *Zeitschrift* are in a satisfactory enough condition they should contribute at least a part of it, to which he agrees. If I received any salary as Redac[k]teur it could be devoted to these extra expenses, but I do not wish this if it would diminish Rank's.

The other question is equally simple. I got a letter from Sophie Durer (the lady you guessed the sex of at the Totem dinner in June)[1] saying that she had written twice to Heller a month previously about the translation of my book, but could get no reply from him. I wrote back saying I was forwarding her letter to him personally, and made the comment to him that his clerks had not been very attentive during his holidays. About the question of translation I quite agree with you that it would help neither ψα not [nor] myself personally, so it is a matter of indifference to me altogether, and purely a question as to whether Heller thinks it worth while for financial reasons. He makes the practical suggestion of translating a few of the less platitudinous articles, and so far as I am concerned he may do either this or nothing at all.

Today there were two agreeable arrivals by the post, your Scientia article, which is wonderfully clear and which whets my appetite for the second part[2]—many thanks—, and the *Zeitschrift*, where I was very proud to see my name;[3] I have not yet had time to read it, but the index looks promising.

Are the Narzissm articles for the *Zeitschrift* or the *Jahrbuch*, and could I hear something about the content?[4] I do not know [if][5] what you have decided about the question of withdrawing from the *Jahrbuch*; so far as I can judge the reasons in favour would be much stronger than those against. I feel that now all hope of reconciliation is over, as well as all wish on our side, the most urgent present need is a clarification of the differences, so that the world may decide whether Zurich represents a "progress" or merely a "watering" through reaction.

We propose to call a preliminary meeting for Oct. 23rd to constitute our group; I will let you know more details later. Meanwhile I have discovered a very serious worker in Syria (!), director of the asylum at Lebanon, and also two more supporters in Scotland.[6] Havelock Ellis refuses to join, on the ground that he belongs to *no* society on principle!

You will surely publish the paper you delivered at Munich?[7] It has stimulated my thoughts on many lines. Think of the brutality and money interests of the Americans, in conjunction with their incapacity to love—regression.

I am happy to hear that Rome was as delightful as ever; it is the right *point d'appui* from which to start another session's work.

Loe will not be in Vienna until about the 21st at the earliest, and begs you to reserve her some hours. She has delayed the flat-furnishing in a most unnecessary way, but what her motive is is too complicated a question for me to unravel, though I can partly guess. She is fairly well, but has taken morphia several times for the period.

Yours very sincerely
Jones.

1. Celebration dinner held on 30 June in honor of Freud (1912–13); see Jones (1955a, p. 355; 1955b, p. 398).

2. Freud (1913j), pp. 165–190]: pt. 1, "The Psychological Interest of Psycho-Analysis"; pt. 2, "The Claims of Psycho-Analysis to the Interest of the Non-Psychological Sciences."

3. Jones, Ferenczi, and Rank are listed on the title page as principal editors of *Zeitschrift*, 1 (1913).

4. Freud (1914c) came out in the *Jahrbuch*.

5. Crossed out in the original.

6. Dr. H. Watson Smith, Lebanon Hospital, Asfurieh, Beirut, and Dr. Leslie Mackenzie of Edinburgh would become members of the London Psycho-Analytic Society; see *Zeitschrift*, 2 (1914): 411. The identity of the second Scot is not clear.

7. Freud (1913i).

145

14 October 1913
69 Portland Court, London

Dear Professor Freud,

Well, I am definitely installed at last in my new residence, and the first letter written there is appropriately dedicated to you. I hope that before long it will prove to be a centre from which much $\psi\alpha$ activity will radiate. The flat itself looks charming; I am very pleased indeed with it, and am already looking forward to entertaining you here sometime as my guest. You will, I think, be pleased to find how well organised it is for work. Loe has been very generous in fitting the flat up, and has been—even for her—extraordinarily efficient.

Many thanks for the Dritte Folge,[1] which I notice is larger than its predecessors. It is a comfort to see those articles rescued from the *Jahrbuch* and *Zentralblatt*, so that they may be read apart from the influence of a contaminating environment. In a short time our literature, supported by the *Zeitschrift*, *Schriften* and *Imago*, will be quite purified and distinct from the wish-wash that unhappily surrounds it, and it will be our chief care to keep it so.

I have no general news to send this time. Our first meeting will be on the 30th, instead of the 23rd, so as to suit Bryan of Leicester. Sachs tells me that at the first Vienna meeting you gave a report of the Munich Congress.[2] How I should have liked to hear it! No doubt you did full justice to Maeder and Seif, not to mention the new star, Schmidt.[3]

I am completely engrossed these days in the emotional task of arranging, or destroying, masses of old letters, documents, etc.. It is painful work, for it unrolls in a pitiless way the story of my past life, which is far from being altogether agreeable. It is a story of much turmoil and turbulence; an unhappy childhood followed by ten years of uninterrupted success, then a series of foolishness and failures, and now gradually settling down to a more substantial basis where, shorn of my illusions, I trust it will enable me to do something sufficiently worth while to justify myself. This year marks a turning-point in my career, and the change will be a *deep* one, both externally and internally. Your lavish good wishes, which I shall try to deserve, are to me the most precious asset, and I thank you again and again.

Yours affectionately
Jones.

1. Freud, *Sammlung*, 3.
2. Freud's report of 8 October 1913 is not contained in *Minutes*, 4:205.
3. Hans Schmid (1881–1932), Swiss psychotherapist, corresponded with Jung in 1915 and 1916 on the issue of psychological types (Jung, 1921); see especially G. Adler (1973, pp. 30–32). Presented "Das Hamletproblem" at the Munich meeting of the International; see *Zeitschrift*, 2 (1914): 407.

146

27 October 1913
69 Portland Court, London

Dear Professor Freud,

Loe has commissioned me to tell you that she has again postponed her departure, and will not be in Vienna until about November the 18th, also to express her regret that she is unable to write herself.

The flat is now practically finished in spite of all delays, and her only excuse is that she wants some free time to herself, to shop in London, to rest, etc.. No doubt there is a mixture of motives, desire to plague me, which she is very successful at, hatred of Lina, which is very strong, but I think the chief one is resistance against going on with the analysis. Yesterday she could not recall the street of the Pension, *Ebendorfer*str., and thought only of *Rotenturm*str.,[1] which might be called a *männliche Protest*.[2] She is physically fairly well, and rarely takes morphia except at the periods. She expresses to everyone a total disbelief in ψα, has the strongest resistance to it, and is irritated by meeting even the most indirect association to it. I am full of concern for her future happiness, especially in reference to marriage, and am afraid you will not have an easy task to do much with her.

Herbert Jones is behaving splendidly, as usual, and is having to face much opposition from his family. McCurdy also, who is strongly homosexual, is doing all he can to prevent the marriage, from motives of jealousy both of Loe and of Herbert, and has composed several letters to you asking that you use your influence against it, though I don't think he has been foolish enough actually to send any of them. He has not written to me at all, being gravely shocked at the revelations Herbert has made to him of my character.

I am sorry to say that the University people in Toronto are making trouble about my not permanently residing there, and it is possible I may have to resign my professorship; I will let you know more as soon as I hear.

You will see that I am not entirely happy in my first time in London, but it is a mirror of life, and one must learn to look at it bravely.

Yours very sincerely
Jones.

1. Street names are underlined by Jones in the original.
2. Adler's concept of masculine protest is likely used here to accentuate Loe's preference for the sexually symbolic erect and vertical "red door" *(Rotentur)* over the "flat village" *(Ebendorf)*.

147

30 October 1913
Vienna, IX. Berggasse 19

My dear Jones,
    Nor am I completely happy at this moment. I scarcely can recall a time so full of petty mischiefs and annoyances as this. It is like a shower of bad weather, you have to wait who will hold out better, you or the evil genius of this time.

I expect Ferenczi Sunday for a conversation on important (sic!) topics related to ΨA. You will soon hear what I intend to do. The enclosed lines please give to Loe if you think they might affect her.

Yours truly
Freud

148

3 November 1913
69 Portland Court, London

Dear Professor Freud,
    Your note to Loe, which came this morning, provoked rather a strong reaction; as no doubt you intended, especially on the point about your not having kept hours for you [her].[1] She speaks of telegraphing to you. I think she will surely be in Vienna on the 18th.

I am eager to hear the result and decisions of yesterday's meeting with Ferenczi, and to know something of the problems that are besetting you. I am extremely sorry that a depressing letter from me should have come at such a time, and am glad to be able to send you a much better report. My depression was chiefly of an internal nature, which is now mending, and you must discount it on that account.

The London Psycho-Analytic Society was duly constituted last Thursday, with a membership of nine,[2] and I have written to Jung applying for admittance into the Vereinigung. Bryan is Vice-President and Eder secretary. I arranged this, because Eder knows the Vienna men and can write German somewhat, and because I would rather be succeeded later by Bryan, who is a very reliable man, than by him. McDougall and Hart have not yet joined, but did not refuse. Our first working meeting will be held on December the 4th.

I have eight patients applying for treatment, some of which will surely come. Other signs as well point to my practice being well assured within a short time, so that your prognosis was more correct than mine. I spoke last week at the Psychiatric Section of the Royal Society and was warmly applauded.[3] I am arranging to make the *Journal of Abnormal Psychology* the official organ of the Psycho-Medical Society here,[4] which will help to bring a wider circle under our influence.

I am feeling personally much happier in every way, and am starting proper work; Rank will tell you that I have already been active in regard to the *Zeitschrift*.

There are a number of technical questions I want to ask you concerning the Zwangsneurose article you are publishing in the next number,[5] but I will wait until you are having a more peaceful time or until I hear from you about the current matters you refer to in today's letter.

Yours always
Jones.

1. It appears as if, at a later rereading, "her" was written in above the "you," which is not crossed out.

2. The society was founded on 30 October 1913. By the time the announcement was published in *Zeitschrift*, 2 (1914): 411, there were fifteen members in all: Douglas Bryan (Leicester), Dr. Davidson (Toronto), Dr. Devine (Wakefield, Yorkshire), M. D. Eder (London), Dr. Forsyth (London), Dr. Graham (Belfast), Bernard Hart (London), Captain Berkeley Hill (Bombay), Ernest Jones (London), Constance Long (London), Leslie Mackenzie (Edinburgh), Maurice Nicoll (London), Colonel Sutherland (Jubbalpore, India), H. Watson Smith (Beirut), Maurice Wright (London).

3. Jones participated in the discussion following the paper by Charles A. Mercier, "The Concept of Insanity," *Proceedings of the Royal Society of Medicine*, 7–3 (1913–14): 3–12; for a summary of Jones's comments, see p. 13.

4. This was accomplished for the period from April–May 1914 through March 1921. The journal still retained its status as the official organ of the American Psychopathological Association in America.

5. Freud (1913i).

149

4 November 1913
69 Portland Court, London W

Dear Professor Freud,

I get Ferenczi's letter this evening, telling me the news, bidding me take action in America, and asking me to send you my opinion.[1] I will waste little time over giving my opinion about the decisions, for you all are in possession of more facts and can come to a more accurate judgement.

(1). *Jahrbuch.* It looks like an unexpected piece of luck that Jung should deliver this into our hands. "Too good to be true", and I fear some trick of his, or some scheme with Deuticke to get you to resign. If it is merely pique on his part, expecting to be called back, then all will go well and Bleuler will probably also retire. I should have suggested Abraham alone as Redakteur, both because he is a member of the committee and because a central redaction is easier to work, but I suppose you wanted an assistant in Vienna. Above all I mistrust Jung's move, which must have something behind it—what, we shall soon see.

(2). *Vereinigung.* I am in favour of dissolving, as you all are, but I do not understand the urgency of acting at once until we can correspond with one another (especially Abraham and myself, being at a distance) and so arrange the most workable plan. Ferenczi says that a dissolution is better than our being forced to resign, but—though of course that is true—it is not in Jung's power to do anything until the next congress. If we have the majority there (as I think) he would have to retire, if he has the majority we must take steps for dissolving before. But why today, *postwendend* [by return post]? Still, you may rely on me absolutely to take whatever steps you think fit.

(3). *America.* Re the New York group, Brill writes to me that Jelliffe, who has been re-admitted as a member, is using every influence to control it, and with considerable success. So we cannot hope for much there.

With the Amer. Association I really do not see that we can do what Ferenczi proposes, and for the following reasons: It meets only once a year, in May, and it would be impossible to get the men together from the different States merely for an extra business meeting—besides which there is no one there (except Brill) who understands the situation. In general the Americans find it very hard to enter into our conflicts. They regard them as merely personal, and rather to be deplored, and do not consider the scientific differences good ground for separating. Putnam told me he followed you in leaving Stekel, out of politeness, but he was very puzzled. Hoch, who is now President, is an old friend and admirer of Jung's, though he does not agree with him scientifically. The Council consists of Brill, Emerson[2] (who knows nothing of the matter), and White,[3] who is Jelliffe's chief friend and is on Jung's side. One could thus depend on Brill and myself out of the five officers. As none of the Americans have ever been present at the Congress and know nothing of the affairs of the Vereinigung, they are quite uninterested in the matter and are immersed in nearer interests. It would be extremely difficult to get them to take such a strong action as Ferenczi proposes. But I will write to them if you think it wise, either to the officers to ask them if they will take the responsibility of acting in the name of the members without the consent of the latter, or to all the members asking for permission to act in their name. In the latter way one might get a majority (I think this probable), but I do not know if it would be legal. They would be very puzzled to understand why a society should be dissolved on the grounds that some of the members cannot get on with the President. For these reasons I am not writing to America tonight, but will wait to hear further from you. If it is urgent, please telegraph to me to write, Plan A to the officers, Plan B to *all* the members.

The London Society is not yet an official constituent of the Vereinigung, and so cannot act.

One point I do *not* agree with Ferenczi about, and that is where he suggests telling the Americans that a new Vereinigung is in prospect. That would mean telling personal friends of Jung's, such as White, Jelliffe, Burrow, etc., and he would certainly refuse to dissolve, so as to retain power and let us, if we wished, be outsiders. If we can numerically *force* him to dissolve, we can force him to resign the Presidency at the next congress, and so need fear nothing. If one told the Americans about a new society, they would certainly say, especially doubtful men like Hoch, "then let those who wish leave the present Vereinigung and found a new one, but that is no reason for destroying the present one".

You will appreciate the difficulty of my situation. When one desires to act and to help, it is very hard when one does not see a clear way of acting, and at present I do not. I hate to write such a negative letter as this, and am trying to think out something more positive. Ferenczi asks if I would advise waiting for the American answer, or acting with Wien, Berlin, and B'pest alone. I would certainly say the latter if it is possible, as it seems to be, judging from his question (although it is only 3 out of the 7 groups), for any support from America in the matter would be lukewarm and doubtful. No doubt you have thought of the possibility of a general referendum amongst the 150 members, issued either by yourself, Abraham and Ferenczi, or by Jung at the request of the three groups. What is your opinion of this? Or could you send a circular to selected members, stating your desire to dissolve, and thus find out whether we had a majority for the purpose, which Jung could not resist?

Hoping to hear soon further details from you, Believe me

Yours as always
Jones.

P.S. No doubt you will forward this letter to Ferenczi.

1. Ferenczi's letter of 2 November 1913 (Archives of the British Psycho-Analytical Society, London) called for the secret committee to go into action to deal with Jung's resignation from the *Jahrbuch*. Jones's response should be read in this context. The entire episode is dealt with in Paskauskas (1988a, pp. 24–29).

2. Louville Eugene Emerson (1873–1939), Ph.D. 1907 Harvard; psychologist in the neurological department, Massachusetts General Hospital.

3. William Alanson White (1870–1937), superintendent of the Government Hospital for the Insane, Washington, D.C., from 1903 and pioneer in psychoanalytic psychiatry; with Jelliffe founded the *Psychoanalytic Review* in 1913.

150
[postcard]

7 November 1913
[Vienna]

L. J.!

Letter just received, excellent, will have moderating effect, is to be sent at once to the friends. Abraham expresses quite similar views. Suspicion regarding *Jahrbuch* of course correct. Matter still pending, shall report details in time. The whole business interfering with work, and disgusting.

Cordial thanks

Yours
Freud

151
[telegram]

8 November 1913
Vienna

Jahrbuch remains with us

Freud

152

11 November 1913
69 Portland Court, London

Dear Professor Freud,

I wrote fully last night to Ferenczi and perhaps he will forward it to you. I enclose Abraham's letter, which seems almost identical with mine in sentiment (willingness to act if necessary, but appreciation of the difficulties and desire not to put ourselves through over-haste into a false position that would only be to our disadvantage).

I now also enclose a letter of Putnam's that came this morning; will you please return it after you have shown it to whomever you wish. You will see from it how unlikely it is that he could be got to take action against Jung, unless there was the strongest objective reason, for he does not share our attitude. And Putnam is more on our side than anyone in America except Brill and McCurdy!

From a letter of McCurdy's this morning I quote the following passage: "Jung is bound to blow up sooner or later and it is my fervent prayer that he won't be too firmly bound to the Internationale Vereinigung when the eruption occurs. (McC. considers J. to be mentally disordered.). It certainly behoves us all to have a sane President for the next Congress." He also gives me the news that they have formed a ψα Verein[1] on Ward's Island, with August Hoch as President and himself as secretary. Their influence will be all on our side scientifically, though I don't suppose we could count on the group for [scientific][2] political action except McC..

I suggested to Ferenczi that we postpone action until after Christmas, and that he, Abraham and I come to Vienna to consult with you all by that time—a full committee meeting. By then I could also have written and got replies from the leading Americans.

Hart has joined the London group.

I wish someone, e.g. Rank, could find time to inform Abraham and myself of the details, especially of the reasons for haste. Did Abraham see my last letter?

Yours very cordially
Jones.

P.S. Many thanks for the telegram about the *Jahrbuch*, which means, I suppose, that you have arranged with Deuticke. It is excellent news, but I shan't be happy until I know what Jung's idea was in resigning.

P.S. I have just received the proof sheets of Jelliffe's *Psychoanalytic Review* (with an O). The first article is by Jung on the "change" in ψα..[3] The *Zentralblatt* is abstracted at greater length than the *Zeitschrift* (Ht. 1)[4] and your own paper in the latter is reviewed in two words "Continued article".!!⁵

*Sie sehen wohl also.*⁶

1. In fact a psychiatric society, not a psychoanalytic one.
2. Crossed out in the original.
3. See Eder, Eder, and Molzer (1913–15).
4. C. R. Payne, abstracts from vol. 2 of *Zentralblatt, Psychoanalytic Review*, 1 (1913): 112–116; L. E. Emerson, abstracts from vol. 1 of *Zeitschrift, Psychoanalytic Review*, 1 (1913): 108–112.
5. *Psychoanalytic Review*, 1 (1913): 108.
6. These you see.

153

13 November 1913
Vienna, IX. Berggasse 19

My dear Jones,

You see your advise and Abraham have prevailed with us. I only called for a council feeling uncertain in these political matters. Ferenczi was the hotspur but he is giving in too. We do not want to lose any position by affective motives.

Jung has already retraced [retracted] his name from the *Zeitschrift*, he is likely to do something more and I expect him to do work for us. It is perfectly clear why he resigned at the *Jahrbuch*. He wanted me and Bleuler to fall off and have it all to himself. The surest proof is that he immediately expressed his readiness to undertake it when Deuticke wrote him under a false impression, that I had produced with him in our first conversation after Jungs resignation. It was not until some days later that I was moved by Rank and Sachs to propose to Deuticke my keeping the *Jahrbuch* and D. had to refuse him and to take from his hands what he considered his booty.

I intend going to Hamburg during Christmas and to pass Sunday 28th of Dec. afternoon from 1h–8h with Abraham at Berlin. If you can be present too I will be very glad, to see you and to talk it over with you. It may be much more easy for you to come to Berlin than to Vienna.

As for Loe I guess from her letter, that she is very angry with me. It must go this way. She seems deep in Morphia but looks for the cause of my unkindness in my personal affairs instead in her own.

(I am getting interrupted)

Sincere love to you
Freud

154

14 November 1913
69 Portland Court, London

Dear Professor Freud,

I enclose part of a letter from Burrow, which may interest you; I know he has written to you. Please destroy it.

Thank you so much for the *Totem und Tabu* book that came this morning. That was a very neat hit at Jung in the preface![1] What is arranged about the English publication of it?[2] I hope this will reach widely in England.

Loe has again postponed her departure, for the last time, and will leave next week. Some of her delays have been unavoidable, others not. She now says there is no reason for her to have treatment, since you do not want it (not keeping the hours), and she doesn't believe in it. But she will depend on your attitude in this.

Yours
Jones.

1. Freud (1912–13, p. xiii).
2. See Brill (1918).

155

17 November 1913
Vienna, IX. Berggasse 19

My dear Jones,

I have been very much amused by your good saying about Jung, but we must not forget, this is our only case of success in the campaign against him, and we are mostly dependent on him for helping us by his foolish ways. If he were clever there would be no chance.

I return Putnam's letter for you, as regards the other—his letter to Meng[1]—it is wandering now, as you suggested, it may be with Ferenczi. I will hunt it up and have it sent to you as soon as possible. There is no doubt all these men incline strongly to Jung or to put it correctly, they tend away from ΨA; it is only your personal influence which may keep them back, doubtful for how long a time. They all seek gratification, not science, perhaps *Erlösung* [deliverance] from their own neurotic charge. Anyone who promises—he need not keep it—will get them.

Burrows' letter is interesting too. I accepted him, not too tenderly, I never show too much happiness when a patient is offering himself.[2]

Now for Loe. She ought not to have expected myself keeping two hours for her, when I was in a stress for time and knew she would not come and she did not write. However she might get her hours when she applies as soon as there is an opening in my crowd, which event is likely to come pretty soon. If she doesnt want I will not urge her. A reproduction of the totem from Rome is waiting for her in any case.

I am glad you are ready for the meeting at Christmas. Abr. writes he is not sure of his being at home Sunday Dec. 28th, so it is possible I stay with him the first of the holidays, Thursday 25th on my going to Hmbg instead of my coming from there. You will hear about it.

Yours sincerely
Freud

1. Heinrich Meng (b. 1887), Swiss psychiatrist; in 1929 headed up with Karl Landauer the newly founded Frankfurt Psychoanalytic Institute.
2. Trigant Burrow. On Burrow's relationship with Freud, see Burrow (1958).

156

19 November 1913
69 Portland Court, London

Dear Professor Freud,

I am hoping that my saying about Jung may be more than a jest. He communicates with Mrs. Eder,[1] whom I saw last night, and they take the view that he would be glad to dissolve the Vereinigung if only he could get your consent! They are bringing pressure to bear on him in this direction, so it is possible that, if we are cautious and silent, what we wish may be brought about from the other side. Jung is probably impatient at the remaining bonds between Zurich and Vienna, and may be glad to go his own way quite independently.

Dr. Constance Long, our fourth London member, and Drs. Young [Omaha] and Hamill [Chicago], of the American Association, are going to Jung to be analysed.[2] He is helped much by his knowledge of English, and also by having an English-speaking woman (Moltzer).

I was impressed by your remark about Putnam, etc., seeking gratification rather than science, and the episode shows how novel and insecure the scientific attitude still is in the world. Your own rigid adherence to it has always called forth my admiration. Progress in culture has always meant renunciation of wish-phantasies, with *courage* in facing and accepting cold reality, and mankind is for the most part nothing if not timid.

I am not sure whether it will be best for me to visit you in Berlin or in Vienna. The distance is not very important. In the former case I see only Abraham, whose attitude seems similar to my own, while in the latter case I see Ferenczi, Rank, Sachs, Hitschmann and Heller, also Loe.

Now some personal news, partly bad, partly good, and the bad first. Namely it is almost certain that I cannot hold my professorship in Toronto any longer. In spite of the Dean's promise to me, the Board of Governors, certainly instigated by malign influences, have decided that to do so I must practise in Toronto for ten months of the year. I have sent in my resignation and it will probably be accepted. The Board were told that I could attend only for the last six weeks of the session, whereas I had offered to come at any time of the year and for as long as I was wanted for my work.[3] Do you think I could retain a "courtesy title" for a short time? In a couple of years I hope to have another one in England. While I regret all this, it has a few compensatory advantages (less expense, continuity of practice, etc.). I shall perhaps visit America for the meetings every two or three years, but not next year.

Six patients more have come to me for treatment, two from America. Only one or two of these are suitable cases, some being paraphrenics, others having no money, but it is very cheering and I feel quite confident about making my way in practice. I seem to be well received here, and have had many letters of welcome; today, for instance, the Secretary of the Neurological Society,[4] whom I do not know well, writes inviting me to dine with him.

Walter Scott, the publisher, has accepted my higher terms for the book in Ellis' series, and I am signing an agreement to produce it before the end of next year. That will mean hard work, for I want to do it well.[5]

I am exceedingly comfortable in my flat, which is now entirely furnished except for an important item—a photograph of yourself. May I beg for a particular one? One taken *about* eight years ago, where you look to the right (a side face) with folded arms and of course a cigar.[6] You know how much pleasure it would give me to have one of you (I have nothing except the *Zentralblatt* copy). If possible I should like a large copy, as I wish to hang it on the wall, framed as a picture (photograph about 12 × 16 cm.).

Loe is a little less angry with you, but is expecting you to "apologise for breaking the agreement". She was leaving definitely this week, but must again postpone it for at least a week because yesterday she burst a vein in her leg and has to stay in bed (obedient for once).

With kindest regards

Yours sincerely
Jones.

1. The letters of this period from Edith Eder to Jones indicate that they knew each other very well. (Archives of the British Psycho-Analytical Society.)

2. Constance Long, M.D. 1896 Brussels, translated Jung (1916b). George Alexander Young, M.D. 1900 Chicago Homeopathic Medical College, specialist in neurology and psychiatry. Ralph C. Hamill, M.D. 1902 Rush Medical College, University of Chicago, later assistant professor of nervous and mental disorders, Northwestern University Medical School. "Omaha" and "Chicago" are written above the two doctors' names.

3. Jones was motivated to continue teaching his six-week course in psychiatry at the University of Toronto in order to retain his title of associate professor. His proposal that he be allowed to do this and live in London the rest of the time was rejected by the university. The board simply felt that if Jones could not live and practice his profession in Toronto, then he should not continue to hold his professorship; see Paskauskas (1985, pp. 218–219).

4. There were two honorary secretaries of the neurological section of the Royal Society of Medicine: T. Grainger Stewart and H. Campbell Thomson.

5. Jones was to do a book on psychoanalysis for Havelock Ellis's contemporary science series; after the war broke out, however, the project was abandoned.

6. See the frontispiece to Jones (1955a, 1955b).

157

22 November 1913
Vienna, IX. Berggasse 19

My dear Jones,

Than[k]s for your letter. That of Jung returns to you. It shows he does not feel quite happy. As for the remark on rumour he at least should be able to recognise the value of a rumour by his own analytical experience. The fact is that he accepted Deuticke's offer the very day it was made to him.[1] He is indeed oversure of his indispensableness, therefore my breaking loose from him is punished by self-destruction. The same as with Stekel, after he had cheated me of the *Zentralblatt* he pitied me for "throwing away my best friends".

It is a pity, this member of yours going to Z[urich] for analysis, he will be lost for you.[2] We know J.s position is a very strong one, our only hope is still he will ruin it himself. You will have to fight him for the influence in England and America and it may be a long and hard struggle. In this course of interests your losing the professorship at Toronto seems to be a blessing in disguise. I can't think you will be able to acquire the position and the patients you want at London, when you are forced to absent yourself for three months during the best season. As for the title you would keep it in Germany and you will remain Prof. J. with us, you know titles stick far more intensily to the person with us than in other countries.

I am flattered you ask a portrait of mine for your flat. That mentioned by you was taken by my son Oliver 7 years ago, enlarged by a Zurich photographer and I possess no sample of the same. But I am in a position to offer you in a few weeks a copper-heliogravure of the other (1909) very much enlarged, and highly satisfying, which is being made by the editors of *"Nos Contemporains"* a French publication. Besides a very able young *"Radirer"* [etcher] is working now to produce an other portrait of my person by the instigation of Heller. So you see in a short time your happiness may be complete and may the other of your wishes be fulfilled as easily!

If you prefer coming to Vienna at Christmas—I expect you will accompany Loe who is bound to look for the dog—I beg you will arrange it so as to be present after the 29th. I am leaving here Christ-evening and coming back Monday morning (29th).

The program of the *Jahrbuch* is nearly settled. I would ask you for your work on the Madonna the elephants and the flatus to be put in there instead into *Imago*, as the *Jahrbuch* is meant to show choice specimens of our workship.[3] Consider upon it! Sachs will write you more.—I am sorry Loe still sticks to one sided obligations and forgets how she has kept her own, more sorry that she is ill again. Be cautious with her about this veinous business.

Yours truly
Freud

1. On 15 November 1913 Jung wrote to Jones in English: "The rumour was spread out, that I made an attempt to take the *Jahrbuch* with me. Deuticke can proof, that this is a lie. I expected that Freud would tell me such a thing directly" (Sigmund Freud Copyrights, Wivenhoe).
2. That is, Constance Long.
3. Jones (1914a).

158

24 November 1913
69 Portland Court, London

Dear Professor Freud,

Would you kindly return Putnam's letters including the one to Mensendieck,[1] as I want to answer him at once; you see he is wobbling.

I shall try to get to Berlin, and shall certainly come either there or Vienna. I am not sure yet about the dates.

I rejoiced at your splendid news about Jung, who evidently over-reached himself by not making sure of Deuticke in his haste. We have an English proverb that may apply to him in relation to the Vereinigung, as well as in other ways: "Give a dog a long enough rope, and he will hang himself".

Yours as always
Jones.

1. Otto Mensendieck (b. 1871), Ph.D., member of the Zurich Psychoanalytic Society.

159

29 November 1913
69 Portland Court, London

Dear Professor Freud,

Well, Loe definitely left London last night, and will reach Vienna, via Holland, on Monday night or possibly Tuesday. The parting was naturally an affective experience for both of us, but I do not doubt that we shall get over it, and then also it is not absolute, for we shall remain to some extent in touch (so far as that is possible with Loe's writing habits). I am very concerned about her future, which does not seem to me to be at all soundly based internally, and am anxious to hear about her relations to yourself. She will call on you, and no doubt reproach you, but if you were to meet her halfway I think she would give in and be manageable.

Our member who goes to Jung is a woman, Constance Long, a virgin of 40, hence in any case not too hopeful. The only Englishman I have hopes of enlisting on our[1] side is Bryan of Leicester; you will hear more of him. Last week I met Stanley Bligh,[2] who visited you last year in Vienna. I judge him to be a bright, active and interesting man, but uncritical through having an untrained and undisciplined mind. He is enthusiastic and is a man of considerable wealth and influence, so he may be useful some time. What was your impression of him?

The next point in your letter is your very kind offer about the photograph; for which I very cordially thank you. It will be an event to look forward to with the keenest pleasure.

I answered Sach's letter about the Madonna *Arbeit*, thanking him and you for the motives whereby it is transferred to the *Jahrbuch*. It is of course indifferent to me whether it appears there or *Imago*, except for one matter, on which I asked his opinion—namely Heller could reproduce the difficult photograph that accompanies the essay better than Deuticke, having a larger page, better paper, and more skilled workmen. This would not weigh against other considerations, but still is to be thought of. Do we edit the second half of Band V, or is this published from material already with the printer from Jung, so that we start a new volume in 1914?

Sachs tells me that Jung is getting out a new journal at Deuticke's, which gives me the following thought. We know Deuticke to be antagonistic in feeling, and be bound chiefly by money considerations. With two competing journals it is in his power to favour one of them by various unconscious actions, choice of printer and proof-reader, delays, etc.. We must be prepared beforehand for this. Have you thought at all of the possibility of amicably transferring the *Jahrbuch* to Heller, which would have the advantages of a common subscription and advertisements of the three journals, mutual exchange of articles if necessary, etc.. By the way, won't

Deuticke object on religious grounds to publishing my essay, just as he did with Storfer's brochure?[3]

Scripture of New York,[4] who helps the ψα cause in about the same way that Stekel does, has just deserted his wife and children and run away with another woman. The latest N.Y. scandal!

I will send you an account of our meeting next Thursday, which I am looking forward to with much interest. How did Ferenczi's demonstration go off in Vienna last week?[5]

With kindest regards

from yours
Jones.

P.S. Practice is very good, and is already paying all living expenses.

1. An *o* is written on top of a *y*, leaving the impression that Jones had first written either "your" or "yur."

2. Stanley Bligh, S.P.M., B.A., was a member of the British Psychological Society.

3. A. J. Storfer, *Marias jungfräuliche Mutterschaft: Ein völkerpsychologisches Fragment über Sexualsymbolik* (Berlin: Hermann Barsdorf, 1914).

4. E. W. Scripture (b. 1864), M.D. Munich 1906, Ph.D. Leipzig; associate in psychiatry, Columbia University, and director of the research laboratory, Vanderbilt Clinic, New York.

5. Ferenczi gave a presentation at the Vienna Society titled "Experiments with Thought-Transference," 19 November 1913, as noted in *Minutes*, 4:215.

160

2 December 1913
69 Portland Court, London

Dear Professor Freud,

I append two extracts for your interest. The first, which you perhaps know already, but which seems to me a very pretty addition to your camel-totem story, is from Porphyry; a description of the Diipolia ceremony in Athens: "They choose some girls as water-carriers, and they bring water for sharpening the axe and the knife. When the axe has been sharpened, one person hands it and the other hits the ox, another slaughters him, others flay him, and they all partake of him. After this they sew up the hide of the ox and stuff it with hay and set it up, just like life, and yoke it to the plough as if it were going to draw it *(Le roi est mort, vive le roi!).* A trial is held about the murder, and each passes on the blame for the deed to another. The water-carriers acuse those who sharpened the knife, the sharpeners blame the man who handed it, he passes on the guilt to the man who struck, the striker to the slaughterer, the slaughterer blames the knife itself; and the knife, as it cannot speak, is found guilty and thrown [in the sea][1] into the sea (castration)."[2] My book adds "All these offices are held in certain families by hereditary right. The whole ceremony clearly points back to days when the ploughing ox was held sacred. The older worship of Attica is all agricultural".

The other is merely taken from Sir George Savage's report in the *Journal of Mental Science* of the International Congress in August. He sketches the different speakers with a word each: "Janet's [His] agreeable and almost courtly manner won a warm place with all of us. Jung was clear and precise in his defence of Freud and in his uncompromising defence [support] of psycho-analysis. [. . .][3] Ernest Jones [Dr. E. Jones, of Canada,] combined the clear-seeing investigator with the unbiassed critic".[4] I don't know which of the three descriptions is the more irrelevant or inappropriate; one might perhaps say that the first is irrelevant, the second untrue, and the third inappropriate (for even if I am unbiassed elsewhere I must have appeared biassed enough at that meeting).

I should be glad if you could find time to correct and modify the review of Jung I sent recently to Rank; the last sentence is certainly not objective enough for the high standards of the *Zeitschrift*.[5]

yours
Jones.

1. Crossed out in the original.
2. From Porphyry, *De Abstinentia*, 2.30.
3. Here a sentence was omitted by Jones: "It was interesting to find out how devout the worshippers of this cult are and their rather emphatic belief that unless one follows their lead one is lost."
4. From *Journal of Mental Science*, 59 (1913): 659.
5. For the review of Jung, see Jones (1914c). The sentence in question may have been dropped, for the last sentence in published form does not seem to be relevant to Jones's comment.

161

4 December 1913
Vienna, IX. Berggasse 19

My dear Jones,

I cannot abstain from sending back Jungs letter, it may be interesting for you after some time. He has learned ΨA in order to bring forward the demand that personal complexes ought to be overlooked. A very nice result. "It is all a mistake" reminds me of something similar recurring saying in Kipling's Phantom Rickshaw.[1]

Your letter contains an excellent piece of news that your practice begins to pay. I am glad to hear you have lost Toronto, you could not succeed in London with that burden.

Something you are wishing for will reach you in the next days although I would prefer to have wished for something else.

I have seen Loe. To be sure she was more kind in my presence than she shows in my absence. I found her not inaccessible to reason and repentence and gave her 2 hours a week to help her in clearing the darkness of the last London events and freeing herself again from Morphia. I know the former sweetness will be banished from our relations, I am not sure that the "new course" will help her.

I am eager to know what your intentions are about meeting at Xmas at Vienna or Berlin. Mine are unchanged.

As regards your doubts on Deuticke's behaviour it may be safely said that he is formally correct and that his only love is for his pocket. Heller was aspiring to the *Jahrbuch* eagerly but we thought it was favourable to lean upon two sticks and to regulate the one by the other. Besides it was a point to keep a position and have the adversary look out for a fresh one.

With sincere love

yours
Freud

1. Rudyard Kipling, "The Phantom Rickshaw," in *Wee Willie Winkie and Other Stories* (London: Macmillan, 1895), pp. 125–169.

162

8 December 1913
Vienna, IX. Berggasse 19

My dear Jones,

I am writing under the eyes of an able young artist who is etching a plate of copper while I am allowed to do as I like.

You will have got my portrait. No thanks please.

The extract about the ox-murder at Athens was known to me from Frazer. I even alluded to some passage of it in *T. & T.* Thank you for taking this pain.[1]

Sir George Savage seems to be a man obliged to say agre[e]able things to every one.

My proposals as to how you could continue your review on Jung will be in your hands at this time. You may use it as you like or not use it at all.

There is a delicious silence about Zürich now. May it last until July 14, when my paper on the "ΨA Movement" in the new *Jahrbuch* will cut definitively all connections between us.[2]

Yours sincerely
Freud

1. Freud actually alludes to Robertson Smith's version of the story; see Freud (1912–13, pp. 137, 152).
2. Freud (1914d).

163

11 December 1913
69 Portland Court, London

Dear Professor Freud,

The portrait arrived safely, and I am very proud. It is a beautiful reproduction. I hope the copper etching will be a success.

You speak of the *Jahrbuch* appearing on only July the 14th. I wondered if this was a mistake for January, but perhaps it means that Jung is completing this volume so that we may start fair on a clean sheet.

I think of leaving here tomorrow week, reaching Vienna on Sunday morning, the 21st, and staying there 5–6 days. If, however, your time will be less occupied after your return than before your departure I could postpone my journey until then; if this is the case I beg you to let me know.

I have been coaching a doctor for the M.D. London, Psychiatry Branch. In the psychology paper four questions only out of six may be answered, and McDougall, the examiner, set four questions on ψα. My man swept the board and I hope may get the gold medal. It will be some time before Berlin, Paris, or Vienna emulate the example of London University in this! On the other side I enclose a programme that shows how the conception of anxiety neurosis is apprehended by an asylum superintendent in London. I made fine play with him at the meeting.

Dr. Hamill of Chicago is coming to study with you in the spring, and I have advised him to be analysed. He is a member of the American Association, but I do not know much of him.

Abraham sent me today his Jung-*Kritik*, and I have just returned it with comments.[1] It is difficult to write on Jung without showing affect; as one reads one gets more and more angry at one stupidity after another. I find Abraham's review very good, a little uneven, but splendid in several lucid passages. I am eager to see what you have added to my review of Jung, and am surprised that you have crossing [crossed] nothing out; it has not come yet.

I am sending your daughter a book of Kipling's that she could not get, also your son Ernst a book that I read recently and which I think will interest him, for I know of his activity at the Zionist Congress in September.[2]

I have had only a note from Loe, and am delighted she has resumed work.

With kindest regards, and looking forward to seeing you soon,

Yours
Jones.

1. Abraham (1914).
2. See *Stenographische Protokolle der Verhandlung des Zionisten Kongresses*, vol. 11 (Vienna, 2–9 September 1913).

164

14 December 1913
Vienna, IX. Berggasse 19

My dear Jones,

I have just finished the 4th edition of the *Traumdeutung*[1] and feel free for a while. So I will be glad to hear to you stick to your plan u [and] be here this day week. I intend to leave Christmas evening for Hamburg.

By "July 14th" I meant the middle of next year. The second half of the 5th vol. will be finished by Jung and may appear in a few days. It contains his resignation in some "affective" words and the announcement of the new era.[2]

I have seen Loe thrice since her arrival and find her in a deplorable condition which makes me sad. She is nearly inaccessible, doesn't know how to profit of her pains, doesnot understand what we want her to do or to find. I incline strongly to the opinion that she will not marry Herbert Jones, but fall ill before and not get free from Morphia. It is a pity she should be so abnormal and so far from help. However I have not given up the trial.

Your review of Jung with my addition you ought to have got long before. But our printers are striking, all our business is upset. May be it is not yet out of the press.

I had an exchange of letters with Putnam about the dissensions with Zürich and did not shrink from strong language regarding Jung. I am tired of leniency and kindness. The motives are too clear and the innovations too stupid. The *"Anpassung"* [adaptation] of our Swiss friends has gone rather too far. Truth cannot, even with a pragmatist, be what brings money.

Gladly awaiting your arrival

yours sincerely
Freud

1. Freud (1900a), 4th ed. 1914.
2. See McGuire (1974, p. 551), which contains Jung's statement of resignation for "personal" reasons.

165

17 December 1913
69 Portland Court, London W

Dear Professor Freud,

I am very grieved at your bad news about Loe. Although she naturally shows me her worst side, I always feared you were too hopeful, and am full of concern about her future. She can be such a wonderful creature at times, that it is dreadfully sad. However, I do not envy Herbert Jones if he marries her.

I meant to stay at the Regina, but last night I got a telegram from Loe, saying she had reserved a room at the pension, so I shall be there on Sunday morning. I am greatly looking forward to my visit.

Yours ever sincerely
Jones.

166

31 December 1913
69 Portland Court, London

Dear Professor Freud,

Enclosed is a document from Putnam, and a letter from Hamill, which he asked me to forward, not having your address; he is a member of the American group, but I know little of him, as he was able to attend only one meeting, his chief, Dr. Patrick, being always away at that time.

I have heard from Abraham; he gives me the light task of reviewing the ψα progress in characterology for the *Jahrbuch*.[1] From Mrs. Eder I hear that Jung has decided not to found a new journal, but has arranged with Deuticke to publish a series of books or brochures.[2] *Sonst nichts neues* [otherwise nothing new].

It was a great pleasure seeing you again personally, and also hearing the fresh ideas. I intend to make regular pilgrimages to Vienna every year at least. Meeting the other men was also of course very enjoyable, and the whole time was profitable.

In the masochism theory[3] there is still a piece not clear to me, which perhaps you will explain. Whence comes the algolagnic[4] phantasies, i.e. whence the pleasure, the wish, that comes to meet the disagreeable trauma, the fear of castration, and which elaborates the latter in so many disguises? One must of course assume a constitutional basis, "femininity", but it feels as though there is something else in between this and the castration idea. Is it impossible that also here an overheard coitus is necessary (thus accounting for the connection between masochism and sadism), but reacted to in a different way from that characteristic of sadism? A Zwangsneurotiker told me this morning he has a horror of women who have some defect, especially a missing hand or arm, or even lameness. He connected it with his mother, who died of tuberculosis when he was five, but who had no deformity. He had an undescended testicle and a small penis, and believed till he was 16 that he had been castrated, confounding castration with circumcision. He has a great horror of blood, which makes him faint, which he connects with his mother's haemoptysis.[5] His father was a drunkard, rough and cruel. That all hangs together well; in the manifest content he is decidedly masochistic.

I suggested to Ferenczi he should write for the *Jahrbuch* a paper on symbolism, theory, practice, and definition, taking perhaps six examples which could be illustrated from different fields, neurosis, dream, folklore, mythology, jokes, etc.. No doubt he spoke to you about it. What do you think of the plan? We should of course all have to help him in collecting material.[6]

Please give my kind regards to your ladies, and accept my heartiest wishes for a Happy New Year and prosperous undertakings.

Yours always
Jones.

1. This did not appear in the *Jahrbuch*.
2. Jung's plans were communicated to Alphonse Maeder, 29 October 1913 (G. Adler, 1973, p. 28): "I shall take care to create for the Zurich people a new organ in the style of the *Jahrbuch*, perhaps called '*Psychologische Untersuchungen*. Works of the Zurich School of Psychoanalysis.' In the event, Deuticke is ready to accept it." The editor notes that the first volume of a series edited by Jung, called *Psychologische Abhandlungen*, containing five essays by Jung's followers, was actually published by Rascher in 1914, and that Jung retained this designation for most of his major works, which are to be found in *C.W.* (p. 28 n. 1).
3. Freud (1905d, pp. 157–160).
4. Sexual excitement in causing or experiencing pain.

5. Spitting of blood.

6. Jones himself published a lengthy paper on this topic (Jones, 1916a). Ferenczi had already published a short piece, "Symbolism," which Jones was to translate (Ferenczi, 1912b).

167

3 January 1913 [1914]
Vienna, IX. Berggasse 19

My dear Jones,

I am very proud of your remarks in continuation of the masochistic business. No doubt you are right, you have hit the very point where the matter must be followed. But it is not yet time to discuss it, perhaps when you come the next time or we meet at another place, it will have advanced so far.

Putnams letter is precious, I could not resolve destroying it, I send it back to you. He is a man of doubt, we know by his self-analysis (you remember the Griselda paper).[1] He does not mention the letter I wrote upon Jung's character. It may produce no good effect with him as he is unable to renounce to an ideal-Sublimirung. I got a letter from him perhaps by the same ship, pretty reserved and of no importance.

Loe has just given in and will take a daily treatment—if not interrupted by Herbert J.'s arrival. She is making no progress in the Morphia struggle.

Ferenczi did not speak to me about your plan for a paper on symbolism. I will communicate with him about the subject. It is hardly ripe, symbolism, but any contribution from F. must be welcome.

I will write and accept Dr. Hamill, who promises to come in March.

I have finished Moses the first day of this year and liked it better while writing than before.[2] The printers' strike is not yet finished.

I am glad to hear from you as from your letter to Loe that you [are] in good spirits. Now help me and our cause in this advancing year as we expect you to do.

Yours truly
Freud

1. Putnam (1913).
2. Freud (1914b).

168

Imago

8 January 1914
Vienna

Dear Jones,

In exchange for your Putnam letter I send you another which seems rather good. His agreement about Jung will appear a strong decision if you remember my terms "brutal, insincere, sometimes dishonest". Even in theory he is making more concessions than we could expect, although to be sure the repressed is coming back by a *"Hinterthür"* [back door]. Please return his letter for answerings sake. I regret the loss of his child but it is not the beloved one, the Griselda.[1]

Loe is rather progressing if I am not mistaken. You will have got Jungs circular on the Congress. Pray do not answer before having communicated with Berlin, Bpest and Vienna. We want to measure our forces with Zürich and act in common. Now what is the way you propose and may bring forward in your group. Will you stick to the decision of the Congress, vote for Schandau[2] and come there with as much members as possible? Or propose something which excludes the Congress and practically puts an end to the meetings? Please consider and give reply to Rank or Sachs, who have put the same question to Ferenczi and Abraham.

Thanks for the interesting passage from Boas. I am working on the *Geschichte der ψα Bewegung*[3] which I try to render as indiscreet and amusing as possible.

Yours truly
Freud

1. See Putnam to Jones, 16 December 1913, and Putnam to Freud, 25 December 1913, in Hale (1971a, pp. 280–281, 167–169).
2. Bad Schandau, near Dresden.
3. Title of Freud (1914d). The German is written out in Gothic characters.

169

9 January 1914
69 Portland Court, London

Dear Professor Freud,

Abraham tells me that Jung has enquired about the place of the next congress, and I wonder if this is not the best moment to suggest a dissolution of the association. If Berlin, Budapest and Vienna (London is not yet an official group, and we have not heard from Jung) combine in this request, Jung may simply get defiant and hold the congress willy-nilly, hoping we will stay away from it. That would leave him in full possession of the field, which would never do at all. Don't you think that you personally could write to him proposing either a dissolution or at least a postponement of the congress for this year, there being no one else with any authority or moral right approaching yours? Then the matter might be submitted to a referendum of all the groups, with individual voting, and this would give us a good chance of winning, for many undecided men, like Eder, would vote for this rather than have the painful farce of last September repeated.

Thank you very much for your encouraging letter that came this week. I am hard at work studying the various problems in question, and have some highly interesting material. One case has made me realise more clearly than before the significance of the castration-complex in women, and its relation to the horror of blood and the humiliation at menstruation (awakening of infantile ideas of being deprived of the penis). It makes me think that much of the curious horror of menstruation shewn in folk-lore may be due to this complex in men; a typical example being the isolation of menstruating women for fear their presence may induce impotence (symbolically, e.g. turn the milk sour, etc.).

I have been chosen as co-referent with McDougall of Oxford for a discussion on the *Sexualtheorie* at a conjoint meeting of the British Psychological Society and the Psychiatric Section of the Royal Society of Medicine, March 10th,[1] also at a discussion of ψα at the British Medical Association, July 30th.[2]

Practice exceeds all expectations. I have eight patients daily, and had to send another one away this week, to Eder. Two pay Kr. 50 each, the others Kr. 25. If things go on this way, and there is no reason why they shouldn't, I shall be able to marry, which I hope will be the next step in my life.

No doubt you got this week the two enclosures I sent you; poor Putnam, I am sorry for him.

As to Loe, I suppose the battle will be fought out on the morphia question as she has chosen that field; she feels that if morphia is not in reserve her boats are burnt. I hope there will be some better news in your next letter; she hasn't written to me since I was in Vienna.

Have you decided to put your name to Moses? Surely!

Yours always
Jones.

1. See note 2 to letter 180.
2. Jones (1914i).

170

10 January 1914
69 Portland Court, London

Dear Professor Freud,

Thank you for this morning's letter. I have little to add to my letter of yesterday about the Congress. Abraham had asked me to vote for Dresden, as being more convenient in case of bad weather, but there are more important considerations than this. Our meeting here is not for three weeks, and by that time you can decide what I am to lay before the members, though probably our opinion is not asked, as Jung has not communicated with us. I am in favour of a referendum vote of the whole Vereinigung on the question whether it should be dissolved, or at all events this year's congress postponed. We should lose nothing by such a vote even if it doesn't go our way (it would be at least a measurement of forces on a favourable ground), and we might gain what we want. The only problem is how to bring this idea to Jung's notice, and I think this would best come from you as President of the Vienna Society.

Putnam [gives][1] takes back with one hand what he gives with the other. I was amused at his peace-offering (two papers) in the postscript.[2] The one good practical point is that we seem to have won him a little away from Jung. He can do no harm by his philosophical speculations, for no one reads them, but it would be another matter were he to ally himself with Jung.

I am glad Loe is going on better, and hope to hear good news again. Is she coming to London?

With kindest regards

Yours
Jones.

1. Crossed out in the original.
2. See Putnam to Freud, 25 December 1913, in Hale (1971a, pp. 167–169).

171

16 January 1914
Vienna, IX. Berggasse 19

My dear Jones,

I am deep in work yet I cannot postpone answering your last two letters in an abrupt way at least.

We will all of us vote for Dresden. I am astonished you got no acknowledgment from Jung as you have a right to it and could vote too. Perhaps you require it from him.

The question of the place does not include the other if the congress should be held at all. Yet we all wonder at your proposal, it being the contrary of what you advised and what was followed by us the last time when we grew impatient of the symbiosis. I think the moment would not be favourable now, our critical papers—yours, Fer.'s Abr.'s—not yet published and mine in the *Jahrbuch* not appearing before July.[1] Besides I would strongly object to addressing him in any matter where I might become subjected to his goodwill.

I am glad you are studying the castration-complex in women and can combine it with the menstruation-taboos. It looks highly promising.

I rejoice in the good news about practice and a little in the triumph of having predicted so. But will you do me the personal favour of not making marriage the *next step* in your life, but to put a good deal of choosing and reflection into the matter since there is no need for you to repeat a story like that of Jephtha's daughter.[2]

Loe I am sorry to say is halting and struggling again, pretty unreasonable and not in good bodily condition. The next event in expectation is the arrival of H. Jones on the 21st January.

I am with best wishes and waiting for more good news

yours truly
Freud

P.S. Why should I disgrace the Moses by putting my name to it? It is a fun and perhaps no bad one.[3]

1. Jones (1914c), Ferenczi (1914), Abraham (1914), Freud (1914c, 1914d).
2. Biblical figure who sacrificed his only daughter; see Judges 11:34–40.
3. "It is a joke, but perhaps not a bad one" is the way this line appears in Jones (1955a, p. 366; 1955b, p. 410), where the episode concerning the anonymous publication of Freud (1914b) is discussed in detail.

172

19 January 1914
69 Portland Court, London

Dear Professor Freud,

I note that Dresden is the place to vote for if we get the opportunity. As our group cannot be legally incorporated into the Vereinigung until the Congress accepts it I suppose we now have no vote, but I am asking Eder, the secretary, who stands better with Jung than I do, to write to Jung demanding one. Still I suppose the voting will be "crossed", and will not represent the relative strength of the two parties.

My attitude on the two occasions does not seem to me so inconsistent as it has apparently struck you. Both times I wish for a dissolution if it can be safely engineered, but I see a great difference in a minority of the groups trying to force it at a time when nothing is happening, and the matter to be opened tentatively now when the other side opens the question of the Congress. Still I am impressed by your point about the reviews producing a situation that would bring things to a head more inevitably than any suggestion at the present time.

I am sorry to hear about Loe's condition, but suppose it is partly due to her state of mind while expecting Herbert Jones. I am eager to hear what will be the outcome of his visit, whether they are coming to London, etc., and am dependent on you for my news, since she does not write to me at present.

As to the very vague subject of my own marrying, I will certainly take your advice about careful reflection and choice, advice which I find both wise and necessary. It has, to be sure, come into my thoughts at various times of late, which is rather natural under the circumstances (settling down, etc.), but I realise that I should become more *"fertig"* [accomplished] with the analysis of my own mental workings before venturing to think of throwing in my lot with that of someone else.

You ask me about Moses. One reason why I hope you will sign it is that, whether you do or not, the authorship will be sufficiently evident from the style and contents, and if you do not, it will set the Zurich people speculating as to what it all means, etc..

I have a queer case at present, rather like Bjerre's case of hysterical paranoia.[1] An unmarried lady of 45 *believes* that the local vicar and his sister make improper remarks to her for the pleasure of seeing her blush, that he—at her mother's instigation—makes references to her from the pulpit, and that another man does not want to meet her because he thinks she is in love with him; one brother has paraphrenia. All this looks very like paranoia, with marked projection, but I feel sure, after a month's analysis, that she is only a hysteric. She responds to analysis like a normal hysteric (rapport, no abnormal insight, etc.), and is already making some progress.

A disagreeable thing has just happened here. Mercier, a celebrated psychiatrist, has written to the *British Medical Journal* a violent letter of vulgar abuse, protesting against the "phallic worship" and "pornography" of "Freudism".[2] Unfortunately he is an annoying antagonist, for he has nothing to do (is retired) except conduct controversies and has such a *Streitigkeit*[s]-complex [quarreling complex] or *Querulantenwahn* [com-

plaint mania] that he generally tires out his opponents who have less time
at their disposal, and again he is entirely unscrupulous and dishonest,
twists words and sentences so as to make verbal quibbles, being entirely
uninterested in getting at the truth; also he has an unusual skilful and
witty pen, for all of which reasons he always "scores" off opponents, especially when he can arouse prejudice on his side.

I went to see Eder, who had already composed an absurd letter ($\psi\alpha$ was
the greatest Mount Pisgah[3] of the centuries, etc.) that would have been
out of place in this connection and only given Mercier plentiful opportunity for his mocking wit. We talked matters over and decided to wait a
week to see if anyone else wrote on either side, and if not, to let the matter
sink into the oblivion it deserves. We shall surely before long have other
opportunities for controversy, and probably more favourable ones, or at
least less degrading. Still if anyone else accepts Mercier's challenge, or
writes to support him, we shall have to step in. What do you think of all
this?

I am working hard, and have done nearly a half of the Ferenczi translation.[4] Abraham wants my contribution for the *Jahrbuch* by the end of
February, but I don't think this will be possible.[5]

Yours always
Jones.

1. Poul Bjerre, "Zur Radikalbehandlung der chronischen Paranoia," *Jahrbuch*, 3
(1912): 795–847.

2. See *British Medical Journal*, 1 (1914): 172–173, 276. Charles A. Mercier, M.B. 1878,
M.D. 1905 London; former lecturer on insanity, Charing Cross Hospital Medical School,
and author of numerous books including *A Text-Book of Insanity* (London: Swan Son-
nenschein, 1902).

3. The biblical mountain east of the Jordan from which Moses beheld the Promised
Land (Deuteronomy 34:1).

4. Jones (1916b).

5. Jones (1914a, 1914h).

173
[postcard]

1 February 1914
[Vienna]

Dear Jones,

Thanks for your sending. Louis is highly interesting and nicely written.—I am writing—writing—and no end of it. Excuse my shortness. Loe is behaving better. The printers' strike is ended.

Yours sincerely
Freud

174

6 February 1914
69 Portland Court, London

Dear Professor Freud,

First as to the enclosed abstracts. They are (1) the translation of a verse by Sappho to a loved object, illustrating beautifully the relation between Libido and Angst by describing the symptoms of an Angstanfall, (2) an extract from the newspaper showing an interesting conception of Hamlet, and (3) the correspondence up to date on the ψα in the *British Medical Journal*, the chief letters being marked by a cross at the side. Will you please return these last. You will see that the paranoic Mercier, the son[1] of a French father who defends "English clean-mindedness" and hates everything from the continent, has drawn a hornets' nest about his head. All the four letters this week, including one from Stoddart, the superintendent of Bethlem asylum and a well-known psychiatrist, are in our favour. The editor, however, has suppressed a letter from Eder (which I wrote) which simply crushed Mercier's quotations from Maeder, and was written in a very suave manner. On the whole, therefore, the situation is pretty good, and there is still some fair play left in old England.[2]

Not hearing from you for so long, I wondered if there were any fresh complications in the situation with Loe, which were taking time to adjust themselves. I am glad to hear she is behaving better, but am eager to hear all that has happened, whether Herbert Jones is still there, what they have decided, whether she is coming to London, etc.. She does not write to me at all.

I was glad you liked Louis, and was afraid you would find him too obvious. It interested me historically, and as shewing that ψα can make some contributions to historical problems, also perhaps psychiatrically (paranoia versus hypochondria).

Jung has sent us a circular, and we shall vote on it at our meeting next Thursday. In the *Journal of Mental Science* for October appears a very remarkable review of Jung's Wandlungen essay, by one Alexander Neuer (unknown to me, and not in the medical directory).[3] He is a follower of Adler, traces Jung to Adler (not historically) and is very perspicacious about Jung's "veiled, but savage attack" on yourself. If you wish, I could procure for you a copy of the number.

I find that Comte's three stages of mental development in mankind (which we searched for in vain last year) are: religious, metaphysical, positivist, so your originality still holds the field. Of the full series animism, mythology, religion, philosophy, science, he omits the first two,—characteristic of his period! I am exceedingly busy at many things, and am glad to hear you are likewise. What are you writing at present? I hope I do not bother you too much.

With kindest regards

Yours always cordially
Jones.

1. This word is almost illegible, and stands out as a dark blot against the rest of the handwritten page.

2. See letters by W. H. B. Stoddart, William Brown, David Forsyth, and Edith G. Collett, *British Medical Journal*, 1 (1914): 340–341, in response to those of Charles Mercier, *British Medical Journal*, 1 (1914): 172–173, 276.

3. Alexander Neuer, "An Attempt to Expound the Psycho-Analytical Theory," *Journal of Mental Science*, 59 (1913): 660–666.

175

8 February 1914
Vienna, IX. Berggasse 19

My dear Jones,

I have heard you complained of not getting any letters from me. The truth is I am writing and utilising every spare hour for the paper on the ΨA movement in the *Jahrbuch*. I am pretty far advanced. I have done with the first rogue to-day and hope I may finish the other next Sunday. I have filled 60 big pages so far.[1]

The strike is over, you will soon feel the wheels turning again. We have every interest in bringing out our critical number.

In the Moses affair I am growing negative again, the last artist I consulted showed me what the way of artists in such matters is and made me afraid of too sharp an interpretation. Meaning is but little with these men, all they care is line, shape, agreement of contours. They are given up to the Lustprinzip. I prefer to be cautious.

News from Loe. She did become more reasonable and accessible to ΨA since Davy's arrival.[2] Their marriage may be arranged. At the same time the problem of her case is cleared. Kaufmann found a good deal of pus in her urine and proclaimed the diagnosis of left side pyelitis. She is feverish sometimes. So she comes out a mixed case; consolated by the concession of organic disease she no more denies the additional hysteria. As she is in a bad phase just now she makes no progress in giving up morphia. She is going to Paris with him for two weeks to meet his younger brother from Chicago. When she returns, the treatment for the kidney will begin if it shows possible. As a nervous case she is very nice, all to be explained by her mother relation.

I made some progress in the question of Sadism-Masochism and the Castration complex, which I think a capital point in the mechanism of neuroses. The choice of the object-sex may be influenced by the sex of the forbidding parent, being opposite to it, and so early sexual inhibition may even play a big part in the determination of Homosex.[3] Pray keep all these things to yourself, and your own work.

Cet. censeo:[4] Be cautious with women and do not spoil your case this time.

Hamill (Chicago) announced himself for March 12th. I got a letter from Bryan about a case of masochistic horse, with good notes. I advised him to keep it for treatment even if the therapeutic chance be bad.

Now deserving again your good news

I am yours truly
Freud

1. Freud (1914d); the rogues are Adler and Jung.
2. Herbert Jones.
3. This sounds a great deal like the "Wolf-Man" analysis (Freud 1918b, pp. 109–110, 111–112), which Freud is said to have begun writing up only in October 1914; see Jones (1955a, p. 277; 1955b, p. 312).
4. "As regards the rest, I think . . ."

176

15 February 1914
69 Portland Court, London

Dear Professor Freud,

You must have received my long letter, with the enclosures, on the day after you sent yours. You are exceedingly kind to write to me so constantly, but I do not want to abuse your time or to set undue claims on you in this way, and should want you to feel as free in this respect as you would want to be. Especially is this necessary at times of concentration on an important work, and I am happy to hear you are giving so much interest to the *Jahrbuch* article, which will be historic as well as historical, and treating it in such a detailed manner.[1]

I was sorry to hear that Loe still has attacks of pus in the urine, as in the old days. The pyelitis was always thought to be on the left side, but the last operation showed nothing visible to the naked eye in the pelvis of the kidney (which was thoroughly explored), so we hoped it was slight; in any case it would account for only a minimal part of the pain. I wonder if she will cross over to London from Paris? Is Herbert going to consult the lawyer about the marriage fiction,[2] or is it dismissed as nonsense? I should like to hear of her marriage plans, etc., when they are definitely made, which I suppose is not yet.

I should much like to know the *reason* why you give me the personal advice about women just at this juncture? I will not say it was not necessary, for I realise the danger of my feeling over-sure in such matters, but I honestly think I have become a very different man in the past two years or so—at least so far as the practical question of self-control and self-knowledge is concerned. I keep in contact with Ferenczi about my analysis and have been able to give him good reports every time.

We had a meeting on Thursday, when Bryan read the case whose notes he had sent you; it evoked a good discussion. He and Forsyth are promising men. Hart was also present, but contributed little. Constance Long was there, having returned from her five weeks' "analysis" with Jung, which she said she greatly enjoyed (Fancy *enjoying* a real analysis!). The case, you will remember, was that of a man thoroughly successful in all the affairs of life, but with a sexual fixation to masochistic phantasies that left him no desire over for relations with women. We learnt that the true explanation was: he was shirking his "task" of having a house of his own instead of living at home, and was concealing this by pretending to suffer from a sexual disability, which was merely symbolic and had only a secondary meaning!! She was so thoroughly stupid, and repeated Jung in such a parrot-like way, that she may do good by discrediting him in the eyes of doubtful men like Eder and Hart.

Sachs has got very excited over a passage from H. G. Wells, which I enclose, and which is said to contain the gist of your tabu theory. I know that Wells held it three years ago, having reached it by putting together the writings of Darwin, Frazer, Robertson Smith, and others, but he does not appreciate the significance of his accidental finding. It is simply one more proof of the inevitability of your theory.

This week's *British Medical Journal* contained no more correspondence about ψα, but a review of Jelliffe's new review, in which they hail Jung's conversion as a "return to a saner view of life".[3] The meaning of his relapse is more correctly diagnosed by our opponents than by himself and his supporters. By the way, did you read a penetrating remark of Stekel's in the [October][4] December *Zentralblatt?* "Es ist eine ebenso feine wie boshafte Rache, die Jung an der [Wiener] Schule nimmt, dass er Sadger als einzigen Vertreter der 'bahn[en]brechenden Wiener Schule' im Jahrbuch paradieren lässt."[5] But he is too polite when he adds "Es gehört dies in das Kapitel der '*un*bewussten Bosheiten'."[6] I was very much annoyed by Stekel's review of some of my articles.[7] He altered every quotation he made, so as to make them absurd or exaggerated; thus "the chief cause" instead of "a possible cause", etc.. In one review he quotes an entire paragraph of 10 lines, supposed to be contained in my article, which I have never written or seen anywhere in my life. I thought of writing an open letter of protest to him, but have renounced the project (with great difficulty), thinking it better to ignore the matter. I suppose this would also be your attitude?

I can give a good report of work. One of my patients has left, being an unsuitable case, another because she had finished, but I have still six hours a day, with some exceedingly interesting material. I feel much more confidence and capacity in the work than ever before, and believe I am successful at it. One case of typical manic-depressive insanity is throwing more light on this condition. It looks to me as if there were no such disease, some cases being psychoneuroses, others paraphrenia (especially paranoia), the prominence of the affective symptoms replacing the other mechanisms of distortion (as they do in dreams sometimes). But of this, more later.

With kindest regards

Yours always
Jones.

1. Freud (1914d).
2. Herbert Jones may well have been worried about the status of Loe Kann's and Jones's relationship in the eyes of British common law.
3. *British Medical Journal*, 1 (1914): 375.
4. Crossed out in the original.
5. "The vengeance Jung takes on the school is as elegant as it is malicious, when he parades Sadger in the *Jahrbuch* as the sole representative of the 'ground-breaking Vienna school.'"
6. "This belongs in the chapter on '*unconscious* malice.'" The *un*- of *unbewussten* is doubly underlined. Quotations are not from the December 1913 issue but from the subsequent one; see *Zentralblatt*, 4 (1914): 179.
7. See Stekel's reviews of Jones (1912–13, 1913g, 1913i), *Zentralblatt*, 4 (1914): 176–177, 180–181, 181–182.

177

Imago

21 February 1914
Vienna

Dear Jones,

I had no special motive to give that famous warning just at the time of my last letter. Only pouring out my mind to you I found this preoccupation amongst the contents of the same and offered it you. I am very glad of your answer.

Loe has since written to you I know, so I have no fresh news to give you but I soon will have when she is able to undergo an examination by the urologist. The behaviour of the young couple is very nice. As far as I can guess much of the future arrangements depends on the condition of kidney to be revealed next week.

I enclose the cuts from the *British Medical Journal* which interested me highly and also the passage of Wells, about which you can easily build a note for the Varia of your Journal the *Zeitschrift*. I find Wells is missing both points: the killing of the father and the origin of the taboos, but as a piece of scientific divination it may pass.[1]

I have now finished the historic and historical Beiträge.[2] Pretty sharp they are and I hope not tedious. The sheets (70 pages!) are now with Ferenczi, will travel on to Abraham, from there to the printer here and you shall get the first proofs coming out. I am afraid of exposing the manuscript to more travelling by land and sea. It will be time to wait for your remarks and proposals.

You are overrating that pig, Stekel by sharing his supposition about Sadger. Jung simply had no other contribution from Vienna and would have accepted any other. If you take my advice you will not mind his critics on your papers.

The great event of last days is the *Rectoralsrede* [rector's address] of Jelgersma (Leiden) on Dream-analysis,[3] his letter to me and his brochure, about which, I am sure, you have heard enough by this time. It is the first official acknowledgment from an university teacher. (14 years!)

I am ready for attacking to-morrow the Narcissm.[4]

Yours with best love
Freud

1. In H. G. Wells, *Mankind in the Making*, rev. ed. (London: Chapman and Hall, 1914), pp. 291–296, there is a mention of taboo as being partly instinctual and partly a developmental phenomenon. Whether this is the reference in question is difficult to determine; in any case, the Wells passage was not included in the *Zeitschrift*. In *The Outline of*

History, 3rd ed. (New York: Macmillan, 1923), pp. 92–105, Wells treats the subject in more depth, mentioning the work of Freud, Jung, and Frazer.

2. Freud (1914d).

3. G. Jelgersma, "Unbewusstes Geistesleben: Vortrag, gehalten zum 339. Jahrestag der Leidener Universität am 9. Februar 1914," published as a supplement to the *Zeitschrift* (1914). See also Jones (1955a, p. 105; 1955b, p. 118).

4. Freud (1914c).

178

22 February 1914
69 Portland Court, London

Dear Professor Freud,

Putnam is incorrigible; he is a woman, not a man.

I have not received any proofs for the *Zeitschrift*, Heft 1, and suppose there will not be time to send them, as we want to get it out as soon as possible. In that case would you kindly add whatever note you like to my review of Jung, so as to save time.[1]

Yours
Jones.

1. Jones (1914c).

179

25 February 1914
Vienna, IX. Berggasse 19

Dear Jones,

Enclosed the famous letter of Jelgersma. Please send it to Abraham.

Another enclosure is Putnam's. Perhaps you are too hard on him. He is over 60 and a doubter by constitution, he is brave for all this. The chief point seems that Jung's authority is pretty well decaying with him. Yet he seems a bit of a fool recognizing that Adler's *Leitlinie* [motto] is nothing but our "fancy" and still preconising it. I understand why you are growing impatient with him.

I had no proof of the *Zeitschrift* myself. *Imago* is already going off. But I cannot except [accept] your generous offer letting me insert into your critic whatever pleases me. You ought to take the responsibility yourself; it is well worth a few days delay.

I am short because again engaged in writing. Narcissm has to be finished.

No news about Loe, she is not yet examined. Yesterday she showed me a nice piece of Verschreiben from a certain person you ought to know. An adress given as had "Frau Prof. Loe K. J."[1] As it was impossible to modify the name there was no other way to deny the change and the loss.

I will try to push Heller and the printers.

Yours truly
Freud

1. It appears that Jones had addressed a letter to Loe as Frau Professor Loe Kann Jones.

180

13 March 1914
69 Portland Court, London

Dear Professor Freud,

I am in the unusual position of having two of your letters to answer, and have much to talk about, so please prepare for a long epistle. The reason is that things have been thrown out of gear by my being ill. I have had a severe cellulitis starting at the back of the neck, and involving all the glands on both sides, deep and superficial, from the skull to the scapulae and to below the clavicles. I saw my patients except on one day, but have not been able to do anything else owing to the pain, etc.. It is now very much better and I shall soon be all right again.

I was on this account prevented from attending McDougall's paper on the sexual instinct, at the Royal Society of Medicine,[1] but I dictated from bed a long contribution, which Hart read at the meeting.[2] It was very crowded. In the discussion two psychologists spoke about instinct in general, and the four other speakers were psycho-analysts, so we had the best of the meeting. [No opposition.][3] I had beforehand organised our debate by dividing up the subject and delegating to each of our men what he could best deal with, so as to cover all the ground and make the maximum impression.[4] This will do much to counteract the *British Medical Journal* onslaught, and we shall soon have other opportunities also. The Mercier attack had not dispirited any of us, and there need be no fear, while a Welshman and a Jew are president and secretary of the society,[5] that such attacks may provoke what we have learned from Zurich to call an "Aryan reaction"; my ancestors were in Europe before the Aryans, which may be a contributory reason for my disbelief in the omniscient pride that "Aryans" vaunt.

Our society met last night, and Mrs. Eder read us a translation of your paper on the Dynamik der Übertragung.[6] It was discussed with intelligence and keenness, showing that the men are learning fast; we are all good friends (except Miss Long) and the meetings are greatly enjoyed. There are now between thirty and forty patients being treated by ψα in London at present.

Abraham's circular arrived this morning, and I have sent him a letter that no doubt will soon reach you. I expect you have by now Jelgersma's letter back again. It was most gratifying to us. I met him in Amsterdam a few years ago, and considered him an honest man.

I have completely re-written my Madonna essay for the *Jahrbuch*,[7] adding both some valuable material and what I think is an important deepening of the theory (relation of flatus to castration); the last part of it was sent to Sachs a fortnight ago. Towards the end an amusing episode occurred. The crocodile part all depended on the fact that these animals, like frogs, have no external genitals.[8] On reading Wallis Budge's book on Osiris,[9] which by the way is very good, I was horrified to read that the Egyptian performed certain rites with the *penis* of the crocodile. I telephoned in a panic to various professors of zoology, none of whom could tell me what I wanted, and the next day went to the Zoological Gardens to investigate the point. None of the keepers knew, so the only thing to do was to turn over an undoubted male crocodile on to his back by means of poles, etc. This proved to be an appallingly difficult task, and created an exciting scene. I found, also later from text-books, that the animal's penis is *entirely* concealed within the cloaca, so that the ψα assumption that it must be invisible from outside proved correct. What a dull life an ordinary doctor leads in comparison with that of a psycho-analyst!

I enclose an interesting document illustrating the nature of American female psychologists.

Flournoy is giving a course on ψα at Geneva, in the Faculty of Sciences; I have asked Claparède to give us an abstract of them for the *Zeitschrift*, but do not know if he will.[10]

Loe's attitude, in her famous letter, was better than it has ever been before (towards ψα). She now admits that the conclusions of ψα are all correct, though they do not help; "it is a science, not a treatment". Has the urological examination taken place yet? Of course I am eager to hear the results. My great fear is that she will reserve to herself the use of morphia, and then exploit this at any future date that a difficulty arises in life. In her letter she says that your youngest daughter has had fever; I hope that this is long a matter of the past.

I have received a great deal of *Zeitschrift* material from Heller. What nonsense Blüher talks;[11] he is only defending his own homosexuality. I see Ferenczi has been in an active mood of late.

Now I come to your letters, answering your points in their order. The Wells passage I will write up for the Varia.[12] You are of course right about Stekel, but it is a good exercise in self-control; this month he has the effrontery to write a paragraph complaining about the distortion of one word by some critic of himself!

I am eagerly looking forward to your *Jahrbuch* paper,[13] and suppose the proofs will come in the next couple of weeks. Could not the *Jahrbuch*, for political reasons, be hurried up and published early in May? How is the Narcissmus article getting on?[14] Could you tell me what special problems you are dealing with in it?

My impatience with Putnam was of course only momentary, for I recognise how much there is to admire and to love in him. But his inability to draw the last consequences from his knowledge, e.g. about Jung, is sometimes trying.

The question of my responsibility for the added passages in my Jung-criticism has been taken out of our hands by fate. After you wrote insisting that I should revise it myself, Rank wrote saying the reverse. Then Heller again reversed this by sending me the proof. I corrected this (there were some mistakes in the translation, but I agree with all the added part) on the same day, but now Rank writes it was too late, as they couldn't wait to get the *Zeitschrift* out.[15] Quite amusing!

If the Verschreiben you quoted was from me, it was not quite unconscious. I have usually addressed Loe with her old title, by which she is probably still called in her environment (Pension), but I suppose I should now cease doing so.

This evening I see a very adverse criticism of my book in the *British Medical Journal*, poking fun at it in the most ignorant way. I know the reviewer from of old, a stupid fellow.[16]

Burrow and Hamill write to me that they cannot leave America just now, for domestic reasons. By the way, I have been meaning to ask you how Frau Hoesch-Ernst is getting on. Is she still in the treatment? She cannot be an easy case.

I close at last, hoping to hear from you soon and with kindest regards

from yours always
Jones.

1. William McDougall, "The Definition of the Sexual Instinct," *Proceedings of the Royal Society of Medicine*, 7–3 (1913–14): 65–78.

2. For Jones's contribution, read by Bernard Hart, see *Proceedings of the Royal Society of Medicine*, 7–3 (1913–14): 83–86.

3. These words are printed in an otherwise handwritten letter and appear to have been inserted at a later rereading.

4. For comments by William Brown, M. D. Eder, David Forsyth, and Charles Mercier, see *Proceedings of the Royal Society of Medicine*, 7–3 (1913–14): 78–83; for McDougall's response, see pp. 86–88.

5. Sir George H. Savage was the president of the psychiatry section, Royal Society of Medicine; honorary secretaries were R. H. Cole and Bernard Hart.

6. Freud (1912b).

7. Jones (1914a).

8. See Jones (1951, pp. 346–350).

9. E. A. Wallis Budge, *Osiris and the Egyptian Resurrection* (London: P. L. Warner, 1911).

10. Not reported in the *Zeitschrift*.

11. Hans Blüher (1888–1955) wrote *Die drei Grundformen der sexuellen Inversion (Homosexualität)* (Leipzig: Max Spohr, 1913), and "Zur Theorie der Inversion," *Zeitschrift*, 2 (1914): 223–243. Blüher's brand of homoeroticism and anti-Semitism in his later work on masculine organizations was highly regarded by the German Youth Movement.

12. Jones's write-up on Wells did not appear in the *Zeitschrift*.

13. Freud (1914d).

14. Freud (1914c).

15. Jones (1914c).

16. Anonymous review of Jones, *Papers*, 1st ed. 1913, *British Medical Journal*, 1 (1914): 597–599.

181

19 March 1914
Vienna, IX. Berggasse 19

My dear Jones,

Is it true that you are ill? Your not writing seems to confirm the rumour. Let me know more about it, I hope it is nothing more than your rheumatism.

I have received today two books, which must be known to you, Lloyd Tuckey's *Treatment by Hypnos* etc. last edition, containing a mention of ΨA in the preface and a special chapter in the text by Const. Long,[1] and Morton Prince's *Unconscious*.[2] The essay by Long does not show the traces of the Swiss infection (perhaps it is written before [you][3] she heard of Jung's gospel),[4] Prince's *Unconscious* is not likely to be the genuine power, we are struggling with for some hours daily. I am sure you will report on both in the *Zeitschrift*.[5]

I have finished both, Beiträge and Narcissm, and feel free for some fresh undertaking. You must not expect me to be enthusiastic about any of the two.[6] Moses has just come from the print,[7] it may be better not to acknowledge this child before the public.

My daughter in Hamburg[8] has been delivered of a boy, Ernst Wolfgang, the 11th of this month, she passed it excellently, is all right now, the boy is not very strong and has not yet displayed his instincts of self-preservation by sucking in what is given him in profusion. I hope he may yet learn it.

As for Loe, we are on excellent terms, I am beginning to understand more of her history which is highly interesting and confess myself a full admirer of her headstrongness and energy, part of which is still directed to irrational aims. She has proved a mixed case as you know, and it is hard to make out what the ratio of the mixture is. Herbert Jones is always behaving nicely, something good may be made out of him by the fates.

Abraham has shown himself an excellent worker in the organisation of the *Jahrbuch*. His proposal is sure to occupy you at this moment.

Lucy Hoesch Ernst left me yesterday for my relief. She is a heavy burden.

Hoping to have your news as soon as possible

yours truly
Freud

1. Constance Long, "An Introduction to Psycho-Analysis," in C. Lloyd Tuckey, *Treatment by Hypnotism and Suggestion*, 6th ed. (London: Ballière, Tindal and Cox, 1913).
2. Prince (1914).
3. Crossed out in the original.
4. The notation "!!" is written in the left margin to indicate the error. The slip is explained in letter 183.
5. Jones does not report on either work in the *Zeitschrift*.
6. Freud (1914d, 1914c).
7. Freud (1914b).
8. Sophie Freud Halberstadt.

182

23 March 1914
69 Portland Court, London

Dear Professor Freud,

I got today your letter, dated the 19th, and see that my last letter must have gone astray or been delayed. I wrote a full one of six pages on the 13th, and posted it on the midday of the 14th. Perhaps it may yet turn up.

I congratulate you sincerely on the birth of your first grandchild, and am sure you feel proud of the event.

I was interested to read your remarks about Loe (I dare say it is easier for you to understand why I loved her so much than why I also hated her), but am eager to know if the urological examination has taken place, and the results of it.

My own illness, of which I gave an account in the lost letter[1] (it is not interesting enough to repeat it) is now entirely over, and I am starting work again with a good heart.

I will review Prince's book on the *Unconscious* (which of course has nothing in common with the real unconscious)[2] and will ask Eder to review Tuckey's.[3] Constance Long's contribution was written before she met Jung, and owes any value it may have to Eder and Bryan, who supplied the examples, etc.. How do you interpret your Verschreiben in regard to this (perhaps it is written before [you][4] she heard of Jung's gospel)?

Before this you will have received my answer to Abraham, unless it also has gone astray (it had the same date as the other letter). I should prefer to wait till the *Jahrbuch* appears. Is there any chance of this been [being] hastened?

Please let me know if my letter does not turn up, because in that case I have to repeat some of the contents (doings in London, etc.).

With kindest regards

Yours
Jones.

1. Jones's letter of 13 March was not lost.
2. See note 10 to letter 7.
3. For Eder's review, see *Zeitschrift*, 2 (1914): 178–179.
4. Crossed out in the original.

183

25 March 1914
Vienna, IX. Berggasse 19

Dear Jones,

Your letter arrived safely the day after I had posted mine. The same morning I could read your clever answer to Abrahams proposal and in the afternoon I learned the particulars of your illness from a report of Lina to Loe. Well I am mightily glad you have recovered so soon and have not been without the help of friends. Promise not to do it again.

Your former letter reminded me that I was mistaken in the belief of having informed you of the result of Loe's examination. As I may suppose that nothing else would interest you more I may begin this letter (intended to be longer than usual as I am suffering of headache, indigestion etc.) by retracing what I have missed. The examen showed some degree of pyelitis (not severe) on both sides, an unexpected measure of cystitis (no symptoms), good function of the left (painful) kidney, *bad* function of the right organ; it gave no explanation for the constant leftsided pain (tortion, cicatrical tissue or hy[steria]?) and did not clear up the condition of the left ureter, supposed to be dilated and fit to retain concrements. The Röntgen picture is said to have shown dark material on a spot corresponding to the accused [spot in the coarse][1] part of that ureter, though of course I could not make out anything in the photograph. She has not been well since the examination, my impression being that she now dives into the neurosis which may prove helpful in the case of postponing marriage.

She now takes a theoretical interest in ΨA lending herself prettily to analysis, while firmly convinced (that means: resolved) that it will change nothing. I know (not she) that she intended to give her father a child, [. . .][2] accumulating[3] the contents of the alimentary channel to that purpose and grew wild raging at the mother, who made her "miscarry", destroyed that child in formation by the daily enemas. The revulsion came after she had taken a husband (you know him) who fulfilled two important fatherly conditions ("helping the father" is one, "showing his penis to the child" the other); she changed into her mother and ever since she and the mother are struggling within her soul.

Now my interesting "Verschreiben" may have aroused your suspicion. But you remember I did not try to conceal it but even called your attention upon it.[4] Some days before I committed the same fault with Rank, with perhaps the same unwished for result. I complained of Reiks unreliability and want of care, and as Rank and Sachs assured me, I uttered "Rank" instead of Reik.[5] Now no reproach would be more injust in the case of Rank. The explication runs otherwise. It is a common trick of my unconscious to supplant a person disliked by a better one (see the first dream on "Irma's Injection").[6] Rank in the place of Reik is equivalent to the thought: Why can he not be like you? It is veiled tenderness, so in your case too. You remember perhaps after the Munich Congress[7] I could never pronouce the name "Jung" but had to replace it by "Jones".

Your letter to Abraham seemed convincing to all of us (Ferenczi being present that Sunday); our thoughts were already engaged in the same lines. The *Jahrbuch* cannot be accelerated, end of July is the next term. Perhaps an attack could be risked from the side of the absolute inactivity and laziness of the Central; there is no trace of a *Correspondenzblatt* since Sept. The only scruple is, we would be unhappy if we got it, so we had better not urge them.

The reports on your activity in your (not lost) letter were very promising and the crocodile episode highly amusing. I am sure a year hence you will be a captain at the head of an army.

Fisher Unwin (I never know whether I give you a piece of news for the first or the second time) is negotiating for the english edition not only of the *"Alltagsleben"*, but also *Totem & Taboo* and *"Witz"*.[8] Federn will have the good chance of going over to America in continuation of a rich mans treatment, he wanted it sadly.

The War Office, Washington asked for my portrait to put it in the collection of the Medical Museum and library. The Etching executed by Heller's order is out now, it is considered excellent by some friends, abominable by the family: Loe ranks among the last.

Now our critical number has appeared let us wait for the effect.[9]

I am with best wishes and regards

yours
Freud

1. Crossed out in the original.
2. Illegible word crossed out in the original.
3. Freud had at first written "accumalating."
4. See note 4 to letter 181.
5. Theodor Reik (1888–1970), Ph.D. 1911 in psychology, University of Vienna; practicing lay analyst, charged with quackery in 1926 but with Freud's help was acquitted; prolific writer who delved into psychoanalytic, anthropological, literary, and autobiographical realms.
6. The first of his own dreams which Freud submitted to a detailed interpretation; see Freud (1900a, pp. 106–121).
7. The International Psychoanalytic Association, 7–8 September 1913.
8. Two of these were put out by Fisher Unwin; see Brill (1914, 1916c).
9. The *Zeitschrift* containing three critiques of Jung: Abraham (1914), Jones (1914c), and Ferenczi (1914).

184

8 April 1914
69 Portland Court, London

Dear Professor Freud,

Thank you very much for your welcome, full letter. I am sorry that the news about Loe could not be better than it was. The left-sided pain must be hysterical. When the left kidney was last operated on, we had all the possibilities in our mind of torsion of the ureter, cicatricial tissue, etc., and could find *nothing* to account for the pain, though since then another stone may possibly have formed. It is an instructive lesson of the indirect organic effects of a neurosis. Hysterical retention of urine, cystitis from infection with the catheter, ascending pyelitis with calculus concretion around this, aided by intestinal toxins due to hysterical constipation.

Some day I should like to learn, for my own benefit, the reason for her hate of me. It preceded going to Canada, so could not have been due to any "unfaithfulness" on my part. I have always ascribed it to the miscarriage (confirmed by what she said in a hysterical delirium in Toronto) in spite of all her denials, and what you say about the relation of the mother to the alimentary canal seems to accord with this view; after that date I became her mother. Is this right?

I am glad that my answer to Abraham's proposal agreed with all your views. It is always unsatisfactory not to arrive at a definite conclusion, but I felt unable to do so. I have hesitations about an attack against the Zentral, for it would be so obviously a pretext that it would be better to come out into the open and fight on the real grounds of opposition. Perhaps we could meet in Berlin on the last Sunday of May, before the groups dissolve for the summer (Sachs will be returning from London at about that time), and discuss the final campaign.

I am very pleased with the work done by the society here, and hope in another year to have four reliable trained men. Not much, but such men are rare enough in our own work. The general interest in $\psi\alpha$ in England is increasing daily, and everything seems satisfactory.

Abraham is most business-like in his editorial duties, and I am sure he will prove highly efficient. I sent him my Therapie-Referat[1] last week; perhaps you will be good enough to criticise the concluding general remarks (it is now with Sachs).

Your portrait was a great shock to me when I opened the roll. The expression seemed more "worried" than thoughtful, the nose was broken, and the lips carelessly done. However, I discovered that when one stood at a distance of M. 3, and remembered that it was an impressionistic etching, not a photograph, it took on another aspect in an interesting manner. I do not consider it particularly good, but it conveys an impression of a certain mood. It is clever, but not excellent.

What is your next step in work? I hope you will continue with the "Ratschläge" [recommendations] series,[2] which are badly needed.

Morton Prince comes to London to lecture next week,[3] and will probably stay with me. He shows up better personally than in what he writes.

Of personal news I have the following: My new step-mother, who is a vulgar person, after quarrelling with my sisters has forced a quarrel on me in such a way as to alienate my father and myself.[4] I am sorry, for I love him in spite of his weaknesses, but perhaps it will have the advantage of increasing my independence. My health is quite restored, and even the rheumatism has quite disappeared. Tomorrow I go to Paris for three days. It will be a pleasant change, and I have friends to visit there.

I have little prospect of writing any articles for some months, as other work will occupy me until then (society contributions, teaching work, translation, etc.). I have sent Rank, however, a few contributions to the Zeitschrift,[5] which is one's first care. Rank must surely be very busy in recovering the ground lost by the printer's strike.

With kindest regards from

Yours always
Jones.

1. Jones (1914h).

2. See Freud (1912e, 1913c, 1914g, 1915a).

3. Prince gave a lecture on his "personal reminiscences of the development of abnormal psychology" before the Psycho-Medical Society, 16 April 1914, London, as noted in *Journal of Abnormal Psychology*, 9 (1914): 296.

4. Edith May Howard was strongly disliked by Jones and his two sisters Elizabeth and Sybil (personal communication from Mervyn Jones, London, 16 January 1990). Jones's father, Thomas Jones, had previously been married to Mary Ann Lewis, who had died in late spring 1909.

5. Possibly Jones (1914d, 1914e, 1914f, 1914g), as well as various reviews by Jones listed in *Zeitschrift*, 2 (1914): v–vii.

185

19 April 1914
Vienna, IX. Berggasse 19

Dear Jones,

Thanks for your letter. I know you will be most anxious to get news about Loe. She is improving steadily and going down in morphia. What you construe about her "hatred" against you is true but not all the truth. I will communicate the essentials of the case to you when treatment is finished. I hope you realize that in spite of that "hatred" you have no truer friend than her, she is always behaving in a glorious way in real matters. So much I may betray that the motive of the aversion against you is identical with that of the attachment. The Jones family is behaving in a very unkind and coarse manner against her. Too much has been spoken on intimate accidents of your common life, it will be better to show less frankness to strangers henceforth.

I agree with your proposal to meet before the Congress,[1] yet I would prefer a term nearer to the date of it. I could not easily go away in May. You will hear more on this point.

I felt pretty tired and unhealthy these last weeks and think I will try to do—nothing at all for some time. Brioni was a splendid enjoyment but too short for recovery; it served only to bring out what was latent of fatigue and weariness.[2]

I was surprised that you too had got my etching. I have heard of the most differing judgments it has met. Ferenczi praised it highly, Abraham took the same position as you. I consider it masterly, though it makes me appear older than I may look.

Two letters (Pfister and Brill) will reach you which I did send into circulation among the C[ommittee]. It is all I have learned about the doings in Zürich.

I know you are very busy but I do'nt believe you will neglect the *Zeitschrift* in the next month.

Your friend Morton Prince I still consider to be a plain ass. I got the visit of one Dr. Garvin of N. Y., who knows you and seems reasonable.[3]

With best love

yours
Freud

1. The Fifth Congress of the International was planned for September 1914, but the war intervened.

2. On Freud's sojourn with Ferenczi and Rank to Brioni (on the Adriatic coast), see Jones (1955a, p. 105; 1955b, p. 118).

3. William C. A. Garvin, M.D. 1903 Columbia University College of Physicians and Surgeons; charter member of the New York Psychoanalytic Society (12 February 1911).

186

22 April 1914
69 Portland Court, London

Dear Professor Freud,

An eventful day today! First your letter, and then the announcement from Jung of his surrender,[1] evidently realising the untenability of his position. So my prediction has come true that "if you give a dog enough rope, he will hang himself", and our Fabian policy is justified![2] I have briefly acknowledged his letter, and now await instructions from you. Will you still postpone our meeting till July, or will it be necessary to appoint a successor sooner for administrative purposes? I would suggest Berlin as a central meeting place, which you can reach over-night, and the day any Sunday. Of the Obmänner the only opponent outside Zürich is Seif, and he would be less likely too to attend in Berlin than in Munich. By the way, why does Jung write of our Verein, instead of Vereinigung?

Thank you for the news about Loe. I gather that she has no plans made as yet. I was indignant to hear about the attitude of the Jones' family, and wonder which members you refer to. You will surely let me know at once if at any time I can do anything to help her, in this connection or any other. In the meantime I had better not mention the matter to her, for she or Herbert might resent my interference. She has not written to me for over two months, but this I suppose is due to her indecision of mind.

You are quite right about Morton Prince. He is an amusing and agreeable companion, but is utterly stupid. I have long since given up the hope of getting him to understand anything of psychology, but I find him useful in several respects.

Garvin I know slightly. He is a steadily-balanced man, sympathetic to us, but chiefly interested in organic psychiatry.

Everything is going on well here, and we are looking forward to Sach's visit.

I see that you have already begun to count the weeks to the vacation. It is a fatiguing time of year, and I hope cordially that you will soon be feeling reinvigorated, e.g. by the news from Küsnacht.[3]

Yours very affectionately
Jones.

1. Jung's circular letter of 20 April 1914 to the presidents of the branch societies announcing his resignation as president of the International Psychoanalytic Association; see McGuire (1974, p. 551).

2. That is, the policy of being patient like the Roman general Fabius Cunctator, after whom the Fabian Society of London was named; his patient and elusive tactics in avoiding pitched battles secured his ultimate victory over stronger forces.

3. Jung's place of residence, just outside Zurich.

187

[postcard]

27 April 1914
69 Portland Court, London

Dear Professor Freud,

I quite agree with your proposal, and add my vote for Abraham's taking over the *Vereinsleitung* [leadership].

In haste

yours
Jones.

188

13 May 1914
69 Portland Court, London

Dear Professor Freud,

I suppose you felt that Sachs would give me all the Vienna news, and he has given me a great deal. So the Vereinigung affair is settled most satisfactorily for the time, but we must be prepared for more possibilities of trouble next. Jung is not slain, only defeated temporarily. He lectures in July before the British Medical Association.[1] He will make a strong appeal in America and perhaps England, where the ψα plant is as yet of tender growth. On such grounds I hope very much that you will not weaken your *Jahrbuch* Referat[2] one iota, for its aim was not only concerned with the Vereinigung.

Sachs tells me that your health is again better, and that Ernst Wolfgang has overcome his original weakness, two pieces of good news, but that your youngest daughter has had difficulty in shaking off her cough; I hope that the sea air in England will remove the last traces of this, if any remain.[3]

I enclose the letters sent to me by Abraham. Affairs do not look very bright in America, though I was glad to see that of the 13 papers announced in the programme of the American Psychopathological Association *every one* was on the topic of ψα, 11 being positive, and only 2 negative.[4] Mac-Curdy, on whom I had built much hope, seems to have shewn a bad side in the Herbert Jones business (surely out of jealousy, for he is very homosexual), and this augurs badly for his ψα activity where character is at least as important as intellect. From Putnam I have not heard for two months, but I have written to him recently—also asking permission to publish his last excellent paper in the *Zeitschrift*.[5]

Loe wrote a long letter this week, after a three months' interval, but I should be glad to hear from you how much effect the sad news has had on her of the death of her aunt, who was really a splendid woman. It was another case of death from ultimately psychical causes (do you remember talking to me on this subject once late at night?), as was that of Scott in the Antarctic expedition,[6] so I discover. Loe's decision about her marriage did not surprise me, as it was the only reasonable course, and I am very glad of it. I cannot be very optimistic about her future, however, since she will not give up the morphia, though I pray with all my heart that she may have some happy years. Does she continue treatment until the end of your working time?

The story of Jekel's *Arbeit* was amusing, though a little annoying. It may spur me to write my Napoleon book for the *Schriften*, perhaps at the end of this year after the congress.[7] Do you think I should sacrifice other work for this?

This summer I spend writing a small book on *The Treatment of the Neuroses* and in translating Ferenczi.[8] Then I have signed the contract to produce next year (before the end) a large work on ψα for a scientific, non-medical public, and this will need an immense amount of work.[9] Besides these tasks I have enough of other smaller ones to occupy the spare time of my evenings.

Sir Ed. Durning-Lawrence has just died.[10] I dined with him a month or so ago,[11] and he assured me that Bacon wrote not only all Shakspere, but also all Spenser and Marlowe (whom he paid in the same way for the use of their names), as well as supervising the translation of the Bible!! Peace to his ashes! By the way, another contemporary set of references has been found in which the name is spelt Shăcksp̱ere,[12] thus confirming what you told me about Jacques-Pierre.[13]

Sachs is writing to you about London, with which he is enchanted. I enjoy having him here.

Yours affectionately
Jones.

1. Jung (1914).
2. Freud (1914d).
3. References are to Freud's nephew, Sophie's son, and to Anna Freud, who was about to visit England.
4. The fifth annual meeting of the American Psychopathological Association was held in Albany, N.Y., 6 May 1914.
5. Putnam (1914b).
6. Robert Falcon Scott (1868–1912), naval officer and explorer, led the ill-fated second expedition to the South Pole (1910–1913); see *Scott's Last Expedition: The Personal Journals of Captain R. F. Scott, C.V.O., R.N., on his Journey to the South Pole*, 2 vols. (London: Smith, Elder, 1913).
7. Ludwig Jekels (1867–1954), Viennese psychoanalyst, wrote a short study of Napoleon (Jekels, 1914). Jones never did publish his planned book-length study of Bonaparte.
8. Jones (1920b, 1916b).
9. See note 5 to letter 156.
10. Sir Edwin Durning-Lawrence (1837–1914), who died on 21 April, propagated a theory that Francis Bacon was Shakespeare; see his *Bacon Is Shakespeare* (London: Gay and Hancock, 1910).
11. In Jones (1957a, p. 429; 1957b, p. 460) the year of the dinner is given as 1913.
12. The *c* is doubly underlined in the original.
13. See letter 20.

189

17 May 1914
Vienna, IX. Berggasse 19

Dear Jones,

I badly want a few hours talk with you. Letter writing is a bad substitute. Be sure I do not think of weakening the tenor of my paper in the *Jahrbuch*,[1] there will be some modifications and additions (not visible in the Fahnen sent to you) but none in the direction of clemency.

It may be that we overrate Jung and his doings in the next time. He is not in a favourable position before the public when he turns against me: ie. his past. But my general judgment on the matter is very much like yours. I expect no immediate success but incessant struggling. Anyone who promises to mankind liberation from the hardship of sex will be hailed as a hero, let him talk whatever nonsense he chooses.

Putnam holds good, see his last paper in the *Journal of Abnormal Psychology* on sex in dream-interpretation,[2] and let aside his exaggerated respect for Adler's fallacies.

But Stanley Hall has proclaimed his adherence to Adler and for personal reasons I felt this accident sharper than others. He may now invite him to Worcester for lectures on the Indiv. psychologie. I picture to myself[3] what they will make out of his preaching.[4]

MacCurdy promised spontaneously to act against Jelliffe if he proposes to take up his journal as an official organ instead of *Zeitschrift*. As a character he seems truly american.

I could not end writing for hours about Loe. She is a charming woman yet she is trying. She will not relent when happy and not obey when miserable. There is rightly room for the question: when should she take "*Lachs mit Mayonnaise*".[5] The marriage is fixed but not the term of it, nor is it sure that she can stay until July. She wants to have done with morphia before she goes but she is going down very slowly.

Do not annoy on Jekels Napoleon. It is good, he has found one of the springs of his character but overlooked the other, yours. It is better not to overhaste your work. Bacon is sure to have been a very extraordinary person! Now enjoy your visitor and think kindly of your affectionate

Freud

P.S. Fisher Unwin writes that the english edition of the *Alltagsleben* will be given out June 3rd.[6] He asks for a list of persons and periodicals, to whom the book may be sent. I will take the liberty to tell him, that you (J.) will provide him with the necessary advice, and have a copy of the book sent to you *en revanche*.

F.

There are transactions going on with F. Alcan (Paris) about french translations which may easily come to something.

1. Freud (1914d).
2. Putnam (1914a).
3. Freud seems to be following the German here: *Ich stelle vor mir*.
4. On Hall's interest in Adler as opposed to Freud, see Ross (1972, pp. 406–407, 409–411). Adler did not speak at Clark University.
5. In an anecdote analyzed by Freud in *Der Witz*, an impoverished individual, who has just borrowed some money, is reprimanded by his benefactor for ordering a delicacy in a restaurant, and retorts: "If I haven't any money I *can't* eat salmon mayonnaise, and if I have some I *mustn't* eat salmon mayonnaise. Well, then, when *am* I to eat salmon mayonnaise?" Freud (1905c, pp. 49–50, 51–52), *G.W.*, 6:51, 53–54.
6. Brill (1914).

190

18 May 1914
69 Portland Court, London

Dear Professor Freud,

The first two batches of proofs have arrived,[1] and we have had a very joyful time reading them. When one knows all the innuendoes and references it is as interesting as it is delightful to mark your delicate rapier thrusts. I am sure the effect will be an excellent one, bracing and invigorating to our side, and what Shaw calls "dismantling" to the other side.

As you may imagine, I have no criticisms to make, but since you asked me to make any remarks that occur to me, I will call attention to a few unimportant details.

The first is a personal one: S. 46 (Fahnen) you write "Alle drei (Brill, Ferenczi and myself) hatten die $\psi\alpha$ in Zürich kennen gelernt".[2] For myself I am afraid I must decline this honour, the facts being as follows: I got your book in 1906 and practised $\psi\alpha$ (imperfectly, to be sure) for a year before the Amsterdam Congress Sept. 1907,[3] where I first met Jung and Otto Gross. In that autumn I was in Munich and learnt there more from Gross than I ever learnt from Jung. On the way home, in December, I spent 5–6 days in Zurich, seeing Jung each day, and thus I got invited to the Salzburg Congress in the following April. Jung presented me to you there, which perhaps gave you the impression that I was his pupil. Since then I have been in Zurich only for two days. I thus constitute a minimal exception to your statement (S. 43) "an allen anderen Orten (ausserhalb Wien und Zürich) ergab diese Zuwendung von Interesse zunächst nichts anderes als eine meist leidenschaftlich akzentuierte Ablehnung."[4]

S. 45. The sense is reversed by omission of the word "not": "Freud's $\psi\alpha$ is now championed and carried out *not* only in Austria, etc.".[5]

[S. 46. The date][6]

S. 55. E. Jelliffe should be "White and Jelliffe". White is a much better man than Jelliffe and should not be neglected.[7]

S. 44. "jenes Charakterzuges von Jung . . . seiner Neigung zum rücksichtslosen Beiseitedrängen eines unbequemen Andern".[8] This is of course absolutely true, and in principle I am in favour of no mercy being shewn in such an important war, but none the less I find this rather strong personally and fear it would weaken, by its personal note, the general effect of the essay rather than strengthen it. One does not want to put weapons in the hands of the enemy. Sachs asks me to add that he is quite of my opinion.

We await the third batch with the keenest interest.

Yours always
Jones.

1. Freud (1914d).

2. The line "All three (Brill, Ferenczi, and Jones) had studied psychoanalysis in Zurich" was dropped; see Freud (1914d, p. 31), *G.W.*, 10:70.

3. In 1910 Jones stated that he became familiar with Freud's work in 1907, and regretfully acknowledged his lack of experience in psychoanalysis. See note 9 to letter 26.

4. "In all other places [outside Vienna and Zurich] this accession of interest at first produced nothing but a very emphatic repudiation, mostly a quite passionate one." See Freud (1914d, p. 27), *G.W.*, 10:65–66.

5. Refers to Freud's use of a passage in English from Havelock Ellis. In the published version he inserts the word *not*; see Freud (1914d, p. 30), *G.W.*, 10:69.

6. Crossed out in the original.

7. Freud made the change: "White and Jelliffe in New York started a new periodical *(The Psychoanalytic Review)*"; see Freud (1914d, p. 48), *G.W.*, 10:91.

8. This passage was dropped. It reads vindictively: "that one character trait of Jung's . . . his tendency to push aside ruthlessly someone else who is in the way."

191

25 May 1914
69 Portland Court, London

Dear Professor Freud,

I am very happy to hear from Sachs that you are again quite well; I had not heard you had been ill. Let me hope that there will [be] no more trouble with this intestinal disorder, and that the holidays will finally put an end to it. Will you let me know what your plans are, if you have made them already. What is the date of the Leiden lecture, and will it be possible for you to come to London after that? I suppose you go to Carlsbad in July?

I quite echo to the full your wish for a talk. My repeated visits to Vienna in the past couple of years have "spoilt" me, and I find five months away from there already more than long enough; I must arrange to pay a visit twice a year. In any case I hope we shall meet before the time of the Congress, especially now that this has been postponed.

Sach's visit is drawing to a close. It has been in every way highly satisfactory. He has enjoyed it greatly, and I have enjoyed it just as much. To live under the same roof is always a good test, and it has succeeded brilliantly in this case. I appreciate his excellent character more highly than before (when I was perhaps a little influenced by Loe's dislike of him), and we have got on together splendidly. Then also there is a good report to give of his address on Swift[1] to our society, which everyone praised most highly. He spoke for 2¼ hours with hardly any notes, and with entire success. There is only one mistake in English that I cannot cure him of—he obstinately confounds the genders (Starfish. *Traumdeutung* identification!)[2]

We have greatly enjoyed the third, and last, proofs of the "Geschichte".[3] I find it superlatively good, *not at all* too strong, and quite final—the last word in the matter. The passage about the "paar kulturelle Obertöne" is magnificent.[4] I wish we could have taken from you the trouble of dealing with these oppositions, but no one else is in a position to say authoritatively the things you have said once for all, so you could not be spared the work. But let us hope you will not find it necessary to leave again the realms of pure science in the positive sense. My wish has long been to form a ring around you of men who will deal with the opposition while you progress with the work itself, and the outlook for such an ideal situation seems highly promising.

As to suggestions on the last proofs, they are all contained in the accompanying page. The first sentence "Wir haben . . . . . . gegangen ist"[5] does not seem to me sufficiently clear on account of its context. The rest of the paragraph is a series of paraphrases of Jung, and some readers may not realise that the last sentence refers to your own views: (Perhaps the word *"früher"* or *"im Gegenteil"* might be inserted).[6]

Then in view of the bad uses to which patients' communications may be put (and to which Jung may retaliate), I would suggest that you insert a word or two before the extract from Pf's letter, indicating that you have reasons to consider the writer a reliable person.[7]

Lastly the word *"schonungsvoller"* stands in *apparent* contradiction to the extracts from the letter, and do not make it quite clear what is meant. I suppose the meaning is that Jung having approached so near to Dubois might make the last step and be kind to his patients?[8]

I think the alteration you mention in today's letter is an improvement on the previous passage that we had commented on, and quite agree with it.

I am writing to Fisher Unwin, but will you please send me a postcard saying what you mean by the *persons* the book is to be sent to. Do you mean as personal gifts from yourself? Books are not sent on approval in England, as in Austria.

Putnam holds staunch, as you will see from the enclosed letter. S. Hall's essay I have not yet had time to read, but will review it for the *Zeitschrift*.[9]

I have bad news of Jung's activity. He has announced a paper for the Internat. Congr. of Neurol. and Psych. at Berne, in September, one before the British Medical Association on July 30, and one on July 24th before the Psycho-Medical Society in London, the last being on the Psychology of Understanding; at these last two I shall have to speak also, which is not an agreeable task to look forward to. They will come just after the appearance of the *Jahrbuch*, and should reveal his reaction.[10] I [am][11] feel quite sure he will not come to Dresden, where I hope we shall have some peace and agreeable work.

I am of course not surprised that you have discovered that Loe can be trying, for I can bear ample witness to the fact. I am afraid she will not give up morphia, even for you and Herbert Jones. I know from Lina that she deceived us all last summer on this point, though I do not know the details, for when Lina (from whom also she had been concealing matters) detected her, she made her promise never to reveal them. Please do not speak of this, [. . .][12] though I am sure it is true. It has been a blow to me to find the extent to which Loe's untruthfulness and exaggeration has proceeded in other directions (especially concerning myself), though I like to think it is mostly unconscious distortion.

From your letter today I learn that she may be getting married at the end of the week. In this she will have no one whose wishes for her future happiness are most heartfelt than my own, and I pray that they may be gratified. Does she stay in Vienna until July?

With all kind regards

Yours affectionately
Jones.

1. "Die Psychologie Swifts," delivered 21 May, noted in *Zeitschrift*, 2 (1914): 412.

2. Jones implies that Sachs is identifying with Freud, who also confused genders. In the discussion of his "Hollthurn" dream, Freud reveals that on a visit to England at the age of nineteen, he picked up a starfish on the shore and exclaimed "He is alive" rather than "It is alive." See Freud (1900a, pp. 455–456, 519–520), and Didier Anzieu, *Freud's Self Analysis*, trans. Peter Graham (Madison, Conn.: International Universities Press, 1986), pp. 328–329.

3. Freud (1914d).

4. The passage in question concerns Freud's attack on Jung and Adler: "The truth is that these people have picked out a few cultural overtones from the symphony of life and have once more failed to hear the mighty and primordial melody of the instincts." See Freud (1914d, p. 62), *G.W.*, 10:108.

5. Refers to last sentence of first paragraph in Freud (1914d, p. 63), *G.W.*, 10:109.

6. Freud did not insert the suggested words ("earlier" or "on the contrary"). The line in question reads: "As we know, however, a neurotic's current conflict becomes comprehensible and admits of solution only when it is traced back to his pre-history, when one goes back along the path that his libido took when he fell ill."

7. Freud does not acknowledge Pfister in the passage he quotes, but does take up Jones's suggestion and adds a footnote about his "informant" as a "trustworthy person"; see Freud (1914d, p. 64 n. 2), *G.W.*, 10:110 n. 1. Pfister, however, is frequently mentioned by name elsewhere in the essay (pp. 37–38, 46, 61).

8. In the published version Freud uses the comparative *schonungsvollerer* (more considerate) rather than *schonungsvoller* (considerate). The passage thus reads: "Dubois cures neuroses by ethical encouragement in a more considerate manner." Freud (1914d, p. 64), *G.W.*, 10:110.

9. Jones (1916–17).

10. The topic "Die Psychologie der Träume," with Jung mentioned as one of the speakers, is listed on the program of the International Congress for Neurology, Psychiatry, and Psychology, Berne, 7–12 September 1914; see *Zeitschrift*, 2 (1914): 403. For the other two papers, see Jung (1914, 1915). For Jones's paper at the British Medical Association meeting, see Jones (1914i).

11. Crossed out in the original.
12. Illegible word crossed out in the original.

192

2 June 1914
Vienna, IX. Berggasse 19

Dear Jones,

I have come back yesterday at night from Budapest, where we—Rank and I and Ferenczi as an interpreter—have helped Loe to become Mrs. Herbert Jones. I am sure it must be hard for you and so it is for me when I remember the series of events from the evening in the Weimar coffeehouse when you offered me her treatment to the moments when I assisted to her wedding with another. It is a most remarkable chain of changes between persons and feelings of such and the most striking points seem to me, that our relations have not been spoiled and that I have learned even to like the other man. As for her, I fully appreciate what I have heard from you as a first description of her person. She is charming, is a jewel as you call her in your noble-minded letter and she is too extraordinarily abnormal to make a workers happiness. She must be judged for herself, measured by a standard fitted to her only self.

Herbert J. though a youth in appearance is a accomplished man in fact and I trust they will enjoy as much happiness as her health will permit for the time coming. The couple will spend some days on the Semmering and then come back to Vienna to stay until I lieve. I have no hope she will get rid of morphia until then but I think it is wiser not to ask of her what she cannot give and I am eager not to loose my interest with her. Take all together, she must disarm the critic and make a friend of him.

Now for the other points of your letter I had taken with me to Bpest to answer it on the field, but I could not. I thank you sincerely for your emendations of my proofs, *all* of which are sure to be regardid. I will insert some lines about Pf., where I know is the most vulnerable link of the harness. I am sorry you follow Jungs moves with too great anxiety. It is unavoidable that he should follow his track, fulfill his mission, produce his impressions and arrive to a personification of some of the resistances, ΨA is destined to meet in her course. I am not in the least afraid of whatever he does, but I affirm that no one can foretell what he will do. Perhaps not even God or the Devil knows it at this moment. I do not consider it necessary for you to follow his steps in England and contradict him on the spot, except perhaps on a single occasion, which you may choose to your pleasure. Let him talk and defy him afterwards in print drily and mercilessly. I have read in these days a "Nachwort" to the second edition of "Inhalt der Psychose",[1] which will appear without connection with the series of the *Schriften*. There he concedes that his "constructive psychology" is *no science* and lands in unveiled adherence to Bergson. So you see he has found another Jew for his father complex. I am no more jealous.

Our summer plans are fixed now. July 12th to Karlsbad, which I need more this time than in former years, with my wife. Aug. 4th to Seis am Schlern (Tyrol) where we meet my sister in law. Sept. 18th departure for Dresden, where I hope to meet my friends of the comité before the congress, 20/21 Congress, 24th Sept. lecture at Leiden;[2] in these days I ex[cept][3] [expect] my girl to come over from England, I have no time to cross spared,—and last some days in Hamburg with her.[4] I may avoid much more travelling feeling somewhat shaken in health.

I enclose Putnam's letter which may not prove the last of his attitudes, brave as he is. The fights for ΨA I must leave to you of the younger generations, for they are just beginning and will not end during my lifetime.

I will not mention Lina's informations about the morphia, but I confess I am only suspicious and not at all sure of the matter.

Thanks for your sending the adresses to Fisher Unwin. If it is not customary to send books to single persons I will make no innovation.

I have seen Sachs, he is full of the praise of London and of yours.

Now excuse this letter which with all its length cannot be expected to be an equivalent for yours and bring forth your reaction to your

affectionate
Freud

1. See Jung (1908, 1915).
2. The advent of the First World War precluded both the congress and Freud's visit to Leiden.
3. Crossed out in the original.
4. With Anna Freud.

193

17 June 1914
69 Portland Court, London

Dear Professor Freud,

Your last letter was eagerly awaited, and even more than usually welcome. Your remarks about Loe's marriage, etc., struck an answering chord in me. You confirm the appreciation of her that I gave you in Weimar, and which probably seemed to you at the time exaggerated. No one in the world can estimate her rare qualities more highly than myself, for I have been the recipient of her wonderful tenderness and charm. That in spite of all this I can honestly say that I am glad we have parted, and that she is married to another, is the best illustration of the intolerable suffering she caused me, about which you can guess only a relatively small part. Now I am *almost* altogether free from her in feeling, and my attitude towards her contains little except the fervent wish that she may be happy.

To me also, the most remarkable of the chain of events is the way in which our relationship has more than stood the strain—even a psychologically interesting matter—and I can only ascribe this, with deep gratitude, to [your]¹ the truly English sense of fairness you have displayed throughout the whole course and your kindly attitude towards me in spite of having a distorted account of my failings presented to you. All this has forged a permanent bond in my feeling towards you.

Your remarks about Jung did me a lot of good, and were evidently needed. You correctly divined that I was too anxious about him, and your letter recalled me to a cooler frame of mind. Now I no longer feel the decision important whether or not to attend his lectures here, and I shall decide later on according to other considerations.

Thank you also for the translation of the *Alltagsleben*,² which has an impressive appearance. It will probably go well. Fisher Unwin has asked me for a book of my own, so now I have four publishers here who are prepared to take up ψα works.

One point in your letter caused me disappointment—you will easily guess which. I had hoped that the Leyden lecture would be earlier in September, and that you would be able to spend some time in London before going to Dresden. But I see that this is impossible, and so must look forward to the pleasure of a visit next year, when we must arrange a regular gathering of friends (? Ferenczi and Rank).

Abraham's Circular letter strikes me as excellent, and in my opinion should be productive of some result.

I am busy proof-correcting for the *Jahrbuch*. Are the proofs of your Narzissmus article yet ready?³ I am eager to read it; Sachs told me a little about it.

This year I shall not take any holiday, except to Dresden and—with your permission—Leiden, but am going to the country every Sunday, which gives me great enjoyment. It is grand being back in England!

Yours affectionately
Jones.

1. Crossed out in the original.
2. Brill (1914).
3. Freud (1914c).

194

1 July 1914
69 Portland Court, London

Dear Professor Freud,

Two presents have arrived, for which I thank you: the "historic" reprint, where the alterations interested me and the Goethe quotation amused me; [1] and the proofs of the Narzissmus article. I will not say anything of this at present, for it is one of your "advanced" articles (like Ch. VII of the *Traumdeutung*) that requires more than one reading. We shall have a good *Jahrbuch* this time that will contrast with the last.

Ferenczi proposes to spend a month in London this summer, and I hope he will carry out the plan.

On Friday I go to Durham, to join in a symposium on "The Rôle of Repression in Forgetting" held by a joint meeting of the British Psychological Society, the Aristotelian Society, and the Mind Association. I have already received the four papers to be read, and will send them to you later. Three of them are very good, one being of a remarkably high order, though critical. You will, I think, be surprised at their quality. [2]

Our latest visitor here was Frink, the President of the New York $\psi\alpha$ Society. [3] He intends coming over next May to be analyzed by you, Abraham, or myself! He seems an honest fellow, but very limited. He gave no special news of America, and seemed fairly satisfied with the N.Y. group.

I heard lately from Abraham, and am eager to hear the result of his bomb, which, however, your reprint may render unnecessary; I suggested he should wait three or four weeks if possible, as Jung may again play into our hands. [4]

Three more people have gone to Jung from here, two of them for three weeks only! Eder's wife, Dr. Nicholl [5]—a rather promising young fellow, but influenced by Dr. Constance Long—and Miss Long's medical colleague, a woman. Jung is staying at Miss Long's for a week this month, and she wanted our society to invite him to address us—which of course I vetoed. [He] [6] Bryan is a great help to me, as I cannot rely on Eder. Bryan is our Vice-President, and will become President in the case of my being made President of the Vereinigung, which matter is I suppose not yet decided. [7]

I do not intend to go to the Bern congress, as I have a great deal of work to do here. Patients still come, and I shall have seven hours analysis a day through the summer.

If it is as hot in Vienna as it is here at present, you will be especially glad to escape, though no doubt you will be glad enough in any case. Your daughter comes to England this month, doesn't she? I shall hope to have the opportunity of seeing her sometime.

You see I have not much news to add to my last letter, things being on the whole quiet just now. I send you my best wishes for a fruitful and beneficial holiday, which I am sure you will enjoy. Please donot forget to send me your Carlsbad address.

Yours always
Jones.

1. The epigraph to part 3 (Freud 1914d, p. 42) is taken from some verses of Goethe in his later years: "Am Jüngsten Tag ist's nur ein Furz" (On Judgment Day it's only a fart).

2. For papers by T. H. Pear, A. Wolf, T. W. Mitchell, and T. Loveday, under the title "The Rôle of Repression in Forgetting," see British Journal of Psychology, 7 (1914–15): 139–165.

3. Horace W. Frink (1883–1935) was analyzed by Freud after the war, and for a short time was considered by Freud and Jones one of the most promising of the American psychoanalysts. After leaving his wife for another woman in the early 1920s, Frink succumbed to mental illness and his life ended tragically.

4. Along with Freud (1914d), Abraham's circular letter, which he prepared in his capacity as interim president of the International Psychoanalytic Association, was aimed at getting the Zurich society to withdraw from the International (which it did 10 July); see letters of July 1914 between Freud and Abraham (H. Abraham and E. Freud, 1965, pp. 181–186).

5. Maurice Nicoll, charter member of the London Psycho-Analytic Society (30 October 1913).

6. Crossed out in the original.

7. Had it not been for the advent of the war, Jones would likely have become president of the International Psychoanalytic Association in September 1914.

195

7 July 1914[1]
Vienna, IX. Berggasse 19

Dear Jones,

It was a bad time for letter-writing, the hottest weather and the most intense work of the year. I am pretty worn out and resolved to shut up next Saturday; our departure has become uncertain by the sudden illness of my sister in law, a bad influenza with bronchopneumonia, she is feverish since a week and as you know, there is no saying what may become of it. My daughter will leave the 7th of this month, pass over to England the 15th and no doubt you will have opportunity to see her in August or before.

As for Loe, the morphia campaign has miscarried; in the trial to get loose from it she developed such a misery that it could not be followed up in the short time before us. She had begun too late, given herself much pain consciously but internal resistance is still too great. As for the last years success it is easy to understand she conceded it only because she was not in earnest. This time she was and had to learn what the difficulties were. I do not think she cheated us more than one single time (known to me) during all the treatment and I presume she is still more reliable than her accuser. I hope she will stick to smaller doses for the next time. The uncertainty about the real nature of her pains was a great obstacle to a consequent treatment. After studying her latest reactions I strongly incline to the solution, that the far bigger part of it is hysterical indeed.

I am glad you will inherit Ferenczi's good society as I am in want of some weeks of secluded life this summer. I have written to Abraham proposing him to put up his circular to the 20th of this month, if no reaction from the Swiss holy men comes up before. I am very glad you show yourself inaccessible to Jung when he comes to London. He might try to flatter and compromise.

Yours with best wishes
Freud

1. This letter may have actually been written a few days before 7 July. See Jones's response in letter 196.

196

7 July 1914
69 Portland Court, London

Dear Professor Freud,

I was very sorry to hear of your sister-in-law's illness, and hope that the next news I get will be much better.

I enclose a rather wobbling letter of Putnam's. His *"Gutmu[ü]tigkeit"* [good nature] is really quite a disease. I shall try to prevent him at all events from becoming mixed up with Adler, and hope to succeed. His corrected paper I will post to Rank.[1]

The enclosed cutting from the *British Medical Journal* reminds me of your remark "Es ist den wenigsten Menschen möglich, im wissenschaftlichen Streit manierlich, geschweige denn sachlich zu bleiben."[2] Still, the editor's remarks are so obviously irrelevant and polemical that the total impression on the reader must be mainly favourable to my attitude, and I regard it on the whole as good luck to have provoked such a foolish reaction on his part.

On the other side I have excellent news to report from the English psychologists, which confirms my expectation that they would prove more accessible than neurologists. The meeting at Durham was an unqualified success. The details I shall write up for the *Zeitschrift*. All the speakers were on our side, and one may say that the conceptions of repression and the unconscious received good recognition amongst English psychologists and philosophers.[3] There remains that of infantile sexuality, which fortunately did not come first in order of consideration. I know of course that acceptance of these two conceptions in the abstract is but a small step towards application of them in the concrete, but still it is a good beginning. With some there was the usual tendency to explain forgetting on the usual principles, and to reserve the ψα explanation for a few cases, but I raised a laugh by saying that before giving our explanations we had first to create a *need* for them (as with infantile amnesia), just as the Salvation Army cannot save souls before they have first created a sense of sin.

After the meeting we had two days' holiday in delightful surroundings. The men were all very intimately known to one another and it made an agreeable family party, into which I was cordially welcomed. ψα was the central theme of discussion throughout, and naturally under such friendly and informal circumstances it was possible to explain difficult points in a satisfactory way. McDougall, of Oxford, asked me to analyse a dream, and we spent one whole morning on it. Plenty of material came out that made a great impression on him as to the correctness of our methods and conclusions. They asked me to take part in their next symposium in November on "Relation of Emotion to Instinct", and also to deliver an address in January on Repression[4] (I had talked for 1½ hours at the meeting on this, and explained I could then cover only a small part of the subject). So at present I have good grounds to be in an elated mood and hope that some men will take up the work. One clever young psychologist, Pear of Manchester,[5] has already done so and confirms the findings for adult life, though not yet for childhood.

You are right in saying that Jung would probably try compromising tactics if we allowed him to speak at our society, which is just the reason why I vetoed the suggestion, especially since we have so few strong members.

Can you tell me anything about the Internat. Congress for Sexuology, to be held in Berlin next October? I miss your name in the list of supporters. Is there some reason for this? The Royal Society of Medicine has asked me to represent it at the Congress, and I have provisionally accepted, though it is not likely I shall go, as I told them.[6]

I was not surprised at what you said about Loe; we can only hope for the best. I suppose I shall see her in another month's time.

Again with best wishes for your holiday and that there will be no reason to delay it.

Yours affectionately
Jones.

1. Putnam (1914b).

2. "Only very few people can remain well-mannered, let alone objective, when engaged in scientific disputes."

3. See note 2 to letter 194. Jones's report did not appear in the *Zeitschrift*.

4. Jones (1915a).

5. T. H. Pear, M.A., B.Sc., after the war was professor of psychology, University of Manchester.

6. International Congress for Sexual Research, 31 October–2 November 1914; see *Zeitschrift* 2 (1914): 293, 400–401. Jones did not attend this meeting.

197

10 July 1914
Vienna, IX. Berggasse 19

My dear Jones,

Many thanks for all your gifts and news. I know that your powers as a speaker are even stronger than those of the writer and rejoice in the report of your success at Durham.

Against my habits I perused the papers on repression in forgetting you sent me and had to judge, what seemed a highly respectable standard among pyschologists was indeed a low level for the analyst. I found no news among many words—such as Hamlet accuses against Polonius—, some few stupidities and much discussions on by-topics which might be settled by reference to a single sentence of mine. Yet we must be contented.

Putnams promise to take arms with us seems formal, but he badly wants a nurse to lead his hand and his steps. He has no idea of Adlers perfidious demeanour,[1] Lou Salomé sent me a letter written by him in 1913 which might have impressed him.

I am glad to announce you that my sister-in-law is on the way of recovery and we need not postpone our departure to take place Sunday evening. She will have to wait one week or more at the Cottage Sanatorium before she can undertake a journey.

The Berlin Congress is not against my line but I see no profit in partaking in congresses. Perhaps you had better go to become better known among the Berlin people.

I will take leave tomorrow from Loe. She recovered instantly after taking more morphia and I see no way to wrench it from her at the moment. She has become no believer in ΨA yet, but she is charming with all her faults, which are more than outweighed by her excellent qualities. There is light and shadow.

The *Traumdeutung* 4th edition has just appeared and will call at yours in a few days.

What is the way, Eder's decision for Jung will show? I am sorry for you, but it is the action of the *"scharfe Löffel"* [sharp spoon], taking away all the insane (unhealthy) tissue.

You have got Bleuler's letter?

My next card to give you my adress at Karlsbad.

Yours sincerely
Freud

1. Several letters between Freud and Putnam of 1914 concerning Adler can be found in Hale (1971a, pp. 173–176).

198
[postcard]

14 July 1914
Karlsbad, Villa Fasolt
Schlossberg

Yesterday arrived. Hope to find good recreation

Yours
Freud

199

17 July 1914
69 Portland Court, London

Dear Professor Freud,

I was very happy indeed to hear of your sister-in-law's recovery, both for her own sake and for its effect in setting free your travelling plans. I hope you will now get all the rest you need at Karlsbad, so that you will be again fresh and eager by September.

I met your daughter yesterday,[1] judging that she had come via Hamburg, and found her looking very well, having greatly enjoyed the little voyage. I saw her and her friend home, as they had to cover a complicated cross-country route, with several changes of trains, etc.. She tells me that you have been shamefully overworking of late; I hope that next year you will show more restraint in your ardour for work, for it must be very exhausting.

Bleuler's letter seemed very satisfactory on the whole, and very characteristic; I have sent it to Abraham. I shall look forward to the *Traumdeutung.* I have not read it since the last edition appeared, which is a long interval for me, and shall be glad of the opportunity of refreshing my memory on various matters as well as studying the additions.[2]

Eder reacted badly to the "sharp spoon", thinking it "undignified, unworthy of you, ungenerous to the valuable work done by Jung", etc., which is a typical example of an affective judgement. His tendency is altogether towards compromise in the matter, but he sympathizes with Jung on religious grounds and is in a curious anti-semitic rebellion—a muddle of personal complexes.

Rank tells me that Ferenczi will come to London, but I have not heard any further from the latter; he is not a ready letter-writer and usually responds only to the second stimulus.

With very best wishes

Yours affectionately
Jones.

1. Anna Freud.
2. Freud (1900a), 4th ed. 1914.

200

22 July 1914
Karlsbad

My dear Jones,

I think it wise from Putnam to have chosen you for his confessor and your answer given in a truly analytic spirit is perhaps the best you could give. But let him try as much as he may, he will never avoid his own hobbies. If he would restrain himself to the saying that there is a striving for sublimation in some of the better individuals we could not contradict, as there is such a thing, but he will spoil that simple fact by mixing it up with some philosophical theory, Hegel's or Bergson's or the like. Yet I am glad he is honest and not likely to do something which is ambiguous.

Jungs abstract is remarkable for his manoeuvers to strike out repression, which I trust will find its place in your paper.[1]

I thank you very much for your kindness with my little daughter. Perhaps you know her not enough. She is the most gifted and accomplished of my children and a valuable character besides. Full of interest for learning, se[e]ing sights and getting to understand the world. She does not claim to be treated as a woman, being still far away from sexual longings and rather refusing man. There is an outspoken understanding between me and her that she should not consider marriage or the preliminaries before she gets 2 or 3 years older. I dont think she will break the treaty.[2]

You will hear or have heard from Abraham that Maeder has nearly proclaimed the exit of the Zürich group; he bade him to wait for something to be printed at Zürich, most likely a pathetic manifesto in answer of my

Beiträge zur Geschichte.[3] Abraham's circular may still accelerate the course of events.[4]

I am glad Ferenczi will come to pass his vacancy [vacation] with you. I am sorry to have him "ousted" (does such a word exist?) for this year, but I need isolation and concentration for the essay in Kraus' *Handbuch*.[5] It is long since I had last leisure to hear my own thoughts.

We have a nice time at Karlsbad though it is very hot, as everywhere in middle Europe. I have finished a technical contribution for the *Zeitschrift* and consider another on the same line.[6]

With best love

yours
Freud

P.S. Putnam's letter returned.

1. Possibly a synopsis of Jung (1914); see also Jones (1914i).

2. Jones's unsuccessful attempt to court Anna Freud is briefly discussed in Young-Bruehl (1988, pp. 66–69).

3. Freud (1914d).

4. In the *Korrespondentzblatt* Abraham announced that on 10 July the Zurich society had voted to withdraw from the International; see *Zeitschrift*, 2 (1914): 483.

5. There is a hint in H. Abraham and E. Freud (1965, p. 309 n. 3) that Freud eventually asked Abraham to make a contribution in his place. But in the end neither Freud nor Abraham nor anyone else from the psychoanalytic camp contributed to Friedrich Kraus and Theodor Brugsch, *Spezielle Pathologie und Therapie innerer Krankheiten*, 12 vols. (Berlin: Urban and Scwarzenberg, 1919–1928).

6. Freud (1914g, 1915a).

201

27 July 1914
69 Portland Court, London

Dear Professor Freud,

The news, which may be false, comes here today that Austria has declared war, and on all sides there are rumours and preparations of a general Armageddon. I naturally wonder how this may affect your sons, Rank, etc., and hope for the best. In any emergency if there is need for your daughter to rejoin you, I could of course act as escort, and you would not hesitate to let me know (or anything else I can do).

I had already fully appreciated what you write about her. She has a beautiful character and will surely be a remarkable woman later on, provided that her sexual repression does not injure her. She is of course tremendously bound to you, and it is one of those rare cases where the actual father corresponds to the father-imago.

I am glad to give you good reports of her, for her health is excellent and she seems to be having a happy time, reacting bravely to her new surroundings. A party of us went on the river on Saturday, and she enjoyed it with the rest. I hope to see some more of her, for I am having no regular holidays this year and it is pleasant to spend a few days with so interesting a companion. Ferenczi will be here next week, and no doubt he will join us also. The family in Arundel[1] is an excellent one, and she could not be in better hands.

Today I hear from Abraham that the official *Austritt* [resignation] has arrived from Zurich, so your article has produced one of its desired effects.[2] I have read Maeder's letter, also Bleuler's and Pfisters, all full of interest. Abraham says he will join you in the Tirol.

Ferenczi proposes I shall continue my analysis with him here, and, as there as [are] still some dark places that I cannot unravel alone (principally in dreams), I shall be very thankful for the opportunity.

Two more patients are coming to me next month from India, which will make nine hours a day. I was not at Jung's lecture on Friday, and am not going to Aberdeen, but I am writing a rapport which Eder will read there (he is one of the secretaries).[3] I had a long talk with Mrs. Eder last week, who has just had a month's analysis with Jung. She discovered that ever since childhood she had been torn in conflict between her leanings to science and to philosophy, that the latter was the strongest part of her nature and must be repressed no longer. You may be interested to learn the latest method of dealing with Übertragung. The patient overcomes it by learning that she is not really in love with the analyst but that she is for the first time struggling to comprehend a Universal Idea (with capitals) in Plato's sense; after she has done this, then what seems to be Übertragung may remain.

I saw Loe yesterday. She had been in bed for some days after pain induced by the vomiting of sea-sickness, but she is now better. On Wednesday she returns to Holland to fetch Trottie.[4] She is trying hard to make mischief with Lina, whom she hates pretty strongly. Why did you tell her my remark about the morphia, which was meant only to give you a hint? Now she is cross with me over it, probably because it was the truth; I do not trust her word so completely as I used to, since I discovered what lies she has told about myself. However I expect things will quiet down, and that one day we shall be good friends. I was amused to hear about your talk with Mac-Curdy, who seems to have crept into the background ever since.

I was so happy to hear that you were benefitting from Karlsbad, and send you all good wishes and love.

Yours always
Jones.

1. Anna Freud's stay in England is discussed in Young-Bruehl (1988, pp. 65–69). The family in Arundel is not mentioned there.

2. A reference to Freud (1914d) and the withdrawal of the Zurich society from the International.

3. See Jung (1915), and Jones (1914i).

4. Loe's dog.

202

3 August 1914
69 Portland Court, London

Dear Professor Freud,

I wonder if you received my letter written a week ago? It is such an anxious time for everyone that the difficulty in communication makes it doubly hard. I am sending three copies of this letter, in the chance of at least one arriving. I have not seen your daughter since I last wrote to you, but have heard from her and from her friend. She seems very comfortable and calm, and does not mention anything about returning to Austria, but that was before the worst news of the general war. If it is necessary for her to return I could certainly get her as far as the Austrian frontier, for there are several ways of doing this, and it will be possible throughout the whole war; but I have no knowledge as to whether railway travelling inside Austria is permitted or how long the traffic will be held up by the demands of the army, e.g. from Trient or Zurich. I await your instructions in this, as in other matters, but in the meantime you may feel safe that your daughter is in good hands and has many friends in England. She is in excellent health.[1]

A letter from Ferenczi tells me he must join the Hussars, but in a medical capacity. A postcard from Rank did not mention the war. You may imagine how eager I am to hear from some of you, and to know what is happening. Do your sons have to serve, and do many of our friends in Vienna?

There is very little feeling in England. We are prejudiced against Germany and also do not like Russia, but the fear of the latter is nearer home than of the former,[2] which will come many years hence. Austria is unpopular for getting everyone into trouble, but her attitude towards the Slav danger is fairly well understood. No one doubts here, however, that Germany and Austria will be badly defeated; the odds are too much against them. The whole business is rather Greek, nations being hurled by a compelling fate into wars that no one seeks, and which must bring inevitable disaster to all. My chief feeling personally is annoyance that America will profit so much to Europe's loss.

Loe has safely smuggled Trottie over, but after unheard-of difficulties and fatigues. She says it was much the worst experience she has had in her life. She is as well as can be expected, and has a comfortable house (her aunt's). Trottie nearly died, but is slowly recovering. Loe is buying up large quantities of morphia to send to foreign armies, because when the supply of morphia runs short it will be given only to those likely to recover, while the hopeless must die in pain. Isn't she wonderful?

Jung unfortunately had a great success in his London lecture, and McDougall was so impressed that he is going to be analysed by him. I did not hear the paper, but have read it, as it was given to me as editor of the *Journal of Abnormal Psychology*. It is a maze of confused thinking, diluted with platitudes; I enclose a sample page. The one progress is that he has a new word "Horme" for Libido, and "prospective psychology" for Ps-A. as conceived by himself.[3]

London is absolutely quiet and indistinguishable from other times except for the newspapers. Grey announced tonight that we should intervene if Germany violates the neutrality of Belgium or if the German fleet attacks the undefended coasts of France.[4] There is a fairly strong feeling here against being drawn into the war, the issues of which are so distant, but our protective attitude towards France is an important factor that may come into play.

I ardently hope to have some news soon from you, and that it will be as good as possible. No doubt you will remain at Karlsbad for some time to come, even if you had the opportunity of returning to Vienna?

yours always affectionately
Ernest Jones.

1. This sentence is written out by hand in an otherwise typed letter.

2. "Latter" and "former" are circled in pen and joined by a line, arrows indicating that they are to be transposed.

3. Jung began to use the term *hormé*, derived from the Greek, in his English texts to avoid misunderstanding, while retaining *Libido* in his German publications; see Jung (1915). He also uses the expression "prospective understanding" as opposed to what he calls Freud's "retrospective understanding" (p. 181).

4. The speech of 3 August 1914 in the House of Commons by the foreign minister, Sir Edward Grey, was published in the *London Times*, 4 August 1914.

203

13 August 1914
69 Portland Court, London

Dear Professor,

I hope that Anna is doing the right thing by going home now, for I doubt whether you would not rather know her safe in England. However, she has struggled hard to make the best decision, and has been very brave in all this crisis.

She will give you the English news, so I need write nothing of it. Personally I feel that my duty is to stay by my post, and go on practising, rather than to join the war service. That has also the advantage that I shall be able to help our Vienna friends (Rank, etc.) financially, which may be rendered necessary by the war; I have tried to send money now, but there are no Austrian notes to be obtained in London.

I am terribly anxious to hear news of you and our friends, and hope you will try to communicate via Bjerre, Van Emden, Pfister, or Assagioli. I shall go to Holland soon to see Van Emden and find out what he knows.

With best love

from yours always devotedly
Jones.

[postcard from L. C. Martin, Sweden][1]

3 October 1914
St. Södergatan 50, Lund

My family is well. My daughter has reached home safely. My eldest son,[2] now Dr. of Law, is in training as a volunteer in the Artillery, and has not yet gone to the front. I hope soon to be able to work, though naturally do not expect many patients. My journals are still appearing—reduced, of course, and at longer intervals. Next week a number of the *Internat. Zeitschrift* and *Imago* will be published. The *Jahrbuch* has for some time been ready, but it is not yet sent out. The friends (?) are all together (?) and will continue the work. Some days ago I visited Abraham in Berlin. We cannot bring ourselves to regard you as an enemy!

S. F.[3]

1. Freud's letter was transcribed and sent to Jones by Louis Charles Martin, a colleague from Jones's Toronto period (Jones, 1959, p. 196) living in Sweden. After the war he was at the Sorbonne in Paris, and later was professor of English at Liverpool.

2. Martin Freud.

3. The appended note from Louis Charles Martin, who complains about Freud's use of Gothic script, reads: "This reached me this morning. Why does he stick to the old way of writing? It is not easy to read, but I think the above is accurate in nearly all particulars. I am sending you two papers with this. We have the *Illustrated London News* and the monthlies—I am just hunting down the *Contemporary Review*, abstracted by the Professor of Economics. All goes well. L. C. M."

204

[postcard]¹

10 October 1914
69 Portland Court, London

Lieber Herr Professor!

Durch Van Emden bekomme ich erfreulicherweise gute Nachrichten von Ihnen, möchte aber gern ein Wort von Ihnen persönlich haben. Loe befindet sich sehr wohl und ist sehr glücklich. Es geht Putnam und Brill gut, mir auch. Ich arbeite 7 Analyse-Stunden täglich, schreibe auch ein wenig. Eder hat uns verlassen. Ich schreibe an Sie auch via Holland und Schweden. Alle meine Briefe sind zurückgekehrt. Wie ist es mit Rank, Sachs und Ferenczi?

Herzlichste Grüsse an Ihre Frau Gemahlin, Anna, und alle andere[n].

Liebe von
Jones.²

1. Sent via Dr. Roberto Assagioli, via degli Alfani 46, Florence.
2. The text reads: "Dear Professor,
"Happily I receive good news about you from Van Emden, but I would like to have a word from you personally. Loe is in good health and very happy. Putnam and Brill are well, so am I. I work 7 hours of analysis daily, also write a little. Eder left us. I am also writing to you via Holland and Sweden. All my letters have been returned. How are things with Rank, Sachs, and Ferenczi?
"My kindest regards to your wife, Anna, and all the others.
"Love from Jones."

205

22 October 1914
Vienna, IX. Berggasse 19

Dear Jones,

One of my friends, a professor of archeology in Rome, is good enough to take this uncensored letter with him to Italy.¹ I received your news via [van] Emden as well as the same via Martin and Assagioli, have replied by the same route and hope that the answer is already in your hands.

I have to send you greetings from all my family, friends and the Society. The latter responded most sympathetically to your efforts to keep in touch. It has generally been decided not to regard you as an enemy!

Regardless of what you read in the newspapers, do not forget that lies are rampant now. We are not suffering from any restrictions, any epidemics, and are in very good spirits. Two of my sons are in the army,² but still in training. None of my closer friends has yet been called up, but the forthcoming enlistment will perhaps tear Sachs or Rank away from their activities. In September I visited Abraham in Berlin; he is working a lot in a military hospital, is very cheerful; we spoke a good deal about you. Issues of the *Zeitschrift* and *Imago* have just appeared. *Imago* contains Jekel's paper on Napoleon;[3] I will ensure that it is sent to you via [van] Emden. But, of course, it is in German and will not be allowed in!

Eder is no loss. Binswanger has come over to us. The seven analytic sessions that you still have probably could not be brought together on the whole continent. I have very little to do.

Ferenczi has so little to do that he has taken a holiday in Vienna. I am working on the third edition of the *Sexualtheorie* and on a difficult case history for the *Jahrbuch*.[4] From America I have only heard from Brill and Payne. I have asked the latter to translate the paper Zur Geschichte der ψα Bewegung for M. Prince's journal, if Brill allows it.[5] With a cordial greeting and in anticipation of your news, despite war and enmity.

Yours truly
Freud

1. Professor Emanuel Loewy; see Jones (1955a, pp. 174, 384; 1955b, pp. 195, 429).
2. Martin and Ernst Freud.
3. Jekels (1914).
4. Freud (1905d), 3rd ed. 1915. Freud's famous case history of the "Wolf-Man" (Freud, 1918b) appeared in *Sammlung*, 4.
5. Actually translated by Brill for Jelliffe and White's journal, *Psychoanalytic Review*; see Brill (1916b).

[card from Freud, translated by J. E. G. van Emden]

26 October 1914
The Hague

Dear Jones,

I answered you through Martin-Lund, more directly is not possible. Thanks for good news concerning yourself and Loe. Two sons are in instruction for artillery; one son[1] and Anna are at home. Medical work is very little. As well as possible I am preparing scientifical works. Correspondence only with Brill. Translation of historical article in the *Jahrbuch*, for *Journal* of Morton Prince is left to Payne if Brill consents. *Zeitschrift* and *Imago* are continued a little reduced and deferred. Anna will try to write to Loe.

Truly yours
Freud[2]

1. Oliver Freud.
2. The appended note reads: "Dear Prof. Jones,
"This is the translation of a card I received for you. If you like I will try to send you

the original. Rank is working much and Ferenczi is passing his holidays with the Freuds. Martin Fr. is coming home with an Icterus. With best wishes and greetings also for 2, Sarse Road

"truly yours
J. v. Emden."

206

15 November 1914
69 Portland Court, London

Dear Professor,

Martin is, I think, leaving for Russia on Nov. 28. He has sent me a postcard from you, as has V. Emden, and I have received the letter from your archaeological friend.[1] Today came from Jekels, via V. Emden, his article on Napoleon,[2] which will interest me very much; will you please thank him for it, as I haven't his address. I should be greatly obliged if you would get the journals, including the *Jahrbuch*, sent for me to V. Emden, and then Dr. Bisschop[3] will call on him and fetch them when he is next in the Haag. Loe and I also exchange all the letters, etc., we receive, so as to get the latest news of you and your family. We shall be especially eager to hear about your sons' welfare, and to know what happens about Rank and Sachs.

I would give a great deal to have an hour's talk with you, which I am afraid must be postponed until perhaps the summer of 1916, and do not know which topic to begin with in a letter. I keenly hope that you will be able to spare some attention from the war, and give it to more productive aims, so that the writings that will result from your increased leisure will to some extent compensate for other things (what Ferenczi calls *nach-kriechende Lust*).[4] What about the *Handbuch* article on Hysteria?[5] Also what are you writing for *Imago?* I have written to Payne offering to help him with the translation of the historical essay, if it is arranged with Brill. You say this is appearing in Prince's Journal, but I thought it was in Jelliffe's *Review*.[6] Janet has republished his paper from the Congress Transactions in both his own *Journal de Psychologie* and in Prince's Journal.[7] He made not the slightest modification of his mis-statements, and so I have written a rejoinder which should appear in the December number of the *Journal of Abnormal Psychology*.[8] As you may imagine, it is quite unsparing, and calculated to affect his reputation in America.

We have had only one meeting of our society since July, a fortnight ago. It was a stormy one. Constance Long read a stupid Jung paper, announcing such discoveries as that a motor-car in a dream symbolised enthusiasm, and when I criticised the paper Eder and his wife behaved very obstinately. I wanted then to postpone further meetings until after the war, or at least for a year (in the hope that the theologians would gradually increase their distance and withdraw), but after an animated discussion it was decided to hold the next meeting at the end of January, when I shall read a paper on Jung's views. The opinion they defend is that Jung's method constitutes a variety, and legitimate evolution, of Ps-A, and that the difference between his views and ours is not great enough to prohibit the possibility of cooperation in work, my opinion to the contrary being regarded as mere obstinacy and dogmatism.[9] Unfortunately there is no one on my side except Bryan, who does not know very much, most of the members being rather passive spectators. However, you may be sure I shall do my best to keep the flag flying.

I get German papers now and then, and so knew that what our papers say about the distress in Vienna and cholera in Galicia was greatly exaggerated. In return I ask you to believe that the Bank of England has not been destroyed by bombs, that Egypt and India have not revolted, and that our coasts have not been bombarded by the German Fleet! There is no feeling here against Austria, the view being that she has been exploited by Germany. An intelligent distinction is made between Prussia and the rest, and there is much resentmen[t] against her bullying arrogance and annihilation of the Hague laws. There is a considerable "sekundäre Bearbeitung" going on, and the worthlessness of German science has been discovered by the war in much the same way as certain people we could mention have renounced their belief in infantile sexuality on equally irrelevant grounds. To me it is very painful to see the lack of objectivity that even scientific men have shewn on both sides on questions relating to the causes, motives, and conduct of the war. Wundt and Eucken one could imagine, but fancy Ostwald![10] It seems to me that here, as elsewhere, the only people who have a real opportunity to display their superiority in this respect are psycho-analysts. I hope we shall be able to learn something about the psychology of nationalism and patriotism as the result of such a good chance to study this important matter, and am sure that much of your attention is going in this direction. As it seems to me I think I could hold the balance pretty well between the arguments brought on either side, and the only real reason [why I][11] that I can give for wanting our side to win is that on the whole the average Englishman is nearer and more sympathetic to me than the average German, especially the average Prussian. It is difficult to see what vital principle is involved in the conflict, which is rather a boyish one of wanting to see which side is the stronger, and not being able to agree on the point without testing it by force. Beyond a tremendous abreaction of pugnacity I don't suppose much will result from the whole war, for obviously Germany cannot win nor can she be really crushed, and even if Bosnia, Galicia, and Alsace are changed over it is not a very important matter. It looks, however, as though Germany will be left with an abiding hatred of England, which is regrettable but apparently unavoidable.

I should very greatly like to hear something of your own attitude towards the war, and to know how deeply your feelings are engaged. The fact that your sons are involved is of course bound to make a big difference.

Of personal news I have not much. Practice is still increasing, but I find time to do some other work. I have finished my book on treatment and am now going on with the translation of Ferenczi's papers.[12] After that comes perhaps Napoleon, the atmosphere being favourable to such topics, and then the big lay book on Ps-A.[13] I see Loe pretty often. She has some physical troubles at present, but is happy and on the whole well; her new house will be ready in January or so. My own health has not been good (toxic arthritis and neuritis) but I hope to remedy that next month by an operation for removal of nasal septum, turbinates, and exploration of antrum; it will mean two weeks in hospital. I am pleased to hear that our circle has decided not to regard me as an enemy, and to see that they have thus been able to correct the irrational tendency to unconscious Verdichtung that might otherwise have made it possible to do so. As for my side, I also have no difficulty in separating personal friendship from national rivalry.

As this letter contains no military secrets I hope it will arrive safely, and shall look forward with eagerness to your next letter. Will you please distribute messages of warm greeting to the Committee and to your family, reserving the warmest for yourself.

Yours always
Jones.

1. A fuller discussion of this early war period is contained in Jones (1955a, pp. 173–174; 1955b, pp. 194–195).
2. Jekels (1914).
3. Possibly Francis R. B. Bisshopp, M.D. 1892 London.
4. In his notes and fragments of 2 November 1932, Ferenczi uses the term *Nachkriechen der Lust* (pleasure creeping in behind the pain); see Ferenczi (1932, p. 277; 1955, p. 265).
5. See note 5 to letter 200.
6. The episode regarding Brill (1916b) is discussed fully by Jones in letter 208.
7. Janet (1914).
8. Jones (1915b); but see also Freud (1916e).
9. Jones had typed "dogmaticness," then crossed out -cness and added -sm.
10. Scholars and scientists on both sides of the war had made a number of declarations throughout October 1914 regarding the righteousness of their respective causes. The German professorial manifesto of 1914, published in the *Frankfurter Zeitung*, 4 October 1914, was signed by ninety-three members of the German intellectual elite, and included the names of Wilhelm Wundt (1832–1920), professor of physiology at Leipzig, founder of experimental psychology; Rudolf Christoph Eucken (1846–1926), professor of

philosophy at Jena, Idealist, winner of the Nobel Prize in literature (1908); as well as Wilhelm Ostwald (1853–1932), professor of chemistry at Leipzig, winner of the Nobel Prize in chemistry (1909). See Klaus Schwabe, *Wissenschaft und Kriegsmoral: Die deutschen Hochschullehrer und die politischen Grundfragen des Ersten Weltkrieges* (Göttingen: Musterschmidt, 1969), p. 22; and also Hermann Kellermann, *Der Krieg der Geister: Eine Auslese deutscher und ausländischer Stimmen zum Weltkriege 1914* (Weimar: Heimat und Welt, 1915), pp. 64–69.

The British response, "Reply to German Professors: Reasoned Statement by British Scholars," appeared in the *Times*, 21 October 1914, p. 10. Jones may have noted, too, some of the reportage on individual scientists. For instance, the *Times*, 5 October 1914, p. 9, ran a short letter by Eucken, sent to America, in which Eucken proclaimed that "certainly never in its history was Germany so united and so great . . . Everything presses forward to take up arms. The feeling of embitterment is strongest against England. It will hereafter always be counted our worst enemy, and our intellectual work together will be ended for an incalculable time." And the *Times*, 31 October 1914, p. 7, reported that Professor Ostwald was visiting Stockholm as a delegate to a new association for the promotion of a German "Kultur" league. In 1910 Ostwald had asked Freud to submit an article for the *Annalen der Naturphilosophie*, but it was never written; see McGuire (1974, pp. 315, 322) and Jones (1955a, p. 78; 1955b, pp. 86–87).

11. Crossed out in the original.
12. Jones (1920b, 1916b).
13. These were not completed.

207

[postcard][1]

29 November 1914
69 Portland Court, London

Lieber Herr Professor,

Hoffentlich haben Sie meinen Brief erhalten. Ich schlage Ihnen vor, die Frage von der [Uber][2] „Geschichte"—Übersetzung zu Brill zu überlassen; er wird am besten wissen, wie es in Amerika steht. (Journal u. *Review*, etc.). Ich möchte sehr gern hören, ob Rank oder Sachs [. . .][3] einrücken müssen.

Hier geht alles gut. Keine Neuigkeiten.
Mit herzlichsten Grüssen an alle Freunde,

Ihr getreuer
Jones.[4]

1. Addressed to "Van Emden, Den Haag," and readdressed to "Berggasse 19, Wien." The card reads:
"Dear Professor,
"I hope you received my letter. I would like to suggest that we leave the question of the '*Geschichte*' translation to Brill; he will know best how things stand in America.

(Journal and *Review*, etc.). I would very much like to hear if Rank or Sachs have to report for military duty.

"All is well here. No news.

"With kindest regards to all friends,

"Your faithful

Jones."

2. Crossed out in the original.

3. Several illegible letters are crossed out.

4. Added notation on postcard by van Emden reads: "Zeitschrifte für Jones habe ich noch nicht von Ihnen empfangen. Viele herzliche Grüsse von Ihrem ergebenen J. v. Emden." (Have not received from you journals for Jones. With kind regards, respectfully yours, J. v. Emden.)

[summary of letter from Freud by J. E. G. van Emden]

14 December 1914
The Hague

Dear friend,

Prof. Freud having the opinion that he cannot answer you directly, he asks me to let you know that:

Rank and Sachs are free; he will urgently try to let you get the *Zeitschrift*; you must make his compliments to Loe and Herbert J. and stimulate them to write to him. The question of the English translation of the ps. a. movement history he has of course ceded to Brill.[1] With New-year an Italian translation of the American lectures on Ps. A. by Bianchini will appear in Naples.[2] The third edition of Sexual theory is in printing.[3] Praxis very feeble; the whole situation is becoming monotonous. He is preparing some articles. Martin and Ernst are still in instruction and write very animated. Anna is occupied with baby-crèche and popular eatinghouse; the old ladies are very well, his wife passed two weeks in Hamburg. Oli is building barracks in the neighbourhood of the spitals. The weather is bad and everybody with catarrh and fever . . .

No news from here. With best wishes

yours sincerely

J. v. Emden

1. Brill (1916b).

2. M. Levi-Bianchini, *Sulla psicoanalisi*, Bibliotheca Psichiatrica Internazionale (Naples: Nocera Superiore, 1915).

3. Freud (1905d), 3rd ed. 1915.

208

15 December 1914
69 Portland Court, London

Dear Professor,

I was glad to hear from Van Emden that my letter to you got through, and am patiently hoping for an answer if it is possible. Since then there is not much fresh news. I have had a long and characteristic letter from Putnam,[1] who seems to be as active as ever in lecturing, writing, etc.. He is of course particularly horrified about the war, and his sympathies are strongly on the side of the Allies (i.e. Entente). Brill, on the contrary, favours the land of his birth, which I suppose is natural. Loe and Herbert were here to tea yesterday. She is very well, and they expect to be in their new home (about ten minutes away from here) at the end of January. My operation is at the end of this week. Work is going forwards with writing, society meetings, etc.; last week I read the report of a case of ereutophobia at a private Psychiatric Club.[2] In January my analysis hours go up from eight to ten or eleven daily, which will be an interesting experience for me. By choice I should never like to do more than seven, but in these uncertain times, when fees are also lower, one must [do][3] take what comes. I intend to have a good holiday in April after a hard winter's work.

There seems to be a little confusion about the matter of the translation of your *Geschichte* essay. This is the state of affairs. When it appeared I was writing to Jelliffe and told him that you had written an article which would, I hope, neutralise the effects of Jung's articles in his (Jelliffe's) *Review*, and I suggested to him that he ask Brill if the translation could not appear in the same journal as Jung's, so as to reach the same audience. I also wrote to Brill with the same suggestion. Brill says that Jelliffe told him I had offered to translate the essay, which of course is not true. Then Jelliffe asked Payne to translate it, he being on the staff of the *Review* and having done much work for Jelliffe, with whom he is friendly. Payne wrote to you, and apparently got the answer that he was to communicate with Brill and that the essay was to appear in Prince's Journal, not in Jelliffe's. When I wrote to you on the point I suggested that you allow Brill to decide whether the *Review* or the Journal was best-suited, as he would know the local situation best. I have never heard from Jelliffe on the matter at all. In Payne's last better [letter] he quotes a remark of your's, that you had heard that I had offered the translation to Jelliffe, which you rightly called an unbelievable rumour; I wonder where you heard it from. Brill's jealousy seems to resent my having mentioned the subject to anyone, and perhaps it would have been more cautious of me if I had said nothing, but I was only prompted by the feeling of satisfaction to think that your essay would soon be available in English to influence the lukewarm Americans. There was of course not the slightest idea of interfering with Brill's prerogatives. I have done my best to put the matter right with him, but he is what we call "touchy".[4]

Since writing this I have heard from Martin that your brother in Manchester had suddenly died.[5] Please accept my deep condolence. I hope it will not be a too severe shock to you, although I know that you had intimate feelings connected with him.

I cordially hope you will have as pleasant a Christmastime as is possible under all these sad circumstances, and that the New Year may bring brighter days. I had thought last Christmas that I should surely be with you again in Vienna this year, but the capacity of human prediction as to human affairs has at present very definite limitations. It is a consolation, however, to think that in time our work must reduce these limitations, perhaps very greatly. If there is ever to be any salvation of the world from these nightmares it will surely be psycho-analysis that will point the way. That is why I feel that if the future of psycho-analysis had to be weighed with the future of my own country I should side with the former.

With warmest greetings and good wishes to your family, our friends, and most of all to yourself

from yours always affectionately
Ernest Jones.

1. Probably Putnam to Jones, 1 November 1914; see Hale (1971a, pp. 283–286).

2. In Jones (1911c) a distinction is noted between ereutophobia, the fear of blushing, and erythrophobia, the fear of red; see Jones, *Papers*, 2nd ed. (1918, p. 226).

3. Crossed out in the original.

4. Concerning Freud (1914d) and Brill (1916b); see also Jones (1955a, pp. 175–176; 1955b, p. 197).

5. Freud's half-brother Emanuel.

209

Internationale Zeitschrift für Ärtzliche Psychoanalyse

25 December 1914
Vienna

Dear Dr. Jones,

Your letter arrived right on Christmas Eve, and, like your earlier attempts to maintain contact, pleased and touched me very much. Through the kindness of Dr. van Emden, I answered you repeatedly, and have had no proof as yet that you received my replies. But if you do not get my replies, how can I let you know that it is not my fault?

The matter of translating my historical article can hardly be disentangled during these times. I think I now finally understand what happened. Naturally, Brill was suspicious and Jelliffe a liar as always. But I think that you too have changed your attitude to the ΨA Review somewhat. On the whole, it does not matter to me where the translation appears and who does it, as long as it does get done. Naturally, I never wanted to encroach on Brill, and as a result left every decision to him.

I have no illusion that the blossoming of our science has now been abruptly cut short, that we are approaching a bad period, and that it can only be a matter of maintaining a glimmer of the fire in individual hearths until a more favourable wind allows it to blaze again. What Jung and Adler left intact of the movement is now perishing in the strife among nations. The Verein is as doomed as everything else that is called international. Our journals are headed for discontinuation; we may succeed in continuing with the *Jahrbuch*. Everything we wanted to cultivate and care for, we now have to let run wild. Of course I have no fears about the final outcome of the cause, to which you are so touchingly dedicated, but the near future, which can only be of interest to me, seems to me hopelessly eclipsed, and I would not blame any rat I see leaving the sinking ship. I am now trying to bring together, in a sort of synthesis, what I can still contribute.[1] It is a work that has already yielded much that is new, but which unfortunately is being disturbed by mood swings.

You write that your "operation" will take place at the end of this week. I naturally do not know what you mean, and conclude that a letter was lost; but judging from your tone, it cannot be serious. As you can imagine, my medical practice has been reduced to a minimum of two to three hours a day. I have never really found a base in Vienna itself; most of those who wanted to come cannot do so. This restriction is actually what I find most difficult to bear because I have been used to extensive work for the past twenty years, and I cannot possibly use more than a fraction of my spare time for my writing.

Strangely, I have heard nothing from Putnam;[2] Trigant Burrow recently offered me refuge in his house in Baltimore!! Pfister writes occasionally; he has left Zurich but has not joined us, and just now I am not in the mood to accommodate the vacillators and half-hearted. The other Swiss, I think, will soon realize that there is no money to be made now from ΨA, and will thus direct their work elsewhere. If we had not been spoiled by the years of triumph, we could be content with the present state of affairs.

As soon as the clamor of war is over and travel permitted again, we must arrange to meet somewhere. But when will that be possible? At the moment one has not even a glimmer of an idea.[3] Such a private meeting will perhaps mean a new beginning of our official activity, but in any case the end of what we have been doing up till now.

Cordial greetings to you, and I thank you on behalf of all my family for your kind wishes. Remain unflinching until we meet again.

Yours faithfully,
Freud

1. The "Papers on Metapsychology" are only partially extant; see Freud (1915c, 1915d, 1915e, 1917d, 1917e), Grubrich-Simitis (1987), and Barry Silverstein, "'Now Comes a Sad Story': Freud's Lost Metapsychological Papers," in *Freud: Appraisals and Reappraisals: Contributions to Freud Studies*, vol. 1, ed. Paul Stepansky (New York: The Analytic Press, 1986), pp. 143–195.

2. The apologetic tone is evident in Putnam to Freud (early 1915), in Hale (1971a, p. 177).

3. The German here is "Es lässt sich bis jetzt nicht einmal ahnen." Freud's use of "ahnen," literally to have a presentiment or foreknowledge, is quite powerful. The word derives from *der Ahn* (pl. *Ahnen*), meaning ancestors, forebears. Also, the German verb *achten* (n. *Achtung*), which means to esteem or respect, has the same Gothic root as *der Ahn*.

210

17 June 1915
69 Portland Court, London

Dear Professor Freud,

I have not heard from you since Christmas—the longest interval for some years—but from other friends (Van Emden, Rank, etc.) I hear that things are going pretty well with you. Letters from Rank, Sachs, and Ferenczi have come, and have been exceedingly welcome in this lonely time, which now promises to last longer than I had hoped. Thank you for the reprints, which arrived safely. The one on Übertragungsliebe[1] interested me greatly, and I should have liked to discuss my experiences of it with you. I have seen all the various outcomes of it that you describe, fortunate and unfortunate. The last *Zeitschrift* I received was the January number; presumably others have since appeared. I trust it will be possible to maintain it, even if *Imago* and the *Jahrbuch* are suspended. Our society has not met since last autumn, owing to Eder's attitude. He is now serving in Malta, and I hope to get him to resign his position so that we can meet without him in October.

My personal news is pretty good. I am extremely well in health, and still busy in practice (8 hours). At Easter I spent two days holiday in Cornwall, and send you two photographs as a souvenir of that. There is a strong call for doctors to join the Army, but I conceive my first duty to be to keep the $\psi\alpha$ flag flying. Still I have offered my half-time services to the War Office, and hope to get some appointment in a London Hospital, probably in mental work. The shock cases in the war are highly interesting. Have you seen any? The war has almost paralysed my productivity—only two articles this year; I have just finished one on War and Individual Psychology.[2] Spare time goes to reading the papers, magazines, and books on history, etc.. I should greatly like to hear from you on the subject of my Napoleon work, of which I wrote to you in my February letter.[3] The secretary of the British Psychological Society, lecturer at University College, London, has come to me for analysis. He was so impressed with the general importance of $\psi\alpha$ that he wished to acquire the technique by being analysed, and he has proved an excellent worker as well as receiving help in his personal problems and inhibitions. It is of course gratifying to me, because I think he will be a staunch and valuable adherent.

Loe is happy and pretty well on the whole; some sciatica and kidney attacks. A skiagram shows a large stone in the left kidney, but there is no talk of operation. She hopes to move to the new house in a month's time. You can imagine her precautions against Zeppelin dangers, including a respirator for Trottie in case of gas. She has become enormously fat, hardly to be recognised. Of course she is bitterly anti-German, as ever, especially as Herbert is so Francophil. Still this does not extend to Austria!

It might interest Anna to know that her friend Mabel Pring is a nurse in the London Hospital since February, and seems very happy there. Her sister Connie is doing Red Cross work at home. Three of the brothers have joined the Army; one, Edward, fought at Neuve Chapelle.

I enclose the programme of the recent meeting of the American Psychopathological Association. The items marked with an asterisk are of $\psi\alpha$ interest, and it would be well to notice them in the *Zeitschrift*.[4] So far I have had only partial reports of the meeting, but there seems to be much swinging from the true principles of $\psi\alpha$—due to individual conceit. You have probably received a copy of Putnam's book;[5] I have not yet read it. At the meeting Stanley Hall in a flattering speech proposed I should be made an honorary member, at which I am pleased.

It is encouraging to hear that you can proceed with productive work in these disturbing times. You know how important that is to us all, and I trust that [the][6] your increase of leisure will benefit us in that way. *A propos* of your work on Narcissism: in a recent book by Shand I came across the following remark on "*amour-propre*" quoted from La Rochefoucauld (*Reflexions*. 1. éd. 1665). "On ne peut sonder la profondeur ni percer les ténèbres de ses abîmes"![7]

I hope very much to get a letter from you soon. Please give my kindest regards to all the members of your family and also of our committee

With all warm thoughts from

Yours always
Ernest Jones.

1. Freud (1915a).
2. Jones (1915a, 1915c).
3. Letter missing.
4. For the program and discussions of the sixth annual meeting of the American Psychopathological Association, New York, 5 May 1915, see *Journal of Abnormal Psychology*, 10 (1915): 263–292; the program was also included in *Zeitschrift*, 3 (1915): 247.
5. Putnam (1915).
6. Crossed out in the original.
7. "We are neither able to probe the depth nor to pierce the darkness of these chasms." Alexander F. Shand, *The Foundations of Character* (London: Macmillan, 1914), p. 79. Jones quotes from Shand's discussion of self-love. The line actually reads: "On ne peut sonder la profondeur de ses projets, ni en percer les ténèbres"; see La Rochefoucauld, *Oevre complètes* (Tours: Editions Gallimard, 1964), p. 318.

211

30 June 1915
Vienna, IX. Berggasse 19

Dear Doctor,

I should have liked to reply to you long ago if the chances of my letter's arriving were better. As you assure me that you had news of Rank and Sachs, I will also try again.

Your news pleased me very much and I can only applaud your resolve to guard the flag of psychoanalysis. When we see each other again after the end of this unfathomable war, our estrangement should be limited to the least possible extent. For quite similar reasons I have not replied to Loe and Herbert Jones.

I thank you for the small enclosures to your letter. While Putnam sent me notice of his book, I have not received it as yet.[1] We are keeping the *Zeitschrift* and *Imago* going; as for the new volumes, the third and second issues respectively are about to be published. *All* my editors are already doing military service; for the time being, Rank is staying in Vienna. My son Martin has been in Galicia since January and is keeping well. Ernst completed his training and is waiting for further orders.

Despite some inner difficulties I have (almost) completed a collection of twelve essays, which is to be published in book form after the war, perhaps with the title *Zur Vorbereitung der Metapsychologie*. The first four of the series will be published in the *Zeitschrift*; "Triebe und Triebschicksale" in Nr. 2 is the first in the series.[2]

Jekel's paper on Napoleon seems to me to have no connection at all with yours; he takes up one of the mainsprings in his character; that should not deter you from refering to the other, which J. is not even aware of. As far as I know, J. is not continuing with his study.[3]

Cordial greetings to you, and I ask you to give my warmest greetings to Loe and Herbert also. The restriction of our friendly relations also counts among the severe privations of these times.

Yours
Freud

1. Freud received Putnam (1915) in early July; see Hale (1971a, p. 188).
2. Freud (1915c) was the first of the series of "Papers on Metapsychology."
3. Jekels (1914). Jones did not publish his study of Napoleon; see Jones (1957a, p. 191; 1957b, p. 204).

212

8 December 1915
69 Portland Court, London

Dear Professor Freud,

Although I have not heard so, I trust that you received my letter which was sent to you in September when you were in Hamburg.[1] Last week I sent to you or Rank a batch of abstracts to help to keep things going. Does *Imago* still run? I hope that at least the *Zeitschrift* will continue all through.

Here everything is as before. Loe's house is not yet ready, though they have gone to live in it. I think she will be miserable when it is finished, it is such a wonderful distraction to her. She is better now, but of late has not been so well, some neurotic symptoms. I see her every two or three weeks, and greatly enjoy doing so. This autumn I have read several papers at various societies, and intend publishing my book on treatment in the New Year.[2] The Ps-A Society has not met, but we have informal meetings of the three or four soundest men; I hope to get Eder out of it. Knowledge of our subject still spreads in England, in spite of the effects of the war. Reversion to repressed and unconfessed tendencies are so evident in all countries at present that it is no longer possible to deny their existence. I find the psychologists here much more accessible than the neurologists, partly, I suppose, because their interests are not so directly threatened. A little indication is the fact that I have recently been elected to the Council of the British Psychological Society, which is satisfactory as it is a very respectable body!

Can I ask you a scientific question arising out of your article on repression,[3] for the reprint of which I thank you? You describe the action of the unconscious in causing part of the repression in a different way from that in which I had conceived it, which was as follows: The attraction of previous, primitive unconscious material involves the newer, associated material in the same orbit of feeling as itself, thus investing it with this feeling and causing it in consequence to be subjected to the same forces of repression as the older material. In other words, the latter involves the newer stuff in its own fate, namely repression, but in both cases the actual repressing force, as is indicated by its name, acts from above, from the "higher" Instanzen (though, of course, not necessarily from consciousness). Am I wrong in this, or can it be reconciled with your different phraseology? In my article on repression and memory, a reprint of which went to you last week, I criticised Jung for a statement which I now find in your recent article on repression.[4] That is very sad, isn't it?

I was delighted to get a letter from Ferenczi not long ago, and postcards come at intervals from the ever-faithful Rank. From Sachs I have heard nothing this year. His domestic news was no surprise after what I had seen in Vienna, and I hope it will be better for both of them, as in my own case. I gather that he is back at home, but am not sure if this means his definite discharge from service. About Rank I am very sad, it is the saddest personal news in the war to me, and I do hope that things will go lightly with him. Is it known how long he will remain with you?[5] Loe tells me that your son Oliver is engaged; will you please congratulate him for me.

It is just two years since we last met, and perhaps it will be another two before we meet again, though I sincerely trust not. I was happy to get good news of you from our valuable friend Van Emden after your meeting together, and trust it still continues, as well as your extraordinary capacity for work in such times as these. It sounds farcical to wish you a "merry Christmas" this year, though at least things might be far worse. I send you my heartfelt wishes for the New Year, and may it bring us all happier times. How different such wishes feel now when contrasted with the more conventional ones in quiet years, and how filled with meaning and desire they are.

Please also convey my kindest regards to your wife and daughter.

yours as always
Ernest Jones.

1. Letter missing.
2. Jones (1915d), and Jones (1920b).
3. Freud (1915d).
4. In his paper Jones suggests that "no psychoanalyst . . . ascribes *any* forgetting directly to the attraction of the unconscious," and then goes on to criticize the statement made by Jung that "it seems as if the mechanism of repression were much more in the nature of a passive disappearance, or even as if the impressions were dragged beneath

the surface by some force operating from below" (Jones, 1915a), *Papers*, 2nd ed. 1918, p. 111. In his metapsychological paper on repression Freud puts forward a similar idea regarding the force of attraction of the unconscious when he emphasizes the importance of "the attraction exercised by what was primally repressed upon everything with which it can establish a connection" (1915d, p. 148).

5. Both Rank and Sachs had been conscripted into the military in July 1915. Sachs was released from service after a short time, and would remain by Freud's side for the greater part of the war years. Rank, however, would depart for Krakow in January 1916, where he spent three years at the *Krakauer Zeitung*. Moreover, Rank was in general prone to bouts of depression during this period. In his biography of Freud, Jones refers to Rank as being "marooned in Cracow," and speaks of his severe attacks of depression, and the fact that Rank's absence from Vienna "was a serious blow to Freud," who was very dependent on him professionally; see Jones (1955a, p. 187; 1955b, p. 210).

213

27 March 1916
69 Portland Court, London

Dear Professor,

Sach's Christmas card told me you had received my December letter. Since then no news from anyone till today, when to my joy a postcard came from V. E. giving good news of you all and telling of Martin's change of fortune. The best news is that Rank is still in Vienna,[1] and that Ferenczi is coming to B-P.. Scarcely an hour of the day goes by without my thinking of you all. I had hoped to see you next Christmas, but now I fear it will be more than twice as long as that; you spoke with right in your article of *dieser ganz unübersehbaren Krieg!*[2]

The tide of war threatened to engulf me recently, as we have conscription now for single men under forty; but the War Office decided I was of more use to the Army at my present work than doing hospital duty in France. I have 10–11 analyses a day (nearly all men), with 3 patients waiting, and besides that many consultations, society and committee meetings, lectures, etc.. There is no doubt that I am now solidly established in London, *fest im Sattel* [firmly in the saddle]. It is of course very hard work, but no one must complain in these times. $\psi\alpha$ is far from dormant in England, and keeps spreading. We have had several society discussions on it. There is much opposition, but you know $\psi\alpha$ thrives on opposition. Several other men besides myself are working seriously at it. With all this experience I am of course learning daily most interesting things, and wish I had time to write more. We are translating a collection of Rank's articles to make a book on dreams.[3] Ferenczi's book is in the press.[4] Payne has finished translating Pfister (with additions from him in the Vienna direction).[5]

Loe is moderately well, but Herbert has chronic bad health, owing to some undiscoverable deep-seated abscess. Lina is still with me, and I am as happy and contented as anyone can be in war time. Trotter has written a book on "Herd Instinct in Peace and War" (with a flattering chapter on yourself),[6] which I should send you if it were possible. From Putnam I hear regularly, from Brill occasionally. In America the "constructive analysis" of Zurich seems to flourish more than here, as perhaps you see from the ψα *Review*. Jelliffe tells me he still cannot see the difference between the two schools!!

I wish I knew what was happening with regard to your Journals, whether there is any use in sending you material, etc.. It is eight months since I got a number.

I am glad to say that the feeling here is all against the Germans, not at all against the Austrians, and we read that this is reciprocated on the other side, which I hope is true.

Thank you for replying about the repression, which is now clear.[7] It was a question of the wording on your side, which I think lends itself to [mis-intepration][8] misinterpretation in Jung's sense, but I am glad to be sure I had read you aright.

I hope Anna is quite well, and all of you.

With kindest thoughts

yours affectionately
Ernest Jones.

1. This was not so; see Freud's reply in letter 214.
2. "This wholly unfathomable war." Freud actually wrote "dieses unabsehbaren Krieges" (see letter 211).
3. "Studies in Dreams and Allied Topics" by Rank, as announced after the war in *Journal*, 2 (1921): 149, was planned, but not completed.
4. Jones (1916b).
5. Pfister (1913).
6. See note 2 to letter 215.
7. Letter missing. After quoting the passage on repression from letter 212 in his biography of Freud, however, Jones states that "in his next letter he [Freud] agreed that my formulation was more precise"; see Jones (1955a, p. 184; 1955b, p. 207).
8. Crossed out in the original.

214

16 April 1916
Vienna, IX. Berggasse 19

To E. J.,

Lieber! I was pleasantly surprised to have news of you again, having given up the possibility of that idea until the end of the war. I was also very delighted that it was good news, as far as these times allow.

I am glad to let you know that the journals continue to exist; they contain some good contributions and are also prepared to accept others. (Pierce Clark concurs.) The first Nr. of the 1916 volume, which has gone to press, has an international content, including *Putnam:* "Allgemeine Gesichtspunkte zur ψα Bewegung"; *Stärcke:* "Aus dem Alltagsleben"; *E. Jones:* "Prof. Janet über ΨA," short pieces, and many reviews by the same Jones.[1]

Rank has been absent for three months editing the *Krakauer Zeitung.* I have only Sachs with me, who has proved excellent. The lectures I gave this term are to be published by Heller in three parts; the third one next year.[2] It is to be hoped the war will be over by then.

Yesterday I received a strange book from America, Holt's *The Freudian Wish,*[3] which I an reading just now. I should naturally like to see Trotter's book as well.[4]

Fortunately there is little to report about my family. My son-in-law was wounded and is at present home on leave.[5] Both my soldiers come to Vienna occasionally, on leave or on duty. Otherwise communication with them is very meager. Oli is employed as an engineer on an important tunnel construction; he got marrried in December, but I have grounds for hope that he will soon be free again.[6] Anna is very successful as a teacher. As always I am greatly interested to have news of Loe and Herbert. I hope that his indisposition will not be serious. You know that I noticed he had *M. Basedowii?*[7]

They wanted to make my sixtieth birthday a festive occasion; in view of conditions, and being separated from so many of my friends, I understandably suppressed all such inclinations.

With cordial greetings and wishes

Yours,
Freud

1. Putnam (1914b); J. Stärcke, "Aus dem Alltagsleben," *Zeitschrift,* 4 (1916–17): 21–33, 98–109; Jones (1915b). Numerous reviews by Jones are listed in the table of contents of *Zeitschrift,* 4 (1916–17).
2. Freud (1916–17).
3. Holt (1915).

4. Trotter (1916).

5. Max Halberstadt.

6. Oliver Freud's first marriage ended unhappily, and he later married Henny Fuchs of Berlin in 1923.

7. Basedow's disease, or toxic diffuse goiter.

215

30 May 1916
69 Portland Court, London

Dear Professor Freud,

First let me congratulate you and send you my warmest wishes on your birthday, which I believe falls this month, though I do not know the exact date. We must have a Festschrift after the war, e.g. 25th anniversary of the "psychischen Mechanismus"[1] or some such suitable date.

It was a great treat to have your letter, especially after so long an interval. I owe a great deal to Van Emden's kindly offices, who makes easy the maintaining of contact. I wish, however, that you had given me more personal news of yourself, about your health, your moods for work, etc..

I cannot understand where the difficulty arises about my getting the *Zeitschrift*, for I get all the other German periodicals with ease. Jelliffe also writes to complain that his exchange copies no longer arrive, or only irregularly. Holt's book I have heard of, but not yet got. Trotter's book was sent you by Loe, and I hope arrived safely. It will interest you, and you will I am sure be amused by the evidences of subjectivity in it (e.g. the sadism he projects on to you, etc.).[2] The alternations between the tone of a detached scientist and the prophet Micah are very startling. The war has quite upset him.

Herbert Jones is better. Loe has had *all* her teeth taken out, which is an affair of many months, so I have not seen her lately, but hear by telephone. The proofs of Ferenczi's book have come at last,[3] and I am just correcting them. A patient of excellent literary capacity is translating for a book a selection of Rank's papers (on dreams chiefly) under my supervision. At present I am doing no original work, for the first time in 14 years, and I feel rather ashamed. But I am busy reading, writing reviews, etc., and also have 11 analyses a day. So much sedentary work I feel tiring, and bad for my rheumatism, so I have been developing the hedonic side of life more. I have bought an auto-cycle with side-car and take off Saturday afternoons for the summer, which gives me a night in the country. I am just buying a country cottage, built in 1627, about 90 km. from London,[4] and hope to see you there some day, as well as other of our friends. I am glad to have the news of Rank, and am writing to him, as also to Sachs.

Hoping to hear again from you before long, and with kindest regards to yourself and your family

Yours affectionately
Ernest Jones.

1. Freud (1893a).
2. For Trotter's critique of Freud, see "Comments on an Objective System of Human Psychology," in Trotter (1985, pp. 48–63). Freud later challenged Trotter's fundamental notion of a primary herd instinct existing on a par with the instincts for self-preservation, nutrition, and sex (1921c, pp. 118–121).
3. Jones (1916b).
4. The Plat, Elsted, Surrey, south of London.

216

14 July 1916
Vienna, IX. Berggasse 19

Dear Doctor,

Many thanks for your good news. When you see Herbert and Loe J., do not fail to give them my cordial greetings. When is the promised first visit to Vienna going to be?

Since the last issue of the third volume and the first issue of the new one, the *Zeitschrift* has been greatly delayed. The first number, which will appear *soon*, will be filled mainly with your works. It really must be possible for you to obtain the *Zeitschrift* in the *same* way as the other archives which you write about.

The first part of my lectures (Fehlleistungen) has already appeared.[1] I regret that I cannot send it directly to you.

Both of my sons are still in the war, so far in good health, one in the north, the other in the south. On 16 July we are traveling to Bad Gastein (probably with Anna). Anything beyond that is uncertain.

I thank you very much for Trotter. ΨA stands rather isolated in the book. I have also received Holt. For many months no letters from America, nor have I sent anything there. Do you want to review the American publications (Putnam, Holt, Trotter)?[2]

May things continue well with you!

Cordially yours,
Freud

1. Part 1 of the *Vorlesungen*. Freud had written *"Vorlesgen,"* thus drawing attention to the slip.
2. Jones did not review Putnam (1915), Holt (1915), or Trotter (1916) for the *Zeitschrift*.

217

31 October 1916
69 Portland Court, London

Dear Professor,

I trust you had a satisfactory holiday in Bad Gastein, and wherever else you went to. I also managed to get three weeks, and went for a motor tour round (and up) the Welsh mountains. I have never seen so much of my own country and of England as in the last two years—a *Nebengewinn des Krieges*.[1]

Loe and Herbert are, I hear, well, but I have only seen her once this year. For a few months she had external difficulties (all her teeth were gradually extracted, etc.), and the effect on Herbert's health of her not seeing me and then of her visit to me made it plain that his neurosis centered round jealousy of me. Whereupon she naturally decided never to see me again. It was a blow to me and I deeply regret the necessity for it, but *che sara sara*.

Through an annoying mistake Constance Long (a Jungite) is to write the section on ψα for a huge new *Encyclopedia of Education*; I am to write on Psychotherapy and on Dream Analysis, and hope to discredit her successfully.[2] I give a few lectures, but write very little as the stimulus is missing now that I have no audience—I hope only a temporary inhibition. The last number of the *Zeitschrift* that I saw was of January 1915, and I cannot find out the reason of the difficulty, for I get all the German periodicals. Will you please tell me the title and publisher of your book?[3] I have just finished the index and last proofs of Ferenczi's book, which should appear before the end of the year. I am also engaged on a collection of Rank's dream papers.[4]

Most Sundays I go to my country cottage, which is very pleasant; the rheumatism is much better. Morton Prince was in England recently. I have not heard from Putnam for some months, and only indirectly from Brill.

I have been three years in England now, and am glad to be able to reassure you finally about any fears you may have had concerning my sexual life. I am a "reformed character", as they say. *Hoch die* ψα.[5]

With kindest regards

Yours always
Ernest Jones.

P.S. Would it be increasing the inhibition you probably feel from the censorship too much to ask you to write in Latin characters? If so please don't trouble.

1. "Incidental gain of the war."

2. See Constance Long, "Psychoanalysis," in *Encyclopaedia and Dictionary of Education*, vol. 3 (London: Pitman, 1922), pp. 1356–57; and Jones (1921–22b, 1921–22a).

3. Parts 1 and 2 of Freud (1916–17) were published separately by Hugo Heller in 1916.

4. See note 3 to letter 213.

5. "Here's to psychoanalysis."

218

15 January 1917
69 Portland Court, London

Dear Professor,

I had looked forward to a letter this Christmas, but probably the postal difficulties and delays are increasing; I hope you got my letter sent early in November. Van Emden kindly sent me the first volume of your lectures, and I cannot tell you how much I enjoyed them. I seemed to hear your voice speaking all through. They are very persuasive, in spite of the initial warning in the first lecture, and ought to have wide success. I am writing articles on Dream Analysis and Psychotherapy for a huge Encyclopedia of Education. Unfortunately, through a mistake, Constance Long (Jung) is writing on $\psi\alpha$, but I hope to checkmate her. Then I have to prepare a second, enlarged edition of my book (Papers).[1] There is formidable opposition here, chiefly focussed in one venomous and unscrupulous man, Mercier, and backed by anti-German prejudice, but I hold my own, being used to standing alone. On the other hand our India office has just submitted to me officially as a test of the value of $\psi\alpha$, the case of a valuable officer, whom they consider incurable; I have been treating him for $5\frac{1}{2}$ months and am hopeful of the result, which if successful would be important.

I have recently parted with Lina, and set her up in a little flat and found work for her. She has been with me for over three years, which is long enough time to spend with such a character. It has been very difficult lately and altogether I feel I have paid heavily for my sin against her and Loe. I now have a housekeeper of 50 who shines with respectability. Loe telephoned to me this week. The morphia had gone up again to 15 gr. (1 grm), and she is now making a final and determined effort to abolish it, in three stages. The circumstances are favourable, as Herbert is now well, and they are happily settled.

I had a postcard from Rank, with not much news. I hope he has been able to keep on his room in Wien, of which he was so proud. I shall be able to help him financially after the war, but when will that be? In two years? Our newspapers are full of the alleged distress in your country, but there are so many palpable lies on both sides, that one can only guess at the truth. Anyhow I pray that you are not seriously incommoded.

How is Anna getting on? Is she more expansive that [than] she used to be? I wrote to her for her 21st birthday, but do not know whether she will feel inclined to write back. Please remember me kindly to her, to all your family, and our friends

and accept my very warmest regards
Ernest Jones.

1. Jones, *Papers*, 2nd ed. 1918.

219

20 February 1917
69 Portland Court, London

Dear Professor,

I have been hoping to hear from you, and trust you are well. I think of you when reading the accounts of tobacco shortage, and hope you have a good stock of cigars laid in.

Since my last letter, written about Christmas time, I have the news to give that I got married last week, and have just returned from a week's honeymoon in West Cornwall—the Celtic end of England. She is Welsh, young (23), very pretty, intelligent, and musical.[1] After taking her degree in music she studied for four years at the Academy and sang at her first and last public concert the week I captured her; she has also composed some promising works. I feel it is a normal choice and we are exceedingly happy. You shall see her as soon as the war is over, which should be this year according to all opinion here (except my own).

I have heard a few times from Loe, who seems to be going on well with her morphia cure; the chances are as favourable as they ever can be externally (happiness and a peaceful, comfortable house).

The Senate of University College, London, has just invited me to give a course of public lectures there on Psychology and War—which will of course follow the lines of your "Zeitgemässiges".[2] My Ferenczi translation has appeared,[3] and I will try to send you a copy. I heard recently from him, also in December from Rank and Sachs. I hope Rank is going on well; what do you think about him?

With my warmest regards

Yours as always
Ernest Jones.

1. Morfydd Owen (1891–1918), a Welsh musician, was actually twenty-five, but had kept this from Jones perhaps to conceal her age. She distinguished herself as a fine composer and singer at the Royal Academy of Music and by 1916 had written about 150 compositions, including orchestral tone poems and incidental music, choral and

chamber works, as well as numerous miniatures for voice and piano. Her marriage to Jones effectively ended her musical career.

2. Freud (1915b).

3. Jones (1916b).

220

6 March 1917
Vienna, IX. Berggasse 19

Dear Jones,

Nice to have news of you again, and even nicer that it is such good news! I will inform Rank of your friendly offer; after a long interval I hope to see him in the next few days.

We are still alive and in decent condition. We are keeping up the Society and the journals as well as can be done. During this time Sachs has been a faithful helpmate, whose worth I cannot praise highly enough. Sadly, Ferenczi is ill with *M. Basedowii*, although not in a severe form, and is recuperating on the Semmering. From friends in America I hear almost nothing. I believe that the *Psychoanalytic Review* is going to publish several of my works, probably translated by Brill after all.[1] There is no communication with the Swiss, only the occasional letter from Pfister.

Please assure Herbert and Loe Jones that even five more years of war will not change our feelings for them.

As soon as travel is possible again, we—the Committee—must meet. I am also getting old and long for each of them. I am particularly pleased to know that your future is so well assured, and I also hope to hear one day that you have been able to find what is still missing.

With cordial greetings

Yours
Freud

[Handwritten note by Anna Freud in Latin script]

Dear Dr. Jones! Now I have to thank you already for 3 birthday letters, which is the clearest indication of how much time has passed since my trip and how little I anticipated the war at that time. This was not *the* birthday, as you surmise in your letter, that won't come for three years. But I have never really yearned for it. Dr. Rank already told me about your little weekend house. Do you too still remember my lovely castle idea with little guest houses, which annoyed Mabel Pring[2] so much at the time? Unfortunately we have not yet achieved anything like that here.

In case you received the ψα journals, it may perhaps be of interest to you that last year I translated your essay against Janet, as well as Putnam's contribution.[3] This year I again attended all of Papa's lectures which you wrote about in your last letter.—Would you give Frau Loe my best wishes as well? Papa and I wrote to her at New Year's, but I do not know whether the letter reached her. I would so very much like to hear from her again.

With best regards, I remain your
Anna Freud

1. Brill (1916b) had come out the previous year, but nothing else of Freud's appeared in the *Psychoanalytic Review* during the war years.
2. A friend of Anna Freud's, also mentioned in letter 210.
3. Jones (1915b) and Putnam (1914b).

221

4 October 1918
69 Portland Court, London

Dear Professor,

I hope you got my cheerful letter sent on July 5,[1] with the best personal news. Now I have to announce that my darling wife died last month, in very tragic circumstances. She was[2] only 25, and a most rare and wonderful being. It is a staggering blow to me, and although I am trying to start work again I am quite overwhelmed inside.[3]

I hope sincerely that you are all well, and look forward to seeing you again within a year. After the war you must come to England for a rest and change.

Yours always faithfully
Ernest Jones.

1. Letter missing.
2. The letter *s* here is doubly underlined and written boldly over another letter, which is illegible.
3. In his autobiography Jones discusses his remorse and the circumstances of Morfydd Owen's death, resulting from a severe attack of appendicitis while the two were vacationing in Wales and the effects of a hurried operation; see Jones (1959, pp. 254–256). Some of the details of Morfydd's last days up to her death on 7 September can be traced in Jones's diaries for August–September 1918 (Archives of the British Psycho-Analytical Society, London). The incident, however, remains mysterious, especially in light of the fact that the death certificate was issued on 25 September, over two weeks after her death. A forthcoming biography of Morfydd Owen by Rhian Davies may shed new light on this tragic life.

222

10 November 1918
Vienna, IX. Berggasse 19

Dear Doctor,

I received the painful news already yesterday from van Emden. I thank you for the opportunity to express at least my sympathy to you directly; I do not want to console you! I had hoped that you had found lasting happiness; I am terribly sorry that it has turned out differently, for the years of separation have done little to change my feelings for you.—

I never received your July letter. By now you probably already know, that Sachs fell ill with tuberculosis and is in Davos, where you can exchange letters with him freely. You will also learn from him that our science has survived the difficult times well, and that fresh hopes for it have arisen in Bpest.

We are all still alive, at least I hope so, for owing to the cessation of the army postal service, we have had no news of my eldest, who was on the Piave. Ernst has gone back to Munich to complete his technical studies. We did not get younger, more cheerful, or healthier in these times. Everything has turned out as you predicted in your letters at the beginning of the war. Even the future is still very somber and ominous.

As peace is unexpectedly drawing so near, I hope that your promise of a reunion "within a year"[1] can be put into effect sooner. It seems to be really unlikely that I should then be the one to travel to England.

I should have liked to hear how Loe and Herbert J. are, but perhaps you yourself are no longer in touch with them.

As soon as communication is easier, Sachs will send you a document that concerns our Committee. Also the long-missed exchange of books and journals will then resume. I am quite without news from America.

Farewell, write again very soon. Do not forget that I am already over sixty-two, and allow me to shake your hand in friendship.

from your
Freud

1. In English in the original.

223

7 December 1918
111 Harley Street, London

Dear Professor,

At last we are allowed to communicate freely again, and I hope it will not be long before we meet. I trust it will be possible for you to come here to stay for a while next Spring, and I hear also that Loe is counting on it. Then we must make plans for an autumn congress for the reorganization of the Vereinigung. I think the time is ripe for an English journal, or edition of the *Zeitschrift* (not identical, of course) owned by the Vereinigung. There is so much to talk over.

You see I can look forward in life, although I have been through hell itself these last three months. It has been an indescribably terrible experience, signifying more even than a tremendous loss—owing to my inner psychical situation and the poignant circumstances of my wife's death. But I am surely winning through, and have learnt very much by it. Yesterday I read your paper on grief and melancholy,[1] which made a great impression on me. Do you remember talking of it to me in Jan. 1914, and saying that would be our next advance? I have much analytic experience of it now, and I agree with all you say except one unimportant particular.

I would give so much for a letter from you.

Yours affectionately
Ernest Jones.

1. Freud (1917e).

224

22 December 1918
Vienna, IX. Berggasse 19

Dear Jones,

Extremely glad to have got your letter. I trust you have heard about all what has happened in Bpest and at the Congress[1] by our friend, who will forward you this letter.

I prefer writing english, however rusty it has become, remembering you could never read my German handwriting which has not improved since. You must not expect me or any of ours in England next spring; it seems quite improbable that we should be able to travel in a few months, peace being put up until June or July. I am sure you cannot conceive what our condition here really is. But you should come over as soon as you can, have a look upon what was Austria, and bring my daughters boxes with you.

I would like to send you the volume IV of my *Sammlung* containing all the papers published during war and a few new ones, but how can I? Needless to say we are all of us impatient to get your contributions to the *Zeitschrift* and see you taking an active part in the new career, opening for "her". *(Zeitschrift)*

There seems to have been something particularly poignant about your loss, which I cannot make out by your hints. Life is harsh you know already. Good bye, dear Jones!

Yours affectionately
Freud

1. Reference to the Fifth Congress of the International Psychoanalytic Association, Budapest, 28–29 September 1918. The rest of the sentence was omitted by Jones in his quotation of this passage; see Jones (1955a, p. 202; 1955b, p. 227).

225

31 December 1918
69 Portland Court, London

Dear Professor,

Your letter of Nov. 10 arrived, after six weeks. It is now permitted to send letters through any friend in a neutral country.

I was *so*[1] glad to see your handwriting again, to know that you are well, and to read your kind words to me. You know that you and ψα are everything to me, especially now when life is otherwise so drear and empty. Tomorrow, New Year's Day, I shall be 40, and life's greatest happiness is past, forever.

But do not fear that I shall lose heart for the work. That I find worth doing. In both England and America it has made great progress of late. Here it arouses general interest in every circle, and is even being taught in one medical school; the younger generation is eager to know more of it. In America several books have appeared, one good one by Frink on *"Morbid Fears and Compulsions"*.[2] I have kept touch with Brill, who seems to be very successful both in practice and in appointments; he is evidently securing recognition in New York. I regret to send you the sad news that dear old Putnam died last month, heart failure during sleep; he was well and at work to the last.

With the many men who do not know German it will be necessary now to have a *Journal* in English. Jelliffe's "ψα *Review*" is of course useless. Tannenbaum of New York arranged last summer to start a new journal, which was ready to appear when I persuaded him to postpone it till after the war, on the ground that we must have an *official* organ of our societies (not a private venture) in touch with the *Zeitschrift* (? mutual translation of articles, etc.) and of course the International Association. That will be one of the many things I want to discuss with you when I am allowed to travel (which I fear *may* not be until after peace, in June), but I mention it now so as to give you time to think it over and send me your views.

I trust that before now Martin will have arrived safely. Please remember me to all your family. I send them and you the best possible wishes for a Happy New Year, and for a successful year in our work with a happy personal and scientific reunion. I hope you will write very soon again.

Yours always
Ernest Jones.

1. Doubly underlined in the original.
2. H. W. Frink, *Morbid Fears and Compulsions: Their Psychology and Psychoanalytic Treatment*, intro. J. J. Putnam (New York: Moffat, Yard, 1918).

226

9 January 1919
69 Portland Court, London

Dear Professor,

Your very kind and welcome letter of Dec. 22nd has done me good. Thank you heartily for it. Yes, for more than one reason I like you to write in English, although I managed to decipher every word of your war letters.

If you can send the *Sammlung* IV to Van Emden I think it will come through, as I have a special licence for ψα work sent to me via Holland. I have your three volumes of *Vorlesungen*, which were "manna in the wilderness" to me, and sent you a long appreciation of them last summer in a letter which seems never to have arrived.[1]

The ψα ferment here is remarkable, and the desire for more knowledge, lectures, literature, etc. very widespread and pressing. I am in doubt whether to wait till I can see you before formulating plans, or to put myself at the head of the movement and guide it now. The immediate question is that of reconstituting our society, which has not met for two years and from which I must expel the Jung "rump". Now I beg you to write at once and state your views as to the new lines along which this should be done. It will of course be a branch of the International. Do you think it expedient to have two classes: members, who have sole control of the business, and a fringe of Associates, who will learn, attend, and discuss? It is essential that we have an *official* journal in English, here or in America—I think better here. If it is not established officially, all arrangements have already been made for an unofficial one, which would be a great pity.

I have sent Sachs my new book and have asked him to translate three of the new chapters for the *Zeitschrift* or *Imago*.[2]

I shall still look forward to the time when you can come to England to rest and recuperate. You would receive a royal welcome.

Yours always loyally
Ernest Jones.

1. Letter missing.
2. Likely Jones (1916a, 1918a, 1918b), Jones, *Papers*, 2nd ed. 1918.

227

15 January 1919
Vienna, IX. Berggasse 19

Dear Jones,

I concede all your predictions about the war and its consequences have come true, but I would be sorry if we could not meet before June this year. A new impulse has been given to ψα activity by the generous gift of one Dr. Anton Freund (Bpest),[1] Rank has been promoted to the dignity and function of leader to an "Internat. ψα Verlag", busy to bring forward books and our periodicals, and in your present state of depression it might do you good to take your part in this new enterprise by editing the english translations of the *Zeitschrift* as you proposed yourself in one of your letters.

I had no news from America these two years and I feel the loss of dear old Putnam grievously. He was a pillar of ΨA in his country and behaved most truly and gallantly against me in opposition to the whimsical, unreliable G. Stanley Hall. I had no notion what had become of the movement there yonder the pond whether ΨA had not been dethroned by Adlerism or some other invention, so I earned some consolation from your favourable report.

These last months are growing the worst we had to endure while this war lasted. My eldest son is still a prisoner in Italy (Abruzzi),[2] his last news containing good reports but dating from the 30th of November. We are all of us slowly failing in health and bulk, not alone so in this town I assure you. Prospects are dark. I am ready to confess, that fate has not shown injustice and that a german victory might have proved a harder blow to the interests of mankind in general. But it is no relief to have his sympathy placed on the winning side if one's wellbeing is staked on the losing one.

We are eager to get your own publications during these years or books and papers, translations, which have appeared in America. I even fostered a childish expectation, one of the members of the American commission or of the english soldiers to be met now in our streets, might be the bearer of such a token of rememberance for me, but it was not.

Vol. IV of *"Sammlg. kl. Schriften z. Neurosenlehre"*, containing two papers not published afore and the second edition of my *"Vorlesungen"* have come out.[3] I am sorry I can send you neither. Come and fetch them.

I hope you will recover and regain your powers by scientific work.

Yours sincerely
Freud

1. Anton von Freund (1880–1920), wealthy patient of Freud, helped to found the Verlag; member of the Secret Committee; died prematurely in January of the following year.
2. Martin Freud.
3. Freud, *Sammlung*, vol. 4 1918; and Freud (1916–17), 2nd ed. 1918.

228

19 January 1919
Vienna, IX. Berggasse 19

Dear Jones,

The next (2d) number of the *Zeitschrift* ought to contain an obituary for good old Putnam. It is to appear in the month April. Now will you be so kind to write it or will you leave it to me?[1] In the *latter* case I must beg you, to send me, as soon as you can, the dates of his birth, life and career, papers etc., until 1910. His name is not to be found in "Who is who in science" of the year 1912 and I have no access to other material (By the by "W. i. W." is a scandalous book). In any case the item should not be too short, warm and highly appreciating on his merits as an adherer to ΨA.

Yours truly
Freud

P.S. My son is at Genova, S. Benigno inferiore (a big *"Kaserne"* [barracks]).

1. See Jones (1919), and Freud (1919b).

229

24 January 1919
Vienna, IX. Berggasse 19

Dear Jones,

I have to answer your letter of the 9th without delay. I have received your book, the second edition of your papers,[1] by the kindness of Nunberg[2] who got it from Sachs on his sojourn at Zürich. I do not know whether it was meant for me or if Sachs sent me his own. In any case I was very glad to have it, found it imposing and learned from the remark in the preface, that British scientists are sometimes very much alike to German ones. I could not yet peruse it at leisure. Sachs proposed that he would translate the paper on symbolism while my daughter ought to do the last one about "anal traits".[3] She is busy on it and took it from me.

Regarding your question 'how you should' arrange matters in the re-born ψα Society I venture to say, your plan seems pretty reasonable, as you work on fresh soil and must throw out the majority of former members. The associates will have the chance or undergo the obligation to be turned into members after due time?

As for the journal, I hope you know, that both periodicals, *Zeitschrift* and *Imago*, have become official with the "european" groups. I hope also you have heard by Sachs, that we are setting on foot a ψα Verlag. Now Rank developed the idea at the same time as you, that you should bring out an english edition of the *Zeitschrift* (or both), all the papers getting translated into the two languages. That means the extension of the Verlag and the forming of an english affiliation. He (R.) will write you soon about this plan and what is more, offer you a meeting in Switzerland to discuss and to decide on this plan, as soon as both of you can do, maybe in February. I will be sorry not to attend to it, but it is impossible for me. Rank is faultless in all these matters.

Vol. IV of the *kl. Schriften*[4] will be posted tomorrow to van Emden and he will be informed by a card, that it is your property.

I am very glad to find motives to write to you so often after so long a break of intercourse.

Yours truly
Freud

1. Jones, *Papers*, 2nd ed. 1918.
2. Hermann Nunberg, member Vienna Psychoanalytic Society, editor (with Federn) of *Minutes*.
3. Jones (1916a, 1918b).
4. *Sammlung*, 4.

230

27 January 1919
111 Harley Street, London

Dear Professor,

Your most welcome letter of the 15th came today; the distance between us is shortening. By this post I send Rank my plan for our *Journal*, which I beg you to consider. More urgent is the question of constituting a new society (purged of Eder, etc.), on which I am anxious for your views. The *Aufschwung* [upward swing] in England is extraordinary; ψα stands in the forefront of medical, literary, and psychological interest. The "Shell-shock" hospitals have ψα societies, lectures are given at medical schools, etc., etc.. I have 10 patients daily, and this month 16 more have applied for my next vacant hour. Do not expect to see much output from me during the war. With the exception of the Ferenczi translation, two articles on psychology of war, and several lectures, all is in the book Sachs has forwarded to you.[1] You will like the preface. I should like to have your opinion on what I consider the chief additions, symbolism, war shock, and anal character.[2]

We read that the English are sending much food to Vienna, but I suppose only a tithe of what is needed. Pfister tells me he can look after you and your family in Switzerland if necessary. Remember how valuable your health is, and make any sacrifices to maintain it. Soon there will be plenty of food and money. I am trying to get a permit to visit Wien before peace is declared, on the ground of investigating work done there on "war shock". I look forward to work and life when I think of you and our friends.

Yours affectionately
Ernest Jones.

1. Jones (1916b, 1915c, 1915d).
2. Jones (1916a, 1918a, 1918b).

231

4 February 1919
69 Portland Court, London

Dear Professor,

I will write the obituary if you wish, but you will do it so much better that I would rather you did it. I have an excellent photograph (have you a copy?), and wonder if it would be better to publish a short note now, and a fuller notice later with photograph, list of ψα writings (not now available without writing to America), etc.? At present what I can find is this: Born 1846. Died aged 72 on Nov. 4/1918 of *Morbus cordis* [heart failure] in his sleep, well and at work the day before. Teacher of Neurology in Harvard Medical School 1872. Professor of Neurology Harvard University 1893–1912. Neurologist to Massachusetts General Hospital, Boston, 1874–1909. Good old New England Puritan family. I have a list of 100 works up to 1905 (mostly on peripheral neuritis). His first article on ψα was 1906,[1] open-minded but sceptical, and I think his real interest in it in a positive sense dated from meeting me, Dec. 1908—when he was 62![2]

Loe is very well, but fiercely anti-German! She makes an exception in your case (and I suppose Rank's) but with no one else. She has been very cruel to her sister Hortense Bubbing of Bonn, who has lost her husband, her only son, and *all* her money—on account of the latter favouring Germany. She may go to America in September for six months.

Rank's plan differs from mine (sent to him 10 days ago) in wishing the English journal to be identical in contents with the German edition. I doubt the advisability of this, but there are advantages in both plans, and such a momentous question should be decided in your presence, not at Davos. You will find my views on the Swiss visit in an accompanying letter to Sachs.

I sent Sachs two copies of my book, in the hope that the second one would find its way where I intended, as I am glad to hear it did. I am honoured by the translations, and such translators. I have had no access to Vienna experience and views of war shock, and shall be glad to learn from you if I guessed right in my chapter on it. It is a historic article,[3] an index of the turning tide in England, as I was asked by the President of the Society to read it (last April) because of the importance of your work. Were you amused by the paragraph on Jung in the preface?[4]

We intend to form a new society this month—nearly 20 members.

It is good to hear regularly from you once more.

Yours always
Ernest Jones.

1. Putnam (1906).

2. Jones met Putnam for the first time when he paid a visit to Boston in December 1908; see note 15 to letter 7.

3. Jones (1918a).

4. Jones speaks of Jung's abandonment of the principles of psychoanalysis as a reactionary gesture and of Jung's preference for mysticism versus science; see Jones, *Papers*, 2nd ed. 1918, pp. vii–viii.

232

18 February 1919
Vienna, IX. Berggasse 19

Dear Jones,

I too enjoy our correspondence sincerely after so long a break of intercourse. Your last letter touched so many points of interest, so I am at a loss where to begin with.

As for good old Putnam I had acted exactly as your letter proposed. Nr. 2 will contain a short notice of his decease now rectified by your giving the date, and promise a full article on his life and merits accompanied by his photo, already reproduced by our care. You are the fittest man to do the article.[1] Dont forget to mention how he resisted Adler's temptings.

As regards your promise: plenty of food and of money in a short time, I will try to believe you, as all your prophesies during this war-time have become true. But it strikes me, that you did not add in clear language, *where* that plentiness should be, with ourselves or in England.

My health is all but perfect, I am growing an old man and am prepared to die a poor man; Martin's captivity is pressing hard on my spirits. Dont you know anyone who is travelling to Genova, where he is detained in San Benigno inferiore?

I derived great pleasure from the perusal of your new papers in that second edition.

Sachs is busy with the "Symbolism", the first half of which I received yesterday by a special messenger, the "anal traits" (to appear in No. 2)[2] have been revised in the proofs this day and the paper on war-shock is remitted to the translator, as a highly valuable [ed][3] addition to the "Discussion über Kriegsneurosen", which will be given out as the first publication of the new "Inter. ψα Verlag".[4] I took the responsibility to decide in this way as we have no time to wait for the return of letters. It is clear and clever and may well have merited its success in England. The first part, the theory of *"Ichkonflict"* is congruous with my utterances on this matter at the last meeting of the ψα Vereinigung.[5] Later on, it seems you are losing the contact with the item of the "Traumatische Neurose", and what you say on the relation to narcisstic anxiety is excellent, hits the point, but it is too short and may not impress sufficiently the reader. Let me propose to you the following formula: first consider the case of the traumatic neurosis of peace. It is a narcisstic affection like dem. pr. etc.. Mechanism may be guessed. Angst is a protection against shock (Schreck).[6] Now the condition of the tr. N. seems to be that the soul had no time to recurr to this protection and is [overrun][7] taken by the trauma unprepared. Its "Reizschutz" is overrun, the principal and primary function of keeping off excessive quantities of "Reiz" frustrated. Then narc. lib. is given out in shape of the signs of "Angst". This is the mechanism of every case of primary repression, a traumatic neurosis thus to be found at the bottom of every case of Übertraggs-neurose.

Now in case of war there is the conflict in the Ego between the habitual and the fresh warlike ideal. The first is subjugated but when the "shell" arrives, this old Ego understands, it may be killed by the ways of the Alter Ego. Its opposition leaves this new master of the Ich weak and powerless, and thus it, the Ego as a whole, gets under the diology of the Tr. Neur. The difference between peace and war is, in the first case the Ego is strong but surprised, in the second it is prepared, but weakened. In this way the

War Neur. is a case of internal narciss. conflict in the Ego, somewhat analogous to the mechanism of Melancholy exposed in the 4th Vol. of the *Schriften*,[8] I sent you by care of Emden.—But I have made no analysis of a case of warshock.

Your intention to purge the London society of the jungish members is excellent.

Your plans about the English *Journal* seem reasonable enough. But the matter cannot be discussed by letters. Try by all means to meet Rank in Switzerland in the *first* half of March. *He* cannot postpone this journey any longer.

To be sure it would be best, nay too good, if we could expect you here at Vienna in the course of April.

Take my best love and let us look forward to a better future.

Yours truly
Freud

1. Jones (1919).
2. Jones (1916a, 1918b).
3. Crossed out in the original.
4. Jones (1918a).
5. Freud (1919a).
6. *Schreck* is written in Gothic script.
7. Crossed out in the original.
8. *Sammlung*, 4; see Freud (1917e).

233

5 March 1919
69 Portland Court, London

Dear Professor,

Your most interesting letter of Feb. 18 came yesterday. In between you have probably had news of me from Rank and Sachs, whom I hope to see within another 2–3 weeks. I am afraid Vienna is as yet impossible, but luckily the peace decisions are being hastened so that probably I shall be able to come by June or July. I cannot help picturing you in England after the war, being well looked after and working in comfortable conditions; I will not pretend there is no personal interest in the picture. Your idea about Martin has also occurred to me, but I can as yet only promise the will to keep it well in mind and to seek some one who may pass that way—perhaps the Eders on their way to Palestine this month can make a detour. Tell Anna I will do my best about her things, and will certainly bring a few things, but luggage and travelling difficulties are so great that the less she expects the less she will be disappointed. I agree to write dear old Putnam's obituary, and have already sent three letters to America to collect proper data; I understand you already have the photograph?

Your stenographic remarks on the war neuroses are very valuable, and I think I can expand them in my mind. As you guess, my interesting analytical experience gives me much more to say than I put in my article, where I only dropped a hint for those who have "ears to hear"; it was given before a non-analytical audience, which fact I hope the indulgent readers will remember when it has the honour to appear in more technical surroundings.

Did you approve of my criticism of Silberer in the symbolism paper?[1] The cloven hoof is there, but it was hard to find and I am not yet satisfied that I have sufficiently defined it. The early part had as paradigm the Priapus-Fest drawing on the cover of "Punch", but they threatened to prosecute me for libel if the reference was not cut out, which it unfortunately had to be; could a footnote (editorial) be added to the translation?[2]

I hear some things from Holland are detained by the Censor, but expect to get them soon, and am looking forward.

Yours always affectionately
Ernest Jones.

P.S. Of course you will have heard from Ferenczi all about the society, which is very promising. I have analysed 6 out of the 11 myself, so am in good contact.

1. Jones (1916a); see especially Jones, *Papers*, 2nd ed. 1918, pp. 178–179.
2. The reference to Priapus is in Jones (1916a, p. 187), *Zeitschrift*, 5 (1919): 252, and in Jones, *Papers*, 2nd ed. 1918, p. 137; 3rd ed. 1923, p. 162; and 5th ed. 1948, p. 95. In all versions there is no explanatory footnote, and the lines in question are identical: "the goat, the ape, and the ass (the animal sacred to the worship of Priapus, with which the figure of Punchinello is constantly brought into association), which are contemned as ridiculous and comic . . ."

234

17 March 1919
Palace Bellevue, Berne

Dear Professor,

It is so wonderful here. If only you were here! There is so much to write about that I am surprised at my courage in attempting a letter, especially as unfortunately my health is very poor, so that there is little energy left. But it is good to feel near you again, with no censorship in between.

First business. Rank will bring Anna's things, which made half the 30 kilos allowed for travelling. Please ask her to write and thank Loe, who was rather disagreeable about it (wanted to know why Anna had not written to her personally with a list of what she wanted, etc.) and may be soothed thereby. Rank met me here on Saturday evening, to my very great joy. Today Sachs came. I spoke with Claparède in Geneva and heard about the two $\psi\alpha$ societies there, besides Zurich![1] We saw Bircher[2] today and will again on Wednesday, but I don't think anything will come of it. *C'est un blagueur.* But I will leave all these explanations for Rank to give you, else there is no end. We go to Luzern Friday, Zurich Monday for the *Sitzung*,[3] then all of us to Geneva. I brought you a new pen, and can easily get the old ones repaired in London and sent on. (The inconsequence of my thoughts go with the lightheadedness of a slight influenza, contracted while travelling.)

Rank I find greatly improved, more independent, self-confident, and manly. I admire his quick brain and sure judgement. We get on splendidly together, and I think you may feel safe in leaving things in our hands; we agree about everything and shall have done a great deal of business before we separate.

In the last week in London I got your 4th *Sammlung*, with great delight, and read the two new articles[4] (the rest I had all read before). There is so much to say about every one. It will interest you that I analysed a girl aged 9, who developed a wolf-phobia at 4 and a Zwangsneurose at 7 (which of course exploited the phobia). She has remained cured now for two years. It was a good example of inf. totemism.

I was most interested in your letter about War Shock. There is so much to say about it. Ferenczi's paper I found disappointing, Abraham's very good descriptively, but deficient on the theoretical side. Simmel also has not much to say, but is no doubt useful propaganda.[5]

I shall hope to spend some of this year's holiday with you, if you allow. With all good wishes

Yours affectionately
Ernest Jones.

1. In addition to Zurich, where a new Swiss Society for Psychoanalysis was to be formed, there were two psychoanalytical groups in Geneva: the Groupe psychanalytique de Genève headed by Claparède, and the Société psychanalytique suisse. See Roudinesco (1986, pp. 362–363), and Mireille Cifali, "Entre Genève et Paris: Vienne," *Le Bloc: Notes de la psychanalyse*, 2 (1982): 91–130.

2. A Swiss publisher operating out of Bern.

3. Jones would attend the inaugural meeting of the newly formed Swiss Society as a guest on 24 March 1919.

4. Freud (1918a, 1918b).

5. Ferenczi, Abraham, and Simmel were the other contributors to *Zur Psychoanalyse der Kriegsneurosen* (Leipzig: Internationaler Psychoanalytischer Verlag, 1919).

235

25 March 1919
Hotel St. Gotthard, Zürich

Dear Professor,

In these days so crowded with incidents after a long isolation you will not wonder that until now I have only written to you once, a letter from Bern which I hope reached you safely. It has been wonderfully good to be again with such sympathetic and lively spirits as Rank and Sachs, and I am full of admiration for their qualities. It is a treat to watch how they turn these stupid and confused Swiss round their little finger. And you can imagine what jokes we all have together.

Last night the Swiss society decided to join the International, unanimously. The best members are Binswanger, a psychiatrist Rhorschach, and Frau Dr. Oberholzer.[1] Pfister you know; he gives trouble in wanting to make the whole world immediately members, being convinced that every one is on the point of becoming a complete ψα. Oberholzer I am sorry to say I don't like, but perhaps more on subjective grounds; this dictatorial, hard, schoolmaster type, with no trace of humour or *Gemütlichkeit* [sociability], is to me very unsympathetic. At the meeting Sachs gave a magnificent address, one of the best I have ever heard in my life, and which could not have been bettered. Rank, who was tired, and I also spoke shortly. I was glad you were not there to hear my German, but perhaps what I had to say about England was of interest.

We intend to see if it is possible to make the English publications independently of any publisher, just as the Verlag does in Wien, and I think it will be possible. I am full of enthusiasm for our future plans. The French plans are not yet settled, though Bircher offers us all we want, but I am rather more in favour of a publisher at Genf or Lausanne—perhaps even independent publishing—and we shall see what the conditions are there. At present nothing can be done with the two comical ψα societies at Genf (I visited Claparède last week), but there may be some younger members. Sachs has the situation well in hand here, and will be invaluable. In my opinion we ought to increase the importance of his position (? Zentralstelle der Vereinigung oder Sekretäriat),[2] because of the immense advantages that Switzerland offers internationally (politically, money, trading, etc.).

My own enjoyment of the experiences in these days has been greatly diminished by personal factors. I think every minute of the day of my dear wife, who had never been abroad, and with whom I planned all the details of this journey with such happiness. It is often very difficult to give proper attention to the outer world when one's feelings are so occupied within. Then also to my other bodily troubles (neuritis, rheumatism) came an influenza, with fever, contracted on the journey hither. That has now led to an otitis, which caused a fall from vertigo yesterday, and for which I am just going to consult a specialist. All this makes it more difficult to put up with the troubles of modern travelling, the repeated waiting for hours at various consulates, police, etc.—a kind of nonsense for which we English never have much patience.

You may imagine how concerned we are about affairs in Hungary, but one can hardly write about political matters which alter from day to day. About England my opinion is on the whole optimistic. I don't think it will come to civil war there, and if it doesn't then the old order will be on the whole maintained—naturally with much better conditions for the working classes.

We are going to Neuchatel on Thursday, and I leave Switzerland the day after. You will soon learn all details from Rank—our opinions and impressions are quite identical on all points. Then I hope to hear news from you when I am in London. I am very happy that Dr. Mackenzie can and will do everything possible for Martin.[3] He is a charming man; tomorrow I am to dine alone with him and his wife and so shall get to know them better—I can do several things for them in London.

In five months I shall surely see you.

Yours always affectionately
Ernest Jones.

1. Hermann Rorschach (1884–1922), Swiss psychiatrist who devised the famous inkblot test for detecting personality traits and disorders. Mira Gincburg (1887–1949), medically trained psychoanalyst in Zurich; married to Emil Oberholzer (1883–1958) of Schaffhausen, a Rorschach specialist, who, along with his wife and Pfister, had founded the Swiss Society the previous evening.
2. "Head office of the Association."
3. Martin Freud was still being detained in Italy, and Jones was likely arranging assistance through Dr. William Mackenzie, who is listed as a member of the British Psycho-Analytical Society (Piazza Meridiana, Genoa) in *Journal*, 1 (1920): 118.

236

2 April 1919
69 Portland Court, London

Dear Professor,

I return to London full of inspiration for the great work in front of us, and on which I think we may build high hopes. Hiller, my faithful assistant,[1] is very enthusiastic, and we trust the congress will empower us to act independently of any intermediary publisher, and we can also start a central *Vertriebsstelle* [distribution outlet], there being no good place here to buy $\psi\alpha$ books without previous ordering. I am confident we shall need no financial assistance from B'pest for our *Journal* or Bibliothek, for we can manage either by endowments here or by forming a guarantee fund by subscription. I am told that the greater part of my second edition (Papers) has been sold already, within four months. That gives an idea! So you can concentrate Freund's power on the German and French movements.

Now I have what I think is an important idea, born of my five years' isolation. The Committee exists not only to direct the external side of the ψα movement, but also to coordinate the internal, scientific side, and so I hold it highly desirable that a couple of weeks before the Congress we have a private congress of our own for about a week, to discuss (1) plans and programmes ready to be submitted to the congress, etc., and (2) purely scientific problems of a more difficult and technical nature than those usually discussed in public. Remember that e.g. Abraham and I have not been in close touch with you, and how important it is to be quite clear amongst ourselves and so present a united front. (Unity of command; the great cry of the Entente for the last two years!).

I pray that things will soon be going better with you.

Yours affectionately
Ernest Jones.

P.S. Did you get my two letters from Switzerland?

1. Eric Hiller would assist Jones with various publishing schemes over the next several years; although he became a member of the British Psycho-Analytical Society, his name disappears from the pages of the *Journal* after 1929.

237

18 April 1919
Vienna, IX. Berggasse 19

Dear Jones,

The first window opening in our cage. I can write you directly and a closed letter! I was extremely glad to hear, that five years of war and separation did not succeed in deteriorating your kind feelings for our crew and very sorry that your health is not the same as your friendship. But I hope the latter will recover as the former will remain.[1]

I am extraordinarily obliged to you for bringing with you so much of my daughters things, she wanted them badly. We have grown hungry beggars all of us here.

But you shall hear no complaints. I am still upright and hold myself not responsible for any part of the worlds nonsense. Psychoanalysis is flourishing I am glad to learn from everywhere, I trust science will prove a consolation for you too.

I agree completely with all your plans and stipulations as far as known to me by Rank. The affairs of ΨA are so well provided by the comité, I may well feel a superfluity, ending to-morrow the 33d year of my medical career.

Sorry to say, Freund, the latest member not the slightest, is ill again and I am not yet sure if I can help him. It is very bad that Hungary is nearly cut off now; there is no assurance to get a letter to or from our friends there, our money is still laid up in a Hungarian Bank, nobody knows how long such a state of things may last and whether it will be relieved by a better one.

Kongress in autumn may well prove impossible under these circumstances, if Ferenczi and Freund cannot leave their country, even a meeting of the comité will be futile. As regards my person I am anxious to meet you, let us say in Holland, but at this moment travelling for one of us is nearly out of question. All our plans depend upon what improvements the next months will bring, if there be improvements.

I thank you very much for having restored to my handwriting its former character. My last two productions "Ein Kind wird geschlagen" and *"Jenseits des Lustprinzips"*,[2] which you will have to criticise one day, were written under bodily pain caused by a bad pen.

Now write me soon and take my best love meanwhile.

Yours truly
Freud

1. Freud's use of "latter" and "former" here should be interchanged.
2. Freud (1919e, 1920g).

238

23 April 1919
69 Portland Court, London

Dear Professor Freud,

I fear you must have been going through a bad time this spring; it will surely be the worst, so that soon times must mend. I want to know your plans as soon as you are able to make them. Shall you go to Switzerland or where, and when? I did not want to break practice again in June—you know how serious that is—then back in July and off again in August, but of course I want to see you as soon as it can be managed—July or August.

I have now got full material from America for Putnam's memoir,[1] which I will soon write and send you at the end of May, after Peace is signed. His daughter likes to think that he was drifting from ψα, but that was not true—only that in his last years his own thoughts on philosophy became more insistent.

In England we are now in the stage that America was in in 1913—everyone talks of ψα. In America it has become a little passé for the sensationalist! These are curious phases. The surprising and sad thing is the remarkably small number of *really* devoted analysts, who identify their [lifes]² lives with the science of ψα. Still I am glad to tell you that my friend and ex-pt Flügel has just finished an excellent book on Family Life,³ which will I think prove a textbook for some time (incest complexes and their various effect[s] on later life).

May I ask you the following questions on War Shock, which I hope will be intelligible even though briefly put. (1) How do you picture the relation of this narc. neurosis (a term which hitherto has been with us synonymous with psychosis) to Dem. pr..? (2) In the peace Tr. Neur. what is the relation to Libido of the Angst produced after the shock as compared with that *normally* produced before a shock? I suppose both are derived from narc. lib., with the same function of deadening stimuli (by the way, how do they do this?). (3) In the War Neurosis do you conceive the conflict to be between the New Ego, non libidinous, and the Old Ego with its self love lib. (as I conceive it) or [between] in what other relation [does] could the lib. stand [in]⁴ to the two ego ideals?

I am glad to say I have new life since seeing my dear friends in Switzerland, and am full of plans.

Yours affectionately always
Ernest Jones.

P.S. I just get [got] a letter from Brill, promising active and cordial support of the plans I sketched to him (and which he had already spontaneously suggested). In N. Y. the society has fallen to 8 members. I gather the movement in America is more widespread and popular, but has few good leaders. How we miss good old Putnam already. Brill makes the strange suggestion that we found an Anglo-American ψα Association, with local branches. I shall not agree to this, not even as regards the *Journal*, for though this will be for Anglo American countries it should belong to the Internat. ψα Assoc.. I have told him he must come to Holland in September. He will write to you soon.

E. J.

1. Jones (1919).
2. Crossed out in the original.
3. J. C. Flügel (1884–1955), British psychologist and active participant in the psychoanalytic movement; wrote *The Psychoanalytic Study of the Family* (London: Hogarth Press, 1921), which remained in print and sold well for many decades; see Woolf (1980, pp. 309–310).
4. The three bracketed words are crossed out in the original.

239

28 April 1919
[Vienna]

Dear Dr. Jones,

I hope to hear soon of your news, intercourse being open. Rank fell ill some days after his return and is recovering slowly. We had a very bad time by the Hungarian troubles, now we are glad our friends and our money [is]¹ are sure. Even spring behaves as if regulated by an international commission.

I wish you good health

yours truly
Freud

1. Crossed out in the original.

240

2 May 1919
69 Portland Court, London

Dear Professor,

It was a pleasure to get a letter from you direct, a sign of the moving times. I shall be very glad to know what your personal plans are likely to be for the summer, whether you stop work as usual in July, if you go to Switzerland, etc.. As to the Congress, it is highly important that it should take place, even if small, and say at Interlaken if Holland is impossible for the Viennese. Otherwise we shall not have the much-needed and essential authority to start the English journal and series; for I rely on the prestige of the Congress in dealing with any difficult Americans. And it is about that that I am now chiefly writing, to ask your advice and decision on the following matter.

Last year Tannenbaum, who is a practitioner of no good standing in N. Y., asked my support for a journal of ps-a which he was quite ready to bring out, saying he even had all the necessary subscribers etc.. My first question was whether it was to be strictly Viennese, to which he answered satisfactorily and sent me articles he had written against Jung. I then begged him to postpone his plans till after the war, saying that there was already Jelliffe's *Ps-A Review*, that there was no more room for a private one, that in any case I hoped as soon as possible to start an official organ, for which we should unite all our forces, and promised him (perhaps rather rashly) that if he joined us his sacrifice would be taken into account; he now claims the fulfilment of this promise.

As I think I told you already, my idea was that I should be assisted by an editorial board consisting of two English and three Americans, the latter being Brill, MacCurdy, and Tannenbaum.[1] On sending this suggestion to Brill he wrote as follows (March 7th): "I am extremely pleased with what you tell me about the journal and I assure you that I'll assist you in everything possible. I spoke to Frink and others who are quite pleased with the idea . . . . As to Tannenbaum I would advise you to leave him out. I am sure the Journal will be harmed through his collaboration. It will certainly keep others away. Tannenbaum is not affiliated with any neurological or psychiatric society. He is associating with a rather questionable crowd, as W. J. Robinson,[2] a Russian Jew of the Bolshevik type who is editing the "Critic and Guide" and similar stuff, a most unscrupulous person, and G. S. Viereck,[3] the German-American writer who has been very notorious during the war. He is undoubtedly a bright fellow and a good writer, but no one has any confidence in him here, and he has hardly—if any—recognition among the better class of physician . . . . I would suggest that there should be a sort of reorganisation of the International V., with an English-American branch located in London and subbranches in all English-speaking countries. It would be very good to keep the Headquarters at Vienna".

(There is of course no need for a London depot of this kind, and my own opinion is that the headquarters should be in Geneva). I then asked him if he thought we could drown Tannenbaum's bad name by having a large list of about twenty. Naturally Brill's opinion on this matter is *massgebend* [authoritative], as he knows the American feeling so well. He replies (April 16th): "I have no doubt at all that we can make the journal a success. I would prefer to have no committee at all, only "Edited for the International Psychoanalytical Association by Ernest Jones". I have no doubt at all that if you should put Tannenbaum's name in it at all it would do harm. Since I wrote to you last I have sounded a number of the men about him by making some remarks as "Well, he understands his work", etc., and they all jumped on me (slang for strong criticism). So I feel that the best solution would be, as long as you have to put him in, to mention no names at all."

Now what do you think should be done. I do not want if possible to make an enemy of Tannenbaum as regards the *Journal*, but I think that Brill's solution (of which I had thought myself) is the only feasible one.

Next week I am lecturing at the University of London on *Alltagsleben* and before a society of shell-shock doctors on how to use dreams in the analysis. Things are very alive here in psychopathology. At present I am acting as chairman, and Flügel as secretary, of the committee of the British Psychological Society, which is being re-organised. A group has been formed for medical psychology, with over a hundred members, who are shewing great interest. Naturally psycho-analysis is well represented in the discussions, as you may imagine, and it is taking good root.

Yours always affectionately
Ernest Jones.

1. Samuel Tannenbaum (b. 1874), M.D. 1898 Columbia; charter member of the New York Psychoanalytic Society (12 February 1911).
2. William J. Robinson (1867–1936), born in Russia, M.D. 1893 New York University; founder and editor of *Medical Critic and Guide*.
3. George Sylvester Viereck (b. 1884 Munich), American editor and writer.

241

28 May 1919
Vienna, IX. Berggasse 19

Dear Jones,

If you press me to inform you, where and when we shall meet this summer or autumn, whether an ordinary congress should be held or a meeting of the comité instead, I cannot but infer that you know nothing of the conditions we live in and get no light on Austria by your papers. Now believe me I have no idea [where and][1] when travelling will become possible for me and no choice where to go for a summer recreation. It may even be I will be glad to stay at home. It all depends on the state of Europe in general and of this neglected unhappy corner in particular, on the signing of peace, on the improvement of our money, the opening of the borders etc. and there is a great probability things will not be better two months hence than they are now. Add to this that my wife is abed with a strong grippe, overcame a pneumonia but shows no good tendency to recover strength and has this very day begun to fever afresh, it is not yet known why, but I hope it may not turn out very serious. As for the other town, Bp, Ferenczi and Freund, indispensable to our meeting, are absolutely cut off for the moment; no prophesy can reveal, what may be their destiny and degree of freedom in the next weeks. As regards the latter, unknown to you, I have reason to fear that you will never be able to make his acquaintance. His life is endangered by a bad recurring growth (he is 40 years old!), and it will be a hard blow to all of us, to the movement and to me personally, if we lose him. Rank is fighting like a lion for the fonds [Fond], Freund created for ΨA, it is still in the grips of the Hung. Government and we could not get it out till now.

I cant remember a time of my life when my horizon was so thickly veiled by dark clouds or if so I was younger then and not [infested][2] vexed by the ailments of beginning old age. I know you had a bad time and bitter experiences yourself and feel extremely sorry, I have nothing better to report and no consolation to offer. When we meet, as I trust we shall this year, you will find I am still unshaken and up to every emergency, but it is so only in sentiment, my judgment is on the side of pessimism.

As regards your plans on the English-American *Journal* you are free to act as you think it best and sure to get all possible support to your authority the chairmen of the societies can give you. By writing, if a meeting proves impossible.

I have not stopped production, or at the worst for some weeks only. I hope these inquiries will interest you greatly. Nr. 1 and 2 of the new "Int. ψα Bibliothek" (*Kriegsneurosen* and Ferenczi's book on *Hy.*)[3] have come out at last. We are living through a bad time, but science is a mighty power to stiffen one's neck.

Take my best love and send your better news to your old friend

Freud

1. Crossed out in the original.
2. Crossed out in the original.
3. See *Zur Psychoanalyse der Kriegsneurosen* (Leipzig: Internationaler Psychoana-lytischer Verlag, 1919), as well as Ferenczi (1919).

242

3 June 1919
69 Portland Court, London

Dear Professor,

I have not had an answer to a letter containing some technical questions which I sent about six weeks ago, and I hope it has arrived safely. I think that in it I acknowledged the very kind letter which your wife was so good as to send me, and expressed my thanks.[1] I hope I may have the pleasure of seeing her and Anna this summer. Is it possible that you may stay in Vienna through the usual holiday time, or do you think it is more likely that you may go to the country or to Switzerland? I know it is impossible to answer such questions definitely in these times, but I should be very grateful to know even only probabilities, for many things hang together with holiday plans.

I have urged Sachs that it is high time we issued notices, especially to America, concerning the Congress. It seems to me better to settle a date and place, and thus give ample notice, even if it may be necessary to counteract it later; the notice would in any case be D. V.![2] Americans have to book their passages long beforehand, and I am anxious that we have a contingent of them over, for it is so important to get unity and support for our publishing plans at the Congress, while the starting of our *Journal* would hardly wait for another year. In other words I think it very important that we make every effort to organise a meeting for the middle of September this year. It is plain that public affairs are not going to be settled for a very long while, so that we cannot wait for that. If peace is signed by then, which I presume will surely be the case, I want very much, with your kind permission, to visit you in August wherever you may then be.

Our society is strong, stable, and fresh, full of hard and genuine workers. I should be proud to shew it to you. Things are in every way very active here, lectures, courses, practice, debates, etc..

Jung is taking part in a symposium here next month,[3] and I fear he will be well received, for he also has his supporters here. It seems impossible to grow flowers without weeds also springing up; the phenomena are interrelated!

My Father is distressingly ill, with a doubtful issue. One has grief enough in life. I am glad to say that my own health is much better and I am very active. Loe is well. I think of you daily and trust that what you have to suffer is already diminishing.

With my very kind regards

yours affectionately
Ernest Jones.

P.S. Please excuse my typing on account of a rheumatic hand.

1. See letter 238; at that time Jones had not yet received the letter from Martha Freud of 26 April 1919 (Archives of the British Psycho-Analytical Society).
2. Possibly *Datum vorbehalten* (date to be announced).
3. Jung (1919).

243

10 June 1919
69 Portland Court, London

Dear Professor,

Your kind but sad letter [28/5][1] came this morning. I am concerned first of all at the news of poor von Freund, of whom I heard such good things when in Switzerland, and whom I greatly want to meet. You do not say that the tumour is malignant, so I trust there is still hope.

You are right, no doubt, in saying that in spite of my efforts to inform myself I am still out of contact with the conditions in Austria, and am extremely sad to think of dear Vienna suffering so. I know that travelling is impossible in Germany, but hoped that your route to Switzerland was still open. Things are not likely to be much better for a while. I therefore suggest that we abandon the idea of a congress this year, and concentrate our efforts on getting together a committee meeting late in August or early in September at the point most accessible to you (? near Vienna or possibly in Switzerland). I will surely visit you at all costs if it is at all possible, and we will see by then who else can come. I will write to Brill to that effect, as I should like him to come if possible.

I trust that your wife has by now recovered her strength. I can imagine how frightfully painful it must be to be unable to give a sick loved one the best conditions possible. Please give her my kindest regards and best wishes.

For the future: having been well loved by mother and wife my confidence is hard to shake, in spite of any judgement, and I also know that you will retain your faith till your last breath. The world is going through a period of bad regression, but our work will last, and will be ready for the world whenever it is ready for it. In the meantime it interests us, and what more can one ask? Science is the only rock that will withstand all these storms. Russia is lost to ψα for some years, but in England things go well for it. As our poet Clough says:

> And not by eastern windows only,
> When daylight comes, comes in the light;
> In front the sun climbs slow, how slowly!
> But westward, look, the land is bright![2]

I hope next time, before long, to hear better news.
With all my devotion

Yours affectionately
Ernest Jones.

1. Appears to have been inserted at a later rereading.
2. See *The Poems of Arthur Hugh Clough*, ed. F. L. Mulhauser (Oxford: Clarendon Press, 1974), p. 206. The passage is also quoted in Jones (1957a, p. 11; 1957b, p. 11). Clough (1819–1861) was a British poet whose work expressed the religious doubt of nineteenth-century England.

244

19 June 1919
Vienna, IX. Berggasse 19

Dear Jones,

I got both your letters of the 3d and 10th June today and hasten to reply. Glad to hear your health has improved and your mind is full of confidence. But let me say, if we try to free judgment from the influence of personal infantile disposition, we must agree that our case here is a very bad one. Mark I never doubted the ultimate chances of our science, although even this may be further off from triumph than my younger friends seem to expect.

As regards our meeting in summertime I made you know by Dr. Forsyth that I *intend* going to Gastein (near Salzburg) alone about the 20th of July and will be glad to see you there in one of the most glorious of alpine surroundings. A meeting of the comité depends on the possibility of throwing open the prison of Ferenczi (and perhaps Freund) by an appeal to the Bpest masters on behalf of Psychoanalysis. The *"Räteregierung"* [communist government] behaved rather kindly against our science so far. Ferenczi has become the first official university teacher on ΨA, (oö. Professor),[1] a success not dreamt before![2] Be assured we will do everything in our power to strengthen your hand in the anglo-american paper business, but at the moment we can neither get nor send a communication to Bpest. A meeting in a neutral country seems excluded, travelling is too hard for most of the concerned and we can get no foreign money in Austria. My wife,—thanks to your inquiry,—is recovering. She means to go to a sanatorium near Salzburg. My son is not yet at home. We are losing much of our spare life-time in waiting. Now it seems the very next weeks ought to bring us the decision for bad or for worse, but we [are][3] were saying so for many months past and are still kept waiting. So wait we must.

Rank is of great help to me in these times. I am afraid we can do nothing for Sachs who clings to Switzerland and evades coming home.

Nr. 1 and 2 of the Int. ψα Bibliothek have appeared. Did you get them?

I wrote a letter to Loe, got no answer, am glad to hear the fault is not with her health.

Take my best love.

Yours as ever
Freud

1. *Ordentlicher öffentlicher Professor* (equivalent to full professor). For a synopsis of events related to psychoanalysis during the brief reign of the *Räteregierung*, see Paul Harmat, *Freud, Ferenczi und die ungarische Psychoanalyse* (Tübingen: Edition Diskord, 1988), pp. 72–76.
2. See note 1 to letter 273.
3. Crossed out in the original.

245

1 July 1919
69 Portland Court, London

Dear Professor,

It is a great joy to get a letter from you within a week, and probably even this time will soon be reduced. We shall not be allowed to go to Austria until peace with her is signed and ratified, and other formalities attended to, and I am beginning to doubt whether that will be in time to enable me to visit you at Gastein, for I understand that you will only be there for four weeks. In any case I will come as soon as travelling is allowed, and if necessary come to Vienna. But Gastein sounds specially attractive.

Dr. F[orsyth] will also come as soon as he can. He told me that you were going to analyse him, which naturally aroused my jealousy, though do not fear that I shall not be able to control this. It may interest you to hear a little about him. He is about 42, very gentlemanly, with a fine and well-balanced mind; not brilliant, but with some originality. He has worked at Ps-A for some five years or so, has not read much of it, but has had a considerable personal experience. He would, I think, count next to me as leader in England, chiefly because of his good personality and the prestige of his position (he is physician to a medical school, equivalent to Professor in Germany and is a children's specialist; he is no neurologist or psychiatrist, but has had great experience of children and has made excellent observations on them from the psychological point of view).

Please congratulate [Prof.]¹ Ferenczi from me if you can write to him; it was splendid news. And tell him that his book (which had some sale in Japan!) is calling for a second edition.² I am thinking of translating his articles of the past five years and taking over the enlarged edition as a member of our monograph series.³ We are hard at work on plans for this series and the *Journal*, of which you will hear more presently, for the scheme to be adopted depends on the success of an appeal for funds now being made.

Do you think Sachs ought to return to Austria? What would he do there? I had been strengthening his resolve to stay if possible in Switzerland if he can support himself there, for he will certainly be very useful there as a liason officer, especially when the international bonds get re-established. From Brill I have not heard for some time, though I am expecting a letter daily; America is now farther away than Austria in time. Is there no use in again asking if you can come to Switzerland? But of course you know the conditions of travelling much better than I can.

yours always affectionately
Ernest Jones.

1. Handwritten above Ferenczi's name in an otherwise typewritten letter.
2. Jones (1916b).
3. The next major series of papers in English appeared much later; see Ferenczi (1926b).

246

8 July 1919
Vienna, IX. Berggasse 19

Dear Jones,

I reckon to be at Bad Gastein, Villa Wassing, on the 15th of this month for a stay of 3 or 4 weeks. We are taking pains to get the permission to pass over the austrian frontier for Ferenczi, his wife and perhaps Dr. Freund too, [for Gastein too][1] if his condition of health agrees with the trip. Ferenczi is engaged by his university lecturing (he is the first *o.ö.* Prof. for ΨA) until August first. Now choose your time. I will be extremely glad to see you. My sister-in-law is with me, going there for her own sake on her physician's command. Suffering as she is she will lead a sedentary life there and we will be free to talk and walk.

Times have not improved since I wrote you last, it may be our last summer as far as I can see. My wife will spend her time at the Sanator. Parsch near Salzburg, my daughter goes to a place not far from Reichenhall (Bavaria), in company of a lady-friend. Afterwards we intend to meet all of us on a small lake between Munich and Garmisch. Parsimony is no[t][2] part of our programm this year, it would not help us.

With kindest regards

yours truly
Freud

1. Written in the margin.
2. Crossed out in the original.

247

20 July 1919
111 Harley Street, London

Dear Professor,

I hope you are enjoying your stay in attractive Gastein and that the change will do you good. I would give a very great deal to be there with you, especially as you have time on your hands, but I am sorry to say it is quite impossible. As you know, the peace treaty has not even yet been handed in full to the Austrian delegates, and it is impossible to get a

passport or permission to enter Germany or Austria until a state of peace
has been declared. An Order in Council will be issued to pass from war to
peace, but I have no idea when, for some people say it will happen as soon
as three Allies ratify the peace with Germany (England will do so [next][1]
this week, but it may be several weeks before other countries do), while
others even say it will only happen when peace has been concluded with
Bulgaria, Turkey, etc.. I imagine the former is the more probable, but there
seems to be an acute phobia lest any one's travelling should precipitate a
new war or something. Nor do the other countries, particularly Switzerland, welcome the idea of a foreigner coming to eat their food, though the
restrictions they interpose can be overcome with patience and tact. I fear
that the Swiss authorities would not allow an Englishman to enter Austria
or Germany without a permit from the British counsul in Bern, even if
one took the risk of breaking our own law. It is heartbreaking nonsense,
the whole business, and I shall not relax any efforts to get information and
try to overcome the official resistances, but I am not too hopeful at present.
Will you please send me your address in Bavaria, and the dates there when
you know them. If I cannot get there I will try to come to Vienna in
September, but I am no longer so sure even of this as I was a little time
ago. Much patience is needed these days with the stupidity of the world,
which is no greater than before perhaps, but which certainly interferes
more with one than it used to.

I am, as you may be sure, very sad to hear of your despondent news and
can only hope that there will be some bright rays somewhere, for at least
it couldn't well get worse. We are having financial difficulties here over
our *Journal* plan and may have to fall back on the help of a regular publisher, as I gather Rank is doing with Birchner [Bircher], but I can tell you
more of this in another couple of weeks. I hope you will be good enough
to write and keep me in touch with your movements, etc., for all possible
contact is needed these times.

With kindest regards

yours affectionately
Ernest Jones.

1. Crossed out in the original.

248

28 July 1919
Badgastein, Villa Wassing

Dear Jones,

I am here since the 15th and I have nearly completely recovered from
the scratches and bruises of this year's life. I intend to stay here until the

12th of Aug. and will give you notice of every change or turn of my plans. The Hollandese invited me for lectures at Leiden, Utrecht and Amsterdam, but as their time is the second week of Oktober, when I will be due at home, it is likely to come to nothing.

I will be very glad to hear of you and extremely disappointed if you cannot make your appearance in Vienna in the course of this autumn. As for business apply to Rank, who is bound to wait for his babe there. He is doing all the work, performing the possible and the impossible alike, I dare say, you know him for what he is, the truest, most reliable, most charming of helpers, the column, which is bearing the edifice. I have given him full power to decide as I recognise his superiority in managing these intricate practical matters.

I read no papers and am forgetting our miseries in a rapid way. The third volume of our "Bibliothek" has just reached me, the *Alltagsleben* in sixth edition.[1] I wrote Rank to send you a sample of it. I am busy on a paper *"Jenseits des Lustprinzips"*[2] but not too busy, as I cannot work, when I am bodily all right, I am ashamed to confess.

Sachs is bent upon staying in Switzerland and I am sure he is right as his health would not hold against a winter [sta][3] at Vienna. I take care however not to influence him, because just now I am unable to help him, sending away all I can spare to my children at Hamburg, bereft of their subsistence by the war. Of my boys only Oli, the engineer, has found some work for a time, Ernest is working at Munich for no salary and Martin whom we expect back in a few weeks, would find himself on the street despite his many medals and decorations, if he had not an old father still at work.

Answer me soon, I am so glad, war did change nothing between us.

Yours with best love.
Freud

1. Freud (1901b), 6th ed. 1919.
2. Freud (1920g).
3. Crossed out in the original.

249

7 August 1919
69 Portland Court, London

Dear Professor,

I was very happy to hear how much the holiday had improved your general state, and I expect that this has also benefitted from the Hungarian news.[1]

I am fully in accord with your opinion of Rank, and have boundless admiration both for his capacity and his character. We are in regular communication over our mutual affairs, and are both confident about them in spite of the difficulties.

It has not seemed advisable to take definite steps in establishing the English Press until I have been abroad again, but I think the delay will be to our advantage. Caution would recommend us to contract with a publishing firm in London, but I am so anxious to have a Verlag here as a filial of the International that I am fighting hard for the possibility; hence the delay.

This is my third letter to Gastein.[2] You should have got the other two, and I trust this will be forwarded.

I am trying to get from our Government a trade permit to visit Germany and Austria as a publisher, and shall know next week if I am successful. I propose to leave here on the 24th for Basel (D. V.!),[3] where I will meet Sachs. Then a week or [so][4] more with him, and a try for Garmisch, accompanying you to Vienna to spend a week there with Rank. That is the ideal! How far it will succeed is not altogether in my hands. In any case I will go to Switzerland, and in the worst event perhaps you could come to Constanz for a couple of days in the middle of September,—it is not far from Munich.

I am re-writing an old book on *Treatment of the Neuroses*,[5] which will be finished tomorrow; it should come in very appropriately just now for the medical profession here, which is shewing great eagerness for our work. There is a great demand for your books in German.

I hope that your wife also has recovered from her unpleasant experiences.

Yours always affectionately
Ernest Jones.

1. A reference to the fall of the short-lived Bolshevik regime of Béla Kun.
2. A letter is missing here.
3. Possibly *Datum vorbehalten* (date to be announced). Jones was likely still unsure of the exact date of his departure.
4. Crossed out in the original.
5. Jones (1920b).

250

1 September 1919
Badersee

Dear Jones,

Gladly taking up your hint[1]—I hasten to write to you from Oberholzer's address, as I do not know whether my last letter, sent to Wengen, reached you there.[2] At the same time, I received news that I can get Marks for my trip to Hamburg and am therefore only now in a position to give firm details about my plans. I also ask you to send word to Forsyth, who telegraphed me twice without my being able to reply (because I had not taken his address with me on the trip).

We are leaving here on 9/September, and I go to Hamburg via Munich, from where I travel back, so that I will cross the German border on 24/9 at the latest. I shall then be in Vienna on the 26th, as there are no express trains in Austria any more. I am sorry to detain you so long, but if I do not get to my children now, I do not know when I will. One should not postpone anything! And if this should result in a longer holiday for you, I can easily take the blame.

I am very glad to see you again. Five years is a terribly long time. Our poverty and inability to receive you and your companions honorably will not make us feel ashamed; we are not to blame for our condition and our cordiality remains unchanged. Give my regards also to Sachs, van Emden, and any of our friends that you meet.

To an early reunion

Yours
Freud

1. First line is in English; letter continues in German.
2. Letter missing.

251

4 September 1919
Hotel du Parc, Locarno

Dear Professor Freud,

Here we are, three miles from the frontier of the forbidden land, but in a lovely country. Still, the more beautiful are the things I see the more desolate and mournful do I feel, especially this week—the anniversary of the fatal illness of my wife, with whom I had so often planned this journey on the way to Vienna.

Sachs is very well, and glad of our company. He must be very lonely. He has been at his best with his humour and wit. We spent two days or so with the Van Emdens in Luzern, and they accompanied us on the boat along the lake to Flüelen. We propose to stay here about a week and then go to Zurich. Before crossing the frontier I have to get my passport signed in Bern by the Austrian consul in the last 24 hours, also by the Swiss. In your telegram to me in London[1] and in your letter to Sachs you say that you expect to be in Vienna [abou][2] in the last week of September. As there are so many arrangements to make, it makes a considerable difference if you mean the beginning or the end of that week, and I beg you to let me know as soon as you can decide.

We heard today from Rank. His wife and daughter, called Helene, are doing well.

We rejoice to think that you are having a pleasant and health-restoring time in the midst of your family, and hope you will be able to get to Hamburg also. If you see Abraham, greet him warmly from me; I have written to him twice this year, but have had no answer yet.

Yours affectionately
Ernest Jones.

1. Telegram missing.
2. Crossed out in the original.

252

7 September 1919

Letter from Forsyth that he is on the way. He must have arrived in Zurich last evening.

Ferenczi and von Freund [wired]¹ telegraphed that they are coming tomorrow in any case, and we are doing everything to secure a *Bewilligung* [permission] and also rooms—till now without success. The wives are also coming.

Greetings
E. J.

1. Crossed out in the original.

253

12 October 1919
Lugano

Dear Professor,

We are here for a week, enjoying not merely a well-earned rest, but great and unexpected happiness. Everything augurs perfectly for a most successful married life,¹ which means for me a new life altogether in both happiness and inspiration to activity.

I need not say what a joy it was to me to see you again, and to find you dealing so nobly with your difficulties. My thoughts will be constantly with you this winter, you may be sure, and we shall both look forward to seeing it a past thing.

About business matters I have written to Rank, and he will doubtless inform you about them. Sachs points out, and I think quite rightly, that as regards the Vereinigung, Ferenczi has only the right to transfer the duties, not however the office—which he could only lay down to either the congress or to the Obmänner. In English this would be expressed by the words "*Acting* President", and perhaps you will be good enough to ask him to write to the Obmänner in this sense.

I want to thank you very deeply for all the trust you have shewn in me, which I appreciate more than anything. You know it will be not misplaced so far as my will goes, and as to capacity I can promise that I will give all my best—more no one can do. I look forward to my responsibilities very seriously, but without apprehension, being well-informed of the general situation and having the best friends around me.

Soon after reaching London I should have a great deal to report, but from Lugano-Paradiso you will not expect a long letter.

Please give my best thanks to your wife and Anna for their kind hospitality and friendliness

and to you I extend, as ever, my loyal greetings

Yours affectionately
Ernest Jones.

1. Jones married Katherine Jokl on 9 October 1919 in Zurich.

254

25 November 1919
111 Harley Street, London

Dear Professor,

I have not heard from you since leaving Vienna, but I suppose you rely on Rank and me to exchange the news; doubtless he shews you my letters.

Forsyth is back, deeply impressed with your technique and the excellence of your English. I am sure you found him a faithful analyst, and consolidated his devotion. He tells me that Rank should be in Holland, so I wired to him that though so far the government here has refused a permit we are still making efforts. I may go to Holland if he can't come here, though practice is a great tie just now. Loe is doing everything for him there, and would cross to meet him if Herbert were not ill (which may prevent their going to America). She has quite turned round, and is most *entgegenkommend* [accommodating] to Vienna, telephoning to me twice a week for news.

An American dentist, Dr. Bieber, came to me from N. Y., a case of obsessional jealousy, but as he had come so far I thought he could travel to Vienna—hence my telegram to you today.[1] He can pay five dollars a time, which is very moderate for American fees. I have had letters from Abraham and Eitingon, but no word from Brill in reply to my famous letter sent eight weeks ago, and no article. Have you heard from him?

Rank asks me to give you my views about Abraham's suggestion—which he only just mentions—of a congress in Berlin in the spring. I am quite opposed to the date, for no Americans at all could be present then (and few English)—which would greatly harm us after our recent autocratic action in their name. The tendency to dissociation there is so marked that it would be mad to offend them gratuitously. I am also doubtful about the place, as against a neutral country, and fear it is another instance of German lack of contact with outside opinion.

Practice here is extraordinary. I have 10 patients a day, and every week send several to other doctors (this week one who came specially from Palestine and one from Baluchistan). I hope the path to Vienna will soon open up now, but it is still difficult for Englishmen.

I dare not ask about the conditions in Vienna, and can only hope with all my heart for the best. I should be very very glad to hear from you.

Yours always affectionately
Ernest Jones.

P.S. The married life is a wonderful and complete success.

1. Telegram missing.

255

8 December 1919
69 Portland Court, London

Dear Professor,

Thank you for your telegram.[1] I hope that Dr. Bieber is now in Vienna. I had of course inquired about fees, but gathered that he could only pay $5 if the period was long.

I write just before the expected advent of Rank. His having to wait in Holland is largely his own fault, but one cannot wonder that so much contact with the political atmosphere of Vienna has impaired his contact with the outer world. We had the pleasure of seeing much of Van Emden and Van Ophuijsen last week here, and introduced them to the members of the committee of our society.

I was greatly distressed to hear the terrible news about poor Von Freund, and also for your sake, for I know something of what it means to you. About death I find there is nothing to say. Nature has omitted to provide us with any means of dealing with the idea. One's attitude is throughout negative.

Loe has been extraordinarily kind about Rank. She would even have gone to Holland to help him over the tedium of waiting, only that her husband is ill. They cannot go to America on account of this. Have you yet heard of her scheme for presenting you with a furnished house in the Hague (Kobus's, he having gone to live in Palestine), if you will consent to live there permanently?

I do not know what to do with the patients who come for treatment, having already filled up the [times][2] hours of all my colleagues. One today, a well-to-do Jew sent to me from Palestine by Eder, has [ma][3] cyclothymia, and I cannot trust any one here to treat such a case. He refused to go to Vienna, although he speaks German well, so I shall have to send him to Van Emden, as he is willing to go to the Hague. If you have any thought of moving to Holland I beg you to telegraph me, which will be in time to keep him for you.

With warmest greetings

Yours affectionately
Ernest Jones.

PS: On account of the Americans returning to work I think it important that the congress be held not later than the 6th of Sept., and it is high time that we notified them so that they can book berths. Will you please let me know if you agree to this? You have doubtless already got my letter about Abraham's Berlin suggestion.

1. Telegram missing.
2. Crossed out in the original.
3. Crossed out in the original. Jones may have started to write "manic depression," then changed his mind.

256

11 December 1919
Vienna, IX. Berggasse 19

Dear Jones,

I *hope*[1] you have seen Rank, so I can write a short letter feeling pretty tired.

Toni Freund is dying a slow and painful death in a sanatorium here. I go to have a look on him every day, but it is not merry.

Proceeding by word-association, the marriage of my son Martin took place Sunday 7th.[2] In the next days the two other boys left home, for Berlin and Hamburg respectively. We are alone and feel lonely.

Dr. Bieber has arrived. He is justified in paying half a price as he is only half of an American. The other half a Hungarian Jew. A case complete in all points, it may take long time to influence him. Not very clever rather a young ass. I preferred Forsyth. Yet 5 Doll. are 750 K!!

Contributions to our journals are flowing in from all sides. The map was never so full, we will have to increase the size of the *Zeitschrift*. I am eager to know how far you have mastered your difficulties. I am nearly helpless and maimed when Rank is away. From Brill I got the translations of Leonardo, Wit and Totem.[3] No letter. Excuse me saying that he is a crazy Jew *(meschugge!)*.[4] But did'nt you make us think that he *had* sent you the money collected?

Give my best thanks to your young wife for her charming letter of introduction. Tell her she is no looser by my not answering it directly in these weeks. The *"Tagebuch eines halbwüchsigen Mädchens"* just published by the Verlag might interest her too.[5] It is long I have heard about her sister.[6]

Hoping you will soon write me again yours

as ever
Freud

1. Doubly underlined in the original.
2. To Ernestine Drucker (b. 1896).
3. Brill (1916a, 1916c, 1918).
4. *Meshugge* is the Hebrew word for "crazy."
5. The diary appeared with a preface by Hermine von Hug-Hellmuth (1871–1924), pioneer in the field of child psychology and member of the Vienna Society. It also included extracts of a letter she received from Freud in 1915; see *S.E.*, 14:341. Two more editions came out in 1921 and 1922, but the book was withdrawn over fears that it may not have been authentic.
6. Freud may have had in mind Katherine's sister Gretel, who lived in Vienna; see note 2 to letter 265 and note 2 to letter 614.

257

23 December 1919
Vienna, IX. Berggasse 19

Dear Jones,

I will write you some lines only, I had postponed my answer until Rank's arrival, who was expected between the 20th and 22d. But he got into the period of suspended railway-*Verkehr*[1] and cannot be here before the 29th or later. So I have to give you the few answers you require.

1) I agree with the date and locality of the Congress as you propose it but I cannot give you the assurance that travelling to Holland will be possible for any one of us as a technical and a monetary problem.

2) I thank you sincerely for sending Dr. Bieber, who now is tormenting me for a second hour daily which he sha'nt get. Subsistance would be warranted, if I had 3 or 4 strangers regularly. But I would not [for sti]² stir for the Palestine cyclothymia however life is bad with us. It is very kind indeed of Loe to offer me her brother's house, yet I intend to stay on my post as long as I reasonably can.

3) Freund is slowly getting estranged to his former being and interests, the bodily dissolution is tardy, but not doubtful.

4) In your remarks on Rank I noticed a harshness which reminded me of a similar mood regarding Abraham. You used kinder language even during the war. I hope nothing is wrong between you and ours.

I am anxious to hear the news Rank will bring about the English *Journal*. No letter from Brill.

Take my best wishes for you and your young wife for 1920 and for ever.

Yours truly
Freud

1. "Railway service." The German word is written in Gothic script.
2. Crossed out in the original.

258

6 January 1920
Vienna, IX. Berggasse 19

Dear Jones,

I had the first conversation on business with Rank this day. I agree with him on all points especially as regards the Congress. It is most important that the Americans gather round the new *Journal*, we should try to conciliate them and render our plans palatable to their taste.

I will struggle with you against Abraham, who is denouncing a congress at the Hague as impracticable and claims it for Berlin, where as you say, English and Americans are sure not to appear. But let us try everything to insure our success with the Western people. I think you ought to treat Brill well, who behaved very nicely in the affair of the contributions, you should propitiate even Tannenbaum and I propose; you should put on the cover of the *Journal* the words

"edited provisionally" by E. J.

although it may mean a sacrifice to you, in order to show them, that no compulsion is intended and all is left to the decision of the Congress. I trust that you will be named sole or principal editor there. The Verlag is in a hard stress, all our force and complete concord is needed.

Affectionately yours
Freud

259

16 January 1920
111 Harley Street, London

Dear Professor,

I was very glad to get your letters dated Dec. 23 (which crossed one of mine)[1] and Jan. 6, which arrived yesterday.

You may rest quite assured, as you must be already from talking with Rank, that I have no trace of harsh feeling towards him or Abraham. Some momentary impatience on my part, of no importance, must have produced the impression on you. I am entirely devoted to every member of our committee (of Eitingon I cannot speak as yet, but I am greatly looking forward to knowing him).

I wonder how poor Von Freund is getting on. It has just been decided that my Father has a carcinoma in the sigmoid flexure (colotomy, and secondary growths), and probably has only a couple of months to live (which makes my visit to Vienna at Easter uncertain). I am very fond of him, so that it is extremely painful, and I am grateful that I have such a dear wife to help me bear it.

Two days ago I had a rather warm letter from Abraham, protesting against the Hague. I am writing to him on the following lines. One has to balance the necessity of enabling the committee members, and those near us, to attend with the great desirability of making it accessible (? passports) and attractive for the Westerners' (explaining the political and financial reasons). Of the two, the former is of course the more important, and would be a decisive reason against Holland if it made their coming impossible. But if it is *possible* for them, one can ask greater sacrifices from them deliberately than from the others, because of their greater good-will and devotion. I put the question to our society last night. They had no personal national feelings against Berlin, but pointed out (a matter that had escaped me) that it would harm the cause greatly in England by reinforcing the view of $\psi\alpha$ as a German decadent science, and not an International movement which we want it to be; they also pointed out many technical objections of an obvious nature. My own opinion is that Holland would be incomparably better for the weal of the Association provided only that it is possible for you and some others to make such a sacrifice.

Of that you must be the only judge, and I hope to hear further from you. In the meantime the Dutch are making their arrangements and I think are counting on the congress to help their local propaganda. I am sure I can put things objectively to Abraham in such a way as to appease him, for he is a very reasonable and clear man.

It lies very near my heart to bring about concord and united force, for that is absolutely vital. What you say about Brill exactly fits in with my inclinations. He may have his peculiarities, but one can never forget that he stands more loyally than any other American for the connection with Europe, and that is a great claim on our gratitude. I have not heard further from him. With Tannenbaum I shall also do my best, but am less hopeful there.

By all means tell Rank to put on the *Journal* "edited provisionally by E. J." I should have thought myself of that. At the same time, I hope the Congress will decide on a central editorship, for the technical difficulties otherwise would be very great.

About Verlag business I will write to Rank. It goes well.

Yours always affectionately
Ernest Jones.

1. Letter missing.

260

[postcard]

17 January 1920
Vienna

Dear Jones,

Dr. Levy Lájos Bpest whom you surely remember, wants to subscribe to the *Lancet* and the *British Medical Journal* from Jan. 1st this year. The numbers to be sent to his address Budapest V Szalay utcza 3, best *care* of British Mission Bpest. He will send the money as soon as transmitting it from Bp to London will be possible.

Ever yours
Freud

261
[postcard]

20 January 1920
Vienna

Dear Jones,

Freund died this evening, a heavy loss for all of us, no better man among us. But we must not pity him!

Is it true that you have got no photograph and desire to get one? Answer at once and you shall have it. I am no potentat and always felt a distinct resistance against giving it away as a present. I received some very nice letters from Brill another has been lost. He is all right. About B. another time, when I know more of his neurosis.

Affectionately yours
Freud

262

25 January 1920
The Plat, Elsted

Dear Professor,

I got your reply in 36 hours after sending off my telegram[1]—quite pre-war communication. The patient, Captain Daly,[2] ca. 30, in the regular Indian Army, is making all arrangements to go next week, provided he gets permission from the India office, and will write to you. I analysed him for a few months four years ago. It is chiefly a question of foolish character-traits, conceit and inferiority, slightly hysterical, rather an ass but easy to manage. I told him you would charge him two guineas. He has a year's leave from the Army, and will find it cheaper to live in Vienna than in London.

A clever man, a doctor, friend of Rivers of Cambridge,[3] has decided to give several years studying psychopathology in different countries,[4] is extremely interested in $\psi\alpha$ of which he already knows something, and begs me to ask you if you can take him for analysis in the first week of April. I think he would also pay two guineas. He seems a very solid, promising fellow, to judge from a single short interview.

Last week I read a long paper before the British Psychological Society on "Recent Advances in $\psi\alpha$"—a Referat, almost entirely of your works.[5] Can you think of your five essays on meta psychology being condensed to a dozen pages? It was, as you will imagine, an extraordinarily difficult task, but I am not ashamed of the way I accomplished it. The title was so attractive that it drew the most brilliant and representative audience I have ever seen in England, practically all the well-known psychologists and psychopathologists from all over the country, Oxford, Cambridge, even Scotland; ten professors. It proved to be very successful indeed, and I can say it produced exactly the effect I intended, namely of heightening their respect for the seriousness, solidity and complexity of our science. It was also for various reasons a specially great personal success, and made me think of your saying: a man is strong so long as he represents a strong idea.

About the Tannenbaum nonsense I have written my views to Rank, who will doubtless communicate them to you. From Brill not a word, and we are waiting anxiously for his article. Forsyth and Bryan have nearly finished theirs,[6] and I hope to forward them next week.

I should like to have some personal news of you, for I am very concerned [about] this weather. How much heating have you?

Yours always affectionately
Ernest Jones.

1. Both communications are missing.
2. C. D. Daly (1884–1950), Peshawar, India, in analysis with Freud for about a year beginning in February 1920. Transcripts of his dreams, which he painstakingly recorded, are contained in the Archives of the British Psycho-Analytical Society.
3. W. H. R. Rivers, St. John's College, Cambridge; associate member, British Psycho-Analytical Society.
4. John Rickman, whose name is noted in the margin, later became an important member of the British Psycho-Analytical Society.
5. Jones (1920a).
6. Only the latter's article appeared; see Douglas Bryan, "Freud's Psychology," *Journal*, 1 (1920): 56–67. Brill did not send one, and Forsyth withdrew his; see letters 271, 276.

263

26 January 1920
Vienna, IX. Berggasse 19

Dear Jones,

I thank you heartily for your kind and conciliatory letters. Now very much depends upon you in the present crisis of ΨA and I am glad to find it confirmed that we did put our trust in the right man.

Poor or happy Tony Freund was buried last Thirsday 22d this month. Sorry to hear your father is on the list now, but we all must and I wonder when my turn will come. Yesterday I lived through an experience which makes me wish, it should not last a long time. My daughter Sophie— perhaps you remember her, or am I wrong to recall that your young wife knew her in school days?—died in Hamburg of rapid *Grippe*-pneumonia, such as are now becoming frequent again in Middle Europe. She was not yet 27, leaves a despondent husband and two boys, the younger a babe of 13 months. My wife wanted to travel to Hambg at once but it proved impossible! If the conditions continue as they are, none of us may be able to attend the Congress. The irregular childrentrains are the only means of conveyance, suppose you can get into one of them.[1]

The decision about this question we may leave to your dealings with Abraham. Try to bring him over to your side, we are ready to undergo all sacrifices we can unless inhibited by sheer impossibility.

Brill is really all right but Tannenbaum is about to issue a $\psi\alpha$ journal of his own with Stekel and Silberer![2] The latter had the impudence to assure us of Stekels friendly intentions toward us in announcing the happy event to the society. He got a convenient answer.

I am deeply distressed and sure of the good feelings of my friends

yours affectionately
Freud

1. *Kinderzüge;* after the war, needy, undernourished children were sent in trains to the country or the North Sea, where they could recuperate.
2. The short-lived *Eros-Psyche;* see Jones (1957a, pp. 35–36; 1957b, p. 37).

264

27 January 1920
111 Harley Street, London

Dear Professor,

So Von Freund has gone, and is relieved of his sufferings. He now belongs to the past, like many noble and beautiful things.[1]

Yes, I should be very grateful of the photograph. Many thanks. What does Brill write to you? I wish I could have a word from him; I wait day by day for news of American affairs, for his article—the lack of which now holds up the *Journal*—and for the money,[1] which we urgently need to buy American books.

I am glad to hear from Daly that he leaves tomorrow for Vienna. You will have got my letter about him already.

I am anxious to publish your *Vorlesungen* (together with the *Fünf Vorlesungen*) as the first volume of our standard edition,[2] and can find reliable translators. Have I your permission to start on this? Brill seems definitely to agree.

Southard, Prof. of Psychiatry in Harvard, has written a long scurrilous article against you in the *Journal of Abnormal Psychology*,[3] which has enraged me. He attacks your *Krieg und Tod*[4] as a deliberate piece of pro-

German propaganda designed to excuse the German atrocities on the ground that all mankind is evil! The yapping cur!

Preger, the Dutch Jew, whose article for the *Journal* you have perhaps seen,[5] seems a very intelligent fellow, and has sent me some interesting material. He is unknown to the Dutch group!

Re your passage on S. 338, Vierte Folge der *Sammlung*, it has doubtlesss occurred to you what a pretty confirmation lies in our view that all *unconscious* symbolism is *concrete*,[6] which I emphasised in my essay on symbolism.[7] (By the way, I have never heard if you have read this, and if you agree with my criticism of Silberer therein). There are so many scientific problems I want to talk over with you.

Yours ever affectionately
Ernest Jones.

1. See note 2 to letter 290.
2. This is the first mention of a standard edition of Freud's writings.
3. Elmer E. Southard (1876–1920), M.D. 1901 Harvard, head of the Boston Psychopathic Hospital, emphasized brain pathology in the aetiology of mental illness; author of "Sigmund Freud, Pessimist," *Journal of Abnormal Psychology*, 14 (1919–20): 197–216.
4. Freud (1915b).
5. J. W. Preger, "A Note on William Blake's Lyrics," *Journal*, 1 (1920): 196–199.
6. Jones refers to Freud (1915e, p. 204), where Freud suggests that the schizophrenic "treats concrete things as though they were abstract."
7. Jones (1916a).

265

2 February 1920
111 Harley Street, London

Dear Professor,

Your news today was a great shock to us both. I have a vivid memory of Sophie, both from Holland and later on two or three occasions in Vienna, and last October I was very interested to see the photographs of her as a beautiful mother. She was just the same age as my first wife, who was as beautiful, and I can imagine the terrible feelings of her poor husband left with such helpless children calling for their mother. Kitty was also deeply moved. She was in the same school class as Sophie. It brought back the memory of [the similar][1] their mutual friend, Herzl's niece, who died of influenzal pneumonia, as did Kitty's favourite young brother, a prisoner in Siberia.[2] She had pneumonia herself last year, and is somewhat apprehensive of the influenza epidemic now beginning again; it was terrible here last year.

Apart from these extensive personal associations, however, all of which enable us to feel the significance of the tragedy, it is yourself and your wife that occupy our main thoughts. I know how exceptionally near to your heart all your children are, and it was a happy relief to me to hear that the war had left them all intact. In the present situation no one knows better than yourself that there is no consolation. It may, however, slightly relieve the desolation—as I know myself—to have the assurance that good friends are sharing your feelings in some degree, and are entering into them with the profoundest sympathy and respect. That conviction you can surely have.

With my warmest regards to yourself and your wife

Yours always affectionately
Ernest Jones.

1. Crossed out in the original.
2. Jones's wife, Katherine (née Jokl), was the youngest of eight children, five girls and three boys. Hans Jokl was the next youngest in the family.

266

8 February 1920
Vienna, IX. Berggasse 19

Dear Jones,

You know of the misfortune that has befallen me, it is depressing indeed, a loss not to be forgotten. But let us put it aside for the moment, life and work must go on, as long as we last.

I have to thank you for two letters, of the 25th and 27th last month. In the first I learned of your daring enterprise to bring metapsychological speculation before a non-analytical audience and I was glad you called it a complete success. It may not have been easily won. Now I may well be declining in power of thought and expression, why not? Every one is liable to decay in the course of time and I have had my full measure of effort perhaps even of success. But I rejoice in your and other friends' performances as if they were my own.

You are providing well for my medical income. Capt. Daly has not yet arrived, only a letter waiting for him. As you describe him I am ready to earn money by his treatment but I spare my interest for that other clever man, whom you announce coming first week of April.[1] Bieber is in a very good condition, not yet cured to be sure. He is a good-natured, illiterate, coarse boy with strong propensities which found no satisfaction in [a] his hard-worked childhood. The milieu is altogether Jewish. The clue of his case is, he did not marry his wife for love; now he strives to love her as a good jewish husband ought to do, but unfortunately his sexual ideal is derived from the mother-complex in the way I described in my "First contribution to Liebesleben".[2] So he wants her to be suspicious in love matters, as he cannot love a woman of another type, and he must be jealous, to find her so. I am anxious he will take to gambling after being cured of his jealousy.

As for Brill, his last letters, although undated were all right. The american post seems to be in a disordered state, I am waiting for other letters from America for some months and cannot get them. Just try to cable to him for his paper.

The photograph will be forwarded to you from my son-in-law in Hamburg.

You have not forgotten that my "Lectures for introduction into ΨA"[3] are being published by my nephew Edw. Bernays in America, prefaced by St. Hall? He assured me that our English rights were not touched by this act, but we ought to inquire the whereabouts and wait for this translation.

I have not seen a paper by Preger and never heard of him. My [essay] trial at impartiality in "War and Death" has brought me many attacks like that you mention. They cannot imagine a man who is neither Pro-German nor *Deutschenfresser*.[4] As regards Symbolism I find I have forgotten what I read in your paper and promise to return to it, as soon as the excitement of these weary days has settled. I have finished a paper on a case of feminine homosexuality[5] and am meditating on *Massenpsychologie* in a slow, hesitating [step][6] way.

Take my best love

yours
Freud

1. John Rickman.
2. Freud (1910h).
3. Freud (1916–17).
4. This may mean "fanatically anti-German," but the image evoked is that of annihilating by devouring.
5. Freud (1920a).
6. All bracketed words in this letter were crossed out in the original.

267

12 February 1920
Vienna, IX. Berggasse 19

Dear Jones,

So your father had not to hold out until he got devoured piecemeal by his cancer as poor Freund was.[1] What a happy chance! Yet you will soon

find out, what it means to you. I was about your age when my father died
(43)² and it revolutioned my soul.

Can you remember a time so full of death as this present one? Cpt. Daly
arrived here Monday, he corresponds very well to your descriptions. When
I handed him a wire waiting for him since the day before, he started and
put it back into my hands. It contained the news, that his mother and
grandmother had both died "yesterday" and urged him to return as soon
as possible. Yet he resolved to stay and begin analysis, ordering a sister-in
law (of the Darwin family) to see and help his sister as his substitute. He
seems somewhat "mixed up". If he succeeds in remaining here you will
hear more of him.

(I will telegraph to the other man that I am ready to take him 12th April,
the week after Easter)

Last week I took a good man of our own country a former Baron, who
had waited for a long time. He had absented himself for this day only, but
in the morning he telephoned to me he must miss some hours more as
his mother had suddenly died, a woman of under fifty. Perhaps it is only
a sample of the well known accumulation of similar facts, but *"Media
vita in morte sumus"*.³

Tell your dear wife, her condolence was one of the most sympathetic
among the many we got, and we thank her affectionately. She is right to
remember the case of poor Minna Herzl; there is even another coincidence
between the two, which I need not name.

Work is going on so very slowly with us, we are handicapped on all sides.
Paper is beginning to fail. The packets from Teschen (Prochaska)⁴ are going
three months, Rank seems to be ill just now (I hope nothing serious), and
so on.

Cpt. Daly brought me two books, one by Havelock Ellis, known to you
I am sure, *"The Philosophy of Conflict"*,⁵ second series, containing an
essay on ΨA or rather on my personality which is the most refined and
amiable form of resistance and repudiation calling me a great artist in order
to injure the validity of our scientific claims (which is all wrong; I am sure
in a few decades my name will be wiped away and our results will last),—
and a second, popular exposition of ΨA, *"Man's unconscious conflicts"* by
Wilfried Lay, 1918.⁶

Can you give me the address of H. Ellis? I will send him a book.

Yours truly in bad times as in good ones

Freud

1. There is likely a missing telegram announcing the death on 5 February 1920 of
Jones's father.

2. Freud's father died 23 October 1896, so Freud (b. 6 May 1856) was actually forty
years old at the time.

3. "In the midst of life we are in death."

4. Teschen, a small town in Czechoslovakia very near the border of Poland, was also not far from Freud's birthplace, Freiberg (Pribor). Prochaska, likely the sender, remains unidentified.

5. Havelock Ellis, *The Philosophy of Conflict, and Other Essays in War-Time*, 2nd ser. (London: Constable, 1919).

6. Wilfried Lay, *Man's Unconscious Conflict: A Popular Exposition of Psycho-analysis* (London: Kegan Paul, 1918).

268

29 February 1920
The Plat, Elsted

Dear Professor,

Thank you for your letters of Feb. 8th and 12th, which I was glad to have. You are right about my Father. It is a significant change for a man to make from a *Sohneinstellung* to a *Vatereinstellung*,[1] but it is being facilitated with me by the circumstance that my wife is now pregnant, at which we both rejoice.

I am familiar with H. Ellis' works and methods of repudiation; they are hard to deal with. His address is not with me here, but I will send it on returning to town. I enclose a review of *Totem und Tabu* by R. R. M., evidently Marett the Prof. of Anthropology at Oxford[2] and leader of the pre-animistic school of religious psychology. Retribution has swiftly overtaken the Harvard Professor, Southard, who dealt so unfairly with your War article, for he has just died of pneumonia, [at 44].[3] Yesterday our dog, a specially valuable creature and one to which we were extremely attached, was suddenly killed in the lift. And so the tale of death goes on.

Mrs. Putnam has given permission for the Press to make a book of her husband's $\psi\alpha$ papers,[4] and even offered to bear part of the cost (which I have gratefully accepted, suggesting a quarter, to be raised by her and his friends).

I have now cabled three times to Brill saying how urgently we need his article, for Rank cannot begin any printing till all the MS is collected. The journal is eagerly awaited and should have a good sale. I am only anxious lest Tannenbaum should steal our title, which would be hard to replace; he is sure to exploit the name $\psi\alpha$. As to Bernays: perhaps my memory has made a tendencious alteration, but it tells me that when I saw you in October you had received B's offer but thought you could alter it in favour of the Press. It is a great disappointment, for, having overcome the main difficulty, with Brill, I hoped we could begin on the projected Standard Edition of collected works, with just the *Vorlesungen* and *Fünf Vorlesungen* as the first volume. Now our scheme is again postponed. Could you at least ask Bernays that the Press receives the sole right to sell his translation in England: I have written to him offering him the American rights of the Press Library at 15%.

Daly's sister, whom I "treated" for two weeks, is one of the most disagreeable and objectionable women I have ever met, and I am not surprised at his wishing to break away from her. The family history is very interesting, as also his pathetic but hopeless attempts to be taken for a gentleman.

I was most interested in the names of the subjects now occupying you. In spite of its great frequency nothing much has been done on homosexuality in women. I feel sure it is not a simple fixation, but a complex product, probably relating to the castration idea. As to the mass psychology, I hope you will take serious account of Trotter's work,[5] which has a great vogue in England, for it is at least an attempt to deal with the nature of the *repressing force*,[6] which we have rather neglected. *If*[7] there is a herd instinct, however, how can one place it in our grouping, for it belongs neither to the ego nor the sex groups, yet has characters of both?

Yours always affectionately
Ernest Jones.

1. From a son's outlook to that of a father.
2. Robert R. Marett, reader in social anthropology, Oxford University; see his review of Freud (1912–13) in *Athenaeum*, 13 February 1920, pp. 205–206.
3. The word here is unclear, possibly "at"; it appears as if the second figure was initially "3" (43), then altered to "4" (44).
4. Putnam (1921).
5. Trotter (1916), 2nd ed. 1919.
6. "Force" is doubly underlined.
7. "If" is doubly underlined.

269

8 March 1920
Vienna, IX. Berggasse 19

Dear Jones,

Glad to hear of your family-news. The grandfather has to be reborn in the grandchild as you know. Wish your dear young wife will have an excellent time until the day of the happy event.

Your letter contains so much for answering. I was surprised to hear that Providence had taken my part against poor Southard so sharply, as I have not been accustomed to her favours. Marett the critic of "*T & T*" is well entitled to say, ΨA leaves anthropology with all her problems as it found it before, as long as he declines the solutions given by ΨA. Had he accepted them he might have found it otherwise. But the joke calling Atkinson's (and mine) hypothesis a just-so story, is really not bad.[1] The man is good, he is only deficient in phantasy.

Edward Bernays, my nephew, cabled me, after I had tried to revoke the permission that he could not stop having already invested $3000 in the matter. So I had to let him go on. But he added expressedly: (Dec. 18th) "Regarding the English rights to the books, I am to-day taking up this matter with your London friends—and we can surely make some arrangements, whereby your friends can bring out the English translations made here, in England."

Edw. was an honest boy when I knew him. I know not how far he has become americanized. So after all not much harm may have been done and you can keep up your intentions. Will you kindly [right][2] write to him? I have not yet got his translation.

The English *Journal* makes no progress I see and I am very sorry T[annenbaum] will beat us by some horses' length. Forsyth's paper was only a note.

Bieber is making a splendid analysis, I begin to like him. He is a child of nature, a gifted savage, the core of him is sound. The essence of his jealousy is indeed the myth of the virginal mother, a [sp][3] glorious dream brought it out just today. But there are complications and so on. I would foretell an excellent result, were it not for the homosexual component which is still behind the scene. I am not so far with the Cpt., who still regrets that I am not you, that I am not familiar with Indian names or English slang etc. and withholds from me the important parts of his life history. But it may be all right in a few weeks. I am anxious about my English, both of them talking an abominable idiom, and long for Forsyth's distinguished correctness.

In fact I could not make the two ends meet if you had not sent this [these] Entente people. Rickman is expected after Easter-time.

As for the herd-instinct I am glad I have devoted a thorough study to Trotters clever book and can see my way through the problems. The herd instinct is not present in the child; I think I can show you where and how it originates. The knowledge of the repressing forces, which we had a right to neglect as long as we could not (and cannot) dissect the Ego, is not greatly promoted by the introduction of the term herd-instinct, as far as I can see. The social instincts are indeed made up of both, libidinous and selfish, components, we always considered them as sublimations of the homosexual feelings. Yet I am sure more can be said on their regard. Palaeobiology may intervene even here.

Of my paper on feminine homosexuality,[4] only remarks attached to the relation of a mild case, I will send you the proofs as soon as I get them from the printer.

Our work is slow here owing to the accumulation of external inhibitions in unhappy Austria. I really doubt, whether it will be possible to keep up one's existence here, if no radical change for the better turns up, and I mean not only money or food.

With sincere love to you and your wife

I am yours truly
Freud

1. See note 3 to letter 517.
2. Crossed out in the original.
3. Crossed out in the original.
4. Freud (1920a).

270

[postcard]

19 March 1920
111 Harley Street, London

We hope to be in Vienna from March 30 to April 9, so I will not write a long letter now. But I want at once to thank you for having the photograph sent to me, of which I am very glad. It is a good one, though rather stern.

E. J.

271

24 April 1920
The Plat, Elsted

Dear Professor,

Please let me thank you again for all your kindness during our stay in Vienna, your hospitality, and the inspiration you gave me during our all-too-few talks. Nothing has taken me back to past days so much as that wonderful evening when you discoursed to me of your new ideas and plans; they will find a fruitful soil in me, you may be sure.

As there is an increased danger of American piracy (Tannenbaum and Jelliffe), will you give us permission to translate and issue your papers on $\psi\alpha$ technique from the Vierte Folge as a separate volume in the Press Library? After that I should like to do the same with the series on metapsychology.[1]

Forsyth's resistances seem to have even increased during the interval, I am sorry to say, and I have loss [lost] all hope of his remaining with us (unless he can continue his analysis). On my return the editor of the *British Journal of Psychology* telephoned to say F. had sent him his long essay on the new-born infant, and noticing it had been read before the ψα Society he wanted to know if he was right in accepting it, as he had thought that such articles belonged to our *Journal*.[2] I thanked him for his courtesy, and said I would sound F. and let him know. On my asking F. at the next society meeting whether this article was yet ready for press, he became very guilty and ashamed and lied by saying "I don't know; I haven't seen it for a long time". I said no more. My impression is that he is not open to any form of appeal, only to direct threats—and that only temporarily. After that came the following correspondence, which speaks for itself.[3] Whether you will write to him or wait for him to write to you, you will of course decide. With regard to his withdrawal of the article now printed for the first number I am strongly of [the] opinion that, having a moral and legal right to it, we should publish it in any case.[4] We have nothing further to hope for from him, and to yield to him would be disastrous as regards his next demands.

May I ask your help in the following difficulty? Rank's salary, which never was a big one, has so diminished in buying-value as to make his existence very precarious, and he has resigned from the Budapest paper so as to have more time for us. By all equity the English Press should pay him a special salary, but there is the obvious difficulty that it has no money for itself. I suggested therefore that he should take £50 a year from me as part of my donation to the Press. He absolutely refused, although I pointed out how much more satisfactory it is for money to come, when possible, from *within* the Committee, for an outside donor (a Mrs. MacCormick)[5] might want to influence our action. Now I think I see a way of forcing him, if you will support me. I want to give to the Press a proportion (about a quarter or fifth) of what my Father left me. I do not yet know the exact amount, but I think it should not be far short of £1000 (the donation, I mean). I told Rank of this, but he remained obdurate, so don't you think the gift could be made conditional on his behaving reasonably?

Loe had a dictatorial neurotic talk with me about your going to Holland. She always wants to arrange everything as she thinks it should be, or not at all. I hope that her visit to Holland to see you will not exclude the possibility of your coming to England for a week or two, which would give my wife and me the greatest possible pleasure.

Yours always affectionately
Ernest Jones.

1. *Sammlung*, vol. 4 1918, and the metapsychological papers were included in *Collected Papers*, 2, 4.

2. The article did not appear in the *British Journal of Psychology* or the *Journal*; see David Forsyth, "The Rudiments of Character: A Study of Infant Behaviour" (read before the British Psycho-Analytical Society, 15 May 1919), *Psychoanalytic Review*, 8 (1921): 117–143.

3. There are about fifteen letters between Jones and Forsyth of February, March, and April 1920 in the Archives of the British Psycho-Analytical Society, London. These indicate that Forsyth was also concerned about Jones's handling of the issue of donations for starting up the *Journal.*

4. This article was not published in the *Journal;* see David Forsyth, "Psycho-Analysis of a Case of Early Paranoid Dementia," *Proceedings of the Royal Society of Medicine,* Psychiatry Section, 13-3 (1920): 65–81.

5. See note 2 to letter 278.

272

2 May 1920
Vienna, IX. Berggasse 19

Dear Jones,

I really cant see what you are thanking [me] for. The fact is that I could do very little for you and your dear wife while here and that I am living to a great extent from such patients as you sent me. The balance is evidently in your favour.

As for Forsyth I regret his attitude sincerely but I have made up my mind not to address him any more unless he applies to me, which is not likely to happen. Leave him alone!

I have succeeded with Rank to make him accept your generous offer, at least provisionally and for this year 1920. Definite arrangements can be postponed until we may be able to judge the life chances of the Press and the *Journal.* You had only one father and [it] is not probable that you will get another inheritance of £1000 next year. I trust I would have been able to act the same way as you when I had grown wealthy but unfortunately fate has never put me to the trial.

I agree with your intention to bring out the papers on technique as a separate volume in English, but you ought to superintend the translation yourself. The metapsych. papers are too hard a reading for your public I should think.[1]

Rank and I had a discussion with one member of the late Hungarian government on the valours you remember. It is not yet decided, but I am pretty sure that we will get a good deal.[2]

With best love to your wife and yourself

Freud

1. Both series of papers came out; see Freud, *Collected Papers,* 2:285–402, and 4:13–170.

2. The problems associated with von Freund's donation to the Verlag and its subsequent devaluation are discussed in Jones (1957a, pp. 32–33; 1957b, pp. 34–35).

273

[postcard]

5 May 1920
Vienna, IX. Berggasse 19

Dear Jones,

You must not believe in the rumour about Ferenczi.[1] I got a letter from him dated April 27th and dont think, Dr. M.[2] could have later news in England. He does not seem to be very reliable. If something had happened I ought to know it here.[3]

—Surprised today by your sendings, you really must drop remembering this day (to-morrow) which is likely soon to recede before another more final date.[4]

Thanks and greetings to both of you.

Freud

1. The complicated issue of Ferenczi's expulsion from the Budapest Royal Medical Association is dealt with in Károly Kapronczay and György Kiss, "Adatok Ferenczi Sándor Egyetemi Tanári Működésével Kapcsolatban," *Magyar Pszichológiai Szemle*, 43 (1986): 111–118. This article is based on data contained in the Semmelweiss Medical Historical Museum and Special Archives, Budapest. After receiving his professorship in psychoanalysis on 12 May 1919, Ferenczi was asked by the dean of medicine to take over the Batizfalvy Sanatorium, which, like all similar institutions, had been confiscated by the Bolsheviks during their brief reign under Béla Kun from the end of March to the beginning of August 1919. In early 1920 Ferenczi was under investigation by the medical profession, the implication being that he had collaborated with the communists in accepting the professorship and taking over the sanatorium. Although Ferenczi denied the charges, the investigative committee in the end recommended his exclusion from the medical society. Moreover, between September 1919 and May 1920, the physicians deliberated on the expulsion of various members who were critical of the medical association. At a meeting of 24 April 1920, it was moved that 22 members be expelled. A final decision was postponed, but at a subsequent meeting of 28 May 1920 these members were indeed expelled. Ferenczi was treated as a special case, and a separate vote was taken: of the 330 members who were present, 266 voted for Ferenczi's expulsion and 54 were opposed, with 10 abstentions. Finally, 30 members felt Ferenczi's case should be investigated further.

2. Possibly Munro, mentioned in letter 275.

3. Ferenczi announced his expulsion from the medical society in a letter to Freud of 30 May 1920; see Jones (1957a, p. 13; 1957b, pp. 13–14).

4. Regarding Freud's sixty-fourth birthday on 6 May 1920. There is likely some missing piece of correspondence from Jones.

274

International Journal of Psycho-Analysis

7 May 1920
London

Dear Professor,

The circumstances that my secretarial wife is in bed after a nasal operation (progressing well) and my fingers are stiff with rheumatism account
for my using the typewriter. I write just today at the request of Mr. James
Strachey to ask if there is any hope of your taking him for analysis. He
would prefer to start now rather than October if you have a vacancy. He
is a man of 30, well educated and of a well-known literary family (I hope
he may assist with translation of your works), I think a good fellow but
weak and perhaps lacking in tenacity. He tells me he can spend £300 on
fees, so doubts if he ought to pay two guineas a treatment if it were possible
to pay less and go on for longer.

I am afraid I bore you with my affaire Forsyth. I will try to take your
advice and leave him alone, if only he will do the same. I am now feeling
distinctly hostile to him for his very scurvy behaviour.

Thank you for the permission to translate your technique papers. Of
course I will attend to them myself, you may be sure. The other ones can
come later; Flugel is at present reviewing them *seriatim* for our society.

I have entrusted some excellent Havanas to two separate messengers
going to Vienna, and hope they will get through safely.

As you mention the question of gratitude I may as well make my own
view of it clear also. To me it is clear that I owe my career, my livelihood,
my position, and my capacity of happiness in marriage—in short everything—to you and the work you have done. Besides those outstanding facts
all the small services I may be able to render must always weigh light in
the balance, and I cannot hope to redress it. But gratitude is an emotion I
can endure well, which as you know is not always the case.

I had a talk with Trotter last night. He was willing to accept the idea
of the primordial beginnings of the herd instinct being called sexual,
probably because they are so unlike such crude phenomena as erection
and emission!

Yours always affectionately
Ernest Jones.

275

13 May 1920
Vienna, IX. Berggasse 19

Dear Jones,

To begin with and to make your heart glad: on the 6th of May a member of the committee (Eitingon) presented me with a new ψα fund to the amount of one million of crowns ($5000) and so put an end to our most pungent fears. Although I proposed myself utmost restriction in spending money in order to secure the future of the two periodicals, yet I may have the "push" to risk something on your English undertakings and begin to feel rich. The more so, when the Hungarian affairs will be brought to an end with a resulting gain for the fund. Now I confess I felt very often miserable about the condition of our business matters. I did not miss the opportunity for improving Rank's position, increasing his monthly salary by 1000 (and Reik's by 500) crs., and hope you as a member of the *G.m.b.H.*[1] will readily consent.

Now for the two inlying letters. The one I got from Tannenbaum is simple insolent. I answered it shortly and sharply as follows: I was sorry I could not enter into the contents of his letter as it would need an *"Abhandlung"* [treatise], to rectify his opinions and show him how utterly impossible it was to assent to his demands. Nor did I feel sure I could impress him by taking these pains. He was calling himself my staunchest friend, adherer, etc., but neither his letters nor his acts confirmed it. So with great respect etc. I dont think we will loose much by his open hostility.

Forsyth's letter I answered far more kindly and opened a discussion with him. I was glad to hear there was nothing serious between you and him, and that there was a good chance of getting over the difficulties either on the Congress or before. I was but dimly aware of the nature of his objections but I thought it might be a matter of principle, the democratic against the autocratic as represented by myself and my adherers. If so I wished to express my opinion that this was perhaps not the matter to be judged by political views. I had a double stand, as a teacher and as a proprietor. In the first place I was one who had to offer a teaching and as such could not be restricted by [pe][2] beginners whose very discernment had to be developed. Science was impossible if decad[e]s of ψα experience ought not to bring an accruement of authority as belonged to the teacher. I hoped he was not a partisan of the *"Schülerrat"* [student council] in public schools. The difference between schoolboys and grown up men was accounted for by the fact, that school instruction is compulsory, while to my teaching only those have to submit who want it. Trusting we had to offer a sound scientific doctrine we determined to start this journal with the provisional consentment of the Anglo-American groups. If this vote should not prove a definite one the journal would be withdrawn or perhaps will have to fight for itself. In the first case a competition between Jelliffe and the new Triad (Tann-St-Silb.) would result, as I did not think the groups were capable to conduct a journal on their own lines.[3] Secondly it was a matter of property too. The English *Journal* was to be sustained *partly* by the funds and by the staff of the *Zeitschrift* and—what meant more—had free legitimate access to its productions. But if he succeeded to bring about an agreement between these views of mine and his demands, still imperfectly known to me, none would enjoy it more than myself who never was an enemy to independent thought but bent on avoiding anarchy in science.

Now this was my letter posted the day before yesterday. I cannot guess if its effect will prove to the good or not. It seemed important to me that he should not find me [flex][4] pliable nor think himself indispensable. It spoils a man's morals.

Now I have omitted to mention that I wrote I considered the withdrawal of his contribution an unkind act towards our journal.—

I hope your dear wife has recovered and you are in good health again. I saw Munro (with two new Havana boxes!) and really got the impression he was not very reliable. Somehow I begin to catch a dislike against members of the Labour Party.[5]

Dont believe in the Ferenczi rumour. Mrs. Levy who is here in treatment got a letter from her husband with no hint at all of such an event, (you know she is Freund's sister).[6]

My health is good, I cannot take another patient until the vacancies, Rickman is excellent, Daly, who offered himself to you for two months after I leave, is a bore and an ass as you said. He is dissatisfied with my person.

My wife is still in Hamburg, Ernest is to be wedded to his bride May 18th in Berlin.[7]

With sincere love to you and your wife

yours
Freud

1. *Gesellschaft mit beschränkter Haftpflicht* = Co., Ltd., or PLC.
2. Crossed out in the original.
3. Reference to Jelliffe's *Psychoanalytic Review* versus *Eros-Psyche* of Tannenbaum, Stekel, and Silberer; see Jones (1957a, pp. 35–36; 1957b, p. 37).
4. Crossed out in the original.
5. Hector Munro, M.B., C.M. Aberdeen 1894, member of the Highland League of Glasgow, which linked up with the British Labour party in 1918. He ran in the general election of 1918 and received 21 percent of the vote. The League ceased activities in the early 1920s.

6. Katä Lévy, social worker, sister of Anton von Freund and wife of Lajos Lévy (1875–1961), director of the Jewish Hospital in Budapest and analysand of Ferenczi.

7. Ernst Freud married Lucie Brasch (b. 1896).

276

18 May 1920
111 Harley Street, London

Dear Professor,

I was delighted to hear the good news of the accession to the strength of the Fond, which will make matters safe for the immediate future. My optimism compels me to believe that sooner or later there will be later windfalls from rich people who have benefitted by Ps-A. Do you think now that we might venture on a noncommercial enterprise, which was the original object of the Verlag? I refer particularly to Roheim's detailed work on Totemism, which seems worthy of publication.[1]

I am most grateful to you for keeping me in touch with the Tannenbaum-Forsyth situation, for it is invaluable to me to know what is going on. I enclose the one letter, but am keeping Tannenbaum's unless you want it, for it contains a useful admission that my promise to him was as I said and not as he later maintained. He will probably be openly hostile after your letter, but what can one do with such a tasteless and tactless person?[2] As to Forsyth, if he does not respond suitably to your tolerance I shall judge him more harshly than before, for he does not deserve such lenience as you shewed. For my part I take his definite refusal to support the *Journal* in any way, and further the unprecedented step of withdrawing his article without reason, as definitely unfriendly behaviour.[3] His remarks about the necessity for more than one "pillar" in this country indicates plainly the nature of his difficulty, and I am glad and very grateful that you made it clear to him that our mode of starting the *Journal* was not at all an autocratic act of mine, but throughout determined by your own judgement and authority. This will probably have more effect on him than anything else, for I am sure he wants your approval above everything, and now you shew him how to get it. If you think there is still a chance of rescuing his article please do so, but of course the decision is in your hands.

A recent postcard from Ferenczi disposed of the disturbing rumour about him.[4] I am glad that Munro arrived safely. I only trusted him with two boxes, for he is an uncertain quantity.

It will be good if you make something out of Rickman; we badly need some good men. I hope I shall be able to avoid Daly.

My wife has made an excellent recovery. She is in the Isle of Wight convalescing, where I join her tomorrow for the Whitsun holidays. Will you please convey to Ernst my congratulations and best wishes. I was speaking about him to Eder a week or two ago, and there seem to be good chances of his being wanted in Palestine.

With my kindest regards,

yours always affectionately
Ernest Jones.

1. Géza Róheim (1891–1953), Hungarian anthropologist, one of the first to apply psychoanalytic theory in anthropological studies.
2. There are five letters between Jones and Tannenbaum of 1919 and 1920, which are contained in the Archives of the British Psycho-Analytical Society. The major issue of dispute was Tannenbaum's wish to be an editor of Jones's *Journal*, in keeping with Jones's apparent promise to Tannenbaum in this regard.
3. See note 4 to letter 271.
4. The postcard is missing, but Ferenczi's expulsion from the medical society did not take place officially until 28 May 1920; see note 1 to letter 273.

277

24 May 1920
Vienna, IX. Berggasse 19

Dear Jones,

Here [is] the reply of Forsyth's, evasive as you see. We must drop the matter and go on without him. Pray consider, he must not be fortified in his disposition to think himself indispensable.

I am glad you agree with my letter to the knave T[annenbaum]. We will be able to stand his attacks. If America really is embracing Jungism as he pretends, she will get what she deserves. Give me some millions (even of Kronen) more and I will nevermore be afraid of an adversary.

I have a high esteem for Roheim's work and am ready to undertake his Australian Totemism in English,[1] especially as he offers in a recent letter to pay part of the expense. Wednesday I will talk the matter over with Rank. There is only the damned question of paper!

Did you know that *nasal* operations during pregnancy are apt to produce abortion? I heard so from Wilh. Fliess and am glad to learn that nothing has happened.[2]

I got the two boxes of excellent stuff from Munro, indeed you must not send any more. My daughter Anna is expected back from Berlin May 26th, my wife is still at Hamburg. I feel tempted to prolong work until July 31st as all the foreigners are sure to stay if I do. I am earning lots of Kronen in this way, but however improbable it may sound, it does not cover half of my wants.

I have just finished correcting and adding to the 4th edition of *Sexual*

Theory and turn now to *"Jenseits d. Lustprinzips"*. B. Low's book arrived today. I think she has "potted" me nicely.[3]

Heartily yours
Freud

1. Róheim (1925).
2. Fliess's support of this theory is briefly discussed in Sulloway (1979, p. 149).
3. Barabara Low, *Psycho-Analysis: A Brief Account of the Freudian Theory* (London: Allen and Unwin, 1920).

278

28 June 1920
111 Harley Street, London

Dear Professor,

I had been missing a letter from you, and only to-day arrived one dated and post-marked Wien, May 24., simultaneously with one from Rank of the same date!

I judge Forsyth more severely than Tannenbaum, for one might have expected a higher standard from one of his upbringing than from an ignorant American. Both deserted us for the same motive of personal jealousy, but T.[annenbaum] at least came out into the open, instead of slipping about like an eel.

My wife, I am glad to say, made an excellent recovery, and is very well. I had inquired first of all about the risk from her obstetrician and the rhinologist, who have had much experience.

There has been no news here of late beyond steady hard work. Hiller has been away ill with influenza for some three weeks, but will soon return. A friend of mine, on a visit here from New York, gave me a very bad account of Bernays, that he is an American "sharper" and quite unscrupulous. That was no surprise to me, after the way in which he had deceived Brill and yourself, so we must watch him carefully.

Pierce Clark has sent an article for the *Journal*.[1] Still no word from Brill. A friend of his, Mrs. MacCormick, sister-in-law of the Zurich one of the same name,[2] came to see me recently. She is on our side, will probably come to the Congress, and may very well help us at some time.

I wonder if there is any hope of your spending a week or so in England after the Congress. It would give us great pleasure, and I think you would find it a pleasant rest, especially in the country.

yours always affectionately
Ernest Jones.

1. Clark (1920).

2. This was the sister-in-law of Edith McCormick. The latter was daughter of John D. Rockefeller, wife of the wealthy and influential Harold McCormick, and a patient of Jung's who spent the period between 1913 and 1923 in Zurich, helping to found Jung's Psychological Club in 1916.

279

4 July 1920
Vienna, IX. Berggasse 19

Dear Jones,

I too had missed your letters these last weeks and I am glad there was no other cause to your silence.

I will continue work until 30th July exhausting the English patients you sent me. I am rather in good condition but will need rest and recovery afterwards.

America seems to pass through a fit of madness just now. The same as you can get no answer from Brill, so I am expecting vainly news from my nephew Bernays about the book, I get neither a copy nor a letter nor money. Yet the book has come out long since. I have seen it advertised in the "Nation" and I got a letter from Allen & Unwin applying for the English edition, joined here. I answered that our Int. ψα Press had the nearest right to it and they should address you. Now if you will undertake the book in spite of the American edition, tell them so; if not *you are entitled to sell it to them*. To be sure the American translation had to be revised carefully and the preface by Stanley Hall substituted by another of yours. Hall may have abused the opportunity offered to him to break a lance for his latest favourite Adler in the wrong place.

I am glad to hear your good wife is well and so I hope are you.

Yours affectionately as ever
Freud

280

9 July 1920
111 Harley Street, London

Dear Professor,

I have just seen the Bernays translation.[1] No translator's name is mentioned, and Bernays plays a Yankee trick by putting on the title page

Authorized Translation
With Preface

By
Stanley Hall.

Hall (who was a pupil of Wundt's) draws a long parallel between you and Wundt, closing with the hope that you will not follow Wundt in parting from your best pupils such as Adler. The translation is loose and rapidly done, full of vulgar Americanisms. You are made to speak in a very unworthy style, so that the reader must get an unfavourable impression of your personality. The translator does not seem to be an analyst, for he makes such mistakes as using "suppression" for "Verdrängung" in spite of our efforts to make "repression" a technical term distinguished from suppression. Still it is perhaps better than Brill's translations, for I have not noticed any performances quite equal to his famous rendering of *halluzinatorische Besetzung* as "an hallucinatory occupation".[2]

I am arranging, I trust with your permission, that an English translation be published in London by the Press and Unwin on the plan of half profits, they providing the capital. We are offering Bernays £25 for the right to use his translation as a basis, but of course it will be re-written. I cannot see the need of any introduction, with the exception, perhaps, of some sentences by me on the paper jacket and advertisements.

Is the enclosed interview authentic?

Could you spare time to give me the answer to a technical question? On S. 282 of the 4. *Sammlung*, and elsewhere in your writings, you speak of the *Anziehung des schon Verdrängten* as a factor in further repression.[3] Do you mean this literally, that a force is exercised [on the part of][4] by the repressed, or would you agree to the following formulation? That material which becomes associated with repressed material becomes thereby subject to the same psychical conditions as the latter, i.e. *also* acted on by the repressing forces exerted from the preconscious? This is how I have always pictured the matter. The result is the same, but the theory is a little different.

yours always
Ernest Jones.

1. *A General Introduction to Psychoanalysis* (New York: Boni and Liveright, 1920) was a translation of Freud (1916–17) by several graduates of Columbia University. See Jones (1957a, pp. 9–10; 1957b, pp. 9–10); and Edward L. Bernays, "Uncle Sigi," *Journal of the History of Medicine and Allied Sciences*, 35 (1980): 216–220. Edward Bernays (b. 1891) was Freud's nephew and a pioneer in the field of public relations.

2. See S. Freud, *The Interpretation of Dreams*, trans. A. A. Brill (London: G. Allen; New York: Macmillan, 1916, p. 435). *Besetzung* is a highly charged German word with a multiplicity of meanings, one of which can be "occupation"; see Ornston (1985b).

Strachey's translation in Freud (1900a, p. 548), *G.W.*, 3:554, is of course "hallucinatory cathexis."

3. The "attraction exercised by what was primally repressed upon everything with which it can establish a connection" is discussed in Freud (1915d, p. 148), *G.W.*, 10:250–251.

4. The bracketed words are crossed out in the original.

281

16 July 1920
Vienna, IX. Berggasse 19

Dear Jones,

I am glad to know you at last got the translation which I still expect and perhaps in vain—as well as letters or money—from my queer nephew. What you utter about the book does not strike me so badly as I could have feared. The translation could have shown other faults than mere lack of elegance, and if St.[anley] Hall did not use the whole of the preface as an ardent plea for Adlers claims it is all right. Yet I know I ought not have given the authorization a year hence.

I willingly conform myself to your plan of bringing out the English edition under your superintendence and on the terms you mention. Just one page of preface out of your pen enough to justify your name on the title-page would do good and serve for distinguishing it from the American edition.

The first number of our *Journal* ought to have come out to-day. Perhaps it did. It appeals to me as very rich and dignified, and nice in outer shape and appearance. Still I regret it developed so slowly under so many retarding influences on both sides of the Channel. There is no stuff for the second number, here a condition which cannot stay. As for Pierce Clark's paper which you sent I will not venture to advise it should be repudiated. But [it] is very bad, worthless Adlerism, based on analysis not reaching into the period of first childhood and therefore most shallow and superficial. I see we cannot rely on American contributors, at least for the next time, and we ought to build up the *Journal* partly on the work of your English staff and partly on good translations from out of the *Zeitschrift*. We ought to provide a stock of this [these] translations ready to be put in as they are wanted. It may prove too much work for the few of your collaborators in London. If you agree we will try to find some Englishman or woman here, who will help you in doing this part of the work, Rank will write you on the matter. To be sure our expenses will grow higher, but there is no help, we want money—money—money—

I think your editorial remark attached to P. Clark's article, emotionally justified, is not strong in itself. Most of his cases are at least Zw + Anx. Hy. [Zwangsneurose and anxiety hysteria]. Can you correct it? I know you felt the stimulus to contradict him.[1]

As for your theoretical question I agree with your second view. Please remember the remark in the *"Sexualtheorie"* on the mechanism of repression. It is compared to the way a tourist comes up to the summit of a great Pyramid, being pushed from one side and drawn from the other.[2]

The interview *(Kuh)*[3] is authentic as regards the two persons and the topic. I gave him some sentences from "Remarks on War and Death". But it is rather a picnic than a report and I have sworn it is to be the last interview I submit for the next ten years.[4]

With kind love to you and Kitty

ever yours
Freud

1. See Clark (1920, p. 160 n. 1), where Jones suggests that all the symptoms mentioned by Clark belong to anxiety hysteria alone.

2. See Freud (1905d, pp. 175–176 n. 2).

3. Literally "cow"; probably an expression of Freud's disdain for journalists, who do not "digest" material properly but, like cows with several stomachs *(Wiederkäuer)*, receive food into the first cavity, then return it to the mouth, where it is chewed over again and swallowed, and then digested in the other compartments. Hence, as Freud says, the interview is a "picnic" and not a "report."

4. Included in Charles J. Rosebault, "Americans Who Were More German Than the Germans," *New York Times* (Sunday), 24 August 1919.

282

22 July 1920
111 Harley Street, London

Dear Professor,

Many thanks for your long letter of July 16th. I have signed the agreement with Unwin for the *Vorlesungen;* Flugel and I will revise it.

I entirely agree with all that you say about the *Journal*. Rank has already seven articles for the 2nd number, but I know the importance of gathering material as far ahead as is possible. When I am definitely appointed editor I can set about collecting a permanent staff of reviewers, translators, etc.. Will you be so good as to substitute something suitable for my remark at the end of Pierce Clark's article. I asked him for the article and so cannot now refuse it, impossible as it is.

You say you agree with the "second view" about the theoretical question. As far as my memory serves, this was the formulation I suggested; please contradict me if this is not so. If so, is not the pyramid analogy possibly misleading to some readers, who might infer that an actual pulling *force* is at work.

I should be glad to have an answer to my questions about the Berlin lectures and the date of the Committee Meeting, for one has to make plans in due time nowadays. Also two points about the Congress, as we are drawing up the programme. Who would you like to preside at the business meeting, yourself, Abraham or myself? I wish you would do it. Have you yet decided the title of your paper, or shall I write *Thema vorbehalten* [topic to be announced]?

The Congress promises well in all respects, good papers and I hope a good attendance; there are sixteen coming from England.

You will be sorry to hear that Col. Sutherland, who called on you once in Vienna,[1] has just died in Calcutta from appendicitis.

Kitty is extremely well and is looking forward to seeing you here in September.

yours always affectionately
Ernest Jones.

1. Colonel W. D. Sutherland visited Freud in March 1911 (see letter 54).

283

2 August 1920
Bad Gastein, Villa Wassing

Dear Jones,

Here I am, amidst the choice beauties of our Alps, pretty well worn out, waiting for the beneficial effects of radioactive water and delicious air. I have brought the material for the *"Psychology of Mass and the Analysis of the Ego"*[1] with me, but my head obstinately refuses so far to take an interest in these deep problems. Therefore I have undertaken a review of the American translation, which I will send you—a rich harvest—later on. You may sell it to my nephew Bernays for the next edition or reserve it for your own improved one. To be sure, I only noticed the faults from my side of the water, nothing on elegance, precision, etc.. I judge it is a slovenly piece of work, but the high strung colloquial tone of the lectures is not badly reproduced.

As for the questions in your last letter, I leave it to Rank to answer them. Poor Rank, so much is left to him! I hope I can manage to reach the Hague on the 6th of Sept., but who can make such a promise nowadays? The Berlin lectures have been given up, as Abraham writes apparently on account of my withdrawing. Really I am not in a condition now, to woo for the affection of the prudish intellectual beauties of Berlin. I see you were right, Prussianity is very strong with Abraham.

As for my paper or rather Vortrag on the Congress let it be *Thema vorbehalten*, if I succeed in giving a lecture. I feel so tired.

I think the presidency in the business meeting ought to alternate between Ferenczi and you. Abraham and I dont come in. Ferenczi is deeply mortified by his expulsion from the Bpest medical Society. We ought to honour him in compensation.

Sutherland has left a kind memory with me. You seem not to be satisfied about the Repression business. You are afraid of conceding a direct pulling (attracting) force to the repressed memories. Yet so we must, all the forgotten things strive incessantly to come to the surface, to present themselves to consciousness etc..

Give my best love to your kind wife, write me hither, where I intend to stay until 28th of this month.

Yours affectionately
Freud

1. Freud (1921c).

284

20 August 1920
The Plat, Elsted

Dear Professor,

We have just arrived here, where I shall be until leaving for Holland, from a tour round Warwickshire, Devonshire, etc., a main object of which, successfully achieved, was to show my wife and make her familiar with the characteristic landscapes and ancient buildings of South England. I wish we knew if there was any hope of seeing you here after the Congress; it would be an enormous pleasure.

I shall be very glad to have your comments on the Bernays translation and will use them for ours. I will bring with me two books on Mass psychology to Holland. I have just read the proofs of your *Jenseits d. L.*,[1] with mixed feelings—deep interest at the contents, and apprehension at the difficulty of translating it, which Rank of course expects me to do on the spot. Of the two main ideas, one is quite clear to me: the tendency of instincts to repeat an old situation and if possible restore an equilibrium (by the way, how would you translate Wiederholungs*zwang?*).[2] The second idea, that this is independent of the Lustprinzip, I have so far only imperfectly digested.

[If you are correcting the proofs you might note the following:][3]

There is still a misunderstanding about my repression question. That the unconscious material is constantly striving for expression, to come to consciousness, is plain enough, also that in so doing it attracts into its domain much preconscious material. But I should not have called the latter process itself repression—only a necessary preliminary to repression, the dragging of previously conscious material into a part of the mind which is subject to repression (from the side of consciousness). What do you think of that formulation?

Rank, Sachs, and I arrive at The Hague on the 5th. I hope it will be possible for you to do the same, as there is much to discuss, and the committee may be rather tired by the end of the Congress, which will be a very busy one. 27 papers were offered! I have heard nothing at all from Brill, and Stern says he (Brill) is not coming to the Congress.[4]

With all good wishes

Yours always affectionately
Ernest Jones.

1. Freud (1920g).
2. *Zwang* is doubly underlined in the original.
3. Crossed out in the original.
4. Sixth Congress of the International Psychoanalytic Association, The Hague, 6–11 September 1920. A summary of the proceedings is contained in *Zeitschrift*, 6 (1920): 376–402.

285
[postcard]

23 September 1920
Hague

Dear Jones,

The Visum for Anna came too late for my dispositions, so I will not come to England this time. I am glad now that I did not retain you here, hope you found your wife allright and that she will remain so to the end of the term. We intend to leave this fat country Tuesday 28th in the morning; passing through Berlin I hope to be back in Wien end of this month. It was a good time and good to have met you again.

Affectiontely yours
Freud

286

1 October 1920
111 Harley Street, London

Dear Professor,

I have transferred the account from Lippmann, Rosenthal to Lissa & Kann, The Hague (they have no address at Amsterdam),[1] have told the latter that you will send them a certified copy of your signature, in case you did not do this while in Holland.

I start next week with Mrs. Rickman. In the meantime Rickman is passing a fortnight with me discussing analytic questions, a semi-analysis of himself. I do not form such a good impression of his character as I did, though he seems to have developed a good many sublimations and reactions of a social kind. I am struck by his inner aloofness from the world, and his inability to love strongly. He must be very difficult to analyse fully, on account of the interesting split in his ego, so that he regards himself almost as an external object, one it is true of the greatest interest. It reminds me of your homosexual girl and her lorgnon attitude.[2] We have just made him an associate member of our society and I have no doubt we shall hear much from him in the future.

Doubtless you got my letter of a few days ago. I hope you have quite recovered from the strain of the congress and the infection you contracted there.

With kindest regards to you and all

yours always affectionately
Ernest Jones.

1. Lippmann, Rosenthal, and Co. was a private banking house founded in 1859 with head offices in Amsterdam. Separate accounts for Jones, Freud, and the Verlag were set up at the smaller firm Lissa and Kann in the Hague. Freud's account served as a kind of tax shelter in order to provide for his wife in the event of his death.

2. See Freud (1920a, p. 163).

287

4 October 1920
Vienna, IX. Berggasse 19

Dear Jones,

By the time this letter reaches you, you may have become already a father or may dwell on the very top of expectation to be so. It is one of the queerest and most exalted situations in life, the beginning of infinite happiness and endless cares. May it prove a blessing to you and your dear wife.

I have come back to Vienna on the last of Sept. at nighttime, having separated from Anna at Osnabrück and passed a day at Berlin to see my widow sister.[1] I was received by an overpowering storm of letters, duties and patients, my hours are all of them taken and I feel pretty tired after the first day's work. Yesterday coming back from a 31 km ride to Tulln (on the Danube) by auto I fixed with Rank and Sachs the contents of our first *Rundschreiben* (circular letter) to the Comittee which is to be sent off every Tuesday.[2] I am eager to learn how this institution will work, I expect it to prove very useful.

I feel very proud of the Congress and as I proclaimed in my improvisation highly relieved by the conviction, that men like you, Ferenczi, Abraham, Rank, etc. are apt and ready to supplant me. The remainder of my time and powers I will have to devote to the duty of providing for my family, that is to say to making money, but if scientific interest, which just now is asleep with me, gets aroused in the course of time I may still be able to bring some new contribution to our unfinished work. Scientific interchange among the members of the Comittee seems a highly important task for the future; [most] too much of our relations [have][3] has been taken up by business interests in these last months.

I have written to Brill the day after my return laughing at his combinations and asking him to send the money back. Will my letter impress him more than yours? The centre of our activity has now shifted to the English affairs and we hope you will behave cautiously and lead us out of the stress we find ourselves in at the moment. We want more money or more reserve.

I am still suffering of my cold; it is a pity you are so inclined to catch ear-disease.

Now in expectation of your next good news I remain with my best wishes

yours truly
Freud

1. Marie Freud (1861–1942) married Moritz Freud (b. 1857 Bucharest), who died in Berlin in 1920. In the original Freud had written "to see my sister widow."
2. The *Rundbriefe* were circulated among the members of the Secret Committee (Jones, Freud, Rank, Ferenczi, Abraham, Sachs, and Eitingon) between 1920 and 1925, and again after Abraham's death among the members of the reconstituted Committee (which included Anna Freud and J. H. W. van Ophuijsen) between 1926 and 1935. There are approximately 350 *Rundbriefe* for the period 1920–1925, and approximately 170 for the period 1926–1935. Many are eight or twelve pages long, and represent about two thousand pages of unpublished correspondence (one third in English, two thirds in German). These documents are located at Butler Library, Columbia University, New York; Library of Congress, Washington, D.C.; Archives of the British Psycho-Analytical Society, London; and Sigmund Freud Copyrights Ltd., Wivenhoe (UK). For a review of the activities of the Committee based on the *Rundbriefe* for the period 1920–1925, see Grosskurth (1991). The very first *Rundbrief*, 20 September 1920, was written by Ferenczi; the next one was from Freud and Rank, 5 October 1920.
3. The bracketed words are crossed out in the original.

288

12 October 1920
Vienna, IX. Berggasse 19

Dear Jones,

So you have become a father nearly at the same time as a president.[1] You are now on the heights of life and with a little σωφροσύνη[2] will never slip down. Give my best wishes to your wife who I am sure behaved bravely and write in time what the baby's weight is and name will be. If you take a deeper interest in the newcomers first action, let me tell you that my eldest daughter exactly did the same thing when first brought to light. Yet I do not remember she was addicted to thumbsucking later on to any remarkable degree.

I got the news that you transferred our account from Lippmann to Lissa & Kann and thank you for it. L.[issa] & K.[ann] wrote me since that you had sent them F 25, I wonder if this sum had anything to do with me.

Your first circulating letter was highly interesting for both of us.[3] As you will learn by our next, the transactions with the man Kola are progressing in a very favourable manner.[4] May be we will soon have our cares behind us and big chances of activity before us. But Rank is rather cool and cautious than enthusiastic in the matter and I dont blame him for it.

I have taken Mr. Strachey at one guinea the hour, do not regret it but for his speech being so indistinct and strange to my ear, that he is a torture to my attention.

The fool Daly is much more reasonable than before. As for Rickman I think your judgment is too severe. His peculiarities are not beyond the measure of any young man getting aware and not yet sure of his powers. He is not conceited and full of passion. I rather like him.

I am now entering into transactions about treatment with another man you sent to me, one Dr. Young[5] of the British Embassy here, a case of erythrophobia etc. Tough cases, but not without good chance.

I have cured my stomach in Vienna, my cold is going its way.

My friend Prof. Pribram tells me I have been expected at Cambridge on Sept. 27th. But I never got a word of invitation as you know.[6] I once had a conversation with Rickman about my visit there but I dropped it hearing that my daughter could not be invited. That was all.

Wishing you a very happy time

Yours affectionately
Freud

1. Referring to the birth of Jones's daughter Gwenith (1920–1928). See letter 520 for the circumstances surrounding her premature death.
2. Greek *sophrosyne* = moderation.

3. Jones's first *Rundbrief* was written 7 October 1920 (Archives of the British Psycho-Analytical Society, London; and Rank Collection, Butler Library, Columbia University).

4. Richard Kola (b. 1872) of Vienna built a huge publishing and financial empire in the early 1920s; see Murray Hall, "Der Rikola-Konzern," in *Österreichische Verlagsgeschichte, 1918–1938*, vol. 2 (Vienna: Hermann Böhlaus Nachf., 1985), pp. 310–357. Kola was attempting to take over the operations of the Internationaler Psychoanalytischer Verlag; nothing came of the negotiations, however.

5. George M. Young (1882–1959) of the British diplomatic service had recently been appointed a temporary secretary in the legation at Vienna to supervise a £2,250,000 loan to Austria made by the United Kingdom.

6. In the *Rundbrief* of 14 October 1920 (Sigmund Freud Copyrights Ltd., Wivenhoe), Freud also reported that Pribram had written that the University of Cambridge was "keen on his work," especially *Totem and Taboo* (Freud, 1912–13).

289

17 October 1920
111 Harley Street, London

Dear Professor,

We were so glad to get your friendly letter about the new arrival, with the kind inquiries. Both the young ladies are blooming and are well pleased with each other. Kitty looks charming as a young mother. The baby weighed 6⅛ English pounds at birth (6 is I think the average for a female child), the same after a week, but in the last three days has gained another $\frac{5}{16}$ of a pound. Her name will probably be Gwenyth; it had to be Welsh to go with Jones.

Perhaps I forgot to tell you that Rivers wrote to me in September expressing the hope that you would visit Cambridge, but it was of course no appointment.

I am using Lissa & Kann for some sums of my own also, as I have a Dutch patient at present, so must be careful of the exact accounts.

Strachey's English should be good, so perhaps his indistinct utterance is part of his general inhibitions and will improve. He offered to help us with translations. Will you or Rank suggest that he does Federn's *Vaterlose Gesellschaft*,[1] which is already partly translated, I believe. I was exceedingly interested to hear that Mr. Young had applied to you. I urged him to, but feared that his complex on the subject of foreigners might be too strong. He was by far the ablest and most interesting man I have ever analysed. He has had a most brilliant career, now interrupted by his neurosis, and is a highly intelligent and cultivated man. Though I could see into the roots of his neurosis (impotence of urethral origin, with an inverted Oedipus-complex), I was never able to break down his resistances, to my keen regret, and I shall rejoice if you will be able to treat him. His speech is clear enough, and he is such a typical Englishman that you would find much interest in observing the English characteristics.

You will have heard from Rank of our success in raising money for the Press, but I will write about that on Tuesday.

With most cordial thanks for your congratulations

Yours always affectionately
Ernest Jones.

1. Paul Federn, *Zur Psychologie der Revolution: Die vaterlose Gesellschaft* (Vienna: Anzengruber, 1919).

290

21 October 1920
Vienna, IX. Berggasse 19

Dear Jones,

Highly satisfied by your good news about the mother and the baby, hope she will soon be able to spell her own name, and so get the better of me.

It is a sign of the present times if remarks on money matters should follow so soon after this congratulation. I was very much surprised at the sudden happy change in your business affairs, cannot understand it,—nor can Rank—and a pardonable doubt still subsists whether the first or the second account is the right one, whether Hiller or you got mixed up in the accounts. It will be matter of correspondence between you and Rank.

Referring to Lissa & Kann I will take the liberty to point out to you that you overlooked one feature of the case. L.[issa] & K.[ann] have not taken the money as a deposit like the Amsterdam bankers but they have opened an account *(Konto)* to me under your name as a cover and they are paying 3% percents at least. Now if you put your money together with mine we will have to divide the interests among us and will not know how to do it. You must either enjoy mine or I yours or we will have to claim the help of a clerk to bring out the legitimate proportion. So I think it would be more convenient if you did return to Lipp.[mann] Ros.[enthal] & Co. and ask them to open an account to you or try some other arrangement. It is a queer thing to throw you out when you were so kind as to lend me your name, but you will see it is better to avoid complications.

I consent to your proposal I should write an introduction to Putnam's book and hope you will be contented if it is a very short one.[1] I am so far from composing now as if I never had written a line for the printer.

None of these foregoing items would have urged me to so rash an answer, had I not got another bit of news for you. I have received a letter from Brill!, a long, tender, crazy letter not mentioning a word about the money but explaining away the mystery of his behaviour. It was all jealousy, hurt sensibility and the like. I will do my best to soothe him and propose you should now put him down as the first of your american coeditors, leave to him the choice of the two others and give him notice of it. The day before he had sent a note to Rank to the purpose that he had transmitted the sum originally sent to Lipp.[mann] Ros.[enthal] & Co. now "to the Deutsche Bank Ernst Fr." which is sheer nonsense, but open to understanding if you read it inversely. I think he meant it the other way and his slip is to be interpreted as a symbol of homosexuality as in a dream.[2]

Now with best wishes for all three of yours I am

yours affectionately
Freud

1. Putnam (1921), and Freud (1921a).
2. This concerns the issue of Brill's contribution and donation of money to the Verlag and the *Journal*. In early 1920 he had sent approximately $600 to Jones and $1,200, according to Freud's instructions, to the account of Ernst Freud at the Deutsche Bank, Munich, which was later returned with no explanation (Brill to Jones, 9 December 1919, 21 January 1920, 17 June 1920, Archives of the British Psycho-Analytical Society). According to Jones's instructions, however, Brill was to send the latter amount to Lippmann, Rosenthal and Co., the Psycho-Analytical Press's account in Amsterdam (Jones to Brill, 15 December 1919), which may in part explain Brill's slip.

291

28 October 1920
111 Harley Street, London

Dear Professor,

Again thank you for your kind messages and inquiries: Kitty is now restored to normal life and of course very happy. Her former *volks-wirtschaftliche*[1] interests are indicated in the choice of the baby's name, for Gwenith is Welsh for "wheat"—also a much-desired object in these days. She has gained ⅞ of a pound in the first three weeks.

Two matters in your letter—the Press finance and the advent or event of a letter from Brill—I dealt with in the London circular letter of two evenings ago, and you will see that I asked for an early answer from you on the latter question. I note that he wrote to you and to Rank, but not at all to me. I hope I have not been drawn into his circle of complexes, but if that were so you would probably have given me a hint which would guide me in dealing with some particular sensitiveness. I think your explanation of the money more likely than Rank's, but we shall soon hear from one bank or other. By the way, I would rather not return to Lippmann after having had to leave them without reason, and would prefer to forego my part of the interest—which will be a small sum. If I get any amount there I will turn it into Dutch oil shares. At the same time, you mustn't have the impression of my not being a good accountant, for I am very proud of my capacity in this direction! It was always a point of emulation between me and my Father who was very talented in such work, and I like to think that I inherit it.

I suppose you heard of the letter from the Oxford professors to the Germans and Austrians. It has caused a rather warm discussion here on both sides. It was got up by our Poet Laureate (a medical man)[2] and I have written to tell him of our congress; I wonder if he will answer.

With my kindest regards

Yours always affectionately
Ernest Jones.

1. Katherine (Jokl) Jones wrote a doctoral dissertation on commercial relations between Austria and England in the nineteenth century, *Die handelspolitischen beziehungen zwischen Österreich und England vom beginn des 19 jahrhunderts bis 1875* (Zurich: Reichenhall, 1920).

2. Robert Bridges (1844–1930), B.A. Oxford 1867, M.B. London 1874, D.Litt. Oxford 1912; leading British poet of the period; poet laureate 1913. After the war he took a leading role in the controversial movement at Oxford which aimed at "reconciliation" among German, Austrian, and English professors in light of the controversies sparked by the outbreak of war in 1914. See note 10 to letter 206; and also "Oxford Letter to German Intellectuals," *Times*, 18 October 1920, p. 8; and "The Poet Laureate on Reconciliation," *Times*, 27 October 1920, pp. 13–14.

292

7 November 1920
Vienna, IX. Berggasse 19

Dear Jones,

I got a letter from Forsyth today explaining his conduct by motives of opposition to you and your "autocratic" moods. I see he is lost for the society, not for the cause I hope and I will try to keep up friendly relations with him in order not to drive him into open opposition. But I can recognise that your position is a difficult one and that you ought more than ever avoid even the appearance of ambiguous dealings. If you will take my advise, bring the affair of the donations to a good end, explain to them, that the money they promised was devoted and spent not for the Press but for the shop, that this last has proved too expensive and therefore a failure, in London as well as in Vienna, as we too have resolved to give up our establishment (in the case of independence) and put us under the wings of a commissionary. After having paid the debts of this experiment, the rest has to be paid back to the donators; Rank will inform you, to what posts we can renounce in order to make this restitution as considerable as possible. Except the case that some of them would like to give a contribution to the ΨA funds, to which no claim of influence could adhere. But you ought not to press it. In any case, whether they give money to the funds or not, I will be glad to consider their wishes—and so will you—concerning the choice of coeditors and of the contents of the *Journal*, but nothing more. We want internal independence as well as external one and even more.

The work of the Press is progressing so very slowly, only one number of the *Journal* having appeared and none of the books. We must insist on drawing the strings closer together. Strachey seems to prove a good acquisition. His translations to me seem excellent, I am ready to give him the "*Jenseits*".

The sense of persecution on the title of Oph.[uijsen]'s papers to be sure should be substituted by the "feeling of p.", as he did it in the text.[1]

I am very busy, no scientific news from my side.

With best love for your family

yours affectionately
Freud

1. J. H. W. van Ophuijsen, "On the Origin of the Feeling of Persecution," *Journal*, 1 (1920): 235–239.

293

International Psycho-Analytical Association
Central Executive

12 November 1920
London

Dear Professor,

I am glad to hear that Forsyth is at last honest; let us hope it may be the beginning of a recovery from his neurosis. I need hardly tell you that I cannot agree with his external diagnosis; so far from exhibiting autocratic tendencies, I have rather laid myself open to the reproach of being too democratic, diplomatic and conciliatory. But I fear he will not be able to work with me as a colleague until some inner change takes place.

I knew that you would be willing to consider the wishes of our society as regards co-editors. They have officially decided on Bryan and Flügel, and I understand that you approve [of] their choice. I am now writing to Brill asking him to choose two men to support him; I am of course very anxious about securing his cooperation and am sure that your personal influence will weigh heavily in the scale with him.[1]

Some time ago Rank sent me the proofs of the *"Jenseits"*, urging me to get it translated as soon as possible, lest the Americans pirate it on its appearance. I did so at once, and now about two-thirds are translated, for I assumed that he was acting with your authority. I hope, therefore, that no confusion will be caused by your offering it to Strachey, whom we can employ usefully enough otherwise.[2]

You say we must insist on drawing the strings closer together because of the slowness with which the Press work is going. I wish I could think of further ways of doing this. The first volume of our Library, Putnam's book,[3] has been in Vienna since last April. It started printing in July and even now not one quarter has been printed. I suppose that no start has been made with the other two books I gave Rank, one in August and one at the Congress. I cannot find out what the delay is due to, but it is inordinate.

In the case of a junction with Kola, could you let us have some general indication of the kind of way in which you propose to spend the Fond? The question has several important bearings, and perhaps you will deal with it in the circular letter.

I am sorry to say that I am not able to bring myself to make the statement to our society in the form that you and Rank suggest. I have always told them the full truth *as I see it*, and I think that Rank has unconsciously altered some of the historical facts. I do not find it accurate, for instance, to say that the donations were either given or spent for the shop, for they were neither given nor spent for this purpose. The premises in New Cavendish St. and the assistance of Hiller, were both engaged last October purely as a branch of the Verlag, i.e. the Press, and purely for *publishing* purposes. This has proved too expensive a way to maintain a branch and we now hope to run the same business from the central office in Vienna. The shop idea was added *later on*,[4] as an additional use for the already existing premises, and this has not cost one penny; on the contrary, it has earned a definite sum.

As for the recent donations, most of which have already been paid, the question of giving them back is rather complicated. They were given purely to the Press, for the sole purpose of continuing the publication of the *Journal* and Library. The members were under the impression that the Press was a branch of the Verlag and would remain so, for at the time Rank [asked] wrote to me [to make][5] about this appeal for further funds he never told me a word of the possible absorption of the Verlag in another, commercial firm. I don't suppose the members would have given the money for the benefit of a commercial undertaking of a strange firm, nor would I have asked them had I known. If, therefore, we join Kola, I think I must offer to restore all of the present funds. But again, the matter is not so simple, for the Press is legally a British firm and can never be part of Kola, for Kola would never submit to the conditions our Government impose on an Austrian firm doing business in England, and especially on one having a branch in England (*e.g.* address of the *Journal*, one without which we cannot produce it). If, therefore, the junction takes place, it seems to me that the Press will have to continue as a separate institution, employing Austrian printers, etc., perhaps at a rate that would not render it profitable or justifiable for us to undertake, for a commercial firm cannot be expected to give us the same advantages that the Verlag can and does in numerous ways. And yet to dissociate the two undertakings would also seem to me disastrous from a scientific point of view, for the collaboration between the *Zeitschrift* and *Journal*, between Rank and myself, are absolutely invaluable, at least to the *Journal*.

I beg you to take into consideration these matters as well as the local points of view, and to represent them to Rank, who perhaps is necessarily engrossed with the latter. I wish with all my heart that I could come to Vienna to talk matters over, but I see no prospect of that at present.

I enclose a letter from my wife in answer to very charming messages from your wife and daughter, which gave us both great pleasure. The mother and child are in perfect health and happiness.

With my kindest regards,

yours always affectionately
Ernest Jones.

1. The title page of vol. 2 of the *Journal* includes these acknowledgments: "Edited by Ernest Jones; with the assistance of Douglas Bryan, J. C. Flügel (London); A. A. Brill, H. W. Frink, C. P. Oberndorf (New York)."

2. The first English translation of Freud (1920g) was by C. J. M. Hubback.

3. Putnam (1921).

4. The Press was the British arm of the Verlag under Jones, who acted as a kind of independent publisher. The shop, operating under the umbrella of the Press, was in effect a small bookstore where one could get German books otherwise unobtainable. See Jones (1957a, p. 36; 1957b, p. 38).

5. The bracketed words are crossed out in the original. The words "wrote to" and "about" are handwritten in an otherwise typed letter.

294

18 November 1920
Vienna, IX. Berggasse 19

Dear Jones,

I return your letter to Brill with many thanks. It is excellent and ought to bring him around if my last letter to him had had some effect. But, as you know, *chi lo sa?*[1]

Yesterday I sent my answer to Forsyth which had to be carefully conceived, after showing it to Rank as I wanted someone to testify how energetically I had shown him the other side of the case. I did not send his letter to you because it was labelled "private".

You seemed irritated in your last circular about our meddling in the Brunswick affair[2] and Rank's distinction between Press and shop. We defended ourselves calmly in the answer composed yesterday and hope you will find out yourself that you overshot the mark. But we are not *"übelnehmerisch"* [resentful] and too sure of your friendly disposition.

The affair Press versus shop appears to me so intricate and full of misunderstandings that I am ready to drop it at once. My impression is that the practical distinction between the two was not made from the beginning but offered itself to Rank in the course of events. Happily the confusion cannot lead to disastrous results. You agree to give up the London business and I think we will have no trouble about the London contributions. We accept Hiller coming over to Vienna where he has to be undertained by your money so as to justify your demands on the members of your Society. There is not the least trace of an intention on our side to dissociate the Press from the Int. Verlag nor can there come any change in our relations, when we join Kola, a possibility which by the way appears neither assured nor very near. But in this case we could easily give you the means to return the contributions, if your members object even to an unofficial contact with a foreign undertaking.

I expect in the course of the next weeks the first *"Bilanz"* [balance] of the Verlag, hope to find it is satisfying and to be able to introduce some improvements even in case we keep our independence. We intend to raise the salaries, to engage Dr. Radó from Bpest as a help for Rank (Reik to be discharged) and to double the authors' fees which now amount to the ridiculous sum of 100 K for the sheet (Bogen).

Let me now propose you another innovation. I think Rank should appear on the titlepage of the *Journal* beneath the other six men as he manages the whole business here. It would be the justification of his getting a salary from the "Press", as he did this year. I am sure he will feel gratified too by this mention.

Business is devouring science I see. *"Die Kunst geht nach Brot"*[3] is more true than ever.

With the kindest regards for you and family

yours truly
Freud

1. "Who knows?" (with a shrug of the shoulders).
2. The Medico-Psychological Clinic, 30 Brunswick Square, operated under James Glover's direction; attempts to make it a permanent psychoanalytic fixture in London never materialized. Issues related to the clinic were debated in the *Rundbriefe* (Jones: 2 November, 9 November, 24 November 1920; Freud and Rank: 4 November, 18 November 1920; Archives of the British Psycho-Analytical Society, London).
3. "Art earns no bread."

295

International Journal of Psycho-Analysis

25 November 1920
London

Dear Professor,

I am glad you approved of my letter to Brill, and will let you know as soon as there is any response.

So your keenness detected the slight note of irritation in my letter, which I had hoped I had succeeded in suppressing altogether. It was a reaction to a number of points in Rank's dictatorial manner and conduct of late which have given me a little difficulty in dealing with internally, I hope with success. As Abraham remarked in his last letter, we must make great allowances for the strain Rank is under at present and for the impatient restlessness of his disposition, which has its advantages as well as its disadvantages.

I think it is an excellent idea to reward Rank with some honour for the work he has done in starting the *Journal*, though I hope he will be relieved of this when Hiller is in Vienna, and I have been planning to get both him and Ferenczi elected as Honorary Members of the British Society. There is much to be said also for your idea of making him one of the assistant editors of the *Journal*, though I am not quite sure that it would be wise policy to increase the foreign associations of the *Journal* just yet until the Americans are selected and our basis more securely established, for there has been much criticism in the public here of the foreign appearance of the get-up of the *Journal* (foreign type of printing and errors, etc.).

As for the Kola business I have not heard any valid arguments in favour of the combination, but I have found a good one for myself—namely, that it will give me a much-needed excuse to withdraw from the business and commercial side of our activities, of which I am quite as tired as you, and devote myself more to the scientific side.

I know Radó fairly well and hope he will be of great use to Rank. He has certainly great activity and capability, though I do not think Ferenczi found it too easy to keep him in order.

It is a pity that Berkeley-Hill's article[1] is not better, but I should be sorry to refuse it altogether, for he is very sensitive and I asked him to write it for the *Journal* (he is a close personal friend of mine); also one should remember that he has done much for psa in India and made a serious financial sacrifice to help the Press in its early days.[2] Would you like me to write to him, suggesting the points you mention which he could investigate further? I should be glad of your opinion on this.

I am overcome with excessive work and am looking forward to a few days at Christmas with my family, whom I rarely see. My wife has had a feverish attack this week, but is better today. I hope you will find Anna well and stronger on her return from Berlin.

With my kindest regards

yours always affectionately
Ernest Jones.

1. O. Berkeley-Hill, "A Short Study of the Life and Character of Mohammed," *Journal*, 2 (1921): 31–53.
2. For a discussion of the historical context of Berkeley-Hill's role in the development of psychoanalysis in India, see Hartnack (1990).

296

24 January 1921
Vienna, IX. Berggasse 19

Dear Jones,

In your last circular you mentioned a letter, in which you had asked me some questions about and proposed some modifications in my preface to Putnam's volume. This letter of yours did not arrive, it perished most likely like others of its kind in our postal strike. If you want to spare a repetition of the same please consider all your modifications as accepted by me in advance.

Our correspondence has got out of its trail somehow in the last weeks, as it is to a certain degree substituted by the Committee letters. I am not sure having thanked you for a precious box of Havannahs, have I? As a rule I agree with you on most relevant points, I do not agree when you get moody and harass Rank about trifles like misprints etc. which can nowhere be avoided. You know the fault of our English Press is in its slowness—not very much relieved by the presence of Hiller, but evidently to be improved by avoiding unnecessary travels from Vienna to London and back.

Anna has just finished translating the first chapter of your book which will go to you to-morrow. I put in some corrections and was consulted on various points. I wondered whether the separation of a fixation-hysteria will be found satisfactory in the (poor) present state of knowledge.[1]

By an "accident" I was able to find out the notice of a new document about Hamlet, which must concern you as much as me. The passage is in a new book by G. Brandes, called *"Miniaturen"*, published 1919 by Erich Reiss, Berlin. It reads like this (p. 137): "G. D. Moore Smith edited 1913 the *Marginalia"* of Gabriel Harvey, which contain the following remarkable passages. "The Earl of Essex praises highly *Albions* England and with good reason . . .",

"The younger generation is enchanted by Shakesp.'s Venus and Adonis but his Lucretia and his tragedy Hamlet prince of Denmark excel by qualities which appeal to the more considerate reader . . ."

"The poem *Amaryllis* and Sir Walter Raleigh's *Cynthia*, how charming productions these are! What a splendid opportunity for competition among Spenser, Constable, D. W., Ch. S.,[2] Shakespeare and the other flowers of our literature! . . ."

Here Brandes takes out the following surprising facts: "This note seems to have been written before January 1599, for Spenser who died about this date is mentioned as if he was living then. [. . .] Essex who too is spoken of as a person alive was executed in February 1601. [. . .] The consequence seems to be, that Hamlet was enacted before the death of Spenser in any case before the death of Essex that is to say much earlier than was believed hitherto."[3]

Now remember Sh.'s father died in the same year 1601![4] Will you think of defending our theory?

With hearty good wishes for you and your family

yours dearly
Freud

1. To Freud's principal categories of the psychoneuroses (conversion hysteria, anxiety hysteria, and obsessional neuroses), Jones adds a fourth, which he calls "fixation-hysteria" (1920b, pp. 19, 198–201).

2. Daniel Werner, Chapman, Silvester.

3. Passages were translated by Freud into English from *Miaturen von Georg Brandes*, trans. Erich Holm [pseud.] (Berlin: E. Reiss, 1919), pp. 137–138. Shakespeare's *Hamlet* was registered at Stationers' Hall on 26 July 1602. The problem of the play's dating is taken up in Jones (1949, pp. 109–110).

4. Freud at this point was adamant about connecting the writing of *Hamlet* with the death of Shakespeare's father; see Freud (1925d, p. 63).

297

28 January 1921
Vienna, IX. Berggasse 19

Dear Jones,

This letter is concerned only with formal interests, neither important nor in itself interesting.

Lissa & Kann are rather fertile in mistakes and confusions these last times, giving false names (Jones instead of Young) stating twice a single payment etc. I use this opportunity in order to renew my proposal that we should not use both of us the same account at their bank. It may become the source of endless and useless muddle. I think we wait until we get the *Abrechnung* [statement of account] for 1920 and then we separate.

You could put your money on the account of—let me say—Dr. Katherine Jones and leave your name to me. Or if you won't, I will have my [items][1] posts put out and transferred to the account of Dr. v. Ophuijsen (or Emden) who, I have no doubt will lend me their names. You know why I need such a "cover". I want to bring money aside, which does not come into the inheritance and will be paid to my wife on her application. Any friend likely to survive me and sure not to rob my widow will do for this, my own name would not.—

Now some news of your patients. Dr. Young was a charming companion in analysis, and a very interesting case, we made the most startling discoveries *viribus unitis* [man to man] and he felt undoubtedly relieved as shown by his behaviour when his lady-friend visited him in Vienna. Unfortunately—but perhaps his resistance had more to do with the change than he confessed—he was called to go to Innsbruck on an official errand some days ago, and so he broke off; he halted where another man perhaps would have [followed][2] hunted down the chance.

Cpt., now Major, Daly has just taken leave from me. His analysis, tedious in its details, was not so bad after all. He got down to the deepest layer of his deposits and grasped his passive attitude to his father, that is the *wish* to be castrated. His mind is still set on practising analysis himself after having served his term in India. He may become qualified in the course of some years for practical educational work, although he surely is not clever.—Dr. Bieber had come back accompanied by his wife November and is about to leave next week. The best work I ever did I could see through the structure of a true delusional Paranoia (Jealousy) down to the "hewn rock" and found some things I will relate at the Committee-meeting in Sept. To be sure I do not know if the result *can* be a definite or a lasting one.

So I have 4 free hours now and would not like to feed on *Mittelmächte-patients* having got the taste of western *valuta*.[3] The next man I expect is Dr. Frink 1st of March. If you have got people willing to live in Vienna while they are treated I am glad to accept them but not at less than 2 guineas. So this letter has outstepped its programm.

With kind regards for you and family

yours truly
Freud

1. Crossed out in the original.
2. Crossed out in the original.
3. The reference is to patients from the Central Powers, who can bring in western currency.

298

International Psycho-Analytical Press

3 February 1921
London W1

Dear Professor,

Your letters of Jan. 24 and 28th telepathically answered the one of mine that never arrived,[1] for it began by expressing my regret that the excellent institution of the *Rundbrief* had the one drawback that it made your letters fewer. My letter contained three other points, those relating to your Putnam preface, which Rank has settled satisfactorily, and a talk about Young and Mrs. Rickman. I hope that Young may still return when he gets into further difficulties, and shall be glad to learn when he does. I am of course very curious to hear which were your chief discoveries about him. In my analysis I had always suspected some infantile urinary scene, but he steadily denied the possibility of it. Some time afterwards, after his return from Russia, he resumed for a short while and one day quite calmly referred to an incident "which I think I told you of"; it was for being reprimanded by his mother for urinating on her in bed. He was one of the most interesting cases, and also personalities, I have ever studied, and I should be grateful to hear something of your views.

Mrs. Rickman is making progress, but *he* is evidently in need of more analysis and the marriage is only partly successful. I find her a very valuable and thoroughly good person, whom one likes the better one knows her, though it is hard to imagine her being sexually attractive. She is very good material. Perhaps you know that she is four months pregnant now.

I am glad to hear that the cigars arrived safely and hope that you find them to your taste. It was a risk, but worth while taking.

I am extremely grateful to you and to Anna for taking so much trouble over the translation of my book[2] and wish it were better worth your time. The arrangement of it should be altered in the next edition, and of course

I should be very glad to [for] any other suggestions; I remember one you made already, about the basis of the obsessional neurosis—perhaps this can be inserted in the German edition.[3]

I make good note of your remarks about my relation to Rank. I am afraid it is inevitable that, working as we both do under great tension and pressure, our relative perspective of importance occasionally fails to coincide, but I think I give myself more self-criticism than I do anything on his side. In any case I am so sure of my feeling for him personally, and I think also his for me, that I cannot imagine any difficulties ever arising important enough to be referred to you.

Many thanks for the Hamlet references, which I will investigate and report on. You know, of course, that Hamlet was played through the nineties in S's company, and the difficulty is to know whether he re-wrote it from Kyd's play gradually or at once. It is thought probable that he made at least some alterations before his final re-writing. I do not find that the passages you quote absolutely prove the date, for they may be written in the "historic present". Every three months or so (literally) I get an evening to devote to my own work, which at present is the re-writing of my Hamlet essay.[4] The chief thing I have discovered from recent reading is that the changes I had supposed S. had made in the old plot were made before him by Kyd, who, however, did not feel the psychological significance of them.[5] S. had a curiously *nachkriechende* [tracking] mind!

I will naturally fall in with your wishes about Lissa & Kann and will remove my money there to another bank as soon as possible. You will not, I hope, mind if this takes a couple of weeks, for I am in the middle of a transaction with them whereby they are buying shares of an oil company for me with fees paid in by a Dutch patient. I have a similar interest in Holland as yourself, for one third of all money paid into my London bank is deducted by the Government to help pay for its adventures in Mesopotamia and elsewhere.

I am to see Daly on Saturday. The Bieber analysis sounds more interesting and will be one reason more to look forward to the September meeting. You have had your way about the Congress, for it is evident that it will not take place in 1921. It would have been simpler if we had all agreed with you from the start, instead of taking months to see the wisdom of the idea.

I will bear in mind what you say about patients. Unfortunately there seems a dearth here at present, whether from the great depression in trade that came on this winter or from the effects of the newspaper campaign I do not know. But these things are very fluctuating and there may be agreeable surprises in store for us all.

Theodore Schroeder has just sent an article for the *Journal*, but I am refusing it as it is purely sociological and doesn't mention analysis, or an analytical point of view.[6]

I lead a pretty harassed life, but get great and constant happiness from my wife and daughter, who are both very well and a source of boundless joy to me and to each other. I have had exceptional fortune in my marriage.

With my kindest respects also to your family

yours always affectionately
Ernest Jones.

1. Letter missing.
2. Jones (1920b).
3. There were no changes made in the German edition of Jones (1920b).
4. For a revised version of Jones (1910a), see "A Psycho-Analytic Study of Hamlet," in Jones (1923a, pp. 1–98).
5. The theme of Thomas Kyd's *Hamlet* as having been written before Shakespeare's play is dealt with more fully in Jones (1949, pp. 106–107).
6. It is not clear which article Jones is referring to here, but in October 1920 Schroeder had published "Conservatisms, Liberalisms and Radicalisms," *Psychoanalytic Review*, 7 (1920): 376–384, containing an explanatory footnote that included a lengthy quotation from one of Jones's letters of rejection to Schroeder (p. 376). Other articles by Schroeder which appeared in the *Psychoanalytic Review* during the period 1921–1922 include "Psychology of One Pantheist," 8 (1921): 314–348, and "A 'Fearless' Opponent," 9 (1922): 84–86.

299

7 February 1921
Vienna, IX. Berggasse 19

Dear Jones,

I am so much pleased by your letter I got today that I begin answering it at once. You shall have no cause to complain that the institution of the Circulars cut short our private correspondence. Perhaps I will have no time to finish it being invited to dinner at the Friends Society this evening.[1] If so I will continue at my habitual [time][2] hour in the night. My people tease me by the promise, I will find there no other dish but "Quaker-oats".

There are so many points in your letter asking for a reply that I had to make notes and number them. 1). *Hamlet.* I agree with you that the proof produced by that Diary is far too incomplete and undirect to settle the matter. I am glad to hear you will keep your eye on it. Yet it is evident that there is much slippery ground in many of our applications from ΨA to biography and literature. I got a similar impression referring to the findings of Reitler on Leonardo (which I inserted into the 2d edition)[3] and if I must not be prepared to retract as well in my own conclusions about this great man, my proliction may be simply and solely the extreme dearth of the material. It is the danger inherent in our method of concluding from faint traces, exploiting trifling signs. The same as in criminal cases, where the murderer has forgotten to relinquish his *carte de visite* and full-address on the *"Tatort"* [scene of the crime].

2). *Your book translated.* To be sure we are glad of an opportunity to show you our friendly intentions, but dont expect the translation coming up to more than a correct reproduction of your thought in readable German. As for niceties Anna is not responsible this time, she has not yet found a good style for sober stuff, as she may develop hereafter. You ought to get the [proofs][4] manuscript in order to insert notes or change a passage here or there. By the way, what is meant by Heterophoria[5] p. 30, 9? I am so much out of modern medicine that I have no idea of it.

3). *Other translations.* Strachey has finished the beaten child[6] and will consult me on some points to-morrow. He is excellent but apt to fall into laziness if not admonished. He is ready to undertake another job which I proposed to him, to translate the 4 or 5 of my *Krankengeschichten* (Dora, Rattenmann, kl. Hans, Schreber and the Wolfmann (russian)), that would give a nice volume of our library,[7] if you agree with the plan. It is true Brill pledged himself to do this work many years ago, but as he has not done it and is not likely to do it now I would have the nerve to discard him. In the circular I will say what my opinion of his case is.

It was Strachey who directed my attention to the indubitable fact that the rendering of Ferenczi's report on my paper on Verdrängg (Review) is a complete failure and has to be remade throughout. The poor translator (Mrs. Porter?) may be excused by the fact that a misprint in the german text of the *"Jahresbericht"* changed Urverdrg [primal repression] into Unverdrgg [unrepressed] and so threw her or him out of his mind and seduced him to renounce any understanding of the matter.[8]

4). *Lissa & Kann.* I thank you heartily for your promise to withdraw your money from the account with Lissa & Kann, it will spare us a lot of complications. When you do so do not forget to claim your share of the interests. May be I felt envious of the big sums you got from your Dutch patients.

I have much leisure now (de Saussure,[9] the Strachey's, two of my old Vienna people, one German) and am still enjoying it immensily. It is quite a new sensation for me, to be idle during a month like February. On the 1st of March two Americans are expected, there are negotiations with other Swiss and American people, mostly pupils, not patients, going on. You know the situation is by no means a serious one, I could get as many patients here as there are hours in a day, but I could not charge more than 500—1000 K an hour (3 sh 6d—7 sh) and it is impossible to live from such fees.

5). *Patients.* I too am sorry that Young left. He is likely to come back but only for a short time and maybe when I will have no free hour. People like he, so well protected behind their fortress dont like to be dislocated so quickly. You were quite correct about the urination scene. He brought it up one day not as a memory but rather as a hypothesis, with no known foundation telling he supposed he had been tickled so intensely that he had to urinate, and was frowned at by the person who had provoked him, but he attributed this doing to his father not to his mother. I am not at all sure it was the case, taking into account the way the scene came up. I suspect it rather to be a screening phantasy behind which the reality is hidden. Of our discoveries several I considered as original ones may have been made during your treatment and not confessed by him. It is hard to pronounce a judgment on an unfinished case, you know how often the prospects change during the course of analysis. Yet I may mention, that his relation to his sister (2–4) had the meaning of a happy marital union (his blushing at the mention of wedding, lawful love etc.) and that a former phase (− 2 years) contained a passive attachment to his father, which unhappily got reinforced by the two homosexual seductions at 10 and 12/13 years. So the passivity or homosex. tendency constitutes the first layer. He was received into the bed of the sister as a reward for not wetting his couch. Blushing is the same flush *hyperaemia*[10] mounting to the head instead to the penis, but the female counterpart to the male act of reaction. He can go two ways to evade the male attitude brought out in erection, either regressing to urination (ejacul. praecox) or jumping to the other trail changing into a female and blushing. He is blushing in the identification with a female (his sister) he always used the important mechanism, when he had to give up an object to make up for the loss by identifying himself with the lost object. But there must be much more in it.

You will [be] highly interested in the case of Bieber. Young is superficially a typical Adler case, in fact rather a complete disproval of his silly theory.

It is late, the visit at the friends was very interesting.

Yours sincerely

with love for mother and child
Freud

1. The Quakers did much to assist Europeans, including the Viennese, in dealing with the conditions of privation in the aftermath of the war. The organization also relied on nonmembers for material and financial support; see Elfrida Vipont, *The Story of Quakerism* (London: Bannisdale Press), pp. 260–262.

2. Crossed out in the original.

3. Freud (1910c, pp. 70–72 n. 3). For a discussion of the historical problems related to this issue, see Sander Gilman, "The Rediscovery of the Body: Leonardo's First Image of Human Sexuality and Disease," in *Disease and Representation: Images of Illness from Madness to AIDS* (Ithaca: Cornell University Press, 1988), pp. 50–62.

4. Crossed out in the original.

5. Absence of parallelism between visual lines.

6. Freud (1919e).

7. The case histories were included in Freud, *Collected Papers*, 3.

8. The error was rectified in the published version (Ferenczi, 1921).

9. Raymond de Saussure (1894–1971), son of the famous linguist Ferdinand de Saussure, was analyzed by Freud and played an important role in the psychoanalytic movement in France.

10. Excess of blood in any part of the body.

300

18 February 1921
Vienna, IX. Berggasse 19

Dear Jones,

In contradiction to your last statement, you would clear out your account at Lissa & Kann after some weeks, I got the intimation that you had already transferred Fl. 1.262.67 to Lippmann, leaving me in full use of your name at the former bank, for what I am really thankful to you. I grew eager to know how I stould [stood] with L[issa] & K[ann] and began to figure[1] out my own account. As I got puzzled about it, I had to turn to yours and see what I detected. It may be a case for psychoanalysis for myself or for you.

Your +		Your −	
4/X	— 24.85	16/XII	—2753.02
10/XI	—1665.51	24/I	—2299.08
13/XII	—1545.22		5052.10
14/I	—1191.75	now	5314.87
8/2	— 887.54		5052.10
	5314.87	Fl —	262.77

So I concluded, you had taken away 1000 Fl more than belonged to your account and made up for it by taking 0.10 less. Have you? In making this enumeration I myself had overlooked the post of Fl 75 (royalties from your oil shares). Have you forgotten this too? And neglected to take your part of the interests up to the end of 1920? Now how is this to be explained? Is the correspondence of the numbers 1.262.67

and 262.77

pure chance or is the analysis correct? Did you moved by conflicting tendencies take away a big 1 and make up for it by a small 1 adding thereto all the interests? Or is the fault with Lissa & Kann who perhaps did not send me all the reports? They made some bad mistakes in the last weeks. In any case I wrote them asking to let me know, what the remainder of the account now amounts to. You should apply for the same information to Lissa & Kann and pray let me know what the true explanation is. According to my control I should be in possesion of Fl 5876.78.

I am [Fr] closing this amusing letter[s] with [by]² the kindest regards

yours sincerely
Freud

1. Freud wrote "my figure" here.
2. The bracketed letters and words are crossed out in the original.

301

The International Psycho-Analytical Press

23 February 1921
London

Dear Professor,

Many thanks for your letters of Feb. 7th and 18th. Let me answer the latter first. The true explanation is much simpler. The probability is that you have mis-read a note from Lissa & Kann (corresponding to one from them to me dated Feb. 15th) in which fl. means florins, which can be mistaken for F. I., the beginning of a thousand florins. If you compare their letter *L* with their figure *I* you will see the difference. They have made no mistake, at least in their acknowledgement of my instructions, and the correct sum was sent to Lippmann & Rosenthal, as shown by their acknowledgement to me. But I will write to Lissa & Kann, as you request, and make sure that your total is confirmed. You are right on one point, that I did not deduct my dividend of Fl. 75. In fact I never knew, till your letter came this morning, that I possessed it. I had written to ask them if a dividend was due, but they never answered, in their usual careless way. I will have this transferred when I write. The interest I did not deduct, as the smallness of the sum is not worth the complexity of the calculation.

I hope you will get Strachey to carry out the plan of translating the papers you mention. It will be very good to have them at last in English. His translation of the Beaten Child, which I am just going through, is very fair (he ranks next to Miss Hubback and Mrs. Riviere as a translator), though it needs a good deal of correction, both as regards German and English. By the way, there is a passage (S. 158, Z. 13 v.u.) about which I should like to make sure: "*darf es aber als Beweis* etc.".¹ From the context I can only think this means that the observed facts of genital excitement are a proof of the existence of the child's dim notion of normal adult sexual goals, but my wife says that grammatically the meaning Strachey has given it is the correct one, that the presence of the *Ahnung* [premonition] is a proof that the genitals have already begun their function. Then, as happens in such cases, I get doubtful and wobble between the two possibilities.

We can never employ Mrs. Porter again after her terrible translation of Ferenczi, which Miss Low corrected and I glanced through.[2] The same applies to Dr. Cole[3] and ought to apply to Bryan were he not an editor. This translation problem is driving me to despair.

You ask me about *heterophoria*, which I suppose is *Heterophorie* in German. I think it refers to disorders of ocular accommodation, functional troubles of the ciliary muscle.

What was quite new to me in your account of Young, in which I was very interested, is the connection between his shyness at marriage and lawful love and his relation to his sister. By the way, he once said to me that he would rather even have the neurosis than be told that he still has any homosexuality, even unconsciously!

My Dutch patient arrived in London without any warning last October and insisted on being treated at once, for three months, although I was full, so I took my revenge by charging her higher fees than I have ever been paid before (or after, I fear). It was a curious situation. A woman of 37, married for 14 years to a man with whom she was anaesthetic (having both the relation of a mother and a daughter towards him), fell in love with a younger man, was sexually satisfied, but could not decide for a divorce. She hesitated for two years, went to Maeder, who urged her to take what I think was a wrong solution, and then came to me, as both men were thoroughly tired of the uncertain situation. Unfortunately I was not successful in freeing her mind, chiefly because her husband interfered so constantly that we could not make much progress with the analysis. She is genuinely attached to him and he is in poor health. At the end I advised her to return to him unless she would consent to go to you for a year's analysis, which she may yet do.

Hiller tells me you wish me to write a footnote to Farnell's weak paper,[4] which of course I accepted only on political grounds. Will you tell me what kind of note you mean? He also says you told him that the author should add a note to the Staircase verses (I see my Fehlleistung; I mean Psychology below Stairs). Stanford Read,[5] the author, did write something, but it was such nonsense that I replaced it by a short note of my own. He is useless. There is no special reason for inserting the verses if you do not like them. My only interest in it was the narcissistic estimation of the female genitals, in contradistinction from two of my present patients with Penisneid who say they cannot comprehend any woman being otherwise than ashamed of her anatomy. I have had rich experience of this complex in the past few years and have learned very much about it.

Before Easter I hope to finish *Das Kind wird geschlagen, Jenseits des Lustprinzips*, and one or two further chapters of the *Vorlesungen;*[6] I think you will be satisfied with them, for they are all having the utmost care.

I am now treating an interesting case of melancholia in a man of 56, with a history extending over the greater part of 20 years. It takes the usual form of personal worthlessness because of masturbation, with fear of ruin, etc., but I cannot avoid the impression that the nucleus is a homosexuality, which is not prominent in your essay on the subject. He turned from his wife because she was anaesthetic and had a miscarriage, and I think the masturbation refers to his son of whom he is extremely fond (Penis equals boy). I should be grateful of any comments on this.

I am happy and well and trust you are the same. My daughter now weighs a stone and so is being introduced to the complexities of English weights and measures!

With our kindest regards

yours always affectionately
Ernest Jones.

P.S. Would you be so kind as to give the enclosed to Strachey, as I haven't his address.

1. See last sentence of page beginning "but we may regard it as a proof . . . " (Freud, 1919e, pp. 187), *G.W.*, 12:207.
2. Ferenczi (1921), trans. Sybil C. Porter.
3. Dr. Estelle Maude Cole, L.R.C.P., L.R.C.S. Edinburgh 1900, member of British Psycho-Analytical Society.
4. F. J. Farnell, "Eroticism as Portrayed in Literature," *Journal*, 1 (1920): 396–413. Frederick J. Farnell (b. 1885), M.D. 1908 Cornell, specialist in psychiatry, Providence, R.I.; charter member of the New York Psychoanalytic Society (12 February 1911).
5. Charles Stanford Read, M.D. 1914 London, specialist in psychological and mental disturbances, member of British Psycho-Analytical Society.
6. Freud (1919e, 1920g), and Freud (1916–17), 4th ed. 1922.

302

[postcard]

26 February 1921
Vienna

Dear Jones,

The main part of my last analysis has become disproved by L[issa] & K[ann]'s information. Now for the rest of it. Why did you leave behind your own interests? Is it generosity?

I am expecting your answer to the project of making Str. translate the five clinical cases to give another volume of the series.[1] Hope you are all right, we miss your news.

Affectionately yours
Freud

1. Freud, *Collected Papers*, 3.

303

International Journal of Psycho-Analysis

11 March 1921
London

Dear Professor,

The points in your postcard of Feb. 26th were answered in my letter of Feb. [26][1] 23rd, which crossed it. I hope you will find time to instruct me about the *Journal* questions I asked. Eder is just returning to Palestine for a few months and has not yet decided whether to stay there or return to London. His wife would like to come to you as soon as possible for analysis till the end of your summer session, and they have asked me to write to you on their behalf and find out if you can take her. They are in very serious financial straits and any money would be a hard sacrifice, so will you forgive me if I ask whether it would be possible for you to take her for one guinea instead of two. As you know, she is much the more intelligent of the two and is a valuable person, though I do not know how she is going to solve her marriage conflict. We should be grateful if you would kindly telegraph on getting this, as they wish to make arrangements before he departs for Palestine.

One of our associate members (whose name I am not sure of, since he has recently joined) wishes to come to you for analysis next autumn. He has a good appearance. I advised him to write to you now, so as [to] secure a place in good time.

I have written to Bernays asking him to send money to L & K instead of to Amsterdam, as I have no account there (except in my wife's name).

With kindest regards

yours always
E. J.[2]

1. Crossed out in the original.
2. Jones's initials are enclosed in a semicircle.

304

18 March 1921
Vienna, IX. Berggasse 19

Dear Jones,

I am answering to your letter of the 11th, which I got from Rank yesterday.

I cannot decide at the moment whether I can take Mrs. Eder, as I am expecting an answer from Dr. Sarasin (Rheinau),[1] who applied long ago and then fixed his arrival at the first of April. As soon as I know I will answer by wire, agreeing to one guinea. I am not sure that her case may be worth my time or her money, being aware of Eder's impotence etc.. It is a good occasion to remind you that Rank is as excellent as analyst as in mythology, he could take such patients whom I must decline, even English ones. He is working now with two Englishmen, one from Australia, the other from Africa and succeeds quite well. I agreed with him that he should lead on two analyses daily, not more, to keep up his touch with the source of our knowledge.

I am 'pretty full now' and busy in rectifying the booklet on *Mass-Psychology* which you know.[2] Your member who wants to come in autumn ought to write me, he will be accepted.

I enclose a dream-analysis sent by Daly from Port Said on his way to India. It is concerned with numbers and rather a good specimen. Will you accept it for the *Journal?*[3]

All the news I get about America I brought to your knowledge by the *Rundbrief* and have little to add. Frink is honest, serious and clever. You ought to write to him directly and appeal to his interest in ΨA to join us. It is puzzling, how little *"Gemeinsinn"* [community spirit] and tendency for organisation there is to be found among the better elements in America, only the robbers and pirates hunt in gangs. Brill is behaving shamefully and has to be dropped.

There are two questions in your letter of Febr. 23d which I have not answered not remembering what they are about. (Staircase verses, Farnell's paper). I think I said to Rank your authors should not indulge in mysterious hinting, that the solutions, the meaning, is evident, but should condescend to write down what these interpretations are. It is a kind of discretion of which we have no use in Analysis. As regards the passage in the "beaten child" your wife is correct in her interpretation; (here I am subject to the illusion of "déjà written"). Your translation is finished, not bad I hope yet it could be better I am afraid; not equal to the care you are spending on my papers. A more fascinating subject would have challenged the ability of the translator to a higher amount of effort.[4]

I am sorry I cannot enter into your scientific talk. Business is devouring science with all of us. Our committee-meeting will be a great recreation.

Take my best love for you, wife and daughter.

Yours truly
Freud

P.S. Pfister wrote [to]day in a kind and conciliatory mood. Your fear was not justified.

1. Philipp Sarasin (1888–1968) studied psychiatry with Kraepelin in Munich and with Bleuler at the Burghölzli in Zurich; between 1916 and 1921 he worked at the Psychiatrischen Klinik Rheinau in the canton of Zurich, after which he seriously took up Freud's work and in 1924 set up psychoanalytic practice in Basel.

2. Freud (1921c).

3. C. D. Daly, "Numbers in Dreams," *Journal*, 2 (1921): 68–70.

4. Jones (1920b), trans. Anna Freud.

305

International Journal of Psycho-Analysis

1 April 1921
London

Dear Professor,

Many thanks for your letter of the 18th. Since then the Eder question has been settled otherwise, as I indicated in a *Rundbrief*. I know she would not go to Rank—I asked her—but I may be able to find other patients for him.

Thank you for the Daly analysis which I will send on to Hiller for the *Journal*. I saw him during his passage through London and found him quite obviously improved, more balanced and grown up. But I am not too enthusiastic about his becoming an analyst.

I was very interested in your remarks about the Americans, which quite tallies with my impressions. Don't you think there is a relation between the lack of *Gemeinsinn* among the successful ones, their fondness for individualism, and just their success? I mean that the quality they lack seems to be related to pressure from without, whether national as with the Jews, Swiss and Celts, or due to other reasons for external unpopularity such as Ps-A. The native-born American feels strong enough without the help of his fellows.

I have observed like you the tendency of our young writers to make such remarks as "the interpretation is obvious", but I think the tendency is not so much one of social discretion as the fear most young writers have to write what they think may be elementary, what other people already know quite well. Is not this the reason why young lecturers are so difficult to follow? It is only assured authorities that dare to be elementary. But in any case I must check the tendency.

Will you be good enough to look through a long article by Berkeley-Hill I am sending to Hiller, from the point of view of its suitability for the *Journal*.[1] If we do not print the *"Jenseits"* there, and Rank seems very much against this, we shall need more material, and I should like to publish B-H's article. It is on anal-eroticism as a character trait among the Hindoos, especially in their religion. Although it has some good Psa comments in it, its value is more from the interesting material he adduces. It is praiseworthy that he should work so hard amid great difficulties and isolation.

I am writing to Rank about the very complicated question of your English translations and rights, and no doubt he will discuss it further with you.

We had a very enjoyable Easter in the country, and I hope you had the same. We spoke of the hope we still cherish of seeing you here some day and of showing you something of our beautiful English countryside, with also what is to be seen within easy reach at Oxford, Winchester, and so on.

Yours always affectionately
Ernest Jones.

1. O. Berkeley-Hill, "The Anal-Erotic Factor in the Religion, Philosophy, and Character of the Hindus," *Journal*, 2 (1921): 306–338.

306

12 April 1921
Vienna, IX. Berggasse 19

Dear Jones,

I know how severely you work and it is a pity I think that you spend your scarce and precious time on my translations as you did for the *"Jenseits"*. I did not know you were doing it yourself. The same feeling applies to your cares on my "Lectures" and the Collected Edition, things quite out of time and not important enough to interfere with your own scientific work. I am glad you take a holiday sometimes but the general impression is, you bear a too heavy burden and should leave minor things to other people. We are looking for translators here, I besides have made up my mind to employ the Americans coming here in the same way as Strachey, there are four of them noted down for Oktober (Polon, Oberndorf, Kardiner and Blumgart).[1] Yet the first attempt made with M. Meyer failed and Frink is too big a man for such work.[2] Frink is *very* good and you ought to write him.

Notwithstanding your praise of Miss H[ubback] I prefer James Strachey should undertake the *"Massenpsychologie und Ich-Analyse"*, as he is near me and I can collaborate with him. Last week I examined the first five lectures of the French translation done by Jankelevitch at Paris.[3] It was excellent and I had to correct only 2 mistakes in 109 pages.

I am very busy and begin to feel tired at last. No half hour left. Will you think of sending patients to Ferenczi, who now experiences how impossible it is to live on home patients?

The article of Berkeley-Hill is interesting enough for publication, although it shows that he can do no more than apply what he has got out of his reading. There is another article by Farnell, which struck me as quite worthless and which is considered simply disgracing by all our authorities here (my daughter, Hiller and Strachey). Could you not wipe it out without any remorse?

The Americans are really "too bad". I would not give a judgment why they are so without better opportunity for observation, I think competition is much more pungent with them, not succeeding means civil death to every one, and they have no private resources apart from their profession, no hobby, games, love or other interests of a cultured person. And success means money. Can an American live in opposition to the public opinion, as we are prepared to do?

On Sunday, April 3d, my son Martin became father to a nice, well developed boy, whose name will be Anton. I expect a girl in the course of summer from my daughter-in law at Berlin, the wife of Ernst.[4]

I hope your family is all right. Your wife seems to be a great help for you. Impossible to work so hard when you feed on adventures.

Did Lissa & Kann notify you the taking out of the Fl 75? I heard nothing about it.

Coriat's pamphlet on Lady Macbeth[5] which I got from him, is a sign of no talent and no honesty.

Affectionately yours

with kindest regards
Freud

1. The first three of these American physicians to be analyzed by Freud graduated from Cornell University Medical College: Albert Polon (b. 1881), M.D. 1910, was a neurologist; Clarence P. Oberndorf (b. 1882), M.D. 1906, was a psychiatrist; and Abram Kardiner (b. 1891), M.D. 1917, was a general practitioner. Leonard Blumgart (b. 1880), M.D. 1903 Columbia, was a psychiatrist. Oberndorf was also a charter member of the New York Psychoanalytic Society (12 February 1911), and by 1922 the others were established members in the society. For personal accounts of this period, see Oberndorf's "Recollections of Psychoanalysis in Vienna, 1921–1922," in his *History of Psychoanal-*

ysis in America (New York: Grune and Stratton, 1953), pp. 138–151, and Kardiner's *My Analysis with Freud: Reminiscences* (New York: Norton, 1977).

2. Munroe A. Meyer (b. 1892), M.D. 1916 Cornell, member of the New York Psychoanalytic Society, went to Vienna (as did Frink) in the autumn of 1919 to be analyzed by Freud.

3. Freud (1916–17), *Introduction à la psychanalyse*, trans. S. Jankélévich (Paris: Payot, 1922).

4. But Ernst and Lucie Freud had three boys: Stephen Gabriel (b. 1921), Lucian Michael (b. 1922), and Clement Raphael (b. 1924).

5. Isador H. Coriat, *The Hysteria of Lady Macbeth* (Boston: Four Seas, 1920).

307

6 May 1921
The Plat, Elsted

Dear Professor,

I have made three inquiries as to which exact day in May your birthday is,[1] but have had to [no] answer to them. Today comes Abraham's letter which shews that the birthday must be in the first week of May. So, although a little late, please allow me to add my warmest congratulations to the others. I hope that the bust, upon which we agreed after anxious discussion, will serve to remind you in a visible form of our devotion to you.[2] I wish I could add such a beautiful present as Abraham did in the way of glowing local news of progress, but I have to admit that Berlin is much in advance of London, though there is no reason to complain of the situation in England.

Since my illness I have had to restrict my correspondence to the most urgent matters, chiefly with Hiller, and I have not yet answered your letter of April 12th.

I inquired of Lissa & Kann about the 75 fl. They had withdrawn them from my account, but forgotten to send them on to my Amsterdam one.

The Farnell article is certainly poor, and I accepted it only because he is one of the oldest-standing analysts in America. I adopted the policy of accepting for the first year or two all articles from well-known American analysts until we should feel strong enough to reject them and risk giving offense, but their superficiality and muddle-headedness undoubtedly try one's patience. I am afraid it would be costly now to omit Farnell's article, as it is already corrected in the Umbruch, but please do if you think fit and give the instructions to Hiller.[3]

I was alarmed at your remark about employing American translators, and would give a great deal to be able to persuade you of how rare it is for anyone to be able to write correct English, of course even rarer in America than in England. Nor is translating a minor matter, for it is by far the chief part of the work for the *Journal* and Library.

As for the translation of your own works, that is a subject, I think the only one, on which I really disagree with you. So far from its being unimportant, as you say, I think it is much the most important task that any of us here can accomplish. No other reading in Psa can ever replace your works, and a garbled, incorrect, and vulgarly written version is almost as bad as nothing. It is all very well for you to say that I should not concern myself in the matter, but all the educated people here hold me directly responsible. I have no answer when I am asked, as I have been countless times: "Why don't you tell Prof. Freud about his English translations? It can't be possible that he does not care".

A great chance was lost to the Press when first the American, and then the English, rights of the *Vorlesungen* were sold to unscrupulous people. I discovered afterwards that Unwin, who like all publishers thinks of nothing but money, was quite prepared to reprint the Bernays version, but fortunately I had made it a condition that his translation was first to be revised to my satisfaction. It was the first *chance* I had had of seeing a book of yours in decent English and naturally I did not neglect it. So now a committee consisting of Mr. Flugel, Mrs. Riviere and myself are re-translating the book, Mrs. Riviere doing the greater part of the work. I understand that Strachey is doing the *Massenpsychologie* and also the *Krankengeschichten*, and so long as I have a chance to revise his work I am satisfied with the arrangement.

You will be glad to hear that our combined efforts have brought James McCann to his knees, as you will see from the accompanying letter from his London agent, Curtis Brown; I enclose also a copy of my reply. Will you please send them back to me sometime.

You may remember the name of Tansley from a paragraph in the Notes in the 3rd number of the *Journal*;[4] perhaps you have also seen my review of his book *"The New Psychology"*,[5] which deals positively with Psa. He has written a very good letter to me asking me to approach you on the matter of your analysing him for four months from next March. I know him personally and can strongly recommend him. I am answering his letter by saying that I had written to you about him and advising him to write to you direct, also to try if possible to secure a longer period.

Did your wife receive the photograph we sent her a couple of weeks ago?

With my deepest wishes for many happy returns of your birthday,

yours always affectionately
Ernest Jones.

1. Freud was born 6 May 1856.

2. A bust of Freud by the Viennese sculptor Paul Königsberger was presented to Freud by Eitingon on behalf of the members of the Secret Committee; see Jones (1957a, p. 25; 1957b, p. 26).

3. The article was not published in the *Journal*.

4. Professor A. G. Tansley (1871–1955), British botanist and plant ecologist, who took

a great interest in Freud's ideas. On 13 October 1920 Tansley gave an address, "Freud's Theory of Sex Considered from the Biological Standpoint," before the British Society for the Study of Sex-Psychology; see *Journal*, 1 (1920): 341.

5. Jones (1920c).

308

8 May 1921
Vienna, IX. Berggasse 19

Dear Jones,

The news of your sickness affected all of us deeply. I could not help feeling that you had no right to fall sick as we could not miss you nor replace you by another. The first sign of your recovery came in the shape of an English journal of art, demonstrating one Moses who clutched his beard with his hand, a subject which could have interested no other man in the United Kingdom but you. You know—a contribution to Rank's myths of the birth of heroes[1]—that this Moses is an illegitimate child of mine, not acknowledged by his begetter; should I be right after all?[2]

On May 6th Eitingon was here in Vienna and presented me a bronce bust of a person very well known and yet not often seen by me by a young Berlin sculptor Königsberger. I had given him some sittings in July last, believing in a naive way that E. wanted the [portrait][3] effigy for himself and not suspecting that it should become my house-mate as I was the possessor of the original. Yet here it is. Besides I got flowers, sweets, books, telegrams etc. to provoke the envy of a primadonna. I am glad you had no part in it and hope your example will be followed by the others if more returns of the day are unavoidable. The emphasizing of my birthday warns me how old I have become and by getting presents one is hopelessly thrown back into the attitude of a child. Yet the two go well together.

The Verlag is doing good work in German books, while the English Press still goes at a very slow pace. Some sheets of my *Massenpsych & Ich-Analyse* have been printed, I expect the whole thing to come out in a few weeks more. Your translation (treatment of the neuroses) is the next book to appear.[4] I am doing too much work and feel tired accordingly. From Oct. next I may restrict the number of my cases to 6 or 7 instead of 9.

As you do not mention wife and daughter I trust they are all right. With kind love to all three of you

Yours
Freud

1. Rank (1909).
2. Freud (1914b) was published anonymously.
3. Crossed out in the original.
4. Jones (1920b).

309

11 May 1921
The Plat, Elsted

Dear Professor,

I enclose a letter from Silberer, with my answer, which I hope you will find correct. You will see that if he sends another letter I have left a loop-hole by having to submit it to you. Would you please return them to me some time.

I should be glad to know if you have anything to say about Bowen and Philadelphia.

Unwin wrote me a letter containing similar remarks from James McCann as those from Curtis Brown. You will be interested to see what Brill wrote to Unwin in the enclosed copy.

I sent you a copy of the *Burlington Magazine* containing a reproduction of an early Moses statue, as I expect that you retain some interest in this subject.[1]

With kindest regards

yours affectionately
Ernest Jones.

1. See letter 499.

310

19 May 1921
Vienna, IX. Berggasse 19

Dear Jones,

I am glad you feel allright again. It was an unpleasant thought.

Had I waited one day more, my last letter of the 10th[1] would have shown another face. So I have to thank you too for your kind wishes. The 6th of May is the day. The bust looks rather stern and imposing, it is much admired by people who understand.

Nothing more about the Farnell paper, as you did so intentionally. As for American translators I thought of engaging some of the analysts who have announced themselves in autumn (Oberndorf, Blumgart, Kardiner, Polon), all of them Germans that is to say Jews; in every case no translation can be printed unless approved by you. The same holds good for Strachey who now is doing the *Massenpsych* and the Wolf-man, his wife the Dora and the Rat-man. I expect the *Massenpsych* will come out in June. Of the *"Jenseits"* I prepared the 2d edition, adding some sentences and a longer passage on the Platonic Theory of Sex sent to me by H. Gomperz (the son of the old famous Th. G.).[2] The new proofs will be forwarded to you shortly.

As for [that][3] those rascals McCann-Tridon I can only admire your energy and diplomacy. I expect we will not get out of them $50. You will have learned from the *Rundbrief* that I had written the publisher a kind letter some weeks before your action, asking only for a copy of the book. I got neither the book nor an answer a good illustration to that passage in his answer where he complains of your harsh handling.

Boni and Liveright, who printed the Bernays translation seem to be no better men. They confessed only to about 600 copies of the book and tried to cheat me for $2019. My nephew got the money from them by paying $100 to a lawyer. More than 4500 copies had been sold in the first year.[4]

The Fl. 75 still figure in Lissa & Kann's *Rekening-Courant* [statement] of April 1st. So they did not take them out.

If you lay so great stress on the translation of my books I cannot but give in to you, but I continue to regret the amount of work it means for you and could be spent better on original research.

A new production by Jung of enormous size 700 pages thick, inscribed *"Psychologische Typen"* the work of a snob and a mystic, no new idea in it.[5] He clings to that escape he had detected in 1913, denying objective truth in psychology on account of the personal differences in the observer's constitution. No great harm to be expected from this quarter.

I got Tansley's letter and answered it in a favouring sense. If all the people who did apply would come I could give 12–14 hours of analysis [a daily][6] [a] day. Instead of I am urged by my friends to restrict my daily task to 6–7 hours. I feel rather tired and worn out by family cares and the general situation.

Hoping to hear more from you personally before we meet

Yours affectionately
Freud

1. Freud likely means letter 308.
2. Freud (1920g, p. 58 n. 1).
3. Crossed out in the original.
4. Freud (1916–17).
5. Jung (1921).
6. Crossed out in the original.

311

International Psycho-Analytical Association
Central Executive

21 May 1921
London

Dear Professor,

Your very kind letter of the 8th came safely, and I thank you for it. I do not think my indisposition has delayed anything in the Press, etc., so I do not feel guilty about it.

In my letter to Frink, which you may have seen, I brought up the matter of American Associate Editors. Yesterday a letter came from Stern enclosing a report of the N. Y. Society in which it is stated that on Feb. 16th that Society "appointed" Frink, Brill, and Farnell as the triumvirate for our *Journal*. Any comments from me are superfluous, and before sending the Report to press I want to know your opinion and decision. I need hardly say that in my request to Brill last October I made it plain that the opinion of the N.Y. Society was only *one* of the factors which you would have to take into consideration in choosing editors, although of course an important one; in fact I intimated that his own opinion was an even more important factor.

I am glad to say that wife and child are blooming like the spring. The child gives promise of being pretty, taking after my wife quite distinctly, and has a wonderful Jewish smile with twinkling eyes.

Yours very affectionately
Ernest Jones.

312

29 May 1921
Vienna, IX. Berggasse 19

Dear Jones,

I herewith enclose the letter I got from Brill after 6 months waiting and imploring, but I did not get it before I wrote in the most plain and brutal way. You will judge for yourself, how deeply he has deteriorated. I intend no answer for the present. Send the letter back after having taken an extract of it.

To be sure the nonsense about the appointing of subeditors is his doing. Let me propose to you, that you should answer Stern that there is a misunderstanding prevalent, that we can give the NY Society no other rights than what proved satisfactory to the London one, that we were glad to accept Frink and Brill, but propose to replace Farnell by Blumgart or Oberndorf, as he (the president) may choose. I had talked over this matter with Frink.

Happy to hear your family is thriving so well and you restored to good health. I am worn out by the excessive heat here.

Affectionately yours
Freud

313

[postcard]

International Journal of Psycho-Analysis

31 May 1921
London W1

Dear Professor,
I hear from Frink that Brill has written to you, but do not know in what tone. If you are in hesitation about accepting him, I should give my vote in his favour, but I should not be surprised if you decide otherwise. I hope that you will substitute Oberndorf for Farnell.[1]

Yours
Ernest Jones.

1. In the end, Brill, Frink, and Oberndorf were listed on the title page of the *Journal*, 2 (1921).

314

International Journal of Psycho-Analysis

6 June 1921
London

Dear Professor,
I will write and make the matter quite plain to Stern, but I must first ask you to make clearer one passage in your letter, where I am to tell Stern that it is proposed "to replace Farnell by Blumgart or Oberndorf as he (the President) may choose". In the *Rundbrief* it says *"ihm vorschlagen"* (i.e. Stern). Whom do you wish to have the choice, Stern, Oberndorf, or the president, who is at present a certain Ames?[1] Or again the Society? I am very sorry to trouble you again in this way, but it is important to avoid

misunderstandings with such touchy people and I want to do exactly what you wish.

May I at the same time ask for help on a few points in the *Jenseits* which I am not sure on? I quote of course from the first edition, for the second has not yet come. (1) S. 49. Z.11 v.u.. *"von Sexualtrieben"*.[2] I suppose this is not a misprint for *"ichtrieben"*? (2) S.52. Last line but one of the footnote. Is *"zeigen"* a misprint for *"zeugen"*?[3] (3) S.57 Last line but two in the footnote. *"treten, der"*. What exactly does *"der"* relate to?[4] (4) S.58. Z.7. Is *"all dies"* general or does it refer to the preceding sentence?[5] I have a copy of this letter, so that your answers can be short, simply numbered.

The proofs of the *Massenpsychologie* that have reached me begin only at Spalte 24 and some are missing even after that, so that it would be foolish of me to comment on it until I can see a complete copy. I will only say that your exposition of suggestion as a *Teilerscheinung des hypnotischen Zustandes "schlägt ein"*.[6]

Brill's lack of insight into himself and also into his relation with the outer world is astounding, almost psychotic. His initial remark about his translations shews that your diagnosis of the aetiology was the right one. About the editorship: you will remember that you and the congress accepted Stern's proposal to ascertain the views of the N.Y. group before you came to a definite decision. Then you wrote and invited Brill to be one of the editors. To reconcile the two things I wrote an official letter about the Congress to Brill, explained what had happened, expressed the hope that he would accept and that he would use his influence to choose the two others according to his own wishes, and made the practical suggestion that he should do as I did in London, first choose and then use one's influence to get the Society to ratify the names put forward. This is what in Brill's mind became "Jones taking an entirely different view"! In any case it is an extraordinary reason for not answering your letters that he had to wait till the society had discussed the matter (and then three months more).

His remark "From all that I gathered I did not feel that I would be missed" is a curious comment on my extravagent flattery of his importance to us, and shews again the impossibility of dealing with narcissism. By the way, no doubt you noticed the Verschreiben of the word "conscious", which I have underlined.

Well, even if he does little for us, which seems probable, I am glad that you decided to accept his name for the *Journal*, in consideration of all he has done in the past, and also that you refuse Farnell after his exhibition in our present number.[7]

I know how you feel in the last month of the year's work and am sure you must be looking forward to a holiday. About the invitation to Edinburgh in September, I am torn between two considerations. On the personal side it would be very delightful to see you in England, and you would be warmly welcomed, not only by our own circle. But at the same time I honestly think that the occasion is not honourable enough to warrant an interference with a much-needed holiday. You would be one speaker amongst others at a congress, whereas you ought to be invited to deliver one or more special lectures at a University and do not doubt that that invitation will come before long.

I am very well and working like a nigger.

With affectionate regards,

yours always
Ernest Jones.

P.S. On Spalte 31, in the middle, Boris Sidis has his name misprinted.[8]

1. Adolph Stern (b. 1878), M.D. 1903 Columbia, specialist in neurology and psychiatry, first of the American analysts to go to Vienna (summer 1919) to be analyzed by Freud. Thaddeus H. Ames (b. 1885), M.D. 1907 University of Michigan, was a neurologist, deeply interested in religion and pastoral psychiatry, and an early supporter of Jung in America (1912). In 1921 he was president of the New York Psychoanalytic Society, but resigned from the society entirely in March 1922.

2. Freud (1920g, p. 52), G.W., 13:56.

3. Freud (1920g, p. 56), G.W., 13:61.

4. Freud (1920g, pp. 60–61 n. 1), G.W., 13:66 n. 1.

5. Freud (1920g, p. 62), G.W., 13:67.

6. See Freud (1921c, p. 128 n. 1), G.W., 13:143 n. 1, where he states that "suggestion is a partial manifestation of the state of hypnosis." For Jones this "hits the nail on the head" (schlägt ein).

7. See note 3 to letter 307.

8. Boris Sidis, whose name is spelled correctly in the published version, is mentioned in Freud (1921c, p. 119), G.W., 13:131.

315

9 June 1921
Vienna, IX. Berggasse 19

Dear Jones,

Jenseits I. p. 49 *"Von Sexualtrieben"*—allright as shown by the *"natür-lich"* in the sentence before.[1]

II. Note *"Zeugen"* is better than *"zeigen"*. You are right, yet the latter is possible too *"zeugen"* would be rather construed by *"für"*.[2]

III. *"Der"* relates to the last noun in the sentence *"Todestrieb"*, as it ought to do.[3]

IV. *"all dies"* relates to *"worüber . . ."* not to the foregoing, is equivalent to *"alles"*.[4]

("Boris Sidis" belongs to the *Mass* Ψ I trust, where the misprint has found correction.)

I have since sent you the notes to the second edition, which itself has not yet appeared. Why they did not send you the *Masspsych* from the very beginning I do not know. Perhaps it got lost.

As for the Americans: You know the NY Society did give the choice to the president, so we have to fall in with them and make him (the president) decide, where we leave it open. I think you might act in my name as you like. If you prefer Oberndorf (or Blumgart) alone to an alternative, say so and I will have endorsed it.

Both of them have fixed themselves to come here Oct. 1st. It is hard work with these analysts. I struggled 6 weeks with Frink, who no doubt is the best man among them, till I got hold of him.

I completely agree with your judgment on Brill, but it is all right now.

I am glad you sympathize with my decision about the invitation to Edinburgh. Yet I would not have been one speaker amongst others. Another man would have said he was too nervous to speak on a Congress, I know I simply will not do so.

I cannot deny I feel tired but I rejoice in your freshness and activity.

Cordially yours
Freud

1. Freud may have reconsidered this later, as his answer does not quite coincide with the published version; see Freud (1920g, p. 52), *G.W.*, 13:56. *Von* and *natürlich* are written in Gothic script in the original.

2. "Als was sie zeigen"; see Freud (1920g, p. 56), *G.W.*, 13:61. *Für* is in Gothic script.

3. "Zum 'Todestrieb' treten, der"; see Freud (1920g, pp. 60–61 n. 1), *G.W.*, 13:66 n. 1. *Der* and *Todestrieb* are in Gothic script.

4. "Aber all dies, worüber das Lustprinzip"; see Freud (1920g, p. 62), *G.W.*, 13:67. *Worüber* and *alles* are in Gothic script.

316

15 June 1921
69 Portland Court, London

Dear Professor,

I have just received a detailed letter from Mrs. Riviere which seems to clear up all the questions very satisfactorily, and I am writing to her accepting all her proposals without reserve. Incidentally it was plain from her letter that I was right in suspecting that your accusations (of cutting down her position and functions, of not letting her correct my revision of her Ms, etc.) were pure misapprehension; there was nothing but the fear that I might do so in the future. I hope now, however, that we shall prove to each other by experience that we can trust each other fully. I hope also that this happy ending will have a beneficial effect on the rest of her analysis and that you will be able to start on your holidays with the feeling of having accomplished a difficult task successfully.

I have been thinking over your suggestion of a little time ago that I should find some official position for Rickman and Strachey. The former has no great gifts for literary work, but it might be well, if I offered him a Co-Directorship with myself of the Press. What do you think of this? The Strachey problem is not so easy to solve at the moment, but it appears less urgent. He has done no work for the *Journal*, or very little, is not even a member of any society, and will probably, so he writes me, not be in England next winter. So perhaps this can wait for further developments.

I am sure you are impatiently waiting for the end of this session's laborious work, and I warmly hope that you will get every benefit from the change and leisure awaiting you.

With my kindest regards

yours always
Ernest Jones.

317

6 July 1921
69 Portland Court, London

Dear Professor,

The Brill mystery is at last solved and his silence of six months accounted for. He has had a bad attack of his old trouble, and is hurt that you and I do not love him enough. I have done my best to calm him down, but these delays are very serious in many respects. He still does not say if he will join in the symposium on psychiatry, so I cannot yet invite Rorschach. I have written to Rank news of the money in Munich and also a contract I am making with Allen & Unwin, so will not repeat this.

I hope that next year's Congress will be in Berlin, and that you will not accept the invitation they have sent to us to lecture there this year. It sounds too much like a staring at lions to please our style, and the Congress next year should give them the advertisement they want. I have written thanking them, but accepting only conditionally.

Are your holiday plans beginning to mature? We hope greatly that you and Anna will be able to come to England for a week or two after the Congress. Should we not arrange about the date of the previous committee meeting? Would it be advantageous to hold this on the German side of the frontier?

yours always affectionately
Ernest Jones.

318

14 July 1921
Vienna, IX. Berggasse 19

Dear Jones,

On the eve of my departure for Badgastein (Villa Wassing) I got hold of the *Mass* Ψ, the first copy of which I am sending you by the means of Mr. Strachey. He is bringing the English translation of the same with him and I beg you to be kind to him and his wife.

I could only go through the first half of the translation shortly before I broke off, the latter is the more difficult one. I found it absolutely correct, free of all misunderstandings and I hope the rest will prove the same. I am no judge of the style, it seemed to me plain and easy, your claims for elegance may be stronger than mine. In any case, dont be too hard on him, it is not easy for us to get efficient translators. Even Miss Hubback whom you praise so much, could not avoid errors and serious misconceptions as Hiller and Anna pointed out to me.

Strachey and his wife might become very useful to you. They are exceptionally nice and cultured people though somewhat queer and after having gone through their analysis (what is not yet the case) they may become serious analysts. Perhaps he is the man to assist you in editing the *Journal* and both would be fit to take an active part in the management of the Brunswick place.[1] This is left to their further development, for the moment their conviction is not yet completely assured. I have to warn you that they are rather sensitive and critical. But they are not to be rebuked, they are good stuff.

I will write you more from Gastein and perhaps expect a letter of yours. The circular correspondence has evidently slain the private one.

With kind love for you and your ladies

yours as ever
Freud

1. See note 2 to letter 294.

319

British Psycho-Analytical Society

22 July 1921
London

Dear Professor,

First my best thanks for your letter and the copy of *Massenpsychologie* which I am devouring with the greatest interest. If I can find [time] to write a paper for the Edinburgh meeting of the Brit. Assoc., which is very doubtful, it will be an exposition of your book, entitled "The Psychology of the Herd Instinct".[1] It is, by the way, curious how steadily Le Bon has deteriorated in the 25 years since he wrote his interesting work.[2] Each successive one has been weaker, till he is now a pure journalist. I enclose a review of his last production,[3] a harsh one, it is true. I also enclose a cutting that will interest you in regard to the *Jenseits*.

The Stracheys came to lunch here yesterday. They have greatly improved since their analysis and should prove to be valuable people. I will of course bear well in mind what you say in regard to them. I could give them enough work to keep them fully occupied, but have a hesitation about overdoing this, as I imagine they also want to earn a livelihood and do work that is remunerative. Later on, when they settle in London, I hope to be able to help them in this respect. In the meantime I gave them an interesting book to review (a Psa of Strindberg).[4] They are both very attractive and cultured people, and I expect to see something of them still this month.

I had most satisfactory interviews with Frink, and we have arranged all manner of details about the *Journal*. He seems very easy to work with, and if only he keeps his promises we shall get great assistance. I suggested that he should be, practically if not officially, the chief American editor, acting as a centre to arrange the abstracting and reviewing of the American literature. I am keeping in good touch with America, and have had the latest news from some Americans passing through London, people interested in Psa. But all this takes time, as does everything else. If only H. G. Well's Time Machine were available I should find things more satisfactory. I once had a slight impotency complex on the subject of insufficient "time", and must take care it does not return under very real provocation!

I was very interested in your re-grouping of the *Sammlung* articles, and wonder if it is definitive or whether I may make a couple of suggestions from the point of view of the English reading public. The main one is this: that there exists here, for some reason that I do not know, a strong association between small books and dilettantism, as though the larger the book the more important its contents; it is a very infantile mode of estimation but it exists widely. I cannot imagine an Englishman issuing such weighty matter as there is in the *Jenseits* and the *Massenpsychologie* in brochure form; it would be either an essay in a journal or else expanded to a larger book. Thus I cannot see why the *Krankengeschichten* should be issued in two small volumes instead of in one respectably large one (still 200 pages less than my *Papers*); no one would ever want to buy one half of them. But perhaps I should begin by recalling to your memory your division, which was: 1. *Einleitungsarbeiten*. S. 194. 2. *Theoretische Abhandlungen*. 287. 3. *Krankengeschichten*. 280. 4. Ditto. 262. 5. *Technik und Metapsychologie*. 260. 6. *Angewandte Psychoanalyse*. 185. Will you allow me to suggest the following modifications? To take two small articles on technique from the *Einleitungsarbeiten* and transfer them to the other technical articles, which could thus be all read chronologically together. To join the *Metapsychologie* with the *angewandte Psa*, for it is largely Psa applied to pure psychology, and the technical to the introductory. The result would then run: 1. Introductory and Technique (which everybody would want to read first). 318. 2. Theoretical. 287. 3. *Krankengeschichten*. 542. 4. Applied and Metapsychology. 321. I shall be anxious to get your opinion about these points. As you know, the work of producing them in worthy form lies near to my heart.[5]

There are endless scientific matters I should like to ask you about, but I will spare you, especially when you are just beginning your sorely needed rest, which I hope you will greatly enjoy. Have you Anna with you? If so, please give her my kindest regards.

As you will guess, I am still in a working mood. Holidays begin with me only on August 13th. We shall probably stay at Elsted until we go to Germany in the middle of September, as I cannot aford the cost of travelling to Edinburgh (if I can write a paper, Flügel will read it there).[6]

With my very kindest regards

yours truly and affectionately
Ernest Jones.

1. The article was not written.
2. Gustave Le Bon (1841–1931), medically trained social psychologist, best known for his *Psychologie des foules* (1895), which is extensively quoted in Freud (1921c, pp. 72–81).
3. Possibly the review of Gustave Le Bon, *The World in Revolt: A Psychological Study of Our Times*, trans. Bernard Miall (London: T. Fisher Unwin, 1921), *New Statesman*, 18 June 1921, p. 310.
4. Strachey reviewed three books on Strindberg in the *Journal*, 4 (1923): 231–233, and *Zeitschrift*, 9 (1923): 107–109: these were Alfred Storch, *August Strindberg im Lichte seiner Selbstbiographie: eine psychopathologische Persönlichkeitsanalyse* (Munich: Bergmann, 1921); Axel Johann Uppvall, *August Strindberg: A Psychoanalytic Study with Special Reference to the Oedipus Complex* (Boston: Badger, 1921); and Karl Jaspers, *Strindberg und Van Gogh: Versuch einer pathographischen Analyse unter vergleichender Heranziehung von Swedenborg und Hölderlin* (Leipzig: Bircher, 1922).

5. Jones's suggestion refers to the structure of the first four volumes of Freud, *Collected Papers*.

6. Jones and Flügel did not attend the meetings of the British Medical Association, 8–14 September 1921 in Edinburgh, according to *British Medical Journal*, 2 (1921): 456–459.

320

27 July 1921
Badgastein, V. Wassing

Dear Jones,

I greatly enjoyed the first of your letters which followed me to this place. I am glad you liked the Strachey's, you will see we can get the best people for ΨA if we only drop the professional condition soon enough, for it will show unavoidable in the long run.

As for Le Bon I know nothing of his later career; it is remarkable that a man who could write so clever a book should have gone down so deeply. The review you enclosed and which I return should not weigh so much, just consider his appreciation of our work!

Frink is a very nice boy. He means what he says and more. If he will prove steady depends on a complete change in his private affairs he is now planning, the success of which is not yet assured. It may interest you to learn that Jelliffe is in Europe, he saw Pfister who announced him to me. Pf.[ister] writes that he is on bad terms with Jung who reproaches him for being a "Freudian". Now Frink is very sharp on Jelliffe, he seems to be the only man he hates. Jllf. [Jelliffe] is described by whom [him] as absolutely reckless, amoral and personally dangerous.

As for the arrangement of the *Sammlung* I lay not stress on any shape and am willing to leave the matter to you and Rank, who both seem so very much interested in it. Allow me only to bring up two or three remarks. First that you must overaccentuate your English habits and whims as the fact of my being a foreigner cannot be denied or concealed. Nor should it be done. I think an element of opposition and innovation will do some good to your chinese rigidity. Secondly I do not think the introductory papers and the technical ones will go together. The first are mostly superannuated while the technique is still up to date. The readers should not be induced to neglect the historical moment. My third point is I would greatly prefer to appear before English readers first as the author of the *Krankengeschichten*, if this can be done. Now Strachey's have nearly finished three of them, perhaps this was the motive for dividing this subject into two volumes. I will send your letter to Rank and please settle it with him.

I have come over to your judgment on the importance of having my papers translated. I see it from literature.

I have a good time here, Anna is at Aussee with my wife and our grand-child from Hamburg 7 years old.[1] Middle of next month all of us meet in Seefeld, Tirol.

It is evident you are sacrificing your personal work to organization and propaganda, the same as Rank is doing for the Verlag. But your excellent reviews in the *Journal* are sure to gain for you the most influential position in English psychology. I hope our week in Sept. will be full of interest for all of us.

With kind love to you and your wife

yours for ever
Freud

1. Ernst Wolfgang (b. 1914), son of Max and Sophie Freud Halberstadt.

321

The International Psycho-Analytical Press

10 August 1921
London

Dear Professor,

Many thanks for your letter of July 27th. I was very glad to hear from Rank that you have already benefitted from your holiday and hope you will get great enjoyment from it.

A letter came from Brill yesterday, *mirabile dictu*, saying that he was leaving on the 23rd for a visit to you and me. I trust this repentance will not be a fleeting one and am sure you will exact conditions before accepting it completely. It comes too late for him to play the chief American part as regards the *Journal*, for, following your instructions, I arranged with Frink that all the editorial work there should pass through his hands. At the same time I am not altogether surprised by the news and am hopeful of good results from it. I am trying to catch Brill on his arrival, for I may have left for Germany before he would be sailing again, which reminds me: could you please let me know the exact date of the Hildesheim meeting,[1] for travelling arrangements, tickets, visas etc. have to be arranged extraordinarily far in advance nowadays. Will it be from Sept. 23rd to 30th? I want to be back in England on Oct. 1st if possible.

I enclose a preface for the translation of the *Jenseits* which I hope you will approve of.[2]

The matter of the American editorship has been very tedious and I will describe it in the *Rundbrief*,[3] but as it is now satisfactorily settled I will not bore you with it further.

Mrs. Riviere consulted me about going to you in January and I advised her to write to you. I fear her motives are not of the best, but we can discuss the matter in September if you wish.

The Stracheys have made an excellent list of words for our projected Glossary and we have discussed the suitable translations of some of them. I shall probably consult you about a few of the most difficult terms; then I propose to publish it in the *Journal* at length with explanatory paragraphs after some of the terms.[4] It will be of great value for translators and will help standardisation. By the way it was hardly fair to judge Miss Hubback's translation from that one example, for the work was done sketchily some five years ago with no thought of publication and has never been even read through again; she has greatly improved since that time.[5] I sent it to Hiller to revise as he wanted some practice in translating and I thought this would be the easiest way, being helped both by having a preliminary sketch and also by having access to Rank.

Your wish that the first volume to be published should be the *Krankengeschichten* will of course be followed, though I suppose it will not be numbered the first.[6] I understand that you do not approve of taking the two Elementary Papers on Technique out of their position in the Introductory Papers and joining them to the older technical ones, but I am not clear whether you mean also that the two series cannot be bound in the same volume. To print the Introductory Papers alone in one volume [is][7] would be making a very small book, and I do not know any other series that would go better with them than the Technique ones; they could of course be separately labelled and clearly distinguished Part I. and Part II. I shall remember your point about our Chinese rigidity, but, as in so many matters, I have to contend with pressure from both sides, so have to strike a balance.

I have only rapidly skimmed through the *Massenpsychologie* as yet, both because I want to finish a lot of work before leaving for the country at the end of this week and also because I want to read it through carefully at leisure in the country to see if it will stimulate me with ideas for a paper on this subject.

I have just finished re-writing my Madonna Essay and have made some interesting new additions.[8] Doing so has brought me some new ideas, which I believe to be important, concerning the psychological distinction between Christianity and older religions. Perhaps I shall be able next year to find time to work them up in a paper.

My wife is very well and is three months on the way to bringing another life into the world.[9]

With kindest regards,

Yours very affectionately,
Ernest Jones.

1. A meeting of the Secret Committee; see Jones (1957a, pp. 80–81; 1957b, pp. 84–85), and Grosskurth (1991, pp. 19–23).

2. Jones (1922a).

3. In his *Rundbrief* of 12 August 1921, Jones summarized the issue of selecting the three American editors for the *Journal* (Sigmund Freud Copyrights, Wivenhoe; and Rank Collection, Butler Library, Columbia University). In the end, Farnell was dropped (see letter 313), and Brill, Frink, and Oberndorf were listed on the title page of the *Journal*, 2 (1921).

4. Jones (1924a).

5. Freud (1920g), trans. C. J. M. Hubback.

6. Freud, *Collected Papers*, 3.

7. Crossed out in the original. The words "would be" are handwritten in an otherwise typed letter.

8. Jones (1914a); see Jones (1923a, pp. 261–359).

9. Mervyn Jones (b. 27 February 1922).

322

18 August 1921
Seefeld i. Tirol, Kurheim

Dear Jones,

You cannot have been more surprised than I by the news of Brill's pilgrimage. I think he has been caught by the current carrying Frink, Blumgart, Oberndorfer and others to Vienna, for assurance sake I will repeat what he writes of his trip. He is to sail on Aug. 23d, to land in Cherbourg Aug. 30th and to depart on Sept. 19th from Cherbourg or Plymouth. He asked me to write him to Paris c/o the American Express Co. So I did to-day and perhaps it will be in time for you to do the same. In my letter I stated that I was likely to stay here during the first half of Sept. I added: as he was to meet you before me you could give him account of my whereabouts in any case. I am not sure where he will go first.

Regarding your question about the term of our private meeting I think it will be the last week of Sept. The same as you I have to be back on the last of this month. I asked Rank to fix the exact day of our meeting in accordance with the Berlin people.

Thanks for the enclosed preface to your translation. It is all right. I appreciate it highly that you undertook this herassing bit of work.

I received Mrs. Riviere's letter and thinking she acted with your compliance I answered kindly and in a positive way. In January I may get some free hours. I am glad you are still utilizing the powers of the Strachey's and accept willingly Miss Hubback's reintegration to her superior rank as a translator.

As for the arrangement of the papers for the *Sammlung* I fully [agree]¹ consent to everything agreed between you and Rank. Your suggestion about separating the two layers by a partition seems practicable enough. It will be the highest triumph of *Massenpsychologie* if it can provoke original contribution to the vast subject most superficially accosted by me from you and others.

The news of your family are delightful, take our most affectionate wishes in return. Did I inform you of the birth of a son called Gabriel to Ernst in Berlin on July 31st? He is the fourth of my grandsons, while I complain the absence of a granddaughter.

I am living here with my wife, Anna and the boy Ernest from Hamburg (now 7½) in very good conditions. It is a *Hochplateau* richly wooded with fine views of the mountains, not far from the Bavarian frontier, ¾ of an hour from Innsbruck by an electric train.

Mit herzlichen Grüssen[2]
Freud

1. Crossed out in the original.
2. "Herzlichen Grüssen" is written in Gothic script.

323

[postcard]

5 September 1921
Seefeld

Dear Jones,
Brill has been with me these last days. He is all right, quite willing to assist us, thoroughly reliable, confessing his neurotic faults. It is a great gain.

I leave this fine place on the 14th, hope to arrive Berlin 15th.
With best love to you and your wife

Freud

324

6 September 1921
The Plat, Elsted

Dear Professor,
The erratic Brill sent me a telegram from Innsbruck asking me to meet him in Zurich, although I had sent an account of my movements to New York, Plymouth and Paris. I suppose he thinks we are as mobile in Europe as they are in America. We return to London on the 9th, leave for Nürnberg via Brussels on the 12th, arriving on the 14th (address there p/a Merck,

Freytagstr. 1.) and staying there till Hildesheim on the 21st. Hiller is coming to Nürnberg, which will have many advantages in organising the *Journal* further.

I have just finished going through Strachey's translation of the *Massenpsychologie*, which is excellently done. As I have also corrected seven chapters of the *Vorlesungen* there has been little time left of my three weeks here to consider writing an article for Edinburgh.[1] But I regret this the less because you give so much food for thought in the *Massenpsychologie* that it will need much digesting before fresh ideas flow. You seem to have written it very easily and confidently, I suppose as a reaction to the difficulty of the *Jenseits*. You could have expanded and illustrated every paragraph of it, but you are rightly leaving such *Hosenarbeit* [dog work] more and more to others. What a library of books that little one will give rise to in time.

It may interest you to know that Bernard Shaw has just written an epic play in which he attempts to deal with the origin of death, and also uses Plato's idea of the origin of sex in connection with Lilith.[2] I will bring the book with me for you. I have just refused an American article for the *Journal*, in which the attempt is made to identify your *Anschauung* [outlook] with that of Bergson.[3] I remarked that it needed to be completed by an indication of the gulf between you. In general I fear that your Life Instinct in the *Jenseits* will lead to your being claimed an adherent of self-creative evolution and vitalism; it will be said that you have found out the error of materialistic determinism. But you are proof by now against misunderstandings, and can also rely on us to correct them for you.

I was glad to hear that Ernst has a son: another gain for Zionism. We are hoping that our second attempt will have the same result next March. In the meantime we are more than pleased with little Gwenith, who is developing in the most normal manner, physically and mentally.

It will be very good to see you again this month, and also our other friends.

I am sorry to say that I have had another spontaneous attack of perforative otitis, but it seems to heal quickly and I am otherwise very well.

yours very affectionately
Ernest Jones.

1. See notes 1 and 6 to letter 319.
2. See *Back to Methuselah* (1918–1920), in *Bernard Shaw: Complete Plays with Prefaces*, vol. 2 (New York: Dodd, Mead, 1962), pp. 3–262. The character Lilith makes an appearance as the being that sundered itself at the beginning of time and gave rise to Adam and Eve; see the end of part 5, "As Far as Thought Can Reach: A.D. 31,920."
3. Albert Polon, "Bergson and Freud: Some Points of Correspondence," was presented at the May meeting of the New York Psychoanalytic Society, as reported by Adolf Stern, *Journal*, 2 (1921): 485. The article appears not to have been published elsewhere.

325

2 October 1921
Vienna, IX. Berggasse 19

Dear Jones,

I am back, as I expected, since Sept. 29th deeply in the preparation for new work, having met all my patients or rather pupils yesterday. I am writing you under the still fresh impressions of our meeting which would have been completely satisfactory had not two darker spots somewhat diminished its splendour. The first was the evident deterioration of Sachs' being and behaviour and the second your condition. I found you easily tired, not lively and bad looking and had to wonder, why you disappeared every day once or twice without explaining your absence. I am in need to be assured that nothing serious is the matter with you. It is likely that I am overanxious on your behalf, and while I hope you will acknowledge my friendship as a motive for my care I am sure you recognise, that my appreciation of your personal importance for our common cause is for much in the matter.

This point apart I have a favour to ask from you. I wrote yesterday to Lissa & Kann to send me no more reports of our account, as the government is likely to spy on letters and to confiscate all foreign valours in posession of an Austrian, also threatens heavy fines on the concealment of such. We are simply in a condition of self-defense—*Notwehr*—against an uncapable and blindly struggling legislation. So I pray you send me a card every time you get a report from L.[issa] & K.[ann], mentioning in slightly disguised words the arrival of some sum from some one. The next I expect is the payment of $997 or Fl. 3.205, sent by my nephew Bernays to Lippmann, Rosenthal & Co. instead [of] to Lissa & Kann, as royalties of the translation. Two lines on an open card, f.e.: Bernays gives the number 3.205, will do and such events cannot occur very often, in no case more frequently than once a month.

Varendonck mentions in a letter that he expected you at Brussels and was very sorry to miss you. I donot know what right he had to wait for you there.

My daughter was very much flattered and pleased by your present. I think she will write you herself.

In a week the Circular Letters will start anew and give you whatever news we have.

With my best love for you and your dear wife

affectionately yours
Freud

326

11 October 1921
111 Harley Street, London

Dear Professor,

I sincerely hope that your cold is now better and that this time it will not leave behind its usual chronic consequences. Next time we must organize matters so that no one brings an infection with him (which is quite easy to do, with a little trouble), for it was the only blot on an otherwise most enjoyable meeting. I do not take so seriously as you seem to the two matters you mentioned, for I hope they are both temporary in nature. Sachs has evidently some infantile regression and has been behaving in Berlin, as I hear, rather like a youth visiting a *Grosstadt* for the first time. As I am intimate with him, I spoke to him about it. I read it as being largely a reaction from years of exile, illness and dependence; his restoration to full life, an important standing, and an unexpectedly strong financial position, has carried him a little off his feet. Before another year is over I trust he will have settled down. My only anxiety is lest his foolishness in keeping late night hours in crowded localities may affect his lungs, and on this point I wonder if you could drop a hint to him against the *spes phthisica*.[1]

For myself I am glad to be able to assure you that my health is excellent, and I live in the best hygienic circumstances (as far as an analyst can!). Your correct observations refer to a quite passing state, partly psychical. The day I joined you all I was thoroughly well and active, but that evening my cold in the head began. Partly for toxic reasons and partly from my intolerance of naso-pharyngeal irritation (erogene Zone, I suppose), this trouble always affects me psychically, in the direction of a slightly hypochondriacal withdrawal, and it is then an effort to remain *gesellschaftsfähig* [sociable] and to retain the proper *Objektsbesetzungen*.[2] This was not made easier by my lack of fluency in languages, having the unpleasant choice [being][3] between trying the attention of my audience by speaking either in broken German or in a foreign tongue; and on account of the cold there was some regression in this respect also. Knowing my propensities I determined from the start not to give in to them and to participate in all the activities at all costs. On the whole I thought I succeeded pretty well, but the effort resulted in much fatigue and occasionally I had to give up some of the sight-seeing and tiring walks. *Voilà tout!* It was also not easy to banish altogether some personal cares. Owing to the unexpected non-appearance of the other women, my wife decided to travel alone from Berlin to London, and I knew she would not be able to get servants for some time (which proved to be true). Also I knew that within four days of my return I would have to provide a large sum of money for the house I was buying and was not [certain]⁴ sure whether I could borrow it from a certain friend (the bank had refused to lend me anything, being under Government orders on the matter, and my savings were unsale-able—having shrunk to *one fifth* of their value in the past six months, owing to the cessation of trade in England). I am glad to say that this difficulty has been overcome for the moment and we are now enjoying the pleasure of arranging our delightful new home. We have at last accommo-dation to invite you to stay in on your long-expected visit to England.

I enter into these personal details at such length in response to your very kind solicitude; I am assured of your interest.

A French lady, Mrs. Philipp, wife of your wife's cousin here, consulted me for epilepsy and nervous symptoms. I propose to take her for a month's trial, as I am not sure whether the fits are organic or psychogenic.

I have had news of Bernays in accordance with your expectation, but will you not ask him to write rather to The Hague direct, which would be simpler?

We stayed in Brussels for 24 hours on the way to Germany and arranged to spend the time with Varendonck, who came from Ghent to meet us. Unfortunately we missed each other at the station, probably because of some delay with my luggage, and went to different hotels.

With my warmest thanks for your kind letter (I trust the Circular Letters will not diminish your correspondence), and with my deepest affection, also greetings from my wife,

Yours always
Ernest Jones.

1. Literally, "hope of the consumptive," in the sense of the beatific denial of death. Sachs had contracted tuberculosis in 1918; a prolonged cure in Switzerland at the Davos sanatorium, however, saved his life. See Jones (1955a, pp. 198–199; 1955b, p. 224).

2. "Interest in people." For a discussion of the issues related to translating *Besetzung*, see Ornston (1985b).

3. Crossed out in the original.

4. Crossed out in the original.

327

6 November 1921
Vienna, IX. Berggasse 19

Dear Jones,

I felt highly gratified by your letter of Oct. 11th as I had taken matters rather seriously and saw the future dark. It may have been the pessimism of old age, which is growing upon me. Now you will be fairly established in your new house and may accept my best wishes for happiness and success while you live therein. What is your new address? You have not changed your medical office?

My wife's cousin Mrs. Philipp is a true epileptic as you will have found out by now. I dont see Frink's case so bad as you do.

The famous husband of Mrs. B. has renounced official persecution which would have shown him in a bad light and the private gossip is likely to fade out shortly, when the parties will have gone to Paris or elsewhere on the continent to go through the formalities of the divorce.[1] I cannot argue with Mrs. B. for her misunderstanding my share in the affair, as in fact I had to assure her of the intensity and genuineness of his affection and to convince him of the presence of those feelings in himself, which he did not dare to confess to himself. To a non-analytical mind this attitude had to appear as an "advise". The case is not bad in a moral sense, as both were unhappy in marriage and had a right to be fond of each other. As usual society does not object to the fact of "adultery" but to the intention to make it good by a permanent union.

I am glad you like Rickman and intend to make him the helpmate you need so much. He is a nice, strong fellow, his narcissism, I expect, a phase on the track of libido from mother-wife to some new, sublimated object. His analysis is just now rather sterile. I make excellent progress with Alix Strachey and expect to succeed with James Str[achey], both of whom may become highly valuable members of your staff.

As I confessed to you some time ago I have become convinced of the importance of bringing out my minor writings *(Sammlung)* in English and gather from your remarks in the *Rundbrief* that you are well provided with translators. Yet I think it would be nice if you could reserve some work in this line for Anna, who now is in excellent health and threatens to go back to her school, if we dont give her work. She could do something with the aid of Hiller, who now has got a secretary to his relief. Consider the matter.

It was very kind of you to inform me of Lissa & Kann's reports as I had requested you to do, but they dont cease to send me the duplicates in spite of my appeal to them and so you ought to spare yourself this additional trouble.

I confess I do nothing besides my daily work.

With kind regards for you and your family

yours as ever
Freud

1. Freud refers to the bank heiress Angelika Bijur and her much older husband, Abraham Bijur, of New York. Mrs. Bijur had become Frink's patient in 1912. They later fell in love, eventually divorced their respective spouses, and were married on 27 December 1922. Their relationship was complicated, however, by Frink's subsequent mental breakdown, and they were divorced in 1925.

328

International Journal of Psycho-Analysis

30 November 1921
London

Dear Professor,

Thank you for your remarks about my letter on the September meeting and for your kindly wishes about our new place of residence. We are very happy here and it is well organised from the point of view of work, with much better arrangements. We have a little garden and overlook the park, the address being 42 York Terrace, Regent's Park, London, N.W.1. It is only three minutes from my room in Harley St., which I still retain.

McCann had finally refused all reparation, and Unwin suggests that the enclosed document be circulated among the leading periodicals and libraries in America. Will you please let me know at your early convenience if I may have permission to add your name to the signatories. I think we should fight the American piracy especially just now when there is every prospect that their laws on the subject will be changed; they are in a state of guilty conscience.[1]

My Treatment of Mrs. Philipp came to a sudden and comical end. After five days she woke up at four one morning with the spontaneous realisation that her husband had been inconsiderate of her in regard to her household difficulties, and she woke him to tell him so. Nothing that I could say could convince her that this was an inadequate aetiology of epilepsy and she regarded herself as cured. Of course she felt better and her husband wrote thanking me for the successful course of psycho-analysis!

After some months' analysis of Rickman's mother I have a chance of comparing her with his wife, much to the disadvantage of the latter, who is really quite devoid of grace and love. He has a very distorted picture of his mother, as of course you will have guessed; she is quite human.

About the Schriften.[2] Most of the Metapsychology and Technique articles are now translated. Egerton promised to attack the non-medical articles in the first two volumes, but I have heard nothing further from him. The only part unallotted, therefore, is the medical part of these volumes, and if Anna would care to undertake these I should like nothing better and be very grateful to her. She could do all the first volume except the French ones, which Meyer has done (very badly).[3] I hope that her health is better now.

I must tell you the latest story of Loe. She replaced Trottie[4] by a more obvious symbol, a cock, who always slept in her bedroom. A time came when she had to go away for a while, so that he had to take his place with the hens in the fowl-coop. Lest, however, he should suffer from fear or loneliness in this unaccustomed environment she had her bed moved there also and slept there with him for the first two nights until he no longer found it strange. Of her health I have no news.

Practice is very full just now and I am trying to steer a couple of patients towards Vienna. I usually work nine hours a day, and only wish I could devote more time to scientific work. But I think none of my duties get seriously neglected, and we even manage occasionally to go to the theatre, not to mention fortnightly visits to Elsted.

With my very warmest regards

yours always sincerely
Ernest Jones.

1. The reference is to a pirated version of Freud called *Dream Psychology*, with a translation falsely attributed to M. D. Eder, published by James McCann of New York. The book was put together from English versions of Freud (1900a) by André Tridon of New York; see Jones (1922i; 1957a, pp. 49, 85; 1957b, pp. 51, 89–90).

2. Regarding Freud, *Collected Papers*.

3. Several articles, originally published in French, were translated by M. Meyer in Freud, *Collected Papers*, 1:42–58, 128–137, 138–154.

4. Loe's dog.

329

International Journal of Psycho-Analysis

7 December 1921
111 Harley Street, London

Dear Professor,

If you have time to look through the enclosed letter from Strachey I should be very glad to hear any comments you may care to make. Incidentally, it may amuse you to see the kind of recreation your English children indulge in.[1]

Yours very sincerely,
Ernest Jones.

1. Jones refers to the important letter on "cathexis" as a translation for the German *Besetzung*; see Strachey to Jones, 27 November 1921, in Ornston (1985b, pp. 393–394).

330

9 December 1921
Vienna, IX. Berggasse 19

Dear Jones,

I am glad you feel so comfortable in your new home, I did not know it was so near to your office.

Life is rich in hardship here. I feel 9 hours of work are too many for me but as yet I see no way of getting a relief. The Americans will stay until end of January or February; the next people I have given a promise are Dr. Asch from N.Y.,[1] Mrs. Riviere who insists on coming here and a Swiss lady doctor who is waiting for many months.

Rickman is hardly pressed in his analysis, in fact I opened your intentions to him in order to stirr up his spirits, as he is a sure man and a good one. James Strachey has not yet overcome his scepticism but his wife is progressing nicely. Among the Americans Oberndorf is the worst, he is still a puzzle to me, he appears to be stupid and arrogant, and yet why should a man who was considered so brilliant and successful, have taken up analysis unless his head or his heart had some share in it. The course of lectures I had arranged for the English people proves a success; Rank impressed all of them immensily. They have invited Abraham, Ferenczi and Roheim to give them 1–2 lectures each. A.[braham] is expected around New Year's day, the Hungarians on Jany 6th. It is a sign of interest and ambition on their side.[2]

The honeymoon of our Verlag-business is now past, we look forward to bad times. I put all the money in I got from Eitingon and would like to get more. We have no appropriate office and the work is very much retarded by this fact. In contrast to these real difficulties our books are selling at a surprising rate. Rank will tell you all about it.

Rickman and Strachey, who now are helping Hiller, are both of them extremely annoyed at the quality of the contributions to Nr. 3/4 and the low standard of the translation contained therein. I donot know what the part of their ambition may be in their criticism, as I did not see the manuscr nor get the proofs. But it is likely they should not be altogether wrong, Hiller and Anna too proclaim Stärcke's paper to be rendered in a very objectionable way.[3] My daughter expressed also the opinion that the paper of Varendonck on his marital misfortunes ought not to have been accepted.[4] Now I lay this matter before you as you are the only one responsible for the level of the *Journal* and I hope you will reduce the reproaches to their due size and try to remedy for what remains.

I hear you will see Hiller in the last week of this year. Rank promised to inform you of all the points to be considered.

It is a good habit of yours to send a private letter to me along with the circular.

With kindest regards to you and family

Freud

1. Joseph J. Asch (b. 1880), M.D. 1902 Columbia; urologist, member of New York Psychoanalytic Society.

2. The lectures are briefly mentioned in *Zeitschrift*, 8 (1922): 106.

3. Stärcke (1921).

4. J. Varendonck, "A Contribution to the Study of Artistic Preference," *Journal*, 3 (1922): 409–429. Freud had written an introduction to Varendonck's *Psychology of Day-Dreams* (1921), and Anna Freud's translation of Varendonck's book into German came out in 1922; see Freud (1921b).

331
International Journal of Psycho-Analysis

15 December 1921
111 Harley Street, London

Dear Professor,

I am sending this letter and a small Christmas parcel by a Mr. Pastor, late of Oxford, now at the University of London as Lecturer. He is an intelligent and much-travelled Spaniard, who has shewn some interest in psycho-analysis, though he does not seem to have the inner need to come closer to it.

The only way to deal with a press of patients is for you to raise your fees still further. Many analysts here, for instance, even unqualified ones, get two to three guineas, and you have surely the right to ask at least five from those who can afford it.

Rickman and Strachey are probably quite right in their criticisms, though they may be sharpened by reasons to do with their analysis. The situation is this. Part 3/4 contains six articles. Two short ones, in fair English and slightly improved by myself, by the Americans Coriat and Van Teslaar.[1] A long one in excellent English by Berkeley-Hill.[2] Three translations.[3] One of Hug-Hellmuth translated into good English by Barbara Low, who is a lecturer on English literature. One by Eisler (pregnancy phantasy) translated by a medical patient of mine, a Cambridge man, son of German parents; I must admit it was not so well translated as I had the right to expect; it was given him as a test. Stärcke's psychiatry one is done by Bryan, and here we come to the difficulties. Of my two assistants, who are certainly the most suitable available at the moment, Bryan works most industrially and has only the one fault of not being an educated man, so that his style and even grammar are exceedingly weak. I have corrected so many of his translations and had so much else to do that I got him to ask Flugel to correct this one. Flugel writes excellent English and is clever, but has two weaknesses. He is rather selfish and only likes doing his own work, not helping other people, and secondly he has not overcome a strong reaction to a sadistic complex the effect of which is to paralyse his efforts to criticise or disagree from anyone else, with very few exceptions. So he feels inhibited when asked to do such work as this (it was the same about correcting the American translation of the *Vorlesungen*) and he sends back the manuscript in very much the same condition as before. A combination of laziness and inhibition. But one must work with the implements at one's disposal and I try to find whatever is most congenial or suitable to him (i.e. very little). To correct Bryan, and many others, properly would mean extensive re-writing of his work, often harder than to do a new translation. I cannot do everything alone, so use my time and powers for whatever I consider the most important. For some time to come this will be the revision of your own translations, *Sammlungen*, etc., in the first place.

You may at all events be sure that I do not underestimate the importance of the linguistic factor in the *Journal*. My fear rather is that you may think that I overestimate it. But it is difficult to overestimate it in England, for the following reasons. A knowledge of good English is almost unbelievably rare here, and of course rarer still in America, and is valued correspondingly highly. It is difficult to convey to anyone not English how completely a man is estimated here by his speech and his writing. The average doctor writes worse English than a poor tradesman writes German in Austria. Last week, for instance, I had the occasion to read for the first time Brill's translation of your Leonardo,[4] and I was deeply shocked time and again to see punctuation as illiterate as that of a servant girl's, with expressions of a similar order. Men of sensitive feeling, taste and education like Rickman and Strachey rightly shudder at such things, though this Stärcke translation is nothing like that and contains at least no gross grammatical errors. In short, what I badly need is someone like Rickman for just this work of revising badly written manuscripts. Until that time I can only struggle on and do what I can myself.

Perhaps I was to blame in accepting Varendonck's article. I was influenced by your high opinion of him, my own being, I must confess, much lower. I am now re-reading his article, but will beg you, if you have the time, to look at it yourself and form an opinion about it (Hiller will be away, but Rank can doubtless find it, or perhaps Anna can).

We have nearly thirty book reviews waiting to be printed, for I am following your advice to make this a strong feature of the *Journal*. One of them, a review of Kempf's imposing work on Psychopathology,[5] I should like you to read if possible before it is printed, lest you may wish to make some alterations in it.

Thank you for your acceptance of the protest I wrote for Unwin. It is being held up for a fortnight, as McCann's agent is making a last effort to bring him to terms.[6] The *Vorlesungen* is ready except for the frontispiece, which Hiller is getting from Germany.

I hope you will have some rest at Christmas and am sure you will enjoy meeting our friends when they come to Vienna. How I wish I could be present.

With my warmest regards to yourself and your family

Believe me, yours always affectionately
Ernest Jones.

1. Isador H. Coriat, "Anal-Erotic Character Traits in Shylock," *Journal*, 2 (1921): 354–360; and James S. van Teslaar, "The Significance of Psycho-Analysis in the History of Science," *Journal*, 2 (1921): 339–353.

2. Owen Berkeley-Hill, "The Anal-Erotic Factor in the Religion, Philosophy, and Character of the Hindus," *Journal*, 2 (1921): 306–338.

3. H. von Hug-Hellmuth, "On the Technique of Child-Analysis," *Journal*, 2 (1921): 287–305; Michael Joseph Eisler, "A Man's Unconscious Phantasy of Pregnancy in the Guise of Traumatic Hysteria," *Journal*, 2 (1921): 255–286; and Stärcke (1921).

4. Brill (1916a).

5. Jones (1922c).

6. In his *Rundbrief* of 12 August 1921, Jones reported that James McCann, the American publisher and pirate of Freud (1900a), had offered the British publisher Stanley Unwin the sum of $250 to continue the piracy (Sigmund Freud Copyrights, Wivenhoe, and Rank Collection, Butler Library, Columbia University). Jones was attempting to intervene and thwart McCann's efforts.

332
[postcard]

19 December 1921
Vienna

Dear Jones,

Very glad to have got your two prefaces (I will try to make you write one more, for Roheim's book, as you do it so well) but will you not correct that false statement that I had given three courses from 1914–17? In fact I lectured *two* years on the *Vorlesungen* winter 1915/16 and winter 1916/17.[1]

Merry Christmas for all of you!

Affectionately
Freud

1. Jones (1922a, 1922b). Jones did not do a preface for Róheim (1925).

333

21 December 1921
111 Harley Street, London

Dear Professor,

This is to introduce a Mr. Barbour, an Oxford man, who is stated to have a serious interest in Psycho-Analysis. I do not know him personally but an old patient of mine has recommended him strongly.

Yours sincerely,
[Ernest Jones]

334

26 December 1921
Vienna, IX. Berggasse 19

Dear Jones,

I cannot put up writing you. There is a rumour started by Mrs. Rickman that you have become father to a son, but we think it untimely and suspect this son to be an incarnation of the child given to the analyst by his patient. We ought to have heard about it from yourself.

I saw Mr. Pastor today and thank you very warmly for the appropriate Xmas present, which I am sorry I did not return, this time not more than former ones.

I appreciate all your difficulties in the translation business and will be glad to send you over Str.[achey] and R.[ickman] as helpmates, as soon as their analysis is finished, that is to say, not very soon. But if an elegant English style means so much to you too, you will have to read German letters in our private correspondence.

I am ready to read your review on Kempf's work and trust I know in what sense you call it "imposing".

On looking through the first two volumes of the *Sammlung* I could not always decide what articles are to be judged as medical or non-medical ones. I will thank you for assigning them to me by name or number. Anna is willing to try at them with the help of Rickman or he with her help. Hiller will be too glad to find himself substituted, as he is very busy here.

Owing to your suggestion I am prepared to take 3 guineas or even 5 for my hours but I expect I will find none to give them.

The Americans are now doing much better, they may be good for something.

I hope you too had a good time in the holidays.

Affectionately yours
Freud

335

29 December 1921
Vienna, IX. Berggasse 19

Dear Jones,

I hope this letter will arrive in time to bring you my kindest wishes for your and your dear wife's welfare in the new year 1922, which is expected to give you the son anticipated by good Mrs. Rickman.

I start the new era by two requests. a) The danger of confiscation of good money has now become imminent with us. I forbade Lissa & Kann to send me any reports of my accounts and so I will be in the dark, whether something has arrived or not. There are only two posts I expect in these days, one of Fl. 25 from a Dutch Society for selling the translation of *Massen*Ψ (which is overdue), and a sum of 1100 French Francs from Payot for some new purchases *(Alltag, Massen*Ψ*,Totem),*[1] this latter just sent off by him. Will you be so kind as to add a note on this matter to the *Rundbrief, after* you have got L & K's report of the *second* post's arrival?

b) The "5 Lectures on ΨA" have now appeared in a new, the 6th edition (unchanged). They have been translated into 7 languages,[2] but the English edition is not accessible as it appeared in the *American Journal of Psychology,* April 1910 and was not given out separately. It was reproduced in "Lectures and Addresses in celebration of the twentieth anniversary of Clark University", Worcester 1910[3] and is still buried there. Do you think, it can be rescued from there and is it worth while to try?

I am waiting for Abraham who is to come on Jany 3d and for Ferenczi who is to substitute him in our house on the 5th.

Cordially yours
Freud

1. Freud (1901b), *Psychopathologie de la vie quotidienne* (Paris: Payot, 1922); Freud (1921c), "Psychanalyse des foules et Analyse du moi," in *Essais de psychanalyse* (Paris: Payot, 1924); and Freud (1912–13), *Totem et tabou* (Paris: Payot, 1923).

2. Freud (1910a), 6th ed. 1922. The translations were: Polish (1911), Russian (1911), Hungarian (1912), Dutch (1912), Italian (1915), Danish (1920), and French (1921).

3. Clark University (1910, pp. 1–38).

336

11 January 1922
69 Portland Court, London

Dear Professor,

Your interpretation of the rumour about my son was of course quite correct, though I hope that it is a happy forecast of what we expect in another six week's time.

We had a very restful Xmas holiday at Elsted and have returned to work with fresh vigour.

I will of course let you know when I hear from Kann.

I have not yet heard from Egerton as to which articles he is translating and have sent him a sharp reminder. But I am practically certain he will do none from Vol. I, so that Anna and Rickman can safely do any from this volume. A propos Rickman, the case I describe in the double number of the *Journal* is from his wife, with of course her consent. Is it not a pretty one?[1]

Of course I think the Five Lectures should be rescued, as you well call it, if possible and on getting your letter I wrote to the American publisher. I trust you will approve of my actions in regard to the McCann piracy.

My wife and I thank you very warmly for your kind New Year's wishes and reciprocate most heartily.

yours always affectionately
Ernest Jones.

1. Jones (1921).

337

International Journal of Psycho-Analysis

17 January 1922
London

Dear Professor,

Dr. Carver of Birmingham,[1] an able man, but distinctly ambivalent in his attitude towards Psa. wanted me to analyse him some time ago, but then withdrew. He now writes to me from Switzerland to ask whether I know if you have any vacancy for someone who wishes to learn technique, but he speaks of only paying a short visit to Vienna for the purpose. I have written to him telling him to write to you direct.

A Mr. Cuming from Egypt, half English and half Greek, with a severe obsessional neurosis and also homosexuality, consulted me but baulked at the fee, so I suggested that he should go to Vienna where he could live more cheaply than in England. Actually he is a well-to-do and extravagant youth who could easily afford three guineas. He begs me to write to you and find out whether you are likely to have any vacancy. He would, if necessary, postpone treatment so as to come to you.

Payot has acted as you expected. Kann tells me there are now 2737 altogether.

I enclose further letters between Unwin and myself.

Yours very sincerely,
[Ernest Jones]

1. Alfred E. A. Carver, M.A., M.D. 1914 Cambridge; specialist in neurology.

338

[postcard]

22 January 1922
Vienna

Dear Jones,

Only to let you know that I fully agree to your steps in the Tridon affair and your answer to Unwin. We are expecting Abraham, who should come to-morrow if not kept at home by a railway-strike. I will write you after he has left.

I did not understand the cipher you gave of Kann's. I have no free hour before Oct. first and have written so to Carver.

Affectionately yours
Freud

339

British Psycho-Analytical Society

22 January 1922
London

Dear Professor,

I thought it might interest you if I told you a few words about your new patient Mrs. Riviere, who is going to Vienna next week, as she plays a considerable part in the society here. It is a case of typical hysteria, almost the only symptoms being sexual anaesthesia and unorganized Angst, with a few inhibitions of a general nature. Most of her neurosis goes into marked character reactions, which is one reason why I was not able to cure her. I am specially interested in the case, for as it is the worst failure I have ever had I have naturally learnt very much from her analysis. She came to me in 1916 and was with me till last June, with about a year's interruptions from tuberculosis and other causes. Seeing that she was unusually intelligent I hoped to win her for the cause, a mistake I shall never repeat. I

underestimated the uncontrollability of her emotional reactions and in the
first year made the serious error of lending her my country cottage for a
week when I was not there, she having nowhere to go for a holiday. This
led to a declaration of love and to the broken-hearted cry that she had
never been rejected before (she has been the mistress of a number of men).
From that time on she devoted herself to torturing me without any intermission and with considerable success and ingenuity, being a fiendish
sadist; my two marriages gave her considerable opportunity for this which
she exploited to the full. The treatment finally broke down over my inability to master this negative transference, though I tried all means in my
power. The situation was complicated by her position in the society, which
gave her a certain personal contact with me. Her dissatisfied reproaches
were equally great whether I limited this as far as possible, which I usually
did, or allowed it, so for two years at least I have seen that the only solution
was to get her to go to you and have finally succeeded in this. Her
symptoms are much better (she can talk fluently at a meeting where she
was once dumb from Angst) and she has a far-reaching insight, but the
main complexes are only intellectually resolved. She has a most colossal
narcissism imaginable, to a great extent secondary to the refusal of her
father to give her a baby and her subsequent masculine indentification
with him. Naturally she comes to you with a strong positive transference
ready, and my only fear is lest there be not time enough to provoke and
work through the necessary negative aspect of this. In that case we should
lose a valuable translator and member of the society, for I think she understands psa better than any other member except perhaps Flugel. Incidently
she has a strong complex about being a well-born lady (county family) and
despises all the rest of us, especially the women.

With most cordial greetings

yours always sincerely
Ernest Jones.

340

International Journal of Psycho-Analysis

26 January 1922
London

Dear Professor,

Another business letter! Dr. William Brown,[1] whom you may know as
one of our unpleasant opponents, who likes to call himself a psychoanalyst when there is no-one present to contradict him, came to me yesterday. I know him well as a scoundrel with a thoroughly bad character. He

will be in Vienna in April and asked me if he could see you as he wanted to discuss some moot theoretical points with you. I told him I was doubtful as you were so busy. I am sure that his sole motive is in order to be able to boast on his return to Oxford "The last time I discussed this question personally with Freud", "On one of my recent talks with Freud I pointed out to him his mistake in thinking" etc., etc.. It would be a pity to give him this pleasure, and in this way to enhance his prestige, and I daresay you will have the boldness to be impolite enough to refuse his request if you feel so inclined.

Kann tells me that his *total* now comes to 2737.

I had a long interview with Unwin yesterday to the following effect. Both Moffatt Yard and he have acted honestly in regard to the *Gradiva.* The only person to whom you could address any remonstrances is Stanley Hall.[2] The translation rights of the *Gradiva* would in any case have lapsed within a few months in all countries by the Berne Convention of ten years from the date of publication.[3] In America they had already lapsed, owing to the state of war, and Moffatt Yard first obtained the assurance from the Congress authorities to that effect. Brill first raised objections, but then is said to have withdrawn them at the second interview he had with Stanley Hall, who then assured Moffatt Yard that all was in order. No doubt Brill saw that nothing was to be done, and perhaps felt his own position insecure as a foreigner at that time. Unwin has bought the American translation to sell in England. He has neither moral nor legal obligations to us or Deuticke, but I have nevertheless extracted from him a written assurance that any future translation of the *Gradiva* we may choose to make will not be regarded as running counter to his copyright, provided it does not appear as a separate work, but in a volume containing other work of [y]ours.[4]

The other matter, that of the Dream Book, is not so satisfactory, and Unwin has asked me to request you to give your decision in the following crisis.[5]

As you know, in America all virtues are measured by dollars, and McKann's [McCann's] offer to pay royalties has changed the position over there. The American agents of both the *Traumdeutung* and *Über den Traum* are said to have expressed their entire satisfaction, and Unwin, after consulting with other American publishers, is convinced that nothing we could do would harm McKann in the eyes of other publishers after his having made this financial offer. The most he has ever secured from an American pirate is money, never a withdrawal of the piracy. His chief concern is to injure McKann, and he thinks to extract money from him would be the only means of doing this. He is therefore inclined to accept the offer, though this involves a note being printed on the title page that although the book was first inadvertently published without your consent, in the circumstances you now accord your consent to its continuation.

To this I opposed the following considerations. Americans are to some extent sensitive of European opinion, as is shown by the new copyright act now before Congress. We have no legal or other weapon against their piracy except the one moral one of expressing our vigorous disapproval of their methods, and publishing this disapproval broadcast, and I cannot believe that this would be without effect on McKann's colleagues and other people concerned. It seems to me, therefore, wrong to throw away our only weapon, the moral one, and to acquiesce with their standards of piracy merely because it is a *fait accompli*. In the second place this particular case is more than one of piracy. It affects your professional reputation by issuing in your name a book made up from cuttings of your writings by a stranger in a form that you would never select yourself, and it has been criticized in the press for this very fault of formlessness. Thirdly, your prestige is injured by having your work presented to the public through a long introduction written by a man, André Tridon, who has an unsavoury reputation, and is an unscrupulous and ignorant exploiter of psycho-analysis, in short the very last man you would choose for such a purpose.

I agreed with Unwin to put the two views before you fairly, and ask for your decision. There is a third alternative, namely, that Unwin and Heinemann should give their consent and accept the royalty without your doing so. This seems to me a poor compromise, but I do not suppose you have any legal right to prevent Unwin from adopting it. He says, however, that he would prefer to continue to work in harmony with us if possible.

I should be very grateful for any comments you would care to make on the enclosed Glossary.[6] By the way, I have not got a clear answer from Abraham about the difference between the meaning of *Position* and *Einstellung* (attitude) (der Libido).[7] Would it be correct to say that both terms describe the same thing from different points of view?—the former from that of fixation and the latter from that of relationship to an object.

I enclose for your considertion an article by a certain Boven, recommended to me by de Saussure, which, in spite of its unnecessary length, I should be inclined to publish in the *Journal* and to recommend to Rank for *Imago*.[8]

No doubt you will communicate the substance of this letter to Rank, which will save me duplicating it to him.

With kindest regards,

Yours cordially,
Ernest Jones.

A Mr. Armstrong, a student at Oxford, has consulted me on account of his bad asthma. Other treatments having failed. I told him I was prepared to analyse him (he is otherwise neurotic), though I explained to him the experimental state of our knowledge on the subject. He now suggests going to Vienna to get your expert opinion as to the advisability of analysis and I am giving him a letter of introduction to you. If you think it a suitable case and have no vacancy yourself, I should be glad to take him and could do so in the middle of February.

1. William Brown, M.A., M.D. 1918 Oxford, Harley Street physician, and Reader in Psychology, King's College, University of London.
2. Freud (1907a) had appeared in English translation in 1917, with an introduction by G. Stanley Hall, and was published in America by Moffat, Yard. A reprint was published in 1921 in England by Allen and Unwin.
3. Jones must have in mind the second edition of Freud (1907a), which appeared in 1912.
4. The "y" here is handwritten in an otherwise typed letter.
5. See note 1 to letter 328, and note 6 to letter 331.
6. Jones (1924a).
7. In Jones (1924a, p. 7) the German word *Einstellung* is translated as "set, attitude (the former is the more technical term, the latter the more general term)." In A. Strachey (1943, p. 18) it is rendered as "attitude" or "position." Jones (p. 11) and Strachey (p. 51), however, also include the German word *Position* in their respective glossaries, and they both translate this as "position."
8. Boven (1922).

341

27 January 1922
111 Harley Street, London

Dear Professor,

This is to introduce Mr. Armstrong, about whom I wrote to you. He would be glad if you would be so kind as to give him an appointment at your early convenience as he does not wish to stay in Vienna longer than necessary.

Yours sincerely,
Ernest Jones.

342

5 February 1922
Vienna, IX. Berggasse 19

Dear Jones,

I have to thank and to answer you for a lot of letters regarding various affairs, first on Mrs. Riviere, whom I expect on the 25th of Febr.; you may imagine how little charmed I was by the prospects opened in your letter.

I will spare myself any further remarks on the subject as you seem to have suffered sufficiently for your mistake. But let us hope that all these adventures belong to the past.

If Dr. Will Brown comes to Vienna and attempts to have a conversation with me it may prove impossible to avoid him or may appear too haughty, but I am warned and will know how to manage him.

In the Unwin-Tridon affair I am with you without any restriction. I will not accept anything but the withdrawal of the book and will not forgo publishing the scandal quite independently whether the two publishers go along with us or suffer themselves to be bribed by the promise of royalties. I am astonished besides that they should put any expectation on these royalties as McCann is sure to cheat them there the same way as they are cheating their own authors, by not confessing the true numbers of copies sold.

Mr. Armstrong did not yet call on me. Boven's manuscript, good, rather *seicht* [shallow], is accepted for *Imago*.[1]

I clearly see that nothing can be done for *Gradiva* but I am anxious the press should not delay the translation of the *Sammlung*, or we could get into new scrapes with the American robbers.

Your Glossary is frequently consulted by Anna and Rickman and when the Strachey's have recovered from their Grippe I am sure they will give their attention to it. I cannot be of much use for it.

I will send you back the Strachey's at Eastertime. Blumgart is leaving here middle of February, you will see him in London. His analysis was excellent, as far as it went, that is to say not deep enough, owing to the short time he spent on it. The next to go is Oberndorf, on Febr. 25th, he has got nothing at all out of his analysis, being an absolutely self-satisfied, inaccessible person, who will never be admitted to the depths of analysis; yet he made an experience with failure which will do him some good. The younger men, Meyer and Kardiner, are much more [hopeful][2] promising.

The course of lectures accentuated by the invitation of Ferenczi, Abraham, Roheim and Sachs, was an unmistakable success. If it can be repeated next years Vienna will become of some importance for America.[3]

I may be more busy than can agree with scientific work or excellent health. General conditions are deteriorating from week to week, life is hard here. Amidst the general ruin and confusion our special work is rather flourishing.

Now take my best wishes for the happy event to be soon expected in your family and give us notice of it as soon as you have got *him*.

Affectionately yours
Freud

1. Boven (1922). *Seicht* is written in Gothic script.
2. Crossed out in the original.
3. This is the same lecture series that was referred to in note 2 to letter 330.

343

International Psycho-Analytical Association
Central Executive

11 February 1922
London

Dear Professor,

Thank you very much for your full letter, which came this morning. You answered all the questions with which I bothered you, except whether Boven should go in the *Journal* as well as *Imago*; they sent it for the *Journal* and want to know.[1] Also about *Einstellung* and *Position*;[2] perhaps my interpretation was correct?

I am not surprised at your decision about McCann-Tridon and will communicate it to Unwin, trying to retain him on our side.

If you pass the enclosed review of Forsyth's book will you be good enough to let Hiller have it. Otherwise will you please let me know your suggestions for alterations.[3]

Westermarck, in the new edition of his *History of Marriage*, attacks you on the incest question, and I have written a strong review,[4] for he gives himself into our hands beautifully.

It is a pity we took Oberndorf for the *Journal*, but I do not see any way now to change him for Blumgart. If only Brill were more helpful in such matters! I was interested in the news of the Americans and shall look forward to greeting any of them who can pass through London.

It must be terrible to live in Vienna just now, but the success of our work there is some compensation, I hope. You are restoring the city to her old pre-eminence as a medical centre.

Thank you for your kind wishes about the new babe whom we expect at the end of the month. In the meantime I enclose some recent photographs of Gwenith, who is a very charming and normal child.

yours always affectionately
Ernest Jones.

1. Boven (1922). This piece did not appear in the *Journal*.
2. See note 7 to letter 340.
3. Jones (1922d).
4. Jones (1922e).

344

International Journal of Psycho-Analysis

13 February 1922
London

Dear Professor,

An important matter has arisen just after I sent off the *Rundbrief,* and in order to save time in dealing with it, I am writing to yourself, Abraham, and Ferenczi for advice. Dr. Bose has constituted an Indian Psycho-Analytical Society and has formally applied for affiliation into the International.[1] He has sent a complete list of their statutes which are modelled on the British ones. Everything is conducted in a most orderly way, and I myself am satisfied to accept them. Would you please let me have a post card by return of post with your opinion.

Yours cordially,
[Ernest Jones]

1. Girindrasekhar Bose, M.B., D.Sc., from 1917 onward taught psychoanalysis at University of Calcutta as lecturer in clinical psychology; founder of the Indian Psycho-Analytical Society on 22 January 1922; see Hartnack (1990).

345

International Journal of Psycho-Analysis

15 February 1922
London

Dear Professor,

I have already refused three or four articles from Schroeder but he keeps sending them, so this time I should like to ask your opinion. This particular article seems to have something in it, but is extremely prolix and American.[1] Schroeder is a lawyer who has defended Psa very sturdily, but not of good judgement.

Yours cordially,
[Ernest Jones]

1. Theodore Schroeder, "Prenatal Psychisms and Mystical Pantheism," *Journal,* 3 (1922): 445–466.

346

[postcard]

20 February 1922
Vienna

Dear Jones,

Today I received Trotter's second edition,[1] as he did not give his adress will you be kind enough to transmit my thanks to him. I have cast a glance on his lines on leadership but I look forward to inquire whether he has found a way connecting the importance of a leader with the nature of a wolf-society.[2]

Yours truly
Freud

He is too much biassed by the war.

1. Trotter (1916), 2nd ed. 1919.
2. See Trotter (1985, p. 16).

347

27 February 1922
42 York Terrace, London

Dear Professor,

You asked me to let you know at once of the son's arrival. It took place this afternoon in 1½ hours. He weighs K. 4.20, is an unmistakably male child, lusty and hearty. Typical *Judenbub* [Jewish lad], but with blond hair and blue eyes. He seems to adapt himself rapidly to his changed life and behaved masterfully at his first meal.

My wife went through the ordeal splendidly, glowing with health and pride and feels very well.

The name will probably be Merfyn (pronounced Merrvin) Ioan (pronounced as German Johann without the h, and with the same meaning) Gower Jones.

Blumgart telephoned this evening. I am to see him in a day or two. Oberndorf is expected on March 6.

I have heard nothing as yet of Armstrong.

You were evidently more successful with G. M. Young than you told me, to judge by his firm public appearances in Vienna. I may have a similar case to send you. Does Mrs. Strachey's illness give you an unexpected vacancy?

With kindest greeting and warm thanks for your interest,

Yours always affectionately
Ernest Jones.

348
[telegram]

2 March 1922
Vienna

Welcome Merfyn

Freud

349

2 March 1922
42 York Terrace, Regents Park

Dear Professor,

My wife and I were very touched by your kind thought in telegraphing your congratulations to us today, and we wish to thank you from our hearts.

I am glad to say that both are progressing perfectly. The youngster is a lusty rascal, very sturdy in every way. He weighed K.4.20, and his grasp when he attaches himself to his mother's breast is such that he can be dislodged only by a lever action of two hands. He resembles myself and my father much more than his mother facially, the reverse of the little girl. The contrast between them is remarkable; no one could mistake their respective sex from the beginning.

always gratefully yours
Ernest Jones.

350

16 March 1922
111 Harley Street, London

Dear Professor,

The kind letter to my wife from you and Frau Professor came this evening and gave us both great pleasure.[1] I am glad to say that she has made an uninterrupted recovery and also that Mervyn, who has acquired a most [more] civilised name than at first flourishes greatly.

Reflection of the matter of names has led me to a conclusion which may give a little trouble to my friends, but which I think I shall act on, unless you send me a hasty protest. It is to amplify my own name to Ernest Beddow-Jones, thus inserting one inherited by my father from his mother (analytically at the same time an affirmation and a repudiation of him). It seems to me a little unfair to expose one's children to the irksome task of gradually distinguishing themselves from the other half a million people called Jones (there are now even three psycho-analysts called Dr. Ernest Jones). Some names like Jones and Smith have lost the first function of a name, that is to separate them from other people, and so it is very customary here to take such a step as I propose.

I have heard nothing more from Armstrong. Did he arrive in Vienna? What did you think about Forsyth?

With kindest regards to you; it was excellent news to hear that you are so well.

yours always affectionately
Ernest Jones.

1. Letter missing.

351

23 March [1922][1]
Vienna, IX. Berggasse 19

Dear Jones,

You have lately developed the habit of joining a private letter to the *Rundbrief* and I hope you will cling to it. It is so very convenient.

I am sorry I did not answer your last but one. Sometimes my (fountain-) pen gets weary. I have so much business-correspondence to do, mostly warning [to][2] patients not to come as I have not the time to treat them, and declining flattering offers to write a paper on such a subject for such a periodical. These are the drawbacks of popularity, I see not much of its blessings.

Now as regards the change or amplification of your name I feel intensely incompetent to give a judgment on the matter. I only know that you will continue to be Dr. Ernest Jones to us. What the effect with strangers may be I cannot imagine. Perhaps it will be similar as if I had tried to avoid the ambiguity of the term "sexual" and employed a new word, say: "hiero-aphroditic" instead. Every reader would have put the question: Now what the deuce does he mean by that new Greek composition, I have never heard of it,—oh it means something like sexual, I see. So people will ask: Who is that Beddow-Jones? I am not likely to confound him with half a million of other Jones', but I know nothing of him. Oh, it is the author of the papers on Psychoanalysis and president of the Inter. ψα Association. Now I know, it is a pity he did not introduce himself by this name from the very beginning. Now perhaps he did not need it.

Forsyth's little book is exceptionally good and full of sound judgment. I acknowledged it in a card to him.

Mrs. Riviere does not appear to me half as black as you had painted her. We agree quite nicely so far. May be the difficulties will come later. In my experience you have not to scratch too deeply the skin of a so called masculine woman to bring her feminity to the light. I am very glad you had no sexual relations with her as your hints made me suspect. To be sure it was a technical error to befriend her before her analysis was brought to a close. No doubt she is very clever and clear-headed.

The Verlag has at last found an abode and I trust it will do good work. I am not so well satisfied by the Press. The sphinx in our coat of arms could be supplimented by a snail to give account of the rate of acceleration in its progress. Maybe its mechanism is too complex, I do not see where the fault lies. As we depend for our subsistence on the sale of the English products we throw on the market—the Verlag cannot pay—it is rather a serious affair. Yesterday I got the first two volumes of the *Journal* in exquisite, nay gorgeous, leather-binding. The contents do not correspond to the cover. My wish is that these offsprings of the Anglo-Viennese alliance shall thrive as do the other two you raise in your house.

Affectionately yours
Freud

1. Freud gives the year as 1923.
2. Crossed out in the original.

352

1 April 1922
111 Harley Street, London

Dear Professor,

Your very welcome letter came safely. As usual, you hit the nail on the head in the matter of the change in name. Such questions are never easy when there is no strong outstanding motive either way, either for or against. Logically I still think the wiser thing to do would be to change, but the decision is so evenly balanced that I haven't enough motive impulse to take the trouble involved in such a change. So I must continue to assimilate the pinpricks involved in being called Jones or E. Jones.

I have not said anything of late about the money from my Father, for it is only this month that the law's extraordinary delays have permitted the definite division of it among the different relatives. Unfortunately the result is far below what I had expected. Owing to the almost complete standstill of trade in England the value of the various stocks and shares is on the average about one fifth of what it was two years ago. It would be madness to turn them into cash by selling at their present value and I have succeeded in carrying through a division of them without doing so. What their value may be in a few years no one can predict. In the meantime, in case of accident, I have inserted into my will a suitable provision for the Verlag, alias Press, on the basis I had already promised.

A day or two ago I received a handsome offer from Mrs. Riviere to take over the revision of translations for the *Journal*. There is no one who could do it as well, and there is no work that I would more gladly be relieved of, for it is physically impossible to do it adequately alone. The delicate problem arises, however, about Rickman, whom I should like to see as assistant editor. He is far easier to work with and will also become a man of standing. But I have also to realise that this particular work he cannot do well. Owing, doubtless, to some remaining infantilism, he makes extraordinary mistakes in spelling and even in grammar, not the mistakes of an uneducated man, but those of a schoolboy, so that his work would all have to be checked carefully. I had known this previously, but forgot it in my urgent wish to find a good fellow-worker, and it was brought vividly to my mind in some recent manuscript he sent me. So Mrs. R. would logically have the better claim to the title so far as work is concerned. On the other hand I should not care to give such a slap in the face to the Americans as to put another lay person on the official staff of the *Journal* immediately after their strong representations to me on the subject of lay analysis. As you know, I am on the side of the lay analysts, but I hope to change the American view by some more persuasive method than this would involve. I also doubt whether Mrs. R. would attach any weight to the title. She speaks a lot about "recognition", but it seems to mean on the part of yourself, myself and a couple of others, rather than on the part of the outside public. I am glad to be able to shift this delicate matter on to your broad shoulders! I will write to her gratefully accepting *your* offer (Verschreiben for "her" because I know it is thanks to you that she has made it), but saying nothing about a title.

I am not surprised that she is shewing her best qualities at present, and she certainly has many, but I only hope that she will have an opportunity to bring out and overcome her bad ones. As she will not be with you in the critical ninth month, when she changed with me, it is a question if it might not be possible later on to regard her as an advanced patient, which of course she is in every respect, and provoke the feelings of disappointment by active therapy? As you remark, the feminine side does not lie far beneath the surface, but that fact I can honestly claim as a result of the analysis with me: the change in such ways, and also in her attitude towards children, has been very great indeed. I was surprised at your suspecting any sexual relations between us and think it must have been a Verlesen of the expression "declaration of love", which was of course on her side only. To satisfy her vanity she has always maintained the theory that I also was in love with her but was not honest enough to confess it, but I have never been able to confirm this in my self-analysis. She is not the type that attracts me erotically, though I certainly have the admiration for her intelligence that I would have with a man. But, speaking more generally, you need never have any fear about me in such respects. It is over twelve years since I experienced any temptation in such ways, and then in special circumstances; even should it arise in the future, which is very unlikely now, I have no doubt at all of my capacity to deal with it.

I am sorry you are not satisfied with the first two volumes of the *Journal*. Looking through the contents I see that of 27 articles half are translations, and of the others three only can be described as poor. Then the reviews have a good standard on the whole. Still it is better to be dissatisfied than the reverse, and I have every hope that by collecting a better staff of helpers we shall be able to improve steadily. Among English and American periodicals we already take a fairly high standing, so I gather.

With the rate of work in the Press I also am very dissatisfied, but I think I can detect where the difficulty lies. In London nothing can be done except to provide manuscripts and correct proofs with the maximum of speed, and this is done already; proofs, for instance, are nearly always returned corrected on the day they arrive. Hiller is an excellent fellow for detailed work, but he is lacking in two important qualities. One of them, *Übersicht über den allgemeinen Zusammenhang*,[1] I can remedy. The other, inability to press other people, only Rank can remedy. Hiller has no capacity to force the printers, to supply the necessary bullying, and also with the other tradespeople, supply of paper, type, etc.. He too readily accepts their assurance that it is impossible and that no more can be done. It is in this respect that Rank is so wonderful, better than anyone I know, and I wish he would not leave this side so much to Hiller. I know he is extraordinarily occupied in his time, but if it were possible for him to devote some of his energy to dealing with the tradespeople concerned with the Press I am sure it would accelerate matters more than anything else. The state of *Jenseits*, for instance, of which only two Bogen have been printed since I sent it to the printers last May, is nothing short of scandalous.

I hear that Armstrong is still on his way to you, and has got as far as Frankfurt. In every town he develops some new illness, asthma, indigestion, etc., which does not negative the diagnosis of neurosis!

Has Tansley started yet? I think he is a very able and careful thinker, and shall be glad to hear your impressions of him.

My family is making excellent progress. Gwenith, who was away in the country, was carefully introduced to her little brother this week. Various emotions flitted over her face and then she decided to react to the situation by offering him her hand to kiss, like a true Viennese lady. Since then she has been remarkably fond of him and has shewn no signs of jealousy on the surface at all events. The youngster is ugly but looks as if he will be intelligent.

With my kindest regards,

yours most affectionately
Ernest Jones.

P.S. I wanted to ask you, if I may take a further demand on your time, for the following advice. Will I be expected to give a general address at the Congress, or to read a technical paper like the others? I want sometime to say something about the relations of Psa to Medicine,[2] which must be done sometime, but do not know if that would be as interesting to continentals as it certainly would in England or America.

1. "Overview of the general picture."
2. A piece on this topic appeared much later; see Jones (1934).

353

6 April 1922
Vienna, IX. Berggasse 19

Dear Jones,

I have a lot of things to talk over with you, which do not go into the Circular. First of all thanks for your good letters which are becoming ever more kind and considerate owing perhaps to the happy turning of your family life.

I answer next to your question if you are expected to give a general address at the Congress.[1] I think it will make an excellent impression if you did—and you should do it in bold dashing German—especially as you are to be reelected for the next period until the Congress in 1924. It is time the herd should become prepared to listen to your voice or Abraham's or Ferenczi's as I am getting old and tired and fond of retirement.

Tansley has started analysis last Saturday. I find a charming man in him, a nice type of the English scientist. It might be a gain to win him over to our science at the loss of botany.

I forgot to mention Mr. Young, about whom you inquired in a former letter. Yes, I think he had been greatly improved by his bit of treatment, and I take it as an infallible evidence, that he did not turn up again. He would have done so, if he felt miserable. It is not nice that he did not call on me, after all, now as he is an official and important personality, for I had been kind towards him and resigned half of the fee, when he complained of his financial straits. Yet there is no matter for surprise or disappointment.

I was glad to inform Mrs. Riviere that you had accepted her offer and would write her so. She seems to be a powerful helpmate and we should bring her to some good use. I further think if she does the work she has a right to claim a title and a position, or she would find no recognition with the other ones. Her own proposal is that she should be named as "translating editor"[2] on the inside of the cover and her address given for all communications regarding translations. I do not think the Americans could object to this way of distinguishing her. (Nor can I lay any stress on the Americans' reluctance. It is well known all through the world of ΨA that Rank the editor of both our Periodicals is a layman.) I am of opinion besides that you owe her a compensation having aggravated her analysis by inconsequent behaviour as you confess yourself. I do not think there will be any need of artificials means to bring up her whims and claims but as long as these last are not more immodest, I am ready to support them with you.

But that is only part of a bigger question. On talking over the subject of the Press' slowness with Rank yesterday I gained the conviction that some reform is unavoidable. The fault does not lie in Hiller's disabilities in certain regards as Rank has recently taken off his shoulders all the outdoor work,[3] for what he seems to be ill fitted. Another wheel in the machinery seems to be wrong and I imagine it is your position in the middle of it and the ceremonial, that prescribes your personal interference in every little step of the process. So I hear, that every Korrektur has to go to you and as there [are] 3–5 men who do the correcting I understand why I get one sheet of *Massenpsych.* in two weeks and see no chance to live up to the finishing of these two poor pamphlets (*Jenseits & Mass.*), let alone bigger things like my *Sammlung.* I know that your time is extremely spare that you cannot do all things for yourself, but I dont see why you should want to do it all alone and suffer yourself to be crushed by the common drudgery of the routine work. As you have seen all the manuscripts and decided on them, it would do if you got a glimpse of the last Korrectur, make it the final one and leave the intermediate phases to Hiller, Strachey, Rickman, my daughter and my niece,[4] who now work all of them for the press. Many months could be spared, if you could be moved to throw down part of the burden, which you as the Editor in chief should not carry yourself. Obviously misprints and arrangement of lines should not be objects of your interest, it means anal gratification as you have pointed out yourself.

Next autumn when the three English will have returned to London, a bit of organization will enable you to make the Press work at a threefold accelerated speed. If you give the supervision of translating to Riviere, the literature to Strachey and Rickman and confide the task of correcting all proofs but the last one to the people here and see your assistants once a week in a *Redactionssitzung* [editorial meeting] you will be served like a master and feel like such.

Rickman and Strachey (if he spends the winter at London) should receive some title and position too, perhaps in a way similar to that resorted to in the case of Riviere. Another question worth[y] of your consideration is whether it were not a profit to strike off the idle names on the cover (Flügel and Bryan) and substitute the real hands for them. Then after a while to do the same with the Americans if a working American committee[5] can be created in New York. I expect Frink here end of April and if his private affairs can be arranged I may urge him to accept the part of a leader for the *Journal.* Brill not being conscientious enough and *"trop arrivé".*[6]

Pardon my meddling with your affairs but they are ours and mine too, and Rank is to[o] meek to oppose you in these quarters. My broad shoulders as you say are better to lift this weight. If you have considered all these points write me upon the matters, do at once, what can be done at the moment and leave the rest for discussion in Sept.

With best love to you, wife and children

affectionately yours
Freud

P.S. I have heard of some danger to be expected from reprinting in English your blasphemous paper on the Holy Virgin. You know where my sympathies go but I think it would be foolish to provoke God and the pious Stupidity of Old England as long as our situation is not better insured in that remarkable island. ΨA has its personal foes and so have you.

1. Seventh Congress of the International Psychoanalytic Association, Berlin, 25–27 September 1922.

2. With the June 1922 issue of the *Journal*, vol. 3, p. 2, Joan Riviere was listed as translation editor.

3. The words "outdoor work" are transposed in the original.

4. Judith Bernays (b. 1885), daughter of Eli Bernays.

5. The words "working American" are transposed in the original.

6. "An arriviste."

354

The International Psycho-Analytical Press

10 April 1922

Dear Professor,

I shan't be able to write the *Rundbrief* until after the Easter holidays, so will not delay in answering your important letter which came this morning, especially as time is of the essence of some of the points raised.

I will do my best to think out an address for the Congress, though I fear it won't be in dashing German; among whatever qualities I may possess linguistic fluency is not one of them, at least in a foreign tongue. But what I should like to know is whether the theme of "The Relations of Psa to Medicine" would be of sufficiently general interest to be suitable; to the English and Americans it certainly would, but I am not sure about the Continentals.

I see that you agree with me that Mrs. Riviere certainly deserves a title if she desires it, and there can be no objection to the proposal she makes. As she makes so many claims that can't be granted it is a pleasure and relief to be able to find some that can. She is, as I told you, a most valuable and capable person (it is this undeniable fact that complicates the situation), but whether she will work as easily for me as she doubtless would for you remains for time to prove; it will depend largely on the result of her analysis. As to your other proposals about sub-editors, they want a lot of thinking over. In the first place I can't shift people about, install them and dismiss them, with the freedom that your commanding position could enable you to, and it is I who should get the odium of any resentment, as with Forsyth and Tannenbaum. My position and age are not secure enough for me to neglect careful consideration of other people's susceptibilities, even if I wished to, which I don't. For instance, Bryan and Flugel are both men of very sound judgement, which I value highly and also find most useful. Then they are certainly the two leading analysts in England. Further Bryan has done twenty times as much work for the *Journal* as Rickman and Strachey together, apart from what these may do in the future. He gives every single minute of his time to it and is constantly improving in his weakness (writing of English), so that I am bound to feel loyal to him. Flugel is certainly not so self-sacrificing, but he does very well what he does and is our best reviewer. On the non-medical sides he is invaluable and uses his influence constantly for Psa. In any case I think that such important changes should be discussed, or at least announced, at the Congress, to give some form to the whole matter. The same applies to the Americans and I think we should consider carefully before making definite promises to Frink. The present staff has only been appointed six months, and I feel we should give it a fair trial of a couple of years before making irrevocable and far-reaching changes, especially after our promises at the last Congress.

Coming now to the working of the Press, I note that Rank agrees with my diagnosis of Hiller's unfitness for the outside relations with printers, etc., and that he is kindly burdening himself with this side. The change is too recent for us to expect results as yet, but I am sure that the main delay lies there, as I have urged months ago to Rank. But, as you say, we must also see what can be done to hasten matters at the London end and there I shall be very grateful for any definite suggestions, for I can think of no more myself at the moment beyond what is already in the process of being done. The only one you make, of leaving all but the final proof-corrections to Vienna, I have already put into force some 18 months ago. Not since the first numbers of the *Journal* have I seen any proofs except the last final "printing-off" ones, and the same is true of all the Press books, from the first to the ones now being printed. Hiller, with occasional help from visitors, has done all this on the spot. Of course I could give up seeing even the final proofs, but the expediency of doing so is rather doubtful; still I should like your opinion on the [matter]¹ point. I don't think Rank would feel happy if he never saw a single proof of the *Zeitschrift* unless he had more trustworthy workers under him than I have. On this matter of proofs, therefore, his information seems very out-of-date, and probably relates to the beginning of the *Journal* when there was no English person in Vienna and the printers were quite unused to the work. At that period, it is true, Hiller and I had to see all the proofs in London, and when we omitted to do so the results were deplorable. But now, and for a long time, I do exactly what you suggest, rapidly look through the final proofs, the first I have seen, and return them on the day of their arrival.

I have no love at all for detailed work of this sort, on the contrary, and have feared I have been too complaining in expressing my strong desire to be relieved of routine work wherever possible. After initiating Hiller into the business side I refused to have any more to do with it and have left him to make all his own arrangements, e.g. with American agents, etc.. Similarly I insist on his attending to all publishing details, arrangement of lines, headings, etc., without consulting me, and I am glad to say I am satisfied with the way he does this kind of work. What trouble I have got into is due rather to my deputing too much. For instance, it was physically impossible for me to revise all the translations that have appeared, and so I deputed some to Flugel, Stoddart, and Miss Low (Mrs. Riviere was not then available, as she was fully occupied with the *Vorlesungen*). The results, as Mrs. Riviere will tell you, were the reverse of promising, but I had to be content with inferior work. Hence my intense sigh of relief when Mrs. Riviere offered to take over this irksome part of the work; I wrote a most grateful letter to her.

So that you see my anxiety coincides with your advice to relieve myself of burdens, and is not at all, as Rank mistakenly thinks, the desire to keep control of details. I had better write fully to him describing the procedure of what happens from the reception of work to its appearance and ask him to suggest some modifications, of which I should be only too [welcome][2] glad.

Coming back now to the actual moment, and the help available in Vienna. I do not know who helps Hiller to correct the proofs. That is his affair and he probably gets whoever is accessible at the moment. The three people should also have enough to do with the work I have given them: Strachey with the *Krankengeschichten*, Mrs. Riviere with the Technik articles and revision of Abraham's book,[3] and Rickman with Einleitungsartikeln,[4] of which he has four, besides the revision of Roheim.[5] I do not know how much *Journal* work I can send Mrs. Riviere while she is in Vienna and must discuss it with her; I do not think there will be so very much just at present. Hiller has long had the *Spiegel*[6] and material for Part II of the *Journal*, which I hope he is having printed already, and we have several articles already for Part III. With regard to the revision of translation I should like to make an exception with your own work and also do not think that Mrs. Riviere would care to undertake the sole responsibility of this, though she might do an intermediate revision. At present I have no fewer than thirteen people translating the *Sammlungen*, scattered from India to America, and progress is being made. By the way I am glad to say that your niece's work is good, though not so good as your daughter's. If Anna shews a liking for the work she could in time supplant Hiller in Vienna and he could return to England, but this is a far subject. You know how sorry I am that your translations are not more advanced, but they constitute a good case in point. You rightly complain about the two brochures, *Jenseits* and *Massenpsychologie*. Well, judge from them. I revised the translation of the former a year ago and sent it to Vienna to be printed last *May*. Since then I have had nothing to do with its existence except to receive last December the first two Bogen (after which a further unbroken peace!) and to make repeated inquiries about its fate. So much for my interfering with details. The only information I can get from Hiller during these [ten][7] eleven months is the repeated message that he has been held up for lack of type or of paper but that he hopes things will soon be better. I am quite helpless except to keep writing him and Rank about it. Similarly with the *Massenpsychologie*. I finished the revision last August, and Strachey took it with him to Vienna. This week I get the first of the proofs. And I have left every detail whatever to Hiller and the others in Vienna, choice of paper, kind of type, etc., beyond expressing my general opinion, such as that the type of the War Neuroses was too small for such a small volume.

I am sorry to trouble you at such length, but the matter concerns us all, and I wanted to put the true situation before you since you have been so good as to take deep interest in it all. You know that it is essentially for you that we are all working, which is why your inspiration and approval means so much to us all. If I can produce a Collected Edition of your works in my lifetime and leave the *Journal* on a soundly organised basis I shall feel that my life has been worth living, though I hope to do more for Psa even than that.

yours devotedly
Ernest Jones.

P.S. I have forgotten to comment on another matter which has made me very uneasy, my Madonna essay. In general Mrs. Riviere is rather timid about the possibility of provoking opposition, but in this case it certainly would. I should not mind this if it had no legal consequences, and believe that our blasphemy laws do not apply to works of this class. But to make sure I am taking legal opinion on the matter. I would not have published the Essays without this chapter, as it is the longest and most original part of the book, especially since I re-wrote and extended it. The book is now half printed, so the position is an awkward one, but we must wait till after Easter and see what the lawyer says before deciding anything.[8]

E. J.

1. Crossed out in the original; "point" is handwritten in an otherwise typed letter.
2. Crossed out in the original; "glad" is handwritten.
3. Freud, *Collected Papers*, 2:285–402. Abraham (1927) was translated by Douglas Bryan and Alix Strachey.
4. Freud, *Collected Papers*, 1:9–283.
5. Possibly the short piece by Géza Róheim, "The Significance of Stepping Over," *Journal*, 3 (1922): 320–326.
6. "Type-grid"; used to speed up the process of typesetting.
7. Crossed out in the original.
8. The revised version of Jones (1914a) did appear; see Jones (1923a, pp. 261–359).

355

[postcard]

Eastersunday [16 April] 1922
Vienna

Dear Jones,

Thank you so much for your kind letter. Afraid I am growing old and moody. You spared me all criticism. We are to have a private meeting on Tuesday evening to discuss the affairs of the Press. The translation of the Lectures has arrived excellently done.[1] Tansley is bringing up enormous resistance.

With affectionate wishes

yours
Freud

1. Freud (1916–17), trans. J. Riviere, intro. E. Jones 1922.

356

11 May [1922][1]
Vienna, IX. Berggasse 19

Dear Jones,

This letter I might have written you some weeks before, only I could not as to the habitual work or overwork was joined the effect of some slight indisposition and the loss of time by the bustle about my birthday, Eitingon's visit etc. Also I had cleared my mind by that card which confessed my being wrong on your account.

The conference with Rickman, Strachey, Rank, Hiller and Mrs. Riviere proved to be a failure in a certain sense. I had wanted to learn what the cause of the incredible delays in the publication of the two essays[2] was and I could not find it out. My first suspicion, that the fault lay with you I had to take back and to apologize to you. It became evident that a great part of the causation had its roots in the "Kinderkrankheiten" [growing pains] of the Verlag and the Press, no rooms, not enough types and no fixed arrangements with the printers, but these obstacles are now nearly all of them removed and have been so for some months. This factor does not seem to cover the effect. I am now inclined to think that Hiller is not very efficient on the whole and I know that Rank is managing him with great care and caution because he is not easy to manage. Yet I do not wish to sow discord between you and him, I am willing to drop the matter and to give up my attempts to interfere[3] with the activity of the Press. I dont think my daughter could be intended as a possible substitute for Hiller, whom I readily acknowledge as indispensable with all his shortcomings.

The other subject treated at this conference appeared much more hopeful. Your countrymen made some special demands and prepositions of which you will now be informed by a letter of J. Riviere. The main result was that all three of them seemed ready to assist you in your work and take upon their shoulders such parts of it as you thought desirable to be relieved of, requesting to consult with you regularly in the meetings of the Committee.

The strongest personality among them is obviously the woman. I think you should not reproach [her][4] you [yourself] for having turned her mind to $\psi\alpha$; she is a real power and can be put to work by a slight expenditure of kindness and "recognitions". To be sure she is a concentrated acid not to be used until duly diluted and she is not yet even with you, but I see no real difficulty. My diplomacy is to be as kind to her as I can and not to spare concessions in order to make her open her mind and disclose the access to the deeper layers. If I am to conclude from my impressions up to now I think you were too hard in criticising her, took her resistance too seriously and could not control her sadism after it came up as it had to do. Apart from the duties of the analyst I feel rather kindly towards her although I am prepared to see the wry sides of her character as you describe them to me. (To be continued)

May 12th

She is ready to give a special interest to the translation of my Collection, thinks that the Americans outsiders like my niece etc. will never do good and that the undertaking was sure to gain in uniformity of style when done by very few people. She did not say she wanted to do it all by herself (with the help of one Miss Baines and the contributions of the Strachey's), but I do think you should favour her and if she selects some special papers as f.e. the Beiträge z. Liebesleben[5] for her own job, take them away from the other people to be reserved for her. I think this translation will play a part in your correspondence with her. By the by I saw yesterday Dr. Egerton (Oxford), who came to the meeting, remembered that you had trusted him with some part of the translation and ventured to ask him if he had done it. He answered no but that he was doing it. I dont expect he will prove reliable, but I could not get his address this time.

One of the points mentioned at the conference, to which I strongly adhere, was that all translations should be duly paid. I am not sure if the Press is supposed to pay me as the author of the books appearing, in that case I am willing to pay the translators myself. If not the money will have to be provided for.

Now I am getting sick of this translating business. I was deeply stirred[6] by your saying that you considered the bringing out of my English books as one of the foremost tasks of your work and hope you will see this in the light of a tender exaggeration produced by some sudden impulse, while your substantial work is sure to aim higher and loose-sight [lose sight] of my narrow personal interests. I still appreciate your words as an expression of your unfailing kindness towards me, which as you know I always intend to return.

My birthday left me one year older and that is all about it. I have accumulated some stuff for work in the vacations, no great discoveries to be sure. I am leaving Vienna on July 1st for Gastein, expect to meet my wife and daughter on Aug. 1st somewhere, the place is not yet known, and to come to Berlin about the middle of Sept. As I have only one (American) patient to eight pupils my work is not so heavy now, but my interest in it is rather declining and my appetite for rest, or rather freedom, increasing.

Dr. Frink has come back for May and June. The death of his rival (by carcinoma) has simplified the state of his affairs and abolished all possibilities of scandal in virtuous America.[7] If he has settled down anew, he may become of great use as a leader to the American movement, he is an excellent man, much more reliable, devoted and serious than Brill. Your Mr. Armstrong turned up one day. I advised him strongly to take an $\psi\alpha$ treatment and had to give him the address of Abraham as he found your fees too high. I have not heared if he has arrived there.

You do not mention your wife and children, so I trust they are all right and progressive according to their promise.

With affectionate regards

yours truly
Freud

1. Freud gives the year as 1920.
2. Freud (1920g, 1921c).
3. Freud wrote "infere" then inserted "ter."
4. Crossed out in the original.
5. Freud (1910h, 1912d, 1918a), trans. J. Riviere, in Freud, *Collected Papers*, 4:192–202, 203–216, 217–235.
6. Freud seems to be following the German here: "deeply stirred" = *tief gerührt*.
7. The husband of Anjelika Bijur, Frink's patient and mistress, had just died; see Jones (1957a, pp. 84–85; 1957b, p. 89).

357

15 May 1922
111 Harley Street, London

Dear Professor,

This is only a note to announce the receipt of 275 florins in Holland. It is nearly mid-night and I have still to start preparing an important address I have to deliver to-morrow evening, so I must postpone writing to you for a more favourable opportunity. Perhaps in the meantime I may get a letter from you.

With kindest regards—I hope your birthday was a pleasant one,

yours affectionately
Ernest Jones.

[undated]
111 Harley Street, London

Dear Professor,

I hear that Emden has received two hundred.

yours cordially
Ernest Jones.

358

[postcard]

17 May 1922
Vienna

Dear Jones,

Mrs. R.[iviere] proposed to me some alterations in the arrangement of the *Sammlung* which appeared to me quite good. I recommend them to you for agreement. I am becoming ever more pleased with her. Will you not transfer to her the whole responsibility for this job, establish her as *redacteur-en-chef* [editor in chief]? I think she would do it well, your final revision would be done on good, uniform work and you might feel it as an immense relief.

Yours affectionately
Freud

359

The International Psycho-Analytical Press

22 May 1922

Dear Professor,

At last I come to write, though I wish there were a wireless telephone between London and Vienna. My secretary has left suddenly and I have in her place a congenital imbecile, which involves double work. I hope the indisposition of which you speak was a slight one and now over, though I am sure you are eagerly looking forward to the holidays. It is too bad that you should be troubled over all these business matters, but you would plunge into them instead of entrusting them to me. You are eager to relieve me, and I you, it seems. But you have worked enough otherwise to be able to leave such matters to your representatives, and I should like to take you at your word as you put it in your letter that you are willing to drop the matter of the Press.

This brings me to a matter I am very loth to speak of, and I will tell you why. I wanted to leave Mrs. Riviere in peace to her analysis without disturbance; also I did not want to risk a further discord being sown between us by your quoting passages from my letters, which has already happened. But it seems impossible to avoid the subject, for she has cleverly managed to introduce into her analysis with you the same difficulty as happened with me, namely the intermixture of analytical considerations with external actual ones; perhaps it was unavoidable on her part. Now, however, it seems impossible to postpone, as I had hoped, the latter set of considerations until her analysis was over. Otherwise it may be too late to remedy matters.

First a few words on the analytic side. Her story of my unkindness is, so far as I can see, a pure myth. She is known in the Society as my favourite, people wonder why I endure her behaviour, and I have never treated any other patient with such consideration, in both feeling and conduct. But every proof of kindness on my part was always ignored or taken as her natural right as a matter-of-course, or even regarded as an insult. One example of the latter out of dozens. When she was ill in a nursing home I called and left her some books to read. This she found to be insulting, for it shewed that that was *all* I was willing to give her. This, of course, after the critical ninth month when the expected child did not arrive. After this time she regressed to identification with her father and treated me (with some exceptions, of course) like her younger brother, whose sole function in life was to admit that he was nothing by the side of her greatness. This attitude continued and, now that she feels sure of your support in all her views and wishes, her letters have become more intolerably dictatorial and harsh than ever. Coming now to the practical effects.

If her position is that of an assistant to me she will never find me, and has never found me, lacking in gratitude for her help, in generosity towards her wishes, and in admiration for her gifts. But it depends on this proviso. When I was thirty I had the experience of cooperating with a domineering woman, you know whom I mean, whose one idea was that every act and opinion of mine was in all details to be dictated by her.[1] I could not endure it then, and I am 13 years older now. It is not easy for anyone to get on well with her unless either he is in a position of acknowledged supremacy, as you are, or else is effeminate like Strachey. Even Hiller, who has more capacity than I have for getting on with hectoring women, writes that he has almost reached the breaking-point, is counting the days before she leaves Vienna, and begs me to come to Vienna to help him. The saying here is that her visit to Vienna will be the final and most severe test of Psa, and people are most curious to see if her disdainful way of treating other people like dirt beneath her feet will undergo any modification.

Why I write this is to indicate that the future path may after all be not so smooth and easy as one could wish, and by no means only in regard to myself. She is put at the head of a translating staff, but the important question of capacity to work with other people is not yet proved. For this reason I am strongly in favour of not extending her position, at least officially, until we see how the present one will work.

With regard to helping in other work, e.g. the *Sammlungen*, I have written to ask her if she would like to undertake the correction of the translations prior to my final revision. I hope she will, for I could then do my part much quicker. She sent me some suggestions about the re-arrangement of the *Sammlung* volumes. They struck me as very good, but I did not think them out carefully because I must first know whether you are prepared to reopen this question. You may remember that I also made a number of suggestions when the list was first sent to me, and that they were nearly all vetoed by yourself and Rank, so I had assumed that the matter was closed. Would you prefer it to remain so, or would you like me to revise it with Mrs. R's assistance? In the latter event I could of course submit a final list to you if necessary.

I had not heard about the death in Frink's environment and am glad to think that his problems will be simplified. Like you, I have great hopes of his future, for he seems to be quite the best man in America. On the other hand he has not fulfilled a single one of the promises he made last year, about abstracting articles there or even writing letters, but one must make allowances for his internal turmoil.

I have to write to you about three people who are going to apply to you for a vacancy in October. One at least is valuable. Money-Kyrle,[2] aged 23, an aristocrat of the highest family and, what is better a first class brain. Young as he is I regard him as a powerful thinker[3] with a very clear grasp of essentials. His line is the modern application of mathematics to the principles of science and he may do much in defining the basis of our science in the future. He came to me because of Angst at using his voice, which proved to be based on an obstinate (manifest) masochistic perversion. He made good progress, but failed at the last when I gave him a terminus at Easter. After leaving he foolishly rushed off and married an older woman in a short time, against my advice. She is the second patient, but I know nothing of her except that she is an anthropologist. Incidentally he can afford to pay at least three guineas. The third person is less attractive, Dr. Riggall[4] a member of our society, who was analysed by me for 18 months. He has no brains and I regret that he went in for the work. Worse than that he has the character traits of being untrustworthy and self-seeking, his real interest in Psa not being very deep. I fear his motive in coming to you (for a couple of months) is little more than *Reklame* [window-dressing].

Dr. Glover[5] proved himself in the paper which I mentioned in the *Rundbrief* to be an extremely close thinker and I am sure you will be pleased with the contributions he has made to your theory of melancholia.[6]

Then I am forgetting Dr. Cole, who I believe has already written to you. She is a loyal well-meaning person, with practical capacity, but no theoretical brain. You may remember her at the Congress from her fat figure and her *outré* manner of dressing in bright colours. I analysed her, but could not completely disperse her asthma though it is much better.

Of myself there is little to say except good. My wife's beauty grows daily in her radiant *Mutterglück*,[7] and her charm and devotion are unsurpassable. I am wise enough to know how to profit from my luck and so am exceedingly happy. The boy is singularly amiable for his age and Gwenith has her mother's charm combined with a determinedness that may stand her in good stead in life, where she will have to win her own way. Both are ideally robust and healthy.

One cannot exhaust all topics, but this letter is already long enough. With my warmest good wishes to you and yours

affectionately yours
Ernest Jones.

1. Jones is probably referring to Loe Kann, but the historical evidence here leaves the issue open.

2. Roger E. Money-Kyrle (1898–1980) would become an associate member of the British Psycho-Analytical Society. He had previously been in analysis with Jones for a short time during 1921–1922, and his analysis with Freud was undertaken for brief intervals between 1922 and 1926. An autobiographical sketch is contained in *International Review of Psycho-Analysis*, 6(1979): 265–272.

3. Jones's insight is cogent; Money-Kyrle's later work, for example, influenced the political thought of Leonard Woolf; see Winslow (1990).

4. R. M. Rigall, M.B. 1907 Glasgow, M.D. London 1915, member of the British Psycho-Analytical Society.

5. James Glover (1882–1926), M.B., Ch.B. 1903 Glasgow; elder brother of Edward Glover (1888–1972), M.B., Ch.B. 1909, M.D. 1915 Glasgow. The two had been in analysis with Abraham at various times during the period 1920–1922 in Berlin. James Glover played a key role in directing the Medico-Psychological Clinic, Brunswick Square, and was an associate member of the British Psycho-Analytical Society; both brothers were elected full members of the Society on 4 October 1922.

6. James Glover, "Notes on the Psychopathology of Suicide," read before a meeting of the British Psycho-Analytical Society, 3 May 1922; author's abstract in *Journal*, 3 (1922): 507–508.

7. "Happiness at being a mother."

360
[telegram]

26 May 1922
London

writing today about *sammlungen*

jones

361
The International Psycho-Analytical Press

26 May 1922

Dear Professor,

I received your postcard concerning the *Sammlungen*, and also a number of heated letters from Mrs. Riviere.

It looks as if, unless the matter is grasped with a firm hand, we may drift into a condition of anarchy about it. At present no one knows from whom to take instructions and different plans keep evolving about the arranging of the volumes, the order of printing and all sorts of technical points. You, Rank, Mrs. R., and I all have our own views, many of which are constantly changing. It is plain that the only satisfactory way of working is to institute one definite head to be responsible for the editing and publishing, the unifying of style and terminology, and for the arrangements that make for order. Otherwise there will reign unterminable uncertainty and delay. We have a saying in English: "Too many cooks spoil the broth".

I had assumed that this role would fall to my part, both as editor of the Press and because I am probably in the best position to form an allround judgement in the many respects that have to be taken into account. I should of course be grateful for any suggestions from Mrs. R., and should doubtless accept most of them. I also hoped, and have written to her to this effect, that she would be willing to undertake the reading through and correcting of the translations before I finally revise them; this I should then be able to do in a much shorter time.

She seems to be under the impression, however, that she is to replace me in this position. If you wish this, then of course I will agree, but I cannot pretend that it will be with indifference. I should not be able to work under her orders because of the impossible tone in which she issues them, and I also much doubt whether Hiller would consent to remain in his post under such conditions, though he works in admirable harmony with me. For years I have dreamed, in spite of many disappointments, of being some day able to issue some of your writings in a form that would satisfy me; and this will be the last chance.

Mrs. R. asked me to allot her certain other articles for translation, which I have done by withdrawing them from three other people who, I hope, will not be offended.

yours always loyally
Ernest Jones.

362

[postcard]

31 May 1922
[Vienna]

Dear Jones,
  Whitsunday is near, on that day I shall compose a long letter consisting of three parts, containing in 1 and 2 some analytic remarks on two interesting personalities, in 3 some practical proposals. Until then make your mind easy about it, there is no tragic element and no break in our relations to be feared. I am allright again.

Affectionately yours
Freud

363

The International Psycho-Analytical Press

31 May 1922
London

Dear Professor,

Will you please advise me whether the enclosed article should go in the *Journal*, in *Imago*, or be returned to the author. I find it has some interesting matter but it is not well arranged; nor are the interpretations closely co-ordinated with Nietzsche's work.

Yours always sincerely,
Ernest Jones.

364

4 June 1922
Vienna, IX. Berggasse 19

Dear Jones,

This is the letter I promised you; the persons subjected to analysis are obviously Mrs. Riviere and—you, my practical remarks will come up in the rear.

Somehow I imagine I guess your opinion of me in this matter. You think Mrs. R. has put on her sweetest face and moods, has taken me in completely and seduced me to defend her against you in a chivalrous manner, so that now I am a puppet in her hands, show her the letters I get from you and give you away to her. I am sure you are wrong and I feel rather sorry there should be a need to point it out to you. But if I have misconstrued your opinion I beg you will pardon me.

A secondary analysis like this is no easy or pleasant task. Special duties were imposed on me which I am to discharge with the least possible damage to the parties concerned. You were not consistent on the matter of her coming over to me, but finally you took the stand that you had sent her for finishing and correcting the analysis she had with you. You confessed to some technical errors in analysis which you regretted in so serious a tone that I was led into a misconception about the nature of your wrong. Now this situation given you must be prepared to my taking her side, defending her interest and even turning against you in favour of her analysis. It means simply doing my duty as an analyst. It would not have worked, had I announced from the very beginning your dissension with Dr. J. must not be mentioned in our analysis or: Be sure, whenever you were at variance with him you must have been wrong and he right, for he

is an old friend of mine, foremost among my pupils and the actual leader
of the psa. movement. Better not to have started her analysis at all! So I
had to go through the matter, to listen to the details and to give you away,
before I could get you back. There was no chance of making her see the
abnormality of her reactions unless she had got the acknowledgment of
your errors where you had committed them.

And in fact I cannot praise the way you handled her. You seem to have
soon lost[1] the analytic superiority especially required in such a case. I may
not dwell on criticizing your ways, if you will not miss it, it may be the
subject of oral conversation between us and in German. You reminded me
yourself of your relations with another powerful woman and made me
remember that in that case too much was due to the faults of your own
demeanour. When Mrs. R. brought up her unpleasant reactions you seem
to have treated her as a bad character in life but you never got behind her
surface to master her wickedness.

Let us turn to Mrs. Riviere. If she were a sheer *intriguante* she would
have insisted on her sweetness with me until she had got out of me all
she needed. Now she did not. She soon became harsh, unpleasant, critical
even with me, tried to provoke me as she had done with you. I made it a
rule never to get angry at her. Now I cannot give you the result of our
analysis, it is not yet definite nor complete. But one important point soon
emerged. She cannot tolerate praise, triumph or success, not any better
than failure, blame and repudiation. She gets unhappy in both cases, in
the second directly, in the first by reaction. So she has arranged for herself
what we call *"eine Zwickmühle"* [a dilemma], ask your wife for the explanation of the term. Whenever she has got a recognition, a favour or a
present, she is sure to become unpleasant and aggressive and to lose respect
for the analyst. You know what that means, it is an infallible sign of a
deep sense of guilt, of a conflict between Ego and Ideal. So the interest in
her case is turned to the narcisstic problem, it is a case of a character-
analysis superadded to that of the neurosis. To be sure this conflict, which
is the cause of her continuous dissatisfaction, is not known to her consciousness; whenever it is revived she projects her selfcriticism to other
people, turns her pangs of conscience into sadistic behaviour, tries to render other people unhappy because she feels so herself. Our theory has not
yet mastered the mechanism of these cases. It seems likely that the formation of a high and severe ideal took place with her at a very early age, but
this ideal became superseded, "repressed" with the onset of sexual maturity and ever since worked in the dark. Her sexual freedom may be an
appearance, the keeping up of which required those conspicuous compensatory attitudes as haughtiness, majestic behaviour etc..

Now I dont know if I will succeed with her better or how far success
may go, but for the time being we are getting on quite satisfactorily and

analysis is full of interest. I confess to a kind feeling towards her, partly based on her intellectual capacity and practical efficiency. I would not give her a bit of chance if she was not possessed of these highly valuable qualities. But so she is and "active therapeutics" could make use of this fact to initiate the reconciliation of her Ideal to her Ego. A due recognition of her ability, while the treatment conquers her incapacity for her enjoying success, is to her advantage as well as to ours.

And here I enter upon the subject of practical measures in regard to the *Journal* as well as to the *Sammlung*. I am sorry I cannot approve of your behaviour in regard to the first. It shows more resentment and less generosity in using your powers than is compatible with your high position in the case. Agreeing to give her function and title of "translating editor" and then cutting it down to the part of a "revising translator", which means nothing, leaves her no responsability and no stimulus for spontaneous work, is either the consequence of being afraid of her or of an inability on your side to delegate some portion of your work to other persons. The first motive I take the freedom to declare a purely imaginative one, it is an absurd idea that your place or function could be usurped either with me or in the movement at large by some one else and that jealousy is not worthy of you. The other explication would imply that you are utterly incapable of organization-work and would soon reproduce that situation of some months ago, when you had to acknowledge our criticism of the badness of the translations and contributions to the *Journal* and to find protection in the rejoinder that you could not do better with the helpmates at your disposal, while with more personal regards for your underlings you could spare your own force for more important work and improve the quality of work actually required. I dare say you need not be more afraid of Mrs. R. than of any other person, she is ready to work under your commands and if you fail with her the same or similar difficulties may arise with Rickman, Strachey etc..

It is not doubtful to me that there is something wrong in the present system of running the *Journal*, and that new methods have to be introduced.

Hiller is a good boy and very devoted to you, but there is a suggestion of sport in the way he works. (His relations to Mrs. R. are by no means as strained as is represented to you. Why should he bring her the articles for revision you send him for print?). I will not enter into details, but there is another point, where I cannot agree with you. You wrote to Mrs. R. that the Press will not pay translators, as it has to save money and to keep the Verlag alive by its gains. Yet if we dont pay translators we have no right to expect translations and cannot bring out the books which might help the Verlag.

However I must leave the affairs of the Press to your own decision, I promised not to meddle. As regards the Collection I may feel more interested in my part as author. Permit me to reassume this question from the beginning. It was your idea to have the *Sammlung* translated and I at first was not too eager on it, fearing it might engage you too much in a work of subordinate value, while you were so busy and kept away from doing original research since we had started the Press and the *Journal*. Then on a sudden I grasped that you were right, that ΨA was better known in England by Jung's work than by my own and that it would mean much to the ψα movement if my collections were accessible to the English public. I became enthusiastic about the plan, thought I discovered that nothing was afoot except Mrs. R.'s translation of the Technique and tried to engage translators here to help you. I caught at least one excellent man, Strachey (and his wife), while others I instigated to do it, Meyer, Kardiner (not Blumgart!), my niece Judith B. proved to be of little or no consequence. (By the way I think you are mistaken on some details. Neither I nor Rank ever engaged Egerton, who now is here and seems to have done nothing. The plan of bringing together the *Krankengeschichten* may have originated with me, and if it is yours, I surely never opposed it.) Referring to the arrangement I can see no difficulty in reopening the question, no single line is yet in print, and a definite order taking into account Mrs. R.'s proposals will be the doing of a quarter of an hour. You will get it in a few days and may decide it in a moment. But the chance of your being able to do all the work yourself is to be measured by the answer you gave Strachey. If he sent you the first *Krankengeschichten* in July you could not return the revision until Dec. or January. Done at that rate I will surely not live to see one volume of the four accomplished. My opinion is you should avail yourself of the rare opportunity Mrs. R. presents you for this bit of work. She is an uncommon combination of male intelligence with female love for detailed work and may relieve you of most of the time-spending drudgery connected with such an undertaking. She will act as a skilled secretary and be the strongest power at work, while you continue to be the directing mind of the whole. I can imagine no better combination if you decide to collaborate with her, giving her as many rights and regards as are requested to render a hard job pleasant to the worker. From her information I gather there is another point where I am sorry to say I have to side with her. She strongly objects to your sending to the printer a revision of her texts before she has seen it and consented to your corrections, and I think any writer is entitled to do so. I surely always did. It is not likely unsurmountable difficulties could arise as a consequence of this concession. By the by, I think Strachey's translations done with the utmost care for style and truthfulness could be permitted to go into print before your revision and I am sure you would not find much to alter when you read the final proof.

Now I think enough has been said on all these matters. Believe me I am not fond of acting the Pontifex maximus and having to interfere between your people and yourself. I would prefer to see them more intensely attached to you than to me and you to have become a master in the art of binding others to his personality.

Regarding the other news in your letters, by which you oblige me, I may mention that none of the three people have yet applied. If they do I will surely refuse Rigall on account of the description you gave of him, as I did refuse Dr. Cole who wanted a treatment of 6 weeks. My argument is that I have resolved to diminish the hours of my daily work guessing from various signs, that 9 hours may soon be too much for my powers. If I take only 6 or 7 cases I may still be able to accept Mr. Kyrle, but not his wife, whom you should send to Rank who is as good an analyst as any man I know. Concomitantly with this decrease of work I intend to raise my fees.

The best part of your long letter was that concerned with your family. It made me very glad to hear of this idyll. May it continue so and assure you of the "*Rückendeckung*" [backing] indispensible for a man in the position of a fighter.

There are not many news from my side. My daughter Anna gave a good lecture last Wednesday and will become a member of the society.[2] She is now deeply attached to the other Lou at Göttingen.[3] We break up the house on July first. Next is Gastein.

Affectionately yours
Freud

P.S. The paper on Nietzsche I got from you is not good. At the most a collection of material and as such it is surely incomplete. (It is a pity Lou Salomé does not easily mention him, from some of her casual remarks I gather that the impression he made was not very favourable.)[4] And it is crudely written, would offend the public and not give some precious bit of truth in exchange. The artistic tact of the writer ought to have provided an introduction accentuating that ΨA did not mean pointing out the abnormalities of a great man, that these complexes were present in every individual and equivalent to the elements in chemistry, that big achievements in some sphere led to expect some particular deviation from the so-called normal average elaboration of these elements etc. etc..

1. The words "soon lost" are transposed in the original.

2. A. Freud (1922). The piece is autobiographical; see "Being Analyzed," in Young-Bruehl (1988, pp. 103–139).

3. For an in-depth analysis of Anna Freud's relationship with Lou Andreas-Salomé (1861–1937), see Young-Bruehl (1988).

4. Andreas-Salomé wrote *Friedrich Nietzsche in seinem Werken* (Vienna: C. Konegen, 1894). He is said to have fallen in love with her in 1882 and made a proposal of marriage, which she rejected.

365

The International Psycho-Analytical Press

10 June 1922

Dear Professor,

Your letter cleared up a great part of the situation and I am determined to do my best with what difficulties may remain. I can begin by assuring you that you misconstrued my opinion of your relations to Mrs. Riviere. I know both Psycho-Analysis and yourself well enough to have been fully prepared that you could not undertake her analysis except by seeing her problems through her eyes, and I have not been concerned at the risk of this vision being adverse to myself. My only fear about you was lest you might involve us all in too many *external* and permanent arrangements without having more than a one-sided knowledge of the actual situation in London (I do not speak for myself alone), in other words that your intellectual judgement might be influenced by information from a biassed quarter. And I am bound to say I do not think this fear was unjustified.

About the analysis itself I need say little. The account you gave of her was very clear to me, and I was glad to have my conclusions confirmed. It is, I am sure you will agree, also in the purely analytic aspects a remarkably interesting and complex case, and, like most character analyses, very difficult.

There is more to say about the current situation. You strongly disapprove of my cutting down the function of "translating editor to the *Journal*" to that of "revising translator". Well, I have puzzled my head about this, and have looked through all the correspondence of the past two months, and I am sorry to say that I have failed to discover what this can refer to. In the copies of my letters to Mrs. R., after my immediate grateful acceptance of her offer, all I can find is the exact opposite, namely, an invitation to her to *extend* her offer to supervise the translations, so that it might also include the arranging with translators (allocation, etc.). I am glad to leave in her hands everything on earth to do with the translations except perhaps the decision of which articles should appear at all, and even here I should welcome her advice. I can only conclude, therefore, that she is under some serious misapprehension here, which I should be glad to clear up.

On the basis of this you conclude that either I must be jealous of her, which, as you rightly say, would be absurd; or else that I cannot delegate work to others, and so am utterly incapable of organization-work and do not show proper personal regard to my underlings. I should be very sorry indeed to think this could be your opinion; I feel pretty sure it is not the opinion of anyone acquainted with my way of working, least of all of anyone who has been in a subordinate position to me.

About the *Sammlungen* you have cleared up my essential point, that someone should have definite charge of the publishing, so that it should not be held up by continual uncertainty. I have not yet received Mrs. R.'s suggestions you speak of, but you may be sure I will give them every consideration. Nor have I yet had an answer to my invitation that she revise the translations before I do, which would save very much time. The only remaining question is whether I should read through these revised translations myself (to read them through in typescript or in proofs takes the same time, but corrections in the latter case would cost much more). The books would of course appear sooner if I never saw them before publication, but I am immodest enough to think that they would not be so good. Even with a first-class translator like Mrs. R. I find many mistakes, made through her not knowing scientific terms, through the influence of her complexes, etc.. The other plan would save me much work, but I should prefer to revise them nevertheless, for it is my ambition that your writings, especially when produced by the Press, should be as well done as is in our power.

Two other details. I did not write to Mrs. R. that the Press will not pay its translators. On the contrary, I agreed with her that this would be desirable, but pointed out that as our means were limited we should not refuse to accept work done for nothing (quoting herself and myself as examples). My idea is simply that until the Press is better established we should accept work that the translator is willing to do for nothing, and in other cases pay for it (i.e. not to make a rule of insisting to pay in all cases, as the *Zeitschrift* does for its articles).

There is a further matter on which you criticise me for an opinion I do not hold; namely, that I should send to the printer a revision of Mrs. R.'s text before she has seen it and consented to the correction. I not only agree with her view, but it has always been my practice; though, incidentally, I doubt if she intends to make the same concession to the people whose translations she revises (at least she did not with the Lectures). So far as I can remember the only manuscript she has sent me since she has been in Vienna has been two Technique articles,[1] and, though I have revised these, they are still here waiting to be typed. When ready they will of course be submitted to her. If my memory is at fault here I should be glad to know about it, so that I may apologize to her.

Finally, I do not think it would be fair to test my powers of dealing with co-workers (or of binding them to me personally) by the exceptional case of Mrs. R. alone. It is true that I shall make every endeavour to bring success to our relationship, but the result will certainly depend more on her than on myself. I can say that I have never yet failed to get on with a co-worker and have made many excellent friends in this way, but I have never yet had to deal with one whose tone was so full of rude and overbearing superciliousness. One would think that ordinary civility was not an unreasonable demand to make from a colleague, but in this case I am making the experiment of dispensing with it; and this quite vitiates your comparison between her and Rickman or Strachey, who surely both have good manners.

About the Nietzsche article I fully appreciate what you say. May I trouble you to send the article back, so that I may return it to him with a further letter. Altogether I am afraid that the *Journal* affairs are occupying an excessive amount of your time, but that belongs to the burden of your position. I am beginning too, in my small way, to feel that leadership has its heavy disadvantages.

Since writing last I hear that Lissa & Kann have received from de Groot 275 and 625 florins (May 8 and June &),[2] from Bernays 2759 florins, and interest 13i florins: also a few sums paid out. Do they notify you of these matters, or should I still do so?

Your very kind remarks about my family were keenly appreciated. They flourish excellently, all of them. The latest production of the little girl (aged 20 months) was to procure some coins, insert them between the thighs and then withdraw them with evident signs that she regarded them as bodily products. As she cannot yet know the food-value of money it shews how primordial this symbolism must be, though one must perhaps remember that she is the child of an analyst and an economist.

With kindest regards,

yours always loyally
Ernest Jones.

1. All of the articles in the "Papers on Technique" section in Freud, *Collected Papers*, 2:285–402, were translated by Joan Riviere with the exception of the one done by James Strachey (pp. 334–341).

2. Perhaps a typographical error for "June 7"; on early typewriters the *&* key is above the 7 key.

366

[postcard]

23 June 1922
London

Dear Professor,
May I remind you of the Nachtrag you said you would write for the English transl. of the *Massenpsychologie* (à propos Trotter's second edition).[1]

Yours ever
Ernest Jones.

1. Regarding Trotter (1916), 2nd ed. 1919.

367

Dear Jones,

I ca'nt know when this letter will reach you. Yesterday a general strike of the officials broke out which may mean the beginning of the final decomposition or be only a forerunner of it.

I think our friendship has gone through a severe test, and has fairly well stood it. I could say it was a triumph were it not for two of your sayings which strike me as insincere or at least exaggerated. The first was your suspicion that Mrs. Riviere wanted to put herself in your place, the second your humble request that at least "the decision which articles should appear at all" should be reserved to you. It sounds like mockery.

The necessities of a "secondary analysis" put me into the unwished for position to criticize and analyse yourself, a task highly undesirable with a friend of whose value you feel sure and whose frailties you are accustomed to forbear. Now what made the case so hard for me was the fact that accuracy and plainness is not in the character of your dealings with people. Slight distortions and evasions, lapses of memory, twisted denials, a certain predilection for sidetracks prevail and whenever I had to examine a case between you and her in detail I had to find, that you were to be doubted while that implacable woman overemphasising the importance of the slightest features yet was right and could not be refuted.

To some more serious errors in handling her you had confessed yourself and so you may guess how fearfully constrained my position was. I hope I have succeeded with you but I cannot say I have much altered the other party. It lasted months before I began to understand the conditions of her case. I am still struggling to find out the technical ways of character-analysis now the time has passed and I dont think I could impress her in a noticeable degree. She intends to come back for a month in Oct.. I fear she will require special care and regards indefinitely. If she had not those inhibitions, analysis would never find a hold on her. It now all lies with you and I may soon drop out of the relation.

As regards Rickman and the Strachey's I send them back to you within a week. Both will prove of great help to you if you treat them generously. I propose the Stracheys should become members (full) of the Society as they have gone through $1\frac{1}{2}$ years of serious analysis, are theoretically well informed and people of a high order. To be sure their conflicts have not been decided, but we need not wait so long, we can only instigate the processus which has to be fed by the factors of life. Becoming full members—as well as Rickman—would bind them to the interests of the Society. Stracheys are likely to remain in England next winter. Do not put back her for him, she is very valuable.

As for me I did not feel tired until now when the gloomy prospects of the political situation became obvious. If I can depart, my address in July will be Badgastein, Villa Wassing.

With affectionate regards for you and your dear family

Freud

368

[postcard]

3 July 1922
Badgastein, Villa Wassing

Dear Jones,

Here I am and hope I may recover from the strain of the last weeks.

I dont think in Trotter's second edition there is any fundamental new turn which would necessitate the note in the *Massenpsych* I intended.

Affectionately yours
Freud

369

[postcard]

17 July 1922
Badgastein

Dear Jones,

You do not mention if the word *"Wiederhol[un]gstraum"* was used by me and *where* I used it. In any case it is not meant to be a technical term.[1]

The German for recurrent dreams is *"wiederkehrende"* Tr. if you dont prefer *"rekurrierende"*.[2] I suppose the *Wiederholungstr* would be a dream repeating an actual experience.

Yours affectiontely
Freud

1. Freud may be replying to a missing piece of correspondence; it is also possible that he was reviewing an early version of the Glossary.
2. "Recurring"; the German word is written in Gothic script.

370

19 July 1922
42 York Terrace, London

Dear Professor,

I must disturb your summer rest with a few business matters, though I hope they are of a simple nature. To begin with the least important, Hiller tells me that you disapproved of an article by Johnson,[1] and I should like your definite decision about this. The article was accepted at the request of the Society, on whom, including Mrs. Riviere, it made a very good impression when it was read. The interest of it seemed to be the attempt to devise an ideal nomenclature, and the evidence that such attempts were strongly influenced by unconscious factors.

Now that the charge of the *Sammlungen* has been left solely to me I have carefully reconsidered the whole question and wish to lay my opinion before you. (I hasten to add that this process does not involve a moment's delay in proceeding with the publishing, which is going on satisfactorily). The matter is not so simple as simply publishing one particular book, for a set of *Collected Papers* has certain characteristics of its own, such as re-arrangement, etc.. One thing I am sure of, that it would make a bad impression on the English scientific public to issue such a collection in small volumes, as had to be done in German. The usual size of such volumes in English would be from 800 to 1200 pages, and though I do not propose anything like this I think the volumes should not be less than 400 pages.[2] In the second place I am satisfied with the grouping of all the sections except one, that entitled *Theoretisches*, which is very mixed in content. I agree with Mrs. R. that the long *Geschichte* article[3] should be taken from this and added to the first section (Einleitung), and that *Die Zwei Prinzipien* and the Narcissism article[4] be extracted and added to the *Metapsychologie*. I would also add the Triebumsetzungen to the latter,[5] and put six others in the Angewandte section (*Tatbestandsdiagnostik, Aufklärungen, kulturelle Sexualmoral, Kinderlügen, Analcharakter,* and *Traum und Telepathie*).[6] That would leave only 65 pages in this section, which I would term Clinical.

Then I would group the whole into three volumes instead of four, which has the great advantage of making each volume unitary in nature. First volume, 527 pages, Einleitung, Clinical, and Technique., all practical medical papers. Second, 542 pages, *Krankengeschichten*. Third, 420 pages, *Metapsychologie* and Angewandte. That is as evenly distributed as I can make it, for I have tried all plans, from three volumes to seven, and all other possibilities gives great unevenness in size as well as other drawbacks.

My plan would be to employ two printers simultaneously for the first two volumes, and I think I could revise articles for press faster than any two Viennese printers, so that there would be no delay on this score. The first one should have started already. The second one cannot start until we have the first article, the Dora one, which Strachey cannot let me have before August. At present, of 71 articles, 27 have been translated, of which I have revised 8. Strachey strongly approves of this plan; Mrs. R. would prefer to subordinate everything else to the pleasure of getting out one small volume before everything else, but I think her judgement in the matter is vitiated by this obviously personal consideration and by her non-medical outlook. In any case, she would agree to my plan.

She and I have spent one long evening talking over matters, and in my opinion the result was very satisfactory. Contrary to your opinion, I thought I could detect some changes in her reactions as the result of her visit to Vienna, and for the better. Or it may be that she is more virulent with a pen in her hand.

I have seen Strachey once and am to spend next Wednesday evening with him. Rickman was here for an evening last week. He has taken a house five minutes from me, which raises fears in me on account of his oriental attitude towards the value of time. I like both men greatly and am looking forward to collaborating with them. What do you think of my suggestion of making Rickman co-director of the Press with myself?

At our next meeting, which will be in October, Rickman will surely be promoted to full membership, which by our rules can only be done once a year, at the annual meeting in October. The Stracheys will also certainly be made associate members, and they shall be made full members if I can over-ride the rule to the effect that members must have been associate members first for at least a year.

The preparations for the Congress are going ahead fairly satisfactorily and a report of them will reach you in a few days in the form of a *Rundbrief*.

I have a bad cold at present, the first since November, but fortunately it has not reached my family. It has been an exceptionally hard-worked summer and I wish I could see my way to a proper holiday. I hope you are enjoying yours and that it will bring you all refreshment.

With affectionate regards,
Ernest Jones.

P.S. Groot fl. 600 July 5
Rickman fl. 403,85 July 14.[7]

1. The visiting Reverend P. Youlden Johnson read "Technical Terms for the Various Dynamic States of Mind" before the British Society, 16 February 1922; see *Journal* 3 (1922): 264 for an abstract of the paper.
2. The number "500" had been typed initially, then "4" was handwritten over the "5."
3. Freud (1914d).

4. Freud (1911b, 1914c).
5. Freud (1917c).
6. Freud (1906c, 1907c, 1908d, 1913g, 1908b, 1922a).
7. The entire postscript is handwritten.

371

[postcard]

25 July 1922
Badgastein

Dear Jones,

I have just got your letter and am glad to leave to your decision everything you like regarding the Collection. Only to my judgment "Triebumsetzungen" and *Analerotik* belong to the Clinical,[1] not to *Metapsych.* or Angewandt. I will send your letter to Rank and make him give his opinion to you directly. As for Rickman and Strachey I rejoice in your way of accepting them and will not interfere with your plans. I am all right and hope you and family will find a way to a thorough recreation.

Yours affectionately
Freud

1. Freud (1917c, 1908b).

372

The International Psycho-Analytical Press

1 August 1922
London

Dear Professor,

I shall be sending the general news in a *Rundbrief* in a day or two, but should like to let you know how the *Sammlungen* are getting on. I had discussed the matter of the arrangement separately with the three Anglo-Viennese, but thought it better to have a joint meeting as well, which we did on Thursday evening. We arranged many of the details satisfactorily so as to secure a uniform plan in such matters as foot-notes, etc.. I submitted to them the enclosed programme of the general arrangement of articles, as I had indicated to you in my last letter. Mrs. Riviere did not like the Early and the Late Clinical Papers appearing in the same volume. Strachey felt strongly against the case of Female Homosexuality[1] appearing with the *Krankengeschichten*. If this is transferred to the Clinical Section as well as the Triebumsetzungen (about which I quite agree with your remark) and perhaps also the Zwang- und *Religionsübung,* the balance is once more thrown out.[2] I am waiting for Rank's criticisms and am in the meantime preparing an alternative scheme which I will submit to Mrs. Riviere before writing to you about it. It is not easy to secure complete agreement among six people with independent views, but I will try to get as near unity as is possible.

I should be glad to have a line from you on the question of Rickman's Directorship and Johnson's article.

Matters for the Congress[3] are proceeding satisfactorily; it will be a heavy undertaking, because of the large number of Papers.

I hope you are having an enjoyable holiday. It is not too hot in London, and we are all very well here.

Tansley is spending the evening with me tomorrow.

With affectionate regards,

yours always
Ernest Jones.

1. Freud (1920a).
2. Freud (1917c, 1907b).
3. Seventh Congress of the International Psychoanalytic Association, Berlin, 25–27 September 1922.

373

10 August 1922
Pension Moritz
am Salzberg bei Berchtesgaden

Dear Jones,

I am living here with the greater part of my family from Berlin and Vienna in something like paradise, yet tired by the cure I got through before.

I fully agree to your intention about Rickman's directorship. Johnson's innovations appeared repelling to me, in any case they are premature. I would inhibit the publication of his article if publishing it meant consenting to it.

Every time you are submerging into the tiresome business of arranging the papers of the Collection I feel deeply touched and somewhat regretful to be the cause of so much trouble. I think no arrangement would prove completely satisfactory unless a purely chronological one, which disregards the other characters of the papers, and I know this cannot be done.

Submitting to your judgment in all points I still must insist on the impression that "Character & *Analerotik*" as well as its continuation cannot be shut out from the Clinical volume, while 18 *(Traum als Beweismittel)* may very well be transported to "Angewandtes".[1] I sympathize with Strachey's criticism, that female Homosex.[2] should not be put into the *Krankengeschichten*. There is the difficulty too, that it had not been translated by the Strachey's. The balance, which you now accentuate so strongly, does not seem so over-important to me.

It is a pity that in the mean time while we debate on order and distribution, no letter can be printed.

If my feeling of fatigue continues, the Congress will be no enjoyment to me, but there are weeks between.

Frink and his future wife are expected to come to Berchtesgaden and I will have to see them as I did in Gastein. I am fond of both, yet still more of my repose.

Hoping you can procure some relaxation of work in spite of the preparation for this Congress,

I am with affectionate regards to the whole family

yours
Freud

P.S. I may stay here 4–5 weeks.

1. Freud (1908b, 1913a).
2. Freud (1920a).

374

15 August 1922
The Plat, Elsted

Dear Professor,

I am spending the time till the Congress here in idyllic surroundings, though three patients I have (two melancholics) would suffice to remind me of work even if I did not have the *Journal* and Congress arrangements. I am sorry to say that Hiller has again been ill, first with bronchitis and then with a sharp attack of gallstones. Otherwise I have only good progress to report.

I suppose you still got my letters to Gastein? Two more comments on the topics in them. There are four sessions at the Congress whose presidency can be allotted. Assuming that you, as at the Hague, would not wish to be burdened with such work, I suggested that Abraham, Ferenczi, Oberholzer (there are 15 Swiss coming to the congress) and van Emden, after considering the claims of Hitschmann and Frink to be less urgent. Abraham insists on Vienna being represented, so we should like your opinion. As an alternative I have suggested that the matter be made informal and only decided at the *Vor*-Congress.[1]

As I indicated in my last letter I submitted yet another arrangement of the *Sammlungen* to Mrs. R., but it had no better fate than my previous ones, so I have agreed to accept her view that we use the one drawn up in Vienna in June. In the meantime no time whatever has been lost with the work itself, and although Hiller's illness will doubtless delay matters we should be able to report something positive by the time of the Congress, for some manuscript has already been sent to the printers.

I was sorry to hear that your cure had proved so exhausting, but trust that the rest with your family will revive your energies completely before long.

This afternoon we motored to the sea in beautiful weather and my wife, who is not very familiar with the seaside, enjoyed it nearly as much as my little daughter.

Please give our kindest remembrances to your family, and accept my affectionte regards,

yours always loyally
Ernest Jones.

1. At the meeting of the Secret Committee prior to the Seventh Congress of the International. For proceedings of the official congress, see *Journal*, 4 (1923): 358–381.

375

22 August 1922
The Plat, Elsted

Dear Professor,

I have just received today a letter from a Mr. Sprott[1] telling me, to my surprise, that he arranged with you last July to lecture at Cambridge next autumn and asking me if I could arrange some public lectures for you to give in London. It would be wonderful to know that you were lecturing in England, but I must first inquire of you about the authenticity of the man, for perhaps he is nothing but a lecture agent. I know nothing about him. I should be glad to get your views on the matter. There would of course be plenty of people in London who would like to hear you, but I do not know if you would care to give a series of lectures merely arranged from within, without any University invitation.

I hope you got my letters at Gastein and one written to Berchtesgaden and trust that you have recovered from the fatigues of the *Kur* [spa].

yours affectionately
Ernest Jones.

1. W. J. H. ("Sebastian") Sprott; translator of Freud (1933a).

376

24 August 1922
Berchtesgaden, Salzberg
Pension Moritz

Dear Jones,

I think I got all your letters, some of them rather late. Dont be annoyed if my answer is a poor one. I am not feeling very strong and am deeply shaken by the death of my best niece, a dear girl of 23, who took Veronal last week while alone at Vienna.[1] The dark prospect of our country and all the uncertainties relating to the time I will have to come back do not improve my mood.

I gladly resign the presidency of a Congress-meeting, but in my opinion you ought to have me let off with a lecture, which all of you refused. As a revenge I have not yet been able to settle my mind on a definite topic.[2] I feel indifferent about the question who should take my place. Frink is still with me at Berchtesgaden and gets an hour of analysis at times. I think it would do him good to be distinguished and impress his future wife who is rich and not mean.

I am glad to hear you gave in to Mrs. Riviere in the matter of the *Sammlung.* The good impression she has made on me did not vanish with her personal presence.

I am still more glad that you have contrived to get a recreation in the country with your wife and family, to whom I send my best wishes.

Affectionately yours
Freud

1. Caecilie Graf (b. 1899), daughter of Freud's sister Rosa (1860–1942) and Heinrich Graf (1852–1908); see Jones (1957a, p. 86; 1957b, p. 91).

2. Freud's paper "Some Remarks on the Unconscious" was never published, but it contained ideas later found in *The Ego and the Id* (Freud, 1923b); see Jones (1957a, p. 87; 1957b, p. 92).

377

30 August 1922
The Plat, Elsted

Dear Professor,

My thoughts are very much with you over this new blow you have received from fate, and I deeply sympathize with you. It seems to me however that we older people lose less from the present state of the world than the younger people who are deprived of all reasonable prospect of success and happiness. We have at least enjoyed life in the days when the world was sane and beautiful.

As for Austria, don't you think that a swift fall this autumn will at least hasten the day when either the Allies or the Little Entente will be forced to make more permanent and *lebensfähige* [viable] arrangements for that unhappy country? The same is true of Germany, though there the matter is complicated by mutual hate so that probably it will take longer. But another two years' time should see better conditions beginning in Europe.

I will not trouble you with business this time, not that there is much going on. The Congress promises to be in every way successful, though I shall be glad when it is over. I see now your wisdom in insisting it should not be every year.

We are all benefitting here from the good country air and life, especially of course the children. It is most interesting to observe the appearance of personality and character traits so early in life, and I think I have some evidence of congenital ideation.

My wife and I send you and Frau Professor our warm sympathy in your grief and in your efforts to sustain it.

Believe me

yours always most affectionately
Ernest Jones.

378

3 September 1922
Salzberg bei Berchtesgaden

Dear Jones,

Mr. Sprott is a young man of excellent manners and good connections, a favourite of Lytton Strachey and friend of Maynard Keynes,[1] a Cambridge student of psychology, who came to invite me for a course of lectures to be given at Eastertime (not autumn, as in your letter). I accepted for the case that I should feel so tired at Easter, that I had to give up work, and yet fresh enough for some other enterprise, which, as you see, is only a polite way of declining. You may be sure I will continue my work as long as I can do any work. Besides we agreed that the question of language would be an obstacle in any case.

I have been deeply impressed by the unfortunate death of a dear little niece of mine, 23 years old, who took Veronal and died of pneumonia on Aug. 18th. She was the only left child of my widowed sister, the boy having been killed in war.

We intend to leave here middle of Sept. for Hamburg and Berlin.

I hope you and your family enjoy yourself in the country,

Affectionately yours
Freud

1. Strachey and Keynes, along with their close companion Sebastian Sprott, were members of the Apostles, a secret society at Cambridge.

379

[?] October 1922
81 Harley Street, London

Dear Professor,

It seems long since I wrote to you in Vienna. I hope that your native air soon completed the cure of your cold, and that you are in a good mood to face the coming session. I wonder what is your opinion of Money-Kyrle? In spite of his lack of discipline I think he has a keen and powerful mind if only it could be clarified and freed of inhibitions.

I trust you were satisfied with my conducting of the Congress. It was not too easy to keep a clear head with so much pressure in all directions, but I enjoyed the experience and had the impression that the Congress was in general a success in spite of the excess of papers. Next time we must weed them out more strictly.

I was glad to hear from the R-Br. [*Rundbrief*] that you liked my Adolescence paper.[1] It created a good impression here, and the Principal of the London Educational Institute so far lost his sense of proportion as to call it the most important contribution to educational theory for many years. But, as I indicated in the previous R-Br., I am not happy about our recapitulation theory and wish we could enlist the services of a good modern biologist. If Tansley were more advanced or experienced I would discuss it with him, but he is not yet sure of the ontogenetic side of the Oedipus complex, let alone the phylogenetic or prehistoric.

I was very distressed at the latest difficulty with Hiller, and should be glad if you could suggest any further action I could undertake. I used all my influence with him in Berlin (twice till four in the morning) but he was at the time upset by your coldness to him there. I fear the root of the matter is that Rank has not succeeded in winning him personally. One cannot forget of course that Hiller is a neurotic and must be treated accordingly to get the best out of him.

I was glad to see Anna and your two sons look so well in Berlin. On my return I found my family flourishing as usual. The youngster, although he is not yet eight months old, is very active and this week performed the feat of walking alone across the room with the aid of a wheel-chair that he pushed.

With my affectionate regards to you,

Yours as always
Ernest Jones.

1. Jones (1922g).

380

6 November 1922
Vienna, IX. Berggasse 19

Dear Jones,

Many thanks for your letter, the first you wrote me since we met at the Congress and the good news you give of your family. I am all right myself and so are my people.

As regards Money-Kyrle I can shape no judgment on his intellectual powers as long as he is exhibiting all his inhibitions and his resistance which he does like any "greenhorn" in his first weeks. His history is clear but his extraordinary reactions to it are by far more conspicuous.

Our present difficulties weigh heavily even with me. I see Hiller is not willing to stay except when his salary is raised to a height, not excessive in itself surely but out of proportion to our actual funds and his efficiency. I dont think my or Rank's behaviour has much to do with his determination. I never was anything but kind to him, but he kept aloof from me, I may say: from us, exclusively footing on his relation to you and aspiring to no personal relation to any of us. I may as well inform you, that he complains bitterly of the treatment he got from you, although I do'nt know it [in] what it consisted.

I am sorry there should exist so many points of disagreement between us at the time. I did not approve your attitude towards Mrs. Riviere nor can I find you are justified in blaming Rank or take your side in the case [of] Hiller. I am of [the] opinion that some aspects of your behaviour with people create more difficulties than you are aware of. As you ask for my judgment on the way you conducted the Congress I will suppress my habitual frankness with old friends and plainly say that you suffered it to drift occasionally with too weak a hand. Your speech at the banquet was a success however.

Do write me again!

Yours affectionately
Freud

381

[postcard]

10 November 1922
Vienna

Dear Jones,

Got today first proofs of the *Sammlung*, congratulate you on it. May I live to see the last of vol. IV (or III).

On page 4 I found a rather important mistake, due to the ignorance of the translator? overlooked by you? "while the upper third and the *middle division* serve the representation of the leg"

It ought to be: the *median* lobe or region on the inner surface ([French][1] text: *mediale Anteil*). Or would it be understood this way in English?

Yours affectionately
Freud

1. Crossed out in the original.

382

19 November 1922
81 Harley Street, London

Dear Professor,

I was glad to hear you are well, though unfortunately I cannot say the same of myself. For a fortnight I have been in severe pain, night and day, from neuritis in both arms, which does not make it easy to keep up good spirits.

The Eitingons arrived on Thursday and I have seen them three times, including most of to-day. Tomorrow evening we are to have a meeting with Rickman and Strachey to discuss the Press situation, about which I will then write at once to Rank. It was a great pleasure to see Eitingon, for I am very fond of him; he is so fundamentally sincere and throughout well-meaning.

So a real start is being made with the great business of the *Sammlungen*, which is a considerable undertaking. I was chagrined to hear of the medical mistake I overlooked in the correction (I suppose I carelessly read *mediale Anteil* as *mittlere Anteil*, not recognising that mediale in this sense is a technical German expression for what we call mesial); though I corrected some dozens that is no excuse for overlooking one, especially one where neurological readers might find something to criticise, so I am very glad you found it and compliment you on your sharp sight.[1]

I was sorry, and also disappointed, to learn that you still think there are disagreements between us. My optimistic temperament had led me to hope, in spite of your changed attitude towards me in Berlin, that they belonged to the past. Indeed I would still hope so but for your expression "at the moment", for your references to them are very general. I refer to them unwillingly, but I cannot make my letters to you artificial, as they would be if I confined myself to external news, which besides is contained in the *Rundbrief*.

The first point you say you disapprove of is my attitude towards Mrs. Riviere. If this relates to anything in the past few months then I am entirely blind to it, for my only feelings towards her in this time have been those of friendliness and gratitude and I was under the impression—which I trust is not an illusion—that my behaviour was in correspondence.

Then you do not think I am right in blaming Rank, though I do not know what for. I do not think I have ever blamed or criticised him in any matter in his own sphere, but I have sometimes had to defend myself against misstatements he has made about me. If you refer to my remark that Hiller and he did not get on well together that is a mere observation, due to a difference in temperament, and there is no question of blaming either for it. It is true that I do not consider Rank to be infallible. For instance, at the present juncture when the Verlag is in a critical position I should have found it wiser of Rank if he had made more efforts for cooperation and a united front instead of doing things that were bound to repel us. I say "us", for since writing my last *Rundbrief*,[2] in which I say plainly what I think I have received the Berlin letter in which Abraham takes up a still sharper position, and also Rickman, to whom I telephoned Rank's message, was not exactly pleased at the cool way in which he had been ignored.

Finally you say you cannot take my side in the Hiller case. I cannot be sure what you conceive my side to be, but to me it appears like this. While defending Hiller a little, so far as I thought it wise, before the Committee, I concentrated my efforts on inducing him to agree to Rank's proposals which I had myself honestly accepted. In this direction I strained my influence with him, working hard over the ground in all my spare time (twice up till four in the morning). The total result was a failure, for he did not or could not carry out the promises he made me. And in the end I have earned your displeasure (I suppose for my failure) and lost his friendship. That is certainly depressing, like all failures, but in the circumstances I knew of no better path to take, nor do I yet know of one that offered a better prospect of leading to success.

As to your own repeated disapproval of me I need not tell you how grievous I find that, for you must know what part you play in my life and feelings. If it lay in my power to alter your attitude through any conduct of mine I would gladly do so; if it is not in my power I must somehow accept the fact. So far I have honestly tried to be true to myself and to act in the best way I could according to the light that is in me, but it may well be that there are dark places which that light does not illuminate. In the latter case I can only wait till I receive some criticism which is concrete enough for me to put to the test and which also corresponds to the facts as they are known to me, but such criticism is rare.

Please forgive me if this letter is not written in too happy a vein; you will not find that surprising if you reflect for a moment on the complexities of my position as it appears to me: health, friends, the future of the *Journal*, work, even practice (my solitary consultation since July has remained solitary and I have several vacant hours). But I will end on two brighter notes: my domestic happiness is all that man could wish it to be, and my spirit has always proved indomitable in the long run. So I cannot doubt that everything will change for the better—you see once more my optimism.

always your loyal friend,
Ernest Jones.

1. The passage was altered to read: "while the upper third and the mesial portion serve the representation of the leg . . ."; see Freud, *Collected Papers*, 1:14.

2. In his *Rundbrief* of 16 November 1922 Jones provided an outline of how Rank, with Hiller, issued orders "behind our backs" to the group secretaries of the branch Societies of the International Psychoanalytic Association (Sigmund Freud Copyrights, Wivenhoe; and Rank Collection, Butler Library, Columbia University).

383

22 December 1922
42 York Terrace, London

Dear Professor,

I hope you received a personal letter I wrote to you about three weeks ago?[1] Hiller brought a message from you, asking, namely, if I agreed to Bose's name being inserted on the *Zeitschrift*. Certainly I do. Bose told me he had gladly accepted your invitation and you will have seen by now that the *Journal* (Nr. 4) has already carried out your excellent Berlin suggestion of printing identical names in the two organs.[2]

I could only see Hiller for one evening on his way through London to his home and, as he forgot to bring his books along and Rickman was unable to come, it was hardly a business meeting. Also so much depends on Rank's answer to my questions in my *Rundbrief* of Dec. 8.[3] I asked for an urgent reply, but have heard nothing as yet. Nor has the Vienna *Rundbrief* of Dec. 15 yet arrived (the Berlin and Budapest ones have). Hiller himself is pessimistic about the Verlag being able to do any of the Press work, even the *Herstellung* [production], but I shall be disappointed if that proves to be so—though I am the only English person who has much hope of it. The outlook will be dark otherwise.

I am glad to be able to assure you personally, as well as in my *Rundbrief*, that your suspicion was not founded about my using Rank as a *Schirm* [screen] for yourself—the reverse would be nearer the truth. Any slight protests I have ever felt inclined to make about your criticisms of me I have made directly and honestly. There is nothing behind that needs to be transferred elsewhere. About you, dear Professor, my only feeling is one of regret that you should think poorly of me, but this feeling has no morbid manifestation or strength, and I sincerely hope that the need for it will before long pass away.

I saw Major Jones, the Anglo-Indian you kindly referred to me, and have sent him to Ferenczi for analysis, for it seemed to me unfavourable that he should be analysed in the same town as his wife lives in. He is a weak character and has behaved very badly to her.

Tomorrow we are going to Elsted for a week. My wife and children are well and flourishing, I am happy to say. My neuritis is still very painful; it has lasted now six weeks, night and day. Practice is a little better this month. Mrs. Riviere tells me you are still more than busy. She made an excellent impression on her return and I think we shall work well together.

With kindest Christmas and New Year greetings to yourself and your family

Yours always affectionately
Ernest Jones.

P.S.[4] Anna's article appears in Part 2 of the *Journal.*[5]

1. Letter missing.
2. Girindrasekhar Bose is acknowledged as an associate editor on the title pages of the *Zeitschrift* (1923) and the *Journal* (1923).
3. In his *Rundbrief* of 8 December 1922 Jones reviewed the financial problems of the Press, which he regarded as "an external legal facade for the English side of the Verlag," and he emphasized the need to continue printing English books in Germany and exporting them in a professional manner (Sigmund Freud Copyrights, Wivenhoe; and Rank Collection, Butler Library, Columbia University).
4. This postscript is written out at the top of the first page of the letter.
5. A. Freud (1922).

384

7 January [1923][1]
Vienna, IX. Berggasse 19

Dear Jones,

I am sorry you should still be suffering and as I felt rather ill myself these two weeks I am full of sympathy for you.

This last year brought a disappointment not easy to bear. I had to find out that you had less control of your moods and passions, were less consistent, sincere and reliable than I had a right to expect of you and than was required by your conspicuous position. And although you yourself had proposed the committee you did not refrain from endangering its intimacy by unjust susceptibilities. You know it is not my habit to suppress my true judgment in relations of friendship and I am always prepared to run the risk attaching to that behaviour.

You are quite right in asking that friends should not treat each other as unrelentingly as fate does, but just imagine how much more satisfactory it is to a friend to acknowledge, to praise or to admire the other man than [you][2] to forgive him.

I cannot understand, why you should have waited impatiently for Rank's decision. You know by my *Rundbriefe* what the general situation is and Rank's opinions and advise you could have learned from Hiller, with whom he had it all talked over before he left. If the matter was considered so urgent with you, Hiller could have discussed it before he went to see his family and not hereafter.

No decision will be made here. It is your turn now. I think the English are bad to collaborate with and the only chance is they should do the work for themselves. You are right to say Mrs. Riviere's attitude has made a great impression on me, but she is a true Englishwoman and Hiller did not react differently.

Wishing for a complete restoration of faith and friendship in 1923.

affectionately yours
Freud

1. Freud gives the year as 1922, as does Jones (1957a, p. 51; 1957b, p. 53).
2. Crossed out in the original.

385

International Psycho-Analytical Association
Central Executive

14 January 1923
London

Dear Professor,

I was very happy to get yesterday the friendly token of a private letter from you and am sure that you too prefer it to the more official task of writing circular letters. I was sorry to hear that you had not been well of late, and trust it is only some passing indisposition. My neuritis is perhaps a little better, for I sometimes get half an hour free from pain; you will remember from neurological days that neuritic pain does not belong to the pleasures of life. I started work last week, but had to break off and spend a few days at the seaside clearing off a bronchitis which was left after my Christmas illness.

Hiller was here for two evenings before going to his family and I saw him on one of these, there being a long Society meeting on the other. Your question about my impatience to hear from Rank at this critical juncture is probably explained in my circular letter of yesterday.[1] We could not decide here about the future, whether to continue with the Verlag, etc., by raising more funds, unless we knew if the Verlag was prepared to continue. It is true that both Rickman and Hiller reported that Rank was tired of the Press and would have nothing more to do with it, but I hesitated to accept this as final, for nothing had altered in the situation since he announced in November his plan of continuing the Press in Germany together with the Verlag (in a letter you do not appear to have seen, for you wrote that there had been *"nie die Rede davon"*.[2] I must now, I suppose, accept this, which coincides also with your judgement, for you say that the only chance is for the English to do the work themselves. In my circular letter I adumbrated a plan by means of which we think we can continue the work, and I hope this will meet with your approval. For my own part, painful as the separation is, I see possibilities of a *nach-kriechende Lust*,[3] to use Ferenczi's term. Unfortunately Rank and I have not found it easy to be business collaborators, for we seem to have different ideas about what such collaboration should consist in, but we have had no such difficulties in scientific and personal fields; therefore I have every hope that our friendship, which is quite unimpaired on my side and I trust also on his, will be restored to its former harmony when the business complications are eliminated.

I want to thank you for your outspokenness to me. You claim the right to say exactly what you think to friends and so far as I am concerned I willingly accord that right. Rank also has exercised it very freely towards me. But may I not claim also a little of the same right? The sole time I have said a critical word in a circular letter[4] I did so after first consulting Eitingon, whose judgement I greatly respect, and he advised me to say simply and honestly what I thought, adding that the members of the Committee ought to be able so to speak to each other. I shewed him my letter before I sent it, and he can assure you that my object, so far from endangering the intimacy of the committee, as you indicate, was to ensure a closer colaboration, which was the only point of my remarks. Unfortunately my object was not attained, for to judge from his subsequent behaviour Rank seems to have been seriously hurt. This I certainly regret, for nothing was further from my intentions, and I must exercise more care for his susceptibilities in the future.

One word about your general judgement of me. It is doubtless true that the fact of my Keltic blood gives me a quick reaction and that I have not the phlegmatic Anglo-Saxon temperament, though I have tried to acquire some of it. It may also be true that I am unduly sensitive; of that I cannot judge. But when you say that I am insincere and not to be trusted, there I am sure, with all respect, that your judgement is at fault. I know my own attitude towards you and towards our common interests so thoroughly that I feel no need to make any protestation, or to reproach myself, or to feel any bitterness or resentment, which I suppose would be one of my reactions if there were any truth in the judgement. I feel nothing but a natural regret that you should think so wrongly of me, coupled with the hope that the future will shew you otherwise.

So let us thus take leave of 1922 and turn to 1923. I was deeply moved by the generous expression of your wish for a complete restoration of faith and friendship in the coming year, which I echo with a full heart; you can imagine that my wish in this direction is no less ardent than yours, for though it is doubtless painful for you to think badly of a loyal friend it is still more painful for the friend.

Yours always affectionately
Ernest Jones.

1. In his *Rundbrief* of 11 January 1923 Jones wrote that he was astonished, not having been informed personally by Rank, that Rank "had definitely rescinded his November plan of continuing the Press in Germany as part of the Verlag." Furthermore, he hoped that this was not "final" and he was still waiting for a personal word from Rank on the matter (Sigmund Freud Copyrights, Wivenhoe; and Rank Collection, Butler Library, Columbia University).

2. "Never any talk of it."

3. "Pleasure creeping in behind the pain" (see note 4 to letter 206).

4. Jones's *Rundbrief* of 1 January 1923 deals with the issue of the future business relationship between Press and Verlag. He was especially annoyed by the fact that Rank had refused to answer his query about the status of that relationship. (Sigmund Freud Copyrights, Wivenhoe; and Rank Collection, Butler Library, Columbia University).

386

15 February 1923
42 York Terrace, London

Dear Professor,

I am glad to tell you that my health is definitely beginning to improve, and I hope that you are in an even better position in this respect.

I was glad to get a personal letter from Rank this week and, if he shews you my reply, I trust that you will both agree with Rickman's and my answer to the question he raised.[1]

Chance has brought me an unusual opportunity from which I hope to learn much. An actively homosexual girl came to be analysed in December, both for her inversion and for neurotic symptoms. Now her feminine partner, who lives with her, has also come. They are both well-educated and highly intelligent persons (in the early twenties), so you may imagine that the analytic work is specially interesting in such a conjuncture.

Practice has once more improved; one has only to wait in the bad times. I wonder how much you have found it possible to make out of Money-Kyrle? What did you find to be the chief cause of his resistance against giving up his symptoms?

Our Society is, I am glad to say, distinctly improving in quality and we now have large meetings with good discussions. Bryan is not moving forwards well and I should judge James Glover to be our best member.

Rickman is of course invaluable on the business side, though he needs constant supervision because of his impulsive judgement, but he does not seem to be very promising in scientific respects. Mrs. Riviere has broadened much and has more interest than she had for theoretical questions.

My boy is a year old next week. He has five teeth and is beginning to walk. He seems to have a happier disposition than his sister, but they are both very dear and promising, and neither of them has yet had a day's illness.

With my affectionate regards to you,

yours always
Ernest Jones.

1. Rank's letter is missing, but Jones's reply of 15 February 1923 contains a discussion about the issue of paying translators for their work; a recommendation that the *Journal* and Verlag share the costs of this is put forward (Archives of the British Psycho-Analytical Society, London).

387

28 February 1923
Vienna, IX. Berggasse 19

Dear Jones,

As I am growing older every day and come to dwell on the idea of my death I am struck by the consideration that the money deposited at Lissa & Kann's would not be available for my wife except by the way of applying to you, and I think this would mean many inconveniences to both parties. So I decided to have my son Dr. Martin Fr. in, who now is in the banking business and give him the right of disposal at L & K. The next thought told me that it was of no use hampering you by getting the receipts and accounts etc., as you are not meant to dispose of that money in any way.

The simplest way out of the situation would be if you wrote to L & K, telling them that you resign from interfering with the account bearing your name and that Dr. Martin Freud, Treuga (Wien),[1] to whom they are sending regular duplicates now, will step into your place. He will send them a sample of his signature, as soon as you have notified the change to me.

There is a possibility that you from any motive may object to lending your name to an account over which you have no control. If so let me know it at once, I will put on another name and request you to inform L & K of two things: 1) that the account is to be transmitted to another name, and 2) that M. Fr. will dispose of it instead of you on equal right as I. If you have no such objection you must not wait for me but write them at once.

In any case I thank you for having done me this service for so long a time.

Yours affectionately
Freud

1. Treuga was the bank where Martin Freud was employed.

388

[postcard]

4 March 1923
Vienna

Dear Jones,
Got your paper in the *Journal of Neurology and Psychopathology*, think it is very clever. Sorry that a mind like Bertrand Russell's should not produce better arguments and objections.[1]

Yours
Freud

1. Jones (1923c) is a critique of an editorial piece, "The Nature of Desire," in the *Journal of Neurology and Psychopathology*, 3 (1922–23): 274–276, which invokes Bertrand Russell's views on psychoanalysis as set forth in *The Analysis of Mind* (London: Allen and Unwin, 1921).

389

6 March 1923
81 Harley Street, London

Dear Professor,
I am glad to confirm the news in my last letter that my neuritis is distinctly better, and hope that you are in the best of health.

I am on the committee of the International Congress of Psychology that is to be held at Oxford on about July 27, and have been requested to ask you if you would honour the Congress with a paper (of course in German). I am sure you would receive a good welcome if you decide to come.[1] We are trying to get the German and Austrian Governments to pay the expenses of those invited from these countries.

This week I finished the feat of comparing every word of the *Erste Sammlung*[2] with the translation, and there must have been very few sentences where I was not able to improve the translation and style, for Mrs. Riviere seems to have lost some of her enthusiasm for detail. The *Zur Geschichte*[3] I hope to do by Easter and then the first volume of your *Collected Papers* will be sent to press; there is every hope of its appearing before the public this summer. May I ask your help with one little point? On S. 226, line 17, does *"an denen"* refer only to *"Faktoren"* or to *"Masturbation oder Pollution"* as well?[4]

One matter that has become quite clear in my three cases of female homosexuality whose lives are so intertwined with one another is the equal importance in both the masculine and feminine types of the identification between the loved woman and the mother, though the mechanism is different in the different types. By the way, one of them has a typical beating phantasy (a mother beats a daughter, both strangers), with the usual guilt, etc.. Hermann B., the husband of one of your patients, is at present complicating the situation by falling in love with one of the three.

I hear indirectly that Loe has returned to London, for Herbert Jones did not obtain the hoped-for benefit by living in the country. He still suffers from obscure abdominal symptoms, and has just produced another book of poor verse.[5]

Anna probably knows from Hiller that her *Imago* article is appearing in the current number of the *Journal*; it has been well translated.[6]

With kindest wishes

yours very affectionately
Ernest Jones.

1. Freud did not offer a paper; but see Jones (1923d).
2. Freud, *Collected Papers*, 1.
3. Freud (1914d).
4. Freud (1906a, p. 272), *G.W.*, 5:150.
5. See Herbert Jones, *Finlay* (London: John Lane, 1923). Other books by Herbert Jones, issued by the same publisher, include *The Well of Being* (1920), *The Blue Ship* (1921), and *Romanel* (1922).
6. A. Freud (1922).

390

8 March 1923
81 Harley Street, London

Dear Professor,

I hasten to answer your letter about Lissa Kann which came today. You should have no doubt that my only wish is to be of as much service to you as is possible. But I am bound to answer your letter before I can write to Lissa Kann, because I do not find your instructions entirely clear.

Perhaps you were hovering between different plans when you wrote the letter.

I had naturally assumed that if you were to die before me I should transmit the money to your wife by whatever route she, probably after consultation with Martin, would decide. Now I understand from you that you have given Martin the right of disposal at Lissa Kann, i.e. on a similar footing to yourself. So far all is clear. You then ask me to write to Lissa Kann informing them that I resign from the account and that "Dr. Martin Freud will step into your (i.e. my) place". In that case I understand I should have no further connection whatever with the account. This also would be perfectly clear, did you not go on in the next paragraph to ask whether I had any objection to lending my name to an account over which I had no control. Of course I have no such objection, but my difficulty is that the remark seems to imply that I would still have some connection with the account. I am therefore not clear what exactly I should inform Lissa Kann, i.e. whether there are to be three names in the account or two (Martin's and yours). If I may trouble you to clear up this point and send me more explicit instructions I will carry them out at once.

Please decide on any plan that seems best to you. You need only consider me in so far as I am at your service for any plan you may choose.

Yours affectionately,
Ernest Jones.

P.S. I hope you approve of my resuming the custom of sending you personal letters with each *Rundbrief*.

391

10 March 1923
Vienna, IX. Berggasse 19

Dear Jones,

While waiting for your reply in the Lissa Kann affair I hasten to answer some of your questions in the private letter and the *Rundbrief*.

The "*an denen*" p. 226 can only refer to "*Faktoren*", [but][1] which is all right.

The biography in the *Encycl Brit* is not signed. Psychoanalysis is mentioned [(not too warmly)][2] in the article "Psychical research" by F. C. S. S. (Ferdinand Schiller, Oxford[)] in a rather stupid way and in another article "Psychotherapy" by E. D. M. (Eric D. Macnamara, Charing Cross Hosp.) more kindly.[3]

As for the invitation to Oxford I do not think of accepting it. I am glad of being for myself during the vacations, I am not attracted to the state of ΨA in England and new personal relations have no value for my age.

I am glad to hear you have recovered, I am at least improving.

With kindest regards

yours
Freud

1. Crossed out in the original.

2. Crossed out in the original.

3. The articles in the *Encyclopaedia Britannica*, 12th ed. (London, 1922), can be found in vol. 6 (unsigned biography of Freud), p. 155, and vol. 32 ("Psychical Research" and "Psychotherapy"), pp. 198–208.

392

12 March 1923
Vienna, IX. Berggasse 19

Dear Jones,

I thank you very much for your kind answer and decision of which I am ready to avail myself. I thought I had been clear, but I see some confusion arose from my mentioning that L & K were in the habit of sending the duplicate accounts to Martin. In fact I had given them his adress in the place of my own as he is in a bank ("Treuga") and letters to him could not look suspicious, but I had not substituted him to you nor sent in his signature. Until now nothing has been changed.

It is the following I request you to write to Lissa & Kann: That you resign your right of disposal of the account, which keeps your name, in favour of Dr. M. F., to whom alone reports should be sent. Martin will send them a sample of his signature from Vienna. That is all. You have made it simple by granting the use of your name.

I had no doubt you would provide the money to my wife at the due time, but it would not be needed at once, only in small lots, and if Martin was not in, every letter had to go from Vienna to you, and from London to the Hague, a nuisance to you and no profit, only delay to my heirs. So I came to the conclusion, I needed nothing of you but your name.

I am glad of your regular separate letters and hope common success may soon wipe out the memory of the latest dissensions. In the affair of Brill's money I had to side with you although your report permitted correction in some points.[1]

Yours affectionately
Freud

1. A reference to Brill's contribution to the Verlag, which, according to Freud, consisted of two parts: the money he had collected from members and other donors, and his own contribution from royalties which he had offered as a gift or loan. Freud had refused the offer because Brill did not make it clear which he really meant. This was the reason why Brill subsequently arranged to give the money to the Press. (Freud to Rickman, 23 February 1927, Sigmund Freud Copyrights, Wivenhoe.)

393

International Psycho-Analytical Association
Central Executive

20 March 1923
London

Dear Professor,

I have received your second letter about Lissa Kann and find it quite clear. I enclose a copy of the instructions I have sent them and hope they are exactly according to your wish.

I was glad you liked my Communication on the Nature of Desire.[1] There are hundreds of occasions to which one could respond by a similar paper, but I only permit myself to react very rarely, for otherwise it wastes so much time.

I am going to ask you a great favour, and an unusual one, namely whether you will be so good as to read through a paper of mine before I publish it.[2] The reason is this: on exploring the subject of auto-suggestion I find one could not avoid dealing with some of the fundamental questions about the *mechanism of healing* in both suggestion and psycho-analysis. It would of course be inadvisable for me to publish it if it contained any serious error on such an important matter, so perhaps I may feel justified in encroaching on your time to this extent. The first part of the paper can be skimmed through rapidly, being mainly of historical interest; it is the last half dozen pages that matter.

Hiller arrived yesterday, but so far I have only been able to see him for a few minutes.

With my best thanks in anticipation,

Yours affectionately,
Ernest Jones.

1. Jones (1923c).
2. Jones (1923b).

394

27 March 1923
Vienna, IX. Berggasse 19

Dear Jones,

I got your letter to Lissa & Kann and thank you warmly for your kind behaviour in this matter. As you may judge from this incident, old age is growing upon me and the idea of the unavoidable exit of life dwells with me more steadily than before.

I read your manuscr.[1] with great interest and dare say I learned quite a lot by it. I had no clear ideas on autosuggestion, suspected that cases like Coué's recent one[2] might easily be revealed as masked suggestion of the common type and felt sure that if it existed it had to be understood on the basis of a temporal fusion of the Ego-ideal with the Ego. Now your remarks made me sure about these points and added a good deal of information I had not possessed. I think your paper is very clever and à propos besides. It is only your remarks on the mechanism of curing by analysis I consider not exhausting and thorough-going enough. The problem appears to be more complex and could be centred in another way.

I propose you should mitigate the ugly *epitheta* you join to the name of Coué.[3] The nonsense of professional writers on psychopathology may make us relent towards the feats of a lay-amateur.

Now what am I to do with your manuskpt? Am I to send it back to you or have you got another copy?

Did you see MacCurdy's *Problems of Dynamic Psychology?*[4] He is as impudent in his praise as in his criticism of my work and person. Lack of manners is a common character of these Americans.

Hoping you and your family are all right throughout,

yours affectionately
Freud

1. Jones (1923b).
2. E. Coué, *Self-Mastery through Conscious Auto-Suggestion* (London: Allen and Unwin, 1922).
3. In the published version of the paper Coué's name is mentioned only once, with no such epithet; see Jones (1923b, p. 300), and *Papers*, 5th ed. 1948, p. 280.
4. MacCurdy (1923).

395

International Psycho-Analytical Association
Central Executive

5 April 1923
London

Dear Professor,

L & K have confirmed my letter to them and have found a way to keep my name associated with the matter. Doubtless you will think of getting Martin to arrange for his powers to be transferred in the event of an accident happening to him, otherwise it might now be very difficult to dispose of the money. (i [I] had foreseen this contingency for myself by instructions first to my wife and secondly to Trotter, to be opened after my death).

I was flattered by your finding some value in my auto-suggestion paper and thank you warmly for the trouble you took with it, but your remarks about the part on the mechanism of analytic healing do not entirely allay my uncertainty. I gather that I made no serious error, for otherwise you would have said so. I know well that the treatment of the matter is far from exhaustive, but I seemed to come to a stop on the lines I was pursuing. If you think of any alteration or modification I ought to make in the statements in this part, I should be very grateful to hear of them. I entirely agree with your comment on the Coué adjectives, and had already felt ashamed of them and had struck them out; in fact I did not read the passage at the meeting. The affect was really misplaced, being directed against William Brown, McDougall's successor at Oxford, who has accepted Coué's work in all its simplicity. In fact I was stimulated to writing my paper by a very offensive one he read at a previous meeting.[1] By the way, please do not trouble to send the MS back, as I have copies here.

I have not yet dipped into MacCurdy's book, but can well imagine its contents. You will, I hope, be amused by the review I shall write of it in good time.[2]

Rickman is proving in many ways useful, but it is not too reliable without control. He has an Oriental idea of time, and turns out to be much weaker in character than he gives the impression of being, very easily influenced; his manner has much of what the Americans call bluff. So far I think Frink is our best addition, not counting of course the redoubtable Mrs. Riviere. Strachey has disappeared into the void so far as I am concerned, but his return to England cannot now be long delayed and we shall see what can be done with him.

Is Money-Kyrle still with you? I wonder how he has turned out? This week I met Hermann B., a pleasing and rather able young fellow, perhaps somewhat simple and distinctly self-centred.

My family are still in the country, which does them all a world of good.

Gwenith's latest *bon mot* (aged 2½) is the following: on being told that I spent so much time in Harley St. because I had to procure milk and food for the family, she reflected a moment and then remarked "But I must have food". She even got a little anxious on my holiday until she was reassured that we had a wekk's [week's] supply and that I would soon go back to Harley St. This in spite of her great fondness for me and desire to be with me all the time.

With my kindest regards to you,

yours always affectionately
Ernest Jones.

1. Although Brown wrote widely on the topic of suggestion in psychotherapy, as for example in *Suggestion and Mental Analysis* (London: University of London Press, 1922), his writings are not mentioned in Jones (1923b); his attack on Jones's paper is contained in W. Brown, "Theories of Suggestion," *British Medical Journal*, 1 (1928): 251–255.

2. This was not done by Jones; see James Glover, review of MacCurdy (1923), *Journal*, 5 (1924): 379–385.

396

[postcard]

[7 April 1923]¹
[Vienna]

Dear Jones,

Who is Israel Levine? I never was so much pleased by a book on a ψα matter as by his *Unconscious*.² A rare bird if he is a philosopher. I want to know the man better.

Yours affectionately
Freud

Yours essays are a stately contribution.³

1. Date of postmark.
2. Levine (1923). Israel Levine (1893–1988) joined University College, Exeter, as lecturer in the department of philosophy in 1923; would become professor and head of the department, and dean of the Faculty of Arts. In his later writings he examined some of the great Jewish contributions to philosophy, including the works of Spinoza, Marx, and Bergson; see his *Faithful Rebels: A Study in Jewish Speculative Thought* (London: Soncino Press, 1936).
3. Jones (1923a).

397

International Psycho-Analytical Association
Central Executive

13 April 1923
London

Dear Professor,

I hasten to answer your card about Israel Levine because you are probably waiting to write to him. His work is a gratifying sign of the wide interest now being taken in psycho-analysis by English psychologists and philosophers. I have not met him personally, but have corresponded extensively with him and will tell you what I know about him.

He is lecturer on philosophy at University College, Exeter, Devonshire, a small provincial College. His race you can guess from his name. It was he who gave the lecture on you at the University of London in the series under the auspices of the Jewish Historical Society of which I reported some time ago in a *Rundbrief*. His present book is partly an outcome of that lecture and is, I think, intended as a graduating thesis, for which purpose I do not doubt it will be successful. I may say that I advised him all through the writing of it and afterwards extensively revised it myself. From the numerous alterations and corrections I had to make I came to the conclusion that the writer was an impetuous young man, rather juvenile and very uncritical, but with the valuable trait of eagerness. I hope he will proceed along the path he has begun and shall of course keep in touch with him.

The copies of my *Essays* have not yet reached London. I think the only part of them with which you are not familiar would be the paper on Ireland and some interesting additions I made to the Hamlet Essay.[1] I shall have to send my Auto-Suggestion paper to the printers in a week or two and so am anxious to know whether you feel inclined to propose any alterations in the last couple of pages about which you wrote. I do not know if you think it worth while publishing in the *Zeitschrift*; if so I would send a fresh copy with some changes in it.[2]

The Double Number of Parts 1 and 2 of the *Journal* should appear before the end of this month and the material for the third, July number, will be sent to the printers in ten days time. So I hope we shall gradually catch up the lost time.

Yours affectionately
Ernest Jones.

1. Jones (1922h); for the revised version of Jones (1910a), see Jones (1923a, pp. 1–98).
2. Jones (1923b) did not appear in the *Zeitschrift*.

398

25 April 1923
Vienna, IX. Berggasse 19

Dear Jones,

After having lost a week or so by illness (operation) I hasten to answer your several questions.

No I have no criticism of your paper to offer and would not like your waiting for my suggestions. I think you are right as far as you go, but you have not gone far enough, as you know. I try not to interfere with the intellectual independence of my friends, and so I push back my criticism on their work unless they have not fallen in gross errors what happily rarely is the case.

Mr. Money-Kyrle is progressing continuously. I think he has learned to listen and even to believe a little. The construction of his prehistoric case is complete and he is wont to lean on it for explanation of present situations. But the fact is, he has not yet penetrated to recollection, all his adherence is only [a] matter of reason and the practical effect of the treatment cannot be guessed. So I am ready to continue work with him, if he returns. He will leave on June 1st for an examination in Cambridge and much will depend on the result of it. I am sure he will call on you.

I detected 2 months ago a leukoplastic growth on my jaw and palate right side, which I had removed on the 28th. I am still out of work and cannot swallow. I was assured of the benignity of the matter but as you know, nobody can guarantee its behaviour when it be permitted to grow further. My own diagnosis had been epitelioma, but was not accepted. Smoking is accused as the etiology of this tissue-rebellion.

Hoping you and your family are all right,

I am affectionately yours
Freud

399

1 May 1923
81 Harley Street, London

Dear Professor,

I was very distressed to hear from your letter of the very unpleasant time you have been passing through. Trouble inside the mouth is so infernally uncomfortable. From your account I may hope that by now it belongs to the past, and I hope it will not leave any disagreeable effects such as restriction in smoking.

Das Ich und das Es arrived this afternoon and looks most thrilling;[1] I shall not go to bed early tonight. Thank you warmly for sending it. I will allow myself to write my impressions later.

With the warmest good wishes

Yours affectionately
Ernest Jones.

1. Freud (1923b).

400

18 May 1923
Vienna, IX. Berggasse 19

Dear Jones,

One day before I got your dear wife's letter I heard of your operation and felt rather struck by the seriality. I expect a permanent improvement of your health to come out of your experience as a patient, while incomplete recovery is all I am entitled to expect from mine. There is so much work before you and so many good claims on life that I prefer to think of your illness as a short,—I hope not too unpleasant—episode.

Affectionately yours
Freud

401

International Psycho-Analytical Association
Central Executive

31 May 1923
London

Dear Professor,

Very many thanks for your sympathetic letter. I was glad to hear from various sources that you yourself are past your trouble, and hope that you are not faced with the choice between letting it recur and giving up smoking; I trust that the golden mean, the British principle of compromise, will be sufficient for the case.

I am still in bed but am looking forward to getting about again, though it will be a few weeks before I am restored to full activity. An abdominal operation is not altogether uninstructive and brings home to one some aspects of life which one does not ordinarily realise fully. But it is a disagreeable experience, none the less.

You can imagine that I have no general news to give you, situate as I am, and I am restricting my business affairs to a minimum. But I want to ask you about one matter which ought to be regularized, namely, about the translation of the *Vorlesungen*. You may remember that a contract was made between the Press and Allen and Unwin, but there has never been a formal one between the Press and yourself. I would suggest that one be arranged on the same terms as we did for the *Jenseits des Lustprinzips* and *Massenpsychologie,* as is also being done in regard to the *Sammlungen*. If you agree with this, would you please arrange it with Rank so that a contract can be drawn up.

I have got an invitation sent to Ferenczi to attend the Oxford Congress in July,[1] but have not yet heard whether he will accept it. It would be very delightful to have both him and Abraham here. For the pleasure of seeing you I must wait a month longer, till the end of August, but I am already looking forward to that greatly.

With kindest regards,

Yours always affectionately,
Ernest Jones.

1. The Seventh International Congress of Psychology; see Jones (1923d).

402

[postcard]

2 July 1923
Villa Wassing, Badgastein

Dear Jones,

I hope you are all right now and deep in work. I have entered into my vacation tired and worn out not only by my operation but more so by the loss of my dear Heinz ($4\frac{1}{2}$ J)[1] the second child of my deceased daughter,[2] by miliary tuberculosis here in Vienna.

Affectionately yours
Freud

1. "*J[ahre]*" = years.
2. Heinz Rudolf ("Heinele") Halberstadt (1918–1923), also called Heinerle, son of Max and Sophie Freud Halberstadt.

403

International Psycho-Analytical Association
Central Executive

2 July 1923
London

Dear Professor,

I have been away for a convalescing holiday in Wales, and am glad to say that I have made an excellent recovery from my illness, with the unfortunate exception of my cursed rheumatism.

It will be an interesting experiment for us to meet in August without your presence, but I trust that you will not regard it as a precedent.

I am sorry to say that Press affairs are going badly, partly because of the difficulty of getting things done in Germany, and partly because there is no suitable man with the time to manage the whole affair. Rickman has the time, but sadly lacks the "push" and energy necessary.

I often wonder how you reply to Day's screeds,[1] for I suppose he writes to you at the same length as to me. Money-Kyrle came to see me recently. I found him very greatly improved in steadiness and confidence, and have no doubt he will complete his cure in the coming year.

I read your *Ich und Es* with enormous interest. You take us into deep waters. It will need another reading and some reflection before I could say anything in the way of comment, except that I am inclined to think the experiment might be tried of extending the repression principle to cover also the *Es* (which must be not only painful but also burdensome if admitted to consciousness).

The Teufelsneurose[2] was charming and obviously aroused your personal interest. It was a happy idea to seek yet another field for confirmation of your theories, like observation of children and study of anthropology. By the way, à propos of your identification of God and devil on S. 14 (ref. to Reik) you will find interesting etymological and other proofs of this in my *Alptraum* (*Schriften* XIV, S. 86, etc.);[3] similarly your suggestion on S. 15 about *Hexenprozesse* [witch trials] I had carried out by making this devil-father identif[i]cation[4] the basis of my incest theory of witchcraft.[5]

I hear today from Ferenczi that he is also coming to the Oxford Congress. It will be a special pleasure to see both him and Abraham in England, and I wish that your long-due visit were not so delayed. We shall of course give them a great welcome, and the Society also is already making arrangements to that effect.

I hope that the stay in Gastein will be as successful as usual in giving you the needed recuperation and that you will derive great pleasure from it as well.

With all my best wishes,

yours always affectionately
Ernest Jones.

1. That is, Daly's prolonged tirades. Freud's correspondence with Daly is briefly discussed in Hartnack (1990, pp. 944–945).
2. Freud (1923d).
3. Jones (1912j, p. 86).
4. "Identifaction" was typed initially, and then the *a* and *c* were transposed, nonetheless leaving the word spelled incorrectly.
5. See Freud (1923d, p. 87 n. 1), where he later partially acknowledged Jones's contribution in a footnote; see also note 4 to letter 449.

404

8 July 1923
81 Harley Street, London

Dear Professor,

I was very much grieved at getting your card this morning and hearing of your little grandson's death. How well I remember your shewing us in Vienna the photographs of him and his brother; it was plain what a deep hold he had on your heart. I think too of the distress the event must have caused your wife and Anna, not to speak of the poor father. Sophie at least has been spared the blow. The boy now lives not only in the memory of his family, but also immortally as the author of the *Fortsein* in your *Jenseits*—unless I mistake.[1]

What occupies me at the moment is the *Journal* and the preparations for the Oxford Congress[2]—quite enough.

With my deepest sympathy, also to your family,

Yours always affectionately
Ernest Jones.

1. Heinz Rudolf was the child who died; it was his brother, Ernst Wolfgang (b. 1914), who was referred to in the now famous *fort/da* episode (Freud, 1920g, p. 15), *G.W.*, 13:12; see Freud's reply in letter 405.
2. "Of psychology" is written in the margin. See Jones (1923d).

405

[postcard]

14 July 1923
Badgastein

Dear Jones,

Thanks for your kind lines. You are indeed mistaken about the personality of the deceased child. It is the younger brother (4½ J) of the boy mentioned in *Jenseits*, who is now 9 years of age.

Affectionately yours
Freud

406

12 September 1923
81 Harley Street, London

Dear Professor,

I had counted on sending you a letter in Rome—but all intentions bow before physical conditions. I have had 12 days of the most severe influenza imaginable (temp. 40°C for three days, pleurisy, intestinal complications, etc.), and am still very weak.

But I do want to send you a line at least to tell you how well you handled the psychological situation at Lavarone.[1] It had been expected that you either wouldn't see us, or else would have simply rated me for being the unwitting cause of so much disturbance. I should of course have borne that, naturally, but it could not have made the best atmosphere for insight—insight which in any case was not easy, for I knew I had been unfairly treated and had much right on my side. As it was, you created the best imaginable atmosphere by your friendliness, directness, and impartiality. You shall see that the help you gave me will bear good fruit, for I am not going to be content with the present unsatisfactory state of my psychology.

I was sorry to find that your health was not what it might be and hope the visit to your old love—Rome—improved matters; also that it will not be long before your health is completely restored.

With my entire devotion and affectionate regards

Yours always sincerely
Ernest Jones.

P.S. On my return I looked up my letter to Brill and found, as I expected, that his account was grossly exaggerated. (The word Semitic, for instance, never occurred in it).[2] I suppose he must have identified me with Frink. I am of course writing to him.

1. A town in the Italian Dolomites, where Freud was staying while the other members of the Secret Committee were meeting nearby in San Cristoforo. Jones alludes to the complex issues centering on his conflict with Rank, the announcement to Freud that the recently removed tumor in his mouth was malignant, and the effect this news had on Rank as well as the others in the group. See Jones (1957a, pp. 55, 92–93, 98; 1957b, pp. 57–58, 97–98, 103).

2. At the time of the San Cristoforo meeting, Jones wrote his wife that Freud would probably not speak to him as "Brill has just been there and told him [Freud] I had said Rank was a swindling Jew (stark übertrieben [highly exaggerated]). Brill of course has gone back to U.S.A. without seeing me" (Jones to Katherine Jones, 26 August 1923, Archives of the British Psycho-Analytical Society, London). In his letter of 28 August 1923 Jones wrote: "The whole committee, after hours of talking and shouting . . . thought I was in Bedlam, decided that I was in the wrong in the Rank-Jones affaire, in fact that I am neurotic. A Jewish family council sitting on one sinner must be a great affair, but picture it when the whole five insisting on analysing him on the spot and alltogether!" Jones went on to say that he was almost forced to resign from the Secret Committee, and in the end was put "on probation" and ordered to resume his analysis with Ferenczi in Budapest. Lieberman (1985, pp. 188–191) charges Jones with anti-Semitism in his treatment of Rank during this episode; and Grosskurth (1991, p. 134) follows a similar line. Gay (1988, p. 424), however, offers a different version.

407

24 September 1923
Vienna, IX. Berggasse 19

Dear Jones,

I am deeply disappointed that you should be ill too thinking it a prerogative of my age and condition. But I expect you will soon have recovered strength and be the former man again or become a still better one.

To your praising my behaviour at Lavaroni I have only to reply that I am too old to give up old friends. If younger people would oftener think of that change in life they would find it easier to keep up good relations among themselves.

Now I hope you will drop the affair and I will do whatever I can to influence Rank in the sense of kindness and tolerance.

I spent a splendid time at Rome in the company of my daughter who did really show to her advantage at this occasion. Yet I am still far from complete recovery and expecting the final judgment of the man who operated on me.

Sept. 26th. It has now been decided that I have to undergo a new operation, a partial resection of the upper jaw as the growth reappeared on this ground.

It is promised I will be able to start work 4–5 weeks later, but you know what it all means.

Another practical item. I have made up my mind to make my nephew Bernays my agent in America and let him mind the American rights of my books. At the same time I bound him to buy the good English translations of the Press and hope I can do some good in this way.[1]

Hoping to hear soon of your complete recovery

yours affectionately
Freud

1. For Jones, Freud's oscillating tactics regarding the copyright of the English translations of his writings were a constant source of irritation; see Jones (1957a, p. 50; Jones 1957b, p. 52).

408

2 October 1923
81 Harley Street, London

Dear Professor,

The distressing news in your letter at least brought from one point of view a certain relief, namely in the knowledge that matters were being dealt with radically. *Sicher ist sicher* [best to be safe], and I happen to know that the prognosis in such cases is entirely favourable if they are dealt with on sound lines. So in a few weeks the trouble will belong to the past, except unfortunately for the great discomfort that you cannot escape for a little time. In this you have my deepest and unbounded sympathy—*how* I wish I could do something to spare you it. Please remember in the bad times that the worst is past and that every day brings you nearer to restored health. How warmly we shall all look forward to that!

What news I have is good. We are securing the survival of the Press by a new arrangement. Mrs. Riviere and I are working excellently together. She is a most helpful and useful colleague. I also get on well with Rickman, though I cannot of course be so enthusiastic about his value. My own health is quite restored.

Enough. You have only one thing to think of—to get better as soon as you can and return to the world of activity where you are so wanted.

With my deepest affection and strongest wishes for your welfare

Yours always devotedly
Ernest Jones.

409

22 October 1923
81 Harley Street, London

My dear Professor,

At last you will, I trust, be in a condition once more to read letters and take an interest in the world outside. It has been an inexpressible joy to receive the excellent reports of your progress—the brilliant success of the operation, the excellent prognosis, and—last but not least—that you have borne the painful situation so courageously. You have set us all an example in fortitude as in so many other things. Personally I felt confident about the surgical aspect of the case, but I feared that the weeks after the operation would be very distressing. The reports seem to indicate that—unpleasant as it must have been—this was less so than in many cases, probably because the disease had not extended far. And now you have the joy of convalescing, every day being an improvement on the last and leading you back to your wonted energy and life-interests. How good to know that!

The news from here, personal and movement, is all excellent with the one exception of the complication to the Press introduced by the question of the American sales. Had it not been for your illness I would have written long since about this matter, though I have been in close correspondence with Rank. As it is a critical and urgent matter I propose to send Mrs. Riviere to Vienna to discuss with you both as soon as your health permits.

I write full of happiness at your good news and with the strongest wishes for a rapid recovery.

Yours always affectionately
Ernest Jones.

410

[telegram]

26 October 1923
Vienna

Visit inconvenient reception impossible no danger for press

Freud

411

27 October 1923
42 York Terrace, Regents Park

Dear Professor,

Your telegram gave the cheerful intimation that you are again able to take an active interest in affairs, even though you are not yet in a position to participate in them directly. Your concluding words about the Press were what one would naturally expect and have put fresh heart in us. But the question is whether *you* realise how great the danger to the Press actually is and how urgent. I tried to make this clear to Rank about ten days ago, and wonder if he has had the opportunity to show you this critical letter.[1] We felt that the only remaining hope was for one of us to travel to Vienna as soon as you are well enough.

With all best wishes

Yours always affectionately
Ernest Jones.

P.S. Rickman and Mrs. Riviere know about your operation, but no other member of the Society.

1. Jones to Rank, 18 October 1923, is a lengthy letter containing Jones's plea for establishing a solid market in the United States, without which the Press would not be able to survive (Archives of the British Psycho-Analytical Society, London).

412

4 November 1923
Vienna, IX. Berggasse 19

Dear Jones,

Your kind bulletins about my state of health were always a bit in advance of reality. It is only in the last few days that I have been regaining my strength, have almost overcome the effect of the operation, and am now waiting for its promised success.

Today I am writing a few words of explanation about my telegram. I never thought that the American sales of the translations of my books (which ones?) could be so vital for the Press. But as you insist on it, I won't dispute it. My private opinion is that the Press has little chance of surviving and that perhaps you yourself would be quite content if you had a good pretext for proclaiming this outcome. But I will certainly not be the one to provide this pretext. That is why I telegraphed "no danger for press."[1] I am prepared to let the Press have the American rights to my books for

a period of two years, that is, until 31 December 1925, provided that during
this period it retains its independence. After that date, if it cannot be
established that it contributed substantially to the distribution of my
books in America, I shall then be at liberty to reclaim the American rights
for myself.

I am sure you understand that the methods of work and production
of the Press have hitherto meant sacrifice for the authors and a loss of
publicity.

A few days ago I would not yet have thought myself strong enough to
receive Mrs. Riviere, much as I like to see her. I am now thinking of
starting work again in two or three weeks' time.

In the hope of hearing soon only good news of you and your family,

Your devoted friend
Freud

1. In English in the original.

413

12 November 1923
81 Harley Street, London

Dear Professor,

It was an enormous pleasure to have a letter again from you and to see
that you are yourself again. The reports received from various sources (the
last one from Hans Sachs to-day) are unanimous in describing how excellently you have endured the painful ordeal.

The offer you make to the Press shows, if I may say so, your characteristic fairness, generosity and shrewdness. I cannot deny the right you have
to be sceptical, and in the circumstances we certainly could not ask for a
better offer than the two year's trial you suggest. I am pretty confident
that we shall have something to show for ourselves within that time.
If not, then the matter is automatically settled. It is, as you say, indeed
a question whether the attempt, much as it has cost us, should not be
given up. The only motive I could have myself for being glad of such a
solution is that it might mean less arduous work. On thinking it over I
am not sure that this would be so, for presumably I should still go on with
the translating whoever published the books. I should certainly be glad to
be relieved of the business complications and confine myself to the scientific side, as I have vainly tried to do for some time past. The part of the
activity to which I do attach the greatest importance is the maintenance
of the *Journal*, and I greatly doubt if we could get any publisher to issue
this for us. If any winding up of the Press is ever decided on I only hope

that you, Rank and myself would be in harmony on the matter, as in all else.

On top of the news that we might lose the American sales of your books came a [proposition][1] proposal from Rank to dispose likewise of the American rights of the other books we are bringing out in our Library (Abraham, Ferenczi, Rank and Reik).[2] The shortest way of explaining my view is by enclosing you a copy of the letter I sent Otto in regard to this. Two of these books are now ready and the other two will be ready before Christmas. As you can imagine, we have expended an enormous amount of labour and also much money in this work and should not like to see it cast away. I trust therefore that Otto will consent to making exactly the same offer as you do (two years), for I really do not think the Press could be made to pay for itself on your books alone or on the other books alone, having regard to the speed at which the different ones can be issued. All the proofs of Vol. I of the *Sammlung* have been corrected so that we are within sight of witnessing its definite appearance. The greater part of the translation work of the other three volumes has been accomplished, but the revising takes so long that we cannot promise to rush them out very quickly.

The upshot of the whole matter is, as I stated to Rank, that it is within the power of either himself or of you to bring the Press to an end. Personally I hold that it would be very unwise to do so, but in any case I wished to leave him in no doubt about what his suggestion would involve. You will of course both discuss the matter together and let us know.

I hear the worst news from various sources in America about Frink, who has succeeded in making himself universally unpopular. He himself tells me for reasons of ill-health he is giving up his activities in regard to the Press, the Society, the *Journal*, and also his private practice. It is a sad blow to us in Europe, but there is nothing to do except face it.

I hope to continue hearing the best news of your recuperation and re-entry into the world of activity.

With most cordial regards,

Yours affectionately,
Ernest Jones.

1. Crossed out in the original; "proposal" is handwritten in an otherwise typed letter.
2. Abraham (1927) and Ferenczi (1926b) were announced in *Journal*, 2 (1921): 149, as was a work by Rank, "Studies in Dreams and Allied Topics," which did not appear in the International Psycho-Analytical Library series. Theodor Reik's *Probleme der Religionspsychologie*, vol. 1, *Das Ritual* (Leipzig: Internationale Psychoanalytischer Verlag, 1919; 2nd ed. rev. 1928) came out as *Ritual: Psycho-Analytic Studies* (London: Hogarth Press, 1931), no. 19 of the Library series.

414

29 November 1923
81 Harley Street, London

Dear Professor,

I was grieved to hear you were not quite through your troubles yet,[1] but trust that by the time you get this letter you will be completely recovered. Perhaps the previous recovery had been too uncannily beautiful; this added a more human touch that gives one a greater feeling of reality and confidence that you are truly free of all the trouble.

I enclose the Preface to the *Sammlung* translation.[2] The proofs of vl. I are long since corrected, and I have finished Dora and Hans of vol II—just starting the *Rattenmensch*.[3]

I am very sad about Ferenczi, for I really feel quite innocent of any wish to slight him and feel sure that his excessive reaction is displaced. To anyone who knows the audience for which the paper was written, and how familiar they are with his theory, his remarks really seem ridiculous.[4] But I will do what I can to assuage his feelings.

With all my best wishes—you know how much we care for your well being.

yours always affectionately
Ernest Jones.

1. In his *Rundbrief* of 15 November 1923 Rank reported that Freud had to undergo a second operation on his mouth that week because of pain experienced in the location where a malignant tumor had recently been removed (Sigmund Freud Copyrights, Wivenhoe; and Rank Collection, Butler Library, Columbia University). See note 1 to letter 406.
2. Jones (1924b).
3. The case histories actually appeared in *Collected Papers*, 3.
4. Ferenczi was upset because he felt he was not given due credit in Jones (1923b) as originator of the libido theory of suggestion. Jones defended himself in detail in his *Rundbrief* of 12 November 1923 (Sigmund Freud Copyrights, Wivenhoe).

415

18 December 1923
Vienna, IX. Berggasse 19

Dear Jones,

I have now familiarized myself with the situation between Verlag and Press, and can assure you that in regard to the four books you mentioned, the Verlag will be no more difficult than I and my American rights. You therefore need not let this uncertainty hold you up in your work.

However, Rank thinks that this point cannot be decided on its own, but is connected with those relations between Verlag and Press, which are to be settled in the contract now under negociation. But I repeat that there is no doubt about his agreement with your wishes.

I am actually recuperating from my various operations, but my prosthesis is not ready yet; I am not master of my time and can therefore not yet resume work.

With cordial greetings to you and your dear family.

Yours truly
Freud

P.S. I informed J. [I.] Levine (Exeter) that we want to publish his *"Unconscious"* in German translation.[1]

    1. Levine (1923).

416

4 January 1924
81 Harley Street, London

Dear Professor,

I was very pleased to hear from Abraham that you are resuming work on January 2nd., and am sure you will feel happier when you are back in the full tide of life.

I was also glad to get your assurance that it may be possible for us to proceed with the Press. It was a surprise to hear that Rank told you he wished to deal with the four books that we have already translated together with the rest of the general contract between Press and Verlag, because he had specifically excluded them from this contract in writing to us and said he would at some future time deal with them separately. We shall be concerned until we know exactly what conditions he proposes. It will be good when all this uncertainty and delay comes to an end.

When Jonathan Cape broke with us last August, we started entering into negociations with three or four other firms. This has all been stopped since last September, the time we had been informed that we might not have the American sales which alone would make the negociations possible. All this time salaries and other expenses have been running on, while we could neither produce nor sell. The result is that all our subscriptions and funds have been exhausted, and we are living on an overdraft at my Bank and Rickman's. We shall feel very relieved when we can hear something definite at last from Rank.

Were you satisfied with the Preface to your *Collected Papers* which I sent you some time go, or do you wish to suggest any modifications?[1]

The conditions in Germany are proving impossible for us. We have had the last two numbers of the *Journal* quite complete for many months, but the difficulties of transport have not yet been overcome.

I spent a very happy Christmas in the country and am glad to say that my family are all well and flourishing beautifully.

With all cordial greetings,

Yours,
Ernest Jones.

1. Jones (1924b).

417

15 January 1924
Vienna, IX. Berggasse 19

Dear Jones,

You heard correctly; I have been at work again since the second of this month, which makes me very content. On the one hand today's letter is to express my thanks and appreciation, and on the other hand my bewilderment at your behaviour concerning a specific point.

The first reactions refer to your introduction to the *Sammlung*, which is written so nicely and to the point, as one could actually only wish for and expect. Now I also have more hope than I had a few months ago to see it fixed in print.

The bewilderment concerns your statement that you still do not know the status of the four books which were taken over by the Press long ago, since Rank reserved the right for himself to deal with them at some point in the future, irrespective of the contract. Rank says, on the contrary, that the matter of the four books has long been settled, and if they are in any way excluded from the contract, it is only because there is no doubt about their status. I told you the same thing in my last letter, namely, that the rights for these books have been left to the Press for a corresponding further period. I therefore cannot understand what difficulties you are creating for yourself; I am tempted to say creating artificially through misunderstandings with which you then want to explain the difficulties of the Press. In short, I do not understand you.

I am glad to hear that you and your family are so well, and greet you cordially.

Yours
Freud

418

International Psycho-Analytical Association
Central Executive

25 January 1924
London

Dear Professor,

It was a great pleasure to have the good news confirmed by you personally that you are again hard at work.

I am glad you were satisfied with the Introduction to the *Collected Papers*. It is intended for the series. All the proofs of the first volume have arrived, but I cannot guarantee that the volume itself will after the bad experiences we have had with the last numbers of the *Journal* which are still held up in Germany. I am hoping to have the next two volumes ready for press before the Congress.

I can understand your being bewildered about the matter of the "other four books", particularly as to why your letter about them was not finally *massgebend* [the deciding factor]. If it were only a question of you and myself the difficulties would long have been over, or would never have arisen. But you must remember that other people are involved, Rank, Storfer, Rickman, Reece, etc.. Your information must all be obtained from Rank and mine from Rickman (since I have handed over the business to him). Unfortunately the two do not always tally. I do not wish to raise the personal questions involved in the relationship of these different persons to one another, but the external facts are these. For various reasons we have concentrated our hopes of making publishing arrangements on Brentano, of New York and London, the books to be actually printed in America. They were naturally most eager to have your works. For a long time we were unable to tell them that we had the American rights of these, and our ambiguous position seems to have aroused doubts and suspicions on their side. They therefore naturally wish to see what agreements and contracts we have. Your assurance about your own works helped greatly, but there is still an element of uncertainty about the exact clauses of the contracts regarding the other books, and these will remain until we have actually seen the contracts. Rank has several times made the suggestion that the American rights of the books be sold separately from English ones, the latter only to go to the Press, and we have had no guarantee from him that his mind is finally made up on this and other points. Permission has been obtained from the authors for a long while, and negotiations have been going on between Rickman and the Verlag since last April. I do not know why—possibly there are delays on both sides—but the fact remains that we have not yet seen any of the contracts. With these *in our hands* we should be in a far stronger position to deal with Brentano, and this is all I meant by my remark that the uncertainty and delay were injuring our chances of success.

I am glad to say that apart from the Press things are going very well in England. I am in good spirits and am working exceptionally hard. This is due in part to the stimulus of having the opportunity of winning new provinces for psycho-analysis, e.g. the sociological and anthropological.[1]

Mrs. Riviere has made excellent progress after her operation and I hope to see her in a day or two.

With my warmest wishes for your enjoyment of activity,

Yours,
Ernest Jones.

1. The lectures that make up Jones (1924d) were delivered in October and November 1923; see also Jones (1924e).

419

9 February 1924
81 Harley Street, London

Dear Professor,

I trust there will be general agreement about the desirability of a Committee meeting before the Congress,[1] i.e. on the Saturday. I see that Abraham has asked you whether this should take place in Salzburg or Vienna. If the latter proves more convenient to you, you know we should of course all fall in with the idea. I do not mind saying, however, that I hope on personal grounds that the former would prove as convenient to you, for to us (my wife is coming too) to travel from Salzburg to Vienna and back would [be] a rather tiring addition to a long and expensive journey (through Switzerland), not to speak of possible complications with her relatives in Vienna (staying only a few hours), and it might well mean giving up work a couple of days earlier. I am sure you will not mind mentioning these considerations, which I do only in the event of your hovering between the two decisions.

You will not have been surprised at the *Rundbrief* news about the Press.[2] The decision was greatly overdetermined. The finances had been allowed to get into a muddle, and I called a company meeting and compelled Rickman to elucidate them, when, as I feared, they proved to be much more precarious than he had assumed. Reece, our agent, has got into a muddle in his sexual life, with the result that he neglects matters badly, constantly changes his address, and may well have to leave the country.

Brentano withdrew their offer. Etc., etc.. There was no bright side anywhere, except that our translations are satisfactory, and it would have been
folly to go on deeper into the mire. My hope now is (1) to keep the Press
in being as a corporate body in the chance of resumming [resuming] at a
future date is [if]³ suitable help is forthcoming, which is likely, (2) to save
the *Journal* at all costs, and keep it in our own hands and (3) to induce a
reputable firm to continue the Library series of books under the same title
and with the same editorship, but at their cost. We should thus still achieve
the esssential aim of the Press, to distinguish between trustworthy psa
books and the rubbish otherwise published, indeed better than before when
Unwin was acting as our sales agent and at the same time publishing bad
books on the subject. I have already approached two good firms on the
matter, and hope soon to let you have good news. Naturally this all means
releasing both the Verlag and yourself from the contractual and personal
arrangements made with the Press, but I trust you will not make any other
plans, e.g. in America, until you have had the opportunity of considering
any scheme we may be able to suggest. After all, the translations are
substantial matters and we have put an enormous amount of work into
them.

It may interest you at this juncture to have my impressions of the three
people you sent me a year or two ago. The most successful has without
doubt proved to be Mrs. Riviere, who I am glad to say has made an excellent
recovery from her operation. After an initial difficulty on her first return,
which did not last long, she has proved a most valuable and loyal
cooperator, has given not the slightest trouble to anyone, and is on the
best of terms with myself. The Stracheys are harder people to get close to,
and have also been away from London a great deal on account of her health,
but behave quite correctly. They have been to dinner a few times, he
oftener, and also for a visit to Elsted, I have sent him a couple of patients
and also some books for review, and recently got him to assist in our
company meetings. He is of course chiefly engrossed in his translation
work, and makes no other contribution, e.g. to the work of the Society.
So the total effect is somewhat neutral, though valuable in some ways.
Rickman has certainly proved the least successful of the lot. He has not
been at all difficult to get on with, and our personal relations have always
been excellent. But he has two qualities that badly disqualify him in serious situations. One is a certain unreliability, in that he promises to do
things and then forgets or postpones them without saying anything more
about them. The other is an extraordinary *Sinn für das Nebensächliche*,⁴
a curious lack of feeling for reality and importance. Then he is distinctly
weak and easily influenced by the last person who spoke to him. On the
other side I must say that he has great energy and working capacity, especially for detail.

I am happy to think of how much you must enjoy being at work again. I wonder what you are writing now. Are you tackling the great task of rearranging the *Traumdeutung?*

With all good wishes,

yours always cordially
Ernest Jones.

1. Eighth Congress of the International Psychoanalytic Association, Salzburg, 21–23 April 1924.

2. In his *Rundbrief* of 2 February 1924 Jones reported regretfully that they would have to face the possibility of "giving up the Press, except in name" (Sigmund Freud Copyrights, Wivenhoe; and Rank Collection, Butler Library, Columbia University).

3. This letter is distinctive in that there is an unusual number of typographical errors, many of which were corrected by hand; only a few are noted here.

4. "Sense for the unimportant."

420

26 February 1924
Vienna, IX. Berggasse 19

Dear Jones,

The committee meeting before the Congress is of course generally desired, and it goes without saying that it is to take place in Salzburg in order to save you the trip to Vienna. Abraham and Sachs are perhaps thinking of traveling to Salzburg via Vienna, and therefore the discussions will already have an earlier start. I hope that all participants will bring their most amicable intentions with them.

Your news about the Press did not of course surprise me. But I am not giving up hope that you will be able to salvage the essential aspects of the undertaking in the manner indicated, and for the time being I will therefore not make any different arrangements for the American rights.

I have absolutely no intentions of changing the *Traumdeutung.* From time to time I write little essays which you will find in the *Zeitschrift.* For the umpteenth time I composed a short history of psychoanalysis for an American collection *History of Our Own Times,* published by the American office of the *Encyclopaedia Britannica.* The translation they sent me was so horribly bad that via cable I stopped it from being printed.

I continue to work without interruption, am still in treatment for improvement of my speech.

With cordial greetings for you and your wife

Yours
Freud

421

3 April 1924
Vienna, IX. Berggasse 19

Dear Jones,

Last week, as a result of my catarrhal influenza, I felt so poorly that I let myself be persuaded to spend Saturday and Sunday at the Semmering Kurhaus, three hours from Vienna. The results were so good that I am repeating the excursion this week and perhaps each week thereafter. Moreover, in my present condition the need for rest and recuperation was demonstrated so unequivocally that I decided to forgo the Salzburg Congress, with all its attendant trouble and excitement, and to spend a week's holiday at the Semmering once again at Easter. I am therefore informing you that I shall not attend the Congress this year. I know this amounts to an admission of my present frailty, but it cannot be avoided.

I hope that my absence will also have the result of showing the gentlemen of the former Committee that, in the interest of the Association and the Movement, they must somehow get along with one another, if they are not to sacrifice a great cause to personal sensitivities.

You may have already heard that Rank is going to New York[1] at Ames's invitation for four or five months immediately after the Congress. He will treat patients there and promote our interests in every respect. You will find it understandable that I do not want to miss this unexpected and rare opportunity to disseminate our literature in America. So, if I may assume that you have so far been unable to do anything about my American rights, I take the liberty to reclaim them and entrust Rank to represent my interests in America.

When Rank returns he will probably be elected in my place as president of the Vienna Society. I am no longer capable of attending the evening sessions and must therefore relinquish this part of my activity as well.

I express the hope that the dissolution of the intimate Committee will reduce the points of controversy and conflict between its members, and that they regain the necessary empathy of being colleagues in the same cause, their greater distance from one another notwithstanding.

I deeply regret that I cannot see you and your wife this time

Yours
Freud

1. Spelled "Newyork" in the original.

422

International Psycho-Analytical Association
Central Executive

9 April 1924
London

Dear Professor,

I was very distressed to hear of your decision not to come to Salzburg and also for the reason you give. The only bright thought is that you are finding recuperation so beneficial and I hope this may continue to be so in still greater measure. Your decision will necessarily cast a gloom over the Congress, but, though nothing can replace your inspiration, you may rest assured that many of us will do everything we can there to consolidating and furthering the progress of your work.

It was a great shock for me to hear from you about the dissolution of the Committee[1] and as I have heard no other intimation in this direction I am quite in the dark about the meaning of it all. I only know I shall still make every effort to re-establish better conditions when we all meet in Salzburg.

I quite understand what you say about Rank taking charge of the literary question in America and will write you more fully on this matter in a day or two. There would seem to be no reason why his function should not be combined with consideration of the work we have already done in the way of translation and publication.

It is hard to foresee when I shall be in Austria next so I should like to take this opportunity of paying you a short visit after the Congress. My wife and I are going to North Italy afterwards, but we could come on direct from Salzburg to Semmering, where I presume you will then be, arriving on Thursday evening, April 24th, and leaving at midday on the Saturday. You will quite appreciate my desire to see you, both on personal grounds and also to discuss the matters of mutual interest. On the other hand, I do not of course wish to intrude if you do not feel well enough to see us. Could I, therefore, leave it this way, that we will arrange to come unless you telegraph to the contrary? We should greatly like to know before leaving London, for it makes some difference in our arrangements. I am notifying Abraham of my request and imagine that he may make a similar one.

With the most cordial wishes for your welfare,

Yours always,
Ernest Jones.

1. In a *Rundbrief* of 10 April 1924 Rank confirmed that the Committee was buried and that he, Ferenczi, and Freud were in agreement on the issue (Sigmund Freud Copyrights, Wivenhoe).

423

International Psycho-Analytical Association
Central Executive

11 April 1924
London

Dear Professor,

I have for some time been meaning to send you a report of our activities
in regard to the Press but the situation kept changing from day to day so
that no suitable moment presented itself. I have been fighting very hard
to induce some leading publisher to establish a "Monograph Series" which
could function as a continuation of our previous one and have interviewed
many of the leading ones. They have practically all turned down the proposal, giving as their main reason the discouraging reports from America
about Psycho-Analysis being a dead subject there (!); Heinemann, on whom
I had set great hopes finally decided in the negative yesterday. The only
firm with whom I am still in negotiation is the Cambridge University
Press, but I have very little hope there.

We have also been working with various American firms to arrange for
purely American sales, and here we have had better luck. Boni & Liveright
have practically agreed to buy two thousand sheets of the *"Group Psychology"* and *"Pleasure Principle"* and to issue them there. The rest of our
stock is derelict, though we shall still persevere with some efforts to sell
it for a small sum. As regards translations, the first volume of the *"Collected Papers"* has, as you know, long been printed in Berlin, though we
have not yet received any actual copy of the book. Our agent seems to
have misappropriated for other purposes money we gave him to pay the
German printer and so we are having delay and difficulty in inducing the
latter to send off the books. The same happened with the last October
number of the *"Journal"*, but I hear that this has now just reached London.
Of Vol:II. more than half is translated and revised. Of Vol:III., the *"Krankengeschichten"*, three-quarters is translated and revised. It would have
been finished long since, but Strachey has not sent me any more material
since Christmas, though he had promised to complete it by that date. He
is extraordinarily slow and inhibited. Translation work has also been begun
on Vol:IV., so you will see that more than half of the whole undertaking
is finished from the translation side.

Rank will now, I understand, arrange for the publication of these *"Collected Papers"* in America. I naturally trust that the sacrifices we have
made will not be thrown away and that it will be possible for him to
arrange that the American publisher acquires our translations and the
material of the book we have already published. There could be no technical difficulty in this.

In the last few years I have personally revised every word of the translation of five of your books and have been only too glad of the opportunity.
As you know it has long been my ambition to put out some of your work
in a worthy form in English and I have even cherished the hope that in
the future it might be possible to come to some arrangement whereby new
translations could be published of the other books as well (*Traumdeutung*,
etc.). Of the latter hope this is not the moment to speak, though I shall
look eagerly for any opportunity of realising it.

If I do not get a telegram from you by midday on Tuesday, I shall change
our tickets so as to be able to proceed via Vienna and Semmering. I am
hopeful that you will not send a telegram to stop me. In case you should
need it, my address in Salzburg will be "Grand Hôtel de l'Europe".

With warmest wishes,

Yours always cordially,
Ernest Jones.

424
[telegram]¹

13 April 1924
Vienna

Leaving Semmering Thirsday twenty fourth glad see you afterwards Vienna

Freud

1. The telegram is addressed to "Doctor Ernest Jones, 81 Harley Street, London."

425
[telegram]¹

14 April 1924
Semmering

for the first time absent I cordially greet all participants and wish their
work complete success

Freud

1. The telegram is addressed to "Psychoanalytischer Kongress, Dr. Jones, Hotel
Europa, Salzburg."

426

International Psycho-Analytical Association
Central Executive

14 April 1924
London

Dear Professor,

The content of your telegram filled us with pleasure and the promptness with which you sent it has saved me much inconvenience. Very many thanks indeed.

We shall arrive in Vienna on Thursday morning, the 24th, and leave Saturday morning. I hope you will be able to keep some time. If I do not hear from you when at Salzburg, I will telephone on the Thursday evening in Vienna.

I have had friendly letters from Abraham and Ferenczi and am still in hopes that something may be done at Salzburg to save the situation.[1]

Yours very cordially,
[Ernest Jones]

1. That is, the dissolution of the Secret Committee. The demise of the Committee is discussed in Grosskurth (1991, pp. 156–174).

427

29 April 1924
Stella d'oro, Padua

Dear Professor,

I want to say how glad I was to see you, better than I had been led to expect, and so full of the keenest activity and interest—also to thank you for devoting time and trouble to me at such a juncture, for which I was very grateful. It will all be very helpful in orienting my views further, and I am sure I made plain to you how I stand in the whole matter.

On leaving Vienna I saw in the *Neue Freie Presse* the news that you had received what we call the freedom of the City of Vienna. It is high time for Vienna to do something to recognise its most distinguished citizen, and I hope it gave you some pleasure.[1]

We are finding interesting by-ways in Veneto and have just got back to the beaten track at Padua. Conegliano is a spot I can recommend in spring or autumn.

I will not tire you with a longer letter at present, but I trust we shall remain in good contact when I am back in London. I have thought over the many interesting things you told me, and find naturally that there are still some points in the same connection on which I should be grateful for your opinion.

I was so happy to find you so active, dear Professor, and only regret you should still have some disagreeable troubles. My keenest wish is that they will get less.

With all my warmest regards

Yours always affectionately
Ernest Jones.

1. Freud had received the honor of *Bürgerrecht*; see Jones (1957a, p. 102; 1957b, p. 107).

428

The International Psycho-Analytical Press

30 May 1924
London

Dear Professor,

As you may imagine I have had an extremely busy time on returning from my holiday. We had a very interesting time alternating between charming cities like Bergamo, Verona and Conegliano on the one hand and lakes and mountains on the other.

At last I am happy to record some satisfactory progress in regard to the Press affairs. I think I told you in Vienna that the arrangement I made with Rank at Salzburg was that we should continue our negotiations in London on the previous lines but not start any fresh ones with other firms until we had heard whether Rank had been able to effect anything with American firms. After a good deal of bargaining we have come to a definite agreement with the Hogarth Press here.[1] They buy from us the stock of six books already published (you doubtless know that 2000 copies of your two books in this series have already been disposed of to Boni & Liveright), and undertake to publish in the same series translations of the *"Sammlungen"*. The first volume of these, which was printed last winter in Berlin, they are acquiring from us at cost price. Future books they will acquire individually from the Verlag according to arrangement. We have thus achieved our main purpose, which at times seemed very hopeless, of securing the continuity of our Monograph Series (The International Psycho-Analytical Library) and as this will continue[2] under my editorship, we have a guarantee as to the quality of the books appearing in it. I have immediately notified Rank of our success and suggested to him that Boni & Liveright might care to negotiate with the Hogarth Press about acquiring unbound sheets of the "*Sammlungen*" in the same way as with the previous books.

I presume that Malinowski sent you a copy of his recent anthropological paper in "*Psyche*". It interested me greatly and helped to embolden me to formulate a theory to which at the moment I am inclined to attach some importance. It is to the effect that the whole system of matriarchy was devised as one means of meeting the difficult Oedipus situation by decomposing the Urvater into a kind paternal nurse and a stern maternal uncle. The same explanation would also account for the supposed ignorance of paternity to which Malinowski like most anthropologists subscribes. As soon as I have any time I shall attempt to work this out and see if it accords with the facts before publishing it.[3] What impression have you of the idea?

I have not heard from Abraham since the Congress though I wrote to him from Italy, so suppose he also must be very busy.

You have doubtless heard of our attempt to save the *Journal*. In case you have not seen the appeal we issued to members, I enclose a copy. I wondered if I might send a copy to Money-Kyrle, but thought I would ask you first, as he is still in the analysis.

I am sure you are already greatly looking forward to the summer vacation, for you really had in the winter no adequate opportunity of completely rallying from the effects of the operation. I hope and fully expect that this summer will see you completely restored to full activity.

With my kindest regards, also to your family,

Yours always cordially,
Ernest Jones.

1. The Hogarth Press was founded in 1917 by Leonard and Virginia Woolf. In his autobiography Leonard Woolf outlines the history of his involvement in publishing psychoanalytic literature, and relates how Freud's *Collected Papers* was one of the most successful of his publications; see Woolf (1980, 307–311). Woolf's letters also reveal his opinions about Freud's work; see Spotts (1989, pp. 287, 359–360).

2. "Continuity" was typed initially, then "ity" was crossed out and "e" was handwritten in its place.

3. B. Malinowski, "The Psychology of Sex and the Foundations of Kinship in Primitive Societies," *Psyche*, 4 (1923): 98–128; and "Psychoanalysis and Anthropology," *Psyche*, 4 (1924): 293–332. See Jones (1925a) for his critique of Malinowski.

429

20 June 1924
Vienna, IX. Berggasse 19

Dear Jones,

Today I am only asking you for information. You wrote to me on 30
May that you had successfully sold the publications of the Press, including
my *Sammlungen*, to Hogarth Press. Rickman told me a few days ago that
the Press *could* sell its works to a firm (I do not know if it is the same
one) if my American rights were sold with them, and he therefore asked
me to give my consent to this. Today Rank writes to me that he has heard
from you that you have already sold the books concerned, as well as the
Sammlungen, to an English firm. These three reports do not tally at all;
there is complete contradiction between the second and the third. According to Rickman's information, I am requested to let my American rights
be sold; according to your letter to Rank, this has already happened. I am
at a loss and request an explanation.

I must ask you to bear in mind that after my last decision I withdrew
the American rights of my books from the Press and handed them over
to Dr. Rank for disposal. You must therefore come to an understanding
with him.

With cordial greetings

Yours
Freud

430

The International Psycho-Analytical Press

24 June 1924
London

Dear Professor,

I am sorry that Rickman felt obliged to bother you with these business
matters, particularly in the unfavourable circumstances of an analysis. It
is obviously impossible for half a dozen people in different parts of the
world to accomplish anything unless plenary powers are delegated somewhere. I understood that you had left the matter entirely to Rank and
myself and have been acting on this assumption. My letter to you of May
30th was only intended to report to you the progress made. It was a precise
decription of the situation, but in answer to your questions I will now
expand it further.

I had a long discussion with Rank at Salzburg and came to a clear understanding with him. I was to initiate no fresh negotiations, but was to continue my efforts with those already inaugurated and then report any success to him direct—which of course I did. He on the other hand was to do the same in New York. His report to me is what I had expected, namely that he has been unable to effect anything in six weeks. I told him he would not find it in the least easy to dispose of a collection of technical papers extending over thirty years, because the demand for proper psychoanalytical literature in America was minimal, and they would only consider popular books on the subject. That has been my experience. The popular success of the *"Introductory Lectures"* a few years ago will certainly never be repeated. The *"Collected Papers"* are an unsaleable article, so I am informed everywhere, unless they are managed as a whole.

I expect you have seen a copy of our agreement with Woolf (Hogarth Press). There is nothing in it about American rights. As a matter of fact, "American rights" are not such a concrete entity as they may seem. Legally they are largely mythical, and the question is one of courtesy and understanding. They are composed of two elements—translation and sales. The Press has of course the sole right of translating the *"Sammlungen"* into English, and I understand that your instructions to Rank were that the standard translation we have made (two-thirds is ready) was the one to be used in any country. That question therefore does not arise. As regards the power of sale in America—owing to a curious copyright law—neither Verlag nor Press possesses legal rights in this matter. Any contract that either Verlag or Press made could be at once nullified by anyone who chose to print a translation in America. There is no legal defence against this, but the matter is usually dealt with on grounds both of courtesy and expediency. I anticipate, for instance, that any publisher whom Rank may manage to interest in the matter will communicate with us or Woolf. It would obviously be to his advantage to secure the translation already made, one of good quality, and to acquire already printed sheets instead of being put to the trouble and expense of doing it all over again in America; it is in fact highly unlikely he would contemplate the latter procedure. I am of course in constant communication with Rank about these technical details.

There are some other matters I want to write to you about, which I will reserve till later. I gather from Abraham that you have changed your plan of going to Switzerland, but hope you will be able to arrange an equally agreeable holiday.

We have been having an anxious time here over the question of saving the *Journal*. It is altogether a critical period.

With my kindest wishes,

Yours always,
Ernest Jones.

431

Brintish Psycho-Analytical Society

9 July 1924
London

Dear Professor,

I am pleased to be able to send you by this post an advance copy, though unbound, of Vol. 1 of your *"Collected Papers"*, which was as you know printed in Berlin. I expect to finish this month the revision of Vol. 2, the more advanced Clinical Papers and Papers on Technique. I hope also to finish by next month the *"Krankengeschichten"*. The "Wolf-Man" I am finishing this week and then there is only the Schreber case, if I can get it from Strachey. Until this week I had not been able to get anything from him for six months. There remains only Vol. 4, Metapsychology and Angewandte, half of which is already translated; I intend to finish the revision of this before Christmas. That will then make seven books of yours, translations of which I shall have revised word by word in the last three years. The next problem will be how to get hold of the older books, *"Traumdeutung"*, etc. and arrange for fresh translations if possible. That is a difficult problem, which must await its turn for solution.

I saw Rickman for a couple of minutes yesterday and was glad to hear that you were well. He did not know when you were leaving Vienna or what your address would be.

With kindest regards,

Yours always,
Ernest Jones.

432

16 July 1924
Semmering, Villa Schüler

Dear Jones,

The first volume of the *Collection,* announced by Mrs. Riviere, was a joy and a surprise for me. I admit to having been mistaken. I underestimated either my life span or your energy. The prospects which your letter open up to me regarding subsequent volumes seem really splendid, but I still doubt whether you can overcome the obstacle that Strachey poses. With these volumes you have taken on an enormous workload.

It is essential that I must not forget to tell you that I find your preface masterly. Every word in it is right and fitting.[1]

I am living here on the Semmering in a remarkable villa, in comfort and undisturbed, even able to work, but still suffering from the awful local torments.

I can make neither head nor tail of your earlier letter about the American rights. I am glad that the matter remains between you and Rank.

With cordial greetings to you and your dear wife

Yours
Freud

1. Jones (1924b).

433

International Psycho-Analytical Association
Central Executive

12 August 1924
London

Dear Professor,

I greatly appreciated your kind letter about the translations. As you must know, the Press has cost me enormous labour in the past few years, as well as nearly £1000 personally, but I have the satisfaction of feeling that a solid start has been made in establishing a nucleus of trustworthy psycho-analytic literature in English. I need hardly tell you also that any credit coming to me should be widely shared. Mrs. Riviere, for example, has done at least as much work as I have and has proved throughout a most loyal co-operator. She has been especially invaluable in attending to details in a way that only a woman can, and I feel nothing but esteem and gratitude towards her. Strachey also, though terribly slow, has improved in his work so much that he now ranks as easily the best translator here or in America, nuch [much] better than either Mrs. Riviere or myself. The only member of the trio with whom I feel any dissatisfaction is Dr. Rickman, who is proving very untrustworthy, but I presume this is due to his special morbid temperament; in fact, I sometimes feel that there may be a psychotic trend present. He will probably be more and more replaced by James Glover, who in any case would appear to be my natural successor.

You will be most amused to hear that at the annual Druid festival in Wales—the National Eisteddfod[1]—the chief bard received his prize for a poem dealing among other things with psycho-analysis. So you see your work is penetrating even into remote fastnesses.

I had an interesting talk last week with Ruth Blumgart, who appears to be repeating Loe's history—I hope with happier results. Her brother-in-law—Leonard—wrote to me recently that he saw no need for the existence of a special psycho-analytical *Journal*, since psycho-analysis should be absorbed in general psychiatry. I answered that I had the same wish, but only on condition that the absorption was postponed for a hundred years. If it happened earlier, it could only be by diluting the significance of our work to an inordinate extent, and I trusted he did not mean this. I have not heard from Rank lately, but from various sources I hear that he is having a great success in New York. This confirms my expectation, for he has three things to offer which Americans most desire: the latest novelty, quick results, and a schematic system which evades the laborious fight with the repressed infantile. Ferenczi and I have exchanged personal letters recently. From the English who visited Buda Pest in May, I hear that the rest of his society have taken advantage of his views to feed their own resistances. And as the Vienna Society seems also rather unstable, and the Dutch and the Swiss are of no great importance in the outer world, that leaves us with Berlin and London as the only staunch defenders of psycho-analysis. I have no doubt, however, that we shall be equal to the task. I am of course in contact with Abraham and Eitingon and we are all agreed in trying to damp the aggressivity of some of the younger Berlin members. I have seen a good deal of Sachs since he has been in London. He has changed a good deal and is much more *schwerfällig* [sluggish]. I hope he will not incline towards melancholy as he grows older. I fear he is working too hard for his temperament.

Had you heard that Frink appears to have succumbed to some psychosis last autumn? I am told that he has been in the Phipps Institute at Baltimore as a patient—another case of *"Die, welche am Erfolge scheitern."* [2] The extent to which you and I backed him has proved an important factor in arousing opposition among the other New York men and I am having some difficulty in dealing with this.

So much for general news. I am leaving town tomorrow for a fortnight's holiday and am well ahead of time with the translation programme; what is still unfinished I shall be able to do during the holiday.

I need hardly say that the various reports which reach me of your continually improving good health and evidently better spirits is the most joyful news that one could have. We may now trust that the anxiety corner has been turned and that you will fully recover all your former vitality. I shall be interested to know what works you have in contemplation at present.

With my kindest regards to your family, also from my wife (who will presently send them some photographs of the children), and affectionate wishes to yourself,

Yours always,
Ernest Jones.

1. Historically the eisteddfod has little, if anything, to do with the Druids.

2. "Die am Erfolge scheitern" (Those Wrecked by Success) is the title of the second section of Freud (1916d, pp. 316–331), *G.W.*, 10:370–389.

434

25 September 1924
Semmering

Dear Jones,

These are the last days of my staying here. On Sept. 30th I will be back in town and see the few people I intend to take for next season. I did not answer your kind letter of Aug. 12th feeling in a peculiar mood of incertainty [uncertainty] and expectation about—you guess about what or whom.[1] (By the by the promised photos of your children did not arrive.)

The final success of the Press is a matter you may be proud of, I had given up all hope of such an issue; I knew what your sacrifices were and feared they would prove a barren expense. I am particularly glad of the praise you give to your helpmates in the case of Mrs. Riviere I see I have been of some use.

What is the use of Americans, if they bring no money? They are not good for anything else. My attempt at giving them a chief in the person of Frink, which has so sadly miscarried, is the last thing I will ever do for them, had I to live the one hundred years you set down for the incorporation of ΨA into Psychiatry. Frink I found a clear head and a fine intellect, I settled all my hope upon his person, yet his reactions during analysis were of a psychotic nature. For a week I had to engage Joe Asch as his nurse and guardian at the hotel in Vienna. He got over it; when he came back to NY one of the very first steps he took was to abuse the powers transferred to him in an unjustified attack on Brill, and when he saw he was not permitted to have free satisfaction to his infantile desires he broke down. It was the same in his relation to his new wife, on account of her hardness in money matters he did not get all the tokens of her affection, he had pressed her for.

My health is much better than I had reason to expect. It is now 10½ months since my last operation and no sign of a relapse. The exertions of Pichler have succeeded at last in a fargoing restorations of the two damaged functions of speaking and eating. My general condition is pretty satisfactory. Yet I am no more what I was. I am subject to feel fatigued in the evening, one of my ears is damaged in a permanent way. I will be obliged to resign the leadership of the Vienna Group at the election next month. The Group will be free to choose my successor.[2]

Rank's letters from America were scarce and cloudy. He had left Europe in a very irritable condition and does not seem to have recovered since. The animosity he partly had experienced from you and the Berlin people and partly imagined had a disturbing effect on his mind, but why his mood should have turned against myself I do not understand. You know the best how far I have sided with him. I am not at all at ease about his next behaviour and afraid your prophecies should come true. It may not be easy to fill up his place. In any case I feel you are right in cultivating the *Entente cordiale* with Berlin. But you should not neglect Ferenczi, who has rather retraced his position from Rank and is under no suspicion of separating.

I did some work of a secondary order in these vacations, a *"Selbstdarstellung"* of my work for the collection of Grote at Halle, a contribution to a Jewish Review, which is to appear at Genf etc..[3] My essay in "These eventful Years" by the *Encycl. Britannica*[4] (published in America) will not have escaped your attention. There is no fresh scientific interest now aloof.[5]

With kindest regards to you and your wife

yours truly
Freud

1. Probably a reference to his relationship with Rank, which had reached a peak of tension in August and September 1924; see Lieberman (1985, pp. 240–246).

2. Freud was again elected president of the Vienna Society at the general meeting of 28 October 1924. As Jones reports, Freud had intended Rank to succeed him, but this was no longer appropriate. Instead, Freud took a leave of absence as president, and Paul Federn as vice president assumed leadership responsibilities. See *Journal*, 6 (1925): 527, and Jones (1957a, p. 107; 1957b, p. 113).

3. Freud (1925d, 1924i).

4. Freud (1924f), "Psychoanalysis: Exploring the Hidden Recesses of the Mind," in *These Eventful Years: The Twentieth Century in the Making, as Told by Many of Its Makers*, trans. A. A. Brill, vol. 2 (London: Encyclopaedia Britannica Publishing Co., 1924), pp. 511–523, was written in October and November 1923; see *S.E.*, 19:190.

5. "Aloof" carries the nautical sense of movement in the windward direction (German *in* or *zu Luv*).

435

International Journal of Psycho-Analysis

29 September 1924
London

Dear Professor,

It was a long time since I had seen your own handwriting, so this feature added to the pleasure of today's letter. Abraham had sent me a good account of your health and spirits after seeing you and this week a letter from Hitschmann reported you as *"frisch und arbeitsfreudig"* [fresh and eager to work], but it was best of all to find this confirmed from your own hand.

I am glad to give you the good news that the *Journal* may be regarded as safe for some years, as the response to the appeal has been excellent. The next thing will be to increase the circulation, especially in America, until it is self-supporting, which I think it will be before long. From Part 3 you will have noticed that we employ a medical publishing firm of good standing (Baillière) to do the work, and that (mainly to please some whim of Rickman's) the name of the Press has been changed to Institute. This Institute has Government powers to do various things, e.g. found a clinic, as soon as we get funds, and we have just decided to make its membership co-terminous with the full *medical* (for political reasons) members of the Society, not Associates; in this we were all agreed, including Mrs. Riviere. What the American representation will be will depend on their wishes, which we shall respect and welcome. Part 4 of 1924 should be out before the end of October.

Mrs. R. and I sacrificed most of our holiday to be in a position to fulfil our contract with Woolf of providing translations of the four *Collected Papers* books by Sept. 1, and I proudly handed them to him on that day. I have now finished the final *revision* of the first three, and am to do the fourth by Xmas, though it is doubtful if this will be possible. We expect every day the proofs of Vol. II. The first two volumes are to appear in public by the end of October, the others only next year. After that comes *Das Ich und das Es*. You do not propose to invent another term (? Greek) for *Es*? It cannot be permanently used in psychology in that form, surely.

Frink has certainly come a bad cropper. After his discharge from the Psychiatric Clinic[1] he has gone to Texas, where he again behaved badly. It is more than doubtful if he will ever return to N.Y.. His wife is applying for a divorce. He has alienated the N.Y. members not so much by his psychosis as by many dishonourable acts, and his name on the *Journal* can do us no good in America; what do you think about removing it?[2]

I understand your attitude towards Americans, and largely agree with it in so far as it relates to the general characteristics of American civilization. But I remember Pitt's saying: "One cannot indict a nation". They are human beings with the same potentiality as others. They vary greatly, and you have had few typical specimens to deal with. Then in fifty years they will be the arbiters of the world, so that it is impossible to ignore them. At all events, I shall persevere in my endeavours to strengthen the slight foothold ψα has there.

The event of this week has been Brill's arrival. He spent the week-end with us and we had a heart-to-heart talk. I find him much improved after an eleven years' interval. He is certainly a gifted analyst, though I cannot agree with some of his technique. His ψα work is interfered with by his psychiatric work as well as hospitals, lectures, etc., but his central position in N.Y. is unquestionable. His resistances against you and me I found to be unimportant and easily cleared away. He admitted his unfortunate Ver-lesen in inserting the word Semitic into my letter to him about Rank (luckily I had kept a copy of it).[3] The sore point was of course his transla-tions, though he is getting used to the knowledge of their being poor. Against me his only grudge was that I had apparently coupled him with Tannenbaum at the inception of the *Journal* (though I had immediately dismissed the latter when Brill answered my inquiry about him). He and Oberndorf seem to be the only two who are uninfluenced by Rank's theories. Many other members, including most of those who were with you in Vienna, evidently find them a valuable outlet for their resistances and are having analysis with Rank.

What shall I say about Rank? What we all feel. There is a man whom we have all been fond of personally, whose unusual capacity no one has ever doubted, and whose position it would be extremely hard to replace. Yet the meaning of the situation cannot be overlooked any longer. The manifest neurosis of 1913,[4] which disappeared in the war, has gradually returned in the form of a neurotic character and is running its normal course—denial of the Oedipus complex [especially][5]. The part played by the father, and the sexual wishes towards the mother, are minimized and re-interpreted. As there is no one he would allow to analyse him, I can see only one outcome, though this may be possibly postponed by compromise.[6] From four or five sources I hear reports of his doings in America and am sorry to say they are none of them agreeable ones. His disparaging remarks about both your person and your work are the most painful, though the most comprehensible—simply a regression of the hostility from the brother (myself, who had been useful in this role for some years) to the father. It is thus not personal against you—only the father imago.[7] Politically I am disturbed by his liaison with Jelliffe and White (he is analysing the latter). To publish the paper he did in their $\psi\alpha$ *Review*,[8] which is the refuge of all malcontents, is something he would never have dreamt of two years ago; he was asked to send it to the *Journal*, but refused. I have much reason to fear that the other members may repudiate the *Journal* in favour of the *Review*, and that his influence will not be used to prevent this. He tried to negotiate with J. and W. that they publish your *Gesammelte Arbeiten* in toto, but the plan fell through.

Ferenczi and I have twice exchanged letters in the vacation, and I shall certainly continue as close contact as possible. I am very fond of him and know him well. I do not trace any suspicion of anti-analytic tendency in his work, but cannot refrain from the diagnosis of narcissism combined with poor judgement. No doubt you saw Tansley's review of his work in the *British Journal of Medical Psychology*.[9]

Sachs left last week after two months in this country, where he made a very good impression. The course of lectures he gave, all of which I attended, were excellent and were highly appreciated.

We were horrified at the dreadful news about Hug-Hellmuth, and fear you must have felt it badly too.[10]

Your capacity for work in the past, dear Professor, has been so extraordinary that it is not fair for you to measure your present output by such a standard. If the quality remains as high, or if possible is even higher, cannot you be content if the quantity is somewhat less.

It is cruel of me to trouble you with such a long letter just when your session is re-opening, but I had so much to say.

With my warmest greetings

Yours always
Ernest Jones.

P.S. I should be interested to know in which year the chapter in *These Eventful Years* was written.

My wife is having some photos prepared and will have pleasure in sending them herself. We are all very well and happy.

1. The previous May, Frink had committed himself to the Phipps Psychiatric Clinic in Baltimore.

2. Frink's name was removed from the title page of subsequent issues of the *Journal*.

3. See note 2 to letter 406.

4. Rank appears to have been in the throes of a deep depression at that time and was in fact considering a personal analysis with Jones. He wrote to Jones on 24 December 1914: "Subjectively, I feel quite badly, and would like to come to you earlier than you expect, if I could" (Archives of the British Psycho-Analytical Society, London).

5. Crossed out in the original.

6. The fact that Rank had considered going to England to be analyzed by Jones is ironic.

7. This sentence appears to have been inserted at a later rereading.

8. Rank (1924a).

9. A. G. Tansley, critical notice of *Versuch einer Genitaltheorie* by Dr. S. Ferenczi, *British Journal of Medical Psychology*, 4 (1924): 156–161.

10. Dr. Hermine Hug-Hellmuth was murdered by her nephew, Rudolph Hug, on 9 September 1924.

436

23 October 1924
Vienna, IX. Berggasse 19

Dear Jones,

Dr. Reik sent me today the proofs of your book reviews of the next issue of the *Journal*. I hasten to direct your attention to a historical error in the

review of Laforgue's[1] (p. 487) hoping I will not be too late for correcting
it. It is the more important as you are about indicting a similar error in
Laforgue's relation in the same passage.

You say: One sentence on p. 8 however is a solid mass of erroneous
statements. It is to the effect that at the Nuremberg Congress in 1910 Jung,
Bleuler, Adler and Stekel separated from Fr., the latter two founding the
Centralblatt pour faire l'opposition à Fr. To be sure you are right in contradicting this extraordinary report. But you add from your own: at the
same time Fr. founded the *Zentralblatt* certainly with no idea of self-
opposition.[2]

Now I am sorry to say, your version of the matter falls short of historical
truth too. The *Zentralblatt* was not founded at the Congress, it was not
founded by myself. The fact is, later when we were back at Vienna, Adler
& Stekel called on me to inform me that they had planned a *Zentralblatt*
and turned to Bergmann at Wiesbaden for a publisher. B. had declined to
do so, unless they did succeed in bringing me in as editor. So they offerred
the editorship of the journal to me and in order to convince me that no
opposition was meant, they assured me I could exercise the right of Veto
against any article to be published. Under this condition I accepted.

I need not say that I enjoyed greatly your criticism of the bad, unrealiable
and misleading biographical pamphlet of Wittels'.[3] Perhaps I could have
wished it to be more severe in its tone and his dependence on Stekel might
have been more conspicuously exposed. But it is a nice and dignified production. Wittels is an author of the immortal type *"Lausbub"* [little ras-
cal].—

My chapter on ΨA in *These eventful Years* was written in Oct.–Nov.
1923 during the intervals of my operations.[4] I since had to do the same
thing over again in a "Selbstdarstellung" (Collection of Grote), which you
will get at due time.

Rank is to come back Sunday 26th and to call on me the same day. I
nourish no illusions on the result of this interview.

My wife is going to Berlin to morrow to see our grandchildren, three of
whom are still unknown to myself.

With kindest regards

yours as ever
Freud

1. René Laforgue (1894–1962), one of the early French psychoanalysts, took up the
presidency of the Paris Psychoanalytic Society when it was formed in 1926.
2. The phrase "at the same time" was replaced by "shortly afterwards"; see Jones
(1924g, p. 487).
3. Jones (1924c).
4. Freud (1924f).

437

British Psycho-Analytical Society

28 October 1924
London

Dear Professor,

I am much obliged to you for correcting the historical errors. It just shows how easily they can creep in when one makes a condensed statement in which similars are treated as identicals. I knew the facts you remind me of, though they were not in my mind when I wrote. The difference between a decision at the time of the Congress and one which was an immediate reaction to it (as a set-off to the *Jahrbuch*) was not great enough to force itself on my consciousness. Similarly, although the idea of the *Zentralblatt* emanated from Adler and Stekel, you accepted the responsibility of appearing before the public as the founder; if matters had gone as we then expected them to, the word *herausgegeben von* would in time have surely been replaced by *begründet von* [*gegründet von*]. However, when I got your letter yesterday I telephoned at once to the printer and was just in time to get the passage altered.

I am glad that my review of Wittels was fairly satisfactory. It was originally more severe, but Mrs. Riviere and my wife both thought it too much so, so I slightly softened it.[1]

We are, as you may expect, sorry that your chapter "In These Eventful Years" had to appear in an American guise. Some of the expressions you are made to use are decidedly undignified, and therefore clash with our conception of you.[2]

Last night I gave the opening address before the Oxford University Psychological Society, about 100 people in the audience, and had a considerable success. The subject was The Relation of Analysis to Determinism, Personality and Responsibility.[3]

Abraham and I are corresponding about the site of next year's Congress. No doubt he has written to ask your opinion about it. What is the likelihood of your attending personally? Your presence would be an inestimable encouragement and pleasure.

With kindest regards,

Yours always,
Ernest Jones.

1. Jones (1924c). Fritz Wittels (1880–1950), Viennese psychoanalyst, had a falling out with Freud around 1910; after Freud's comments on the biography (Wittels 1924) he became active in the psychoanalytic movement, especially in New York from 1928 on.

2. Freud (1924f).

3. Jones (1924f).

438

5 November 1924
Vienna, IX. Berggasse 19

Dear Jones,

I am sorry to hear that you disapprove of several passages in my contribution to *These Eventful Years*. If you indicate these passages to me, perhaps I can send you the German text, so that we can divide the blame between author and translator. But I think it will not be worth your trouble.

Abraham has not written to me about the choice of venue for the Congress. Perhaps he will still do so. Perhaps he thinks, and rightly so, that this choice is of little interest to me, given that my attendance at the Congress is rather unlikely.

I have just heard today from Mrs. Riviere how far along you are with preparing the *Collection*, and how much work it has been for all of you. Naturally, the volume or two volumes will be welcomed here with great satisfaction.

Now an official report. Eitingon and Ferenczi were here on 31 October and 1 November in order to confer with me and Rank, who has returned at last, about the necessary changes in the Verlag and *Zeitschrift*. It was decided that Rank will resign from his post as editor of the *Zeitschrift* and director of the Verlag. Together with Sachs, he is to retain his editorship of *Imago*. Storfer has been appointed head of the Verlag and will also be granted some editorial influence. The editorial office itself will be moved to Berlin and entrusted to Radó, who will be assisted there by Eitingon and by Ferenczi in Budapest. The pillar in the new organization is, of course, Eitingon, who has proved himself extraordinarily in this crisis. Rank was in absolute agreement with these new arrangements; he intends to go to America again, even before Christmas, and stay for several months.

Now to more intimate matters: as you see, an open breach has been avoided. Rank himself did not intend one, and a row is not in our interest either. But all more intimate relations with him have come to an end. We cannot explain his behavior; however, this much is certain: he discarded us all with great ease, and is preparing a new existence for himself independent of us. In order to make this decision easier for himself, he has to maintain that I treated him badly. That he has done, and when cornered refuses to give any information. On the other hand, he declares the reports of his own unfriendly remarks to be gossip and fabrication. Not only I but also the other two have found it very difficult to regard him as forthright and to give credence to his statements. I am very sorry that you, dear Jones, have been proven right to such an extent.

This solution naturally does not take the scientific value of his alleged discovery into consideration. We are not yet in a position to formulate a judgment, as he stubbornly denies using a special analytic technique, and analysis, as we practice it, does not lead to such results. Naturally our assessment of his character also colors his theory, and we do not expect it to result in much that is new or of value. But we must, so to speak, wait for further information from him. Until now he has observed a secretiveness that is not customary in scientific activity. When we have the material, we want to keep the objective examination as free as possible from our subjective impressions.

With cordial greetings to you and your family

Yours
Freud

439

International Journal of Psycho-Analysis

7 November 1924
London

Dear Professor,

I am sending you today Vol. I of the *"Collected Papers"*. Vol. II is also ready, but for some reason I have not heard, Mr. Woolf has changed its date of actual appearance from Nov. 3rd to Nov. 25th. You will naturally get a copy in due course.

A Mr. Farrow, with whom you are in correspondence, has sent me a rambling auto-biographical article. From the content of it I should suspect him of suffering from dementia praecox, though Tansley who knows him does not think so. I am trying to get the article re-written in a form possible of presentation.[1]

With kindest regards,

Yours always,
[Ernest Jones]

1. See Farrow (1925), and also Freud (1926c).

440
British Psycho-Analytical Society

11 November 1924
London

Dear Professor,

In "These Eventful Years" there can be no question of the author's responsibility. I was only referring to the slang Americanisms (such as "Right now I want to say", etc.) which occur in it.

I was very glad to hear that the Verlag and *Zeitschrift* changes had been brought about so smoothly. It had given me anxious thought, for otherwise awkward possibilities stood in sight in the future as no one but you could have the authority to deal with the matter. In the new arrangement I entirely concur. How much trouble Rank will give me in America (by opposing Jelliffe's *Review* to the *Journal*) is another question; I have trouble enough as it is with the numerous malcontents there, and am now placing all my faith in Brill to help us.

I know well what a grievous blow this must all have been to you, dear Professor, and can only wonder at the noble fortitude with which you have borne it. Nor must I pass it by without a word about poor Rank. Although his loss bears most of all on you, I can genuinely say that I am as sorry I was right as you are yourself. Your words were, it is true, no surprise to me, for bearing the brunt of his neurotic behaviour in these last years forced me to think deeply about him and to recognise the situation. My one hope was that you should never know, and my endeavours to prevent this cost me dearly in many ways. But I was throughout very fond of Rank, and among the foremost to praise his valuable qualities, so that I too suffer an intense regret at the course fate has chosen. I still wish him well in his future life, though I fear he has not chosen an easy path.

To turn for a moment to a happier topic. Working through your writings has called my attention to many interesting early passages in which were foreshadowed later developments. Of these I may mention four: (1) Unconscious sense of guilt is mentioned in *Zwangshand. und Religionspsych.* 1907.[1] (2) Phallic stage of inf. gen. organization is clearly described in the last paragraph of *Disp. z. Zwangsn.* 1913.[2] (3) Active therapy in phobias, *Zukunftige ψαTher.* 1910.[3] This has since been quoted, I think, by Ferenczi. (4) *Strafbestreben des Ichs* in hysteria comes in Das Unb. 1915.[4]

The best news came today from Eitingon, via Abraham. It was that you were very well and active.

Yours always devotedly
Ernest Jones.

1. Freud (1907b, p. 123).
2. Freud (1913i, pp. 325–326).
3. Freud (1910d, p. 162–164).
4. The expression as employed by Freud is *Strafbestreben des Systems BW* ("endeavor towards punishment of the system *Cs*"). See Freud (1915e, p. 184); *G.W.* 10:284.

441

16 November 1924
Vienna, IX. Berggasse 19

Dear Jones,

I am pleased to hear that you are in agreement with the changes in the Verlag and *Zeitschrift*. I hope you are in regular contact with Berlin, and this arrangement is good, for I see myself that not much can be done with Vienna.

The first volume of the *Collection* has arrived. Very nice! And respectable! My only reservation, that these outdated works are not a good introduction for the English public, is offset by the news that the second volume will follow in a few weeks. Then, it is to be hoped, also the case histories, to which most weight is attached. I see that you have achieved your aim of establishing a secure position for the psychoanalytic literature in England, and I congratulate you on the result which I had almost ceased to hope for.

You must not take Mr. Farrow for a fool. I know him through Tansley and from a personal conversation. He is an odd man, but a very able, "shrewd"[1] one, who had no luck with two analysts and has since then undertaken a self-analysis and is coming up with quite serious findings.[2] To be sure he is a bit of a grumbler, but both analysts (near you) really made technical mistakes with him.

The Rank affair is now coming to an end. Radó arrived today to relieve him of business duties. You must not think that the affair affected me very deeply or will have long after-effects. That is perhaps surprising when one considers the role Rank has played in my life during the last decade and a half. But I know of three explanations for my feeling of indifference. First, it may be a consequence of old age which no longer takes losses so much to heart. Second, I tell myself that the relationship has in these fifteen years amortized itself, as it were; it is not the same thing if a person breaks faith after two or three years, or only after having rendered excellent service for so long. Third, and "last [but] not least,"[3] perhaps I am so unperturbed because I feel in absolutely no way to blame for this outcome. How he will fare in America cannot be foreseen. Once it becomes known that he has turned away from us, it will certainly be just as much to his disadvantage as it is still at present to his advantage.

With cordial greetings to you and your family

Yours
Freud

1. In English in the original.
2. See E. P. Farrow, *A Practical Method of Self-Analysis* (London: Allen and Unwin, 1942); and Freud (1926c).
3. In English in the original.

442

The International Psycho-Analytical Press

24 November 1924
London

Dear Professor,

I am glad to be able to send you by this post a copy of Vol. ii of the *"Collected Papers"*. You will see that it contains translations of your latest papers belonging to 1924. Vol. III—"Case Histories"—has already gone to the printer and is due to be published in March. Vol. IV is not due to be published until next Autumn. We were to have finished the revision of the manuscript by this Christmas, but Mrs. Riviere tells me that it will be impossible to do so before March; that will, however, make no difference to the date of its publication.

I was glad to hear from you about Mr. Farrow. Tansley is revising his manuscript and we shall publish it in the *Journal*.[1]

Storfer has sent me a list of corrections you kindly inserted in my Wittels' review.[2] Many thanks.

I read a paper before our Society last Wednesday on the problem of Matriarchy, where I expounded the view that mother-right was one of the secondary institutions erected to defend against father-son hostility; decomposition into kind father and stern uncle is of course clear. I hope to write the paper out fully and publish it in the April number of the *Journal*.[3]

With kindest regards,

Yours always,
Ernest Jones.

1. Farrow (1925).
2. Jones (1924c).
3. Jones (1925a).

443

International Journal of Psycho-Analysis

1 December 1924
London

Dear Professor,

In a *Rundbrief* from Berlin this morning there is mention of one from you. I do not know if a copy was sent to me, but I had not received one.

Several Americans have spoken and written to me of the disadvantage to the *"Journal"* in America of Frink's name remaining on it and today I got an official request from Brill and Oberndorf that his name should be removed. They say he is still in hospital and "will probably remain there indefinitely". They also speak of some scandal approaching when his wife's divorce case comes on. I think they are quite right and therefore am asking you for permission to act in that sense. Would you be good enough at the same time also to let me know whether Rank's name remains on the cover of the *"Zeitschrift"* and, if so, in what form?—for we ought to bring the *"Journal"* as much into line as possible with the *"Zeitschrift"* in such matters.[1]

With kindest regards,

Yours cordially,
Ernest Jones.

1. Rank's name was removed from the title page of both journals.

444

British Psycho-Analytical Society

18 December 1924
London

Dear Professor,

In your *Rundbrief* which arrived today you ask for an extra letter on the subject of Associated Memberships. In London, we are unreservedly pleased with this system, which gives us many advantages. Associate Members are elected year by year and thus can be released if they are not satisfactory. It gives a probation period to test whether they deserve promotion and membership and it affords an opportunity to have associated with us a few workers in other sciences who are seriously interested in psycho-analysis without wishing either to practise or to profess a thorough knowledge of it. It occurs to me on the other hand that the need for such an arrangement may not be so urgent in a Society like that of Berlin, where the *Lehrinstitut* [training institute] affords ample guarantees for training and control.

Natrually [naturally] my curiosity is piqued by your reference to Rank as I have no clue to its meaning.[1] My first thought was that he had given up analysis and accepted a position in a bank; my second that he had decided to settle in America. But the latter would be more *erfreulich* [pleasing] to you than to me.

I enclose an abstract from a letter of Brill's a month or two ago.

With all good wishes,

Yours cordially,
[Ernest Jones]

1. In his *Rundbrief* of 15 December 1924 Freud had written that "in the Rank matter a surprising change occurred which is a delight to each of us" (Sigmund Freud Copyrights, Wivenhoe).

445

6 January 1925
Vienna, IX. Berggasse 19

Dear Jones,

I absolutely wanted to await your reaction to the turn in the Rank affair.[1] But, in the end, I must write to you first. I can imagine that the incident runs quite counter to your expectations. Indeed, it was a great surprise to me, too. But, after all, it is gratifying that we were both proved right, and not you alone; particularly you, of course, in stressing his neurosis, which lies behind the whole incident. He was really in a manic state when he caused all that trouble, and I saw him in the depression which resulted in the clarification and restoration of his former personality. I have obtained full insight into the development of the whole story and can reveal to you that he paid dearly and suffered much. I am inclined to regard him now as being in the process of being cured and assured against a relapse. I understand very well that he really cannot impart everything to his former friends, so that his explanation leaves something to be desired. But he told me, and I may say that it was a sad and grave story.

Although I know you have been at variance with him for some time, I nevertheless expect, from your understanding and human kindness, that you put an end to this now, forget the past, and allow him fresh credit. I think we shall not be disappointed. On the whole, it is surely a gratifying outcome that we do not again have to abandon one of our own along the way as an apostate or marauder, but can hope that, after a period of recuperation, he will fight bravely with us in our ranks. Tomorrow he is on his way to America and will try to repair the damage he caused through his earlier behavior. I anticipate that it will not be easy, but I insisted that he make the attempt and asked Brill to support him in this.

I will save our minor news for the *Rundbrief*, which you will receive soon. The times are otherwise peaceful, nothing unpleasant has happened.

With cordial wishes to you and your dear wife

Yours
Freud

1. After splitting with Freud and the other members of the Secret Committee, Rank apologized to the group in a letter of 20 December 1924; see Lieberman (1985, pp. 248–250), and Grosskurth (1991, pp. 165–167).

446

British Psycho-Analytical Society

10 January 1925
London

Dear Professor,

I was very glad to get your letter this morning and quite echo the sentiments you express in it. In the meantime, perhaps Rank has shown [you] the letter I wrote to him, and I hear from Berlin that their letter to him was also couched in similar tone. I am sure that none of us have any hesitation in feeling generously and cordially towards him and also that we will do all we can to help him in the difficult path he has now entered upon. At the same time, you will not be surprised to hear that I also share the purely intellectual reserve expressed by our Berlin friends and am bound indeed to be distinctly sceptical about the security of the future. This, however, in no way affects our attitude of willing helpfulness as well as of personal sympathy, so we will all hope for the best. Local news, which is all good, will be reported in the next *Rundbrief*.

We spent a happy holiday in the country, but I am sorry to say that since then my wife has gone through some unpleasant experiences. First, she slipped on the stairs and sustained a Pott's injury to the ankle (fortunately, no bone was fractured, though the lateral ligament was), and then a few days ago, she had to go through the experience of having her tonsils dissected out. The operation passed off smoothly, but she is still having a miserable time from the pain and discomfort involved.

I trust that you and yours are in the best of health.

With renewed greetings for the New Year,

Yours always affectionately,
[Ernest Jones]

447

British Psycho-Analytical Society

5 February 1925
London

Dear Professor,

I was very happy to learn in a recent letter from Eitingon the cheerful news of your continued good health and that your working capacity is first-rate. He says that your tone contradicted *auf[s] lebhafteste* [most emphatically] your occasional pessimistic remarks.

I am afraid I am not likely to be able to take Daly within the time suitable for his purposes, though it is often very hard to predict one's future vacancies.

By next week we shall have finished correcting the proofs of Vol. iii *(Krankengeschichten)*, so that it should appear at the appointed time. In revising the translation of the *Teufelsneurose*, I came across the following point and wish to ask you whether you would like to rectify what I imagine could only have been a temporary oversight. On Page 423 *(Ges. Schr. X.)* you quote Reik in reference to the original identity of God and Devil; in the essay on *Der Teufel* in my *Alptraum*,[1] 1912, I had fully emphasised this original identity on both historical and etymological grounds. On Page 425 you write: "Wenn man sich getraut, die Idee des Teufels als Vaterersatz kulturgeschichtlich zu verwerten, so kann man auch die Hexenprozesse des Mittelalters in einem neuen Lichte sehen".[2] It was this point of view, with the Oedipus constellation relating to it, which formed the basis of my chapter on the *Hexenprozesse* in the same book.[3] Would you like to make any modification or addition to the English translation now being prepared? I need hardly assure you that if you think the matter too unimportant, I shall quite concur.

My wife has quite recovered from her tonsil[l]ectomy operation and I from my perforative otitis (the second within a month), and we are hard at work.

With kindest regards,

Yours always
Ernest Jones.

1. Jones (1912j); see also Jones (1931b, pp. 154–189).
2. "If we are bold enough to apply this idea of the Devil as a father-substitute to cultural history, we may also be able to see the witch-trials of the Middle Ages in a new light." See Freud (1923d, p. 87 n. 1).
3. Jones (1931b, pp. 190–236).

448

11 February 1925
Vienna, IX. Berggasse 19

Dear Jones,

I have to agree that you are absolutely right: I always used to read the publications of our Verlag, and formerly those of Deuticke, at the proof stage. In a way that is no longer comprehensible to me today, but probably due to overwork in those days, I unfortunately neglected to check your *Nightmare.* I distinctly remember that I read only the introductory chapters. The following suggestion may repair the damage, as far as that is possible. I invite you to add a note to the English translation of the *"Teufelsneurose,"* in which you say that, at my express wish, you have added from your work the corrections you consider necessary.

I do not view my condition as optimistically as Eitingon does, but I readily admit that, apart from the continuing dissatisfaction with my prosthesis, I cannot complain about my health.

I received a letter and telegram from Rank informing me that he is making good progress in pacifying the analysts there and clarifying the situation for them. Rumor has it that he will still be returning this month.

It's time the Janus temple of your family ailments were shut.

With cordial greetings to you both.

Yours,
Freud

449

British Psycho-Analytical Society

17 February 1925
London

Dear Professor,

Thank you very much for your kind letter. Your explanation about the *"Alptraum"* was very interesting and it awakened a chord in my memory. I recollect that the criticism you passed on the book to me at the time was that it was the sort of work which did not greatly interest you because it was too much a question of simply making translations from the unconscious.[1] I remembering thinking at the time that, though the criticism was doubtless justified, it would have been more apposite if it had been confined to the first couple of chapters. These, for certain reasons, had to be purely interpretative, but the main point of the book which came out later had, I hoped, contained work of a somewhat different kind. My theme was

to show that the *Hexenepidemie* [witch craze] which raged for two centuries achieved its intensity through the temporary fusion into one delusion of half a dozen different constituents which existed independently of
one another before that time and after. Analysis showed that each of these
constituents was a presentation of the Oedipus conflict and I thus tried to
deal, doubtless inadequately, with the historical reasons why they had
fused in this extraordinary fashion for a given period.

I will obey your kind command to insert a couple of additional notes,
but I find it most difficult to guess just what you yourself would like to
say. The only thing I can suggest is something as follows and I will ask
you to be good enough to send me any criticisms.

Beginning of chapter, footnote: The author expressly desires two additions to be made to the English translation, which appear within square
brackets.[2]

Ges. Schr. X. S. 423, fn. 2. [citing Ernest Jones, *Der Alptraum in seiner
Beziehung zu gewissen Formen des mittelalterlichen Aberglaubens,*
1912] (Reik does so on p. 139 of his book. E. J.)[3]

S. 425, addition at end of footnote: [as was done by Ernest Jones in
the Chapter on *Die Hexenepidemie* in his *Der Alptraum in seiner
Beziehung zu gewissen Formen des mittelalterlichen Aberglaubens,*
1912][4]

I was delighted to receive this morning your *Selbstdarstellung* and have
already read with the highest interest the biographical introduction. It will
be of great value in regard to points which are often raised, and I was
pleased to read the reference to Janet.[5] I am glad you realise that, particularly after the publication of the Wittels book,[6] that your mental development cannot be isolated from psycho-analysis as a whole and that you
have been willing to repeat the sacrifice of your own privacy already undertaken in the *Traumdeutung.*

Is there any hope of your attending the forthcoming Congress?[7]

I am glad to say that our health here has been fully restored and I trust
that the same satisfactory condition rules in your house.

Yours always,
[Ernest Jones]

1. See letter 70.
2. The brackets in the next two paragraphs were inserted by hand in an otherwise
typed letter.
3. T. Reik, *Der eigene und der fremde Gott: zur Psycho-Analyse der religiösen
Entwicklung* (Leipzig: Internationaler Psychoanalytischer Verlag, 1923).
4. The published versions of these recommended changes are similar; see Freud
(1923d, p. 72 n. 1; p. 86 n. 1; p. 87 n. 1).

5. See Freud (1925d, pp. 13, 19, 30–31), where he explicitly dissociates himself from Janet.

6. Wittels (1924).

7. Ninth Congress of the International Psychoanalytic Association, Bad Homburg, 3–5 September 1925.

450

22 February 1925
Vienna, IX. Berggasse 19

Dear Jones,

I endorse your suggestion of both footnotes for the Teufelsneurose. I would only ask you to add to the sentence: "The author expressly desires . . ."[1] my regret that this was omitted from the German text. The footnotes themselves could well be more detailed.

I am feeling fairly well, and I am still looking for improved function of the prosthesis which my doctor is busy modifying continuously. Whether I attend the Congress depends on various circumstances, which at present are still indeterminate. In principle I would like to come. But listening to lectures for hours on end is no longer in my power. However, I will do my utmost to see that my daughter does not miss this Congress.

Anticipating the *Rundbrief,* I notice that I am indeed the agency that decides on the arrangement of the title page of the *Zeitschrift.* The names mentioned there are those of the Obmänner of the individual groups.

In the matter of Miss Newton[2] you misunderstood one point. It is not correct that transferring members automatically become members of the other group. They only enjoy full rights there, but make payment to their group, and must effect a formal transfer in order to belong to the new group.

Cordial greetings.

Yours,
Freud

1. In English in the original.

2. Caroline Newton (1883–1975), a wealthy American from Berwick, Pennsylvania, presented a paper, "Anwendung der Psychoanalyse auf die soziale Fürsorge," before the Vienna Psychoanalytic Society on 27 February 1924 and was subsequently elected a member; see *Zeitschrift,* 10 (1924): 244, and *Journal,* 5 (1924): 510. She was also the translator of Ferenczi and Rank (1924).

451
British Psycho-Analytical Society

27 February 1925
London

Dear Professor,

Many thanks for your letter. It is splendid news to hear that you are seriously thinking of coming to the Congress. Of course, no one could expect you to listen to the papers. I think that you and I held a record at both the Hague and Berlin Congresses as being the only ones to listen to every paper, but neither of us is masochistic enough to wish to repeat the experience!

You will have received the Swiss correspondence I forwarded. Of course, I entirely approve of Abraham's actions in the matter and think he is to be highly commended for his combination of tact and firmness.[1]

You are right in correcting me in the matter of Miss Newton. The Rule I was thinking of was formulated by yourself at the Hague to the following effect; "Election to membership of a foreign group shall be subject to the consent of the Central Executive".[2] It is doubtful whether my conception of it necessarily follows, though perhaps it does. It would appear doubtful whether Miss Newton's election in Vienna is legal. At all events, some fuller exposition of such questions should be considered at the next Congress.

I note your remark about the *Zeitschrift* title-page. It is difficult to keep up-to-date with the New York changes which are so frequent. I did not know that Stern was President, for the last I heard was from Brill that he was debating whether he would accept the Presidency.[3]

With cordial greetings,

Yours always,
[Ernest Jones]

1. The reference is to Abraham's dealings with the Swiss Society, which wanted the Ninth Congress of the International to be held in Geneva; see Jones (1957a, p. 109; 1957b, p. 115).

2. The rule in question is documented in *Zeitschrift*, 6 (1920): 388, and *Journal*, 1 (1920): 209.

3. Adolf Stern was president of the New York society in 1924, having succeeded Horace Frink, who had been president since January 1923.

452

International Journal of Psycho-Analysis

23 March 1925
London

Dear Professor,

Just a line to give the latest news of the rapid transformation in America. Brill is now the President of the New York Society instead of Stern, and Coriat of the American Society, so I suppose that *Zeitschrift* and *Journal* will act accordingly as regards to the titlepage.[1]

With cordial greetings,

Yours always,
[Ernest Jones]

1. The title page of subsequent issues of these journals did not reflect any of these changes in administration.

453

1 April 1925
Vienna, IX. Berggasse 19

Dear Jones,

Looking at the 7 volumes on my shelf—three more to be expected—I feel amazed what a big lot I have written during my short life.[1] I cannot find out where the utterance you quote may be sought.[2] Nor is it necessary you should attend to it. It must belong to the period preceding *Totem and Taboo* and has since lost its importance.

I feel rather tired by 6 months of strenuous work or what appears to me as such in my present condition. The concomitant treatment for my plate—never to be finished it seems—is for something in the effect.

Cordially yours
Freud

1. Freud's collected works, *Gesammelte Schriften (G.S.),* began to appear in 1924.
2. Appended to Jones's typewritten *Rundbrief* of 16 March 1925 is a handwritten note inquiring where Freud made the remark that "the father's place in the family signified *der bedeutsamste Fortschritt in der Kulturentwicklung* [the most important progress in cultural development]." In Jones (1925a) this passage is quoted without a citation to Freud's writings; see Jones (1951, 2:173).

454

26 April 1925
Vienna, IX. Berggasse 19

Business!
Dear Jones,

I admit that I am unable to understand anything of your communication in the *Rundbrief* about the apportionment of the fee for the *Collection*, particularly as no figures are mentioned. I therefore ask you for a clear explanation. Everything that I know so far comes from the following notification from the International Verlag of 24 March. "From the Institute of Psycho-Analysis we have just received for the translation rights of the *Collected Papers*, vol. 1 (1,500 copies) and vol. 2 (1,000 copies):

26 pounds 18s. 5d.,

i.e., half of the amount due to us by contract. We therefore assume that the Institute of Psycho-Analysis will pay the other half directly to you or will credit you."

Cordially yours,
Freud

455

British Psycho-Analytical Society

30 April 1925
London

Dear Professor,

I am sorry the account I gave in the *Rundbriefe* was not quite clear and so will expand it. There are two separate matters to be kept distinct, only the second one of which concerns you directly; the first I described as a matter of general interest and information.

1. Woolf will pay us £200 for the four volumes. From this we have to pay various expenses such as typing, etc., royalties to the Verlag and yourself. There will remain a sum of about £40 (I do not yet know the precise figure) and we decided to allocate this in the proportions of five-eighths to Mrs. Riviere and three-eighths to the Stracheys.

2. Now as to the royalty due to you. The sum for the first two volumes is the same as for the Verlag, namely £26-18-5. For the second two volumes, due only when they appear (we have not yet been paid by Woolf), it will be £30-13-9. I understand that you have been good enough to allocate this money to the translators, but a certain confusion arises from the cir-

cumstance that in one letter you had said it was to be divided between Mrs. Riviere and Mr. Strachey, and in another between Mrs. Riviere, Strachey *und anderen* [and others]. Will you please let either Mrs. Riviere or myself know your final decision about the persons to whom you wish the money paid and the respective proportions?

Yours always cordially,
[Ernest Jones]

456

10 May 1925
Vienna, IX. Berggasse 19

Business!
Dear Jones,

I thank you for your detailed information. So now I know that I have 26 pounds 18s. 5d. at my disposal. It was always my intention that the translators should be paid for their efforts. But I learn with satisfaction from your letter that this has already been done to some extent at your end.

I have therefore decided to dispose of the amount in question in such a way that one-half is to be paid to Mrs. Riviere and the other half to my daughter Anna, who indeed also has a certain share in the translation. The deposit for Anna can be paid into her account at the Anglo-Austrian Bank Ltd., London, Piccadilly.

When my royalties for the two other volumes arrive, I ask you to divide them equally between Mrs. Riviere and the Stracheys, without asking for further instructions from me.

With cordial thanks.

Yours,
Freud

457

20 May 1925
Vienna, IX. Berggasse 19

Dear Jones,

The correspondence with McDougall was very interesting. Your polemical reply was, as always, striking in every sense. Now the only remaining question is why did he write such things, if he is so conciliatory and so free of affect? There's something wrong here.

I thank you for sending Anna the cheque. Piccadilly was really my mistake. I meant the head office on Lombard Street. But that the bank denied having an account for Anna is not my fault. It does exist and the cheque has reached it again via a detour. We complained to the bank.[1]

Cordial greetings.

Yours,
Freud

1. This letter may be in response to a note or letter sent by Jones with a check directly to Anna Freud. The correspondence with McDougall is brought up in Jones's *Rundbrief* of 15 May 1925.

458
British Psycho-Analytical Society

25 May 1925
London

Dear Professor,

The Bank sent an apology for their mistake which I at once forwarded to Anna.

Many thanks for your comment on the McDougall matter. I fancy that the key to his letter was the last sentence in which he expressed the hope that the *Journal* would review more favourably the second half of his book on *Psychology*.[1] He seems to be struggling with a great deal of respect for psycho-analysis. In the meantime, however, since writing to you last, I find that he has published two more papers directly on psycho-analysis in the *Journal of Abnormal Psychology* and the *British Journal of Medical Psychology* respectively.[2] They both show strong signs of emotion and so I shall continue my castigation of him.[3]

With kindest greetings,

Yours cordially,
[Ernest Jones]

1. The first part of the book had been reviewed in Jones (1924h).
2. McDougall (1925a, 1925b).
3. See Jones (1927b).

459

British Psycho-Analytical Society

27 May 1925
London

Dear Professor,

The American Psycho-Analytical Society which was of course founded as a branch of the international seems to have undergone some irregular 'Declaration of Independence' during the war and ever since there has been much doubt about its status. The practical result was that the members, except those who happened to be members of the New York Society, felt themselves under no obligation to subscribe either to the *Journal* or to the International Association funds. Ever since I heard of this state of affairs I have been exercising pressure to remedy it and I now hear that at the annual meeting of the Society this month they agreed to regard themselves as a branch of the international with the corresponding obligations. The council of the Society is predominantly composed of men favourable to us, but as a sign of their ambivalence they have elected as President Dr. Trigant Burrow,[1] who is very vague and muddle-headed, far more Jungian than Freudian. Logically his name should now appear with those of all the other Society Presidents on the title page of the *Zeitschrift* and the *Journal*, and this is the delicate question I am submitting for your consideration.

I am also sending a copy of this letter to Abraham.

With cordial greetings,

Yours sincerely,
[Ernest Jones]

1. Burrow, replacing Coriat, was elected president at the annual meeting of the American Psychoanalytic Association, 12 May 1925, Richmond, Virginia.

460

9 June 1925
Vienna, IX. Berggasse 19

Dear Jones,

If the members of the American P. A. Society have really fulfilled their obligations, then I think the name of their president should also have the same distinction as that of other groups. But first let them subscribe, in other words pay. Not long ago I had some correspondence with Trigant Burrow regarding a confused story of psychical relativity which he had sent me.[1] By the way, I will point out to the editors of the *Zeitschrift* that the president of the other American group is not Stern but Brill.[2]

Several days ago I received new separate offprints of my *Selbstdarstellung*, and I am sending you three of these today, with the request that you send two of them to Lord Balfour and Lord Haldane,[3] to whom I owe thanks for an honorable mention. I am not doing it from here because I know neither the addresses nor the proper titles of the distinguished gentlemen. As for the third copy, perhaps you yourself can find an addressee.

With cordial greetings.

Yours,
Freud

P.S. Your last review was again very gratifying.

1. See Burrow to Freud, 3 April 1925, in Burrow (1958, pp. 94–98).

2. Brill had replaced Stern as president of the New York Psychoanalytic Society in January 1925.

3. Arthur James Balfour (1848–1930), British statesman, prime minister (1902–1905), and foreign secretary (1916–1917); his declaration of 1917 expressed official British approval of Zionism. Richard Burden Haldane (1856–1928), lawyer, philosopher, and prominent British statesman. Both men had publicly acknowledged Freud's outstanding contribution to modern thought and culture; see Jones (1957a, pp. 109–110 and n. 137; 1957b, p. 116 and n. 3), in which he quotes a *Rundbrief* of 15 May 1925 that is incorrectly cited as a letter of his to Freud.

461
British Psycho-Analytical Society

17 July 1925
London

Dear Professor,

The good news concerning your health continues to reach me from various sources. I am sure, however, that you must have greatly welcomed the change from work and are thoroughly enjoying your rest on the Semmering. We are eagerly looking forward to seeing you at Homburg.

Your son, Martin, lunched here a few days ago to our great pleasure. He speaks English with a very pleasing accent and has a pretty good knowledge of it.

Eitingon tells me the good news that Rank intends to read a paper at the Congress. It will surely be listened to with special attention by everybody.[1]

Melanie Klein has just given a course of six lectures in English before our Society on 'Frühanalyse'.[2] She made an extraordinarily deep impression on all of us and won the highest praise both by her personality and her work. I myself have from the beginning supported her views about early analysis and although I have no direct experience of play analysis I am inclined to account her development of it as exceedingly valuable.[3] It has been arranged that Roheim should come here in September to give a course of lectures.

If you have had time to read it I should be interested to know your opinion of the theory of Mother-right I expressed in a paper I sent you some time ago, which I hope arrived safely.[4]

My wife and children left this morning for the sea-side in Wales. I finish work on July 25th and join them there for six days. After that we spend a week at our cottage in Sussex and leave the children there while my wife and I join the two Glovers and their wives in a party that intends to reach Homburg by automobile. Our itinerary, if there are no breakdowns, will be from Havre through Rouen, Orleans, Tours, Limoges, Grenoble, Geneva, Strassburg and Heidelberg. Afterwards we return through Belgium to Ostend. I will get letters which reach London up to August 3rd. After that they will wait until they can be sent to me at Geneva which I reach on August 26th.

With all kind wishes,

Yours always affectionately,
Ernest Jones.

1. Rank (1925).

2. The lecture series on "early analysis" had been announced in Jones's *Rundbrief* of 19 June 1925 (Sigmund Freud Copyrights, Wivenhoe). A most interesting account of the events that led up to Klein's lectures that summer is to be found in the letters between James and Alix Strachey; see Meisel and Kendrick (1985, pp. 247–291).

3. The interchange between Freud and Jones about Klein is scattered: several letters in 1925 (letters 461–463), eight in 1927 (502–506, 508–510), a single letter in 1928 (519), a handful for the years 1931–1932 (519, 578, 580–582), and another handful for 1935 (633–637). For a critical discussion of this aspect of the correspondence as background to the Klein-Freud disputes in the British Society, see Steiner (1985). The actual "Controversial Discussions" of the 1940s are contained in King and Steiner (1991).

4. Jones (1925a).

462

22 July 1925
Semmering, Villa Schüler

Dear Jones!

I was pleased to hear of your nice summer plans. This year we are enjoying our stay on the Semmering very much. You will not see me in Homburg.

I thank you for the kind welcome you extended to my son Martin. Your remark about his English being good is surely flattering.

Rank informed me that he will be here tomorrow, in order to discuss his Congress paper. Melanie Klein's works have been received with much skepticism and opposition here in Vienna. As you know, I myself don't have much of an opinion on pedagogical matters.

Naturally I have read your paper on matriarchy with interest. I was very pleased with your correction of Malinowski's statement about the sexual ignorance of his Australians. It is also in complete agreement with a remark of mine in *Totem und Tabu*.[1]

Some time ago I sent you several offprints of the *"Selbstdarstellung"* with the request that you send them to Lord Balfour and Lord Haldane. I have heard nothing more about this.

With cordial greetings.

Yours,
Freud

1. Malinowski's claim that primitive peoples are ignorant of the causal connection between sexual intercourse and pregnancy is challenged in Jones (1925a); see Jones (1951, 2:154). See also Freud (1912–13, p. 144) for his comment on matriarchy.

463
British Psycho-Analytical Society

31 July 1925
London

My dear Professor,

I was exceedingly disappointed to hear of your change of plans as regards the Congress, for your letter was the first intimation I had and I had fully counted on meeting you there. It is fifteen months since I saw you last and I will try to make it possible for me to come to the Semmering either before or after the Congress.

I knew that Melanie Klein's work has met with considerable opposition in Vienna and also in Berlin, though more at first than later. I regard the fact as indicating nothing but resistance against accepting the reality of her[1] conclusions concerning infantile life. Prophylactic child analysis appears to me to be the logical outcome of psycho-analysis.

I sent of course the copies of the *'Selbstdarstellung'* to Lords Balfour and Haldane. A formal acknowledgement came from the former but nothing from the latter.

With my best wishes for a pleasant and beneficial holiday,

Yours always,
Ernest Jones.

1. "Her" is crossed out and "your" is written in the margin in an otherwise typewritten letter.

464

British Psycho-Analytical Society

19 September 1925
London

Dear Professor,

We all greatly missed you at Homburg, but you could not have given us better consolation for your absence than the one you did in the form of that charming paper which Anna read beautifully.[1] Had I not expected to see you at Homburg I would not have arranged my elaborate holiday in the way I did, but afterwards the arrangements were so complicated that I could not break off in the middle. So I shall have to postpone the pleasure of seeing you until Christmas or Easter. We had a pleasant holiday, full of rich experiences.

You will want to know my impressions of the Congress. Socially it was a great success and proved once more the enormous advantage of personal contact among workers in different countries. Scientifically perhaps it was not up to standard, largely owing to a considerable number of feeble contributions from the Anglo-Saxon countries, a feature which I will do my best to remedy by the next Congress. I thought the best papers were by Alexander[2] and Reik.[3] Ferenczi was in a slightly ambiguous position, trying against his will to modify his former extreme attitude as regards active therapy. (By the way, I wish someone would invent a more descriptive word for this procedure.)[4] He looked very well and young and we were all delighted to see him and enjoyed his company. Poor Abraham was evidently suffering still, but in spite of his difficulties he performed his duties with excellent judgement and skill.

Sachs also made a good impression and it is evident that continued co-operation with the Berlin group has greatly improved him. The main credit for the Congress should, I think, fall to Eitingon who was in every way a great success.[5] He is developing his personality more freely and is in every way exceedingly valuable. Rank, I am sorry to say, did not make a very good impression. His paper[6] was very confused and he is evidently again in a state of chronic hypo-mania, evolving with his old energy vast plans for future works that shall embrace gigantic spheres. He spoke to his old friends about scientific questions but evidently had no personal feelings of friendliness to express. Our attitude, therefore, must necessarily be one of reserve.

You will have heard that in the business meetings, the main question was the differences arising between the American and Vienna groups.

Although I disagree with some of the American attitude I was bound to side with them in the main question, for it is certain that in Vienna and to some extent in Budapest there has been a lack of consideration for the efforts made by our American colleagues to keep up the standard among psycho-analysts there. Eitingon enthusiastically supported my proposal, which was also adopted by the Congress, to the effect that an International Commission be constituted to deal with the problems of analytic education. It seems to me urgently desirable that, even if it is difficult to secure proper control in these matters, there should at least be contact between the various groups in regard to questions affecting more than one group and I hope that the Commission will prove the first step in this direction.

Roheim is in London at present giving us a course of lectures on some anthropological matters.[7] He has apparently quite recovered from his temporary attack of *Geburtstrauma* and is proving a welcome source of incitement to our members. He is also to read a paper before the Royal Anthropological Institute in a couple of weeks' time.[8]

Tansley, who is the last man to welcome polemics, has nevertheless been drawn into a controversy in a weekly magazine where he had been extensively attacked.[9]

We shall be beginning our Session next week and the spirit of our colleagues appears to be good and active.

It was delightful to hear on all sides how much you were enjoying your holiday and how much fresher you felt. I hope you will be in the mood to welcome the work awaiting you in Vienna, but will add my entreaty to those of other friends not to undertake more than you are absolutely compelled to.

With my kindest regards,

Yours always affectionately,
Ernest Jones.

1. Freud (1925j).

2. Alexander (1926). Franz Alexander (1891–1964), born in Budapest, undertook medical studies in Göttingen, then after the First World War took up intensive work in psychoanalysis in Berlin.

3. Theodor Reik, "Der Ursprung der Psychologie" (The Origin of Psychology), abstracted in *Zeitschrift*, 11 (1925): 513, and *Journal*, 7 (1926): 127.

4. Ferenczi (1926a). The expression "active intervention" has also been employed; see Stanton (1991).

5. See Max Eitingon's important report and proposals regarding psychoanalytic training in *Zeitschrift*, 11 (1925): 515–520, and *Journal*, 7 (1926): 130–135.

6. Rank (1925).

7. The lectures were not reported in the *Zeitschrift* or the *Journal*.

8. Possibly G. Róheim, "Hungarian Calendar Customs," *Journal of the Royal Anthropological Institute*, 56 (1926): 361–384.

9. The polemics appeared in the *Nation*; the episode is discussed in more detail in Jones (1957a, p. 113; 1957b, p. 119).

465

25 September 1925
Semmering

Dear Jones,

I am sorry that my absence at the Homburg Congress disappointed you, but I have the impression that I prepared you for this repeatedly. Perhaps I was not explicit enough. For a long time I had hoped that my condition would improve sufficiently to make it possible for me yet to attend the Congress; but I have long since realized that I am not equal to the tasks there. Whenever you come to Vienna, be it Christmas or Easter, you will be welcome and can see for yourself that I neither overestimate nor underestimate the extent of my capabilities.

I thank you for giving me your impressions of the Congress, which correspond broadly with those from another quarter. The attempts to keep in touch with the American group are certainly laudable. We also readily concede that the acceptance of Miss Newton in Vienna was an infringement of our own rules. But the demands of the Americans seem to me to go really too far and are dictated too much by narrow-minded, egotistical considerations. Their position is also incorrect in that they resist lay analysis altogether instead of making the thorough training of both lay-people and doctors the crucial point. Of course they cannot demand more from their laypeople, since they cannot make the funds available to anyone for training in analysis. On the question of lay analysis I did not keep my decided opposition a secret from the Americans.

I hope that the work which I will start in about a week will not be taxing for me. I will endeavor to keep it within certain limits. You are, of course, apprised of my latest publications. A little booklet, "*Hemmung, Symptom und Angst,*"[1] is to go to the printer at Christmas. It is good to hear that you are content with the Londoners and are looking confidently forward to the work of the next few years. Personally I am looking forward to the fourth volume of the *Collected Papers*, which I may expect soon. I have been invited by the *Encyclopaedia Britannica* to write an article on psychoanalysis,[2] which is intended for the next supplementary volume. I find it very boring to deal with the same subject time and again, have sent them something that does not please even me, and added that if they do not want this essay, they may turn to you to write another one for them.

With cordial greetings to you, and may your family thrive.

Yours,
Freud

1. Freud (1926d).
2. Freud (1926f).

466

[postcard]

4 October 1925
Vienna

Dear Jones,

By some accident I found out that I did not possess part 4 of vol. IV of the *Journal*. Cannot imagine by what neglect it got lost. Will you kindly send me another copy?

Yours as ever
Freud

467

British Psycho-Analytical Society

30 November 1925
London

Dear Professor,

This is to commend to your kind attention Mr. Earl F. Zinn, the American gentleman about whom I wrote to you some time ago. He is, you will remember, Secretary of the Committee for the Study of Sex appointed by the National Research Council in America.

With kindest regards,

Yours sincerely,
[Ernest Jones]

468

British Psycho-Analytical Society

5 December 1925
London

Dear Professor,

I have not heard directly from Berlin for a little time, but Eitingon tells me that Abraham is in hospital facing the possibility of a gall-bladder operation. We shall all be happy when this painful illness comes to an end.[1] I am myself at present in bed for a few days, a thrombosed haemmorrhoid having complicated in a painful way a severe influenza cold. I hope that you at least are in good health. I had hoped to come to Vienna at Christmas, but shall have to postpone it till the Spring, when I will surely come to see you.

In my Congress letter to you, I omitted any reference to the film affair,[2] but it has now become actual in England, so I should like to define my standpoint. It is, I am glad to say, identical with your own. I regard it as unprofessional to depict one's own medical work in any such way before the public. Also to link up one's scientific work with commercial transactions opens the way to unforeseen possibilities of trouble. I think, and very many with me, that Abraham committed an error of judgement in acceding to the Ufa request. He forgot for the moment the responsibility of his official position. I cannot blame him, for not only did it happen at the onset of his illness, but the error was dictated by just that innocence and optimism which are otherwise such valuable traits in his character. The other people concerned I cannot regard as so blameless. I spent many hours at the Congress discussing both in company and individually the whole matter with Sachs, Storfer and Bernfeld. Storfer is a pathological personality who has to be humoured, so there is no more to be said. But I was disappointed to find that both Sachs and Bernfeld allowed their artistic ambitions and jealousies to triumph in a most narcissistic way over other considerations, and nothing that I could do was able to influence them.

There was a great deal of adverse criticism of the matter at the Congress and there will, I am afraid, be more. Some newspaper notices suggesting that the film might appear in England also led to a heated discussion at our Society meeting this week. It was not easy to quell the feeling, which wanted to express itself in the form of some precipitate action. The members unanimously complained, and with some justice, that they had been forced by the President of the Association, without their knowledge, to bear the odium of a situation of which they themselves disapproved. It is certain that if the film appears in England there will be much justified criticism of the methods of psycho-analysts. The newspaper notices all say that you have arranged the film because of the failure of psycho-analysis to get accepted by other means. We shall at least take steps to dissociate you from the undertaking.[3]

Now to turn to pleasanter topics. It is with great pleasure that I am despatching today to you the Fourth Volume of your 'Collected Papers'. Both it and Part IV. of the 'Journal' had been ready for a month but could not be issued before because of some strike. The undertaking must have seemed to you slow, but at least it had the merit of being sure, which you sometimes doubted. I am also having despatched to you from Paris a copy of the French translation of my 'Papers', which has just been published.[4]

Can you tell me anything about the progress of a Dr. Power, whom I saw on her way to Vienna some time ago? I have a patient whose life is somewhat involved with hers.

I will finish with an amusing anecdote. A certain George Smith,[5] one of the keenest interpreters of Assyrian characters, had to wait impatiently for some days before he could examine an important tablet which was being cleaned. Then as soon as he finished interpreting it, he jumped up in a state of excitement and, to the astonishment of the bystanders, began to undress. It is a neat confirmation of the pairedness of the instincts, is it not?

With kindest regards,

Yours always,
[Ernest Jones]

1. Abraham's fatal illness resulted from a series of complications that began with an infection of the lung caused by a foreign object during a visit to Holland the previous May (H. Abraham and E. Freud, 1965, p. 382 n. 1).

2. *Geheimnisse einer Seele* known in English as "Secrets of the Soul," was produced by Neumann Produktion G.m.b.H. on behalf of Universum Film-Aktiengesellschaft (Ufa) and directed by G. W. Pabst. Although Freud did not give his authorization, Abraham nevertheless supported the project; see H. Abraham and E. Freud (1965, pp. 382–385, 399). The film's release caused a commotion among analysts, which is detailed in Jones (1957a, pp. 114–115; 1957b, pp. 121–122).

3. As Jones later pointed out, the association of Freud with this film was indeed quite marked at this time. Jones (1957a, p. 115; 1957b, p. 122) contains this passage from *Time:* "Every foot of the film, *The Mystery of the Soul*, will be planned and scrutinized by Dr. Freud."

4. Jones (1925b).

5. George Smith (1840–1876), British Assyriologist, deciphered the Chaldean account of the Flood from Layard's tablets.

469

13 December 1925
Vienna, IX. Berggasse 19

Dear Jones,

I have now received the fourth volume of the *Collected Papers*, am very pleased that the work is completed, and thank you warmly for this achievement, the realization of which I had really doubted. I shall not be surprised if this book makes its influence felt only very slowly, but at least we did everything we could. The French translation of your *Papers* has not yet arrived.

This month we do not feel like writing a *Rundbrief*. Abraham's illness has us all holding our breath, and we are very unhappy that the news is so vague and therefore so uncanny. You doubtless know that the gallbladder operation has already been performed. But it showed nothing that might explain his pain and fever attacks. Dr. Felix Deutsch[1] went to Berlin last Sunday. He will probably bring us as much enlightenment as is at all available now.

It seems to me that you have confused the candidate for the chair of psychoanalysis in Jerusalem, Leo Kaplan of Zurich, with a Dr. Kaplan of Vienna, who has not been seen around for years. They are not related to each other.[2] The one from Zurich has even written to me, expecting me to support his application with the local influential chief rabbi, Dr. Chajes. I declined. I do not know Kaplan personally, only from his writings, which contain nothing erroneous, but are dull and boring.[3] I think it would be very regrettable if Kaplan were to get this post. He is a man without originality, necessarily without much practical experience of analysis, and is certainly no inspiring lecturer. Eder would certainly be a better man, and Bernfeld, with his fascinating personality, sharp sense and powers of oratory, even better. But I am just as doubtful as you that such a chair will be founded in the near future.

I hope that we shall see each other again in the spring in good health. I was very sorry about your news that you have had ailments lately. I too had my bad weeks; first, as a result of dental surgery, which, however, has nothing to do with my troubles (lower jaw on the other side), and now as a result of a severe catarrh, which is widespread in Vienna at this time of the year.

This business of making a film I disliked from the beginning. But I did not want to impose my feelings on the others by laying down the law. When they pursued me with the argument that if they did not do it someone else would, I desisted from emphatically stopping Abraham, Sachs, Bernfeld, and Storfer, and only insisted that I myself not be part of it. Now the affair has taken an unexpectedly favorable turn in that it has procured for Abraham a contribution to the costs of his protracted illness. Perhaps we are all too conservative in this matter; one really ought to have made some sort of concession to the film fever.

I hope that your health is restored and that your wife and children are well.

With cordial greetings.

Yours,
Freud

1. Felix Deutsch (1884–1964), Viennese psychoanalyst, on occasion Freud's personal physician in the early 1920s.

2. Freud is responding to Jones's *Rundbrief* of 19 November 1925, in which the issue of a chair of psychoanalysis at the University of Jerusalem is raised (Sigmund Freud Copyrights, Wivenhoe). Leo Kaplan (1876–1956) was born in Russia and later settled in Zurich. He was trained in mathematics and physics, and his writings attempted to deal with the theoretical problems of psychoanalysis and the philosophical issues of the time, as expressed especially in the works of Hegel, Marx, Schopenhauer, and Sartre. Michael Kaplan of Vienna is listed as a member of the Vienna Psychoanalytic Society in *Journal*, 3 (1922): 280, and *Zeitschrift*, 10 (1924): 120, as well as in *Journal*, 8 (1927): 130.

3. Consider, however, that Leo Kaplan's *Gründzuge der Psychoanalyse* (Leipzig: Deuticke, 1914) and *Psychoanalytische Probleme* (Leipzig: Deuticke, 1916) were highly thought of by Freud's friend Lou Andreas-Salomé; see Pfeiffer (1972, pp. 57, 223 n. 83).

470

16 December 1925
Vienna, IX. Berggasse 19

Dear Jones,

Your French translation arrived today.

I expect you to know all about Abraham's condition. Felix Deutsch who had gone to Berlin to see him says this week will be the critical period and we ought to be prepared for the worst. It is a gloomy prospect, but as long as he [is] alive we may cling to the hope that his affection [affliction] often gives a chance of recovery. In case of emergency I will not find it in my powers to come to Berlin. I think Ferenczi will go and I would like to know if your health permits you to do the same. I intentionally abstain from picturing the consequences if that fatal event occurs. I am sorry Eitingon stays at Taormina and is not likely to return before March. Rank is expected back in a few days, he may already have arrived at Paris. Your creation—the comittee—has fallen to pieces you see. If we are to lose Abraham we will have to consider the matter anew.

Writing in deep affliction

affectionately yours
Freud

471

British Psycho-Analytical Society

18 December 1925
London

Dear Professor,

Thank you very much for your kind letter. Like you I have not felt in the mood for writing a *Rundbrief* when Abraham's life is hanging by a thread. The latest news gives one again ground for hope, provided that exhaustion does not supervene. Until Sach's terrible telegram *"Abrahams Zustand hoffnungslos"* [1] which came on Tuesday morning, I had heard nothing from either of them since the October *Rundbrief*, though I had written twice to both for news. The only rumours that had reached here were vague but very satisfactory, including news of the operation. The thunderbolt this week was therefore all the more overwhelming. I need say nothing about my feelings, because your own will be the same. There is of course general consternation among our group here, where Abraham is so much loved and respected.

The chief news from London, which I will relate to you as it is good, is that an old patient of mine has given two thousand pounds to our Institute, a sum which will probably enable us to start a clinic early in the New Year. We are all very happy at the news, though it will mean more work.[2]

A Mr. Earl Zinn will probably ask you for an interview before long, so I will say a word about him. Personally he makes a very capable, shrewd and fair-minded impression. He has had a partial analysis himself and is very favourably inclined. He is in the interesting position of being perhaps the first representative despatched by orthodox science to form a bridge to psycho-analysis. He is Secretary of an important Committee for the Study of Sex which has been formed by the National Research Council of America, and they have gone about their work in an altogether praise-worthy manner, a manner showing nothing American about it beyond the feature of spending much money. He has been deputed to investigate the possibility of our methods, work and conclusions being presented in such a way as to conform to the canons of regular scientific principles more closely than it might at first sight appear to do. I shall be glad to co-operate in achieving this very interesting task.

Our only thought at present is the hope that Abraham's condition will allow us to spend a rejoicing Christmas.

With kindest regards,

Yours affectionately,
Ernest Jones.

1. "Abraham's condition hopeless."
2. The London Clinic of Psycho-Analysis, 36 Gloucester Place W1, was officially opened on Freud's seventieth birthday, 6 May 1926, but full work did not commence until the following autumn. The benefactor was Pryns Hopkins (b. 1885), who received a Ph.D. at the University of London for his psychoanalytically oriented treatise *Fathers or Sons? A Study in Social Psychology* (London: Kegan Paul, 1927).

472

British Psycho-Analytical Society

19 December 1925
London

Dear Professor,

I hasten to answer your second letter which came today and to express my sympathy with you for what you must be going through. Abraham has been even nearer death than you appear to have been told, but the latest news does at last give one reasonable grounds for hope. It is evident that the surgeons made a bad mistake and very nearly killed him.[1]

In answer to your question, of course I am ready to go to Berlin at once for the purpose you mention or for any other purpose where I could be of any help. I very nearly went last Tuesday on getting the first telegram and was chiefly restrained by the thought that my appearance from a distance might seem ominous to Abraham. I only wish I could have some say on the medical questions involved, but there is already such a multiplicity of advice that I had to renounce this desire. I am in constant communication with Sachs by telegrams and letters and he will let me know if my presence in Berlin could be of any assistance. He has behaved splendidly this week. I was surprised to hear from you that Eitingon was still in Sicily. Probably he has left since then.

My Committee, as you call it, will I hope survive any blow. The need for it will always give it life, though the loss of Abraham could never be replaced. When he is better I am going to make another determined attempt (he refused me this Summer) to insist on his living under conditions that will completely restore him before he resumes work, and this time I hope he will listen.

I feel with you, dear Professor, with all my heart.

Yours always,
Ernest Jones.

P.S.: If for any reason you yourself wish me at any time to go to Berlin, you have only to telegraph me.

1. See Jones (1957a, pp. 112, 115–116; 1957b, pp. 118, 122).

473

21 December 1925
Vienna, IX. Berggasse 19

Dear Jones,

For once this is good news in dismal times. I have always said that America is useful for nothing but giving money. Now it has at least fulfilled this function. Of course, not for me or my purposes, but I am happy that it happened for London, and I am convinced that once you have initiated something, it will not founder. My best wishes for the thriving of your institute!

No news of Abraham today. The last sounded reassuring. As we saw with Mrs. Strachey, lung abscesses offer hope, even when the case seems very severe. If he only has the strength to survive the operation that will be necessary later. His heart is said to be undaunted.

Ferenczi is supposed to come here during the holiday. I will speak to Rank tomorrow. My catarrhs are still troublesome. I sent the printer a small pamphlet with the title *"Hemmung, Symptom und Angst"*.[1]

With cordial greetings to you all for this Christmas.

Yours,
Freud

P.S. Dr. Deutsch just telephoned, having returned from Berlin today. He left Abraham in satisfactory condition, with a temperature of 37.6, but learned later this afternoon, through a call from Radó, that there has been a great change for the worse; a renewed fever attack as high as 39.5, etc.. He has been requested to return there immediately, as Abraham sets great store by his presence. His own depleted state is perhaps the reason why he sounded so pessimistic on the telephone just now.

1. Freud (1926d).

474

25 December 1925
81 Harley Street, London

Dear Professor,

What is to be said about today's frightful news? You know that I share your feelings to the full. It seems as if very little is to be spared you in the way of suffering—and I too know what suffering means. There is no way of meeting this blow: it cannot be dealt with, for nothing can ever cure it—not even time. Karl was my best friend, and his wife one of my wife's best friends. We all understood each other completely. The loss is quite irreplaceable, both personally and to the movement. Nothing could have better illustrated the senselessness and meaninglessness of the universe, its awful blindness. And yet I am equally oppressed with the appearance the whole course of events gives of diabolical deliberate aim—from the trivial start to the terrible end, the selection of the best and most valuable man we know, even the choice of Christmas day, the rejoicings of which will increase his wife's poignancy to the end of her life.

To you, dear Professor, I have only two things to say; to tell you again how completely I share your affliction, and to assure you that nothing shall ever make me swerve from following, however imperfectly, the ideals for which Abraham worked and fought so clearly. You can count on me, now as ever.

Presuming that the funeral will be on Monday or Tuesday I wired to Sachs and Mrs. Abraham that I will arrive on Sunday evening. I asked him to let me know if it was on Sunday, in which case I should leave tonight, but there has been no reply. I suppose that Ferenczi, Eitingon and Van Emden will also be there. Both my children have acute bronchitis (temperature just under 40°C, but I do not think their state will prevent me from travelling tomorrow, as they have passed the worst stage and are also in good hands.

If the question of succession to the Presidency comes up I shall vote for Eitingon and imagine you will do the same.

There is no more to say.

in deepest distress and grief yours
Ernest Jones.

475

30 December 1925
Vienna, IX. Berggasse 19

Dear Jones,

I can only repeat what you said: Abr.'s death is perhaps the greatest loss that could have hit us, and it has hit us. In letters I jokingly called him my *"rocher de bronze"*; I felt safe in the absolute confidence he inspired in me, as in everyone else. In the brief obituary I wrote for him for the *Zeitschrift* (Heft 1, 1926)[1]—a full-length appreciation will doubtless come from another quarter; Heft 2 is being reserved for it[2]—I applied to him the line from Horace:

"Integer vitae scelerisque purus."[3]

I have always found exaggerations at death particularly embarrassing and have taken care to avoid them, but with this quotation I feel I have been truthful.

Who would have thought, when we met that time in the Harz, that he would be the first to depart this irrational life. We must work on and keep together. No one can personally replace our loss, but then for our work no one can be indispensable. I shall soon depart; the others, I hope, not until much later, but our work must continue; in comparison with its greatness, all of us put together are insignificant.

I am certainly in favor of Eitingon as president; we have owed him this honor for a long time, but he does not intend to return till March; his ailing wife requires too much of his time. Of what use to us is an absent president? I hope that you and he, together with Ferenczi and van Emden, have now arranged everything in Berlin for the best.

I clasp your hand with a deep feeling of fellowship.

Yours,
Freud

1. Freud (1926b).
2. Jones (1926a).
3. "He whose life is blameless and free of guilt" (Horace, *Odes*, I, xxii, 1).

476

25 February 1926
81 Harley Street, London

Dear Professor,

It was very delightful, and gave me great pleasure, to gather from your semi-humoristic *Rundbrief* that you are in good spirits. It was like a ray of sunshine, which in these last years has not been too frequent—thus all the more welcome.

You are doubtless right, as usual, when you say that I am too much oppressed by the telepathy matter, for in time we shall overcome the resistance it evokes just as we do all others. But you are lucky to live in a country where "Christian Science", all forms of "psych. research", mingled with hocus-pocus and palmistry do not prevail as they do here to heighten opposition to all psychology. Two books were written here trying to discredit ψα on this ground alone. You also forget sometimes in what a special position you are personally. When so many things pass under the name of ψα, our great answer to inquirers is "ψα is Freud", so now the statement that ψα leads logically to telepathy etc. is more difficult to meet. In your private political opinions you might be a Bolshevist, but you would not help the spread of ψα to announce it. So when *"Ru[ü]cksichten der äusseren Politik"* [considerations of external policy] kept you silent before, I do not know how the situation should have changed in this respect. Your first communication on the subject in *Imago* seemed to me to cover the ground adequately,[1] to defend the *Traumtheorie* from being altered even if telepathy were proved, so the second one seemed to me only irrelevant and harmful.[2] At all events it gave me a new and unexpected experience in life, that of reading a·paper of yours without a thrill of pleasure and agreement.[3]

Incidentally, the consolation you offered me was no news, for it was I who got you made an Honorary Member of the British Psychological Society, and you may be sure it was not done as a reward for your telepathy paper which had not then appeared. Other members of the Council had offered opposition on two previous occasions, but I kept insisting till they felt ashamed of their attitude.

You may be sure I am writing Abraham's biography[4] with the greatest care, but before it is published I should be grateful if you would read it through, for it raises in places delicate questions of taste or judgement where your opinion would be decisive. The bibliography Rado sent me proved of little value, as it was full of inaccuracies and omissions, so I have spent a fortnight getting it into proper form.

I have been indisposed for a fortnight with painful rectal trouble and was four days in bed, but today it shows good signs of mending again. Yesterday I saw Money-Kyrle on his way to you and thought the auspices looked favourable for a final result. What became of Dr. Power, the American lady?

I am greatly looking forward to May. My wife will also seize the opportunity to visit her family in Vienna, and on account of these arrangements as well as several others it would be a great convenience if you could indicate to me *which* days and how many you will make use of for the Committee gathering, etc.. Shall you be in Vienna or Semmering at the time?

With kindest regards

Yours always affectionately
Ernest Jones.

1. Freud (1922a).
2. "The Occult Significance of Dreams," in Freud (1925i, pp. 135–138).
3. This episode and Freud's position on telepathy are dealt with more fully in Jones (1957a, pp. 394–396; 1957b, pp. 422–424).
4. Jones (1926a).

477

6 March 1926
81 Harley Street, London

Dear Professor,

Very many thanks for the latest book.[1] It will create general gratitude to you for writing it and joy at the proof of your continued energy. I have read it through rapidly and will record a few of my first impressions, which will of course be deepened later.

I do not think I ever enjoyed a book of yours more, which is saying very much indeed, as you must know. It is exactly the kind of book of yours that gives me a special pleasure, with that fine dissection of clinical findings, the constant clarifying of confused issues, and the repeated emerging of useful generalisations. I could not refrain from thinking also how Abraham would similarly have delighted in it. One misses him at every moment.

Have you noticed how your last four or five books have regularly alternated in style? One very abstruse and difficult is followed by one easy and flowing—generally misleadingly easy, for it is just as rich and deep as the other kind.

So far as I have apprehended the content at this first reading I find it entirely persuasive and convincing. I could at once agree with all the arguments and conclusions, though it reveals how much more there is for us to ascertain and elucidate. I especially liked the lovely generalisation contrasting repression and outer *Gegenbesetzung* with regression and inner *Gegenbesetzung* (S. 113),[2] the description of how the ego gets reconciled to symptoms, the setting up of Abwehr as a general term with its sub-divisions, relation of Angst to Symptombildung, and of course the tracing of Angst to the ego instead of to the Libido. I say 'of course' in the last instance because this is one of the few matters in which I have never been able to feel satisfied with your formulations, and so long ago as in 1910 when I wrote my exposé of the pathology of morbid anxiety[3] I felt bound to take the opposite view and maintain that Angst was generated from the ego in response to the dangers brought about by libidinal demands. I remember at least twice discussing the matter with you (before the war, and again at The Hague Congress), but was never able to convey my argument with success. Indeed I still see no reason why the same explanation could not be applied to the more primitive case (S. 88) (infancy and actual neurosis) which you distinguished so beautifully from the case of danger signal.[4] Incidentally it occurred to me that an analogy between the traumatic and the danger situations (S. 126)[5] was shewn in 1914 when Germany declared a general state of *Kriegsgefahr* [war threat], an institution which I do not think exists in any other country; it was of course followed by the *trauma* of war itself.

There follow a few disjointed comments. I can confirm through a particular patient your connection between the phenomenon of isolation and *Berührungsscheu* [avoidance of touching] (S. 60).[6] She complained prominently of not being able to associate any idea with the ideas that would logically follow from it, and this proved to be a radiation of forbiden onanism. The mechanism is not quite the same as in the isolation of the obsessional neurotic (it was a case of hysteria), but the effect and symbolism are very similar.

Your statement (S. 39) that Angst makes the repression not vice versa,[7] which would surely agree with your old description of Urverdrängung as a Fluchtversuch, wouldn't it? Flight is biologically *secondary* to the perception of danger (Angst signal).

I am not entirely satisfied with the decision whether the Abwehr is primarily against the *Libido* or the *hostility* connected with the latter (S. 65 etc.),[8] or with the escape from the dilemma by pointing to the libidinal component of what you term the sadistic aggression against the father (S. 36)[9] what speaks in favour of your view is that one sees less repression if the attitude towards the rival is one of pure hate (e.g. a stranger), but when one thinks of the early history of mankind, [it would] [10] when there would not be so much love for the Urvater as in later times (much of it is a secondary reaction-formation), it would seem more natural to regard the first repressions as due to fear [of] [11] on the part of the son that his hostility would provoke dangerous reprisals from the father.

Your clear account of the *series* of danger situations solves a problem that has occupied me in my analyses of female homosexuals, namely what in the female corresponds with castration in the male as the resolver of the Oedipus complex? After working through various layers I found as the deepest with them the dread of being disapproved of and *deserted* by the father, because this meant the loss of all hope of penis and child. But in the more normal woman why is the dread of the mother so great. What can the mother do? (Perhaps seperate daughter and father?). At all events the development from *Verlassenheit* [abandonment] to castration is most illuminating. It can also be confirmed on the other side, the reactions of the parent. I have good examples of castration reactions in the mother after weaning her child. And my wife produced a neat illustration of Angst after leaving children last year when she unwillingly parted from them to go abroad. We slept the first night on board ship and she woke me up with a startled cry "Ernest, where are the children, I can't find them"; there was a strong wish-illusion of their being in the room.

My last comment, for the moment, is that you provide a fourth, and perhaps most important, reason in addition to the three you related to me at the time of why you were not more disturbed by the difficulty with Rank. It is now clear that you were wise enough to do what none of us others could do, namely to learn something from it all by allowing Rank's views to work on you in a stimulating and fruitful way. What a splendid reaction to a depressing difficulty—*alle Ehre* [hats off]!

Again thank you a thousand times for what will be a permanent source of inspiration to further thought and work.

Yours always gratefully
Ernest Jones.

1. Freud (1926d).

2. Freud (1926d, p. 159), *G.W.*, 14:191. *Gegenbesetzung* is translated as anticathexis by Strachey. In the present context, however, we might consider the expression "withdrawal of interest," as employed by Freud in his first extant letter to Jones; see note 3 to letter 5.

3. Jones's seminal paper "The Pathology of Morbid Anxiety" is one of his few significant contributions to psychoanalytic theory (Jones, 1911e). In this piece Jones reworked Freud's earlier view of anxiety as being derived from repressed sexuality. Rather, Jones posited that anxiety is "a reaction against repressed sexuality, a reaction derived from the instinct of fear" (Jones, *Papers*, 1st ed. 1913, p. 171). As Harold Stewart has observed,

Jones's explanation of the problem of anxiety as put forward in 1911 is akin to Freud's later view of signal anxiety as outlined in *Inhibitions, Symptoms, and Anxiety* (Freud, 1926d); see Stewart's paper "The Scientific Importance of Ernest Jones," *Journal*, 60 (1979): 379–404. Jones rightfully claimed precedence for this theoretical contribution to psychoanalysis in "The Psychopathology of Anxiety" (Jones, 1929a; *Papers*, 5th ed. 1948, p. 298) and in his biography of Freud (Jones, 1957a, p. 255; 1957b, pp. 275–276).

    4. Freud (1926d, p. 141), *G.W.*, 14:172.

    5. Freud (1926d, pp. 166–167), *G.W.*, 14:199–200.

    6. Freud (1926d, pp. 121–122), *G.W.*, 14:152.

    7. Freud (1926d, p. 109), *G.W.*, 14:137.

    8. Freud (1926d, pp. 125ff.), *G.W.*, 14:155.

    9. Freud (1926d, p. 106), *G.W.*, 14:135.

    10. Crossed out in the original.

    11. Crossed out in the original.

478

7 March 1926
Vienna, IX. Berggasse 19

Dear Jones,

I am writing to you from the Cottage Sanatorium, to which I retired the day before yesterday because I had several attacks of cramp in the street and my friend, the internist Braun, diagnosed a heart condition that calls for care.[1] The prognosis is favorable, and I expect to be discharged within a few weeks. I get heart therapy here, conduct three analytical sessions a day, and, on the whole, feel subjectively very well. This incident will naturally reinforce the tendency to restrict to the utmost all formalities connected with the date 6 May. I should like to leave Vienna, but that cannot be done. Consequently, I shall stay here and, as the sixth falls on a Thursday, will devote the following days, including Sunday, to my friends and visitors.

I very much regret that my views on telepathy have plunged you into new difficulties. But it really is difficult not to offend English sensibilities. I sometimes really felt I should not have written *Das Ich und das Es*, for *das Es* cannot be rendered into English. There is no likelihood of my placating English public opinion, but to you I do want to explain my seeming inconsistency in the question of telepathy.

As you remember I already expressed a favorable bias toward telepathy during our trip to the Harz. But there was no need to do so publicly; my conviction was not very strong, and the diplomatic aspect of preventing psychoanalysis from drawing too close to occultism very easily retained the upper hand. Now, the revision of *Traumdeutung* for the collected edition gave me the impetus to reconsider the problem of telepathy. In the meantime, however, my personal experience through tests, which I undertook with Ferenczi and my daughter, have attained such convincing power over me that diplomatic considerations had to be relinquished. Again I was presented with an instance where, on a very much reduced scale, I had to repeat the great experiment of my life; namely, to admit to a conviction without considering the resonance of the world around me. So it was then inevitable. If anyone should bring up my Fall[2] with you, just answer calmly that my acceptance of telepathy is my own affair, like my Judaism and my passsion for smoking, etc., and that the subject of telepathy is not related to psychoanalysis.

That I am indebted to you for being honored by the Psychological Society naturally divests the event of its symptomatic value; it would not have had any other significance for me anyway. Despite telepathy, I hope you will not wholly lose confidence in me.

I hope that your physical ailments will not bother you anymore and greet you cordially.

Yours,
Freud

1. Freud's friend Dr. Ludwig Braun had diagnosed angina pectoris, and Freud eventually agreed to spend a few weeks at the luxurious Cottage Sanatorium just outside Vienna; see Schur (1972, p. 390).
2. The German here is *Sündenfall*, literally, "the Fall (of Man)."

479

11 March 1926
81 Harley Street, London

Dear Professor,

I was very distressed to hear of your new bodily trouble and like to think it will be only a passing one. I wonder if it has to do with smoking and whether this will have to be restricted. At all events it is good to hear that what you once called "the inner man" feels well and is also engaged in work.

Eitingon wrote to ask my opinion about his inviting representatives of the various societies, clinics, institutes, etc. to visit you in May. I answered emphatically that the matter could be left to them, and that there would be quite enough strain put on you without his making any efforts to increase it.

I have said all I have to about the telepathy question. You were right in assuring me not to take it too seriously. Your remark about my trust in you was truly superfluous. In the meantime you will have got my letter saying how highly I appreciated your last book. I did not understand your difficulty about *"Das Ich und das Es"* in English. Are you not satisfied with *"Id" = "Es"*. To me it is as good, but obviously neither word is a good technical term.

Except for the revision, I have finished writing the Abraham obituary,[1] which is very full. I asked Anna if she would be kind enough to translate it and expect her answer soon. To portray the personality and thought of a friend to an audience of psychoanalysts is [a h][2] to set a high standard, especially when absolute truth must be combined with discretion about intimacies and consideration for the living. It is a high aim and I wonder how I have succeeded. For these reasons, and for more general critical ones, I shall be grateful if you would read it through before it is published and should of course be glad if you would make any alterations or modifications that occur to you.

My bodily troubles are of a disagreeable kind and have interfered with my freedom of movement. Last week I was unable to give my lecture and I shall be relieved when the course is finished. I take three days holiday at Easter, which will I hope do good.

Next time I hope to have better news of you. I have the memory of visiting the Cottage Sanatorium more than once in your company; if one has to lie up it is a pleasant enough place compared with most such places.

Yours always
Ernest Jones.

1. Jones (1926a).
2. Crossed out in the original.

480

21 March 1926
Vienna, IX. Berggasse 19

Dear Jones,
Anna has now translated your obituary [of Abraham], which was beautifully and sympathetically written, and I revised it. I have comments to make on several points and the translation will have to be modified accordingly.

(1) On page 1 you say: "We have once before lost by death a president of a branch society," but I think that is a mistake. I know of no such case. Will you let us know what you mean?

(2) On page 6 I should prefer not to mention that he held the chair longer than any other society's president, as it is unimportant and doubtful.

(3) On page 7 you state erroneously: "The opposition to Jung at the Weimar Congress . . ."; that, of course, was Munich, not Weimar.

(4) Further below on the same page, I suggest that you alter the reference to the disturbance owing to the war, for in 1914 it was not Dresden but Holland that was contemplated. Dresden was not proposed until 1918 and was replaced at the last moment by Budapest.

(5) We must first obtain confirmation for the editorship of the *Zeitschrift* mentioned on page 8. We are in the sanatorium and do not have the literature at hand.[1]

The rest seems all in order; we are waiting impatiently for the continuation. The translation of the first part will be sent off to Storfer tomorrow.

In haste and with cordial greetings.

Yours,
Freud

1. Freud's questions refer to Jones (1926a).

481

International Journal of Psycho-Analysis

25 March 1926
London

Dear Professor,

I was very glad indeed that you like the first part of the OBITUARY and so may venture to hope that you will like the personal part at the end which is naturally most significant. I am grateful for your comments and will mention them in order.

1. Reginald Allen was President of the American group when he was killed in the war. See Proceedings of the Hague Congress, *Zeitschrift* 1920, S. 381.[1]

2. The record of length during which Abraham was President is, as you say, unimportant and can well be omitted.[2]

3. The mistake about Weimar and Munich came about as follows: At the end of the Weimar Congress Jung talked to me about the time when he would stand higher than you. I was very astonished and naturally asked him why he did not analyse his father complex instead of trying to live it out in such an inappropriate way. His mystical answer "It is my fate" showed me which way things were moving. As you know, I was closely identified with Abraham in the opposition to Jung at Munich, but my opposition really began from Weimar.[3]

4. My memory was correct here, for I was in correspondence with

Abraham over the choice of place for the 1914 Congress. There is an official notice in the *Korrespondenzblatt* announcing that it would be held at Dresden on the 20th September, 1914.[4] About the discussion that preceeded the choice of Budapest in 1918 I know nothing.

5. You will find that these points about the editorship are also correct as is recorded in the various volumes.[5]

6. The second part was dispatched on Tuesday, so that it should reach Vienna today or tomorrow and the final part accompanies this letter. The retyping, correcting and revising have been more considerable work than might appear, but I can assure you that I have not lost a single moment from the beginning of the undertaking. Everything else has been put aside for it.

Yours always,
[Ernest Jones]

1. Jones (1926a); see Abraham (1927, p. 9). The sentence referred to by Freud in the previous letter was left intact.

2. Jones (1926a); see Abraham (1927, p. 13). The sentence was altered to read: "He held the Presidency of the Society from its foundation until his death."

3. Jones (1926a); see Abraham (1927, p. 14). The error was corrected accordingly. (The Third Congress of the International Psychoanalytic Association was held in Weimar, 21–22 September 1911; the Fourth Congress in Munich, 7–8 September 1913.)

4. *Zeitschrift*, 2 (1914): 407. The reference to Dresden was left intact (Jones, 1919); see Abraham (1927, p. 14). Moreover, the choice of Dresden for the Congress in 1914 came up several times in the letters between Freud and Jones of early 1914.

5. Jones (1926a); see Abraham (1927, p. 15).

482

6 April 1926
Vienna, IX. Berggasse 19

Dear Jones,

Donna de Ortuzar, a Chilean adventuress of noble birth, is the wife of Dr. Gilchrist, whom, as I told you, I sent away after three weeks.[1] They are a bad lot, but perhaps one should recall Macaulay's comment about the ten thousand pickpockets in the London of his day.

I thank you for your letter giving your reasons and corrections. You have been very much on my mind lately because, together with Anna, I translated your obituary notice while in the sanatorium, which I left the day before yesterday. However, we found it impossible to finish the whole job in the short time before Storfer needed it, and therefore called on Reik for help; he was in the same sanatorium with his wife, who has fallen ill again. He has very willingly taken over the middle part—the most difficult, in fact—while the beginning and end will come from us. I only regret that we did not have enough time to devote as much care to your work as it deserved. It is thorough, exhaustive, extremely gracious, almost altogether to the point, and, in several places, rises to profound insights. In other instances we noticed that you did not sufficiently avoid repetition. It is remarkable that, despite all his simplicity and clarity, Abraham's character was really difficult to grasp; as you rightly indicate, there was something impenetrable about him. I can well believe that your work on Abraham gave you much trouble, but you have done the association a great service.

I know that I may expect to see you again in a few weeks' time; in the meantime, I send my cordial greetings to you and your family.

Yours,
Freud

1. In a *Rundbrief* of 17 March 1926 Jones writes: "A certain Donna de Ortuzar is practising psycho-analysis in London and says she has studied under Freud and Rank and has 'all diplomas.'" John Stirling-Gilchrist, M.B., Ch.B. 1915 Glasgow; B.A., LL.B. 1920 Cambridge; in a *Rundbrief* from Freud and Anna Freud, 15 November 1925, it is noted that he is unqualified to practice psychoanalysis (Sigmund Freud Copyrights, Wivenhoe).

483

10 April 1926
81 Harley Street, London

Dear Professor,

I was very happy to read your kind words about the Abraham Obituary and thank you very warmly for them. You can imagine that much of it was written for the small circle of friends nearest to him. I was also very glad to hear that you were supervising the translation, particularly of the first and last parts. The middle part, although a labour for Reik, is straightforward, but with the other part the question of form and style is naturally more important and therefore I was especially pleased to know that that will be rendered at its best.

I had four days' holiday at Easter and feel refreshed for further work. The next piece will be my paper on Psycho-Analysis and Religion for the International Congress of Psychology.[1] They asked me to let them have it in February, so that it is distinctly overdue. As the Congress is at the end of August, however, it should be in good time.

I was glad to hear recently from Eitingon that you[2] have benefitted from the visit to the Riviera,[3] so that you should be able now to endure better the birthday *Strapazen* [stress and strain].

Yours always affectionately,
[Ernest Jones]

1. Jones (1926b).
2. "He" has been penciled in in place of "you."
3. The reference is to Freud's recent stay at the Cottage Sanatorium.

484

19 April 1926
Vienna, IX. Berggasse 19

Dear Jones,

Very saddened to hear the reason for the distress in your family. By the time you receive this letter I hope that at least all concern will be over and that you will at once write me a few lines of reassuring news.

Regarding your trip to Vienna, I should like to ask you to start a day earlier, because in consideration of the many circumstances I had to decide to be available already on the fifth, and I naturally wanted to make sure of our discussions before the birthday celebrations.

Many thanks for your enclosure; the comment is very interesting, although it sounds somewhat distorted, "queer."[1]

Cordial greetings to you.

Yours,
Freud

1. In English in the original.

485

British Psycho-Analytical Society

19 April 1926
London

Dear Professor,

I am glad to say that my children are going on satisfactorily but I shall not like to be away from them long even in a fortnight's time. The train service also is not so convenient as I could wish and so I am afraid I shall have to limit my stay in Vienna to three nights and two days, arriving on Wednesday evening, May 5th, and leaving on the Saturday morning.

In these circumstances would it be possible for you to arrange the Committee Meeting for some time on the Friday for I suppose Thursday will be taken up socially?

With kindest regards,

Yours always,
[Ernest Jones]

486

23 April 1926
81 Harley Street, London

Dear Professor,

Your letter must have crossed one from me in which I gave the good news that my children are progressing most satisfactorily. I hope to take them to the country before I leave for abroad so that they may have a fortnight there before resuming school. Thank-you for your kind enquiries.

I am altering the travelling time, as you suggest, and shall arrive at the Regina late Tuesday night, the 4th, leaving again on the Saturday morning.

With all good wishes,

Yours affectionately,
[Ernest Jones]

487

24 April 1926
81 Harley Street, London

Dear Professor,

As I wrote to you last Monday I planned to reach Vienna at 6.30 Wednesday evening. That would make it easily possible to have an evening meeting if you so wished. The express train leaves only three times a week so that for me to come earlier and arrive on Tuesday night would mean starting a day and a half earlier, which has various disadvantages. However, on getting your letter yesterday saying that you would like to see us on Wednesday I immediately changed my tickets to the earlier slow train. This morning I get a letter from Eitingon saying that he had arranged with you by telephone that our meeting was to be on the Friday, May 7th, so that my change of plans would appear to be unnecessary. I am therefore once more reversing them and now propose to reach Vienna at 6.30 on Wednesday.

I trust that this will be convenient to you. But if you would prefer for us to meet in the afternoon rather than the evening please do not hesitate to let me know and I will come by the earlier train.

With all good wishes,

Yours always,
[Ernest Jones]

488

[postcard]

15 August [1926][1]

A wonderful holiday with quite perfect weather and beautiful scenes. We send you our warmest greetings.

Ernest Jones.

Kindest regards to you and your ladies.

Katherine Jones

1. The postcard was sent from France; the front shows a picture of a sixteenth-century castle and reads "Azay le Rideau—Le Chateau National."

489

30 August 1926
Semmering

Dear Jones,

Very sad! I hardly knew him, but the general opinion of him leaves no doubt that he was your best man.[1] We really are not favored with luck, have more losses than gains, and the relationship between those remaining leaves much to be desired. At the same time the ideas of psychoanalysis are spreading in ever-wider circles and are freeing themselves from their first proponents: also one way in which fate fulfills itself.

Here at last beautiful summer days, which, my condition being quite tolerable, I am also enjoying. If the weather more or less permits, we want to remain here until the end of September.

Ferenczi spent a week with us—before his departure for New York. During this time we had occasion to enlighten Dr. Frankwood Williams[2]— an influental person from New York, who was analyzed by Rank and was one of his hopes—about Rank's distortion of analysis. The fight against him is unavoidable; I do not like to think that you were so right in your assessment of him.

You seem to be engaged in a trip around Holland. Cordial greetings to you and your wife.

Yours,
Freud

1. Freud is referring to the death of James Glover, 25 August 1926. There is likely a missing letter or telegram informing him of Glover's death.
2. Frankwood Williams (1883–1936), M.D. 1912 University of Michigan; psychiatrist and medical director of the National Committee for Mental Hygiene (1922–1931).

490

23 September 1926
81 Harley Street, London

Dear Professor,

I had the latest news of you last night from Rickman and was happy to think that it was good. Either he or Mrs. Riviere will take Glover's place on the Council of the Society. The vacancy at the Institute and Clinic will be filled by Edward Glover. I am to open the Clinic next Tuesday.[1]

When I was reading your most interesting book on Lay Analysis I planned to write you a long letter on the subject.[2] After finishing the book, however, I find there is so much I should like to say that I have written to Radó asking him if he would like me to review the book.[3] While you have left a few things unsaid, you have given a totally different perspective to the whole problem, a perspective which we must all feel to be of vast importance. The thing I think you have settled beyond all doubt is that it would be very injurious to our movement to forbid lay analysis. There will be lay analysts, and there must be because we need them. The necessity for training is of-course obvious. The wider question of how far we should aim at making analysis an independent profession, having only certain links with the medical one, is extraordinarily interesting, and I find there is much to say about it. In all probability, however, it will not be settled by us, but by fate.

The Laforgues are in London this week. He told me that Rank told him in June of this year that he was on most amicable terms with you *(im besten Einvernehmung)*, in proof of which he cited the fact that he had recently given you a present that cost $300. Your interpretation of the Nietzsche Symptomhandlung was thus confirmed.

The practice here is very busy and we are nearly all occupied. I have, of-course, additional work through Glover's death, but at present feel well and fresh enough to undertake it. How I shall feel at the end of the Winter is another question.

With kindest regards,

Yours always,
[Ernest Jones]

1. Prior to his death, James Glover had been appointed assistant director of the newly formed London Clinic of Psycho-Analysis.
2. Freud (1926e).
3. Jones (1927a).

491

27 September 1926
Semmering

Dear Jones,

We are leaving for Wien after some delightful weeks in this place.

I very much appreciate your last remarks on *"Laienanalyse"*. Glad to know I have at least made some impression on you. I expected you to take the other side of the question. Of course you are invited to give your judgment in a report on my booklet, to be published in the *Zeitschrift*. Perhaps others will do so too and the ensuing discussion may be of interest for all of us. You have justly guessed what my real intention is, but I saw no obligation to proclaim it to the public at this moment. To be sure fate will decide over the ultimate relation between ΨA and medicine, but that does not imply that we should not try to influence fate, attempt to shape it by our own efforts.

I am always glad to see Rickman. Regarding my health I dare say I am now better than I appear while it was the contrary before. I am suffering much less from the plate but my speech is more inhibited—by technical difficulties—than it used to be.

You too may have been puzzled by the lack of logics in Rank's statement that he is on the best of terms with me adducing as a proof that he made me a costly present. The conclusion would have been justified, if I had given the present to him. As it was, his gift sprang from a mixture of different motives, the oppressing feeling of owing so much to me, even in money, a reaction of gratitude or rather against gratitude, a tendency to boast of his newly acquired riches and a self-destructive impulse to spend all he is earning, which appears also in other doings of his. I am not at all sure what the final result of his career may be, he does not belong to those easy-going scoundrels, to whom success in life is assured.

Although absent from the opening of the Clinic to-morrow, I am all with you and feel the importance of the day.

With kindest regards for you and your family.

Freud

492

20 November 1926
Vienna, IX. Berggasse 19

Dear Jones,

So, is it really twenty years since you joined the cause? You have really made the cause quite your own, for you have achieved everything that could be made of it: a society, a journal, and an institute. What you have meant to it may be left for historians to ascertain. I certainly expect that you can accomplish even more, once the many activities which you still have to contend with have been relieved by a smooth routine. Then you will find the leisure time in which to use your accumulated experience to do more for your colleagues and the new generation.

We may well be satisfied with each other. I myself have the impression that you sometimes overestimate the importance of the disagreements ("dissensions")[1] that occurred also between us. Indeed, it is difficult to achieve complete satisfaction with one another; we all find something missing in the other, become somewhat critical. You yourself have pointed out that even Abraham and I had certain differences—it is much the same as with one's wife and children. Only speechmakers at funerals deny such traces of reality; the living may believe that such deviations from the notion of an ideal do not spoil their enjoyment of reality.

You will be surprised to discover the reason why my correspondence with you is hindered. It is a classic example of the petty restrictions to which our nature is subject. I find it very difficult to write German in Latin script, as I am doing today. All facility—inspiration is reserved for greater matters—deserts me at once. But you have often told me that you cannot read Gothic script, thus leaving me with only two means of communication, both of which interfere with one's intimacy: either to dictate a letter to Anna on the typewriter or to use my clumsy English.—

As a result of your reminder, I have reread your paper on the superego[2] and confirmed my first impression. All the obscurities and difficulties that you point out really do exist. But one cannot remove them, even with the criteria that you stress. It does require fresh examination of accumulated impressions and experiences, and I know how difficult they are to obtain. It is, after all, an obscure beginning in a complicated matter.

My state of health is turning me away from work—I rather think forever. Better not to deceive oneself. I feel as though life were giving me *"Gnadenbrot"*[3] a little longer. Your wife, to whom I send my kind regards, can translate this for you.

Cordially yours,
Freud

1. In English in the original.
2. Jones (1926c).
3. Literally "bread of charity."

493

22 December 1926
81 Harley Street, London

Dear Professor,

In writing to wish you a pleasant Christmastime I want also to thank you warmly for your cordial letter, with its kind allusions to myself. I will treasure its words of wisdom. What a pity Vienna is so far from London; there are so many things I should like to discuss with you.

Your judgement about my Überich paper did not surprise me, for it was also my own—but I only meant to ask you one single point in it, whether you would agree that hate of the object is as essential as love of that object before it can be incorporated as a super-ego? Perhaps some time you will tell me this, if I have made the question clear enough for it to be answered in a line.

Things here all go well, except that first-class analysts are too rare—as they seem to be everywhere. One must be patient and wait for the next generation. I am sure the chief reason is not the lack of *potentially* excellent analysts, but the difficulty of getting fairly normal people to join us. The capable brains find easier paths in life. Things will be better when we have more "official" contacts, and our chief political problem is how to obtain these without making any scientific sacrifice; for die Sache itself must of course always come first.

When I told you of my difficulty in reading Gothic, did I not tell you that there was one exception—namely your own handwriting? I do not pretend it is easy for me, but it is possible. Perhaps my omission was due to my fondness for your English, which is very attractive.

Please give my kindest greetings to your wife and to Anna, who I hope is flourishing, and accept all good wishes yourself

From yours always affectionately
Ernest Jones.

494

British Psycho-Analytical Society

27 January 1927
London

Dear Professor,

I hasten to answer your question about the translation arrangements, though I cannot help regretting that you did not ask it before the fatal deed was done. I would ask you to cast your mind back to the rather similar situation in regard to the *"Vorlesungen"* and to the agitated cabling through which some of the situation was then salvaged. Today, however, it can no longer be remedied in any such way.

The facts, as I explained them then, are indeed quite simple. A translation in England gives no rights in America, though one in America can and usually is registered in England also. No publisher in England, therefore, would consider issuing a translation unless he was assured that one was not to appear in America. The only exceptions are if (a) the sale would be likely to be large in England and (b) there was some arrangement to prevent the American one entering into England. Both these conditions could be fulfilled in the case of the *"Vorlesungen"*, but not in the case of any other book. Your private influence with your nephew was enough to gain his consent to any exporting into England being stopped,[1] whereas we know nothing of the publishers who are acting for Clark. The *"Vorlesungen"* made a very popular book, and the time was at the height of the temporary boom in psycho-analysis. The *"Hemmung"* book[2] has, of course, no popular appeal, and in any case the boom is long since past. The net result of all this is that no publisher in England would consider issuing a translation of the *"Hemmung, etc."* unless he were very heavily subsidised (perhaps several hundred pounds). Even the Abraham book,[3] which should have a considerable sale in both England *and* America cannot be published until we personally add another fifty pounds to the hundred pounds already donated from your Fond.

The other considerations you[4] also know well—to translate a book of yours satisfactorily needs a correct knowledge of English, which is a comically rare possession, together with a reasonable knowledge of both German and psycho-analysis. Pierce Clark's English would be distressing if it were not amusing and I do not think that the other bases of necessary knowledge are at their best. In the course of years we have gathered in London three or four people who can do such work adequately. They have the disadvantage of being slow workers and not well blessed financially, but they have two other features, those of being scrupulous and capable, which seem to me to outweigh the disadvantages. At all events, no [appearance][5] sign of an adequate translation has yet appeared anywhere except in their hands.

I had hoped, particularly after giving the *"Collected Papers"* such an established position in our "Library" series, that things were at last on a sound basis as regard this most important question of translation. The enterprise of our official "Library" series and *"International Journal"* has survived many storms and difficulties, including even Rank, and has always tried to produce the best quality work. Pierce Clark, refusing to support either us or the Association starts a separatist tendency of a purely individual nature. In this you have unwittingly supported him at our cost.

Mrs. Riviere's comment, when I told her the news on the telephone, was "And this is how we are treated after years of work!"

If I have left anything still unexplained in the situation you have only to ask me.

Yours always sincerely,
Ernest Jones.

1. "Being stopped" is inserted by hand in an otherwise typewritten letter.
2. Freud (1926d).
3. Abraham (1927).
4. "You" is handwritten.
5. Crossed out in the original; "sign" is inserted by hand.

495

1 February 1927
Vienna, IX. Berggasse 19

Dear Jones,

I am very sorry that my permission to P. Clark to translate *"Hemmung, Symptom und Angst"* distressed you so much, as is evident from the tone and content of your letter. "I meant no harm."[1] Even the tragic note in Mrs. Riviere's exclamation seems to me hardly warranted. You must bear in mind that you only very rarely let me have news of the works and plans of Hogarth Press and that, until your last letter, I was really under the impression that the English rights had nothing to do with the American rights, that translations of the former would not interfere with those of the latter. Your letter is the first corrective, with its valuable information that an English publisher will not readily publish a translation of a book if a translation of it is already circulating in America. I will act accordingly and immediately stop my endeavors to obtain American translations of the *Selbsdarstellung* and *Laienanalyse.*

However, this brings up another question to which I request an early reply. What is the position regarding American translations of books that Hogarth Press has already published in England? Would you or they be just as opposed if a translation of *Massenpsychologie,* for example, were to be planned in America? Naturally, I would yield to you in this case too, but would ask you to consider what that means. As our excellent English translators work with unnatural slowness, the first concession already involves the risk that the English-speaking readership will be deprived of access to the writings in question for too long. *Laienanalyse,* for example, is a piece addressing a specific issue, probably of no interest in several years' time. By then the question may well have been settled. For the second restriction we must have proof that Hogarth Press can find a market in America as well; otherwise it would be tantamount to sabotage of my writings in America and would certainly do our cause no good.

I have no financial interest in the English translations. You know that I get nothing from Hogarth Press, and the profit from the American translations has to be shared between the translator there and the Verlag in Vienna, and is not worth mentioning. If I am mistaken on the first point, or my memory is playing a trick on me, I am sure you will correct me. On the whole I only want to be clear about the whole matter; I do not wish to offend you or our translators, but do the most expedient thing for the publicity. I very much dislike seeing your bad mood directed toward me; perhaps it will have improved by the time you reply. Cordial greetings.

Yours,
Freud

1. This sentence is in English in the original.

496

9 February 1927
81 Harley Street, London

Dear Professor,

Your kindly and soothing letter had an instantaneous effect on the little that was left of my *"schlechte Laune"* [bad mood] (which with me is always mobile and never very serious), and I thank you for it.

My infrequent news about our publishing activities is solely due to the infrequency of the activities themselves; when there is news I invariably include it in the *Rundbrief*. As regards the only two remaining books of yours the position is this: Strachey has already translated most of the *Selbstdarstellung*, and the only reason for delay is that the funds (of both the Institute and the Hogarth Press) have been strained to their limits by publishing three books this winter (*Ich und Es*, Ferenczi, and Abraham).[1] I will let you have further news as soon as it is available. The question of the *Laienanalyse* is more complicated, first by the fact that no commercial sale can be expected from it and secondly by the point you make of its actuality. In these circumstances, much as I desire to secure as many of your works as possible for our Library series, I hardly feel justified in asking you to refuse any American offer you may have for the book. I say this most unwillingly, but I see that you would be disappointed if its appearance were delayed—which it probably would in England.

Your other question implies (unjustifiably, as I think) that I am indifferent to the propaganda in America. I make no distinction between Great

Britain and America in this respect, and mean both when I speak of an 'English' translation. Of the six books of yours in our series (4 *Coll. Papers, Mass Psychology* and *Pleasure Principle*) we have sold *more* in America than here. I do not say we have sold more there than an American firm could have done, on the contrary, but this has been a difficult technical question. So far we have failed in getting any American firm to take up the sale of the books, in spite of many efforts, and so have had to sell them from here. Last week your nephew, Bernays, wrote to the Hogarth Press on this matter, and I hope they will make some arrangement. It is, however, a purely business affair in which we should not interfere. The H. Press have [pu]² bought from the Verlag the legal rights of the *sole* authorised translation, with the sales all over the world, including America. They can of course sublet, as it were, the American sale to a firm in that country. It is true that, as no book published in Europe secures copyright in America, any American can issue a 'pirated' edition, but this very rarely happens with scientific books and so the Hogarth Press took the risk. I gave them at the same time [that]³ the moral understanding that at least no other *authorised* translation would appear in America to compete with theirs. I can assure you that I am deeply concerned with this question of sale in America, and shall be glad to find any way of improving it.

I hope that these remarks clear the situation still further.

I have been ill for three weeks with severe influenza and complications (bronchitis and otitis), but am again better; I only missed two days' work. I hope you all escaped the epidemic.

With kindest regards

yours always
Ernest Jones.

1. Freud (1923b), Ferenczi (1926b), and Abraham (1927).
2. Crossed out in the original.
3. Crossed out in the original.

497

15 February 1927
Vienna, IX. Berggasse 19

Dear Jones,

I am pleased to learn from your gracious letter that, together with your health, your good mood has also returned. Thank you for giving further explanations about the matter in question.

It will not have escaped you that the whole topic of English and American translations is, so to speak, on the periphery of my interest and that I was always prepared to let others make the decisions. I now notice that on behalf of Hogarth Press you waive your rights to the translation of *Laienanalyse.* I am therefore also resuming negotiations over this little piece with America. After a discussion with Storfer I must draw your attention to a rather specific circumstance regarding the *Selbstdarstellung.* As you know, the *Selbstdarstellung* does not belong to the Verlag, but to the Leipzig firm Felix Meiner. It was only with difficulty and financial sacrifice that we obtained their permission to reprint it in the *Gesammelte Schriften.* Storfer now informs me further that Meiner has decidedly refused to leave the English rights to him. He could only obtain the translation rights restricted to America. Storfer sees the reason for this in the fact that Meiner is counting on an offer for the translation of the whole series in England, but not in America. For the time being there is therefore absolutely no chance of Hogarth Press publishing a translation of *Selbstdarstellung,* and our Verlag can give England neither a refusal nor permission for anything. Given this situation I regarded it as expedient not to break off negotiations with America for translating the *Selbstdarstellung.* But I suggested to the publisher there (Brentano) I could possibly make it a condition that B. acquire an English translation to be provided by us. This, of course, would be one by Strachey, which would have to be finished quickly. I am now asking you for an answer, possibly by telegram, as to whether Strachey is prepared to sell his translation to America. I will keep you regularly informed about the further development of the matter.

I was also delighted with a letter from Mrs. Riviere, who had not written me for a long time. I am glad that these small business matters have been cleared up so quickly and greet you cordially.

Yours,
Freud

498

British Psycho-Analytical Society

21 February 1927
London

Dear Professor,

I was not able to telegraph because a simultaneous letter from Storfer showed me that the situation is even more complicated than you had depicted it. I have had a talk with Strachey and will try to make our points as clear as possible. *1.* Strachey is willing to sell his translation of the

"*Selbstdarstellung*" to Brentano with the only condition that he correct
the actual proofs (so as to make sure that it is not distorted). 2. He is also
willing to undertake a translation of the "*Lay Analysis*" for Brentano on
the same conditions. 3. We suggest that Meiner be asked to buy a copy of
Strachey's translation from Brentano whenever he wishes to issue a publication in England. Something about this eventuality should be said to
Brentano in the preliminary programme with him.

Now I come to the main difficulty. Storfer tells us that Brentano's intention is to publish the two books in one volume. As Meiner refuses to
release the English rights over the first book that means that neither can
ever be sold in England without his consent. This would be a calamity to
us and can only be avoided by some sort of preliminary arrangement with
Meiner.

Before we consider the solution of this difficulty let me clear up another
point. You will remember my expressing the opinion that Woolf (the
Hogarth Press) would not be likely to undertake the rapid publication of
both these books, since he is already straining his resources to publish
three others this winter for us. It was, of course, solely on this ground that
I felt I could not press you to withdraw from the American negotiations
about the "*Lay Analysis*". Now, however, that, according to the latest
news, the "*Selbstdarstellung*" is not available to us, it reopens the question
of our publishing the "*Lay Analysis*". It is naturally a matter on which I
should have to consult Woolf before saying anything definite, but you will
see that the situation has altered in this sense. It is true that not having
the American rights would make Woolf even less inclined to publish the
book, and further that if he did it would constitute a double bar against
the admission of Brentano's book into England.

The matter would be greatly simplified if Brentano would consent to
publish the two books separately and I would suggest that he be pressed
to do so. If, for commercial reasons, he does not agree to this, then the
question arises whether he should be given the rights of the English sale
of the "*Lay Analysis*". It would be useless to him in any case because his
book could not enter England, but a clause might be inserted into the
agreement with him to the effect that the Hogarth Press could buy at a
fixed rate from him the loose sheets of the book ("*Lay Analysis*" only)
with the idea of their publishing it in England. Obviously Woolf would
only agree to this, for the limited English sale, if the rate to be agreed on
is extremely cheap; inasmuch as, for the reason given above, the rights of
sale in England are worth exactly nothing to Brentano, he might very well
agree to a rate that would make the plan possible.

As regards the "*Selbstdarstellung*" the only hope is that your influence
might induce Meiner to consent to our issuing an English translation on

condition that it be available to him if the time ever comes for him to publish his collected work.

You may imagine how loth we are here to see one after another of your books slipping through our fingers. To change the metaphor, it seems to be always a question of salvaging something out of the wreckage. Our beautiful plan of a worthy English translation of your collected works recedes further and further away in the light of one complication after another.

Yours always,
[Ernest Jones]

499

[postcard]

3 March 1927
Vienna, IX. Berggasse 19

Dear Jones,

Was it you, who sent me—years ago—a number of the *Burlington Magazine* containing a representation of a 12th century Moses who is grasping his beard just the same way I interpolated into the statue of Michelangelo? Please answer me at once. I have written a short supplementary note to my essay, which is to appear very soon in the new French psychoanalytic Journal.[1]

Yours affectionately
Freud

1. See letter 309. In Freud (1927b) Jones's contribution is explicitly acknowledged; a photograph of the statue in question is included in *S.E.*, 13 (facing p. 237). Freud's piece first appeared as "Appendice (1927) au Moïse de Michel-Ange," trans. E. Marty, rev. M. Bonaparte, *Revue française de psychanalyse*, 1 (1927): 148.

500

7 March 1927
81 Harley Street, London

Dear Professor,

I am afraid my memory is not quite clear on the detail you mention about the *Burlington Magazine*, but I think it most probable that it was I who got hold of it. All I can be quite sure of is that at that time I gave you a good deal of material of the sort, including a number of photographs which I brought back from Rome.

May I suggest that we should welcome any expression of opinion from you in the *Rundbrief* concerning the discussion between Alexander and Reich. It seems to me that both are in the right, because there is a good deal of *Aneinanderreden* [altercation]. I only hope that Alexander may not go too far in the Adler direction of making the super-ego into a *dummer August* [halfwit], but the *economic* side of the *Strafbedürfnis* certainly needs clearing up.[1]

Yours always affectionately,
Ernest Jones.

1. In the dialogue "Strafbedürfnis und neurotischer Prozess" (Need for Punishment and the Neurotic Process), Reich challenges Alexander's theory of personality based on the hypotheses of a death instinct, the repetition compulsion, and the need for punishment as the basis of neurotic conflict, and Alexander replies in turn. See Wilhelm Reich, "Kritische Bemerkungen zu neueren Auffassungen des Neurosenproblems," *Zeitschrift*, 13 (1927): 36–46, translated as "A Criticism of Recent Theories of the Problems of Neurosis," *Journal*, 9 (1928): 227–240; and Franz Alexander, "Entgegnung auf Reichs kritische Bemerkungen," *Zeitschrift*, 13 (1927): 47–53, translated as "A Reply to Reich's Criticism," *Journal*, 9 (1928): 240–246.

501

[postcard]

[7 April 1927][1]
Genoa

Dear Professor,

Greetings from an old haunt of yours.[2] My lecture[3] to the French group was very successful and I had a good impression of them. We are now going to Genoa.

Yours always
Ernest Jones.

1. Date of postmark.
2. Although the card is postmarked Genoa, the scene depicted on it is of the west facade of Notre-Dame cathedral in Paris.
3. Jones (1927e).

502

16 May 1927
81 Harley Street, London

Dear Professor,

Though the gratitude I owe you for many years is too great to be adequately expressed, I have from time to time indicated it in both words and actions. And I am writing today to express once more some of it, the recent debt being by no means the least. It concerns my children. Since September they have, with the exception of some weeks of holidays and illness, been analyzed, and I expect it will be finished in another two or three months.[1] The changes already brought about are already so striking and so important as to fill me with thankfulness towards the one who made them possible, namely yourself.

Though we had brought them up as wisely as we knew how, neither child escaped a neurosis, which analysis showed, as usual, to be much more serious than appeared. The symptoms of moodiness, difficulties with food, fears, outbursts, and extensive inhibitions seemed to make it worth while, and now I am extremely glad.

The girl proved to have a severe castration complex, intense guilt and a definite obsessional neurosis. The boy was very introverted, lived in a babyish dream world, and had an almost complete sexual inversion. They have responded excellently to treatment, are in every way freer, and are constantly gay and happy. It is plain that they were helplessly struggling with infantile conflicts that otherwise could only have ended in an unsatisfactory compromise, at considerable cost to the personality.

These and several other experiences have convinced me that early child analysis is the logical conclusion of $\psi\alpha$ in general. Just as prophylaxis is in general better than cure, both easier and more effective, so in regard to the neuroses it is surely more sensible to deal with them when they are being formed, still in a plastic state, than after the mind has become set and organized on an unhealthy basis and at great cost. I do not know what exactly you think about it, but there are no doubts at all in my own mind. The purely theoretical and academic objections sometimes raised, e.g. about the stability of the child's super-ego, etc., are completely answered by the test of experience, and I wonder if they are not sometimes displaced from a lingering doubt about the *reality* of the phenomena and the richness and capacity of the child's mind. All our experience shows how right were your conclusions in attributing to the infant a far greater maturity than had been suspected.

It is a pain to me that I cannot agree with *some* of the tendencies in Anna's book,[2] and I cannot help thinking that they must be due to some imperfectly analyzed resistances;[3] in fact I think it is possible to prove this in detail. It is a pity she published the book so soon—her first lectures, but I hope she may prove as amenable as her father to further experience. This hope is strengthened by my admiration for all her other qualities— also analytic ones.

May I ask you if you have made your plans for September? Is there any chance of your visiting the Congress? If not, I shall try to visit you immediately afterwards? Semmering.

I am very well and full of energy, as is all my family.

With my kindest regards

Yours deeply grateful and affectionate
Ernest Jones.

P.S. There were some serious mistranslations in my contribution to the Symposium, so if you read it I hope it will be in the corrected version.[4]

1. Freud would have understood that Jones's children were being analyzed by Melanie Klein. The comments regarding this letter generally, and this passage in particular, in Grosskurth (1986, pp. 171–172) are highly tendentious and distort the historical context of Jones's relationship to Freud.
2. A. Freud (1927a).
3. On Freud's analysis of his daughter Anna, see Young-Bruehl (1988, pp. 103–139).
4. See Jones (1927c) for his contribution to the "Discussion on Lay Analysis."

503

31 May 1927
Vienna, IX. Berggasse 19

Dear Jones!

Thanks for your unusually cordial letter. First, my reply to your questions. On 16 June we are going to the Semmering to the same house, Villa Schüller. It seems to me well nigh impossible that I should attend the Congress. I shall be very pleased if you want to visit me immediately afterwards. After all, remember that perhaps you will not be the only one to make this stop on the way back. I have reasons for assuming this.

Now your comments on child analysis. I am very glad that it was so beneficial for your two youngsters. I also gladly acknowledge that, on the most important points, namely the scope, the effectiveness of analysis,[1] and the content of infantile neurosis, there is full agreement between the two authorities concerned. I therefore think that one need not overemphasize the differences between Mrs. Klein and Anna regarding technique and theoretical views. Naturally, as far as possible, I maintain an impartial position; on the one hand, because Anna is my daughter, and, on the other, because she has done her work quite independently of me, basing it on her personal experience only. In any case, I can reveal one thing to you: Mrs. Klein's view of the behavior of the ego-ideal in children seems quite impossible to me and is in contradiction to all my postulates.

I will make only one comment on the polemical part of your letter. When two analysts have differing opinions on some point, one may be fully justified, in ever so many cases, in assuming that the mistaken view of one of them stems from his having been insufficiently analyzed, and he therefore allows himself to be influenced by his complexes to the detriment of science. But in practical polemics such an argument is not permissible, for it is at the disposal of each party, and does not reveal on whose side the error lies. We are generally agreed to renounce arguments of this sort and, in the case of differences of opinion, to leave resolutions to advancements in empirical knowledge.

Reading the discussions on lay analysis has shown me that my small pamphlet was not superfluous after all.[2] I already know that I have not convinced anyone who did not already share my view, but certain extreme attitudes seem to be wavering or intimidated, and the way is perhaps opened wider for an objective treatment of the question.

In the meantime, I cordially greet you and your wife.

Yours,
Freud

1. *"Der Analyse"* is handwritten in an otherwise typed letter.
2. "Discussion on Lay Analysis," *Journal*, 8 (1927): 174–283; and Freud (1926e).

504

British Psycho-Analytical Society

20 June 1927
London

Dear Professor,

Many thanks for your recent letter. I should like to return to one sentence in it of extreme importance, namely, where you say that you find Melanie Klein's views about the super-ego quite incompatible with your own. I would seem to be suffering from a scotoma, for I do not perceive this at all. The only difference I was aware of is that she dates both the Oedipus conflict and the genesis of the super-ego a year or two earlier than you have. As one of your chief discoveries has been the fact that young children are much more mature than had been generally supposed, both sexually and morally, I had regarded the conclusions reached from Frau Klein's experience as being simply a direct continuation of your own tendencies. May I therefore ask you to help me clear up the point? You know that I do not without reason give you trouble, especially during holiday time, but in this case I feel justified in asking for a letter on the point. My position, as you know, gives me considerable influence and I am anxious that none of this should be used in any mistaken or erroneous way.

About your warning concerning polemics, I am glad to say it was in no way necessary. What I wrote to you was purely private and personal and had no connection with any sort of public arguments.

Ferenczi's visit has been a great success here, though I am not so sure about the success of his American visit. It becomes clearer that his value lies essentially in the inspiration of his personality rather than in his intellectual judgements, for the latter are sometimes too strongly influenced by his phantasy. It was a very great pleasure having him here and I need hardly say that we are on the most excellent possible terms.

By now you will have started your well-deserved holiday and I hope you will thoroughly enjoy it. I shall make every effort to come to Semmering after the Congress.

With all my kindest regards,

Yours always,
Ernest Jones.

505

6 July 1927
Semmering

Dear Jones,

My reply to your last letter was delayed because of my poor health during the last few weeks.[1] The prosthesis was torturing me so much that I felt unable to meet all my obligations. It now seems to have been overcome once and for all, I hope.

The fact that Melanie Klein makes children more mature than we used to think is indeed in agreement with my ideas. But even that has its limits, and is no proof in itself. Otherwise I would have to agree a priori if it were maintained that small children speculate about epistemology. I should like to oppose Mrs. Klein on the following point: she presents the superego of children as being similarly independent as that of adults, while Anna seems to me to be right in stressing that the child's superego is still under the direct influence of its parents. On the whole I prefer to be pleased by the far-reaching agreement between the two researchers and gladly leave it to posterity to settle their differences.

Ferenczi also expressed to me his great satisfaction with the welcome he received in London and with his stay there, regretting only that he did not obtain more far-reaching agreement[2] with you on the lay question. You know that he fully shares my viewpoint; I know that you do not. I think one does not need to defend medical analysis—or that was our endeavor hitherto—and it is now secure enough. But the other part of analysis is endangered and I have therefore taken its side. I have written a short supplement for discussion, which naturally contains nothing new.[3] Originally I wanted to have a more detailed discussion with the New Yorkers, who betray just as low a level in this question as in other matters, but I gave it up as fruitless. Let us now see what the Congress will decide.

This year we are having an unusually beautiful summer, family visits, Oliver came with wife and child from Berlin, no patients until September. As far as my physical state permits, I am also very content with everything.

I hope you are enjoying this beautiful time as well with your wife and children, and greet you all cordially.

Yours,
Freud

1. First sentence is written in Gothic script; letter continues in Latin characters.
2. "*Auss*" is crossed out in the original: "*weitergehende [Auss] Einigung*" (more far-reaching agreement).
3. Freud (1927a).

506

18 July 1927
81 Harley Street, London

Dear Professor,

I appreciate very highly your kindness in writing about difficult topics at the most precious part of your holiday—the start. The content of what you had to say was also most welcome.

About the *Kinderanalyse* I was relieved to see that the differences you had mentioned are of degree only, and not of principle, so that—as you say—we may safely leave them to experience.

Our difference about the Lay Analysis does not arise from one of aim, for we both want the best *medical and lay* material for our analysts, but of method in reaching this. You find lay analysts need defending, while I think they are safe except in America (and there only temporarily). On the other hand I believe that the plan of telling candidates they need not study medicine could only end in $\psi\alpha$ being lay, and separated from medicine altogether—to the disadvantage of both. My reasons for this are given in my essay in the *Journal*,[1] which I should like to think you have read.

I spent yesterday in The Hague with Eitingon. We were shocked to find van Emden in hospital with a pyloric trouble that is in all probability carcinoma. He has dismissed the possibility from his mind and refused operation for months. We did something to influence him in this direction, and I hope he will now consent to it. His wife knows.

I urged Eitingon to accept the Presidency at the Congress[2] and hope you approve of this. He is universally acceptable, whereas—especially at present—Ferenczi might not bring the harmony we need. I hope we shall find a place for Anna in the Executive Council—certainly if Ferenczi goes to Budapest, for then we must have a Viennese—, but I suggested that Ophuijsen as secretary and Anna as Treasurer would work better than the reverse.

I wonder if Federn has sent you the latest New York explosion. I deplore their action just before the Congress discussion, and had sent Brill last week a strong letter urging compromise (that they should admit lay members, but in small numbers).[3]

My children have just had *Keuchhusten* [whooping cough], which was certainly influenced beneficially by the analysis. The psychical side of childrens' illnesses seems even more important than that of adults.

I look forward to seeing you the day after the Congress.

With all good wishes for the holiday benefit,

Yours always.
Ernest Jones.

1. Jones (1927c).

2. Tenth Congress of the International Psychoanalytic Association, Innsbruck, 1–3 September 1927.

3. Earlier in the year the New York society had drafted a set of resolutions on lay analysis excluding nonmedical personnel from treating patients but allowing them to seek "psychoanalytic instruction" to further their education. The society's official position was published as part of the "Discussion on Lay Analysis," *Journal*, 8 (1927): 283. The campaign against lay analysis was increasingly stepped up as a result of Brill's annoyance with Rank and Ferenczi, who both vigorously campaigned for the acceptance of lay analysis in the United States, and also as a result of the fact that a "new medical practice act . . . in N.Y. is very definite on the subject. You cannot possibly be associated with people who are not *M.D.s*" (Brill to Jones, 4 August 1927, Archives of the British Psycho-Analytical Society, London).

507

20 August 1927
Wales

Dear Professor,

I have ordered the Russell book and will bring it with me if it has appeared before I leave.[1] Eitingon and I will come to Semmering on Sunday,

Sept. 4, (Hotel Südbahn) and are greatly looking forward to the pleasure of seeing you.

The Americans threaten a secession from the Association, but I hope we shall be able to manage them at the Congress.

Yours affectionately
Ernest Jones.

1. Probably Bertrand Russell, *Why I Am Not a Christian* (London: Watts, 1927). It is interesting to note here that in the following year Jones would bring out his psychoanalytic study of Christianity (Jones, 1928c). Freud's copy of this book, a gift from Jones, contains the inscription: "To Professor Freud with respects of a fellow infidel Ernest Jones" (Freud Museum, London).

508

23 September 1927
Vienna, IX. Berggasse 19

Dear Jones,

When I think that a few days ago I had the opportunity to talk to you personally, I have to regret that two events did not occur somewhat earlier. Discussions by letter are a poor substitute.

The first is a letter from Brill, the first in I do not know how many years. He does not spare me the reproaches that he feels justified in making. But he assures me that he and they all "shall remain absolutely loyal to you and your principles".[1] Furthermore, he has heard that *I* intend to force the N.Y. Society out of the Association, but "J. should feel very sorry if anything like this should occur".[2] I sent a friendly but sharp and candid answer, pointing out to him how he has disappointed me and of us. With a clear conscience I could dispute that I intended to force the Americans to withdraw, but I made no secret of my conviction that we should lose nothing as colleagues, or on a scientific or material level, if they wanted to secede. Perhaps he will be offended now, but, in any case, he already was. When he overcomes his touchiness, which stems from a guilty conscience, a good relationship may still ensue. In any case, I am changing my own tactics late enough as it is; instead of coaxing anyone who is disaffected, I will not suppress my personal dissatisfaction.

I am also writing to you with such an aim in mind. I do not understand your attitude in this matter. At the Congress it was you who threatened with the secession of the N.Y. Society. But you were also in favor of publishing the arguments in my supplement,[3] which were sure to offend the N.Y. Society, and which I had written only for friends *without* the intention of making them public. Are you pursuing a particular aim or are you yielding to your inclination to make yourself unpleasant?

In addition there is something else. In London you are organizing a regular campaign against Anna's child analysis, accusing her of not having been analyzed deeply enough, a reproach that you repeat in a letter to me. I had to point out to you that such a criticism is just as dangerous as it is impermissible. Is anyone actually analyzed enough? I can assure you that Anna has been analyzed longer and more thoroughly than, for example, you yourself. The whole criticism is based on an irresponsible assumption which, with some good will, could have been avoided. From a remark of Anna's to a child, which is aimed at stimulating the child to find the material by itself, Mrs. Klein concludes that Anna is avoiding the Oedipus complex in her analyses,[4] and she concludes this without knowing anything else about this particular analysis. The whole attack is built on this conviction. At the Congress Mrs. Klein makes this reproach to Anna, and, to her counterquestion "What else should I analyze in a child if not the Oedipus complex?" Mrs. Klein admits her misunderstanding. But that is the attack to which you want to give the widest publicity: a complete translation in the *Zeitschrift* and publication of it by the Verlag as a separate pamphlet.[5] In this symposium such an otherwise clever person as Riviere lets herself be carried away by theoretical assumptions, which run counter to everything that we know and believe, and which indicate a new path to the derealization of analysis.[6] What does all this mean? I believe I may ask for an explanation. The difference of opinion between two child analysts regarding superego development in the child and the technique of analysis are really not so drastic that one could not leave them to historical development, that they have to produce such a premature, passionate, and unfair reaction. Is this directed against me because Anna is my daughter? A nice motivation among analysts, who demand that others control their primitive impulses.

In reality, Anna's views on child analysis are largely independent of mine; I share her views, but she has developed them out of her independent experience.

This second incident has left me with an unpleasant impression and has aroused the need to understand more about the mental processes in the English Society, especially in you.[7] If it can be explained briefly, you ought not to withhold from me the solution to this puzzle. I have learned to bear much, and have no illusions about a golden age in which the lamb grazes next to the wolf; and I know how to get over much of the roughness of life. I think you will also welcome the opportunity to speak out more freely than hitherto.

With cordial greetings.

Yours,
Freud

1. In English in the original.

1. In English in the original.
2. In English in the original.
3. Freud (1927a).
4. Klein (1927b, p. 341).
5. For papers that Melanie Klein and Anna Freud presented at the Tenth Congress of the International Psychoanalytic Association, Innsbruck, 1–3 September 1927, see Klein (1927c) and A. Freud (1927b). Klein's paper was not published in the *Zeitschrift*.
6. Riviere (1927).
7. The German here is "mehr von den seelischen Vorgängen in der Englischen Gesellschaft, speziell bei Ihnen zu verstehen." Freud is referring to the British Psycho-Analytical Society, as the expression "Englische Gesellschaft" would normally be written "englische Gesellschaft" if it referred to English society in general. But there is likely a play on words here too which should not be overlooked.

509

International Psycho-Analytical Association

30 September 1927
London

Dear Professor,

I was just contemplating writing to you about the latest news and to express my pleasure at seeing you on the Semmering when your letter arrived with its rather painful contents. It is, as you say, an enormous pity that we could not have discussed these matters together when we met. Correspondence is a very imperfect mode of communication, especially when it is a question of explaining and describing a psychological atmosphere. However, I will try to compensate for this by writing as fully as possible.

When I read your little essay[1] in the Hague I expressed the opinion to Eitingon that I did not think either the tone or the content would offend Americans. To this I made a reservation of three sentences which I suggested omitting. Otherwise it was to me simply interesting, and I had no other motive for expressing the desire to see it published than the general one that applies to all your writings. The incident had not the slightest importance to me otherwise and I find it impossible to connect it with any other matter. You may, of course, be right in thinking that it would offend the Americans, but when I read it it did not produce that impression on me.

You ask what my aim is in regard to the American situation. It is nothing at all else than to restore as much harmony as possible between them and us by trying to diminish the factors that have reduced that harmony. Everything I have said and done has no other meaning than that, even though you may, of course, not agree with the particular *means* I advocate. I should regret their secession much more than you apparently would, but for no other reason than that it would, in my opinion, impair the extension of psycho-analysis in America; consequently I am prepared to make some effort to understand their grievances. A secession is certainly possible, but I do not think it at all likely, and I am sure we could easily prevent it with some goodwill if we think it worth while to do so. Kardiner, whom I met recently in London, said they were very disappointed with the results of the Congress and spoke again of a secession. One of the things which, in his opinion, would certainly bring it about would be the official acceptance of the new Ferenczi lay group in New York.[2] I assured him that we had had no official overture from this group, which he thought we had, and that Eitingon was in the highest degree unlikely to take any such decided step before the next Congress. Incidentally, it is really untrue to say that I threatened the meeting with an American secession. This can only emanate from a misunderstanding and distortion of a sentence of mine committed by Ferenczi, which I publicly rectified at once at the meeting.

The two means I proposed for diminishing the tension between the two continents were exactly as follows. The first relates to the conditions for admittance of candidates to membership. The view I expressed was that, though every effort should be made to secure identity of these conditions in different countries, where this proved to be temporarily impossible it would be wiser for the majority to grant the individual societies (as has always hitherto been the practice of the International) the right to make their own conditions according to their knowledge of the local laws and general social situation rather than to attempt to impose an artificial unanimity which would not exist in reality. In this view I was not supported by the general feeling of the Congress, though no vote was taken on it.

The second means I wished to propose did not come to expression because Rado, by a rather scurvy trick which we much resented and against which Anna herself publicly protested, prevented the question from being raised. I am in complete agreement with Eitingon's theory and practice that we should be stringent in the selection of candidates for training, of course equally so with the medical and lay. I wished to suggest that some further steps be taken towards tightening up the conditions of training, largely because if this were done most of the dissatisfaction under which the Americans and, to a less extent, the English suffer would be removed. I refer to the matter of what I called *wilde Ausbildung* [wild training], i.e. very unsuitable candidates being taken in an irresponsible manner for a short time by individual analysts. I found that only Berlin and London have a rule in the Society which forbids training of candidates except under the complete auspices of the *Unterrichtsausschuss* [training committee], and even Berlin does not apply this law to foreign candidates. I am convinced that much more discrimination needs to be made in this matter, preferably by a responsible body. Here also I know that, as you told me recently, I am not in accord with you, but I can only ascribe this to your not coming into direct contact with the practical consequences of the opposite policy. I am fully convinced that if more goodwill and responsibility were shown in this matter on the Continent the tension with the Anglo-Saxon countries would rapidly diminish and I should be entirely hopeful about the future. You may not agree with the means I propose, but you cannot mistake my aim.

A third means I have in mind seems too chimerical in the present state of feeling. It is that better relations and contact be established among the Training Committees (or their secretaries) in the different countries over this question of foreighn [foreign] candidates. I do not see, for instance, why the names of the candidates coming from one country should be withheld from the training committee of that country as Eitingon did recently when the New York group approached him on these lines. This, however, is a matter which I do not think was raised at the Congress, except perhaps in private talk.

All this naturally does not mean that I am blind to the faults of the Americans and I have made myself pretty unpopular with them by telling them what I think of their attitude. The rigid resolutions passed by the New York group, for example, last May,[3] before even there was an opportunity of proper discussion of the questions at issue, was most tactless and unwise, indeed even discourteous. Their blind obstinacy is also shown by their not attending the Congress in larger numbers or in preparing any reasoned statement of their case, which it would be easy to do. Even after they passed their resolutions I sent a strong eleventh-hour appeal to Brill and Oberndorf begging that they give way at least on the principle of lay analysts, even if they restricted their numbers in practice. Brill's answer I showed you at the Semmering.

It is plain that if I consulted for a moment my personal interests I should have refrained from lifting a finger in the matter. But I had no hesitation in risking this when I felt that two sets of people were drifting apart in mutual misunderstanding and that I was in a peculiar position of being able to appreciate the points of view of both.

Turning now to the second and much more painful matter, I hope to be able to show you that your complaint about my arranging a definite campaign against Anna and publishing an illegitimate criticism of her does not tally with the actual facts, and I will also give, as you request, a full account of the situation in London. It is best to begin at the beginning. For many years there has been a rather special interest taken in the problems of childhood in London, perhaps more than elsewhere. I suppose the reason is that we have a number of women analysts, Miss Low, Miss Searl,

Miss Chadwick, Miss Sharpe, Mrs. Isaacs, Miss Lewis, Miss Terry,[4] etc., who have done a good deal of child-study and child analysis. I have taken a benevolent interest in the matter, for the reasons I set forth in my recent contribution to the discussion,[5] dating probably from two very successful results I had myself with analyses in the latency period. About three years ago we had a thorough discussion of the question of how far analytic methods can be pushed in childhood, particularly to what extent and to how early an age.[6] Various doubts and hesitations were voiced on much the same lines as those recently expressed by Anna, and the fact is worth mentioning because it shows you how familiar they were to us long before this recent occasion. The outcome of our discussion was a progressive one. We decided that only experience could prove whether the young child's ego was capable of enduring repressed material in the same way that we know an adult's ego can by the help of analysis, and that this should be more important than any theoretical reason to the contrary. Some time after this Mrs. Klein came to London, first to lecture and then to work. There is general confidence in her method and results, which several of us have been able to test at the closest quarters, and she makes the general impression of a sane, well-balanced, and thoroughly analysed person. We were somewhat astonished to learn with what little sympathy her work has been regarded on the Continent, but decided to give her work a fair hearing and form our own judgement about it. This has been so favourable that we have come to regard her extension of psycho-analysis into this new field as not only a valuable addition to our powers, but as opening up the most promising avenue to direct investigation of the earliest and deepest problems. Holding such an attitude, we could, as you will well understand, only regard any attempt made to close this avenue as unfortunate.

Such is the pre-history of the situation, which proves demonstratively that our general attitude about deep child analysis was formed without the slightest personal reference to either yourself or to Anna. Anna's unexpected attack on her could therefore only evoke a reaction of regret here. Mrs. Klein's new method, which seems so valuable to us, was repudiated as untrustworthy, early analysis, i.e. below the latency period, was condemned, and an extremely conservative attitude was recommended throughout. A book issued by the Verlag and bearing the name it does could not fail to carry exceptional weight,[7] in spite of the fact, which I well recognise, of Anna's personal independence from yourself; and that it has this weight is shown by the extent to which Mrs. Klein's work is thought on the Continent to [be][8] have been discredited by it. My own reaction, which I did not hesitate to communicate to you at once, was simply one of regret that Anna had been so hasty as to publish her first lectures in such an uncompromising form and on such a slender basis of experience. I felt she might regret it later and that taking so decided a step would make it harder to adopt later on a more advanced position.

When Anna read her paper at Berlin Mrs. Klein, who was still at that time a member of the Berlin group, sent a written contribution to the discussion, but this was suppressed.[9] Rado had previously barred the "*Zeitschrift*" to her, and so she came to me to ask what opportunity there was for her to defend herself against this attack on her life's work. I wrote to Rado asking if Anna's book could be simultaneously reviewed, as has been done before, by two people from different points of view, and his reply indicated that only a favourable review of it could be published.[10] There remained only the "*Journal*". I should, of course, publish the "*Zeitschrift*" review in translation in the "*Journal*",[11] but I promised Mrs. Klein that our pages would also be open to any contribution of hers defining the points at issue between her and Anna and generally clearing up the situation. You may well imagine that it never once occurred to me that Anna would claim immunity from criticism of her writings, still less that [she] you would expect any such immunity for her.[12] Extremely important scientific issues were at stake and an open discussion on all sides seemed the obvious course. I certainly could not sympathise with the possibility of one side of the case being artificially blocked, especially when it was the one that seemed to me to be the more progressive and promising of the two.

So the matter stood when in the natural course of things a review of Anna's book was read before the Society by my Miss Low. It was an excellent and comprehensive review—almost a translation. The discussion that followed had to be continued to the next meeting, but was not in any way organised or influenced. I did not myself parteke [partake] in the discussion on either evening (my own contribution was written afterwards as a sort of summing up) and I exchanged very few words with anyone on the subject. It was certainly noteworthy that people so dissimilar and independent of one another as Edward Glover and Mrs. Klein, Mrs. Riviere and Miss Searl, should agree in deprecating the check that Anna's attitude was felt to impose on the development of early analysis.[13] Though Anna's book was the topical occasion of focussing the subject once more in our attention, the whole range of child analysis and cognate problems were widely discussed, and so many definite points of view and considerations were adduced from diverse angles that we thought it worth while to publish the discussion as a whole, in the same way that has several times been done previously by other societies.[14] It was thought that definite contributions had been made to the problems of child analysis which it was worth while to print. Everyone was invited to partake in this discussion and of course there were no special invitations or selections. That they agree in certain respects is a fact, but not, as you suggest, an arranged fact. What you refer to as the haste in publishing it (three months after the discussion) was simply due to our having very little other material at the time for the number of the *"Journal"* that was then needed, whereas to hold it over would bring us into the flood of the Congress contributions.

Owing to the rush of the holidays Mrs. Riviere and I divided the work of correcting the material, she attending to Mrs. Klein's contribution which she had translated, and I to all the rest. If there is any illegitimate criticism of Anna in Mrs. Klein's paper I am of course technically responsible, though it happens that I did not read it until after your letter came this week. It seems to me that any question of possible misunderstanding would best be left by us to the two people most directly concerned. Anna must know that any reply or contribution from her would be received with welcome by the *"Journal"* and esteemed as an honour. I was not myself aware of any *illegitimate* criticism in what Mrs. Klein said at the meeting nor do I observe that any have been inserted into the written account. In saying this I naturally cannot make myself responsible for or defend everything she writes—it is her own affair and all I have as Editor to see to is that the tone and content of such a contribution is within the usual bounds of scientific controversy. In this case I trusted Mrs. Klein and Mrs. Riviere and I do not see any reason for thinking that they abused my trust. As regards the Oedipus complex, the point you mention, what Mrs. Klein criticises is Anna's hesitation to explore this unsparingly to its depths, especially in young children. So far is the criticism from being based on a misreading of a single remark, that Anna gave a series of reasons defending this attitude, all of which are dealt with *seriatim* in the criticism.

This letter is already too long for me to discuss here Mrs. Riviere's views, expressed in her characteristically uncompromising and rather vehement fashion. All that matters in the present connection is that, instead of their being due to her being *'hingerissen'* [swept away] by the recent incident, they long ante-dated it and arose quite independently of child analysis [in general][15] at all.

As regards publication in German, naturally I think it reasonable that some of our contributions, and particularly Mrs. Klein's defence, should appear also in that language. I told Rado about our discussion, as about everything else the *"Journal"* is doing, and he replied that the *"Zeitschrift"* had no space for papers on child analysis. He offered, however, to publish a two-page abstract of the discussion and made the suggestion that it be published in brochure form by the Verlag. I reported to Eitingon my conversation with Rado, of which this was only a part, but have not spoken of it to anyone else, nor indeed, thought of since.

This history of a perfectly natural and spontaneous order of development will, I trust, convince you that the situation here is much more objective than you thought and did not arise from any personal feelings about either Anna or yourself. The mood here is one of entire devotion to your personality and fidelity to the principles of psycho-analysis. I am glad to be able to affirm[16] that I do not know of a single exception to the whole-hearted truth of this statement.

Long as this letter is, I take the opportunity of adding what news there is since my return. There has been a correspondence in the *"Saturday Review"* on your supposed melancholia (dictated by Viereck's interview) and I have just sent them a contradicting letter.[17] Last Monday I attended for the first time the Committee of the British Medical Assoction on Psycho-Analysis and received a not unfavourable impression. In all probability the final report will contain nothing denunciatory, the only difficulty being to clear up the confusion with the so-called allied analytic methods (Jung, etc.). The few hints dropped on the subject of lay analysts gave me the hope that the Committee may prove amenable on that matter, so that there may be some chance of regularising their position.[18]

I enclose two cuttings in support of what I said about the religious situation in England. The Bishop in question got his Fellowship of the Royal Society for mathematics.[19] The doctor, whose paper on "Psycho-Analysis and Religion" was read before the British Association for the Advancement of Science last July, is personally unknown to me.[20]

I have just been through Strachey's translation of your *Selbstdarstellung*, which is as usual excellent.

I cannot expect you to agree with many things I have had to say in this letter, but I trust nevertheless that it will afford you sufficient reassurance about our attitude. Please convey my greetings to Anna and tell her that, in spite of our unfortunate scientific differences which I hope one day will be resolved, I entertain the highest respect for her and am looking forward with pleasure to co-operating with her in the work that we have to do together.

Yours as always,
Ernest Jones.

1. Freud (1927a).

2. One of the results of Ferenczi's trip to America (autumn 1926–spring 1927) was the formation of a group of lay analysts who sought official acceptance by the International Psychoanalytic Association. But their efforts were unsuccessful, and the group dissolved in early 1928. See Jones (1957a, pp. 294, 297; 1957b, pp. 316, 319).

3. The report of the New York society's committee on policy regarding their opposition to lay analysis was approved on 24 May 1927; see *Journal*, 8 (1927): 453. See also note 3 to letter 506.

4. Handwritten in the margin are the words "all lay." Of this group, those who were

full members of the British Psycho-Analytical Society included Susan Isaacs (1885–1948), a pioneer researcher in the field of child development; Barbara Low (1877–1955), educator and lecturer; and Ella Freeman Sharpe (1875–1947), teacher and lecturer in psychoanalysis. Isaacs, Low, and Sharpe would later play important roles in the "Controversial Discussions" between 1941 and 1945; see King and Steiner (1991). Mary Chadwick, M. G. Lewis, and N. Searl are listed as associate members in *Journal*, 8 (1927): 123–124, while E. M. Terry's name, as an associate member, appears in *Journal*, 10 (1929): 556.

5. Jones (1927d).

6. See *Journal*, 6 (1925): 238–239, 359–360.

7. A. Freud (1927a).

8. Crossed out in the original; "have been" is handwritten in an otherwise typed letter.

9. As reported in *Zeitschrift* 13 (1927): 367, Anna Freud delivered a paper, "Zur Technik der Kinderanalyse," in March 1927 before the German Psychoanalytic Society, Berlin, of which Melanie Klein was still a member; the latter's election to the British Psycho-Analytical Society did not take place until 2 October 1927.

10. Radó's review was the only one that appeared; see *Zeitschrift*, 14 (1928): 540–546. The "Symposium on Child Analysis" was reviewed but not published in German; see Fenichel (1928).

11. This did not appear in the *Journal*.

12. "She" is crossed out; "you" and "for her" are inserted by hand.

13. The contributors to the discussions of 4 and 18 May 1927, which were published as the "Symposium on Child Analysis," *Journal*, 8 (1927): 339–391, were Melanie Klein, Joan Riviere, M. N. Searl, Ella F. Sharpe, Edward Glover, and Ernest Jones. Barbara Low's review did not appear.

14. "Vienna" is handwritten in the margin.

15. Crossed out in the original; "at all" is handwritten."

16. Here the following phrase is crossed out: "that I do not know of a single member of our Society."

17. Viereck's interview with Freud is contained in his *Glimpses of the Great* (London: Duckworth, 1930), pp. 28ff.; see Jones (1957a, p. 126; 1957b, p. 133) and Strachey's note in *S.E.*, 21:168.

18. See British Medical Association (1929).

19. See note 2 to letter 513.

20. W. R. D. Fairbairn, "Religion and Fantasy," is abstracted in *British Association for the Advancement of Science: Report of the Ninety-Fifth Meeting*, 31 August–4 September 1927, Leeds, p. 397. Ronald Fairbairn (1889–1964) was to become one of the most important British psychoanalysts of the post–World War II era. Born and educated in Edinburgh, he was a philosopher and physician by training; though influenced by both Freud and Anna Freud, he later developed a systematic object relations theory in his *Psychoanalytical Studies of the Personality* (1952), which involved a significant modification of classical psychoanalytic theory.

510

9 October 1927
Vienna, IX. Berggasse 19

Dear Jones,

I am naturally very happy that you replied so calmly and extensively instead of declaring yourself to be highly offended; and I would like to select from your communications what is useful for resolving and placating the situation. Just a few points will then remain, which your letter did not deal with. Then we will leave the whole thing to the test of time.

On the American question I have hardly anything to add, particularly as your own opinion condemns the behavior of New York, and I am relying on Brill to send you my letter to him. I agree with your wish that the training committees should have a uniform procedure and impose strict requirements. The whole organization is after all still young and untested.

I can assure you that it never occurrred to me or Anna herself to ask that her book and opinions should be exempt from criticism. If anyone barred Mrs. Klein from expressing her views—it is not my fault that she is so unpopular in Berlin—I will personally see to it that she is given free access. I also knew that the attitude of the English to child analysis was already fixed, even before Anna's appearance. On the other hand, it is unjust to give prominence to the nature of the attack on Mrs. Klein in her book. She has simply, on the basis of her own very extensive experience, developed her views and very reluctantly brought forward some polemical points. In the behavior of the English toward Anna, two points remain inexcusable: the reproach, which is not customary among us and offends against all good practice, that she was not analyzed sufficiently—put forward by you publicly and in private—and Mrs. Klein's remark that she believed Anna is avoiding the Oedipus complex on principle. With more good will, this misunderstanding could easily have been avoided.

More disconcerting to me than these tempests in a teapot are the theoretical statements of Riviere, especially because I have always had such a high opinion of her understanding. Here I must reproach you with having carried tolerance too far. If a member of any of our groups expresses such mistaken and misleading basic views, that is good reason for the group's leader to give that person a private lecture, but not a case for which one seeks to ensure the widest publicity, without critical comment. The editors in Berlin may also have thought along similar lines.

I am writing to Mrs. Riviere herself about this, for I would like her to appreciate her blunder for herself.

Both statements about religion are very interesting.

Only this for today, to close both matters. We shall soon resume the *Rundbrief.*[1]

Cordially,
Freud

1. The German here is uncharacteristically *Rundverkehr*, literally, "circular traffic."

511

International Psycho-Analytical Association

18 October 1927
London

Dear Professor,

I was glad to get your letter. There is only one point in it which I wish to answer, especially as I had not dealt with it in my previous one. It is your reproach that I neglected my part as leader in respect of Mrs. Riviere. I think you will see from the following considerations that this is not so.

To begin with, I did not find her views untrue in themselves,[1] though they are presented in a one-sided and therefore misleading way. This I certainly endeavoured to influence to the best of my ability, but you know that she is a person of considerable determination and in any case there was no question of refusing to publish them. She gave way to the extent of modifying or omitting a great number of her expressions, but she could not agree with me that to present one side of the matter emphatically would have a misleading effect on the reader. There are two main points in her views, both of them related, and I think I can express them shortly. She insists that the child's unconscious picture of the parents to which it reacts in such manifold ways is far from being a photograph of them, but is throughout coloured by entirely individual contributions from the child's own component instincts, e.g. the idea of the parent may be much more sadistic than the reality, etc. etc.. This I should have thought was common ground in psycho-analysis; if not, it is in my opinion easily demonstrable. It also seems to me worth insisting on because of the tendency at times to identify the growing super-ego with the *actual* parents rather than with the child's particular picture of them. Naturally Mrs. Riviere would not deny the influence of real attributes to the parents in this compound, and I told her she was making a mistake in dwelling only on what might be called the phantastic half of the picture.

The second point is that repression, with the accompanying formation of guilt, super-ego, etc., is not effected simply as a response to external oppression,[2] threats, etc., but is in large part an *internal* necessity of the child to defend itself against the intolerable distress induced by the non-gratification of various wishes which *in the nature of things* cannot be gratified, e.g. cannibalistic wishes, etc. etc.. I also agree with this view, but again I think it mistaken to ascribe the whole process to what may be called the inner factor alone. I am not sure how far she would go in this matter, but I am inclined to think she might wish to reduce the whole situation to primary intolerance of thwarted desires. What percentage of the process is internal and what percentage external seems to me a most important problem for further research.

I am, of course, curious to know what exactly you found so heretical in her contribution, or whether you could have misunderstood her way of presenting her views. I hope that in these few sentences I have succeeded in defining the issue in a simple manner.

With kindest regards,

Yours always,
Ernest Jones.

1. "Themselves" is handwritten in an otherwise typed letter.
2. "Repression" had been typed here, then "op" was written in to replace "re."

512

22 October 1927
Vienna, IX. Berggasse 19

Dear Jones,

You have made it very easy for me to reply to your question. In fact you say it all yourself, and so clearly that there is nothing for me to change or add. I learn that your assessment of Mrs. Riviere is exactly the same as mine. Naturally I criticize her for denying half the facts, while the other—what you call "the phantastic half"[1]—is alone proclaimed; incidentally, in an excellent way. This makes her viewpoint "heretical," contains an unfortunate similarity to Jung's, and, like his, is an important step toward making analysis unreal and impersonal. The clarity of her style precludes any misreading of her meaning. Just read the last paragraph of her article again.[2] If she has experienced a case which proved to her the importance of the phylogenetic imago, then only a greater number of cases can be useful to me to put the influence of real, personal factors beyond any doubt. It is remarkable that people find it most difficult to recognize overdetermination and the multiplicity of etiological factors. All our apostates always grasped part of the truth and wanted to declare it as the whole truth.

Incidentally, Mrs. Riviere's logic and perspicacity are revealed even in her error; she has quite rightly discovered the theory which alone fits Mrs. Klein's technique.

Guilt feelings are a different matter; here you cannot speak of "heresy,"[3] for we are not yet agreed on the genesis of guilt feelings. I believe—again like you—that Mrs. Riviere is not right here. Frustration certainly plays an important role, but cannot be the only source. Just think of the proletariat, whose life is an accummulation of frustrations. The result of this is not a particularly great guilt feeling but, as is much more evident, an unappeased hunger for satisfaction, with a tendency to ruthless rejection of moral precepts.

Is it not time to end this not altogether agreeable episode? I should be sorry if Mrs. Riviere continued to be discouraged or estranged.

Cordially yours,
Freud

1. In English in the original.
2. Riviere (1927, pp. 376–377).
3. In English in the original.

513

International Psycho-Analytical Association

26 November 1927
London

Dear Professor,

Thank you very much for sending me the new book which appeared sooner than you had expected in September.[1] I found it most interestingly written and need hardly say that I am in accord with every word of it. I trust I may assume that you will give us the translation rights. Rickman is writing to the Verlag on the business side of this. The Hogarth Press is willing to bring out the translation at once, especially as it will be of topical interest in view of the religious controversy now going on in England started by the Bishop of Birmingham. It is not over his views on evolution, which are generally accepted by the clergy, but over his talk on the Catholic influence in the Church of England in which he points to the anthropological origin of belief in Transsubstantiation at the Mass.[2] I have found a new translator, a man of literature who has been a patient with me for three years, but both Strachey and I will revise the translation as well.[3]

Ad Gegensinn der Urwörter⁴: *'Nebe'* in Middle High German signifies both 'nephew' and 'uncle'.⁵

With kindest regards,

Yours always,
Ernest Jones.

1. Freud (1927c).

2. Ernest William Barnes (1874–1953), English clergyman, Cambridge mathematician, fellow of the Royal Society, and bishop of Birmingham since 1924, whose controversial book *Should Such a Faith Offend?* (London: Hodder and Stoughton, 1927) upset the conservative-minded, especially the Archbishop of Canterbury, Randall Davidson. In Jones (1957a, p. 138; 1957b, pp. 146–147) this episode is linked to the urgent need to translate Freud (1927c).

3. Freud (1927c), trans. W. D. Robson-Scott 1928.

4. Jones echoes Freud (1910e).

5. *Nebe* in the standard Middle High German dictionaries is synonymous with *Neve*— or *Neffe* in modern German—and means "nephew." The source for Jones's assertion is not clear.

514

1 December 1927
Vienna, IX. Berggasse 19

Dear Jones,

I am satisfied that the new book pleased you¹ and, after the last discussion, am naturally prepared at once to concede the translation rights to Hogarth Press, if, as you promise, they do not delay publication indefinitely; but I prefer James Strachey as translator to anyone unknown to me. I already arranged the translation with him when he visited me at Semmering, and I have sent him a copy; unless he has reconsidered it since then.

Everything here is otherwise the same, except for news of the *Rundbrief.*

Cordially yours,
Freud

1. After the opening phrase here, the verb *ziehe* is crossed out in the original. Freud then employs *vorziehen* a little later to complete the sentence: "ziehe aber als Übersetzer James Strachey jedem Unbekannten vor" (but I prefer James Strachey as translator to anyone unknown to me).

515

International Psycho-Analytical Association

5 December 1927
London

Dear Professor,

Your two wishes, that Strachey should do the translation himself and that it be done quickly, have a certain incompatibility. His intolerance of work, about which you doubtless know more than I do, has not been improved by his having eight patients a day. Recently he ungraciously objected to being put on the James Glover Memorial Sub-Committee, because it would involve giving up part of an evening every two or three months and it is hardly possible to get out of him a book review or any other contribution. Woolf accepted the book for the Hogarth Press on condition that it appeared quickly, and both you and I have the same wish. Knowing nothing of Strachey's interview with you last September, I saw him together with Mrs. Riviere about your new book but they were equally disinclined to undertake the work. After half-an-hour's pressure all I got from him was a promise that he would try dictating the translation of one chapter as an experiment to see if it would be less laborious that way. Just after that, it happened that Robson Scott, who has been three years in analysis with me for an obsessional neurosis (and who is therefore scrupulously meticulous) showed me some translation work he had done from the German. His work is purely literary and he is in some ways more gifted than Strachey in felicitous expression. So I asked Strachey if he would like some help from him. Greatly relieved he begged that Robson Scott should do the translation on the condition that he revised it, which I shall of course also do myself. You may be sure, therefore, that it will be both skilfully and accurately done and I hope that you will not press your condition, for getting translation work done in England is difficult enough in any case.

I hope you will find some points of interest in a reprint I am sending you by this post.

With kindest regards,

Yours always,
Ernest Jones.

516

11 December 1927
Vienna, IX. Berggasse 19

Dear Jones,

If Strachey has withdrawn the willingness he expressed to me, I naturally agree to your new proposal.

Cordially yours,
Freud

517

13 February 1928
81 Harley Street, London

Dear Professor,

I enclose a little booklet which I think you will like if you have time to read it. It attempts to place $\psi\alpha$ in a general setting of science.[1]

Some time ago I sent you a reprint of my Congress paper. As it contains two new conclusions, one general and one specific, I am naturally eager to know how they impress you.[2]

The translation of the 'Zukunft' is almost finished and is excellent. Robson-Scott is a welcome addition to our limited band of translators. It might interest you to know that he is a cousin of Andrew Lang and of 'Just So' Atkinson.[3]

I hope the world is going well with you. Do you know of the efforts being made to secure you the Nobel Prize?

Yours always affectionately
Ernest Jones.

1. Most likely Jones (1928a).
2. Jones (1927f).
3. Freud (1927c), trans. W. D. Robson-Scott 1928. Andrew Lang (1844–1912), Scottish scholar, poet, and man of letters, with serious interests in psychical research, especially known for his work on myths; he dealt with the origins of totemism in *Social Origins* (London: Longmans, 1903), which was printed together with Atkinson (1903). "Just So" echoes a comment by Marett on Freud's *Totem and Taboo*, see letter 269 and note 2 to letter 268.

518

18 February 1928
Vienna, IX. Berggasse 19

Dear Jones,

I hasten to thank you for your sending the science primer on ΨA before reading it, promising to give you my impression of it hereafter. A tedious conjunctivitis at one eye interferes with my facility of reading and writing, just at a time when I have the proofs of the translation of *Selbstdarstellung* and *Laienanalyse*, both done by Princess Marie, on hand. (Their titles in French are "Ma vie et la PsA" and "La PsA et la médicine".)[1]

Apart [from] this trouble I am all right. We had a good deal of correspondence about the Swiss *"Sturm im Wasserglas"* [tempest in a teapot]. C. G. Jung is to give a public lecture here, on Wednesday next, I do'nt think I will attend it. So I will miss an excellent opportunity of hearing about the Structure of the Soul from a first-rate source.[2]

No, I know nothing of efforts to secure me the Nobel Prize and I do not appreciate them. Who is fool enough to meddle in this affair?[3]

Affectionately yours
Freud

1. The French translations of Freud (1925d, 1926e) appeared in Marie Bonaparte, *Ma vie et la psychoanalyse: La psychanalyse et la médecine* (Paris: Gallimard, 1928).
2. Jung's lecture "Struktur der Seele," as reported in the *Neue Freie Presse*, 23 February 1928, was delivered before the conservative group Kulturbund.
3. Heinrich Meng spearheaded the campaign on this occasion; see Gay (1988, p. 456).

519

22 February 1928
Vienna, IX. Berggasse 19

Dear Jones,

I am able to read again, and the first project was your essence of psychoanalysis.[1] To have undertaken so difficult and thankless a task is of great merit. I will not withhold several minor criticisms from you.

The end of the first paragraph made a fearful impression on me. The truth lies in the middle, they say. But both extremes are an equally gross condemnation of analysis.[2]

I seem to remember that you were repeatedly uncertain when you described Breuer's case. This time it is a mistake to say that she had to revive a forgotten memory "in a waking state";[3] it always happened only under hypnosis.[4]

Your requirement "that the analysis of children be a real one, quite independent of any educative measures,"[5] seems to me just as unfounded in theory as inappropriate in reality. The more I learn of these things, the more I believe that Melanie Klein is on the wrong track and Anna is on the right one.

Everything we know about early female development seems to me unsatisfactory and uncertain. I see only two points clearly: that the first representation of sexual intercourse is an oral one—sucking on the penis, as earlier, at the mother's breast; and giving up clitoral masturbation on account of the painful realization of the inferiority of this organ. On everything else I must reserve my judgment.

Cordial greetings,
Freud

1. Jones (1928a).
2. The extremes mentioned are that psychoanalysis is "nothing but the translation into high-sounding jargon of platitudes that are well known to every writer about human nature" and that "it consists of a number of statements and conclusions that would be in the highest degree repellent were it not that the fantastic improbability of them prevents their being taken seriously." See Jones (1928a), rev. ed. 1949, p. 7.
3. In English in the original.
4. The error was corrected in the revised edition; see Jones (1928a), rev. ed. 1949, p. 18.
5. In English in the original. See Jones (1928a), rev. ed. 1949, p. 79.

520

7 March 1928[1]

Dear Professor,

Your very kind telegram moved me greatly.[2] Although I know that, to my deep regret, I have not found much favour in your eyes of late years, it showed that you retained some affection for me.

When you lost Sophie you wrote to me [and][3] that you wished you could die too. At the time I only partly understood this, but now I do so fully. I am finding it hard, and as yet impossible, to discover enough motive to go on living and to endure the present and future suffering that this blow has brought. My dear wife feels this even more so. Our boy is happy and sunny and certainly does not need us. It is strange how little consolation he is in spite of our love for him. The politics and personalities of ψα work have brought more pain than pleasure in the last years, and what else is there?

I thought I had tasted ten years ago all that the suffering of grief could bring,[4] but life always knows some trump card with which to destroy such illusions. To lose one's first-born, one's only daughter, when one is nearly fifty and cannot begin again, is in itself a fearful blow, but two other features have here combined to make it a crushing one.

The child had the rarest qualities that wound deeply round our hearts. With a wonderful sweetness and vitality she had the poignancy that, as you once told me 16 years ago, is only developed in its highest and most touching degree as a reaction to a neurotic character. A magnificent fidelity and tenderness, with a rare courage and fortitude. A deep suspicion of the cruelty of life, but a strong love of life. Physically she was very healthy and strong and last Christmas at Andermatt astonished the Swiss by a feat of endurance on skis in the High Alps in a snowstorm. But she was what the Scotch call "fey"—not for this world, and we always felt this. Two years ago she startled us by saying she would die when she was seven, as she did.

The illness lasted 18 days. After five days of influenza with excessively high fever, she developed double broncho-pneumonia and this showed no signs of resolving till the 13th day, the day she died. For nine days she breathed at 70 to the minute, which is rarely possible for more than two days, and this went with an incessant hacking diaphragmatic cough that wore her out. For ten days she had no sleep, an active and most distressing insomnia that no drugs could influence. We had seven doctors and on three occasions they gave her only a few hours to live, but her vitality survived crisis after crisis. Transfusion of blood was tried twice, and venesection when her heart began to fail. At the end she was unconscious for two hours and the respiratory centre gave out. I cannot picture to you the agonies of alternating fear, despair and painful hope we experienced, but it left us little able to bear the final blow.

My writing at such length to you tells you how I feel towards you. A word from you might help us.

I know your wife will be grieved. She loves children so, and always was interested to hear of ours.

Your broken
Ernest Jones.

1. Jones had written "Feb. 7," with "Feb." doubly underlined. "March" and "1928" were penciled in later. The letterhead "Tanton's Hotel, Bideford, North Devon" is crossed out.

2. Freud had likely responded to a telegram or short note from Jones informing him of his daughter's death. Both are missing.

3. "That" is written directly above "and"; neither word is crossed out.

4. Jones refers to the death of Morfydd Owen; see letter 221.

521

11 March 1928
Vienna, IX. Berggasse 19

Dear Jones,

True, in the last few years I have criticized much about you and have occasionally lost touch with you. But we did not need this last sad occasion to realize that it was only a case of family discord, as when one strains against a bond which one feels to be unbreakable. It would, of course, be better to desist from that as well, but unfortunately we have the gift to create for ourselves unnecessary difficulties in addition to those that are unavoidable.

My painful sympathy stems from my own experience. I realize that the draught was set before me in two portions, which you had to drain all at once. Sophie was a dear daughter, to be sure, but not a child. It was only three years later, in June 1923, when little Heinele died,[1] that I became tired of life permanently. Quite remarkably, there is a correspondence between him and your little one. He too was of superior intelligence and unspeakable spiritual grace, and he spoke repeatedly about dying soon. How do these children know?

You and your dear wife are of course young enough to regain your feeling for life. I should like to do something to distract you, but I do not know whether or not I have already spoken to you about this. My memory does occasionally become unreliable. Therefore, let it seem as if I were touching on the subject for the first time. Through your study of Hamlet you are, of course, the one closest to the Shakespeare problem. I am again impressed by a book that, after a year, I have read for a second time. *Shakespeare Identified*, a book by someone called *Looney*, was published in America in 1920, but the author is obviously an Englishman. The book makes it seem probable that *Edward de Vere, seventeenth Earl of Oxford*, is the author of Shakespeare's poetry and plays.[2] Until now I was a convinced Stratford supporter and dismissed particularly the Bacon hypothesis as being absurd. But now, I must confess, I am very impressed by Looney's investigations, almost convinced. If this aristocrat, of whose life much is known and even more can become known, really was Shakespeare, then we have much to modify in our analytic constructions, perhaps also much to gain. It would surely repay an analyst's interest to look into the matter. How was Looney's book received in England? How did they react to the strange interpretation of the sonnets, etc.? Would you not like to look into whether a reliable analysis of Shakespeare can be constructed on the basis of this new hypothesis?

A further request. I hear that the English edition of Abraham's writings, for which I made a contribution from the birthday endowment, has already been published.[3] I should very much like to own it, or purchase it, if under the new conditions you do not receive complimentary copies. I hear, too, that American publishers are interested in the *Zukunft einer Illusion*.

Thinking of you fondly.

Yours,
Freud

1. See note 1 to letter 402.
2. See Looney (1920), Trosman (1976), Holland (1966), and Jones (1957a, pp. 428–430, 457–458; 1957b, pp. 460–461, 487–488). Freud supported this theory of authorship to the end of his life (1925d, pp. 63–64 n. 1; 1940a, p. 192 n. 1).
3. Abraham (1927).

522

29 April 1928
81 Harley Street, London

Dear Professor,

My delay in thanking you for your very kind letter is a sign of the mental paralysis which has restricted my activity to only the most urgent things. The only meeting I have brought myself to in the past weeks was that of the ψα Committee of the British Medical Assoc.,[1] where of course my presence was quite indispensable, but from this week I am resuming attendance at the ψα Society which Glover had taken over. When in Mentone[2] I went carefully through the excellent translation of the *Zukunft einer Illusion*, which Strachey had previously revised; it goes to the printer tomorrow. That, with patients and a few letters, is the whole record of my external activities in this time.

My main problem is my wife. While the catastrophe affected me as deeply and as painfully as her, it has had a more disintegrating effect on her. It is not only the loss of something ineffably precious and wonderful, but of something that for complicated psychological reasons was vitally *necessary* to her existence, or at least mental stability. Brave as she is, and trained by bitter experience to endure, she is finding it barely possible to face our bleak future (for as far as one can tell further children would appear to be out of the question). This naturally reacts on me, for my own vitality and hopefulness have suffered such a blow as to diminish my powers of helping her. The painfulness of the Trauerarbeit is made excruciating by the horrible memories of what the child suffered, and our spasms of hope to the last; one can only pray that the *Usur* of time[3] will be effective in at least this aspect.

You see it is hard for me to write about any other subject than the one that engrosses my energy. Grateful as I was for the warmth and thoughtfulness displayed in your letter, I missed something in it, some expression of *"tiefe Lebensweisheit"* [deep wisdom] which no one can utter so well as you. It was as though all my efforts had failed to convey to you our desperate need for some such support.

Actually your offer of practical help was well aimed, except that it was much too early to think about *"Ablenkung"* [diversion]. I like to think that your choice of theme was dictated by the wish to combine my wife's literary and my analytic interests, for in the future I hope something of the sort may be possible. Now a word about the subject. Yes, I well remember your telling us all about Looney in May 1926, and our admiration at the keenness you could devote to such a theme at two a.m.. As a result I gave Sachs a present of the book (though I never heard whether he read it) and studied it carefully myself. It gave me the feeling that Shakespeare was probably interested in De Vere and well informed about him, but the main thesis did not seem to be probable. So many books consist in the first half of excited promises to reveal and prove something, and in the second half of triumph at what they think they have proved. It could not have made much impression here, else I would surely have heard of it. The only literary man I spoke to about it was disparaging, largely on the ground of the contemporary evidence about S's identity, which by now is really very considerable. However, some day I shall look into the matter more thoroughly.

I was shocked to learn that you had shared my own fate of having no copy of the Abraham book and will remedy it the first time I speak to Rickman. It is one little example of the result of my deputing the Press work to him. I used always to get the 6 copies due to us of the 'Library' books and to dispose of them suitably (you, author, translator etc.). Without saying a word to me he gave orders that they were to be sent to him to be disposed of, which he has not always done very wisely or fairly. However, if there is one thing more useless in life than another it is complaining. Wasn't it Disraeli who said "Never explain and never complain", which I think is not a bad motto.[4]

I am writing at this date so that you shall not get a sad letter on your birthday, and I hope you will spend a happy one.

Yours ever gratefully
Ernest Jones.

P.S. I am happy to think that the affairs of the Association are in excellent hands with Eitingon, so that the absence of inclination to be concerned in them coincides with the absence of need.

1. See British Medical Association (1929).
2. Jones had a villa in Menton near the Italian border in the south of France.
3. Jones echoes Freud's comment in letter 510 *"Das Ganze wollen wir dann der Usur durch die Zeit überlassen"* (then we will leave the whole thing to the test of time).

4. "And how is the old complaint?" was Disraeli's standard way of covering up when greeting a person whose name he had forgotten. Jones is blocking the name of John Rose Bradford, professor of medicine, Jones's mentor during his early years, who used the expression to comfort Jones in times of crisis; see Jones (1959, pp. 83–84, 151).

523

3 May 1928
Vienna, IX. Berggasse 19

Dear Jones,

Glad to have got at last an answer of yours.[1] Your silence was beginning to become uncanny to me. If I did not write what you had expected, it was for good reasons. I know of only two avenues of consolation in such a case. The one is bad, because it devalues life itself, and the other, more effective, is of use only to the elderly, not young people such as you and your poor wife. You can easily guess what this second one is. I therefore wrote you what I know was untimely only in order to keep in touch with you.

Let me continue in this vein, for, as an unbelieving fatalist, I can only sink into a state of resignation when faced with the horror of death. I was dissatisfied with your information about Looney. I recently read his book again and this time I was even more impressed by it. I believe it is unfair to say that he only triumphs after making promises, like so many other riddle solvers. The explanation of the sonnets and the contributions to the analysis of Hamlet seem to me—besides others—to justify his conviction well. Of course I did not know that recent research has added so much to our knowledge of the man from Stratford; that would change the state of affairs. Can you tell me *where* one can find information about this? In any case, the existence of de Vere provides material for new investigations which can yield interesting positive and negative results. We know Lady Oxford remarried after her husband's death, but do not know the date. What would our position be if this justified the reproach of unseemly haste which Hamlet makes to his mother? And many similar things.

You touch on the fact that in a few days I shall be seventy-two years old. I am expecting my Ernst, his wife, and Eitingon for this occasion, and I am writing you today in view of the fact that I may not get around to it for a while. As you know, I have decided that until my seventy-fifth birthday I shall not celebrate any others, and you can readily appreciate the hidden expectation behind this. Nevertheless, I may assume that on this day the Verlag will present me with volume XI of my *Gesammelte Schriften*. And I can still put up with that.

"Young" and "old" now seem to me the most significant opposites that the human soul can harbor, and an understanding between the representatives of either group is impossible. I lack the necessary information to understand many of the allusions in your letter to the condition of your wife. If I should be allowed to grace this earth a little longer, I expect to hear for certain that you both will have overcome the cruel blow as young people do.

With heartfelt sympathy.

Yours,
Freud

1. The first sentence is written in English in the original.

524

17 June 1928[1]
Semmering

Dear Jones,

Thank you for the translation of *Illusion*.[2] It seems quite good. You will be interested to hear that the censors in Russia—as Eitingon told me—banned a translation that was planned there.

That it is very hot you probably know from feeling it yourself. Otherwise tranquillity and great inertia.

Greetings to you and your wife.

Cordially,
Freud

1. The date is written on the envelope.
2. Freud (1927c), trans. W. D. Robson-Scott 1928.

525

23 June 1928
42 York Terrace, Regents Park

Dear Professor,

Though I am late in answering I want to thank you very warmly for your second letter, which helped me very considerably. We are finding our way day by day, but life is unattractive and our pain very bitter to bear. What more is there to say? You know I shall not fail in my duties and work, but will not expect much creative activity from me for some time. My wife struggles on. She is going to Vienna next Monday to visit her mother.

I hope you will have a pleasant holiday and will find energy to write on the interesting theme you mention (young v. old).

Yours always
Ernest Jones.

526

1 July 1928
Semmering

Dear Jones,

We had your[1] dear wife here with us and were very delighted with her visit despite the sad history of the preceding period. She was so cordial, unaffectedly natural. I did not speak to her about her bereavement; on such occasions I feel only my impotence. But I heard that she spoke about it freely with the women and expressed her undiminished grief.

The lateness of spring has afforded us a particularly beautiful time here. We are glad to be up here and are thinking of staying on for the whole of July and August. You will only understand this last remark when I divulge a little secret to you, which, however, should remain a secret.

Pichler's efforts to make a better prosthesis for me caused me much suffering last year, and the result is not very satisfactory. So, in the end, I yielded to pressure from all sides to turn to someone else. This was not easy for me, as it basically means turning away from a man to whom I already owe four years' prolongation of my life. But I could not continue. Last week Prof. Schroeder of Berlin sent his assistant here to examine me, and promised that he would make something better for me in about four weeks. We arranged that I should go to him in Berlin in September, under the pretext of visiting my children there. Discretion, please![2]

Cordially yours,
Freud

1. The first three words, "Wir haben Ihre," are in Gothic script; letter continues in Latin characters.

2. For the role of Hans Pichler in attending to Freud's surgical needs between 1923 and 1938, see Schur (1972, pp. 347ff.), and Pichler's "Surgical Notes," in Jones (1957a, pp. 468–495; 1957b, pp. 497–521). Hermann Schroeder was the director of the Dental Institute at the University of Berlin; for his role in this episode, see Schur (1972, pp. 405–406).

527

19 July 1928
81 Harley Street, London

Dear Professor,

It was kind of you to send me those friendly remarks about my dear wife. The visit to Austria has certainly benefitted her, and given her a little more courage in facing life. She specially enjoyed her visit to you all at the Semmering.

I was glad to hear that you were not resigned to your discomfort and are

determined to make further efforts to diminish it. Surely it is to be pre-
sumed that Pickler [Pichler] would be glad if you can be helped further,
even if not by him. Why shouldn't he be a decent person?

The publishers were very slow in issuing *The Future of an Illusion*, but
you will have seen it before this letter and I hope it will please you. I think
it is the best translated of any of your works. I do not ask you, but if you
feel inclined to send a line to the translator it would be a great event in
his life. I will of course let you know of any interesting reviews of the book.

We are beginning to plan arrangements for the next Congress, which
will be at Oxford. Perhaps the experience of the Berlin journey, and some
good results from it, may yet decide you to favour England.

I am only taking a short holiday, three weeks in Brittany and a couple
of days in the country.

With all good wishes to you

Yours affectionately
Ernest Jones.

528

11 October 1928
Berlin-Tegel
Sanatorium Schloss Tegel

Dear Jones,

You know that I came to Berlin to have a more tolerable prosthesis made
by Prof. Schröder. I do not know yet if it will be successful, but think hope
is justified. I will probably have to stay here until the end of this month.
Anna is with me; I found the most gracious reception at Simmel's Sanatorium.[1] It is half an hour by car from the city center, but beautiful and
quiet, situated in a park a few minutes from Lake Tegel. The weather has
been very good, the treatment quite exhausting. Before I leave for home,
I will write you again as to what I have achieved, if anything.

I enclose a short paper for the *Journal* by my student Ruth Mack-
Brunswick[2] and greet you and your dear wife cordially.

Yours,
Freud

1. Ernst Simmel (1882–1947), influential in setting up the psychoanalytic training
curriculum at the Berlin Psychoanalytic Institute; in 1927 founded the Psychoanalytic
Clinic at Tegel Sanatorium outside Berlin, where Freud stayed periodically to have work
done on his prosthesis; went to Los Angeles in 1934.

2. Ruth Mack-Brunswick, "Eine Beobachtung über die kindliche Theorie des Coitus
a tergo," *Zeitschrift*, 15 (1929): 500–502; translated as "A Note on the Childish Theory
of Coitus a Tergo," *Journal*, 10 (1929): 93–95.

529

15 October 1928
81 Harley Street, London

Dear Professor,

This is only a line to acknowledge the safe receipt of Ruth's manuscript and to thank you for your letter containing what I hope will prove to be very good news of yourself. I intend soon to write to you a long personal letter.

With best wishes,

Yours always,
[Ernest Jones]

530

20 October 1928
81 Harley Street, London

Dear Professor,

First I am glad to hear today from Eitingon that there are good prospects of your getting substantial relief as the result of your visit to Berlin. If good wishes had the power they deserve there would be no doubt of the gratifying result. I shall look forward to hearing good news soon.

I have been asked to write a Biography of you for the *Encyclopaedia Britannica*.[1] If there is time I will send you a copy to correct, but feel I should be competent for even this responsible task. I wonder if you can remember *when* it was that Breuer first told you of Anna O? I assume it must be about 1884. After much correspondence I obtained a confidential copy of the article on ψα for the new edition of the *Encyclopaedia Britannica* and want to be sure it is authorised by you. It is signed by your name, but it has been written by a Prof. Wolf who compiled it from your previous article *(These Eventful Years).*[2] It has no serious mistakes, but the perspective is not good, and it is in several respects not as you would have written it. Will you reassure me that they have your permission to do this.

I am sending you a packet of reviews of *The Future of an Illusion*.[3] There are one or two good ones, but mostly they can be described as stupid though respectful. They will at all events show you that I was right in saying that no one in England would be shocked on religious grounds.

My paper on ψα and Folklore aroused intelligent interest at the Folklore Congress in London last month.[4] The resistance there mainly takes the form of scepticism about any unitary psychological explanations, after their disastrous experiences with Max Müller,[5] solar myths, etc.. It seems to be my destiny to be the first to present ψα to professional audiences. I think this is true in folklore, anthropology, psychology, pedagogy, and perhaps general medicine (though not of neurology or psychiatry).[6]

Coming to more personal matters I think I can tell you that work and time have had a slightly analgesic effect on our minds, perhaps more on mine than on my poor wife's. She is now struggling to take an interest in the study of Norwegian, which certainly seems far enough away; she also took some interest in arranging a new study-sitting-room for herself. But life is very bleak and we manage to get on by sheer repression of the intolerable, not by any sort of philosophic assimilation of it. I ask myself if my extensive experience of grief does not enable me to make any contribution to our understanding of it. I have lost by death my father and mother, three out of my four closest friends, a wife and an only daughter. Of course the last two were in a quite different category from all the others. There cannot be much I do not know about grief on the conscious side, the variety, quality and conditions of its pain, and so on; but the connections with the unconscious are a more obscure matter. Of this too I know more than I can write in a letter, but I will mention one point. You have often raised the question of the extraordinary intensity of the pain in the Trauerarbeit, which you describe as a withdrawal of the Libido. But this withdrawal is not necessarily in itself painful, cf. for instance simply ceasing to be in love with someone. Here the fact that it is sharply against one's will is evidently important and must re-activate castration fears. It seems to me that the Unc. cannot conceive of another person's death except in terms of murder, so that when [one][7] it is demanded of one to "accept" the terrible *fait accompli*, this to the Unc. means being asked to consent to the murder of the loved one. We know in this connection the guilt that often follows death, the searchings of heart, self-reproach and other more indirect consequences of guilt. Perhaps I have been better able to see this now just because my attitude towards my daughter was a purer non-ambivalent love than in any of my other experiences. The two features I have mentioned, castration (thwarting) and murder-guilt are obviously connected in more ways than one.

This leads on to ideas about grief and neurosis, and grief and religion. I find, for instance, that intense grief leads to either more devotion to religion than before or to more repudiation of it (usually the latter).

This letter is long enough. Once again I express the regret that the journey between London and Vienna is so long; I have lost much in life from this simple fact.

With all my good wishes and profound respect

Yours always devotedly
Ernest Jones.

1. Jones (1929f). He also wrote a piece on abnormal psychology for the same edition; see Jones (1929e).

2. "Psychoanalysis: Freudian School," *Encyclopaedia Britannica*, 14th ed. 18:672–674.

3. See Kiell (1988, pp. 712–713) for an extensive list of reviews of Freud (1927c).

4. Jones (1928b).

5. Friedrich Max Müller (1823–1900), German-born British philologist, Oxford professor of modern European languages and comparative philology, and curator of the Bodleian Library; gave up professorial duties in 1875 to edit *Sacred Books of the East* (51 vols.) and to devote himself to comparative mythology and comparative study of religions; extremely influential in Oriental linguistic and mythological scholarship.

6. For example, see Jones (1928b, 1924e, 1915a, 1910f, 1911g).

7. Crossed out in the original.

531

27 October 1928
Tegel

Dear Jones,

You are right in assuming that Breuer's reports of his case date from about 1884.[1] Our relationship began gradually about 1882; in 1885 I went to Paris.

I am very glad to hear that you will write the biographical essay for *Encyclopaedia Britannica*. However, I am very surprised that the editors want to replace my own presentation of ΨA by another, which is to be signed by me, *without my knowing anything about it or having given my consent.* If you could protest on my behalf, I would be very pleased.

I have not yet received the reviews of *Illusion*.

We are traveling to Vienna on the thirty-first. I am bringing with me an improvement, which I hope will ease my performance considerably. However, one cannot speak of an elimination of the complaint, and my speech is "far from perfect."[2] They only promise that it will yet improve. Eitingon's optimism obeys an inner need and is far removed from reality.

If London and Vienna were really closer, I should certainly have asked you several questions about your and your wife's mourning, which a letter cannot accommodate. Renunciation has become a habitual practice with me in the last few years.

Regarding your comment on the mechanism of the Trauerarbeit, I should say that we are not very much at variance. My question was just, why is withdrawal of libido *in mourning* so painful, whereas it succeeds so easily under other circumstances? My answer was that one has to bring recognition of the reality principle to every single point of the libido, and this, in fact, is in agreement with your formulation: against one's own will. I envisaged that, in each individual case, one then has the choice of dying oneself or of acknowledging the death of the loved one, which again comes very close to your expression that one kills this person. I should not like to link guilt feelings with mourning; I believe that this appears only when ambivalence or some hostility was actually present. But here too I have not got the last word or a definitive insight.

Write to me again soon; correspondence is really not to be despised as a means of reducing distance.

Cordial greetings to you and your dear wife.

Yours,
Freud

P.S. I notice only now that I became unfaithful to my resolution not to write to you in Gothic script. Phenomenon of calcification of feelings in old age!!

1. Freud learned of the case of Anna O. on 18 November 1882, which he reported to Martha in a letter dated the following day; see Jones (1953a, p. 226; 1953b, p. 248).
2. In English in the original.

532

4 November 1928
Vienna, IX. Berggasse 19

Dear Jones,

Thanks for the biography.[1] Allow me several trifling comments.

—Substitute "zoology" for "botany."

—(1) I was with Charcot for only ½ year. Charcot had no interest in a psychological study of hysteria.

—"The immediate disproval"[2] must refer to the time after I settled in Vienna.

(2) No longer 3; the French *Revue* and the new Brazilian *Rivista brasileira* have been added.

—Eitingon mentioned not long ago 400 as the number of official adherents (members) of the I.P.V.

(3) A word about my having lived and worked in Vienna as a doctor since [18]86.

—The Spanish collected edition deserves mention.

—Having returned a few days ago, I have hardly settled in again. The new prosthesis is proving to be a big gain, but the remaining discomfort is "zu tragen peinlich" (*Faust* II).[3] It is, incidentally, no means "of rejuvenation";[4] I remain an old man, without the desire for productive work. Let us be content.

I am hoping for plenty of news from you and greet you and your dear wife cordially.

Yours,
Freud

1. Jones (1929f).
2. In English in the original.
3. "Painful to bear"; see Goethe's *Faust,* pt. 2, l. 11,955.
4. In English in original.

533

12 December 1928
81 Harley Street, London

Dear Professor,

It was very happy news to hear from you—and since then from Anna and from Roheim—that you received considerable benefit from your visit to Berlin and that you have regained something of your former spirits. I wonder what you are writing? You spoke some time ago of the contrast between youth and age; will that be the theme? Incidentally I wonder to which I belong, for on the first of the next month I shall be fifty years old. I suppose that seems young to you, but it is old enough when I think of how much work I still wish to accomplish. I feel in many ways young enough still, but my rheumatic body tells me the truth. The chief difference I see in growing years is in regard to hope for the future—or rather expectation; one expects less and less.

You asked me for personal news, so I will run on. The pain about our daughter is less sharp—through pure repression rather than through philosophy, though the regret and longing is still dominating in life. The effect of the tragedy on my wife's psychology has been very unfortunate, and this in its turn reacts somewhat on me. So there is little happiness to report. Work helps somewhat, but physical limits give me no chance to react via productivity. Ten patients a day, with four control analyses, the *Journal,* Society, Institute and endless committee meetings leave neither time nor energy over.

My son finished his analysis today (18 working months) and the results have exceeded even my expectations. It is appropriate that he should be the first young child to be analysed in England.[1]

I was glad you found I had made some contribution to the difficult grief problem. Of course, as you say, it is in full harmony with your previous conclusions. I wonder why you feel there is some other unknown factor besides the guilt? You say that if I were in Vienna you would like to ask me some questions about my personal experiences. Perhaps you could do it by letter, for any gain to be got from my suffering could only lessen it.

I regret that the *Rundbrief* circulation has again mysteriously stopped, for private letters do not entirely replace it. I am in active communication with Eitingon and van Ophuijsen, but have not heard from Ferenczi for a long time.

An associate member here, Dr. Warburton Brown,[2] died this week from exhaustion following pneumonia.

Groddeck is here lecturing and does not make a good impression on the sober English.[3] He has very little knowledge of ψα and it is a pity he was admitted to the movement, for he certainly does it more harm that [than] good. It is plain to us that his philosophical *id* is little else than an introjected God.[4]

Though I have written *two* letters of polite protest to the Editor of the *Encyclopaedia Britannica* (about your contribution) he has not deigned to reply, which looks like a bad conscience. Do you think I should write a third time or will you write yourself? Thank you for the corrections to my bibliographical notice,[5] which I will insert when I get the proofs. The Spanish translation is not mentioned because they wanted references only to the original and to English translations. I was in doubt about the number of trained specialists, for certainly not all members of the I.ψα.V. can be so called.

I wonder what you thought of the *Future of an Illusion* reviews? They are mostly stupid, but at least they will dispel your idea that the English would be shocked on religious grounds. They show that the book would have made more impression if you had dissociated your new contribution more distinctly from the "rationalism" of the eighties.

With all good wishes and regards

Yours affectionately
Ernest Jones.

P.S. If it would not be too much trouble, perhaps Anna would be kind enough to return the review cuttings which we should like to keep in our collection.

1. Mervyn Jones's own comments about the analysis indicate that he remembers very little about it; see M. Jones (1987, p. 14).

2. J. Warburton Brown, dental surgeon, captain R.A.M.C. 1914–1919; his single psychoanalytic paper as well as an obituary appear in *Journal*, 10 (1929): 5–28, 102.

3. G. Groddeck, "Remarks on the Embryonal Time in Relation to Later Life," was read before a meeting of the British Psycho-Analytical Society, 5 December 1928, as reported in *Journal*, 10 (1929): 529.

4. Groddeck (1923).

5. The work in question is Jones (1929f), which was a "biographical" piece, not a "bibliographical notice." This is an interesting slip, for Jones made none of the corrections, nor did he insert any of the additional points mentioned by Freud in letter 532.

534

1 January 1929
Vienna, IX. Berggasse 19

Dear Jones,

I am writing to you *on*[1] your fiftieth birthday instead of *for* it, as an enemy of all celebrations and formalities. Since I cannot put the letter off, I am obliged to make excuses for it, because I feel rather weak and incapacitated by influenza (not feverish), and the heightened narcissism of this condition will have been revealed to you through my reverting to Gothic script at the beginning of this letter.

Much that I could have written in reply to your letter must therefore be left unsaid. Not, however, the assurance that I have always counted you as one of my closer family members, and will continue to do so, which indicates—beyond all the discords that are seldom lacking within a family and have also not been lacking between us—a fund of tenderness that one can draw on time and again. I believe it began when I accompanied you once to the train station (in Worcester?). To be sure, I am not in the habit of expressing such affection freely, so that I easily seem indifferent, but my family knows better.

No, I will not write anything about youth and old age. Perhaps I shall not write anything at all, for the ease of conceptualization, which was once characteristic of me, has deserted me in old age and I am intelligent enough not to force myself. I readily acknowledge the great relief in my existence since Berlin, but something in me longs for further amelioration, and I am hopeful I will obtain it soon.

The reviews of *Illusion* have been placed in the archives run by Storfer. If you repeat your wish, you may have them. Your prognosis regarding the reaction in England was certainly right.

With most cordial wishes for your next decade.

Your faithful
Freud

1. The first four words, "Ich schreibe Ihnen *an*," are in Gothic script; letter continues in Latin characters.

535

Dear Professor,

I am writing to ask your opinion on the following proposal. The Professor of Philosophy at Harvard University has asked me to edit, and write an Introduction for, what in America is known as a "source book" of your writings. The idea is that I should go through them all and reduce them, by making suitable omissions, to one-ninth of their present size, a very considerable piece of work as you may imagine. The publishers, Scribner's, will of course deal with the question of copyright and royalty. Before deciding, I should like to have your opinion on the advisability of the proposal. I should say that they have already done this for various of the ancients, e.g. Plato, Schopenhauer, etc. and are now intending to do the same with a few modern great men in the same series.

With my best wishes to you all for the coming New Year,

Yours always,
[Ernest Jones]

536

Dear Jones,

Our letters crossed each other very nicely! I must now quickly answer your inquiry.

The reply will not be easy for me, however. I will not get beyond a pro and contra; fortunately the decision does not rest with me.

Basically, the whole matter is quite distasteful to me as being typically American. You may rest assured that once such a "source-book"[1] is available, no American will ever consult a primary source. But perhaps he will not do that anyway, but continue to draw his knowledge from the murkiest popular sources. So that is in its favor. On the other hand, if you undertake it, it will be a wearisome, laborious task and one not quite worthy of you. After fifty, you should be entitled to direct your energies to more original work. As your friend, I can only dissuade you from it.

The counterargument is that the publisher will certainly not be restrained by your refusal, if he imagines to have found something profitable for himself. He will give the job to someone else, and God knows what he will do with it. Quite certainly he will not do it as well as you.

These are the opposing considerations. A voice rises above them saying that it is actually quite irrelevant for the course of the world whether the Americans get a good or bad source-book of my work.

I think I was honest. And I shall not be offended to hear that you have declined the proposition.

Most cordially yours,
Freud

1. In English in the original.

537

21 January 1929
42 York Terrace, Regents Park

Dear Professor,

You may be sure I would have written earlier to thank you for your two letters, but it has required all my energy to cope with the immediate exigencies of life. Things are now going better, I am glad to say. My wife's pneumonia proved to be a mild one and she is already out of bed. I have been ill and sleepless from pain, but am beginning to recover; since Christmas I have not been able to walk farther than the front door. But it will soon all be a thing of the past.

Your letter gave me the greatest possible pleasure and I thank you for it with all my heart. It will always be kept as a treasured memento of what has made my life most worth living, my relationship to you and your work. Yes, I remember well the talk at Worcester Station, exactly what you said and what I replied. Shall I ever write an autobiography,[1] I wonder? I could relate many interesting things.

Your most characteristic answer about the American "stunt" amused me greatly, it was like a gem. Your arguments were so much what I had expected that I asked myself why I had bothered you about it [at] all. I suppose I was more loth than you to have it done badly, was impelled to accept it for that reason, but feared you would disapprove of my doing so. I have written a non-committal reply, pointing out the difficulties in the way (also of the unequal translations, etc.) and will see what happens next.

In the meantime another American wants me to describe the pure psychology of $\psi\alpha$ in 10,000 words for a volume called "Psychologies of 1930"—a successor to "Psychologies of 1925." They are a queer busy people. No wonder they never do anything. I am trying to get Flugel to do this instead.[2]

The British Medical Association is drawing up its report[3] (to be ready by April) and it is giving me the greatest anxiety. It means fighting step by step against an invincible opposition.

I hope to see you in June, dear Professor, either in Vienna or Semmering, and shall greatly look forward to this.

With all my most grateful thanks and best wishes

Yours always loyally and affectionately
Ernest Jones.

1. Jones (1959) was published posthumously.
2. J. C. Flügel, "Psychanalysis: Its Status and Promise," in *Psychologies of 1930*, ed. Carl Murchison (Worcester, Mass.: Clark University Press, 1930), pp. 374–394, was included in pt. 11, "Analytical Psychologies," which also contained pieces by Pierre Janet and Alfred Adler. The rest of the volume included a distinguished list of contributors such as William McDougall, Edwin G. Boring, Wolfgang Köhler, I. P. Pavlov, and John Dewey, among others. The second volume referred to by Jones is *Psychologies of 1925*, ed. Carl Murchison (Worcester, Mass.: Clark University Press, 1928).
3. British Medical Association (1929).

538

28 May 1929
81 Harley Street, London

Dear Professor,

At last, after a long interval, I take up my pen to write to you. I had fixed in my mind to do so as soon as the British Medical Association Committee should come to an end, so that I could report on its results. But this has been adjourned again and again and my expectations repeatedly disappointed until yesterday. I will say no more on this subject because I am circulating an official statement on it which should reach Anna the day after this letter.

At all events I contributed to the peace I know you like on your birthday. We celebrated it here and I hope it passed off as satisfactorily as we all wished from this distance.

The past months since Christmas have been among the hardest in my life. The record is soon told. Private sorrow from the year before, a very painful illness, two attacks of influenza, a basis of ten analyses daily which I have not missed once, endless Society business and committee meetings, two scientific papers, one for the Royal Society of Medicine here, the other (in French) for the Sorbonne last month,[1] a week on the Riviera, and above all the harrassing anxiety and almost daily labour of the B. M. A. Committee which has at last met with as much success as could be expected in the circumstances.

We leave here on June 15, motoring to Vienna, and are looking forward to the pleasure of seeing you in Berchtesgaden a few days after that date. I am eagerly looking forward to this and to having a good talk with you.

With all my kindest regards

Yours always devotedly
Ernest Jones.

1. Jones (1929a, 1929b).

539

2 June 1929
Vienna, IX. Berggasse 19

Dear Jones,

I am very sorry to hear how much hard work is behind you, and I know that you are not exaggerating. You will not be surprised to read shortly that I have also pointed out publicly your extraordinary capacity for work and how indebted we are to you. But at least you have achieved something, and section V of the report that you sent Anna is easily recognizable as your work, with its precision and correctness.[1]

On 15 June I shall finish my work in Vienna and on the seventeenth or eighteenth we should arrive in Berchtesgaden. I will therefore see you and your dear wife there soon after our arrival, and if our house should not yet be in order and I cannot show you proper hospitality, this will not affect the warmth of the welcome. Naturally I am also very eager to discuss many things with you, particularly your siding with the Americans in the lay question, which, considering your other views, I do not understand, and which seems to me very dangerous for the survival of our I.P.V. I hope to convince you.

To an early reunion!

Most cordially yours,
Freud

1. British Medical Association (1929, p. 263).

540

7 June 1929
81 Harley Street, London

Dear Professor,

Thank you very deeply for your kind letter. Mrs. Riviere had hinted to me that you had written some personal words for my Festheft,[1] but I felt it more seemly to restrain my curiosity, as I have done in the whole affair. When I read it my gratification will doubtless be all the greater.

I shall certainly look forward to your attempt to convince me about the Americans. At present I am under the impression of being one of the few people with an open mind on the subject, so let us put it to the test.

We shall get to Berchtesgaden in the late afternoon of either the 22nd or 23rd, but I will telegraph to Anna from about Kitzbühel as she has kindly promised to book a room for us. We are very disappointed that she cannot visit us at Elsted after the Congress.

Looking forward to the pleasure of seeing you soon,

Yours always devotedly
Ernest Jones.

1. Freud (1929a).

541

4 August 1929
Berchtesgaden

Dear Jones,

I am extremely happy that the Congress proceeded in such a conciliatory fashion and that the New Yorkers reached a clear rapprochement with our standpoint. You remember my apprehensions and my determination in case of a different outcome. The credit for allaying this danger is certainly due to you and Brill.[1] I have already thanked him and now thank you too. You also surely admit now that we shall not lose America if we insist on the recognition of lay analysis. It was a case where conquering the external world seemed more justified than adapting to it.

Anna also reported to me how much effort the English group put into the Congress, and how amiably the guests were received.

With cordial wishes for your and your dear wife's remaining summer.

Yours,
Freud

1. At the Eleventh Congress of the International Psychoanalytic Association, Oxford, 28 July 1929, Brill had agreed to modify the New York society's previous unyielding position on lay analysis. Freud, earlier in the year, had put forward the recommendation to the Secret Committee that a separation between the American and European societies be enacted if no arrangement could be made to allow non—medically trained psychoanalysts to practice in America. See Jones (1957a, pp. 298–299; 1957b, pp. 320–321).

542

20 August 1929
81 Harley Street, London

Dear Professor,

Thank you most cordially for your warm and kind letter, which gave me great pleasure. I need hardly say that I also was very happy at the smooth [progr][1] course of the Congress and share your pleasure at it. I am hopeful about the future, though I recognise that Brill will have a hard fight in New York and that we must not be disappointed if his success is not immediate. I am sure, from various indications, that we cannot rely on Oberndorf in the matter, but I should judge that his influence is very limited.

One sentence in your letter tells me that you have not yet understood my attitude. You write: Sie geben jetzt gewiss zu, dass wir Amerika nicht verlieren, wenn wir auf der Anerkennung der Laienanalyse bestehen.[2] This I have never doubted, provided only that we changed our tactics. My pessimism arose from the alternate ignoring and berating of the Americans, giving them so much reason to complain. Once I induced Eitingon and the others to treat them more humanly, to approach them personally and to treat them friend[l]ily, I was entirely hopeful that we should succeed. I kept writing the strongest letters to Brill in particular, for he is always easy to manage when one can get him face to face. This time he behaved really splendidly in every way and he deserves every praise.

Anna doubtless gave you a full account of the Congress, also of the special efforts the British Society made in its organization, but I am sure she did not relate one interesting item, namely that her Vortrag[3] was certainly the most interesting and the most applauded of all; everyone was full of admiration for her gifts.

A woman, Dr. Wilson, American but of English extraction, has applied for membership of our Society, saying she was analysed by you in 1920 and has recently done control analyses with Anna. What are we to do about her? She does not want to practise in England.

I have been back at work for a week. My wife joins me in wishing you all an enjoyable time in your delightful *Erdenwinkel* [corner of the earth].

Yours always
Ernest Jones.

1. Crossed out in the original.
2. See letter 541, the sentence beginning "You also surely admit . . ."
3. A. Freud (1929).

543

25 August 1929
Berchtesgaden

Dear Jones,

Thanks for your good letter. I hasten to let you know that neither Anna nor I can recall ever having analyzed or controlled one female Dr. Wilson. You may doubt the reliability of my memory although its weakness would not show first on matters of analysis, but Anna's is unimpeachable and she is quite sure of not knowing such a person. So it may be a fraud, a mistake, or we did meet her under another name.

Middle of September we (Anna and I) leave again for Berlin; if it is possible we will stay at Tegel like the other times. But the situation of the Sanatorium seems to be endangered by debts. It may have collapsed at the time. I expect to pass 3–6 weeks at Berlin.

My booklet *"Das Unglück in der Kultur"* (or so) is now finished, not yet ripe for print. Will your press claim it for a translation?[1]

With kind wishes for you and your wife

affectionately yours
Freud

1. Freud (1930a), trans. J. Riviere 1930.

544

International Psycho-Analytical Association

27 August 1929
London

Dear Professor,

I was thrilled to hear about your new booklet and of course wish to enter at once a claim for the translation.

What you say about Dr. Wilson surprised me and gives a very puzzling problem. I saw her recently (before getting your letter) and had a definite impression of an honest person. She is a woman of sixty-eight and quite an interesting personality. She said she had been analysed by you for four or five months in 1920 and had worked with Anna, I think in January or February of this year. It is true that Americans sometimes regard two or three conversations as constituting "working with", or even "conducting a control analysis", but I was puzzled that Anna could not remember meeting her at all.

I did not gather from Simmel and Spitz[1] at the Congress that the situation at Tegel was so hopeless or desperate as you evidently think, and I hope it may still be saved.

London is proving quite tolerable in August, but I am alone here and am looking forward to the return of my colleagues within the next week or two. Dr. McCord is coming to London at the end of next week and I shall be pleased to see him.

With my kindest regards,

Yours always,
Ernest Jones.

1. René A. Spitz (1887–1974), born Vienna, M.D. 1910 Budapest; in analysis with Freud 1911; became a prominent psychoanalyst and developmental psychologist; member of the Vienna Psychoanalytic Society; would soon join the German Psychoanalytic Society in Berlin, then depart for Paris in 1932.

545

[30 September 1929][1]
Berlin-Tegel

Dear Jones,

I also believe we would be doing the right thing if we tried to preserve this instrument for our movement and made it available for future work. Even if at some future point I can stay no longer as a guest in Dr. Simmel's villa, the house will still be valuable for other analysts. Therefore join in the relief work.

Cordially yours,
Freud

1. This note is the postscript to a letter from Ernst Simmel to Jones, 30 September 1929, regarding the precarious state of Simmel's psychoanalytic clinic at Tegel Sanatorium outside Berlin. The clinic had opened in April 1927, was in a state of bankruptcy between 15 September and 20 October 1929, and finally closed down at the end of August 1931; see Brecht et al. (1985, pp. 46–49). In Jones (1957a, p. 129; 1957b, p. 136) the date of the clinic's opening is given incorrectly as November 1926.

546

14 October 1929
81 Harley Street, London

Dear Professor,

I hope that your visit to Berlin proved as successful as possible and that you return to Vienna with both that benefit and the recuperation of the holiday.

I am engaged on the arrangements for carrying out your kind offer that your latest book[1] should appear in the official International Psycho-Analytical Library. (How proud I should be if all your works were in it!) I learn from Mr. Woolf that there is danger of a hitch with the Verlag in regard to the rights and I am writing to remind you that appearance in our Library series includes both the American and the British rights. I need not go over again the reasons I gave you some time ago why this has to be so. You will remember that it was your not realising the necessity for the two rights being combined that led to the Anglo-Saxon world being condemned to a bad American translation of *"Hemmung, Symptom und Angst"*,[2] for we were thus prevented from making an English translation. I am writing by this post to Storfer to make sure that there is no misunderstanding.

I got your note attached to Simmel's circular letter about Schloss-Tegel and was glad to see that there was some chance of saving it. I have already written to Simmel giving him two suggestions for making his appeal more effective in non-German countries and you may be sure I will do anything I can to help the matter.

As I wrote to Anna some time ago, I am probably accepting an invitation to go to New York to give an address on the occasion of the opening of the new Psychiatric Institute there.[3] I think the occasion is important enough to warrant the great sacrifice this involves and I shall, of course, take the opportunity to help Brill in his campaign with the New York group. You will be glad, by the way, to know that I had this week a favourable letter from him.

We are busy here revolutionising the relation between the Society, Institute and Clinic. Everything goes smoothly except for Rickman who, being in the middle of his analysis with Ferenczi, is naturally in a very difficult and ambivalent mood. We have at all events succeeded in passing rules admitting all lay members to work at the Clinic, whether on the permanent staff (in the case of full members of the Society) or as assistants (candidates, etc.). There is no doubt that this signifies an important step in the consolidation of the new profession of psycho-analysis.

With my kindest regards,

Yours always,
Ernest Jones.

1. Freud (1930a).

2. Freud (1926d), trans. supervised by L. Pierce Clark, preface by S. Ferenczi (Stamford, Conn.: Psychoanalytic Institute, 1927).

3. Jones spent only three days in New York and delivered a paper (Jones, 1929d).

547

19 October 1929
Tegel

Dear Jones,

I am still here, but hope to be able to leave in the course of next week with a fairly big improvement of the prosthesis. I have read your comments in reply to Simmel's letter and found them very reasonable.

I do not know why there should be difficulties with the Verlag on account of the translation of the new *Unbehagen in der Kultur*.[1] I regarded the matter as settled since your last explanation about the English rights. We have long given up expecting mountains of gold from translations in America.

Your trip to New York after such a long absence will certainly be very interesting for you and important for us. Your support of Brill in the fight against all the American medical quarter-, eighth- and sixteenth-analysts will make an impression. It is again an instance where "resistance"[2] is more necessary than "adaptation,"[3] which is the only thing they esteem there.

The periodic distinctions between holidays and work-time are already disappearing for me behind the slow and steadily declining curve of life. I think I am entitled to a rest.

When do you leave for New York?

With cordial greetings to you and your dear wife.

Yours,
Freud

1. Freud (1930a).
2. In English in the original.
3. In English in the original.

548

1 January 1930
81 Harley Street, London

Dear Professor,

Thank you very much for the copy of your latest book, with its kind inscription.[1]

I had read it last week in Mrs. Riviere's proofs and was on the point of writing to you to congrarulate [congratulate] you on it. There is so much that one could say that I hardly know where to begin. Of course I was delighted with all the part concerning civilisation, and instructed by the more technical part on the theory of guilt. I fully accept what you say about the [specifically]² close relationship between this and hostility and indeed have been teaching that for some time, though I do not think I have formulated it so sharply in any writing. My only difference with your views still remains my uncertainty about the Todestrieb. My difficulty does not come from either of the two kinds of resistance you indicated. Both psycho-analysis and life have shown me amply the amount of hostility in human nature and I should certainly have stated this to be, as you have done, the essential obstacle to civilisation. Nor does it arise from any preference for the idea of bipolarity in love for I have no special preference for bipolar views in general in comparison with pluralistic ones. I fully agree with your philosophical conclusions on the levelling of energy in the earlier part of the *"Jenseits"*, but felt that you took a jump when you identified these principles with the clinical observations of aggressivity and death wishes in the psycho-analytical realm. I still do not see why one cannot regard the function of these latter as being to remove the obstacles to pleasure, in which case they would come under the heading of what are called "reactive" instincts. This is the view I tried to represent in my Congress paper.³ At the moment I feel, by the way, that this paper is my best effort and I hope that it may have carried the problem of anxiety a step further, though I am doubtful of your agreement on the point. If you can afford the time I should be very grateful for your opinion about it, especially over points with which you may not agree.

We are having a considerable discussion about the English title of *"Das Unbehagen"* and should be glad if you have any suggestions to offer. The old English word "dis-ease" would be admirable for it, but for obvious reasons is no longer possible. There is a rare word in English, "unease". I have also suggested "malaise", though I do not greatly like it. "Discomfort" seems to be hardly strong enough: "discontent" seems too conscious.

I hope you had a pleasant Christmas time and also hope that you were able to cheer up poor Eitingon on his visit to you. I am sending you no personal news because they are all contained in the recent *Rundbrief*.

With all kind wishes and regards,

Ernest Jones.

1. Jones's copy of Freud (1930a), located in the library of the British Psycho-Analytical Society, London, contains the following inscription by Freud: "Seinem Lieben—Ernest Jones der Verf[asser]" (literally, "For his dear—Ernest Jones the author"). In Jones (1955a, p. 148; 1955b, p. 158) the inscription is reported incorrectly as "Meinem Lieben [for my dear]—Ernest Jones."

2. This word, which is typed, appears to have been inserted at a later rereading.

3. Jones (1929c).

549

26 January 1930
Vienna, IX. Berggasse 19

Dear Jones,

At last a day when I can give you my long-postponed reply. I just finished a letter to Brill, in which I apologized in full for the same neglect by mentioning everything I have had to do these last few weeks. For you I add further the admission of my growing love for idleness.

Your paper "Fear, Guilt and Hate"[1] I have read; incidentally, a second time for this letter. I agree with your assessment. I cannot see that it takes the concept of anxiety beyond my viewpoint in *"Hemmung, Symptom und Angst,"* but I find the description of the three "layers"[2] and the emphasis on the regressive nature of the last formation very pertinent and instructive. As a whole, and in individual points, I see a far-reaching correspondence of our views on these difficult questions. In the phenomena of traumatic primal anxiety, I should like to distinguish an automatic, that is, economically enforced reaction which—as with everything—later finds an appropriate application. To be sure, this paper of yours does not touch on the problem of the aggressive or death drive. The details proposed in your letter seem to me inadequate. I can no longer manage without assuming this basic drive, either psychologically or biologically, and I think one need not give up hope that you will yet find the way to it.

Of course all the factual news in your *Rundbrief* interested me very much. You know that Anna declined the pressing invitation to attend the Congress for Mental Hygiene in May; she did so without my direct influence, but I believe she did the right thing. Her time will come later, when everything is more favorable. I have no confidence in Fr. Williams, who is a student of Rank's, and in my reply to his letter, which emphasized the invitation to Anna, I even told him so point-blank.

It pleased me very much that you are in broad agreement with the *Unbehagen.* To be sure, it is also drawn from a shared source; as you are an expert on my writings (cf. the introduction *"Collected Papers"*), the singular character of this latest one will not have escaped you. It is an expansive, actually dilettantish foundation (as it deals with nothing exhaustively), from which a finely tapered analytic examination arises. But one notices that sort of thing only when it is finished and can no longer be changed.

I will not rack my brains over the translation of the title, which is certainly difficult. Incidentally, I have already received two offers for

American editions, which I referred to Hogarth Press in accordance with my contract.

With cordial greetings to you and your dear wife.

Yours,
Freud

P.S. I suppose you cannot suppress the advertisements for books by Jung and Adler that were inserted in our *Journal?*

1. Jones (1929c).
2. In English in the original.

550

International Psycho-Analytical Association

5 April 1930
London

Dear Professor,

I would have written earlier to thank you for your very interesting and welcome letter of a month or so ago but for my painful illness. As it is, this will serve as a birthday letter to you, for you know I have the practice of not burdening your budget on the day itself, though I shall certainly think of you when that day comes round. I hope you will receive the expected help from your coming visit to Berlin and that it will be even greater than before.

I have just finished going through the translation of *"Das Unbehagen"* and enjoyed the book more than ever. Mrs. Riviere found a good deal of difficulty in the second part of it, which therefore is not so fluently done as the first part, but you may be sure that at least the accuracy can be guaranteed.

A propos of the book, the editors of an encyclopaedic work entitled *"Sex in Civilization"* will no longer be able to write, as they did, of your work: "Despite the magnificent sweep of this entire approach, and the brave adventurousness embodied in its challenge, it has seldom, in a deep sense, risen beyond the pathology of the individual".[1]

By the way, are you familiar with Edward Carpenter's *"Civilisation, its Cause and Cure"?*[2] I enclose a couple of quotations on the subject of dreams from a book called *"The Terrors of the Night"* written by Thomas Nashe in 1594.[3]

I got this week a very human document from a man who has just emerged from a convict prison in England. It might be entitled "Psycho-Analysis under Difficulties". One of the other persons was an amateur analyst who worked through the material of dreams, free association, etc. which my correspondent wrote in his cell the night before. Ultimately the matter was discovered and the authorities were so puzzled with the meaningless flow of associations that they were inclined to call in a doctor to inquire into the man's mental condition when, to their relief, they detected a number of obscene words scattered through the material and so decided that he was not insane but wicked. He had to pass several days on bread and water as expiation for this scientific adventure.

A Japanese by the name of Yabe,[4] of whom you may have heard, has founded a very promising Society in Japan and has been entrusted by the Japanese Government with the mission of spending two or three months in Europe investigating generally the subject of psycho-analysis. He has been working with Glover and myself privately in London and I find him an exceptionally intelligent and well-informed man, most trustworthy in every way. His attitude is throughout sound and understanding and he has an astonishing knowledge of the work. He proposes on his return to Japan to send us two or three of the younger members to go through the thorough training. He himself is Psychologist to the Government Railways of Japan, having resigned a University position there in Experimental Psychology. He speaks English fairly well, but has not much German or French. He is, of course, very eager to meet you on his return and I wish to commend him strongly to you. He will probably be in Berlin when you are there, otherwise he had of course, planned to go to Vienna.

Strachey read a very excellent and original paper recently on the "Psycho-Analysis of Reading".[5] Altogether he is proving distinctly the best of the three helpers you sent me some ten years ago.

Now I have given you all the news except that I have reserved the best to the end, namely that my wife expects the appearance of a baby towards the end of this month.

With my kindest regards to yourself and your family, I am,

Yours always affectionately,
Ernest Jones.

1. V. F. Calverton and S. D. Schmalhausen, eds., *Sex in Civilization*, intro. Havelock Ellis (New York: MacCaulay, 1929). The quoted passage is from the editors' preface (p. 8).

2. Edward Carpenter, *Civilisation, Its Cause and Cure, and Other Essays* (New York: C. Scribner's Sons, 1921).

3. During the Toronto years Jones had also sent Freud some passages from Nashe (1594); see note 4 to letter 70 and letter 72.

4. Y. K. Yabe founded the Japanese Psychoanalytic Society in Tokyo.

5. Strachey (1930).

551

9 April 1930
Vienna, IX. Berggasse 19

Dear Jones,

I hasten to reply to your letter.[1] It was very full of content; I was not very happy to hear that you have been ill, but the news with which you end had a refreshing effect on me, aroused all my sympathy. That is the proper way to take revenge on cruel fate, and I hope it will meet with good success. At the end of this month—in other words at the time when your child is expected—I hope to be able to go to Berlin. I will stay again in Tegel with Anna.

Most cordial wishes to you and your dear wife.

Yours,
Freud

1. First sentence is in English.

552

7 May 1930
Tegel

Dear Jones,

The first news that Eitingon gave me on my arrival in Berlin was of the happy birth of your daughter.[1] Like Anna, who is with me, I hasten to express to you both our great joy over this event. May your intention of maintaining your rights against fate now succeed in all other things as well!

Most cordially yours,
Freud

1. Nesta May Jones.

553

[postcard]

8 May 1930
Vienna, IX. Berggasse 19

Dear Jones,

To introduce Dr. Smiley Blanton[1] to you. A nice man, chiefly interested in child's guidance (Vassar College). He had 6 months personal analysis with me, I think he goes home an honest adherer of PsA. He will stay at London only a few days, sailing on May 12th or so.

With affectionate greetings on this occasion,[2]

Freud

1. One of Freud's analysands; see S. Blanton, *Diary of My Analysis with Freud* (New York: Hawthorn, 1971).
2. In German in the original.

554

8 May 1930
81 Harley Street, London

Dear Professor,

My wife and I were both very much moved and pleased at receiving from you such a warm and hearty message of congratulation. Thank you, and also Anna, very much indeed. I am happy to say that the two people most concerned are thriving well. Nesta May is a lusty child and well versed in ψα lore. She promises to play her part with great success.

I heard a rumour (from Yale) that you were confined to a sanatorium in Vienna, but am hoping from your letter and a long telegram from Eitingon—neither of which indicate anything—that this is some misunderstanding. I wrote to E. and hope to have full news from him soon.

With our united thanks, and good wishes for a beneficial visit to Berlin

Yours always affectionately
Ernest Jones.

555

12 May 1930
Tegel

Dear Jones,

In the second half of April my heart, stomach, and bowels failed me so much that I actually went to the Cottage Sanatorium in Vienna. There I soon discovered that I had acquired a total intolerance to cigars, and, by giving up this long-accustomed pleasure, I procured a rapid and extensive improvement, which is lasting. Only my stomach is still not functioning without trouble. Otherwise I feel better than I have for a long time. Waiting for the new prosthesis will probably keep me in Berlin until after the middle of June.

I am pleased that the first news of Nesta May sounds so favorable. In any case, she was received on this planet not quite without sympathy.

Cordially yours,
Freud

556

15 May 1930
81 Harley Street, London

Dear Professor,

I read your personal news with mixed feelings, but the outstanding fact is the gratifying one that the outcome is so satisfactory. It is sad to think of your deprivation from tobacco, for I know how much that means. I suggested to Eitingon that he might be able to procure some de-nicotinised cigars in Berlin and perhaps he has done so. I am trying to find some here, but so far have only come across de-nicotinised cigarettes and am doubtful whether those would prove acceptable.

I saw Dr. Blanton yesterday and had a fair impression of him. No doubt he will be of some positive value to us, but I am still looking forward to the day when some young American will spend three years in Europe deepening his knowledge to the desirable degree. I advised him of course to apply for membership to the New York group.

With renewed wishes for a successful visit to Berlin,

Yours always,
Ernest Jones.

557

19 May 1930
Tegel

Dear Jones,

I think you will answer the enclosed letter better than I, and I therefore pass it on to you. I do not know whether he is the American who will finally meet your ideal requirement of the three years.

Many thanks for being sympathetic about my abstinence. But yesterday I made a shy attempt at my first and, for the time being, only cigar per day.

Is your new guest behaving herself properly?

Cordially yours,
Freud

558

26 May 1930
81 Harley Street, London

Dear Professor,

I have answered the American's letter you enclosed at the same time as an identical one he had addressed to me. I get a number of such enquiries from America but it is seldom that anything further happens.

Yours always
Ernest Jones.

559

3 July 1930
81 Harley Street, London

Dear Professor,

Presumably you are some time back from Berlin where I hope the visit proved very successful in procuring greater comfort for you. I wonder what your summer plans are! Will it be Berchtesgaden again? The baby ties us this year to this country and I shall spend a quiet month in Sussex.

I should like to send you a copy of an interesting book called *"The Story of San Michele"* by Dr. Axel Munthe,[1] but as I think it very likely that you already have it I should ask you first. The description of life in Paris under Charcot would be particularly interesting to you, and altogether the author's personality is one of unusual interest. So far as I can estimate he seems to have been about two years after you in Paris.

We are all well here, the baby in particular. The session of the Society is drawing to a successful close.

With kindest regards to you all,

Yours always,
Ernest Jones.

1. *The Story of San Michele* (London: J. Murray, 1929), by Axel M. F. Munthe (1857–1949), Swedish physician and writer, practiced in Paris and Rome.

560

13 August 1930
Grundlsee, Rebenburg

Dear Jones,

I gather with pleasure from a letter by McCord that you had invited him to write a review for the *Journal* of the splendid book by Healy.[1] He enclosed a copy of it for me, and I ask you, if you make any alterations, not "to take off the edges."[2] Healy is a wicked liar and deserves to be kicked.[3]

We are staying in unusually beautiful surroundings and in a comfortable house, but it rains, rains "every day,"[4] not only in Grundlsee, by the way.

I hope you and your family, which is now complete again, are benefiting from the rustic solitude in which I assume you to be.

With cordial greetings.

Yours,
Freud

1. C. P. McCord, review of W. Healy, A. Bronner, and A. M. Bowers, *The Structure and Meaning of Psychoanalysis* (1930), *Journal*, 11 (1930): 500–510.
2. In English in the original.
3. William Healy (1869–1963), American psychiatrist. For the exchange of letters between Freud, Jones, and Healy regarding Healy's book, see George E. Gifford, Jr., ed., *Psychoanalysis, Psychotherapy, and the New England Medical Scene, 1894–1944* (New York: Science History Publications, 1978), pp. 265–269.
4. In English in the original.

561

26 August 1930
The Plat, Elsted

Dear Professor,

I was glad to see your handwriting. Only yesterday I heard from Eitingon the excellent news of the Goethe Prize, at which I was greatly joyed. Best congratulations, and may it give a stimulus to the lagging Swedes!

I was not so enthusiastic about MacCord's [McCord's] review of Healy as you are. Of course I share your opinion about the gentleman, but it should be possible to put him in his place without betraying so much lack of personal self-control. I shall have to edit MacCord, in his own interest, but will of course bear in mind your instructions.

I hope your long stay in Berlin was well worth while. Last month I acquired a dental 'prothese' and the minor discomforts and re-adjustments connected with it helped me to realise more fully how much you must have been plagued in these last years.

You do not appear to have got a letter from me, early in July, in which I asked if you had already got a fascinating book by Axel Menthe ('San Michele'). I presume you have, but if not I should like to send you a copy.

With the exception of a few days in Wales my holidays have been spent in Sussex, where a wonderful rose-garden and a very charming new baby have been the chief sources of interest to us. I say 'have been', for alas I return to work at the end of this week. The holidays were also broken by the Congress for Sex Research in London. It was composed almost entirely of biologists, who had to listen to an hour's address from me on ψα and Biology[1] and to hear how they had overlooked the greatest advance in their subject since 1859.[2] The Laforgues, who were there, stayed with us in Elsted afterwards. I like them greatly. My next work is on the ψα of Chess,[3] a game which has always occupied me.

With warmest greetings to yourself and your family

Yours always affectionately
Ernest Jones.

1. Jones (1930a).
2. That is, since Darwin's *Origin of Species*.
3. Jones (1931a).

562

30 August 1930
Grundlsee

Dear Jones,

I fully agree with you concerning McCord's review, and also hoped that you would revise it. If you refer to my letter, I only asked you not to tone the review down; I did not have a single word of praise for it.

The Goethe Prize caused much uproar in Germany. Anna represented me in Frankfurt,[1] tells me that the ceremony was very dignified, and that the people there express respect and sympathy for analysis. I do not think that this surprising episode will have further consequences, either for the Nobel Prize or for the general attitude toward analysis in Germany. On the contrary, I would not be surprised if, after this unexpected letdown, the resistance thrust forward with renewed force.

I read the book by Axel Munthe in Tegel; it seemed to me to be fiction and truth, the first component having the higher percentage. I did not hear his name in Paris (1885/6, which proves nothing; Charcot died in 1894).

I am sorry that you too are bothered with prostheses, but I would not want to allow comparisons, for your sake.

If possible I should like to extend our stay here into September. It is very nice and (not yet?) too hot. The Laforgues are supposed to be coming today.

Cordially to you and all yours.

Freud

1. Freud's address in acceptance of the prize was read by Anna Freud on 28 August (Freud, 1930e).

563

10 September 1930
81 Harley Street, London

Dear Professor,

The sad news is in tonight's paper and I hasten to express to you my deep sympathy. You have had experience in bearing the blows death can deal, but this one must have a peculiar poignancy of its own.[1] How clearly I can picture seeing her a year ago as she sat enjoying the news of her son. I will tell you something that probably you never heard. When we were discussing your operation in S. Cristoforo the question came up of what to do in the event of your refusing to undergo it. Someone, I think it was Eitingon, asserted that the final and most potent appeal that could be made to you was "for your mother's sake".[2] To our relief, however, you acted without hesitation.

You have many who feel for you in this moment, but not many who do so more warmly than

Your affectionate friend and pupil
Ernest Jones.

1. In the biography of Freud the death of Freud's mother, Amalie, is reported as having taken place on 12 September; see Jones (1957a, p. 152; 1957b, p. 162).
2. In Jones (1957a, p. 93; 1957b, p. 98) the version put forward is that it was Rank's idea, not Eitingon's.

564

15 September 1930
Grundlsee

Dear Jones,

Many thanks for your condolences on the death of my mother. However, I will not hide from you that my reaction to this event, as a result of special circumstances, has also been a particular one. To be sure, "there is no saying"[1] what such an experience may cause at deeper levels; on the surface, however, I feel only two things: the increase in personal freedom I acquired, for it was always a forbidding thought to me that she should experience my death; and second, the satisfaction that she obtained at last the deliverance to which she had earned a right after such a long life. Otherwise no mourning, as is displayed so painfully by my brother,[2] who is ten years younger than I. I was not at the funeral; again, Anna represented me, as in Frankfurt. Her importance to me can hardly be increased.

You may have heard, or read yourself, that foreign newspapers are print-ing alarming reports on my state of health. I believe they result from the Goethe Prize, which the hostile public cannot accept without a show of resistance. So they are swiftly killing me off. Well, they will be right eventually. Such predictions do come true. For the time being, I can still warmly thank all those who are dear to me.

Yours,
Freud

1. In English in the original.
2. Alexander Freud (1866–1943).

565

18 November 1930
Vienna, IX. Berggasse 19

Dear Jones,
You have heard of my illness, a bronchopneumonia occurring after an insignificant operation in the region of the scar. I am now myself again, though not much stronger than before.

The motive of this letter was given me by the receipt of N. 4 of your *Journal* whose contents left to me a pleasant impression of the standard arrived at. But at the same time I noted that I did not possess No. 3 nor the four supplements mentioned in the advertisements. The number I may have lost in the transports to and from Grundlsee. I am rather sure I never got the supplements. I hope you will remedy this defect, it makes no difference, whether you make me pay for them or think they are due to me.

I hope your wife and children are allright, it is long since I had direct information from you.

Affectionately yours
Freud

566

20 November 1930
81 Harley Street, London

Dear Professor,
I had written to Eitingon and Anna to get news of your health, but without success, so it was a shock to hear from your letter that you had had such an unpleasant experience as broncho-pneumonia. It tests the

strength of the heart, and it is gratifying to see from the tone of your letter [that you]¹ how successfully you have overcome the strain.

Your kind remark about the *Journal* is encouraging and I will transmit it to Mrs. Riviere who is always in despair at what she calls our low achievements (the *Zeitschrift* she thinks has sunk to hopeless depths!). The missing numbers will at once be forwarded to you (of course at our expense). I think you will find that each of the supplements represents some very solid work.

Things are proceeding here quietly and satisfactorily. We have sixteen candidates in training—as many as our small numbers can manage—and some of them are of very good quality. We do not make much outside propaganda. This week I read at the Society a paper on the ψα of Chess, which I will send to *Imago*.² Tomorrow I am lecturing at Oxford on ψα and Religion,³ and want to write a book on this. At present I am engaged on a book 'On the Nightmare', about twice the size of my old *Alptraum*.⁴ I wonder if the Deuticke 'Schriften' series has come to an end? Perhaps it has been replaced by the 'Imago Bücher'. Because one section in my book— a ψαal study on etymology—entitled 'Die Mahre und die Mähre' might make a suitable number for such a series.⁵ The Verlag is considering a book by my wife 'Gesprächbuch für Psychoanalytiker'⁶ which should be useful for furthering communication between German and English speaking analysts. She is very well and extraordinarily happy with the new baby, who is a huge success—healthy, sweet-dispositioned and intelligent. I enclose a few photos taken in August by Mme. Laforgue.

With all good wishes for continued recovery in strength and with my kindest regards to you and your family

Yours always affectionately
Ernest Jones.

1. Crossed out in the original.
2. Jones (1931a).
3. Jones (1930b).
4. Jones (1931b, 1912j).
5. See "The Mare and the Mara: A Psycho-Analytical Contribution to Etymology," in Jones (1931b, pp. 241–340).
6. This was not published by the Verlag.

567

25 November 1930
Vienna, IX. Berggasse 19

Only a few words to thank you for promising the missing issues and to say that my family welcomed the photographs with heartfelt delight.

Yours,
Fr.

568

International Psycho-Analytical Association

31 December 1930
London

Dear Professor,

You have probably heard from Eitingon of our meeting in Paris which we both found extremely agreeable. He was in a very clear and active mood and we had not the slightest difficulty in agreeing on every point of discussion. We also had a useful general talk about the progress of the movement, though I was grieved to hear of the amount of friction that apparently exists in the Berlin group. This is doubtless due both to the absence of a leader and to the group being of such heterogeneous sources, so we may hope that both these reasons will pass with time.

My family is very well, but I paid for my visit to Paris by contracting some infection which culminated in a severe otitis, so that most of the holiday was spent in bed. I got the tympanum pierced yesterday so should soon mend now. I wish I could join Eitingon in Nice. The weather in [Nice][1] London for the last month has been too filthy for words and we have rarely seen the sun.

A patient of mine, Mr. Robson-Scott is paying a visit to Vienna and has written to ask me for a letter of introduction to you. I am sending him one, saying at the same time that I do not know whether you are at present receiving visitors; he will probably write to enquire. He has been in analysis for some years and has proved one of the most difficult cases I have ever had to handle. It is a case of obsessional neurosis, with a basis of melancholia, but the main analysis has been a characterological one. He has throughout shown the most implacable hostility I have ever known and this has been coupled with the typical negative therapeutic reaction to progress. Nevertheless I still have confidence of a satisfactory final result. I expect the main object in wishing to see you is to obtain reassurance.

I have no other immediate news except that I saw the Princess and Laforgue in Paris who gave very satisfactory accounts of their activities. With my best wishes to you all for the coming New Year,

Yours always,
Ernest Jones.

1. Crossed out in the original; "London" is handwritten in an otherwise typed letter.

569

4 January 1931
Vienna, IX. Berggasse 19

Dear Jones,

I sincerely regret that you paid for your trip to Paris with otitis, but I may assume from your remark that you are now well again. Your relationship with Eitingon pleased me very much. You, he, and Ferenczi are indeed the crucial individuals in the I.P.V., whose future will depend mainly on unanimity among you.

I hope you will not be annoyed if I do not receive Robson-Scott. I am turning away all visitors, and do not think that because of his bad behavior he deserves to be an exception. Through his visit he probably wants to gather fresh material for difficulties in his analysis.

Despite continuing torments with the prosthesis, my health is not bad; in Berlin and here I have gained a total of $6\frac{1}{2}$ kilos in weight. The pleasure of smoking will always remain restricted.

Recently I received the Japanese translation of *Alltagslebens*,[1] but not from Yabe. I am afraid I caused a slight confusion there.

It is not yet too late to wish you and your reconstructed family all the best for 1931.

Cordially yours,
Freud

1. K. Marui, translation of Freud (1901b) (Tokyo: Ars, 1930).

570

12 January 1931
Vienna, IX. Berggasse 19

Dear Jones,

Just to let you know that I was invited (through D. Forsyth) to give this year's Huxley lecture in London. I was really sorry that I had to decline.[1]

Cordially yours,
Freud

1. See Jones (1957a, p. 155; 1957b, p. 165).

571

15 January 1931
81 Harley Street, London

Dear Professor,

The news of your invitation to give the Huxley Memorial Lecture was in yesterday's papers and was followed to-day in the *'Times'* by the usual rumour about your ill-health which I have contradicted. I can well understand your regret at deciding to refuse the invitation. It happens to be one of my few remaining ambitions to receive a similar invitation myself some day, Huxley having been the chief hero of my youth. As you doubtless know, he was nicknamed "Darwin's bulldog", and you would perhaps agree that my identification with him has not been entirely fruitless.

I am happy to be able to tell you that your wish is being gratified which you expressed in your last letter about the spirit of unity subsisting among the three most active leaders. Ferenczi had been behaving very neurotically in the past few years towards both Eitingon and myself,[1] and all our endeavours to deal with his resistances were in vain. You know it is not my custom to speak to you about such difficulties among colleagues, but rather to attempt to deal with them myself. I mention them now only because there is good hope that they are at an end. They appear to have been mainly due to my action in proposing that Eitingon be confirmed in the Presidentship, which he had been holding in the interim following Abraham's death. I still think it would have been offensive to him to do otherwise and do not at all regret my action, but Ferenczi appears to have felt otherwise. Now, however, I hope that is a matter of the past. I wrote him a letter at Christmas notifying him of our intention to propose him at the next Congress and he has, to my great pleasure, replied with a most friendly letter. Incidentally, he now forgives me for the *"Groll"* [resentment] which he, not I, had been feeling!

I am not sorry that you did not see Mr. Robson-Scott, for probably it would have increased rather than diminished the difficulties of his analysis.

To have translated the *"Alltagsleben"* into Japanese must have been a hard task, but presumably they chose Japanese examples. You may have lost your interest in such things, but I will relate an amusing example that happened last week with one of my patients who had just received her monthly account from me. She mis-read a passage in my book referring to "Freud's extensive researches" as "Freud's expensive researches".

My convalescence is proceeding slowly, which seems to be a characteristic of the infections this year. One ear is still painful and quite deaf, which, as you unfortunately know, does not make analytic work any easier. The rest of the family, I am happy to report, are blooming with health and happiness.

With all good Wishes[2]

Yours always
Ernest Jones.

1. See note 3 to letter 613.
2. This line and the following one are handwritten in an otherwise typed letter.

572

19 January 1931
Vienna, IX. Berggasse 19

Dear Jones,

I enjoyed your letter up to the one point that your recovery is so slow. All is full of *"Grippe"* with us; I myself feel tired and moody but not feverish. My jaw and my plate do not agree with each other.

There is no saying how glad I would be to hear that you have been invited to give the Huxley Lecture. I expect you will be some day, but I do not expect to last so long. At about your present age I was called to Worcester, as you remember. Our analysis has since made some progress in the esteem of the public but not enough.

Affectionately yours
Freud

573

23 January 1931
81 Harley Street, London

Dear Professor,

Thank you very much for your kind letter. I am gradually pulling round again, inspite of some minor complications, but I have a strong wish that London was not so distant from the South of France where it would be very pleasant to spend a week or so at present.

The following anecdote may entertain you. A certain Kronbach, apparently a lecturer at a Hebrew theological college in Cincinnati, has written a book on the psycho-analysis of Judaism and has sent me a few pages of it for me to correct any errors in the account he gives of psycho-analysis itself. From them I should judge that he has a very slender acquaintance, especially of understanding, with the subject, but to my great astonishment the opening sentences of his final chapter are: "The one conclusion [persuasion] to which we are inevitably impelled is that there should be generous financial provision for psychoanalytic research. . . . . . Liberal subventions are needed enabling gifted analysts to devote themselves entirely to investigations along rigidly scientific lines."

That he is a born optimist is shown further by the following quotations: "Who knows but, aided by psychoanalysis, we might reckon more successfully with such problems as Temple attendance, satisfactory devotions and sermons, inspiring religious instruction, Jewish loyalty, social mindedness or whatever else may be the conundrum that the religious worker is expected to solve. . . . . The person who will contribute money for religio-psychoanalytic inquiry will have entered upon the way *par excellence* in which religion can be furthered by money."[1]

Next week I am sending a circular to the members of the International Training Sub-Commission[2] with which I hope you will be in full agreement.

With my kindest regards,

Yours always,
Ernest Jones.

1. See Abraham Cronbach, "The Psychoanalytic Study of Judaism," *Hebrew Union College Annual*, 8–9 (1931–32): 605–740; quoted passages from pp. 728, 728–729, and 731.

2. This committee had been formed during the Eleventh Congress of the International Psychoanalytic Association, Oxford, 27–31 July 1929; see *Journal*, 10 (1929): 525.

574

[postcard]

Easter Sunday [7 April 1931][1]
Scilly Isles

A greeting from the Arthurian land of Lyonnesse, where I am trying to recuperate from the winter's infections. My wife is with me—the children in Sussex.

With best wishes to all of you,

Ernest Jones.

1. Date of postmark.

575

[postcard]

13 April 1931
Vienna

Dear Jones,

With the help of my atlas I shared your pleasure on your Easter trip. With cordial greetings.

Yours,
Freud

576

2 May 1931
81 Harley Street, London

Dear Professor,

I generally send my congratulations a few days before your birthday, so as not to add to the crush on that day. I am not proposing to come in person, chiefly because my rheumatism makes me far less *'beweglich'* [mobile] than in earlier years, when to travel to Vienna [for][1] to spend a day or two there would have been a light matter. Also you have never kept it a secret that ceremonial occasions give you no pleasure and that you much prefer to see friends at informal times; in fact I expressed the hope to Eitingon that no one would accompany him except presumably Ferenczi. We have all taken here special interest in the fact that this is your seventy-fifth birthday and our members wish me unofficially to express to you their congratulations, esteem and good wishes for health and happiness, in all of which you know no one joins more heartily than myself.

My wife and I greatly appreciated your card à propos of our novel holiday in the Scilly Isles, which we enjoyed enormously. Today is the first birthday anniversary of our little daughter. She leaves nothing to be desired in health, development, appearance and—most important of all—in disposition, which tells you that she has brought great joy into our life. Mervyn was first in his class this term, and is in every way promising.

There is no startling news about the society or movement here. The progress is solid and satisfactory in all respects. We are getting older, but younger members are coming on in a gratifying fashion. You will have heard that Roheim contemplates settling in London. I think it would be a wise decision and have told him he would be very welcome.

Please convey our kindest greetings to your family and enjoy yourself [your]² the well-earned esteem and affection that surrounds you and streams to you from all over the world—from nowhere more than

Yours always affectionately
Ernest Jones.

1. Crossed out in the original.
2. Crossed out in the original.

577

2 June 1931
Vienna, IX. Berggasse 19

Dear Jones,

Perhaps you already know that, since you wrote on 2 May for my birthday, I not only turned seventy-five years old, but underwent yet another operation and a slow convalescence, which is still incomplete. I answered a great number of letters, and today, almost at the bottom of the pile, I finally came across your letter, which I am answering belatedly, but gladly.

On the whole, there is actually not much left to say. The fact that my strength is gradually diminishing cannot contradict any expectations.¹ My last illness put an end to the security that I enjoyed for eight years. Everyone generally advises me not to focus on this particular path to leave life. I appreciate the justness of this warning, but can do nothing about it.

Since the Goethe Prize last year the attitude of my contemporaries towards me has changed at least into a somewhat reluctant recognition, just to show how unimportant it actually is. Rather like a tolerable prosthesis which did not want to be an end in itself or the chief purpose of existence.

What I found especially pleasing was the news that your family is thriving so well. Cordial greetings to you and all your family from

Your
Freud

1. The opening words of this sentence in German are interesting: "Dass es allmälich mit mir weniger wird" (literally, "That it gradually becomes less with me").

578

25 October 1931
Vienna, IX. Berggasse 19

Dear Jones,

Your book[1] was a pleasant surprise for me. I will read it thoroughly in my leisure hours and take pleasure in all its viewpoints.

It just so happens that I cited you during the last few weeks; however, in doing so I had to impugn you. For I used my improved health during the summer to write two short papers, which you will read very soon in the *Zeitschrift*.[2] In one of them, on female sexuality, I had to mention that your views diverge from my findings.[3]

I hope things are going well with you and your family.
With cordial greetings.

Yours,
Freud

1. Jones (1931b).
2. Freud (1931a, 1931b).
3. Jones (1927f) is challenged in Freud (1931b, p. 243).

579

15 November 1931
81 Harley Street, London

Dear Professor,

Thank you for your kind words about my book. It was re-written for my personal interest, and I have no idea what impression it will make on others. The third Part was destined originally for the *Schriften zur angewandten Seelenkunde* under the title *Die Mahre und die Mähre: ein psa-etymologische Versuch*.[1] I suppose it is hardly worthwhile publishing it in German now, for I take it that the *Schriften* series is no longer continued?

I am greatly looking forward to your *Zeitschrift* papers, which are presumably clinical. Although I have ten patients a day, I find it hard to be sure that any generalisations I make are not based on too narrow material, and that one needs to practise for several centuries to get enough experience! ψα itself as a movement will certainly need that time to make a social impression. The view of the Unconscious at close quarters is so different from any conscious description that one sometimes despairs at being able to convey it to the outer world, so we must wait till the individuals of that world are, one by one, analysed! But I suppose we shall establish gradual contact between the two worlds.

There is no special news of the Society, which means that they are all working satisfactorily and zealously. Rickman has returned, but he does not make the best impression in spite of all Ferenczi's efforts; there must be a very abnormal primary constitution.

My wife and I had hoped to take a short holiday in January in Vienna and Semmering, but the economic crisis, which reverses the old relation between the two shillings, has made such plans uncertain. I am finding the English winters increasingly trying as I grow older, especially in respect of uninterrupted pain from rheumatism. My family is extremely well, and we have the great joy of that very rare phenomenon—a normal infant who enjoys life to the full.

From various sources I have heard that your health is much better than in last spring and I will also hope that your discomfort will get less as the local condition gets better adapted.

With the warmest personal regards

Yours affectionately
Ernest Jones.

1. "The Mare and the Mara: A Psycho-Analytical Contribution to Etymology," in Jones (1931b, pp. 241–340).

580

10 January 1932[1]
81 Harley Street, London

Dear Professor,

Things are quiet these days, and there is little news either here or abroad. Economically things are bad here, and I suppose they are no better on the Continent. I wonder if the Congress will be held this year. I hope so, although we must expect it to have a much smaller attendance than hitherto. I am afraid our hoped-for visit to Vienna in January must be postponed, perhaps till immediately after the Congress, but I am still hoping to break the winter by a fortnight's holiday towards the end of January.

Your stimulating essays in the *Zeitschrift*[2] gave me food for thought during the Christmas interval. The first of them, which one would like to see expanded, will set many people wondering to which type they belong. It would be interesting to study whether there is any correlation between these types and the character types based on pathology, e.g. anxiety, compulsion, etc..

The longer essay will of course occupy me more, as I am specially interested in its problems. As you can imagine, it was a surprise to find that my work and experience in them could be dismissed in a couple of sentences,[3] and I think there must be some misunderstanding between the clitoritic and the phallic phases in your apprehension of what I wrote. It was, however, gratifying to find you laying stress on the prolonged early mother attachment in women with a strong father-fixation (in my experience the same is true in cases, which perhaps you do not see so often, of strong father-aversion) and on the early aggressivity towards the mother, for in London we have for some time been emphasizing these two points. But we do not find that this stage is entirely a matter between the girl and the mother *alone*, the phantasy of the father (especially of his penis in her womb) playing also a part of some importance. I remember years ago you remarked to me about Jung's long paper in 1913: "Previously (in his *Die Bedeutung des Vaters f. d. Schicksal d. Einzelnen*)[4] he forgot the mother, and now he has forgotten the father". Hitherto you have laid such stress on the father and male side (owing to the obscurity of the female) that I hope some passages in your essay discounting the father and the triple Oedipus situation in the young girl will not influence some analysts to proceed to a similarly one-sided view as you then indicated.

Probably you are right in anticipating that some of your remarks may not please the more feminist of the psycho-analysts. Personally I do not feel impelled to take sides in such a difference of opinion, but the effect of your essay is to re-double my curiosity to know the full truth on the various problems in question. I feel that some useful work could still be done in stating the problems more explicitly, and I shall try to do this. It is, for instance, not quite clear whether the differences can be brought to a definite issue on some points, or whether they are all simply differences of accent—of relative importance of various factors. Perhaps this task may give me the occasion for a Congress paper.

Both Mrs. Klein and Mrs. Riviere are in distinctly poor health at present—for the past few months—but they should soon mend. Otherwise we are all well, including also my family, and I trust the same is true of you all.

With the best of wishes for 1932 and with the warmest greetings from

always yours
Ernest Jones.

1. The year indicated is that of the typed version. The original handwritten letter was dated incorrectly as 1931.

2. Freud (1931a, 1931b).

3. Freud (1931b, p. 243).

4. Jung (1909).

581

23 January 1932
Vienna, IX. Berggasse 19

Dear Jones,

I not only expected but also hoped that my new study on female sexuality would induce you, too, to deal with the subject again. It is so important and still so obscure that it really merits this. Both of your objections seem to me unwarranted. My essay is explicitly presented as one contribution among others, and only touches on the confirmation or contradiction from other quarters. A full appraisal of these other authors is not intended. That I am supposed to have forgotten the father is generally not like me. I state that the father does not yet play a role, or only a negligible one, in a certain developmental phase. It seems to me that in your circles this chronological order is neglected, and that too many disparate elements are thrown onto the same plane, probably under the influence of Kleinian interpretations, whose justification I dispute in accordance with my latest experiences. As you see, there is still much to be ascertained and determined.

However, I also sense a misunderstanding between us. Can it be that what you denote as the phallic phase in the girl means something different to us; that you make a distinction between phallic and clitoral, which mean the same to us? It seems to me to be so.

We were certainly sorry to hear that we missed a visit from you and your wife in January. But we would really much rather see you in summer and welcome you in a garden. We rented the same house as last year in Poetzleinsdorf, and we are all longing to stay there from the end of May until September, so peacefully beautiful, near the town but away from its noise, in greenery and sunlight. It was like that last year, when the wretched weather made all enjoyment virtually impossible.

With cordial greetings to you and yours.

Freud

582

12 February 1932
81 Harley Street, London

Dear Professor,

I was very sorry to hear from Anna that she had had what sounded like a severe attack of influenza, but I hope that by now it has quite disappeared without leaving any sequelae. The older one gets the more one perceives the benefits of the summer and the more objection one has to the months from December to March!

I have sent to Eitingon my vote to hold a Congress this year but raised the possibility of its being held in a less expensive country than Switzerland.[1] Storfer sent me the news of his resignation, but I know nothing about the cause. At all events we are lucky to have such a pleasant and reliable colleague as Martin in this post.[2]

Thank you for your answer to my letter about your *Zeitschrift* papers. You put your finger exactly on the misunderstanding to which I alluded. Your criticism of my supposedly wrong chronology was based on the very natural assumption that by 'phallic phase' I meant the same as you. And indeed at the time I also thought I did, otherwise I should of course have made the distinction clear. Now I see that I have wrongly taken for granted a distinction which I should certainly wish to establish—namely, between the 'clitoritic phase' (with, as you point out and I can confirm, its masculine impulses towards the mother) and the 'phallic phase' later on when the child has been brought into the problem of its relation to male beings and [after][3] has regressed defensively to the clitoris-phallus position. The latter we probably agree is much more secondary and komplexbedingt than the former. Whether all[4] girls have a phase of clitoris primacy I do not know. It seems likely, but there is also the accompanying oral attitude to remember which perhaps in the more feminine type may equal or surpass the clitoris. So much for the present, but you have stimulated me to more work.

With kindest regards, also to your family

Yours always
Ernest Jones.

1. Twelfth Congress of the International Psychoanalytic Association, Wiesbaden, 4–7 September 1932.
2. Martin Freud took over as managing director of the Verlag, a post held by Storfer since 1924.
3. Crossed out in the original; replaced by "has."
4. Doubly underlined in the original.

583

21 April 1932
81 Harley Street, London

Dear Professor,

You may be sure that the impressive communication you have sent round to the various Presidents will receive all the attention it deserves. My wife and I are translating it. I am circularising a copy of it to all our members so as to give them time to reflect on it before we discuss it at the next Meeting.[1]

On the general principle of maintaining the Verlag if possible I think there will be unanimous agreement, but the discussion will begin over the question how. In order to tackle this it will be essential to have some concrete details of the sums of money necessary, both at the moment and in the future. I had already written to Eitingon on this point and am sending him another urgent message.

It is not easy to be optimistic over any matter involving the raising of funds during the present terrible times. You know better than I do how bad things are in Austria, and now it is the turn of the English to be the poor cousins—since the currency relationship is the reverse of what it was ten years ago. Everyone here is having great difficulty in dealing with the immediate necessities of life. One is accustomed to look to America, but all that I hear from there is that the situation is terribly bad, with no immediate prospect of betterment, and in addition the economic depression has had a profounder psychological effect in producing apprehension there than in older countries better fortified to cope with misfortune. My chief hope is that Brill may know of some rich man who could solve the problem.

I am entirely in agreement with your suggestion that the International Association should take over as much responsibility as it can in this matter, with of course the proviso that they would exercise some control to secure a more efficient working than has previously been possible. In this direction I had already made the suggestion to Eitingon that in the worst case the Association could acquire the rights and responsibilities of at least the official organs.

You are right in assuming in your circular that some prejudice may be voiced on the score of the Verlag having in the past been too exclusively German in its outlook and insufficiently international. As you know, I have endeavoured in English-speaking countries to further the same object that you describe as being the Verlag's, namely to stamp a body of literature as being entirely distinct from the medley of rubbish all around. In pursuit of this aim we have been considerably hampered by the encouragement repeatedly given in the most official way to rival and inefficient undertakings, publishers, translators, other journals, etc. It has been an uphill fight against the difficulties from within and without, but we have accomplished something. As you will remember, my own wish has always been for a closer cooperation, so that all the undertakings would be entirely and jointly international.

I will of course report to you the results of our discussion as soon as it has taken place and will also write to Brill in support of your proposals to see what concrete scheme we can devise.

Apart from this, news has been scarce of late. The level of scientific work in our Society is very satisfactory and in spite of our small numbers we are training more and more candidates. The number of first-class analysts is still deplorably small, and I imagine this is true in all countries.

My family is, I am happy to say, very well and flourishing, and I trust the same is true of yours.

With my kindest regards and best wishes for our mutual success in the present difficult undertaking,

Yours always,
Ernest Jones.

1. See note 1 to letter 586.

584

26 April 1932
Vienna, IX. Berggasse 19

Dear Jones,

I am pleased that you received my *Rundbrief* sympathetically. The demand for a detailed statement of the Verlag's position is fully justified. Martin is busy preparing one. It will soon be in your hands. The answers from Sarasin and Ferenczi, too, are evidence of their great willingness. I do not deceive myself about the difficulties.

It is superfluous to comment on the general international situation. Perhaps we are only repeating the ridiculous act of rescuing a birdcage while the house is burning down. As foolhardy as it may seem, one can only act by making optimistic assumptions.[1]

The best news in your letter is that you and your family are well.

Cordially yours,
Freud

1. The extraordinary power of the German here cannot readily be conveyed in English: "Aber der Handelnde muss doch immer so leichtsinnig sein, von einer optimistischen Möglichkeit auszugehen."

585

5 May 1932
81 Harley Street, London

Dear Professor,

I hasten to send you news which, so far as it goes, is very good. I had translated and circularised your communication, so that there was a specially large attendance at the Meeting. Unfortunately I had nothing more to lay before them, since Martin was not able, in spite of my entreaties, to send me any data in time for the Meeting. Your communication had had exactly the effect you desired and the members took the fullest and entirely positive interest in the situation. Many alternative proposals were made of a general nature, with which I will not trouble you in detail at present. We appointed a strong Sub-Committee to consider the question further when we had some concrete data to study. In the meantime, however, the spontaneous wish was expressed, without any suggestion from myself, that even at this preliminary meeting a resolution be passed (which was carried unanimously) expressing the intention of the Society to do its utmost to save and maintain the Verlag.

My own impression is that it should prove possible, by annual subscriptions [and]^1 or otherwise, to secure enough money that would support the Verlag indefinitely, provided that it was made more internationally oriented^{x2} and that it was supervised by a sufficiently representative committee. Today, however, my optimism has received some set-back by receiving Martin's communication when I was appalled at the size of the sum that has to be collected before September. I really do not know what to say about this possibility at the moment and think it will have to depend on the goddess Fortune—let us hope that she still lives in America! I am going to Berlin after Whitsun where I will have an opportunity of discussing the whole matter, together with Congress business, with Eitingon.

Another interesting piece of news, also favourble in direction, is the following. The Radio in this country is a [well-managed]^3 Government institution with great prestige. It has hitherto wisely avoided the subject of psycho-analysis and all the surrounding debatable ground (Adler, etc.), and my own name was on a black list as a morally dangerous person, together with Bertrand Russell's (something like the old Austrian P.U.). They have now judged that the situation has ripened and have decided to give a course of lectures on Psychology next autumn, divided into two equal parts, the first part, on Consciousness, to be delivered by a modern and capable Professor of Psychology (incidentally, one of our own members, Cyril Burt),^{4} and the second part, on the Unconscious, by my-

self.[5] My name was taken off the black list by the Archbishop of York![6]
With best wishes for the success of our latest campaign

Yours always
Ernest Jones.

P.S. Would you please give Anna the enclosed note.

1. Crossed out in the original; "or" is handwritten in an otherwise typed letter.
2. On the bottom of the second page of the letter Jones appended a note referring to this last point: "*Incidentally, you were not correct in saying that the JOURNAL can [entirely] freely dispose of papers published in the ZEITSCHRIFT. This is a desideratum I have long striven for, but in vain." "Entirely" is crossed out; "freely" is handwritten.
3. Crossed out in the original; "Government" is handwritten.
4. Cyril Burt (1883–1971), generally regarded as Britain's first professional psychologist.
5. For the published version, see Cyril Burt, "The Conscious Mind," in C. Burt, E. Jones, E. Miller, and W. Moodie, eds., *How the Mind Works* (London: Allen and Unwin, 1933), pp. 17–58; and Jones (1933b).
6. The remainder of the letter, including this line, is handwritten. The archbishop of York at this time was William Temple (1881–1944), who later became the archbishop of Canterbury. Jones repeats the story of being taken off the blacklist of the British Broadcasting Corporation in his biography of Freud (Jones, 1957a, p. 171; 1957b, p. 182). The Written Archives Centre of the BBC, Reading, however, contains no record of such a list.

586

28 May 1932
81 Harley Street, London

Dear Professor,

Eitingon has probably reported at length to Martin the results of our long talk in Berlin, so I need not repeat the details. Our "Verlag's Sub-Committee" in London has met again since my return and we are making a report to the meeting of the Society next Wednesday asking them to accept a resolution cordially supporting your appeal and offering to make the same subscription as the Vienna group has recently done.[1]

Even if this favourable standard is widely maintained, however, I am afraid it will only bring about half the total sum required. We have therefore still to count on the unknown American uncle. We must be prepared to consider an extensive reorganisation of the system under which the Verlag will be conducted in the future, for it is plain that the past system is simply impossible. I suppose the wisest thing will be for the Congress to appoint a small representative Committee who will have full powers, and also full data of the donations by that time, to deal with the situation which will then be imminent.

I am also in communication with Brill who is doing all he can in the matter.

With my kindest regards,

Yours always,
Ernest Jones.

1. Jones reported to the Verlag subcommittee on 18 May 1932, moving that the British society support Freud's appeal that the Verlag be transferred from private hands to those of the International Psychoanalytic Association, and recommending a subscription fee of fifteen shillings per member. The general principles of the motion were accepted unanimously, with minor amendments being proposed regarding the subscription. Recorded in *Scientific Minutes* (October 1929–May 1939), Archives of the British Psycho-Analytical Society, London, pp. 81–82.

587

1 June 1932
[Vienna] XVIII
Khevenhüllerstr 6

Dear Jones,

Thank you for your earnest endeavours on behalf of the Verlag! I hope we will be able to save it.

The demand for supervision of the management is fully justified. It remains to be decided whether one should simply transfer it to the current executive of the I.P.V. or appoint a special supervisory committee for it. The Verlag's management ought to retain a certain measure of independence.

Out here since 15 May, we have enjoyed a beautiful spring.

Cordially yours,
Freud

588

2 June 1932

Dear Professor,

I am glad to be able to send you the best news about the response of our members to your appeal. The strength of their response had only gathered weight in the days that had elapsed since receiving it. Our special Sub-Committee discussed the whole matter very thoroughly, both before and after my visit to Berlin. At a representative meeting held last night the accompanying resolution was passed unanimously. I am now sending out forms to secure the signed promises of the subscriptions and do not doubt that many members will state a larger sum than the minimum officially agreed on, which is approximately the same sum as that agreed on by the Vienna and Berlin groups.

I am very concerned about both the fact and the form of the new American publishing undertaking, *The Psychoanalytic Quarterly*.[1] It is in direct competition with the official English-speaking organ, the JOURNAL, and, since we are dependent on American subscriptions, it may even constitute a threat to our existence. That this should have been done without consultation with me, who has been officially responsible for catering to the English-speaking public, or without letting me know what was the nature of their dissatisfaction with my efforts, is unfortunate, as is still more the fact that they have the official approval and blessing of the leading authorities in all coutries, including all the other officers of the International Association. I shall of course have to bring the matter up at the Congress, and should be only too glad if I could find some amicable arrangement.

I hope you are pleased with the special Roheim double number, which is meant to be a worthy memorial both of his work and of the Princess's far-sighted generosity.[2] All other material had to be postponed, so that you[r] last ZEITSCHRIFT papers are appearing in our July number. In the meantime this American QUARTERLY has already published one of them, and, before taking this matter up with them, I should be glad to know if it happened with or without your consent.[3]

I have for some time been meaning, as I see you so rarely nowadays, to report to you about the three colleagues you trained and sent to me some ten years ago. Of the three there is no doubt that Mr. Strachey proves the most successful. He is not very enterprising but all his work is very thorough and reliable and his judgement is remarkably balanced and of the greatest value. Mrs. Riviere has also been extremely useful, both in her advice and in the actual work which you know she has accomplished. Unfortunately in the last year or two she has shown unmistakable signs of reverting to her earlier troubles; nothing can please her, whatever efforts are made by us all, and I think *"difficile"* is a very fair word to use in connection with her. The least satisfactory by far, however, has been poor Rickman. We had hoped very much of the work he must have done during his three years with Ferenczi, and it has been a great disappointment to realise that this has not been successful. Ever since his return, in spite of all encouragement and help, he has behaved in the most extraordinary and negative fashion; I am afraid that the underlying psychosis must be regarded as incurable.

We have a good supply of younger members now making progress or being trained and although there is a poverty in the generation immediately succeeding Dr. Glover, Dr. Payne,[4] and myself, etc., I think that the third generation will prove adequate to its future tasks. The level of the discussions at our Meetings is consistently high and even my critical spirit sees ample reason for gratification at the work accomplished by the Society.

With my kindest regards and, once more, the best wishes for the success of our latest campaign together,

Believe me,

Yours always,
Ernest Jones.[5]

P.S. This letter was delayed in the posting and in the meantime your kind note has come to hand. In reply to your question I would advise that the committee in question be a specially selected one, not the official Executive of the Association. I have in mind men like Sarasin and van Ophuijsen,[6] though I wish I could think of a suitable man in Vienna who would be in more immediate contact with the business direction.

1. See Jones (1957a, pp. 168–169; 1957b, p. 180).

2. Géza Róheim's fieldwork between 1928 and 1931, primarily undertaken in Central Australia, New Guinea, and Arizona, had been financed by Princess George of Greece (Marie Bonaparte, 1882–1962), and was documented in his "Psycho-Analysis of Primitive Cultural Types," *Journal*, 13 (1932): 1–224.

3. Freud (1931a), trans. E. B. Jackson, *Psychoanalytic Quarterly*, 1 (1932): 3–6. The piece also appeared in the *Journal*, 13 (1932): 277–280, trans. Joan Riviere.

4. Sylvia M. Payne (1880–1976), M.B., B.S. 1906 London, distinguished member of the British Psycho-Analytical Society; for the important role she played in holding the Society together during the years of controversy, see King and Steiner (1991).

5. The typed copy of this letter has been preserved in full. The second-to-last page of the original typed version is signed and underscored by Jones; the last page contains the postscript. The first two pages of the original are missing.

6. J. H. W. van Ophuijsen (1882–1950), born in Sumatra, M.D. 1909 University of Leiden; postgraduate training (1909–1913) at the Bürgholzli under Bleuler. Served as president of the Dutch Psychoanalytic Society between 1927 and 1933, and was a member of Jones's reconstituted Secret Committee; in 1935 he joined the teaching staff at the New York Psychoanalytic Institute.

589

8 June 1932
Vienna, XVIII

Dear Jones,

I am very happy about the proposed measures, which, I too believe, should make it possible to save the Verlag. If you wish to have a special supervisory board appointed over its management, I have no objections. But I am opposed to Ophuijsen, who has the bad habit of burdening himself and others with disputes over formalities. Whereas the Verlag and the editors are together in Vienna, I think the supervisory committee should be international in composition and not contain a Viennese member, whose proximity might put him in an advantageous position. As members I suggest: you yourself, so as to look after the interests of the English publisher as well; *Eitingon* (if he will accept!!), Princess Marie, and an American, Brill as first choice.

I do not share your concerns about the *Quarterly*. The new organ will bind American PsA. closer to that in Europe, and compete significantly with the *Ps. Review* and Jelliffe's journal, which are really overflowing with psychoanalytic contributions. I too am sorry that no one informed you of the intended founding, but it shows how little the Americans feel themselves tied to England. A friendly agreement would certainly be very desirable.

Next time I will tell you about a new work that I have started to write.

Cordially yours,
Freud

590

13 June 1932
81 Harley Street, London

Dear Professor,

Thank you for your letter. I am glad to know you are enjoying the spring. With us it has been a cold one and the last two days have been the first when it was pleasantly warm to be out of doors. May is one of the many months in which the Vienna climate is preferable to the London one.

Although of course it is for the Congress to decide, I am very glad of the opportunity to discuss with you the suitable composition of the future committee.[1] I think, in spite of the distance, we must have an American representative and that no one other than Brill could be considered. I notice you do not mention Sarasin. I do not know him very well personally, but Eitingon seems to think very well of him and has recently suggested that he act as Treasurer for the foreign money until it is needed in Vienna. I understand your feelings about Ophuijsen, although I get on very well with him personally. The bad habit you mention amuses me and is, I am sure, not dictated by any malice. After all, his endeavour to introduce some order into the laxity of our affairs is not altogether disadvantageous. In Paris either Laforgue or the Princess would obviously be suitable. It might be advantageous to have Eitingon from the point of view of continuity with the past, but I am not sure that his name would inspire universal confidence. I was interested in your idea that there should be no Vienna member on the committee and quite see the advantages of it. By the local Viennese *Direktion* I take it you meant no one but Martin; I think we are very lucky to have secured his services.

The matter of the new American *Quarterly* is actually not so simple as you appear to hope, and I want to say something more about it. First I must remove a little misunderstanding. It is not the case that they failed to communicate with me before beginning the new undertaking. On the contrary, they pressed me to let my name appear in the long list of patrons they have secured. This I naturally had to refuse, on two grounds; first that I think psycho-analytical publications should be regularised by official arrangements instead of being wild private ventures, and secondly because it would be paradoxical for the editor of one journal to support another which is destined to replace his own, without there being some good reason for it. I am sure that if someone suddenly announced in Leipsic [Leipzig] or Frankfurt that he intended to duplicate the *Zeitschrift* by a parallel magazine the editor of the *Zeitschrift* would take the same view. What I really complain of is that the authors of the new undertaking failed to consult beforehand with people who are obviously affected. This shows no spirit of cooperation. After all, it is being published in more or less the same language as the *JOURNAL*, which hitherto has been officially recognised as adequate to publish both contributions and reports in English of what is going on in the psycho-analytical world. I have tried to cater for the Americans as well as for other countries in the *International Journal* (in spite of Mrs. Riviere's stern veto on American contributions). If the Americans had explained to me in what respects they regarded the *JOUR-NAL* as inadequate to fulfil its function I am sure I should have been glad to cooperate with them or make any concessions they wished, e.g. enlarging the size of the *JOURNAL*, having an American co-Editor, a special section reserved for American contributions, or in any other way.

Much more serious than any of this, however, is the fact that the *Quarterly* now directly threatens the existence of the *JOURNAL*. It happens that we are dependent for more than half our income on American subscriptions, and it is not to be supposed that America will continue to subcribe to the *JOURNAL* when they have a cheaper corresponding periodical near to hand. Further, it requires no gift of prophecy to foretell that once it is established the *Quarterly* will demand recognition as an official organ of the Association, which will be hard to refuse in view of the fact that they are supported by the leading analysts in all countries, who seem to me to have given their support without reflecting on the consequences. When that happens, all the American members will transfer their obligatory subscription from the *JOURNAL* to the *Quarterly*, and the *JOURNAL* cannot exist as a purely English periodical. I am sure we should not be able to subscribe among ourselves the large deficit which would ensue.

The direct competition is openly announced in the first number as well as by the steps which, to my knowledge, they have already taken in the way of securing the contributions of German writers, the translations of which used to be published in the JOURNAL. It is sheer nonsense and waste of energy for the same things to be translated twice over in the same language. The JOURNAL has a legal contract with the ZEITSCHRIFT and Verlag whereby no translations may be published within twelve months without permission from the JOURNAL. This contract has been openly violated in the first number of the Quarterly.[2] And to whom are we to protest? Martin would naturally say he knew nothing about it, the Redaktion of the ZEITSCHRIFT no longer exists in any responsible fashion since Rado's removal to New York, and the senior member of the Verlag is the author who has apparently given permission for this very thing to happen.

As to the Psychoanalytic Review, I regard its existence as superfluous as you do, but I am bound to say thay [they] have always behaved quite honourably in respect of the JOURNAL and have never encroached on its domain. Jelliffe and I came to an understanding which has been friendlily respected on both sides. If, as you think, the aggression of the Quarterly is meant to be directed against the Psychoanalytic Review, it would have been quite easy for the Americans to have cooperated with the JOURNAL in extending it in America for that purpose.

Your inference that the Americans do not feel related to England I should modify by saying this is only true of the foreigners recently arrived in America, who have lost their own civilisation and not acquired any other. Zilboorg, who is a completely wild Russian, is the real centre of this piece of activity. I admire his energy, but wish it could be somewhat directed and controlled. The upshot of the whole situation is that a few people have behaved inconsiderately, and a number of other people thoughtlessly; whereas the consequences in two or three years' time are likely to be quite perilous to the existence of the Journal. That in itself is of no tragic import, but what we have done in London in the past fifteen years to establish a good standard of representative and carefully translated presentation of the work of our European colleagues would seem to us to have deserved encouragement rather than discouragement.

I wish there were someone else than you [to][3] whom I could trouble with these reflections, but you know there is not. We lost our last leader with Abraham.

With my best wishes for a pleasant summer,

Yours always,
Ernest Jones.

1. The committee which took over control of the Verlag was appointed at the Twelfth Congress of the International Psychoanalytic Association, Wiesbaden, 4–7 September 1932, and consisted of Brill, Jones, Oberndorf, van Ophuijsen, Spitz, and Sarasin; see *Journal*, 14 (1933): 179.

2. Regarding Freud (1931a), in *Psychoanalytic Quarterly*, 1 (1932): 3–6.

3. Crossed out in the original.

591

16 June 1932
42 York Terrace, Regents Park

Dear Professor,

I am glad to say that within the first week of sending out our subscriptions forms £500 has been promised for the Verlag fund, although not half of the members have yet replied.

Yours very sincerely,
[Ernest Jones]

592

17 June 1932
Vienna, IX. Berggasse 19

Dear Jones,

I am the more ready and willing to do everything to maintain excellent relations between us, the less easy you so often make it for me.[1] It is only with this in mind that I am replying in detail to your letter, the affective background of which I acknowledge as indeed justified.

First, with regard to the supervisory committee. It is only a suggestion of mine which you need not follow. You can draw up a list of members independently of me and have it confirmed by the Congress. It is of course a little strange that I left out two persons who are particularly dear to me. Sarasin is close to me as a student of mine, whom I would also recommend for any position of trust; but he is quite lacking in any business sense. With Ophuijsen we maintain close personal contact, but his constant harping on principles and his pedantic adherence to the letter of the law are not only amusing but also tiresome and dangerous. I listed Eitingon only as a possibility, if he wishes it himself; I want to avoid offending him, especially in his present state. I prefer by far the Princess to Laforgue, all advantages are on her side. I resent the fact that Laforgue makes big promises so easily which then come to nothing, as in the case of Tegel. Naturally

I endorse Brill; the number of members should be limited, otherwise the committee works all too sluggishly.

You wrote in your letter of 2 June: "That this (the founding of the *Quarterly*) should have been done without consultation with me . . ." Naturally I concluded something from these words that contradicts your description today. Unfortunately, misunderstandings between us occur too often these days. You are certainly right in saying that all the Americans who gravitate to Berlin rather than London are immigrants (*recte:* Jews), but let us be fair enough to admit that the contributions by the native-born would fill neither the columns nor the cash-boxes of the *Journal*. Here in Vienna we did not endorse the *Quarterly* quite recklessly, not without consulting Brill first and making our support dependent on his approval. After all, we had the right to regard Brill as our representative in America. And here I cannot spare you a reproach. If you learned of the founding of the *Quarterly* and considered it a danger to the *Journal*, you should have written to warn us and drawn our attention to the danger. It is your responsibility and not ours to attend to the interests of the *Journal*. Your silence and Brill's approval led us to believe that we were aiding our cause by supporting the Q. As far as I myself am concerned, I have heard so many reproaches for having left the English translation rights of my works once and for all to your Press; it has been drilled into me so often that the English rights are not the American rights, that the latter remained free, that I have become used to acting accordingly.

Once again one feels the collapse of the Committee and the cessation of the *Rundbriefe*, which maintained contact among the members, to be a severe disadvantage. Since then Ferenczi has isolated himself; since then the English group has gone its own particular way and is losing sight of what is happening on the Continent. I have gradually become tired of the strain to hold together such diverse and uncooperative individuals. You are right, if Abraham were still alive, he probably would have succeeded in doing so. I cannot bring him back to life,[2] only regret that no replacement has been found for him.

At present, since there is very little analytic work to do, I am working on the *"Ergänzenden Vorlesungen zur Einführung."*[3]

With cordial greetings.

Yours,
Freud

1. This is a difficult sentence in German: "Ich will umso bereitwilliger alles für ein ausgezeichnetes Einvernehmen zwischen uns thun, je weniger leicht Sie es mir oft machen." Freud appears to be underlining his annoyance by reversing the usual sequence of comparative phrases; also, the words "weniger leicht" (less easy), rather than "schwieriger" or "schwerer" (more difficult), add an awkwardness that could have been avoided.

2. The German here is "Ich kann ihn nicht aufwecken," literally, "I cannot wake him up."

3. Freud (1933a).

593

21 June 1932
81 Harley Street, London

Dear Professor,

Many thanks for your full letter of 17th June. You were right in reproaching me for not having written to you about the *Quarterly* at an earlier date and I see it was a mistake on my part. Actually at the time I heard only that the *Quarterly* was being supported by Eitingon, Anna and Ferenczi, not by yourself, and you may be sure I lost no time in defending the interests of the *JOURNAL*. I wrote strong letters at once to Feigenbaum, Lewin, Zilboorg,[1] Brill and Eitingon. There was no point in writing to Ferenczi, whose attitude about American affairs is apt to be somewhat vague, and I assumed Anna was in touch with Eitingon, acting as Secretary and President of the Association respectively. I am sorry to say I was not able to get any satisfaction from Eitingon either from correspondence or during my visit to Berlin. He will never see what he does not want to see. I still find it deeply shocking that the President of the Association should have given his support to the enterprise of a small coterie in their competition with the Official Organ of the Association without first consulting with the Editor of that organ; apart from his official position, I should have expected that much loyalty from him as a friend. Then a rumour reached me that they were printing one of your papers in the first issue and I at once wrote to you to find out if they were doing this without your consent.[2]

So much for the actual history of the events, but it is also true that there are deeper reasons which would have made me more disinclined to approach you immediately in such a matter, quite apart from the fact that at the time there did not seem to be any definite reason for doing so. These other reasons are a constitutional dislike, bred from schooldays, against referring to a senior authority difficulties and disputes with colleagues of one's own generation. It is in my nature to postpone doing this so long as is possible until I am compelled by circumstances, such as when the authority, as here, himself seems to be taking sides. It seems to me disgraceful to have to admit that we cannot arrange such things among ourselves amicably, as I am sure we should be able to. I have evidently too much trust in the good will of my generation. There is an obvious further reason why I should think it unkind to plague you, who have suffered so much, with troubles from which you should be spared. I made the same mistake in the Rank affair and concealed from you for a long period how badly he was behaving in the vain hope that I might be able to smooth him down, but the only result was that you had to listen to all his complaints about me and none of myself about him. You can very well reply that you are not spared in the long run, so that we may as well begin with you. I see that, and although I am not ashamed of that trait in my nature, I recognise that it often leads to unsatisfactory results in practice, especially to myself.

Coming back to the present situation, why I wrote to you so fully in my last letter was in the hope that you might have some helpful suggestions or advice about dealing with it. That you did not shows me that you find it hard to think of any, and so do I now [that] one is presented with a *fait accompli*. Nevertheless the situation seems to me so ridiculous that we should have two organs in the same language competing with each other and translating the same work that it is surely imperative to come to some sort of understanding or arrangement. I am of course continuing to do all I can with the "Americans", but a word from you would carry enormous weight and would be perhaps the only way of inducing them to consent to discuss the situation openly with me.

There was one passage in your letter the meaning of which I was quite unable to get. You were speaking of having been reproached for having given the English translations once for all and then follows the phrase "so oft wurde mir eingeschärft, dass die englischen nicht die amerik. sind, dass die letzteren frei geblieben sind".³ I have no idea at all what this refers to, but from the tone gather that you feel there is some unsatisfactoriness or possibly even injustice in the difference between English and American translations about which I know nothing at all. I should be glad to be enlightened here; then perhaps I can do something about it.

I was very interested in hearing about your additions to the *"Einführung"*. This has been your most successful book from the point of view of beginners and outsiders, and I was glad to hear that you are thinking of extending it.⁴ Have you any view about the vexed question of translation?

I shall be very grateful for any help in the disagreeable situation that has been forced on me.

Yours always
Ernest Jones.

1. Three of the principal editors of the *Psychoanalytic Quarterly* were Dorian Feigenbaum (1887–1937), Viennese psychoanalyst, who settled in New York in 1924; Bertram D. Lewin (1896–1971), M.D. 1920 Johns Hopkins; and Gregory Zilboorg (1890–1959), Russian-born, M.D. 1926 Columbia. All three were members of the American Psychoanalytic Association and the New York Psychoanalytic Society.

2. See note 3 to letter 588.

3. "It has been drilled into me so often that the English rights are not the American

rights, that the latter remained free, that I have become used to acting accordingly."
"Sind" is handwritten in an otherwise typed letter.

4. In letter 592 Freud was referring to his *New Introductory Lectures on Psycho-Analysis* (Freud, 1933a), which he considered extensions of his previous set of lectures Freud (1916–17).

594

[postcard]

28 August 1932

Greetings to you and all the family out of the French Wales, where we have just spent a couple of weeks.

Ernest Jones.

Alles Liebe und beste Wünsche![1]

Katherine Jones

1. "Kindest regards and best wishes."

595

9 September 1932
The Plat, Elsted

Dear Professor,

I seize the first peaceful moment to write to you. In the first place will you allow me to express my sympathy over the difficulty that has arisen with your oldest and dearest analytical friend. I know that you will not be tempted to copy the old Kaiser *("mir bleibt . . . .")*[1] because your calibre is too tough, and you are surrounded both by affection and by followers whose acceptance of the unconscious is unbreakable. Nevertheless, how painful it must be I can imagine. To Eitingon it came as a shock of surprise, to you probably less so. To me not at all, for I have followed F's evolution (including the pathological side) closely for many years, and knew it could only be a question of time before this denouement arrived. Abraham and I drew him forcibly back from the precipice at the Rank time, and lately Rickman's regular reports of his analysis showed me clearly the direction things were going. His exceptionally deep need of being loved, together with the repressed sadism, are plainly behind the tendency to ideas of persecution. My reaction was therefore very simple: first the cause, then everything to keep him with us. The first excluded the possibility of his being President—in that I agreed with the firm attitude of Eitingon and van Ophuijsen. But the second made me oppose both these two and also Brill. They wanted at all costs that Fer. be asked to withdraw his Vortrag[2] and to postpone as long as possible the expression of his ideas—to avoid scandal. On the contrary I insisted that there would be less scandal if we kept it inside the Vereinigung and that we were quite strong enough to digest the ideas ourselves without harm coming. It would have fed the pathological ideas to have told him that his Vortrag etc. was too wicked to be presented to us, and that might end in his publicly withdrawing from the Vereinigung. I gained my point, and so far as I can judge the advice was successful, for Fer, finding himself welcomed and listened to, visibly expanded and day by day identified himself ever more with the interests and plans, business, etc., of the Vereinigung; he felt himself one of us, which is what I intended and which I am confident will do us no harm. He is, I am afraid, a sick man—also physically—and the impression he made was very pathetic.[3] To me personally he was affectionate, and I think I was able to help both him and his wife. It is terrible—but also unprofitable—to make comparisons with the brilliant past. One can only accept the facts, do the little possible to help, and again to learn how one underestimates the difficulties in the way of retaining a full acceptance of the reality of the unconscious; most people seem to have a limit to their power in this respect.

As for the Presidency, I thank you for the kind message of congratulation you sent through Anna. To speak plainly, the task was not quite welcome to me. I had thought that if I ever accepted the position again, it would be in some years' time after I had given up some work (Clinic, Institute or *Journal*) which my group still wants me to function; how that will be possible now I do not yet know, but a few months' reflection may show that it would be wiser to divide up the work in London—as has always been done in Berlin and Vienna. Of course I feel quite happy about being able to carry out the duties of the [Verein][4] International, which are so familiar to me. And I am confident that it will be a pleasure to work together with Anna, for we always understand each other easily; I am very glad she consented to continue.

My impression of the Congress was throughout excellent. I have rarely known one with a better *Stimmung* [mood], friendly and confident. The scientific part was well maintained, if not remarkble. In my opinion no outstanding paper, eight excellent ones, three poor ones (Schneider, Steiner and Fr. Behn. Eschenburg), the rest good.[5] Of the personalities, Brill was in splendid form and was most helpful, Rado has improved, Alexander very accessible, Eitingon as usual, ditto van Ophuijsen, Laforgue rather quiet in the background, Weiss much improved scientifically and otherwise, Roheim very good indeed—of the rest *nichts neues* [nothing new]. You know already of Harnik.[6] The paranoia is very advanced, fully manifest and very disturbing to the peace of the congress. It is a great pity, for he was a very talented fellow. On the other side I had a most delightful impression of the three young Viennese you have chosen as editors. I saw a great deal of them, and it was easy to plan out cooperation which I hope will be fruitful. A stroke of great luck to have these three, and I expect great improvements from them which we have needed.

Of the Verlag Martin will tell you everything. He made a most excellent impression throughout, in capacity and character, and we all feel we can safely rely on him. It proved impracticable, for various reasons, to make a committee as small as you and I wished, but this will be no loss as the administrative sub-committee is exceptionally small (especially in practice).

After a strenuous time I am resting two or three days in the country, and hope you are enjoying your holiday.

affectionately yours always
Ernest Jones.

1. The words *"mir bleibt (auch) nichts erspart"* (I am also spared nothing) were allegedly spoken by Kaiser Franz Joseph I after the murder of the heir apparent, Franz Ferdinand, and the outbreak of the First World War.

2. Ferenczi (1933). See letter 613.

3. See note 3 to letter 613.

4. Crossed out in the original.

5. See "Report of the Twelfth International Psycho-Analytical Congress," in *Journal*, 14 (1933): 138–180, especially Ernst Schneider, "The Psycho-Analysis of Tics," p. 152; Maxim Steiner, "What Does the Specialist in Sexual Diseases Owe to Psycho-Analysis," pp. 143–144; and Hans Behn-Eschenburg, "Contributions to the Pre-history of the Oedipus Complex," p. 144.

6. J. Hárnik, member of the German Psychoanalytic Society, who presented "The First Post-natal Phase of Libidinal Development," *Journal*, 14 (1933): 146.

596

12 September 1932
Vienna, IX. Berggasse 19

Dear Jones,

Thank you for your first letter as President! I was sorry that Ferenczi's obvious ambition could not be satisfied, but then there was not a moment's doubt that only you have the competence for the leadership.[1] To be sure, Ferenczi's change is most regrettable, but there is nothing traumatic about it. For three years already I have been observing his increasing alienation, his unreceptiveness to warnings about his technical errors, and what is probably most crucial, a personal hostility toward me for which I have certainly given him even less cause than in previous cases. Except perhaps for the fact that I am still here. Unfortunately in his case the regressive intellectual and affective development seems to have a background of physical decline. His perceptive and good wife let me know that I should think of him as a sick child.[2]

This is contrasted by the fact that everything else at the Congress went so satisfactorily. I am told it is unmistakable that the movement is making itself independent of the influence of individuals, and is apparently in the position to survive the loss of this or that personality quite well. The understanding, based on the bond to the common cause, the best guarantee for the future, is said to be excellent.[3]

I am glad that you agree with the choice of my young people (Kris, Hartmann, Wälder,[4] Martin). Martin is still enjoying a few days' holiday in Switzerland; consequently I do not yet know the details of the arrangements concerning the Verlag or their scope. Once the Verlag has shaken off its dependence on the committee of creditors, the supervisory committee will, I hope, prove to be a wise adviser and not a burdensome steward of the court.[5] Unfortunately the future of the Verlag depends on political developments in Germany; if this *Hitlerei* succeeds still further not many psa. books will be bought. The fate of my *"Ergänzende Vorlesungen"*,[6] which have just gone to press, will be very enlightening.

With cordial wishes for your good health, which is now of common interest to all members.

Yours,
Freud

1. The German here is "dass nur Sie zur Leitung berufen sein können," literally "that only you could be called" (or "destined") "for the leadership."
2. Gizella Palós (1863–1949) had been married to Ferenczi since 1 March 1919. They had no children, but she had a daughter, Elma, from a previous marriage, who had been Ferenczi's patient. There is strong evidence in *Sándor Ferenczi/Georg Groddeck: Correspondance* (Paris: Payot, 1982), as well as in Ferenczi's letters to Freud, that suggest Ferenczi had been in love with Elma, and that he resented Freud for having sanctioned his relationship with Gizella but not with Elma.
3. Here *"unverkennbar"* (unmistakable) is crossed out in the original; it had been employed already in the opening part of the previous sentence.
4. Ernst Kris (1900–1957), Ph.D. 1922 University of Vienna in art history, curator of the Kunsthistoriches Museum; also took up psychoanalysis professionally. Heinz Hartmann (1894–1970), M.D. 1920 University of Vienna; would become the leading theoretician of ego psychology. Robert Wälder (1900–1967), Ph.D. 1921 University of Vienna in physics; later turned to psychoanalysis; coeditor (with Kris) of *Imago*.
5. The German word here is *"Hofmeister."*
6. Freud (1933a).

597

15 September 1932

Dear Professor,

Thank you for your letter about the Congress, etc.. I am writing at the moment in reference to your last sentence about the new *Vorlesungen* being ready for printing, to ask your views about translation. As I have explained to you before, England and America are for scientific publications as inseparable as Germany and Austria. Every publisher in both countries reckons on the sale in both countries, and it is the rarest thing in the world to find a publisher in either country who would consent to publishing a scientific book if the sale was restricted to one country. That means in effect that the book can either be translated and published in America or England, but not in both. I need hardly say that we are prepared to undertake the work of making a first class translation—an offer which I do not think you can honestly receive from America—and should esteem it an honour to be allowed to include the volume in our International Psycho-Analytical Library series, the only one that exists in English—as the Verlag series are the only ones that exist in Germany. If you agree to this perhaps you would also mention any wishes about the financial terms, which you may be sure we will do everything to meet.

With kindest regards,

Yours always,
[Ernest Jones]

598

11 November 1932
Vienna, IX. Berggasse 19

Dear Jones,

This letter, although addressed to me, belongs to you.

I just got over *Grippe* with otitis media; still quite weak. How are you?

Cordially yours,
Freud

599

10 January 1933

Dear Professor,

I waited to read your book before writing to thank you for your kindness in sending me a copy. It was a very great pleasure to enjoy again your rich personal style—one could hear you talking—as well as the always interesting content. You will not be surprised to hear that my skin is too tough to be much affected by your plea for telepathy.[1] I have had of course many similar examples to the one you quote, and a large number of striking ones were sent in by correspondents after my radio talks. It is really curious that no one ever gets the opportunity of investigating these phenomena at the time, so that one is always driven back on to speculative probabilities where of course free play is left to the subjective. I wish you had added some analytical considerations on the nature of the tendency to believe or disbelieve in such matters: there is much to say there that is interesting. The chapter I enjoyed most was the final one and this I feel sure will belong to the classics. The whole chapter is truly magnificent, and I don't think I have in my life read a page with which I was in more complete accord than S.222.[2] I wonder if you remember a talk we had some time ago whether the greatest danger to psycho-analysis came from the materialistic, anti-psychological tendencies in science, particularly in medicine, or from the anti-natural tendencies of religion and its later derivatives. I remember taking strongly the ground that the latter was the only serious enemy, but you were more doubtful.[3]

I am happy to tell you we have secured a very good translator for the book,[4] and both Mr. Strachey and myself will see to the revision.

You cannot, I am sure, be content with the progress made in regard to the Verlag, but I think that everything possible is being done. Certainly no one else could have achieved half so much as Martin has done.

We are expecting to present our little girl with a playmate next May. That is the chief personal news, and there is nothing else going on worthy of note. The word 'news' reminds me of my last *Rundbrief*, à propos of which I should from pure curiosity like to ask you a question. What, in your recollection, was the duration of your *Vortrag* on *Zwangsneurose* at the Salzburg Congress? I find an enormous discrepancy between Sadger's memory and my own.

I hope that 1933 will be a pleasant year to you and that we shall accomplish a good deal in our common interests.

With warmest regards to you and your family,

[Ernest Jones][5]

P.S. I enclose a letter from Berkeley-Hill that will interest you.

1. Freud (1933a, pp. 36–39, 55).
2. See Freud (1933a, p. 160), where science is given a dominant position over religion and philosophy.
3. See letter 65.
4. Freud (1933a), trans. W. J. H. Sprott.
5. The extant version of this letter is not signed, nor is Jones's full name typed out in the usual manner.

600

13 January 1933
Vienna, IX. Berggasse 19

Dear Jones,

The splendid news that you and your wife are expecting in May deserves, without delay, warm congratulations from us all. If it is to be the last—the last are not exactly the least, as you can see from my family.

It was very agreeble for me that you liked something about the new *Vorlesungen* without reservation. Regarding telepathy, you are taking the easy way out. It is not a question of psychological consistency. Until a few years ago I had the same thoughts as you have now. Also your argument of a delayed revision no longer holds. For instance we observed and tested again (repeated twice) the case of the gold coin. Incidentally, I make no secret of demanding further proof in order to be fully convinced.

Otherwise there is not much that is new here either. One gets older, the functions of life become more difficult, less pleasurable.

As far as I remember, that lecture of mine in Salzburg lasted a terribly long time: $1\frac{1}{2}$–$2\frac{1}{4}$ hours?[1] I could no longer do that today.

With particular affection.

Yours,
Freud

P.S. Enclosure.

1. In Jones (1955a, p. 42; 1955b, p. 47) the session on the subject of Freud (1909d) is reported to have lasted a total of five hours.

601

15 January 1933
Vienna, IX. Berggasse 19

Dear Jones,

A brief addition to my last letter. Feigenbaum invited me, pressingly and urgently, to permit my name to be included in the list of contributing editors. I sent him a noncommittal reply by cable. As you know, I am on the title page of the *International* as some sort of editor. I do not know how the *Quarterly* settled matters with our English journal and do not want to give you further cause for dissatisfaction. I therefore ask your opinion as to whether I should oblige Feigenbaum.

Cordially yours,
Freud

602

18 January 1933
81 Harley Street, London

Dear Professor,

I thank you for your friendliness in asking my opnion about Feigenbaum's latest proposal, and could only wish that some of our other Continental colleagues had shown the same sense of loyalty. You say you do not know what arrangement the QUARTERLY has come to with the JOURNAL. I know no more than you, for I sent you a copy of my final letter to Feigenbaum which completely defined the situation; if it is not accessible I enclose another copy of it.

My standpoint seems to me perfectly clear and simple. Feigenbaum admits that the QUARTERLY has no special function—such as concentrating American contributions, etc.—but that its aim is identical with that of the JOURNAL. This can only mean that in his opinion the JOURNAL does not adequately fulfil its purpose and needs to be supplemented. If I knew what the basis of this criticism is, I should be only too happy to co-operate with anyone who wished to remove the supposed defects, or else to be replaced by someone who could better fulfil the task. Instead of discussing this, however, Feigenbaum launched an enterprise which can only have one effect—that of increasing whatever defects there are in the JOURNAL. By his activity he restricts the number of contributions available to us, so that the level of what we publish must necessarily be lower than before, as there is not the same field from which to choose the best. And since few of his subscribers will also subscribe to the JOURNAL we are deprived of a certain number; we are so dependent on American sales that if the QUARTERLY succeeds the JOURNAL may well have to cease publication. In short, co-operation is replaced by competition.

You are the Herausgeber of the INTERNATIONAL JOURNAL and entrusted me as Editor with the task of supplying the English-speaking people in all parts of the world (from Japan to California) with the best contributions made by authors in every country in the world and in every language. That task seemed to me a quite definite one and I have done my best to carry it out. If now you were to agree with Feigenbaum that I am not carrying it out and that you wish officially to support a rival whose activities tend to displace me, then I should have nothing left but to ask you to accept my resignation and to appoint someone with whom you would be more satisfied. I hope I should not take this contingency too personally, though I should naturally ask for information about the alleged deficiencies. More important to me would be the effect on the international movement, to which I have entirely devoted myself.

I hear that several colleagues have already regretted their impulsive response to Feigenbaum's methods, which I will not more nearly characterise. From Brill I hear this week that the internal dissensions and jealousy in New York about the QUARTERLY are so great and so distressing to him that he is seriously thinking of resigning his positions and retiring from the whole field. In fact he says that the only thing deterring him from doing so is his consideration for you and for me. It does not surprise me that an enterprise founded on ill-will should have dissension as its result.

With my kindest regards,

Yours always,
Ernest Jones.

603

24 February 1933
Vienna, IX. Berggasse 19

Dear Jones,

I hope that the printing of the translation of my new *Vorlesungen* is not so far advanced that the correction of an error could not be permitted.

On p. 227 of the last *Vorlesung* I quote a famous dictum by Kant. But this quotation is wrong and does the philosopher an injustice. I will obtain the right wording and in a few days will send you a different version of this passage for the use of your translator. Thanks!

Cordially yours,
Freud

604

1 March 1933
81 Harley Street, London

Dear Professor,

The translation is not yet complete, and will be subsequently revised, so there is plenty of time for you to send in any corrections you may wish.

I am expecting this week reprints of my Congress paper.[1] I know you will disagree with parts of it, but hope you will find it suitable for the purpose of stimulating thought and further research.

We are very well here and hope you are the same. You must be glad that Austria is not a part of Germany.

With kindest regards,

Yours always,
Ernest Jones.

1. Jones (1933a).

605

1 March 1933
Vienna, IX. Berggasse 19

Neue Vorlesungen p. 227 (instead of lines 5–8): In a famous dictum the philosopher *Kant* points to the starry heavens above us and the moral law within us as being the two things which should fill us with ever new and increasing admiration and awe. Believers will certainly be prepared to claim these two elements of creation as the strongest testimony to the greatness of God. Strange though etc.[1]

Freud

1. The note in Freud (1933a, p. 163 n. 1) refers to the original version of this passage, which was pared down in later editions.

606

7 April 1933
Vienna, IX. Berggasse 19

Dear Jones,

Among the noticeable symptoms of these times is also the disinclination to write, which is generally spreading, although one knows that letters to England, unlike those to Germany, are not exposed to the danger of being opened. I am overcoming the inhibition in the interest of Abraham's heirs, for I want you to count on my assistance when you and Ophuijsen do something to provide for Hilde and his widow. Admittedly I can do no more than contribute money.

I am quite prepared to disperse the little I have gathered in riches. My unemployed son, Oliver, whom I have been supporting for a year, is coming to Vienna tomorrow to discuss his future. There is little doubt that he will never find a job again in Berlin. (He is a civil engineer.) Ernst too is thinking of emigrating, perhaps to Palestine; because of his wife he is, however, more secure.

Despite all the newspaper reports of mobs, demonstrations, etc., Vienna is calm, life undisturbed. We can expect with certainty that the Hitler movement will spread to Austria, is indeed already here, but it is very unlikely that it will present a similar danger as in Germany. It is much more likely that it will be bound[1] through the alliance with the other rightist parties. We are in transition toward a rightist dictatorship, which means the suppression of social democracy. That will not be an agreeable state of affairs and will not make life pleasant for us Jews, but we all think that legal emergency declarations are impossible in Austria because the terms of our peace treaty expressly provide for the rights of minorities, which did not happen in the Versailles Treaty. Here legalized persecution of the Jews would immediately result in the intervention of the League of Nations. For Austria, however, to annex herself to Germany, in which case the Jews here would be equally without rights, is something that France and her allies will never allow. Besides, Austrians are not inclined to the German brutality. In such a way we lull ourselves into—relative—security. In any case, I am resolved not to budge an inch.

I have not forgotten that May is to bring you a birthday as well and greet you cordially.

Yours,
Freud

1. The verb here in German is "wird . . . gebunden werden," the infinite being "binden," literally, "to bind" or "to combine with," as in a chemical reaction, thereby providing the sense of an arrested process that is rendered harmless.

607

10 April 1933
81 Harley Street, London

Dear Professor,

It was a special pleasure to get a personal letter from you, and to hear again your manly and firm tones in these difficult times. So far as I can judge, my opinion about the situation in Austria is the same as yours, though I should attach more value to the national-patriotic desire of the *Heimwehr* people[1] to retain the personality of old Austria; they must have noted how swiftly Bavaria allowed herself to be swallowed by Prussia. I am in touch with the Austrian Embassy here and know how strong a fight they are opposing to the Nazi-Anschluss movement.

I was deeply moved by your offer, even in these difficult days, to help the Abraham family,[2] and am sure that we shall be able to do something practicable in this respect. I have had to be extremely careful in what I write to them, but I told her in a recent letter that she could always find shelter with us. I am negotiating with a friend of Eder's to find work for the boy and with van Ophuijsen over the girl's future. I should imagine it impossible for Mrs. Abraham to continue with her pension, both because of the flight of all guests and because of her brother's ruin. She appears to have no other friends or support in Berlin, so that presumably she may also come to England. There are formidable difficulties in the way, both as regards admission to residence in England, especially when earning a living, and even to leaving Germany. The German solution for what they regard as superfluous Jews appears to be, not to send them away, but to keep them in a cage until they starve. At the same time their guilt gives them a certain sensitiveness to outside opinion. I know, for instance, that an interview between Lord Reading[3] and the German Ambassador here produced a deep impression. Therefore the furor will surely die down. But in the meantime the positions in medicine and law will be occupied by Gentiles, so that the harm cannot be undone. There is intense indignation in this country among all classes, and I should think also among many Germans.

The Abraham problems seem to me the most urgent.[x4] Eitingon will of course stand firm and his Polish nationality should give him security; in the worst case he should find a good home in Paris. So many of the others have already left the country that their problems are of a different nature. We are at the moment trying to get permission for Schmideberg[5] to live in England, and hope to be able to do the same for two or three other colleagues from Germany. Our Society is unanimous in wishing to help in every way it can. In the meantime we must all remain in good contact and send any information that may be useful. I need hardly say that letters here are never opened.

With my warmest greetings,

Yours always affectionately
Ernest Jones.

1. "Home defense forces."

2. Karl Abraham's widow, Hedwig, and son Gerd; as well as his daughter Hilde (later Hilda) Abraham (1906–1971), who, after emigrating to England, became a prominent member of the British Psycho-Analytical Society.

3. Rufus Daniel Isaacs (1860–1935), first Marquess of Reading, politician, Lord Chief Justice of England (1913–1921), and diplomat; served a brief term in 1931 as foreign secretary in Ramsay MacDonald's coalition government.

4. At the top of the page Jones wrote by hand the words: "[x]With the exception of personal ones: my wife has two sisters and a brother in Berlin!"

5. Walter Schmideberg (1890–1954), who had arrived in England the previous year, was the husband of Melitta Schmideberg (1904–1983), the daughter of Melanie Klein. Both Schmidebergs were psychoanalysts and were actively involved in the affairs of the British Society; see Grosskurth (1986) and King and Steiner (1991).

608

3 May 1933
42 York Terrace, Regents Park

Dear Professor,

Two[1] birthdays are the occasion of this letter. One, the most recent, came about this morning: a strong boy, called Lewis Ernest. Mother and son are very well, though the birth was not easy. Because of an acetonemia we had to induce artificial labour at midnight, and that made the course of events more painful and longer. Now all seems well. It is an optimistic event in these days, but surely the world economics will be better regulated before he grows up.

The other of course is your own. I hope you are spending [it] in enjoyable surroundings, *'in Lilazeit'* [lilac time], even if there are dark thoughts about the world. My wish to you is that you live to see the beginnings of happier changes, so that you will feel happier about relatives, friends and our work.

I fully realise the set-back we have had, and that we even yet may not know the full consequences. But, as you said on your seventieth birthday, you have no illusions about the extent of our progress, and therefore can have fewer disappointments. I think $\psi\alpha$ is more securely based in England than in any other country, and feel we can quite safely all adopt the motto 'slow but sure'.

I enjoyed reading your 'Einstein' book and shall review it myself for the *Journal*.[2] I am trying to write a book on $\psi\alpha$ and World Problems (government, politics, nationality, economics),[3] and you may be sure it will have no 'tendencies'.[4]

Since Anna and I correspond so much, my news reaches you *via* her. But let me take this opportunity of a renewed expression of my devotion to you, and loyalty to our common work, with the best and warmest wishes to you and all your family

Yours always affectionately
Ernest Jones.

1. Here a line links the word *"two"* with a sentence written out at the top of the page: "Really three, for today was also Karl Abraham's birthday."
2. Jones (1933c).
3. The book was not written.
4. See letter 72, where Jones speaks of checking "wrong tendencies" and getting "control of various wrong tendencies."

609

7 May 1933
Vienna, IX. Berggasse 19

Dear Jones,

Now that the flood of receptions has receded, the first reply naturally belongs to you because there was nothing in the other letters that was equally nice and important, and because here is an opportunity to reciprocate a greeting of congratulation with one that has a better justification. Given all the uncertainty of life that we are familiar with, one may envy the parents their joy and hopes that will soon attach themselves to the new human being, whereas in the case of the elderly person one has to be content if one can more or less balance one's inevitable need for ultimate rest with the desire to enjoy the love and friendship of one's family a little longer. I believe I have discovered that the yearning for final rest is nothing basically primary but the expression of the need to free oneself from the feeling of inadequacy that assails one [den Alten], particularly in all the small tasks of life.

You are right that, compared to my seventieth birthday, my worries are no longer focused on psychoanalysis. It is secure, and I know it to be in good hands. But the future of my children and my grandchildren is bleak and endangered, and my own impotence is painful.

With cordial greetings to both parents and all the children.

Yours,
Freud

610

16 May 1933
81 Harley Street, London

Dear Professor,

Thank you very warmly for your kind greetings to the new arrival. I am glad to say that both mother and child are doing very well.

I was very much interested in your discovery about the longing for rest, which I hope you will publish. It appeals to me as being much more humanly comprehensible than a naked, unexplained, wish for death itself. I can also give a slight confirmation from a minor sphere. It is this. Periodically I have had the same wish to retire from work as I remember your having at my age, and I have always noticed that these moods coincide with a feeling of inadequacy in respect of one's work. Instead of [its][1] work being a positive expression of one's wishes, it has for the time being reverted to the sense of obligation and duty no doubt originating in the need to assuage primal guilt.

We are of course anxious about your political situation. Will you or Anna give due warning if you think there is any risk of letters being censored. I have just heard, from the Embassy, that Mussolini is planning with the Pope and perhaps with France to engineer a Catholic movement that would result in Bavaria joining Austria and in the Rhineland being made autonomous. That would be a wonderful thing for the peace of the world, but I fear it is a fanciful project.

We have many applications, including one from Reik, to come to work in England. We quite warmly welcome such applicants, but the external situation is decidedly unfavourable. Those who venture to [come][2] apply personally will probably have a better chance.

With kindest greetings to you all,

Yours affectionately
Ernest Jones.

1. Crossed out in the original; "work" is handwritten in an otherwise typed letter.
2. Crossed out in the original; "apply" is handwritten.

611

25 May 1933
81 Harley Street, London

Dear Professor,

We have to condole with each other over the latest sad news.[1] It can unfortunately[2] no longer be said that the event is a blow to the movement itself, but I am sure the shock will have revived in you—as it did in me—the memory of many happy days in the past and the thought of an inspiring figure whom we all loved so much. I am more glad than ever that I succeeded at the last Congress in keeping him within our circle. Your work is now so disseminated over all the world that nothing can prevent its ultimate progress, and in England we have an Institute and a body of workers which would seem to be as firmly based as anything can be in this unpredictable world.

With my warmest sympathy to you,

Yours always affectionately
Ernest Jones.

1. Jones refers to the death of Ferenczi the previous day.
2. Here it appears as if "un" was crossed out (uncharacteristically with an X rather than a straight line as usual), and then underscored with a line of dots to indicate that the phrase should read as typed initially, suggesting a moment of highly charged ambivalence for Jones.

612

29 May 1933
Vienna XIX. Hohe Warte 46

Dear Jones,

We have indeed every reason to condole with each other. Our loss is great and painful, one aspect of that change that overthrows everything in existence and creates room for the new. Ferenczi takes a part of the old era with him; then, when I step down, a new one will probably begin, in which you will still be prominent. Fate, resignation, that is all.

To be sure, the loss was not a new one; for years Ferenczi has no longer been with us, indeed, not even with himself. It is now easier to comprehend the slow process of destruction to which he fell victim. During the last two years it expressed itself organically in pernicious anemia, which soon led to severe motor disturbances. Liver therapy improved the condition of his blood, but had no effect on the other symptoms. In his last weeks he could no longer walk or stand at all. Simultaneously a mental degeneration in the form of paranoia developed with uncanny logical consistency. Central to this was the conviction that I did not love him enough, did not want to acknowledge his work, and also that I had analyzed him badly. His technical innovations were connected with this, as he wanted to show me how lovingly one has to treat one's patients in order to help them. These were indeed regressions to his childhood complexes, the main grievance being that his mother had not loved him—a middle child among 11 or 13—passionately or exclusively enough. So he himself became a better mother, even found the children he needed, among them a suspect American woman to whom he often devoted 4–5 hours a day (Mrs. Severn?).[1] After she had left, he believed that she influenced him through vibrations across the ocean, and said that she analyzed him and thereby saved him.[2] (He thus played both roles, was mother and child.) She seems to have produced a *pseudologia phantastica*; he credited her with the oddest childhood traumas, which he then defended against us. In this confusion his once so brilliant intelligence was extinguished. But let us keep his sad end a secret between us.

Cordially yours,
Freud

P.S. I hope your little son is thriving.

1. Elizabeth Severn, a dancer and writer, who had been in analysis with Ferenczi from about 1926 and was an important collaborator with Ferenczi regarding his pioneering experiments in mutual analysis. She figures significantly in Ferenczi's clinical diary as the patient "R. N." (Dupont, 1988).

2. Severn's interest in telepathy, the teachings of the Yogis, as well as communication

by means of bodily vibrations, was long-standing; see her study *The Psychology of Behaviour* (New York: Dodd, Mead, 1917), pp. 70, 103, 307.

613

3 June 1933
81 Harley Street, London

Dear Professor,

It was distressing to hear of the bad time that poor Ferenczi must have gone through, but I hear from Roheim that the end was unexpectedly sudden and without suffering. Presumably there was degeneration of the spinal cord which sometimes accompanies pernicious anaemia. I will of course keep secret what you told me about the American lady, but I am afraid the paranoia is public news:[1] it was sufficiently obvious to all analysts from his last Congress paper,[2] and it is about this I am now writing. Eitingon did not wish to allow it to be read at the Congress, but I persuaded him. I thought at the time of asking you about its publication in the *ZEITSCHRIFT* and whether you would add any Anmerkung der Redaktion. I hoped that Ferenczi himself would not publish it, but when I received the proofs of the *ZEITSCHRIFT* I felt he would be offended if it were not translated into English and so asked his permission for this. He seemed gratified, and we have not only translated it but set it up in type as the first paper in the July number. Since his death I have been thinking over the removal of the personal reason for publishing it. Others also have suggested that it now be withdrawn and I quote the following passage from a letter of Mrs. Riviere's, which [with] which I quite agree: "Now that Ferenczi has died, I wondered whether you will not reconsider publishing his last paper. It seems to me it can only be damaging to him and a discredit, while now that he is no longer to be hurt by its not being published, no good purpose could be served by it. Its scientific contentions and its statements about analytic practice are just a tissue of delusions, which can only discredit psa and give credit to its opponents. It cannot be supposed that all *JOURNAL* readers will appreciate the mental condition of the writer,[3] and in this respect one has to think of posterity too!" I therefore think it best to withdraw the paper unless I hear from you that you have any wish to the contrary.

We have been able to give Ernst some good introductions and he has fully lived up to his reputation of a *Glückskind* [fortunate son]. You need have no anxiety about his making his way. We shall be delighted to have him in England, though I have wondered whether his vivacious personality would not be more suited to France.

Frau Dr. Maas[4] has a clever scheme for running a hostel in England for a number of Jewish children from Germany whose parents can still afford to pay for them to be brought up in a happier environment. She is coming over next week with Hilde Abraham for a visit. It is likely that there may be work for Frau Dr. Abraham in connection with the scheme. I greatly hope so, because the poor woman's situation in Berlin is quite hopeless, both financially and psychologically. Gerd is having a very hard struggle to get a footing in England and we cannot yet say whether it will be successful. Our Government unfortunately is strictly excluding all it can. I am sure, however, that we shall have several analysts and we shall give them every welcome.

With kindest regards,

Yours always,
[Ernest Jones]

1. In a letter to Brill 20 June 1933, Jones uses the term "paranoic" (with "lucid intervals") to describe Ferenczi's condition (Archives of the British Psycho-Analytical Society, London).

2. Ferenczi (1933).

3. It appears that Jones was convinced that Ferenczi was undergoing a mental deterioration of the greatest proportions during his last years. Thus in his biography of Freud, Jones refers to Ferenczi's mental state by using terms such as "his latent psychotic trends," "his final delusional state," his "mental disturbance," or his "violent paranoic and even homicidal outbursts" (Jones, 1957a, pp. 176, 178; 1957b, pp. 188, 190). Some commentators suggest that Jones "concocted" these allegations (Roazen, 1974, p. 357), but in fact Jones felt he had corroborating evidence supporting his position, and not just from Freud. Freud's diagnosis (see letter 612), to cite Peter Gay (1988, p. 586), was actually one of a series of reports which Jones had been obtaining over the years, for example, from Eitingon (letter 571), Rickman (letter 595), and, as can be seen here, from Joan Riviere.

4. Dr. Hilde Maas was elected an associate member of the British Psycho-Analytical Society in November 1933.

614

17 July 1933
81 Harley Street, London

Dear Professor,

In the first place I want to say how glad I was to get the excellent photograph with which Ernst presented me. It is extremely lifelike and I must congratulate Ruth Brunswick about it.

Last week my servant surprised me by suddenly announcing that Professor Freud would like to see me. I said calmly: "By all means. Show him in!" There appeared a man of about thirty-five who said his name was Marzel Freud, that he was a nephew of yours, that he was a famous German

painter and Professor der Bildenkunst [*bildende Künste*, visual arts] in the
Academy at Karlsruhe. His story was that he had been expelled from Germany at twenty-four hours notice on account of pacifism, that he wished
to give an exhibition of his oil paintings in England, and that in order to
defray the Customs duties (which actually do not exist with oil paintings),
he was selling some copper etchings. These were very good, so I bought
three—though at a very high price. Ernst denies all knowledge of him and
we are making some police investigations. It is very delightful having
Ernst in London. His vitality is inspiring to all those in contact with him
and I am sure he will make his way successfully. He is also being very
helpful to other *emigrés*.

Gerd Abraham is still here, but has not yet found the possibility of
getting a permit to work. I shall be very relieved when he does. Hilde
Abraham has just heard that her hope of finishing the medical course in
Berlin is quite fruitless. She is continuing her analysis there, but will
probably have to emigrate and become a doctor's secretary or assistant.

Strachey is going through Sprott's translation of the *Neue Vorlesungen*,[1]
and I have just been making some revision of the first chapters. The MS.
should all reach the printers by the end of this month and the book should
therefore appear some time in the autumn.

My younger son is thriving excellently and appears to be the only child
taking after me in appearance. My wife's sister, Valerie Merck, is here from
Berlin, and we are trying to make plans for her. When I see you next I
must tell you a wonderful story about the other sister's (Gretel) final scene
on being dismissed from her position in the *Bundesgenossenschaft*.[2] Personally I am still plagued with osteo-arthritis and am on a strict diet. I
propose to go through a cure in Scotland next month and then spend the
rest of the holidays with my family in Sussex.

I have been very happy at receiving recently good reports of your health
and hope you are enjoying the more peaceful time away from town life.

With kindest regards,

Yours always affectionately,
Ernest Jones.

1. Freud (1933a).

2. Katherine Jones's sister Gretel (née Jokl) Mayer worked in Vienna up to the time
of Hitler's rise to power, then left with her husband for America. Her sister Valerie left
Berlin and settled in London in 1933; she was an actress, and later also a journalist and
writer.

615

23 July 1933
Vienna, IX. Berggasse 19

Dear Jones,

It is a relief to have a chat with you in these wretched times. My son Ernst is right, I have no nephew called Marcel. He may be called Freud; the name is not as rare as one might wish. Even in Vienna there is a Prof. Freud, who is not related to us. Incidentally, if the etchings were good, the fraud is almost forgivable. Worse things are happening these days.

I like to hear that you predict success for my son Ernst in London. He certainly seems decided on settling there. His youngest, Clemens, a delightful fellow with whom he last visited us, said literally: "How different things would be for me today if I were an Englishman!" It would be nice if this wish were granted to him.[1]

I have read Ophuijsen's letter to you as well as your reply. Your counsel to maintain diplomatic calm is certainly justified, but W.-N.'s behavior remains disgusting and may well embitter such a serious man as Ophuijsen.[2] The poor exiles never have it too easy anywhere.

We too will get our fascism, party dictatorship, elimination of opposition, applied anti-Semitism. But we should retain our independence, and the peace treaty makes it legally impossible to strip minorities of their rights. It won't be pleasant, but we will be able to stay in Austria. Of course the future still depends on what will develop out of the witch's cauldron in Germany. You probably already know that v. Hattingberg obtained the lectureship in psychotherapy in Berlin. An aristocrat, Aryan, fool, blockhead, and a bad sort, in other words in every respect the right man for the post. (Enclosure!)[3] It will probably depend on his mercy what kind of existence if any analysis will lead in Germany. Perhaps you remember him from the Munich Congress in 1913.[4]

Sprott is probably the darling of Lytton Strachey who visited me once in Gastein. I am not writing anything at the moment, was never before so far from producing anything. I want to keep August totally free. "Too bad"[5] that you are working with so much rheumatism and arthritis. My health is, so to speak, not bad; I mean it does not deserve the name. I am sure your youngest one will have an easier life.

I have before me the galley proofs of "Die phallische Phase"[6] which demand to be read in August.

Cordial greetings to you and everyone.

Your
Freud

1. Clement Rafael Freud (b. 1924) is at this writing a Member of Parliament and a fixture of British public life on television and in publications as a humorist and a celebrated cook.

2. A. J. Westerman-Holstijn, member of the Dutch Psychoanalytic Society, who greeted with disdain the arrival in Holland of the Jewish psychoanalyst Karl Landauer from Frankfurt. This issue, together with the ongoing conflicts in the Dutch society, resulted in van Ophuijsen's resignation as president in September, and the formation on November 1 of a second organization, the Society of Psychoanalysis in Holland, of which Landauer became a member; see *Journal*, 15 (1934): 366, 371–372. For excerpts from the relevant correspondence between Westerman-Holstijn and Landauer, see Brecht et al. (1985, pp. 56–57).

3. "*(Beilage!)*" is written in the margin.

4. Hans von Hattingberg (b. 1879) had presented "Zum analerotischen Charakter" at the Congress of the International Psychoanalytic Association, Munich, 7–8 September 1913; see *Zeitschrift*, 2 (1914): 407. It later appeared as "Analerotik, Angstlust und Eigensinn," *Zeitschrift*, 2 (1914): 244–258. In 1914 he established a practice as a psychotherapist in Munich, was largely critical of psychoanalysis, joined the medical faculty of the University of Berlin in 1933; see Cocks (1985, p. 69).

5. In English in the original.

6. Jones (1933a).

616

23 August 1933
Vienna, XIX. Hohe Warte 46

Dear Jones,

As an exception, I will for once not write about the bleak misery of these times which at present stifles all more meaningful activity for me. I am glad to have an occasion to preoccupy myself with an admittedly smaller but tangible matter.

I hear little from you, feel as though I am isolated and stranded, perceive as if from afar that unpleasant things are brewing in the I.P.V., and I am almost prepared for the eventuality that our organization will also perish in the current world crisis. Berlin is lost, Budapest devalued by the loss of Ferenczi, and one cannot tell in which direction they are drifting in America. Of course we shall put up a resistance, and you as president will organize this resistance.

With the death of Ferenczi the post of vice president is also vacant, a gap torn in the executive. As you know, Eitingon is going to Palestine and will therefore be inaccessible to some extent and recede into the background. I think one should find a replacement. After a year's absence Princess Marie is with me again, and this leads me to suggest that she be moved into Ferenczi's place. Not only because one can make an impression with her abroad. She is a person of high intelligence, has the working capacity of a man, has done nice work, is fully devoted to the cause, and as you know, is also in a position to give material help. She is now 50 years old, will presumably turn increasingly away from her private interests and devote herself to analytic work. I need not mention that she alone holds the French group together and pays for the *Revue Française*. Her good practical sense and charming, sociable manner will make her a delightful colleague on the executive.

I assume that an actual replacement for Ferenczi can only be made by election at the next Congress. But is it not in your power to appoint her provisionally as Beirat, with the intent of having her confirmed later by the plenum at the Congress? And a further aspect; the appointment of a layperson to the executive of the I.P.V. would be a clear demonstration against the undesirable arrogance of the physicians who like to forget that psychoanalysis is after all something other than a part of psychiatry.

Hoping to hear only good news of you and your family,

Cordially yours,
Freud

617

[postcard]

14 September 1933
Durley Dean Hotel
Bournemouth

Dear Professor,

I have been moving about (Scotland, Wales and Sussex) and my secretary also has been away, so I get only today your interesting letter of August 23. I need hardly say that I agree with it, but will write to you fully on Monday from London. *Es ist viel zu sagen.*[1]

Immer Ihr
Ernest Jones.

1. "There is much to say."

618

18 September 1933
81 Harley Street, London

Dear Professor,

I have just come back from an enjoyable holiday. The rheumatism cure, like most of these cures for organic troubles, was not very successful. It

gave considerable temporary relief, but the trouble soon came back afterward. However, there are much more important things to talk about.

First of all, please let me say that it is perhaps possible to exaggerate the
blow to our work caused by recent events in Germany. It is easy in Germany, or perhaps even in Austria also, to forget the rest of the world.
Deplorable as the whole affair has been, particularly in its personal rever-
berations among our friends, I am confident that we shall survive it as we
have other blows. Nothing can lastingly set back the progress of our work.
Its effect on our organization is another matter, which needs careful consideration. We shall certainly miss Eitingon very much. I see this much
advantage in von Hattingberg's appointment by Hitler, namely, that his
calling himself a psycho-analyst will have the result that psycho-analysis
will not be forbidden in Germany.[1] There will of course be a tendency to
dilute it with other material, and it is there that we shall have to fight.
Boehm has sent me a letter of which I enclose a copy and you will of course
perceive the significance of the passage I have marked. We have good
reason to be suspicious of him, but I want to explore the situation and so
am accepting his invitation to meet him in Holland (next week). I am
making the condition that van Ophuijsen, as Beirat, should also be present
at the discussion.[2]

Coming now to your proposal about the Princess, my opinion of her is
that she has the highest technical ability, admirable energy, and self-less
devotion to our cause. The fact of her being non-medical would also, as
you say, be an advantage to an official position. I think, however, that her
judgements are apt to be impulsive and to need a steadying influence. We
are good friends and it will be a pleasure to cooperate with her more fully.
You have, however, forgotten one technical point in the rules of the Association. A Beirat can only be an ex-President. At the last Congress an exception to this rule was specially made by resolving that the President of the
Pan-American Association should also be a Beirat.[3] If it were a question
simply of nominating an official I should certainly take the responsibility
of doing so and would ask the Congress to ratify it subsequently. It would
be exceeding my powers, however, to abrogate an official rule without first
asking the permission of the Congress. I shall come to see you before the
next Congress and we can arrange this as well as other matters.

I am very distressed at the suffering caused to our colleagues in Germany,
but not despairing at the blow dealt to our movement, which I am sure
we shall survive. Ever since Abraham's death the *niveau* [level] of the
German Society had steadily deteriorated, both from emigration and from
internal dissensions. Two other matters give me almost as great concern.
One is that several Societies, notably the Dutch and French, contain a
majority of members who are evidently opposed to international coopera-

tion. The other matter, and perhaps the gravest of all, is the tendency towards quarrelling and internal dissension in so many Societies. I think in the first place here of the New York Society where the little *Quarterly* group, flushed by their early and unexpected triumphs, have now grown so troublesome as to paralyse the good working of the Society and to [en]force[4] the retirement of the steadier influences. I have a great deal of influence with Brill, but on this occasion seem to have failed in moving him from his decision to resign. I feel sure this would be a fatal blow to the Society, and would therefore suggest that you make a personal appeal to him to continue his efforts to steer it until at least the paranoiac Zilboorg be eliminated.[5] I am afraid that nothing other than an appeal from you would be successful. Rado is in a position where he could do much. Unfortunately, I have the best of reasons for deeply doubting his trustworthiness. He has of late been behaving with tact and skill, but I am afraid that his future aims will prove to be of an intriguing nature.

The British Society continues to be one of the bright spots on the horizon, and I do not think Brill exaggerates when he says in a recent letter that it is "the real bulwark of the psycho-analytic movement". We have checked any slight tendency to the formation of cliques, and work together very harmoniously. The intellectual level of the work and discussions is very gratifying and we are slowly consolidating some prestige in the profession, etc., outside.

You must have wondered often why psycho-analysis has not been more successful among analysts themselves. I find three reasons for this. First, that so many were originally neurotic and have chosen the career as a method of holding their neurosis at bay. Secondly, that continued work all day in the realm of the unconscious imposes a strain which only the most balanced natures can sustain. Many analysts are sufficiently well analysed for other activities in life, but not for doing analytic work. Thirdly, and last not least, is the fact that so very few of them are adequately analysed. One sees, and I have experienced it myself personally, how difficult it is to secure enough analysis when one has attained a senior position, with intimate contact with many colleagues. Yet we must find some method for securing what [must][6] may be called post-graduate analysis. I think this can be done only by insisting on a still higher standard of analysis among the beginners and introducing them to the idea that they must continue their analysis from time to time later on.

Brill tells me that the American woman who was the evil genius in Ferenczi's later days was Clara Thompson.[7] I am sure you must miss him very much, though there again we have actually lost less than it might appear.

I am glad to say that my family is very well and happy. The latest arrival promises to be a lusty fellow. I have left them at the seaside now, but they return to London in another week.

With my kindest personal regards to you and your family,

Yours always affectionately
Ernest Jones.

1. Psychoanalysis did suffer severely under the Nazis; see Cocks (1985) and Brecht et al. (1985).

2. The meeting regarding an order prohibiting Jews from sitting on scientific councils is discussed in Jones (1957a, pp. 183, 185; 1957b, pp. 195, 198). Felix Boehm (1881–1958) was president of the German Psychoanalytic Society between 1933 and 1938.

3. Brill, president of the newly formed (1932) Federation of American Psychoanalytic Societies (the reorganized American Psychoanalytic Association) was given a seat as vice president on the Central Executive of the International Psychoanalytic Association; see *Journal*, 14 (1933): 177.

4. "En" is crossed out in the original.

5. Brill did not resign his post as president of the New York Psychoanalytic Society and was reelected in 1934; Zilboorg, who was secretary in 1933, was not reelected in 1934. See *Journal*, 14 (1933): 523 and 15 (1934): 379.

6. Crossed out in the original.

7. Clara Thompson (1893–1958), M.D., American psychoanalyst, member of the Washington-Baltimore Psychoanalytic Society, Ferenczi's patient between 1928 and 1933; later helped found the William Alanson White Institute in New York. She was an "evil genius" through her participation in Ferenczi's researches into active therapy. See Stanton (1991).

619

5 October 1933
81 Harley Street, London

Dear Professor,

The latest reports of your progress are good and I am looking forward to receiving another one from Anna soon. I enclose a copy of a magnificent speech that Einstein made before ten thousand people here this week.[1]

Our four German psycho-analysts in England have received the necessary permissions they need and are already hard at work. Two more are expected this autumn.[2] We are starting our new session with a good spirit.

With kindest personal regards,

Yours ever
Ernest Jones.

1. See Otto Nathan and Heinz Norden, eds., *Einstein on Peace* (New York: Simon and Schuster, 1960), pp. 236–243.

2. The British Society's list of members for 1933 included Franz Cohn and Melitta Schmideberg, as well as the associate members S. H. Fuchs (later Foulkes), Paula Heimann, Hilde Maas, Kate Misch (later Friedlander), and Walter Schmideberg; see

Journal, 14 (1933): 530–531. Barbara Lantos (see Brecht et al., 1985, p. 64) and Wilhelm Reich (see Steiner, 1988, pp. 313–319) may have been among those expected.

620

15 October 1933
Vienna, IX. Berggasse 19

Dear Jones,

I am out of bed, have already worked to a modest extent for the past week, feel " 'moderately' well,"[1] but have still not overcome the consequences of the thrombosis, and an initial attempt to climb the stairs cost me a thorough relapse. I thank you for the letters that I received from you during this time, and for all the news of your activity, particularly for the poor refugees.

Here it almost looks as though we need not fear a takeover by German fascism. What we shall get instead we do not know, only that it won't be anything particularly pleasant. We shall be satisfied if we can only remain here in peace.

I appreciate your argument about the Prince[ss].[2] Admittedly Brill was already an exception, and Oph, whom you invited to the German conference "as Beirat," was also never president.

For years I have been advocating your idea of a "Postgraduate Analysis,"[3] and am also trying to put it into effect. I find such supplementary analyses unexpectedly interesting and helpful. Therefore, in this instance I am stressing my priority!

Particularly glad to hear that your little family is thriving so well.

Cordially yours,
Freud

1. In English in the original.
2. The German here is "Prinz" (Prince), without a period. Freud is referring to Prinzessin (Princess) Marie Bonaparte.
3. In English in the original.

621

26 November 1933
Vienna, IX. Berggasse 19

Dear Jones,

I am writing these lines not quite spontaneously, however, not against my will or interest. They concern Th. Reik, who is at present in Vienna, very discouraged and without prospects, and who absolutely demands that

I interest you in his fate. It is true that he made a particularly valuable contribution in his application of analysis to a certain field. This is the basis of his claim for material help, so that he can continue his work. One should note that the exigencies of these times have not had a very favorable effect on his mental peculiarities. Naturally it would be primarily my responsibility not to let him founder, but you know how limited my means are, how they are disappearing under the financial pressures, and how uncertain I am about the time span in which I can continue to earn a living. It would therefore be very welcome if you as president of the I.P.V. can find a way of helping him. I am recuperating slowly, and hope you and your family are well.

Cordially yours,
Freud

622

1 December 1933

Dear Professor,

Reik has addressed a long letter to me, and I can best answer your letter about him by enclosing a copy of my answer to him. If only one knew of some way of finding him a research post. He is in every way unsuitable for therapeutic work, where his irresponsibility towards his patients and unscrupulousness towards his colleagues have so often been demonstrated. Can you think of any practical suggestion towards getting him such a post?

I have been wondering if there would be any point in trying to raise a fund for our colleagues in distress. Obviously we should get nothing from Germany, Holland, France and Hungary. There remains Austria, England and America. Analysts have strained themselves recently for the Verlag and would, I fear, wish to devote the small sum that could now be raised to the distressed analysts in their own countries. The nett result would be perhaps a couple of pounds each for the refugees which would be more of an insult than a help. Many people are doing much by their individual initiative and would probably prefer this method.

It was very gratifying to hear that you are keeping your health. We shall soon have the spring to look forward to and I am very much looking forward to seing you personally in the summer.

With kindest regards,

Yours always,
[Ernest Jones]

623

4 December 1933
Vienna, IX. Berggasse 19

Dear Jones,

Received your *Reikbriefe*. Can only endorse every one of your sentences. It is difficult to help.

Cordially yours,
Freud

624

14 January 1934
Vienna, IX. Berggasse 19

Dear Jones,

Do you have space in the *Journal* for this odd *Mutterliebesgedichtchen?*[1] Perhaps you can have a few comments made about it.

Cordially yours,
Freud

1. "Little poem on mother love."

625

16 January 1934
81 Harley Street, London

Dear Professor,

Many thanks for the interesting sonnet which we will insert in the next number.[1]

I was shocked to hear of Martin's painful illness. It reminded me of my numerous experiences with Loe. I hope he is now on the road to recovery.

Yours always cordially,
[Ernest Jones]

1. This did not appear in the *Journal*.

626

26 March 1934
42 York Terrace, Regents Park

Dear Professor,

I do not often have occasion to consult you about a patient, let alone a member of your own family. Yesterday we were in the country and took the opportunity of calling on Lucie[1] in Yeovil. I had better give you the full story as I understand it. On the momentous motor trip she was disturbed by the fact that the man was not able to drive and very apprehensive, with right, about the woman's driving. She begged a man to take her place in driving, but this could not be done. Five minutes before the accident she sent off a postcard at a stopping place and thought to herself it would probably be the last postcard she would ever send; I think it was to her mother. This seems to me already excessive. When the accident happened she went off into a pleasant dream that everything was all right and she was very happy. I read this as a strong Reizschutz with vigorous denial of reality, based on the assertion that her infantile fears (? danger from the mother) [might][2] could never come true in reality. She was in fact astonishingly well and only the bleeding from the ear revealed that there was trouble. The Doctor, whom I saw at the hospital yesterday, told me he was astonished to find that there was much greater shock on the second day than on the first. After this, however, she rapidly improved for two or three weeks. Now in the last ten days comes the problem of once more facing life and she has been very depressed, frequently crying, feeling she is not equal to her duties in life, reproaching herself on this score, and suffering very great weakness and giddiness when she gets up. Moreover, when she gets up she has severe pain on one side of the head as though it had been struck by a blow, i.e. delayed response to the accident. There can at present be no possible organic explanation, for even the weakness goes beyond what might be expected in the circumstances. I am very concerned lest she be laying the basis for a traumatic hysteria, of a quite classical kind, and I am afraid we shall have something to face in this respect in the future.

A practical question was whether to allow her to remain in bed for a much longer period or to encourage her to face the inevitable psychological reaction on once more coming back to life. I should have been in favour of the latter, for she is in a very invalid atmosphere at present, but for the unfortunate fact that to move her involves a journey which would certainly re-activate the Trauma. The train journey to Dartington where she was very anxious to go to see the boys takes four hours with two changes, and a motor car two and a half hours. I did not like this idea, and so suggested to Ernst that the boys be brought over from Dartington for a day or two at Easter, then going back again there for the holidays, and that she be brought direct to London, by a simple train journey, the week after Easter, i.e. six weeks after the accident. This he will probably do. But he told me that various authorities in Vienna stated that in such a case there was less likelihood of psychological after-effects if the patient was allowed to remain in bed for a very long period. This I find hard to believe and should specially like your opinion about.

We are all happy to think of the coming spring. Anna tells me that you have not yet found a house, but I can well imagine that you are longing to get away from the Berggasse. You know I intend to visit you in August; I am very greatly looking forward to this pleasure.

I need not give you any Association news for Anna doubtless keeps you informed of its ups and downs.

With kindest regards

Yours always
Ernest Jones.

1. Ernst Freud's wife, Lucie (née Brasch).
2. Crossed out in the original; "could" is handwritten in an otherwise typed letter.

627

29 March 1934
Vienna, IX. Berggasse 19

Dear Jones,

Thank you very much for your letter and the friendly interest it demonstrates. It contains a great many details which were unknown to me, that is, were concealed from me, and alter the interpretation of the situation in your sense. It does not seem to me connected with a worsening of the prognosis. I was still very concerned about the possibility of residual organic disturbances. I know nothing of the advice given by Viennese authorities for long bed rest. I hope Ernst will take your advice. Dr. Lampl[1] is perhaps right in thinking that an examination by an ear specialist can remove the doubts about the nature of the giddiness and thus open the way to certain practical measures.

I shall be very pleased when I can see you in Vienna in August. Probably *with* your dear wife, I hope? I still do not know where we shall receive you; we are just searching. It gives me great satisfaction to hear from Anna that you both work together so well.

Times are bleak and life is no longer easy.

With cordial greetings.

Yours,
Freud

1. Hans Lampl (1889–1958), Viennese physician, interested in anatomy, serology, and bacteriology; began psychoanalytic work in Berlin in 1921, married the psychoanalyst Jeanne de Groot in 1925, and returned to Vienna with his family in 1933 after Hitler came to power.

628

12 June 1934
42 York Terrace, Regents Park

Dear Professor,

I have just heard that Groddek has died after a ten days' illness with heart disease.[1] Please accept my condolence for I know you specially esteemed him. The only consolation is that he did not die in Ferenczi's lifetime.

On the other hand, I have the pleasant domestic news that my boy aged twelve has just won a scholarship of £500 at a modern public school (not co-educational) in Derbyshire. He will be going there in September, the first step into the outer world.[2]

We have seen Ernst and Lucie several times lately, she seems to me to be better, but older. Naturally she cannot feel settled till Ernst gets some good work here. I daresay his prospects are satisfactory when he gets a chance, but it is very hard to make the first start.

It is good to hear how much you are enjoying this lovely weather in your pleasant surroundings, which must make a wonderful change from the Berggasse; I shall see you now in a couple of months time and am greatly looking forward to it.

Yours always affectionately
Ernest Jones.

1. Georg Groddeck (1866–1934), German physician, specialist in psychosomatic medicine, colleague of both Freud and Ferenczi, whom he treated at his Baden-Baden clinic.
2. See M. Jones (1987, pp. 19–40).

629

16 June 1934
Vienna XIX. Strassergasse 47

Dear Jones,

Am pleased about the fine success of your son (Joan, isn't it?). May he remain a good omen for the future.

Rumor has it that in the end Groddeck was committed because of mental disturbance. The announcement of his death states that he died in Zurich; what was he doing in Zurich? Was he therefore in Burghölzli?[1] The times demand sacrifices. People die, perhaps more willingly than before. We learned yesterday that Mrs. Stella Zweig, Martin's invaluable assistant at the Verlag, died from an attack of poliomyelitis (Landry's form). A great predicament for the Verlag.

It is beautiful here in Grinzing, but one does not enjoy life. The foundations are rocking. Perhaps at this very moment the intriguer M. in Venice is selling us to the captain of the thieves H.[2] I will be happy to see you (and your wife?) with us in the summer. But what will it look like here then?

Cordially yours,
Freud

1. Prior to his death Groddeck had been writing strange letters to Hitler, and had suffered a severe heart attack. He had also gone to Zurich to read a paper on 2 June 1934 before the Swiss Psychoanalytic Society. He died shortly after at Schloss Knonau in the canton of Zurich.

2. The German is "*Räuberhauptmann H.*" It is tempting to posit an allusion here to Friedrich Schiller's play *Die Räuber* (1781) and to the German writer Gerhart Hauptmann (1862–1946), which might imply that literature was also imperiled by the political dealings that were being concocted in the encounter between Mussolini and Hitler, which took place 14–15 June 1934.

630

20 June 1934
42 York Terrace, Regents Park

Dear Professor,

Thank you very much for your congratulations about my boy. You remember his name correctly but we always call him by his Welsh name Mervyn. He will come to Switzerland with his Mother and myself in August but I shall leave them in Zürich during my short visit to Vienna. His relatives will not be in Vienna at that time of year and we have the intention of taking both him and his little sister for a week's visit to Vienna next Easter.

I was dreadfully sorry to hear about Frau Zweig's death. I saw during Martin's illness what a valuable and competent person she was and am sure that he will miss her very seriously.

I hope you are getting some amusement out of the current correspondence between Anna and myself in dealing with this truly embarrassing situation of the surplus of Congress papers.[1] It is at all events gratifying to see how much scientific activity is proceeding still in these troublous times.

With my kindest regards

Yours always
Ernest Jones.

1. Thirteenth Congress of the International Psychoanalytic Association, Lucerne, 26–31 August 1934.

631

International Psycho-Analytical Association

19 February 1935
London

Dear Professor,

I do not think I have written to you since I saw you last. My letters to Anna seem to convey all the news and I have no doubt it is passed on to you. There is at present rather a lull in the doings of the Association, but presumably the various problems will soon surge up again.

Federn and Weiss have notified me of the *Jahrbuch* they intend to bring out with your approval.[1] I had thought you had agreed with me last summer that it was time these official organs were regulated by a responsible committee, and I got the Lucerne Congress to appoint a special committee for that purpose. I hope that Weiss will consent to discussing his plans with the committee. As to the idea itself it seems to me a laudable one, but difficult of attainment at the moment. My own impression is that once a year is too frequent to provide useful summaries of our literature, but I would attach very great importance to such summaries of various aspects of Psycho-Analysis, if only we could get them well done. We have at present, however, no great surplus of energy at our disposal.

An excellent sign of the respect paid to Psycho-Analysis in this country is that I was recently elected an Honorary Member of the British Psychological Society. As they previously had an informal rule that no British subject could be so elected until he had reached the age of seventy, I am in doubt whether to regard this exception as a personal compliment or as an exaggeration of my advancing age!

I am glad to send you good personal news. My family is in excellent health and my rheumatism greatly benefitted from a twelve days' visit to the Engadine. We are all, except the baby, greatly looking forward to spending a week in Vienna at Easter. I wonder if you will have already moved from Berggasse at that time.

With kindest greetings

Yours always affectionately
Ernest Jones.

1. Edoardo Weiss had founded the Italian Psychoanalytic Society in 1932, as well as the journal *Rivista di psicanalisi.* It is not totally clear what he and Federn may have had in mind here, but Jones probably succeeded in quashing their plans to publish a psychoanalytic yearbook.

632

24 February 1935
Vienna, IX. Berggasse 19

Dear Jones,

From afar it seems to me too that your election to honorary membership of the British Psychological Society is a good sign. I just read that you are to give a lecture there in March.[1]

The prospect of your visit to Vienna at Easter makes me feel glad, as well as wistful. As a result of the restrictions of old age I know that I will be able to meet my obligations as host only very inadequately. Our Wolf, too, who once behaved in such an unfriendly manner towards you, is now an old gentleman and as old as I am in his canine context, i.e., over eleven years old.

I can only approve your decision in the matter of Eduardo Weiss. He is, incidentally, a particularly good fellow and I should like to accommodate him as much as possible.

With cordial greetings. *Auf Wiedersehen.*

Yours,
Freud

1. See Jones (1936).

633
International Psycho-Analytical Association

12 March 1935
London

Dear Professor Freud,

I am to give a public lecture next week under the auspices of the British Psychological Society, the title being 'Psycho-Analysis and the Instincts'.[1] For this purpose I am naturally re-reading many of your writings and I should be very grateful if you could give me answers to the following two questions, which all relate to passages from *'Das Ich und das Es'* (1923 edition).

(1) I do not quite understand the sentence beginning 'Beide Triebe' on Seite 49, L. 18,[2] specially in connection with the preceding sentence. I am referring only here to Eros. When you speak of the Wiederherstellung brought about by Eros do you mean simply the physical re-union of living substance or have you something else in mind? If so, how do we know that life began by dividing anything rather than by amalgamating simple molecules into more complex ones?

(2) The sentence, Seite 51, L. 4, 'Wir erkennen . . . . .' does not easily combine with the footnote on Seite 58.[3] In another place you speak of the musculature of multi-cellular organisms being a device whereby the dangerous death-instinct directed inwards becomes more safely directed outwards.[4] Are we to understand that Eros, perceiving the advantage of this path already laid down, takes advantage of it to flow outward from the narcissistic reservoir? In that case Eros would be making use of the death-instinct, exploiting it or subordinating it to its purpose. But in the footnote one would rather gather that the death-instinct would not of itself be flowing outwards unless it were directed thither by the outward flow of the libido. My question really is which precedes the other? Perhaps it cannot be answered in chronological terms.

With kindest regards

Yours very sincerely
[Ernest Jones]

1. Jones (1936).
2. See Freud (1923b, p. 40), *G.W.*, 13:269, sentence beginning "Acting in this way, both the instincts . . ."
3. Freud (1923b, pp. 41–42, 46 n. 3), *G.W.*, 13:270, 275 n. 1.
4. Jones may be referring to Freud (1920g, pp. 49–52).

634

15 March 1935
Vienna, IX. Berggasse 19

Dear Jones,

Gladly prepared to answer!

ad (1) Nothing else is meant than the union of living masses to form greater units. That life began with a disintegration is only a deduction, just based on the general nature of a drive. Since one observes that Eros wants to establish larger living units, one concludes that such a state existed at the beginning and was destroyed with the start of life. In no way do I overestimate the conclusiveness of this construction. Another way out is welcome.

ad (2) All your conceptions are correct. The chronological question seems to me irrelevant and cannot be answered with certainty. The train of thought would be something like this: It would be in the nature of Eros to turn outwards, as it seeks union with something else. Such a tendency would not be in the nature of the Todestrieb, since it would only be intent on destroying its own living mass. It is therefore assumed that the direction outwards originates from Eros. The Todestrieb which is also taken along outwards would thus become the Destruktionstrieb. Result: through this change the living organism protects itself against self-destruction. Of course, all this is tentative speculation—until one has something better.

Cordially yours,
Freud

635

International Psycho-Analytical Association

2 May 1935
London

Dear Professor,

It was a pleasure of the highest order to see you looking so well and to enjoy talking with you again. You can imagine however that my wish for the latter is not easy to satisfy and I hope to have the privilege of indulging it further as soon as it can be managed.

The great question of whether we in England have advanced your theory further or whether we have made a rather serious mistake still remains an open one so far as I am concerned. That I am anxious to thresh it out in a friendly discussion I have already shown. What we need next is for some penetrating critic from Vienna to come here and criticise our work on a similar basis.[1] I have already spoken to Federn and Anna about this and hope it will be arranged before long. What we most need is to study some concrete material together, for generalities do not carry one any further. I was grateful for your friendly reception of what I had to say and am going next week to report the points in our discussion to a small circle here.

I was glad you liked my Instinct paper,[2] but was very astonished at your thinking I had made such a mistake as to suppose you had used any of Melanie Klein's work as a starting point for any thoughts of yours. Of course I know very well that your exposition on the matter actually preceded her writing at all. I do not think I have ever known you to be influenced by anyone else, certainly least of all Melanie Klein. So I turned with curiosity to my paper and think I have found the sentence that puzzled you. It comes after an exposition of the super-ego and its severity and runs as follows:

"Detailed analytic studies, particularly those carried out on young children by Melanie Klein and others, have thrown a great deal of light on the sources of this severity and have led to the conception of a primitive aggressive instinct, non-sexual in character."

To avoid the least chance of ambiguity I will rewrite this sentence before publishing it.[3] It does, it is true, come rather as an interpolation in the argument, but I wanted to deal with all the contributions made by Psycho-Analysis, not only your own. When writing it I was not actually thinking of you because I should not ascribe to you the belief in a primary aggressive instinct (that is rather my own view); yours I should describe as a belief in an internal Todestrieb which is *secondarily* exteriorised into an aggressive impulse.

In any case there can hardly be a risk of misunderstanding, since [almost][4] the next sentence runs:

"But, strangely enough, it was not by this conception and the studies I have just outlined that *he* arrived at his present view of the duality of mental structure."[5]

Then I go on to your work about the Wiederholungszwang, '*Jenseits des Lustprinzips*' etc..

Our visit to Vienna made the deepest impression on all of us from the oldest to the youngest. Mervyn in particular will always treasure the precious gift you were so good as to give him.[6]

With my kindest regards

affectionately yours
Ernest Jones.

1. A week previously Jones had presented a paper outlining the differences between London and Vienna on various issues such as early female sexuality, the genesis of the superego, child analysis, and the death instinct; see Jones (1935). Robert Wälder was chosen to address the British Society; see note 4 to letter 637. The entire episode is discussed in Jones (1957a, pp. 196–197; 1957b, p. 210).

2. Jones (1936).

3. In the published version "particularly" is replaced with "strikingly confirmed by," and "aggressive instinct" is italicized; see Jones (1936, p. 281), and *Papers*, 5th ed. 1948, p. 162.

4. "Almost" is inserted by hand in an otherwise typed letter.

5. This sentence as typed was left intact in Jones (1936, p. 281). The emphasis was added to "he" by hand.

6. This was "an Etruscan statuette of exquisite beauty"; see M. Jones (1987, p. 17).

636

26 May 1935
Vienna, XIX. Strassergasse 47

Dear Jones,

At present I am affected by a communication[1] from the Royal Society of Medicine informing me that I have been unanimously elected an honorary member. As this cannot have happened "because of my beautiful eyes," it must be proof that respect for our psychoanalysis has made great progress in official circles in England. I thanked them most emphatically. Does not this appointment give one the right to add a whole string of letters after one's name, such as:

H.F.R.S.M.?[2]

Your cordial letter for my birthday was the proper continuation of your visit, which we all still recall with pleasure. (Incidentally, I have seldom seen two such delightful children as yours, each in their own way.)

I do not underestimate the differences in our theoretical views, but if there is no underlying malice, there can also be no bad consequences. I may insist that we in Vienna did not accompany our opposition with any feelings of hatefulness; whatever injustice Melanie Klein and her daughter committed in this respect to Anna has been set right by your kindness. To be sure, I am of the opinion that your society followed Mrs. Klein on a wrong path, but I am unfamiliar with just that sphere of observations which she draws upon and hence have no right to a firm conviction.

Your proposal that the discussion you initiated in Vienna should be continued by a guest in London has met with general approval. As I hear, Dr. Wälder is intended for this task.

Many thanks for explaining the point in your lecture on instinct which misled me. But you admit that the connection was "rather misleading."[3]

With patience and deeper reflection we will surely get over our current theoretical differences. We—London and Vienna—must hold together; the other European groups hardly play a role, and the centrifugal tendencies in our International are very strong at present. And it would be a pity if it were not to outlast my own existence.

With cordial greetings to you and your wife.

Yours,
Freud

1. Here *"Zeit"* is crossed out in the original and the sentence continues with *"Zuschrift."*
2. Honorary Fellow of the Royal Society of Medicine.
3. In English in the original.

637

International Psycho-Analytical Association

27 June 1935
London

Dear Professor,

It was such a pleasure to receive your kind letter a couple of weeks ago. I am sure you are right in the inference you draw from the Royal Society of Medicine's action which we were all very delighted to hear of. This is confirmed by the fact that it was a spontaneous action on their part, no analyst being concerned in it, and that the proposal was quite unanimously accepted. Though it does not add to the actual number of letters after your name we shall be able to print on the next book 'Hononary'[1] Fellow of the Royal Society of Medicine'.

This brings me to the immediate purpose of my letter, namely, to ask you whether you will agree to sell to the Hogarth Press for inclusion in our International Psycho-Analytical Library series the English rights of your *Autobiography* and *'Hemmung, Symptom und Angst'*.[2] I have seen your excellent postscript of the *Autobiography* and presume that Strachey will deal with it.[3] The *'Hemmung, Symptom und Angst'* would of course need a proper new translation before we publish it and I hope that we should be able to persuade Strachey to undertake this also. So by and by we shall recover the lost ground in providing a worthy translation of your work; it seems strange that we should be behind Spain in this respect.

I think Wälder was wise in postponing his visit to London till the autumn so as to have more time for a full preparation.[4] It is puzzling me to know what will happen if he *'geht versichert weg'*—an allusion I am sure you will understand—but I suppose the contingency is not very likely to arise.[5]

Ernst is occupied at present in, amongst other things, designing a new wing for my cottage in Sussex. Although it is a small matter it is surprisingly complicated and that gives me an opportunity for the highest admiration of his extraordinary ingenuity and masterly efficiency. It is a rare treat to come across such a high standard of capacity in any work.[6]

I am looking forward to seeing Anna and Eitingon at the Paris Conference next month,[7] for these days we need more than ever as close contact as possible.

With kindest regards

Yours always
Ernest Jones.

1. The same error is made in the two typed versions of the letter.

2. Freud (1925d), trans. James Strachey, and Freud (1926d), trans. Alix Strachey 1936.

3. Freud (1935a), trans. James Strachey.

4. Robert Wälder presented "Problems in Ego-Psychology" to the British Psycho-Analytical Society, 18 November 1935.

5. If he "goes away insured" implies that Jones felt Wälder might run the risk of being converted to the London side of the issues, dealt with in Jones (1935). The allusion is to the story of the pastor and the insurance salesman in Freud (1915a, p. 165): The insurance salesman, a freethinker, lay at the point of death, and his relatives insisted on bringing in a man of God to convert him before he died. The interview lasted so long that those who were waiting outside began to have hopes. At last the door of the sick-room opened. The freethinker had not been converted, but the pastor went away insured ("geht versichert weg"; see *G.W.*, 10:314).

6. The preceding two paragraphs were added to a second version of this letter, after being sketched out in Pitman's shorthand at the end of the first version. Both versions are signed by Jones. (Jones had learned to use the shorthand system of Isaac Pitman [1813–1897], the noted English educator and inventor, as a student in the late 1890s.)

7. A reference to a planned meeting of the International Training Committee in July, which in the end had to be canceled.

638

7 July 1935
Vienna, IX. Berggasse 19

Dear Jones,

I am most delighted that you intend to include the *"Selbstdarstellung"* and *"Hemmung, Symptom und Angst"* in your Ps.a. Library, and I have asked Martin to contact you regarding the realization of this plan. J. Strachey is certainly the translator who would suit me best.

Your recognition of Ernst's capacity for work is balm to my paternal heart. I wish my other son in Nizza [Nice] also had a fatherland and a livelihood again.

Wälder is a great intellectual force and will certainly represent us well. Your endeavors to smooth out the differences which arose during a period of "splendid isolation" have my fullest sympathy. We still speak of Nesta's "charm."[1]

Now, a further word from behind the scenes. I have been told that you are planning a special celebration for my 80th birthday. Well, apart from the possibility that it will not take place at all, and considering a telegram of condolence to be the only proper reaction to it happening, I think that neither the situation within analysis nor the general state of the world justify holding a celebration. If the need for such a display cannot be suppressed, it should be channeled into something involving a minimum of expense, commotion, and work. Perhaps something like an album with photographs of the members.

But warm thanks for your intentions!

Yours,
Freud

1. In this paragraph the words in quotation marks are in English in the original.

639

International Psycho-Analytical Association

13 July 1935
London

Dear Professor,

We were very pleased to get your permission to acquire the English rights of the two books in question and I have asked the Hogarth Press to enter in communication with Martin. Strachey has volunteered to translate the 'Hemmung, Sympton und Angst', which is very gratifying. He and his wife are doing very useful work at present in an extensive revision of our Glossary.[1]

I am reluctantly inclined to think you are right about my proposal of a Gedenkbuch. It would be useless to think of any proposal that would not give you pleasure, and I dare say you can guess that the risks of invidiousness in my proposal might result in considerable jealousy and ill feeling. We shall probably fall back on the photograph suggestion, which strikes me as a very interesting one, with many possibilities in it. Fortunately for you Eitingon will not be President at the time of your birthday. I think you know that I share more fully your quiet attitude about ceremonial occasions.

McDougall gave three lectures on you recently at University College,[2] obviously proceeding from hurt homosexual vanity; their theme was how little you had taken his important work into account. You had appropriated his theory of suggestion without acknowledgment and had now given up all your back views, e.g. the Unconscious, the Oedipus complex, etc., reverting to a level of knowledge which he could have conveyed to you a quarter of a century ago! A philosopher called Joad gleefully took up the theme for his own purposes and published an extremely muddled and absurd article in the *New Statesman* a couple of weeks ago.[3] The editor wanted me to write an article in reply, but I contented myself with a pointed letter of reply. I have heard since that in the first week after the article appeared, the editor received no fewer than 193 letters, every single one of which was on your side.

With kindest regards

Yours always
[Ernest Jones]

1. A. Strachey (1943).
2. McDougall (1936).
3. Cyril Edwin Mitchinson Joad, "Psychology in Retreat," *New Statesman and Nation*, 9 (1935): 956–957.

640

21 July 1935
Vienna, XIX. Strassergasse 47

Dear Jones,

I admit that I have reason to be pleased by the fact that you are at the helm of the ΨA bark, not only because of the "Gedenkbuch." You met my concerns with such understanding that I now have the courage to go a step further.

So let us bury the Gedenkbuch or the "Sammelband" and such like. Turning to my own suggestion of the album, I confess that it now pleases me just as little, indeed, it thoroughly displeases me. Aside from the two objections that it would also involve much effort and afford no guarantee that I will live until that date, I now disapprove of the aesthetic monstrosity of some four hundred pictures of mostly ugly people, more than half of whom I do not know at all, while a considerable number of them do not want to know anything of me. No, the time is not right for a celebration, neither *"intra Iliacos muros nec extra."*[1] The only admissible course, it seems to me, is to give up the idea of any concerted action. Whoever thinks he must congratulate me may do so, and whoever does not need not fear my vengeance.

And a further argument! What is the secret meaning of these celebrations of the big round numbers in one's life? Merely a modicum of triumph over transience, which, as we never forget, is ready to devour us. Then one rejoices with a sort of mutual feeling that one is not made of such frail stuff after all, that one of us has withstood the hostile effects of life victoriously for sixty, seventy, or even eighty years. One can understand and allow that, but obviously the celebration has a meaning only when the survivor can participate as a man indeed,[2] despite all the wounds and scars; it loses this meaning when he is an invalid whom one cannot show off. And as the latter is the case with me and I bear my fate alone, I should like my eightieth birthday to be treated as my private affair—by my friends.

Cordially yours,
Freud

1. "Neither inside the walls of Troy nor outside." The Latin passage on first encounter sounds as if it might be from Virgil's *Aeneid*, but it is not to be found there.

2. The German here is "als ein ganzer Kerl mitthun kann," the verb *mittun* being written in the old style.

641

International Psycho-Analytical Association

25 July 1935
London

Dear Professor,

I was very interested in your human document of July 21st and find the arguments in it very convincing. I should like to add to them the desire to express one's pleasure at the co-existence of someone one loves, which one can do more decidedly on a selected occasion than in everyday life. A birthday seems a natural occasion for this, it being a celebration of one's gladness at their birth, and there are obvious reasons why the desire comes to the forefront specially in reference to childhood and old age. In any case, however over-determined the desire may be, there is no doubt that it loses all sense if it does not give pleasure to the recipient. So you may be sure we shall respect your definite wishes in this matter.

Would you please tell Anna that I had a letter today from Eitingon in Trieste and have communicated with him in Paris. I saw Oberndorf last night, who presented me with a sad picture of the state of analysis in America. I am trying to arrange an informal meeting between several of us and Eitingon.

I hear the summer weather in Vienna has been rather overdone and hope it is now behaving in a more moderate fashion.

With kindest regards

Yours always
Ernest Jones.

642

[postcard]

29 October 1935
Vienna

To my great joy, received *"Autobiographical Study."*[1] Heartfelt thanks to you and J. Strachey.

Yours,
Freud

1. Title is in English in the original.

643

[postcard]

30 October 1935
Vienna

Just to say that yesterday I expressed my thanks to you and Strachey for the publication of the translation of *"Selbstdarstellung,"* but sent it to the wrong address, 42 York Terrace.[1]

Cordially yours,
Freud

1. That is, to Jones's home rather than to his business address.

644

International Psycho-Analytical Association

27 February 1936
London

Dear Professor,

It must be a long time since I have written a letter to you personally, but I always regard my constant correspondence with Anna as being communications with yourself. I am glad to learn from her that you have got over the lastest trouble and you must now be looking forward very greatly to the coming of spring and the life in Grinsing [Grinzing]. You were in my mind specially vividly last night when I gave a public address at Oxford on the history of the analytical movement,[1] including a description of your personality. You would, I am sure, have been interested, as was the audience. The general atmosphere in England is much more friendly and respectful than it was ten or fifteen years ago.

In connection with the history I wanted to ask you two little questions. Could you remember in which year it was (a) you replaced hypnotism by the Bernheim device[2] and (b) when you replaced the tracing of symptoms by general free association? Also when does the word 'psycho-analysis' first appear in your writings?

Mrs. Pierce Clark tells Leonard Woolf that her husband had only the American rights for the translation of 'Hemmung, Symptom und Angst'. She is under the impression that we have the English rights. May I assume that this is so? You doubtless know that Strachey is at present engaged on a translation, which is badly needed. By the way, is Stefan Zweig's remark, referred to in a letter from Leonard Woolf which I enclose, as unfounded as the passage I have underlined about the Nobel prize in his book review which I also enclose?[3]

I am also sending on to you a very sad lucubration by McDougall which shows how thoroughly upset he is at your refusal to love him. I may say that the lectures that make up the book produced here an impression highly unfavourable to himself.[4]

At the moment we are relatively free from illness, but it is an unpleasant time of year. Our chief enjoyment is watching the wing grow which Ernst has in a masterly way devised for our Sussex house. It is so attractive that it would tempt me to go there to live if only I had the means—an unlikely contingency.

I shall of course be in Vienna on May 6th. It seems impossible to damp down all ceremonies, but I am using my influence to reduce them to a reasonable minimum. In any case some of them will take place in the Berggasse when you are safely ensconced in Grinsing.

With my kindest regards and best wishes, also to the family

Yours always affectionately
Ernest Jones.

1. Jones's diary entry for 26 February 1936 reads: "4.45 to Oxford. History of P.A. Psych. Soc." (Archives of the British Psycho-Analytical Society, London.) It appears as though the Psychological Society at Oxford may have been a band of undergraduates who met irregularly. See also Jones (1924f).

2. The reference is to the technique of posthypnotic suggestion employed by Hippolyte

Bernheim (1840–1919), leader of the Nancy School, who held that hypnosis was the effect of "suggestion," in opposition to Charcot, leader of the Salpêtrière School, who advocated the theory that hypnosis was a pathological condition found only in hysterics. Freud had translated two important works by Bernheim; see Freud (1888–89, 1892a), and Jones (1953a, pp. 238–239; 1953b, pp. 261–263).

3. Further attempts to secure the Nobel Prize for Freud are mentioned in Jones (1957a, p. 207; 1957b, p. 221).

4. McDougall (1936).

645

3 March 1936
Vienna, IX. Berggasse 19

Dear Jones,

Your letter, about which you had asked Anna on the telephone, came yesterday. Of course I learn everything from your correspondence with her.

I am *very* pleased to hear that you will be in Vienna for the house-warming of our new home.[1] As far as the celebration of my birthday is concerned, I really do deserve consideration. My heart responds to physical stress of any kind with disagreeable sensations. Analytic work does not bother me.

The matter of translating *"Hemmung, Symptom und Angst"* I handed over to Martin.

I can only give approximate answers to your questions about the history of PsA. The replacement of hypnosis by free association happened before the *Traumdeutung*, between 1895 and 1900; simultaneously I began to use the term *psychoanalysis*. When it first appeared in print would have to be ascertained by painstaking research—if it were worth the trouble.[2]

St. Zweig must know more about the Nobel Prize affair than can be gathered from the newspaper cutting, for it was he himself who once endeavored to get the prize for me. His text was probably distorted by the editor of the daily newspaper. What he says about a religio-historical work which I am preparing is not without foundation. Last year I wrote a work entitled *"Der Mann Moses, ein historischer Roman"*[3] and told Zweig about it during his last visit. But the title already betrays why I have not published this work and will not do so. I lack historical verification for my construction, and since my results seem very important to me, containing as they do a denial of the Jewish national myth, I do not want to expose them to the facile criticism of opponents. The book would create quite a furor, and I am not in a position to guarantee the reliability of its assumptions. Only a few people have read the thing: Anna, Martin, Kris.

One really cannot do anything with McDougall. For him, the Unbe-wusste is really a *façon de parler*.

I am pleased that you are all healthy now, and greet you cordially.

Yours,
Freud

1. New quarters had been arranged at Berggasse 7 for the Verlag, as well as the Vienna Psychoanalytic Institute and Clinic; see Jones (1957a, pp. 188, 202–203; 1957b, pp. 201, 216–217).

2. Freud first used the term *"psycho-analyse"* in an article published in French (Freud, 1896a); in German *Psychoanalyse* was first used in Freud (1896b), *G.W.* 1:379–403; prior to this he employed the terms "analysis," "psychical analysis," "psychological analysis" and "hypnotic analysis" in Freud (1894a). See J. Laplanche and J. B. Pontalis, *The Language of Psycho-Analysis*, trans. D. Nicholson-Smith (London: Hogarth Press, 1973), p. 367.

3. Freud (1939a).

646

International Psycho-Analytical Association

2 June 1936
London

Dear Professor,

Anna tells me you want my opinion about the enclosed communication. I cannot imagine any reason why you should not accept what is decidedly an honour. The Royal Medico-Psychological Association is an old body, perhaps a hundred years old, to which all asylum psychiatrists belong. Your work is being increasingly studied and accepted among the younger psychiatrists in England. There has been a very decided change in this respect in the last ten years.

An ex-patient of mine has put forward your name in connection with the Foreign Membership of the Royal Society itself. You doubtless know that membership of this Society (with the letters F.R.S. after one's name) is by far the highest honour that any scientific man can attain.[1] You probably remember the various anecdotes associated with its being founded by Charles the Second.

I have been glad to hear that you have rallied well from the birthday exertions and even that you are experiencing a sort of *Nachlust* [after-pleasure] at the knowledge of their being over. I hope you noticed that I did not treat you in the way the Bürgermeister of Ischl[2] is reputed to have treated your Mother on a similar occasion. I refer to the story of his telling her that in future he would pay a ceremonious visit only every ten years instead of every five years.

We intend motoring to the Tatra after the Congress and from there via Budapest to Grinsing.

With my kindest regards

Yours always affectionately
Ernest Jones.

1. See Jones (1957a, p. 206; 1957b, p. 220).
2. Mayor of Ischl, the town in which Freud's mother had lived.

647

4 July 1936
Vienna, IX. Berggasse 19

Dear Jones,

So I really have become For. Mem. R. S., a great honor indeed.

A letter that arrived simultaneously from someone at St. John's College, Cambridge, whose name I read as "Jeffreys," connects me with the person who proposed me. So now I know that your influence is behind it, and I thank you warmly. But I should also like to know who this J. is. Would you like to write me a couple of lines about this?

Your old
Freud

648

International Psycho-Analytical Association

6 July 1936
London

Dear Professor,

Please accept my warm congratulations. You have achieved the highest scientific honour in England and, I should suppose, in the world.

Harold Jeffreys is a Cambridge professor—I think of geo-physics.[1] He was in analysis with me for a couple of years, and later with Miss Sharpe. The remarkable feature of his case was a combination of the highest intellectual capacities with a very low degree of ordinary social capacities, such as *savoir faire*, common sense, etc.. I think the success of the analysis was only moderate. He has an astounding facility for rapidly acquiring the profoundest knowledge of any subject, e.g. botany, higher mathematics, physics, etc., and has made himself world famous through his mathematical researches into physics and the structure and movements of the earth, on which he has written some heavy books. He is himself a F.R.S., an honour also bestowed a couple of years ago on Trotter for his experimental work on sensation, so now psycho-analysis has received the highest possible recognition as a branch of pure science.

With kindest regards

Yours always
Ernest Jones.

1. Sir Harold Jeffreys (1891–1989) fellow of St. John's College, Cambridge, from 1914; elected fellow of the Royal Society 1925; distinguished scientist with professional interests in astronomy, mathematics, and geophysics. For amusing comments on Jeffreys by James Strachey, see Meisel and Kendrick (1985, pp. 219, 223–224).

649
[telegram][1]

4 August 1936
Vienna

Thanks for thinking of me greetings to friends and colleagues the same in old age.

Freud

1. Addressed to Ernest Jones at the Fourteenth Congress of the International Psychoanalytic Association, Marienbad (2–7 August 1936).

650
[postcard]

11 November 1936
Vienna

We are happy to confirm that Nesta is charming. Many cordial wishes to you and your family.

Fr.

651

International Psycho-Analytical Association

23 February 1937
London

Dear Professor,

My letters to you nowadays are much scarcer, but whenever I write to Anna I always think that I am writing to you as well. Your generous gift to the Eder Memorial Fund was highly appreciated. Between the two funds (the Zionist and the Analytical) we shall probably get about £500—a sum with which one can really do something. Professor Weil, the librarian in Jerusalem, has asked me to undertake the choice and buying of suitable books, and I shall of course enlist the services of the Verlag for those in German.[1] Some people, e.g. the Hungarians, are not allowed to send money but intend sending books, so we must be careful not to duplicate them.

Things in the analytical world seem to be pursuing a more even tenor than usual at present, so there is nothing startling to report. It is undeniable that there has been a heavy shift of accent to America from Europe, a fact which none of us can welcome. Our Society here is becoming distinctly *verdeutscht* [more and more German], there being some seventeen members who have reached us from abroad in the last few years. There is urgent need for an analyst in South Africa (preferably a Training analyst), but so far I have not been able to find one. Bernfeld is in London for two or three months pending his overcoming the formalities about going to America, where he intends to settle in San Francisco. Dr. Cohn of Berlin, who is in London, has recently spent three or four months in Los Angeles with Simmel intending to settle there, but he has returned here and gives a not very encouraging account of the local situation. He thinks that both Simmel and Frau Deri have been subjected to the usual American flattening influence.[2]

My personal news is good. The children thrive and we are all in good health. Nesta May, who has a passionate Viennese temperament, has a pathological jealousy of her little brother and is being analysed by Dr. Winnicott[3]—our only man [child][4] analyst. Mervyn is precociously sitting for his Matriculation examination in the summer, having by then reached the ripe age of fifteen. I intend to send him abroad for a year for languages between the school and the university, i.e. when he is seventeen. My wife and I are spending three weeks' holiday at Easter at Florence and Rome, where she has never been. It will bring back to me the memory of your Moses among many other things. How the world has changed since those peaceful days, yet I cannot complain personally since my life is much happier now than it was then. Ernst and Lux[5] are coming to the country with us next week. He seems to be getting on most satisfactorily.

I close this tittle-tattle of local news with my kindest regards to you and the expression of my joy that you made such a good recovery from the unpleasant operation in December.[6] You will not have long to wait now for your beloved Grinzing[7] in the spring.

Yours always affectionately
Ernest Jones.

1. A sum of over £600 was finally collected toward the establishment of a memorial library at the Hebrew University in Jerusalem; see *Journal*, 18 (1937): 487.

2. Siegfried Bernfeld (1892–1953), psychoanalyst active in Berlin from 1926 until 1932; after short stay in Vienna left for the South of France, then with third wife, Suzanne, emigrated to America in 1937. The two contributed to biographical scholarship on Freud's early intellectual and scientific development. Franz Cohn, former member of German Psychoanalytic Society in Berlin, joined British Psycho-Analytical Society in 1933. Frances Deri of Los Angeles, member of Vienna Psychoanalytic Society.

3. Donald W. Winnicott (1896–1971), leading British paediatrician, child psychiatrist, and psychoanalyst. At this time he was an advocate of Melanie Klein; for his role in the "Controversial Discussions" of the early 1940s, see King and Steiner (1991).

4. Inserted by hand in an otherwise typed letter.

5. Ernst Freud's wife, Lucie.

6. See Jones (1957a, p. 210; 1957b, p. 224), and Schur (1972, pp. 485–486).

7. "Grinsing" was typed initially then altered by hand.

652

2 March 1937
Vienna, IX. Berggasse 19

Dear Jones,

Your last letter pleased me especially, precisely because there was no real reason for it and it obviously sprang from an emotional need. It was nice to hear only good news of you and your family. I do not regard Nesta's analysis as one of the unfavorable ones; it will not harm her charm. Anna tells me that Dr. Cohn is one of those dissatisfied types whose opinions should not be regarded as a yardstick. Wulf Sachs[1] is here just now and making himself very agreeable. He has been most helpful to my son-in-law Halberstadt, and now insists that Ernstl should follow his father as soon as possible because immigration to South Africa is beginning to be difficult too.

Thanks to the fact that I may smoke again—to a modest extent—and no thanks to the other, that my analytic practice has quite fallen off, I am beginning again to write shorter works. In view of your—envied—travel plans it will interest you that one of them, which was finished for *Imago*, deals with Moses again. It is entitled "Moses ein Aegypter" and is a fragment of a larger work which has been preoccuping me for three years and which I do not want to publish, because its results are very significant while I cannot provide adequate historical proof.[2]

Our political situation seems to become more and more gloomy. The invasion of the Nazis can probably not be checked; the consequences are disastrous for analysis as well. The only hope remaining is that one will not live to see it oneself. The situation is similar to that in 1683, when the Turks were outside Vienna. At that time military reinforcements came over the Kahlenberg; today—nothing like that is to be expected. An Englishman has already discovered that they have to defend their border on the Rhine. He should have said: outside Vienna. If our city falls, then the Prussian barbarians will swamp Europe. Unfortunately, the power that has hitherto protected us—Mussolini—now seems to be giving Germany a free hand. I should like to live in England like Ernst, and travel to Rome, like you.

With cordial greetings.

Yours,
Freud

1. Wulf Sachs (1893–1949), born in St. Petersburg; member of British Psycho-Analytical Society, founder of the psychoanalytic study group in South Africa.
2. Freud (1939a).

653

18 May 1937
Vienna, XIX. Strassergasse 47

Dear Jones,

I have just received a diploma, full of pomp, as honorary member of a "Royal Medico Psycholog. Association, London." Will you let me know in a couple of lines what sort of thing that is and how I am expected to react?

Did you notice that after eighty I no longer express my thanks for letters of congratulations?

Cordially yours,
Freud

654

International Psycho-Analytical Association

22 May 1937
London

Dear Professor,

It was good to see your handwriting and even better to hear to-day from Dr. Kris, who is spending the weekend with us, that the last operation was not so bad as had been expected and that you are now in much better health. I know what May in Grinzing is like and I am sure you must be enjoying the freedom and beauty. Here, unfortunately, we have had a very cloudy May, but the flowers are always wonderful.

The Royal Medico-Psychological Association is the official Group of Psychiatrists in Great Britain, chiefly of course Asylum doctors. I have forgotten the exact name of the corresponding German Society, *etwa Deutsche Psychiatrische Vereinigung*.[1] The honour in question is a considerable one. Actually, it must have been bestowed on you some time ago because I remember referring to it in my last Congress address.[2]

The question of birthday wishes is a complicated one but you must know that in all circumstances the wishes are throughout positive. Even with your restricted life we hope that you are able to extract some enjoyment from various aspects of it.

I hear you have a paper in the forthcoming *Zeitschrift*, and shall look forward to receiving the Fahnen.[3]

With kindest regards,

Yours always affectionately
Ernest Jones.

1. Actually the Deutscher Verein für Psychiatrie, founded in Frankfurt, 1864; its official journal was the *Allgemeine Zeitschrift für Psychiatrie und psychisch-gerichtliche Medizin*.

2. Jones mentioned it at the Fourteenth Congress of the International Psychoanalytic Association, Marienbad, 2–7 August 1936; see *Journal*, 18 (1937): 95; see also letter 646.

3. Freud (1937c).

655

International Psycho-Analytical Association

1 November 1937
London W1

Dear Professor,

Undeterred by your letter to him Herr Daiber[1] of Stuttgart wrote a 40 page answer which he sent to me together with his other writings. I am afraid I could not find anything substantial in them and judge him to be a philosophical paranoiac with a pregenital basis trying to break through. I gave him the address of Kris as a *Kunsthistoriker* [an art historian], but hope he will not trouble him too much.

The news we get of you continues to be good. I am sure you are bearing the life in the Berggasse with fortitude although you must already be thinking of next spring's lilac in Grinzing. I have always envied Eitingon his ability to travel so freely, especially to Vienna, but this year's experience inclines me to change my mind. For the first time in my life I spent my holidays under my own roof and indeed seldom went out of the garden. The experience was extraordinarily pleasant and restful.

With my kindest regards,

Yours always affectionately
Ernest Jones.

1. Possibly the German architect Hans Daiber (1880–1969), who at this time was living in Stuttgart; see *Attempto*, 31–32 (1969): 40–43.

656

International Psycho-Analytical Association

6 December 1937
London

Dear Professor,

I sent you recently two paper cuttings which I hope interested you. There have been wild rumours here of your having published two large volumes on the Bible. I hear from Martin that they are grossly exaggerated. We should, of course, like to publish the *Imago* and *Zeitschrift* Papers in the *Journal*; in fact one of them *"Die endliche und die unendliche Analyse"* is in the October number.[1] I am specially looking forward to the two I have not seen.

With kindest regards,

Yours always,
Ernest Jones.

1. "Moses an Egyptian," pt. 1 of Freud (1939a), in *Journal*, 19 (1938): 291–298; Freud (1937d), *Journal*, 19 (1938): 377–387; and Freud (1937c), *Journal*, 18 (1937): 373–405.

657

9 December 1937
Vienna, IX. Berggasse 19

Dear Jones,

So both "cuttings"[1] were from you. I have received others of a dreadful sort (*"Sunday Chronicle"* and *"Sunday Referee"*) which I should have thought possible only of American journalism. Behind the whole uproar is nothing other than a foreboding about the second essay on Moses, which will appear quite soon in the fourth issue of *Imago*. It is actually a historical study and may seem out of place in the *Internat. Journal.* But, as you decide.

Cordially and with greetings to your wife and children.

Yours,
Freud

1. In English in the original.

658

International Psycho-Analytical Association

13 December 1937
London

Dear Professor,

I have been reading with the utmost pleasure your second Moses Essay. Your writings have always been one of my chief enjoyments in life, but I have never been more delighted than over this one. It combines the delicacy of the *Gradiva*, the charm of the *Kästchenwahl*,[1] and the grandeur of *Totem und Tabu*.

My wife is also greatly taken with the two Essays and has claimed the honour of translating them.[2]

It is a far cry from the famous little Moritz (*"sagt sie"*)[3] to the fundamental question of the genesis of religions! I have the impression that Moses himself must have belonged to the *Gottmensch* [God-man] type, which would go some way to excusing the mistake over the "chosen people". You do not say anything about the ten plagues. I wonder if this is an *Umkehrung* [reversal] of the tortures the orthodox Egyptian priests inflicted on Amenhotep's followers, including the Jews.

There is a wonderful picture of Moses' psychology in the wilderness, particularly in regard to the ingratitude of his followers, in Stanzas IX, X and XI of Browning's poem called "One Word More".[4] I rather think I once presented you with a copy of Browning many years ago, but if you have not one I should be pleased to send you a copy of the poem.

Yours in admiration and affection

Ernest Jones.

1. Freud (1913f).
2. Katherine Jones (1939).
3. The allusion is to a well-known Jewish joke utilized in *Vorlesungen:* when the intelligent Jewish boy is asked who the mother of Moses was, he answers, without hesitation, the princess. But no, he is told, the princess only took Moses out of the water. That's what *she* says [sagt sie], he replies, and thus proves that he has found the correct interpretation of the myth; see Freud (1916–17, p. 161), *G.W.,* 11:163. See also Jones (1957a, pp. 362–363 and 363n.; 1957b, pp. 388–389 and 389n.), where the connection of "der kleine Moritz" to the issue of the Egyptian princess as the real mother of Moses is discussed in the context of Freud (1939a).
4. Browning (1895, p. 362).

659

[postcard]

14 February 1938
Vienna

Warm congratulations on the fourth edition.[1]

Freud

1. Jones, *Papers,* 4th ed. 1938.

660

23 April 1938
Vienna, IX. Berggasse 19

Dear Jones,

Among the many who have turned to you concerning entry into England is also Dr. Maxim Steiner.[1] I beg you to take up his case. I cannot claim that he is important as an analyst, but it should be considered that he is a special friend of mine, has been our specialist (dermatology) for many years, and moreover is one of the oldest, i.e., earliest members of the Vereinigung.

We are finding, of course, that the winding up of our affairs here is proceeding very slowly.

With cordial greetings and the wish to see you soon.

Yours,
Freud

1. Maxim Steiner, member of the Vienna Psychoanalytic Society since 1908. Freud (1913e) is a preface to his book. For his role as Freud's physician, see Schur (1972, pp. 350–351). Steiner emigrated to London and became a full member of the British Psycho-Analytical Society in 1939. He died shortly thereafter in 1942.

661

28 April 1938
Vienna, IX. Berggasse 19

Dear Jones,

The fact that two letters from you came today with the erratic post, for Anna and for me,[1] both so refreshingly gracious, moves me as well to write you today without any external reason but from an inner impulse.

I am sometimes disturbed by the idea that you might think we believe that you simply want to do your duty, without our valuing the deep and honest feelings expressed in your activity. I assure you that this is not the case, that we recognize your friendship, rely on it, and fully reciprocate it. This is a rare expression of feelings on my part, for among beloved friends much should be taken for granted and left unsaid.

I shall be heartily delighted to see you again at Victoria Station. Do not be surprised if this does not happen as soon as you expect. The delay is truly not our fault, but is connected with the settling of finances and property, and is characteristic of this transitional period, in which the officials are not yet certain by which regulations they should work. It is true that several individuals have already effected their exit, but these are exceptions, and one does not know how they came about. In general, one has to be patient and still wait for weeks, perhaps months. At the moment emigration applications are not being processed at all; Kris's application was returned unprocessed after four weeks. Our application could not be filed until Monday (25th).

Meanwhile—needless to say, it is a difficult time. Martin is in the sanatorium in Baden, recovering well. My brother has me very worried; he is bearing the loss of his business very badly—in critical physical condition.[2] The women are the most capable; Tante Minna is learning to see again, should be very contented, but cannot yet use her new glasses properly. I am suffering from the lack of active engagement, help a little with sorting the library and the *Sammlung*.[3] I also find an hour daily to continue working on Moses, who plagues me like a "ghost not laid."[4] I wonder if I shall still manage to pull together this third part despite all external and internal difficulties. For the time being I cannot believe it. ¿But *quien sabe?*

With cordial greetings.

Yours,
Freud

1. Jones's letter to Freud is missing.
2. See Freud to Alexander Freud, 19 April 1938, *Letters*, p. 442.
3. Here *Sammlung* refers to all of Freud's own writings.
4. In English in the original.

662

13 May 1938
Vienna, IX. Berggasse 19

Dear Jones,

Anna tells me she concludes from your last letter that you expected a reply to your letter for my birthday,[1] and I am therefore writing to you, but also because I am sitting here in my study being absolutely idle and otherwise useless. We had decided to disregard this birthday and to postpone it to 6 June, July, August, etc., in short, to a date after our liberation, and indeed, I have not acknowledged any of the letters, telegrams, etc. that arrived. Now it seems that we shall land in England in May after all. I say "it seems" for, despite all promises, uncertainty is the all-controlling factor. Two days ago Princess Marie, with her touching devotion, telephoned that she intends to come to Vienna on Monday (that is, 16 May) to escort us across the border as far as Paris; yesterday we had to ask her to lower her hopes, as we still cannot specify the date of our departure.

Another reason for not answering you is my general inhibition to write these days. You may remember that I once traced the so-called "physiological feeblemindedness of women" (Moebius) to the fact that women were forbidden to think about sexual matters.[2] As a result they took a dislike to thinking altogether. How such a restriction must affect me, who has always been used to expressing what I believed. But how very much your cordial letter pleased me would have been the first sentence that you would have heard from me at Victoria Station.

I wish I could arrive in England in better condition. To be sure I am traveling with my personal physician, but I am in need of several doctors, and soon after my arrival I will have to find an ear specialist and consult the jaw specialist, whose name Pichler gave me. Sometimes one even tells oneself *"Le jeu ne vaut (plus) pas la chandelle,"*[3] and although one is right, one must not admit that one is right. The advantage that emigrating will bring Anna is worth all our petty sacrifices. For us old people (73, 77, 82),[4] emigrating would not have been worthwhile.

Anna is untiringly active, not only for us but for countless others as well. I hope that she will also be able to do much for analysis in England, but she will not obtrude herself.

Perhaps we shall see each other soon again after all.

Cordially yours,
Freud

1. This letter is missing.

2. Paul Julius Möbius, *Über den physiologischen Schwachsinn des Weibes* (Halle: C. Marhold, 1907); see Freud (1908d, p. 199; 1927c, p. 48).

3. The expression is "Le jeu n'en vaut pas la chandelle," in this context meaning "life is not worth living." Freud adds a different dimension by saying life is "no longer" worth living.

4. The ages, in reverse order, refer to Freud, his wife, Martha, and her sister Minna Bernays.

663

1 November 1938
20 Maresfield Gardens
London

Dear Jones,

I very much regretted yesterday that your cold obliged you to stay away from me, and then I was greatly dismayed to hear that you would not be able to finish the translation of my Moses before February or March. I know your time is very valuable, your conscientiousness very great, and that you have all sorts of other things to do which are at least just as important. But I remember that you took on this new burden voluntarily, without my requesting you to do so. To be sure, I regarded your undertaking as a special kindness to me and as a mark of respect for the book.

The prospect of a delay is unwelcome to me in more than one respect. First of all, a few months mean more to me than to someone else, when I cling to the understandable wish that I myself may still see the book finished. On the other hand, we have to count on the impatience of the American publisher (Knopf, N.Y.), from whom we have already accepted payment. The general uncertainty of the international situation is a further consideration. I therefore hope that you will find it understandable that I cannot accept a delay of the publication in English without resistance. To

resolve the difficulty, I suggest that you commission someone else to translate the remainder who will pledge to finish the work by the end of this
year. I hope that it will not be difficult for you to find someone else, and
it will not be an impossible task for this other person to deal with a fraction
of the third essay in two months. Naturally I very much regret the loss of
uniformity in the English text, but a postponement to a date that might
easily coincide with *ad calendas graecas* [never] is even more undesirable
for me.

With kind regards to your wife whom up to now I regarded as the actual
translator,[1] and best wishes for your early recovery.

Your faithful
Freud

1. Katherine Jones (1939).

664

2 November 1938
42 York Terrace, Regents Park

Dear Professor,

I also was for several reasons sorry to be unable to see you on Monday,
but I hope to do so next Saturday or Sunday.

As regards the matter of translation I would say this. I have the English
habit, which is found so annoying on the Continent, of being reluctant to
promise anything I cannot well see my way to perform. Therefore we never
gave any date by when we could complete the translation, the typescript
of which—as you will remember—we received towards the end of August.
Early in October Mr. Woolf asked me if it could be ready by the end of
that month and, of course, I told him it was out of the question.[1] He then
reminded me, which I well knew, that there were certain fixed publishing
seasons in the year with definite dates on which travellers were sent round
the country beforehand and told me that the next date when this could
happen would be February 1st, asking if we could get the translation ready
for press by then. I replied that we would make our best endeavour to do
so and we are hopeful of succeeding. From the publishing point of view
there would therefore be no point at all in having the translation ready by
the end of next month as you suggest. If, however, you want it for personal
reasons finished next month, i.e. a month before Mr. Woolf's date, then
we are, of course, quite willing to hand it over to any other translator you
would suggest. I should tell you, however, that it would be very difficult
to find a translator. In our *Journal* and other work we have two competent
translators, who are paid for their work, and for different reasons they have

both failed us at the moment so that we have no one left. Among analysts only Mrs. Riviere and Mr. Strachey would come into consideration and all my experience of their work is that it is a good deal slower than the rate at which my wife and I work. It is, of course, possible that Mr. Woolf would be able to recommend some professional outsider, but you probably know that you have the reputation of not being the easiest author to translate.

Auf baldiges Wiedersehen.[2]

Yours,
[Ernest Jones]

1. Further details regarding the problems associated with bringing out Freud (1939a) can be found in the letters between Leonard Woolf and Freud, and Woolf and Jones; see Spotts (1989, pp. 333–336).
2. "See you again soon."

665

14 November 1938
42 York Terrace, Regents Park

Dear Professor,

My bronchitis is gradually improving and I hope that before long it will be safe for me to visit you—perhaps this week.

My wife is in hospital for a week with a slight operation, but she devotedly spends her time there in pushing on with the translation.

In the meantime there are two small points I might ask you about, both raised by Strachey, whom Woolf got to read the book. They are both in the third part. On page 22 you speak of Egypt having been free from volcanoes, which so far as I know is correct and is relevant to your argument. You also say, however, that it is free from earthquakes, which I do not think is very relevant to the argument. Strachey points out that one of the pair of Colossi of Memnon at Thebes was broken in half by the earthquake of 27 B.C., (and repaired 200 years later by Septimius Severus). Actually an earthquake at Cairo was announced on the wireless a week ago.[1]

The other question is to know definitely about your choice of the English or American spelling for the great monotheist. Strachey writes "the usual English spelling is undoubtedly "Akhenaten", the "e" being the indeterminate sound (Alexander Gardiner, Petrie, Davies, Newberry, Pendlebury, British Museum Catalogue, English Official Guide to Cairo Museum, etc.).[2] The only time the spelling "Ikhnaton" occurs in English is in the *Cambridge Ancient History* and that is only because the chapters there were written by Breasted of Chicago,[3] whom the Editors would, of course, not think of correcting. In either case we could, of course, insert a footnote on the point.

I trust that the bone trouble is rapidly drawing to an end.

With kindest regards,

Yours always,
[Ernest Jones]

1. The statement that Egypt is free from earthquakes was dropped; see K. Jones (1939, p. 55), and Freud (1939a, p. 34).

2. Jones cites the distinguished Egyptologists Sir Alan Henderson Gardiner, Sir William Matthew Flinders Petrie, Norman de Garis Davies, Percy Edward Newberry, and John Devitt Stringfellow Pendlebury. "Akhenaten" (the Egyptian heretic king figures very prominently in Freud, 1939a) is the spelling employed by Strachey; see his explanation in S.E., 23:6.

3. Freud's use of "Ikhnaton" was retained in K. Jones (1939), who follows (p. 38 n. 2) James Henry Breasted; see chapters 3–4 on ancient Egypt in J. B. Bury, S. A. Cook, and F. E. Adcock, eds., The Cambridge Ancient History, vol. 2, The Egyptian and Hittite Empires: to c. 1000 B.C. (Cambridge: Cambridge University Press, 1924), pp. 40–195.

666

15 November 1938
20 Maresfield Gardens
London

Dear Jones,

I am glad to hear that your and your wife's illnesses are less lasting than mine, and therefore hope to see you soon.

Regarding the earthquakes in Egypt, I realize that I am in error and ask you to delete the word from the text. (I remembered having read somewhere the suggestion of a fool that pyramids should be built in countries afflicted with earthquakes as protection against them. His argument was that earthquakes do not occur where there are pyramids, that is, in Egypt.)

I think the second point has already been decided by the text of the second German essay. There I decided on the name Ikhnaton, and it really will not do that there should be a different spelling in the English edition. This essay (Imago IV, p. 392) also contains an explanatory footnote, but it is too short, not quite accurate, and can be replaced by another.[1]

With cordial greetings.

Yours,
Freud

1. The footnote in fact incorrectly describes the use of "Ikhnaton" as typically English. Strachey points out, as does Jones, that this is Breasted's (American) version; see Freud (1939a, p. 23 n. 1).

667

16 November 1938
81 Harley Street, London

Dear Professor,

Many thanks for the two decisions which we will at once attend to.

It has occurred to me that on Seite 43 it would be interesting if you inserted a passage about Mythra. It is where you say that the man who showed us the guilt should logically have been the murderer himself, which is, of course, Mythra's role when he slays the bull *(vide "Totem und Tabu")*.[1]

Yours,
[Ernest Jones]

1. The suggestion is followed, and Jones is acknowledged; see Freud (1939a, p. 87 n. 1). Jones alludes to the mention of Mythra's role in Freud (1912–13, p. 153).

668

12 December 1938
81 Harley Street, London

Dear Professor,

When you told me the story yesterday about your eccentric colleague,[1] I was puzzled to understand his motive for coming, because I was quite sure that there was not the slightest idea of really being analysed. On thinking it over afterwards I realised the only explanation could be that he was tempted to repeat the experience with me of which I told you. Then after a dozen or so interviews he would be writing and lecturing all over the country about his analytic work with you, which would certainly do us all a great deal of harm because of his prominent position. Even as it is I shall not be surprised to hear him before long referring to an important discussion he had with you about the theory of free will, etc..

It was very good to see you looking so decidedly better yesterday.

Yours always,
[Ernest Jones]

1. "William Brown" is handwritten in the margin of an otherwise typewritten letter, apparently at a later rereading.

669

31 January 1939
20 Maresfield Gardens
London

Dear Jones,

You criticized a comment on Napoleon which appears in the paragraph on the great man. I am not sure whether I told you that this was deleted in the German edition.[1]

Cordially yours,
Freud

1. Likely Freud (1939a).

670

7 March 1939
20 Maresfield Gardens
London

Dear Jones,

It is still quite remarkable how unsuspectingly we human beings approach the future. When you told me shortly before the war about founding an analytic society in London, I could not foresee that a quarter of a century later I would be living so near to it and you; I would have thought it even less possible that despite this proximity I would not be able to take part in your celebratory meeting.[1]

But our impotence forces us to accept everything that fate brings.[2] Consequently I have to content myself with sending your jubilant society a cordial greeting and hearty congratulations from afar but yet so near. The events of recent years have so ordained that London has become chief venue and center of the psychoanalytic movement. May the society discharge the functions thus devolving upon it in the most brilliant manner.

Your old
Sigm. Freud

1. The reference is to the banquet held in celebration of the twenty-fifth anniversary of the founding of the British Psycho-Analytical Society.

2. The German reads "Aber wir sind in unserer Ohnmacht [gezwungen] alles so hinzunehmen, wie das Schicksal es bringt." The verb *gezwungen* was added in the British typescript, although not in Freud's original.

671

International Psycho-Analytical Association

3 September 1939
London

Dear Professor,

This critical moment seems an appropriate one for me to express once more my personal devotion to you, my gratitude for all you have brought into my life and my intense sympathy for the suffering you are enduring. When England last fought Germany, twenty-five years ago, we were on opposite sides of the line, but even then we found a way to communicate our friendship to each other. Now we are near to each other and united in our military sympathies. No one can say if we shall see the end of this war, but in any case it has been a very interesting life and we have both made a contribution to human existence—even if in very different measure.

With my warmest and dearest regards

Yours always affectionately
Ernest Jones.

List of Correspondence

References

Glossary

Index

List of Correspondence

Key

—	Missing item
Anna	Appended letter in German from Anna Freud, handwritten in Latin characters
cc	Additional carbon copy
E	Letter from Freud in English
G	Postcard from Jones in German
hws	Handwritten, signed
I	Initialed by Jones, underscored with ⟶
I-tel	Telegram from Freud in Italian
L	Letter from Freud in German, in Latin characters
L.C.M.	Letter from Freud transcribed by L. C. Martin
Loe	Appended letter from Loe Kann, handwritten in English
nI	Initialed by Jones, not underscored with ⟶
nJS	Not Jones's signature, signed "Ernest Jones" and initialed by secretary
nS	Signed by Jones, not underscored with ⟶
pc	Postcard
sI	Secretary's initials only
T	Typed original, signed
Ta	Additional typed copy
Tc	Typed copy, signed
Tcu	Typed copy, unsigned
tel	Telegram

| Tu | Typed original, unsigned |
| van E. | Letter from Freud transcribed by J. E. G. van Emden |

Letters

	Jones		*Freud*	
1.	13 May 1908		—	
			—	
2.	27 Jun 1908			
3.	26 Sep 1908			
			—	
4.	8 Nov 1908			
5.			20 Nov 1908	E
6.	10 Dec 1908			
7.	7 Feb 1909			
			—	
8.	17 Feb 1909			
9.			22 Feb 1909	E
10.			28 Feb 1909	E
11.	19 Mar 1909			
12.	8 Apr 1909			
13.			18 May 1909	E
14.	18 May 1909			
15.			1 Jun 1909	E
16.	6 Jun 1909	nS		
17.	5 Aug 1909	nS		
18.	17 Oct 1909			
19.			23 Oct 1909	
20.			31 Oct 1909	
21.	3 Nov 1909	pc		
22.	18 Dec 1909			
23.	2 Jan 1910			
24.			11 Jan 1910	L

	Jones		*Freud*	
25.			27 Jan 1910	E
26.	12 Feb 1910			
27.	14 Feb 1910			
28.			10 Mar 1910	E
29.	30 Mar 1910			
30.			15 Apr 1910	E
31.	20 Apr 1910			
32.	4 May 1910			
33.			22 May 1910	E
34.	3 Jun 1910			
35.	19 Jun 1910			
			—	
36.	28 Jun 1910			
37.			3 Jul 1910	E
38.	25 Jul 1910			
			—	
39.	2 Aug 1910			
40.	10 Oct 1910			
41.			6 Nov 1910	E
42.	6 Nov 1910			
43.	19 Nov 1910			
44.			20 Nov 1910	E
45.	2 Dec 1910	nI		
46.			18 Dec 1910	E
47.	1 Jan 1911			
48.	3 Jan 1911	nS		
49.			22 Jan 1911	E
50.	7 Feb 1911	tel		
51.	8 Feb 1911			
52.			12 Feb 1911	E,pc
53.			22 Feb 1911	E,pc
54.			26 Feb 1911	E
55.			2 Mar 1911	E,pc
56.	8 Mar 1911			

	Jones		Freud	
57.	17 Mar 1911			
			—	
58.	30 Apr 1911			
59.			14 May 1911	E
60.	22 May 1911			
61.	1 Jun 1911			
62.			25 Jun 1911	E
63.	13 Jul 1911	T		
64.			9 Aug 1911	E
65.	31 Aug 1911	T		
66.	17 Oct 1911	nS		
67.			5 Nov 1911	E
68.	26 Nov 1911	T		
69.	7 Jan 1912			
70.			14 Jan 1912	E
71.	20 Jan 1912	T		
72.	30 Jan 1912	T		
73.			24 Feb 1912	E
74.	15 Mar 1912	T		
	—			
75.			28 Apr 1912	E
76.	7 May 1912	T,nS		
77.	10 May 1912	T,nS		
78.	18 Jul 1912			
79.			22 Jul 1912	E
80.	30 Jul 1912			
81.			1 Aug 1912	E
82.	7 Aug 1912			
83.			11 Aug 1912	E
84.			18 Aug 1912	E
85.			22 Aug 1912	E,pc
86.	28 Aug 1912			
87.			3 Sep 1912	E
88.	4 Sep 1912			

	Jones		*Freud*	
			—	
89.	6 Sep 1912			
90.			7 Sep 1912	E
91.	12 Sep 1912			
92.			14 Sep 1912	E
93.			16 Sep 1912	E,pc
94.	18 Sep 1912	Loe		
95.			22 Sep 1912	E
96.			28 Oct 1912	E
97.	30 Oct 1912			
98.	6 Nov 1912			
99.			8 Nov 1912	E
100.	13 Nov 1912			
101.			14 Nov 1912	E
102.	14 Nov 1912			
103.			15 Nov 1912	E
104.			16 Nov 1912	E,tel
105.	17 Nov 1912			
106.			21 Nov 1912	I-tel
107.	5 Dec 1912			
108.			8 Dec 1912	E
109.	23 Dec 1912			
110.	24 Dec 1912	nI,pc		
111.			26 Dec 1912	E
112.	29 Dec 1912			
113.			1 Jan 1913	E
114.	30 Jan 1913			
115.			10 Feb 1913	E
116.	17 Feb 1913	pc		
117.			5 Mar 1913	E
118.	18 Mar 1913			
119.	26 Mar 1913			
120.			9 Apr 1913	E
121.	25 Apr 1913			

	Jones		*Freud*	
122.	3 Jun 1913			
123.			8 Jun 1913	E
124.	11 Jun 1913			
125.	17 Jun 1913			
126.			20 Jun 1913	E
127.	25 Jun 1913			
128.	8 Jul 1913			
129.			10 Jul 1913	
130.			11 Jul 1913	E,pc
131.	22 Jul 1913			
132.			23 Jul 1913	E
133.	8 Aug 1913			
134.			10 Aug 1913	E
135.			15 Aug 1913	E,pc
136.	15 Aug 1913			
137.	18 Aug 1913			
138.			22 Aug 1913	E
139.	22 Aug 1913			
140.			29 Aug 1913	E
141.	13 Sep 1913			
142.			21 Sep 1913	E
143.			1 Oct 1913	E
144.	4 Oct 1913			
145.	14 Oct 1913			
146.	27 Oct 1913			
147.			30 Oct 1913	E
148.	3 Nov 1913			
149.	4 Nov 1913			
150.			7 Nov 1913	L,pc
151.			8 Nov 1913	E,tel
152.	11 Nov 1913			
153.			13 Nov 1913	E
154.	14 Nov 1913			
155.			17 Nov 1913	E

	Jones		Freud	
156.	19 Nov 1913			
157.			22 Nov 1913	E
158.	24 Nov 1913			
159.	29 Nov 1913			
160.	2 Dec 1913	T		
161.			4 Dec 1913	E
162.			8 Dec 1913	E
163.	11 Dec 1913			
164.			14 Dec 1913	E
165.	17 Dec 1913			
166.	31 Dec 1913			
167.			3 Jan 1914	E
168.			8 Jan 1914	E
169.	9 Jan 1914			
170.	10 Jan 1914			
171.			16 Jan 1914	E
172.	19 Jan 1914			
173.			1 Feb 1914	E,pc
174.	6 Feb 1914			
175.			8 Feb 1914	E
176.	15 Feb 1914			
177.			21 Feb 1914	E
178.	22 Feb 1914			
179.			25 Feb 1914	E
180.	13 Mar 1914			
181.			19 Mar 1914	E
182.	23 Mar 1914			
183.			25 Mar 1914	E
184.	8 Apr 1914			
185.			19 Apr 1914	E
186.	22 Apr 1914			
187.	27 Apr 1914	pc		
188.	13 May 1914			
189.			17 May 1914	E

	Jones		*Freud*	
190.	18 May 1914			
191.	25 May 1914			
192.			2 Jun 1914	E
193.	17 Jun 1914			
194.	1 Jul 1914			
195.			[7] Jul 1914	E
196.	7 Jul 1914			
197.			10 Jul 1914	E
198.			14 Jul 1914	E,pc
199.	17 Jul 1914			
200.			22 Jul 1914	E
201.	27 Jul 1914			
202.	3 Aug 1914	T		
203.	13 Aug 1914			
			3 Oct 1914	L.C.M.
204.	10 Oct 1914	G,pc		
205.			22 Oct 1914	
			26 Oct 1914	van E.
206.	15 Nov 1914	Tc,nS		
207.	29 Nov 1914	G,pc		
			14 Dec 1914	van E.
208.	15 Dec 1914	T		
209.			25 Dec 1914	
	—			
210.	17 June 1915			
211.			30 Jun 1915	
	—			
212.	8 Dec 1915	T		
			—	
213.	27 Mar 1916			
214.			16 Apr 1916	
215.	30 May 1916			
216.			14 Jul 1916	
217.	31 Oct 1916			

	Jones		Freud	
218.	15 Jan 1917			
219.	20 Feb 1917			
220.			6 Mar 1917	Anna
	—			
221.	4 Oct 1918			
222.			10 Nov 1918	
223.	7 Dec 1918			
224.			22 Dec 1918	E
225.	31 Dec 1918			
226.	9 Jan 1919			
227.			15 Jan 1919	E
228.			19 Jan 1919	E
229.			24 Jan 1919	E
230.	27 Jan 1919			
231.	4 Feb 1919			
232.			18 Feb 1919	E
233.	5 Mar 1919			
234.	17 Mar 1919			
235.	25 Mar 1919	nS		
236.	2 Apr 1919			
237.			18 Apr 1919	E
238.	23 Apr 1919			
239.			28 Apr 1919	E,pc
240.	2 May 1919	T		
241.			28 May 1919	E
242.	3 Jun 1919	Tcu		
243.	10 Jun 1919			
244.			19 Jun 1919	E
245.	1 Jul 1919	T		
246.			8 Jul 1919	E
247.	20 Jul 1919	T,nS		
248.			28 Jul 1919	E
	—			
249.	7 Aug 1919			

	Jones		Freud	
			—	
			—	
250.			1 Sep 1919	
251.	4 Sep 1919			
252.	7 Sep 1919	nI		
253.	12 Oct 1919			
	—			
254.	25 Nov 1919			
			—	
255.	8 Dec 1919			
256.			11 Dec 1919	E
	—			
257.			23 Dec 1919	E
258.			6 Jan 1920	E
259.	16 Jan 1920			
260.			17 Jan 1920	E,pc
261.			20 Jan 1920	E,pc
	—			
			—	
262.	25 Jan 1920			
263.			26 Jan 1920	E
264.	27 Jan 1920			
265.	2 Feb 1920			
266.			8 Feb 1920	E
	—			
267.			12 Feb 1920	E
268.	29 Feb 1920			
269.			8 Mar 1920	E
270.	19 Mar 1920	I,pc		
271.	24 Apr 1920			
	—			
272.			2 May 1920	E
273.			5 May 1920	E,pc
274.	7 May 1920	T		

	Jones			*Freud*	
275.				13 May 1920	E
276.	18 May 1920	T,nS			
277.				24 May 1920	E
278.	28 Jun 1920	T			
279.				4 Jul 1920	E
280.	9 Jul 1920	T			
281.				16 Jul 1920	E
282.	22 Jul 1920	T			
283.				2 Aug 1920	E
284.	20 Aug 1920				
285.				23 Sep 1920	E,pc
286.	1 Oct 1920	T			
287.				4 Oct 1920	E
288.				12 Oct 1920	E
289.	17 Oct 1920				
290.				21 Oct 1920	E
291.	28 Oct 1920				
292.				7 Nov 1920	E
293.	12 Nov 1920	T			
294.				18 Nov 1920	E
295.	25 Nov 1920	T			
	—				
296.				24 Jan 1921	E
297.				28 Jan 1921	E
298.	3 Feb 1921	T,cc			
299.				7 Feb 1921	E
300.				18 Feb 1921	E
301.	23 Feb 1921	T,cc			
302.				26 Feb 1921	E,pc
303.	11 Mar 1921	T,nI,cc			
304.				18 Mar 1921	E
305.	1 Apr 1921	T,cc			
306.				12 Apr 1921	E
307.	6 May 1921	T			

	Jones		Freud	
308.			8 May 1921	E
309.	11 May 1921	T		
310.			19 May 1921	E
311.	21 May 1921	T,cc		
312.			29 May 1921	E
313.	31 May 1921	T,pc		
314.	6 Jun 1921	T,cc		
315.			9 Jun 1921	E
316.	15 Jun 1921	T		
317.	6 Jul 1921	T		
318.			14 Jul 1921	E
319.	22 Jul 1921	T,cc		
320.			27 Jul 1921	E
321.	10 Aug 1921	T,cc		
322.			18 Aug 1921	E
323.			5 Sep 1921	E,pc
324.	6 Sep 1921	T,cc		
325.			2 Oct 1921	E
326.	11 Oct 1921			
327.			6 Nov 1921	E
328.	30 Nov 1921	T,cc		
329.	7 Dec 1921	T		
330.			9 Dec 1921	E
331.	15 Dec 1921	T,cc		
332.			19 Dec 1921	E,pc
333.	21 Dec 1921	T,nJS		
334.			26 Dec 1921	E
335.			29 Dec 1921	E
336.	11 Jan 1922	T		
337.	17 Jan 1922	T,nJS		
338.			22 Jan 1922	E,pc
339.	22 Jan 1922	T,cc		
340.	26 Jan 1922	T,cc		
341.	27 Jan 1922	T		

	Jones		*Freud*	
342.			5 Feb 1922	E
343.	11 Feb 1922	T,cc		
344.	13 Feb 1922	T,nJS		
345.	15 Feb 1922	T,nJS,cc		
346.			20 Feb 1922	E,pc
347.	27 Feb 1922			
348.			2 Mar 1922	E,tel
349.	2 Mar 1922			
			—	
350.	16 Mar 1922	T		
351.			23 Mar [1922]	E
352.	1 Apr 1922	T,cc		
353.			6 Apr 1922	E
354.	10 Apr 1922	T,cc		
355.			[16 Apr] 1922	E,pc
356.			11 May 1922	E
357.	15 May 1922	T		
	[undated]	T		
358.			17 May 1922	E,pc
359.	22 May 1922	T,cc		
360.	26 May 1922	tel		
361.	26 May 1922	T,cc		
362.			31 May 1922	E,pc
363.	31 May 1922	T		
364.			4 Jun 1922	E
365.	10 Jun 1922	T,cc		
366.	23 Jun 1922	pc		
367.			25 Jun 1922	E
368.			3 Jul 1922	E,pc
	—			
369.			17 Jul 1922	E,pc
370.	19 Jul 1922	Tc,cc		
371.			25 Jul 1922	E,pc
372.	1 Aug 1922	T,cc		

	Jones		*Freud*	
373.			10 Aug 1922	E
374.	15 Aug 1922	T		
375.	22 Aug 1922	T		
376.			24 Aug 1922	E
377.	30 Aug 1922			
378.			3 Sep 1922	E
379.	[?] Oct 1922			
380.			6 Nov 1922	E
381.			10 Nov 1922	E,pc
382.	19 Nov 1922	T,cc		
	—			
383.	22 Dec 1922			
384.			7 Jan [1923]	E
385.	14 Jan 1923	T,cc		
386.	15 Feb 1923	T,cc		
387.			28 Feb 1923	E
388.			4 Mar 1923	E,pc
389.	6 Mar 1923	T,cc		
390.	8 Mar 1923	T,cc		
391.			10 Mar 1923	E
392.			12 Mar 1923	E
393.	20 Mar 1923	T,cc		
394.			27 Mar 1923	E
395.	5 Apr 1923	T,cc		
396.			[7 Apr 1923]	E,pc
397.	13 Apr 1923	T,Ta		
398.			25 Apr 1923	E
399.	1 May 1923			
400.			18 May 1923	E
401.	31 May 1923	T,cc		
402.			2 Jul 1923	E,pc
403.	2 Jul 1923	T,cc		
404.	8 Jul 1923			
405.			14 Jul 1923	E,pc

	Jones		*Freud*	
406.	12 Sep 1923			
407.			24 Sep 1923	E
408.	2 Oct 1923			
409.	22 Oct 1923			
410.			26 Oct 1923	E,tel
411.	27 Oct 1923			
412.			4 Nov 1923	T
413.	12 Nov 1923	T,cc		
414.	29 Nov 1923			
415.			18 Dec 1923	T
416.	4 Jan 1924	T,cc		
417.			15 Jan 1924	T
418.	25 Jan 1924	T,cc		
419.	9 Feb 1924	T,cc		
420.			26 Feb 1924	T
421.			3 Apr 1924	T
422.	9 Apr 1924	T,cc,cc		
423.	11 Apr 1924	T,cc		
424.			13 Apr 1924	E,tel
425.			14 Apr 1924	tel
426.	14 Apr 1924	T,nJS		
427.	29 Apr 1924			
428.	30 May 1924	T		
429.			20 Jun 1924	T
430.	24 Jun 1924	T,cc,cc		
431.	9 Jul 1924	T,cc		
432.			16 Jul 1924	T
433.	12 Aug 1924	T,cc		
434.			25 Sep 1924	E
435.	29 Sep 1924	hws,nS,Ta		
436.			23 Oct 1924	E
437.	28 Oct 1924	T,cc		
438.			5 Nov 1924	T
439.	7 Nov 1924	T,nJS		

	Jones		Freud	
440.	11 Nov 1924			
441.			16 Nov 1924	T
442.	24 Nov 1924	T,cc		
443.	1 Dec 1924	T		
444.	18 Dec 1924	T,nJS,cc		
445.			6 Jan 1925	T
446.	10 Jan 1925	T,nJS,cc		
447.	5 Feb 1925	T,cc		
448.			11 Feb 1925	T
449.	17 Feb 1925	T,nJS		
450.			22 Feb 1925	T
451.	27 Feb 1925	T,nJS,cc		
452.	23 Mar 1925	T,nJS		
453.			1 Apr 1925	E
454.			26 Apr 1925	T
455.	30 Apr 1925	T,nJS,cc		
456.			10 May 1925	T
457.			20 May 1925	T
458.	25 May 1925	T,nJS,cc		
459.	27 May 1925	T,nJS		
460.			9 Jun 1925	T
461.	17 Jul 1925	T,cc		
462.			22 Jul 1925	T
463.	31 Jul 1925	T,cc		
464.	19 Sep 1925	T,cc		
465.			25 Sep 1925	T
466.			4 Oct 1925	E,pc
467.	30 Nov 1925	T,nJS		
468.	5 Dec 1925	T,nJS,cc		
469.			13 Dec 1925	T
470.			16 Dec 1925	E
471.	18 Dec 1925	T		
472.	19 Dec 1925	T,cc		
473.			21 Dec 1925	T

	Jones		*Freud*	
474.	25 Dec 1925			
475.			30 Dec 1925	
476.	25 Feb 1926			
477.	6 Mar 1926			
478.			7 Mar 1926	T
479.	11 Mar 1926			
480.			21 Mar 1926	T
481.	25 Mar 1926	T,nJS,cc		
482.			6 Apr 1926	T
483.	10 Apr 1926	T,nJS		
484.			19 Apr 1926	T
485.	19 Apr 1926	T,nJS		
486.	23 Apr 1926	T,nJS		
487.	24 Apr 1926	T,nJS		
488.	15 Aug [1926]	pc,nS		
	—			
489.			30 Aug 1926	
490.	23 Sep 1926	T,nJS		
491.			27 Sep 1926	E
492.			20 Nov 1926	L
493.	22 Dec 1926			
494.	27 Jan 1927	T,cc		
495.			1 Feb 1927	L
496.	9 Feb 1927			
497.			15 Feb 1927	T
498.	21 Feb 1927	Tu,sl,cc		
499.			3 Mar 1927	E,pc
500.	7 Mar 1927	T		
501.	[7 Apr 1927]	pc		
502.	16 May 1927			
503.			31 May 1927	T
504.	20 Jun 1927	T		
505.			6 Jul 1927	L
506.	18 Jul 1927			

	Jones		Freud	
507.	20 Aug 1927			
508.			23 Sep 1927	L
509.	30 Sep 1927	T		
510.			9 Oct 1927	L
511.	18 Oct 1927	T,Ta		
512.			22 Oct 1927	L
513.	26 Nov 1927	T		
514.			1 Dec 1927	L
515.	5 Dec 1927	T		
516.			11 Dec 1927	L
517.	13 Feb 1928			
518.			18 Feb 1928	E
519.			22 Feb 1928	L
	—		—	
520.	7 Mar 1928			
521.			11 Mar 1928	L
522.	29 Apr 1928			
523.			3 May 1928	L
524.			17 Jun 1928	L
525.	23 Jun 1928			
526.			1 Jul 1928	L
527.	19 Jul 1928			
528.			11 Oct 1928	L
529.	15 Oct 1928	T,nJS		
530.	20 Oct 1928			
531.			27 Oct 1928	
532.			4 Nov 1928	L
533.	12 Dec 1928			
534.			1 Jan 1929	L
535.	1 Jan 1929	T,nJS		
536.			4 Jan 1929	L
537.	21 Jan 1929			
538.	28 May 1929			

	Jones		Freud	
539.			2 Jun 1929	
540.	7 Jun 1929			
541.			4 Aug 1929	
542.	20 Aug 1929	nS		
543.			25 Aug 1929	E
544.	27 Aug 1929	T		
545.			[30 Sep 1929]	L
546.	14 Oct 1929	T		
547.			19 Oct 1929	L
548.	1 Jan 1930	T		
549.			26 Jan 1930	L
550.	5 Apr 1930	T		
551.			9 Apr 1930	L
552.			7 May 1930	L
553.			8 May 1930	E,pc
554.	8 May 1930			
555.			12 May 1930	L
556.	15 May 1930	T		
557.			19 May 1930	L
558.	26 May 1930	T		
559.	3 Jul 1930	T		
560.			13 Aug 1930	L
561.	26 Aug 1930			
562.			30 Aug 1930	L
563.	10 Sep 1930			
564.			15 Sep 1930	L
565.			18 Nov 1930	E
566.	20 Nov 1930			
567.			25 Nov 1930	
568.	31 Dec 1930	T		
569.			4 Jan 1931	L
570.			12 Jan 1931	L
571.	15 Jan 1931	T		
572.			19 Jan 1931	E

	Jones		*Freud*	
573.	23 Jan 1931	T		
574.	[7 Apr 1931]	pc		
575.			13 Apr 1931	pc
576.	2 May 1931			
577.			2 Jun 1931	L
578.			25 Oct 1931	L
579.	15 Nov 1931			
580.	10 Jan 1932	hws,Tcu		
581.			23 Jan 1932	L
582.	12 Feb 1932			
583.	21 Apr 1932	T,cc		
584.			26 Apr 1932	L
585.	5 May 1932	T,cc		
586.	28 May 1932	T,cc		
587.			1 Jun 1932	L
588.	2 Jun 1932	T,Tcu		
589.			8 Jun 1932	L
590.	13 Jun 1932	T,cc		
591.	16 Jun 1932	T,nJS		
592.			17 Jun 1932	L
593.	21 Jun 1932	T,cc		
594.	28 Aug 1932	pc,nS		
595.	9 Sep 1932			
596.			12 Sep 1932	L
597.	15 Sep 1932	Tcu		
598.			11 Nov 1932	
599.	10 Jan 1933	Tcu		
600.			13 Jan 1933	L
601.			15 Jan 1933	L
602.	18 Jan 1933	T,Ta		
603.			24 Feb 1933	L
604.	1 Mar 1933	T		
605.			1 Mar 1933	
606.			7 Apr 1933	

	Jones		Freud	
607.	10 Apr 1933	T,cc		
608.	3 May 1933			
609.			7 May 1933	L
610.	16 May 1933	T		
611.	25 May 1933	T		
612.			29 May 1933	L
613.	3 Jun 1933	T,nJS,Ta		
614.	17 Jul 1933	T,cc		
615.			23 Jul 1933	L
616.			23 Aug 1933	L
617.	14 Sep 1933	pc		
618.	18 Sep 1933	T,cc		
619.	5 Oct 1933	T,nS		
620.			15 Oct 1933	L
621.			26 Nov 1933	L
622.	1 Dec 1933	Tcu		
623.			4 Dec 1933	L
624.			14 Jan 1934	L
625.	16 Jan 1934	T,nJS		
626.	26 Mar 1934	T,cc		
627.			29 Mar 1934	L
628.	12 Jun 1934	T		
629.			16 Jun 1934	L
630.	20 Jun 1934	T		
631.	19 Feb 1935	T,cc		
632.			24 Feb 1935	
633.	12 Mar 1935	T,nJS		
634.			15 Mar 1935	
635.	2 May 1935	T,cc		
636.			26 May 1935	L
637.	27 Jun 1935	T,Tc		
638.			7 Jul 1935	L
639.	13 Jul 1935	T,nJS		
640.			21 Jul 1935	L

	Jones		*Freud*	
641.	25 Jul 1935	T,cc		
642.			29 Oct 1935	pc
643.			30 Oct 1935	pc
644.	27 Feb 1936	T,cc		
645.			3 Mar 1936	L
646.	2 Jun 1936	T,Tcu		
647.			4 Jul 1936	L
648.	6 Jul 1936	T,cc		
649.			4 Aug 1936	tel
650.			11 Nov 1936	L,pc
651.	23 Feb 1937	T,cc		
652.			2 Mar 1937	
653.			18 May 1937	L
654.	22 May 1937	T		
655.	1 Nov 1937	T		
656.	6 Dec 1937	T		
657.			9 Dec 1937	L
658.	13 Dec 1937	T		
659.			14 Feb 1938	pc
660.			23 Apr 1938	
	—			
661.			28 Apr 1938	L
	—			
662.			13 May 1938	L
663.			1 Nov 1938	L
664.	2 Nov 1938	T,nJS		
665.	14 Nov 1938	T,nJS		
666.			15 Nov 1938	L
667.	16 Nov 1938	T,nJS		
668.	12 Dec 1938	T,nJS		
669.			31 Jan 1939	
670.			7 Mar 1939	
671.	3 Sep 1939			

References

⚜

Works by Sigmund Freud

1886e. Translation of J.-M. Charcot's "Sur un cas coxalgie hystérique de cause traumatique chez l'homme," under the title "Über einen Fall von hysterischer Coxalgie aus traumatischer Ursache bei einem Manne." *Wiener medicinische Wochenschrift* 36:711–715, 756–759. (Incorporated in Freud 1886f.)

1886f. Translation with preface and footnotes of J.-M. Charcot's *Leçons sur les maladies du système nerveux* (vol. 3, Paris, 1887), under the title *Neue Vorlesungen über die Krankheiten des Nervensystems insbesondere über Hysterie*. Vienna. English trans., "Preface to the Translation of Charcot's *Lectures on the Diseases of the Nervous System*." *S.E.* 1:19–22.

1888–1889. Translation with Preface and Notes of H. Bernheim's *De la suggestion et des applications à la thérapeutique*, Paris, 1886, under the title *Die Suggestion und ihre Heilwirkung*, Vienna. (English trans. of preface to the translation of Bernheim's *Suggestion*, *S.E.* 1:73–87.)

1892a. Translation of Bernheim's *Hypnotisme, suggestion et psychothérapie: études nouvelles*, Paris, 1891, under the title *Neue Studien über Hypnotismus, Suggestion und Psychothérapie*, Vienna.

[with J. Breuer]. 1893a. "On the Psychical Mechanism of Hysterical Phenomena: Preliminary Communication." *S.E.* 2:3–17.

1894a. "The Neuro-Psychoses of Defence." *S.E.* 3:43–61.

[with J. Breuer]. 1895d. *Studies on Hysteria. S.E.* 2.

1896a. "L'hérédité et l'étiologie des néroses" [in French]. *S.E.* 3:142–156.

1896b. "Further Remarks on the Neuro-Psychoses of Defence." *S.E.* 3:159–185.

1896c. "The Aetiology of Hysteria." *S.E.* 3:189–221.

1900a. *The Interpretation of Dreams. S.E.* 4, 5.

1901a. *On Dreams. S.E.* 5:631–686.

1901b. *The Psychopathology of Everyday Life.* In *S.E.* 6.

1905c. *Jokes and Their Relation to the Unconscious. S.E.* 8.

1905d. *Three Essays on the Theory of Sexuality. S.E.* 7:125–245.

1905e. "Fragment of an Analysis of a Case of Hysteria." *S.E.* 7:3–122.

1906a. "My Views on the Part Played by Sexuality in the Aetiology of the Neuroses." *S.E.* 7:270–279.

1906c. "Psycho-Analysis and the Establishment of the Facts in Legal Proceedings." S.E. 9:99–114.

1907a. *Delusions and Dreams in Jensen's "Gradiva."* S.E. 9:3–95.

1907b. "Obsessive Actions and Religious Practices." S.E. 9:116–127.

1907c. "The Sexual Enlightenment of Children." S.E. 9:130–139.

1908b. "Character and Anal Erotism." S.E. 9:168–175.

1908c. "On the Sexual Theories of Children." S.E. 9:207–226.

1908d. " 'Civilized' Sexual Morality and Modern Nervous Illness." S.E. 9:179–204.

1908e. "Creative Writers and Day-Dreaming." S.E. 9:142–153.

1908f. [Preface to Stekel 1908.] S.E. 9:250–251.

1909b. "Analysis of a Phobia in a Five-Year-Old Boy." S.E. 10:3–149.

1909d. "Notes upon a Case of Obsessional Neurosis." S.E. 10:153–320.

1910a. "Five Lectures on Psycho-Analysis." S.E. 11:3–56.

1910c. *Leonardo da Vinci and a Memory of his Childhood.* S.E. 11:59–137.

1910d. "The Future Prospects of Psycho-Analytic Therapy." S.E. 11:140–151.

1910e. "The Antithetical Meaning of Primal Words." S.E. 11:154–161.

1910f. "Letter to Dr. Friedrich S. Krauss on *Anthropophyteia*." S.E. 11:233–235.

1910h. "A Special Type of Choice of Object Made by Men (Contributions to the Psychology of Love I)." S.E. 11:164–175.

1910k. " 'Wild' Psycho-Analysis." S.E. 11:220–227.

1911a. "Additions to the Interpretation of Dreams (Wholly Incorporated in *The Interpretation of Dreams*)." S.E. 5:360–366, 408–409.

1911b. "Formulations on the Two Principles of Mental Functioning." S.E. 12:215–226.

1911c. "Psycho-Analytic Notes on an Autobiographical Account of a Case of Paranoia (Dementia Paranoides)." S.E. 12:3–79.

1911e. "The Handling of Dream-Interpretation in Psycho-Analysis." S.E. 12:90–96.

1912a. "Postscript to the Case of Paranoia." S.E. 12:80–82.

1912b. "The Dynamics of Transference." S.E. 12:98–108.

1912d. "On the Universal Tendency to Debasement in the Sphere of Love (Contributions to the Psychology of Love II)." S.E. 11:178–190.

1912e. "Recommendations to Physicians Practising Psycho-Analysis." S.E. 12:111–120.

1912f. "Contributions to a Discussion on Masturbation." S.E. 12:241–254.

1912g. "A Note on the Unconscious in Psycho-Analysis." [In English.] S.E. 12:257–266.

1912–13. *Totem and Taboo.* S.E. 13:1–162.

1913a. "An Evidential Dream." S.E. 12:268–277.

1913c. "On Beginning the Treatment (Further Recommendations on the Technique of Psycho-Analysis I)." S.E. 12:122–144.

1913e. "Preface to Maxim Steiner's *Die psychischen Störungen der männlichen Potenz* (1913)." S.E. 12:345–346.

1913f. "The Theme of the Three Caskets." S.E. 12:291–301.

1913g. "Two Lies Told by Children." S.E. 12:304–309.

1913i. "The Disposition to Obsessional Neurosis." S.E. 12:313–326.

1913j. "The Claims of Psycho-Analysis to Scientific Interest." S.E. 13:164–190.

1913m. "On Psycho-Analysis." [In English.] *Australian Medical Congress.* (Transactions of the Ninth Session, Sidney, New South Wales, September 1911.) *S.E.* 12:206–211.

1914b. "The Moses of Michelangelo." *S.E.* 13:211–238.

1914c. "On Narcissism: An Introduction." *S.E.* 14:69–102.

1914d. "On the History of the Psycho-Analytic Movement." *S.E.* 14:3–66.

1914g. "Remembering, Repeating, and Working-Through (Further Recommendations on the Technique of Psycho-Analysis II)." *S.E.* 12:146–156.

1915a. "Observations on Transference-Love (Further Recommendations on the Technique of Psycho-Analysis III)." *S.E.* 12:158–173.

1915b. "Thoughts for the Times on War and Death." *S.E.* 14:274–302.

1915c. "Instincts and their Vicissitudes." *S.E.* 14:111–140.

1915d. "Repression." *S.E.* 14:143–158.

1915e. "The Unconscious." *S.E.* 14:161–204.

1916d. "Some Character-Types Met with in Psycho-Analytic Work." *S.E.* 14:310–333.

1916e. "Footnote to Ernest Jones's 'Professor Janet über Psychoanalyse.'" *S.E.* 2:xii–xiii n. 2.

1916–17. *Introductory Lectures on Psycho-Analysis. S.E.* 15, 16.

1917c. "On Transformation of Instinct as Exemplified in Anal Erotism." *S.E.* 17:126–133.

1917d. "A Metapsychological Supplement to the Theory of Dreams." *S.E.* 14:219–235.

1917e. "Mourning and Melancholia." *S.E.* 14:239–260.

1918a. "The Taboo of Virginity (Contributions to the Psychology of Love III)." *S.E.* 11:192–208.

1918b. "From the History of an Infantile Neurosis." *S.E.* 17:3–123.

1919a. "Lines of Advance in Psycho-Analytic Therapy." *S.E.* 17:158–168.

1919b. "James J. Putnam." *S.E.* 17:271–272.

1919e. "'A Child Is Being Beaten': A Contribution to the Study of the Origin of Sexual Perversions." *S.E.* 17:177–204.

1920a. "The Psychogenesis of a Case of Homosexuality in a Woman." *S.E.* 18:146–172.

1920f. "Supplements to the Theory of Dreams." *S.E.* 18:4–5.

1920g. *Beyond the Pleasure Principle. S.E.* 18:3–64.

1921a. Preface [in English] to J. J. Putnam's *Addresses on Psychoanalysis. S.E.* 18:269–270.

1921b. Introduction [in English] to Varendonck, *The Psychology of Day-Dreams*, London. *S.E.* 18:271–272.

1921c. *Group Psychology and the Analysis of the Ego. S.E.* 18:67–143.

1922a. "Dreams and Telepathy." *S.E.* 18:196–220.

1923b. *The Ego and the Id. S.E.* 19:3–66.

1923d. "A Seventeenth-Century Demonological Neurosis." *S.E.* 19:69–105.

1924f. "A Short Account of Psycho-Analysis." *S.E.* 19:190–209.

1924i. "Letter in *Jewish Observer and Middle East Review*" 3, 23 (June).

1925d. *An Autobiographical Study. S.E.* 20:3–70.

1925i. "Some Additional Notes on Dream Interpretation as a Whole." *S.E.* 19:125–132.

1925j. "Some Psychical Consequences of the Anatomical Distinction between the Sexes." *S.E.* 19:243–258.

1926b. "Karl Abraham." *S.E.* 20:277–278.

1926c. " 'Foreword' to E. Pickworth Farrow's *A Practical Method of Self-Analysis.*" *S.E.* 20:280.

1926d. *Inhibitions, Symptoms, and Anxiety. S.E.* 20:77–175.

1926e. *The Question of Lay-Analysis. S.E.* 20:179–250.

1926f. "Psycho-Analysis" [article in *Encyclopaedia Britannica,* 13th. ed.]. *S.E.* 20:261–270.

1927a. "Postscript to *The Question of Lay-Analysis.*" *S.E.* 20:251–258.

1927b. "Supplement to 'The Moses of Michelangelo.' " *S.E.* 13:237–238.

1927c. *The Future of an Illusion. S.E.* 21:3–56.

1929a. "Dr. Ernest Jones (on his 50th Birthday)." *S.E.* 21:249–250.

1930a. *Civilization and Its Discontents. S.E.* 21:59–145.

1930e. "Address Delivered in the Goethe House at Frankfurt." *S.E.* 21:206–212.

1931a. "Libidinal Types." *S.E.* 21:216–220.

1931b. "Female Sexuality." *S.E.* 21:223–243.

1933a. *New Introductory Lectures on Psycho-Analysis. S.E.* 22:3–182.

1933b. *Why War? S.E.* 22:197–215.

1933c. "Sándor Ferenczi." *S.E.* 22:226–229.

1935a. "Postscript (1935) to *An Autobiographical Study.*" *S.E.* 20:71–74.

1937c. "Analysis Terminable and Interminable." *S.E.* 23:211–253.

1937d. "Constructions in Analysis." *S.E.* 23:256–269.

1939a. *Moses and Monotheism. S.E.* 23:3–137.

1940a. *An Outline of Psychoanalysis. S.E.* 23:141–207.

1945a. Foreword [in English] to J. B. Hobman, *David Eder: Memoirs of a Modern Pioneer* (London: Victor Gollanz, 1945).

1950a. *The Origins of Psycho-Analysis. S.E.* 1:175–397.

Works by Ernest Jones

1904. "The Healing of the Tracheotomy Wound in Diphtheria." *British Journal of Children's Diseases* 1:153–158.

1905a. "The Onset of Hemiplegia in Vascular Lesions." *Brain* 28:527–555.

1905b. "Multiple Bilateral Contractures Simulating Pseudo-Hypertrophic Muscular Paralysis (An Aberrant Form of the Nageotte-Wilbonchewitch Syndrome)." *Brain* 28:585–586.

1905c. "A Case of Extreme Microcephaly, with Ape-Like Movements." *British Journal of Children's Diseases* 2:214–215.

1907a. "La vrai aphasie tactile." *Revue neurologique* 15:3–7.

1907b. "Eight Cases of Hereditary Spastic Paraplegia." *Review of Neurology and Psychiatry* 5:98–106.

1907c. "A Simplified Technique for Accurate Cell Enumeration in Lumbar Puncture." *Review of Neurology and Psychiatry* 5:539–550.

1907d. "The Clinical Significance of Allochiria." *Lancet* 2:830–832.

1907e. "The Precise Diagnostic Value of Allochiria." *Brain* 30:490–532.

1907f. "Mechanism of Severe Briquet Attack as Contrasted with that of Psychasthenic Fits." *Journal of Abnormal Psychology* 2:218–227.

1907g. "Alcoholic Cirrhosis of the Liver in Children." *British Journal of Children's Diseases* 4:1–14, 43–52.

1907h. "The Occurrence of Goitre in Parent and Child." *British Journal of Children's Diseases* 4:101–103.

1908a. "The Symptoms and Diagnosis of Juvenile Tabes." *British Journal of Children's Diseases* 5:131–140.

1908b. "The Significance of Phrictopathic Sensation." *Journal of Nervous and Mental Disease* 35:427–437.

1908c. "The Variation of the Articulatory Capacity for Different Consonantal Sounds in School Children." *Internationales Archiv für Schulhygiene* 5:137–157.

1908d. "Rationalisation in Everyday Life." *Journal of Abnormal Psychology* 3:161–169.

1909a. "The Pathology of Dyschiria." *Review of Neurology and Psychiatry* 7:499–522, 559–587.

1909b. "The Differential Diagnosis of Cerebellar Tumours." *Boston Medical and Surgical Journal* 161:281–284.

1909c. "Psycho-Analysis in Psychotherapy." *Journal of Abnormal Psychology* 4:140–50; and Prince et al. (1910, pp. 107–118).

1909d. "Remarks on a Case of Complete Autopsychic Amnesia." *Journal of Abnormal Psychology* 4:218–235.

1909e. "Psycho-Analytic Notes on a Case of Hypomania." *American Journal of Insanity* 66:203–218.

1909f. "An Attempt to Define the Terms Used in Connection with Right-Handedness." *Psychological Bulletin* 6:130–132.

1909g. "The Differences between the Sexes in the Development of Speech." (Read at the Sixth International Congress of Psychology, Geneva, 2–7 August 1909.) *British Journal of Children's Diseases* 6:413–416.

[with George W. Ross] 1909h. "On the Use of Certain New Chemical Tests in the Diagnosis of General Paralysis and Tabes." *British Medical Journal* 1:1111–1113.

1909i. [Comments on case reported by] W. G. Heggie, "Glioma of the Optic Thalamus." *Dominion Medical Monthly* 33:96–98.

1909j. "The Pathology of General Paralysis." *Dominion Medical Monthly* 33:127–136; and *Alienist and Neurologist* 30:577–588.

1909k. "Cerebrospinal Fluid in Relation to the Diagnosis of Metasyphilis of the Nervous System." *Bulletin of the Ontario Hospitals for the Insane* 2:15–39.

1909l. "A Review of Our Present Knowledge Concerning the Sero-Diagnosis of General Paralysis." *American Journal of Insanity* 65:653–688.

1909m. "Modern Progress in Our Knowledge of the Pathology of General Paralysis." *Lancet* 87(2):209–212.

1909n. "The Proteid Content of the Cerebro-Spinal Fluid in General Paralysis." *Review of Neurology and Psychiatry* 7:379–391.

1909–10. "The Dyschiric Syndrome." *Journal of Abnormal Psychology* 4:311–327.

1910a. "The Oedipus-Complex as an Explanation of Hamlet's Mystery: A Study in

Motive." *American Journal of Psychology* 22:72–113. Trans.: "Das Problem des Hamlet und der Oedipus-Komplex," *Schriften* 10.

1910b. "The Question of the Side Affected in Hemiplegia and in Arterial Lesions of the Brain." *Quarterly Journal of Clinical Medicine* 3:233–250.

1910c. "The Psycho-Analytic Method of Treatment." *Journal of Nervous and Mental Disease* 37:285–295.

1910d. "Freud's Theory of Dreams." (Read before the American Psychological Association, Boston, 29 December 1909, *Review of Neurology and Psychiatry* 8:135–143.) Expanded version in *American Journal of Psychology* 21:283–308.

1910e. "The Practical Value of the Word-Association Method in Psychopathology." *Review of Neurology and Psychiatry* 8:641–672.

1910f. "Psycho-Analysis and Education." *Journal of Educational Psychology* 1:497–520.

1910g. "Some Questions of General Ethics Arising in Relation to Psychotherapy." *Dominion Medical Monthly* 35:17–22.

1910h. "Freud's Psychology." *Psychological Bulletin* 7:109–128.

1910i. "Simulated Foolishness in Hysteria." (Read before the Detroit Society of Neurology and Psychiatry, 3 February 1910.) *American Journal of Insanity* 67:279–286.

1910j. "The Mental Characteristics of Chronic Epilepsy." (Read before the National Association for the Study of Epilepsy, Baltimore, 7 May 1910.) *Maryland Medical Journal* 53:223–229.

1910k. "A Modern Conception of the Psychoneuroses." (Read before a meeting of the Canadian Medical Association, Toronto, 2 June 1910.) *Interstate Medical Journal* 17:567–575.

1910l. "The Relation between Organic and Functional Nervous Diseases." *Dominion Medical Monthly* 35:202–207.

1910m. "On the Nightmare." *American Journal of Insanity* 66:383–417.

1910n. "Bericht über die neuere englische und amerikanische Literatur zur klinischen psychologie und Psychopathologie." *Jahrbuch* 2:316–337. Trans.: "Review of the Recent English and American Literature on Clinical Psychology and Psychopathology," *Archives of Neurology Neurology and Psychiatry* 5:120–147.

1910o. "The Differential Diagnosis of Paraplegia." *Canadian Practitioner and Medical Review* 35:1–8.

1910–11a. "The Action of Suggestion in Psychotherapy." *Journal of Abnormal Psychology* 5:217–254. [Expanded version of Jones (1911), "The Therapeutic Effect of Suggestion." (Read at the first meeting of the American Psychopathological Association, Washington, D.C., 2 May 1910; and at the First International Congress of Medical Psychology and Psychotherapy, Brussels, 7–8 August 1910.) *Canadian Journal of Medicine and Surgery* 29:78–87.]

1910–11b. [Report on First International Congress of Medical Psychology and Psychotherapy, Brussels, 7–8 August 1910.] *Journal of Abnormal Psychology* 5:290–291.

1911a. "The Deviation of the Tongue in Hemiplegia." (Read at the Thirty-Seventh Annual Meeting of the American Neurological Association, Baltimore, 13 May 1911.) *Journal of Nervous and Mental Disease* 38:577–587.

1911b. "Remarks on Dr. Morton Prince's Article 'The Mechanism and Interpretation of Dreams.'" *Journal of Abnormal Psychology* 5:328–336.

1911c. "Some Instances of the Influence of Dreams on Waking Life." *Journal of Abnormal Psychology* 6:11–18.

1911d. "Reflections on Some Criticisms of the Psycho-Analytic Method of Treatment." (Read before the Chicago Neurological Society and Chicago Medical Society [Joint Meeting], 18 January 1911.) *American Journal of Mental Science* 142:47–57.

1911e. "The Pathology of Morbid Anxiety." (Read before the American Psychopathological Association, Baltimore, 10 May 1911.) *Journal of Abnormal Psychology* 6:81–106.

1911f. "The Relationship between Dreams and Psycho-Neurotic Symptoms." (Read before the Wayne County Society, Detroit, 15 May 1911.) *American Journal of Insanity* 68:57–80.

1911g. "The Psychopathology of Everyday Life." (Read at the Detroit Academy of Medicine, 16 May 1911.) *American Journal of Psychology* 22:477–527.

1911h. "Syphilis of the Nervous System." *Interstate Medical Journal* 18:39–47.

1911i. "Darwin über das Vergessen." *Zentralblatt* 1:614.

1911–12. [Review of Bleuler 1910.] *Journal of Abnormal Psychology* 6:465–470.

1912a. "The Therapeutic Action of Psycho-Analysis." (Read before the Detroit Society of Neurology and Psychiatry, 7 December 1911.) *Review of Neurology and Psychiatry* 10:53–64.

1912b. "The Value of Sublimating Processes for Education and Re-Education." (Read before the American Psychological Association, Washington, D.C., 29 December 1911.) *Journal of Educational Psychology* 3:241–256.

1912c. "A Forgotten Dream (Note on the Oedipus Saving Phantasy)." *Journal of Abnormal Psychology* 7:5–16.

1912d. "Zwei interessante Fälle von Versprechen." *Zentralblatt* 2:33–34.

1912e. "Analyse eines Falles von Namenvergessen." *Zentralblatt* 2:84–86.

1912f. "Ein klares Beispsiel sekundärer Bearbeitung." *Zentralblatt* 2:135.

1912g. "Unbewusste Zahlenbehandlung." *Zentralblatt* 2:241–244.

1912h. "Die Bedeutung des Salzes in Sitte und Brauch der Völker." *Imago* 1:361–385; 454–488.

1912i. "Ein ungewöhnlicher Fall von 'gemeinsamen Sterben.'" *Zentralblatt* 2:455–459.

1912j. "Der Alptraum in seiner Beziehung zu gewissen Formen des mittelalterlichen Aberglaubens." *Schriften* 14:1–149. Trans. in pt. 2 of Jones (1931b, pp. 55–240).

1912–13. "Einige Fälle von Zwangsneurose." *Jahrbuch* 4:563–606, 5:55–116. "Analytic Study of a Case of Obsessional Neurosis," abridged version, in *Papers*, 2nd ed. 1918, pp. 515–539.

1913a. "The Treatment of the Neuroses, Including the Psychoneuroses." In *The Modern Treatment of Nervous and Mental Diseases by American and British Authors*, ed. William A. White and Smith Ely Jelliffe. 2 vols. Philadelphia: Lea and Faber, 1:331–416. (See Jones 1920b.)

1913b. "Die Beziehung zwischen Angstneurose und Angsthysterie." *Zeitschrift* 1:11–17. ("The Relation between Anxiety Neurosis and Anxiety Hysteria."

[Read before the International Society for Medical Psychology and Psychotherapy, Zurich, 9 September 1912.] *Journal of Abnormal Psychology* 8:1–9.)

1913c. "A Simple Phobia." *Journal of Abnormal Psychology* 8:101–108.

1913d. "The Interrelations of the Biogenetic Psychoses." (Read at the opening ceremony of the Phipps Psychiatric Clinic, Baltimore, 18 April 1913.) *American Journal of Insanity* 69:1027–32.

1913e. "Die Bedeutung des Grossvaters für das Schicksal des Einzelnen." *Zeitschrift* 1:219–223.

1913f. "Andrea del Sarto Kunst und der Einfluss seiner Gattin." *Imago* 2:468–480.

1913g. "Der Gottmensch-Komplex; der Glaube, Gott zu sein, und die daraus folgenden Charactermerkmale." *Zeitschrift* 1:313–339.

1913h. "George Meredith über Träume." *Zentralblatt* 3:54–55.

1913i. "Hass und Analerotik in der Zwangsneurose." *Zeitschrift* 1:425–430. Trans.: "Hate and Anal Erotism in the Obsessional Neurosis." (Read before the American Psychopathological Association, Washington, D.C., 9 May 1913.) In *Papers*, 2nd ed., pp. 540–548.

1913j. "[Report on] Internationaler Kongress für Medizin. London, August 1913." *Zeitschrift* 1:592–597.

1913k. "The Phantasy of the Reversal of Generations." (Read before the Psychiatric Society, Ward's Island, New York, 8 February 1913). In *Papers*, 2nd ed. pp. 658–687. Trans. (abridged): "Generations-Umkehrungsphantasie," *Zeitschrift* 1:562–563.

1913–14. "The Case of Louis Bonaparte, King of Holland." (Read before the American Psychopathological Association, Washington, D.C., 8 May 1913.) *Journal of Abnormal Psychology* 8:289–330.

1914a. "Die Empfängniss der Jungfrau Maria durch das Ohr: Ein Beitrag zu der Beziehung zwischen Kunst und Religion." *Jahrbuch der Psychoanalyse* 6:135–204. Trans. and rev.: "The Madonna's Conception through the Ear: A Contribution to the Relation between Aesthetics and Religion." In Jones (1923a, pp. 261–359; 1951, 2:266–357).

1914b. "Die Stellungnahme des psychoanalytischen ärztes zu den aktuellen Konflikten." (Read before the Fourth International Psychoanalytic Congress, Munich, 8 September 1913). *Zeitschrift* 2:6–10. Trans.: "The Attitude of the Psycho-Analytic Physician towards Current Conflicts." In *Papers*, 2nd ed., pp. 312–317.

1914c. [Critique of Jung 1913b.] *Zeitschrift* 2:83–86.

1914d. "Bemerkungen zur psychoanalytischen Technik." *Zeitschrift* 2:274–275.

1914e. "Frau und Zimmer." *Zeitschrift* 2:380.

1914f. "Zahnziehen und Geburt." *Zeitschrift* 2:380–381.

1914g. "Haarschneiden und Geiz." *Zeitschrift* 2:383.

1914h. "Die Technik der psychoanalytischen Therapie." *Jahrbuch der Psychoanalyse* 6:329–342.

1914i. "The Unconscious and Its Significance for Psychopathology." (Read in Jones's absence before the British Medical Association, Aberdeen, 29–31 July 1914.) *British Medical Journal*, 2 (1914):966–967; and *Review of Neurology and Psychology* 12:474–481.

1915a. "The Repression Theory and Its Relation to Memory." (Read before the

British Psychological Society, Durham, 30 January 1915.) *British Journal of Psychology* 8:33–47.

1915b. "Professor Janet on Psycho-Analysis: A Rejoinder." *Journal of Abnormal Psychology* 9:400–410. Trans.: "Professor Janet über Psychoanalyse," *Zeitschrift* 4:34–43.

1915c. "War and Individual Psychology." *Sociological Review* 8:167–180.

1915d. "War and Sublimation." (Read before the British Association for the Advancement of Science, Section of Psychology, Manchester, 10 September 1915). In Jones (1923a, pp. 381–390; 1951, 1:77–87).

1916a. "The Theory of Symbolism." (Read before the British Psychological Society, 29 January 1916.) *British Journal of Psychology* 9:181–229. Trans.: Hanns Sachs, "Die Theorie der Symbolik," *Zeitschrift* 5:244–273, and 8:259–289.

1916b. Translation of Sándor Ferenczi, *Contributions to Psychoanalysis*. Boston: R. G. Badger.

1916c. "The Unconscious Mental Life of the Child." *Child-Study* 9:37–41, 49–55.

1916–17. [Review of Stanley Hall, "A Synthetic Genetic Study of Fear," *American Journal of Psychology*.] *Zeitschrift* 4:55–60.

1918a. "War Shock and Freud's Theory of the Neuroses." *Proceedings of the Royal Society of Medicine* 11:21–36. Trans.: "Die Kriegsneurosen und die Freudsche Theorie." In *Zur Psychoanalyse der Kriegsneurosen*. Leipzig: Internationaler Psychoanalytischer Verlag, 1919, pp. 61–82.

1918b. "Anal-Erotic Character Traits." *Journal of Abnormal Psychology* 13:261–284. Trans.: Anna Freud, "Über analerotische Charakterzüge," *Zeitschrift* 5:69–92.

1919. [Obituary of J. J. Putnam.] *Zeitschrift* 5:233–243. Trans.: "Dr. James Jackson Putnam," *Journal* 1:6–16.

1920a. "Recent Advances in Psycho-Analysis." (Read before the Medical Section, British Psychological Society, 21 January 1920.) *British Journal of Medical Psychology* 1:49–71; and *Journal* 1:161–185.

1920b. *Treatment of the Neuroses*. New York: Wm. Wood; London: Baillière, Tindall, and Cox. [Based on Jones 1913a.] Trans.: *Therapie der Neurosen*. Leipzig: Internationaler Psychoanalytischer Verlag, 1921.

1920c. [Review of A. G. Tansley, *The New Psychology and Its Relation to Life*.] *Journal* 1:478–480.

1921. "Persons in Dreams Disguised as Themselves." *Journal* 2:420–423.

1921–22a. "Dream Analysis." In *Encyclopaedia and Dictionary of Education*. Vol. 1. London: Pitman, pp. 493–494.

1921–22b. "Psychotherapy." In *Encyclopaedia and Dictionary of Education*. Vol. 3. London: Pitman, pp. 1371–72.

1922a. [Preface to Freud 1920g.]

1922b. [Preface to Freud 1916–17.]

1922c. [Review of Edward J. Kempf, *Psychopathology*.] *Journal* 3:55–65.

1922d. [Review of D. Forsyth, *The Technique of Psycho-Analysis*.] *Journal* 3:224–227.

1922e. [Review of E. A. Westermarck, *The History of Human Marriage*.] *Journal* 3:249–252.

1922f. "Notes on Dr. Abraham's Article on 'The Female Castration Complex.'" *Journal* 3:327–328.

1922g. "Some Problems of Adolescence." (Read before a joint meeting of the General, Medical, and Education Sections of the British Psychological Society, 14 March 1922.) *British Journal of Psychology* 13:31–47.

1922h. "The Island of Ireland: A Psycho-Analytical Contribution to Political Psychology." (Read before the British Psycho-Analytical Society, 21 June 1922.) In Jones (1951, 1:95–112).

1922i. [Review of S. Freud, *Dream Psychology*.] *Journal* 3:114–115.

1922j. "A Psycho-Analytic Study of the Holy Ghost Concept." (Read before the Seventh Congress of the International Psychoanalytic Association, Berlin, 27 September 1922.) In Jones (1951, 2:358–373).

1923a. *Essays in Applied Psycho-Analysis*. London: International Psycho-Analytical Press.

1923b. "The Nature of Auto-Suggestion." (Read before the Medical Section of the British Psychological Society, 22 March 1923.) *Journal* 4:293–312.

1923c. "The Nature of Desire." *Journal of Neurology and Psychopathology* 3:338–341.

1923d. "Classification of the Instincts." (Read before the Seventh International Congress of Psychology, Oxford, 31 July 1923.) *British Journal of Psychology* 14:256–261.

[et al.]. 1924a. *Glossary for the Use of Translators of Psycho-Analytical Works*. Supplement no. 1 to *Journal* 5:1–16. (Additions and corrections in *Journal* 6.)

1924b. "Editorial Preface." In Freud, *Collected Papers* 1:3–4.

1924c. [Review of Wittels 1924.] *Journal* 5:481–486.

Ed. 1924d. *Social Aspects of Psycho-Analysis: Lectures Delivered under the Auspices of the Sociological Society*. London: Williams and Norgate.

1924e. "Psycho-Analysis and Anthropology." (Read before the Royal Anthropological Society, 19 February 1924.) *Journal of the Royal Anthropological Institute* 54:47–66.

1924f. "Free Will and Determinism." (Read before the Oxford Psychological Society, 27 October 1924.) In Jones (1951, 2:178–189).

1924g. [Review of R. Laforgue and R. Allendy, *La psychanalyse et les névroses*.] *Journal* 5:486–487.

1924h. [Review of McDougall 1923.] *Journal* 5:496–498.

1925a. "Mother-Right and the Sexual Ignorance of Savages." *Journal* 6:109–130.

1925b. *Traité théorique et pratique de psychanalyse*. Trans.: S. Jankélévich. Paris: Payot. (Translation of *Papers*, 3rd ed.)

1926a. [Obituary of Karl Abraham.] *Journal* 7:155–189; and *Zeitschrift* 12:155–183. In Abraham (1927, pp. 9–41).

1926b. "The Psychology of Religion." (Read before the Tenth International Congress of Psychology, Groningen, 7 September 1926.) *British Journal of Medical Psychology* 6:264–269.

1926c. "The Origin and Structure of the Super-Ego." *Journal* 7:303–311. Trans.: "Der Ursprung und Aufbau des Über-Ichs," *Zeitschrift* 12:253–262.

1927a. [Review of Freud 1926e.] *Zeitschrift* 13:101–107; and *Journal* 8:87–92.

1927b. [Review of McDougall 1926.] *Journal* 8:421–429.

1927c. [Contribution to the "Discussion on Lay Analysis."] *Journal* 8:174–198. Trans.: *Zeitschrift* 13:171–192.

1927d. [Contribution to the "Symposium on Child Analysis."] *Journal* 8:387–391.

1927e. "La conception du surmoi." (Read before the Paris Psychoanalytic Society, 5 April 1927.) *Revue française de psychanalyse* 1:324–336. Trans.: "The Development of the Concept of the Superego," *Journal of Abnormal and Social Psychology* 23:276–285.

1927f. "The Early Development of Female Sexuality." (Read before the Tenth Congress of the International Psychoanalytic Association, Innsbruck, 1 September 1927.) *Journal* 8:459–472.

1928a. *Psycho-Analysis.* London: E. Benn. Rev. ed.: London: Allen and Unwin, 1949.

1928b. "Psycho-Analysis and Folklore." (Read before the Jubilee Congress of the Folk-Lore Society, 25 September 1928.) *Scientia,* 55:209–220; and Jones (1951, 2:1–21).

1928c. *Zur psychoanalyse der christlichen Religion.* Leipzig: Internationaler Psychoanalytischer Verlag.

1929a. "The Psychopathology of Anxiety." (Read before the Psychiatric Section of the Royal Society of Medicine and the British Psychological Society, 9 April 1929.) *British Journal of Medical Psychology* 9:17–25.

1929b. "La jalousie." (Read at the Sorbonne, 21 March 1929.) *Revue française de psychanalyse* 3:228–422.

1929c. "Fear, Guilt, and Hate." (Read before the Eleventh Congress of the International Psychoanalytic Association, Oxford, 27 July 1929.) *Journal* 10:383–397.

1929d. "Psychoanalysis and Psychiatry." (Read at the Psychiatric Institute, Columbia University, 4 December 1929.) *Mental Hygiene* 14:384–398.

1929e. "Abnormal Psychology." *Encyclopaedia Britannica,* 14th ed. 1:50–56.

1929f. "Freud, Sigmund." *Encyclopaedia Britannica,* 14th ed. 9:836–837.

1930a. "Psycho-Analysis and Biology." (Read before the Second International Congress for Sex Research, London, 7 August 1930.) In Jones (1951, 1:135–164).

1930b. "Psychoanalysis and the Christian Religion." (Read before the Lotus Club, Oxford University, 22 November 1930.) In Jones (1951, 2:198–211).

1931a. "The Problem of Paul Morphy: A Contribution to the Psychology of Chess." *Journal* 12:1–23; and Jones (1951, 1:165–196).

1931b. *On the Nightmare.* London: Hogarth Press and Institute of Psycho-Analysis.

1933a. "The Phallic Phase." (Read before the Twelfth Congress of the International Psychoanalytic Association, Wiesbaden, 4–7 September 1932.) *Journal* 14:1–33. Trans.: "Die phallische Phase." *Zeitschrift* 19:322–357.

1933b. "The Unconscious Mind." In C. Burt, E. Jones, E. Miller, and W. Moodie. *How the Mind Works.* London: Allen and Unwin, pp. 61–103.

1933c. [Review of Freud 1933b.] *Journal* 14:418–420.

1934. "Psycho-Analysis and Modern Medicine." (Read before the Paddington Medical Society.) *Lancet* 226:59–62.

1935. "Early Female Sexuality." (Read before the Vienna Psychoanalytic Society, 24 April 1935.) *Journal* 16:263–273.

1936. "Psychoanalysis and the Instincts." (Read before the British Psychological Society, 22 March 1935.) *British Journal of Psychology* 26:272–288.

1945. "Reminiscent Notes on the Early History of Psycho-Analysis in English-Speaking Countries." *Journal* 26:8–10.

1949. *Hamlet and Oedipus.* New York: W. W. Norton; London: V. Gollancz. Reprinted: New York: W. W. Norton, 1971. [Rev. version of Jones (1910a) and "A Psycho-Analytic Study of Hamlet" (Jones, 1923a, pp. 1–98).]

1951. *Essays in Applied Psycho-Analysis.* 2 vols. London: Hogarth Press. Reprinted: *Psycho-Myth, Psycho-History: Essays in Applied Psychoanalysis.* 2 vols. New York: Hillstone, 1974.

1953a. *The Life and Work of Sigmund Freud.* Vol. 1. *The Formative Years and the Great Discoveries, 1856–1900.* New York: Basic Books.

1953b. *Sigmund Freud: Life and Work,* Vol. 1. *The Young Freud, 1856–1900.* London: Hogarth Press. New ed. 1954.

1954. "The Early History of Psycho-Analysis." *Journal of Mental Science* 100:198–210.

1955a. *The Life and Work of Sigmund Freud.* Vol. 2. *Years of Maturity, 1901–1919.* New York: Basic Books.

1955b. *Sigmund Freud: Life and Work.* Vol. 2. *Years of Maturity, 1901–1919.* London: Hogarth Press. New ed. 1958; reprinted 1967.

1957a. *The Life and Work of Sigmund Freud.* Vol. 3. *The Last Phase, 1919–1939.* New York: Basic Books.

1957b. *Sigmund Freud: Life and Work.* Vol. 3. *The Last Phase, 1919–1939.* London: Hogarth Press.

1959. *Free Associations: Memories of a Psycho-Analyst.* New York: Basic Books. New ed., intro. Mervyn Jones. New Brunswick, N.J.: Transaction Publishers, 1990.

Works by Other Authors

Abraham, H. C., and E. L. Freud, eds. 1965. *A Psycho-Analytic Dialogue: The Letters of Sigmund Freud and Karl Abraham, 1907–1926.* Trans. B. Marsh and H. C. Abraham. London: Hogarth Press.

Abraham, Karl. 1909. "Traum und Mythus: Eine Studie zür Völkerpsychologie." *Schriften* 4.

——— 1911. "Giovanni Segantini: Ein psychoanalytischer Versuch." *Schriften* 11:1–65. Trans.: "Giovanni Segantini: A Psychoanalytic Essay." In Abraham (1955, pp. 210–261).

——— 1914. [Critique of Jung 1913b.] *Zeitschrift* 2:72–82. Trans.: "Attempt at a Representation of Psycho-Analytical Theory." In Abraham (1955, pp. 101–105).

——— 1927. *Selected Papers of Karl Abraham,* trans. D. Bryan and A. Strachey. London: Hogarth Press.

——— 1955. *Clinical Papers and Essays on Psychoanalysis,* ed. H. Abraham, trans. H. Abraham and D. R. Ellison. London: Hogarth Press.

Adler, Gerhard. ed. 1973. *C. G. Jung: Letters,* in collaboration with Aniela Jaffé, trans. R. F. C. Hull, vol. 1, *1906–1950.* London: Routledge and Kegan Paul.

Alexander, F. 1926. "Neurose und Gesamtpersönlichkeit." *Zeitschrift* 12:334–347. Trans.: "Neurosis and the Whole Personality," *Journal* 7:340–352.

Alexander, F., and S. T. Selesnick. 1965. "Freud-Bleuler Correspondence." *Archives of General Psychiatry* 12:1–9.

Andreas-Salomé, Lou. 1965. *The Freud Journal of Lou Andreas-Salomé*, trans. S. A. Leavy. London: Hogarth Press.

Atkinson, J. J. 1903. *Primal Law*. London: Longmans.

Barnes, Julian. 1989. "Morceaux de bois littéraires." In *Le désir biographique*, ed. P. Lejeune, pp. 291–297. Cahiers de Semiotique textuelle 16. Paris: Université de Paris X.

Bettelheim, Bruno. 1982. "Freud and the Soul." *The New Yorker* (1 March), pp. 52–93. And *Freud and Man's Soul*. New York: Alfred A. Knopf, 1983.

Bleuler, Eugen. 1910. "Die Psychoanalyse Freuds: Verteidigung und kritische Bemerkungen." *Jahrbuch* 2:623–730.

———— 1911. "Dementia Praecox, oder Gruppe der Schizophrenien." In Gustav Aschaffenburg's *Handbuch der Psychiatrie*. Leipzig: Deuticke. *Dementia Praecox, or the Group of Schizophrenias*. Trans. J. Zinkin. New York: International Universities Press, 1950.

Boehlich, Walter, ed. 1990. *The Letters of Sigmund Freud to Eduard Silberstein, 1871–1881*. Trans. A. J. Pomerans. Cambridge, Mass.: Harvard University Press.

Bourdieu, Pierre. 1986. "L'illusion biographique." *Actes de la recherche en sciences sociales 62/63*, pp. 69–72. Paris: Editions de Minuit.

Bourke, J. G. 1891. *Scatologic Rites of All Nations*. Washington, D.C.: W. H. Lowdermilk.

Boven, William. 1922. "Alexander der Grosse." *Imago* 8:418–439.

Brecht, Karen, Volker Friedrich, Ludger M. Hermanns, Isidor, J. Kaminer, and Dierek H. Juelich, eds. 1985. *"Hier geht das Leben auf eine sehr merkwürdige Weise weiter . . .": Zur Geschichte der Psychoanalyse in Deutschland*. Hamburg: Michael Kellner.

Brill, A. A. 1908–9. "Psychological Factors in Dementia Praecox: An Analysis." *Journal of Abnormal Psychology* 3:219–239.

———— 1909a. Translation of Freud, *Selected Papers on Hysteria and Other Psychoneuroses*. New York: Journal of Nervous and Mental Disease Publishing Company, Monograph Series, no. 4., 2nd ed. 1912.

———— 1909b. "Freud's Conception of the Psychoneuroses." *Medical Record* 76:1065–69.

———— 1910a. "Dreams and Their Relation to the Neuroses." *New York Medical Journal* 91:842–846.

———— 1910b. "The Anxiety Neurosis." *Journal of Abnormal Psychology* 5:57–68.

———— 1910c. Translation of Freud, *Three Contributions to the Sexual Theory*, intro. J. J. Putnam. New York: Journal of Nervous and Mental Disease Publishing Company, Monograph Series, no. 7.

———— 1911. "Freud's Theory of Wit." *Journal of Abnormal Psychology* 6:279–316.

———— 1912a. *Psychanalysis: Its Theories and Practical Application*. Philadelphia: W. B. Saunders; 2nd ed. 1914.

———— 1912b. Translation of Freud, "Wild Analysis." In Brill (1909a), 2nd ed. 1912, pp. 201–206.

———— 1913. Translation of Freud, *The Interpretation of Dreams*. London: G. Allen; New York: Macmillan.

————— 1914. Translation of Freud, *Psychopathology of Everyday Life*. London: Fisher Unwin; New York: Macmillan.

————— 1916a. Translation of Freud, *Leonardo da Vinci*. New York: Moffat, Yard.

————— 1916b. Translation of Freud, "The History of the Psychoanalytic Movement." *Psychoanalytic Review* 3:406–454; and New York: Nervous and Mental Disease Publishing Company, Monograph Series, no. 25, 1917.

————— 1916c. Translation of Freud, *Wit and Its Relation to the Unconscious*. New York: Moffat, Yard; London: Fisher Unwin, 1917.

————— 1918. Translation of Freud, *Totem and Taboo*. New York: Moffat, Yard; London: Routledge, 1919.

British Medical Association. 1929. "Appendix II: Report of Psycho-Analysis Committee." *Supplement to the British Medical Journal*, London, 29 June 1929, pp. 262–270. (*Report of the Committee on Psychoanalysis*, Archives of the British Psycho-Analytical Society, London.)

Brome, Vincent. 1983. *Ernest Jones: Freud's Alter Ego*. New York: W. W. Norton.

————— 1984. *Freud and His Disciples*. London: Caliban Books.

Browning, Robert. 1895. *The Complete Poetic and Dramatic Works of Robert Browning: Cambridge Edition*. Boston: Houghton Mifflin.

Burnham, John Chynoweth. 1967. *Psychoanalysis and American Medicine (1894–1918): Medicine, Science, and Culture*. New York: International Universities Press.

————— 1983. *Jelliffe: American Psychoanalyst and Physician & His Correspondence with Sigmund Freud and C. G. Jung*, ed. William McGuire, foreword by Arcangelo R. T. D'Amore. Chicago: University of Chicago Press.

Burrow, Trigant. 1958. *A Search for Man's Sanity: Selected Letters of Trigant Burrow*. New York: Oxford University Press.

Carotenuto, Aldo. 1982. *A Secret Symmetry: Sabina Spielrein Between Jung and Freud*, trans. Arno Pomerans, John Shepley, and Krishna Winston. New York: Pantheon Books.

Clark, David R., and James B. McGuire, eds. 1989. *W. B. Yeats: The Writing of Sophocles' King Oedipus*. Philadelphia: American Philosophical Society.

Clark, L. Pierce. 1920. "A Study of Primary Somatic Factors in Compulsive and Obsessive Neuroses." *Journal* 1:150–160.

Clark, Ronald W. 1980. *Freud: The Man and the Cause*. New York: Random House.

Clark University. 1910. *Lectures and Addresses Delivered before the Departments of Psychology and Pedagogy in Celebration of the Twentieth Anniversary of the Opening of Clark University, September 1909*. Worcester, Mass.

Cocks, Geoffrey. 1985. *Psychotherapy in the Third Reich: The Göring Institute*. New York: Oxford University Press.

Collins, Joseph. 1910. "The Psychoneuroses: An Interpretation." (Read before a meeting of the Canadian Medical Association, Toronto, 2 June 1910.) *Medical Record* 78:87–92.

Crawley, A. E. 1902. *The Mystic Rose: A Study of Primitive Marriage*. London: Macmillan.

Davies, T. G. 1979. *Ernest Jones: 1879–1958*. Cardiff: University of Wales Press.

Decker, Hannah S. 1977. *Freud in Germany: Revolution and Reaction in Science,*

1893–1907. Psychological Issues, Monograph 41. New York: International Universities Press.

De Mijolla, Alain. 1989. "Images de Freud au travers de sa correspondance." *Revue internationale d'histoire de la psychanalyse*, pp. 81–200. Paris: Presses Universitaires de France.

Dupont, Judith. ed. 1988. *The Clinical Diary of Sándor Ferenczi*. Trans. Michael Balint and Nicola Zarday Jackson. Cambridge, Mass.: Harvard University Press.

—— 1989. "La relation Freud-Ferenczi à la lumière de leur correspondence." *Revue internationale d'histoire de la psychanalyse*, pp. 81–200. Paris: Presses Universitaires de France.

Eder, David. 1911. "A Case of Obsession and Hysteria Treated by the Freud Psycho-Analytic Method." *British Medical Journal* 2:750–752.

—— 1913. "The Present Position of Psychoanalysis." *British Medical Journal* 2:1213–15.

Eder, Edith, and M. D. Eder, and Mary Moltzer. 1913–1915. [Translation of Jung 1913b.] *Psychoanalytic Review* 1:1–40, 153–177, 260–284, 415–430; and 2:29–51.

Ellenberger, Henri F. 1970. *The Discovery of the Unconscious: The History and Evolution of Dynamic Psychiatry*. New York: Basic Books.

Evans, Richard I. 1964. *Conversations with Carl Jung and Reactions from Ernest Jones*. Princeton: D. Van Nostrand.

Farrow, E. P. 1925. "A Castration Complex." *Journal* 6:45–50.

Fenichel, O. 1928. [Review of "Symposium on Child Analysis," *Journal* 8:339–391.] *Zeitschrift* 14:546–561.

Ferenczi, Sándor. 1909. "Introjektion und Übertragung." *Jahrbuch* 1:422–457. Trans.: "Introjection and Transference." In Ferenczi (1916, pp. 35–93).

—— 1910. "The Psychological Analysis of Dreams." *American Journal of Psychology* 21:309–328; and Ferenczi (1916, pp. 94–131).

—— 1912. "On Symbolism." In Ferenczi (1916, pp. 253–281).

—— 1913. "Entwicklungsstufen des Wirklichkeitssinnes." *Zeitschrift* 1:124–138.

—— 1914. [Review of Jung (1913d).] *Zeitschrift* 2:86–88.

—— 1916. *First Contributions to Psychoanalysis*, trans. Ernest Jones. London: Maresfield Reprints, 1980. (See Jones 1916b.)

—— 1919. *Hysterie und Pathoneurosen*. Leipzig: Internationaler Psychoanalytischer Verlag.

—— 1920. "Further Extension of the Active Technique in Psycho-Analysis." (Abstract of a paper read at the Sixth International Psychoanalytic Congress, The Hague, September 1920.) *Journal* 1:354–355.

—— 1921. [Review of Freud 1915d.] In *Bericht über die Fortschritte der Psychoanalyse in den Jahren 1914–1919*. Leipzig: Internationaler Psychoanalytischer Verlag. Supplement to *Zeitschrift*, pp. 103–105. Trans.: Sybil C. Porter, *Journal* 1:306–308.

—— 1926a. "Kontraindikationen der aktiven psychoanalytischen Technik." (Read at the Ninth International Psychoanalytic Congress, Bad Homburg, 3–5 September 1925.) *Zeitschrift* 12:3–14.

—— 1926b. *Further Contributions to the Theory and Technique of Psycho-Analysis*, compiled by John Rickman, trans. J. I. Suttie, C. M. Baines, O. Edmonds, E. G. Glover, and J. Rickman. London: Hogarth Press.

—— 1932. "Infantilismus infolge Angst vor realen Aufgaben." In *Bausteine zur Psychoanalyse*, vol. 4. Zurich: Internationaler Psychoanalytischer Verlag, 1938, pp. 276–277. Trans.: "Infantility resulting from anxiety concerning real tasks." In Ferenczi (1955, pp. 264–265).

—— 1933. "Sprachverwirrung zwischen den Erwachsenen und dem Kind." (Read before the Twelfth Congress of the International Psychoanalytic Association, Wiesbaden, 4–7 September 1932.) *Zeitschrift* 19:5–15. Trans.: "Confusion of Tongues between Adults and the Child," *Journal* 30:225–230.

—— 1955. *Final Contributions to the Problems and Methods of Psychoanalysis*, ed. M. Balint, trans. E. Mosbacher et al., intro. Clara Thompson. New York: Basic Books.

Ferenczi, Sándor, and Otto Rank. 1924. *Entwicklungsziele der Psychoanalyse: Zur Wechselbeziehung von Theorie und Praxis*. Leipzig: Internationaler Psychoanalytischer Verlag. Trans.: Caroline Newton, *The Development of Psychoanalysis*. New York: Nervous and Mental Disease Publishing Company, 1925.

Fichtner, Gerhardt. 1989. "Les lettres de Freud en tant que source historique." *Revue internationale d'histoire de la psychanalyse*, pp. 11–78. Paris: Presses Universitaires de France.

Frazer, J. G. 1910. *Totemism and Exogamy: A Treatise on Certain Forms of Superstition and Society*. 4 vols. London: Macmillan.

—— 1911–1915. *The Golden Bough: A Study in Magic and Religion*. 3rd ed., 12 vols. London: Macmillan.

Freud, Anna. 1922. "Schlagephantasie und Tagtraum." *Imago* 8:317–332. Trans.: "The Relation of Beating Phantasies to a Day Dream," *Journal* 4:89–102.

—— 1927a. *Einführung in die Technik der Kinderanalyse*. Leipzig: Internationaler Psychoanalytischer Verlag. Trans.: L. Pierce Clark, *Introduction to the Technique of Child Analysis*. New York: Nervous and Mental Disease Publishing Company, 1928.

—— 1927b. "Zur Theorie der Kinderanalyse." (Read at the Tenth Congress of the International Psychoanalytic Association, Innsbruck, 3 September 1927.) *Zeitschrift* 14:153–162. Trans.: "On the Theory of Analysis of Children," *Journal* 10:29–38.

—— 1929. [Abstract] "Ein Gegenstück zur Tierphobie der Kinder." (Read before the Eleventh Congress of the International Psychoanalytic Association, Oxford, 28 July 1929.) *Zeitschrift* 15:518. Trans.: "A Counterpart of the Animal Phobias of Children," *Journal* 10:499.

Freud, E. L., L. Freud, and I. Grubrich-Simitis, eds. 1985. *Sigmund Freud: His Life in Pictures and Words*. New York: Harcourt Brace Jovanovich.

Freud, Martin. 1957. *Glory Reflected: Sigmund Freud: Man and Father*. London: Robertson.

Friedländer, A. A. 1911. "Hysteria and Modern Psychoanalysis," trans. H. Linenthal. *Journal of Abnormal Psychology* 5:297–319.

Gay, Peter. 1978. *Freud, Jews and Other Germans: Masters and Victims in Modernist Culture*. New York: Oxford University Press.

—— 1987. *A Godless Jew: Freud, Atheism and the Making of Psychoanalysis.* New Haven: Yale University Press.

—— 1988. *Freud: A Life for Our Time.* New York: W. W. Norton.

—— 1990. "Freud and the Man from Stratford." In *Reading Freud: Explorations and Entertainments*, pp. 5–53. New Haven: Yale University Press.

Gilman, Sander L. 1991. "Reading Freud in English: Problems, Paradoxes, and a Solution." *International Review of Psycho-Analysis* 18:331–344.

Girard, Claude. 1972. *Ernest Jones: Sa vie; son oeuvre.* Paris: Payot.

Graf, M. 1911. "Richard Wagner im *Fliegende Holländer:* Ein Beitrag zur Psychologie künstlerischen Schaffens." *Schriften* 9.

Groddeck, G. 1923. *Das Buch von Es: Psychoanalytische Briefe an eine Freundin.* Leipzig: Internationaler Psychoanalytischer Verlag.

Grosskurth, Phyllis. 1986. *Melanie Klein: Her World and Her Work.* Toronto: McLelland and Stewart.

—— 1991. *The Secret Ring: Freud's Inner Circle and the Politics of Psychoanalysis.* Toronto: MacFarlane, Walter & Ross.

Grotjahn, Martin. 1967. "Sigmund Freud and the Art of Letter Writing." *Journal of the American Medical Association* 200:13–18.

Grubrich-Simitis, Ilse, ed. 1987. *A Phylogenetic Fantasy: Overview of the Transference Neuroses: Sigmund Freud*, trans. Axel Hoffer and Peter T. Hoffer. Cambridge, Mass.: The Belknap Press of Harvard University Press.

Hale, Nathan G. Jr., ed. 1971a. *James Jackson Putnam and Psychoanalysis: Letters between Putnam and Sigmund Freud, Ernest Jones, William James, Sándor Ferenczi, and Morton Prince, 1877–1917*, trans. Judith Bernays Heller. Cambridge, Mass.: Harvard University Press.

—— 1971b. *Freud and the Americans.* Vol. 1. *The Beginnings of Psychoanalysis in the United States, 1876–1917.* New York: Oxford University Press.

Hart, Bernard. 1909–10. "The Conception of the Subconscious." *Journal of Abnormal Psychology* 4:351–371.

—— 1910. "The Psychology of Freud and his School." *Journal of Mental Science* 56:431–452.

—— 1912. *Psychology of Insanity.* Cambridge: Cambridge University Press; New York: Putnam's Sons.

Hartland, E. S. 1909–10. *Primitive Paternity: The Myth of Supernatural Birth in Relation to the History of the Family.* London: D. Nutt.

Hartnack, Christiane. 1990. "Vishnu on Freud's Desk: Psychoanalysis in Colonial India." *Social Research* 57:921–949.

Hinckle, Beatrice M. 1916. Translation of Jung (1911–12). *The Psychology of the Unconscious: A Study of the Transformations and Symbols of the Libido: A Contribution to the History of the Evolution of Thought.* New York: Moffat, Yard.

Hitschmann, E. 1911. *Freuds Neurosenlehre: Nach ihrem gegenwärtigen Stande zusammenfassend dargestellt.* Leipzig: Deuticke. Trans.: C. R. Payne, *Freud's Theories of the Neuroses*, intro. E. Jones. New York: Journal of Nervous and Mental Disease Publishing Company, Monograph Series, no. 17, 1913.

Hoch, August. 1910. "On Some Mental Mechanisms in Dementia Praecox." *Journal of Abnormal Psychology* 5:255–273.

Hoche, Adolf. 1910. "Eine psychische Epidemie unter Ärtzten." *Medizinische Klinik* 6:1007–10.

Holland, Norman N. 1966. *Psychoanalysis and Shakespeare*. New York: McGraw-Hill.

Holt, Edwin B. 1915. *The Freudian Wish and Its Place in Ethics*. New York: Holt.

Hughes, Athol, ed. 1991. *The Inner World and Joan Riviere: Collected Papers 1920–1958*. London: Karnac.

———— 1992. Letters from Sigmund Freud to Joan Riviere. In press.

Janet, Pierre. 1914. "La psycho-analyse." *Journal de psychologie* 11:97–130. Trans.: "Psychoanalysis," *Journal of Abnormal Psychology* 9:1–35, 153–187.

Jekels, L. 1914. "Der Wendepunkt im Leben Napoleons I." *Imago* 3:313–381. Trans.: A. Ratisbonne, "The Turning Point in the Life of Napoleon I." In Jekels (1952, pp. 1–73).

———— 1917. "Shakespeares *Macbeth*." *Imago* 5:170–195.

———— 1952. *Selected Papers*. New York: International Universities Press.

Jones, Katherine. 1939. Translation of Freud, *Moses and Monotheism*. London: Hogarth Press and Institute of Psycho-Analysis.

Jones, Mervyn. 1987. *Chances: An Autobiography*. London: Verso Editions.

Jung, C. G. 1907a. *The Psychology of Dementia Praecox*. *C.W.* 3:1–151.

———— 1907b. "On the Psychophysical Relations of the Association Experiment." *C.W.* 2:483–491.

———— 1908. "Inhalt der Psychose." *Schriften* 3. Trans.: "The Content of the Psychoses," *C.W.* 3:153–178; supplement: "On Psychological Understanding," *C.W.* 3:179–193.

———— 1909. "Die Bedeutung des Vaters für das Schicksal des Einzelnen." *Jahrbuch* 1:155–173. Trans.: "The Significance of the Father in the Destiny of the Individual," *C.W.* 4:301–323.

———— 1910. "The Association Method." *American Journal of Psychology* 21:219–269. *C.W.* 2:439–465.

———— 1911. "Morton Prince, M.D.: The Mechanism and Interpretation of Dreams: Ein kritische Besprechung." *Jahrbuch* 3:309–328. *C.W.* 4:56–73.

———— 1911–12. "Wandlungen und Symbole der Libido: Beiträge zur Entwicklungsgeschichte des Denkens." *Jahrbuch* 3:120–227, and 4:162–464; and Leipzig: Franz Deuticke, 1912. Trans.: Hinckle (1916); revised: *Symbols of Transformation, C.W.* 5.

———— 1912. "America Facing Its Most Tragic Moment." *New York Times* Magazine Section, 29 September. Reprinted: *C. G. Jung Speaking*, ed. William McGuire and R. F. C. Hull. Princeton: Princeton University Press, 1977, pp. 11–24.

———— 1913a. "General Aspects of Psychoanalysis." (Read before the Psycho-Medical Society, London, 5 August 1913.) *C.W.* 4:229–242.

———— 1913b. "Versuch einer Darstellung der psychoanalytischen Theorie." *Jahrbuch* 5:307–441. Trans.: "The Theory of Psychoanalysis," *C.W.* 4:83–226; and Edith Eder and M. D. Moltzer (1913–1915).

———— 1913c. "On the Doctrine of the Complexes." (Paper contributed to the Australasian Medical Congress, Ninth Session, Sydney, September 1911.) *C.W.* 2:598–604.

———— 1913d. "Contribution à l'étude des types psychologiques." (Read in German before the Fourth Congress of the International Psychoanalytic Association, Munich, 7–8 September 1913.) Trans. and rev. by author in *Archives de psychologie* 13:289–299.

———— 1914. "On the Importance of the Unconscious in Psychopathology." (Read at the Eighty-Second Annual Meeting of the British Medical Association, Section of Neurology and Psychological Medicine, Aberdeen, 29–31 July 1914.) *British Medical Journal* 2:964–966. *C.W.* 3:203–210.

———— 1915. "On Psychological Understanding." (Read before the Psycho-Medical Society, London, 24 July 1914.) *Journal of Abnormal Psychology* 9:385–399. *C.W.* 3:179–193.

———— 1916a. "Psychoanalysis and Neurosis." *C.W.* 4:243–251. Revised: "On Psychoanalysis," *Seventeenth International Congress of Medicine*, London, sect. 12, pts. 1 and 2. London: Henry Frowde, 1913. (Revised version of paper read before New York Academy of Medicine, 8 October 1912.) *C.W.* 4:243–251.

———— 1916b. *Collected Papers on Analytical Psychology*, ed. Constance E. Long. London: Baillière, Tindall, and Cox.

———— 1919. "On the Problem of Psychogenesis in Mental Diseases." (Read before the Royal Society of Medicine, Section of Psychiatry, 11 July 1919, London.) *C.W.* 3:211–225.

———— 1921. *Psychological Types*. *C.W.* 6.

———— 1973. *Experimental Researches*. *C.W.* 2.

Jung, C. G., and F. Peterson. 1907. "Psychophysical Investigations with the Galvanometer and Pneumograph in Normal and Insane Individuals." *C.W.* 2:492–553.

Jung, C. G., and C. Ricksher. 1907–8. "Further Investigations on the Galvanic Phenomenon and Respiration in Normal and Insane Individuals." *C.W.* 2:554–580.

Kafka, Franz. 1946. "The Great Wall of China." In *The Great Wall of China and Other Pieces*, pp. 81–94. Trans. Willa and Edwin Muir. London: Secker and Warburg.

Kiell, Norman. 1988. *Freud without Hindsight: Reviews of His Work (1893–1939)*. Madison, Conn.: International Universities Press.

King, Pearl. 1973. "The Contributions of Ernest Jones to the British Psychoanalytic Society." *Journal* 60:280–284.

———— 1983. "The Life and Work of Melanie Klein in the British Psychoanalytic Society." *Journal* 64:251–260.

King, Pearl, and Riccardo Steiner, eds. 1991. *The Freud-Klein Controversies: 1941–1945*. London: Routledge.

Klein, David. 1981. *Jewish Origins of the Psychoanalytic Movement*. New York: Praeger.

Klein, Melanie. 1927a. "The Psychological Principles of Infant Analysis." *Journal* 8:25–37.

———— 1927b. [Contribution to "Symposium on Child Analysis."] *Journal* 8:339–370.

———— 1927c. "Early Stages of the Oedipus Conflict." (Read at the Tenth Congress of the International Psychoanalytic Association, Innsbruck, 3 September 1927.) *Journal* 9:167–180.

Levine, Israel. 1923. *The Unconscious: An Introduction to Freudian Psychology*.

London: L. Parsons; New York: Macmillan. Trans.: A. Freud, *Das Unbewusste.* Leipzig: Internationaler Psychoanalytischer Verlag, 1926.

Leys, Ruth. 1981. "Meyer's Dealings with Jones: A Chapter in the History of the American Response to Psychoanalysis." *Journal of the History of the Behavioral Sciences* 17:445–465.

Lieberman, James. 1985. *Acts of Will: The Life and Work of Otto Rank.* New York: Free Press.

Looney, J. Thomas. 1920. *"Shakespeare" Identified.* London: C. Palmer.

MacCurdy, John T. 1923. *Problems in Dynamic Psychology: A Critique of Psycho-Analysis and Suggested Formulations.* Cambridge: Cambridge University Press.

McDougall, William. 1923. *An Outline of Psychology.* London: Methuen.

—— 1925a. "A Great Advance of the Freudian Psychology." *Journal of Abnormal Psychology* 20:43–47.

—— 1925b. "Professor Freud's Group Psychology and His Theory of Suggestion." *British Journal of Medical Psychology* 5:14–28.

—— 1926. *An Outline of Abnormal Psychology.* London: Methuen.

—— 1936. *Psycho-Analysis and Social Psychology.* London: Methuen.

McGuire, William, ed. 1974. *The Freud-Jung Letters: The Correspondence between Sigmund Freud and C. G. Jung,* trans. Ralph Manheim and R. F. C. Hull. Princeton: Princeton University Press. Trans.: *Sigmund Freud–C. G. Jung Briefwechsel,* ed. William McGuire and Wolfgang Sauerländer. Frankfurt: S. Fischer Verlag, 1974.

Mahony, Patrick J. 1984. "Further Thoughts on Freud and His Writing." In *Psychoanalysis and Discourse.* London: Tavistock Publications, 1987, pp. 145–158.

—— 1987. *Freud as a Writer: Expanded Edition.* New Haven: Yale University Press.

Masson, Jeffrey Moussaieff, trans. and ed. 1985. *The Complete Letters of Sigmund Freud to Wilhelm Fliess, 1887–1904.* Cambridge, Mass.: The Belknap Press of Harvard University Press.

Meisel, Perry, and Walter Kendrick, eds. 1985. *Bloomsbury/Freud: The Letters of James and Alix Strachey, 1924–1925.* New York: Basic Books.

Meng, Heinrich, and Ernst L. Freud, eds. 1963. *Psycho-Analysis and Faith: The Letters of Sigmund Freud and Oskar Pfister,* trans. Eric Mosbacher. London: Hogarth Press and Institute of Psycho-Analysis.

Meyer, Adolf. 1910a. "The Dynamic Interpretation of Dementia Praecox." *American Journal of Psychology* 21:385–403.

—— 1910b. "The Nature and Conception of Dementia Praecox." *Journal of Abnormal Psychology* 5:274–285.

Nashe, Thomas. 1594. *The Terrors of the Night, or, a Discourse of Apparitions.* London: printed by John Danter for William Jones.

Ohtsuki, K. 1931. Translation of Freud 1901b. Tokyo: Shunyodo.

Ornston, Darius Gray. 1982. "Strachey's Influence: A Preliminary Report." *International Journal of Psycho-Analysis* 63:409–426.

—— 1985a. "Freud's Conception Is Different from Strachey's." *Journal of the American Psychoanalytic Association* 33:379–412.

———— 1985b. "The Invention of 'Cathexis' and Strachey's Strategy." *International Review of Psycho-Analysis* 12:391–399.

———— ed. 1992. *Translating Freud.* New Haven: Yale University Press.

Oster, Daniel. 1989. "Bien sûr que oui." In *Le désir biographique,* ed. P. Lejeune. Cahier de Sémiotique textuelle 16. Paris: Université de Paris X.

Paskauskas, R. Andrew. 1985. "Ernest Jones: A Critical Study of His Scientific Development." Ph.D. diss. University of Toronto.

———— 1988a. "Freud's Break with Jung: The Crucial Role of Ernest Jones." *Free Associations: Psychoanalysis, Groups, Politics, Culture* 11:7–34.

———— 1988b. "The Jones-Freud Era: 1908–1939." In *Freud in Exile: Papers on the Origins and Evolution of Psychoanalysis,* ed. Edward Timms and Naomi Segal. New Haven: Yale University Press, pp. 109–123.

———— 1989. "Freud's English: Style, Charm, and Ideology." Paper presented at a conference titled "Translation in Transition: The Case of Sigmund Freud and James and Alix Strachey" (Institute of Germanic Studies, University of London; Austrian Institute; Goethe Institute; German Academic Exchange Service, and Institute of Psycho-Analysis, London, 28–29 April 1989).

Pearson, Karl. 1900. *The Grammar of Science.* 2nd ed. London: A. and C. Black.

Pfeiffer, Ernst. 1972. *Sigmund Freud and Lou Andreas-Salomé: Letters.* New York: W. W. Norton.

Pfister, Oskar. 1910. "Die Frömmigkeit des Grafen Ludwig von Zinzendorf: Ein psychoanalytischer Beitrag zur Kenntniss der religiösen Sublimierungs-Prozesse und zur Erklärung des Pietismus." *Schriften* 8.

———— 1913. *Die psychoanalytische Methode: Eine erfahrungswissenschaftlichsystematische Darstellung.* Foreword by S. Freud. Leipzig: Klinkhardt. Trans.: C. R. Payne, *The Psychoanalytic Method.* New York: Moffat, Yard, 1917.

Pines, Malcolm, Riccardo Steiner, Darius Gray Ornston, Jr., Alex Holder, and Helmut Junker. 1988. [Contributions to Part III "Problems of Translation."] In *Freud in Exile: Papers on the Origins and Evolution of Psychoanalysis,* eds. Edward Timms and Naomi Segal. London: Yale University Press, pp. 177–219.

Prince, Morton. 1908–9. "The Unconscious." *Journal of Abnormal Psychology* 3:261–297, 335–353, 391–426; and 4:36–56.

———— 1910a. "Dreams: Their Mechanism and Their Interpretation." *Journal of Nervous and Mental Disease* 37:305–309.

———— 1910b. "The Mechanism and Interpretation of Dreams." *Journal of Abnormal Psychology* 5:139–195.

———— 1911. "The Mechanism and Interpretation of Dreams—a Reply to Ernest Jones." *Journal of Abnormal Psychology* 5:337–353.

———— 1914. *The Unconscious: The Fundamentals of Human Personality, Normal and Abnormal.* New York: Macmillan.

Prince, Morton, Frederick H. Gerrish, James J. Putnam, E. W. Taylor, Boris Sidis, George A. Waterman, John E. Donley, Ernest Jones, and Tom A. Williams. 1910. *Psychotherapeutics: A Symposium.* Boston: Richard G. Badger; and *Journal of Abnormal Psychology* 4:69–199.

Putnam, James Jackson. 1906. "Recent Experiences in the Study and Treatment of Hysteria at the Massachusetts General Hospital; with Remarks on Freud's

Method of Treatment by 'Psychoanalysis.'" *Journal of Abnormal Psychology* 1:26–41.

———— 1909–10. "Personal Impressions of Sigmund Freud and His Work, with Special Reference to His Recent Lectures at Clark University." *Journal of Abnormal Psychology* 4:293–310, 372–379.

———— 1910a. "Personal Experience with Freud's Psychoanalytic Method." (Read at Thirty-Sixth Annual Meeting of the American Neurological Association, Washington, D.C., 2–4 May 1910.) *Journal of Nervous and Mental Disease* 37:657–674.

———— 1910b. "On the Etiology and Treatment of the Psychoneuroses." (Read before the Canadian Medical Association, Toronto, 2 June 1910.) *Boston Medical and Surgical Journal* 163:75–85. Trans.: "Über Ätiologie und Behandlung der Psychoneurosen," *Zentralblatt* 1:137–154.

———— 1911. "A Plea for the Study of Philosophic Methods in Preparation for Psychoanalytic Work." *Journal of Abnormal Psychology* 6:249–264.

———— 1912. "Comments on Sex Issues, from the Freudian Standpoint." *New York Medical Journal* 95:1249–54, 1306–9.

———— 1913. "Bemerkungen über einen Krankheitsfall mit Griselda-Phantasien." *Zeitschrift* 1:205–218. Trans.: "Remarks on a Case with Griselda Phantasies." In Putnam (1921, pp. 175–193).

———— 1914a. "Dream Interpretation and the Theory of Psychoanalysis." *Journal of Abnormal Psychology* 9:36–60.

———— 1914b. "On Some Broader Issues of the Psychoanalytic Movement." *American Journal of the Medical Sciences* 147:389–406. Trans.: "Allgemeine Gesichtspunkte zur psychoanalytischen Bewegung," *Zeitschrift* 4:1–20.

———— 1914c. "The Present Status of Psychoanalysis." *Boston Medical and Surgical Journal* 170:897–993.

———— 1915. *Human Motives.* Boston: Little, Brown.

———— 1921. *Addresses on Psycho-Analysis.* Preface by S. Freud. London: International Psycho-Analytical Press.

Rank, Otto. 1909. "Mythus von der Geburt des Helden." *Schriften* 5.

———— 1910. "Ein Traum, der sich selbst deutet." *Jahrbuch* 2:465–540.

———— 1911a. "Die Lohengrinsage: Ein Beitrag zu ihrer Motivgestaltung und Deutung." *Schriften* 13.

———— 1911b. "Ein Beispiel von poetischer Verwertung des Versprechens." *Zentralblatt* 1:109–110.

———— 1912. *Das Inzest-Motiv in Dichtung und Sage.* Leipzig: Deuticke.

———— 1924a. "The Trauma of Birth and Its Importance for Psychoanalytic Therapy." *Psychoanalytic Review* 11:241–245.

———— 1924b. *Das Trauma der Geburt und seine Bedeutung für die Psychoanalyse.* Leipzig: Internationaler Psychoanalytischer Verlag. Trans.: *The Trauma of Birth.* London: Kegan Paul; New York: Harcourt Brace, 1929.

———— 1924c. *Eine Neurosenanalyse in Träumen.* Leipzig: Internationaler Psychoanalytischer Verlag.

———— 1925. "Zur Genese der Genitalität." (Read before the Ninth Congress of the

International Psychoanalytic Association, Bad Homburg, 3–5 September 1925.) *Zeitschrift* 11:411–428. Trans.: "The Genesis of Genitality," *Psychoanalytic Review* 13:129–144.

Rank, Otto, and H. Sachs. 1913. *Die Bedeutung der Psychoanalyse für die Geisteswissenschaften.* Wiesbaden: Bergmann. Trans.: C. R. Payne, *The Significance of Psychoanalysis for the Mental Sciences.* New York: Journal of Nervous and Mental Disease Publishing Company, 1916.

Rieff, Philip. 1960. *Freud: The Mind of the Moralist.* London: Gollancz.

Riviere, J. 1927. [Contribution to "Symposium on Child Analysis."] *Journal* 8:370–377.

Roazen, Paul. 1974. *Freud and His Followers.* New York: New American Library.

Róheim, G. 1925. *Australian Totemism: A Psycho-Analytic Study in Anthropology.* London: Allen and Unwin.

Ross, Dorothy. 1972. *G. Stanley Hall: The Psychologist as Prophet.* Chicago: University of Chicago Press.

Roudinesco, Elisabeth. 1986. *La bataille de cent ans. Histoire de la psychanalyse en France. 1: 1885–1939.* Paris: Seuil.

Sachs, Hanns. 1945. *Freud: Master and Friend.* London: Imago.

Schrötter, K. 1912. "Experimentelle Träume." *Zentralblatt* 2:638–646.

Schur, Max. 1972. *Freud: Living and Dying.* London: Hogarth Press.

Sidis, Boris, and H. T. Kalmus. 1908–9. "A Study of Galvanometric Deflections Due to Psychophysiological Processes." *Psychological Review* 15:391–396, and 16:1–35.

Smith, W. Robertson. 1894. *Lectures on the Religion of the Semites.* Reprinted: London: A. and C. Black.

Spotts, Frederic, ed. 1989. *Letters of Leonard Woolf.* London: Harcourt, Brace, Jovanovich.

Stanton, Martin. 1991. *Sándor Ferenczi: Reconsidering Active Intervention.* London: Free Association Books.

Stärcke, August. 1921. "Psycho-Analysis and Psychiatry." *Journal* 2:361–415.

Starobinski, Jean. 1970. "Hamlet et Oedipe." In *L'oeil vivant,* 2:286–319. Paris: Gallimard.

Steiner, Riccardo. 1983. Unpublished paper on the Strachey's translation given at a special meeting of the British Psycho-Analytical Society.

——— 1985. "Some Thoughts about Tradition and Change Arising from an Examination of the British Psycho-Analytical Society's Controversial Discussions (1943–1944)." *International Review of Psycho-Analysis* 12:27–71.

——— 1987a. "Die Weltmachstellung des britischen Reichs. Some Notes on the Notion of 'Standard' in Freud's *Standard Edition.*" In *Freud in Exile,* ed. E. Timms and N. Segal. New Haven: Yale University Press.

——— 1987b. "A World-wide International Trade Mark of Genuineness?: Some Observations on the History of the English Translation of the Work of Sigmund Freud, Focusing Mainly on His Technical Terms." *International Review of Psycho-Analysis* 14:33–102.

——— 1988. "'C'est une nouvelle forme de diaspora . . .': La politique de l'émigration des psychanalystes d'après la correspondence d'Ernest Jones avec Anna

Freud." *Revue internationale d'histoire de la psychanalyse* 1:263–321. Trans.:
"'It is a New Kind of Diaspora . . . ,'" *International Review of Psycho-Analysis*
16:35–78.

———— 1991. "'To Explain Our Point of View to English Readers in English Words.'"
International Review of Psycho-Analysis 18:351–392.

Stekel, Wilhelm. 1907. *Die Ursachen der Nervosität*. Vienna: Paul Knepler.

———— 1908. *Nervöse Angstzustände und ihre Behandlung*. Intro. S. Freud. Berlin:
Urban and Schwarzenberg. Trans.: Rosalie Gabler, *Conditions of Nervous Anxiety and Their Treatment*. London: Kegan Paul, Trench, Trubner, 1923.

———— 1909. "Rechts und Links im Traume." *Jahrbuch* 1:466–473.

———— 1911. *Die Sprache des Traumes*. Munich: Bergmann.

———— 1912a. *Die Traüme der Dichter*. Munich: Bergmann.

———— 1912b. *Die Onanie: Vierzehn Beiträge zu einer Diskussion der Wiener psychoanalytischen Vereinigung*. Wiesbaden: Bergmann, pp. 29–45.

———— 1913a. [Review of Jones 1912g.] *Zentralblatt* 3:257.

———— 1913b. [Review of Jones 1913d.] *Zentralblatt* 3:456.

Storfer, A. J. 1911. "Zur Sonderstellung des Vatermordes: Eine rechtsgeschichtliche und völkerpsychologische Studie." *Schriften* 12.

Strachey, Alix. 1943. *A New German-English Psycho-Analytical Vocabulary*. London: Baillière, Tindall, and Cox.

Strachey, James. 1930. "Some Unconscious Factors in Reading." *Journal* 11:322–331.

———— 1963. "Obituary of Joan Riviere (1883–1962)." *Journal* 44:228–230.

Sulloway, Frank J. 1979. *Freud, Biologist of the Mind: Beyond the Psychoanalytic Legend*. New York: Basic Books.

Trömner, Ernst. 1911. "Vorgänge beim Einschlafen (Hypnagoge-Phänomene)."
(Read at the First Annual Meeting of the International Society for Medical Psychology and Psychotherapy, Brussels, 7–8 August 1910.) *Journal für Psychologie und Neurologie* 17:343–363.

Trosman, Harry. 1976. "Freud and the Controversy over Shakespearean Authorship." In *Freud: The Fusion of Science and Humanism*, ed. John E. Gedo and George S. Pollock. Psychological Issues, Monograph 34/35. New York: International Universities Press, pp. 307–331.

Trotter, Wilfred. 1908. "Herd Instinct and Its Bearing on the Psychology of Civilized Man." *Sociological Review* 1:227–248.

———— 1909. "Sociological Application of the Psychology of Herd Instinct." *Sociological Review* 2:36–54.

———— 1916. *Instincts of the Herd in Peace and War*. London: T. Fisher Unwin;
2nd ed. 1919.

———— 1985. *Instincts of the Herd in Peace and War: 1916–1919*. Intro. Douglas Holdstock. London: The Keynes Press, British Medical Association. (Includes Trotter 1908, 1909, 1916, 1919.)

Waterman, G. A. 1910. "Dreams as a Cause of Symptoms." *Journal of Abnormal Psychology* 5:196–210.

Wilson, Emmett. 1987. "Did Strachey Invent Freud?" *International Review of Psycho-Analysis* 14:299–315.

Winslow, Ted. 1990. "Bloomsbury, Freud, and the Vulgar Passions." *Social Research* 57:786–819.

Wittels, F. 1924. *Sigmund Freud: Der Mann, die Lehre, die Schule.* Leipzig: E. P. Tal. Trans.: Eden and Ceder Paul, *Sigmund Freud: His Personality, His Teaching, and His School.* New York: Dodd Mead; London: G. Allen and Unwin.

Woolf, Leonard. 1980. *An Autobiography*, Vol. 2. *1911–1969.* Oxford: Oxford University Press.

Yerushalmi, Yosef Hayim. 1991. *Freud's Moses: Judaism Terminable and Interminable.* New Haven: Yale University Press.

Young-Bruehl, Elisabeth. 1988. *Anna Freud: A Biography.* New York: Summit Books.

Glossary

ψα (ΨA): psychoanalysis
Abwehr: defense
Allmacht der Gedanken: omnipotence of thoughts
Ambivalenz: ambivalence
Angewandt(-e, -es): applied psychoanalytic writings
Angst: anxiety, fear
Angstanfall: anxiety attack
Angstträume: anxiety dreams
Angstzustand: anxiety state
Anmerkung der Redaktion: footnote, annotation of the editorial staff

Band: volume
Beirat: vice president
Beiträge: contributions
Berührung: touch, contact; contiguity
Bewegung: movement
Bewusste: the conscious
Bibliothek: I.P.V. Library series
Bogen: sheet (of paper)

Deckerinnerung: screen memory, cover memory
Destruktionstrieb: destructive instinct (drive)
Dritte Folge: third issue, installment, series

Einleitung: introduction
Erkenntnistrieb: instinct (drive) for knowledge
Ersatzformation: substitute formation

Fahnen: galley proofs
Fehlleistung: failure, mistake; slip
Festheft: commemorative booklet, pamphlet, brochure
Fluchtversuch: flight reaction, attempt at flight
Folge: series
Fond[s]: fund, capital

Gedankenübertragung: telepathy
Gedenkbuch: commemorative (jubilee) volume
Gegensinn (der Urworte): antithetic meaning (of primal words)
Gleichungen (symbolische): equation (symbolic)

Hälfte: half
Heft: booklet, pamphlet, brochure
Herausgeber: director
Honorar: royalties

Ichkonflikt: ego conflict
Instanz: (psychical) agency
Internationale ψα (ΨA) Vereinigung: International Psychoanalytic Association
Inzestscheu: fear (horror) of incest
I.P.V.: Internationale Psychoanalytische Verlag

Komplexbedingt: conditioned, determined by the complex
Korrektur: proof (sheet)

Lustprinzip: pleasure principle

Minderwertigkeit: inferiority

Nachtrag: postscript
Namenvergessen: forgetting of names
Nervösität: nervous condition

Obmann: chairman, head man
Ortsverein: local psychoanalytic society

Partieltriebe: component instincts
 (drives)
Penisneid: penis envy
Platzangst: agoraphobia, fear of open
 places, or space(s)

Rapport: report, notice
Realitätsprinzip: reality principle
Redakteur: editor
Redaktion: editorial staff
Redaktionssitzung: meeting of the edito-
 rial staff
Referat: review, abstract
Reiz: stimulus; stimulation, irritation,
 excitation
Reizschutz: protective barrier against
 stimuli

Sache, die: the cause (psychoanalysis)
Sammelband: omnibus volume
Schreck: fright, shock
Schrift: writing; book; publication; paper
Seite (S.): page
Sekundäre Bearbeitung: secondary elab-
 oration
Sonderabdruck: separate impression;
 offprint
Spalte: column
Sublimierung: sublimation
Symptombildung: symptom formation
Symptomhandlung: symptomatic act,
 action

Todestrieb: death instinct
Trauerarbeit: work of mourning

Traumatische Neurose: traumatic
 neurosis
Traumgedanken: dream thoughts
Trieb: instinct; drive, impulse, urge
Triebkomponente: component instincts
 (drives)
Triebumsetzung: instinctual transposi-
 tion, transformation, transmutation

Übertragung: transference
Übertragungsneurose: transference
 neurosis
Umbruch: page proof
Unbewusste: the unconscious
Urlibido: primal libido
Urvater: primal father
Urverdrängung: primal repression

Verdichtung: condensation
Verdrängung: repression
Vereinigung (Verein): short form for Inter-
 national Psychoanalytic Association
Vergessen: forget
Verlag: publishing house
Verlesen: to misread, to read wrongly
Verschiebung: displacement
Verschreiben: to make a mistake in writ-
 ing; a slip of the pen
Versprechen: to make a mistake in
 speaking; a slip of the tongue
Vorbewusste: the preconscious
Vorrede: introduction, preface
Vortrag: lecture, address, talk

Wandlungen: transformations
Wiederherstellung: restoration
Wiederholungszwang: repetition compul-
 sion
Wunsch: wish
Wunscherfüllung: wish fulfillment

Zentral(e): Executive Committee, Inter-
 national Psychoanalytic Association
Zwang: compulsion, obsession
Zwangsneurose: obsessional neurosis
Zwangsneurotiker: obsessional neurotic

Index

✣

Note: Numbers refer to correspondence numbers.

Abraham, Gerd, 613, 614

Abraham, Hilde, 614

Abraham, Karl, 4, 5, 11; Jung critique by, 163; fatal illness of, 468, 469, 470, 471, 472; death of, 474, 475; obituary of, 476, 479, 480, 481, 482, 483; *Selected Papers of Karl Abraham*, 494; provision for the heirs of, 606, 607

Acher, R., 63, 64

Acquired characters, transmission of, 82

"Action of Suggestion in Psychotherapy, The" (Jones), 52

Active therapy, 440, 464, 618

Actual neurosis, 25, 477

Adler, Alfred, 30, 33, 54, 57, 59, 62; dissension with, 64; "Das organische Substrat der Psychoneurosen," 89; on masculine protest, 121, 146; Freud's attack on, 191

Aehrenthal, Aloys Lexa von, 6

Affectivity, 25

Agoraphobia *(Platzangst)*, 68

Alexander, Franz, 464, 500

Algolagnic fantasies, 166

Allen, Alfred Reginald, 32, 481

Allied analytic methods, 509

Alptraum work (Jones), 97, 403, 447, 449

Alter ego, 232

America: interest in psychotherapy in, 7, 10; sexual attitudes in, 7, 8; psychoanalysis in, 60, 238; Freud's impressions of, 304, 305, 306; translators in, 310; choice of editors in, 311, 314, 321; piracy of Freud's writings in, 340; psychoanalytic

literature in, 430; Freud's attitude toward, 434; book sales in, 496; source book of Freud's writings in, 535, 536

American Journal of Insanity, 14, 47

American Journal of Psychology, 10, 18, 23, 31

American Neurological Association, 14, 32, 60

American Psychoanalytic Association, 4, 32, 51, 54, 60, 149, 459, 618; Boston meeting of, 76

American Psychopathological Association, 7, 23, 32, 60, 148, 188, 210

American Therapeutic Society, 7

Ames, Thaddeus H., 314

Amnesia, 61

Anaesthesia, 4, 5

Anal complex, 42, 77, 118

Anal eroticism, 42, 44, 45, 305

Analysis: of prominent psychoanalysts, 82; advice in, 142; training for, 509. *See also* Child analysis; Lay analysis

Analytic education, 464

Andreas-Salomé, Lou, 197, 364, 469

Animal magnetism, 32

Animism, 113

Anna O. case, 530, 531

Antithetic meaning *(Gegensinn)*, 61, 62, 513

Anxiety *(Angst)*, 58, 97; relation to desire, 136; relation to libido, 174; as a protection against shock, 232

Anxiety attack *(Angstanfall)*, 174

Anxiety conditions, classification of, 4
Anxiety dreams *(Angsttraüme)*, 4, 6
Anxiety hysteria, 4, 296
Anxiety neurosis *(Angstneurose)*, 6, 23, 163
Anxiety state *(Angstzustand)*, 4
Aphasia, 132
Art, psychoanalytic view of, 98
Asch, Joseph J., 330
Assagioli, Roberto, 17, 22, 24, 63
Association method, 1
Associations, 7. *See also* Free association
Atkinson, J. J., 127
Aural conception, 120. *See also* Madonna essay (Jones)
Auto-eroticism, 66
Auto-suggestion, 39, 393, 394

Bacon, Francis, 136
Baldwin, James Mark, 31
Balfour, Arthur James, 460
Barker, Llewelys Franklin, 32
Barlow, Sir Thomas, 74
Barnes, Ernest William, 513
Barrier against stimuli *(Reizschutz)*, 232
Becker, W. F., 140
Bergmann, J. F., 33
Berkeley-Hill, Owen, 43, 61, 82, 141, 148; "Short Study of the Life and Character of Mohammed, A," 295; "Anal-Erotic Factor in the Religion, Philosophy, and Character of the Hindus," 305, 306, 331
Berlin Psychoanalytic Institute, 528
Bernays, Edward, 266, 269, 278; *General Introduction to Psychoanalysis, A,* 280
Bernays, Emmeline, 28
Bernays, Judith, 353
Bernays, Minna, 83
Bernfeld, Siegfried, 651
Bernheim, Hippolyte, 644
Besetzung, 5, 280, 329; *Libidobesetzung,* 94; *Objektsbesetzungen,* 326; *Gegenbesetzung,* 477
Bestiality, 61
Beyond the Pleasure Principle (Jenseits des Lustprinzips), 237, 248, 284, 293, 314
Bezzola, Dumeng, 32
Bieber, Dr., 254, 255, 256, 257, 266, 269, 297, 298
Bijur, Angelika, 327, 356
Binswanger, Ludwig, 40, 235

Birthplace symbolism, 80
Bisexuality, 21, 22, 58
Bisshopp, Francis R., 206
Bjerre, Poul, 49, 172
Blanton, Smiley, 553, 556
Bleuler, Eugen, 25, 41, 43, 51, 54, 89
Bligh, Stanley, 159
Blüher, Hans, 180
Blumgart, Leonard, 306, 342
Boccaccio, Giovanni, 136
Boehm, Felix, 618
Boltzmann, Ludwig, 15
Bonaparte, Princess Marie, 518, 588, 616, 618, 620, 662
Bose, Girindrasekhar, 344, 383
Boven, William, 340, 342, 343
Bradford, John Rose, 522
Brandes, Georg, 296
Brasch, Lucie, 275, 306, 626, 651
Braun, Ludwig, 478
Bridges, Robert, 291
Brill, Abraham Arden, 4, 7, 20, 22, 34, 60; "Freud's Theory of Wit," 26; translations by, 207, 208, 209; contribution to the *Verlag,* 290, 392; choice of American editors and, 314; *Leonardo da Vinci,* 331; as president of the New York Psychoanalytic Society, 452, 460
British Medical Association: Psychoanalytic Committee of, 509, 522, 537
British Psycho-Analytical Society, 508, 509, 618, 619, 670
British Psychological Society, 240; Freud's honorary membership in, 631, 632
Brodman, Korbinian, 16
Brown, J. Warburton, 533
Brown, William, 340, 342, 395, 668
Browning, Robert, 12, 97, 658
Bryan, C. A. Douglas, 141, 148, 194, 354, 386
Budge, E. A. Wallis, 180
Bulletin of the Ontario Hospitals for the Insane, 6, 40
Burrow, Trigant, 51, 154, 155, 209, 459, 460
Burt, Cyril, 585

Campbell, Charles Macfie, 2
Canadian Medical Association, 34
Carpenter, Edward, 550
Carver, Alfred E. A., 337
Castration, 180; fear of, 166, 530

Castration complex, 169, 171, 175, 502
Castration reactions, 477
Catatonia, 1
Cathartic method, 38
Causal analysis, 66
Centralblatt, 30, 436. See also Zentralblatt
Chadwick, Mary, 509
"Character and Anal Eroticism" (Freud), 44, 371
Character formation, 31, 33
Charcot, Jean-Martin, 1, 644
Chase, Harry W., 22
Chicago Neurological Society, 69
Child analysis, 234, 463, 502, 503, 506, 519; controversy over, 508, 509; Riviere's views on, 511, 512
Childhood: night terrors in, 29; symbolism in, 36; genital excitement in, 301; Oedipus complex in, 508, 509; superego in, 511
Child illness, psychical side of, 506
" 'A Child Is Being Beaten': A Contribution to the Study of the Origin of Sexual Perversions" (Freud), 237, 299, 301
Christianity, Jones's study of, 507
Christian mythology, 105
Circular letters (Rundbriefe), 287, 288, 289
Civilization and Its Discontents (Freud), 543, 546, 547, 548, 550
"Claims of Psycho-Analysis to Scientific Interest, The" (Freud), 144
Clarke, C. K., 3, 60, 63
Clifford, W. K., 29
Clitoric phase, 580, 581, 582
Cocaine use, 2
Co-conscious, 7
Cohn, Franz, 619, 651, 652
Cole, Estelle Maude, 301
Collected Papers (Sammlungen), 370, 371, 372, 374, 381; Collection, 356, 364, 373, 432, 439, 442, 454; Jones's preface to, 416, 417, 418, 432; publication in America, 423
Collins, Joseph, 32, 33, 34
Complexes: oral, 42; psycho-sexual, 51. See also Anal complex; Castration complex
Component instincts (Triebkomponente), 118
Condensation (Verdichtung), 16, 127
Conscious, the (Bewusste), 51
Constructive analysis, 213

Constructive psychology, 192
Conversion hysteria, 26, 296
Coriat, Isador H., 32, 306, 331
Correspondenzblatt, 63, 64. See also Korrespondenzblatt
Coué, Émile, 394, 395
Cronbach, Abraham, 573
Crucifixion, as a rebirth fantasy, 98
Cushing, Harvey, 51
Cyclothymia (manic-depressive psychosis), 71, 255

Daiber, Hans, 655
Daly, C. D., 262, 266, 267, 275, 297; "Numbers in Dreams," 304, 305; correspondence with Freud, 403
Davidson, Frederic J. A., 65, 148
Dearborn, George V. N., 7
Death: from psychical causes, 188; guilt associated with, 530; Freud on, 609
Death instinct (Todestrieb), 548, 633, 634, 635
de Groot, Jeanne, 627
Delusion, 98
Delusions and Dreams in Jensen's "Gravida" (Freud), 340
Dementia praecox, 1, 2, 4, 7, 18, 66
de Ortuzar, Donna, 482
Dercum, Francis X., 47, 63, 64
Deri, Frances, 651
de Saussure, Raymond, 299
Desire, and relation to anxiety, 136
Detroit Neurological Society, 71
Deutsch, Felix, 469
Deutscher Verein für Psychiatrie, 654
Devil-father identification, 403
Devine, Dr., 148
Dirnenliebe complex, 51
Displacement (Verschiebung), 16
Donley, John E., 32, 67
Dream analysis, 22, 36, 43
Dream Psychology, 328
Dreams: interpretation of, 13, 189; as wish fulfillment, 23; egocentricity and, 23; masochistic, 26; posthypnotic suggestion and, 73; recurrent, 369. See also Nightmares, Jones's work on
Drei Abhandlungen, 29, 36, 47, 63, 82
Drucker, Ernestine, 256
Dubois, Paul-Charles, 16
Durer, Sophie, 144

Durning-Lawrence, Sir Edwin, 188
Dutch Psychoanalytic Society, 588, 615
"Dynamics of Transference, The" (Freud), 180

"Early analysis" lecture series (Klein), 461
Eder, Edith, 156, 166, 201, 303, 304
Eder, Montague David, 64, 65, 80, 82, 131, 141, 148
Eder Memorial Fund, 651
Ego, angst and, 477
Ego and the Id, The (Das Ich und das Es), 376, 399, 478, 479
Ego complex, 32
Ego conflict (Ichkonflict), 232
Ego-ideal, 503
Ehrlich, Paul, 68
Eighth Congress of the International Psychoanalytic Association (Salzburg), 419
Eisler, Michael Joseph, 331
Eitingon, Max, 308, 382, 438, 464, 475, 593; Jones's relationship with, 568, 569
Eleventh Congress of the International Psychoanalytic Association (Oxford), 541, 573
Ellis, Havelock, 64, 137, 139, 144, 156; Philosophy of Conflict, and Other Essays in War-Time, The, 267
Emerson, Louville Eugene, 149
Emmanuelism, 14, 32
Encyclopaedia Britannica: articles on psychoanalysis in, 391; entry on Freud in, 530, 531
Encyclopedia of Education, 217, 218
England: interest in psychoanalysis in, 184; Freud's immigration to, 661, 662
Ereutophobia, 208
Eros und Psyche, 64, 65, 263, 275
Erythrophobia, 288
Eucken, Christoph, 206
Exhibitionism, 44

Fabian Society, 186
Fairbairn, W. R. D., 509
Falconer, Robert Alexander, 51
Farnell, F. J., 301, 306, 307
Farrow, E. P., 439, 441
Father complex, 22, 127, 192
Father: murder of, 127; fixation, 580
Father-son hostility, 442

"Fear, Guilt, and Hate" (Jones), 548, 549
Fear of incest (Inzestscheu), 76
Federation of American Psychoanalytic Societies, 618
Federn, Paul, 64, 289, 434
Feigenbaum, Dorian, 593, 601, 602
Female development, 519
Female Don Juanism, 136
Female sexuality, 635
"Female Sexuality" (Freud), 578, 581
Female symbols, 58, 59, 61
Feminine homosexuality, 266, 268, 269, 386, 389, 477
Ferdinand, Maximillian, 40
Ferenczi, Sándor, 13, 16, 29, 90, 121; Jones's analysis with, 122, 124, 125, 128, 201; "On Symbolism," 166; as university teacher of psychoanalysis, 244, 245; expulsion from Budapest Royal Medical Association, 273, 276, 283; lay analysis and, 509; "Confusion of Tongues between Adults and the Child," 595; death of, 611; mental deterioration of, 613
Ferrier, Sir David, 74
Fifth Congress of the International Psychoanalytic Association (Budapest), 224
First International Psychoanalytic Congress (Salzburg), 1
"Five Lectures on Psycho-Analysis" (Freud), 335, 336
Fixation hysteria, 296
Flatus, symbolism of, 45. See also Anal eroticism
Fliess, Wilhelm, 21, 277
Flournoy, Henri, 137, 180
Flournoy, Théodore, 137
Flügel, J. C., 238, 537
Forel, Auguste, 15, 88
Forgetting, psychoanalytic explanations for, 196
Forgetting of names (Namenvergessen), 60, 61, 63
"Formulations on the Two Principles of Mental Functioning" (Freud), 68
Forsyth, David, 131, 148, 245, 250, 254, 271, 272, 274, 275, 276, 292
Fort/da episode, 404
Fourteenth Congress of the International Psychoanalytic Association (Marienbad), 649, 654

Fourth Congress of the International Psychoanalytic Association (Munich), 131
France: psychoanalysis in, 70; psychoanalytic movement in, 299
Frank, Ludwig, 38
Frankfurt Psychoanalytic Institute, 155
Frazer, James George, 74, 97, 127
Free association, 644, 645
Freud, Alexander, 564, 661
Freud, Amalie, 563
Freud, Anna, 83, 199, 200, 201; relationship with Lou Andreas-Salomé, 364; *Introduction to the Technique of Child Analysis*, 502; on the superego, 505; child analysis and, 508; "Counterpart of the Animal Phobias of Children, A," 542
Freud, Anton, 306
Freud, Clement Raphael, 306, 615
Freud, Emanuel, 75, 208
Freud, Ernst, 205, 248, 275, 306, 615, 637, 638, 644
Freud, Gabriel, 322
Freud, Lucian Michael, 306
Freud, Lucie Brasch, 275, 306, 626, 651
Freud, Marie, 287
Freud, Martin, 49, 203, 205; wartime service of, 211, 227, 232, 235, 248; marriage of, 256; as manager of the *Verlag*, 582
Freud, Marzel, 614
Freud, Mathilde, 8, 83, 87, 90
Freud, Moritz, 287
Freud, Oliver, 205, 212, 214, 248
Freud, Stephen Gabriel, 306
Freud-Breuer cathartic method, 38
"Freudism," 29, 32, 172
"Freud's Psychology" (Jones), 26
"Freud's Theory of Dreams" (Jones), 31
Friedländer, A. A., 34, 40, 42
Frink, Horace W., 194, 225, 304, 306, 319, 433, 434, 435; Freud's opinion of, 320; mental breakdown of, 327; scandal involving, 443
Frustration, guilt and, 512
Fuchs, Henny, 214
Fuchs, S. H., 619
Functional psychiatry, 7
Furtmüller, Carl, 119
Future of an Illusion (Freud), 527, 530, 533

Garvin, William C. A., 185, 186
Gaupp, Ernst W. T., 19

Geld complex, 42
German professorial manifesto, 206
German Psychoanalytic Society, 618
Germany, pre–World War II conditions in, 618
Gerrish, Frederick Henry, 7
Glover, Edward, 359, 490, 509
Glover, James, 359, 386, 433; death of, 489
God complex, 118
God-men, 112
Goethe Prize, 561, 562
Goldenweiser, Alexander A., 116
Gordon, Emma Leila, 51
Graf, Caecilie, 376
Graf, Max, 30, 65
Graham, Dr., 148
Grey, Sir Edward, 202
Grief: Jones's views on, 530; guilt and, 533
Groddeck, Georg, 533, 628, 629
Gross, Otto, 1, 2, 35
Group Psychology and the Analysis of the Ego (Freud), 283, 304, 306; English translation of, 318, 324
Guilt: unconscious sense of, 440; genesis of, 512; association with death, 530
Guilt complex, 72

Hacker, Friedrich, 71
Halberstadt, Ernst Wolfgang, 320, 404
Halberstadt, Heinz Rudolf, 402, 404; death of, 521
Halberstadt, Max, 83, 402
Halberstadt, Sophie Freud, 83, 181, 402; death of, 263, 265, 521
Haldane, Richard Burden, 460
Hall, G. Stanley, 10, 14, 15, 64, 71, 189
Hamill, Ralph C., 156, 163
Hamilton Medical Society, 32
Hamlet literature, 15, 18, 20, 22, 26, 27, 29, 31, 44, 63, 298
"Handling of Dream-Interpretation in Psycho-Analysis, The" (Freud), 71
Harnik, J., 595
Hart, Bernard, 1, 28, 29, 30, 40, 80, 148
Hartland, E. S., 74
Hartmann, Heinz, 596
Healing by touch, 98
Healy, William, 560
Hecht, D'Orsay, 32, 69
Height phobia, 36
Heller, Hugo, 99, 143, 159

Helmann, Paula, 619
Herd instinct, 213, 268, 269, 274, 319
Herzl, Minna, 265, 267
Hesnard, A., 70
Heterophoria, 299, 301
Hiller, Eric, 236, 278, 379, 380, 382
Hitschmann, Eduard, 56
Hoch, August, 7, 32, 34, 40, 60, 107, 118,
    152
Hoche, Alfred E., 37, 38
Hoesch-Ernst, Lucy, 131, 132, 137, 141,
    180, 181
Hogarth Press, 428, 495, 497, 498, 513, 637
Hollitscher, Mathilde Freud. See Freud,
    Mathilde
Holt, Edwin B., 23, 214
Homosexuality, 9, 29, 66, 109, 111; deter-
    mination of, 175. See also Feminine
    homosexuality
Hopkins, Pryns, 471
"Horme," 202
Hostility: civilization and, 548
Hubback, C. J. M., 293, 306, 318, 321
Hug, Rudolph, 435
Hutton, Edward, 109
Huxley Memorial Lecture, 570, 571
Hyperaemia, 299
Hypnoidization, 7, 71
Hypnosis, 40; as a sexual rapport, 136; sug-
    gestion and, 644
Hypomania, 4, 18
Hysteria, 1, 4, 7; manifestations of, 16
Hysterical illness, 184, 195
Hysterical paranoia, 172

Imago, 64, 70, 73, 74
Incest, 76, 80
Incest complexes, 238
Incest myths, 63
Incest theory of witchcraft, 403
India, development of psychoanalysis in,
    295
Indian Psycho-Analytic Society, 344
Individual psychology, 66
Infantile dreams, 43
Infantile fixations, 102
Infantile narcissism, 118
Infantile neurosis, 503
Infantile sexuality, 88, 102, 125, 196
Infantile theory, 57, 59, 61, 62
Inferiority (Minderwertigkeit), 118

Inhibitions, Symptoms, and Anxiety
    (Hemmung, Symptom, und Angst), 465,
    473, 494, 495; American translation, 546
Inkblot test, 235
International Congress for Sexual
    Research, 196
Internationaler Psychoanalytischer Ver-
    lag, 49
Internationale Zeitschrift für
    Psychoanalyse, 98, 101, 103, 105
International Journal of Psycho-Analysis,
    240, 247, 281, 293, 295, 352, 354, 435
International Psycho-Analytical Library,
    428, 546
International Psycho-Analytical Library
    Series, 413, 419, 637
International Psychoanalytic Association
    (Vereinigung), 28, 60, 149, 170; Jung's
    resignation as president of, 186
International Society for Medical Psychol-
    ogy and Psychotherapy, 66, 88, 91
International Training Committee, 637
International Training Sub-Commission,
    573
Interpretation of Dreams, The (Traum-
    deutung), 3, 5, 63
Introductory Lectures on Psycho-
    Analysis (Vorlesungen), 227, 264, 266,
    401, 494
"Irma's injection," Freud's dream of, 108,
    183
Isaacs, Rufus Daniel, 607
Isaacs, Susan, 509
Italian Psychoanalytic Society, 631

Jackson, J. Hughlings, 136
Jahrbuch, 149, 153, 157, 159
James, William, 7, 57
James-Lange theory of emotions, 7
Janet, Pierre, 1, 4, 38, 68, 133, 134
Japanese Psychoanalytic Society, 550
Jeffreys, Harold, 648, 649
Jekels, Ludwig, 188, 205, 206
Jelgersma, G., 177, 179
Jelliffe, Smith Ely, 77, 149, 152, 189, 208
Joad, Cyril Edwin Mitchinson, 639
Johnson, P. Youlden, 370, 373
Jokl, Hans, 265
Jones, Edith May Howard, 184
Jones, Gwenith, 288, 289, 291, 352, 359;
    death of, 520, 522, 526

Jones, Herbert, 115, 122, 123, 124, 133, 137, 139, 175, 188, 214, 389; marriage to Loe Kann, 192
Jones, Katherine Jokl, 253, 265, 291
Jones, Lewis Ernest, 608
Jones, Mary Ann Lewis, 184
Jones, Mervyn, 321, 347, 349, 628, 630; analysis of, 533
Jones, Morfydd Owen, 219, 221; Jones's reaction to the death of, 223, 235
Jones, Nesta May, 552, 554, 651
Jones, Sybil, 26, 36
Jones, Thomas, 184
Journal für Psychologie und Neurologie, 16
Journal of Abnormal Psychology, 4, 22, 148
Journal of Educational Psychology, 26
Journal of Mental Science, 160
Journal of Nervous and Mental Disease, 22, 43
Judaism, psychoanalysis of, 573
Jung, Carl Gustav, 1, 2, 18; "Transformations and Symbols of Libido" (Wandlungen), 67, 68, 75, 88, 95; dissension with, 79, 88, 95, 152, 153, 155; exclusion from the secret committee, 81; New York lectures ("Theory of Psychoanalysis, The"), 94, 131; new concept of the libido, 97; views on psychoanalysis, 102, 107; Freud on, 108; criticism of Freud, 111; resignation from Jahrbuch, 149; Freud's attack on, 191; "Content of the Psychoses, The," 192; method of, 206; Psychological Types, 310
Jung, Emma, 92, 94

Kann, Louise Dorothea (Loe), 6, 56, 57, 63, 94; illness of, 66, 70, 129, 164, 165, 175, 183; attitude toward psychoanalysis, 68, 74, 146, 154, 180; Freud's analysis of, 99, 100, 111, 114, 115, 120; break with Jones, 122, 125; marriage to Herbert Jones, 139, 189, 192
Kaplan, Leo, 469
Kaplan, Michael, 469
Kardiner, Abram, 306, 342, 509
Kaufmann, Rudolf, 129
Kirschmann, August, 3
Klein, Melanie, 461, 462, 463, 502, 503, 607; views on the superego, 504; child

analysis and, 508; differences with Anna Freud, 508, 509
Kleinpaul, Rudolf, 97
Kola, Richard, 288, 293
Königsberger sculpture, 307, 308
Korrespondenzblatt, 54, 57
Kraepelin, Emil, 1, 7
Krankengeschichten, 299, 307, 319, 320, 364, 423
Kraus, Friedrich S., 43, 115, 200
"Kreuzlingen gesture," 79
Kris, Ernst, 596
Kuh, Sidney, 51

Laforgue, René, 436, 490
Lamarckian principle, 82
Lampl, Hans, 627
Landauer, Karl, 155, 615
Lang, Andrew, 516
Lantos, Barbara, 619
Latency period, 131
Lawrence, D. H., 1
Lawrence, Frieda Richthofen, 1
Lay, Wilfried, 267
Lay analysis, 465, 490, 491, 496, 503; controversy over, 505, 506, 509; American position on, 539, 541
Le Bon, Gustave, 319
Left- and right-handedness, 19, 21, 22
Leiden lectures, 191, 192, 193
Leonardo da Vinci and a Memory of His Childhood (Freud), 28, 29, 30
Lesage, Alain-René, 42
Leuba, James H., 116
Levi-Bianchini, M., 207
Levine, Israel, 396, 397, 415
Lévy, Lajos, 260, 275
Lewin, Bertram D., 593
Lewis, M. G., 509
Libido: Jung's work on, 75; Jung's concept of, 97, 139, 202; relation to angst, 174; mourning and, 531
Libido theory, 95
Libido theory of suggestion, 414
Liebesbedingungen articles, 51
Literature: applications of psychoanalysis to, 299
"Little Hans" case, 4, 7, 12, 14, 15
Lloyd, J. H., 63, 64
Local psychoanalytic society (Ortsverein), 43; American, 45

Loewy, Emanuel, 205
Lombroso, Cesare, 31
London, Jones's career in, 137, 148, 161, 169, 213
London Clinic of Psycho-Analysis, 471, 490
London Psycho-Analytical Society, 1, 141, 144; founding membership of, 148
London Society of Psychical Research, 54, 57
Long, Constance, 148, 156, 157, 159, 181, 194, 206, 217, 218; analysis with Jung, 176
Looney, J. Thomas, 521, 522, 523
Low, Barbara, 277, 331, 509

Maas, Hilde, 613
Macbeth studies, 63
MacCurdy, John T., 51, 57, 146, 152, 188, 394, 395
Mack-Brunswick, Ruth, 528
Mackenzie, Leslie, 144, 148
Mackenzie, William, 235
Madonna essay (Jones), 180, 321, 353, 354
Maeder, Alphonse, 17, 61, 63, 89, 119, 166
Maier, Hans Wolfgang, 91
Male hysteria, 1
Malinowski, Bronislaw, 428, 462
Manic depression, 18
Manic-depressive insanity, 176
Manic-depressive psychosis, 71, 255
Marett, Robert R., 268, 269
Marie, Pierre, 2
Marriage, Jones's views on, 172
Martin, Louis Charles, 203
Masculine protest, 121, 146
Masochism, 5, 166, 175
Masochistic dreams, 26
Mass psychology, 266, 268, 304
Masturbation, 27, 28
Matriarchy, 81, 127; Oedipus complex and, 428; father-son hostility and, 442
Mayer, Gretel Jokl, 614
McCann, James, 307, 309, 331, 336, 340, 343
McCord, C. P., 560
McCormick, Edith, 271, 278
McDougall, William, 80, 141, 169, 639, 644; on sexual instinct, 180; analysis of, 196; correspondence with, 457, 458
Medicine: psychosomatic, 77; relation of psychoanalysis to, 352, 354

Medico-Psychological Clinic (Brunswick Square), 294, 359
Melancholia, 301, 359
Meng, Heinrich, 155, 518
Mensendieck, Otto, 158
Menstruation taboos, 169, 171
"Mental Characteristics of Chronic Epilepsy, The" (Jones), 32
Mental development, stages of, 174
Mental disorders, classification of, 1
Mercier, Charles A., 172, 174, 180, 218
Merck, Valerie, 614
Meredith, Sir William Ralph, 65
Meyer, Adolf, 7, 22, 31, 32, 33, 51, 57
Meyer, Munroe A., 306
Meyers, Campbell, 65
Mills, Charles K., 47
Mirror writing, 29
Misch, Kate, 619
Möbius, Paul Julius, 662
Modena, Gustavo, 20, 22, 24
Moll, Albert, 38
Moltzer, Maria, 111
Money-Kyrle, Roger E., 359, 379, 380, 398
Morbid anxiety, 477
Morichau-Beauchant, R., 70, 71, 73
Moses and Monotheism (Freud), 645, 652, 656, 665, 666
Mosso, Angelo, 15
Mother complex, 27
Mother-right theory, 461
Motor aphasia, 132
Mott, F. W., 34
Mourning, work of (Trauerarbeit), 522, 530, 531
"Mourning and Melancholia" (Freud), 223
Müller, Friedrich Max, 530
Münchhausen psychology, 131
Munro, Hector, 273, 275
Münsterberg, Hugo, 7
Munthe, Axel M. F., 559, 561, 562
Mute-death symbolism, 80
Mutual analysis, 612
Mythology, 5; Christian, 105
Myths, theory of, 4

Nancy School, 644
Napoleon studies, 63, 71, 97, 119, 137, 210
Narcissism articles (Freud), 143, 144
Narcissistic anxiety, 232
Narcolepsy, 39

Nashe, Thomas, 70, 72, 550
Nationalism, psychology of, 206
Natural selection, 82
"Nature of Auto-Suggestion, The" (Jones), 394, 395, 397
"Nature of Desire, The" (Jones), 393
Nazis, 606, 607; psychoanalysis under, 618; invasion of Austria by, 652
Nervous condition *(Nervösität)*, asexual, 23, 25, 27
Neuer, Alexander, 174
Neurasthenia, 4, 23, 25; related to masturbation, 27, 28
Neuron theory, 15
Neurosis. *See* Obsessional neurosis
New German-English Psycho-Analytic Vocabulary, A, 639
New Introductory Lectures on Psycho-Analysis (Freud), 592, 593, 614
Newton, Caroline, 450, 451, 465
New York Psychoanalytic Society, 4, 57, 194, 240, 452, 460, 506, 508; opposition to lay analysis by, 509; Brill's presidency of, 618
Nicoll, Maurice, 148, 194
Nightmares, Jones's work on, 40, 47, 63, 65
Night terrors, 29
Ninth Congress of the International Psychoanalytic Association (Bad Homburg), 449, 465
Nunberg, Hermann, 229
Nuremberg Congress, 26, 28

Oberholzer, Mira, 235
Oberndorf, Clarence P., 306, 330, 342
Obsessional neurosis *(Zwangsneurose),* 15, 43, 97, 148, 296, 298, 502
Obsessions, 4, 42
Occultism, 45, 136
"Occult Significance of Dreams, The" (Freud), 476
Oedipus complex, 14, 62, 71, 127, 504; in children, 508, 509
"On the History of the Psycho-Analytic Movement," 168, 191, 200, 207, 208, 209
On the Nightmare (Jones), 29, 566, 578, 579
Onuf, Bronislaw, 43
Oppenheim, Hermann, 16
Oral complexes, 42
Organic neuropathology, 13

"Origin and Structure of the Super-Ego, The" (Jones), 492
Osler, William, 64, 65
Ossipow, M. E., 24
Ostwald, Wilhelm, 206
Oxford University Psychological Society, 437

Palós, Gizella, 596
Papers (Jones), 218, 229; French translation of, 468, 469
"Papers on Metapsychology" (Freud), 209, 211, 271, 272
Paranoia, 41, 44, 46, 66, 95
Paraphrenia, 95
Paris Psychoanalytic Society, 436
Parricide, 49
Pater, Walter, 29, 30, 109
"Pathology of Morbid Anxiety, The" (Jones), 66, 67, 477
Patrick, Hugh T., 51
Payne, Charles R., 56
Payne, Sylvia M., 588
Pear, T. H., 196
Pearson, Karl, 29
Penis envy *(Penisneid),* 301
Pfister, Oskar, 14, 15, 30, 43, 65, 191; *Psychoanalytic Method, The,* 137
Phallic phase, 440, 580, 581, 582
"Phallic Phase, The" (Jones), 615
Phallic symbols, 61
Philadelphia Neurological Association, 47
Phipps Psychiatric Clinic, 118, 121
Phobias, 4; concerning height, 36; active therapy in, 440
Picard, Émile, 15
Pichler, Hans, 526
Pierce Clark, L., 102, 278, 281, 494, 495
Pitman, Isaac, 637
Pleasure principle *(Lustprinzip),* 68, 70. See also *Beyond the Pleasure Principle*
Polon, Albert, 306, 324
Pope, Curran, 56
Post-graduate analysis, 618, 620
Posthypnotic suggestion, 73, 644
Preconscious *(Vorbewusste),* 51
Preger, J. W., 264
Prescott, William Hickling, 127
Press, 293, 294, 365, 412; problems with, 383, 403, 411, 419; relations with the *Verlag,* 415, 416; success of, 434

Priapus, 22

Primal libido *(Urlibido)*, 88

Primal repression *(Urverdrängung)*, 477

Primitive bisexuality, 58

Prince, Morton, 4, 6, 7, 9, 23, 55, 56, 57; on
the subconscious, 11; Monograph Series
of, 131; *Unconscious: The Fundamentals of Human Personality, The*, 181,
182; on abnormal psychology, 184

Pring, Mabel, 210, 220

"Problem of Paul Morphy: A Contribution
to the Psychology of Chess, The" (Jones),
561, 566

"Prospective psychology," 202

Prostitution fantasy, 136

Psychasthenia, 4

Psychiatric Society, 80

Psychical conflict, 27

Psychical shock, 7

"Psycho-Analysis and Folklore" (Jones),
530

"Psychoanalysis and the Christian Religion" (Jones), 566

"Psychoanalysis and the Instincts" (Jones),
633, 635

"Psycho-Analysis in Psychotherapy"
(Jones), 7, 25

Psychoanalysts, first international meeting of, 1

"Psycho-Analytic Notes on an Autobiographical Account of a Case of Paranoia
(Dementia Paranoides)," 46

Psychoanalytic Quarterly, 588, 589, 590,
592, 593

Psychoanalytic Review, 77, 149, 152, 190,
220, 275, 298, 590

Psychoanalytic writings, popular, 74

Psychogalvanic reflex, 7

Psychological Bulletin, 22, 26

Psychological Club (Jung), 278

Psychological mechanisms, 16

Psychological types, 145

Psychologies of 1930, 537

Psychologische Abhandlungen, 166

Psychology and war lectures (Jones), 219

Psycho-Medical Society, 148

Psychoneurosis, 4; sex origin of, 7;
symptoms of, 60; categories of, 296. *See
also* Obsessional neurosis

"Psychopathology of Anxiety, The"
(Jones), 477

*Psychopathology of Everyday Life, The
(Psychopathologie des Alltagslebens)*,
26, 61, 569, 571

Psycho-sexual complexes, 51. *See also*
Complexes

Psychosomatic medicine, 77

Psychotherapeutics, 22

*Psychotherapy: A Course of Reading in
Sound Psychology, Sound Medicine,
and Sound Religion*, 6

Putnam, James Jackson, 7, 18, 19, 32, 46;
"Freud and Bergson's Theories of the
Unconscious," 22; on Jung's views, 109;
Griselda complex of, 139, 141; self-
analysis of, 167; "Dream Interpretation
and the Theory of Psychoanalysis," 189;
Human Motives, 211; death of, 225, 227,
231, 233, 238; *Addresses on Psycho-
Analysis*, 268, 290, 293

Question of Lay Analysis, The (Freud), 490

Radio lectures on psychology, 585

Ramón y Cajal, Santiago, 15

Rank, Otto, 18, 19, 41, 51, 54, 99, 294, 295;
Lohengrin saga by, 66; illness of, 123;
conscription of, 212; Jones's relations
with, 298; "Mythus von der Geburt des
Helden," 308; discord with, 382, 435,
438, 441, 445; resignation from
Zeitschrift, 438

"Rat Man" case, 15

Reaction formation, 477

Read, Charles Stanford, 301

Reality principle *(Realitätsprinzip)*, 68, 70

"Recent Advances in Psycho-Analysis"
(Jones), 262

Recurrent dreams, 369

Régis, E., 70

Reich, Wilhelm, 500, 619

Reik, Theodor, 183, 413, 621, 622

Reincarnation, 71

"Relation between Anxiety Neurosis and
Anxiety Hysteria, The" (Jones), 100, 105,
111

"Relationship between Dreams and
Psycho-Neurotic Symptoms, The"
(Jones), 60, 61

Religion, 29; psychology of, 64; Jones's
interest in, 65; psychogenesis of, 67;
Freud's work on, 74

Religious fanaticism, 6
Repetition compulsion
(Wiederholungszwang), 284, 635
Repressed sexuality, 477
Repression (Verdrängung), 1, 80, 81, 82, 91;
Jung on, 212; versus suppression, 280;
angst and, 477; in children, 511
"Repression" (Freud), 212
"Repression Theory and Its Relation to
Memory, The" (Jones), 196
Resistance, 32
"Rest cure," 7
Restoration (Wiederherstellung), 633
"Retrospective understanding," 202
"Return of Totemism in Childhood, The"
(Freud), 81
Review of Neurology and Psychiatry, 26
Revue neurologique, 77
Rickman, John, 262, 266, 269, 286, 288, 316;
analysis of, 330; translations by, 352
Rickman, Mrs., 298, 334
Rigall, R. M., 359
Riklin, Franz, 57
Rivers, William H. R., 262
Riviere, Joan, 70, 307, 316, 351; Jones's
analysis of, 339; translations by, 352,
353, 354; discord with Jones, 359, 361;
Freud's analysis of, 364, 365; success of,
419; views on child analysis, 511, 512
Robinson, William J., 240
Robson-Scott, W. D., 515, 516, 568
Rochester, Haydon, 23
Róheim, Géza, 276, 277, 354, 464, 588
"Rôle of Repression in Forgetting, The,"
194
Rorschach, Hermann, 235, 317
Rosenstein, Gaston, 119
Royal Medico-Psychological Association,
646, 648, 653, 654
Royal Society of Medicine, 80; Freud's
honorary membership in, 636, 637
Russell, Bertrand, 388, 507

Sachs, Bernard, 32
Sachs, Hanns, 64, 325, 326; conscription
of, 212
Sachs, Wulf, 652
Sadger, J. Isidor, 42, 51
Sadism, 166, 175
Sanford, E. C., 18
Sarasin, Philipp, 304

Savage, Sir George H., 133, 160, 162, 180
Schauer, O., 40
Schaulust, 44
Schizophrenia, 95
Schmid, Hans, 145
Schmideberg, Melitta, 607, 619
Schmideberg, Walter, 607, 619
Schreber, Daniel Paul, 41
Schriften series, 42, 43
Schroeder, Hermann, 526
Schroeder, Theodore, 298, 345
Schrötter, K., 73
Schwab, Sidney I., 32
Scientific attitude, and Freud, 156
Scott, Robert Falcon, 188
Scripture, Edward Wheeler, 60, 159
Searl, N., 509
Second International Psychoanalytic Con-
gress (Nuremberg), 26, 28
Secret committee, 81, 236, 287, 307, 321,
374, 541, 588; San Cristoforo meeting of,
406; dissolution of, 421, 422, 426
"Secrets of the Soul," 468
Seif, Leonhard, 66, 89, 94, 112
Selbsdarstellung, 495, 496, 497, 498
Self-analysis, 6, 22, 36, 37, 42, 68, 80, 131,
352
Self-love, 210
Sensory aphasia, 132
"Seventeenth-Century Demonological
Neurosis, A" (Freud), 403
Seventeenth International Congress of
Medicine, 74
Seventh Congress of the International
Psychoanalytic Association (Berlin),
353, 372
Seventh International Congress of
Psychology, 401
Severn, Elizabeth, 612
Sex: hysteria and, 16; pain and, 166
Sex in Civilization, 550
Sextheorie, 28
Sexual anaesthesia, 339
Sexuality, left- and right-handedness and,
22. See also Infantile sexuality
Sexual liberty, defense of, 142
Sexual motives, 7
Sexual selection, 82
Shakespeare, William, 18, 20, 188, 521
Shand, Alexander F., 210
Sharpe, Ella Freeman, 509

Shaw, Bernard, 56, 68, 97, 324
Shock cases, 210, 230
Sidis, Boris, 7, 23, 71
Signal anxiety, 477
Silberer, Herbert, 51
Simmel, Ernst, 528, 545
Sixth Congress of the International Psychoanalytic Association (Hague), 284
Sixth International Congress of Psychology, 6, 17
Slip of the pen *(Verschreiben)*, 77, 179, 180, 182, 183
Slip of the tongue *(Versprechen)*, 66
Smith, George, 468
Smith, H. Watson, 144, 148
Smith, W. Robertson, 127
Snake symbolism, 61, 98
Society for Psychical Research, 73, 74, 112
Society of Psychoanalysis (Holland), 615
"Some Problems of Adolescence" (Jones), 379
Somnambulism, 136
Southard, Elmer E., 264, 268
Sperber, Hans, 112
Spiller, William Gibson, 32
Spitz, René A., 544
Sprott, W. J. H., 375, 378
Stärcke, August, 330, 331
Starr, Moses Allen, 75, 77
Steiner, Maxim, 660
Stekel, Wilhelm, 3, 4, 7, 33, 54, 58, 59, 62, 96, 176; separation from, 98, 99, 103, 107
Stern, Adolph, 314, 451
Stewart, T. Grainger, 156
Stigmata, 5
Stirling-Gilchrist, John, 482
Stoddart, W. H. B., 174
Storfer, A. J., 49, 159, 468; as head of the *Verlag*, 438; resignation from the *Verlag*, 582
Strachey, Alix, 354, 639
Strachey, James, 274, 288, 515; translations by, 292, 306, 307, 433; meeting with Jones, 319; "Some Unconscious Factors in Reading," 550
Strohmayer, W., 8
Subconscious, the, 7, 11
Sublimation, 68
Substitute formation *(Ersatzformation)*, 16
Suggestion, 29, 52, 77; libido theory of, 414; hypnosis and, 644. *See also* Autosuggestion

Suicide, 61
Superego, 492, 493; Klein's views on, 504; in children, 511; genesis of, 635
Supernaturalism, 65
Sutherland, W. D., 43, 54, 57, 59, 148; death of, 282
Swiss Psychoanalytic Society, 14, 234, 235, 451, 629. *See also* Zurich group
Switzerland, psychoanalytic groups in, 234
"Symbolic Significance of Salt" (Jones), 26
Symbolism, 26, 42, 43, 58, 74, 80; "Theory of Symbolism, The" (Jones), 26, 61, 166, 233, 264; in childhood, 36; phallic, 61; stereotyped, 71; unconscious, 264. *See also* Female symbols
Symbols, theory of, 4
"Symposium on Child Analysis," 509
"Symposium on Freud's Theory of the Neuroses and Allied Subjects," 47
Symptom formation *(Symptombildung)*, 477
Szecsi, Stephan, 17

Taboo, 177
Tannenbaum, Samuel, 240, 268, 275, 276, 277, 278
Tansley, A. G., 307, 352, 353, 435, 464
Tausig, Paul, 29, 34, 41, 42, 44
Taylor, E. W., 7
Tegel Sanatorium Psychoanalytic Clinic, 528, 543, 544, 545, 546
Telepathy, 57, 58; Freud's views on, 476, 478, 599, 600; Severn's interest in, 612
Temple, William, 585
Tenth Congress of the International Psychoanalytic Association (Innsbruck), 506, 508
Tenth International Congress of Psychology, 483
Terry, E. M., 509
Teufelsneurose, 403, 447, 448, 450
These Eventful Years, 436, 437, 438, 440
Third Congress of the International Psychoanalytic Association (Weimar), 57
Thirteenth Congress of the International Psychoanalytic Association (Lucerne), 630
Thomas, Henry M., 51
Thompson, Clara, 618
Thomson, H. Campbell, 156

Thomson, James, 70, 72
Three Essays on the Theory of Sexuality (Drei Abhandlungen), 29, 36, 47, 63, 82
Toronto, opposition to Jones in, 56
Toronto Asylum, Jones's dismissal from, 63
Toronto General Hospital, 65
Totem and Taboo, 68, 73, 120, 125
Totemism, 74, 276, 516
Touch, power of, 98
Training Committees, 509, 510
Transference *(Übertragung)*, 99, 113, 180, 201, 210, 339
Trauma, 7
Traumatic neurosis *(Traumatische neurose)*, 1, 232
Treatment of the Neuroses (Jones), 188, 249; translation of, 296, 298
"Treatment of the Neuroses, Including the Psychoneuroses, The" (Jones), 76, 137
Tridon, André, 328, 340, 342
Trömner, Ernst, 66
Trotter, Wilfred Batten Lewis, 58, 60, 124, 213, 215, 268; *Instincts of the Herd in Peace and War*, 346
Tuckey, C. Lloyd, 181
Twelfth Congress of the International Psychoanalytic Association (Wiesbaden), 582, 590
"Two Lies Told by Children" (Freud), 125

Unconscious, the *(Unbewusste)*, 7, 30, 51
Unconscious forces, 105
Unconscious psychological mechanisms, 16
Unconscious suicide attempts, 61
Unconscious symbolism, 264
United States. *See* America
University of Toronto: Jones's resignation of professorship at, 146, 156, 157; Jones's psychiatry course at, 156

van Emden, J. E. G., 78, 205, 206, 506
van Ophuijsen, J. H. W., 287, 292, 588, 589
van Teslaar, James S., 331
Varendonck, J., 330, 331
Verlag, 293, 385; effect of Depression on, 583; subcommittee to save, 585, 586, 587, 588; supervisory committee of, 590, 592. *See also* Press
Vienna, post–World War I conditions in, 241

Vienna Psychoanalytic Society, 1, 113, 434
Vienna school, Jung's vengeance against, 176
Viereck, George Sylvester, 240
Vogt, Oskar, 66, 88
von Freund, Anton, 227, 237, 241, 243; death of, 255, 256, 261; donation to the *Verlag*, 272
von Hattingberg, Hans, 615, 618
von Hug-Hellmuth, Hermine, 256, 331, 435

Wälder, Robert, 596, 635, 636, 637, 638
"War and Individual Psychology" (Jones), 210
War neuroses, 232, 233, 238
Warren, Howard C., 29, 30, 31
War shock, 230, 232, 234, 238
Washington-Baltimore Psychoanalytic Society, 618
Waterman, G. A., 7
Weir Mitchell, S., 7
Weismann principle, 82
Weiss, Edoardo, 631
Wells, H. G., 176, 177
Westerman-Holstijn, A. J., 615
White, William Alanson, 77, 149
Williams, Frankwood, 489
Williams, Tom A., 7
Winnicott, Donald W., 651
Wish fulfillment: in children's games, 5; dreams as, 16, 23
Wish-fulfillment fantasies, 4
Wish-fulfillment hypothesis, 129
Wittels, Fritz, 436, 437, 442, 449
"Wolf-Man" analysis, 175
Wolf phobia, 234
Women: contempt for, 12; castration complex in, 169; sexuality in, 266, 268, 269, 386, 389, 477, 635; as analysts, 509. *See also* Feminine homosexuality
Woolf, Leonard, 428, 498, 515; correspondence with Freud and Jones, 664
Worcester lectures, 18, 24, 30
Word-associations method, 71
World salvation, psychoanalysis and, 208
World War I, 201, 202, 203, 206; effect on psychoanalytic movement, 209; psychoanalytic publications during, 210; Oxford professors' response to, 291
Wright, Maurice, 148
Wundt, Wilhelm, 206

Yabe, Y. K., 550
Young, George Alexander, 156
Young, George M., 288, 289, 297, 298, 299, 301, 353

Zangwill, Israel, 80
Zeitschrift. See *Internationale Zeitschrift für Psychoanalyse*
Zentralblatt, 33, 54, 57, 63, 64, 96, 99, 436; Freud's resignation of the directorship of, 100

Ziehen, Theodor, 16
Zilboorg, Gregory, 593, 618
Zurich group, 49, 144, 158, 234; severing of connections with, 162, 194, 200; dissensions with, 164
Zurich School of Psychoanalysis, 166
Zur Psychoanalyse der Kriegsneurosen, 234, 241
Zweig, Stella, 629, 630